A HANDBOOK OF
PRACTICAL AUDITING

A HANDBOOK OF
PRACTICAL AUDITING

[For the Students of B.Com., M.Com., Professional Course of C.A., C.S., I.C.W.A. and Professionals of Financial Institutions]

B.N. TANDON
M.A. Econ., L.L.B., (Agra) M.A. Com., (Cul),
B. Com., (Hon), Ph.D. Econ. (Munich)
Formerly Professor and Head of the Department of Commerce and Business Administration, Delhi Polytechnic, Delhi

Revised By

S. SUDHARSANAM
M. Com., M. Phil., AICWA, Ph.D.
Reader in Commerce,
D.B. Jain College, Chennai-97

S. SUNDHARABAHU
M.Com., B.L., F.C.A. D.I.S.A (ICA).,
Chartered Accountant
Mayiladuthurai

FULLY REVISED AND ENLARGED FOURTEENTH EDITION

S Chand And Company Limited
(ISO 9001 Certified Company)

S Chand And Company Limited

(ISO 9001 Certified Company)

Head Office: D-92, Sector–2, Noida – 201301, U.P. (India), Ph. 91-120-4682700
Registered Office: A-27, 2nd Floor, Mohan Co-operative Industrial Estate, New Delhi – 110 044
Phone: 011-49731800

www.**schandpublishing.com**; e-mail: **info@schandpublishing.com**

Marketing Offices:

Chennai : Ph: 23632120; chennai@schandpublishing.com
Guwahati : Ph: 2738811, 2735640; guwahati@schandpublishing.com
Hyderabad : Ph: 40186018; hyderabad@schandpublishing.com
Jalandhar : Ph: 4645630; jalandhar@schandpublishing.com
Kolkata : Ph: 23357458, 23353914; kolkata@schandpublishing.com
Lucknow : Ph: 4003633; lucknow@schandpublishing.com
Mumbai : Ph: 25000297; mumbai@schandpublishing.com
Patna : Ph: 2260011; patna@schandpublishing.com

First Edition 1958
Subsequent Editions and Reprints 1960, 61, 63, 65, 68, 69, 70, 71, 72, 74 75, 76 (Twice), 78, 79 (Twice), 80, 81, 82 (Twice), 83 (Twice), 85 (Twice), 86, 87, 88, 89, 90 (Twice), 91, 92, 93, 94, 96, 97, 98, 99, 2001, 2002, 2003, 2004
Revised and Enlarged Edition 2006
Reprints 2007, 2008, 2009, 2010, 2012, 2013 (Twice), 2014, 2015, 2018 (Twice), 2019, 2020 (Twice), 2021, 2022, 2024

Reprint 2025

ISBN : 978-81-219-2041-4 **Product Code:** H8AUD48AUDT10ENAN06O

PRINTED IN INDIA

By Vikas Publishing House Private Limited, Plot 20/4, Site-IV, Industrial Area Sahibabad, Ghaziabad – 201 010 and Published by S Chand And Company Limited, A-27, 2nd Floor, Mohan Co-operative Industrial Estate, New Delhi – 110 044.

Dedicated to the sacred memory of

Late Shri. K. M. Tandon

&

Late Smt. Dhan Devi Tandon

(parents of Shri. B. N. Tandon)

Revision Dedicated to the memory of

Late Shri. B. N. Tandon

&

Smt. and Shri. K. Alagar,

Smt. and Shri. A. Aravamudhan

(our great grand-parent and grand-parent)

Fourteenth Revision Edition Dedicated to the memory of

Sri. A. Srinivasan

(our affectionate Father)

PREFACE TO THE FOURTEENTH EDITION

It is our pleasurs to present to our dear readers the comprehensively revised and enlarged fourteenth edition of Shri B.N.Tandon's "A Hand Book of Practical Auditing". In this edition, we attempted our best to familiarise the students with the basics of auditing more technically. We added ten new chapters to provide good insights into the basics of the technical expertise of auditing-starting from audit planning to reporting, considering various matters, issues along the lines of which the auditing process is normally woven through. The appreciation of these facets of the auditing process, in our opinion, would prepare the readers to gain the grip of how to learn of a subject like auditing.

We have completely revised the chapters on auditing of insurance companies. The opening of insurance sector to private companies and passing of IRDA Act, 1999, have added new dimensions to the audit of insurance companies. The chapter on it is fully recast in the light of new provisions. The chapters dealing with cost audits, audit of government accounts, management auditing, have been changed. The chapters on audits of limited companies have also been revised. The requirements of reporting under CARO 2003 have been adequately discussed.

For better appreciation of the perspective of auditing issues, we have arranged the chapters in four parts- part I - Basics; Part II - Auditing procedures Part III Audit of entities and special audits and Part IV-Others.

We brought this revision with dedicated efforts, which our mentor and father Sri.A.Srinivasan always wished of us. We place down this completely revised, enlarged edition at his lotus feet for his gracing. The humane radiance he spreads around him fills every iota of every nerve of us. His thoughts had been ever filled with concern for good of others. We cannot repay for his pure love nor do we forget his message of selfless service, simple life and high thinking. We move with his memories in mind and his lofty virtues at our heart.

We repeat what we have said in our Eleventh edition- "We do not claim that we have given the students all that they must learn of auditing, though we certainly attempted on it. We humbly feel that we have shown them how to learn the technical subject of auditing. If this mission is achieved, we feel that we are accomplished". We do hold and carry the same message now too.

We are thankful for all the encouragement the readers have shown to us over the decade. We are thankful to their kind responses and would welcome them as our treasure.

We record our thanks to the Publishers for their encouragement and support. Our thanks are due to the Managing Director and every staff of the company for their yeomen service in academics.

We hope that this book will be well received by all students - collegiate and those pursuing professional courses.

With greetings to one and all.

Sudharsanam
&
Sundharababu

PREFACE TO THE FOURTEENTH EDITION

It is our pleasure to present to our dear readers the comprehensively revised and enlarged fourteenth edition of Shri B N Tandon's "A Hand Book of Practical Auditing". In this edition, we attempted our best to familiarise the students with the basics of auditing more technically. We added ten new chapters to provide good insights into the basics of the technical expertise of auditing-starting from audit planning to reporting, considering various matters, issues along the lines of which the auditing process is normally woven through. The appreciation of these facets of the auditing process, in our opinion, would prepare the readers to gain the grip of how to learn of a subject like auditing.

We have completely revised the chapters on auditing of insurance companies. The opening of insurance sector to private companies and passing of IRDA Act, 1999, have added new dimensions to the audit of insurance companies. The chapter on it is fully recast in the light of new provisions. The chapters dealing with cost audits, audit of government accounts, management auditing, have been changed. The chapters on audits of limited companies have also been revised. The requirements of reporting under CARO 2003 have been adequately discussed.

For better appreciation of the perspective of auditing issues, we have arranged the chapters in four parts - part I - Basics; Part II - Auditing procedures Part III Audit of entities and special audits and Part IV-Others.

We brought this revision with dedicated efforts, which our mentor and father Sri A Srinivasan always wished of us. We place down this completely revised, enlarged edition at his lotus feet for his graceing. The humane radiance he spreads around him fills every iota of every nerve of us. His thoughts had been ever filled with concern for good of others. We cannot repay for his pure love nor do we forget his message of selfless service, simple life and high thinking. We move with his memories in mind and his lofty virtues at our heart.

We repeat what we have said in our Eleventh edition: "We do not claim that we have given the students all that they must learn of auditing, though we certainly attempted on it. We humbly feel that we have shown them how to learn the technical subject of auditing. If this mission is achieved, we feel that we are accomplished." We do hold and carry the same message now too.

We are thankful for all the encouragement the readers have shown to us over the decade. We are thankful to their kind responses and would welcome them as our treasure.

We record our thanks to the Publishers for their encouragement and support. Our thanks are due to the Managing Director and every staff of the company for their yeomen service in academics.

We hope that this book will be well received by all students - collegiate and those pursuing professional courses.

With greetings to one and all.

Sudharsanam

&

Sundharababu

PREFACE TO THE FIRST EDITION

I think, I owe an explanation for bringing out yet another book on auditing when there are so many already in the market. I have taught this subject for many years and have always felt the need for a book which will not only be useful to the students for examination purposes but will also be useful from practical point of view.

This book does not claim any originality in regard to matter and facts since I had to depend for these on standard books published in India and outside on the subject. I have, however, tried to present the facts in such a way as to make it easy for the students to comprehend them.

I have taken special care to incorporate the latest Companies and other Acts as they refer to auditors and auditing. Legal cases have also been discussed at length. At the end of each chapter, questions set by universities and professional bodies are given. I hope the book will prove to be useful not only to the students who are to take university examinations but also to candidates who take professional and competitive examinations in the subject.

I take this opportunity to thank my esteemed colleague and friend Mr. A. Dasgupta, Head of the Commerce Department, Delhi Polytechnic and Professor of Business Administration, Delhi School of Economics, Delhi University, without whose encouragement it would not have been possible for me to bring out this book.

Suggestions for the improvement of the book from practising accountants, teachers and students will be very much appreciated.

AUTHOR

CONTENTS

Chapter 1

Introduction

Origin of Audit

The origin of audit may be traced to middle ages, but the audit in the present sense can be traced to aftermath of large scale production in consequence of industrial revolution during the eighteenth century. Goods produced for hand to mouth levels were started to be mass-produced for reaping the economies of scale and technology. As at and after industrial renaissance the following concepts and practices had begun to evolve - (a) appropriate funding of the business capital, (b) Managing the business by objectives rather than on the score of one owning it, implying that the management is a profession by itself and it would imply that there is marked preference for separation of class of investors as one type and managers/captains of industry as the other, (c) mushrooming of a plethora of auxiliary and facilitator services like banking, financing agencies, warehousing, stock market, depositories, risk managers, dispute resolution agents, factors, intelligence providers, Information technology system, Information technology enabled services etc. (d) Strict societal and governmental expectation of compliance to laid down norms like Acts, rules, orders in a scene of complicated entanglement of law to cite only a few. These called for-

(*i*) a creation of monitoring authority to ensure a review and correction mechanism, a system to effect, extract accountability from the mangers of the business- a sine quo non for the trust reposed on them for allowing the custody of societal funds including investors money, bank's finances, and in general all what the societal milieu and environment allowed them for to operate with and around, and

(*ii*) a paradigm of power-penalty suite to see that the appraisal agency accomplishes its task as is expected of it and it suffers for what it fails to do.

As a result, therefore, Auditing as an independent and professional medium emerged, not a part of industrial and business services- but as one separate, unique, independent, a class by itself, a par excellence, with robes of technical education, expertise, experience and self-regulated discipline for ensuring standards of quality of work befallen onto its shoulders.

Definition of Audit

The word "audit" is derived from the Latin word "*audire*" which means "to hear". In olden times, whenever the owners of a business suspected fraud, they appointed certain persons to check the accounts. Such persons sent for the accountants and "heard" whatever they had to say in connection with the accounts. It was an Italian, Luca Pacialo, who first published his treatise on double entry system of book-keeping for the first time in 1494. He mentioned and described the duties and responsibilities of an auditor. Since then, there have been lot of changes in the scope and definition of audit and the duties and responsibilities of an auditor.

As has been stated above, the original object of an audit was principally to see whether the accounting party has properly accounted for the receipts and payments of cash. In other words the object of audit was to find out whether cash has been embezzled and, if so, who embezzled it and what amount was involved. Thus, it was only an audit of cash book, but as will be seen later on, the principal object of modern audit is to see whether the Balance Sheet exhibits a true and fair view of the state of affairs of a company and whether it is drawn up according to the Companies Act, in the case of the audit of a company. Detection of fraud is an incidental object of modern audit. Since the Balance Sheet incorporates all personal and impersonal accounts and the balances of Profit and Loss Account, which in its turn, incorporates balances of nominal or fictitious accounts, we may safely say that the Balance Sheet for a particular period incorporates all the transactions, which took place during the period for which the Balance Sheet is prepared.

Spicer and Pegler, have defined Audit as "such as examination of the books, accounts and vouchers of a business, as will enable the auditor to satisfy himself that the balance sheet is properly drawn up, so as to give a true and fair view of the state of the affairs of the business, and whether the Profit and Loss Account gives a true and fair view of profit or loss for the financial period, according to the best of his information and the explanations given to him and as shown by the books; and if not, in what respect he is not satisfied."

F.R.M. de Paula, an English authority on auditing literatue, describes auditing as "the examination of a Balance Sheet and Profit and Loss Account prepared by others, together with the books, accounts, and vouchers relating thereto in such a manner that the auditor may be able to satisfy himself and honestly report that, in his opinion, such Balance Sheet is properly drawn up so as to exhibit a true and correct view of the state of affairs of the particular concern, according to the information and explanations given to him, and as shown by the books". He further continues that an "audit of a Balance Sheet involves the verification of the Profit and Loss Account, as the balance of that account must be included in some form or other in the former..."

J.R. Batliboi, a renowned authority on accounting and auditing defines auditing as "an intelligent and a critical scrutiny of the books of account of a business with the documents and vouchers from which they are written up, for the purpose of ascertaining whether the working results for a particular period, as shown by the Profit and Loss Account, as also the exact financial condition of that business, as reflected in the balance sheet are truely determined and presented by those responsible for their compilation"

The Institute of Chartered Accountants of India in its publication of Auditing and Assurance standard (AAS 1): Basic Principles Governing an Audit (AAS 1) describes audit as "the independent examination of financial information of any entity, whether profit oriented or not, and irrespective of its size or legal form, when such examination is conducted with a view to expressing an opinion thereon".

Montgomery, a leading American accountant, defines: "Auditing is a systematic examination of the books and records of a business or other organisation, in order to ascertain or verify, and to report upon the facts regarding its financial operations and the results thereof".

On a reading of these definitions, one can appreciate the following points as reflected in them:

(*a*) Auditing is to express an opinion on the quality of financial statements. Financial statements generally mean the balance sheet and profit and loss account. The financial statements of any entity may be subject to audit so that credence is added to them. The entity may be business organisations with profit motive or organisations with non-profit motive. They may be of any forms of organisation- companies or co-operatives where audit is compulsory or sole proprietorship or partnership where auditing is sought after by the entities voluntarily.

(b) The opinion on financial information is expressed after careful examination of books of account, documents, records and vouchers. That is, before an opinion is pronounced evidence is gathered and tested to form the basis for framing an opinion.

These views reflect various aspects of one of the dimensions of auditing, perhaps, as it was traditionally and essentially it is even today. But auditing is not all that. The contemporary auditing is not confined to attest function of financial statements. The scope of auditing has extended to various realms. Auditing is not concerned with review of financial data alone. It extends to review of such areas as systems, operations of any entity. In this connection, it is interesting to take note of the description of auditing by the Institute of Chartered Accountants of India in its "General Guidelines on Internal Auditing' (1983). It describes auditing as "a systematic and independent examination of data, statements, records, operations, and performances (financial or otherwise) of an enterprise for a stated purpose. In any auditing situation, the auditor perceives and recognises the propositions before him for examination, collects evidence, evaluates the same and on this basis formulates his judgement which is communicated through his audit report." This definition has shown the wider coverage of modern auditing - auditing extending to review of operations and performances connected with non-financial areas also. The purpose of audit need not necessarily to be expression of opinion about the quality of financial statements alone; it may be for any stated purpose like giving expert advice for improving efficiency, productivity of an enterprise or systematising the operations.

It is relevant, in this connection, to study the view of auditing as it is with reference to audit of government accounts.

The book "*An Introduction to Indian Government Accounts and Audit*", third edition, issued by Comptroller and Auditor General of India, defines audit: "Audit" is an instrument of financial control. It acts as a safeguard on behalf of the proprietor (whether an individual or a group of persons) against extravagance, carelessness or fraud on the part of the proprietor's agents or servants in the realisation and utilisation of his money or other assets, and it ensures on the proprietor's behalf that the accounts maintained truly represent facts and that expenditure has been incurred with due regularity and propriety. The agency employed for this purpose is called an 'auditor'. This view highlights ascertainment of financial propriety in auditing the funds of government.

From the above discussion, it is clear that the term audit generally implies audit of financial statements. In such an audit, the expert opinion of auditor is given about the quality of such statements or he merely attests the truth of the statements. In its widest scope, the term audit implies audit of non-financial matters as well, like audit of operations, efficiency etc. In such of those audits, the auditor tenders his expert advice also. *Hence it can be concluded that the audit means critical and intelligent examination of facts-financial or otherwise, to give in the form of certificate or report an attestation, an expert opinion or an expert advice.*

Difference between Book-keeping, Accountancy and Auditing

Before we proceed further, it is considered necessary that one should understand the difference between Book-keeping, Accountancy and Auditing:

1. Book-keeping is an art of recording the business transactions in the books of original entry and the ledgers. This work, to a great extent, is being done by junior clerks or by machines in Western countries. This work is of mechanical nature which does not require a knowledge of the principles of accountancy. On the other hand accountancy means the compilation of accounts in such a way that one is in a position to know the state of affairs of the business. The man who performs this work is called an accountant. His work is to interpret and review the accounts and draw conclusions with a view to guide the management in chalking out the future policy of the business. But auditing means the verification of book entries and accounts to find out their accuracy. It is neither book-

keeping, nor accountancy. His work is to find out whether the final accounts exhibit a true and fair view of the state of affairs of the concern or not and to report his findings to the shareholders.

2. The spade work is done by the book-keeper and the accountant while the finishing touch is given by the auditor or, as has been said, that where the work of an accountant ends, the work of an auditor begins.
3. Sometimes an auditor is asked to prepare from a set of books the trial balance, profit and loss account and balance sheet in which case he would be acting as an accountant and he would not be required to give his certificate at the foot of the balance sheet. He has simply to put his signature in token of his having prepared such a profit and loss account and balance sheet. On the other hand, an auditor has not to prepare the trial balance, profit and loss account and balance sheet. He is to report whether the profit and loss account and the balance sheet prepared by the accountant exhibit a true and fair view of the state of affairs of the concern and in the case of a company, they are drawn up according to the Companies Act.
4. A book-keeper and an accountant has to record the transactions in the books of accounts while an auditor has to check and verify such transactions and accounts and send a report to the persons who appointed him.

Auditing and Investigation

Sometimes students get an impression that auditing and investigation mean the same thing. There is a lot of difference between the two. Investigation means a searching enquiry into the profit-earning capacity or the financial position of a concern or to find out the extent of the fraud if there is any suspicion about it and so on.

1. Audit is conducted to find out whether the balance sheet is properly drawn up and exhibits a true and fair view of the state of affairs of a concern while investigation is carried out with a certain object in view, e.g., to find out the profit-earning capacity, or the financial position of a concern or a fraud and the extent thereof.
2. Investigation covers several years, say, 3, 5 or 7 years to find out the average earning capacity, financial position, etc., of a concern while audit usually relates to one year.
3. Investigation may be carried out on behalf of outsiders while audit is conducted on behalf of the proprietors only. However, investigation may also be carried out on behalf of proprietors in some cases where fraud or defalcation is suspected.

We shall, however, deal with this topic in detail, in the chapter on "Investigation".

Objects of an audit

"The Auditing and Assurance Standard: Objectives and Scope of Audit of Financial Statements–AAS 2" of the Institute of Chartered Accountants of India specifies that the objective of an audit is to express an opinion on financial statements. To give the opinion about the financial statements, the auditor examines the financial statements to satisfy himself about the truth and fairness of financial position and operating results of the enterprise. There are certain inherent limitations of audit examination. It would not be possible for auditor to discover all errors and frauds, in the financial statements due to the limitations of his checking. The AAS 2 of the Institute of Chartered Accountants of India, states that 'such discovery is not the main objective of audit." In this light, the objectives of audit can be categorised into (*i*) Main objectives (*ii*) secondary objective and (*iii*) specific objectives.

The main objective of audit is to express expert opinion on financial statements. The secondary objectives are (*i*) detection and prevention of errors and (*ii*) detection and prevention of frauds.

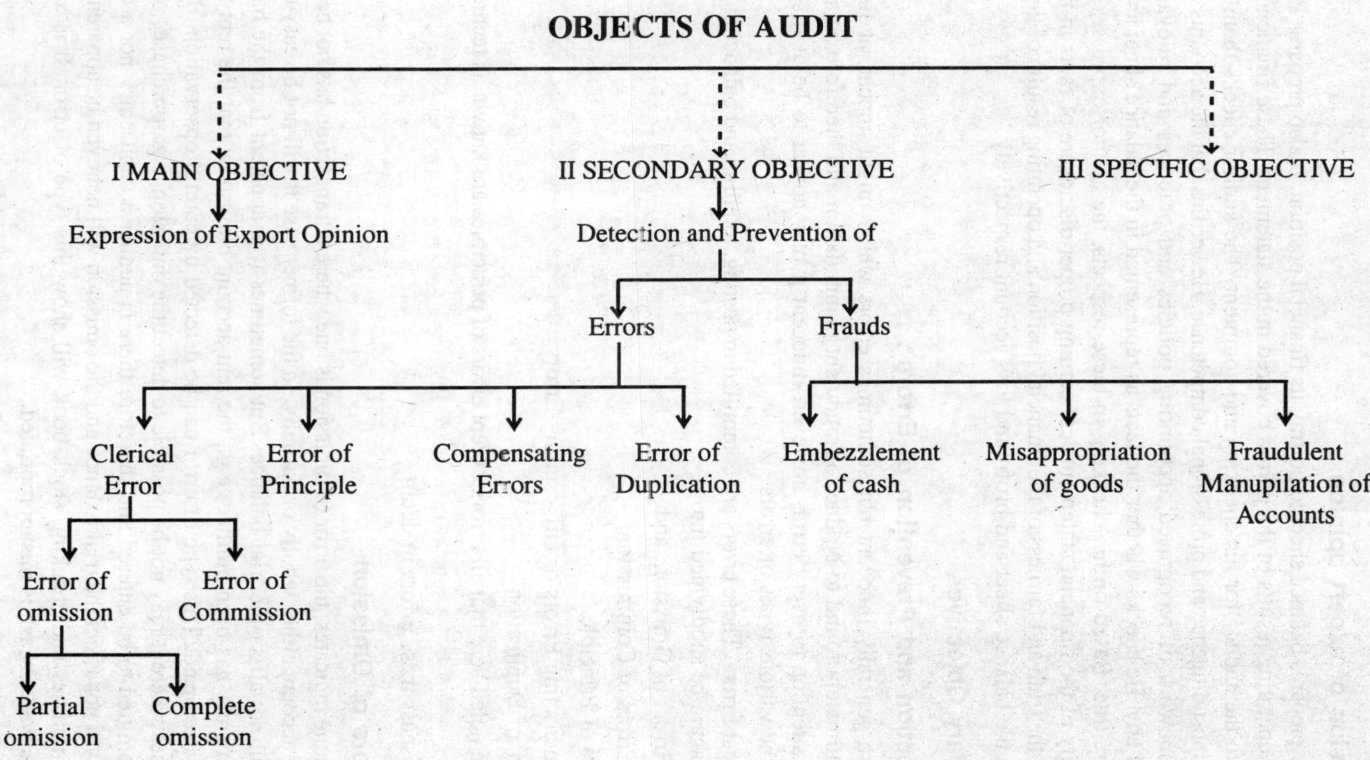
OBJECTS OF AUDIT
I MAIN OBJECTIVE
II SECONDARY OBJECTIVE
III SPECIFIC OBJECTIVE
Expression of Export Opinion
Detection and Prevention of
Errors
Frauds
Clerical Error
Error of Principle
Compensating Errors
Error of Duplication
Embezzlement of cash
Misappropriation of goods
Fraudulent Manupilation of Accounts
Error of omission
Error of Commission
Partial omission
Complete omission

I. Main Objective

Expression of expert opinion :

An entity prepares balance sheet to portray its financial position. It also prepares P&L account to disclose the operating results of the period covered in the statement. These financial statements are submitted to the auditor for his checking and comment. The auditor checks them in a careful manner with utmost diligence and professional competence. He verifies that the accounts are prepared within the framework of recognised accounting policies and practices and relevant statutory requirements if any. He checks whether the facts as represented in the balance sheet and profit and loss account are true. Based on his checking in these respects, the auditor expresses his opinion about the quality of the financial statements concerning proper disclosure of facts in the financial statements and the truth and fairness of the financial position and operating results of the enterprise, as disclosed in the balance sheet and profit and loss account respectively.

II. Secondary Objectives

(*i*) Detection and Prevention of Errors :

Errors are generally innocent but sometimes errors which might appear, at first sight, as innocent are ultimately found to be due to fraudulent manipulation and therefore an auditor must pay particular attention to every error, however, innocent it may appear to be at first sight. The following are the various types of errors

1. Clerical Errors. These errors are committed in posting, totalling and balancing. Such errors may again be subdivided into —
   (a) Errors of Omission; and
   (b) Errors of Commission.
2. Errors of Principle.
3. Compensating Errors or Off - setting Errors.
4. Errors of Duplication.

It may be noted here that all errors except errors of principles are known as technical clerical errors.

Let us discuss these errors in detail.

1. (*a*) Errors of Omission

As the name indicates, the error of omission is one where a transaction has not been recorded in the books of account either wholly or partially. In the former case it will not be easy to detect the error and it will not affect the trial balance. But sometimes it is apparent from the balance of an account that an entry has been omitted, e.g., the rent account may show that the rent for the 12th month has not been paid. This type of error can be detected by careful observation. But there are many other cases where it may not be possible to detect the omission, e.g., purchases or sales have entirely been omitted to be entered and therefore there is neither a debit entry nor a credit entry. Such an error will not affect the trial balance and the omission will not even be apparent. However, vouching of purchases and checking stock book will show this type of error. It is a method by which goods as well as cash is misappropriated.

But if one aspect of the purchases or sales has been entered in the books, it will affect the trial balance and the omission will be easily detectable. It may be due to the fact that the item has not been posted although the entry has been made in the books of original entry. If a transaction has been intentionally omitted to be entered in the books of account, it will affect results shown by the accounts and affect the ultimate profit or loss.

(*b*) Errors of Commission

When a transaction has been recorded but has been wrongly entered in the books of original entry or posted in the ledger, error of commission is said to have been made, e.g., a purchase invoice for Rs. 1,250 was entered in the purchase book as Rs. 1,520. Such an error may be intentional or un-intentional. The underlying idea may be to mis-appropriate cash, in league with the seller of the goods. Therefore, vouching should be done very carefully, in order to detect such an error or fraud. Other errors of commission are, wrong castings, calculations, postings, extensions, carry forwards, etc. Some of such errors will be detected by the non-agreement of the trial balance. On the other hand, if a mistake has been committed in the invoice for the sale of goods, the error will not be detected, as the mistake will appear, both in the original books as well as in the ledger.

2. Errors of Principle

Such errors arise when the entries are not recorded according to the fundamental principles of accountancy, e.g., wrong allocation of expenditure between capital and revenue, ignoring the outstanding assets and liabilities, valuation of assets against the principles of book-keeping.

Such errors may be committed either intentionally, or unintentionally. If they are committed intentionally, the object is to falsify and manipulate the accounts either to show more profits or less profits than they actually are. Such errors ultimately affect the profit and loss account and the balance sheet. Therefore, it is very important for an auditor to pay particular attention towards this type of error. Such an error is not disclosed by the trial balance or by routine checking. It can be detected only by a searching inquiry and independent checking.

3. Compensating Errors or Off-setting Errors

A Compensating error or off-setting error is one which is counter-balanced by any other error or errors, e.g., if A's account was to be debited for Rs. 100 but was debited for Rs. 10 while B's account which was to be debited for Rs. 10 was debited for Rs. 100. Thus, both the accounts have been debited for a total sum of Rs. 110 which amount ought to have been debited or a sale of Rs. 10 to A is posted to the debit of B as Rs. 5, and the purchases book is over-cast by Rs. 5. Again, an over-casting of an account may be counter-balanced by the under-casting of another account to the same extent. These errors are most dangerous and are difficult to guard against. This type of error will not be detected by the trial balance. Such an error will not affect the trial balance and will not be detected easily. This error may or may not effect the profit and loss account.

4. Errors of Duplication

Such errors arise when an entry in a book of original entry has been made twice and has also been posted twice.

Location of Errors

The question is how to locate an error if the trial balance does not agree and the auditor is called upon to locate the error although it is not his duty to do so. If the following steps are taken, there will be no difficulty in finding out an error:

1. Check the totals of the trial balance.
2. Compare the names of the accounts in the ledger with the names of the accounts as have been recorded in the trial balance. It is possible that balance of some accounts might not have been transferred to the trial balance especially in the case of the balance of cash book, purchases and sales book, bills books, etc.
3. Total the lists of debtors and creditors and compare them with the trial balance.

4. If the books are maintained on the self-balancing system; see that the total of different accounts agrees with the total of these accounts with the balance of accounts as recorded in the trial balance.
5. Compare the items of the trial balance with the items of the trial balance of the previous year to see if any item has been omitted.
6. Whatever be the difference in the trial balance, halve it and see if there is any item of this value. This is done to avoid the putting of the debit balance on the credit side of the trial balance or *vice versa*.
7. It is possible that the totals of some subsidiary books, e.g., Cash Book, Purchases Book, Sales Book, etc., might not have been transferred to the trial balance. Re-check the totals of these books.

If in spite of the above steps the error cannot be located the error may be due to the following causes:

1. An error say of Rs. 1 or 10 or 100, etc., i.e., a round sum may be due to wrong totalling. If the difference is in rupees and paise, it may be due to wrong posting or extracting a wrong balance.
2. An error which is divisible by 9 may be due to misplacement or transposition of figures, e.g., 32 for 23, 52 for, 25,or 54 for 45 and so on.

It may be remembered that in spite of the fact that the trial balance has agreed, it does not mean that there are no errors.

II. Detection and Prevention of Fraud

Having dealt with the detection and prevention of errors, let us now proceed to discuss the detection and prevention of fraud.

Fraud means false representation or entry made intentionally or without belief in its truth with a view to defraud somebody.

Detection of fraud is considered to be one of the important duties of an auditor. As a matter of fact, originally audit was conducted mainly with a view to detect fraud whenever it was suspected. The system of internal check aims at the prevention of fraud. If the auditor finds that the internal check system is defective and will not prevent the commission of frauds, he should suggest a better system.

The following are the chief ways in which fraud may be perpetrated:

1. Embezzlement of Cash;
2. Misappropriation of Goods; and
3. Fraudulent manipulation of Accounts.

1. Embezzlement of Cash

There is a greater possibility of defalcation of money in a big business house than in the case of a small proprietary business where the proprietor has a direct control over the receipts and payments of cash. In a big business house, the system of receipt and payment of cash should be such that the work of one clerk is automatically checked by another clerk. Such a system is known in auditing as "Internal Check" system which will be dealt with in detail later on. It is easier to misappropriate cash, and, therefore, the auditor will do well to pay particular attention towards cash transactions.

Cash may be misappropriated by

(*a*) omitting to enter any cash which has been received; or
(*b*) entering less amount than what has been actually received; or

(c) making fictitious entries on the payment side of the cash book; or
(d) entering more amount on the payment side of the cash book than what has been actually paid.

In order to discover fraud under (a) and (b) above, the auditor should check the debit side of the cash book with rough cash book, salesmen's reports, counterfoils of the receipt books, agents returns and other original records while the fraud under (c) and (d) can be discovered by reference to the vouchers, wage sheets, salary book, invoice, etc.

2. Misappropriation of Goods

Again, fraud may be in respect of goods, *i.e.*, misappropriation of goods. This type of fraud is very difficult to detect especially when the goods are less bulky and are of higher value. Proper methods of keeping accounts in regard to purchases and sales, stock taking, periodical checking of stocks, comparing the perçentage of gross profit to sales of two periods, necessity for collusion will help to avoid misappropriation of goods.

3. Fraudulent manipulation of Accounts

This type of fraud is more difficult to discover as it is usually committed by directors or managers or other responsible officials with the object of

(a) showing more profits than what actually they are (i) so that if they get commission on profits, they may get more commission; or (ii) their service may be retained by showing to the shareholders that because of their efficiency they have shown more profits and thus maintain the confidence of the shareholders or (iii) if they hold shares, they may sell them at high price by declaring higher dividends; or (iv) to obtain further credit by showing the financial position of the business better than what actually it is; or (v) to attract more subscribers for the sale of the shares of the company, etc.; or

(b) showing less profits than what actually they are (i) in order to purchase shares in the market at a lower price; or (ii) to reduce or avoid the payment of income tax; or (iii) to give a wrong impression about the success of the business to competitors, etc.

Falsification of accounts may be resorted to

(a) by not providing any depreciation or providing less depreciation or providing more depreciation ; or
(b) by under-valuation or over-calculation of assets and liabilities; or
(c) by showing fictitious sales or purchases or returns in order to show more profits or less profits whatever the case may be; or
(d) by the utilization of secret reserves during a period when the concern has made less or no profit, without disclosing that fact to the shareholders; or
(e) by sharing revenue expenditure to capital account, or *vice versa*; or
(f) by crediting the revenue account with the income which will be received next year or not crediting the profit and loss account with the income which has accured but which has not been received.

Such frauds are difficult to detect as they are committed by the people at the helm of affairs who are presumed to be trustworthy, honest and responsible, and, therefore, no suspicion falls on them. They are very cleverly made and, as such, the auditor should be very careful in detecting such frauds. He should carry out the routine checking and vouching most carefully and make searching, tactful and intelligent inquiries.

Position of auditor in regard to errors and frauds affecting financial statements

The auditor carries out necessary checks before expressing his opinion on the truth and fairness of financial position and operating results of an entity as reflected in financial statements. The auditor seeks to ensure that there is no material misstatement of financial information arising from errors or frauds. However, there is possibility that some material misstatement of financial information resulting from errors or frauds may creep in the financial statements. The misstatement may be subsequently found out. Can such subsequent discovery of the happening of errors or fraud point to the fact that the auditor has not performed his audit properly? Is auditor liable for his omission to unearth the errors or frauds?

The auditor is an expert in his own field. He must have adequate expertise to testify the financial statements as to their truth and fairness. Definitely he must have at his disposal specialised skills to unravel the mess of errors and frauds. He is not to be merely written off as mere "adder - upper and subtractor". He must bring to bear upon in discharge of his duties such skill and diligence that he holds out to possess. He must, with utmost duty of care, skill of expertise and professional diligence, check the accounts to ensure that there is no material misstatements of financial information arising from errors or frauds.

But, it is to be remembered that there are certain limitations as to the audit. The auditor cannot check every item of the financial transactions. He applies test checking of material items. The test nature of audit involves inherent risks associated with it. Secondly, the evidence he relies are only indicative and not conclusive in many of the cases. Thirdly, it is the responsibility of the management to introduce such in-built control system in the operational and accounting system as to reduce the chance of happening of errors or frauds. Even the management cannot completely eliminate the happening of errors or frauds; they can only reduce their occurrences. Fourthly, the management may, sometimes, flout its good conscience and make false representation to the auditor in respect of matters for which auditor has no other means of checking. Finally, frauds committed with ingenuity is difficult to be detected within a limited period of audit checking. The instances like these hinder the auditor in his checking to detect errors or frauds that may affect the financial information materially.

Then what is expected of the auditor in such a circumstance? The auditor is not expected to apply in his duty nothing more than reasonable skill and diligence as would be exercised by a professional of his category. He is expected to do the audit according to the generally accepted auditing practices (more details of this are discussed in chapter II). With necessary skill, diligence and care, if he expresses his opinion, he is relieved of any misstatement in financial information resulting from errors or frauds. What is the requisite degree of skill, care and diligence is a matter of specific factual circumstances of individual instances.

As observed by the learned judge in a famous Kingston Cotton Mills case (1896), the auditor is only a watchdog and not a blood hound. However, when there are circumstances arousing his suspicion, he must be doubly alert. He must so modify or enlarge his audit procedure and extent of checking to ascertain the truth. He must not recklessly leave unattended the grounds of suspicion when he encounters them. It was said in the judgement of the case Armitage vs Brewer and Knott (1932). "That one piece of paper raised a grave suspicion. It was of critical importance. It was by little things like that forgeries and frauds were found out." In the case *State Street Trust Co., vs Ernest* (1938), it was said that the auditor is acting not properly if there is "a refusal to see the obvious, a failure to investigate doubtful, if sufficiently gross".

The position of the auditor in regard to errors and frauds can be summarised as follows:

1. It is the responsibility of management to prevent errors and frauds.
2. The auditor is not liable for any subsequent discovery of misstatement of financial information resulting from errors and frauds, if he carried out his duty according to the generally accepted auditing practices.
3. If he discovers any errors or frauds during his audit, he must see that the errors are corrected and the effect of fraud on financial information of the financial statements is

properly reflected. He must also bring to the notice of the concerned, the occurrence of fraud at the earliest time.

4. The auditor need not sniff for errors and frauds. But, if he smells something about it, he should not leave them carelessly. He must enlarge his extent of checking and modify checking procedures to suit the occasion.

III. Specific Objectives

We have emphasised that the term audit should not be taken to imply financial audit alone, in the definition' topic. The audit may encompass such other areas like review of operations, performance management policy, cost records and so on. Accordingly, there will be specific objective in respect of each type of such specific audits. For example, in operational audit, the aim of audit is to evaluate the existing operations of the entity in order to give expert advice to improve their efficiency. The cost audit is to check the cost records of the entity in order to make a report on the proper ascertainment of cost of production of goods or services. Depending upon the nature of specific audit engagement and terms of engagement, there may be different objective in respect of each specific audit.

Different Classes of Audit

The audit may be classified into

(*a*) On the basis of legislative control-statutory audit, Government audit, private audit.

(*b*) On the basis of relation of auditor vis a vis management-external audit, internal audit.

(*c*) On the basis of periodicity of audit-continuous audit, interim audit, periodical audit, occasional audit.

(*d*) On the basis of subject matter of audit-financial audit, operational audit, cost audit, management audit.

(*e*) On the basis of coverage of audit-complete audit, partial audit.

(*f*) On the basis of manner of checking-standard audit, balance sheet audit, post and vouch audit.

A. Legislative Control :

Where the appointment of auditors, manner of audit, contents of audit report etc., are specifically mentioned in any enactment, the audit conducted with reference to them is called statutory audit. Statutory audit is a compulsory audit and is to be carried out each year by an auditor called 'statutory auditor'. In India, the accounts of joint stock companies, banking companies, insurance companies, co-operative societies, trust institutions are subject to compulsory (statutory) audit. The Companies Act, for example, contains provisions dealing with the appointment of auditor, rights and duties of auditor, matters to be included in audit report and so on. The Banking Regulation Act of 1949 deals with the audit of banking companies. Co-operative societies Act, Public and charitable trust Acts of various states deal with the audit of these entities. Similarly the life and general insurance audits are governed by special enactments concerning these entities.

The audit of accounts of Union of India, States, Government departments, undertakings, local bodies are done by government auditors. The appointment of auditor is as per the articles of the Constitution of India. Under article 148 of the constitution, the President of India shall appoint 'the Comptroller and Auditor General of India (C&AG), who is the prime authority in the audit hierarchy of government accounts. Each state has its auditor general. To audit the accounts of municipalities, universities and other government institutions, local fund auditors are appointed. The C&AG submits the audit report of accounts under his jurisdiction to the President. The audit report of the C&AG is laid before the parliament for a debate on it. Similarly the state legislature considers the audit report of the accounts laid before them. With regard to the audit of government companies and

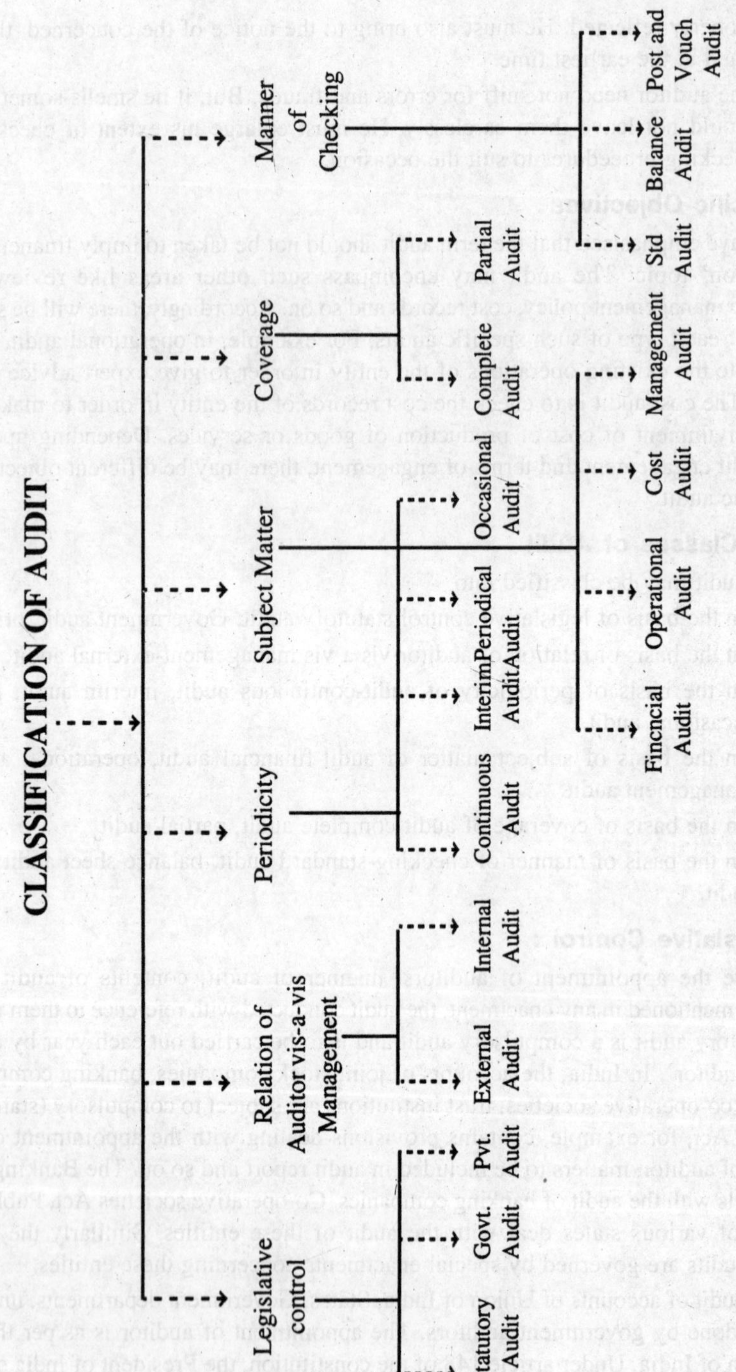
CLASSIFICATION OF AUDIT
Legislative control
Relation of Auditor vis-a-vis Management
Periodicity
Subject Matter
Coverage
Manner of Checking
Statutory Audit
Govt. Audit
Pvt. Audit
External Audit
Internal Audit
Continuous Audit
Interim Audit
Periodical Audit
Occasional Audit
Fincncial Audit
Operational Audit
Cost Audit
Management Audit
Complete Audit
Partial Audit
Std Audit
Balance Audit
Post and Vouch Audit

public sector undertakings, the auditor is appointed by central government on the advice of C&AG. The C&AG shall have power to give directions to the company auditor; he can conduct supplementary audit also. The auditor submits his report to C&AG who comments on it and cause it to be placed before parliament.

In case of private audit, there is no statutory or constitutional compulsion to get the accounts audited. For example, the sole proprietors, partnership firms get their accounts audited without compulsion in view of advantages of having audit.

B. Relation of Auditor vis a vis Management

The audit is said to be external if the appointment of auditor is made by persons other than those whose performance is evaluated by auditor. For example, the directors of the company are responsible for the activities of the company. They present an account of company's performance to the shareholders through P&L account and Balance sheet. The statutory auditor is said to be external auditor because he is appointed not by the management but by the shareholders. The external auditor is an independent person. The scope of his audit cannot be curtailed by the management. The external auditor submits his report to the appointing authority, say, shareholders in case of joint stock companies. Generally, the external auditor verifies the truth and fairness of financial information as reflected in financial statements of the entity.

On the other hand, an audit is said to be internal when the auditor is appointed by persons who are responsible for the performance of the entity. An internal auditor is usually appointed by management of the company. In many cases the internal auditor is in regular employment of the entity. In few cases, external audit firms are engaged to conduct internal audit. However their terms of appointment, remuneration and scope of audit work etc are determined by the management. The internal auditor is not complelly independent. The scope of his work can be controlled by the management. The internal auditor submits his audit report to the chief of management team. The internal auditor generally extends his review to non-financial areas as well. Besides verifying financial data generated in accounting system of the entity, the internal auditor evaluates the existing systems, operations and policies to suggest improvement in respect of them. The internal audit report is more in the nature of management information report. The management is at liberty to take appropriate action on internal audit report.

C. Periodicity of Audit

Based on the frequency with which the audit is conducted, the audit is classified into continuous audit, periodical audit, interim audit, and occasional audit.

I. A Continuous Audit or a detailed audit as it is sometimes called is an audit which involves a detailed examination of the books of account at regular intervals of, say, one month or three months. The auditor visits his clients at regular or irregular intervals during the financial year and checks each and every transaction. At the end of the year he checks the profit and loss account and the balance sheet. A continuous audit is not of much use to a small concern as its accounts can be audited at the end of the financial year without much loss of time.

Businesses where Continuous Audit is Applicable

1. Where it is desired to present the accounts just after the close of the financial year, as in the case of a bank.
2. Where the volume of the transactions is very large.
3. Where the statement of accounts is required to be presented to the management after every month or quarter.
4. Where no satisfactory system of internal check is in operation.

Advantages of Continuous Audit

1. *Easy and quick Discovery of Errors*: Errors and frauds can be discovered easily and quickly as the auditor checks the accounts at regular intervals and in detail. If he were to check the accounts after one year, it would be difficult to locate an error. As the auditor visits his clients, say, after a month or two or so, the number of transactions will be small and hence the errors will be detected easily and quickly.
2. *Knowledge of Technical Details:* Since the auditor remains more in touch with the business, he is in a position to know the technical details of it and hence can be of great help to his clients by making valuable suggestions.
3. *Quick Presentation of Accounts:* Most of the checking work having been already performed during the course of the year, the final audited accounts can be presented to the shareholders soon after the close of the financial year at the annual general meeting.
4. *Keeps the Client's Staff Regular*: As the auditor visits the clients, at regular intervals, the clerks will be very regular in keeping the accounts up-to-date. They will see that there is no inaccuracy or frauds as it would be detected by the auditor at his next visit.
5. *Moral Check on the Client's Staff*: If the auditor pays surprise visits, it will have a considerable moral check on the clerks preparing the accounts as they do not know when the auditor may pay a visit to check the accounts. The moral check will be more than in the case of Interim Audit described in the following pages.
6. *Efficient Audit*: The auditor, having more time at his disposal, can check the accounts with greater attention and in detail and his work will be more efficient.
7. *Preparation of Interim Accounts*: Where the directors of a company wish to declare an interim dividend, continuous audit will help in the preparation of the interim accounts without much delay.
8. *Audit Staff can be kept busy*: The audit staff may be sent to other clients after having finished the work for one client. Thus whole of the staff can be kept busy throughout the year.

Disadvantages of Continuous Audit

In spite of the above-mentioned advantages of a continuous audit, there are certain drawbacks of such an audit which are as under:

1. *Alternation of Figures*: Figures in the books of account which have already been checked by the auditor at his previous visit, may be altered by a dishonest clerk and the frauds may thus be perpetrated.
2. *Dislocation of Client's work*: The frequent visits by the auditor may dislocate the work of his client and cause inconvenience to the latter.
3. *Expensive*. It is an expensive system of audit.
4. *Queries may Remain Outstanding*: The audit clerk may lose the thread of his work and the queries which he wanted to make may remain outstanding as there might be a long interval between the two visits.
5. The staff of the client may depend upon the audit staff to help other out of difficulties in the course of their work, e.g., to discover an error which they could not discover and thus entail upon the time of the audit staff.
6. Extensive note taking may be necessary in order to avoid any alteration in the figures after the audit.

These disadvantages and dangers are perhaps more theoretical than real. However, they may be avoided by taking the following precautions:

1. No alteration should be allowed to be made after the entries have been checked by the auditor, without his permission.
2. If any alteration has to be made, it should be done by means of a rectifying entry in the journal.
3. Checking of a book should be complete as far as possible at one visit to avoid loose ends. However, if this is not possible, the auditor should check the transactions up to a particular date and make a note of it in his diary and, if possible, he should make a note of the totals up to that date in his diary or note-book and compare them at his next visit.
4. Well drawn-up programme by the auditor will prevent any loose ends.
5. A note should be made in the Audit Note Book regarding any queries which have not been satisfactorily answered. However, efforts should be made to get the matter settled rather than carry forward such queries the precise significance of which might be forgotten at a later date.
6. If any alteration in a figure has already been made, the auditor should put a secret tick against such a figure. He may enter inset, in the coloured pencil, the correct figure or he may rewrite the correct figure in a different coloured ink and tick it as usual.
7. Before he begins the work, the auditor should glance over any alteration, which does not bear any secret tick.
8. The audit of Impersonal, General or Private Ledger should be conducted at the time of final audit as there is a greater possibility of fraud being committed by making fictitious entries in the nominal accounts which affect the personal accounts.
9. He should pay surprise visits so that the clerks of the client may not know the exact date of the visit of the auditor.

II. Periodical Audit or Final Audit or Complete Audit. Periodical audit is one which is taken up at the close of the financial or trading period when all the accounts have been balanced and a Trading and Profit and Loss Accounts and the Balance Sheet have been prepared. It may also commence before the final accounts are prepared and continue till the audit is completed even after the close of the financial or trading period. The only thing is that the audit is completed in one continuous session. At this jucture, the auditor gets hold of the books and checks the accounts. He is in possession of the full facts relating to accounts for the year under review. In the case of such an audit, the auditor visits his client only once a year and goes on checking the accounts until the audit work for the whole of the period is completed.

The Final Audit lacks the advantages which result in the case of Continuous Audit. If the auditor has several clients whose financial year ends on the same date, it may be difficult for the auditor to finish the work of all his clients. But the advantages are that there is less danger of manipulation of figures after they have been checked. Moreover, the auditor has not to maintain a big establishment for the purpose. Preparation of the time table for audit for the audit staff is made easy.

Though his type of audit is sometimes called Complete or Detailed Audit the expression is erroneous because each and every transaction is seldom checked in a big business house. Therefore, these expressions are misleading.

This type of audit is satisfactory especially in the case of small concerns. This class of audit is usually adopted by almost all concerns. But in the case of large concerns, it takes more time to complete the audit and hence presentation of accounts to the shareholders is delayed. The shareholders are usually very anxious for the dividends which cannot be declared until the final accounts have been prepared and audited.

III. Interim Audit. Some writers opine that an audit which is conducted in between the two annual audits, with a view to find out interim profits to enable to company to declare an Interim

Dividend, should be called Interim Audit. It is a kind of audit which is conducted between the two Periodical or Balance Sheet Audits.

Advantages of Interim Audit

1. This type of audit is good where the publication of the interim figures are necessary.
2. The final audit can be completed very soon, if there has been an interim audit.
3. Errors and frauds can be more quickly found and detected during the course of the year.
4. There is a moral check on the staff of the client as the accounts are checked say, after three or six months.

Disadvantages of Interim Audit

1. Figures may be altered in the accounts which have already been audited.
2. It will mean that the audit staff will have to prepare notes when they finish the interim audit.
3. This means additional work.

Lest the students might confuse the Interim Audit with Continuous Audit, we give below the points of distinction between the two types of audits.

Distinction between the Continuous Audit and Interim Audit

1. In the case of Continuous Audit, the work of audit is carried on up to any date according to the convenience of the auditor and his client while in the case of Interim Audit, the work of audit is up to a definite date according to the instructions of the client.
2. In the case of Continuous Audit, the verification of assets and liabilities is done after the balance sheet has been prepared at the end of the accounting period while in the case of Interim Audit the assets and liabilities are verified when such an audit is conducted.
3. In the case of Continuous Audit, no trial balance is prepared though the totals of certain accounts may be noted while in the case of Interim Audit the trial balance has to be prepared or checked.
4. In the case of Continuous Audit, the object is not to know the profit or loss while the Interim Audit is conducted with the object of finding the profit or the loss.

The question often asked is, what type of audit is satisfactory which may be adopted, as both the continuous and periodical audits have advantages as well as drawbacks.

It is suggested that a continuous audit followed by the final audit conducted by another independent auditor is the most satisfactory type of audit although it is very expensive. The type of audit to be adopted depends upon the magnitude of the business.

IV. Occasional Audit. As the name indicates, this type of audit is conducted once a while whenever the need arises and the client desires it to be carried out. This is possible only in case of proprietor concerns such as a sole-trader's business or a partnership business.

D. Subject matter of Audit

On the basis of subject matter of the audit, the audit may be classified into financial audit, cost audit, operational audit and management audit.

I. Financial audit is examination of financial statements to express opinion on the truth and fairness of financial condition and operating results of the entity. The statutory or external audit is generally financial audit.

II. Cost audit is audit of cost records of the company. It is checking of cost accounts and costing techniques, methods, system followed by the entity. The cost audit seeks to verify the truth and fairness of cost of production of goods or rendering of service by an entity. The Companies Act contains reference to cost audit in section 233B. It lays down that the central government may, by order, direct that the cost records maintained by the company be subject to cost audit. The cost audit is generally carried out by cost accountants within the meaning of Cost and Works Accountants Act 1959. In case of companies the cost auditors are appointed by board of directors. The cost audit report is submitted to the management and to the central government, in case of cost audit of companies.

III. Operational audit is review of operations of an entity. It is generally carried out by internal auditors. It involves intelligent examination of various operations of functional areas of the business viz production, marketing, stores etc, observing weakness, lapses, inefficiency in the operations and suggesting ways to strengthen the system, for averting lapses and for improving efficiency and profitability of the operations.

IV. Management audit is critical review of policy and practices of management. It involves review of various process of management. For example, the audit involves checking of objectives for their relevance, clarity and dissemination downward the structure in understandable terms; the examination of organisational hierarchy-authority-responsibility relationship, departmentation; the quality of control techniques; the style of direction practised by management etc.

E. Coverage of Audit

On the basis of coverage of audit, the audit may be complete audit or partial audit. In complete audit, there is no restriction placed on auditor in the matter of coverage of audit. The auditor checks up all books of accounts with connected records to express opinion on the final financial statements. The client cannot put any restriction with regard to coverage of audit in case of statutory audit. Therefore it is an example of complete audit. In case of partial audit, usually the areas to be covered in audit are delimited by specific agreement to this effect. For example, the auditor may be asked to carry out the cash audit alone, to ensure that there is no falsification of cash account. Or the auditor may be asked to limit his checking only with respect to purchases effected during a particular month when the proprietor suspects certain irregularities during the period in respect thereof. When the auditor accepts partial audit, he should clearly mention in his report that he has performed only partial audit as per instructions of his client.

F. Manner of Checking

On the basis of manner of checking the audit may be classified into standard audit, balance sheet audit and post and vouch audit.

I. Standard Audit :

Mr. Irish of Australia defines Standard Audit in his book *Theory and Practice of Auditing* as "This embraces a complete check and analysis of certain items and, contingent upon effective internal check, appropriate test checks on remaining items, the whole of the work being in accord with general auditing standards quite adequate to justify un unqualified opinion."

From the definition it would appear that certain items in the accounts are thoroughly checked and analysed and appropriate test checks are applied to other items provided there is a good and effective internal check in operation.

II. Balance Sheet Audit :

Balance Sheet Audit is of recent growth as compared to other types of audits which we have already dealt with. This type of audit is more popular in U.S.A. than in England or other countries. With the development of industries and consequently the establishment of larger economic units, Balance Sheet Audit will be more widely used in future. The term "balance sheet audit" means verification of the values of assets, liabilities, the balances of reserves and provisions and the amount of profit earned, or loss suffered by a firm during the year. Prof. Howard F. Stettler is of opinion that even the audit which concentrates on the balance sheet must include some review of operations, e.g., repair and maintenance expense accounts should be reviewed to ascertain whether any expenditure of a capital nature has been improperly expensed. However, as mentioned earlier the item Profit and Loss Account does appear in the balance sheet and hence the auditor who conducts balance sheet audit does review the transactions which appear in the profit and loss account.

Procedure to conduct Balance Sheet Audit:

1. The auditor should examine the minute book of the concern, especially those items which have a bearing on the accounts.
2. He should examine and compare the profit and loss account with that of the previous year to see whether there is any material difference between the two.
3. He should compare the increase or decease in the expenses between the two periods with the turnover, making necessary adjustments regarding allowances, sales tax or any other variations during the period under reviews.
4. He should investigate into the cause of any variation in the gross profit and pay attention to the valuation of closing stock.
5. He should see whether there has been any change in the rate of depreciation charged during the current year and if so, what is its effect on the revenue account.
6. He should investigate into the items of non-recurring nature, *e.g.*, profit made or loss suffered on the sale of a fixed asset.
7. He should pay attention to any substantial change in the fixed assets as compared to the previous year especially regarding the valuation of assets.
8. Similarly any variation in the current assets as compared to previous year should be inquired into.
9. If there is any material alteration in the pre-payments and the accruals, he should pay attention to such a variation.
10. He should pay attention to other items of the balance sheet for any substantial change from the normal figure.
11. He should verify the assets held and liabilities owing.
12. He should ascertain whether any capital commitment exists and whether there is any item on which a subsequent loss may arise and whether any provision has been made therefor.

Position of Auditor in the case of Balance Sheet Audit

When the auditor checks only the items appearing on the balance sheet under this system, naturally he does not check all the transactions taking place but Section 227 (3) requires him to state in his report *inter* alia, "whether the balance sheet and the profit and loss account dealt with by the report are in agreement with the books of account and returns". Hence how can he honestly say so. Thus it may be inferred that he has not performed his duty honestly when he signs such financial statements. Of course, law does not prescribe any procedure or lays down any method by which the audit of a firm is to be conducted. However, if he is satisfied that he has discharged his duties and responsibilities by conducting the balance sheet audit, he may do so.

Under this type of audit, the audit is commenced from the balance sheet working back to the books of original entry and the relative documents, etc. The conventional method of vouching and casting, posting, etc., are dispensed with.

The Australian accountant, Mr. Irish, in this book *Practical Auditing* states on page 222. "Balance Sheet Audit" is an American term which is capable of two meanings:

1. It means limited audit in which all the balance sheet accounts are verified and tests imposed only on those profit and loss items which are directly related to the assets such as repairs

and maintenance, depreciation or bad debts. Accounts such as these are analysed, but otherwise no detailed audit is conducted.

2. In such a balance sheet audit tests are imposed on internal control but generally for a specific period. In any case, the transactions for the closing months of the year are closely scrutinised. Further tests include scrutiny of records, comparison of income and expenses, investigation of material fluctuations and analysis of appropriation accounts.

Balances Sheet Audit can prove to be more efficient when there is a good system of internal check or control in operation. This type of audit can prove to be more efficient (a) in big business concerns where the volume of transactions are very large, (b) where there is a good and efficient system of internal check and control, (c) where qualified accountants are employed, and (d) where mechanised accounting system is in operation. In Balance Sheet Audit, the audit work like vouching and casting which is considered necessary under the normal audit, is dispensed with.

III. Vouch and Post Audit

Vouch and post audit is that where the auditor checks each and every transaction right from its origin in the books of prime entries till they are posted. This system of audit has become obsolete in the case of large firms where the number of transactions run into millions and where a good internal check system is prevalent or where the mechanised system of accounting has been introduced. The auditor relies on the examination of some of the transactions scientifically selected at random.

Procedure

How to proceed with the work will depend upon the circumstances of each particular case. The method of work varies with the training, experience, and knowledge of the auditor. Some general points are given below:

Distinctive ticks of different colours for, say, additions, postings, ledger balances, carry forwards, etc., should be adopted. The significance of these ticks should not be made known to the clerks of the client. The same kind of 'tick' should not be used for every firm and for the same kind of transactions or for all the visits. As far as possible the work of checking of one book should be completed at one sitting for if it is not done, some fraudulent alterations may be made by the clerks after the audit clerk has left the office for the day. On the next visit, the audit clerk should see that there has been no alteration by rubber or by scratching of the work he had already checked on the previous visit. If it has been done, he should get an explanation and check the whole of the work again. If any adjustment is found to be necessary, it should be made by a journal entry and no alteration of a figure should be allowed. Special ticks should be used for figures which had already been erased. The auditor should write the correct figure with his own ink just close to the erased one and tick his own figure or he should put a circle around the erased figure with a coloured pencil. Pencil figures should not be accepted. It sometimes happens that the clients put the total figures with pencil. The auditor should refuse to commence his work until these figures are inked. The audit clerk should not balance the books. It is not his duty. Sometimes he is asked to balance the books, in which case he will be acting in the capacity of an accountant rather than an auditor. Frequently, the auditor is asked to begin the audit work even before the balancing of books, so that the audit may be completed sooner. However, this procedure should be discouraged as there is a danger of the errors being overlooked because there has been no clerical test like the preparation of the trial balance. No transaction should be passed unless he understands it, for an auditor must not certify what he does not believe to be true.

The auditor should not discuss anything in regard to the meaning of different 'ticks', etc., lest the clients's staff should know about the secret meaning and defraud the auditor. Vouching should be carried out by two clerks, the senior examining the voucher and calling out the amount and the junior comparing the amount and placing a special tick against the item in the Cash Book. When speaking out the figures, the audit clerk must be very clear in speaking out the figures, otherwise mistakes may crop in, e.g., when one clerk calls out the figure as Rs. 60. P.9, he might be understood as Rs. 69. Therefore the clerk should make a pause between 60 and 9. Similarly there might be confusion between ninety and nineteen, eighty and eighteen, etc. It would be advisable to pronounce ninety as ninetie and so on.

Advantages of an Audit

On account of the following advantages people get their accounts audited especially in case where audit is not compulsory:

1. Errors and frauds are located at an early date and in future no attempt is made to commit such frauds or one is rather careful not to commit an error or a fraud as the accounts are subject to regular audit.
2. The auditing of accounts keeps the accounts clerks regular and vigilant as they know that the auditors would complain against them if the accounts are not prepared up-to-date or if there is any irregularity.
3. In case of fire, the insurance company may settle the claim on the basis of the audited accounts of the previous years.
4. Money can be borrowed easily on the basis of previous audited balance sheet.
5. If the business is to be sold as a going concern, there will not be much difficulty regarding the valuation of assets and goodwill as the accounts have already been subject to audit by an independent person.
6. Income-tax authorities generally accept the profit and loss account which has been prepared by a qualified auditor and they do not go into details of the accounts.
7. The management may consult the auditor and seek his advice on certain technical points although it is not the duty of an auditor to give advice.
8. If the accounts have been prepared on a uniform basis, accounts of one year can be compared with other years and if there is any discrepancy, the cause may be enquired into.
9. Audited accounts are considered more or less correct by the sales tax authorities.
10. It would facilitate the settlement of the accounts of a deceased partner.

Sole traders or partnerships are under no legal obligation to get their accounts audited but because of the advantages derived, they generally have their accounts audited.

Different Classes of Audits and their Advantages

A. The audit of the accounts of a private individual or a sole-proprietor and the advantages derived from it.

When an auditor is asked to audit the accounts of a private individual or a sole trader, he must get clear instructions in writing from his client as to what he is expected to do. As he is appointed by an individual or a sole trader under an agreement, his duties and the nature of the work will depend upon such an agreement. The drawing up of the agreement defining the scope of his work is very important because if later on any charge of negligence is levied, he can produce the agreement as to what he was asked to do. In the case of an auditor of joint-stock companies, this question does not arise as his duties are defined by the Companies Act itself. Sometimes an auditor is appointed by an individual to prepare the accounts or sometimes he is asked to prepare the accounts for the purpose of presenting them to the income-tax authorities. Therefore, it is very essential that he must know his exact duty and the nature of the work he is called upon to perform.

If he is called upon to perform the full audit, he must see that the accounts are properly prepared and that the balance sheet is correct. It is possible that his client might propose to take a loan on the basis of the balance sheet signed by him. In such a case if the lender later on finds that the balance sheet does not represent the true and correct financial position of the individual, the auditor might be held responsible to the banker to make good the loss as was decided in the case of *State Street Trust Co. vs Ernst*, in 1938. When the court said:

"A representation certified as true to the knowledge of the accountants when knowledge there is none, a reckless misstatement, or an opinion based on grounds so flimsy as to lead to the conclusion that there was no genuine belief in its truth are all sufficient upon which to base liability. A refusal to see the obvious, a failure to investigate doubtful, if sufficiently gross, may furnish evidence leading to an inference of fraud so as to impose liability for losses suffered by those who rely on the balance sheet. In other words, heedless and reckless disregard of consequence may take the place of deliberate intention."

In short, he must act strictly according to the instructions of his employer.

In addition to the advantages of an audit in general as enumerated above, the following are the particular advantages which an individual derives by getting the accounts of his business audited.

Advantages

1. The individual is assured that his accounts are properly maintained and that he is not being defrauded by his employees. This is specially important when the proprietor is a landlord who has a large establishment and consequently cannot have proper control over it.
2. The audited books of a deceased are very helpful to the executors and administrators for such accounts will form the basis for the preparation of the death duty accounts.
3. Where agents are appointed, it is difficult to keep a check on their accounts and if the auditors are appointed, the agents will keep proper accounts. If they has committed any defalcation, etc., these can be easily discovered by the auditors.
4. Wealth tax can be properly assessed.

B. The Audit of the Accounts of a Firm

It is not necessary that the accounts of a firm should be audited but since there are many advantages of getting the accounts audited, many a firm generally makes a provision for audit in the Partnership Deed.

The audit of the accounts of a firm will be dealt with in detail in the chapter "Audit of Partnership Accounts".

C. The Advantages derived by a Joint-Stock Company in getting the accounts audited

1. The Shareholders of a company have no access to the books of account and therefore if the accounts which have been maintained by the directors are audited by an auditor who is an independent professional accountant, they are assured that they have not been defrauded.
2. An audit acts as a check upon the dishonest employees whose number may be very large.

In addition to the above-mentioned particular advantages a company derives all the advantages which are usually derived in getting the accounts audited as stated earlier.

Distinction between the audit of a Joint-Stock Company and a Partnership or firm

1. The audit of joint-stock companies is compulsory under the Companies Act while that of a partnership is not.
2. The duties, powers, rights, etc., of an auditor of a joint-stock company are defined by the Companies Act while in the case of a partnership they depend upon the agreement between the auditor and the firm.

3. In the case of a joint-stock company, its auditor must be a qualified auditor as is laid down under Section 226 of the companies Act., while in the case of a partnership, its auditor need not hold those qualifications.

D. The Audit of Trust Accounts

Trusts are created for the benefit of some institutions, widows, minors, etc. The trustees look after the property left over by the testator.They collect the rents of the property, dividends on the shares, etc., and distribute the income to the beneficiaries according to the terms of the Trust Deed. As the widows, minors, etc., for the benefit of whom these trusts are created, are not in a position to have access to the books of account or criticise them, they may be defrauded by the trustees. There have been cases where the trustees have misappropriated large sums of trust money without the knowledge of the beneficiaries. Sometimes the trustees themselves do not know how to keep accounts or sometimes they do not do so at all, not because they are dishonest but because they are ignorant of the trust laws and the fundamentals of book-keeping. To avoid such a thing, sometimes, a provision is made in the Trust Deed for the appointment of auditors to check the accounts of the trust. This step will avoid the misappropriation of money by the trustees. If the accounts are audited by a qualified auditor, it will help both the trustees as well as the beneficiaries. Trustees will be benefited because there will be no unnecessary criticism against them. The beneficiaries will also be benefited because they will be assured that the accounts have been properly maintained and that there has been no misappropriation of trust money or fraud.

It may be mentioned here that certain states have enacted laws to make it compulsory to get the accounts of a Trust audited by a Chartered Accountant, e.g., under the Bombay Public Trust Act, 1950, the accounts of a Public Trust must be audited by a Chartered Accountant. The powers and duties of the auditor are laid down by that Act.

QUESTIONS

1. Define an "Audit" and state the various objects of an audit.
(*Osmania, Cal., Guwahati B. Com.*)

2. "Accountancy is a necessity while Auditing is a luxury." Comment. (*Rajasthan B. Com.*)

3. Discuss the main classes of errors and frauds found in auditing of a firm's accounts. Is the auditor responsible for the detection of such errors and frauds? (*Lucknow 1971*)

4. What are the different types of frauds in connection with accounts? Give three examples of frauds and state how the auditor can detect and prevent such frauds?
(*Cal. B. Com. Hons. 1968*)

5. Give the objectives of audit of government accounts and compare them with those of the audit under the Companies Act, 1956. (*Guwahati M. Com. 1969*)

6. "Auditing begins where accountancy ends." Explain. How does Accountancy differ from Auditing? (*Lucknow B. Com.*)

7. "Fraud does not necessarily involve misappropriation of cash or goods." Discuss giving illustrations. (*Poona B. Com. 1965*)

8. What is meant by continuous audit and to what type of business is it specially applicable? State the merits and demerits of such an audit.
(*Agra B. Com. 1964; C.A. Int. 1967; N.D. Com.1967; Rajasthan, 1970*)

9. "The auditor of an individual or a firm has no statutory obligation to comply with." Discuss briefly the implications and limitations of the statement. (*Jabalpur, Cal. B. Com.*)

10. What are the advantages of having the accounts audited by an independent professional auditor? (*Madurai B. Com.*)

11. Is it part of an Auditor's duty to trace and locate any difference in the books he is auditing? What steps he should take to trace an error? *(Poona B. Com. 1964)*

12. Explain and illustrate the classes of errors that may exist in the book-keeping records of a business stating the effect of such errors on the agreement of the Trial Balance. *(Madurai B. Com.)*

13. Explain clearly the difference between Book-keeping, Accountancy, Auditing and Investigation. *(Annamalai B. Com. 1961, Agra B. Com. 1966)*

14. What are the essential qualities required of an auditor apart from the statutory qualifications? *(Guwahati B. Com. 1965)*

15. What do you mean by "routine checking" and "Vouching"? How will you vouch the Sales Book? *(Nagpur 1962)*

16. Make out a case that audit is essential whether it is a sole trader's business or partnership or a limited company or a Government corporation. *(Nagpur B. Com. 1965)*

17. Write short notes on the "Method of Work" and "Check Marks" or "Ticks" generally adopted during audit.

18. Give examples of errors which might still exist in a set of books after the Trial Balance had been agreed, and state the steps an auditor would take to detect them.

19. Distinguish between Continuous Audit and Balance Sheet Audit. What are the disadvantages of Continuous Audit and how will you guard against them? *(Marathwada B. Com. 1960)*

20. Among the principal objects of an audit are the detection of (1) technical errors, and (2) errors of principle.

Discuss and illustrate your answers with examples. *(C.A. Inter 1961)*

21. What is meant by Balance Sheet Audit and give a suggested programme to be followed in such an audit. *(C.C.A.)*

22. "Audited accounts are free from all errors and fraud, if any, committed during the period is duly got exposed out of audit" — Can you endorse this statement without any reservation? Clearly put down your views in this respect.

23. Differentiate the following :

(a) Statutory audit vs private audit
(*b*) Internal audit vs external audit
(*c*) continuous audit vs periodical audit
(*d*) financial audit vs cost audit
(*e*) audit of joint stock company *vs* audit of partnership firm.

24. "Audit is critical and intelligent examination of facts-financial or otherwise, to give in the form of certificate or report an attestation, an expert opinion or an expert advice". Elaborate this statement bringing out clearly the different dimensions of modern auditing and its scope.

An Overview of Auditing

Generally accepted Auditing Practice

Auditing is a process by which a competent, independent person accumulates and evaluates evidence about various assertions contained in financial statements of an entity for the purpose of determining and reporting the quality of disclosure of financial information, judging them against the back drop of established criteria. Auditing is as equally concerned with what is found out as how it is found out. Auditing is not sweaty search with any foregone conclusion. Nor does it end abruptly with any accidental catch in the audit mesh. *Essentially auditing is a process, a professional exercise, conforming to the quality parameters of generally accepted auditing practices.* What is "generally accepted auditing standards" cannot be easily defined. Yet it is important one must have understanding of what the term may connote. It implies, among other things, the following:

(*a*) Only competent and independent person carries out the audit:

(*b*) In performing audit the work is well-planned and supervised.

(c) Sufficient and appropriate audit evidences are gathered and tested before an opinion is framed.

(*d*) Proper judgement is made of financial statements under audit in the light of professional knowledge of auditor concerning generally accepted accounting practices, special enactments affecting the financial statements, pronouncements of professional bodies having bearing on them.

Competence, Independence and Confidentiality

Audit should be conducted by competent persons only. The competence is obtained by pass in the prescribed course after undergoing practical training prescribed. In India, Chartered Accountants are competent auditors. A Chartered Accountant is a person who is a member of the Institute of Chartered Accountants of India. To become the member of the Institute, one must undergo practical training and pass the prescribed examination stipulated in the Chartered Accountants Act and Chartered Accountants Regulations. The competence is updated by continuing education programme of the institute.

Besides competence the auditor must have independence. Unless an auditor is independent, his opinion is no more reliable than the financial statements prepared by the management itself. It is often said that an auditor must be ready to resign rather than to sign a document which he does not approve of. Independence, then, implies acting without any fear or favour. In order to protect the independence of the auditors, enactments contain various provisions. For example Section 226 (2) of Companies Act lays down that the following persons cannot be appointed as auditor of a company even though they are otherwise qualified :

(*a*) An officer or employee of the company.

(*b*) A person who is partner or who is in the employment of an employee of the company.

(*c*) A person who is indebted to the company for an amount exceeding Rs 1000.

Thus the relation of employee, debtor are envisaged as constraints affecting independence of auditor. In order to protect auditors who give adverse opinion, it has been laid down in the Act that an auditor cannot be removed without prior approval of central government. An auditor who is sought to be removed has the right to make representation to shareholders of his stand. Sometimes, it is suggested periodical rotation of auditor may enhance independence of auditor. But it is highly a debatable issue.

An auditor should keep the information concerning his clients confidentially. He should not disclose these to others unless there is legal or professional duty to divulge information.

Audit Planning and Supervision

In any audit assignment, an auditor must be very clear about what he is required to perform. Without any slight ambiguity he must understand audit aim in any situation. He must know whether he is to give any opinion on financial statements or to certify accuracy of any data or to give his expert advice on certain matters. Bearing in mind the audit aim, he must programme his work, schedule them, depute staff, divide work among them, co-ordinate their work, supervise the progress of the work and make review of their findings before giving his opinion/certificate or advice. Elaborate discussion on audit planning and supervision follows in the next chapter.

Audit Evidence

An auditor must gather sufficient and appropriate audit evidence and test them to make judgement of opinion. In gathering evidence to support his assertions, the auditor is often confronted with two issues: What evidence will be relevant to assess an assertion with greater reliability? How much evidence is to be obtained?

To obtain sufficient and appropriate evidence the auditor performs (1) compliance procedures and (2) substantive procedures.

1. Compliance procedures : In big organisations, transactions may be voluminious and repetitive. If these transactions occur systematically, within in-built checks and balances, it would be unnecessary to verify all the transactions to assess what these transactions signify. Quite a few transactions, if checked would tell what all transactions of the type seek to signify. In case of such a systematised environment (i.e. where what is known as internal control system operates) sufficiency of evidence can be restricted at a percentage less than full checking. Besides restricting the quantum of checking, the auditor will be entitled to assume that the evidence generated in the systemised environment will be highly reliable. But the auditor must satisfy himself that the internal control system is in effect in the organisation. To check this he performs compliance test. Compliance tests are tests designed to obtain reasonable assurance that those internal controls on which audit reliance is to be placed are in effect. Compliance procedures seek to test

(*a*) that the internal control exists

(*b*) that the internal control is effective

(*c*) that the internal control has so operated throughout the period of audit with continuity.

An auditor carries out compliance procedure by observation of the system, eliciting responses to his enquiry from clients, making critical look of the facts against the back drop of control criteria.

2. Substantive procedure : By performing compliance procedures, the auditor finds out the efficacy of internal control system. If for instance, the internal control system is found to be effective, can auditor take that all assertions given by the financial statements are true and fair? While existence of good internal control system adds reliability to audit evidence, it can not dispense with checking audit evidence to substantiate data generated within the system. Substantive procedures are designed to obtain audit evidence as to completeness, accuracy and validity of data produced by the accounting system. Accounting system of an organisation generate various data concerning various transactions. Their effect reflect in P & L account and balance sheet. These transactions communicate one or more of the following assertions in financial statements viz.

(*a*) Existence : that an asset/liability exists

(*b*) Rights and obligations : that the enterprise has right over the asset or has obligation over the liability

(c) Occurrence : that a transaction happened during the period, say, sales of so much rupees occurred

(*d*) Completeness : that all transactions/asset/liability find place in financial statements without omission

(*e*) Valuation : the monetary values attached to asset or liability is correct or fair

(*f*) Measurement : that a transaction is recorded in proper amount. For e.g. freight paid to bringing machinery is included in transaction pertaining to installation. Revenue or expense is properly allocated to the period; e.g.: pre-paid expense, accrued income.

(*g*) Disclosure: data is disclosed according to accounting convention, statutory requirement.

These seven assertions of financial data may be correct or not. A financial statement may depict a leasehold right as a freehold right. The auditor has to check to get assurance that these assertions are fairly represented in the financial statements. To do this, he performs substantive procedure.

In doing substantive procedure of obtaining evidence, the auditor may use one or more of the following popular methods viz inspection, observation, inquiry, confirmation, computation and analytical review, Using these methods, substantive procedures seek to obtain evidence as to details of various transactions of an entity or critically test the data in its entirety or otherwise as to their correctness or completeness.

Gathering audit evidence :

We have seen that a auditor seeks to obtain evidence to check the assertions viz effective functioning of internal control system (compliance procedure) and existence, rights and obligations, occurrence, completeness, valuation, measurement and disclosure of financial information (substantive procedure). According to SAP-5 of ICAI, an auditor may obtain evidence for these from different sources. The evidence may be available within the entity itself. Or it may be obtained from sources *outside the entity*. For example sales invoices, reply by the staff etc., constitute internal evidences. Purchase bills, confirmation by debtors etc., constitute external evidences. Whether the source of origin is internal or external the evidence are of the following types viz *written, oral, events, physical existence, system, analytical tools*. Written evidences are in the form of documents, records, vouchers, ledgers, subsidiary books, confirmation, written reply etc. Oral evidences are in the form of verbal reply in person or over phone or in a meeting and so on. Physical evidence are possible in cases of tangible assets. For example factory building, cash, investments etc may be physically checked. Certain fixed assets can not be physically inspected. For instance, the existence of electrical system concealed within the walls cannot be physically checked. That a bulb lights in a corner of a room is a proof that the room is electrically connected with the main. In certain cases direct access to physical existence of an asset is impossible. Only circumstantial evidence can make the point clear. Existence of good internal control system is established by obtaining evidence in compliance procedure. Once the existence of good system is determined, it itself proves to be an evidence as to reliability of financial data within the system. Analytical tools are often used to check completeness, and correctness of data. For instance, by comparing gross profit ratio over a period of time, it can be inferred that purchases/sales/stocks had been manipulated if the ratio varies abnormally year to year without justification.

Besides, *events occurring after balance sheet date* may provide certain evidence. For example that a debtor of the company has become insolvent after balance sheet date may point to uncollectibility of dues of the company as on the date of Balance sheet.

What is the best evidence for a particular assertion can not be said. It is a matter of facts and convenience.

The evidence are obtained by following methods viz

(*a*) inspection (*b*) observation

(*c*) inquiry and confirmation (*d*) computation

(*e*) analytical review.

Inspection consists of examination of records, documents or tangible assets. Vouching, scanning, verification of asset are general auditing techniques used for inspection.

Observation means taking part in a process as a witness. The Auditor may witness the stock taking process to check that the system of stock-taking is fair.

Inquiry is to solicit information by putting questions. Confirmation consists in getting corroboration for facts supplied.

Computation consists of doing arithmetical exercises like totalling, balance extraction, preparing reconciliation etc.

Analytical review consists in computing critical ratios, comparison etc.

Auditing in Depth

Taylor and Perry define Auditing in depth as "It implies the examination of the system applied within a business, entailing the tracing of certain transactions from their origin to their conclusion, investigating at each stage the records created and their appropriate authorisation".

Another writer has defined it: 'It is a method according to which a few selected transactions are subjected to a thorough scrutiny in forming an opinion as regards the accuracy of the data so scrutinised."

From the definitions given above, it would appear that the auditor has to examine a few transactions in detail, *i.e.*, from the origin of the transactions to their conclusion. Thus certain transactions are traced through various stages from the beginning to their end. Every record maintained relating to a particular transaction is scrutinised. The object is to see whether a very efficient internal check and control system is in operation.

To illustrate "audit in depth", let us take an example of the purchase of goods. The auditor should follow the technique detailed below:—

1. He should inquire whether there was a demand from the storekeeper or the godown keeper to the administrative officer or the purchase department that such and such goods having reached the minimum or the ordering level should be purchased.
2. Whether the tenders were invited for the purchase of the goods.
3. Whether the order was placed by an authorised person.
4. He should examine the delivery note.
5. He should examine the inspection report by the technical supervisor that the goods are according to the order placed and the invoice from the suppliers of the goods.
6. He should examine the invoice.
7. He should see whether the goods were entered in the stock register and the bin cards (if in use) by the storekeeper or the godown keeper.

8. He should examine the necessary entry regarding the purchase in the purchase journal, ledger and the relative vouchers.
9. He should see whether the account of the supplier had been credited with the correct amount according to the invoice.

The principle of "auditing in depth" is possible in large firms but is not suitable for the small firms as in the latter case internal system is not in existence in which case all the entries in the books of account have to be checked by the auditor. The auditor should resort to in-depth auditing only when he is satisfied with the efficacy of the internal check system prevalent in the business. The extent of the efficiency of internal check system will enable the auditor to decide how far he should apply the technique of auditing in depth. He should, therefore, select especially those transaction which are material in relation to the affairs of the company as a whole. But he should also select a number of entries at random. As to how many entries should be checked will depend upon the size of business, taking into consideration the importance of the entries and the nature of the business.

Such a system will enable the auditor to satisfy himself as to the efficiency or otherwise of the system of internal checks in operation and which subject will be discussed in another chapter. He will also be in a position to know whether the procedure for the receipt and payment of cash, purchase and sale of goods, etc. as prescribed has been properly followed or not. He will also be able to find out the weak points of the existing procedures for making entries in the books of account and he may, therefore, suggest to the management a better procedure for recording the transactions to avoid any loopholes for committing frauds.

Test Check

Professor Meig defines: "Testing and test checking means to select and examine a representative sample from a large number of similar items".

In big business houses where the number of transactions to be checked is very large and the time at the disposal of the auditor is little, a few transactions may be checked at random. Such a check is called test check. All the transactions need not be checked. The method of checking the accounts will minimise the work of the auditor.

For example, while vouching the credit sales, a few transactions, say, for a week per month, may be checked or the transactions for a few months selected at random may be checked. Again, the auditor may check all the transactions for any month or dealings with a particular concern may be checked. If the transactions so checked are all correct and there is no suspicion of any error or fraud, the auditor may presume that all the other transactions may be correct. With the increase of business transactions and the establishment of big business houses, test checking has become more in vague. Most of the auditors minimise their work by applying test checks.

It must be remembered that if later on it is found that a few errors or frauds have remained undetected as the auditor did not check each and every transaction for he depended upon the Test Check, he would be held responsible for showing negligence in the performance of his duties.

Therefore, the auditor should be very careful in relying upon the Test Check. He should apply these checks if he is fully satisfied that the internal check system prevalent is efficient and no suspicion arises in his mind.

Precautions to be taken while applying Test Checks

1. Entries of every description should be checked.
2. Selection of entries to be checked should be at random.
3. Periods and entries selected for test check should be different at each audit, e.g., if the credit sales for the months of July and December were checked during the year 1994,

credit sales for other months except July and December should be checked for the year 1995.

4. A large number of entries of the first and the last month of the audit period should be checked.
5. The test check should be so arranged that the work done by every clerk is checked.
6. Test check should not be applied to cash book, where every transaction should be checked.

Factors determining Size of Sample:

(*a*) *Internal control system:* If good internal control system operates within the entity, the auditor can restrict the size of sample to a minimum.

(*b*) *Nature and volume of business:* If the transactions are voluminous and repetitive, the auditor has to resort to small sampling only.

(*c*) *Time:* depending upon the audit schedule, the auditor may select the sample size.

(*d*) *Audit aim:* If correctness of the data is to be vouchsafed entire transactions are to be checked. If opinion is to be given on fairness of the statements, the auditor may select such audit sample as would give him satisfaction for framing judgement of opinion.

(*e*) *Risk tolerence level :* If the risk in not checking an item is high, auditor may not leave checking it. If risk is insignificant he may ignore checking it.

(*f*) *Previous history :* Previous audit history of the entity may throw light on areas requiring large audit sampling.

(g) *Analytical review :* By making critical review of financial statements, auditor can find out areas where errors have crept or manipulations have been made. He may increase the size of audit sample in those areas.

Compliance to Accounting, Auditing Standards and Enactments

Generally accepted accounting practices :

Auditing of financial statements seeks to ensure that the financial statements are prepared with due regard to accounting conventions. Called accounting conventions, concepts or doctrines, these give uniformity in presentation of financial data. Important concepts in this connection are :

(*a*) Double entry system of accounting.

(*b*) Going concern concept-that current assets are valued at their realisable value and fixed assets are valued at cost less depreciation.

(*c*) Accrual concept: Income is to be recognised if right to receive it has occurred irrespective of actual collection of it. Expense is to be accounted if it has occurred irrespective of actual payment of it.

(*d*) Distinction between capital expenditure and revenue expenditure.

(*e*) Conservatism : All losses-present or probable are to be provided. Income is to be recognised only if it is not unreasonable to expect its ultimate recovery at the time of its occurrence.

While all entities have to follow these conventions in preparation of financial statements, there are few accounting policies where entities can choose one for the other, for e.g., depreciation method-straight line policy or written down policy. In selecting accounting policy, entities are to be guided by the following factors viz, materiality, prudence and substance over the form.

According to Accounting standard 1 of the Institute of Chartered Accountants of India, financial statements are assumed to be prepared and presented on the basis of the following assumptions *viz:*

(*a*) going concern : That the enterprise has neither necessity nor intention to close the operations in foreseeable future

(*b*) consistency : accounting policy followed in the last year is continued to be followed this year also (*c*) accrual: Revenue and expenditure are accounted on due basis irrespective of collection or payment.

If these fundamental accounting assumptions are vitiated, if the business is to be closed or changed accounting policy is followed during the year or any expense or income is accounted on cash basis, these deviations are to be specifically disclosed by way of notes in the accounts.

Accounting/Auditing Statements, Guidance notes and Standards

The Institute of Chartred Accountants of India has issued from time to time many statements/ guidance notes/standards on matters of accounting and auditing. The statements have been issued with a view to securing compliance by auditors. Hence statements are mandatory in character. If the financial statements deviate from what is said in any accounting standard or if the auditor is not able to carry out the audit as per the requirement of an auditing standard, such deviation or departure is to be highlighted in the audit report. Auditing and accounting guidance notes are issued to provide guidance to auditors in certain accounting or auditing contingency. Guidance notes are recommendatory in character. Accounting standards and Auditing And Assurance Standards (AAS) are issued to ensure that the financial statements are prepared according to generally accepted accounting practice and auditing is carried out according to generally accepted auditing practice. They are mandatory from the dates notified. Similarly International Accounting Standards (IAS) are issued by International Accounting Standards Committee. International Auditing Practices Committee of International Federation of Accountants issue International Auditing Guidelines (IAG). These international pronouncements, though not binding on members, are of useful guidance to the auditors.

Besides, various enactments regulate the presentation of financial statements and auditors' liability in their duty. Companies Act, Banking Regulation Act, The Chartered Accountants Act etc., are illustrative pieces of enactments in this regard. The auditor has to ensure compliance to the provisions of these enactments in relevant circumstances.

Auditing in a Computerised Environment

The accounting system of business entities is increasingly being computerised. Speed of processing data, accuracy, economy, compact storage of data, facility of putting the data for multi-various requirements at easy retrieval etc., gain score for computerised system over manual accounting system. Yet computerised accounting process changes the storage and processing of accounting data to a greater extent. This manner of change in storage and processing of data results in changes in organisational procedures and control systems. Accordingly auditing in a computerised environment must recognise this vital fact.

In a manual system of accounting each transaction is supported by a basic voucher. The transaction is entered in a prime register. Postings are made from prime registers to ledgers. P & L account and balance sheet are prepared from the trial balance. At any point of time, the data used in final financial statements can be traced and checked as they are stored. The process of preparation of financial statements can be checked at each stage viz from origination (from voucher), entry (from subsidiary registers), compilation (from trial balance). But in a computerised system, the origin of a transaction may not be adequately documented.For example, in an on-line system of computer, invoices may be fed into computer as and when sales are effected. The computer processes these input instantaneously and effects necessary changes in debtors balance, stock balance, sales figure, and so on. The '*trail*' of a transaction cannot be followed up post mortem. Mainly absence of adequate storage of input for checking and invisibility of 'trail' contribute certain difficulties in auditing of the data in such an environment.

In conducting audit in a computerised environment, the auditor has to adapt his auditing techniques suited to the system. He has to bear in mind the following:

For any output in a computer, the input must be correct and duly authorised. If garbage is in then garbage is out. The auditor has to evaluate the control system operating in a computerised accounting system, viz. what controls exist in feeding data, what controls exist to check that the data fed are processed according to pre-determined criteria, what controls exist in obtaining, storing and presentation of output. To ensure that the auditing is progressed following the links in input, process and output, the auditor may require the client to take out intermediate outputs such as necessary subsidiary records, trial balance or statements as may be required by him. The auditor has two options in doing audit in a computerised environment. He can audit 'around the computer' or audit 'through the computer'. 'Auditing around the computer' implies that the auditor conducts the audit in his traditional way, yet adapting his techniques to check the efficiency of the system. He insists on obtaining as many intermediate statements as he may require to move forward in his auditing in his traditional style. 'Auditing through the computer' on the other hand, involves use of computer itself for performing compliance and substantive procedures. The auditor may make use of test data to check the programmes put to use by the client. The checking reveals whether the programmes used by the client can be relied or not. Again the auditor can also make use of the computer of the client to make critical analysis of the financial statements of the client by calculating various ratios, comparisions, with the aid of programmes or packages available with the client or with him. Whether an auditor is an expert in computer applications, or not, he continues to be responsible for his opinion on the financial statements.

QUESTIONS

1. "Auditing is a process, an organised exercise, carried out by independent and competent professionals" -elucidate.

2. What do you understand by the concept "generally accepted auditing practices"?

3. Mention few ways to guard the independence of an auditor.

4. Explain the compliance procedure and substantive procedure in gathering audit evidence.

5. List down the assertions which the financial information signify in annual financial statements.

6. What are the different types of audit evidence?

7. Explain the important methods employed by an auditor to collect relevant audit evidence.

8. What is meant by auditing in depth? Explain with an illustration how a transaction can be audited in depth.

9. Can an auditor check all transactions of a large sized entity? If he cannot, suggest a suitable accepted auditing technique to overcome this problem.

10. Why test-checking of transaction is often resorted to by auditors?

11. Does test checking of transactions preclude the application of auditing in depth?

12. Explain the significance of test checking in auditing. Also, mention its limitations and suggest precautions to be taken in test checking.

13. Explain the significane of checking as to adherence to accounting conventions in preparation and presentation of financial statements.

14. What are fundamental accounting assumptions signified in financial statements?

15. Mention the factors that must guide the management of an entity in selection of a particular accounting policy in the place of other alternative.

16. Explain briefly the relevance of accounting and auditing standards, guidance notes issued by I.C.A.I in the work of an auditor.

17. As an auditor, what problems you encounter in auditing the computerised accounts? How will you try to sort them out?

18. What is meant by audit trail? What is relevance of it in cases where it cannot be preserved?

19. What are the important factors which must be taken into account in fixing an appropriate audit sample?

20. As an auditor how will you deal with the following:

(*a*) An entity accounts its sales only if the amount is collected from the debtors. Otherwise, the sale value of goods sold during the year is shown in a suspense account under liability side of the balance sheet.

(*b*) During the year it becomes imminent that the business of the entity is to be closed altogether immediately after a brief period once the accounts for the year are closed.

(*c*) Till previous year, the company is following straight line method of depreciation. It wants to change it to written down value method.

21. While Checking audit evidence, you confront the following situations. State how will you decide and justify your answer.

(*a*) Bank balance as per the cash book of the entity is Rs. 10,500. Balance as per pass book of the bank is Rs 17, 800.

(*b*) The outstanding balance from Mr. X is Rs 18,700. He gives written confirmation of balance for Rs 17,800 only.

(*c*) As on the date of audit (i.e., after the date of balance sheet) it comes to light that a debtor of the company has become insolvent. The management of the company represents to you that the debtor is quite solvent as on the date of balance sheet and they had no reason to expect its uncollectibility as on that date. The subsequent insolvency, according to management, is accidental and is not traceable to any unfavourable conditions existing as on the date of balance sheet.

(*d*) The gross profit rate is 20% on sales for all the past five years. When you calculate this for this year it comes to only 8% on sales.

Chapter 3

The Auditor

The Auditor

The person doing the audit and who is ultimately responsible for the results of the audit is called Auditor. Auditor multiplies his hand through employing the assistants for doing the work. Still, he alone is responsible for what he does and others do for him.

The Auditor occupies roles which are unique in themselves as he wears the different mantles suited to the engagement he is called for to associate with. He is involved in audit in relation to financial statements. He is also involved in audit in relation to other assignments.

Even in relation to his work with reference to financial statements, sometimes, he does the "audit" and gives an opinion on financial statements; sometimes he merely certifies them; in some other context, he makes a review only; in a different occasion he merely compiles the accounting work. Any reference to the role and the responsibility of the auditor should be meaningful only when it is talked of in relation to what he is supposed to be in a given assignment. But the term audit is very widely and loosely used to connote the varying functions of auditor though they may not bear the same reference levels.

Auditing of Financial statements and Auditing of other areas.

The Auditor is concerned with the financial statements of an enterprise. He is also involved in providing his expert services in areas like tax planning, tax compliance, cost reduction, information system. The auditor generally does one or more of the following functions besides auditing of financial statements-

(*a*) Tax auditing

(*b*) Management and operational auditing

(*c*) Cost auditing

(*d*) Internal auditing, concurrent auditing

(*e*) Information system auditing

(*f*) Quality auditing

(*g*) Energy auditing etc.

It would be interesting to note a matter of reference in Part II of the Schedule VI to the Companies Act 1956. It mentions various items to be specified in Profit and Loss Account of a company. One item in this payment to company's Auditor as fees, expenses reimbursement. The Act says that the amount should be shown for services rendered

(*a*) As auditor

(*b*) As an advisor or in any other capacity for taxation matters, company law matters or management services

(c) In any other manner.

The reference is drawn to emphasis the point that the law itself used the term auditor commonly for different roles- **auditor** in a capacity of *auditor* and **auditor** in a capacity different from auditor, say advisor.

Auditor in audit of financial statements.

Financial statements refer to Profit and loss accounts and Balance sheet of an enterprise. These two statements are statements depicting financial results of operations of the enterprise for a period and financial status of the enterprise as as on a date.

Essentially, as it is his traditional realm, and still is his dominant forte, unless we specifically talk of any different assignments, we refer the auditor only as one who is concerned with the financial statements.

In relation to financial statements auditor's role is not the same. He

(*a*) "audits" them or

(*b*) renders the services other than "auditing".

The Statement issued by the Institute of Chartered Accountants of India "Framework of Statements on Auditing and Assurance standards and Guidance Notes on Related Services: distinctly call these two functions in relation to financial statements as-

(*a*) " auditing" and

(*b*) " related services".

The related services that an auditor performs are-

(*a*) Review

(*b*) Agreed upon procedure

(*c*) Compilation

Audit function of an auditor in regard to financial statements

While "auditing" financial statements an auditor expresses an opinion. The opinion establishes a positive assurance on assertions expressed by financial statements. The positive assertion is signified by the use in unambiguous terms that the financial statements exhibit a true and fair view of the results and status. These statements portrays different assertions to the readers. For example, P&L account would assert that so much is the profit for a period from xxx to period yyy and the profits are earned after booking such revenues and charging such expenses as are recorded. If the financial statements do not exhibit true and fair view, the opinion is straight and in a positive fashion it openly states that the accounts do not show true and fair view; or it says that the accounts show true and fair view except the specified defects. The tenor of the expression and tone of the opinion seek to establish whether the assertions that the financial statements speak are right or wrong. The opinion tells the answer that it is right or that it is wrong. It would not say that the accounts may "not be wrong", when they are correct. Similarly the opinion in an audit would not say that accounts may "not be right" when they are wrong. An audit would call a spade a spade. The duty of audit is complete only upon expressing an opinion – favourable or unfavourable in a positive fashion.

The expression of opinion by the auditor is after gathering of evidences to vet the assertions of financial statements; weighing the evidences as to their reliability and forming an opinion thereafter.

The expression of opinion provides to the readers an assurance as to the reliability or otherwise of the assertions in the financial statements. The assurance as it comes from such a high person as an auditor, assumes a high level. Very high and dependable assurance that it is, yet it is not an insurance or a guarantee that all is well about the financial statements. Much about the limitations attached to it, we will be appreciating as we proceed deep into and along the subject.

Reference is invited to AAS 28 "The Auditor's report of financial statements". It specifies the standards on the form and contents of an auditor' report on financial statements.

Auditor as a Reviewer - Review of financial statements:

The objective of review of financial statements is to provide an opinion about the truth and fairness of the accounts. But the tenor and tone the expression is different from what they are in " audit". The expression of opinion here is not positive or straight. The expression of opinion seeks not to satisfy the readers with a positive answer of right or wrong ; but it seeks to pacify the readers with the limited version of opinion that nothing has to come to auditor's notice that would warrant him to say that the accounts are not prepared in a true and fair manner. An auditor doing the review says that the accounts may not be called wrong because he has not come across anything to say so. An auditor is reluctant to say, then, that the accounts show true and fair view because he has not gathered such evidences as to establish that they are so.

Generally quick review of the accounts are made for intermediate financial periods say half year closing, quarterly closing and auditor expresses a limited opinion of whether accounts may be taken to be wrong or may not be taken to be wrong.

The opinion of auditor in review does have a good degree of assurance; but it is low in level; it does not have the same fervor and ferocity as an opinion in auditing obtains of.

Auditor as a doer of an Agreed upon Procedure:

The assignment of "agreed upon procedures" is carried out by an auditor in accordance with an agreement with the entity and or select third party on the one hand and the auditor on other The agreement stipulates the auditor to present actual findings after carrying out such audit procedures as are agreed upon. He does not provide any opinion after performance of agreed procedures. He binds himself to carry out agreed procedures and he presents the facts (findings) . He does not interpret and opine what the findings would mean. It is for the readers to make their opinion based upon the findings. An auditor would not be expected to give his opinion in a case the procedures of audit routines are matters of agreement with other party. Similarly an alien to the agreement too cannot make any meaningful opinion as he may not be aware of the procedures employed and the limitations to which the checking is subjected to.

For example, the auditor may be asked to check all sales invoices above Rs. 10,000 with sales day book and may be asked to give discrepancies. An auditor would not express any opinion as to the truth and completeness of the sales accounting as the audit procedure he employs is not as what he may choose appropriate as per his planning and wisdom.

The level of assurance as to auditor's opinion is nil as he never expresses any opinion at all.

AAS 32 provides for the standards on professional responsibilities of an auditor when he undertakes an agreed upon procedure audit.

Can "audit" be carried out as agreed upon?

"Audit" (i.e. audit proper or say a statutory audit) is an exercise culminating in expression of an independent opinion on the financial statements examined by an auditor. The expression of an opinion is based on the evidences gathered to test the veracity of the assertions explained in the financial statements. The auditor uses such auditing techniques and undertakes such audit procedures as are appropriate and relevant to the circumstances of the case. His right to information and right to carry out the audit in accordance his audit plan are fundamental to his audit process. Any abridgment or curtailment either by agreement or by arrangement effecting cut in rights, procedures shall be void against the accepted auditing standards. Similarly, when an audit is carried out in accordance with and under a statute, say, The companies Act 1956, the appointing authority cannot usurp on to themselves any right to curtail the powers and duties of an auditor as enshrined in the Statute. To the extent that it does not result in any inconsistencies and conflicts, the powers and duties may, in appropriate circumstances, be enlarged subject to mutual agreement.

Auditor as a compiler – Compilation function of an Auditor

An auditor may be asked to collect, classify and compile the financial transactions. He would identify himself as a compiler. His association with the financial statements as a compiler or an accountant would add a credence that the compilation may be proper. It is in no way offers any assurance as to the truth and fairness of what had been compiled.

AAS 31 prescribes the standards on professional responsibility of an auditor when he acts an accountant and the form and contents of the report of compilation.

Auditors association with financial statements- Extent of responsibility

Auditor holds out that he is responsible to the third party only when he attaches a opinion on the financial statements or allows his name to be linked to any financial statements about which he is aware of. An auditor is liable for giving out a reckless or untrue opinion on the financial statements to the persons who might have reasons to rely them. An auditor may be estopped from denying his liability when he allows his name to be associated with any financial statement. To deny the liability he must prove that he is unaware of such use or he must have taken steps to stop such use on his becoming aware of it or must have informed the third party about the unauthorised use of his name.

The Different Engagement of Auditor in Audit of Financial statements-Statutory Auditor, Branch Auditor and Joint Auditor

The auditor in doing the audit function of the financial statement may be rendering his services as a statutory auditor. As a statutory auditor, he may be doing the attest function of the whole entity or may be doing the attest function of a unit or branch of the entity. In the latter case, he will be called a branch auditor. The auditing of branches by a person different from the auditor of the whole entity would call for matters meriting attention. For example, when the branch of a company entity is audited by a person other than company auditor, Section 227 (3) (bb) of the Companies Act, 1956 envisages the matters of reporting as to how the company auditor had dealt with the reports submitted to him by the Branch auditor. Similarly when the audit of entity is done by more than one auditor (not being branch auditor), there will be issues related to the conduct of such joint audit.

AAS 10 deals about the standards of audit in connection with the using the work of another auditor (i.e. branch auditor) by a principal auditor.

AAS 12 lays down the standards of audit in case of a joint audit of an entity.

Integrity, Objectivity and Independence of Auditor

Basic Principles Governing an Audit (AAS 1) requires that an auditor to be straightforward, honest and sincere in his approach to his professional work. He must not allow prejudice or bias to mar his objectivity. He must be and appear to be free of any interest that might be incompatible with integrity and objectivity.

Independence is a state of mind in which the pangs of pride and prejudices do not detract the vision of approach and wisdom of judgment of the auditors. An independent auditor ploughs his furrows straight against the star of giving an unbiased and just the right opinion.

Certain safeguards to uphold independence of auditor

To ensure the independence of auditors various safeguards such as the following are put into field-, (*a*) Rotation of the auditors over a period of time,

(*b*) Non-indebtedness of the auditor with the client,

(*c*) Bar to holding any office of profit other than auditor,

(*d*) Ceiling on number of audits,

(*e*) Regulation on charging contingent fees,

(*f*) Avoiding taking professional assignments that conflict the duties of the auditor,

(*g*) Disclosure of substantial interest if the auditor audits a client in which he holds substantial interest.

The Companies Act 1956 in regard to Independence of Auditor

Section 226

The Companies Act 1956 provides for disqualifications of an auditor. According to it a person shall not be eligible to be appointed as auditor of a company if he is

(*a*) an officer or employee of the company

(*b*) a partner or employee of an officer or employee of a company

(*c*) indebted to the company for a sum exceeding Rs. 1,000

(*d*) a guarantor for any debtor of a company for a debt exceeding Rs. 1,000

(*e*) a s provider of security to the company for a debtor for a debt exceeding Rs. 1,000

(*f*) a holder of security- i.e. shareholder of shares carrying voting rights.

Section 314

Section 314 places restriction on the persons who are relatives or partner to a director to hold offices of profit (*i.e.* position carrying pecuniary benefits) in the company. If any such person is to be appointed, a special resolution in s general meeting needs to be passed. It had been so interpreted that post of auditor is also an office of profit for the purposes of this section. Hence a person who is a relative of or who is a partner of a director cannot be appointed as an auditor of a company without getting the consent of the shareholders obtained by way of a special resolution.

For example when a partner of a Chartered Accountants firm is a director in a company, another partner of the firm will attract the provisions of section 314 if he is offered appointment of auditor. That whether he could accept the assignment or not would depend on the harmonious reading of section 226 and section 314 and also the restriction prescribed by code of conduct of Chartered Accountants.

Code of Ethics

Clause 10 of Part I of Schedule I

The Chartered Accountants Act, 1949 (in schedule first, part I clause 10) deems it a misconduct if a Chartered Accountant charges the fees for any professional work which are based on a percentage basis or dependent on the findings or results of the work.

For example think what a hell effect it would result in if a chartered Accountant were to be paid fees for his certifying fees as a percentage of profits he certifies.

Clause 4 of Part I of Schedule I

Clause 4 as referred to above requires an auditor to disclose in the report his interest, when he expresses an opinion on financial statements of an entity in which he or his partner or a firm has substantial interest.

The Council of Institute of Chartered Accountants had notified that auditor of specified entities shall be guilty of professional misconduct if he accepts any other work than audit while he is an auditor of the entity- for a remuneration which is more than the fees for doing statutory audit.

The specified entities are public sector undertaking/ Government companies/ listed companies, public companies having a turnover of Rs 50 crore or above.

Qualities of an Auditor

AAS 1 of ICAI – Basic Principles Governing an Audit- stipulates that an auditor should possess the following qualities-

(*a*) Integrity, Objectivity and Independence

(*b*) Skills and Competence

(*c*) Ability to maintain Confidentiality

The following are the general traits that an auditor should possess.

Qualities of an Auditor

1. It is very important for an auditor to be well-versed in the fundamental principles and theory of all branches of accounting, *e.g.*, general accounting, cost accounts, income-tax, etc. It is not possible for a person to audit the accounts unless he himself knows how to prepare them. He should be aware of the latest development of the technique of accounting so that he may modify his procedure of work.
2. He should not pass a transaction unless he knows that it is correct. This is possible only when one knows thoroughly well the principles of accounting.
3. He should be able to grasp quickly the technical details of the business whose accounts he is auditing. If possible, he should pay a visit to the works of his client, before he commences his work.
4. He should be prepared to seek elucidation on technical questions rather than show a false pride or fear of displaying his own ignorance.
5. He should be quite familiar with the Company and Mercantile Laws and must be a complete master of the principles of auditing.
6. He must be tactful and scrupulously honest, as Lord Justice Lindley has said: "An auditor must be honest, i.e., he must not certify what he does not believe to be true, and he must take reasonable care and skill before he believes what he certifies is true."

   (*In re London and General Bank, 1895*).
7. He must not be influenced, directly or indirectly, by others in the discharge of his duties.
8. Sometimes he is put in a very awkward position, when his duty to his client is opposed to his own interests, in which case he must have the courage to carry out his duty faithfully and honestly, even if such a step harms him. In the long run, this policy will be of immense value to him. He will acquire a reputation for his honesty, which will bring more business to him.
9. He must be prepared to resign, rather than sign a balance sheet, which he knows does not exhibit a true and fair view of the state of affairs of the concern and thus give a false report.
10. He should not disclose the secrets of his clients.
11. He must have the tact to put intelligent questions to extract full information.
12. He must not adopt an attitude of suspicion.
13. He must be prepared to hear arguments and must be reasonable.
14. He must be vigilant, cautious, methodical and accurate.
15. He should have the ability to write the report clearly, correctly, concisely and forcefully.
16. He should have an understanding of the general principles of economics.
17. He should have thorough training in business organisation, management and finance.

18. Last but not the least, he should have 'Common Sense'.

The following *Obiter dicta* of famous Judges have been made from time to time, in regard to the qualities of an auditor: —

"An auditor is not bound to be a detective, or to approach his work with suspicion, or with the foregone conclusion that there is something wrong. He is a watch-dog but not a blood-hound. He is justified in believing tried servants of the company, and is entitled to rely upon their representations, provided he takes reasonable care." (Lopes, L.G. in *re Kingston Cotton Mills case, 1896*).

"An auditor is not bound to assume when he comes to do his duty that he is dealing with fraudulent and dishonest people... if circumstances of suspicion arise ... it is his duty to probe them to the bottom." — Lord Alverstone, C.J. *The London Oil Storage Co., Ltd., vs. Seear Hasluck and Co.* (1904).

"If in the course of these long and arduous audits the auditor has in even one instance fallen short of the strict duty of an auditor, he cannot, I apprehend, be excused merely because in general he displayed the highest degree of care and skill." — Romer J., in **The City and Equitable Fire Insurance Co., Ltd. (1924)**.

"He is a watch-dog and not a blood-hound". — Lord Justice Lopes.

"He is not an insurer; he does not guarantee that the books do correctly show the true position of the company's affairs." — Lord Justice Lindley.

QUESTIONS

1. Why is it important for the auditor to be independent? How is the independence of the auditor ensured by the Indian Companies Act?

2. Can auditor accept the full fees as advance before completion of the audit?

3. State the important qualities of a person to be a good auditor.

4. What are the differences in role playing when auditor

(*a*) audits (*b*) reviews and (*c*) compiles the accounts.

5. Can the audit responsibilities of an auditor in auditing be lowered by mutual agreement?

6. What is meant by doing audit as per "agreed upon" procedures?

Audit Planning and Audit Control

The auditor has to conduct the audit in a planned manner. Elsewhere, we have said that the audit is not a groping in the dark, a sweaty exercise, an accidental catch of stray findings in an audit-fish net, a luxury sojourn with as much an abrupt start as an indiscreet end. It is with a mission, a planned performance, meaningful and well-covered reporting and with a senses of time, cost and above all quality. An auditor, not a toddler that he is- knows where and how to begin, go about and bid adieu. An auditor must be equally well aware of what is found as how it is found. He confirms himself with conviction based on his professional work and has with him adequate documentation to prove the manner how he is convinced. Not only he plans in these areas, but he does control the performance as well to conform to his plan and quality.

AAS 1 Basic principles governing an audit states that the auditor should plant his work to enable him to conduct an effective audit in an efficient and timely manner.

AAS 8 governs the standards of auditing respecting audit planning.

The audit plan should cover the following areas -

1. Clear fixings of what the audit engagement is about, What the objectives and scope of the audit are.
2. Gaining knowledge of client's business
3. Gaining knowledge of client's internal control system
4. Consideration of laws governing the entity of the client
5. Considerations as to initial engagement
6. Obtaining of Terms of engagement
7. Planning for nature and extent of audit procedures, audit programming and scheduling
8. Man power planning and quality control plan
9. Coordinating the work to be performed by others
10. Documentation

In the present chapter we will know about the audit planning generally. The chapters that follow deal at length about each component discussed above.

Audit planning – a continuous and permeating exercise

The students should not approach the practice of audit in a water-tight sheds of several processes like planning, performance, reviewing and reporting. The approach is a holistic one. An audit planning permeates audit performance and vice versa. An auditor plans and performs and as he performs, modify his plan to make his planning conform to the situations of exigencies that emerge. An audit planning is, therefore, a continuous exercise. Essentially it comprises of two dimensions- (*a*) developing an overall audit plant-guiding the matters of audit objectives, scope, time-framework, reporting requirements etc. and (*b*) developing an audit programme showing the nature, timing and extent of audit procedure. The former is a master charter and the latter is an audit-specific check list of procedures. Both the overall plan and audit programming may get changed if there are changes in conditions or unexpected results of audit procedures. The planning will be adaptive always to obtain the best possible results.

Benefits of audit planning.

1. Appropriate attention to important areas : When an audit situation is well visualized and audit areas are well thought out, it is possible that appropriate attention is devoted to each area. Otherwise, the attention will be lop-sided and devoid of merits.
2. Potential problems promptly identified: Audit planning helps the audit to go smooth even when a problem strikes the work. A well conceived audit plan, in fact, takes note of emergence of such a problem and would have provided for solution to move about it. The audit would not slip a problem down its hands; or when confronted with it, the audit would not waste time with lack of action plan to hit it.
3. Time bound progress and completion: An audit plan ensures that the work is carried out expeditiously with less cost and high quality.
4. Man power utilisation: The audit plant is an logistical management of audit staff for optimum utilisation. It avoids heaping in an audit engagement the persons not required and making the audit engagement dry of competent persons when required. The resultant benefit is not only in cost but in effectiveness of audit performance as well. Will not too many cools spoil the broth ?
5. Coordination of work of auditor and experts: An audit often envisages situations when the audit environment is alight with the association of different experts and more than one auditor. The responsibility of issuing audit report still rests with the auditor of the entity. The auditor of the entity would be concerned with issues of prompt and smooth obtaining of the benefits of pooled expertise to sub-serve the audit mission without any conflicts from rights-responsibility syndrome. Again issues related to the manner, timing and extent of obtaining and relying expertise would call for careful planning.

Factors affecting audit planning :

Audit plan can not be charged out sitting in isolation. It is a brain storming exercise. It is a brain child of wisdom, foresight, professional knowledge, previous experience, knowledge about the industry, knowledge about the entity, its business, management people, management and operating system, legal, economic milieu. The audit plan is often subject to revision in the light of new experiences encountered as one performs. The overall audit plan takes into consideration the following aspects-

1. The terms of engagement
2. Statutory duties connected with audit
3. The nature of report, timing for submission
4. Legal and statutory milieu
5. Accounting policies followed by the entity, any change effected thereon
6. The effect of new accounting or auditing pronouncements by the governing body
7. Identification of significant and special audit areas
8. The setting of materiality level for audit purposes
9. The probability of misstatements appearing in financial statements due to fraud or errors

10. Related party transactions- the transactions of the entity with those persons who are intimately related to the management
11. The nature and veracity of audit evidences obtainable
12. The extent of participation in audit work by other people, - internal auditor, experts, joint auditors,
13. The element of surprise, shift contemplated in matters and areas of audit.

Audit Programming

The audit programme would be developed satisfying optimally the constraints of time and cost without in any way compromising the quality of audit. Audit Programme is a plan of action translated into specific areas of audit works with check list of actions to be performed. An audit programme becomes well knit when time units and personal responsibility are embroidered on to the specific areas of work assigned. An audit programme thus entails the following-

1. Specific listing of audit area components in terms of related procedures : For example, the overall audit procedures of an entity may consist of the following, components-vouching of cash book, bank book, sales day book, purchase day book, scrutiny of journals, debtors ledger, creditor ledger, general ledger, inventory verification, checking trial balance, grouping of balances, disclosure of items in P&L account and Balance sheet, critical and overall analysis etc. Each such component is sub-divided into procedures. For example in cash book vouching-vouching of receipts, vouching of payments are two major division. Again receipt vouching is listed in terms of procedures say - (*a*) vouch 15 days receipts in each month (*b*) Scan all receipts in excess of Rs. 50,000 (*c*) Check total of last two months (*d*) trace the cash balance on the last day with the trial balance etc. (*d*) final review of the work as a whole
2. Staff positioning: The staff who would do the specific procedures are also specified. For example, continuing with our example of cash book receipt vouching above, Mr. Bahu, a junior would do the procedure (*a*) and Mr. Sudhar would do the scanning in procedure (*b*) and again Mr. Bahu would do the (*c*) and (*d*). Mr. Vasan would supervise the whole work.
3. Timing built in : The audit programme specifies the time or date by which the work should have been completed,
4. Sequencing : Audit programming also fixes up the time values in such a way that the overall completion of the audit is not hampered for want of performance of initial and routine audit procedures. For example, the works or routine vouching of cash book, day books are planned immediately after the completion of the financial year followed by ledger scrutiny and consolidation work is taken at a later stage. The auditor should understand the critical path in which he cannot brook any delay. Within that he shuffles and reshuffles his man-power. Again, he does not have discretion to timing in relation to certain audit procedures. For instance, the verification of cash balance as at the year end cannot be postponed to any later date.
5. Responsibility fixing : The auditor assigns the duty to different staff. In token of their having done the job, they are required to sign the plan paper against the work area allotted to them with dates.
6. Documentation: The audit programme is often written and is filed (or in a book form) and kept as an evidence that –the work is well planned, carried out in accordance with plan.

Advantages of audit programme :

1. The audit programme acts a guide and it ensures that all audit areas have been duly attended to without any omission.
2. Since the audit programming has time units for works to be carried out, the auditor is in a position to know about the progress of the work at any point of time.

3. The audit programme helps as a base which provides minimum insights for chalking the future audit planning for the years to come.
4. Since the audit programme documents the stage of work at any point of time, it is possible to pick the thread at any stage even if one staff to leave the assignment in the middle.
5. As the audit programme dovetails the duty with the persons who should perform it, responsibility is tightened for errors/omissions.
6. Audit programme is an effective communication of direction of auditor to the people at audit work.
7. As the audit programme includes in it details of audit staff deployment, it is possible to assess the training and experience of the staff in any audit area.
8. The preparation of audit programme is mandated by the pronouncements of AAS No. 8. The maintenance of audit programme with due noting of the work done by audit staff is an evidence of planning and performance of the audit. It will be of good use for reference as to any doubt as to whether a particular area of the work had been attended to or not.
9. Final review of the work performed can easily be made with reference to the audit programme.
10. Audit programme brings into play a play of orderliness in the place of haphazard audit play in the work situations.
11. The record of training of the articled clerks with the auditor can easily be compiled for the audit programmes of the different entities for the years during which the clerk has spend his time with the auditor.

Limitations of the audit programming

1. Sometimes, an otherwise bright and ingenious audit staff loses his spirit if the method and manner of what he must do is mandated by the specific check list of the audit programme.
2. A pious adherence to rigid audit programme may sometimes betray an auditor and the audit planning may fall a petty prey to non-appreciation of emerging areas of the audit needs during the process.
3. The audit programme may be used by lower level of audit staff as a defence. They may like to flee quite content with that they have done what is required of them as per letters of the check list. They may fail to appreciate the substance over the form the programme.

Audit Control

If it were to do some good, the audit plan must be complemented by a good audit control. An audit control is an exercise to ensure that the audit plan is actually carried out in the lines it is thought out to be; that the audit plan is appropriately modified and adapted to meet appropriately the real life situation; the deviations in performance is promptly signaled out the corrective measures are taken for conforming; direction, supervision and review required of the auditor are duly forthcoming.

The auditor exercises the control over his assistants, coordinates the work by his interaction with the client, other experts involved in the business of the client in so far as they may relate to his audit work and subsequently taking note of the progress of the work. Simultaneously, the auditor builds up proper files of the audit matters and events to create the documentation for his plan and action.

Audit Control over Assistants

The control over audit assistants is exercised with the following aims :

(a) the audit work is performed by the assistants as per programme

(b) the work is progressing per time schedule

(c) to provide necessary training and guidance to the assistants in carrying out the work

(d) to appreciate the practical difficulties in actual performance of work and to sort out the problems by remedial action

(e) to update the audit programme in the light of new experiences narrated by the audit assistants

(f) to decide on important matters involving his expert knowledge, or concerning his responsibilities.

The control over the assistants is exercised by asking them to meet the auditor at periodical intervals. Generally weekly reporting of assistants at the auditors' office is insisted. The assistants are encouraged to maintain diary of work performed by them during the week. Their diary sheets are put to scrutiny by auditor. The auditor conducts meeting, discussion with the assistants and reviews their work for correction and guidance. The auditor makes surprise visits to the client's office to obtain first-hand information about the actual state of audit.

Audit Control over the work performed by others

In audit, the auditor quite often makes use of the work performed by other auditors or other expert. In case of work performed by assistants, the auditor exercises supervisory role over them as it is a case of delegation of work by him. But in cases of work performed by other experts, it cannot be said, of hand, whether the expert could be brought under his supervision or not. It depends on the facts whether the expert is being employed by the auditor or by the client. Whatever be the terms of engagement, if the auditor desires to make use of the work of such experts in his work, he is required to evaluate the findings of expert in so far they relate to any base for framing his opinion on financial statements.

There are many circumstances during audit where an auditor makes use of the work of an expert. For instance, for determining measure of depreciation, the useful working life of the asset is to be assessed. An engineer's opinion in this regard may have to be relied. Or for ascertaining present liability on account of gratuity to the employees on their reaching superannuation, the work of actuary may have to be utilised. Quite often, legal opinions are sought from advocates for interpreting provisions of any statute or agreements or for determination of rights and liability over certain property etc. While making use of the work of experts in his audit, the auditor must take into consideration the following precautions. He must ensure the skills and competence of the expert. If the expert is a paid regular employee of the client, or is related to the client, or has substantial interest in the business of client, the auditor has reason to infer that the objectivity may suffer. In such a case, he must be cautious in evaluating his work before using it. The auditor must communicate with the expert to understand the area of his work, type and nature of information made available to him by the client, and general methodology of his doing work. Accordingly the auditor must verify that the information provided to him are correct and are relevant. If the expert opinion is based on any assumption, the auditor has to check the validity of such assumption. The auditor must take such necessary steps to ensure whether the work of expert could be relied or not. If the work of expert, according to the opinion of the auditor, could not be relied, then he must indicate his disagreement with the opinion of expert appropriately, with due regard to the professional competence of other expert.

Co-ordinating the work of other Auditors

The auditor has to rely on the work performed by other auditors in certain circumstances. Cases of joint audit, Branch audit, and internal audit provide examples where the auditor has to liaise with other auditor. In case of joint audit more than one auditor are appointed. The auditors have to plan division of work among them. The work may be divided according to units of operation or areas of checking. Where the auditors have agreed to have division of audit according to units of operation, each auditor has to control the audit work of the unit which has been allotted to him. He must plant to devise auditing procedures, extent of checking and programme suited to the audit work of his division. He alone is responsible for the audit of the unit. Where audit is allotted to each of the joint auditors according to the areas of financial data, say, assets or liability or income or expenditure each will be responsible for the work performed by them. Division of work may be made on the basis of parts of period covered under audit. Many a time, joint auditors make joint report. It is a professional obligation that each auditor must bring to the notice of co-auditors any matter observed by him which may have significant bearing on the truth and fairness of financial information.

In case of Branch audit, the statutory auditor is entitled to regard the branch auditor as an expert in respect of branch audit. As such, he is entitled to rely the work of expert-branch auditor. However, the statutory auditor has right to visit branch, make enquiry, and have access to records of the branch. The statutory auditor must plan to have good liaison with branch auditors to ensure that the degree of reliance on branch audit is high.

Where the entity has internal audit conducted by other auditor , the statutory auditor must evaluate the efficacy of internal audit. The statutory auditor must plan to advantageously utilise the work of integral auditor by so arranging his audit programme, manner and extent of checking that duplication is avoided. Detailed discussion on areas of co-ordination between statutory auditor and internal auditor is presented in the next chapter. It is necessary that the auditors must,have good liaison with each other to improve the efficiency of each one's job.

Quality Control for audit work

AAS 17 establishes audit standards on the quality control policies and procedures. The standard deals with-

1. quality control policy and procedures of an audit firm regarding audit work generally
2. quality control procedures regarding the work delegated to assistants on an individual audit.

Quality Control Policy for an audit firm

The audit firm should implement the quality control policies and procedures designed to ensure that all audits are conducted in accordance withe Auditing and Assurance Standards in relation to the audit generally.

The relevant quality control objectives are-

1. Professional requirements: This is a quality objective that insist that all personnel adhere to the principles of independence, integrity, objectivity, confidentiality and professional behaviour. A culture of professional behaviour must prevail in the audit firm. The professional behaviour is a word of wider significance and it would require personnel to maintain a high degree of moral, ethical and work standards, whether in or about or away the work.
2. Skills and competence: The staff must be adequately attained the professional competence and skills required of them to perform the duty of auditor.
3. Assignment: Audit work is to be assigned to the personnel who have the required technical training and proficiency required in the circumstances.
4. Delegation: Delegation of audit assignment from the auditor to his assistants does not operate in vacuum of giving nod to start and work and of taking the audit report upon completion. A delegation must be spirited in the sense that there must be sufficient direction, supervision and review of the work delegated to ensure quality standards.
5. Consultation: The auditor should have arrangements for access for consultation within and outside the firm with those who have appropriate expertise.
6. Acceptance and retention of a client: Decision as to accept a prospective client or retain an existing client should be based on the considerations like the firm's independence and the

ability of the firm to serve the client properly. Vexing clients, or the clients who may jeopardize the firm's independence or clients who may prove to be while elephants to serve should be pruned on an ongoing review as part of retention policy.

7. Monitoring: The audit firm should ensure that quality control policy, procedures are continued to be monitored for their adequacy and effectiveness in their implementation.

The quality objectives, policy, procedures should be adequately communicated to the audit staff so that they can understand them properly and attempt to conform to them in their practice.

We have seen that an audit firm is to be guided to achieve quality of excellence in audit performance with a mission and commitment to achieve the goal of total quality. We have listed areas of relevance for quality parameters in relation to-

1. Audit staff- (*a*) Skill set, (*b*) mental attitude set (*c*) expertise-enrichment (*d*) oversight of staff in the form of direction, supervision and review.
2. Work performed-appropriateness of match between people and work delegated, oversight in the form supervision, direction and review of work
3. Client-prospective as well as existing- (*a*) adequacy of service in the light of expectation for and supply of service (*b*) pruning the client profile
4. Quality awareness: Continued on-field exercise without excuse and with improvement Quality Control in an Individual audit

Quality Control in an Individual Audit

The total quality policy of the firm specifies, *inter alia*, that the quality control is to be implemented in relation to the individual audit work.

1. Staff deployment :

The auditor should ensure that the delegation of work to the assistants is done after considering the professional requirements of the work and the professional skills of the audit people to be at work.

2. Direction of work delegated :

Direction involves in leading mentally the audit assistants to the work situations with a prior sense of how and when to do audit procedures. Direction involves- (*a*) informing audit assistants about the what procedures (nature) they are to perform, (*b*) what their responsibility are in relation to them, (*c*) what objectives the procedures seek to attain, (*d*) what possible problems or audit issues in such area they may encounter, (*e*) a standard solution if possible to them or if not, the reference level to solve issues, (*f*) nature of audit situations in the light of uniqueness of business, accounting system, (*g*) vulnerable areas of slip, pitfall in internal control system (*h*) timing of the audit procedures- time of start, sequence of doing and element of surprise (*i*) extent of audit procedure and so on. The direction is conveyed to the audit people at work through audit programme, overall audit plan and time budget.

3. Supervision

Supervision by the auditor is a link exercise between direction and review. The auditor cannot wait to find that things had gone away at a review stage. If he finds that the directions are misunderstood or disregarded by the staff, he could use the exercise of supervision to set things correctly at a possible earliest opportune time or to modify the set of directions to address appropriately to the need of the situations. It is tool to ensure that audit programming is followed in substance over form. Supervision involves

(*a*) monitoring the progress of the work to ensure that the skills set of the audit staff are appropriate to the requirements of real work.

(*b*) monitoring the work to ensure that directions have reached the audit staff in correct sense

(*c*) monitoring the work to ensure that the work is carried out in accordance with overall audit plan and programming.

(*d*) getting to know about the accounting and audit questions raised during the audit, analyzing their significance, providing appropriate further direction or modification of programme to suit them appropriately.

(*e*) resolving the differences of professional judgement between personnel and considering the level of consultation where differences in judgement are sharp and require of deeper insights.

4. Review

The review is the final stage of quality testing process of audit work. But it does not mean that it is finally done. Reviews are often made at stages which may by themselves constitute certain levels of finish. Though linked to supervision, the review distances itself in that review looks at things in whole or in specifics from a distant perspective of time and work completion. While supervision is an on-field monitoring and support tool to get things close to what they must be, review is an evaluation of the things that had happened. Both seek to ensure the work to meet the quality parameters.

The person who should review the work should be the person who has competence at least equal to the competence of the person who performed the work. That is peer or higher-ups are competent to perform review. Review of work of junior audit clerks is done by senior clerks, the work or employee chartered Accountants' work is done by another employee or by principal auditor as the case may be.

Review involves considering that

(*a*) work had been completed as per audit programme

(*b*) work performed and the results obtained have been adequately documented

(*c*) the significant audit matters have been resolved

(*d*) where significant matters remain not resolved or they otherwise require of disclosure they are reflected in audit conclusions

(*e*) the objective of audit procedures have been achieved

(*f*) the audit conclusions are based on the results of the work performed and there is no inconsistency in drawing the audit conclusions from them.

(*g*) the audit opinion expressed is backed by audit conclusions and there is no inconsistency between the two;

In short, the review seeks to ensure that the links between audit opinion expressed and the audit performance and planning have been consistently and appropriately operated.

The timely reviewing is necessary about

(*a*) the adequacy, appropriateness of overall audit plan and programming;

(*b*) assessment of the inherent and control risks and also the results of the tests of control, modification needed in audit plan and programme as a result of findings of tests of control

(*c*) documentation of the results of the substantial audit procedures, the drawing of conclusion therefrom and results of consultation if any in connection therewith.

(*d*) Financial statement and proposed adjustment in the financial statements in the light of auditor's examination or proposed audit report.

QUESTIONS

1. Explain the importance of good audit plan and control.

2. Mention the important areas of audit planning.

3. **What are the factors that affect audit planning?**
4. **State how audit programme helps in audit planning and audit control.**
5. **Though auditor delegates the work to the assistants he still remains responsible for the opinion he gives. As such, he expects his assistants to work the way he himself would do. Suggest the ways how an auditor could ensure this.**
6. **Illustrate few cases where the auditor may make use of the work of other expert. What precautions he takes the auditor may make use of the work of other expert.**
7. **Mention the circumstances in which the auditor may have to liaise with other auditors in the course of his audit duties. Explain how good coordination among them will be of mutual benefit to both.**
8. **What are the general ways by which the work of joint auditors are divided ? How each one's responsibility is determined for the work ?**
9. **How will you perform in this case ?- The Managing director of Amudhan Lubricants Limited ventilates his feeling thus- The internal auditing department of his company is doing all the checking as you, as an external auditor do. As such it seems that the resources are not properly utilised. He requests you to liaise with the internal audit department to finalise the area of their checking with regards to accounts and suggest new thrust areas which may be put to their critical analysis.**

Audit Objectives and Scope of Audit of Financial Statements

Auditing by Objectives

Auditing is a planned exercise. It is guided by the mission of objectives and guarded by standards of procedures of performance and requirements of reporting. We have in a briefly discussed about the various audit objectives in chapter I to give the readers a preliminary view about the audit function. This chapter is elaborately devoted to present an extensive discussion on this.

AAS 2- of ICAI deals about the Objective and Scope of Financial Statements.

Audit objective- Exclusion clause.

In this chapter we are studying the audit objective of audit of financial statements. We are not concerned with audit of other areas e.g. internal audit, Operational audit etc., . Nor are we concerned with the auditor's role as regards financial statements in matters of compilation or agreed upon procedures. We deal solely with the objective and scope of the "*audit*" of *financial statements*.

Expression of opinion- the objective of the audit

Opinion

The objective of the audit is to express an opinion on financial statements. The opinion is an expression of conclusion based on a performance of standard (not uniform) procedures upon the financial statements. The conclusion is a matter of conviction based on satisfaction in a positive manner that the things are well with what the financial statements seek to portray. The conclusion cannot be a mere conjecture or based on surmise. Auditor is not only to be convinced that nothing has come to his notice to hold that the financial statements portray any misstatements. He ought to be fairly and positively positioned to make a frame of mind to pass a judgment that the financial statements do portray the assertions truly and fairly.

Opinion as to the truth and fairness of the financial statements

Financial statements – Revenue statements and Position statement depict the results of the operations of the entity over a period and status of the entity as on a date. If a Profit and loss Statement tells the reader that so much is the profit or so much is the loss for the period, the matters of interest do not get restricted to that figure alone. It is not enough that the figure of profit or loss is correct. Though it might be correct finally, it is to be properly arrived at; it must appear to be properly arrived at. Not merely the truth of the figure alone would suffice to be a matter of interest to the reader. The fairness of it is very much a matter of concern to the readers. The judgment of fairness requires a finer assessment of several aspects. For example the figure profit in a revenue statement asserts the following-

(*a*) the profit is arrived at after application of appropriate accounting policies;

(*b*) the profit is arrived at arithmetically correct; and is properly arrived after providing for expenses related to the period and related to the earning of the profit reported

(*c*) the profit is relevantly related to the period specified in the revenue statement

(*d*) the profit is completely measured without omission or spill over for the prior or next period relevant to the period of audit

(*e*) the manner of computation of profit – in terms of its components viz. revenues involved therein, expenses and provisions comprised therein, are adequately disclosed to the readers

There are assertions in a balance sheet or revenue statement which are to be true and fair in the substance and form. Where inadequacies have crept in, the auditor shall express his opinion of satisfaction besides highlighting the inadequacy. If he is fully satisfied, he will be expressing a clear or clean opinion of satisfaction. If he is fully dissatisfied, he will be expressing an adverse or negative satisfaction or dissatisfaction.

Expression of opinion – misconceptions dispelled

While an audited financial statements adds to the credence of the financial statements, it is not to be taken to be an all panacea for what the entity has failed to do or a pointer to what it may do. The expression of the truth and fairness cannot be indefinitely and indiscreetly stretched to relate to the efficacy and efficiency of the management operations while earning profit. The expression of opinion is not an assurance as to the future viability of the enterprise.

The auditor's role as regards financial statements should be clearly understood as beginning with and ending on expression of opinion on financial statements prepared by the management. It is the management who is primarily and solely responsible for the preparation of financial statements. Auditor expressing a positive or negative opinion on the financial statements does not take on to his shoulders anything concerning their preparation. For the purposes of dispelling any misconceived notion by a reader or even the management, it is expressly clarified that-

(*a*) it is the management responsibility to maintain adequate and complete accounting records

(*b*) it is the management responsibility to select and apply appropriate accounting policies

(*c*) it is the management responsibility to maintain adequate internal control

(*d*) it is the management responsibility to safeguard the assets of the entity.

The audit function of the financial statements does not relieve the management of its responsibility mentioned above.

Scope of the Audit of financial statements

Expression of opinion about the truth and fairness of the financial statements is the objective of audit of financial statements. The expression emanates after performance of audit procedures. The scope of audit refers to the identification or delineation of audit related aspects in regard to say, the objective of audit, procedures, areas to be covered etc. The scope of audit is governed by-

(*a*) the terms of engagement

(*b*) relevant statutory provisions

(*c*) relevant Institute pronouncement

However, the term of engagement cannot restrict or lower the scope of the audit in relation to matters which are prescribed by legislation or Institute pronouncements.

The scope of audit relates the auditor's concern in the following conjoints of financial statements-

(*a*) underlying accounting records and source documents

(*b*) financial statements themselves

The auditor aims at checking the

(*a*) sufficiency and relevance of information contained in underlying accounting records and source documents;

(*b*) proper disclosure of relevant information in financial statements

To check the sufficiency and relevance of information contained in underlying accounting and source records, the auditor should study the existence of internal control and accounting system, and test them to decide the nature, extent and timing of other audit procedures.

To determine the proper disclosure of relevant information in financial statements, the auditor compares the transactions, events represented in source documents and underlying accounting records with the financial statements and check that they are properly summarised, carried down to the financial statements and adequately disclosed. In other words, the auditor checks that

(*a*) the trial balance reflects the proper summary of balances and transactions,

(*b*) the financial statements reflects the fair disclosure of events and transactions by proper grouping of balances, events, transactions,

(*c*) Information reflected in the financial statements adequately convey the messages required by narration and notes as may be desired by statute, pronouncements or requirement of the context.

(*d*) judgement of the management is fairly made in matters where they are inherent and implied - for e.g. estimation involved in making provision, or selection of particular accounting policy among available alternative policies (like in depreciation methods)

Inherent limitation of audit

(*a*) Absolute certainty not possible

The Auditor's work involves exercise of judgement - for e.g. judging reasonableness of estimates made by management . Again much of the evidence available to the auditor enables him to draw reasonable conclusions only and not absolute certain decisions. As such one cannot take that audit ensures a finality or an assurance. Absolute certainty is rarely attainable.

(*b*) Test nature of audit and weakness of internal control system

The constraints of volume of business transactions, availability of time at the disposal of the auditor and the like would force the auditor to resort to test checking of items. This is a serious inherent limitation of the audit. Again however strong and wide the internal control mechanism of the entity might be, there are still inherent limitations as to it. Cost, circumventing of the control, collusion, ingenuity of the fraud perpetrator, lack of adaptability of the system to changing scenario etc. contribute to the weakness of the internal control system. Test nature of checking coupled with inherent limitations of the internal control system of the business would throw open for certain material misstatements remaining undetected even after the conclusion of the audit. An auditor would have to extend his procedures of audit where there is any indication as to existence of errors or frauds when he audits as a professional man of wisdom and skepticism. But he can not do the audit to the core of ensuring that there are no errors or frauds in the areas he had audited.

(c) Materiality

An auditor is concerned with items that are material either individually or as a group to the affairs of the enterprise. What is material is a question of fact dependent on many factors. It is a matter of decision of an auditor based on his expertise and experience. It is likely that an auditor might have winked at immaterial items and would not have bestowed his attention on such insignificant items.

(*d*) Matters beyond the scope of the audit

Auditor 's scope of work and reporting is conditioned by the terms of engagement subject, however to the mandatory requirements stipulated by statute, if any, and pronouncements of the Institute. An auditor would not naturally lend himself to be liable for not doing any work or reporting in relation to the matters which are beyond his scope of work and reporting.

(*e*) Constraints on audit

Some times, certain constraints may be fall in audit milieu which inhibits the auditor's ability to express an opinion. For example, he might not have received the confirmation of balance from a big debtor which he would have liked to test. In such a circumstance an auditor cannot bury himself with an all out effort to the core to get at any cost the information he would have required. He would have to still proceed expressing his opinion, yet clearly expressing the restraint which had disabled him in a particular area of his work. Such expression of constraints may take a disqualification or a disclaimer in his audit report depending on the circumstances of the case.

QUESTIONS

1. What are the audit objectives of general financial statements?
2. Is an audit an insurance against the risk of appearance of misstatements in financial statements?
3. Can the fact that the audit has been carried out be claimed as a defence for any error in preparing the financial statements by management?
4. Why an audit cannot be taken to be a fool-proof system for detection of errors appearing in financial statements?
5. Explain the audit objective – expression of opinion as to the truth and fairness of financial statements.
6. State any three important constraints that impede the efficacy of audit function.

The Auditor's Responsibility to Consider Fraud and Error in Audit of Financial Statements

Recognising the inherent risk of errors and frauds in financial statements

We have stated the objective of the audit of the financial statements is expression of opinion on the truth and fairness of the assertions in the financial statements. One important and inherent element that an auditor comes across in audit of financial transactions of an entity is the existence or possibility for existence of an crror or fraud in such transactions or events. In a financial statements, the relevance of attestation of events, transactions and the balances therefore stem from the fact that errors or frauds might have interfered in their compilation or reporting. If financial accounting and reporting were to be error-free and with zero-fraud incident, why at all audit is to be conducted? The possibility for eruption of errors and for happening of frauds is but natural and inherent. On the other hand, one cannot suspect that the errors and frauds *have* occurred unless detected and proved.

Hence, an auditor has to take into account the risk of material misstatements in financial statements arising from errors and frauds in the following stages of his audit-

(*a*) Planning the audit work

(*b*) Performing the audit procedures

(*c*) Evaluating audit findings

(*d*) Reporting audit conclusions.

Error, Fraud- described

Misstatements in financial statements may arise from errors or frauds.

The term error refers to unintentional misstatement in financial statements including an omission of an amount or a disclosure. Error is said to be present when-

(*a*) There is a misstatement in financial statement

(*b*) There is no misstatement but a material statement (fact) or amount is omitted to be stated.

(*c*) The misstatement or omission to state was done without any intention of malice. The stating of misstatement or non-stating of a material statement is due to slip or ignorance.

The error may thus be error of omission, error of commission or error of principle. The effect of error may be telling or just compensating. Errors for example may be of – errors in gathering data (say Rs. 986 of purchase accounted as Rs. 896 from purchase bills) ; errors in processing the data (total purchases wrongly cast and credited to suppliers' account); errors in making accounting estimates; errors in application of accounting principles.

On the other hand, fraud refers to intentional act by one or more individuals among management, those charged with governance, employees or third parties. Fraud is committed using the method of deception in order to gain an unfair or illegal advantage. According as to who initiates the fraud, the fraud may be of management fraud, employee fraud or a third party fraud.

Fraud involves a motivation to deceive and perceived opportunity to commit fraud. A person may resort to intentional false reporting of financial data as there might be motivation in the form of pressure to achieve results and there might be avenues to false accounting due to weakness in accounting and internal control system of the entity.

Error and Fraud compared

Fraud and Error differ from each other on the score of element of the intention and deception present in the former and absent in the latter. Both are alike in causing misstatements appear in financial statements.

Fraud is a very broader legal crime with which an auditor is not fully concerned with. The auditor concerns himself with such elements of fraud that have resulted in material misstatement in financial statements.

Errors and Fraud categorised

Errors are of many types- such as error of commission, error of omission, error of principle, Frauds may be of fraudulent financial reporting and fraudulent misappropriation of assets.

Fraudulent financial reporting may involve –

(*a*) deception or cheating by fabricating, falsifying, manipulating, or altering accounting records or supporting documents; or

(*b*) misrepresentation of events, transactions or significant information in financial statements; or

(*c*) intentional omission to record significant information, events or transactions in financial statements; or

(*d*) intentional misapplication of accounting principles relating to measurement, recognition, classification or presentation or disclosure

Fraudulent misappropriation of assets means theft of entity's asset- tangible or intangible. For example, embezzlement of cash, or accounting against a false voucher of expenses without the expense incurred at all or not for the entity,

AAS on Auditor's Responsibility to Consider Fraud and Error in Audit of Financial Statement

AAS 4 –(Revised) deals with standards on the auditor's responsibility to consider fraud and error in financial statements. The standard deals with the auditor's concern in the matters of-

(*a*) Responsibility of auditor as against the responsibility of those charged with governance and management of the entity

(*b*) Professional skepticism for understanding the risk of material misstatements resulting from the errors and frauds in financial statements

(*c*) Audit preliminaries for gaining knowledge about any susceptibility of misstatements arising from fraud.-Audit planning with audit team, audit enquiry of management; Discussion with those charged with corporate governance, identification of fraud risk factors

(*d*) Audit Response when fraud risk factors are identified to be present- Considering modifying substantive procedures to reduce detection risk

(*e*) Circumstances indicative of presence of misstatement resulting from fraud, identification of misstatement

(*f*) Determining the effect of misstatement in financial statements, tagging it with fraud, documentation, communication and reporting

The Responsibility for prevention and detection of Fraud

The questions here are-

Who is responsible for detection and prevention of fraud?

What is the responsibility of the auditor as regards the material misstatements appearing in financial statements arising from the frauds and errors?

Those charged with the governance and management are responsible for perpetrating a system of internal control, accounting system and financial control to ensure integrity. Those charged with governance shall infuse a code of ethics in the entity and encourage honesty and integrity within the entity. They shall have to see that necessary preventive and corrective organs for monitoring risks (sensors), control mechanism like internal control system, accounting system, financial control are well conceived of and are in place in the entity. The management shall establish and see that they are implemented properly. The conception and implementation of control mechanism shall reduce, if not completely eliminate, the risk of misstatements arising from frauds or errors. But there may still be room for eruption of frauds and errors. Those charged with governance and management alone shall bear the cross for the residuary errors and frauds not taken care of by conception and or implementation. The first question is thus answered that it is the primary responsibility of the management to take steps to detect and prevent frauds.

As regards the role of auditor in sharing the responsibility the answer is not simple. The fact audit had been conducted does not in any way guarantee that the financial statements are purged and are pristine pure. The fact of audit does not point to complete certainty in absolute terms about the truth and fairness of the financial statements. We have elsewhere specified about the inherent limitations of the audit. Audit uses test nature of checking; Audit evidences are persuasive rather than conclusive; Collusion and management tacit approval for perpetuation of fraud may deter auditor to detect material misstatement effectively. The risk of not detecting material misstatement arising fraud is all the more higher when the management is involved in committing fraud. Hence on the mere score of not detecting fraud (which had come to light subsequent to audit), it cannot be concluded that the audit failed to obtain reasonable assurance; lacked professional competence; inadequately planned and inefficiently performed the audit; failed to conduct the audit according to generally accepted auditing standards. When audit is conducted with proper planning, performance, documentation and according to generally accepted auditing standards, there is no reason why an auditor should be made a scapegoat for any misstatements appearing in financial statements arising from fraud. An auditor should always approach the audit, of course with a professional skepticism which is not a cynicism, the usual favorite of a Cassandra of kismet. What is then a professional skepticism?

Professional skepticism Vs cynicism

It is an attitude to identify and properly evaluate and report something that smells bad. The auditor does not start to suspect, does not elongate his nose to sniff, but keeps his nostrils alert to smell matters, circumstances and evidence that point to foulness near and around what and where he works. The professional skepticism is both conceptual and also practical. It is conceived before hand in a mentally simulated scene and also practised in real life situation of audit. It goes well with in a planning as well performance stages of auditing. He cannot let loose and ignore (*a*) the matters that increase risk of material misstatement in financial statements resulting from fraud (e.g. operating characteristics of business, management characteristics, control environment)

(*b*) circumstances that make the auditor suspect that material misstatements are there

(*c*) evidence obtained (his prior knowledge as to a fraud from his previous audit, a case paper he chanced to peruse in his audit work etc.). In the absence of a circumstance in which evidence reveals to the contrary, the auditor is supposed to accept and not suspect that records and documents are genuine. The auditing does not in any way contemplate the authentication of documentation. Nor the auditors are experts in authenticating the documentation.

Understanding of the susceptibility of the entity to material misstatements resulting from fraud.

(*a*) **Audit Planning discussion**: The auditor shall discuss with the audit team to obtain knowledge of and appraise of the audit team about the error-prone areas, the potentials for perpetuating frauds. Areas of special attention, additional procedures to be applied, the persons who shall be assigned the area, the type of enquiries to be made, the manner and content of sharing the result of enquiry with the team member etc. will be planned for in the discussion.

(*b*) **Inquiries of the Management**: The auditor may make inquiries of the management to gain an understanding of management perception of risk of misstatement in financial statements as a result of fraud and the existence of the accounting and internal control system in the entity to address to such risk The enquiry of management shall also address itself to know whether the management is aware of any fraud that has occurred; or whether the management suspects a fraud which the entity is investigating.

(*c*) **Discussion with those charged with the Governance:** The auditor may also hold discussion with those charged with the governance of the entity. In an entity where the practice of the corporate governance is well developed, those charged with the governance may have assumed the responsibility for monitoring risk, financial control and compliance with the law. Discussion would them throw insights for the auditor to understand how the entity stands in relation to these matters. It would also be possible for the auditor to have a sharing of views in matters about the nature, extent, and frequency of the management's assessment of the accounting and Internal control systems to prevent or detect fraud, the failure of the management to address to the material weakness in internal control identified during a prior period audit, the auditor's evaluation of the control system, competence and integrity of the management. The discussion would benefit both the auditor and the persons charged with the governance to gain a better understanding of the susceptibility of the entity to the risk of misstatements in financial statements as a result of fraud.

(*d*) **Identification of fraud risk factors**: AAS 6 (Revised) on "Risk Assessment and Internal Control" describes auditor's assessment of inherent risk and control risk and how those assessment affect the nature, timing and extent of audit procedures. In making the assessment the auditor considers how the financial statements might be misstated as a result of fraud or error. The auditor may identify events or conditions that provide an opportunity, motive, a means to commit fraud or indicate that a fraud might have occurred. Thus the auditor is concerned with identification of a set of events and conditions prevailing in the entity. The back drop of planning discussion, inquiries with the management and discussion with those charged with the governance may help him in identifying the set of events and conditions conducive to or indicative of committing frauds. This set of events and conditions is referred to fraud risk factors. The presence of fraud risk factors in an entity may affect the auditor's assessment of inherent risk and control risk. The gamut of fraud risk factors is not a standardized one and it would vary depending upon the size, complexity, and ownership pattern of the entity. The presence of fraud risk factors, *ispo facto,* does not indicate that there is a high degree of audit risk. The higher the fraud risk factors, the more is the caution required for an auditor. However based on his assessment of control mechanism to combat the fraud risks, the auditor may choose to fix up the control risk at a level less than high. In view of all these, it is not possible to make a ranking of fraud risk factors and factor analysis could not result in a predictive model of foretelling audit risk.

Examples of fraud risk factors

We know that fraud risk factors are set of conditions and events that point to susceptibility of the enterprise to the risk of misstatement resulting from fraud. We give below few examples of such conditions or events which point to the presence of fraud risk in an entity -

Fraud risk factors relating to misstatement resulting from *fraudulent financial reporting-*

(*a*) Management characteristics and management influence over the control environment –

- There is motivation for management to indulge in fraudulent financial reporting like-
- Management compensation is linked to aggressive targets for operating results, financial position etc.
- Management is interested in resorting to inappropriate means to minimise reported earnings for any tax motivated reasons.

(*b*) Failure on the part of management to display and communicate an appropriate attitude regarding internal control- like

- Lack of attention for the advice to strengthen the internal control by previous auditors.
- Frequent and aggressive violation of laws
- There is high turnover of management counsels and board members

(*c*) Industry related conditions like high degree of competition, increasing business failures etc.

(*d*) Conditions relating to operating characteristics and financial stability like continued cash losses, bad solvency position, significant related party transactions etc.

Fraud risk factors relating to susceptibility of assets to misappropriation

Entity's assets may likely be misappropriated and misstatements arising therefrom are likely to appear in financial statement depending on-

(*a*) The nature of assets the entity possess- like high balances of cash on hand, easily negotiable instruments like bearer cheques, small sized inventory with high values like say diamonds etc.,

(*b*) Nature of control environment – like lack of supervision, non-balancing of books daily, lack of record keeping, non-segregation of duties, poor custodial responsibility etc.

Audit response to reduce detection risk when fraud risk is perceived

After gaining an understanding and assessing the inherent and control risks affecting the entity (*i.e.* set of fraud risk factors- inherent in the entity and control risk of dealing them by the system of internal control) , the auditor should design substantive procedures to reduce to an acceptably low level, the risk of misstatement, resulting from fraud and error that are material to the financial statements taken as a whole, will not be detected. Depending upon his assessment of fraud risk factors, the auditor may adapt his audit responses. The audit response in the light of this may be-

(*a*) The auditor may judge that audit procedures- test of control and substantive procedures already planned are sufficient;

(*b*) The auditor may modify the nature, extent and timing of audit procedures; the response may be overall or may be specific to particular account balance, class of transaction or assertion. The auditor response may be combination of modifications aimed at appropriately dealing with overall as well as specific areas of financial data.

The judgement of the auditor that there is fraud risk in an audit of financial statements may affect the auditor in the following ways-

(*a*) *Professional skepticism:* The auditor may increase his sensitivity to the audit environment. He may increase his sensitivity in selection of nature and extent of documents to be examined in support of material transaction. He may like to corroborate more the management explanations and representations concerning the material matters. He would bestow more attention in the manner of auditing such matters.

(*b*) *Assignment of members of audit team:* The auditor may also consider that the skill, ability of the members of the audit team are commensurate with the auditor's assessment of the level of risk in the audit engagement. The auditor shall relook into these matters. He may also think appropriately in the matters of increased or modified supervision of the audit team.

(*c*) *Increased attention to the selection of accounting principles and policies:* The auditor may consider to judge more deeper and further in matters of selection and application of accounting policies, principles particularly those related to revenue recognition, asset capitalisation versus expensing. For example, management perceived to be plagued with the interest to show more profit, may choose to capitalise an interest expense to an asset when it may not be proper to do so. It would try all means to write in asset the expenditure rather than expending them in P&L account. It would try all means to book all items to revenue when sometimes it may not be correct to do so.

(*d*) *Premium on control risk:* The auditor would be sensitive to reassessing the control risk especially when he otherwise feels that the control risk is not very high. He would doubly think and consider whether it would be appropriate for him to take the control risk (*i.e.* risk of internal control failing to detect fraud) at a level he planned for. It is not that he always increases the level of control risk in a fraud risk affected financial system. In spite of presence of fraud risk, he may stick to the level of control risk as he perceived already in view of what he appreciates about the presence and practice of control mechanism effectively in the entity.

(*e*) *Modification of the nature of audit procedure:* The auditor may consider the need for changing the nature of audit procedures in the light of his assessment of fraud risk in the entity. He may like to place importance for getting more of external evidences rather than internally generated documents as evidences.

(*f*) *Modification of timing of audit procedure:* The auditor may consider also the timing of audit procedures to be carried out. For example, he may like to do certain audit procedures at or very close to the year end rather than postponing them to a later stage.

(*g*) *Modification of extent of audit procedure:* The auditor may consider that his sample size, contents and criteria for selection of samples may have to be suitably adjusted to address to the need that he may perceive in the light of presence of fraud risk factors.

(*h*) Specific focus approach: When an auditor understands that there may be presence of fraud risk factors, the auditor may analyse their effects- whether it would result in fraudulent financial reporting or fraudulent misappropriation of assets. According to what he perceives, he would deploy such audit procedures specifically aiming at tackling these issues. For example, when fraudulent financial reporting may happen, the auditor may like to confirm- revenue recognition is properly and fairly made or inventory valuation does not get manipulated or accounting gimmicks are not resorted to by passing non-standardised journal entries at the top management levels. For example,

(*i*) in matters of revenue recognition, the auditor may like to dwell in length in appreciating terms of contract of sales, services, (in case of perceived doubt as to accruing of revenue to the entity) or the pronouncements of the court order, (in case a revenue is taken in the light of a judgement) or

(*ii*) in matters of fraudulent financial reporting via inventory manipulation, the auditor may like to examine the value and quantity pattern of inventory, locationwise, productwise, agewise etc.

(*iii*) in matters of fraudulent financial reporting by passing fictitious or malicious journal entries the auditor may like to assess every non-standardised and last minute pre-pared unusual journal entries authenticated by top level management as to their impact on the financial statements.

If fraudulent misappropriation of assets is perceived to be present, the auditor may like to address his audit approach focussing to specific balances of account, class of transactions where susceptibility to fraud is perceived.

Determination of misstatement

An auditor may come across circumstances that may be indicative of presence of material misstatement appearing in financial statements resulting from fraud. The fraud risk factors point to the presence of potentiality of the entity to get into the risk of its financial statements affected by fraud driven misstatements. The professional skepticism of the auditor, together with his understanding of entity specific knowledge, enables him to devise an appropriate audit net where the incidents of fraud may get caught. Now, the prevalence of the not too good circumstances would point to the higher probability of misstatement appearing in the financial statement as a result of perpetuation of fraud. For example, -

Unrealistic time schedule to finish audits, reluctance of management to engage in frank communication, undue restriction on rights and powers of auditor, conflicting audit evidences, information not forthcoming timely, unreconciled suspense and total accounts, long outstanding debit balances in receivables unsupported transactions, unauthorised entries, incongruent results with those obtained by analytical procedures- all may point to the auditor to draw an inference that the financial statements may contain material misstatement due to fraud or error.

The auditor shall perform sufficient and appropriate audit procedures to confirm or dispel the suspicion that financial statements contain material misstatements. The presence of fraud may not be an isolated factor. It may have repercussion and connection with other several areas. The auditor needs to redevise his audit procedures to take care of all these.

Determining the misstatement-fraud nexus and disclosure in report.

When an auditor finds that the financial statements contain misstatement, the auditor has to see that there is tag between the misstatement and fraud. He has to see that any indication of fraud could be linked to that. If so, he should consider, evaluate the implication of such indication in every sphere of his audit including the area of evidence collection especially the management representation. The auditor would decide whether a misstatement is confirmed or is one about which he could not conclude. Based upon his judgement as to materiality, the auditor would disclose this aspect in his report either by qualification or adverse remark as he deems appropriate.

Documentation, communication of fraud.

Documentation

The auditor should document audit evidences about the facts he across concerning the errors and frauds and his judgement process. He should document the fraud risk factors identified and the audit responses he made to deal with them appropriately.

The auditor should obtain a management representation letter for his files. The management representation shall-

(*a*) acknowledge that it is the responsibility of the management to devise the accounting and internal control systems to detect and prevent errors and frauds.

(*b*) acknowledge that it believes that the effect of uncorrected misstatements in financial statements (which have been pointed to them by the auditor) is not material individually or taken as a whole.

(*c*) Acknowledge that it has disclosed to the auditor the facts of any fraud known to it.

(*d*) Acknowledge that it has disclosed to the auditor that the results of its assessment of the risk that the financial statements may be materially misstated as a result of fraud.

Communication

When an auditor comes across a misstatement resulting from fraud or error or suspected fraud, he should consider his responsibility to communicate that information to the management, those charged with the governance and to the law enforcing or regulating authorities.

The auditor must use his professional judgement to decide the level of management to whom the matter of fraud should be brought to the attention. This depends on nature, frequency, amount of fraud etc. The auditor should bring the matter to a higher level of the management than the one in which fraud has occurred and the communication must be timely so that it could operate as a deterrent.

The auditor must select the items of misstatements that would require of the attention of the persons charged with the governance. Such items may be of – frauds involving management people, doubts about the integrity of the management, material misstatement arising from fraud/error, misstatements indicative of weakness in the internal control system concerning its design, operation or financial reporting system, misstatements pointing to the future that financial statements may materially be misstated.

An auditor owes the duty of confidentiality to the client. Therefore whether he is required to communicate any fraud to the law regulating/enforcing authority, would depend on whether any duty is cast on him by any law or directives which would supervene his duty to maintain confidentiality. For example, the RBI directs the auditors of banking companies to report the frauds which the auditor has come across during the audit to its department. Similarly there is a requirement with audit of NBFCs. Again CARO 2003 requires the company auditor to mention in his report under section 227-4A about the frauds on or by the company.

When contacted by the incoming (new) auditor, the previous auditor who has come across the fraud would owe a professional duty of responding to the communication of the incoming auditor appropriately. He should tell him the professional circumstances which led him to leave the previous engagement. When the previous auditor had been constrained to divulge the facts of fraud and other internal matter of the entity, the auditor should appropriately indicate this to the incoming auditor.

QUESTIONS

1. Is detection of fraud a main objective of audit?
2. Who is responsible for devising the system for detection and prevention of fraud?
3. Can the audit be taken to be an insurance against the risk of financial statements being subject to the effects of misstatements arising from fraud?
4. Define fraud and error. Differentiate them.
5. Explain the following–

   (*a*) the misstatements arising from fraudulent financial reporting and

   (*b*) misstatements arising from fraudulent misappropriation of assets.
6. What are fraud risk factors? Illustrate your answer,
7. How the audit response should be when the fraud risk factor is identified to be present in an audit situation?
8. Should an auditor of a company report the occurrence of fraud in his report to the shareholders?
9. What matters that you may like to be included therein when management issues a letter of representation regarding their concerns about the fraud in the entity?

Chapter

7

Gaining Knowledge About the Business of the client

Gaining knowledge of the business

It is true that while auditing the financial statements the auditor expresses an opinion as to the truth and fairness of assertions in the financial statements. It is a misconception that he is concerned with the accounting data and their presentation in the reporting documents. If not for extending his professional edge as a consultant of suggesting ways for doing good business, an auditor basically requires a good understanding of the business of the client even for doing the attest function of financial statements effectively. An auditor whose knowledge about the business is bleak runs the risk of reduce being misled in vouching the assertions of the financial statements in a proper perspective. The appreciation as to the fairness of the disclosure would suffer a lot in the altar of ignorance of the knowledge about the business. The insights about the proper accounting treatment as to revenue measurement, the provisioning for expenses and liabilities, the segregation of extra ordinary transactions from the ordinary transactions etc. disclosure requirement would get blurred if the auditor attests financial statements after a mundane passing of entries devoid of the history of facts behind each of them.

AAS 20 sets a standard that in auditing of financial statements, the auditor should have or obtain knowledge of the business sufficient to enable the auditor to identify and understand the events, transactions and practices that, in the auditor's judgement, may have significant effect on the financial statements or on the examination or audit report.

The auditor should have knowledge of the business, as such knowledge would affect him in–

(*a*) appreciation of the financial statements presented for audit

(*b*) examination of the assertions contained in the statements

(*c*) reporting of the audit conclusions

The knowledge of the business is used by the auditor in assessing the inherent and control risks and in determining the nature, timing and extent of audit procedures to be carried out in any audit.

Level of knowledge of business:

The auditor is a professional who is concerned with the attest function of financial statements. He requires to obtain and have such level of knowledge as would place him in a comfortable position to do his job. He is not a business man in that field and certainly, therefore, his level of knowledge would be less than that possessed by the management. The level of knowledge an auditor possess should go beyond that concerned with the operating of the business by the entity.

The auditor may have to possess general knowledge about the economy and the industry in which the entity operates.

An illustrative list of matters about which the auditor is to be knowledgeable-

A. General economic factors

- General level of economic activity- boom or recession
- Interest rate, availability of finance,
- Inflation, monetary policy,
- Fiscal policy
- Trade and export and import policy

B. The Industry

- The market, competition
- Changes in product technology
- Adverse conditions affecting industry
- Key ratios and operating statistics
- Specific accounting treatment and problems
- Unique practices
- Legislation and regulatory framework

C. The Entity

1. About ownership and management characteristics

- structure of the entity- private, public, government
- Beneficial owner, related parties
- Capitals structure
- Organisation structure
- Management objectives, philosophy, strategy
- Persons charged with governance- composition, experience, independence, code of conduct for governance etc.
- Operating management – key persons, turnover rate (change in person), experience, competence, management information system, compensation package and whether it is linked to profits or results
- Internal audit function – expertise, functioning
- Internal control environment

2. The entity's business- products, markets, suppliers, expenses and operations

- Location of the production facilities, warehouses, offices
- Employment (by location, supply, wage, union contracts, pension commitments, government regulation etc.
- Products or services or market- (major customers, profit margin, warranty terms, export, delivery pattern, after sales service commitments etc.)
- Inventories (location, quantity, custody)
- Franchises, licenses, patents,
- Important expense category (like for banks- interest on deposits and establishment)
- Research and development
- Information systems

3. Financial performance-

- Key ratios and operating statistics

- Trends
- Debt structure- terms, covenants, restrictions

4. Reporting requirements

- Legislation
- Regulatory environment and requirements
- Taxation-direct and indirect
- Measurement and disclosure issues peculiar to the business- for e.g., revenue measurement for a contract business, disclosure requirement of a banking business
- Auditing reporting requirement
- Users of the financial statements

Obtaining the knowledge-

Prior knowledge, updating, accumulation and vetting

Initial knowledge of the business is acquired before accepting the engagement. Initial knowledge of industry, ownership, management and operations of the entity is gathered. Following he acceptance of the engagement, more information is gathered and the initial knowledge is refined, modified, updated and accumulated. The auditor relates the knowledge he obtains with the audit evidences he gathers. In continuing audits, the auditor re-evaluate the information gathered in the light of his past experience and new pointers in the audit scenario. Changes that have taken place since the last audit are identified and updates are made.

Sources for obtaining the knowledge

The auditor obtains the knowledge about the industry and entity from a number of sources-

- Previous experience with the entity or the industry
- Discussion with the people with the entity
- Discussion with internal audit department and review of internal audit reports
- Discussion with other auditors, professional like lawyers who have association with the entity or the industry
- Discussion with persons knowledgeable in the field like economists customers, suppliers
- Publication related to the industry
- Legislation and regulations that significantly affect the industry, entity
- Visits to the entity- premises and plant facilities
- Documents produced by the entity- memorandum of association, articles of association, previous reports and accounts, offer documents, minutes, case papers, promotion literature, budgets, office manual, survey reports etc.

Using the knowledge

The knowledge of the business is a frame of reference within which the auditor exercises his professional judgement. The auditor benefits if he could appropriately use the information with him in—

1. Assessing risks and identifying problems
2. Planning and performing the audit effectively
3. Evaluating audit evidences
4. Providing better service to the client..

An auditor makes many a judgement throughout the audit process. The knowledge of the business would be of great relevance to him in such situations. For example,

- Assessing inherent and control risks in the entity

- Considering the business risk and management response to it
- Considering the fraud risk factors of the entity
- Developing overall audit plan and audit programme
- Determining materiality level and assessing whether materiality level chosen is appropriate
- Assessing audit evidences to vet the assertions contained in financial statements
- Evaluating accounting estimates and management representation
- Identifying special audit areas where attention is required
- Considering the appropriateness of the accounting policies and disclosure requirements
- Identifying related party transactions
- Recognising conflicting information and assessing their validity

Action plan for gaining and using knowledge of the business

1. The auditor should devise plan and procedures to obtain, enrich or modify his knowledge of the business.
2. He Should communicate the information to the audit staff and require them to correlate them with the audit transactions, events and practices of the entity.
3. He should require the audit staff to be alert to the signaling of any additional or new information as they do the audit.
4. The additional information should be shared with the principal auditor and other audit staff.
5. The knowledge of the business should be in the back of auditor's judgement process. The auditor should be well versed to consider how they could affect his judgement of the financial statements taken as a whole or any of their assertions he is vetting for.

QUESTIONS

1. How the knowledge about the client business helps the auditor in his planning and performance of audit?
2. State the few sources from which the auditor can obtain/enrich his knowledge of the client's business.
3. Is an auditor required to be as trained and knowledgeable as the doer of the business? If you feel that it is not so required, state how an auditor could perform effectively his work.
4. State few instances where the knowledge of the business would enter the audit judgement process.
5. Gaining knowledge helps auditor to do his work confidently. Besides, it is a value addition to his services- Elucidate

Consideration of Laws and Regulations in an Audit of Financial Statements

The Laws and regulations

The entity operates in a milieu of plethora of laws and regulations that may affect the operations and preparation of financial statements. Laws and regulations vary considerably in their relation to financial statements. Some laws and regulations prescribe the form and content in which the financial statements are to be prepared. For example, the Companies Act, 1956 prescribes in section 210 read with schedule VI, the form and content of final accounting statements of the company. Some laws and regulations determine the amount to be recorded in the financial statement for certain disclosure. For example, the Income Tax Act, 1961, determines the amount of tax payable by an entity on its earnings. The amount of provision for tax shall require the computation in compliance with the provisions of the Income Tax Act. There are laws which stringently enforce the regulations subject to which only an entity can operate. For example, banking companies, sugar industry or pharmaceutical industry are subject to stringent supervision of monitoring mechanism of the legislature. Still more, there are laws which prescribe the conditions in relation to the operating activities of the enterprises. For examples, there are laws which prescribe the mandatory welfare, hygienic conditions of working atmosphere. Again there are regulations which delimits the area of authority for the entity to do business. For example, the memorandum of association covenants to the public that the company is established to do the business in furtherance of the objectives specified in the object clause of the memorandum and nothing further.

AAS 21 establishes the standards on the responsibility of the auditor regarding the consideration of laws and regulations in an audit of financial statement.

Non-compliance of laws and regulations –meaning

The term non-compliance as used in AAS refers to acts of omissions and commission by the entity being audited either intentional or unintentional, which are contrary to the prevailing law or regulations. Such acts include transactions entered into by or on behalf of or in the name of the entity. For the purpose of this AAS, non-compliance does not include personal misconduct of the employees or management people. To decide that a particular act constitutes non-compliance is beyond the professional competence of the auditor. It is the experts of law (lawyers) who can opine as to whether a particular act would constitute a non-compliance. It would be the Courts of law which could pronounce that a particular act in fact, does constitute a non-compliance. But, however, the auditor's training, experience and understanding of the entity, industry may provide a basis for recognition that some acts coming to the knowledge of the auditor may constitute a non-compliance of law and regulations.

Is detection of non-compliance of laws an aim of the audit of financial statements?

The aim of the audit of financial statement is to express an opinion on the truth and fairness of the financial statements. When they are materially misstated, it is the duty of the auditor to bring the fact of it in his audit report. When planning and performing audit procedures and in evaluating and reporting the results thereof, the auditor should recognise that non-compliance by the entity with laws and regulations may materially affect the financial statements. However, the auditor cannot be expected to detect non-compliance of all laws and regulations.

Responsibility of management for the compliance with laws and regulations.

It is the responsibility of the management that laws and regulations as applicable to the entity are complied with. It has to rcognise this and develop a monitoring system to instill the philosophy of compliance, detection of non-compliance and correction and prevention of non-compliance. The management may have to build a register or manual listing the laws to be complied with and action guides for the benefit of employees. The involvement of internal audit department, legal section and audit committee in this direction will be of immense help.

Auditor's duty as to non-compliance of laws and regulations

1. The auditor cannot be held responsible for preventing non-compliance. The audit may, at the best, instill a moral fear and may act as a deterrent for non-compliance of laws and regulations.
2. Regarding detection of non-compliance, it is to be acknowledged that the audit is subject to certain limitations. Though the audit is conducted properly, there might remain certain material misstatements without detection. This is due to various facts including- intentional suppression of facts by staff, misrepresentation of facts by management, persuasive not conclusive nature of audit evidence, top management's involvement in circumventing the laws etc. Hence there is inherent risk that all misstatements arising from non-compliance of laws may not be exposed to the auditors.
3. But the auditor cannot turn a blind eye everywhere. The auditor should plan and perform the audit recognising that the events or conditions he may encounter during audit may throw certain light for him to question whether certain laws have been complied or not.
4. The financial statements the auditor certifies might have to be prepared in accordance with specific legal format. For example, the Companies Act, 1956 specifies the form and content of the financial statements of the companies. Again, there might be industry specific requirements. The Banking companies Act may require certain additional information/ modifications in financial statements for a company engaged in banking business. Similarly RBI may be empowered to issue guidelines for provisioning for bad and doubtful debts of a bank and determination of a performing asset in relation to banking and other specified companies. The auditor should have knowledge of these funedamental laws that might have a bearing on the material amounts of financial statements and disclosure. There might be certain laws, the compliance of which is fundamental to the very existence of sub-stratum of an entity. For example, obtaining of incorporation certificate for a company, obtaining of license for a banking or non-banking financial company from RBI before commencement of business are important aspects to be complied with by an entity. The auditor should gain an understanding of these laws. The existing knowledge of the entity, industry, discussion with the management etc. may help the auditor to obtain a common understanding of these types of laws affecting the entity. These are the laws about which alone the auditor is expected to be vigilant to ensure that material misstatements do not appear in financial statements arising out of non-compliance as regards them.

5. Again, as auditor performs his audit, he may encounter events or conditions that may necessitate him to make certain enquiries with the management, or lawyers as to the susceptibility of the entity to non-compliance of the laws and regulations. For example, in doing substantial vouching, the auditor may come across situations warranting him to enquire about the noncompliance of the laws. The reading of minute books of directors, claim files, taxation files, correspondence with lawyers, legal fees scrutiny etc. might bring forth certain points to the notice of the auditor.
6. In circumstance narrated in point 5, the auditor may obtain a written representation from the management that they have disclosed to the auditor all acts of non-compliance whose effects may affect the financial statements. The auditor may rely the representation and believe it to be true in the absence of any evidence to the contrary.
7. When auditor comes across evidences of non-compliance of laws, he has to examine the nature of non-compliance, the circumstances in which it occurred, the effect of it in financial statements. The nature of non-compliance may, sometimes, be serious as to affect the very fundamentals of the entity itself. For example, the doing of illegal business might affect the substratum of the entity itself. The circumstances for non-happening may throw certain insights as to the efficacy of the internal control operation in existence. It may prompt the auditor to question the integrity of the management when the management is actively involved in non-compliance. In such a circumstance, the representation given by management cannot be relied with such force as it would merit in normal circumstances. The effect of the non-compliance on financial statements should be considered by the auditor. For example, the quantum of potential fines, penalties, threat of discontinuance of the operations etc. should be considered and auditor should judge about the adjustment of the financial statement balances or providing of disclosures that are appropriate to the circumstances.
8. When the auditor is unable to obtain the information in relation to a non-compliance known to him, the auditor should consider the effect of lack of audit evidence in relation to the matter before finalising the report.
9. The auditor should document the matters, events and audit judgment in relation to non-compliance he considered.
10. The fact of non-compliance must be reported to the management timely depending on the seriousness and materiality of the non-compliance. When the non-compliance involves top management, the auditor must bring to the notice of the next higher management – say, Board, audit committee, about the fact of non-compliance.
11. The users of financial statements should be informed of the non-compliance when they affect the financial statements in material amounts or in their disclosure needs. The auditor should judge issuing a qualified opinion or adverse report or disclaimer depending on the individual case and facts.
12. The auditor may find that he is precluded from informing the breach of law to any third party including regulatory and enforcement authority in view of his duty of confidentiality to the client. However he may have to disclose the non-compliance to the regulatory or enforcing authority when he is specifically mandated by such authorities by a law to reveal this to them. For example, RBI requires the company auditor to report the non-compliance of RBI directives in relation to acceptance, repayment of public deposits by a company.
13. When non-compliance, though not affecting the financial statements, is, in auditor's opinion, of such nature that cast aspersion on the integrity and good conduct of top management of the entity, or not corrected at the instance of auditor's specific pointing

out the same, the auditor would find that it is wise and in good professional ethics to withdraw from being auditor to the entity.

QUESTIONS

1. Who is responsible for the initiation and implementation of the system for ensuring compliance to laws and regulations?
2. There are certain laws the knowledge of which are fundamental to the audit function of the entity- Explain.
3. How will auditor respond when he comes across situations or conditions in which it appears that the laws may be non-complied?
4. Is auditor duty bound to disclose the non-compliance of laws to the enforcing and regulatory authorities?
5. Is non-compliance of laws to be disclosed in audit report to the users of financial statements?

Chapter 9

Audit Engagement

I ENGAGEMENT FOR AUDIT

Determining Scope of Audit-Audit Engagement Letter :

An auditor acts in different capacities while offering his professional service to clients. Sometimes he acts as an accountant, sometimes as an expert consultant and many times as an auditor in its strictest sense of the term. Even while acting as an auditor, he may be required to give his opinion on certain matters or he may be required to certify certain facts. In his audit work, the auditor may be expected to cover certain facts. In his audit work, the auditor may be expected to cover what is generally expected of in such as engagement or he may be expected to cover certain special matters in addition to it.

Misunderstanding the position by auditor or wrong conception of role played by the auditor by the client or users of financial statements often results in avoidable litigations. In Wilde and others vs Cape and Dalgleish (1897), the plaintiffs sued the auditors for certain negligence in their audit duty while the defendent auditor contended that they were engaged to prepare P&L accounts and Balance sheet. The Learned judge observed misunderstanding between plaintiffs and defendent-auditor with regard to role to be played by the defendant. The case was compromised with auditor having been asked to pay certain damages. In famous Leech Vs stockes Bros & Prim (1937) case, the plaintiffs instructed the defendant audit firm to prepare annual profit and loss accounts for submission of them to tax authority. At a later date, the plaintiff sued the auditor for not finding out certain defalcations. They urged that the defalcations would be revealed during routine auditing. The court held that the auditors were not liable as there was difference between role of an accountant and role of an auditor. An auditor wearing the mantle of an accountant is no more or no less than the accountant himself only.

In discharging his attest function, an auditor is not always guided by single audit aim. The audit aim for his reporting is different from the audit aim for his certifying. His audit aim is entirely different for his role as an advisor. In reporting on financial statements under Companies Act, for example, the auditor opines on the truth and fairness of the financial statements whereas in certifying a financial document, he asserts the veracity of the document in terms of truth and *correctness* as against *fairness*.

An auditor takes the audit expectations of him from the enactments governing the audit or from generally what is expected in such an engagement. A client cannot expect the auditor to cover special areas in his audit unless these are explicitly made known to the auditor as audit expectations.

Misconception of role of auditor could be avoided, audit aim could be pin-pointed, audit expectation could be detailed, if the auditor and his client come to know of these areas of understanding in unambiguous terms. The issuance of audit engagement letter by the auditor to his client is an arrangement in this direction. It is a clarificatory document detailing the areas of auditing, its objective and responsibilities of auditor in connection therewith. The audit engagement letter defines the position of auditor, describes the audit aims and delimits the audit expectations by specifying audit limitations.

AAS 26 lays down the standards on-

1. Agreeing terms of engagement with the client and
2. The auditor's response to a request by a client to change the terms of an engagement to one that provides a lower level of assurance.

Audit Engagement letter

In the interest of both client and auditor, the auditor should send an engagement letter before the commencement of the engagement. The engagement documents and confirms the auditor's acceptance of the appointment, the objectives and scope of the audit and the extent of auditor's responsibilities to the client.

The principal contents of the audit engagement letter are-

- The objective of the audit of financial statements.
- Management responsibility for the financial statements.
- Management responsibility for selection of appropriate accounting policies, implementation of applicable accounting standards, explanation for material departure from those accounting standards.
- Management responsibility for preparing the accounts on a going concern basis.
- Management responsibility for making judgements and estimates for true and fair compilation of financial statements.
- Management responsibility for maintenance of adequate accounting records and internal control.
- The scope of audit including reference to applicable legislation, regulations, and the pronouncements of the Institute.
- The fact that certain material misstatement resulting from fraud (and sometimes from error) may remain undetected even after the audit in view of inherent limitations of the audit.
- The right of unrestricted access to records and information needed by auditor for conducting audit.
- The fact that the audit process may be subject to peer review under the Chartered Accountants Act, 1949.
- Besides these the engagement letter may also include-
  - ☐ Arrangement regarding planning of the audit
  - ☐ Expectation from the management of receiving written confirmation concerning representation made in connection with the audit.
  - ☐ Basis on which the fees for audit is to be computed and billing arrangements.
  - ☐ Request for the client to acknowledge the duplicate copy of engagement letter as a token of his acceptance to the terms set therein.
  - ☐ Arrangement for involvement of other experts, auditors, internal auditors etc. where deemed necessary for the audit.
  - ☐ Arrangement for any reference or otherwise with the predecessor auditors where the engagement is a new one.
  - ☐ Any restriction to the auditor's liability, if it could be and is restricted.

Issuance of engagement letter for recurring audits

The audit engagement letter is issued at the commencement of initial engagement. It contains a clause that it shall remain in force unless otherwise modified. Hence, it would not be necessary to issue audit engagement letter each time during repetitive audit to the same client. However, the auditor may consider the necessity of issuing engagement letter again if it he feels so. The following may be circumstances in which the auditor may consider appropriate to issue a fresh engagement letter-

- ☐ When it appears that the client has misunderstood the objective and scope of the audit.
- ☐ A change in the composition of the management, board of directors or ownership and it would be pertinent to remind them of the terms fresh
- ☐ Any revised terms in engagement letter either by addition, deletion or modification of original terms.
- ☐ A significant change in nature or size of the business of client, say, warranting inclusion of terms regarding certain arrangements for audit
- ☐ Legal requirements or pronouncement of the Institute affecting the existing terms or necessity for inclusion of new terms.

Acceptance of change in terms of engagement letter

Audit is commenced after issuance of audit engagement letter. Sometimes it may happen that the client may request the auditor to change the terms of audit engagement letter which substitutes the level of assurance to a lower level. In chapter III we have indicated that auditor's role differs depending on the engagement for e.g., audit, review, agreed upon procedures, or compilation. In each of the situations he expresses his opinion in the form of assurance. In **audit** the assurance level is high (assurance in a positive fashion-financial statements exhibit true and fair view/ or they do not exhibit true and fair view/ or exhibit true and fair view subject to the list of misstatements). The level of assurance is moderate in **review** , where the assertion is given in a negative fashion-(assurance in the style- *nothing* comes to the notice of the auditor to believe that the financial statements are infected with misstatements). In agreed upon procedures, the auditor lists down the procedures performed and findings. He gives no assurance and it is left to the readers to make their own assessment based on facts of work done and findings reported. In compilation auditor indicates that he took part in preparation and no assurance is given in any form.

The client may request the auditor who commenced the work in accordance with an engagement letter to revise his objective of giving assurance to a lower level than what he planned for and communicated originally. This might be necessitated by-

- ☐ Change in circumstances affecting the need for services of the auditor
- ☐ Misunderstanding as to nature of an audit or related services.
- ☐ Restriction on the scope of the audit either imposed by management or caused by circumstances.

Now the question arises whether it is correct for the auditor to accept a new role (in reference to the assurance level to be changed).

1. The auditor should not agree to a change in engagement letter when there is no reasonable justification for doing so. Where change relates to information which is incorrect, incomplete or otherwise unsatisfactory, the auditor should not accept to change. Also, where during the audit, the auditor finds lack of evidence (for e.g., there is no confirmation for debtors and hence auditor is to issue a qualified report) and the client suggests that the audit of the debtors be so changed and accordingly indicated to be review of debtors), the auditor may not be justified for agreeing to such a change.

2. The auditor should not do agree to change where there is restriction on scope of his audit function. If the restrictions place fetters on his free play for effectively discharging his functions in accordance with any statute, or pronouncements of the institute, he may have to desist from agreeing to such change.
3. Where there is justification for change in terms of engagement, he may agree to such change. Where change is due to change in expectation of auditor's services or due to misunderstanding to the nature of audit and related services (as review, agreed upon procedures or compilation etc.), the auditor may agree for change. Before agreeing for change the auditor should weigh the legal or contractual implications if any, of such change.
4. Where the auditor who originally performed audit finds it agreeable to change a role for a related service, he may issue report in the light of changed level of assurance expected based on the *audit* work he performed provided-
   - The report issued is appropriate for the revised terms of engagement.
   - The report does not contain any reference to the original engagement.
   - The report does not contain any reference to the procedures that may have been performed in original engagement. However, if the changed engagement is one of agreed procedure, the report may contain reference to such procedures performed which are the procedures as agreed upon in revised engagement and which ordinarily become part of the report of revised engagement.
5. If the auditor is not agreeable to change in terms of engagement and he is not permitted to continue with the original engagement, he should withdraw from the engagement. He should consider whether it is necessary to inform the circumstances which prompted him to withdraw from the engagement to the board of directors or shareholders.
6. When the auditor agrees to change, he should get a letter of acknowledgement of the acceptance of the client for revised terms so that mutual acceptance is established without confusion.

II ENGAGEMENT FOR COMPILATION OF FINANCIAL INFORMATION

Sometimes, the auditor may be asked to compile the financial information of an entity. In such a case, he acts as an accountant rather than an auditor. AAS 31 lays down the standards of assurance in an engagement to compile financial information.

The objective of a compilation engagement is for an accountant to use accounting enterprise, as opposed to auditing expertise, to collect, classify and summarise financial information. The procedures employed are not designed and do not enable the accountant to express any assurance on the financial information. However, the users of the financial information derive some benefit as the compilation engagement entails the participation of professional accountant.

Management responsibility for financial information

In compilation engagement, it is the management who is responsible for ensuring that the financial information generated in the entity is correct, complete and reliable. The management should maintain adequate accounting and other records and ensure internal control. It is responsible for selection and application of appropriate accounting policies. The management should ensure adequate safeguarding of assets and monitor for detection and prevention of frauds, non-compliance with laws and regulations. The professional accountant who complies the financial information does not assume responsibility for these and disclaims them in his report.

Issuing letter of engagement for compilation

It is in the mutual interests of both accountant and client to have the terms of engagement reduced to writing. The engagement letter issued by the accountant to the client should include the following terms among other things-

- nature of the engagement,
- a clarification that the compilation is not audit or review,
- the fact that no assurance will be expressed,
- management responsibility for matters specified in the paragraph above,
- basis for billing of fees,
- acknowledgment from the client for acceptance of the terms.

Accountant's Report- compilation report

In all the circumstances where the accountant name is associated with financial information compiled by him, the accountant should issue a report. The Report should be titled as Accountant's Report to make clear that it is not Auditor's Report. The Accountant's duty is to compile and not to verify the information supplied to him. However, where the Accountant becomes aware of any material misstatements- e.g., mistake in application of identified financial frame work (for e.g., for company client, the format of Schedule VI is mandated; if there are mistakes in application of the data in the format) or omission of disclosure in accordance with identified financial framework or departure from accounting standards, the Accountant should see that the departures are disclosed in notes to the financial statements compiled and also in Accountant's Report. Similarly the Professional accountant should ensure that estimates are properly made by management for provision of expenses and income. If the estimates are subject to material errors, he may require the management to amend the data. If the same are not properly adjusted, the Accountant may consider withdrawing from the engagement rather than compiling with data known to him to be materially wrong.

III ENGAGEMENT TO PERFORM AGREED UPON PROCEDURE

AAS 32 lays down standards and provide guidance on the auditor's professional responsibilities when an engagement to perform agreed-upon procedures regarding financial information is undertaken. In an engagement to perform agreed upon procedures, the auditor is engaged by client to issue a report of factual findings, based on specified procedures on specified subject matter of specified elements, accounts or items of a financial statements. For e.g. an auditor may be engaged to scrutinise the receivables with the following procedures- check the confirmation, verify reconciliation where the confirmed balances and book balances differ, check that proper adjustments are made for items appearing in reconciliation list, report the findings;

The engagement to perform the agreed upon procedures is not an engagement of audit or review. There is no opinion expressed on the findings. The report merely specifies the nature of procedures adopted, the items checked, and findings. It also specifies that the engagement should not be taken to be an audit or review. It also cautions the readers that the findings are to be read only in relation to the use for which it is intended to be used as agreed between auditor and the client or other party. It cautions that had audit or additional procedures been carried out, other matters might have come to the notice of the auditor which he would have reported. The report also delimits that the engagement is limited to application of agreed upon procedures to items specified and not to the entire gamut of financial statements.

It is in the interests of both the auditor and the client to get the terms of engagement reduced to writing incorporating among other thing- the list of agreed upon procedures, the items to be checked, the fact that the engagement is not to be construed as audit etc.

Considerations at the commencement of new Audit

An audit is generally conducted with some definite objects in view. This object should be constantly kept in mind in the initial stages of the audit.

1. He should see that his appointment in case of a joint-stock company is in accordance with the previsions of the Companies Act. If he does not do so, he will be held liable. If he has been appointed in place of another auditor, he should enquire from the retiring auditor, the reasons for the changes. (*U.C. Majumdar* vs. *J.N. Saika, 1954*).
2. He should obtain definite instructions from the clients about the nature and scope of his work and duties; whether he is to do the accountancy work or audit work or both: by which date the work is to be completed; his honorarium, time by which the report is required, etc. Usually an agreement between an auditor and a client is made verbally but it will be better if the auditor sends a letter of confirmation embodying the terms of contract, scope of work, when the work is to be done, audit fee payable and so on to avoid any dispute later on. This question will not arise in the case of audit of accounts of a joint-stock company as his duties, rights, powers, liabilities, etc., are all laid down by the Companies Act itself.
3. He should examine the system of accounting employed by his client. If he finds any weak point he must study it thoroughly and make recommendations to his client to remove these weak spots.
4. He should then obtain a list of all the books maintained in the office, together with the names of the keepers of such books and their specimen signatures. Such a list should be duly signed by a responsible official of the company. If this is not done, it is possible that he may not have examined some books which had a bearing on the balance sheet. Moreover, he is, in case of joint stock companies, required by the Companies Act to state in his report that proper books have been kept by the company. Again he is also required to state that the balance sheet and the profit and loss account are in agreement with the books of account and (in the case of branches) returns. Thus, the auditor runs a great risk, 'if he omits to examine any of the books which has a bearing on the accounts. He should arrange appointments with key personnel.
5. If internal check system is in operation he should get, if possible, a written statement to that effect and examine that system.
6. He should get a list of the officers of the company containing particulars about their duties, powers and their specimen signatures.
7. If the business is of a technical nature, he would do well to visit the works, acquire technical knowledge to some extent, before he actually commences the work so that he may be able to put intelligent questions to his clients and may not appear to be ridiculous by putting absurd questions and may not be deceived by the clerks who may take undue advantage of his lack of technical knowledge.
8. He should ask the clients to balance the books, prepare the final accounts and the balance sheet, file the vouchers in order of occurrence of the transactions, prepare the schedules of the debtors—good, doubtful and bad debts, creditors, important legal papers, contracts, list of securities, etc., if this has not been done so far. He should never begin his work until the books have been balanced.
9. He should obtain the previous year's audited balance sheet, it any, and see that the accounts during the current year have been opened with those balances which appeared in the previous balance sheet.
10. He should get the report of the auditor, if any, relating to the accounts of the previous year for information regarding the state of the affairs of the company during that year.

11. He must read those clauses of the Memorandum of Association and the Articles of Association of the company which have a bearing on the accounts or the Articles of Partnership of the firm whose accounts he is auditing or Will or Trust Deed in case of an audit of a Trust or Special Acts of Statutes in case of a public utility concern, etc.
12. If it is the first audit of a company, he must also go through the prospectus, contracts with the vendors, promoters etc.

QUESTIONS

1. What is an audit engagement letter? State the advantages of issuing an audit engagement letter.
2. State few important matters that should find place in an audit engagement letter.
3. Can an auditor accept to the terms of engagement be so modified as to require auditor to express a lower level of assurance after the audit has been commenced in terms of original engagement letter?
4. How does the engagement letter to compile financial information differ from audit engagement letter?
5. The engagement to perform agreed upon procedures is a prototype audit in relation to certain components of financial statements-Do you agree?
6. What are the considerations to be kept in mind before taking up a new audit?

Audit Evidence and Audit Procedures

In chapter II on overview of Auditing, we have seen that the auditor should gather sufficient and appropriate audit evidence and test them before expressing any opinion on financial statements. AAS 1 "Basic Principles Governing an Audit" states that the auditor should obtain sufficient and appropriate audit evidence through the performance of compliance and substantive procedures to enable him to draw reasonable conclusions therefrom on which to base his opinion on financial information.

Compliance procedures are tests designed to obtain reasonable assurance that those internal controls on which audit reliance is to be placed are in effect. It is a test about the framework of internal control. Substantive procedures are designed to obtain audit evidence as to the completeness, accuracy and validity of the data produced by the accounting system. It is test about the financial data themselves. The subsubstantive tests are of two types- (a) tests of details of transactions and balances and (b) analysis of significant ratios and trends including the resulting enquiry of unusual fluctuation and items. The tests of transactions are checked by means of vouching of each class of transaction viz. cash receipts, cash payments, purchases, sales etc. The balances are tested by checking of opening balances, scrutiny of debtors' balances, creditor's balances, general ledger balances. The analytical review of the financial information is carried out to find out unusual or unexplained items or amounts. It may entail computations of significant ratios, doing comparative analysis with previous years figures etc.

AAS 5 amplifies the basic principles of audit evidences.

Sufficient and appropriate audit Evidence

It is stated that the auditor should obtain sufficient and appropriate audit evidence. Sufficiency refers to the quantum of audit evidence to be obtained. Appropriateness refers to the relevance and reliability of the evidence. Sufficiency seems to be focused on quantum of audit evidence and appropriateness is related to quality of the audit evidence. Relevance means pertinence or aptness. It is concerned with what type of evidence is apt to confirm an assertion of a financial transaction or a balance. For example, for example mere physical verification of land may not be relevant to confirm the ownership of a land by the client. It would be apt to check that the title deeds are in the name of the client. The reliability of the evidence refers to the degree of confidence that the auditor can place as to the genuineness of the audit evidence checked. The physical verification of cash by the auditor himself on the close of the financial year is a better and more reliable evidence than the accepting of the certificate from a cashier that the balance existed on the closing date.

Thus the auditor is concerned with –

1. the testing of enough volume audit evidence

2. the testing of relevant audit evidences
3. the testing of reliable audit evidence.

Judgement of sufficiency and appropriateness of audit evidence

It is a matter of judgement for auditor to decide what constitutes a sufficient and appropriate audit evidence for a given transaction or a balance or an assertion. No hard and fast rule can be laid down in this regard. The judgement of auditor is influenced by a variety of factors. Few of them are-

1. the degree of risk of misstatement which may be affected by-
   - nature of the item: If the item is vulnerable to fraud, say item of cash, the certificate from the custodians may not be appropriate evidence.
   - the adequacy of internal control : If the internal control is weak, the sufficiency of transactions to be checked will be at a higher level.
   - the nature or size of the business carried on by the entity: If the business is controlled and operated by the owner himself – a proprietary concern- with limited number of outside staff, the risk of misappropriation of assets may be considered to be less.
   - situations which may exert an unusual influence on management-If managerial remuneration is related to sales volume, the complete vouching of last few months may be appropriate.
   - the financial position of the entity: The risk of misstatement by window dressing may be present in a banking company when its key financial data are not good.
2. the materiality of the item- e.g., for significant items, the auditor may like to get more reliable evidence.
3. the experience gained in previous audit: e.g., if the auditor is of firm opinion that internal control is good or believes in integrity of the management, he may place reliance on internal evidence.
4. the results of auditing procedures including fraud, or error which may have been found- if the environment of the entity is suspected to be fraught with fraud, the auditor may place less reliance on the evidence gathered from such sources.
5. the type of information available: e.g. if the total of a schedule of debtors is done electronically, the risk of the figure being not accurate is less and the evidentiary value of the total being correct is more.
6. the trend indicated by accounting ratios and analysis: e.g. the unusual gross profit rate is indicated by ratio, it may prompt to raise the reliability standards of evidence more for inventory valuation.

Assurance of audit assertions by audit evidence

1. The audit evidence obtained from compliance procedure is intended to assure that the assertion that-
   - the internal control exists,
   - that the internal control is operating effectively and
   - that the internal control has so operated throughout the period under audit
2. Audit evidence obtained from substantial procedure is intended to assure the assertions in respect of a transaction or a balance about the existence, rights and obligations, occurrence, completeness, valuation, measurement and presentation and disclosure . Refer chapter 2 for a detailed discussion in this regard.

Reliability of audit evidence

The reliability of audit evidence means the credential value of the assurance the evidence provides about the assertions. When audit evidences collected from different sources and in different forms or nature point to same assurance without conflict, the cumulative effect of effect of assurance level is high. Where they point to inconsistent assertions, the reliability of the evidences is doubted and more evidence needs to be gathered to resolve inconsistency.

Generally-

1. The external evidences are more reliable than internal evidence
2. Internal evidence is more reliable when related internal control is satisfactory.
3. Evidence in the form of documents and written representations is more reliable than oral representation
4. Evidence obtained by the auditor himself is more reliable than that obtained through the entity.

Evaluative criteria for selection of audit evidence

The auditor's aim is to frame a judgement of mind to express an opinion as to the truth and fairness of assertions in a financial statement. The judgement cannot be made intuitively, but based upon careful evaluation of evidences in support of forming an opinion.

The following factors should be borne in mind in gathering evidences.

1. Relevance
2. Reliability
3. Sufficiency
4. Cost effectiveness
5. Convenience
6. Preservation
7. Materiality of the assertion to be tested.
8. Need for corroboration or resolution of inconsistency
9. Accepted Auditing standards / agreed upon procedures to obtain specified evidence.

Depending upon cases, the auditor should seek for specific type of audit evidence. It is a more a matter of practice than of a set of hard and fast rules.

Audit Procedures, Methods to obtain evidence

Basically, there are two types of procedures for obtaining audit evidences. They are compliance procedure and the other is substantive procedure. Substantive procedure consists in procedures to test the balances and events and analytical review with analysis of deviations in amounts or items. Whatever be these, the procedures are carried out by means of employing certain methods called techniques. If vouching is a procedure of carrying substantive checking, the procedure of vouching is accomplished by various methods or techniques like *examination* of documentary vouchers, *inquiry*, *computation* etc. A transaction of payment of cash for purchases is substantially checked by examination of purchase bill, totalling the amounts in various columns of the invoice, checking the posting, inquiring with supplier for a confirmation etc.

The following are the methods of obtaining audit evidences

- ☐ Inspection
- ☐ Observation
- ☐ Inquiry and confirmation
- ☐ Computation
- ☐ Analytical review

Inspection

Inspection consists of examination of documents, records or tangible assets. The documents and records may be of the following types-

- documentary evidence emanating from and held by third parties
- documentary evidence emanating from third parties and held by the entity
- documentary evidence emanating from the entity and held by the entity
- documentary evidence emanating from entity and held by third party.

The reliability of audit evidence varies with each type of these documents.

Observation

Observation consists of witnessing a process or procedure without actually doing it by the auditor. If inventory are counted by the client' staff, the auditor may choose to remain in the place as a witness rather than involving in actual physical counting.

Inquiry and Confirmation

Inquiry consists of seeking appropriate information from sources inside or outside the entity. The sources may be operating personnel or management or owners or experts or persons having dealing with the entity. It may even be interacting with an electronic information system with a search and query language. When sources from outside entity are inquired with regard to data of the entity, the implications of impairment of confidentiality of the client are to be so carefully taken care of. Responses to the inquiry may provide for additional information, or dispel the doubts clouding the information, or may corroborate the information.

Confirmation is more a response to the auditor's technique of inquiry, though loosely described and commonly understood to be an auditing technique. Confirmation consists of the response to an inquiry to corroborate an information. It may be about any fact affecting financial statements. For e.g., the debtors may be requested to confirm the balances as per their records with the balances as per the entity's records. Or the consignee may be asked to confirm that the stocks lying with him do belong to the entity only.

Computation

Computation consists of checking arithmetical accuracy of the source data, or accounting data of the entity. It may include addition, subtraction, multiplication, division, checking the carry over, brought down, comparing the totals of both sides, posting checking, extraction checking, reconcilation.

Analytical Review

Analytical review consist of –

- studying significant ratios, and trends
- Investigating unusual fluctuations and items.

Nature, Extent and Timing of Audit Procedures

The techniques or methods described above are not isolated specifics mutually excluding the other in one's use. The employment of one technique may necessarily involve the use of other technique on to or along with it simultaneously. For example, the analytical review may entail computations; examination of documents may involve inquiry or computation. The nature, extent and timing of audit procedures to be deployed would depend on auditor's judgement as to various factors like the assertion to be tested, the environment in which he operates including the internal control, accounting system, the management culture, reliability of the audit evidence, materiality of the item, the time availability, the timing of audit, the timing of availability of the evidence etc. The decision as to use of appropriate nature, extent and timing of the evidence is crucial.

Nature of certain audit procedures

Let us discuss about the nature of certain audit procedures elaborately viz., about-

- ☐ Tests of control – compliance procedure for testing internal control (already discussed)
- ☐ Tests of details- test of transactions and tests of balances –substantive procedure(already discussed)
- ☐ Analytical procedures
- ☐ Review of Events occurring after balance sheet date for its evidentiary value

Analytical Procedures

Analytical procedures include means the analysis of significant ratios, trends including the resulting investigation of fluctuations and relationships that are inconsistent with other relevant information or which deviate from the predicted amounts. The two important components of tools of analysis of analytical procedures are comparative analysis and relational analysis. The utility of analytical procedure lies in proper investigating the findings of relational and comparative analyses.

The auditor may apply analytical procedures at all stages of audit and should apply them necessarily at the planning and overall review stages of audit.

AAS14 lays down standards on the application of analytical procedures during an audit,

Nature of Analytical Procedures

Analytical procedures include-

- ☐ Consideration of comparison
- ☐ Consideration of relationship

Comparison of the item of audit checking is made with-

- ☐ Comparable information for prior periods
- ☐ Anticipated results of the entity such as budgets or forecasts
- ☐ Predictive estimate prepared by auditor-for e.g., amounts of depreciation calculated, tax provision computed etc.,
- ☐ Similar industry information-e.g., comparison of trade debtors as a percentage of sales with industry average

Relation of the item of audit is studied with other elements to ensure that they conform to audit expectations.

- ☐ Inter-relation of financial information may be made- e.g., the ratio of gross profit to sales.
- ☐ Intra-relation of Financial and non-financial information may also be made. e.g., the quantum of good x sold and sale value of good x. This would check the audit expectation that the per unit realization should be within the allowable lower range of maximum selling price.

Purpose of analytical procedures

Analytical procedures are used -

1. As a planning tool
2. As a substantive procedures
3. As an overall review

Analytical procedures as a planning tool

Analytical procedures are used in planning the nature, timing and extent of audit procedures to be applied in an audit situation. The use of analytical procedure during planning stage may indicate the auditors the aspects of business and accounting information of which he may not be aware. It would help him in allocating the time and attention in tune with the audit risk needs. For example, before auditing the financial statements of a bank, it would be interesting for the auditor to see from a previous profit statement of a bank that interest on deposits constitute major expenses head. Accordingly he would plan for his audit programme to vouching of major deposit heads with more attention. Similarly, in checking a consolidated financial statements, an auditor can decide on extent of checking of financial details of the select components.

Analytical procedures as a substantive procedure

An auditor faces the detection risk when he does the substantive checking. The detection risk implies that a material misstatement may lie without detection even after the doing of the audit. An auditor cannot completely reduce the detection risk to nil always, yet, he can reduce it to an acceptable level. To reduce the level of detection risk, the auditor makes use of tests of details- i.e., tests of balances and tests of transactions, and analytical procedures. Analytical procedures may be used to complement as well as to supplant the tests of details. It is used as a *complementary* one to corroborate the results of the tests of details. It is used to *supplant* the tests of details when in the opinion of the auditor, the results to be obtained from the analytical procedure would be effective and efficient. That how it is used is a matter of professional judgement.

Analysis by auditor or by entity

The analytical procedure may be done by the auditor himself or by the entity at the instance of the auditor or otherwise. In the latter case, the auditor may restrict himself with the analysis of the results to the required audit needs. He must be cautious that the analysis is properly made by the entity and the data- financial or non-financial made use of therein are reliable; the methodology are validated.

Considerations for making use of analytical procedures as a substantive audit procedure.

1. **Objectives of analytical procedures**
   The auditor needs to know what he plans to make use of the findings of analytical procedures. He must be clear whether he applies the analytical procedure to obtain primary evidentiary value or corroborative evidentiary value. Again, if the analytical procedures are employed as a basis for deeper investigation, the nature of the analytical procedures would accordingly vary.
2. **Extent of reliance on analytical procedure**
   The analytical procedures generally ground on the premise that a relation does exist among data. The degree of relation is tested by these procedures which throw to light the aberrations or exceptions. However, the auditor should recognize that there is always a risk that material misstatement may remain still undetected even in spite of the relation being established properly. If the auditor's assessment of such risk is at low level, the results of the procedures may not mislead. If the auditor perceives that such risk at a higher level, the auditor needs to mitigate them with performing of other or additional audit procedures. The extent of reliance that the auditor places on the results of the analytical procedures depends on the following-
   - □ **Materiality of the item involved**- If the item to be tested is material and hence the detection risk assumes importance, then the auditor may not exhaust the substantive checking of the item with the analytical procedures alone. For example, where the inventory value is material in balance sheet, the auditor may not just calculate the inventory turnover ratio and stop with it if the findings conform to the expected results. Rather he may have done other substantive procedures of observation, examination of inventory records etc.,

- □ **Analytical procedures supplemented by other procedures.** Sometimes, the doubts raised by analytical procedures may get dispelled by the findings of other audit procedures. The doubt as to collectibility of the trade debt beyond a specified time period (as obtained by analytical procedures) may be dispelled by review of cash receipts in respect of the same debts subsequent to balance sheet date. The procedure of review of subsequent events thus adds credence to an assertion of collectibility of debt which was otherwise portrayed by another audit procedure.
- □ **The vulnerability of findings to prediction .** The findings of the analytical procedures should lend themselves to a meaningful and relevant comparison with predetermined predicted results. For e.g. it may not be expected that each expense shall bear an expected relation with sales. While the gross profit may generally bear a predicted ratio with sales, it may not be the same with net profit.
- □ **The degree of inherent and control risks.** If the internal control and accounting control are weak, the information used for analytical procedure may be subject to limitations of reliability. In such a situation, more reliance needs to be placed on tests of details.

3. **The ease with which information may be disaggregated.** The results of the analytical procedures will be not effectively revealing unless the information is easily amenable to be disaggregated. To check the correctness of interest expenditure for a bank one may like to compute the interest cost. In this connection for e.g., the ratio of interest to total deposits may not be that useful as the ratios of category-wise interest expenditure to category-wise total deposits. If the information is not easily compilable in different forms as the auditor may require, the use of analytical procedures will be limited.
4. **The availability, reliability, comparability of variety of financial and non-financial information.** Depending on the availability of the information within and without the entity, the use of analytical procedures will be wide. Similarly, the nature, source, comparability, and reliability of data influence the use of analytical procedures.
5. **Knowledge gained in previous audits** The knowledge on hand with the auditor will guide him in making use of analytical procedures. The problems he encountered, the investigation he made in resolving inconsistency in predicted results and findings of the procedures will all be of help in use of the procedures in a repetitive situation.

Analytical procedure as an overall review tool

The analytical procedure should be used at or near the end of the audit when forming an overall conclusion as to whether the financial statements as a whole are consistent with the auditor's knowledge of the business. The analytical procedure may indicate, for e.g., the profit may not be more than a limit. If the actual profits are not conforming to this, it would suggest that there are certain errors somewhere or it would suggest that further analysis would be required to spot the factors causing variance.

Investigation of unusual items

The findings of the analytical procedures point to significant fluctuation or inconsistent relationship with other relevant information or deviation from the predicted results, the auditor needs to investigate further the cause of aberrations. He may inquire the reasons for these with the management. Sometimes, the auditor needs to modify or apply additional audit procedures to remove the anomalies unexplained.

CONSIDERATION OF EVENTS OCCURRING AFTER BALANCE SHEET DATE

Accounting Standard 4(AS 4) and Auditing and Assurance Standard19(AAS 19) deal with auditor's concern about events occurring after Balance sheet date. AS 4 deal with the accounting standards concerning the adjustments of accounts and disclosure in response to the **events occurring after balance sheet date**. AAS 19 lays down the standards of auditing as regards **subsequent events**.

AS 4 defines the events occurring after Balance Sheet date as those significant events, both favourable and unfavourable, that occur between the balance sheet date and date on which the financial statements are approved by the Board of directors in the case of a company and by the corresponding approving authority in the case of any other entity. Two types of events are identified by AS4.

1. Those which provide further evidence of conditions that existed at the balance sheet date
2. Those which are indicative of conditions that arose subsequent to the balance sheet date.

(*a*) Adjustments to assets and liabilities are required for events occurring after the balance sheet date that provide additional information materially affecting the determination of the amounts relating to the conditions existing at the balance sheet date. For example, the event of insolvency of a debtor subsequent to the balance sheet date may provide additional evidence as to the assertion as to the realisability (i.e., in this example that the debt is not realisable) of the debt. Accordingly, the value of the debtor needs to be suitably adjusted by making provision for bad debts expected as on the balance sheet (which in fact had so become after balance sheet date but before the accounts are approved).

(*b*) Adjustments of assets and liabilities are not appropriate for events occurring after balance sheet date, if such events do not relate to the conditions existing at the balance sheet date. For example, the land is accounted at the cost of purchase. Subsequent to the balance sheet date, the purchase cost had lowered or increased, it is not appropriate to substitute the original cost of asset with the current cost obtained during the period after the balance sheet date but before approving of the accounts. Because, the event does not relate to the condition existing at the balance sheet date. If subsequent events point to *providing of additional information* for deciding the conditions existed at the balance sheet date, the accounts are adjusted. If subsequent events constitute a different condition with respect to different specific time point, the adjustment of accounts in such case is not appropriate.

(*c*) There may be events which do not relate to the condition existed on balance sheet date. They may be so significant that they may be disclosed in report of the approving authority e.g., director's report. For e.g., the destruction by fire of a godown subsequent to balance sheet date but before the date of approving the accounts, may require a mention of the fact in director's report. Since these do not affect the amounts in the balance sheet date, no disclosure would be required in the accounts.

(*d*) Certain events which occur after balance sheet date may require adjustment in accounts by reason of specific requirement in law. For example, the dividend becomes payable only upon and after its declaration in annual general meeting. But a provision for it needs to be made because schedule VI of the Companies Act requires a specific disclosure for the same.

(*e*) The events which occur after balance sheet date may provide, sometimes, information as to the appropriateness of the going concern assumption. Generally, an entity is assumed to carry on its business from period to period. The important implication of this assumption is that current assets are meant for immediate realisation and fixed assets are held without intention of selling them, but with the intention of carrying on the business upon or with them. Hence is the accounting treatment of recording the current assets at carrying cost or market price and fixed assets at their cost less depreciation. If the subsequent events point to the fact that the going concern assumption is vitiated, it would require consideration as to whether it would be proper to have prepared the accounts with the assumption. For e.g., the event of complete nationalisation of the entity that had occurred subsequent to balance sheet date (but before approval of accounts) would merit consideration of management and auditor regarding the appropriateness of the going concern assumption implied in the preparation of the accounts.

Audit procedures for gathering audit evidence from subsequent events

The auditor should perform procedures designed to identify sufficient and appropriate audit evidence of subsequent events. It would be incumbent upon auditor to check whether the information obtained of these events are adequately used for the adjustment or disclosure in financial statements where it is appropriate to do so. Subsequent events are defined in AAS 19 as events occurring after balance sheet date but before the date of auditor's report.

1. The review of subsequent events to the balance sheet date is in addition to what auditor has to perform normally for transaction vouching of routine nature. For example, the concept of cut-off procedure would dictate that a line of demarcation should be established for certain pending transactions which hang on the balance sheet date. For e.g., good received note may have been prepared for goods received within the balance sheet period but invoices might have reached late after balance sheet date. As at year end, the auditor initials the last Goods Received Note (GRN). Hanging transactions (subsequently finished) upto the last number of GRN so identified alone are considered. The review of subsequent events contemplated under AAS 19 is in addition to these review of routine nature.
2. The auditor should review the procedures that the management has established for identification of subsequent events.
3. The auditor may find it useful to read the minutes of meeting of shareholders, the board, and executive committees held after balance sheet date,
4. The auditor may also inquire about the matters discussed in meetings for which minutes are not yet prepared.
5. The auditor may also study the latest available budgets, cash flows, performance appraisal and other interim reports prepared by the entity after balance sheet date for the subsequent periods to know about any developments connected with the conditions existed as at the balance sheet date.
6. Inquiring with the entity's lawyers for any pending litigation, claims etc.
7. The auditor may inquire with the management in specific areas like- the current developments in contingent matters, any occurrence of events which may question the appropriateness of certain accounting policy or assumption adopted, the availability of any additional information on matters which were earlier accounted based on preliminary or inconclusive data etc.
8. The auditor should satisfy himself that the subsequent events is appropriately considered to adjust or provide disclosure in accounts. If the auditor is not satisfied, he may decide the qualifying of the report accordingly in regard to such matters.

Extent of checking audit evidence-Census versus Sampling

The extent of checking denotes both quantum of items to be selected for checking and the length of stretching the checking plan for an item selected.

There may be temptation for census checking in which all the transactions are checked cent percent. There may appear that checking of all vouchers in cash payment, for instance, may provide a sense of relief that detection errors are reduced to the maximum level possible. But, the case may not correspond to this notion. It is not always correct that more quantum of checking means detailed checking. It may happen one may loose quality in the altar of ceremonial counting of number of items checked. Lack of discretion may one to slip in dangers of quagmires of misstatements and omission. A sample may provide for an alternative. But ill conceived sample plan may cause detection risks at high level. The auditor should make a professional judgement on the quantum of items to be checked, the methods of choosing samples and projection of sample findings onto the population.

Audit sampling

AAS 15 lays down standards on a) design, b) selection and c) evaluation of sample results.

Audit sampling means the application of audit procedures to less than 100% of the items within an account balance or class of transactions to enable the auditor to obtain and evaluate audit evidence about some characteristic of the items selected in order to form or assist in forming a conclusion concerning the population.

Design of the sample

Designing audit sample is an important task. The checking of all items of the population is not sample. Again, checking all items within a portion of population having a particular characteristic does not constitute sampling for that portion. Again such a testing cannot be construed to be sample testing for the population of which it is a part. Because, the items tested are those with a predetermined characteristic and cannot be assumed to be representative of the entire population.

When designing audit sample, the auditor should consider-

- Specific audit objective
- Population from which the sample is chosen
- Sample size

Specific audit objective

The auditor should be clear about the specific audit objective in relation to an audit exercise and what audit procedures are to be applied for achieving the audit objective. For e.g. when the auditor wants to ensure that all items required to be disclosed in accordance with a statute are so disclosed in a balance sheet, it would be inappropriate to select a random sample of few items and to confirm their proper disclosure. Again, tests of efficacy of internal control would seek to ensure that all documents, say purchase invoices, are properly processed before their accounting. In such a case, the amount of invoice is not a concern for auditor in his checking of the completeness of the working of the system. On the other hand, while doing the substantive checking for getting an assurance of the value of the purchases of the year, the auditor may choose to select items of purchases with values above a limit.

Population- Base, Sample units and Stratification

The population is the base from which the auditor selects sample to draw conclusions. The appropriate identification of the population for achieving audit specific objective is crucial. For e.g., for testing the correctness of interest expenditure debited by a bank in its P&L account, the relevant population would be listing of interest debits, the listing of all deposits. The auditor may select certain items from the interest schedule and check them for their accuracy. He may select few items of deposits and check that interest is provided for them. So at least two base population he requires in situation of the type in the instance.

Apart from deciding on population base, the auditor must decide on sample units. The sample units are individual units which make up a population. For e.g. in a population of total debtors balance, the sample unit may be a set of several individual invoices or a set of several balances of different customers. The auditor must choose how he must go about in picking the sample units- in this case, customer-wise, or invoice-wise.

To design a sample effectively, the auditor may choose to sub-divide the big population into various sub-populations each sub-population possessing a defined characteristic unique to it alone. For example, the population of customer balances may be so stratified into balances range of different amounts. The stratification helps the auditor to reduce the population size smaller and also vary the sampling plan suited to different strata depending on the audit objective and detection error considerations.

Sample Size

When determining sample size, the auditor should consider –

- Sampling risk
- Tolerable error
- Expected error

Sampling risk

Sampling risk or sampling error arises from the possibility that the auditor's conclusion, based on sample, may be different from the conclusion that would be reached if the entire population were subjected to the same audit procedure. On the other hand, non-sampling errors arise not because that a conclusion projected from sample findings may turn out to be different; it arises when the auditor uses any audit procedures and is common and present whether or not sampling technique is made use of. Non-sampling errors connote wrong conclusion due to the reasons - the audit evidences are persuasive in nature and not conclusive; inappropriate audit procedure may mislead results; incorrect interpretation may have been drawn from the evidences assessed.

The sampling risk may result in – risk of under reliance or over reliance in tests of control. The risk of under reliance suggests that the sample result does not support the auditor's assessment of control risk but the actual compliance rate would support such an assessment. The Risk of over reliance suggests that the sample result supports the auditor's assessment of control risk, while the actual compliance rate would not support such an assessment.

Again, the sampling risk may results in- risk of incorrect rejection or risk of incorrect acceptance in substantive procedures. The risk of incorrect rejection means when in fact, the account balance or a class of transaction is not misstated, the sample results supports the conclusion that they are misstated. In other words, it is akin to accepting a statement as false while it is true. The risk of incorrect acceptance means when in fact, the account balance or a class of transaction is misstated, the sample results supports the conclusion that they are not misstated. In other words, it is akin to accepting a statement as true when in fact it is false.

The risk of under reliance and risk of incorrect rejection affect audit *efficiency*. The performance of additional procedures either by the auditor or the entity may establish that initial conclusions drawn from the sample were incorrect. The risk of over reliance and risk of incorrect acceptance affect the audit *effectiveness.* They may lead to an erroneous opinion on the financial statements. The likelihood of such eruption of such error is higher in these risks than what they are in risk of under reliance and risk of incorrect rejection.

The size of the sample is affected by the risk perception of the auditor with regard to the sampling risk. The lower the risk of sampling error that the auditor is willing to undertake, the greater should be the size of the sample.

Tolerable error

The tolerable error is the maximum error in the population that the auditor would be willing to accept and still conclude that the result from the sample has achieved the audit objective.

In compliance audit procedures, the tolerable error is the maximum rate of deviation from the prescribed control procedure that the auditor would be willing to accept, based on the preliminary assessment of control risk. In substantive procedure, the tolerable error is the maximum monetary error (i.e. materiality level) in an account balance or class of transactions that the auditor would be willing to accept. If the error rate or range of error in tests of control or test of details and balances are well within the tolerable error rate or tolerable error amount, the auditor would still be able to conclude that the financial statements are not materially misstated.

The smaller the tolerable error that the auditor is willing to accept, the greater should be the sample size.

Expected error

The expected error is the level of error predicted to be present in sample. The probability of error in the population is indicated by the auditor from his past experience, nature of item to be checked and the audit procedures and entity's control procedures. If the error in achieving specific audit objective is nil, a small sample would be adequate. Where the population is expected to be infected with greater or more errors, the sample size should be adequately large enough.

To summarise, the size of the sample is affected by the error perceptions of the auditor. The sampling errors refer to the risk where the auditor may conclude with an erroneous opinion when either the actual or sample results indicate otherwise. The tolerable error is the auditor's allowance for prevalence of errors even when he concludes that financial statements are not materially misstated. The expected error is the probability of occurrence of errors in a population.

Selection of the sample

The auditor should select the sample units from the sample in such a manner that sample as a whole can be expected to be representative of the population. This requires that all items in a population have an opportunity of being selected.

The commonly used sampling selection methods are-

- Random selection- simple random or stratified random
- Systematic selection
- Haphazard selection

In random selection, each unit has equal chance of being selected. The random number table may be used to select units. For example, in a population of invoices, it may be so laid that invoices numbers 15,24,37,76,121 etc., may be randomly listed for examination. In a stratified random sample, the population is divided into sub population and random selection is resorted with respect to each sub population. The invoices may be subdivided into 12 strata with reference to each month.

Systematic selection involves selection of sample units by using a constant interval- say every 50th invoice number from an initial invoice (randomly selected) say invoice number 13. Then the invoices listed for selection would be 13, 63, 113 and so on.

In haphazard selection the units are selected according to the auditor's whims with no rule of random or system. There is a danger of bias in selection prompted by convenience.

Evaluation of sample results

- The auditor carries out appropriate audit procedure on each sample item.
- He analyses any errors detected in the sample.
- He projects the errors found in the sample to the population and
- He reassess the sample risk

Analysis of errors

From the sample findings, the auditor analyses the errors. For this the auditor should have a prior definition of what constitutes an error with reference to each specific audit objective. What *seemingly* portray to be an error may be confirmed whether it is in fact so, by examination of alternative audit evidences. The analysis of both quantum and quality of errors must be made. The qualitative analysis may point to nature, cause and effect of the errors on the audit objective, other areas of audit procedures. The errors may, sometimes, bear a common characteristic. For e.g., The vouching of sales invoice on select sample may point that the invoices of the last month alone are erroneously accounted. This may prompt the auditor to constitute a strata of the last month in the population of invoices and apply a larger sampling in that sub-population. This may also qualitatively signal the auditor to other areas of audit objective like examining the overstatement of sales in the last month etc.

Projection of errors

The auditor projects the error results of the sample to the population. The projection should appropriately be made. The projection technique should be consistent with the methods used to select sample. The auditor should not conclude with the results by the projection results made statistically. The qualitative factors hidden behind the errors should not be missed sight of.

Reassessment of sampling risk

The auditor compares the projected population error with the tolerable error. If the projected population error exceeds the tolerable error, the auditor reassess the sampling risk. If the sampling risk is unacceptable to him, he would consider extending or modifying the audit procedures to gain assurance about his opinion on the financial statements.

Timing of audit procedures

The time when an audit procedure is to be performed depends on variety of factors. Certain audit procedures are performed by or very close to the year-end. Sometimes certain procedures are done surprisingly. Some procedures are performed after doing of certain other procedure additionally. Some procedures are substituted in course of audit. Some procedures of gathering audit evidence is done when it is best available.

The specific audit objective, the nature and extent of audit procedure, the materiality of the assertion, the nature of contingency, the need for corroboration, the resolution of inconsistency in assertions of audit evidences, the audit environment including internal control, the availability of time etc.,- all of these do affect the decision of the auditor about the timing of the audit procedures.

Surprise checking

Surprise checking implies an element of surprise as to the timing of the audit procedure. The surprise checking affects the audit efficiency in a number of ways-

- □ The tests of efficacy of internal control is best done when the working of the control system is checked surprisingly.
- □ The opinion as to the reliability of the data- accounting or management information processed by a computer system can be well formed when the system-check is done surprisingly. This would ensure that computer system is operated in accordance with laid down procedures and with authorised programmes only.
- □ Surprise check is relevant for ensuring that timely entries are made in certain statutory registers and prime books like cash and other day books.
- □ Surprise check is appropriate style of doing checking with reference to certain assets which are vulnerable to fraud and misappropriation, e.g., cash, jewels, inventory .

- Surprise checking is resorted when an entity is wide with operations in different locations. The element of surprise would reduce the chances of misstatements due manipulations by way of inter-division adjustment of assets.
- Surprise checking is done to instill a sense of moral fear among the employees.
- Surprise checking would help auditor to make assessment about fraud risk factors prevalent in an entity.

The auditor should document the findings of surprise checking and report them to the management. If the findings affect the financial statements materially, the auditor should decide on disclosure of the effect of the findings suitably in his audit report.

Audit risks and Materiality

Audit risk. Audit risk is the risk that the auditor may give an inappropriate opinion when the financial statements are materially misstated. Audit risk has three components- inherent risk, control risk and detection risk.

Inherent risk means the susceptibility of an account balance or class of transactions to misstatement that could be material either individually or when aggregated with misstatements in other balances or classes assuming that there were no related internal controls. The aim of internal control is to reduce (if not to eliminate) the misstatements in balances and transactions due to error or fraud. Assuming that there is no internal control the entity will run a risk of misstatements due to errors and frauds. This is called inherent risk. The inherent risk is a dependent function of many factors- viz., item of balance, or nature of class of transaction, technology used in processing the data about the balance or class of transaction, the sophistication of level of knowledge required in processing the data(e.g., estimation for provisioning), the business environment etc.

Control risk means the risk that a misstatement, that could occur in an account balance or class of transactions and that could be material, either individually or when aggregated with the misstatements in other balances or classes, will not be prevented or detected and corrected on a timely basis by the accounting or internal control systems. The inherent risk is risk of misstatement in a control-free situation. The internal and accounting control systems seek to reduce it. Still there is risk that such a system may not capture the misstatement due to variety of reasons (the inherent limitations of internal controls). The perception of the auditor about such risk is termed as control risk factor.

Detection risk is the risk that an auditor's substantive procedures will not detect a misstatement that exists in an account balance or class of transactions that could be material, either individually or when aggregated with misstatements in other balances or classes. Knowing that the financial statements may be misstated in view of inherent and control risks and having assessed by compliance procedure the extent of reliance that could be placed on the functioning of internal control, the auditor applies appropriate substantial procedures- tests of balances, tests of transactions and analytical procedures. There may be chances that such substantial procedures may fail to detect some misstatements. The reasons may be-inadequacy of the extent of audit procedures, in appropriate audit procedures, insufficient sampling, misinterpretation of sample findings etc.

Materiality

AAS 13 lays down standards on concept of materiality and its relationship with audit risk. Information is material if its misstatement (erroneous statement or omission) could influence the economic decisions of the users taken on the basis of the financial information. Materiality is the threshold or cut off limit with reference to which the misstatements are considered. It may be the size- frequency, amount, or nature of item. For e.g., Errors constituting in one expense, say not more than 5% of the total amount of expense may be considered to be not material. Or nature of item omitted to be disclosed explicitly may be that its disclosure is mandated by a statue. For e.g., the remuneration to directors may have to be specifically disclosed. Its amount judged from total salary of the staff may be negligible. But the nature of the item would make it material for misstatement.

The materiality is perceived with reference to the individual items or aggregate items. Some items which are not by themselves material may cumulatively result in material significance. Some items though by size not material, may relate to legal or statutory matters the non-compliance of which make the financial statements materially misleading. Certain other items may qualitatively present material misstatements. For e.g., inappropriate application of accounting policy may result in material misstatements either in current period or may affect material misstatements in financial statements that follow the period.

The relationship between materiality and audit risk

While planning the audit, the auditor plans to keep the audit risk at a lower level. He decides the materiality level related to specific account balances or class of transactions. This helps him in deciding the items to be selected, the sample to be chosen, the audit procedures to be applied on them.

There is inverse relationship between materiality level and audit detection risks. If the materiality level is high, the audit risk is low. If the auditor chooses to lay materiality limit of few hundred rupees for the truth and correctness of profit figure, the likelihood that audit carried out may fail to detect the errors within such a narrow range may be higher. The auditor, in such cases, reduces the audit risk by a comparatively extensive or more appropriate checking of control systems and balances and transactions. The auditor lays strictly a lower control risk (which alone he would tolerate) and carry out additional or elaborate tests of control. Similarly he lays down a lower detection risk (which alone he would tolerate) and carry out additional or other appropriate substantial procedures. These two, in combination, would help the auditor in reducing the total audit risk to the level he desired, in spite of his fixing tolerable materiality level at a lower level.

Materiality and Audit risk in evaluating audit evidence

The auditor may lay for himself a materiality level at the planning stage, which however, may change as he proceeds along the audit. The knowledge gained in audit, or change in the circumstances may prompt the auditor to revise the materiality level to a higher or lower side. Keeping in mind the materiality level for financial statements as a whole, the auditor fixes up materiality levels for auditing of individual transactions or balances at a lower level. The fixing up of low level of materiality for substantial checking would necessitate the auditor to perform a extensive audit checking of transactions and balances. And hence the auditor may come across a large number of cases under his cover which upon checking would place him in a better position for making overall conclusion with a margin of safety for audit risk.

In forming an opinion about the financial statement, the auditor should consider whether the effect of aggregate uncorrected misstatements on the financial information is material. The aggregate of uncorrected misstatement comprises of specific misstatement identified by auditor during this audit, the net misstatements brought down from previous period without correction, the projected misstatement where misstatements are projected from a sampling tests of balances and transactions. The management should correct and adjust the financial information in reference to the misstatements portrayed to them. The adjustment may involve, for e.g., application of appropriate accounting policy, providing disclosure where it was conspicuous by absence, complying with the statute for matters affecting financial statements, rectification of error, undoing, suitably, by disclosure or otherwise, the effect of fraud, etc. If the auditor could not find the effect of material misstatements within materiality level fixed for the financial statement as a whole (tolerable level), he may decide to express a qualified or adverse opinion about the financial statement appropriately.

QUESTIONS

1. What are the assertions tested by substantive procedure of checking audit evidences?

2. Differentiate the tests of control from tests of balances and transactions.

3. What is an analytical procedure of checking? How it is useful in different stages of audit?

4. The utility of analytical procedure lies in examination of deviations. Elucidate.

5. State the important factors on which the sufficiency and appropriateness of audit evidence test.

6. State the different methods of collecting audit evidence.

7. Explain how the reliability of audit evidence changes with the nature of audit evidences.

8. How sampling testing could help auditor in his substantive checking of audit evidences? Explain different types of sample selection.

9. Differentiate a sampling error from non-sampling error.

10. State few appropriate circumstances in which the surprise checking as a tool for examination of audit evidences would be relevant.

11. What is audit risk? How is related to materiality level.

12. Explain- (*a*) inherent risk (*b*) control risk (*c*) detection risk

13. How the auditor could guard himself for exposing himself to a high audit risk by choosing a low materiality level?

14. How the events occurring after balance sheet date affect auditor in his audit conclusion?

Coordinating the Work of Others

Auditing, as a planned professional exercise of expressing opinion on financial statements, encompasses the issues, in such process related with consideration and using of the works of experts and other co auditors AAS 9 lays down the standards of audit in relation to the work of an expert. AAS 10 deals with the standards on using the work of another auditor..AAS 7 deals with the auditing standards connected with the relying on the work of an internal auditor. AAS 12 specifies auditing standards in relation to the work of joint auditors

(I) USING THE WORK OF AN EXPERT

The auditor is an expert in profession of auditing. He is educated and trained to possess expertise in his field of auditing. It could not be expected of him that he possesses expert knowledge in other fields which may matter in his work, and are the domain of specific other experts. For example, the auditor cannot be supposed to bear technical competence of a lawyer, an engineer, or an actuary in matters of specialisation that concern them. Quite often an auditor comes across the need to make use of the work of such experts in this work of auditing. An expert in this context means a person possessing specialised knowledge, skill and experience in a particular field other than accounting and auditing. An expert may be engaged by or employed by the client or the auditor.

Determining the need to use the work of an expert

The auditor may require the statements, opinion, reports from experts during the course of his audit. Instances of such requirements may be-

- Valuation of certain type of assets like land, building etc.,
- Determining estimates of physical stock keeping of certain assets like minerals remaining undepleted in quarry, petroleum in tankers etc. Useful life of plant and machinery
- Determining the valuation of liability for terminal benefits like gratuity by actuarial valuation
- Legal opinion an various matters including about any contingent liability
- Determining the degree of completion of works in a contract accounting.

When determining the need to make use of experts's work in an audit, the auditor should weigh the materiality of the item to be tested with expert knowledge, the availability of other evidences nature and complexity of the item warranting the use of expertise.

While planning to make use of the work of experts as an audit evidence, the auditor should assess the skill set- professional qualification, experience, training etc of the expert, the objectivity of the expert. The assessment as to the objectivity of the expert will become all the more crucial when the expert is an employee or is engaged by the client or is related to the client. The auditor should assess whether it would be appropriate to take the work of expert as an audit evidence free from any impairment caused due to bias

Evaluating the work of an expert

1. The auditor should assess the skill set of the person whose work he may rely as expert opinion in the form of audit evidence.
2. The auditor should also assess the independence of the expert.
3. The auditor should examine the terms of expert's engagement such as-the scope of the expert's work, the general outline of expert report, the confidentiality of the expert's work including the possibility of communication to third party including the auditor, confidentiality of the client's information used by the expert.
4. The auditor should seek reasonable assurance that the expert's work constitutes appropriate audit evidence in support of financial information. He should consider the (*a*) the source data used (*b*) assumptions made by expert (*c*) methodology used for findings and (*d*) consistency and logic in deriving conclusions..
5. The auditor may do certain audit procedures to satisfy himself that the work of expert constitutes sufficient and appropriate audit evidence. He may inquire the client as to how he has satisfied himself that the source data is sufficient, reliable, and relevant. The auditor may also do certain test checking of input of data supplied to the experts. For example when the actuary is supplied with the data as to age, date of joining of the personnel, pay structure etc., the auditor may obtain the copy of such details and test check them with the employee's files as to the correctness of the data supplied. The auditor's knowledge is limited in matters related to examining the relevance and appropriateness of the assumptions, tools used in work, opinion derivation process. However. where it appears grossly unreasonable, having regard to the auditor's general knowledge of the business and experience of his audit contexts and transactions, the auditor should refer his point to the expert..
6. Where the expert's work does not constitute appropriate and reliable audit evidence or where the expert's opinion does not support the financial information, the auditor should consider checking other audit evidence including the consideration as to making use of the work of another expert and also ways to resolve inconsistency.
7. If after performing additional procedures, the auditor is not satisfied that the work of expert does not constitute sufficient and appropriate audit evidence or the results of the expert is inconsistent with the information in financial statement, the auditor should issue an opinion other than unqualified opinion. It may be adverse, qualified or disclaimer.
8. Where the auditor is satisfied and issues an unqualified opinion, he should take the responsibility for his expression of opinion and he should not refer to the work of expert. On the other hand, where he issues an opinion other than unqualified, he should consider whether it would be good to refer to the opinion of expert in reference to matters which are subject matters of reservation. If he decides to so refer, he should obtain the prior consent of the expert, if his identity were to be disclosed in the auditor's report.

(II) USING THE WORK OF ANOTHER AUDITOR

Quite often, in auditing of financial statements of multi-locational or multi-divisional entities, the auditor comes across the issues connected with dealing with other auditors.

AAS 10 (Revised) lays down the professional auditing standards in connection with the using the work of another auditor.

Principal auditor and other auditor.

The auditor reporting on the financial information of the entity is called principal auditor. The auditor who reports on the financial statements of financial information of one or more components included in the financial information of the entity is called other auditor. Component means a division, branch, joint venture, associated enterprise, or other entity whose financial information is included in the financial information audited by the principal auditor. The relationship *inter se*, between the joint auditors (who are the principal auditors in their own right) and the relationship between the current auditor and his predecessor are not covered by this standard. The branch auditor stands in the relation of other auditor to the statutory auditor of the whole entity.

Acceptance as principal auditor

Interestingly it would concern an auditor that whether it would be appropriate to consider himself as a Principal auditor. For example, where all the principal divisions are audited by the auditors (who we may take in our example as other auditor) and the person (whom we may consider as Principal auditor) is a mere adder upper of the financial information, it would concern whether the person could at all be called as principal auditor with ultimate responsibility for the expression of opinion on whole set of financial information. The auditor should consider whether the auditor's own participation is sufficient to be able to act as the principal auditor. For this purpose, the auditor would consider-

(*a*) the materiality of the portion of the financial information which the principal auditor audits;

(*b*) the principal auditor's degree of knowledge regarding the business of the components;

(*c*) the risk of material misstatements in the financial information of the components audited by the other auditor;

(*d*) the performance of additional procedures as regards the components audited by other auditor, thus increasing the significant participation in such audit of component by the principal auditor.

Principal auditor's procedures

- **Access to the books and records of the component-** In certain situations, the statute governing the entity may give to the principal auditor a right of access to the books and records of the component. Where another auditor is appointed to audit the financial information of the component, the principal auditor is normally **entitled** to rely on the work of the other auditor, unless there are special circumstances to make it essential for him to visit the component or examine the books and records of the components.
- **Examining the professional competence of other auditor-** Before planning to make use of the work of other auditor, the principal auditor should consider the professional competence of the other auditor in the context of specific assignment, if the other auditor is not a member of the Institute of Chartered Accountants of India.

  Where the financial information of the component is audited by a person not professionally qualified to be auditor (for *e.g.* where the component is situated in a foreign country and the local laws allow for the audit of the component by a person who is not professionally qualified) the principal auditor should consider performing additional audit procedures before he could make use of his work as an audit evidence.
- **Performing certain procedures to ensure the adequacy of other work -** The principal auditor should perform procedures to obtain sufficient appropriate audit evidence that the work of the other auditor is adequate in the specific context. When using the work of other auditor, the principal auditor should ordinarily perform-the following procedures-

  (*a*) **Communication-** The principal auditor should advise the other auditor about how the other auditor's work or report would get reflected in his audit work of the entity as a whole. The other auditor should stand to know how the entity's financial information would get weighed by his work and report. The principal auditor should also communicate with the other auditor about the inter- components transactions. The time schedule for completion of the audit work should also be previously informed to the other auditor.

The principal auditor may also inform the other auditor about the significant accounting, auditing and reporting requirements, areas where special attention needs to be bestowed upon etc.

(*b*) **Review the audit procedures/ findings-** The principal auditor may discuss with the other auditor about the audit procedures to be applied. He may even review the audit procedures employed by the other auditor and also his audit findings. He may use the checklist or questionnaire for this purpose. The principal auditor may dispense with the review if the principal auditor had already concluded that quality control policies and procedures are complied with in the conduct of audit by the other auditor.

(*c*) **Consideration of audit findings of other auditor-** The principal auditor should consider significant findings of other auditor. The principal auditor may discuss the audit findings with the other auditor, the management of the component. He may decide carrying out supplementary procedures or tests in relation to matters affecting the findings. Such tests may be carried out by the principal auditor himself or by the other auditor.

(*d*) **Documentation-** The principal auditor should document the in his working papers the components whose financial information are audited by other auditors; their significance to the financial information of the entity as a whole, the names of other auditors, their findings, the way he dealt with their reports etc.

(*e*) **Reporting-** When the other auditor issues a qualified or adverse opinion in his report, the principal auditor should consider whether it would be necessary for him to issue a qualified or adverse opinion on the financial information of the entity as a whole. It is a matter of professional judgement to be decided having regard to various relevant factors including the materiality of the financial information of the component in relation to the financial information of the entity as a whole. In cases where the principal auditor finds that the work of other auditor could not be relied on and he has not been able to perform additional procedures regarding financial information of the component, he may decide to issue a qualified or disclaimer of opinion.

(*f*) **Indication of division of responsibility-** Where the financial information of the component is audited by other auditor and his report has been considered in expression of opinion of the financial information of the entity as a whole by the principal auditor, he should indicate the extent to which financial information of components audited by other auditor had been included in his report. For example, the Principal auditor may state that so many number of branches audited by branch auditors have been included in the financial information of the entity as a whole.

(III) RELYING UPON THE WORK OF AN INTERNAL AUDITOR

Internal audit is an important component in the internal control system. It seeks to determine whether the internal control are well designed and properly operated. AAS 7 lays down the auditing standards when the work of internal auditor is relied by the external auditor.

Generally, the internal audit function operates in the following areas –

- Review of accounting system and other related internal controls.
- Examination for management of financial and operating information
- Examination of the economy, efficiency and effectiveness of the operations including non-financial controls of an organisation.
- Physical examination and verification of tangible assets of the organisation.

Internal Audit vis a vis External audit

The internal audit is a management tool to report on the effectiveness efficiency of control mechanism and also of the operating function of the organisation and also the reliability of data generated for managerial decisions. The internal auditor is employed or engaged by management. On the other hand, the external auditor is an independent reviewer of the financial information of the organisation who derives his position from a statute. He is an independent man and who only is responsible for the expression of opinion on the financial information of the organisation. Though operating on different site, both internal audit and external audit draw certain similar exercises in achieving their respective objectives. It is this common ground from where the external auditor could reap certain advantages by way of relief from duplication of certain procedures. The external auditor is thus concerned with the work of internal auditor in determining the nature, timing and extent of audit procedures that he must carry out in his audit.

Evaluation of internal audit function

The external auditor is concerned with the internal audit work in determining the nature, extent and timing of audit procedures to be carried out by him. Before relying on the work of the internal auditor, the external auditor should evaluate the internal audit function generally and also the internal audit work he relies specifically.

General Evaluation of internal audit function

The external auditor should consider the following-

(*a*) Organisational status- Whether the internal audit is undertaken by the outside agency or by the internal department. To whom the internal audit head reports to; The rights and limitations in carrying out the audit-These will affect the status in which the audit function is positioned in an orgnisation.

(*b*) Scope of function- The depth and coverage of areas brought within the fold of internal audit

(*c*) Technical Competence- The skill content of the operating personnel in the internal audit function.

(*d*) Due professional care- The planning, and performance of internal audit function as evidenced by audit programme, manual, working papers, documentation, reporting etc.

(*e*) Consideration of internal audit report- The weight given by management to the reports of internal auditors.

Evaluation of specific audit work

Where the external auditor plans to rely the work of internal audit work, he should evaluate the specific internal audit work carried out by the internal auditor.

(*a*) The auditor should examine the scope of the work as evidenced in the audit programme

(*b*) The auditor should review that the internal audit work is well planned and carried out properly. The work must be properly directed, supervised and reviewed by the competent internal audit staff.

(*c*) Sufficient and appropriate audit evidence has been gathered to afford reasonable basis for conclusions.

(*d*) Conclusions are derived from the work results that are properly documented.

(*e*) Exceptional or unusual matters are disclosed. The findings are discussed with management and remedial actions are taken

Sole responsibility of external auditor for his opinion

The external auditor is alone responsible for the expression of opinion on the financial information of the orgnaisation. The reliance he placed on the work of internal auditor could not be pleaded as a defence. It is a matter of his judgement for his convenience whether it would be appropriate for him to rely the internal audit work in determining the nature, extent and timing of audit procedures.

For determining the reliance, the auditor may *observe* internal audit functioning, *test check* the work done by internal auditor *review* the reports of the internal auditor.

(IV) RESPONSIBILITY OF JOINT AUDITORS

In audit of large entities, more than one auditor is appointed. This is to cope with the requirement of work load involved in auditing of large volume of transactions. AAS 12 deals with the professional standards in relation to joint audits. The joint auditor is to be distinguished from "the other auditor" (as discussed in AAS 10-Using the work of another auditor). The other auditor is an auditor to report on the financial information of a component and he is *appointed* as auditor of component as such. The audit of component is not given to the "other auditor" in pursuance of an agreement to divide work among joint auditors. AAS 12 does not deal with the relationship contemplated in AAS 10.

Division of work

The joint auditors mutually divide the work among themselves by discussion. The division may be in terms of audits of -identifiable units (*e.g* branchwise, locationwise, departmentwise) or specified areas, or items of assets/ liabilities/ income / expenditure heads. Certain areas of work may not be divided and would be carried out jointly due to nature or importance of the work involved. The division agreed among the joint auditors should be documented.

Responsibility of joint auditors

- **Individual responsibility-** In respect of the audit work carried out by each joint auditor as per division arrangement, each joint auditor is responsible for the work allotted to him. Unless the nature, timing and extent of audit procedures to be applied are agreed by a common understanding, it is the responsibility of individual auditor concerned to determine the appropriateness of the nature, timing and extent of procedures to be carried out in relation to the audit work to be performed by him.
- **Joint responsibility-** All joint auditors are jointly and severally responsible -
  - (*a*) **Joint work-** in respect of the audit work which is not divided among themselves and is carried out by all of them.
  - (*b*) **Decision as to appropriateness of nature, timing and extent of audit procedures-** in respect of decisions taken by all the joint auditors concerning the nature, timing and extent of the audit procedures to be performed by any of the joint auditors. The joint and several liability extends only to the appropriateness of the common decision taken as regards the audit procedures to be applied by each joint auditor. The actual performance of the audit procedure is the specific responsibility of the individual auditor concerned who has been allotted the assignment.
  - (*c*) **Matters brought to the common notice-** In respect of matters which have been brought to the notice of the joint auditors by any of them and on which there is agreement among the joint auditors.
  - (*d*) **Matters concerning disclosure requirement-** In respect of matters concerning examination that the financial statements comply with the disclosure requirement of any statute concerning the entity
  - (*e*) **Matters concerning audit report-** In respect of matters relevant for ensuring that the audit report complies with the requirements of relevant enactment, if any.
- **Duty to disclose matters concerning the responsibility of other joint auditors-** Where in the course of his work, a joint auditor comes across matters which are relevant to the areas of responsibility of other joint auditors, or which deserve their attention, or which require disclosure or which require discussion with or which require application of

judgement by other joint auditors, he should communicate the same to all the other joint auditors in *writing*. This should be done by a report or note *before* finalisation of the audit. If the matter is brought to the attention of the other joint auditors after the audit report has been submitted, the other joint auditors are not responsible for those matters.

- **Joint responsibility for obtaining information/ explanations-** A significant part of audit work involves obtaining and evaluating management explanations. It is the staturtory duty of auditors also to frame opinion after obtaining necessary information for any matters concerning the financial information. It is the joint responsibility of all the auditors to obtain sufficient and satisfactory information and explanations, unless this part of work is otherwise distributed to any of them. However, where the audit work is divided in terms of units, zones etc., the duty to obtain information and explanations regarding matters concerning the unit/zone shall lie only with the auditor to whom such division is made.
- **Entitled to assume professional competence of other joint auditors-** Each joint auditor is entitled to assume that the other joint auditors have carried out their part of audit work in accordance with the generally accepted audit procedures. It is not *necessary* for a joint auditor to review the work performed by other joint auditor or perform any tests in order to ascertain whether the work has actually been performed in such a manner. Each joint auditor is entitled to rely upon other joint auditors for bringing to his notice any departure from generally accepted accounting principles or any material error noticed in the course of audit.
- **Entitled to presume the truth and fairness of financial information of divisions audited by a joint auditor-** Where the financial information of any division/branch are audited by a joint auditor, the other joint auditors are entitled to assume that the financial statements of the division/ branch audited by the other joint auditor complies with the relevant requirements of statute or professional pronouncements regarding disclosure, presentation etc. He is also entitled to presume that the financial information as provided in the statements audited by the other joint auditors exhibit true and fair view of the operations/financial status of the entity subject to any observations that might have been communicated to them by the other auditor.
- **No rule of majority in reporting-** The joint auditors are able to come to an agreement generally and hence they issue a common report. However, where they are in disagreement, each will issue a separate report setting out his opinion. The joint auditors are not bound by majority view.

QUESTIONS

1. Give few instances where an auditor is concerned with the relying on the work of an expert.
2. How can the work of an expert be evaluated by the auditor before he decides to rely on it?
3. Can an auditor mention the identity of the expert when he reproduces his opinion in his report in circumstance where he disagrees with it?
4. What an auditor should do when client refuses to elaborate any further than his opinion relation to the work of an expert in view of constraint of confidentiality of the expert work.
5. Who is a principal auditor and who is "other auditor" in terms of AAS 10?
6. Is principal auditor entitled to rework on the areas of work audited by the other auditor?
7. Can a supplementary test be required of other auditor in line with what the principal auditor decides?
8. How should the principal auditor demarcate the line of responsibilities between him and other auditor in his audit report?

9. How should the principal auditor determine that his participation in audit of the entity is sufficient enough to be called himself as principal auditor?

10. Is principal auditor bound to qualify his report when the other auditor issues a qualified report?

11. Is external auditor relieved of his responsibility in areas covered by internal auditor if he discloses that such areas are covered by the scope of internal audit of the entity?

12. How the internal audit function be appraised generally and specifically?

13. Suggest ways how the internal audit function be used to relieve the work load of the external auditor? Is there any word of caution on this score?

14. Suggest how the work of joint auditors be segregated?

15. Is a joint auditor duty bound to pass over to other joint auditors the information that comes to him affecting financial information with which only the other auditor is concerned?

16. When are joint auditors jointly and severally liable?

17. Are joint auditors bound by the rule of majority in reporting the conclusions of the audit?

18. Is branch auditor of a company a joint auditor?

Documentation

Remember that the auditing is a professional exercise conforming to the quality parameter of generally accepted auditing practices. The process of auditing is as much equally concerned with the means of achieving objective as with the attainment of objectives. It is not enough that auditor has opined fairly on the financial information; it must equally appear that he acted fairly to gain such satisfaction. It is in this background that the documentation of auditing process assumes relevance. AAS 3 lays down standards connected with documentation.

Importance of audit documentation

Documentation means reducing to writing the audit matters and manner and their proper upkeep. The writings of audit matters and manners are called working papers. The working papers are prepared or obtained by the auditor. Its form varies through from entries in scribbling pads, extracts, photocopy of documents, representation from management and so on. The documentation functionally encompasses the generation of working papers, in the first instance and its proper upkeep to meet the purpose of reference at any point of time. In the latter part of its function it covers filing and indexing, pruning of the working papers. The documentation is vital because-

(1) Adequately documented plan and control of audit work evidences the practices, procedures followed in audit and important findings.

(2) It acts as a manual of reference for planning the audit for future and also in similar types of new audit engagements.

Audit note book

An Audit Note-Book is a book which is maintained by the audit clerk. During the course of audit, the clerk comes across several difficulties or new points which he has to discuss with his senior or the auditor. He makes several inquires which, he thinks, have not been satisfactorily answered. Least he might forget these points, he noted down these in a book which is called by different names such as Audit Note Book or Audit Memoranda. Such a book is a written record of queries made, replies received thereto, correspondence entered into, etc. This book may be of great help to the auditor preparing his Audit Report from such a record. A separate Audit Note Book is maintained for each concern.

Contents of an Audit Note-Book

Some of the points which are noted down in an Audit Note book are given below :

1. A list of books of account maintained by the client;
2. The names of the principal officers, their powers, duties and responsibilities;

3. The technical terms used in the business;
4. The points which require further explanation and clarification;
5. The particulars of the missing vouchers, the duplicates of which have to be obtained;
6. The mistakes and errors discovered;
7. Totals or balances of certain books of account, Bank Reconciliation statement;
8. Notes and queries which might be required at a subsequent audit;
9. The points which have to be incorporated in the Audit Report;
10. Any matter which requires discussion with the senior or with the auditor;
11. Accounting method followed in the business;
12. Dates of commencement and completion of the audit;
13. Provisions in the Articles and Memorandum of Association affecting the accounts and audit.

The following is an example of notes made in the Audit Note Book :-

28-8-95 Entry in Cash Book Folio 63 for Rs. 500 wrongly debited to Freehold Land and Building instead of Leasehold Improvement—Accountant advised.

29-8-95 Receipt for Rs. 1,000 paid to Messrs. XYZ *vide* C.B.Folio 69, not available.

2-9-95 Receipt for Rs. 1,000 paid to Messrs. XYZ, seen and cancelled.

Value of an Audit Note Book

If notes have been properly made in the Audit Note Book, it might prove of great value to the auditor later on, in case a suit is filed against him for negligence or misfeasance. Such a book will be a documentary evidence in favour of the auditor even after several years by which time the auditor might have forgotten everything about that particular audit. The importance of such a Note Book was emphasised by Lord (then Mr.) Justice Vaughan Williams in the *London and General Bank* case. Similarly the Audit Note Book which contained detailed information was of great assistance to the auditor in the case of the *City Equitable Fire Insurance Company*.

Such a book should be clear, concise and complete so that it may be quite Intelligible to the clear who audits the accounts of the same concern next year. In fact it would be a guide to such a clerk.

Form and Content of working papers

As one traverses along the entire gamut of working papers, it should provide a good road map of audit site starting from engagement to audit reporting and thereafter too. Essentially it exhibits what the plan was about, what were the nature, extent and timing of audit procedures performed, what was the conclusion reached in an audit exercise.

The form and content of working papers are affected by-various matters. It cannot be expected that the auditor keeps documenting each and every matter of his audit moves. Such exercise is neither practicable nor of any value - The volume of working papers is a dependent function of host of many factors. Essentially it is matter of judgement of auditors as to what and how the documentation should be with him. Sometimes it is conditioned by client's reservations as to the need for and relevance of auditors concern to keep them. (for *e.g.* while vouching payment of royalty for patents, if the auditor chooses to document the patent formulas of the client!) The form and content of the working paper are dependent on such factors as - nature of engagement, the form of auditor's report, the nature and complexity of client's business, the nature and condition of client's records and degree of reliance on internal controls, the need in particular circumstance for direction, supervision and review of work performed by assistants. The Auditing and Assurance Standards on various audit matters/issues require documenting of certain significant matters discussed in those standards.

Although the generation of working papers is engagement-specific, it would do good to standardise them in general and a plus for variation. The standardised working papers in the form of check lists, programmes, engagement letter, management representation letters on routine audit issues may help auditors in time saving. The duly filled in documents shall become working papers for the relevant engagement.

As regards content, all significant matters which require the exercise of judgement of auditor should invariably be documented. The documentation should portray the compliance tests, substantial procedures carried out. The analytical review of the findings by the auditor should find place in the working papers. It may be in the form of significant ratios, comparatives etc. The auditor insists on the preparation of various working schedules to be prepared by the client himself to substantiate disclosures in balance sheet and P&L account.

Filing of working papers

The utility of working papers lies in its ability to answer the query requirement of auditors in various emerging situations. The quality of working papers get increased when the time for search any audit issue is short and also the information provided is complete and bear cross references to related issues. It is in this context, a good filing and indexing of working papers assumes importance.

In case recurring audits, working papers are filed into current audit file and permanent audit file.

A permanent audit file normally includes-

- Information concerning legal and organisational structure of the entity. For *e.g.* in case of a company, the memorandum, articles of association, any amendment updates, any particulars as to license for functioning etc.
- Extracts of important documents concerning significant matters like legal documents, agreements, arrangements, minutes etc.
- A record of study of internal and accounting control of the entity. This may be in the form of descriptive narration, flow chart or questionnaire or in combination of these.
- Copies of management letters issued to auditors
- Copy of the communication with the retiring auditors
- Copies of audited financial statements of the previous years
- Analyses of significant ratios and trends
- Notes on significant accounting policies
- Significant audit observations of earlier years.
- Updates of the current year which will be of continuing importance to succeeding audits

The current file stores information relating primarily to the audit of a single period. It includes-

- Correspondence relating to acceptance of annual engagement.
- Extracts of important matters in the minutes of Board or General meeting which are relevant to the current year audit
- Audit programme
- Analyses of transactions and balances- significant queries, explanatory schedules etc.
- Record of nature, timing and extent of audit procedures carried out, results thereof.
- Evidence that the work of assistants had been supervised and reviewed.
- Copies of communication with experts, other auditors or other third parry.
- Copies of letters or notes on audit matters communicated to the client, or discussed with the client, including terms of engagement / material weakness in internal control.
- Letters of representation/confirmation received from the client.

- Conclusions reached on significant audit matters- how exceptional or unusual matters have been adjusted or resolved or reported.
- Copies of financial information reported on; audit reports issued on such information.

Responsibility, Protection and Preservation of Working Papers

Whosoever is in possession of Working Papers should be responsible for their safe custody. They should in no case be shown to a third party except with the permission of the client.

After the audit Report has been prepared and delivered to the client, these papers may be filed and preserved for a period of five to ten years or even more.

Ownership of Working Papers, Audit Note Books, etc.

A question arises as to who is the owner of these Working Papers. The client claims that these Papers belong to him because the auditor acts as his agent in making such queries, entering is to correspondence with the debtors and creditors, etc., while on the other hand, the auditor claims the ownership of the Working Papers on the ground that such information has been collected by him for the purpose of discharging his duty. It is further argued that such Papers should not be handed over to the client even after he ceases to be the auditor of the concern. These are the Papers which might come to the help of the auditor in future in case the client files a suit against the auditor for negligence, etc. The auditor will have no evidence in his possession to defend himself, after he hands over these Papers to his client.

It is sometimes argued that as a matter of professional etiquette the out-going auditor should hand over these Working Papers to the in-coming auditor, especially when his appointment has come to an end in amicable circumstances so that the latter may get help from such papers during the course of audit in future.

In any case, if the auditor has the slightest doubt or suspicion that fraud has been committed or facts have been concealed, he should refuse to part with such Papers even to his successor.

The question of lien in regard to the Working Papers arose in the case of *Sockockinsky* vs. *Bright Grahm & Co.*(1938) in England. The question was whether the auditors had a right to retain the Working Papers as if it were their own property even after the payment of the audit fee. The court gave judgement in favour of the auditors on the ground that they were independent contractors and not agents of the clients.

Again, in *Chantry Martin & Co.* vs. *Martin* (*The Times,* London: 15th July 1953), quoted by Spicer and Pegler, it was held that the Working Papers prepared by an accountant for the purpose of producing a balance sheet on behalf of a client for audit purposes belonged to the accountant and not to the client. The Court held on the other hand that the correspondence between an accountant and the Inland Revenue concerning a client's taxation liabilities belonged to the client.

Working papers are the property of the auditor. The auditor may, at his discretion, make portions of or extracts from his working papers available to his client.

The auditor should take reasonable precautions for custody and confidentiality of his working papers. He may keep them for such length of time as is required of him based on considerations as to needs of his professional practice and related legal or professional requirements in connection therewith.

QUESTIONS

1. Why is it essential to document matters and manners of audit?
2. What is an audit note book? How is helpful to auditors?
3. The utility of audit papers lies in its discreete generation and classified filing- Do you agree?

4. What is a permanent audit file?
5. What are Filed in current audit file?
6. What are the factors that affect the form and content of working papers?
7. Is standardised format of maintaining working papers desirable?
8. To whom the working papers belong? Can a client claim the return of working papers to him on the ground of- his (*a*) superlative ownership (*b*) confidentiality
9. Does ownership of working papers confer superior ownership to auditors to deal with them with unfettered privileges?

Chapter 13

Audit Report

Introduction

The audit Reporting is the communication of audit conclusions after having carried out the audit process in accordance with audit plan. The statutes prescribing audit requires the auditor to submit his report specifying matters to be included therein. The audit report is the summarised expression of certain facts and opinions regarding the conduct of the audit and conclusions with reference to it. The AAS 28 lays down the standards to be complied with in connection with the audit reports. The enactments governing the preparation and presentation of financial statements of the entity also lays down the requirement of an audit report. For e.g., Section 227 of the Companies Act specifies the matters to be included in audit report of a company. Similarly section 233B deals with matters of report of a cost auditor.

Basic Elements of an Audit Report.

The audit report should, generally, be in the following lay out-

(*a*) Title

(*b*) Addressee

(*c*) Opening or introductory paragraph- (*i*) identification of financial statements audited and (*ii*) a statement on the responsibility of the entity's management and that of auditor.

(*d*) Scope paragraph - (*i*) a reference to the auditing standards generally accepted in India and (*ii*) a description of work performed by the auditor.

(*e*) Opinion paragraph - (*i*) a reference to the financial reporting framework used to prepare the financial statements and (*ii*) expression of opinion on the financial statements

(*f*) Date of the report

(*g*) Place of signature

(*h*) Auditor's signature.

Sometimes, the governing enactments may require inclusion of certain statements or matters in or with the auditor's report. In such cases, the auditor's report should include all those matters in addition to the matters as specified in AAS above.

1. Title

The title indicates the nature of report. The title should be like- "Auditor's Report" or Branch Auditor's Report". The title distinguishes this report from other reports like Director's report of an Accountant report on compilation of the accounts etc.

2. Addressee

The auditor's report should address the person to whom it is meant to be forwarded. The requirements of the engagement or the relevant statute may determine the person to whom the report should be submitted. Generally the report is submitted to the person who appoints the auditor.

3. Opening or Introductory paragraph

The introductory paragraph should identify -

1. the financial statements with respect to which audit opinion is given- Financial statements are identified by title, period covered, the entity to which it relates etc.
2. the clear marking of the responsibility between management and auditor- The report should state that the financial statements are the responsibility of the management; the auditor's responsibility is limited to expression of opinion thereon. The preparation of the financial statements involves making of significant accounting estimates, determination of appropriate accounting principles and methods used in preparation of financial statements. These determination will have to be made appropriately by the management having regard to the reporting frame work of financial statements, as chosen by or is required to be complied with, by the management.

4. Scope paragraph

The scope paragraph specifies the work performed by auditor. The scope of audit work is governed by the terms of engagement, statutory provisions and the pronouncements of the institute. The scope of the audit as affected by the statute or the pronouncements of the ICAI, cannot be modified or whittled down by the terms of engagement, agreement or any arrangement between auditor and auditee. The auditor should specify in the scope paragraph that auditing has been conducted in accordance with the established auditing standards. This is both an expression of auditing procedures carried out as well as an expression of assurance to the readers that the auditing conducted could be taken to be one in accordance with what AAS have mandated auditors to do in audit situations.

The scope paragraph should indicate that auditor had planned and performed the audit to obtain reasonable assurance whether financial statements are free from material misstatement. Specifically the scope paragraph describes the audit as including-

(*a*) examining on a test basis, evidence to support the accounts, disclosures in financial statements.

(*b*) assessing accounting principles used in the preparation of financial statements.

(*c*) assessing the significant estimates made by management in preparation of financial statements.

(*d*) evaluating the overall financial statement presentation,

The report, besides describing what an audit is, should mention that the audit has provided reasonable basis for expression of opinion.

5. Opinion Paragraph

The opinion paragraph of the report should indicate the financial reporting framework used to prepare the financial statements and state the auditor's opinion as to whether the financial statements give a true and fair view in accordance with that financial reporting framework and comply with the statutory disclosure requirements. In addition to the opinion on true and fair view of the financial statements, the auditor may be required to express opinion on specific matters required by statute. In such cases, besides, expressing opinion on the truth and fairness of financial statements, the auditor should specify his opinion on such additional matters as well. For e.g. the

Companies Act, 1956 requires auditor in terms of section 227(2) to express whether in his opinion, the said accounts give information as required by the Act.

6. Date of the report

The date of report indicates the date on which the auditor signs his report. It indicates that the auditor has considered the effect on the financial statements and also on his reports of events occurred upto that date. Again this date should not precede the date on which the financial statements were approved by the management. Because, the auditor's responsibility is to express opinion on the financial statements as prepared by the management.

7. Place of report

The town in which the audit report is signed should be indicated.

8. Auditors signature

The report should be signed by the auditor in his personal name. Where the firm is auditors of the entity, the signature should be in the personal name of the partner signing as well as in the firm name. The membership number of the individual signing the report should invariably be mentioned.

Specimen of a clean auditor's report

We have audited the attached Balance Sheet of ABC as at 31st March 2005 and also the Profit and Loss Account for the year ended on that date. The financial statements are the responsibility of the entity's management. Our responsibility is to express an opinion on these financial statements based on our audit.

We conducted our audit in accordance with auditing standards generally accepted in India. Those standards require that we plan and perform the audit to obtain reasonable assurance whether the financial statements are from material misstatements. An audit includes examining, on a test basis, evidence supporting the amounts and disclosures in the financial statements. An audit also includes assessing the accounting principles used and significant estimates made by the management as well as evaluating the overall financial statement presentation. We believe that our audit provides a reasonable basis for our opinion.

In our opinion and to the best of information and according to the explanations given to us, the financial statements give a true and fair view in conformity with the accounting principles generally accepted in India

(*i*) in case of the Balance sheet, of the state of affairs of ABC as at 31st March 2005 and

(*ii*) in case of Profit and Loss Accounts of the profit / loss for the year ended 31st March 2005/

For A. SRINIVASAN and Co.,

Chartered Accountants

A. Srinivasan

(name of the auditor with membership number)

Place - Chennai

Date - 25.04.2005

Kinds of Audit Report

Clean or unqualified report

An auditor issues an unqualified report when he concludes that the financial statements give a true and fair view in accordance with the financial reporting framework used for the preparation and presentation of financial statements. An unqualified opinion or clear report indicates that

1. the financial statements have been prepared using the generally accepted accounting principle. These have been consistently applied from time to time.
2. the financial statements comply with the relevant statutory requirements and regulations.
3. there is adequate disclosure of all material matters relevant to the proper presentation of the financial information, subject to statutory requirement if any,
4. changes in accounting method if any, is in accordance with what is permissible and the same have been properly determined, the effect measured and disclosed fairly in financial statements.

Modified report- qualified, disclaimer or adverse report

An auditor's report is considered to be modified when it includes

(*a*) matters that do not affect the auditor's opinion
- emphasis of matter

(*b*) matters that do affect the auditor's opinion
- Qualified opinion
- Disclaimer of opinion
- Adverse opinion

Modified opinion for emphasis and not affecting auditor's opinion

Sometimes, the auditor may find it useful to incorporate reference to certain matters which have been properly disclosed in the financial statements for the benefit of the readers. Such reference is indicated before opinion paragraph. The mentioning of such matters in auditor's report is to highlight the importance of such facts the conjoint reading of which will be beneficial for the better understanding of the report. It is not to be taken as any reservation on the part of auditor in relation to the opinion he expresses beneath. AAS requires two items to be highlighted as modified opinion for emphasis. When there is "going concern problem"* (**i.e.* generally accounts are prepared based on the concept of going concern. That is, the entity will be carried out in future. This implies current assets are held for realisation and hence are to be valued at lower of cost or market price; fixed assets are held for carrying operations on them and hence they are to be valued at cost less depreciation. But when the going concern concept is impaired due to imminent threat to continuity of the entity, the accounting of transactions and balances would require consequent changes. For e.g. all asset are to be valued at realisable values.) and it is not resolved as to the appropriateness or otherwise of the going concern, the fact should be indicated in the report about the doubt. Again, when there is an uncertainty about a matter, which has been disclosed in the financial statements and about the effect of which, it is not possible to determine and which is beyond the control of the management, the same should be emphasied in the audit report. But if the effects of uncertainties are of multiple nature and the magnitude may be such (of course uncertain) as to vitiate the opinion, the auditor may choose, instead of reporting it as a matter of emphasis, to mention it by way of disclaimer.

Modified opinion-disclaimer, qualified and adverse opinion

An auditor expresses "other than unqualified" opinion - which may be "disclaimer, qualified or adverse" opinions when either of the following circumstances exist and in the auditor's judgement, the effect of the matter is or may be material to the financial statements-

(*a*) there is a limitation on the scope of the auditor's work

(*b*) there is disagreement with management regarding the (*A*) acceptability of the accounting policies selected (*B*) the method of their application or (*C*) the adequacy of financial statement disclosures.

The limitation on the scope of work may necessitate auditor to issue a qualified or disclaimer of opinion.

The disagreement as specified in (*b*) may necessitate auditor to issue a qualified or adverse opinion.

(A) A qualified opinion should be expressed when the auditor concludes that an unqualified cannot be expressed but that the *effect of disagreement with management is not so material and pervasive as to require an adverse opinion or the limitation on the scope is not so material and pervasive as to require a disclaimer of opinion.* A qualified opinion is expressed as being "subject to" or "except for" the effects of the matter to which the qualification relates.

The qualification should clearly indicate the reasons for the qualification and the impact of the qualification in profits/losses and also on the financial position of the entity.

Note that the qualified opinion is given in cases of disagreement with management regarding the (*a*) acceptability of the accounting policies selected, (*b*) the application of such policies, or (*c*) the adequacy of disclosure. The wrong policy chosen or applied cannot escape from the auditor's qualified report on the pretext that such wrong policy is adequately disclosed as a note to the financial statements. The (*a*), (*b*) or (*c*) warranting issue of qualified report operates in a mutually exclusive plane.

Examples

1. Limitation on scope of audit- Non availability of confirmation of balances of major debtors, non-verification of stocks at the year end etc.
2. Disagreement with management

Accounting policy- e.g. Providing of retirement benefits on cash basis without accrual accounting; non - provision of depreciation

Wrong application of accounting e.g. Capitalising interest expenditure on loan for erection of machinery after installation.

Inadequate disclosure- omitting to furnish quantitative details of purchases, sales, stock as per schedule VI requirements, omission to separately show the managerial remuneration etc.

(B) A Disclaimer of opinion should be expressed when the possible effect of limitation on the scope is so material and pervasive that the auditor has not been able to obtain sufficient appropriate audit evidence and is accordingly unable to express an opinion on the financial statement. The disclaimer is expressed when forming of an overall opinion about the financial statements. The opinion-forming process is inhibited by non-availability of material supporting for an assertion. If the non-availability of evidences relates to only partial segment of audit matters which is considered to be not material, the auditor would limit his "other than unqualified opinion" to "qualified opinion". For example, when he is not able to observe the stock taking of the entity, he may opine the truth and fairness of financial results and position adding a term " subject to the non-observance of the stock taking by us due to the reason......" On the other hand, if the financial records are not at all produced to him in view of the seizure of the same by Income tax authority, the limitation is so pervasive and grave that the auditor will disclaim to give opinion as to the truth and fairness of the financial results and position. Again, when the limitation imposed on auditor is designed to curtail or take away the rights and duties of auditor as enshrined in enactments, or pronouncements of ICAI, the auditor will refrain from taking up such audit, instead of accepting the assignment and expressing disclaimer.

(C) An Adverse opinion is expressed when the effect of disagreement is so material and pervasive to the financial statements that the auditor concludes that a qualification of the report is not adequate to disclose the misleading or incomplete nature of the financial statements.

QUESTIONS

1. What are the components of an audit report?
2. What is a clean report?
3. What are "other than unqualified" opinions?
4. When a qualified opinion is and is not sufficient?
5. When a qualified opinion is not sufficient, but an adverse opinon is necessary?
6. What is the significance of dating of the report?
7. Distinguish the Scope portion of the report from opinion portion.
8. What is a modified opinion without affecting auditor's opinion?
9. Distinguish a qualified opinion from an adverse opinion.
10. Give a model clean audit report for a small non-corporate entity.

Chapter 14

Internal Control

As the size of the operations of an entity increases and nature of activities become complex, it becomes difficult for the manager of the entity to control the operations of the entity by his direct and close supervision. Control under his nose is impossible for every activity and even if possible, it would prove to be very costly in terms of time and efficiency. What the management in such a circumstance is interested is to devise a system which in its efficient operation provides desired control-effects. An efficient system of control is established by the management as a matter of convenience and effectiveness.

Internal Control—Meaning, Importance

Spicer & Peglar, a famous authority on auditing literature, defines the system of internal control as "Internal control is best regarded as the whole system of controls, financial and otherwise, established by the management in the conduct of a business including internal check, internal audit and other forms of control".

This definition implies the following

(*a*) The internal control is a *system* of controls.

(*b*) Controls are established over *financial* and *non financial* areas

(*c*) The mechanism of controls may manifest itself in the forms of *internal check* or *internal audit* or other forms.

The Statement on Auditing Practices (SAP-6) of the Institute of Chartered Accountants of India describes internal control as "the plan of organisation and all the methods and procedures adopted by the management of an entity to assist in achieving management's objective of ensuring, as far as possible, the orderly and efficient conduct of its business, including adherence to management policies, the safeguarding of assets, prevention and detection of fraud and error, the accuracy and completeness of the accounting records and timely preparation of reliable financial information. The system of internal control extends beyond those matters which relate to the functions of accounting system".

This definition throws light on the complete realm of internal control. The internal control, according to this definition, implies the following:

Internal control is a prescription and practice of a system by management.

The system encompasses plan, methods and procedures prescribed for and practised by the internal constituents of an entity.

The aim for prescription and practice of such a system is to ensure control over accounting and other administrative areas in order to bring forth efficiency and orderliness.

Internal Control—Accounting, Administrative Controls

We have seen that the internal control areas spread over accounting and non-accounting spheres. Internal control, as it applied to accounting system, implies control over accounting system with the aim of achieving the following objectives:

(*a*) Efficient and orderly conduct of accounting transactions

(*b*) Safeguarding the assets in adherence to management policy

(*c*) Prevention of error, detection of error

(*d*) Prevention of fraud, detection of fraud

(*e*) Ensuring accuracy, completeness, reliability and timely preparation of accounting data.

On the other hand administrative controls seek to achieve the aim of management in efficient and orderly conduct of transactions, in non-accounting areas. It seeks to ensure the adherence to management policy in various areas of business operations. For example in a manufacturing system of a business enterprise, the internal control may be established to ensure the adherence of management policy as to quality (quality control), safeguarding assets (control over wastages, ABC control over raw materials) prevention of errors (monitoring production methods, maintenance programme for machines), prevention of frauds (security system), timely supply of reliable management information (MIS).

An auditor is mainly concerned with good accounting control of internal control system. If good internal control system exists in accounting system, an auditor can put greater reliance on the financial data generated in the system with test checking of select items. If the accounting control is not strong, the auditor may have to resort to detailed checking of transactions, events, and practices in the accounting system. With regard to administrative controls, the auditor may evaluate those part of administrative controls as may have bearing on the financial information of the entity. For example before certifying the valuation of stocks, the auditor may refer to the reports of consumption patterns prepared by manufacturing segment to administration, if the auditor feels material discrepancy in physical quantity of stocks. On the other hand, he may not be concerned no more than a matter of general interest with the quality report of chemical A used in operation X.

Internal Check

We have seen that internal check is one of the modes of executing internal control. As applied to accounting system internal check is a method of organising the accounts system of a business concern or a factory where the duties of different clerks are arranged in such a way that the work of one person is automatically checked by another and thus the possibility of fraud, or error, or irregularity is minimised unless there is a collusion between the clerks, e.g., the receipt of cash is entered by the cashier on the debit side of the cash book; this entry is carried to the ledger by another clerk; the statement of account relating to this transaction is sent to the customer by a third clerk and so on. Thus, we see that the same transaction has passed through three different hands, and the work of one is checked automatically by the other. It is a kind of division of labour. This minimises the possibilities of frauds and errors unless all the three join hands in defrauding their employer. Again if an error or fraud has been committed, it will be detected very soon by another clerk while the transaction is being automatically checked.

L.R. Dicksee defines Internal Check as "such an arrangement of book-keeping routine that errors and frauds are likely to be prevented or discovered by the very operation of the book-keeping itself."

F.R.M. de Paula defines it as "Internal Check means practically a continuous internal audit carried on by the staff itself, by means of which the work of each individual is independently checked by other members of the staff."

Professor Arnold W. Johnson, in his book, *Auditing Principles and Case Problems*, defines internal control system as one wherein the accounting work of the employee is complemented and verified by the work of another employee–both employees working independently and without duplication of each other's work.

"Internal Check—a system under which the accounting methods and details of an establishment are so laid out that the accounts and procedures are not under the absolute and independent control of any one person—that, on the contrary, the work of one employee is complementary to that of another— and that a continuous audit of the business is made by employees." *Special Committee on Terminology, American Institute of Accountants, 1949*.

Under this system, the clerk incharge of a book of prime entry should not have access to the ledger and *vice versa.* Self-balancing ledger system, time-recording clocks regarding wages or automatic tills for recording cash receipts, are some of the devices by which the commission of fraud may be prevented. No one is allowed to deal with one book throughout the year. Therefore the work of the members of the staff should be changed from time to time and if it is found expedient they should be encouraged to take leave. In such a case it will be easy to detect an error or fraud committed by the absentee member of the staff. Under this system wage sheets are prepared and chacked from different records by different clerks. In case of cash sales, the salesman does not receive the money from the customer, nor does he deliver the goods to him. Cash is received by the cashier; the goods are delivered by the gate-keeper, and all the three, viz., the salesman, the cashier and the gate-keeper, send their own statements regarding the sales, receipt of cash and the delivery of goods, in the evening to the General Manager who compares these statements and if he finds any discrepancy, he makes an investigation. Under such a system, unless all the three join hands, there is no possibility of fraud.

Similarly when the goods are purchased on credit, entries are made regarding the purchase by the gate-keeper, who records the name of the supplier, the quantity of goods and the date on which they were received; another entry is made by the keeper of the purchases book, the godown-keeper, etc. Thus, the same entry is recorded by different clerks and the possibility of fraud or mistake is reduced to the minimum.

The applications of some of the automatic devices, e.g., cash registers, time recording clocks, book-keeping and calculating machines, etc., prevent the commission errors and frauds. The clerks should be transferred from one department or job to another department or job from time to time without any prior notice. Members of the staff should be encouraged to go on leave as in case frauds, if any, committed by the clerk may come to light.

From the above definitions and discussion, it would be apparent to the readers that the work is sub-divided amongst many persons and hence the internal check system can be usefully employed by big concerns. In a small concern, this system is not practicable as a clerk has to handle assets as well as the records.

The aim of the application of internal check is the prevention and alternatively the early detection of frauds, errors, and misappropriation. But it must not be presumed that where the internal check is in operation, there cannot be an error or a fraud. The internal check system minimises or makes difficult the chances of committing frauds, thefts or irregularities.

The advantage of the existence of good and efficient internal check is that in that case the auditor can rely upon the accuracy of the accounts. Even though he finds a very efficient internal check system in operation, he should not be negligent but must be alert. He should apply test checks to a few items selected at random, e.g., in case of payment of wages, he should compare the attendance of the workers with the gate-keeper's record, foreman's record, the wages sheet and the cash book. On the other hand if he finds that the internal check system in the business is not satisfactory he should be very careful and test checks should be extensive and thorough and he should mention that fact in his report.

Evaluative Criteria for Good Internal Check

A good internal check system must provide in-built checks and balances while the operations are being performed. To achieve this end, the following control mechanism may be introduced:

(*a*) **Division of Work:** No one should be allowed to have right to perform the work from origin to end. For example, a transaction of sale may have to be split into display of article by a staff, the preparation of invoice by another, the receipt of cash against the invoice by a third clerk, the delivery of article against the proof of receipted invoice by another clerk, checking of outward movement of article against delivery order by a clerk and so on. In big business houses, such specialised tasks increase the speed of work and automatically introduce internal check.

(*b*) **Job Rotation :** No individual clerk should be allowed to occupy a particular area of operation for long. Familiarity with and exclusiveness in a position offers a person greater flexibility to attempt manipulation with the system.

(*c*) **Authority Levels:** There must be clear cut authority levels for according sanctions to various transactions. Commensurate to the authority vested, responsibility must be extracted. Existence of authority levels result in review of operations of subordinates.

(*d*) **Separation of Custody & Recording :** There needs to be effective control by way of separation that the persons handling an asset cannot make entries for the transactions without any counter check. For example in a bank the payments effected by cashier are entered in his rough cash chits. Simultaneously the officer authorising payments maintain a scroll of payments authorised.

(*e*) **Accounting Controls :** In order to ensure internal check with regard to recording of transactions in accounting records various cross checks must be introduced to ensure that the accounting records reflect reliable information. Use of control accounts, self-balancing system, preparation of reconciliation statements etc add checks to the system.

Internal Checks for various Transactions

The auditor must know general internal checks that must operate in respect of various types of transactions. Specifically, these checks may vary to suit the peculiar circumstances of actual case. The general checks in respect of cash transactions-receipt, payment and trading transactions-purchases, sales, stock keeping etc are detailed in the chapter vouching of cash transactions, (chapter v) and vouching of trading transactions (chapter vi). The readers may refer to the relevant sections in the chapters.

Internal Audit

As discussed in definition of internal control, the control is exercised in the form of internal check and internal audit. Internal check is concerned with so devising the form and flow of operations of an entity that automatic checks are carried out as the transactions occur. On the other hand, internal audit is a critical appraisal of functioning of various operations of an enterprise including the functioning of the system of internal check. Exceptions from normal functioning of internal check system are exposed in internal audit. Accuracy, completeness, reliability and timeliness of accounting information are tested and reported for remedial action. Non-accounting areas viz. operational side of enterprise are critically studied, analysed and weakness of the system or practice - viz., inefficiency, wastage, frauds etc - are brought to the notice of the management. Suggestions for increasing the effectiveness of the system, for improving the productivity and profitability of business practices are offered. That part of internal audit dealing with operational side of the entity to improve efficiency is termed as operational audit. That part of internal audit aiming at improving the effectiveness of accounting and administrative and other operational systems are called system audit.

"Internal audit is the independent appraisal of activity within an organisation for the review of accounting, financial and other business practices as a protective and constructive arm of management. It is a type of control which functions by measuring and evaluating the effectiveness of other types of control." Professor Walter B. Meigs of America says: "....internal auditing consists of a continuous, critical review of financial and operating activities by a staff of auditors functioning as full-time salaried employees." "Internal audit is an independent appraisal activity within an organisation for the review of accounting, financial and other operations as a basis for service to the management", definition by the Institute of Internal Auditors, Inc., New York in the published statement Responsibilities of Internal Auditors, under the heading "Nature of Internal Audit". Internal audit implies an audit of the accounts by the employees of the business. The work is done by a separate set of staff who may or may not have professional audit qualifications. The function of an internal auditor is practically the same as that of an auditor. In addition to that an internal audit has to see that there is no wastage and the business is carried on efficiently, e.g., when purchasing furniture whether tenders were invited; when waste materials were sold, whether they were sold by auction or by inviting tenders and so on. Again if an internal auditor finds that as a result of the inefficiency of the management, the concern has suffered a loss, it is his duty to report that fact. He has to report to the management whether the policy and plans of activities prescribed by them have been implemented; whether the internal controls and checks established were adequate; whether the actual results obtained were varying from the estimates,etc., to enable the management to achieve the objective of the company in the planned manner. It is a kind of continuous audit but conducted by the staff of the concern. In the case of large concerns like banking or insurance companies or local bodies, they have a separate Internal Audit Department. If such a Department is working independently and efficiently the auditor may depend upon the checking undertaken by such a Department.

Internal Audit and Statutory Audit

We have seen the meaning of internal audit in the foregoing paragraphs. Let us now see what is meant by Statutory Audit. When an audit is conducted under the statute, it is called Statutory Audit, e.g. the audit of joint-stock companies.

Distinction between Internal Audit and Statutory Audit

Let us see the points of distinction between the two audits:

1. *Appointments*. Internal auditor is appointed by the management while the statutory auditor is appointed by the shareholders except in certain cases when he is appointed by the directors of the company or the Government.

   Appointment of internal auditor is optional while that of the statutory auditor is obligatory. Again appointment in the former case is according to the decision of the management while that of the statutory auditor is according to the Companies Act.
2. *Qualifications*. Internal auditor need not posses the qualifications as are laid down under Section 226 of the Companies Act while a statutory auditor must have those qualifications.
3. *Status*. Internal auditor is an employee of the company while the statutory auditor is an independent person.
4. *Conduct of Audit*. An internal audit is a kind of continuous audit while a statutory audit is generally conducted after the preparation of the final accounts.
5. *Scope of Work*.The scope of the work by the internal auditor is determined by the management while the scope of the work by and the responsibilities of the statutory auditor are determined by law.

6. *Objective.* An internal auditor has the primary duty to find out whether any error or fraud has been committed while the statutory auditor has to report whether the balance sheet and the profit and loss account of a company have been drawn up in conformity with law and whether they show true and fair view of the state of affairs of the company. Detection of errors and frauds are incidental duties of a statutory auditor.
7. *Determination of Duty.* The scope and duties of an internal auditor can be reduced while it is not so in the case of a statutory auditor.
8. Internal auditor has to make suggestions to the management as to how to run the business efficiently and to avoid wastages but a statutory auditor need not do so unless he is specifically asked.
9. Internal auditor has to check all the transactions while the statutory auditor may apply test checks.
10. *Report.* Internal auditor has not to submit any report to the shareholders while a statutory auditor has to do so.
11. *Application of Chartered Accountants Act.* Internal auditor cannot be prosecuted for professional misconduct unless he is a Chartered Accountant while a statutory auditor can be prosecuted.
12. *Removal.* Internal auditor can be removed by the management or the directors while a statutory auditor can be removed only by the shareholders and not by the management or the directors.
13. The internal auditor acts as a watch-dog for the directors while the statutory auditor has to act as a watch-dog for the shareholders.
14. Internal audit is carried out for the satisfaction of the management of the concern while the statutory audit is carried out for the satisfaction of the shareholders and third parties for the financial data.
15. *Remuneration.* Remuneration of the internal auditor are fixed by the management while for the statutory auditor they are fixed by the shareholders.
16. *Attendance at Meetings.* Internal auditor has no right to attend a meeting of the shareholders while a statutory auditor has such a right.
17. The activities of the internal auditor are continuous while those of the statutory auditor are periodic, usually for a year.

The internal audit is not made compulsory under Companies Act. However it is desirable to have internal audit. Under section 227-4A the company auditor has to make specific comment on various matters covered under an order notified by central government. (called MAOCAR order-more details can be seen in chapter on audit of companies). In it, the statutory auditor is required to evaluate the efficacy of internal audit system in cases of companies whose paid up capital exceed Rs. 25 lakhs or whose turnover on an average during the period of three years preceding financial years cross Rs 2 crores.

Using the work of Internal audit by External Auditor:

The auditor can effectively make use of the work performed by internal auditor by planned co-ordination of his work. The auditor must judiciously use his work to his advantage. As regards to accounting system of the enterprise, the internal audit covers almost all areas of checking covered under external audit. However, the external auditor expresses his opinion on the truth and fairness of financial statements. Therefore the auditor has to evaluate the internal audit and decide whether its coverage of checking can lessen the extent of checking. The auditor has to evaluate the efficacy of internal audit system by assessing the professional competence of internal auditor, their independence in the organisation, audit coverage, actual work performed by them as evidenced by their working files, reports etc. Depending upon the degree of reliance that he could place on it, the auditor can devise his nature, extent and timing of audit work. By liaisoning with internal auditor, the external auditor can have the co-operation of internal auditor in areas of routine checking, asset verification, checking of certain schedules, statements etc. For instance if the internal auditor vouches sales of certain months, the external auditor can ask his assistants to check certain other months and so on.

Limitations of Internal Control

The existence of internal control system in any entity provides good clues that aims of internal control viz., adherence to policy, safeguarding of assets, detection and prevention of errors/frauds, reliability and completeness of accounting data-might be achieved. One must not forget that clues that they are and not assertions guaranteeing the fulfilment of control objectives. Essentially, there are certain inherent limitations attached to internal control. SAP-6 of ICAI points out certain possible limitations. For instance, the internal control may not adequately cover all areas in view of cost considerations, it cannot foresee control mechanism for transactions of unusual nature, it cannot stand against deliberate circumvention of control procedures by management, false manipulation of transactions by the entity with tacit approval of management or ingenious breach of controls by staff by collusion or controls may become obsolete in changed scenario. Recognising this vital fact the auditor should proceed to evaluate the internal control.

Evaluation of Internal Control

The auditor has to decide whether he can place reliance on the internal control. If internal control is adequate, he can restrict nature, timing and extent of his checking accordingly. If not, he is left with no alternative but to resort to detailed checking.

The auditor makes use of compliance procedure and substantive procedures in gathering evidence as to reliability of internal control system and data generated in accounting system. The methods of compliance procedure, and substantive procedures had been elaborately discussed in chapter II- (An Overview of Auditing). By resorting to compliance procedure, the auditor seeks to find out whether there exists good internal control system and whether such a system has operated with continuity throughout the period covered under audit. For this, the auditor studies the system in operation. He gains understanding as to how a transaction is processed and how the assets are handled. He evaluates the actual operation of the system against certain control criteria that must exist. Accordingly he decides whether the design of the system is adequate or not. Now he is concerned whether the system actually works out without break. For this he inspects documents flowing in the system. He makes enquiry with the persons involved in operation of the system. He tests the completeness, accuracy and validity of data generated in the accounting system of the entity by adopting substantive procedure. By inspection, enquiry or other methods the substantive checking point to actual practising of the system effectively or otherwise. The reliance the auditor can place on internal control is affected by badly designed system or ineffective operation of a good system.

If the auditor finds out weakness in design or operation of internal control system, he reports them to the management in what is called "letter of weakness". The letter of weakness lists down the areas of weakness in the system and offers suggestions for improvement. It helps management to revise the system or to insist its strict implementation. It also acts as good defence for the auditor for any liability as it throws light on important limitation of his audit environment.

The manner of evaluation of internal control may be in the following lines: making preliminary evaluation of the system to test the design of the system, compliance procedures to evaluate the adequacy and continuity of the system in practice and supplementing the compliance procedure with limited substantive procedures. For making preliminary evaluation, the auditor makes use of the following techniques viz., narrative method, questionnaire method or flow charting. Narrative method describes the actual working of the internal control system in an essay form. The audit assistants prepare their observation of the system. Narrative method of evaluation has certain limitations. It is lengthy. It may lack specificity and miss certain areas. It is not uniform and may vary according to persons preparing them. On the other hand, Internal control Questionnaire method makes use of well-structured specific questions covering each and every area of operation (like purchase, sales, stock-keeping, wage payment). Each question is framed with the aim of assessing the strength of control at various stages of an operation. Generally the questions range over authorisation of transaction, flow of transaction, documents made use of in the flow, recording of transaction, division of work aiming at internal check, handling of assets, reporting of transactions to management, and review of operations. Each question seeks responses in terms of `Yes' or `No' or `Not applicable'. The questionaire are filled by responsible officials or by the auditor himself after having specific comments for each question from the staff or after having observation of the working of the system. The flow charting technique of preliminary evaluation gives out graphical description of the flow of each transaction, control points, forms used etc. It depicts the direction of flow of transaction by marks of arrow, describes documents by figures with title, (indicating the points of their origin, route, storing or destruction) and indicates control points with symbols. Flow chart gives good visual description of sequence of transaction, inherent controls in it and documentary evidences generated in its occurrence. Next, for doing compliance and substantive procedures for testing the actual operation of the system, the auditor makes use of any one of the methods viz., - inspection, observation, inquiry, computation, analytical review suited to the occasion.

QUESTIONS

1. Define internal control. Explain its objectives.
2. "The system of internal control extends beyond those matters relate to the functions of accounting system". (I.C.A.I). Explain the statement pointing out the matters in accounting as well as non-accounting system with which the internal control is concerned with.
3. State the aims of instituting control mechanism in a) accounting system and b) administrative system of an entity.
4. "Internal control in its whole gamut includes importantly the two forms of control devices viz., internal check and internal audit". Discuss this, bringing out the inter-relationship among internal control, internal check and internal audit.
5. What is meant by internal check? What important points are to be borne in mind in devising good internal check system?
6. Is internal check synonymous with internal control?
7. Illustrate how internal check could be introduced in respect of sales transactions of a business entity.
8. Define internal audit. What are the aims of having internal audit?
9. The management of XYZ co., Ltd., being a manufacturing company informs you that since the review of accounts, any way, is to be taken up by its statutory auditors, it feels unnecessary to create internal audit department. Moreover, creation of internal audit department entails permanent overhead costs. Convince them about the utility of having internal audit. Present them the benefits of having an external auditor as its internal auditor on a retainer basis.
10. The manner and extent of checking by an auditor is affected by the existence or otherwise of good internal control system- Discuss. Also set out the limitations of internal control system.
11. How an auditor evaluates the efficacy of internal control system?
12. What is a letter of weakness? Why is it issued?

Chapter 15

Auditing in an EDP Environment

The adoption of computer for accounting, auditing and administration has lent new dimension to the approach of auditing in such an EDP environment. While, the auditing is greatly facilitated by the use of computer in accounting and auditing functions, the control risks associated therewith have significantly increased which need to be carefully managed.

The computer has given the accounting and auditing a large number of benefits. The computer has increased the capacity of accounting facet of the administration to receive, store, retrieve, correlate, compare, analyse large volume of data to suit different requirements. Any type of statements, analytical reviews, arrangements which would be difficult in manual handling of data have now become possibility of easy and quick finish.

Problems in an EDP Environment

1. Absence of Supporting Vouchers:

In conventional accounting, there are basic documents duly authorised by officers to originate a transaction. For example, the sales invoices may be prepared by a person which may duly be signed by a responsible official. On the other in a computerised environment of a high degree, many transactions may be fed directly into computer without authorisation record in the conventional form of vouchers. Similarly, the price calculations, discount, interest and other arithmetic manipulations may be done by computer according to the parameters of such arithmetic already set in the programme. These definitely would pose certain difficulties in checking from outside what and how these are recorded.

2. Lack of Visible Audit Trail:

In a manual accounting, the origination of data follows an apparently visible auditing sequence to culminate into final output of the accounting system. For example, sales value before figuring in profit and loss account originates in pieces of sales invoices which are chronologically written in sales day book, which again are posted to general ledger and debtors ledger and which is reflected in financial statements after proper grouping and disclosure. The computer environment may not allow such intermediary stages of output and data may after subjecting themselves to required manipulations reach the final output. The audit trail may not be so elaborately and so understandably available as they are in manual accounting system. The manipulations undergone by the final output may not be easily listable unless the programme allows for such a listing. The tracing of such manipulations, if possible, may last only for limited period of time in many cases.

3. Vulnerability to Manipulations:

The computer input, processing, and output may be subject to easy manipulations. The computer obediently and faithfully does what is dictated. As is active, it is passive. Unless it is told of persons to whom must it be loyal, it obeys all and sundry. The restriction of access to computer is serious concern of the management. It involves issues like levels of authorisation, exhibition unusual or material manipulations computed in the computer, throwing out of exceptional transactions with due comparison with standards and so on.

4. Garbage in Garbage out:

It is the entry that is inputted into computer that undergoes processing and reflects in final output. Any entry wrongly or erraneously read by computer would only be wrongly written by it. In successive manipulations and ununderstandable highly complex and comprehensive logical sequence, it may not serve purpose if the correction is attempted at an inappropriate place of processing.

5. Storage Problem:

The program, data recorded in the computer are stored in the hard disc and other storing devices like disc, floppy etc. These are to be carefully stored. They are to be guarded against risks of loss of physical devices, manipulations, and inflection of virus.

6. Coding Problem:

The computerised accounting makes extensive use of codes in the place of self-explanatory accounting heads employed in manual accounting. The designing and operating of coded accounting version of business transactions requires care and experience.

7. Computer Frauds:

The computer frauds are of different types and may even defy conceivable imagination. The frauds may range from simple unauthorised use of computers, to physical manipulation of framework of system, to theft of confidential output, to taping, intercepting and editing final output different from what is logically expected of given a set of input in a prima facie known environment of programmes and processes. The frequent auditing of the system itself is often called for to ensure that the system does function according to the normal expected way at all levels of input and at all times.

8. Computer Virus

Another recent phenomenon connected with computer is the computer getting sick or even becoming dead with the infection of computer virus. Computer virus is the mischievous attempt on certain pre-targetted area of computer. It is a programme that affects the working of target area of the computer. It gains entry into computer in many ways. For example, use of pirated programmes or discs, or floppy used in another computer etc. often carry these criminal and install them in the system. The computer viruses are sometimes innocent and does no harm more than simple inconveniences; sometimes they are so lethal as to make the system dead,; sometimes they operate for a while at specified date and disappear later; sometimes they target only certain programmes and leave the others in tact; whatever their style in causing effect, they do cause concern and the system needs to be guarded against them. Use of vaccine programmes, use of expertise of technical personnel, controlled use of disc, programme in the system are certain ways out for minimising infection and curing of computer viruses.

Control in an EDP Environment:

The problems enumerated with the installation and operation of computer in accounting would require installation and implementation of adquate internal control system to gain control over the problems inherent with the computerised environment. The control should aim at presenting a reliable, effective fool-proof system and also providing timely, authorised and required data from the system so controlled. Thus control over the system in a general way and also the application of the system in particular are essentially called for.

1. Division of Responsibilities:

The clustering of all duties in hands of few would throw open enormous chances for making frauds. The concept of internal check requires that the duty listing should be so drawn up that the work of one is, in the course of performance of duties, checked by another and commiting of fraud is not possible unless collision exists. Thus duties connected with the computer operation should be clearly specified and duties must be so defined as to fix up specific responsibility and to require review of operations of others. The duties must be properly divided among different staff. This would minimise the happening of errors and also committing of frauds.

2. Control Over Development, Maintenance of Software:

Systems software and application software must be acquired or developed in accordance with the pre-determined standards. Use of sub-standard software may, besides posing threat to reliability, endanger the system itself. Various criteria should be carefully fixed for acquisition and or developing programme and other software packages. The procedure for developing new systems and required documentation should be clearly spelt out. A manual incorporating such requirements should be prepared and updated. The systems manual should provide for various requirements as to the input content, the form in which such data may be narrated, the periodicity of gathering such data, the form and content of master file, the manner and the requirements of processing and the output requirements. Similarly, the programming requirements should also similarly, the programming requirements should also be documented in the form of a manual. The programme manual should provide a base for programmers as to the approach to be followed in a programme, the control parameters to be taken care of, the listing of instructions to operators, data content and the results of testing. The system should become functional only if it is certified by competent authority as to its implementation. Similarly programmes made use of in the system should be carefully reviewed and pretested for all eventuality. The programme files may be corrected with the authorisation of competent authority level. The programmes must be properly preserved and protected.

3. Control Over Operators:

The allocation of work assignments among operators should be properly planned and carried out. The sequencing of work should be so arranged that the work is carried out smoothly and time is not wasted and required output could be obtained at appropriate time without waiting. The scheduling of work, the shift allocation, and job rotation etc. require to be handled adequately in this connection.

4. Data Access and Programme Access:

Authorisation commensurate with the levels of authority should be defined for the system to accept the data, manipulation in programming. Use of pass words for accepting a transaction in the system is an example in implementing authorisation in feeding entry into computer. The secret keeping of passwords and its periodical changing and fixing up responsibility for users of the password are matters of concern in this direction.

5. Control Over Editing:

When outputs are altered from what is inputted, it is to be ensured that the editing is but to correct the errors unintentionally crept into. It is also to be ensured that whether corrections speak of any lagging in the systems design, programming or applications. Any correction should be incorporated under the express authorisation of the authority and the statement of the corrections edited should be obtained as an output to ensure the tolerability of corrections.

6. Storage Control:

The floppy or other storage devices used in the system should be properly and distinctly labelled. This is essential because the operator himself may unintentionally make use of the protected storage devices and data or programme may destroy in processing. The storage devices and data or programme may destroy in processing. The storage devices such as magnetic tape, floppy discs etc. must be protected against the risk of fire and other damages. The programmes and date files must be preserved and stored within and outside the computer system. The taking of adquate distant back-up file in the system and also taking copies of files in the floppy and other storage devices outside the computer are called for.

7. Control Over Functioning of Equipment (hardware control):

The output obtained from the equipment is reliable if the equipment consisting of various mechanical and electronics parts responds properly to the dictates of input, process and output commands. Therefore, certain controls to ensure that there is no error in the system due to any fault in functioning of equipment is called for. Reduntant or parity character, duplicate processing, echo check, validity cheek and equipment check are certain controls in this direction. Under parity check, whenever a data is entered, a bit is added to make the total odd to ensure odd parity check. when the data is moved in the computer, the bits are counted to ensure that total remains odd. Duplicate processing involves performance of the process twice to compare the results of the two performance to find out discrepancies if any in them. The echo check consists in reading and comparing of the data by the system. If data processed is different from what is read, then the computer gives out signal. Validity and equipment checks are also developed in the system to ensure the control over proper functioning of hardware.

APPLICATION CONTROLS:

The application controls aim at devising adequate internal control to ensure that the input fed is authorised, reliable and are recorded in the manner intended and the processing is done thereon completely, timely, and accurately so that the output obtained is true and correct reflection of transactions recorded.

(A) Control Over Input:

If only correct input is fed, the output will be correct. The input may be wrongly coded or recorded in the originating department itself. Or the input may get manipulated in its handling; or the computer may, read the input wrongly.

1. The input is to be complete and should contain all relevant particulars. The data should be entered in a well defined field. For this purpose, the design of the input document should be structured to suit the requirements and convenience of the user department and also operation department of computer section.
2. The input documents should be authorised by a responsible official so that only authorised documents we recorded in the system.
3. The input documents should be reviewed and verified by another person after preparation so that error does not creep into system once the input is recorded in the system.
4. There must be hardware control to ensure that the equipment processes only the data it has read.

5. The check digits say total of financial information contained in the documents or hash total-like total of invoice numbers or debit accounting codes used or any such totals may be used as a control tool. The data processor after finishing processing upto certain stages, computes the identified control totals and compares them with the totals to be. Any discrepancy between than highlights omission of data to be fed into computer or reference to serial control of any other accompanying document may be used as a control tool, the lack of serial order is immediately signalled out by the system.

(B) Control Over Processing:

The data recorded in the computer is moved about, added to the file by way of updatation, manipulated, analysed, computed, compared and so on. The final output will be accurate, reliable if the data is accurate, software in which it undergoes changes is efficient, the hardware supporting it is efficient and there are in-built controls to ensure control over processing.

1. Run to Run Control:

It is to be ensured that each step of the programme is correctly written and is executed accordingly for example, when data is fed and merge process happens, the data gets added to the opening balance of the file and the control should check that the closing balances of the file equals the opening balance and aggregate updation recorded. This would ensure that the merge process is accurately carried out.

2. Generation of Computer Log:

The exhaustive computer log should be obtained from the system which would detail out the various moves, manipulations, the transaction path - source area, destination, total of documents recorded, direct manipulations attempted etc. This would provide complete history of day's transactions with regard to inputting, processing, outputting of data into and from the computer.

3. Efficiency of Software Testing;

The software should at periodical intervals be audited to ensure that it is efficient. Two test systems relevant in this connection are - contrived systems test and real systems test. The contrived systems test contains deliberate faults and errors introduced into the system to test the validation and control procedure. For example, alpha character in numeric field, wrong batch totals, impossible codes, dates, values etc., may be introduced along with certain correct data to check how the system responds to correct and incorrect input. On the other hand, real system test makes use of a representative data which have already been analysed or computed before-hand to make comparison of functioning of software.

4. Hardware Controls :

Adequate in-built hardware controls like parity check, echo check etc. should be installed to ensure that the equipment responds correctly while processing the data.

5. Editing of Data:

By editing the data, it is meant here the editing of data by the processor itself to ensure the validity of the data communicated to it for processing. The processor verifies the validity of the data against certain in-built control tools.

(*a*) Check digit verification ensures verification of validity of the data by protecting against the transcription errors. An extra number which is passive in operation is added as a self checking number. The numbers so added is defined by certain arithmetical operation upon all digits. The processor checks the compatibility of such a check digit number in the light of the definition of such number and if the input is recorded wrongly, then the self checking number will be incompatible and this would he thrown to light.

(*b*) Valid coding is another control tool that checks the correctness of grouping and accounting of a data in the relevant classification. For example, sundry debtors may contain codes ranging from 5000 to 6000 and the entry any sub-entry which should find in the list of sundry debtors cannot have codes beyond this range.

(*c*) Limit checking ensures that data recorded falls within the reasonable limits set out for each of the category. For example, in pay roll accounting, the number of hours including over time cannot exceed 12 hours if the limit is fixed for as 12 as 12. The entry involving labour hours worked by a single worker beyond 12 hours would be thrown out for verification.

(*d*) Format checks ensures that the characters are in alpahabetic or in numeric and are of specified lengths only (say 8 digits or so) and field size are in speeified format.

(*e*) Sequence checking ensures that the master files and transaction files follow sequences and no gap occurs.

(*f*) Missing data test finds out all data field relevant in coding the transactions are filled in and no field is left without information recorded.

Thus using editing control tools, it is ensured that the data recorded are processed in the manner desired of them.

Control Over Output:

The effectiveness of control over input and processing cannot relieve that the output will be correct always. It is always desirable that the output is compared in the light of analytical review. The reasonableness of the findings and facts recorded in the output should be critically examined as to its correctness and fairness. The output should be distributed in the format required of to various users departments and feed back should be obtained from them to ensure the quality of the output generated.

Audit approach in An EDP Environment:

The computerisation of accounting does not change the basic objective and scope of auditing. It remains the same as expression of opinion of the truth and fairness of the financial documents reviewed by the auditor. However, the computerisation has brought out changes in organisation, procedures, manner of storing information and processing them. This entails serious concern with regard to control elements. Basically auditor had to do audit in an environment with little or no audit trail, primary records and non-visible output.

These changes in an EDP environment requires certain modifications in his conventional testing of compilance test and substantive test. The auditor would do well to lay more emphasis in evaluation of internal control in generation of data in computer environment. But equally important as to his testing of internal control over the storing, processing of date in a computer environment is the checking of accurary, validity and completeness of data recorded and processed in the computer.

The auditor may not vouch each and every transaction especially when the audit trail is absent. However he must perform overall analytical checking to ensure that the picture presented does not show any distorted version of the transactions of the entity and is true and fair representation of events and results of the entity for the period under review.

If upon checking the compilance test the auditor is satisfied with the efficacy of internal control and its continued functioning during period under review, the auditor can pay reliance upon the arithmetical accuracy of data generated in the system. He must ensure that periodical systems audit and methods compilance review are carried out by internal audit personnel duly qualified in an EDP environment. If auditor finds out any weakness in internal control procedures, he must bring out the matter to the attention of the management through a letter of weakness.

Auditing in an EDP Environment :

With this philosophy in the background, the auditor should programme his audit functions to cover the following steps-

(1)Review of internal control.

(2)Examination of records produced by the system

The auditor should bring to bear upon his duties the basic principles connected with compliance and substantive tests. The auditor should use various techniques like flow charting, discussion with the staff, questionnaire, test-checking etc. to ensure that-there exists adequate and appropriate internal control in the entity; it actually functions in the entity during the period under reivew: Based upon his checking, the auditor should draw up a conclusion as to the degree of reliance he can place on the effectiveness of internal control system. If he is satisfied he would proceed to ensure the accuracy, validity and completeness of the data through substantive checking.

The auditing in an EDP environment may be carried out by auditing around the computer or auditing through the computer. Auditing around the computers means the carrying out of audit in a traditional manner by comparing the print-outs generated in the system. The auditing through the computer makes use of computer in auditing. It also involves auditing systems and programmes used in the entitly by the auditor. Technqiues which use the computer itself for audit purpose are known as "computer-assisted auditing techniques" (CAAT)

Computer Assisted Auditing Techniques:

Techniques which make use of computer system in auditing are known as Computer assisted auditing techniques. Certain important computer assisted are given hereunder.

Test Data:

This test aims at testing the effectiveness of the programme made use of in the system. The auditor prepares a set of input and applies them in the programe in use in the system. The input so prepared consists of different varities of transactions involving valid and invalid conditions. The invalid conditions are specifically created to test how the programme responds to such invalid conditions. The results of the computer are checked against the predetermined solutions. The deviation of results obtained from computer throws open the ineffectiveness of computer in such of those situations. This test is known as contrived test. On the other hand, the auditor may pick up certain representative transactions from real situation of the client's business and test the effectiveness of the programme in handling such transactions.

In checking this the auditor usually determine the areas where he may like to test. The input fed in the computer either in the contrived test or real test, may update and manipulate the records of the client. The auditor should carefully note to document the input fed, the computation, calculations, comparisions etc done in the system, the results obtained. This documentation is of good use to him to evaluate the efficacy of the internal control system and also to report the weakness found in the system to the management. More importantly, the auditor has to erase the effect of his test applications from the records of the computer so that the data stored in the system is as it were before his testing.

Controlled Processing:

This method consists in auditor's checking the efficacy of particular programme by insisting on its putting to use in his presense. When a set of particular transactions are processed, the auditor may present himself in the system department to do observation of the processing. Alternatively, after processing is over, the auditor may require the processing to be repeated in relation to the programme which he wants to test.

Computer Audit Programmes :

Another area where computers are often made use of in auditing are putting them to use to provide auditing information required by the auditor for making judgement and drawing conclusions. The use of computer in planning, conducting and concluding audit will be of great help to the auditor. It saves time, reduces monotony of work, enhance reliability and lowers audit cost in appropriate cases. However, the use of computer in auditing requires the expert knowledge of the system. It is also necessary that there should exist an awareness that the computerised auditing assistance is only to provide help to the auditor and not to substitute his professional judgement. The following are certain areas where the use of computer in auditing may be relevant-

(1) preparing detailed audit programming;

(2) preparing audit planning, schedulling and assignment of available manpower to different assignments in hand;

(3) retrieving requaired key informations from the files for making comparison with the set of standard information;

(4) doing arithmetical computations and checking the arithmetical computations;

(5) doing analytical review of the data by way of comparison, ratio analysis, trend analysis, tests of reasonableness and so on;

(6) checking of validity, consistency and reasonableness of entries;

(7) reviewing the internal control of the system;

(8) selecting representatives for vouching, vertfication - debtors acconnts may be planned to be listed if they comply certain predetermined criteria;

(9) flow-charting;

(10) preparation of audit reports, documenting working papers; writing other communication etc.

The use of CAAT in auditing is of immense help to the auditor. However, the adoption of such techniques should be appropriate to the audit handled. Too elaborate or too simple audit techniques planned in the pack may prove to be inappropriate in terms of cost, coverage and timing. The auditor should weigh the audit demands before he decides on the contents of CAAT he makes use of. The use of CAAT requires computer knowledge and experience of the auditor. The auditor should also be familiar with the system in vogue in the client's place. Appropriateness and relevance must be established with the client's system and the auditor's test pack. He should also ascertain whether his test pack can be accbmodated in the facility offered by his client and whether required co-operation would be forthcoming without any inconvenience to the client in regard to offering of expert personnel for assistance and making available the system for checking. The checking is to be carried out in smoother way without any inconvenience to the client and also without loosing sight of checking areas desired to be checked by the auditor. Again, certain data of client which are desired to be auditor may not last long in the machine. If such of those data enter in the checking scope of the auditor, the auditor would first discuss these areas with the client and arrange timing of his checking accordingly.

TYPICAL QUESTIONS

1. Explain auditing through computer?
2. In an EDP environment, the auditor has become more of an information technologist rather than an auditor in his own right according to conventional meaning of the term - Do you agree.

3. List down few important are as which pose problems for audit or in adapting himself to computerised accounting environment?
4. What are audit risks associated with computerised accounting environment?
5. Suggest programme for checking the efficacy of internal control of the computerised accounting?
6. Discuss the internal control components of an EDP accounting system?
7. Has audit approach been altered in a computerised accounting milieu?
8. What is meant by computer assisted auditing techniques?
9. Discuss few illustrative techniques made use of in CAAT ?
10. What pre-cautions are called for in making use of CAAT's in an auditing situation?

Substantial Procedures-Vouching of Cash Transactions

The main objects of the audit of the cash book may be summarised thus :

1. To ensure that all receipts are accounted for;
2. To ensure that no fraudulent payments have been made;
3. To know that all receipts and payments have been properly recorded; and
4. To verify the cash in hand and at bank.

Vouching : Its Meaning

A voucher is a documentary evidence in support of a transaction in the books of account. The act of establishing the accuracy and authenticity of entries in the account books is called vouching. Ronald A. Irish of Australia defines vouching as "vouching" is a technical term which refers to the inspection by the auditor of documentary evidence supporting and substantiating a transaction. Vouching is considered to be the essence of auditing and therefore the auditor should be very careful while vouching. Vouching means to substantiate an entry in the books of account not only with any documentary evidence such as agreements, receipts, counterfoils of a receipt book or paying-in-book, contracts, but also to see that the transaction has been properly authorised, recorded and entered in the books of account, e.g., verification of the entries in the invoice book with the invoices, checking of the cash receipts with the counterfoils of the receipts book, the checking of the cash payments with the receipts issued by the payee and so on. Vouching means testing the truth of items appearing in the books of original entry. The success of an auditor in vouching depends upon his intelligence, critical bent of mind, common sense, observation and tact with which he handles his work. He should go beyond the books of account and go to the source of a transaction. If he simply compares the entry say, on the credit side of a cash book with the voucher, it is possible that he might be deceived, e.g., the purchase might not have been for the business or the receipt might have been for the previous year. If it is a receipt side entry and if he compares the entry with the counterfoil of the receipt book, it is possible that less amount might have been entered on the counterfoil than the money which has actually been received. Again a person might have sent two or three amounts but only one receipt for all the amounts might have been issued while the three amounts might have been shown on three different counterfoils of the receipt book. The second or the third blank receipt might be issued to other persons who have sent money–which might have been misappropriated. Clever frauds can be discovered only by proper vouching. Therefore, it is very important that the auditor should vouch the items with great care and intelligence. It is through vouching that an auditor can satisfy himself as to the authenticity and completeness of transactions in the books of accounts. In case he is negligent, he will be held guilty as was decided in the case of Armitage vs. Brewer & Knott.

Vouching also means checking of additions, ledger postings, extracting of balances in the ledger, etc. The extent to which the auditor should check will depend upon the size of the business, the accounts of which he is auditing. If it is a big business, efficient internal check will be in operation and hence the auditor will be justified in relying upon a few test checks, while in a small business, internal check may not be in operation and hence the auditor will have to check every entry. To be on the safe side, the auditor will do well to check the entries in detail because the curtailment of work not in any way reduce his responsibility.

Voucher

As explained above, a voucher is a documentary evidence in support of a transaction in the books of account. It may be a receipt, counterfoil of a receipt book, an agreement, resolution passed by the Board of Directors or shareholders and as recorded in the minute books, an invoice, bank paying-in-slip, Bought Note, Sold Note, correspondence, gate-keeper's books, wages book, order book and so on.

While examining the vouchers, following points must be borne in mind:

1. All the vouchers are consecutively numbered and filed in order of the entries in the accounts. If the client has not done so, the auditor has a right to ask him to do so. If they are not properly arranged, much valuable time will be lost in finding out a particular voucher to check it.
2. He should pay attention to the dates, which must correspond with the cash book, name of the party to whom the voucher is issued, the name of the party issuing the voucher and the amount, etc.
3. The vouchers inspected should be cancelled by a stamp lest they may be produced again. Subsidiary documents such as statements, invoices, etc., relating to such a voucher should also be cancelled. In case stamp is not available, the audit clerk should affix his initials or put a tick right across the face of the voucher. Such a mark of stamp should be put in the centre of the voucher to avoid its removal by a dishonest clerk if it has been put in a corner.
4. Special attention should be paid to those vouchers which are in the personal name of one of the partners, directors, manager or secretary, etc., as such a voucher may not relate to the business. In such a case, original invoice, inward book, etc. should be examined to find out whether the goods were purchased for the business or for the individual to whom the voucher is addressed. He should ask the client to issue instructions to the suppliers not to address the vouchers to any individual of the firm or the company. If on enquiry it is found that the goods were meant for one of the officers, personal account of such an officer should be debited.
5. He should see that every voucher is passed as in order by a responsible officer. The signature of the officer should be noted. If the receipt is a printed one or it bears a rubber stamp of the name of the firm, the voucher should be taken as a genuine one.
6. He should also note, whether the voucher is stamped, if the amount of the voucher is above twenty rupees.
7. He should also find out the nature of Payment as to whether it relates to the business.
8. He should see as to which account the payment is posted — revenue or capital. This is important as wrong posting will affect the profit and loss account and ultimately the balance sheet.

9. Attention should be paid to the amount both in words and figures. If they differ, the matter should be investigated. Amount mentioned only in figures should be particularly taken care of as a cypher or figure may be easily added to a figure by a dishonest employee which will make a lot of difference.
10. Note should be made of any item which requires further elucidation or information or evidence which is available from Partnership Deed, Contracts, Article of Association, Minute Book, Leases, etc.
11. If duplicate voucher for a missing one is produced, it should be properly scrutinised to avoid any fraud. List of missing vouchers should be prepared and reason and explanation for their loss should be obtained from the client and if the auditor is not satisfied with the explanation, he should mention this fact in his report. Transactions relating to such vouchers should be carefully examined. Sometimes vouchers may not be available for certain types of payments such as salaries, wages, petty expenses, etc. Such payments can be verified by reference to salaries book, wages book, petty cash book respectively.
12. The audit clerk should not take the help of any members of the staff of the client for an explanation, while vouching receipts.
13. Receipted invoice should not be accepted as a voucher because there is a danger of the payment being made twice — once as a crédit purchase and again as a cash transaction against the receipted invoice.
14. Sometimes business houses issue their own printed receipts to be signed by the payee, which receipts are considered as vouchers. The practice must be discouraged, as the dishonest employees of the client themselves may fill up such receipts and forge the signatures of the supposed payees. In case this has been done, the auditor should get more documentary evidence such as statement or invoices, etc., which should be attached with such a receipt, before he passes such a voucher.
15. While examining the vouchers for insurance, rent, rates, and taxes, etc., the audit clerk should note the period for which the payment has been made. If the payment is made for some months in advance, proper adjustments should be made.

Internal Check as regards Cash

Before the auditor starts the vouching of the cash book, he should enquire about the system of internal check in operation, There are lot chances of misappropriation of cash if there is no well-organised system of internal check. He should enquire as to the duties of the cashier, and whether he has access to the ledger and other books of original entry. If it is so, there are chances of fraud and therefore he should be vigilant. In case of big concerns the question will not arise as the cashier will have no time but to write his cash book. This danger is usually in small concerns where a clerk is assigned two or more jobs. The following system of internal check as regards receipt and payment of cash is suggested:

1. When cash is received, it should be acknowledged by means of a printed receipt which should have a counterfoil or by a carbon receipt. Cashier should not sign receipts and counterfoils. The receipts should be consecutively numbered. The unused receipt book should be kept under lock and key. Spoiled receipts should be cancelled and must not be detached from the counterfoils. No blank counterfoils should be accepted.
2. As soon as cash is received, it should be entered in a rough cash book or diary.
3. Remittances should be opened by the cashier in the presence of a responsible officer who should not be connected with the cashier's office. All cheques received should be crossed 'Not Negotiable—A/c Payee only.'

4. Automatic tills or cash registers are very useful for checking receipts. Some cash registers or tills are so made that a receipt is issued only when money is deposited in the till, which device is very useful.
5. All the receipts of the day should be deposited in the bank at the end of the day or the next morning.
6. Bank reconciliation statement should be prepared frequently by the cashier and also by some one else.
7. The cashier should not have any control over the ledgers.
8. Petty cash should be organised under the Imprest System.
9. Before a cheque is issued, it should be presented along with the account of the payee to a responsible officer, who should not have any access to accounting records or securities, for his signature. Cheques should be crossed 'A/c Payee only', before they are despatched. Unused cheque books should be kept under lock and key by a responsible official lest they may be used by forging the signature of the officer.
10. Castings of cash book should be independently checked.
11. Internal control over the preparation of wages sheets to prevent fraud and manipulation should be exercised.
12. All payments as far as possible, except for petty cash, should be made by cheques.
13. If travellers are permitted to collect money on behalf of the company, the issue of receipts by them and deposits of such moneys into the bank should be carefully controlled. As far as possible the system of collection by the travellers should be discouraged. Fidelity insurance policies should be taken out as an additional protection to the business if travellers are allowed to collect money. The travellers should be given receipt books having three copies — one to be given to the customer; another to be sent to the head office and the third to be retained by them.
14. The method of recording the cash sales has been dealt with below in detail. This should be so organised that chances of misappropriation are reduced to a minimum.
15. Cashier should not sanction the payments of special nature. Directors should do so.

Procedure in regard to vouching the debit side of the Cash Book

After satisfying himself that there is a good internal check system regarding the receipts and payments of cash, the audit clerk should now proceed to vouch the debit side of the cash book. It is rather very difficult to vouch the receipt of cash as some entries might have been omitted altogether and therefore only an indirect evidence is available. He should check a few items at random and if he finds that they are in order, he may assume that the others will be correct but he must not omit to compare the rough cash book or the diary with the cash book. If he fails to do so and later on a fraud is detected, he might be held responsible. If he finds that there is a time-lag between the two dates, he should go deeper into the matter as it is possible that money might have been received in between the two dates and misappropriated.

Sometimes it is argued that the auditor is not responsible if he does not check rough cash book or dairy because such books are not included in the 'books of account'. The argument may appear to be sound to some extent, but if such books are a part of the system of account books maintained by the company, the auditor will be failing in his duty if he does not compare the rough cash book or dairy with the cash book. The duty of an auditor is not only to examine the books of account but also to go beyond them which means that he should examine the memoranda books, and other evidence available in support of the correctness of the books of account. Some of the important items which usually appear on the debit side of the cash book and the duty of an auditor in that connection are given below:

1. Opening Balance

This should be compared with the balance shown in the duly audited balance sheet of the previous year. This is done to see that the actual balance has been brought down.

2. Cash Sales

There are greater chances of fraud under this head. The salesman may sell goods and may not make an entry in the cash book and thus misappropriate the money. The following system should be adopted to avoid fraud. The salesman should neither deliver the goods to the customers nor receive cash for the goods sold. He should prepare three carbon copies of the cash memo when goods are sold to a customer, to whom two copies of the cash memo are handed over. The goods are in the meantime sent to the cashier. The customer goes to the cashier and hands over the cash memos. The cashier who receives the price of the goods, hands over the goods and a copy of the cash memo duly stamped as 'cash paid', while the other copy of the cash memo is retained by him. Sometimes four copies of the cash memo are prepared. The fourth copy is retained by the gate-keeper who hands over the goods to the customers instead of by the cashier. At the end of the day, the salesman, the cashier, and the gate-keeper prepare the summaries and send them to the General Manager. The summary sent by the salesman shows the quantity and value of the goods sold; one sent by the cashier will show the cash collections against the cash memos and one sent by the gate-keeper will show the goods delivered. All the three summaries must tally. If there is any discrepancy, it will mean that some fraud has been committed by some one. The auditor should check here and there a few items from the salesman's summaries, cashier's summaries and the gate-keeper's extracts. If the auditor does not do so, he will be held liable for any fraud which remained undetected as was decided in the case of *Pendlebury's Ltd.vs. Ellis, Green & Co.in 1936*.

Where automatic tills are in use, the entries in the cash sales book and in the cash book should be verified from the till records.

In some business houses cash memos are issued against goods sold on credit. The reason advanced is that this system ensures prompt payment. In such a case, there may be so many cash memos against which there may be no cash. Therefore, it would be rather impossible to vouch cash. The auditor should disown his responsibility in such a case. Such a system should, however, be discouraged.

The auditor should compare the dates on the cash memos and the cash book. If cash discount has been allowed on sales, he should see that a uniform policy and rate of discount has been followed. The cancelled cash memo should not be detached from the book. He may also compare a few items of sale with the stock.

3. Receipts from Debtors

The auditor should vouch cash received from debtors to whom goods had been sold on credit in the past. The only evidence available on account of this item is the counterfoils of the receipts issued to the debtors. But this evidence is not very reliable as less amount might have been issued inserted in the counterfoils than what had actually been received from the customers to whom a receipts for the full amount might have been and less amount recorded on the debit side of cash book.

Teeming and Lading Method of Frauds

Another method of committing fraud in connection with the receipt of cash from debtors is what is known as the process of "*teeming and lading*" or "*lapping*". Professor Meigs says "Lapping" may be defined as the "concealment of a shortage by delaying the recording of cash receipts." Under this method, when cash is received, say from A, no entry is made in the cash book by the cashier and he misappropriates this money. Later on when cash is received from B, the amount is recorded on the debit side of the cash book by crediting the account of A. Again, when money is received later on from C, the amount is credited to B, and so on. Later on the cashier replaces the money he has so far used without any authority and credits the account of the debtor whose account he had not credited so far. Of course no misappropriation of money has been committed, but this type of fraud should be prevented as it may encourage the cashier to commit such a type of fraud often and of bigger amount. It is possible that he may not be able to replace the amount. Similarly when a cheque is received, it is not credited to the customer and the proceeds is misappropriated. Later on when another customer sends a cheque it is credited to the first customer's account and so on. Of course this type of fraud is difficult to commit though not impossible, e.g., when the cashier has a control over the cash received on the accounts of the customers, receipts to be issued by him, etc.

How to detect such a fraud

1. The auditor would scrutinise the debtors accounts especially those accounts which show part payments from time to time although such debtors have been making full payments in settling the accounts in the past.
2. If there is any suspicion that a fraud had been committed, the auditor should compare the amount deposited in the bank with the entries made in the counterfoil of the paying-in-slip to see whether full amount had been deposited in the bank or whether some money has been misappropriated.
3. He should compare the carbon copies of the receipts or the counterfoils of the receipt book with the entries in the Cash Book and he should pay special attention to the amount and the date of the receipt of the money and the date on which the amount was deposited in the bank.
4. In case he is still suspicious about some account, he should get the balances of the customers confirmed by them. The statement of accounts sent to the debtors for confirmation should be prepared under the supervision of a responsible officer. The correctness or otherwise of the statement of account should be sent direct to the auditor. Such a request should be made to the customer.
5. Above all, before he commences the checking, he should find out the system of internal check regarding the receipt of cash from customers and deposits into the bank and the preparation of Bank Reconciliation Statements from time to time.

Again, if cash had been received from a debtor, a receipt might have been issued from the unused receipt books unless they had been kept under lock and key. He should compare the counterfoils or the carbon copies of the Receipt Book with the counterfoils of the Pay-in-slips to see whether full amount has been deposited or not.

Particular attention should be paid to discount allowed to customers. The method of granting discounts should be enquired into as there are chances of manipulation, e.g., a customer sends Rs. 95 and is allowed Rs. 5 as discount. The cashier may make an entry in the cash column amounting to Rs. 90, and enter Rs. 10 in the discount column. The receipt issued to the debtor will be for Rs. 100 and counterfoil will show as if Rs. 90 had been received and a discount of Rs. 10 had been allowed. As a matter of fact, the company has been defrauded to the extent of Rs. 5. The auditor will do well to devote his attention to such items as there are chances of fraud. He should check in detail such items and enquire into the method of granting discounts. He should ask for the general rate of discount. Any unusual bigger discount should be noted and an explanation should be demanded from a responsible official. He should enquire as to who sanctions the discount.

The same remarks apply to 'bad debts' written off. The dishonest clerk may either write off the whole of the debit balance or a part of it as bad debts after he has received the whole of the amount. In case a debt is written off as bad, the auditor should enquire as to who is responsible to write off debts as bad. He should examine the correspondence in this connection. In no case the cashier should be allowed to do so.

Wherever possible, after taking permission from his clients, a statement of accounts should be sent to the debtors to confirm the balances show in the statements so sent. If this is done, debtors should be instructed to send letters of confirmation direct to the auditor. If any fraud has been committed, it would be brought to light by adopting this method.

4. Income from Interest, Dividends, etc.

Interest received on account of fixed deposits in the bank should be vouched with the bank pass book. Sometimes a fictitious Pass Book is produced. Care must be taken to see that it is a genuine one.

Dividends received can be vouched with the counterfoil of "tops" of the dividend warrants or the letters covering the cheque. Interest received on securities can be vouched from the securities themselves or from the tax deduction certificate issued by the Reserve Bank, or from the Investment Ledger as to the date of the receipt of interest, the amount, the rate, etc. Care should be taken to adjust the outstanding interest. The auditor should check the receipt of such an interest in the beginning of the subsequent year. Interest received for any particular fund like Provident Fund, should be credited to that fund and not to the revenue account.

If the interest has been received on account of the loan granted, agreement with the borrower should be inspected to ascertain the rate of interest, the date for the payment of interest, etc.

If divident warrants or securities, etc., are deposited with the bank for the purpose of collection of interest and dividends, bank pass book must be referred to. If the investments have been sold 'ex-dividend' or bought 'cum-dividend', the auditor should examine broker's Sold and Bought Notes respectively and should see that dividend is received subsequently. He should also see in such a case that proper allocation is made between capital and revenue.

5. Loans

The receipt of loan should be vouched with the agreement with the lender. He should see whether his client is entitled to raise loan. He should examine the rate of interest payable, the terms of repayment and the security offered which should be examined. The security offered should be indicated in the balance sheet. The interest due but not paid at the balance sheet date should be adjusted in the accounts.

6. Rents Received

The auditor should examine the Lease Deeds and agreements to ascertain the amount of rent payable, the due date, and provision regarding the repairs, etc. Rent received may also be compared with the 'rent rolls' if they are maintained or list of various properties as in the case of owners of large estates. If receipts are issued to the tenants for the rent paid, the counter foilds of the receipts would be a good evidence. If rents are collected by agents, their accounts must be examined.

Particular attention should be paid towards 'rent-outstanding'. It is possible that rent might have been received but misappropriated while it may be shown as 'outstanding'. In such a case, if the 'outstanding' is a heavy one, with the permission of the client, the auditor should write to the tenants requesting them to confirm the amount of the arrear of rent outstanding against their names. Provision should be made for the doubtful outstanding rents. Similar consideration must be paid towards properties shown as "unlet". The auditor should get a list of such "unlet" property duly signed by a responsible official.

7. Bills Receivable

Bills Receivable Book should be compared with Cash Book and the Pass Book to see that the amount has been received on the due date. Inquiries should be made regarding the bills which have matured but the amount has not been received for them. Such bills might have been dishonoured or retired. It is also possible that such bills might have been paid and the proceeds might have been misappropriated by the cashier. To discover this type of fraud, the auditor should examine the bills. If they had been paid, they would not be available. Contingent liability should be shown on the balance sheet in respect of bills receivable discounted but which have not matured at the date of the balance sheet.

8. Commission

Commission account should be checked with the accounts of the parties from whom commission has been received. Agreement with the parties regarding the rate of commission should be inspected. Counterfoils of the receipts should be checked with the amount in the cash book. To see the accuracy of the amount, calculations should be made.

9. Sale of Investments

The amount received on account of the sale of investments should be vouched with the Broker's Sold Note. If they have been sold through the bank, examine the bank advice. If they have been sold 'cum-dividend' he should see that dividend is subsequently received and that the sale proceeds is properly apportioned between capital and revenue. If investments have been sold 'ex-dividend', the auditor should see that the dividend has been received subsequently. If any investment has been sold, in respect of any earmarked fund, any profit made or loss suffered should be credited or debited to that particular fund.

10. Bad Debt Dividends

The amount received from debtors, who have become bankrupt, should be vouched with the dividend warrants received from the Official Receiver or Assignee indicating the total debt and the rate per rupee payable as dividend or any correspondence which might have passed between the debtor or the Official Receiver and the client in regard to the amount paid, the number of instalment and the balance due.

11. Subscriptions

Subscriptions received by a club or school, etc., should be checked with the Register of Subscribers and the counterfoils of the receipts.

12. Insurance Claim Money

Insurance money received against a claim from an insurance company should be checked with correspondence passing between the client and insurance company, the account rendered by the insurance broker or company.

13. Share Capital

For this item reference may be made to the Chapter on 'Audit of Limited Companies', where this item has been dealt with in greater detail. In the case of firms, the Partnership Deed should be examined to find out the amount of capital contributed by each partner.

14. Sales of Fixed Assets

This item may be vouched with correspondence, auctioneer's account, sale contract, minute book of the Board of Directors or any other evidence available. He should see that the proper asset account has been credited with the amount. If there is any profit, that should be credited to the Capital Reserve Account which is not available for distribution to the shareholders. If any expenses have been pre-paid in respect of that asset, e.g., pre-paid insurance and the benefit of such an expense will be derived by the purchaser, a part of the proceeds should be credited to the Insurance Account.

The auditor should also see that the sale of such a property has been properly sanctioned.

15. Income from Hire-purchase Agreement

Where money is received on account of the instalment relating to goods sold on hire-purchase system, the auditor should examine the agreement. It should be remembered that the instalment includes interest also. The auditor should see that the whole of the amount is not credited to sales account. Proper allocation between sales and interest should be made.

16. Miscellaneous Receipts

Correspondence, contracts or any other document will help auditor to vouch such transactions.

Credit side or the Payment side of the Cash Book

When the auditor has finished the vouching of the debit side of the cash book and having satisfied himself that there is a good internal check system, he should now proceed to vouch the cash payments which means that he should satisfy himself that the payments have been actually made —

(*a*) to the right persons or parties;

(*b*) for the business itself;

(*c*) have been sanctioned by a person holding some authority; and

(*d*) have been properly recorded in the books of account.

The detection of misappropriation of money depends largely upon an intelligent and careful vouching of this side of the cash book.

Some of the important items which usually appear on the credit side of the cash book and the duties of an auditor thereto are given below:

1. Payments to Creditors

Money paid to creditors on open accounts can be vouched with the receipts issued by the creditors acknowledging the receipt of money. Money due to them can be compared with the accounts of the creditors and the actual invoices received from the suppliers of the goods. The auditor should enquire whether periodical statements are submitted by the creditors and are compared with the creditors' accounts. He may have to refer to minutes, contracts, and other evidences before he passes an entry.

In regard to cash purchases, cash memos and Goods Inward Book should be compared with the entries in the cash book. Special attention should be paid to trade discounts which should be deducted from the purchases and only net amount should be carried to the books of account.

If any voucher is missing, he should insist upon getting a duplicate copy of it. He should vouch such an item with any other possible documentary evidence.

2. Wages

Another important entry, which is usually a big one, is that of wages. There are many chances of misappropriation of cash under this head. Before the auditor proceeds with his work, he should make a thorough investigation regarding the internal check system which is in operation. He should satisfy himself that the arrangement for the preparation of wages sheets and the system of payment is adequate so as not to leave any loophole for fraud. If he finds that there is any loophole, he must disown his liability. The chances of fraud or errors are:

(*a*) the inclusion of fictitious names of 'dummy workers' in the wages book;

(*b*) errors or fraud in time and piece-work records;

(*c*) possibility of clerical errors;

(*d*) the names of the employees who have resigned or whose services have been dispensed with, may have been included in the wages sheets;

(*e*) over-stating of rates of wages;

(*f*) over-stating the hours of work or days of work put in by the workers;

(*g*) conversion of unpaid wages;

(*h*) over-footing of pay roll sheets;

(*i*) understatement of deductions.

All the above may mean withdrawal of more money than is actually needed for payment to the workers.

The following internal check for the payment of wages is, however, suggested to avoid fraud. The system will be of great help to the auditor. Of course, the best system applicable will vary in each particular case.

(*a*) Time Records

If the wages are to be paid according to the time spent by the workers, correct record of the time spent by them in the factory should be recorded. For this purpose, Time Recording Clocks should be installed at the gate. Each worker is given a card. When he enters the gate, he inserts his card in the slot of the Time Recording Clock. The date and the time of the entry is recorded on the card. Similarly when he leaves the factory, he gets the data and time recorded. This will be a good evidence of the time spent by the worker in the factory.

In case there is no Time Recording Clock, the gate-keeper should record the time of each worker in the Gate Register. So that the workers may not waste their time, the time of their arrival and departure should also be recorded in each department by means of another Time Recording Clock or by the foreman of the department. These two records, viz., one maintained by the gate-keeper and the other by the foreman of the department, should be compared. A responsible officer should sometimes pay a surprise visit and check the Gate-Keeper's Register and the Foreman's record with the number of workers actually, working in a department.

(*b*) Piece-work Records

Where the wages are to be paid according to piece-wage system, each worker should be given a card which should record the amount of work done by the worker. This card should be signed by the worker, foreman of the department and the store-keeper to whom the goods are delivered when they are ready to be recorded in the Production Register. If any fine is to be imposed on account of faulty goods, it must be recorded.

(*c*) Preparation of Wages Sheets

Information regarding the time record and piece-work record available now should be entered in the wages sheet or wages book (separate wages sheets should be prepared for time workers) which should have the following columns:

(*i*) Worker's number, name, occupation and rate of wages per day or month or per unit of goods manufactured.

(*ii*) Time: ordinary and overtime.

(*iii*) Gross amount payable.

(*iv*) Deductions on account of fines, contributions towards provident fund, employees state insurance, etc.

(*v*) Any advance of wages.

(*vi*) Net wages payable.

(*vii*) Signature or thumb impression of the worker.

Whole of the above information should be collected by different clerks from the gate-keeper's record, foreman's record, etc., and if there is any discrepancy, it should be inquired into. All the clerks who have to do something in the preparation of the wages sheets, should initial the sheets so that the responsibility may rest upon them individually if any error is discovered later on. All the wages sheets should be countersigned by the Works Manager, a Partner or a Director.

(*d*) Payment of Wages

The Wages Sheets should now be handed over to the cashier who should have nothing to do with their preparation. The cashier should then withdraw the exact amount which is shown under the column 'Net wages payable', plus the amount payable to the Employees State Insurance Department, etc. This amount should be deposited in a separate bank account from which it may be drawn whenever the wages have to be paid. The foreman of each department should be present at the time of payment to prevent impersonation for any absent worker. Wages of the absentees should be paid to a worker only when he has brought a letter of authority, but due frecaution should be taken in such a case. In no case should they be paid to foreman or a fellow, worker. The wages of the absenters should be paid during the following few days after getting satisfactory explanation from the persons entitled thereto. The Works Manager or some responsible officer should be present at the time of payments. All the officers, namely, the cashier, the foreman and the Works Manager, should sign the wages sheet as certificate of correct payment having been made. If it is not possible to get the signature of each payee, the foreman of the department should certify that the workman has put his thumb impression. Wages should not be paid by the petty cash keeper as in that case payment might be made twiceÅonce by the petty cash keeper and again by the cashier in the regular course of business. If the above system is followed the evidence of the foreman, the cashier, and the Works Manager will be sufficient proof of the payment having been made to the workmen who are entitled to get the payment.

The employment of casual labour and the payment of wages on the spot presents problems. Names of dummy workers might have been included and thc payment to such workers might. To misappropriated. To avoid any such fraud; the officer authorised to employ such casual labour should not be connected with the payment of wages to such workers. The pay clerk should pay wages and the foreman or the officer who employed such labour should certify that the worker had been employed and that he was employed on proper authority.

A list of the "Unpaid Wages" should be prepared and signed by the cashier, foreman of the department concerned and the Works Manager.

Auditor's Duty as regards Wages

1. He should see whether the Internal Check System as detailed above is satisfactory and that there is no loophole for any fraud. If he finds any loophole he should probe into it and disown his responsibility.
2. He should check the casts of the wages sheets or wages book.
3. He should check a few items of the wages sheets here and there to see that the calculations are correct. If he does not do so, he would be held responsible if later on it is found that the wages sheets were incorrectly prepared and overpayment had been made.
4. He should check the total amount of wage payable with the amount of cheques drawn to see that more money has not been withdrawn than was needed. In case of unpaid wages, the amount should be deposited in the bank.
5. He should check the names of some of the workers as mentioned in the wages sheets with the job cards and the gate-keeper's and the foreman's register to see that no "dummy" workers are included. Sometimes the fictitious names, i.e., the names of the ex-employees are entered in the wages sheets. This method is known as "Padding".
6. He should also see that the wages sheets are properly initialled or signed by all the persons responsible for the preparation of the wages sheets.

7. He may pay a surprise visit on the day of payment of wages to see that they are paid according to the method suggested above, though it is not his duty in the ordinary course of business. He should see that wages are paid to the workers by showing the Identity Card.
8. He should compare the sanctioned strength of the workers with the wages sheets. If the number of the workers is more than the sanctioned strength, the authenticity of which should be verified by reference to the files of the Personnel Department.
9. The number of workers as recorded in the wages sheets should be compared with the Employees State Insurance Cards, deduction for Provided Fund, etc., because the names of the ghost workers will not appear on the register for they do not contribute anything.
10. Wages sheets of the previous months should be compared with the current month and if there is any increase of the number of workers, enquiry must be made.
11. The total wages of each department should be compared with the original estimate made by the Costing Department.
12. He should see that the receipt is duly signed or bears the thumb impression of the workers and that it is duly stamped if the amount exceed twenty rupees.
13. Leave register should be examined to find out whether leave was granted with or without salary.
14. Compare the signatures of the workers of two or three periods to examine their genuineness.
15. He should see that the name of the same person does not appear often in the list of the unpaid wages or that the wages payable have not been adjusted against an "advance payment" again and again.
16. Examine the system of employment of casual labour. If there is any loophole, go into details.
17. Test check the signatures and thumb impressions of some of the workers with the previous months.

In short the duty of an auditor in verifying the item of wages is to see that the wages as recorded in the cash book have actually been paid and that they were actually due and that they were properly authorised.

3. Capital Expenditure

Capital expenditure means money spent on acquiring fixed assets. The duty of an auditor in this connection is to see that the payment is in order, that it is duly authorised and that the money spent has been properly capitalised. Such expenditure requires special attention. The question as to which documentary evidence is required will depend upon the circumstances of each particular case. We shall take up some of the fixed assets and deal with the duties of the auditor in vouching such expenditure in each case.

(*a*) Freehold and Leasehold Property and Buildings

The agreement for the purchase of property, or the Lease Deed, Conveyance and Title Deeds, showing the money paid, should be examined. If the property has been purchased through a broker, his statement or account should be examined. He should see that the Board of Directors have sanctioned the purchase (Section 292). If is has been purchased at an auction, auctioneer's note or account will be a good evidence. The auditor should see that the property has been registered in the name of his client under Section 17(1) of the Transferer of Property Act. He should also see that the title of the transfer has been duly verified by a solicitor. In case a building has been constructed, Architect's certificate, Builder's contract and his receipt should be examined. He should examine the minute book of the Board of Directors sanctioning the purchase.

Expenses incurred in acquiring the fixed asset, e.g., auctioneer's commission, brokerage, registration fee, architect's fees or solicitor's charges, which can be vouched by their respective accounts, should be capitalised.

In some cases the staff of the client and his materials are used in construction of the building. In such a case, proper allocation of materials and wages to the building account is necessary."

(b) Plant and Machinery

Same considerations apply as in the case of Land and Building. Invoice of the supplier of the machinery should be examined to see the price paid for it. In case some expenses have been incurred in erecting and fixing up the plant he should see that such expenses are capitalised.

(c) Patents

In case a patent has been purchased, the auditor should examine the patent and the receipt acknowledging the purchase consideration. Any expense incurred in acquiring it should be capitalised. In case the patent has been secured by making experiments and research, the expenses incurred on experiments and research should be capitalised. If the patent has been acquired through an agent, the auditor should see that his commission is capitalised. It should be remembered that the renewal fee is not capitalised but treated as revenue expenditure.

(d) Investments

Payments for the purchase of shares, securities, etc., should be vouched with the Broker's Bought Note. If possible, he should actually examine the investments. If they have been purchase-cum-dividend, the auditor should see that the dividend accrued is received subsequently and that the expenditure is properly allocated between capital and revenue.

In case of a new issue, letter of allotment and the Banker's receipt for the instalment paid should be examined. Bank Pass Book should also be examined in case payment has been made through the bank. He should see that the investments have been purchased by a resolution of the Board of Directors (Section 292). He should also see that the investments are registered in the name of the company (Section 49).

In case of inscribed stocks, a certificate from the bank in whose books the stock is inscribed, should be examined.

(e) Payments under Hire-purchase and Instalment Agreements

The auditor should examine the agreement regarding the Hire-Purchase or instalment. For every instalment paid, he should examine the vouchers. Those instalments which have been paid include interest also, and, therefore, the should see that such interest is not capitalised but is transferred to revenue account.

4. Loans

He should examine the receipt given by the borrower and the loan agreement, Pro-Note or Bill of Exchange. He should read carefully terms of loan regarding the rate of interest, the dates on which interest has to be paid and the date of repayment of the loan. He should make inquiry whether his client is authorised to advance loans. If the loan has been advanced against certain securities, he should examine those securities. If that loan has been advanced against mortgage, he should examine the Mortgage Deed and the Title Deeds, etc.

In case of loan to the Directors, Managing Agents and officers of a company, he must see that the provisions of the Companies Act are complied with for details, the reader should refer to the chapter on 'Audit of Limited Companies'.

5. Salaries

Salaries book should be examined. He should see that the total for the salaries book for a particular month agrees with the cheque drawn for salaries or the item in the cash book under the cash column.

There may be some variation in the salary of an employee during the course of the year, possibly because of the increment which falls due in a particular month or some special increment or allowance might have been given to him. The auditor should see whether the increment was actually due or it is a fictitious entry. To ascertain this he should examine the agreement or a copy of the letter of appointment or the minute book of the Board of Directors, etc. He should see that necessary deductions for Provident Fund, Income Tax, etc., have been made. If any loan or advance has been made to an employee, the amount should be deducted from his salary.

Salaries may be verified with the Annual Returns submitted to the Income Tax Department regarding the payment of salaries.

6. Agents' and Travellers' Commission

The agreement with travellers and the agents should be examined to ascertain the terms of the appointment regarding the rate of commission. Calculation should be made and the receipt given by the traveller or the agent should be examined and compared with the cash book.

The auditor should test the payment of commission by examining the orders received through the travellers.

7. Travelling Allowance

He should see the rules and regulations regarding the payment of travelling allowance. Calculations should be made. If there are no such rules, he should recommend to the management to frame such rules. He should examine the vouchers which should be countergned by a responsible official. An extraordinary travelling expenses should be authorised by the Board of Directors. The directors are not allowed any travelling expense to attend the meeting of the Board of Directors unless the Articles of Association permit it. He should examine the Directors' Attendance Register or the Minute Book whether the director attended the meeting. He should see that such expenses were incurred by the directors in the interest of the company.

Where fixed travelling expenses are allowed, no calculation is necessary. He should see that the travelling bills have been duly checked by a responsible official."

8. Insurance of Premiums

In case of a new policy, the cover note or the receipt from the insurance company and the policy itself should be examined. In case of a renewal, the renewal receipt for the premium should be examined. A schedule of insurance policies, if their number is large, should be called for and examined. Such a schedule should give details of the polices, e.g., the number of the policy, the amount, the date of maturity, the amount of the premium payable, etc. If he finds that a policy has lapsed, he should enquire under whose authority it has been allowed to lapse.

9. Bills Payable

Returned bills duly cancelled should be examined. It would be a sufficient evidence of the amount having been paid. Reference may be made to the Bank Pass and Bills Payable Books.

10. Bills Receivable Discounted and Dishonoured

Bills Receivable which has been discounted with the bank and which have been dishonoured can be vouched with the entry in the Bank Pass Book. The auditor should see that the account of the acceptor or the previous endorser is debited with the amount of the bill, noting charges and other expenses, if any.

If the bill had been sent to the bank for collection and had not been discounted, the bank would credit the client's account in the first instance. When the bill is presented for payment and is disbonoured, the bank will debit the account of the client. These entries can be vouched with the Bank Pass Book, Bills Payable Book, Cash Book and correspondence. The dishonoured bill should be examined.

11. Freight, Carriage and Custom Duties

The statements of account regarding the payment of freight and carriage, submitted by the shippers, clearing or forwarding agents, together with the receipts issued by them, should be examined to see that the payment has been duly made and accounted for. He should see that allowances in respect of rebates have been brought into account.

12. Bank Charges

Bank charges such as commission, interest on overdraft and loan, etc., should be examined with the Pass Bank. He should check the calculation of interest.

13. Partner's Drawings

Partnership Deed should be examined as to what is the maximum amount and the time for which a partner can draw money and whether he is to be charged any interest on drawings. He should vouch this entry with the Parnter's Drawing Book or Account and see that the signature of the partner is there against such entry.

14. Postage

The postage book should be compared with the Cash Book or the Petty Cash Book and the balance of stamps in hand should be counted. Where a franking machine is in use the receipts issued by the post office for the payments made should be examined.

15. Petty Cash

There are greater chances of misappropriation of cash as there are no vouchers for a number of petty payments. He should, therefore, make an enquiry into the internal check system of petty cash payments. The petty cash book should be maintained on the imprest system. To ensure a fairly frequent inspection of the petty cash book by the cashier, the fixed round sum or 'float' should be as low as possible. The cashier should check the petty cash at frequent intervals. He should stamp the vouchers at the time of checking and replenishing of the funds to prevent their presentation later on in support of a fictitious entry in the petty cash book. The amount of petty cash in the hands of the petty cashier should be according to the requirement of the business. The auditor should check the receipt of money by the petty cash keeper with the cash book and also compare the dates. In certain cases, a certain sum is advanced to the petty cash keeper who is not subjected to any check by the cashier. The profit and loss account is debited at the end of the month or the year with the total amount spent by the petty cash keeper. It is very seldom that the auditor or cashier checks the petty cash book. The procedure is very defective and the auditor should disown his responsibility. He should recommend the adoption of the columnar petty cash book which should be maintained on the imprest system as explained above. No employee of the concern should be allowed to borrow money from the petty cash keeper except under very special circumstances. Postage may be compared with the Postage Book. He should insist upon having vouchers for every expenditure, say, above Rs, 2 or so. Those vouchers should be properly arranged and consecutively numbered. In certain cases, it may not be possible to have vouchers, say for bus fare, charity, entertainment (cigarettes, tea, etc.) in which case the docket system should be introduced. According to this system a slip showing the amount of expenditure should be signed by the officer who has spent that amount. This docket or slip should be countersigned by a responsible officer. The amount in the docket should be both in words as well as in figures to prevent any alteration in figures after the docket has been signed. It should be seen whether figures and words have been over-written or erased. If a docket cannot be prepared, a list of all such expenses for which a docket or voucher could not be had, may be prepared in the evening and signed by a responsible person. The purpose for which money was spent should also be stated. The auditor should check a few items at random. He should also cast the individual columns to see whether the additions are correct and the total of each column is carried to the appropriate account in the ledger.

Postage can also be dealt with like the petty cash. A definite amount of stamps should be handed over to the despatcher who will keep the records of the letters, etc., sent out. Whenever he wants more stamps, he will have to get his postage book checked. Thus, there will be little chance of embezzlement. Even if cash is advanced to him by the petty cashier, it should be done on the imprest system. The petty cashier should advance money to the despatcher only after having checked the Postage Book.

The auditor should count the petty cash balance on the balance sheet date. If he is not in a position to be present on that day he should instruct the client to deposit the balance in the bank or return it to the cashier. If that has also not been done, he should check the expenditure from the date of the balance sheet to the date of checking and should count the petty cash balance in hand on that date. The counting of petty cash balance in hand is very important. If he does not do so and if there is any discrepancy in the balance as per the petty cash book, and actual cash in hand, will be held responsible to pay damages as was held in the case of London Oil Storage Company Ltd. vs. Sear Hasluck & Co., in which case it was held that in not vouching the existence of petty cash in hand, the auditor had committed a breach of duty. The balance as shown by the books in this case amounted to £ 796, while actual cash in hand amounted to £ 30 only.

At the time of counting the petty cash balance the auditor should see that it does not include any I.O.U's. If there are such acknowledgments, he should get confirmation, especially in the case of I.O.U's by high officials of the concern because there have been cases where a dishonest petty cash clerk having embezzled the money, covered it up by forged I.O.U's presuming that the auditor would not care to get these I.O.U's verified from the high officials. Petty cash keeper should not be allowed to lend money out of petty cash to any employee of the company.

16. Directors' Fee

As a general rule the directors of a company cannot claim any remuneration unless the articles expressly provide for it. In any case they are not entitled to get any monthly salary."

He should examine the Articles of Association to find out the fee payable to the directors. He should also examine the minute book or the attendance register of the Board of Directors or the resolution passed at a general meeting sanctioning such a payment to ascertain the number of meeting attended by them, and to calculate the fee payable to the directors. He should examine the vouchers too.

Where the commission payable is to be calculated as a percentage on profits, he should examine the agreement and find out the basis of the calculation of the profits which should be according to Section 349, 350 and 351 of the Companies Act.

It must be remembered that according to Section 211 (2) of the Companies Act, it is incumbent that the remuneration paid to the directors either by way of fees or commission, etc., must be shown separately in the Profit and Loss Account. If this has not been done, the auditor must make a mention of this fact in his report, The total amount paid to all the directors must be shown and not the amount paid to individual directors. According to Section 200 (1) of the Companies Act tax-free payments are prohibited.

If a director has foregone his fee, the auditor should refer to the minute book of the directors. This is necessary to avoid any misappropriation.

17. Miscellaneous expenses, such as rent, rates, taxes, advertising, lighting, etc.

He should examine the vouchers as usual and see that the expenditure is properly appropriated between the periods where necessary.

18. Bank Account

During the course of the year, cash or cheques are sent to the bank for deposit or collection and money is withdrawn from it frequently. Therefore such receipts and payments are to be vouched."

These transactions in the Cash Book should be compared with the Pass Book. Payments into the bank should be vouched with the counterfoils of the paying-in-book. Sometimes customers pay directly to the client's banking account. Such a transaction may be vouched from bank's advice notes of amounts having been credited to the client's account. Intimation from the client having deposited the money may be another proof in support of this entry. Payments out of the bank can be vouched with the counterfoils of the cheques issued. In case the client has ordered the bank to transfer a certain amount to a creditor or to a society or association as subscription, counterfoils of the cheques may not be available. In such a case the receipt from the payee and a copy of the advice to the banker for such a transfer will be sufficient proof of the payment. For some items such as Bank Charges, Interest, Incidental Expenses, etc., there will be no proof except the Bank Pass Book or a letter from the Bank to this effect. Particular attention should be paid to dates. Sometimes it so happens that the cashier records the transactions on the payment side as if the money has been sent to the bank but actually it is not sent and the cashier utilises the money for some time and deposits it later on. Though no misappropriation of money in such a case has taken place yet this course is undesirable. In some cases, there might be difference between the dates in the cash book and the pass book which might be due to the fact that cheques sent to the bank might not have been collected and hence the account might not have been credited on the same date."

It may be very difficult to check all the items where cheques drawn are numerous. In such a case, the auditor will do well to apply 'test cheek', i.e., few transactions may be checked at random.

With regard to the balance at the bank, the bank reconciliation statement should be prepared by the client to verify the balance. A copy of such a Reconciliation Statement should be retained by the auditor as his working paper for future reference. A question often arises as to whether the balance, as shown by the cash book, or the balance as shown by the pass book, should be carried to the balance sheet. Supporters of the first view hold that as the auditor has to give a certificate that 'the Balance Sheet exhibits a true and fair views of the state of the company affairs' and 'as shown by the books of the company' naturally balance as per cash book should be shown. While on the other hand some people hold that whatever the actual balance is and which is shown by the bank books should be shown, as that is the actual balance in the hands of the company's bankers on the balance sheet date. Both the views have some force in them.

In any case it would be better if a certificate from the bank about the balance should be obtained directly, but this step may be taken with the permission of the client. There have been cases when fictitious pass books have been produced.

If the client has a banking account in a foreign country, the balance should be converted at the rate of exchange prevailing on the date of the balance sheet. A certificate confirming the balance should be obtained from the bank abroad.

Some banks supply the modern form of loos-leaf Pass Book. The auditor should handle such a pass book carefully as there is a danger of the client misplacing the sheets or fraudulently substituting one. To avoid such a danger, the auditor should get directly from the bank a confirmation of the balance. Such a pass book has the advantage of being up-to-date and the auditor will have to wait until it is written up.

QUESTIONS

1. What is the object of vouching the Cash Book? Discuss in brief the method of vouching the items of cash receipts under different heads. (*Rajasthan B. Com. 1962*)

2. (*a*) As auditor of a pubic company how would you verify the following payments.

(*i*) Compensation paid to director for loss of office.

(*ii*) Contribution of Rs. 50,000 to the Staff Pension Fund.

(*ii*) Secret payments aggregating Rs. 1,00,000 certified by the directors personally.

(*iii*) Commission paid to sole selling agents Rs. 15,000. A partner of the firm (selling agents) was also a partner of managing agents till :31st March, 1966.

(*Gauhati M. Com. 1969*)

3. State the evidence you would require to vouch the following:-

(a) Dividends received on investments;

(b) Commission paid or payable to Sole Selling Agents.

Your client is a company and no investments were purchased or sold during the year.

(*C.A. Int. 1966*)

4. The cashier of a company of which you are the auditor has control of all the financial books. Besides, he is authorised to open all letters and acknowledge receipt of letters and cheques. Enumerate the possible frauds likely to be committed by a delinquent cashier in respect of both receipts and payments and the checks you would exercise to detect such malpractices.

(*C.A. Inter. Final 1957*)

5. Indicate how would you vouch any two of the following in the ease of a limited company:"

(*a*) Foreign travel expenses of the Managing Director.

(*b*) Loss on account of defalcation.

(*c*) Dividend income of an investment company. (*C.A. Final, 1971*)

6. Give examples of vouchers you would refuse to accept, although properly stamped and signed. Explain clearly the reasons for your refusal.

7. You are auditing the accounts of a firm and you discover that it is the practice of the travellers of this firm to collect Debtors Accounts, deduct their commission and remit the balance to the head office. What precautions would you take to ensure that all collections were accounted for?

8. How would you vouch the following items and to what special points would you direct your attention while doing so?

(*a*) Cash Sales;

(*b*) Payment against purchase of investments;

(*c*) 'Directors' Fees; and

(*d*) Receipt against realisation of an insurance claim. (*Cal. B. Com. 1963*)

9. In the audit of the accounts of a company having a considerable volume of transactions with its bankers, it is sometimes considered unnecessary to check all entries in the Cash Book with Bank Pass Book, and therefore, you are asked to decide a form of "test check" which would, in your opinion, result in saving of time without, loss of efficiency.

Would you agree to the proposal? Give reasons.

10. During the cash verification of Messrs. Jayantilal & Co. Pvt. Ltd., on 30th September, 1971 (the date of closing of their annual accounts) you, as the auditor, find the following:—

(*i*) Rs. 2,300 have been advanced to various members of the staff against slips sent by them. These payments are, however, not recorded in the cash book and as such this amount is part of the cash balance.

(*ii*) Sum of Rs. 10, 570 has been shown as having been paid as salaries. These amounts are, however, found to be lying with the cashier in sealed envelopes bearing the names of the employees concerned.

(*iii*) Cash includes cheques amounting to Rs. 975 not deposited in bank and postage stamps of Rs. 235.

What action will you take in respect of each of the above matters? (*C.A. Inter.1971*)

11. What is vouching? How would you vouch the cash book ? (*Agra B. Com. 1964*)

12. State briefly the important features in a system of internal control relating to amounts received in respect of sales ledger accounts. (*C.A. Inter, England, 1963*)

13. How would you verify the correctness of the wages paid in a Cotton Textile Mill? Explain the extent of the internal check which you would expect to come across in the case of a well-managed mill. (*Bombay B. Com. 1960*)

14. Describe the salient features in the vouching of wages in an industrial concern. (*Madurai and Delhi B. Com.*)

15. "In vouching payments, the auditor does not merely seek proof that money has been paid away." Discuss fully this statement. (*Cal. B. Com. Hons. 1967*)

Substantial Procedures-Vouching of Trading Transactions

Having examined the cash book, the auditor may now. proceed to check the trading transactions. Let him begin with the purchases. One of the objects of auditing is to check and prevent misappropriation of goods. The auditor should see that the client pays for only those goods which have actually been ordered and received. Before the auditor begins his work, he should examine the internal check system regarding the purchases on credit, returns outward, etc.

Internal Check as regards Purchases

The system of internal check will depend upon the size of the business and the staff available. If he finds a bad or inefficient system the auditor should exercise great care and check exhaustively the purchases book and the ledger. Whenever goods are required in a particular department, the head of such a department should send the 'Purchase Requisition' which should show the quantity, quality, if possible the price or the maximum price at which they may be purchased, the time by which the goods must be supplied, etc., to the Purchasing Department which should invite tenders or quotations from suppliers. The auditor should inquire about the procedure for opening and acceptance of the tenders. The lowest tender should be accepted. A responsible officer in addition to the storekeeper should be present when the goods are received and unpacked to see the accuracy of the quality and quantity of the goods.

1. All the orders sent out should be recorded in the Purchases Order Book which should have two carbon copies-one to be sent to the supplier of the goods and the other to be retained for reference purposes.
2. When the goods are received, the gatekeeper or the storekeeper should make a record in the Goods Inward Book after having checked the quantity, weight, etc.
3. The invoice should then be checked with the Goods Inward Book maintained by the storekeeper and the delivery note, if any, to see that the goods received are correctly recorded in the Stock Register, according to the invoice.
4. Another clerk should check the invoice regarding calculations, etc.
5. After this, the invoice should be sent to the head of the department who placed the order for the goods to see that the prices and qualities, etc., are correct.
6. The departmental head will then pass over the invoice to the clerk who will record the same in the Purchases Book.
7. Every person who has to deal with the invoice and the goods should initial the invoice.

Duty of an Auditor in connection with Credit Purchases

After having satisfied himself that there is a good internal check system regarding the purchases, the auditor should now proceed to vouch the Purchase Book. Entries in the Purchases Book or Invoice Book or Bought Book, as it is called by the different names, should be vouched with the Invoices relating to the purchases, and the Goods Inward Books maintained by the gatekeeper and the godownkeeper and the delivery notes, if any. He should see that the name of the creditor is the same as has been entered in the `Particular' Column of the Purchases Book. Only credit purchases are entered in this book.

While examining the invoices, the auditor should pay attention to the following points:-

1. Whether the invoice is in the name of his client, as sometimes invoices have been produced for goods which have never been purchased for the *Business* or goods might have been purchased by an official of the company for his personal use while the payment is made through the company.
2. Who is authorised to place orders for goods? Only a responsible officer should be allowed to do so.
3. The date of the invoice should relate to the period under review. This is done to prevent the production of old invoices for which the payments had already been made.
4. Whether the clerk, who has checked the invoice with the Order Book to see that only those goods have been sent for which the order was placed and that the rates and quantities are correct, has signed the invoice. He should also see that only those goods which are dealt with by the client have been purchased.
5. The auditor should also see that the goods mentioned in the invoice are not capital goods. If they are capital goods, they should not be carried to the Purchase Book but should be carried to the fixed asset account,
6. He should, as a 'test check', compare some invoice with the Goods Inward Book or the Gatekeeper's Inward Book in order to see that the goods have been actually received. This would prevent the inclusion of fictitious invoices or the duplicates as "original" ones.
7. The auditor should check the casts and crosscasts of the Purchases book.
8. He should see whether trade discount has been deducted from the invoice before making the entry in the Purchases Book. Expenses as freight, custom duty, octroi duty, etc., which have been incurred in connection with the purchase, should be debited to the Purchases Account.
9. He should compare the Goods Inward Book and the Stock Sheets with the Purchases Book to ensure that all goods taken into stock have been entered in the Purchases Book. In order to inflate profits, the management sometimes includes the goods in the closing stock while no entry is made in the Purchases Book. In this connection he should pay particular attention to the purchases made at the close of the year to see that they are included both in the Purchases Book as well as in the Stock Book, otherwise he will be held responsible to pay damages as was decided in the case of *Smith vs. Offers and Others*. In case the goods have not been received but the invoice only has been received, no entry should be passed through any book. Similarly if the goods have been received but the invoice has not been received, goods should not be included in the Stock Book. In short, if an entry is made, it should be made both in the Purchases Book as well as in the Stock Book.
10. The auditor should stamp the invoice or cancel it after he has compared it with the entries in the Purchases Book to prevent its being produced again.
11. Sometimes the officials of the company purchase goods through the company in order to take advantage of the trade discount. In such a case, the account of the official should be debited and goods account credited. If this is not done, it would mean the company pays for the goods purchased by the officials.

12. While examining the invoices, if the auditor comes across invoices marked `copy' or `duplicate', he should satisfy himself that they were obtained in respect of only those invoices which have been actually lost or mislaid and that they have not already been entered anywhere else in the Purchases Book.
13. In order to be sure that all the invoices are included, the auditor should ask his client to write to all the creditors to send their Statements of Account direct to the auditor who will compare them with ledger accounts.
14. If an invoice runs into several pages, the auditor should see that the grand total is correct.

Purchases Returns

When the goods are returned to the seller, being not according to the sample or of inferior quality, a credit note should be obtained if the price has already been paid. If the price has not been paid, a note should be sent to the cash department to send less amount to the seller.

The he auditor should compare the credit note with the purchases Returns Journal or Returns Outward Book and the GateKeeper's Outward Book or the stores records. Particular attention should be paid to the entries in the Purchases Returns Journal for the first portion of the following period as in order to manipulate accounts, fictitious purchases might have been entered and the same written off in the following year as if the goods were returned to the suppliers.

He should pay particular attention to heavy returns at the beginning or the close of the year as such entries might have been passed to adjust a fictitious purchase in the past.

Credit Sales

The auditor should now proceed to vouch the Day Book or the Sales Book which records only credit sales. The auditor has to be more careful in the case of vouching sales, as documentary evidence is not as conclusive as in case of purchases. He should enquire into the internal check system regarding the sales which may be outlined as below:

Internal Check regarding Credit Sales

1. Whenever an order is received, it should be recorded in the Order Received Book, giving details regarding the date on which the order was received, the name of the customer, the particulars about the goods, date of delivery, mode of transport, etc.
2. The order or a copy of it is sent to the Despatch Department.
3. When the Despatch Department has packed the goods, another clerk should compare the goods so despatched with the order to see that the whole of the order is complied with or another list is prepared showing the goods in the package which list is sent to the Counting House.
4. A responsible official will now mark the rate at which the goods are to be charged.
5. A clerk will now make the extensions.
6. The invoice will then be prepared in duplicate or triplicate by means of carbon papers.
7. One copy of the invoice will be sent to the invoice clerk who enters it in the Sales Book and later on this is sent to the customer, another copy will be sent to the gatekeeper who will record in the Goods Outward Book that such and such goods left the premises; the third copy will be retained for further reference.
8. If orders are received through the travellers, they should be given order books with triplicate copies-one copy to be handed over to the customer, the second to be sent to the Head Office for necessary compliance and the third one is to be retained by the traveller for his record.

The Duties of an Auditor in connection with Credit Sales

1. He should see that the internal check system is efficient. If it is not so, he should disown his responsibility. If it is efficient, he should apply a few 'test checks'.

2. He should compare the data of the copy of the invoice with the data in the Sales Book.
3. He should see that the sales arc not omitted from being entered in the Sales Book. If it is done, it is possible that when the customer sends cash or cheque in payment of the goods sold, such an amount may be misappropriated. The fraud will not be detected because no entry was made when the goods were sold and, therefore, if no entry is made when the payment is received, it will not affect the accounts at all whereas cash has been misappropriated. Fraud can be detected in such a case when comparison is made with original records, e.g., copies of invoices, Order Received Book, Goods Outward Book, Gatekeeper's Outward Book, Delivery Note duly signed by the purchaser, receipts issued by the transport company or the railways.
4. He should further see that the sale of an asset is not treated as ordinary sale, otherwise profit will be inflated. If an old asset has been sold, purchaser's account should be debited and particular asset account should be credited.
5. With the permission of the client, the auditor should send Statements of Account to the customers to confirm the accuracy of the balance. This method will prove the accuracy of the credit sales as well as the receipts from debtors and is very effective to check frauds.
6. He should check the Sales Book for the last days or weeks of the financial period and the Returns Inward Book for a few days or weeks after the close of the period in order to see whether fictitious sales or returns had been recorded to inflate profits.
7. He should check the casts and cross casts of the Sales Book.
8. The cancelled invoices should be checked with the duplicate copy of the invoice.
9. Sales tax, insurance charges, etc., which are recoverable from the customers should be debited to the customer's account and credited to the appropriate accounts.
10. Sales to allied or sister concerns should be carefully examined as they may be fictitious entries with a view to inflate profits.
11. If there is a significant difference of trade discount allowed to two different purchasers, he should inquire into the reason of such a distinction.

Sale Returns

When the goods are returned from customers, being defective or on account of any other reason, they should be entered by the gatekeeper in the register known as Gatekeeper's Returns Inward Book and the Stock Register. The goods returned should also be recorded in the Sales Returns Book and a credit note should be prepared to be sent to the customers. Such a credit note should be signed by a responsible official. There are lot of chances of fraud in connection with the sales returns, e.g., the goods might not have been returned but a credit note has been sent to the customer. The auditor should, therefore, pay particular attention to such transactions. The auditor should also pay attention to heavy returns inwards at the beginning or at the close of the year to detect any bogus sale.

Sometimes the customers attempt to return the goods if there is a fall in the prices after the purchase has been made. The auditor should pay attention to such a return of goods. If there is time-lag between the sale and return the auditor should see whether the returned goods were in good condition or they have become stale. Returns from allied or sister concerns should be carefully examined to see their genuineness.

The auditor should vouch these transactions with the Gatekeeper's Returns Inward Book and with the carbon copies of the credit notes sent, to customers or the debit note received from the customers. He should further see that such returns, just before the date of balancing the books, are recorded both in the stock as well as in the Sales Returns book. If they are taken into stock but are not entered in the Sales Returns Book, a fictitious profit will be shown.

Goods sold on Sale or Return System

Sometimes goods are sold to customers on approval, i.e., the goods are delivered to customer on condition that if he does not approve of the goods, he can return them within a particular period. Until the customer approves of the goods they cannot be treated as sales. It may so happen that on the date of the balance sheet, some of the goods might be with the customers who might not have sent their approval. In such a case, these goods cannot be treated as sales. If such goods are treated as sales and in the beginning of the following year, such goods are returned having not been approved, profits will be inflated. The auditor should, therefore, see that until the approval, such goods must be shown as `goods with customers' and deducted from sales of the current period and from the list of the debtors. He should ask his client to prepare a schedule of goods in the hands of the customers.

In case such transactions are numerous, the auditor should recommend the use of 'Goods on Sale or Return Journal' to avoid any confusion between such sales and credit sales. The auditor should vouch journal with any documentary evidence such as correspondence, invoice, etc, which may be available. The goods, which have not been approved of on the date of the balance sheet, should be marked at cost price or the market price whichever is lower and shown in the balance sheet as 'Goods with Customers'.

Goods sent on Consignment

When the goods are sent out to agents to be sold at the owner's risk, a separate book called 'Consignments Outward Journal' should be maintained if the number of such transactions is large. This book should be vouched with the copies of the proforma invoice, correspondence, account sales, and contracts with consignees. If the goods were sent on consignment at a higher price, proper adjustments should be made at the time of finding the profit or loss. The unsold goods with consignees should not be treated as sales but should be shown in the balance sheet as `goods on consignment' or included in the stock. Such unsold goods should be marked at cost price plus proportionate expenses incurred in connection with consignment outward. Provision should also be made for any probable loss which might occur.

Packages and Empties

When customers are supplied with packages, e.g., casks, jars, bags, crates, cans, etc., which the customers have to return, a good system of record should be adopted. It would be better if a separate column is provided in the sales journal for `Packages and Empties'. When the empties are purchased, the Empties Account should be debited with the cost and when they are sent to customers, the Empties Account should be credited and purchaser's account debited with the cost of empties. But sometimes customers resent this system. Therefore, a memoranda system should be adopted. The customer should be debited with the cost of such empties and credited when they are returned. The cost of empties should not be included in sales. They should be entered in the Sales Return Book under a separate column headed as 'Empties or Packages'. They snould also be recorded by the gatekeeper in the Empties Returns Inward Book. The auditor should check a few entries. The return of such packages should not be treated as "Sales Returns".

At the date of the balance sheet, the value of the empties in the hands of the customers should be deducted from the gross amount of the debtors, and such empties should be included in the 'Empties and Packages on hand' at cost price less depreciation.

When the empties are not charged to the customers but are charged only when the customers do not return them, the sales ledger should have packages column and the customer's account should be debited when packages are sent to them and credited when they are returned. If it is not practicable, separate quantity accounts showing issues and returns should be maintained. At the end of the year, the accounts will show the number of packages with the customers. If the packages and empties are with the customers for a long time, the debt may be considered as doubtful or bad.

They should be properly valued for the purpose of balance sheet. He should see that proper provision is made for depreciation in respect of Empties and Packages in hand and with the customers.

Journal

All those entries which cannot be passed through any other book of prime entry are passed through the journal. The use of the journal will depend upon the size of the business and consequently the number of entries, e.g., where very few entries relating to bills of exchange take place, there will be no necessity of having separate books for Bills Receivable and Bills Payable. Similarly where there are few transactions relating to returns inwards and outwards, there will be no necessity for maintaining Returns Inwards and Outwards Books. In such a case all such entries are passed through the journal. The following transactions ave usually passed through the journal:

1. Opening entries.
2. The acquisition of different assets or liabilities taken over from the vendors.
3. The issue and allotment of shares.
4. Forfeiture of shares.
5. Adjusting entries such as provision for bad and doubtful debts, outstanding, prepaid expenses, depreciation, interest on capital, rectification of errors.
5. Closing entries, i.e., transfer from the nominal accounts to the Profit and Loss Account.
6. Entries relating to consignments.
8. Entries relating to dishonour of bills, etc.

From the above, it will appear that these entries are of a variety of nature. They affect the profit and loss account. The auditor should insist upon narration being given after each entry. There are lot of chances for committing frauds through the journal, e.g., writing of a good debt as bad and misappropriating the cash received in respect of such a debt. Hence the auditor should pay particular attention to the transactions passed through the journal. While vouching the entries in the journal, the auditor should see that (*a*) the transaction has been properly authorised (*b*) the transaction is within the power of the company, and (*c*) the transaction is supported by documentary evidences.

The evidence to vouch each transaction will depend upon the nature, e.g., the opening entries will be vouched with the previous year's audited, balance sheet or the working papers of the previous years; the acquisition of assets and taking over the liabilities from the vendors can be vouched with the contract entered into with the vendor; the issue and allotment of shares can be vouched with the prospectus, directors' minute book, application and copies of allotment letters; forfeiture of shares can be vouched with the prospectus, Articles of Association, minute book of the Board of Directors, correspondence, etc. He should check the totals of journal entries consisting of more than one item.

The auditor should not pass any entry in the journal until he is quite satisfied with regard to its validity and correctness.

Bought Ledger

The auditor should now proceed to check the bought ledger, i.e., the ledger which contains the creditors' accounts. The opening balance of different accounts in the Bought Ledger should be checked with the previous year's audited balance sheet or the schedule of the creditors duly checked by the previous auditor. This ledger can be vouched with the help of the audited balance sheet of the previous year, Purchases Journal, Purchases Returns Book, Cash Book, Journal, Allowances Book, Bills Payable Book, etc. The castings of the accounts in the Bought Ledger should now be checked with the balances as shown in the schedule of creditors which has been supplied to him by his client. If the books are maintained on 'self-balancing system', the total of the balance shown in the `Creditors Ledger Adjustment Account' in the General Ledger should agree with the total of the schedule of creditors. It is possible that some of the goods purchased at the end of the year might not have been entered in the accounts of the creditors. He should see that it is done.

In spite of the above checking, frauds may remain undetected, e.g., cash might be shown to have been sent to the creditor but actually it might not have been sent and the cashier might have misappropriated the amount. To avoid such a contingency, it would be better to invite the statements of the creditors and compare the balances shown in the schedule of creditors and the statements sent by the creditors. But still some statements of accounts may not agree with the schedules as creditors might have sent the goods and debited the account of the client who in his turn might not have credited the account of the creditor as the goods might not have been received by the time the books were closed.

In such cases, the auditor should check the transactions before the balance sheet date and see that if goods have not been received, they should neither be entered in the Stock Book, nor in the Purchases Book.

Another course of disagreement of the statement may be due to the fact that certain accounts are in dispute. He should check such accounts with correspondence and make provision for such contingent liabilities in the balance sheet. If inadequate provision for bad and doubtful debts has been made, he should suggest to his client to increase it. If unsuccessful he should refer the matter in his report.

Some Bought Ledger balances may be debit balances, e.g., for goods returned or allowances for defective goods for which payment had already been made. If such balances are standing for a long time, he should see whether they are bad or doubtful debts. If they are so, he should see that provision is made for reserve.

The debit balance in the Bought Ledger may also be due to the cash having been paid in advance to the seller but the goods might not have been received either because they are still with the seller or they are in the course of transit. In both these cases, the auditor should ascertain whether the property in the goods has passed to the buyer or not. If it has, an entry 'Goods in transit' or 'Goods with the seller' should be made. Where the property in the goods has not passed to his client, the amount may remain as a debit balance. It is also possible that the 'advances' might be a loan to the other party. The auditor should see whether it is a custom to send advance for the purchase of goods.

If the auditor finds that the debit balance in the Bought Ledger is a *bona fide* balance, he should see that such a balance is shown on the Asset side of the Balance Sheet along with the other debtors. In no case should such a balance be deducted from sundry creditors. Where provision has been made for "Reserve for Discount on Creditors", the auditor should see that the provision is not excessive. Such a provision for "Reserve for Discount" should not be made unless a provision for "Reserve for Discount" on debtors has been made.

Sales Ledger

Having checked the bought ledger, the auditor should now proceed to check the sales ledger, i.e., the ledger which contains the accounts of the debtors.

The opening debit balances will be checked from the previous audited balance sheet or the schedule of debtors duly checked by the previous auditor. The accounts in this ledger will be checked from the previous audited balance sheet and subsidiary books, such as Sales Journal, Sales Returns Book, Cash Book, Journal, Allowances Book, Bills Receivable Book, etc. The castings of the accounts in the Sales Ledger should now be checked with the Balances as shown in the schedule of debtors which has been supplied to him by his client. Such a schedule must be certified by the manager, secretary, or any other responsible official. He should pay special attention to the credit entries in the Sales Ledger as there is a possibility of committing fraud by passing fictitious entries in respect of credit notes, cash discounts, allowances and bad debts.

It is possible that there may be some credit balances in the Sales Ledger which may be due to the omission of the record of invoices in respect of goods supplied. In such a case, necessary adjustments should be made. It must be remembered that such a credit balance must not be deducted from the amount of debtors but should be shown on the liabilities side of the balance sheet along with sundry creditors.

If credit balance is due to the fact that an advance is made on account of an order placed, it must be shown under a separate head as "Advance against goods on order" and should not be included amongst" Sundry Creditors.

To avoid any fraud, it would be better if the auditor, in consultation with his client, sends the Statements of Account to all the debtors to confirm the balance. The replies from these debtors must be sent direct to the auditor so that the clerks may not make any alteration in the statements so received. It is possible that the balances as confirmed by the debtors may not agree with the balances as shown by the ledger. In such a case reconciliation account may be prepared to see whether any amount received from a debtor might not have been credited to his account or a sale might not have been debited to his account in order to suppress the sales.

After being satisfied that the debit balances as recorded in the Sales Ledger are correct, he should ascertain the value of these debts. Of course, it is difficult to lay down any set rules to find out the value of book debts with exactitude. The terms of credit differ from business to business and in the same business from one customer to another. Again the terms of the credit are not always rigidly adhered to in every case. The auditor has, therefore, to use his discretion in each case.

For the purpose of valuation of debts, he should ask his client to supply him a list of good, doubtful and bad debts. It may be mentioned here that even if such a list of the debtors (good, doubtful and bad) duly signed by a responsible official of the company is handed over to the auditor, he should not presume that it is quite correct. He would not be free from his liability if later on it is found that the list was incorrect. He should scrutinie such a schedule. He can verify this list by applying the following tests to each account:

1. If the account is regularly settled and the advantage of cash discount taken by the debtor, the debt is good.
2. Whether the debt is outstanding beyond the period of credit allowed. If so, it *may* mean that the debt is doubtful.
3. Whether the payments are on account and the balance tends to increase. If it is so, it means the party is doubtful.
4. Whether an old balance is being carried forward and the new goods are supplied for cash. If so, it means, the debt is doubtful. It is also possible that the old balance may be due to a dispute. The possibility of the old balance having been paid and the cash misappropriated should also be considered in such cases.
5. Whether a cheque or a bill received against a debit balance has ever been dishonoured. If it has been the case, it shows the party is not financially sound, and that the debt may be doubtful or prove bad some day.
6. Whether any remark regarding nonpayment, like 'account stopped', 'in solicitor's hands', 'in bankruptcy', 'in liquidation', or 'disappeared and address unknown', etc., is made on the ledger account. In such a case, he should scrutinie the case thoroughly to find out whether the debt is doubtful or bad. If in case of insolvency, a final composition is paid, the balance of the debts due should be written off as 'bad' only by a responsible official in order to prevent the possibility of misappropriation being concealed by the creation of fictitious 'bad debts'. If any debt had been written off as bad in the past and if any composition or dividend is received later on, such an amount should not be credited to the debtor's account as there is

now no corresponding debit entry. It should be credited to the Bad Debts or Bad Debt Dividend Account.

7. The Law of Limitation allows three years to recover a debt and if the debt is outstanding for a longer period, it means the debt is bad.
8. If the bills are constantly renewed, the party is financially weak and the debt may be treated as doubtful.
9. If payments are irregular, the debt may not be good, and may become bad some day.
10. Whether there is any unusual item of discount or allowance. If so, he should probe into the matter.

It would be better, if a list of all the debtors with four columns, viz., 'good', 'doubtful', 'bad', and 'remarks', is prepared when each debt is discussed with a responsible official. It may be extended in the appropriate column, and totals cast. Now it will be easy for the auditor to form an estimate as to what will be the amount of 'good', 'doubtful' and 'bad' debts and reserve made accordingly. It should also be noted that out of the good debts, some of them may also prove doubtful or bad and provision, therefore, should also be made for such debts.

The above method to scrutinise the debts as good, doubtful, or bad is very cumbersome or laborious and, therefore, some companies or firms provide reserve on percentage basis, which method is not recommended. The auditor in such a case should scrutinise thoroughly to find out estimated amount of reserve to be provided.

If no effort is made to find out doubtful and bad debts and no provision or inadequate provision is made for reserves, the result will be .that the balance sheet will not show the correct position of the concern. The debtors will be shown as more than what they are actually worth. The profits will also be overstated as the debtors represents sales which have been credited to the Trading Account, but for which no payment has been made or is expected. Instead of such sales representing a profit, they represent a loss. Therefore, it is very important that correct estimates of debts be made. The only method of arriving at such an estimate will be to adopt the method described above.

If the auditor finds that the reserve provided for bad and doubtful debts is inadequate, he should persuade the directors to raise the amount. If he is not successful, he should refer the matter in his report, otherwise he will be held guilty of negligence and breach of duty as was held in the case of *London and General Bank Ltd*, in 1904.

Total Accounts and Sectional Balancing

In big business houses where there are large numbers of transactions, it will be difficult to prove the accuracy of the balances of the Bought and Sales Ledgers. To do so the 'Total Debtors' and Total Creditors' Accounts with have to be prepared. The total debtors' or creditors' accounts will contain all the items appearing on the debit side and the credit side of the accounts in the Sales and Purchases Ledgers.

In case the client maintains the ledgers on the self-balancing system, the chances of error will be minimised. The auditor should apply a few 'test checks' and if he finds that there is no mistake, he may presume that everything is all right. Of course, responsibility for any inaccuracy of fraud will still rest upon him.

QUESTIONS

1. The accounts of a company of which you are the auditor show a fall of 15% in the gross profits during the year under review. Suggest the possible reasons for the decrease and state what steps you would take to ascertain the cause in a particular case.
(*Jabalpur; Gauhati B.Com. 1969*)

2. Explain the points you would keep in view while auditing the sales. (*Delhi B. Com.*)

3. Suggest an internal control system regarding purchases of raw materials in a large manufacturing company and explain the significance in the context of the recent "social audit order" issued under Section 227 (4A) of the Companies Act. *(C.A. Inter Nov. 1976)*

4. You are the auditor of a private limited company. The audit notes submitted by your assistants disclose the following:
   (*i*) Purchases, total Rs. 1,54,000 are not supported by vouchers.
   (*ii*) Certain advances given to suppliers amounting to Rs. 50,000, still continue to be shown as advances although the final bills of such suppliers have been settled after deducting such advances.

   State how you will deal with the above mentioned matters. *(C.A. Int. 1971)*

5. A manufacturing concern of which you are the auditor has suffered a loss as a result of frauds perpetrated in the following manners:
   (*a*) Fictitious purchases were entered in the books and duly posted to the personal accounts. Subsequently, cheques purporting to be in payment of the accounts were drawn, endorsed and cashed and divided by and between the staff.
   (*b*) Fictitious entries for goods returned were passed through the books and posted to the credit of the personal accounts, the cash being misappropriated as and when received.
   (*c*) Dummy men were included in the wages sheets and the amount divided between certain members of the staff.
   (*d*) The cashier has misappropriated funds by "teeming and lading" process.

   State the steps you would take to detect such frauds.
   (Sardar Vallabhbhai Vidyapeeth, 1961)

6. How would you discover fictitious sales in the course of an audit?

7. What are the advantages of keeping Personal (Debtors' and Creditors') Ledger on self-balancing system? Are there any advantages accruing to the auditor as well?

8. In the course of an audit, you find that the item "Sundry Debtors" include changes made for packing cases and the like. Discuss the correctness or otherwise of this.

9. For what purpose is the Journal utilised? How is it audited? *(Poona B. Com. 1964)*

10. What is the legal position of the auditor of a company regarding the adequacy of Reserve for Bad and Doubtful debts? Quote the relevant case law in support of your answer.

11. In the annual Balance Sheet of a limited company the creditors are under-stated, in consequence of goods purchased not having brought them into the Purchase Day Book and the Ledger, though the goods were included in the Stock. Could an auditor, under such circumstances, be held responsible for not discovering the omission? Give reasons for your reply.

    What check can an auditor apply to avoid such errors?

12. Describe the duty of an auditor in regard to book debts, indicating how far you would accept a responsible official's views as to what debts should be written off as irrecoverable.
    (Guahati B. Com. 1969)

13. Your client, a manufacturer, intends to mechanise the sales ledger section of his Accounts Department and you are asked to suggest safeguards for its efficient operation, so as to facilitate your own audit. Suggest accordingly. *(C.A. Final 1966)*

14. Many difficulties which may arise where accounting records are mechanised are those resulting from:
    (*a*) the absence of primary records, or
    (*b*) difficulty in ascertaining the composition of debtors' balances.

    Discuss the problems which may arise from these two courses and suggest how they may be overcome. *(C.A. Final)*

Chapter 18

The Audit of Impersonal Ledger

Having checked the Bought and the Sales Ledgers, the auditor should now pay his attention to the Impersonal ledger or General Ledger or Nominal Ledger as it is called by different names. Such a Ledger contains accounts from which Trading and Profit and Loss Accounts and the Balance Sheet are prepared. In other words, the Impersonal ledger has two kinds of accounts, viz., nominal accounts which relate to the trading and profit and loss and real accounts which record assets. If the accounts in the General Ledger are incorrect, they will affect the Profit and Loss Account and the Balance Sheet. The certificate which an auditor will sign, will, therefore, be incorrect. As there are not many entries in the nominal ledger, except in the case of very big business concerns, the auditor will do well to check all the transactions. The procedure will not only ensure the correctness of the profit and Loss Account but also the Total Personal Account as well, "since one of the commonest methods of concealing manipulations in personal accounts is to make a corresponding fictitious entry in Impersonal Accounts."

We have already dealt with the transactions relating to purchases, sales, purchases and sales returns, wages, etc., which appear in a Trading Account.

We now propose to deal with the transactions in the Impersonal Ledger which relate to profit and loss account. These transactions will be recorded either from the cash book or the journal or the totals of the subsidiary books of prime entry. The Impersonal Ledger, therefore, will be vouched as follows:-

1. The vouching of cash transactions relating to profit and loss has already been dealt with in connection with the audit of cash transactions. The auditor should check the posting of such transactions to the impersonal ledger.
2. Many important transactions of impersonal nature such as transfers and adjustments from one impersonal account to another are passed through the journal. He should see that each entry is supported by sufficient evidence. Particular attention should be paid to such transactions as they materially affect the final accounts.

Check the total of the subsidiary books. The balances in the Impersonal Ledger should be checked and verified with the Trial Balance.

Outstanding Assets and Liabilities

Even though the balances in the Impersonal Ledger may be arithmetically correct, the profit or loss so arrived at may be incorrect because certain expenses which ought to have been incurred during the current year have not been debited to Profit and Loss Account. Similarly, certain income which ought to have been credited to Profit and Loss Account has not been credited. Such a type of expenditure and income must be incorporated in the current year's Profit and Loss Account in order to arrive at the correct profit or loss. Adjusting entries, therefore, must be passed through the journal to arrive at correct profit or loss. It would be convenient if an outstanding memorandum book is maintained. This book should be certified by a responsible official. It will not be out of place to mention here that the auditor will not be relieved of his responsibility if there is any mistake in the outstanding memorandum book or because he relied upon such a book even though it was signed by a responsible official. He must, therefore, compare the expenses of the closing month with the corresponding month of the previous year. If there are outstandings naturally the expenses for the closing month will be less while those of the succeeding month will be more. If there is a large variation between the two periods, he should make inquiry. He must, therefore, exercise reasonable skill and diligence while examining such a book. The auditor will find such a book very useful as he can compare the outstandings of the two periods and easily find out as to what are the outstandings which require adjustments during the year under review. In this connection, it may be mentioned that such adjustments do not vary very much from year to year. Therefore, if intentionally or unintentionally, any item of income or expenditure has not been incorporated in the accounts, it will be easily detected. Another advantage of maintaining such a book is that adjusting entries can conveniently be made in the Impersonal Ledger directly from such a book.

However, if no outstanding memoranda book is maintained, adjusting entries should be passed through the Journal and a narration should be inserted.

Let us deal with some of the outstanding assets and liabilities in detail and see what are the duties of an auditor in this connection.

Outstanding Assets

Outstanding assets or intangible assets as they are sometimes called may be:

(*a*) Income Receivable;

(*b*) Prepaid Expenses; and

(*c*) Deferred Revenue Expenditure.

(*a*) Income Receivable

Income might have accrued but might not have been received at the date of the balance sheet, e.g., rent might have accrued but the tenants might not have paid it; dividend by a company might have been declared but it might not have been received; the borrower might not have paid the interest due at the date of closing the books; commission, shipping rebates, taxation claims, etc., might not have been received. As these incomes had accrued during the current year, it is but fair that the profit and loss of the current year must be credited with the amount even though it has not been received at the date of the balance sheet, with a view to arriving at the correct profit. But the auditor in such a case should see that the accrued income is brought into account only when it is likely to be recovered, e.g., a banker who has lent money to a customer should not credit the profit and loss account with the accrued interest if the customer has ceased to make the payments or has become bankrupt.

(*b*) Prepaid Expenses

Arnold W. Johnson defines prepaid expenses as "Prepaid expenses are unconsumed services receivable or inventories of expense commodities which will convert into expense as the expenditure is consumed.... They are expected to be used up as costs of the revenues of future income periods."

In certain cases, expenses are paid for a definite period but a part or whole of such expenditure may be for the subsequent period and which is not covered by the period under audit. Therefore, to debit the profit and loss account for the current year with the whole of the amount will be unduly burdening the profit and loss account and the net profit or loss arrived at, without any adjustment will be incorrect. The whole of the expenditure should not, therefore, be debited to profit and loss account of the current year but a part of it paid for the subsequent years should he deducted from the total expenditure. Examples of such prepaid expenses are insurance premium, rent, rates and taxes, subscriptions, telephone rent, etc. If, for example, insurance premium is paid on 1st October for one year and the books of account are being closed on 31st December, the profit and loss account of the current year should be debited with only one-fourth of premium paid and the three-fourths of the premium paid in advance should be treated as "prepaid expense" which should be shown on the assets side of the balance sheet. Such prepaid expenses are to be treated as current assets.

A question arises as to how to apportion such an expenditure between two periods. Professor Johnson has made the following suggestion for the apportionment of prepaid expenses:

1. On a time basis, i.e., the cost is consumed proportionate to the passage of time.

2. On a revenue basis, i.e., the cost is consumed proportionate to the revenue produced by the expenditure.

3. On the inventory basis, i.e., the cost is consumed proportionate to the physical consumption of the assets. The prepaid expense (on the balance sheet) is the value of the physical inventory of the expense item at cost. The write-down of the balance of the prepaid expense account on the books to this inventory value is the amount consumed, *i.e.*, the amount converted into expense."

1. Prepaid Insurance, Prepaid Property Tax, Prepaid Rent.
2. Prepaid Advertising. Prepaid Commission, Prepaid Royaties.
3. Automobile Supplies, Truck Supplies, Boiler Room Supplies, Factory Supplies, Office Supplies, Sales Department Supplies.

The suggestion made by Professor Johnson in regard to No. I is quite reasonable and practicable. In regard to suggestion No. 2, lot of' calculations will have to be made. In fact, Professor Johnson himself admits and says: ".... but detailed accuracy is not really necessary or worthwhile." In regard to suggestion No. 3 in our opinion, when depreciation is provided, there seems to be no necessity of apportioning the expenses.

However, prepaid expenses should be ignored when the amount is so small that it would not appreciably affect the accounts.

The auditor, in the case of prepaid expenses, should examine the nominal accounts, the demand notes, receipts, etc., and see that proper adjustment for unexpired period is made in the books of account at the date of the Balance Sheet. The amount so paid in advance should be shown on the assets side of the Balance Sheet as explained above.

(c) Deferred Revenue Expenditure

Professor Arnold Johnson defines Deferred Charges as "non-recurring expenditures which are expected to be of financial benefit to several accounting periods of indeterminate total length."

Expenditure which, though of revenue nature, is spread over a number of years because its benefit is derived during those years. Such an expenditure is called Deferred Revenue Expenditure.

Sometimes heavy expenditure is incurred, the advantage of which will be derived in subsequent years, e.g.,

(*a*) Expenditure incurred in launching an advertisement campaign;

(*b*) Development expenditure in the case of mines and plantations;

(*c*) Experimental expenditure:

(*d*) Research expenditure;

(*e*) Plant rearrangement and removing costs;

(*f*) Exceptional repairs of non-recurring nature, e.g., overhauling of the plant.

(*g*) Discount allowed on the issue of debentures, and so on.

The whole of such expenditure should not be debited to profit and loss account of the year in which such an expenditure has been incurred but a part of it should be carried over. If a part of such an expenditure is not carried over to subsequent years and whole of it is debited to the year in which it is incurred, the profit and loss account of that year will be unnecessarily burdened although the advantage of such an expenditure would be derived in subsequent years also.

In order to inflate the profits, the legitimate expenditure of a year is spread over a number of years as if it were deferred revenue expenditure, *e.g.*, improvements to leased property. Such an expenditure should be added to the cost of capital expenditure. The auditor should, therefore, investigate into the circumstances which led to the carrying forward a part of the expenditure to see whether it is really applicable to the following years. The auditor should also see that the unwritten portion of the deferred revenue expenditure is shown on the assets side of the balance sheet until it is entirely written off.

Exceptional losses suffered, *e.g.*, loss by fire when the property was not insured or loss by earthquake or riots, etc., are recouped out of the future profits. Such losses must not be confused with Deferred Revenue Expenditure.

The following are some of the instances of the deferred revenue expenditure and we shall discuss as to how such an expenditure is to be treated in the books of accounts:

I. Advertising

When a new article is introduced in the market, abnormally heavy expenditure is incurred for advertising or in the establishment of a new department or business. Such expenditure is, in fact, in the form of capital expenditure. This should, however, be written off within a period of a few years and the profit and loss account should be debited with the amount to be written off every year and the balance shown as an asset until it is completely wiped off. There are certain writers who do not subscribe to this view. They say that such expenses are chargeable against current income. However, the auditor should verify these expenses by examining contracts, invoices, vouchers, etc. He should see that the expenditure is spread over a reasonable period.

II. Preliminary Expenses

Heavy preliminary expenditure may be incurred in connection with the formation of a company or the establishment of a new department. In such a case the whole of the expenditure should not be debited to the profit and loss account of the year but it should be spread over a period of say 3, 5 or 7 years. Such expenditure is of capital nature but as it is not represented by any assets, it should be written off as stated above and profit and loss account of such years should be proportionally debited.

III. Alterations and Heavy Repairs to Plant, etc.

Sometimes heavy expenditure is incurred to make alterations to plant and machinery or getting it overhauled to suit the changed conditions of the business. Strictly speaking such expenditure is not capital expenditure but it improves the earning capacity of the business. This type of alteration is not an annual feature and hence all such expenses should not be debited to the profit and loss account of the year in which they are incurred. Such expenses should, therefore, be spread over a number of years provided there is no provision for repairs or renewal funds against which it may be debited. Where an old plant is scrapped and a new one is installed in place of the old one the treatment will be the same.

Outstanding Liabilities

In order to arrive at the correct profit or loss, it is necessary, that all known liabilities are brought into account. If any liability in respect of any expense is not included in the Profit and Loss Account of the current year, the net profit arrived at will be more than what actually it is. It is, therefore, the duty of an auditor to see that all such liabilities are brought into account before ascertaining the net profit or loss for the current year. If he fails to do so, he will be held liable as the dividends will have been paid out of capital because of the omission or under-statement of certain liabilities as was held in the case of *the Westminster Road Construction and Engineering Company, Ltd*, 1932. But it may not be easy for an auditor to know whether all liabilities have been brought into account or not. Some of the expenses might have been suppressed and this may not be clear from the books of account. If the auditor refers to the payment side of the cash book after the close of the audit period, he may find out the existence of such a liability. But there are some outstanding liabilities, e.g., expenses of a regular nature like the rent which usually occurs and, therefore, the auditor can easily find out such liabilities. Moreover, an auditor will learn about the existence of such outstanding liabilities by experience. It will be better if he gets a certificate from a responsible official that there are no expenses incurred which have not been brought into account during the period under audit.

In any case he should scrutinses the nominal accounts like wages, salaries, interest, discount, taxes, etc., to verify that all expenses accrued up to the date of the balance sheet have been duly accounted for. He should compare the total expenditure with the previous year and if there is an appreciable difference, he should make an enquiry. He should also examine the purchases book to find out whether there has been any suppression of purchases.

Some of the outstanding liabilities may be in respect of:

1. Unearned Income

Income might have been received though a part or the whole of it is not applicable to the current year but will be earned during the following year, *e.g.*, rent received in advance. Such an income which is not applicable to the year under audit should not be credited to the profit and loss account of the current period but should be shown as a liability in the balance sheet.

The auditor should examine the vouchers to find out how much amount is to be credited to the profit and loss account the current year and how much is to be carried forward and which will be earned during the following period.

2. Unpaid Expenses

Expenses incurred during the year but for which payment has not been made and will have to be made next year are called "Unpaid Expenses". In such a case, profit and loss account should be debited with the amount and credited with the unpaid expenses account and shown as a liability in the balance sheet.

The auditor should examine vouchers, receipts, invoices, demand notes, etc., to ascertain whether the expenses ought to have been debited to the current year's profit and loss account and that no payment has been made.

Some of the common forms of outstanding liabilities are given below:

(*a*) Purchases

It sometimes happens that goods are purchased at the close of the year and are entered in the Stock Book when received but as the relative invoice has not been received, no entry is made in the Purchase Book. A schedule of such purchases should be prepared and the total debited to purchases account and credited to outstanding liabilities account.

The auditor should compare the Goods Inward Book with the Purchases Book for the last few days of the year. He should also compare the creditors' statements with their accounts in the Bought Ledger. Any heavy debit balance of creditors must be enquired into.

(*b*) Rent, Rates, Taxes. Electricity, Water, etc.

In order to arrive at the correct profit or loss, provision for all liabilities for rent, rates, taxes, etc., which have accrued but for which no payment has been made by the time the books are closed, must be made. In other words, outstanding liabilities must be brought into account. If this is not done, the profit arrived at will be more than what actually it is. If for example, a concern closes the books of account on 31st December, and any tax is payable by 1st April, it must make provision for tax for nine months in its books of account although the tax has not been paid so far. If this is not done, the profit and loss account will be debited with less amount and, consequently more profit will be shown than actually what it is.

The duty of the auditor in such cases will be to inspect the ledger accounts, demand notes, receipt, etc., to find out what period is covered so that he should adjust the account for amounts payable during the year under audit.

(*c*) Wages and Salaries

The books are generally closed on the last day of the month and the wages and salaries are paid on the first day of the following month. In such a case the wages and salaries will not be debited to the profit and loss account of the year under audit as no payment has been made. Therefore, the profit arrived at would be more than what it actually is. It is, therefore, but proper that such wages and salaries must be brought into account before arriving at the correct profit. In such a case, wages and salaries account should be debited and outstanding liabilities account should be credited for the wages and salaries payable. The auditor should see that profit and loss account has been debited with twelve months' wages and salaries.

(*d*) Audit Fee

The question is whether the audit fee payable to the auditor at the balance sheet date should be treated as an outstanding liability or not. On the one hand, it is argued that as the audit work has not commenced before the close of the books, audit fee should not be debited to the profit and loss account or should not be treated as an outstanding liability. It is further argued that since the audit work by the auditor will be performed in the next financial year, it should be debited to the profit and loss account of the next year and not to the current year. On the other hand, it is argued that as the auditor is to be paid for the audit of the accounts for the year under review, it is but proper that the profit and loss account of *that* year should be debited with the audit fee payable even though it has not been paid as yet or even though the work of the audit has not commenced till the date of the balance sheet. It is argued that an auditor is appointed under the Companies Act to "hold office until the conclusion of the next annual general meeting." His duty is to report on the balance sheet and profit and loss account laid before the general meeting which has to discuss the annual accounts. Therefore, it is argued that the fee payable to him for his work should be debited to the profit and loss account. If such a fee has not been paid, it should be shown as an outstanding liability.

Both the arguments appear to be sound. It will be fair to debit the profit and loss account of the year under review if the work of audit has commenced before the closing of the books and the audit fee payable should be brought as an outstanding liability. In case the books have been closed and the auditor begins his work after that date, the audit fee should not be debited to the profit and loss account of the year under audit but should be debited to that of the subsequent year during which period the auditor checks the accounts. In any case, he should see that the revenue account is not debited with double the amount.

(*e*) Freight and Carriage

Sometimes the clearing and forwarding agents do not send the account regarding the freight, carriage, commission, etc., before the close of the annual accounts. It is, therefore, necessary that an estimate should be made of such charges which should be debited to the profit and loss account and brought as an outstanding liability. The auditor should compare such outstanding with the corresponding period of the previous year. It will practically be the same if the business is of a regular nature. He should examine the statements of account rendered by the clearing and forwarding agents during the subsequent periods to find out the accuracy.

(*f*) Travellers' and Agents' Commission

The auditor should examine the commission account and see that any commission earned by the travellers and agents but not paid at the date of the balance sheet is brought into account and shown as an outstanding liability. It sometimes so happens that travellers are paid some money in advance. At the date of the balance sheet, it should be seen what amount is due to traveller after deducting the advance and, therefore, only that amount should be shown as an outstanding liability. If the advance is more than the commission payable, it should be shown as a loan to the travelling agent on the assets side. In case it is treated as a loan, reserve for doubtful or bad debts should be made as some of the travellers may not clear the accounts before they give up the job. If such an amount is outstanding for a long time provision should be made for doubtful or bad debt.

Sometimes travellers are allowed to collect dues from the customers and to set off their commission against such collections. There are dangers in such a practice. The traveller may not inform the head office of the collection and may misappropriate the money so collected. To guard against such a danger, the traveller should be instructed to prepare three carbon copies of the receipt — one to be given to the customer, the second to be sent to the head office and the third to be retained by him for his record. Thus the head office will have up to date information as to how much money is with the traveller. He should be instructed to send the money to the head office if the amount collected exceeds a certain figure or such collection should be remitted every week.

Another danger of collections by the travellers and setting off these against their commission is that the profit and loss account may not be debited for their commission. This system should be avoided as far as possible. However, if this system is in existence, whatever has been collected from the debtors should be creditors to Sundry Debtors' Account and Commission Account or Profit and Loss Account should be debited for the commission paid or payable.

In case of *del credere* agents, commission is payable to them at a higher rate, but the arrangement is that if a customer does not pay or the goods are returned, no commission is payable to the traveller. It may also happen that at the close of the year, commission might have been debited to profit and loss account but the customer might have become insolvent in which case no commission is payable to the agent. If this is the case, such commission should he deducted from the commission account if the amount has already been debited to the commission account.

Again, the arrangement with the traveller might be that commission is payable only after the customer has paid the price of the goods sold through the traveller. Sometimes a part of the commission is payable at the time of the despatch of the goods and the balance is paid when the price of the goods is paid by the customer. In case of such arrangements, the auditor should see that proper provision is made for such a liability at the date of the balance sheet.

(*g*) Commission to Sales Manager

Commission paid to the Sales Manager should be verified as usual, i.e . by referring to the agreement with the sales manager regarding the rate of commission, the sales should be verified from the sales book, commission paid should be verified by making calculation; the receipt issued by the sales manager; the counterfoil of the cheque book; cash book etc.

If a fraud is suspected, the auditor should take the following steps: —

1. He should compare the sales with the stock book to see whether the goods have been dispatched or it is a fictitious sale.

2. He should compare the stock as shown by the balance sheet with the stock book at the end of the year.
3. He should physically check the closing stock.
4. He should examine the dates of the sale of goods and see whether there has been any entry in regard to the return of goods after the sale had been effected. The idea is to see that there has been no fictitious sale or goods might have been sold on 'sale or return' basis. This procedure has to be followed especially in the case of sale at the close of the year.
5. He should see that the sales in respect of which the goods have been returned either before or after the close of the year are not included in the sales for the purpose of calculating the commission to the sales manager.

(*h*) Interest Payable

Interest payable at the date of the balance sheet should be shown as an outstanding liability. The auditor should examine the ledger account to find out how much interest is to be paid. He should calculate the amount.

Allocation between Capital and Revenue

When expenses are incurred they may be of revenue nature or capital nature. If no distinction is made between the two, it will affect the profit or loss of the concern and ultimately the balance sheet. If on account of wrong allocation, more profit is paid to the shareholders of a company, the auditor as well as the directors of the company might be held responsible for the payment of dividend out of capital. But before we discuss this point, let us see what is capital and revenue expenditure.

(*a*) Capital Expenditure

It is that expenditure which is incurred in purchasing new property which will help the production of goods or which will increase the earning capacity of the business or acquiring a valuable right or increasing the life of an asset. This type of expenditure is "incurred in acquiring assets for the purpose of earning income, or increasing the earning capacity of the business". If the existing property is permanently improved or enlarged or extended in order to increase the earning capacity of the business or its efficiency or reduce the normal expenses of production or administration, such an expenditure will be classified as capital expenditure, *e.g.*, construction of a new shed, adding more looms and spindles in a textile mill, purchase of motor lorries to replace horse carts, initial expenditure incurred or losses suffered in the development of a plantation; interest paid out of capital during the course of construction of works subject to the conditions laid down under Section 208 of the Companies Act, etc. In short the benefit of the capital expenditure extends over a number of accounting periods. In all these cases earning capacity of the asset is increased either by effecting large output or by reducing the cost. Other examples of capital expenditure are installation of fans and lights, acquisition of patents, copyrights, patterns, designs, etc. Again, if heavy expenditure is incurred on repairs which ultimately increase the efficiency of the plant or machinery such an expenditure is of capital nature. Similarly expenses incurred in erecting plant and machinery should be capitalised as such expenses increase the cost of machinery. The correct allocation between capital and revenue will be determined after taking into consideration all the relevant facts.

Sometimes a wrong idea is formed that if a heavy expenditure is incurred it is capital expenditure and when a small expenditure is incurred it is revenue expenditure. It may or it may not be so. It depends upon the circumstances of each particular case.

The auditor should, therefore, see the basis on which the expenditure has been allocate between capital and revenue and should not be guided by the amount of expenditure alone.

Again, sometimes a particular nature of expenditure is considered to be revenue expenditure, *e.g.*, repairs which may be capital as well as revenue expenditure. If repairs are effected in the ordinary course of business, it is revenue expenditure but if such repairs are effected to increase the life of the asset it is capital expenditure. So the demarcation depends upon the purpose for which the expenditure is incurred.

(*b*) Revenue Expenditure

It is the expenditure which is periodically incurred to maintain the revenue-earning capacity of the business, *e.g.*,

(*i*) Expenditure incurred to maintain the value of any existing asset, *e.g.*, ordinary repairs, white washing of the building, etc.;

(*ii*) Expenditure incurred in the ordinary conduct and administration of the business, *e.g.*, rent, advertising, salaries, wages, etc.

(*iii*) Expenditure incurred in connection with the administration and distribution of the goods manufactured or sold, e.g., commission, travelling expenses and so on.

(*iv*) Expenditure incurred exclusively in earning the revenue of a particular accounting period, and is wholly consumed and written off during that period, e.g., the expenditure incurred for the purchase of goods for resale.

Importance of distinction between Capital and Revenue Expenditure

The correct allocation of expenditure between capital and revenue is of great importance as it will affect the Profit and Loss Account and Balance Sheet of a concern. It is not easy to classify a particular expense as revenue expenditure, e.g., wages during the ordinary course of a manufacturing business will be of revenue nature, while on the other hand wages paid for erecting and fitting a new machinery in the same manufacturing business will be of capital nature. In the latter case, the General Wages Account should be credited and the machinery account debited, if the regular workers of the concern were directed to erect or fit the new machinery and their wages had been debited to the General Wages Account. If this is not done, the Profit and Loss Account will be unduly burdened and less profit will be shown. In such a case, proper data should be obtained as to the number of workers employed for the erection of the plant and machinery, number of days they worked, rate, and so on. Such a data should be certified by the wages clerk regarding the calculation of wages; by the foreman of the works regarding the nature of the work done and by the works manager about the correctness of the allocation. If such a certificate is not obtained, the auditor might be deceived as to the correct allocation of the expenditure between capital and revenue. Similar considerations apply to materials used for a particular asset, *e.g.*, in case of building contractor, if cement or steel has been used out of the stock for constructing his own building, personal account of the contractor should be debited and Materials Account should be credited. The Store-keeper and the Works Manager should certify as to the proper allocation and the cost of the materials. Similarly, carriage paid for buying a new machinery, interest paid during the construction of works, legal charges incurred in purchasing a building, etc., all such expenses will be considered as expenses of capital nature and will be debited to the particular asset account. On the other hand carriage expenses, interest on money borrowed or debentures, etc., will be classified as revenue expenditure and will be debited to the Profit and Loss Account.

Where new plant is purchased with a view to replacing an old one, the expenses incurred in pulling down the old plant will be treated as revenue expenditure whereas cost of erecting the new one will be treated as capital expenditure.

If capital expenditure is debited to profit and loss account, the particular asset will not be debited with that amount. The result will be that the particular asset will be undervalued and a secret reserve will be created to the extent of the undervaluation of that asset. The creation of secret reserve by a public company is prohibited under the Companies Act, as we shall see later on. Moreover, the profit and loss account will be unnecessarily burdened and it will show less profit or it might show even a loss.

If revenue expenditure is debited to the capital account, profit will be inflated. In such a case dividend will be paid out of capital which payment is against the provisions of the Companies Act. The auditor might be held responsible for such payment and might be asked to refund that amount.

Improper allocation of expenditure between capital and revenue will have far-reaching result on the accounts of a concern. The auditor should see very carefully that proper allocation is made. He should get a certificate regarding the allocation of expenditure between capital and revenue from a responsible official and mention that fact in his report, especially when the expenditure involved is very heavy. He should state in his report that he has relied upon the certificate from a responsible official about the allocation of expenditure between capital and revenue.

Contingent Liabilities

The duty of an auditor is to see that all known and unknown liabilities are brought into account at the date of the Balance Sheet. There may be certain liabilities which may or may not arise after the preparation of the balance sheet. It is, therefore, necessary that provision should be made for such unknown liabilities. Such liabilities are called contingent liabilities. A contingent liability has been defined as one which may or may not arise at a future date. A contingent liability has been defined by another writer thus: "A contingent liability in a balance sheet is a possible future liability arising from one or more business acts preceding the date of the balance sheet", e.g., the result of a litigation; about the assessment of damages; a bill receivable which has been discounted may be dishonoured on the due date and hence it may amount to a liability because the amount will have to be paid to the banker with whom the bill was discounted; calls on partly paid shares which have been purchased; liability under a contract of guarantee; liability in respect of unfinished contracts; forward contracts, etc. Montgomery says: "The term 'contingent liability' should be used in the accounting sense to designate a possible liability of presently determinable or indeterminable amount which arises from past circumstances or action which may or may not become a legal obligation in the future, and which, if paid, gives rise to a loss or an expense or an asset of doubtful value."

Prof. Walter B Meigs says, "Contingent liabilities may be defined as potential obligation which may in the future develop into actual liabilities or may dissolve without necessitating any outlay." The uncertainty as to whether there will be any legal obligation differentiates a contingent liability from an actual liability A contingent liability may or may not involve the payment of money. As already stated above, if a bill receivable has been discounted with the banker, one is not sure whether the liability will arise not. If the bill is honoured, the will question of liability will not arise.

Kinds of Contingent Liabilities

Contingent liabilities may be of two kinds, *viz.*,

1. A liability involving an ultimate loss, *e.g.*, a liability in a disputed case where damages may have to be paid; guarantee given by a company for loans or overdrafts granted to managed companies; speculative transactions on the stock exchange; forward contracts, etc.
2. A liability which will involve in the acquisition of an asset of corresponding value, *e.g.*, when goods have been purchased for future delivery or under an agreement of service. No note should be made in the balance sheet in respect of this type of contingent liability but if the amount involved is considerable, a note should be inserted at the foot of the balance sheet

The auditor can find out such liabilities during the course of the audit while going through the books of account, correspondence, minute books, etc. He should consult the solicitor of his client to assess the value and genuineness of such liabilities. He should inquire from the bank where the bills receivable have been discounted and as to the number of bills which have not matured as yet. He should see which shares are held by his client on which calls have to be paid. Again, he should find out the amount of dividend payable to cumulative shareholders. He should also find out whether his client has stood as a guarantor for any loans or overdrafts granted to any managed company, etc. If possible he should get such a statement in writing from the solicitor especially when the transaction appears to be illegal.

The amount of the contingent liability may be definite or may not be so. The example of the first is that of a bill received which has been discounted and which might be dishonoured at the date of maturity. The example of the contingent liability, the amount of which is not definite, is of a suit for damages against the company which is pending at the date of the balance sheet.

Similarly a contingent liability may be certain or uncertain. Example of the first is when a suit has been filed against the company for the infringement of the patent and the company knows that it has infringed the patent right while, on the other hand, when the company knows that it has not infringed that patent rights, the contingent liability is uncertain.

The auditor should divide the contingent liabilities into two main categories according to Part I of Schedule VI of the Companies Act, viz.

1. The liabilities in respect of which a provision has been made in the balance sheet, *e.g.*, where the directors think that the liability will definitely arise in connection with a suit filed against the company though the amount may be uncertain. These are shown under the heading "Current Liabilities and Provisions", and
2. The liabilities in respect of which no provision has been made in the balance sheet but merely a note has been inserted at the foot of the balance sheet, *e.g.*, bills receivable which have been discounted and which have not matured at the date of the balance sheet, arrears of fixed accumulated dividends, etc. If the company has a number of suits pending against it but the company is advised by its legal adviser that the ultimate legal and financial responsibility in regard to such suits is very negligible in relation to the total assets of the company, the amount is not extended in the money column.

The auditor should see that the requirements of the Companies Act regarding the contingent liability are complied with in the Balance Sheet on the liability side as stated above.

The information required to be given under any of the items, or sub-items in this form if not included in the Balance Sheet because they are numerous, should be furnished in a separate schedule or schedules to be annexed to and form part of the Balance Sheet.

Contingent Assets

Usually no mention is made at the foot of the Balance Sheet on the assets side about a contingent asset such as "an option to apply for shares in another company on favourable terms", "Refund of octroi paid for goods which have been sent out later on", "Claim for money from a previous endorser of a bill receivable which had been discounted but which might be dishonoured", "Uncalled share capital of a company," "A legal action for infringement of a copyright", etc., probably because of conservatism, *i.e.*, to show the position of the company worse than what it is. It is but fair that if a contingent liability is shown, a contingent asset must also be shown at the same time. The danger in not showing the contingent asset but showing the contingent liability only will mislead the outsiders about the prosperity of the company. Although the Companies Act provides that contingent liabilities should be provided in the Balance Sheet of a company, it does not require the contingent assets to be disclosed.

QUESTIONS

1. How would you ascertain that all outstanding expenses and all income received in advance have been provided for in the accounts? What effect would it have on the final accounts if these provisions are not made?

2. What is meant by 'Outstanding Assets' and Outstanding Liabilities and explain the duties of an auditor in regard thereto? *(Punjab B. Com. 1964; Cal B. Com. Hons. 1967)*

3. What are the principles of allocating expenditure between capital and revenue? Describe how you would apply such principles to each of the following items: —

(*a*) Additions to factory buildings.

(*b*) Repairs to plant.

(*c*) Heavy advertisement expenses.

(*d*) Renewals of licences. *(Agra B.Com. 1966)*

4. It is said that the contingent liabilities may be divided conveniently into two main classes. Give your views and if you also think so, state an example of each class. State also how each of them should be dealt with in the Balance Sheet of a company.

5. What are the contingent liabilities? Give five examples of such liabilities. What is the method by which you would satisfy yourself at the time of audit that all contingent and outstanding liabilities have been disclosed in the balance sheet? *(Delhi B. Com.)*

6. Explain the meaning of "Deferred Revenue Expenditure". Give three examples of deferred revenue expenditure and describe the Auditor's duty with regard to this item of expenditure. *(Bombay B.Com. (1969)*

7. State whether the following items should be classified as capital or revenue, giving reasons for your decision:

(*a*) Cinema advertising of a new product;

(*b*) Research expenditure on a project subsequently abandoned;

(*c*) Wages to workers employed on repairs to factory following a storm damage.

(Cal. M. Com.)

8. An audit implies more than ascertaining the arithmetical accuracy of the books of account. Set out ten debit items of the Profit and Loss Account stating the sources from which the accuracy of the charges can be verified. *(CA. Inter)*

9. When preparing the Balance Sheet of a Limited Company on 31st December, 1965, the Directors seek your advice on the following:

(*a*) Bills receivable Rs. 15,000, discounted but not due until 30th April next.

(*b*) Rs. 10,000 invested in another company in shares of Rs. 100 each, Rs. 75 per share has been called up.

How should you advice them?

10. At the date of the Balance Sheet, a manufacturing concern has outstanding forward contracts for the supply to it of its principal raw materials at a price substantially higher than the market price. No reference to the matter appears in the Profit and Loss Account and the Balance Sheet presented to you for audit. What would you do?

11. As an auditor, how would you satisfy yourself that the following have been duly provided for:

(*a*) Reserve for doubtful Debts,

(*b*) Outstanding Liabilities for expenses and Provision for Depreciation?

(Andhra Public Service Commission)

12. How do you define (*a*) Capital Expenditure, and (*b*) Revenue Expenditure? As an auditor how would you deal with structural alterations? (*Andhra Public Service Commission*)

13. Your note in the course of your audit that the accountant has treated following transactions a capital expenditure:

(*i*) The construction of a new staircase by replacing the old one;

(*ii*) Interest paid for delay in payment of acquiring a lease of colliery;

(*iii*) The cost of repairs to a Plant incurred during the course of its removal to a new and convenient site.

Give your opinion with brief explanation. (*N.D. Com.1962*)

14. (*a*) Discuss the general principles to be applied when allocating expenditure as between Capital and Revenue.

(*b*) State with reasons how the following expenditure should be treated in the final accounts of a business firm:

(*i*) Rs. 4,000 paid for removal of stock of goods to a new site which will be more convenient for various reasons.

(*ii*) Second-hand furniture worth Rs. 6,000 was purchased and the repairing of the furniture cost Rs. 1,500. The furniture is installed by the firms' workmen. Wages paid to them for this purpose being Rs. 300.

(*iii*) Fire insurance, Rs. 1,200, was paid on 1st January 1966 for one year. The accounts of the firm are closed on 31st March each year. (*Gauhati M. Com. 1968*)

15. What are the auditor's duties regarding contingent liability? Illustrate your answer with two examples explaining their treatment and verification. (*Gauhati M. Com. 1969*)

16. Explain the meaning of the work "Contingent Liability". As auditor how would you consider the same for treatment in accounts? Name some items you will regard as 'Contingent liability' giving reasons for the same. (*Bombay B. Com. 1969*)

Chapter 19

Verification and Valuation of Assets and Liabilities

Meaning of Verification

Verification means 'proving the truth', or 'confirmation'. The student is warned at this stage not to confuse verification with vouching the expenditure in connection with the acquisition of an asset. One of the most important duties of an auditor in connection with the audit of the accounts of a concern is to verify the assets and liabilities appearing in the balance sheet. He has not only to examine the arithmetical accuracy and *bona fide* of the transactions in the books of account by vouching only, as has already been explained in one of the previous chapters, but he has also to see that the assets as recorded in the balance sheet actually exist. The fact that there is an entry regarding the purchase of an asset and which entry has been found to be correctly recorded, is not a proof that the asset is in the possession of the concern at the date of the balance sheet. It is possible that after the asset had been acquired and all the necessary entries made in the books of account, the asset might have been disposed of or pledged or mortgaged and no entry had been made regarding these facts in the books of account before the closing of these books. He has, therefore, to see whether a particular asset as recorded in the balance sheet on the day of the closing of the books of account exists or not. If he fails to verify the asset, he will be held liable as was decided in the case of *London Oil Storage Co. Ltd vs. Sear Hasluck Co.* (1904), when Alverstone, C.J., said, "It is the duty of the auditor to verify the existence of assets stated in the balance sheet and he will be liable for any damage suffered by the client if he fails in his duty ...."

The verification of assets involves the following four points:

1. Comparing the ledger accounts with the balance sheet.
2. Verifying the existence of the assets on the date of the balance sheet.
3. Satisfying that they are free from any charge or mortgage.
4. Verifying their proper value.
5. Assets were acquired for the business.

Having satisfied himself that a particular asset does exist either by actual inspection or otherwise and that it is free from any charge, he has to proceed further to find out whether the assets are properly valued.

Of course, it is not possible for an auditor to inspect each and every asset, *e.g.*, stock. If this duty was imposed on him it may take weeks and months for him to actually inspect every asset. It was held in are *Kingston Cotton Mills* case that "it is no part of an auditor's duty to take stock. No one contends that it is. He must rely on other People for the details of the stock in trade in hand...."

But in the light of the decision in *McKesson* and *Robins*' case in 1939, it would appear that the auditor must physically inspect some of the assets. Wherever possible, the documents of tile such as negotiable instruments, shares and securities, debentures, etc., should be examined on the last day of the financial period. If it is not possible and the auditor visits his client after that date, he must examine the transactions which took place between the closing date and the date of his visit to ensure that any adjustments or alterations which have been made are *bona fide* and are supported by proper evidence. But in the case of stock-in-trade the auditor has some documentary evidence, *e.g.*, the Purchases Book, the Invoices, the Gate Keeper's Inward Book, the Stock Book and so on. Thus, although law does not require an auditor to take stock, indirectly he is asked to verify the stock by referring to the Stock Book and other books.

Problems in the Valuation of Assets

The accuracy of the balance sheet and the estimated profits of a concern depend upon the correct valuation of the assets and liabilities. The valuation of the assets made by the proprietors or officials of the company or the firm. The auditor has simply to apply certain tests regarding the valuation of the assets. He is entitled to rely upon the certificates of competent persons such as valuers, surveyors, etc. If he does so he must mention this fact in his report. He cannot be expected to possess the technical knowledge to find out the value of the assets. Under such conditions, he should also refer to the invoices to find out the price at which such assets were acquired. Of course, he cannot guarantee the correctness of the valuation of the assets.

We have also to consider the question whether the assets should be valued at replacement or realisable value, in other words, the amount which would be required to purchase such an asset or the price at which it would be sold. 'Replacement value' is the amount which would be required to purchase another asset of the same type to replace the existing one. 'Realisable value' is the amount which the existing asset would fetch if it is sold in the open market. 'Breakup value' or `Scrap value' is the amount which would be realised if a particular asset is sold when it has become unserviceable. The auditor has simply to apply the accepted principles of valuation. If he is not satisfied with the mode of valuation, he must mention that fact in his report. It must also be remembered that the assets are not to be valued for the purpose of balance sheet at their breakup values as if the business were closed. They should be valued as for a *goingconcern*. Therefore, the assets are valued taking into consideration (*a*) their original cost, (*b*) the probable working life of the assets, (*c*) the wear and tear of the assets, (*d*) break-up value of the assets, and (*e*) the chances of the assets becoming obsolete. The duty of the auditor in such a case is to see that the basis of valuation and the calculations are correct and that all contingencies are provided for.

It must have been seen from the above discussion that the object of the valuation of assets is to show that the balance sheet represents a true and fair view of the state of affairs of the concern and that there is no manipulation of accounts to inflate the profits. Let us see what are the accepted principles regarding the valuation of assets for the purpose of balance sheet. For this purpose, the assets are generally classified into `fixed assets', and 'circulating assets' or 'floating assets' or current assets'. Some writers divide the assets into (a) `intangible assets' such as goodwill, copyrights, trade marks etc., which cannot be seen or touched, (b) 'wasting assets' such as mines, quarries, etc., a part of which is extracted and sold during the period of their operation, and (c) 'fictitious assets' such as payment made in advance or heavy expenditure incurred while launching a campaign, e.g., heavy expenditure incurred to advertise an invention or new article introduced in the market and the expenditure of which is to be spread over a number of years. There are others who classify the assets as fixed, current and unrealisable assets. They define unrealisable assets as "items of expenditure of a capital nature, such as discount and commission on the issue of shares and debentures, preliminary expenses and preacquisition losses'. Let us deal with these assets in detail and see how they are valued.

Valuation of Assets during Inflationary Period

A problem which confronts an auditor is as to how to value the assets during the Inflationary period, e.g.,

1. The value of stock is not sufficient to meet the cost of replacing the same quantity of stock.

2. The depreciation charges based on the historical cost of the fixed assets will not provide sufficient amount required to meet the cost of replacing those assets if they are needed to be replaced later on.

3. If depreciation is provided on the historical cost of the assets and similarly if the stock-in-trade is also valued accordingly, the profits shown by the profit and loss account will not reflect an increase or decrease in terms of the purchasing power of the money.

To solve the above problems, the following suggestions have been made:—

1. The replacement cost method of dealing with the fixed assets should be followed, i.e., the fixed assets should be valued at replacement cost.

2. The fixed assets should be written up according to the market price of the assets prevailing on the balance sheet date.

4. The stock-in-trade should be valued at the market price and depreciation should be provided on the value of the stock so arrived at.

5. The index method of adjusting the accounts to reflect the changes in the purchasing power of money should be followed.

Fixed Assets

Fixed assets are those which are acquired for permanent equipment and not for resale in the ordinary course of business. They are not consumed in the very process of manufacture. They are more or less of permanent nature and are acquired by a concern for the purpose of earning profits. Cohen Committee on Company Law Amendment in England suggested the definition of fixed Assets as "assets not held for sale or conversion into cash". This definition was incorporated in the Act. Statement on Auditing Practices issued by the Institute of Chartered Accountants of India states: "A convenient working rule is to regard as fixed assets as those acquired for the purpose of use in the business with the object of earning revenue and which are not intended for resale at a profit and conversion into cash in the ordinary course of *business*". These assets are of permanent or semi-permanent nature. Of course it is not easy to say which assets are fixed and which are circulating. That depends upon the nature of the particular asset and the use to which it is put. Machinery is fixed asset for a cotton mill but it is a floating or current asset for a concern dealing in machinery. A motor van may be fixed asset for a concern carrying on business as carriers but it will be a floating asset for a deer in motor vans. Stock,shares, securities, etc., are fixed asset for a trust company as these investments are acquired to earn profits and to retain them permanently, but in the case of a finance company, the investments are to be treated as floating assets as they are acquired with a view to reselling them and to make profit on their resale.

Mode of Valuation of Fixed Assets

Fixed assets should be valued at cost price less total depreciation in their value by constant use. They are to be valued at original or historical cost less total depreciation written off up to the date of the balance sheet. They are valued at what is known as a "going concern value" or "conventional value" or "token value". The reason for this principle is that these assets are acquired for running the business and not for the purpose of resale. No notice is taken of any fluctuation in their price as the fluctuation does not effect the earning capacity of the assets of the business. They are valued, from the point of view of their utility to the business. They are not valued at the saleable value. In other words such assets are valued at their estimated present value to the *business*.

The valuation, of course, is arbitrary as the amount of depreciation is only an estimate. As mentioned above, current replacement or realisable value is not taken into account while valuing the fixed assets. Therefore, they should not be valued at the price they would fetch at the date of the balance sheet, if they are sold.

Floating Assets or Current Assets and the Mode of their Valuation

Floating Assets are those which are acquired for resale or produced for the purpose of sale or converting them into eash, e.g., stock, semi-manufactured goods, book debts, cash, bills receivable, etc. They are either cash or acquired with a view to converting them into cash later on. They are valued at the date of the balance sheet at original or historical cost price or the market price whichever is the lower, as they are held with a view to converting them into cash. They should never be valued at more than their original cost, as it would mean taking into consideration a fictitious profit at the date of the balance sheet bacause they have not been sold as yet. Moreover, it is possible that later on when they are sold, the market price may be lower. In the valuation of the floating assets, we do, take into consideration the market fluctuations.

The guiding principle in the valuation or the floating assets should be to be rather conservative in estimating the profits. It is safer not to take estimated profits into account, but if on the other hand there is an expected loss, that should be taken into account. The reason is that if anticipated profits are taken into account, it may so happen that the expected profit may not be realised when the asset is sold. At the date of the balance sheet, the expected profit has not been realised and hence it is not available for distribution.

Wasting Assets

Wasting assets are those fixed assets which are depleted gradually or exhausted in the process of working, such as a mine, a quarry, an oil well, etc. Distinction between the decrease in the value of a fixed asset and a wasting asset must be clearly understood though both of them are fixed assets. In the case of a fixed asset, the decrease in its value is due to wear and tear or obsolescence while decrease in the value of a wasting asset is due to the operation of extracting a part of it and selling it out, or exhaustion.

But it is very difficult to know how much of the mine is exhausted and how much mineral remains more. Thelefore, the cornmon method followed in the valuation of this asset and also as recommended by the Institute of Chartered Accountants of England and Wales is to show it in the balance sheet at its original cost and provision is made for depreciation and depletion according to the estimated exhaustion of such an asset.

Intangible Assets

Intangible assets are those assets which cannot be seen or touched, e.g., goodwill, copyright, patents, trade marks. In his examination of such assets, the auditor should determine the following:—

1. The basis on which such assets were originally valued.
2. The reasonableness and adequacy of the amortization programme or the write-off procedure.
3. Fair and adequate balance sheet presentation.
4. The accuracy, completeness and proper control of the income arising from the ownership of such an asset as leasehold and patents.
5. He must also determine whether such assets represent some benefit or privilege at the date of the balance sheet.
6. He should see that such assets are recorded on a basis consistent with generally accurate accounting principles.

7. He must see that such assets are shown properly and fairly in the financial statements.
8. They should be shown separately.

Valuation of Intangible Assets

1. They should be shown at cost price unless they had been acquired in a non-cash transaction in which case they must be shown at a fair market price.
2. They are the least liquid of all assets since most of them are unsaleable unless the business or a part of it is sold.

Auditor's Position as Regards the Valuation of Assets

From the above discussion it must have been clear to the reader that the correctness of the profit and loss account and the balance sheet depends to a great extent on the correct valuation of the assets which is, however, a difficult problem. As has been pointed out above, the auditor is not a valuer or a technical hand to estimate the value of an asset. He has to depend to a great extent on the valuation by the directors, partners, experts, surveyors, etc. But does it mean that he is absolved from his liability if assets are overvalued by the directors, etc., and if he has entirely depended upon them? Does he guarantee the absolute correctness of the balance sheet under such circumstances? The answer is 'no'. He must see that the assets are valued according to certain principles of accountancy. In certain cases, the market value of assets may be available, e.g. in, case of investments, when he should see that the assets are valued accordingly. If he is satisfied with the method of valuation of the assets he is freed from his liability. Further, as has already been pointed out, the depreciation provided for is only an estimate and, therefore, the audited balance sheet can never be claimed by an auditor to be absolutely correct. However correct the estimates of the value of assets may be, it merely shows the fairest possible etimate of the position of affairs according to the accepted principles as checked and estimated in every reasonable manner. The auditor has to see whether the valuation is according to the accepted principles of accountancy. Where the values of assets such as shares, stocks, etc., are available he must see that the assets are valued accordingly. Again, if there is the slightest suspicion regarding the valuation, he should probe into the matter.

Verification and Valuation of Different Kinds of Assets

Having discussed the general principles of verification and valuation of asset and the duty of an auditor in relation thereto, let us proceed further to discuss the verification and valuation of various types of common assets which usually appear in the balance sheet and the duty of an auditor in connection with each particular asset. It may again be pointed out than an auditor does not guarantee the accuracy of the valuation of any asset.

1. Cash-in-hand

Sometimes the accountants accept a certificate from the management regarding the amount of cash in hand. This procedure is objectionable. Recently there was a case when the auditor was asked by the Council of the Institute of Chartered Accountants to explain why he did not check the cash balance of a company, but his explanation was: "So far we are aware, it is normally the practice of the profession to rely on the certificate of cash on hand in case of private limited companies in the absence of suspicion or doubt, and we are not unaware of cases even of public companies having sufficiently large funds where reliance is placed on the certificate of management by the auditor in regard to cash on hand." The Council's comment was : "The Council feels that this is not a correct appreciation of an auditor's responsibility in regard to the verification of cash. Therefore, the auditor should actually count the cash on hand".

The auditor should visit the business house at the close of the financial period or on the following morning and actually count the cash in hand and compare it with the balance in hand as shown by the cash book. This should be done in the presence of the cashier and if there is any shortage his certificate should be obtained, if there are different kinds of cash balance, e.g., petty cash balance, cash in till, etc., they should be counted simultaneously so that shortage in one account may not be up from cash in hand from other account,ie., one cash balance may not do 'extra duty'. He should also acount cash, stamps, I.O.U's. in hand. As a matter of fact, the use of I.O.U's. should be discouraged as there is a possibility of fraud being concealed or fictitious or forged I.O.I's. placed in the cash box to make up the deficiency in cash. He should accept the I.O.U's only when he is satisfied with their genunes, *i.e.*, when he knows that the signature is genuine. If there are any I.O.U's. which represent cash advanced for expenditure, such expenditure should be brought into books and if they represent any authorised loan, it should be carried to the personal account of the borrower. If there are cheques and drafts in hand, the auditor should see that a receipt for them has already been issued. Where a small balance of cash in hand is held by a director or a responsible official, an acknowledgment by them should be obtained.

If it is not possible for the auditor or his assistant to pay a visit to actually count the cash in hand he may pay a visit on a subsequent date and count the cash in hand and exhaustively vouch the petty cash and cash book up to date and compare the cash in hand with the balance as shown by the books of account. In case of continuous audit, all balances should be counted frequently, say at an interval of a month or so.

Another method of verification of cash in hand is to ask his client to deposit the whole of the cash in hand, including petty cash, etc., into the bank on the closing day and then drawing a cheque on the following day for expense, etc., to reopen the cash book with cash drawn from the bank. In this way the whole of the cash in hand will be automatically counted and the auditor will be saved of the cumbersome task of counting the cash in hand. The difficulty in such a case is that stamps, I.O.U's., etc., cannot be deposited in the bank.

The drawback in the method of verifying cash in hand as described above is that when the cashier knows that the auditor will pay a visit on the closing day or on the opening day, he will borrow the necessary amount to make up the shortage and after the auditor had checked the cash book and cash in hand, he might repay the amount to the lender and thus may conceal the embezzlement for a number of years in this way. To prevent this thing, the auditor should towards the close of the period, not necessarily on the last working day, pay a surprise visit and actually count the cash in hand and petty cash so that the cashier may not have time to borrow money and make up the deficiency which was due to embezzlement in the past.

Keeping of large sums of money in hand should be discouraged unless it is absolutely necessary as in case of banks, because it will be very difficult to count whole of the cash balance. Usually the auditor counts currency notes, cheques, etc., while nickel and copper coins are weighed in such cases.

As regards cash in hand at different branches, the auditor should get certificates from the auditors of these branches to that effect and mention in his report that he has relied upon the certificates from the local auditors. If local auditors are employed, they should actually count the cash in hand at the branches. If local auditors are not employed, he must pay a visit to the branch and actually count the cash in hand or ask the branch managers to deposit the balance in the bank. Sometimes it may not be possible for the auditors to visit the branch, in which case the branch should be instructed to deposit the cash in the bank on the balance sheet date.

With regard to cash with agents or in transit reference may be made to documentary evidence which may be available. He should also see whether entries have been made in the books of account when such money is received.

Even if an efficient system of internal check is in existence, the auditor will not be absolved of his responsibility if he does not verify the cash balance.

2. Cash at Bank

To verify cash at bank, the auditor should examine the Bank Pass Book and compare it with the balance as shown by the bank column of the cash book. If he does not do so, he will be held liable as was decided by the Court in the case of *Fox & Sons. vs. Morris Grant & Co.*, in 1918. There may be still a difference as some of the cheques sent out for collection might not have been encashed and some of the cheques issued, though recorded in the cash book, might not have been presented for payment at the bank and so on. For the purpose of comparison the auditor should prepare a bank reconciliation statement as has been explained in one of the previous chapters. Even if the pass book balance agrees with the cash book, it is no proof of the correctness of the bank balance as there have been cases where fictitious pass books have been presented to the auditors although it was found later on that real pass book showed less balance. To prevent this type of fraud, the auditor will do well to get a certificate regarding the balance at the bank directly from the bank or actually inspect the bank ledger. Of course, the auditor should take this step with the permission of his client. Here again, the danger is that the cashier might borrow money to deposit the same in the bank a few days before the year closes in order to conceal the misappropriation which he had committed in the past. Thus, even if a certificate is obtained from the bank, the fraud will not be disclosed as happened in the case of the *Brighton Eden & Empire Syndicate Ltd., vs London & Country Bank Ltd.(1904)*.

Another precaution which an auditor must take is that the balance as shown by the cash book should be brought into the balance sheet as `Cash at Bank' and not `Balance as shown by the pass book', so that no adjustment in respect of the cheques not yet credited or not paid out may have to be made.

The auditor should also see that the 'cheques outstanding' and cheques not yet collected' are genuine and not made up in order to conceal the deficiency. If some of these cheques are more than six months old, he should make inquiries.

Cash on Fixed Deposits with the bank can be certified by examining the deposit receipt, or getting a certificate from the banker as described above. In cash the audit is undertaken after the financial year is over, the auditor should pay particular attention to the date mentioned in the deposit receipt as it is possible that the receipt may be relating to the current year and not to the previous year.

If there are more than one bank account such as Dividend A/c, 'Charity A/c.' etc., all such accounts should be checked and the balances should be verified certified up to the same date. Information regarding their balance should also be obtained from the bank directly.

If the bank account shows a debit balance, and the client has deposited any security for the overdraft, the auditor should enquire from the bank the particulars of the security for the overdraft, the auditor should enquire from the bank the particulars of the security and the amount of the interest charged.

3. Loans

Loans may have been advanced —

(*a*) Against the security of land and property; or

(*b*) against the security of stock and share; or

(*c*) against the security of goods; or

(*d*) against the security of insurance policies; or

(*e*) against the personal security of the borrower, etc.

We shall take up these separately in detail and discuss the duty of an auditor in connection therewith. The auditor should see that the loans are shown in the balance sheet according to the Companies Act.

(a) Loans against Security of Land and Property

(*i*) The auditor has not only to examine the loan account in the ledger, but he has to examine the documents relating to the security, viz., promissory note or bond, acknowledgements by the parties, etc.

(*ii*) If the land or property has been mortgaged, the auditor should examine the mortgage deed and find out whether the mortgage is properly executed in favour of his client.

(*iii*) If it is a second mortgage, he should see that the first mortgagee has been duly informed of the creation of the second mortgage.

(*iv*) He should also examine the title deeds relating to the property.

(*v*) In case of the second mortgagee the title deeds will be with the first mortgagee, in which case the auditor should ask the first mortgagee whether he has got the title deeds relating to the property.

(*vi*) The amount of the loan and the date should be inquired into. The amount advanced should not be more than two thirds of the value of the property. If he thinks that the marg in is small or if he is not satisfied with the security he should report accordingly. To find out the value and sufficiency of the security, the auditor should examine the valuer's certificate.

(*vii*) He should enquire the rate of interest and the date on which it is payable. If the loan has been outstanding for a long time, he should make inquiry, especially when the interest has not been paid and has been added to the principal amount. If after adding the interest, the margin between the loan and the security has become very small, further security must be demanded. If further security is not given, sufficient provision for doubtful or bad debt may be made.

(*viii*) He should also see that the property is insured against fire and examine the last receipt for the premium paid. If the property is not insured, the danger is that if the property is destroyed by fire, the loan becomes unsecured and the lender might lose the money

(*ix*) In case of loan on mortgage of leasehold land the auditor should see that the ground rent has been regularly paid by the lessee (borrower) on the due dates, and, therefore, the last receipt for the payment of the ground rent paid should be examined.

(*x*) He should see whether the mortgager has the power to mortgage the property and borrow money.

(*xi*) He should see that the mortgage is duly registered. In the case of a company he should examine the certificate from the Registrar of Company regarding the registration of charge.

(*xii*) There have been cases where part of the loan has been repaid but the repayment has not been accounted for in the books of account. Therefore, the auditor should get the amount of the loan confirmed by the borrower.

(b) Loan against Security of Stock and Shares

(*i*) The auditor should get a list of such stock and shares which have been held as security.

(*ii*) He should see that such shares, etc., are transferred to his client.

(*iii*) He should inspect such shares, etc., and see that they do not belong to his client.

(*iv*) The auditor should get a written acknowledgement from the borrower regarding the amount of loan on the date of the balance sheet or examine the agreement.

(*v*) Partly paid shares should not generally be accepted as security because as soon as they are transferred to a person, such a person will have to pay the uncalled amount whenever the company makes a call.

(*vi*) He should check the valuation of securities and find out the margin between the loan and the present value of the security. If he finds that the margin is small, he should ask his client to demand more security.

(*c*) Loans against Security of Goods

(*i*) Where loan has been advanced against a Godown-keeper's Receipt, such a receipt should be examined. If the goods are at docks or in a bonded warehouse, the dock warrant or the warehouse receipt duly endorsed in favour of his client should be examined. In case the dock warrant or the warehouse receipt has not been issued, delivery note in favour of his client should be examined.

(*ii*) He should see that the warehouse rent has been paid by the borrower; and in case it has not been paid, the amount should be added to the loan and the margin between the security and the loan should be ascertained. If the margin has become small, more security must be demanded.

(*iii*) Where it has been advanced against goods in transit, railway receipt or *bills of lading together with letter of hypothecation, insurance policy and invoices, as the case may be, duly endorsed in favour of his client, should be inspected.*

(*iv*) *The value of the goods may* be ascertained from market quotations, invoices, etc., in order to find out the value of the security.

(*v*) He should examine the inspector's report from time to time regarding the quantity of goods.

(*vi*) If the goods are of perishable nature, he should examine the turnover of the stock.

(*d*) Loans against Insurance Policy

(*i*) Last receipt for the payment of the premium paid should be examined. If the premium has been paid by his client to prevent the policy lapsing, the auditor should see that the amount has been debited to the Loan Account.

(*ii*) The Uditor should see that the notice of assignment of the policy has been given to the insurance company.

(*iii*) The valu of this form of security should not be takes as the assured sum but the surrender value of the policy — which value can be ascertained from the insurance company — should be taken as the value of security. The reason is that if the borrower does not pay the premium, the policy will lapse and the amount payable by the company at that time will be only the surrender value as the assured sum is payable only at the death of the policy-holder or when the policy matures.

(*e*) Loans against Personal Security

In case the loan has been granted against the personal security, the auditor should make an inquiry regarding the financial position of the surety as the value of such a security depends on his financial position. He should also see that no charge in the terms of loan has been made as such a course will discharge the surety and the client loses that security.

4. Bills Receivable

The auditor should examine the Impersonal Ledger or Bills Receivable Book with the bills receivable in hand. Some of the bills might have been sent out for collection in which case an inquiry should be made from the bank. It would be better if the auditor prepares a list of the bills thus:

(*a*) Thouse which have been discounted earlier and the date of the maturity of which has not arrived at the date of the balance sheet in order to find out contingent liability, if any.

(*b*) Those which have not been discounted should be entered in the second column and compared with the bills in hand.

(*c*) Those sent for collection to the bank should be entered in the third column and verified from correspondence or certificate from the bank, etc. The auditor should see that a note in regard to contingent liabilities against the bills discounted is made at the foot of the balance sheet.

While examining the bills, the auditor should see that they are properly drawn, stamped, duly accepted and that they are not overdue. In case there is a doubt about the payment of the bill on the due date, sufficient provision should be made.

If the auditor has paid a visit after the date of the balance sheet and if in the meanwhile any bill has been retired, the renewed bill should be examined.

Bills which have been dishonoured before the date of the balance sheet should not be included as 'bills receivable in hand' as they are no longer assets. The acceptors who had dishonoured such bills should be shown as 'debtors' as they owe the amount of the bills. The auditor must examine the dishonoured bill as it is possible that the bill might have been paid, but a fictitious entry might have been made to show that the bill had been dishonoured to conceal misappropriation. If such has been the case, the dishonoured bill will not be available.

In case a bill received from a previous endorser had been discounted and dishonoured, the account to the previous endorser should be debited. The auditor should see whether a notice of dishonour had been given to the previous endorser to hold him liable for the dishonored bill.

Sometimes the auditor pays a visit after the date of the balance sheet in which case some of the bills might have matured and honoured before the auditor comes. In such a case the auditor should vouch the cash received in the Cash Book and the Pass Book.

Where transactions in bills are numerous and a large number of bills are discounted, it is the practice to apportion the discount on the bills which are to mature after the date of the balance sheet. This discount relating to the period after the date of the balance sheet should be shown as an asset under the head Rebate on Bills discounted not yet due'.

5. Investments

If there are a large number of investments, as in the case of banks and insurance companies, the auditor should ask for a schedule of investments held by his client. The schedule should give full particulars of the investments, e.g., name of the investment, the cost price, the market price, book value, date on which the investment was acquired, rate of interest payable and the dates of the payment of interest, tax deducted and so on and compare these with the records in the books of his client.

In the case of the purchase of stock and shares for which no certificate has been issued till the date of verification, the transfer deed will be a good evidence for the purchase. If new shares have been applied for, the receipt for the applicaton money or the allotment letter should be examined.

The auditor should examine all the investments simultaneously and compare them with the schedule. If the number of the investments is large and they cannot be inspected at one sitting, the investments which have been checked must be locked and sealed in a box so that they may not be produced against at the time of the next inspection. I he key and the seal must be retained by the auditor. If these investments are held by any trustee on behalf of the company, the Trust Deed executed by such a nominee should be examined. If there is no Trust Deed, he should get a certificate from the Trustee that the latter holds those securities in trust and that they are free from any charge, and that they are in favour of the nominee or any other persons. In such a case, he should advise his client that a Trust Deed should be obtained as soon as possible.

In the securities have been entrusted to the bankers for safe custody, the auditor should get a certificate from the bank that so many securities are held by it for safe custody and that they are free from any charge; but will such certificate be sufficient in all cases? The answer is, in most cases it will be sufficient, but in the light of the judgment in the City *Equitable Fire Insurance*

Company Ltd., (1924), where a large number of treasury bonds were held for safe custody by the company's Stock Brokers, Eills & Co., who in their turn pledged these bonds, it would be better to go beyond this. Their lordships in this case were of opinion that in all cases an auditor should personally inspect all securities, wherever or by whomsoever held. Their lordships said that had the auditor not depended upon the certificate by Ellis & Co., and had he demanded the actual production of the securities, the fraud might have been detected as Ellis & Co. could not have produced the bonds which had already been pledged by them. It may be mentioned here that their lordships said that the brokers were not the proper persons with whom securities are lodged for safe custody. Had the securities been lodged with a bank and if the auditor had obtained a certificate to that effect the auditor would not have been held guilty of negligence.

If such securities are kept in the custody of the Secretary of the company, they should be held by him jointly with some other officer of the company. Such securities should be registered in the name of the company as is required by Section 49 of the Companies Act. At the end of the year these securities should be compared with the schedule showing the particulars of securities, their numbers, cost price, etc.

If at all a certificate is to be accepted, the auditor must examine the date and inquire whether it is usual to deposit such securities with such companies for safe custody.

If some of the investments have been sold since the date of the balance sheet but prior to the date of audit the auditor should vouch the proceeds either in the cash book or the bank pass book.

While auditing the accounts of a banking company, the auditor should inspect all the investments of the bank at the same time, i.e., investment of the bank and the securities *lodged with the bank as securities against loans and advances*.

If the bank has lodged its investments with some other party, receipt given by such a party for investments lodged should be accepted with great care. It is possible that the investments have been lodged with such a party not for safe custody but against a loan to the bank. However, such a receipt may be accepted after taking the following precautions:

1. The certificate or the receipts should state whether the securities lodged are free from any charge.
2. He should see that the provisions of the Banking Companies Act, 1949, are complied with.
3. He should compare the details of the investments with the Investment Register maintained by the bank.
4. He should see that if the investments are held by the nominee of the bank, the former should clearly state that he holds these investments on behalf of the bank. He should examine the Transfer Deed in such a case.
5. He should see whether the investments are properly valued and shown in the balance sheet according to the Banking Companies Act. The reader should see the *pro forma* of the Balance Sheet of a bank given at the end of the chapter on "The audit of Banking Companies".

Investments may be —

(*a*) Registered Debentures, Stocks and Shares, Government securities;

(*b*) Inscribed Stock; and

(c) Bearer Bonds and Share Warrants.

We shall discuss these different kinds of securities in detail as to how the auditor should verify each type of investment in the following paragraphs.

(*a*) Registered Debentures, Stocks and Shares, Government Securities.

The term 'Registered' means that the name of the holder of debentures, stock, shares, securities, etc., is registered in the Register of the Company or the Reserve Bank of India which has issued such scrips and that a certificate of title has been issued in the name of the holder.

The auditor should examine such a certificate and should see that is properly executed, sealed and stamped and that it is made out in the name of his client.

If any share or debenture, etc. has been sold out before the date of the audit, the auditor should examine the broker's Sold Note. If certificates have been lodged with the broker, a receipt from him should be obtained. If the delivery has been effected, the cash received should be vouched. If the broker has purchased other shares, etc., out of the sale proceeds of the investments sold out, the auditor should examine the broker's Sold Note and Bought Note in support of the double transaction. If a part of the shares, etc., held have been sold out and no new certificate has been issued the auditor should examine the 'Balance Certificate' from the company issuing such shares relating to the unsold portion. The Balance Certificate or the `Interim certificate' is issued by a company until the new certificate can be prepared. Sometimes companies do not issue Balance Certificates, in which case the auditor should examine a certificate from the company certifying the balance held by his client. In some cases the companies simply endorse the original certificate.

Where shares, etc., have been purchased a few days before the date of the balance sheet and the transfer deed has been lodged with the company which has not issued the fresh certificate, a certificate by the company that so many shares have been transferred by the seller to his client, will be sufficient evidence of the purchase. The auditor should inspect the broker's Bought Note also.

In case new shares have been purchased but no share certificate has yet been issued by the company, the auditor should examine the letter of allotment and banker's receipt for the payment of application and allotment money.

(*b*) Inscribed Stock

Inscribed stock is that type of stock where no certificate by the issuing authority is issued to the purchaser of such a stock. A stock receipt is issued to the purchaser giving the nominal amount purchased and the amount received but his name is inscribed in the register of stock maintained by one of the Joint Stock Banks, Crown Agent for the Colonies, etc., or the Reserve Bank of India. Those stocks are known as Consols, War Loan, India 3%, Colonial Stocks, Municipal Stocks, etc.

Where such inscribed stock is sold by a holder to any person, the Stock Receipt need not be handed over to the buyer. Therefore, the auditor should not assume by inspecting such a receipt that his client holds the Inscribed Stock. Similarly a certificate by a broker or a banker or any other agent that stocks purchased by his client have been duly inscribed has no value. Such a receipt has no value as a document of title. The question is, then, how is the auditor to verify the existence of such a stock at the date of the balance sheet? In such a case, the auditor should send an application on a prescribed form to the bank where the stock is registered giving full particulars regarding the nature of the stock, the name of the person to whom it is inscribed, the date of the inscription and the name of the auditor to whom the certificate is to be sent. The bank charges a small fee, and if the particulars given in the application are correct, it signs the application and returns it to the auditor if so required by the holder. As a matter of fact, such a certificate should always be sent direct to the auditor to prevent any alteration in the figures. This will be a good evidence of the amount of Inscribed Stock held by his client.

The auditor should note the date of issue of such a certificate as the certificate is not a definite proof of the ownership but only a record that the person named therein held the stock on that particular date of the certificate and before the date of the balance sheet the stock might have been sold out. Such a type of certificate should be obtained at the time of each audit.

The auditor should also find out whether the interest on these stocks is paid after deducting the income tax or without the deduction of income tax at the source. In the latter case, he should see that provision in made in the accounts for the payment of such income tax.

The auditor should obtain a certificate from the place of inscription that no party has any charge on such a stock held by his client.

It may be mentioned here that all the formalities relating to inscribed stocks, are being relaxed now and after some time regular stock certificates might be issued and the inscribed stock may become non-existent.

To value such a stock, the auditor should refer to the officials quotations issued by the Stock Exchange.

(*c*) Bearer Bonds and Share Warrants

The auditor should actually inspect such securities. If they have been deposited with the banker for safe custody, the auditor should get a certificate from the banker. He must see that the coupons for the next payment of interest or dividend are attached. Sometimes dividends are not payable at any fixed date. In such a case the coupons will not bear any printed date.

Where the full amount of the shares or bonds has not been paid, no certificate or bond will be issued. In such a case, the auditor should examine Letters of Allotment, the banker's receipt for the payment of money in respect of application, allotment, first call, etc., as the case may be.

If an interim certificate has been issued by the company before the date of the Balance Sheet, all moneys paid in respect of application or allotment or first call, etc., are endorsed on the back of the interim certificate which is exchanged later on with the full-fledged share certificate.

Valuation of Investments

Having verified the existence of the investments, the auditor should now proceed to find out whether they are properly valued at the date of the balance sheet. Let us now see what are the various methods by which the valuation of such investment is made.

Strictly speaking, there is no depreciation, in the real sense of the term, in the case of investments, except investment in the shares of mines and plantation companies.

The basis of the valuation of investments in the balance sheet will, to a large extent, depend upon the purpose for which they are held. If they are held by a Trust Company, the object of which is to earn dividends and interest and distribute such dividends and interest amongst the shareholders, such investments are to be treated as fixed assets and, therefore, even permanent fall in their value may be ignored, of course, subject to Articles of Association and the Memorandum of Association of the Trust Company.

On the other hand, if the investments are held by a Finance Company as current assets to be sold whenever found necessary, the basis of their valuation should be 'cost price or the market price, whichever is the lower'.

For the underwriters, if they have to purchase the shares, which had been underwritten by them, the 'cost price will be the face value less the underwriting commission'.

If shares and debentures have been issued to his client in consideration of any services rendered, the cost of such shares and debentures will be equivalent to the approximate cost of the services and, therefore, such securities must be marked at such a cost. If, however, such services cannot be measured in terms of money, a separate account for such shares, etc., may be opened as usual and the value of these investments may be shown as agreed upon.

As mentioned above, the investments should be valued at cost price which can be ascertained from the broker's Bought Note. If there is a temporary fluctuation in the price of these assets, it should be ignored. If there is a permanent fall in their price, depreciation should be provided. If no reserve has been created in respect of a permanent fall in the value of assets, he should refer this fact in his report. Where investments are shown at cost price in the balance sheet and no provision is made for a fall in market value a note should be made in the balance sheet showing the current price if there is a difference between the book value and the market value.

If the investments represent a temporary investment of the surplus funds, they should be shown at cost price or market price, whichever is lower. If the total market value of the investment is less than the total cost price, the whole of the difference may be debited to Depreciation Account and credited to Investment Fluctuation Account. Depreciation Account should be debited to the Profit and Loss Account while the Investment Fluctuation Account should be deducted from the original cost of the investments on the assets side of the Balance Sheet thus showing the net figure in the outer column. Sometimes Investment Fluctuation Account is termed as Investments Depreciation Account. The present value of investments can be ascertained from the official list of the Stock Exchange published on the date of the balance sheet. The price of the stocks and shares which are not quoted in the official list of the Stock Exchange, may be obtained from the financial papers which will give a fair idea of their value.

Where the quotations regarding the value of such investments are not available either from the official list of the Stock Exchange or from the financial papers, some difficulty will be experienced. In such a case the auditor should write to the Secretary of the company whose shares are held by his client asking for the latest quotations at which the shares were transferred. But the reader is warned here that this is not a correct criterion of the value of the shares. The auditor should, therefore, examine the balance sheet of such a company and enquire the rate of dividend paid in order to have a rough idea of the value of such shares.

Whatever method of valuation is followed, the auditor should see that the investments are never valued at a higher price than the cost, crediting the estimated increase to the profit and loss account except in very special circumstances, e.g., where there is a change in the partnership or where the business is being sold away. Even under such circumstances, other investments must also be revalued so that if there is an increase in one form of investments, and a decrease in the value of other investments, both may be .set off against each other. This method of valuation seems to be more fair in case it is considered absolutely necessary to write up certain assets. Balance Sheet must make clear whether the valuation is at 'cost', 'market price' or at 'cost less reserve'.

In case of investment which are not fully paid up and which fact is not apparent from the description of investments in the balance sheet, a note should be appended that there is a contingent liability for such and such amount in respect of such and such shares.

The auditor should see that the different types of investments are classified in the Balance Sheet according to the Schedule VI, Part I of the Companies Act. He should also see that the mode of valuation of the investments is clearly shown in the balance sheet according to the Companies Act. He must see that the provisions of Sections 49, 77, 292, 293 (c) and 372 in connection with the purchase of investments are complied with. The reader should for this purpose see the pro forma of the Balance Sheet given at the end of the chapter on "The Audit of Limited Companies".

Regarding the valuation of investments of a bank, the auditor should see that the mode of valuation of investment—cost or market value—is stated in the balance sheet as is required by the Banking Companies Act. Such investments are generally shown either "at cost" or "below cost". Where the value of the investments shown in the outer column of the balance sheet is higher than the market value, should be shown separately in brackets.

6. Stock-in-hand

General Consideration

The correctness of the profit and loss account of a concern depends, to a great extent, upon the correctness of the value of the stock of goods in hand at the close of the period. The auditor has, therefore, not only to verify the existence of the stock in hand but he has also to see that it is valued according to certain accepted principles of accountancy. The auditor will not find any difficulty if proper stock accounts are maintained but in a large number of cases this is not done. It is also very difficult for the auditor to physically verify each and every item of stock in hand as he may not possess technical knowledge and moreover he has no time to do so. Justice Lindlay in the case of *Kingston Cotton Mills Co., Ltd.* (1896) said: "It is no part of an auditor's duty to take stock. No one contends that it is. He must rely on other people for details of Stock-in trade." Again in the *Irish Woolen Mills* case the learned Judge observed: "There was certainly no duty cast on the auditor to take stock. What he did was to have the calculations checked in his office and this was done with proper care".

The auditor cannot, therefore, be expected to take stock or value it. He cannot with certainty say that the stock in hand as mentioned in the balance sheet is quite correct. He has to see that the stock-taking method as followed by his client is correct and, therefore, there is no risk of any mistake. If possible, he must prepare a rough stock accounts, if it has not already been prepared by his client, showing the quantity of stock at the beginning of the year, purchases and sales during the course of the year and the balance. This will show the quantity of stock in hand at the close of the year, of course, making provision for shrinkage, evaporation, etc. To be on the safe side, he should get a certificate from the client that the quantity of stock as mentioned in the stock sheets is correct. On the other hand, the auditor was held liable for damages for not detecting the over-valuation of the work-in-progress in spite of the fact that sufficient data was at his disposal (in *re Westminster Road Construction Company*). In another case the auditor was found guilty of recklessly attempting to induce investment of money by producing a balance sheet and prospectus which falsely stated the assets (work-in-progress)— *Wake & Bean, Ltd.*, (1954). In regard to the duty of an auditor in connection with the Stock-in-trade, we shall deal with this topic later on. The auditor should insist upon the maintenance of stock book, if it has not already been maintained. Let us see in the first instance what method is generally followed in taking stock.

Method of Stock-taking

Stock is taken on the last day of the business year. A clerk goes to the godown and calls out the number of items of each class of goods while another clerk goes on writing on sheets of papers the particulars of the goods and their quantity in the other column. These sheets are known as Stock Sheets. When all the goods in the godown are recorded, another batch of two clerks check the work of the first batch to see that there is no mistake.

The stock sheet is now sent to a responsible official of the concern who jots down the rate of each item of goods at which they are to be valued.

Another clerk now calculates the value of each class of goods in hand. The calculations and castings are now checked by another clerk to avoid any miscalculation.

Every clerk and official who has a hand in the preparation of the stock sheet must put his initials for the work performed by him so that if later on any mistake is found in the stock sheet, the official concerned may be held responsible for the mistake.

The stock sheet is now signed by the General Manager or the Managing agent or the Partner, as the case may be.

Sometimes the balance as shown by the stock book is entered in the stock sheets as closing stock. The auditor should not accept such a stock figure. The auditor should compare the stock sheets with the stock book, entry in the Trading Account and the Balance Sheet.

Precautions to be taken while Taking Stock

It may be that there are some goods which may not be in the physical possession of the client but legally his client is the owner of the goods, *e.g.*, goods might have been purchased, the invoices passed through the books of account but the goods might not have been delivered. The client is legally the owner of such goods and hence they must be included in the stock sheets. If they are not included in the stock sheets, the consequences will be that more purchases will be shown while closing stock shown at the date of the Balance Sheet will be less. The business will, therefore, show less profit than what actually is the case. Such goods must be treated as 'goods in transit'.

Similarly stock which is at the branches or goods which are with the consignees or which are sent out on approval, or sale or return contract and when the buyer has not sent his approval or which are in the course of transit or are lying at the stock, etc., must be included in the stock sheets.

Again, it may so happen that the goods might have arrived but the relative invoice has not been passed through the books of account as it might not have been received by the time the books are closed. In such a case, such goods must not be included in the stock sheets unless the property in the goods has passed to his client when care should be taken that the corresponding liability is also included in the books of account, i.e., the invoice is passed through the books of account.

Goods which have been sold, but which have not been delivered to the buyer at the date of the balance sheet should not be included in the stock sheets. Similarly, goods which are held by his client as consignee should not be included in the closing stock.

If the precautions enumerated above are not taken, errors are certain to occur and, therefore, the whole of the work of stock taking should be done under the supervision of a responsible official.

The Basic Principles of the Valuation of Stock-in-trade

If stock is not properly valued, it would affect the profit and loss account. If the stock is overvalued, it will result in artificial, false and misleading profits. This type of manipulation may be done by the General Manager or Managing Directors, employees, etc., who get bonus or commission on the profits earned by the concern or where there is less profit or no profit it is done with a view to show more profits. If the stock is undervalued, it may be with a view either to create a secret reserve or to show less profits to artificially lower the price of the shares of the company in the market.

No particular method of valuation of stock-in-trade is suitable for every type of business. However, the auditor should see that the same principle of valuation of closing stock is followed year after year. If this is not done, it will not be possible to compare reliably the results of the various years of trading.

Stock is a floating asset and is meant for resale. The accepted basic principle of accounting is to value floating assets at cost price or the market price, whichever is the lower. It is a sound accounting maxim that losses should always be anticipated but no account should be taken of the expected profits which may not be realised. In no case should stock be valued at a higher price than the cost price even if the rise in the price is a permanent one. The reason is that profits are taken into account only when the goods are sold. Although on the date of the balance sheet, the market value of the stock is higher than the cost price, profit and loss account cannot be credited with the difference as the goods have not been sold as yet. Moreover, the unsold stock when sold in the subsequent period after the date of the balance sheet may not be sold at a regular price either because the prices have gone down or the goods have gone out of fashion, etc.

On the other hand, if there is a fall in the price of the goods, it must be valued accordingly. As stock is a floating asset, it must be brought into account at its realisable value at the date of the balance sheet, if it is lower than the cost price. It may be questioned that when we ignore the realisable value of the stock which is higher than the cost price on the date of the balance sheet why should not realisable value which is lower than the cost be ignored in this case. It is submitted that the goods have been bought for the purpose of selling at a profit and if there is any probability or possibility of a loss on the date of the balance sheet, it must be taken into account.

As the price has gone down, there is a probability or possibility of a loss during the subsequent period and it must be provided for out of the profits of the current year by bringing such stock into account at its reduced value. It must be mentioned here that even if the price has gone down due to obsolescence or staleness, that fact must be taken into consideration The effect of valuing the stock-in-trade on the principle "cost price or market price whichever is lower" is to take into consideration the expected loss but no credit is taken for unrealised profit

The auditor should not lose sight of slow moving and obsolete stock at the balance sheet date. Of course, it will be difficult for him to ascertain the existence of such stock. Being a non-technical person, he cannot be expected to discover such stock. He should ascertain the method of identifying, reviewing and valuing the slow moving or obsolete stock in order to find out whether the method adopted is adequate and correct and whether such stock has been cor r correctly valued

We may summarise what we have said above:

1. 'The auditor should compare the prices with the original and independent data.
2. Discounts, duties, freight and insurance, should also be taken into consideration.
3. Ascertain that obsolete, damaged or slow moving stock has been properly valued.
4. He should investigate material changes, if any, in the inventory from the commencement and the close of the year.
5. He should check the computation of extensions.

The term 'cost price' has been often used in the foregoing paragraphs. 'the term has been interpreted in many different ways. It may mean *(a)* actual cost, *(b)* average cost, *(c)* first-in-first out cost, *(d)* lost in first out cost, *(e)* base stock method, *(g)* standard cost method, *(h)* adjusted selling price method. The accountants have not defined the word 'cost' and hence there is confusion in the minds of many an accountant. 'Therefore, the auditor must have a definite idea about the cost price and the market price in order to value the closing stock properly. 'The following are the different methods of finding out the cost price of the stock of goods:

1. Unit Cost Method or Actual Cost Method

If goods have been purchased in diderent lots and the present stock can be identified as to which consignment it belongs to, there will be no difficulty in finding out the cost price of such stock as the invoices or the cash memos will show the cost price of different consignments which have remained unsold on the date of the balance sheet. This method is known as 'Unit Cost'. According to this method, each article, batch, parcel of consignment is valued at its individual cost. The difficulty under this method is that it may not be practicable in respect of bulk stock and partly manufactured goods or finished goods where the individual units of goods lose their identity.

Again a difficulty might arise to find out the cost because expenses such as freight, octroi, sales tax, etc., incurred in connection with the purchase of such materials are debited to the profit and loss account rather than the materials account.

In regard to the semi or finished goods the cost of the materials cannot be measured with exactitude. Allocation of overhead charges is only an estimate. Some concerns allocate these expenses according to direct labour charges while others do so according to the time and so on.

2. Average Cost Method

Where goods have been purchased from time to time and they are so mixed up that it is not possible to identify a particular consignment, e.g., oil purchased from time to time and stored in bulk in tanks. In this case the following method may be adopted to find out the cost price of such an unsold stock:

Stock may be valued at the average cost of various consignments purchased from time to time during the course of the year, plus the cost of opening stock, less the sales. The average should be "weighted average" by taking into account quantity and cost. It should not be arithmetic average, *e.g.*,

In Stock,	100	Kilos @ Rs. 4,	400
Purchases,	200	Kilos @ Rs. 6,	1200
	300		1600

Average cost = $\frac{1600}{300}$ *i.e.*, Rs. 5.33 per Kilo.

This method has the merit of taking into consideration the violent fluctuations in the purchase price of the goods from time to time during the year under audit. Such a method is suitable in respect of manufacturing concerns where several processes are involved.

3. First in, First out (Fifo) Method

The whole of the stock is valued at the rate of the latest consignment purchased or up to the quantity which is in hand at the time of taking the stock on the assumption that the latest purchases have not been sold, i.e., the goods are sold in the order in which they are purchased. This method is known as the 'first in first out', for short, the 'fifo' method. Under this system the unsold stock has a reasonable close relation to the replacement price. But the difficulty is that during the inflationary period the closing stock will be valued at a higher rate with the result that more profit will be shown. If more profit is shown, the workers will demand more bonus; the managing directors or managers who get commission on profits will have to be paid more commission; more dividend will be paid; more income-tax will have to be paid and so on. Moreover it is difficult to apply this method in case of manufacturing or producing concerns.

4. Last in, First out (Lifo) Method

The whole of the stock is valued at the rate at which the earliest purchases made on the assumption that the latest purchases are sold first and the unsold stock represents the earliest purchases. This method is known as the 'last in first out', or '*Life*' method. This method does not appeal to common sense. Every businessman would try to sell those goods which were received first so that they may not become stale. Another defect of the 'Lifo' method is that the stock appears in the balance sheet at a figure which has no relation to replacement cost or its realisable value. Those who advocate this method of the valuation of stock do not claim that in actual practice, the closing stock represents those goods which were purchased in the beginning of the year. They also admit that a businessman will always try to sell out the earliest purchases. However, they say that when there is a trend for the prices to rise, if this method is adopted, false money profit being shown will be avoided. This method is very little used in the United Kingdom. Income computed on 'Lifo' basis is not acceptable to Income Tax authorities in the United Kingdom and Canada, while on the other hand this method is widely used in the U.S.A. where it had been accepted by the Income Tax Authorities in the case of *Anaconda American Brass Ltd., vs. Minister of National Revenue in 1952*.

5. "Base Stock" Method

Under this method it is supposed that a certain minimum or basic quantity of the material for carrying on the business is always essential to be in stock and that the quantity remains the same almost every year except when there are abnormal times. This quantity of stock is more or less fixed just like plant and machinery or any other such asset. The advocates of this method of valuation of stock say that such stock should not be valued at "cost price or the market price whichever is lower" method but should be valued at "normal long period price" as if it were a machine. In case, the quantity of the stock is more than the "basic quantity", the excess of the quantity may be valued at "cost price or market price whichever is lower".

Advantages of this Method

(*a*) If the stock is valued year after year at the "basic price", there would be no violent fluctuations in the gross profits even though there may be changes in the price level of the materials.

(*b*) Comparison of gross profit of two periods separated by a long time can give a true picture of the business.

(*c*) Even if on account of rise in the price of stock, the stock is valued on the "Base Stock" method, the balance sheet will not show the position of the concern better than what it is. Hence there is no harm if the closing stock is valued at the "Base Stock" method.

(*d*) Lot of calculations will not have to be made every year.

Disadvantages of this Method

(*a*) This method of valuation is not possible for every class of industry where variety of raw materials are used in the process of manufacture.

(*b*) This system of valuation of stock is mostly followed in America but has not found much favour in England. This method is more or less like the "*Lifo*" method.

6. "Standard Cost" Method

Under this method, the stock is valued at a pre-determined or budgeted cost per unit. This method of valuation of stock is finding favour with the manufacturers who produce goods on large scale.

7. "Adjusted-Selling Price" Method

Under this method, the stock at the close of the year is valued at the market price out of which the normal profit and the cost of disposing of the goods are deducted. The remaining balance is the value of the stock for the purpose of trading account and the balance sheet.

To find out the cost price of the finished or unfinished goods the accepted formula is that these goods are marked at work cost if it is lower than the market value. By "works cost" we mean the cost of the raw materials and the factory overhead charges. The raw materials used in the manufacture of goods are valued by any one of the methods described above. The overhead charges allocated to these jobs include the following:

(*a*) Wages and direct expenses.

(*b*) Factory overhead charges or indirect charges, e.g., factory rent, depreciation of machinery, electric charges, etc., which are calculated according to the 'direct wages'.

Care must be taken to see that administrative, selling or distributive expenses are not included in the cost of the manufactured or semi manufactured goods.

We give below the summary of the paper and findings entitled "Accounting and Audit Approaches to Inventory in Three Nations", issued by the International Study Group which was jointly formed by (1) the American Institute of Certified Public Accountants, (2) the Indian Institute of Chartered Accountants, and (3) the Institutes of Chartered Accountants of England, Scotland and Ireland:

1. The amount to be attributed to inventories is of fundamental importance in the preparation of financial accounts of most trade undertakings.
2. The maintenance of adequate inventories records is a primary responsibility of management who must also ensure that inventories are managed and safeguarded under an efficient system of internal control.
3. Inventories should be physically inspected under proper supervision at appropriate intervals.

4. Attendance to observe physical inspection of inventories is the most significant audit verification procedure which should be adopted as internationally recognised standard procedure.
5. In general, inventories should be valued on a consistent basis from year to year at the lower of the cost (including the overheads considered appropriate) and market, as in America; or the lower of the cost and net realisable value as in the United Kingdom and Canada. The accounts should state the basis of valuation adopted. The effect on the accounts of any material change in the basis of valuation between one year's end and the next year should be noted. The auditors should carry out such audit tests on the inventories as they think necessary. The differences of emphasis which exist as regards recognised basis of inventory valuation among the three nations is a subject for further study, research and discussion.

Market Value

Having discussed the method of ascertainment of the cost price, let us now see how the 'market price' is found out. Ordinarily, it would appear that the 'market price' would be the same as that of the similar goods in the market. But it is not so simple. There are two aspects of the Market Value, viz.,

(*a*) *Replacement Value*, i.e., the amount which would be required to purchase the same kind of goods which are in stock at the date of the balance sheet, i.e., the cost of replacing the stock at the date of the balance sheet should be considered as the 'market price' of the goods. It is applied only when Replacement Cost would be less than the actual cost.

(*b*) *Market Value*, i.e. the estimated net amount that the goods would realise when sold, after deducting the estimated expenses such as allowances, selling and distributing charges, etc., would be the 'market value' of the stock or in other words realisable value.

While discussing the formulas to be adopted, as explained above, one has to take into consideration the purpose for which stock is held, viz.,

(i) Whether the goods are held in stock for use; or

(*ii*) Whether such goods are regularly sold or they are not to be replaced when sold out.

At no time the market value be used, when it is in excess of the cost.

Methods used in the Valuation of Different Kinds of Goods

Goods may be divided into (*a*) Raw Materials; (*b*) Semi-finished Goods; (*c*) Finished Goods; and (*d*) Stores.

(*a*) Raw Materials

These are the materials which are purchased for the purpose of manufacturing goods. Such materials must be valued at the net invoice price, i.e., the cost price plus a reasonable proportion of freight, duty, etc., in connection therewith. Sufficient provision should be made for any fall in the value of these materials. If such raw materials have been purchased in different lots and they can be distinguished from one another, there will be no difficulty in assessing their value. But if the different lots cannot be identified from one another, an average price may be taken as has been explained previously. Care must be taken that such raw materials should never be valued at a higher price than the market price. If the price of the finished goods, in which such raw materials are used, goes down, calculation should be made by taking into account the expenses of manufacture and find out whether it would result in a profit. If not, the depreciation of raw materials should be written off.

Some materials generally appreciate in value with the passage of time, *e.g.*, wine, timber, tobacco, rice, etc., and therefore, they are valued at a high price than the cost price in order to cover the storage charges, interest on capital locked up in such goods, and the better quality which is the result of passage of time. To value such goods at a higher price than the cost price seems to be reasonable. But the auditor should see that they .are not valued at a very high price and that they are not valued at a high price than the market price of similar goods of similar quality. This principle does not apply in the case of obsolete, out for fashion, unsaleable, and damaged goods.

(*b*) Semi-manufactured Goods

It may so happen that at the date of the balance sheet, some goods might be in the process of manufacture, i.e., they have not been completely manufactured. In such a case, they are valued at cost price of the raw materials used, plus a proportionate amount of wages and a percentage to cover establishment charges relating to manufacture as per the certificate given by the departmental manager. The auditor should also examine cost sheets.

The term 'work-in-progress' is used in connection with the contract work which has not been completed at the date of the balance sheet. This topic will be dealt with at the appropriate place.

(*c*) Finished Goods

The cost price of the finished goods which have been purchased is the purchase price, i.e., the invoice price and the direct expenditure, *e.g.*, carriage inward, custom duty, dock charges, etc.

The goods which have been manufactured by the concern, are valued like the semi-manufactured goods as explained above, i.e., the cost of the raw materials and proportionate expenses of manufacture. The auditor should refer to the Cost Accounts if they are maintained. He should also see that such finished goods are not valued at a higher price than the price of such goods prevailing in the market. Sometimes it so happens that the cost of manufacture is very high in the initial states of the establishment of a factory and consequently the cost of production of such goods may be higher than the same kind of goods available in the market. As mentioned above, such goods must be valued at the lower price, i.e., the market price.

The overhead expenses on finished or semi-finished goods are apportioned according to the 'Direct Labour' of either (*a*) the last month, or (*b*) the time spent in the manufacture of the goods, or (*c*) the average wages of the year, or (*d*) the volume of production.

(*d*) Stores

There are goods, other than those described above, which may be in hand at the date of the balance sheet. Stores are not held for sale in the original form. Such goods are oil, tallow, grease, dyes, fuel, etc. These stores must not be included in the list of the stock-in-hand. They should be shown separately and those stores which had been consumed during the process of manufacture must be put on the debit side of the Manufacturing Account of the particular period to arrive at the correct cost of production.

As regards the valuation of such stores, it may be pointed out here that the general practice is that they are valued at cost price. If the market price of such stores had gone down, it is suggested by some accountants that they must be written down. There are others who say that the stores should be valued at cost price even if their market price has gone down in order to find out the actual cost of production of goods.

Spare Parts

The spare parts are used for the upkeep of the plants and machinery. The auditor should get a list of such spare parts from the Works Manager. Whenever such parts are used, the Plant and Machinery Account should be debited. Spare part should not be included in the Stock Sheets. They should be valued at cost price and need not be written down to the market value if that value is lower at the date of the balance sheet.

Goods on Consignment

Sometimes goods are sent out to agents to be sold on behalf and at the risk of the consignor. It may so happen that at the date of the balance sheet, the whole of the consignment or a part of it may not have been sold. In such a case the unsold stock has to be verified and valued for the purpose of incorporation in the balance sheet of the consignor. The auditor should ask for a certificate from the consignee to ascertain the amount of stock with him if he is not satisfied by examining the Account Sales.

Having satisfied himself about the quality of the unsold consignment he should find out the basis of its valuation. It should be valued at cost price plus the proportionate expenses, e.g., freight, dock dues, custom duty, godown rent, etc. If any expenses has been incurred to sell out any part of the consignment, e.g., auctioneer's commission, it should not be allocated to the unsold stock.

The unsold consignment of goods, as mentioned above, should be valued at cost price, plus proportionate expenses, etc., but in no case it should be valued at higher price than market price of similar goods. The anticipated losses, however, should be taken into consideration while valuating such stock of goods.

Sometimes the consignor, while sending out the goods, marks them at the selling price so that the consignee may not know the cost price. In such a case, the auditor should see that necessary adjustment is made in regard to the closing stock with the consignee. If that were not done, the stock would be valued may at higher price than the cost price.

The auditor should particularly see that the consignment received by his client is not included in his stock as it does not belong to him.

Goods on Approval

If the goods have been sent out on approval and they have not been approved of till the date of the balance sheet, they should not be treated as 'sales' but should be considered as 'stock with the customers' or 'stock on approval'. If the date, by which the customer ought to have sent his approval, has expired and he has not sent his approval, the goods may be treated as sold. In such a case, the auditor should inspect the contract with the customer. The unapproved goods must be valued at cost price less damages, if any, caused during the course of transit. In no case should such goods be valued at higher than the market price.

The auditor should also see that if his client has received any goods on approval, and has neither sent his approval nor has the date by which the approval ought to have been sent expired, they are not included in the stock.

Stock of Plantation Products

In the case of plantations, e.g., tea, rubber, coffee, etc., the annual accounts are usually prepared after the crop is sold out.

The companies usually value the closing stock at an expected sale price in the subsequent year less the estimated selling expenses. The object is to know the profit or loss on the crop although it might not have been sold at the date of the balance sheet. If this basis is adopted, the fact should be clearly indicated in the accounts.

The Duty of an Auditor in connection with Stock-in-trade

The duty of an auditor in connection with the stock can be summarised as follows: (1) to verify the existence of stock (2) to check the ownership of the stock (3) to see that the stock is properly valued.

The auditor must be cautious that no manipulations have been made by the management in accounts by resorting to undesirable practices with regard to determination of physical quantity of stock, or inclusion of stock over which the entity does not have ownership or incorrect valuation of stock. The following methods may be used to distort the true and fair value of stocks :

(*a*) Incorrect additions and calculation in the Stock Sheets.

(*b*) Incorrect valuation of the closing stock in the Stock Sheets.

(*c*) Inclusion of such stocks of goods in Stock Sheets as have been purchased but the relative invoices for which have not been passed through the purchases Book.

(*d*) Inclusion of such goods as tools, furniture, etc., in the Stock Sheets.

(*e*) To overvalue the stock, by not providing depreciation on obsolete, damaged, out-of-fashion goods, etc.

(*f*) Inclusion of those goods in Stock Sheets which have been sold and passed through the Sale Book but which have not been delivered to the buyer.

In order to guard against these, the auditor must devise his audit checks carefully to cover the following areas viz., ensuring correct physical stock taking, ensuring ownership of the entity over the stocks included in accounts and ensuring correct valuation.

1. Physical verification of stocks :

Physical verification of stocks is the prime responsibility of the management of the entity. Justice Lindlay in the case of *Kingston Cotton Mills Co.*, Ltd., (1896) said it is no part of an auditor's duty to take stock.If one were to relay on the decision of this case, it would be quite fair for the auditor to get the certificate from the management about the physical quantity of the stock lying with the entity at the year end and the auditor need not be unduly concerned about the physical existence of stocks. As a matter of disclosure, the auditor may state in his report that the stock is accounted as valued and certified by the management.

The question is whether such a report will absolve the auditor of his responsibility if it is found later on that in fact so much stock did not exist or it was not properly valued. The answer is given in the judgment of P. Chakravarti, C.J. in the case of *Deputy Secretary, Ministry of Home Affairs* vs. *S.N. Das Gupta*, which is given below:

"With regard to the first finding which relates to the failure to verify the cash in respect of the years 1942 and 1943, Mr. Sen contended that since the respondent stated in his special report that he had not verified the cash, he absolved himself from liability. I am afraid the argument was entirely misconceived... the lapse is constituted by his failure to perform a duty without which an audit is meaningless and it is not excused by giving information of the omission to the shareholders... If Mr. Sen's arguments were correct, an auditor might do nothing at all nor even look into the account and yet say with complete immunity in his report to the shareholders that he had done nothing and assumed no responsibility whether for any inaccuracy or untruth in the balance sheet or profit and loss account. The absurdity of such a contention if advanced would be obvious."

Therefore, it would appear that even such a qualified report in regard to stock-in-trade will not relieve the auditor of his liability.

Spicer and Pegler in their book on auditing in 1961 Edition wrote: "... the decision in the case of *Kingston Cotton Mills* was taken more than a century back. At that time the of skill and care required of an auditor probably was not very exacting standard as it is today." In England the Companies Act was amended in 1948 according to which the auditor has *to state in his* certificate that the balance sheet and the profit and loss account represent a *true and fair* view of the state of affairs of the company which means that the assets (which include stock also) are neither over-stated nor under-stated.

F.R.M. de Paula in his book, *The Principles of Auditing*, Eleventh Edition, writes: "... but, in the author's opinion, an auditor today would be running considerable risks if he acted too literally upon this decision. (*Kingston Cotton Mills*) which is an old one, and opinions and practice have changed greatly since this case was decided. For, if the auditor were to accept, say, the manager's certificate, without in any way checking or testing the stock, the audit will be a little short of farce, for although every other item in the balance sheet many be tested and checked in every way, yet if the auditor merely relies upon a certificate as regards the stock, it means that the official responsible for the valuation of the stock can make the account show whatever results he pleases..." Again, "... a too literal construction should not be placed upon the ruling in the Kingston Cotton Mills case.""

"The standard of reasonable care and skill are, with expert advice, more exacting today than it prevailed in 1896 when the leading case of *Kingston Cotton Mills Co.* was decided", said Mr. Justice Peunyenick in re *Thomas Gerrard & Sons, Ltd.* (1967).

American accounts have not accepted the principle laid down in the *Kingston Cotton Mills* case that it is no part of the duty of an auditor to take stock since the decision in the case of *McKesson and Robins* in 1939 when fictitious entries were made in the Stock Sheets to the extent of $10 million.

The foregoing discussion can be summarised as under :

(*a*) The Kingston Cotton Mills case (1896) held the view that the auditor has no duty with regard to stock taking. It could then imply that the auditor can rely on the figures of stock as certified by the management of the entity.

(*b*) Subsequent decisions in England, U.S.A., and India have relegated the decision of the *Kingston Cotton Mills* case as view of past. It was considered to be professional absurdity to pass over a representation of management to the readers of the financial statements without checking its veracity if the checking is within the power and competence of the auditor.

Now the interesting question arises. Whether physical verification of stock is within the power of auditor and if the auditor has power to inspect the stocks what is the manner in which he can perform it commensurate to his competence and professional requirement?

There is no provision in the Companies Act to empower the auditor to physically examine the assets (cash, investments, stock-in-hand) with a view to discharge his duties honestly. The only power which is given to an auditor in this respect is given S. 227 which lays down:

(*a*) The auditor of a company has a right of access, at all times, to the books and accounts and vouchers of the company...

(*b*) The auditor of a company is entitled to require from the officers of the company such information and explanation as the auditor may think necessary for the performance of his duties as auditor.

From the above it will be clear that the auditor has no power according to law to physically inspect the assets, including the stock-in-hand, of the company.

Though the accepted practice of the American Accountants has not been accepted in India and, therefore, an auditor may or may not physically verify the stock-in-trade but according to the Companies Act, 1956, he has to give a certificate which implies that he has physically checked the stock. For instance S. 209 of the Companies Act lays down: "Every company shall keep ... proper books of account with respect to:

(*a*) all sums of money received and expended by the company and the the matters in respect of which the receipt and expenditure take place;

(*b*) all sales and purchases of goods by the company; and

(*c*) the assets and liabilities of the company.

We have italicised the word "*shall*" to show that it is mandatory for a company to maintain such books which record purchases and sales. Moreover, the work "assets" includes stock-in-trade. Thus it is necessary for an auditor to check those books which record stock-in-trade. If he fails to do so he would be held liable as was decided in *re. Westminster Road Cinstruction and Engineering Co. (1932)*. Unless he has physically checked the closing stock how can he give a certificate that the books of account give a *true and fair* view of the state of the affairs of the company. Again S. 541 (2) lays down : " ... it shall be deemed that proper books of account have not been kept in the case of any company, if there have not been kept.

(*a*) * * * * *

(*b*) Where the business of the company has involved dealings in goods, statements of the annual stock-taking and (except in the case of goods sold by way of ordinary retail trade) of all goods sold and purchased, showing the goods and the buyers and sellers thereof in sufficient detail to enable those goods and these buyers and sellers to be identified.

Part II of Schedule VI of Companies Act lays down that the figures for the opening and closing stocks must be given. Part I of this schedule lays down that the mode of valuation of stock-in-trade shall be stated.

Again, according to S. 227 (2) (*ii*) (*c*) an auditor has to report whether the company's balance sheet and profit and loss account dealt with by the report are in agreement with the books of account and returns. Therefore, unless he is satisfied with the quantity of stock-in-hand, he cannot give such a report.

Moreover, when other assets like cash, investments, etc., are subject to physical verification, there seems to be no reason why the stock-in-trade should not be physically checked. Of course, it is very difficult to do so but a test check of the stock-in-trade and a certificate from the third parties with whom a part of such stock may be, in the absence of any suspicious circumstances, will relieve the auditor of his responsibility.

It is relevant here to have a look at the requirements of CARO 2003 under section 227 (4A) of the Companies Act (for details refer the chapter on Audit of Limited Companies—Auditor's Report). The order requires the auditor's comment on the actual physical verification of stock during the year, the adequacy of procedures adopted for physical verification etc. If the auditor has to effectively comment on these, it would be necessary for him to concern himself with the physical verification of stocks.

Now it follows that the auditor is concerned with ensuring that fair physical verification of stocks has taken place. If so, the next question arises as to the manner in which the auditor has to satisfy this.

The Institute of Chartered Accountants of India has issued a guidance note on audit of inventories. Among other things, it suggests three methods for ensuring physical existence of stocks. They are (*a*) attendance of the auditor at stock taking (*b*) examination of records and (*c*) confirmation from third parties.

(*a*) Attendance of auditor during physical verification of stocks:

According to the guidance note, it would be appropriate for the auditor to present himself or depute his assistants at the time of physical verification of the stocks. Such attendance will give the auditor an opportunity to evaluate the efficacy and adequacy of physical verification of stocks. The auditor should see that the physical verification of stock is conducted in a systematic manner. Necessary written instructions must be given to the persons engaged in stock taking regarding the procedures and methods to be followed in stock-taking. These written instructions must preferably be drafted in consultation with the auditor. The auditor should observe that the instructions are followed by the persons while doing stock-taking. The auditor may, himself, perform certain test counts of stocks in respect of stocks of higher value. During stock taking the auditor must ask the client to stop movement of goods till the completion of the physical verification. If it cannot be ensured, the movement should be distinctly monitored. The auditor should ensure that those stocks over which the entity does not have ownership are segregated. During stock taking itself, the damaged or obsolete stocks should be identified and noted. The auditor should document his test checking in his working papers.

(*b*) Examination of records:

The auditor should study the internal control prevailing in the organisation regarding purchases, sales, maintenance of stocks and stock-taking. It is necessary that good internal checks should be introduced for stock taking. The store keepers should not be asked to physically verify the stocks for checking discrepancies. The physical count sheets should be signed by the person who counted the stocks. Alterations in the physical count sheets should be authenticated by initials. All the physical count sheets should be collected and classified summary sheet with valuation should be prepared by some other responsible person. The discrepancy between physical stock and balances as per bin card/stores ledger must be ascertained and serious discrepancies must be inquired into. Adjustment entries for shortage or excess should be passed by the responsible official after due warning to the custodians of stocks. The auditor must evaluate that good internal control operates in the entity. He must check the additions, multiplications, carry-over etc in the stock sheets. He may compare the physical count sheets with his working papers in respect of stocks which he test-counted. He must check the calculations in summary sheet and compare the balances with such accounting records as bin cards, stores ledgers etc. He must vouch entries for shortages/excess of stocks, provision for obsolescence with necessary supporting evidence. He may critically examine the correctness of stock figure with the use of gross profit ratio.

(*c*) Verification of confirmation

Sometimes, stock may lie with third parties in which case the physical verification may not be easily possible. For example, goods may lie with fabricators for certain processing or with consignee etc. In such case, the auditor should see that it is within usual business of the entity to have the stocks lying with such parties. The auditor should obtain confirmation from the party that the stocks are lying with them on behalf of the entity in good condition and with no encumbrance. The value of the stocks should also be ascertained. The auditor should check the confirmation and reconcile the figure with the figures as per records kept by the entity.

2. Ensuring the ownership over the Stocks :

The auditor should verify that the stocks reflected in balance sheet belong to the client. Stocks held by the entity as consignee or agent of another person should be excluded from value of stock. The auditor should pay particular attention to cut-off transactions. That is, he must check goods inward notes and invoices of certain days prior to and subsequent to the date of closing of accounts. It may so happen that goods would have been received and goods received notes would have been prepared before the close of accounting period. But the relative supplier's bills might be recorded for the period after the close of accounting period. In such cases, if the goods received without bills are included in stock, necessary liability for pending bills should also be created by way of provision. Sometimes things may happen otherwise. The delivery notes or documents of title to goods (say lorry receipts, ship bills etc) would have been made out in favour of the entity on dates prior to closing of accounts. But the goods would not have reached the entity. In such cases, the entity may account such goods as `goods in transit' after accounting or creating provision for bills in this respect. With regard to sales, the entity would have raised sale invoices and gate passes/delivery notes on dates prior to closing of accounts. But the goods would not have been moved out from the entity prior to closing of accounts. In such cases, the stocks sold but still lying with the entity should not be taken as the stock of the entity. Again, the entity may have certain encumbrances with regard to the ownership of the stock. A common example would be the stocks being given as security to bank by way of hypothecation for the borrowings of the entity. Such claim of others over the stock should be ascertained carefully and the fact should be disclosed in the balance sheet.

3. Valuation of Stocks

The basic principles for valuation of stocks are detailed in Accounting Standard 2 (AS-2) of the Institute of Chartered Accountants of India. Accordingly the stocks must be valued at the lower of cost and market price. Certain inventories like spares, maintenance supplies etc may be valued at cost, however. The cost of the goods must be ascertained correctly. In case the goods are manufactured by the entity, the cost should include all direct expense and relevant portion of production overhead only. The comparison of cost and market price may be made for individual items of stock or on aggregate items of stocks (global method). As far as possible the cost and market price of each and every item of stock must be compared and the least of them should be taken as rate for valuation. In case of similar or interchangeable items of stocks the global method of valuation of stocks may be followed. That is, the cost prices of stocks are applied on quantities of stocks and total cost of the stock is aggregated. Similarly aggregate market value of total stocks is ascertained. The aggregate cost and aggregate market value of stocks are compared and the lower of them is taken to be the value of the stocks. Again according to AS-2, the valuation should be consistently followed year after year. If the valuation method is changed, it should be disclosed in the accounts, indicating the impact on the profit /loss of the entity. The duties of the auditor with regard to valuation of stocks are summaried hereunder:

1. The auditor should see that the goods are properly valued. For the purpose of finding out the cost price, he will have to refer to the original invoices, cost accounts and market prices, which can be ascertained from the financial papers, etc. He should see that the basic principles regarding the valuation of the stock as mentioned previously are followed correctly.
2. He should find our whether the calculations, additions and castings in the Stock Sheets are correct.
3. He should also see that proper provision is made for depreciation of the damaged, obsolete, out-of-fashion stock, etc., in order to find out the exact value of stock in hand.
4. He shold see that the same basis of valuation is followed year after year to enable comparison of profit of different years. It is adviable that he should get a certificate to this effect from his client.
5. He should see that the Stock Sheets are signed by a responsible official and a certificate is appended to the Stock Sheet thus: "I certify that the quantities, prices and calculations by which the stock-in-hand amountng to Rs ... on the ... day of ... 19 .. has been arrived at, are correct. The prices are reasonable and are taken at cost price or market price whichever is lower at the date of stock-taking.All goods included in the stock are the sole property of ....and invoices in respect of all goods included in the stock have been entered in the books as purchases prior to the date of stock-taking." The auditor is entitled to rely upon such certificate, the trusted servants and employees of the concern, in the absence of anything which may otherwise arouse his suspicion. But the auditor should not take it for granted that the Stock Sheets are correct because they have been signed by a responsible official.
6. He should see that the goods with the consignees or at branches or sent out on approval, etc., are not valued at selling prices. If this is the case, the stock will be over vauled and the unrealised profit will be included in the year's profits.
7. He should compare the percentage of gross profit to turnover for the previous two or three years and inquire into any considerable fluctuation, if any.
8. He should compare the Stock Sheet of the previous year with the current year and if there is a considerable difference in the closing stock of the two periods he should enquire into the matter.

9. He should examine the Purchases and Sales Books, Goods Returned Inward and Outward Books and the Stock Book for the last one week or so to ascertain that the goods purchased and sold before the close of the financial year are recorded both in the Purchase and Sales Books as well as in the Stock Book.
10. The auditor should see that the stock-in-trade is shown in the balance sheet of a company according to Schedule VI, Part I of the Companies Act, i.e., (a) the mode of valuation of stock-in-trade and work-in-progress should be stated, (b) the amount of raw materials, as far as practicable, be stated separately, (c) whether there is a change in the mode of valuation of the stock from the previous year.

Valuation of Fixed Assets

The usual method of the valuation of fixed assets is the cost price less depreciation. But the problem may arise when it is desired to replace the assets during the inflation period. It has been suggested that during the inflationary period, the replacement cost method should be followed while valuing the assets on the balance sheet date, i.e., they should be valued according to the amount required to replace that asset. The object of the replacement cost method is to charge the revenue account to provide the amount needed to meet the cost of replacement. Under this method, provision for replacement would be made instead of the usual rate of depreciation on the historical cost to amortise the cost of the fixed assets over their useful life.

This method was in vogue in the past. It was followed by the public utility undertakings.

Difficulties under this method

Unless the asset is to be replaced within a short period, it is difficult to accurately estimate the replacement value of the asset after a very long time. Moreover many calculations will have to be made. Again, new methods of production and new and better type of machinery and plant, due to technological development , may bee airlable in the market, which the management might like to purchase but the price of which cannot be predicted, makes it very difficult to estimate the amount required to replace the asset.

7. Book Debts

The auditor should see that the debts as shown in the balance sheet are recoverable. If they are doubtful, provision should be made for them. If they are bad, i.e., they are irrecoverable, they should not be shown on the assets side. If the auditor does not pay any attention to these points, the balance sheet which he certifies to show a "true and fair view" may be wrong and he might be held liable for damages.

In the case of the balance sheet of an individual or a firm, no prescribed form to show the book debts is laid down but the Companies Act has prescribed the form of the balance sheet *vide* Schedule VI, Part I, according to which the sundry debts should be shown as under:

(*a*) Debts considered good and in respect of which the company is fully secured;

(*b*) Debts considered good for which the company holds no security other than the debtor's personal security;

(*c*) Debts considered doubtful or bad; and

(*d*) Less Provision.

Debts due by directors or other officers of the company or any of them either severally or jointly with any other person or debts due by firms or private companies respectively in which may director is a partner or director or member are to be separately stated.

Debts due from other companies under the same management should be indicated with the names of the companies (*vide* S. 370). If any debt is due from a subsidiary company, the auditor should find out whether it is genuine. Confirmation by the subsidiary company regarding the debt may not be a good proof. In such a case the auditor should examine the agreement or any other documentary evidence available to see the genuineness of the debt.

The maximum amount due by directors or other officers of the company at any time during the year should be shown by way of a note.

It is not possible for an auditor to know the financial position of the debtors of his client. Then how can he certify the balance sheet showing the amount of book debts? Still if he applies the tests mentioned in Chapter IV as to how to find out whether a debt is good, doubtful or bad, he would have done his duty and would be free from any lability. Therefore, the auditor should apply these tests. After he has done that, he should see that sufficient provision is made for doubtful or bad debts. For debts which have been written off, he should examine the correspondence, counterfoils of the dividends paid and any other relevant documentary evidence available.

Debts due from foreign countries should be converted in home currency. If accordingly less amount is there due provision should be made for the deficiency.

If the customers have purchased goods on hire purchase system from the client and some instalments are still to be paid, they should not be treated as book debts as the customers have the option to return the goods. But if the date of the payment of the instalment has expired, the amount should be treated as debt. In such a case provision should be made for a possible bad debt."

8. Endowment Policies

Sometimes Endowment Policies are taken out to provide funds for redeeming some liability falling due at a later date or to replace an asset later on. The most common form of such policies is Sinking fund Policies for the redemption of Debentures. The auditor should physically inspect the policies and see that the premium payable has been paid and that the policy has not lapsed."

9. Patent Rights and Trade Marks

The Patent Rights and Trade Marks are verified by examining the certifiers granting such rights or marks. If they have been purchased the auditor should examine the assignment deed and see that they have been duly registered in the name of his client.

If the client holds large number of patents or trade marks the auditor should ask him to prepare a schedule giving (*a*) the description of the patent, (*b*) registered numbers, (*c*) the dates on which they were acquired, and (*d*) the unexpired period. The auditor should examine the receipts for the payment of the fees. He should also see that the renewal fee has been paid each year at the right time. If is has not been paid, the patent will lapse. A patent has 16 years of life, unless the term has been extended. After the expiry of that period the right automatically lapses. If a patent has been allowed to lapse, the resolution of the Board should be examined.

With regard to the valuation of these assets, it may be mentioned here that with the lapse of time, they lose their value, i.e., they are subject to the depreciation. The causes for the depreciation are (*a*) lapse of time, (*b*) obsolescence and (*c*) the patented article going out of fashion, etc.

Under the above circumstances such assets should be revalued at the date of the balance sheet. They must be depreciated as mentioned above. Their value may be estimated according to the unexpired period. In no case should they be valued at a higher figure than the amount at which they were purchased even though its present value may be higher than the cost price."

The fees paid for purchasing or taking out such rights are in the nature of capital expenditure and therefore they should be debited to the Patent Account or Trade Mark Account, as the case may be, while the renewal fees are of revenue nature and should, therefore, be debited to the profit and loss account.

If the client has created the patent by doing some research work, the money spent for the research work should be capitalised. The auditor should see that only the cost incurred in doing the research work should be debited to the Patent Account.

10. Copyright

This is a sole right to produce or reproduce a book or an article. The life of copyright is the lifetime of the author and fifty years after his death. Excepting this all the remarks relating to patents apply to this type of assets. Actually the value of the copyright is not very firm because they lose their value by the lapse of time. Copyrights, therefore, must be revalued at the date of the balance sheet. If the publication does not command any sale, the copyright should be written off.

11. Assets in a Foreign Country

If documents relating to property in a foreign country are at the head office, the auditor should examine them. However, if they are not available, a certificate from the local auditor should be sought for and examined. The auditor should see that the certificate discloses in clear terms that the assets are free from any charge. The auditor should mention this fact in his report.

12. Furniture and Fixtures

The auditor should verify this item with the help of invoices. Any additions made during the year should be verified in the usual way. Any expense incurred in the purchase of this asset should be debited to the Furniture Account. The auditor should see that proper depreciation is provided and that the net figure is shown in the balance sheet. The amount of depreciation will depend upon the use to which it is put, e.g., depreciation of furniture will be more in the case of an hotel than in an office. Repairs to furniture during the year should be debited to revenue account.

The auditor should see that whenever a piece of furniture is purchased an entry is made in Furniture Stock Register. Every piece of furniture should be numbered to avoid the risk of pilferage. Demaged and unserviceable furniture should be written off by a responsible officer.

13. Plant and Machinery

This item is also verified by reference to the original invoices, correspondence, etc. Expenses incurred on custom duty, freight, erection of machinery, etc., should be debited to Machinery Account while repairs should be charged to revenue account. The auditor should see that plant and machinery is properly depreciated . As the auditor is not a technical hand, it may not be possible for him to find out the rate at which depreciation is to be provided; he may have to depend upon the advice of the Works Manager or the engineer. If Plant Register is maintained, much difficulty will be minimised. Plant and Machinery Account should be shown in the balance sheet at cost less depreciation after making necessary adjustment regarding purchases of machinery made and sale of some parts effected during the year by the concern itself. If plant and machinery is kept abroad, the auditor should get a certificate from the local auditor with regard to the machinery.

14. Loose Tools, Patterns, Dies, etc.

Such assets have short useful life and the value per unit is also low. Hence no separate account is maintained for each unit. There is a danger of pilferage of such assets and therefore proper supervision over these should be exercised. The auditor should examine the list of the loose tools. He should see that the list has been certified by a responsible officer. This type of asset comprises items like small tools, dies, jigs, moulds, etc. Some of them are liable to be lost and some of them consumed very rapidly. Hence the conventional method of depreciation is not applied to them. Montgomery suggests: "charging the cost of replacement of such items to maintenance in lieu of depreciating them is usually a satisfactory alternative." The suggestion is very reasonable."

Where the concern makes its own tools, the auditor should see that they are not valued in excess of the cost.

15. Property

The auditor is not competent to examine the title deeds relating to a property. In such a case he should insist upon the client to get a certificate regarding their validity from the solicitor. A certificate from an architect, surveyor or an engineer will also serve the purpose of the valuation of the property.

The property may be (*a*) Freehold property, and (*b*) Leasehold property. Let us see how each class of property is verified and valued.

(a) Freehold Property

The auditor should examine the title deeds relating to the property. If it has been purchased, correspondence and broker's or auctioneer's account should be examined. If it has been built, the Builder's or Contractor's and Architect's certificates should be examined. If the property has been mortgaged and the title-deeds are with the mortgagee, the auditor should get a certificate from the mortgagee, regarding the possession of the title-deeds and the amount of the loan. If the title-deeds are with the solicitor or bankers for safe custody, it is better to get a certificate from the custodians lest the title-deeds might have been kept with them as security for a loan. The auditor should see that the property is in the name of his client. He should see that the conveyance deed has been duly registered in accordance with Section 17 (1) of the Indian Registration Act. The auditor should get a certificate from the legal adviser of his client regarding the validity of the litle-deeds relating to the property.

If any property has been purchased during the year, it should be vouched. The property Account should be shown in the balance sheet at cost including the legal and registration charges, less depreciation up-to-date.

While valuing the land and building, it should be remembered that no notice of appreciation or fall in their market value is taken into consideration. But if the management decides to appreciate the value of the asset, the auditor should see that the appreciated adjustment is disclosed in the balance sheet for a period of five years as is required by the Companies Act.

It should be seen that there are separate accounts for building and the land on which it is constructed because depreciation has to be provided for building while there is no depreciation of land. IF there are no separate accounts, the valuer or the architect can find out the cost of the building and the land unless some documentary evidence is available showing the cost of land.

(*b*) Heasehold Property

Lease deed should be examined to find out its value and duration. He should see that the lease has been duly registered with the Registrar if it is for a period of more than one year as per the requirements of section 107 of the Transfer of Property Act. The lease money paid should be capitalised. Any legal expense or other expenses incurred in acquiring the lease should also be capitalised.Lease rent should be debited to the revenue account. The lease money and other capitalised expenses should be spread over the number of years of the lease and debited to revenue account. In case of a lease of building, depreciation, insurance against fire, necessary repairs, etc., should be debited to revenue account. He should also examine the last receipt for the payment of the lease rent.

16. Goodwill

Goodwill is defined as the assessed value of the reputation of a business or as the difference between the purchase price and the net assets which are purchased and the excess amount so paid, represents the goodwill acquired by the business. It is an intangible asset. Its value depends upon the earning capacity of the business and fluctuates accordingly, i.e., it increases with the rise in profits and decreases with the fall of profits. However, it is not valued at the date of the balance sheet like other assets. In case the Directors have debited the profit and loss account and credited the amount to the goodwill account, the auditor should object to this step especially when the action taken is likely to prejudice the interest of any class of shareholders. He should mention this fact in his report to the shareholders if such a step has been taken. It does not depreciate even with the lapse of time.

If it is shown in the books of account, the auditor should verify it by referring to the contract with the vendors to find its value.

Sometimes, goodwill is created by incurring very heavy expenditure in introducing a new invention in the market. Such expenditure is capitalised and this is called `deferred goodwill'. The auditor should enquire into the reason for doing so. Sometimes when the current expenditure is unnecessarily high, the management capitalises some of the expenditure by debiting the goodwill account to conceal the high expenditure. This is a wrong method. The auditor should see that regular revenue expenditure is not capitalised. Deferred goodwill must be clearly shown in the balance sheet to differentiate it from the `purchased goodwill'. Such a goodwill must be written off within a reasonable time.

The company law does not compel a company to show goodwill at its realisable value. It is usually shown at cost less any sum written off. Legally goodwill need not be written off according to the judgment in Wilmer vs. McNamara case but from the sound financial point of views, it must be written off within a reasonable period out of the current profits or reserves, etc. The auditor should see that the goodwill is never appreciated in the books of a company.

Verification of Liabilities

General

Verification of liabilities is also as important as the verification of assets. If the liabilities are overstated or understated the balance sheet shall not represent a true and fair view of the state of affairs of the company. Similarly the profit and loss account will be incorrect. For example if some expenses have been incurred but they have not been entered in the books of account, the profit and loss account will be incorrect and will show more profit and the balance sheet will not show such a liability (Westminister Road Construction and Engineering Co.). The auditor should, besides verifying the liabilities as shown in the balance sheet, should get a certificate from the management that all the liabilities for purchases as well as for expenses or on any other account have been included in the books of account and that the contingent liabilities have been shown by way of a foot-note to the balance sheet or have been provided for."

The verification of the liabilities is much easier than their valuation. Let us see how different items on the liability side of the balance sheet are to be verified and valued.

1. Capital

Although capital is not the liability of a company, still it should be verified to enable an auditor to give a certificate in regard to the correctness of the balance sheet.

If it is the first audit of the company, the auditor should examine Memorandum of Association and the Articles of Association of the Company. He should examine the Cash Book, Pass Book and Minute Book of the Board of Directors to find out the number and the different classes of shares issued, the amount received on each share and the balance due from the Memorandum and Articles of Association, and Minute Book of the Board of Directors should be examined. The auditor should see that the issue of capital is according to the Memorandum and Articles of Association. If any shares have been issued to the vendors the contract between the vendors and the company should be examined.

If it is not the first year of the life of a company, there will be no difficulty as the figures regarding capital will be the same as they were during the previous year unless more capital has been issued during the course of the current year. He should see that the provisions in Schedule VI of Part I of the Companies Act are complied with in disclosing the share capital. For details, reference may be made to the Chapter on the Audit of Limited Companies.

In regard to the capital of a sole trader or a firm, the auditor should examine the Partnership Deed or Agreement, the Cash Book and the bank Pass Book in the year of the establishment of the business. In subsequent years the capital of the proprietor or the partners will increase or decrease according to the profits earned,losses, withdrawals, additions of capital, etc. The auditor, in such a case, should examine the cash book, pass book, partnership agreement, etc.

2. Reserve Accounts and Funds

For the audit of these two items, reference may be made to the Chapter on Reserves.

3. Debentures and Mortgages

The auditor should enquire into the powers of the company to borrow money. (For details, reference may be made to the Chapter on Audit of Limited Companies).

4. Trade Creditors

The auditor should ask for a schedule of the creditors and check it with the Purchases Ledger which in its turn may be checked with the books of original entry with the Purchase Invoices, Credit Notes, Goods Inward Book, Returns Outward Book, Bills Payable Book, Cash Books, etc.

The Auditor should see that all purchases during the year have been included in the purchases and especially purchases made at the close of the year. He should find out whether all purchases made at the close of the year have been credited to the suppliers' accounts by referring to the Goods Inward Book and the Purchases Book. If he deems it necessary, he may ask for statements of account from the creditors to check the accuracy of the amounts. He should compare the percentage of the gross profit with that of the previous years. If there is any appreciable change, he should enquire, If the debt has not been paid for a long time, enquiry should be made. It is possible that instead of paying to the creditor, the amount might have been misappropriated.

5. Bills Payable

The auditor should verify this item from the Bills Payable Book and the Bills Payable Account. The Bills payable already paid should be checked from the Cash Book and examine the returned bills payable. To see the genuineness of the bills payable in hand on the date of the balance sheet, the auditor should check the cash book of the succeeding year as to whether any payment has been made in respect of such bills. In case of suspicion he should ask for the confirmation from the drawers of the bills. If any charge has been created on any asset of the concern by accepting the bill, the fact should be disclosed in the balance sheet.

6. Outstanding Expenses

The auditor should get a certificate from a responsible official to see that all expenses for the current year are included and that the payment for each expenses such as interest, discounts, salaries, wages, legal expenses, which have not been paid are included.Some of the expenses which ought to have been debited to the current year may be apparent, e.g., rent of twelfth month, or salaries payable or electricity charges for the last month, etc. Chapter V may be referred to for details.

7. Loans

Reference may be made to the agreement and correspondence for getting the loan. If interest on the loan has not been paid, he should see that it is shown as a liability. If loan has been secured by mortgaging any property, it should be indicated in the balance sheet. If possible, the auditor should get a confirmatory letter from the party who has advanced the loan regarding the amount of loan, interest due and the security offered, if any. In case the client is a joint-stock company, he should see whether the company is empowered to borrow money according to the Memorandum and Articles of Association and the Companies Act. He should also see that the mortgage has been registered with the Registrar of Companies and an entry has been made in the Register of Mortgages.

In case of bank overdraft, the agreement with the bank and the security offered should be examined.

8. Contingent Liabilities

This topic has already been dealt with in detail in Chapter on "Audit of Impersonal Ledger" and therefore reference may be made to that chapter.

QUESTIONS

1. You are the auditor of a company which prefers to change the method of valuation of stock. So far they were valuing stock at Prime Cost only, but now they intend to add proportional indirect expenses over and above the prime cost. How will you satisfy about the change and what disclosure will you require to be made in the final accounts? *(C.A. Inter., 1971)*
2. In examining the sales ledger balances what points will you take into consideration to satisfy yourself regarding the sufficiency of bad and doubtful debts reserves? *(Poona B. Com. 1964; Delhi B. Com. 1961; Bombay 1968)*
3. What is meant by the term "Verification of Assets"? How does it differ from the term "Valuation of Assets"? State the importance of verification and valuation of assets from the point of view of an auditor of a Limited Company. *(Marathwada, Nagpur and Bombay. B.Com.) (Andhra, Pb. Serv. Commission)*
4. In auditing the Balance Sheet of a limited company, state what steps you would take to verify Sundry Debtors and Creditors and what your duties are regarding these. *(Madurai, Cal. B. Com.)*
5. A Cotton Mill Company places before you their Stock Sheets showing the stock at the end of the year. State how would your proceed to check them and what information would you call for before including the figures of the Stock in the balance sheet before you are called upon to sign. *(Punjab Pb. Serv., Commission 1963)*
6. "An auditor is not a valuer". "An auditor is intimately connected with values". Explain fully how these two statements can be reconciled. *(Cal. M. Com., Poona, Lucknow B. Com.)*
7. As auditor of a public company, how would you verify the following :—
   (*i*) Securities furnished by the employees.
   (*ii*) Increase in the remuneration of the Managing Director.
   (*iii*) Allotment of shares for consideration other than cash.
   (*iv*) Loans given by the company to other companies under the same management *(C.A. Inter. 1971)*
8. When examining the stock sheets of a manufacturing business you notice three items which appear to you to be unusual, viz.,
   (*a*) Goods on Consignment Outwards—valued at market price to which 5% has been added as representing a proportion of the profit which will be made when the goods are sold.
   (*b*) Goods on Consignment Inwards—valued at invoice price.
   (*c*) Goods sold but not delivered—valued at selling price.

What special inquiries would you make in regard to each of the three cases, and if you do not agree with the methods of treatment, how would you suggest the items should be shown?

9. A large engineering company finds itself unable to undertake physical verification of its inventories (which covers more than 100 items of consumable materials) and mainly relies on its stock ledgers for the inclusion of closing stock in its final accounts and undertakes such physical verification once in three years. Upon such verification, you find substantial differences in the actual stock as compared to the stock shown by its stock ledgers. Discuss how you, as auditor, would consider this matter. *(C.A. Final, 1971)*

10. How would you verify the following liabilities appearing in the Balance Sheet of P and Y, a partnership firm: —

(*i*) Bank overdraft of Rs. 74,600, which is secured against bills drawn by the firm. The overdraft is also guaranteed by Shri Yashwant, a partner of the firm; and

(*ii*) Unsecured loans from various parties amounting to Rs. 81, 360 @ 12% interest ?

(C.A. Inter., 1971)

11. (*a*) As auditor, what records would you expect to find out the value of goods sent out on approval?

(*b*) To what points would you pay attention in checking the value of goods included in the Balance Sheet as "on approval"?

12. What is the liability of an auditor of a Public Company with regard to the stock-in-trade of manufacturing business? *(Andhra Pub. Serv. Commission 1962)*

13. Valuation of investments depends largely upon the objects for which they are held. Discuss the statement describing the procedure of valuation to be adopted under different circumstances. *(Delhi B. Com. 1964)*

14. After vouching has been done to the satisfaction of the auditor of a public Limited Company, do you think it is necessary for him to consider the question of valuation and verification of assets? What consequence might follow if valuation and verification are not carried out by auditors in respect of the assets appearing in the Balance Sheet to be certified?

(Calcutta B. Com. 1960)

15. What are the duties of an auditor regarding the valuation and verification of stock-in-trade of a manufacturing concern? State the facts of and judgement in *Kingsten Colten Mills* Co. case heading upon the duties of auditor in regard to stock-in-trade. *(Rajasthan B. Com.)*

16. How would you verify the following assets and liabilities : —

(*a*) Provision for taxation.

(*b*) Leasehold property.

(*c*) Contingent liabilities. *(C.A. Inter Nov. 1976)*

17. At the date of the Balance Sheet,a manufacturing concern has outstanding forward contracts for the supply to it of its principle raw materials on a price substantially higher than the market price. No reference to the matter appears under the Profit and Loss Account and the Balance Sheet presented to you for audit. What would you do?

(Annamalai B. Com.; Cal M. Com. 1968)

18. How would you verify and treat the following transactions:

(*a*) Payment of Interest out of Capital;

(*b*) Preliminary Expenses.

(*c*) Remuneration to Managing Agents. *(Annamalai M. Com. 1961)*

19. State how would you verify any two of the following liabilities of a limited company:

(*a*) Provision for accruing liabilities on account of gratuity.

(*b*) Provision for taxation.

(*c*) Sundry creditors for goods supplied. *(C.A. Final 1971)*

Chapter 20

Depreciation

General Definition

The word 'Depreciation' is derived from a Latin word *Depretium*. If we analyse this word, *de* means decline and *pretium* means price. Thus it means decrease in the value of fixed or capital assets. Depreciation has been defined as the decrease in the value of an asset on account of natural wear and tear or effluxion of time. It may be argued that sometimes the value of a fixed asset increases by effluxion of time (whether the asset is in use or not) as during the period of inflation. Again, the value of a fixed asset depreciates though less even if the asset is not in use. One writer has, therefore, defined it as "gradual diminution, loss or shrinkage in the utility value of an asset due to wear and tear in use, effluxion of time or obsolescence."

B.G. Vickery defines it "permanent decrease in the value of an asset through wear and tear in use, or passage of time". Cropper, Marsis and Fission define "Depreciation is a term employed by accountants to indicate the gradual deterioration both in the value and the usefulness of these assets which, by reason of their nature and uses steadily decline in value." Again it has been defined as a permanent and continuing decreases in the value of any asset from any cause.

De Paula says, "In practice, the term 'depreciation' is commonly used in a very wide sense, covering diminution in the value of assets caused by outside fluctuations in realisable and replacement values, and also the amortization in the cost of an asset over the period of its use".

It must be remembered that depreciation as used in accountancy is not the same thing as physical depreciation. Montgomery, the famous American Accountant, in this connection says, "Physical depreciation of property, plant and equipment is generally understood to be the loss in useful life or efficiency caused by wear and tear from operation and by deterioration resulting from chemical reactions from air, water, gas, or other elements. In varying degrees it takes place whether plant and equipment is operated or is idle, whether it is well cared for or neglected, whether it is built from materials of good quality or constructed from scrap."

The Committee on Terminology of the American Institute of Accountants has defined depreciation accounting as —

"Depreciation accounting is a system of accounting which aims at distributing the cost or other basic value of tangible capital assets, less salvage (if any) over the estimated useful life of the unit (which may be a group of assets) in a systematic and rational manner. It is a process of allocation, not of valuation. Depreciation for the year is the position of total charge under such a system that is allocated to the year. Although the allocation may properly take into account occurrences during the year, it is not intended to be a measurement of the effect of all such occurrences."

From the above definitions, it will be found that depreciation is usually in the case of fixed assets and results on account of the following viz,

(*a*) wear and tear

(*b*) effluxion of time

(*c*) obsolescence

(*d*) exhaustion (in case of wasting assets like minerals)

(*e*) effects of weather and other elements

Difference between Depreciation and Fluctuation

Before we proceed further, let us find out the differences between depreciation and fluctuation.

Accountants have sometimes described depreciation as 'Internal Depreciation' and fluctuation as 'External Depreciation'.

1. Depreciation is due to internal causes, i.e., cause inherent in the asset itself, *e.g.*, by constant use of an asset affecting its earning capacity and, therefore, it is a charge against the profits of the year while fluctuation on the other hand is due to external causes which do not affect the earning capacity of the business and, therefore, it is not a charge against the profits of the year. These outside factors, i.e., changes in the market price of the asset, do not affect the earning capacity of the asset and hence such a change is ignored. Moreover such an asset is acquired not for resale.
2. Depreciation always means *decrease* in the value of an asset while fluctuation may mean *either increase or decrease* in the value of an asset.
3. Depreciation is always, *a permanent decrease while fluctuation* is *a temporary* rise or fall in the market value of an asset.
4. Depreciation is a charge against the profits while fluctuation does not affect the profits and hence it is not taken into consideration.
5. Depreciation is in connection with fixed assets while fluctuation is in connection with current assets.

Objects of and necessity for providing Depreciation

1. The depreciation is to be determined and provided in the accounts to find out the correct cost of production. As an asset is put to use for earning profit, it loses its value over a period of time. That is, part of the asset is consumed year after year in the process of its usage. As such, it is like any other expenditure incurred for manufacture of goods. A true and correct cost of production should, therefore, include this diminution in value of assets. Otherwise the cost of production will be wrong and therefore the profit ascertained will be overstated.
2. If depreciation is not provided, the asset will appear in the balance sheet at a value higher than its worth. Hence, the balance sheet will not show the true and fair view of the financial position of the company.
3. The real object of providing depreciation is to keep the capital intact. By charging depreciation in profit and loss account, the amount of distributable profit (i.*e*. net profit) is reduced. The amount of depreciation set apart, accumulate year after year. The accumulated amount can be used to replace the asset when the asset is scrapped. Had the depreciation not been provided, more profits would have been distributed to shareholders and when the asset is scrapped, the whole cost of the asset would represent a capital loss. This capital loss implies reduction in capital. It also implies payment of dividend over years from capital.

4. Lastly, it is necessary to provide depreciation legally in case of company. Under section 205 of the Act, dividend can be declared only after providing for depreciation. In cases of non-corporate entities like proprietorship or partnership, though there is no legal predicament to distribute profit without providing depreciation, it is unadvisable to do so in view of financial prudence.

Basis of Depreciation-Original cost vs Replacement Value

We have said the object of depreciation is to amortise the original cost of the asset over a period of time so that the correct cost of production is ascertained each year. We have also said that the object of depreciation is to replace the asset when it is worn out and to keep the capital intact. It is perfectly correct to calculate depreciation with reference to original cost to find out true cost of production, according to conventional accounting. If amount is set apart for depreciation with reference to the original cost, can the entity be left with adequate amount to replace the asset at future date especially during the period of inflationary trend? Is it not necessary to set apart such amount of depreciation as wold be equal to replacement value of the asset at the time it is scrapped? It is for this reason, there are views that the depreciation should be provided on the basis of replacement value of the asset and not with reference to the historical original cost.

However there are certain objections to providing depreciation with reference to replacement value. Importantly, the following are few among them:

1. The companies Act and Income Tax Act specifies methods of providing depreciation with reference to original cost only. The practice of providing depreciation with reference to replacement value lacks statutory sanction.
2. Providing depreciation on the basis of replacement value without statutory sanction would result in auditor's comment in his report.
3. No suitable basis has been determined to find out the replacement value because the value of currency fluctuates.
4. If depreciation alone is to be charged with reference to replacement value and other items of financial data are not adjusted to inflationary trend wherever necessary, the rate of return for different years cannot be compared.
5. The chief aim of charging depreciation in P & L account is to ascertain cost of production. The provision of sum for replacement of the asset is consequential.
6. Providing depreciation on inflated value of assets will result in excess provision and creation of secret reserve in the guise of depreciation provision.
7. Replacement cost cannot be defined, as the owner may not purchase the same type of asset. Moreover due to improvement, in technology, much sophisticated model may be available and that too, at a reduced rate, perhaps.
8. Providing depreciation with reference to replacement value is a piece-meal method of adopting inflation accounting. It would be redundant to depreciate the value of fixed assets alone with reference to replacement value, leaving every other assets and liabilities without required adjustment for inflationary pressures.

Hence it is suggested that the depreciation should be provided with reference to original cost of the asset only. It is however, emphasised that nothing prevents the management from creating replacement reserves for adequate amount to purchase the asset when old one become scrap. What is required is that the replacement reserve should not be described as provision for depreciation in the accounts. Amount calculated with reference to cost be shown as a charge for depreciation in P & L account and the amount if any required in excess of it can be shown as an appropriation towards replacement reserve.

Measure of Depreciation:

We have seen that adequate amount of depreciation is to be provided in P&L accounts of each year. It is neither to be high nor to be low. If more amount of depreciation is provided, it is no more a provision but is a reserve. If inadequate amount of depreciation is provided in the accounts, it amounts to releasing more distributable profits without taking care of legitimate expense of the business, thereby implying dividend payment out of capital.

The Institute of Chartered Accountants of India has issued Accounting standard (revised) 6 (AS-6) dealing with depreciation accounting. According to it, depreciation is charged in each accounting period, by reference to the extent of depreciable amount, irrespective of an increase in market value of the asset. Thus it has been set at rest, that depreciation is to be provided with reference to historical cost and not with reference to market value of the asset. Now the question is how the depreciable amount for each year is to be determined? The following are the important factors that determine the quantum of depreciable amount for any accounting year:

(1) Original cost of the asset
(2) Expected useful life of the depreciable asset
(3) Estimated residual value of the depreciable asset
(4) Methods of providing depreciation
(5) Requirements of statutes.

(1) Original Cost of the Asset :

The original cost of the asset means money spent for acquiring, installing, commissioning the asset and subsequent addition or improvement cost associated therewith. The asset may be purchased from outside or it may be fabricated from within the entity. If the asset is purchased from vendors, the original cost represents the purchase price. If trade discount or cash discount is allowed from purchase price, the original cost is to be taken net of such deductions. Certain expenses, which are normally considered as revenue, are incurred usually in connection with acquisition and installation of capital assets. For example, freight charges are incurred for bringing the asset from the place of vendor to the place of factory of the entity. Such revenue expenses must be capitalised and added to the original purchase price. If the asset is fabricated from within the entity, the construction-cost should be properly ascertained. The time spent by labourers, the materials and stores used, and other direct and relevant overhead expenses are to be accumulated properly to ascertain the original cost of the asset. Besides, purchase price or constructioncost incurred for acquisition of the asset, its installation and commissioning expenses are to be added to the original cost. For instance, the amount spent for raising platform around the machinery, fencing in front of the machinery would represent the original cost of the machinery. Similar is the case with expenses for commissioning the asset. Such expenses incurred for setting up the asset for the very first time ready for working, making a trial run of machinery would represent commissioning expenses and therefore they are to be added to original cost.

Sometimes no money outlay is involved in acquisition of asset. For example the property would have been acquired in exchange of certain assets, or by way of gift. In such case, the property is to be valued and the valuation would represent original cost.

Quite often, the government or other developmental agencies grant subsidy to the businessmen for making investment in capital assets. One has to study the purpose and nature of such subsidy. If the subsidy is for and is relatable to investment in asset, it is a capital grant. The original cost of the asset should be reduced to the extent of such capital grant.

If the assets are acquired from utilising borrowed money, can interest paid on borrowed sum be added to the original cost? The answer is yes, but all interest cannot be added to the cost. Interest amount pertaining to the period from the date of loan to the date of putting the asset ready for commercial use alone can be added to the capital cost of the asset. Interest pertaining to the period thereafter should be treated as revenue expense and is to be charged off to the P&L account.

Now another interesting question arises. Capital assets like machinery may be purchased from foreign country. In such a case, long term liability in foreign currency would be involved. This would get changed year after year due to fluctuations in foreign currency. Can these increase or decrease in liability on account of exchange fluctuation be treated as representing cost of the asset? Definitely yes. The original cost of the asset is to be suitably increased or decreased by corresponding increase or decrease in liability on account of fluctuation.

The original cost, besides historical cost of acquisition, installation, commissioning and certain finance expenses, would also include expenses incurred for subsequent additions or improvements to the original asset. The addition may either get merged with original asset or keep its identity and separate use. If the addition is a part and parcel of the original asset, the amount of addition is added to the original cost. But it is advisable to enhance the depreciable amount so suitably to write off the cost of addition within the remaining period of useful life of the original asset. On the other hand, if the addition represents separate asset by its identity and capability of serving the use even after the life of the original asset, it is to be treated as a separate asset by itself and the cost of addition is not added to the original cost of old asset but is separately taken to be fresh original cost of new asset added.

If the expenses are incurred for improving the efficiency, productivity, or profitability of the original asset they can be treated as capital expenditure on account of improvement and therefore be included along with original cost of the asset. If the expenses incurred are just to maintain the existing level of efficiency, productivity or profitability of the asset, they are no more than mere revenue expenditure and should never be treated as representing original cost of the asset.

(2) Estimated residual value of the asset:

After the asset ceases to be of use it is disposed of. But it may have some realisable value, even if it is a junk. The amount of scrap value is to be estimated at the time of acquisition of the asset. If only very negligible amount would be realised, the scrap value can be taken to be nil. On the other hand, significant amount can be realised on disposal, the amount is to be assessed approximately. The determination of scrap value for an asset is a difficult exercise.

The amount of original cost of the asset less its scrap value determines the total quantum of depreciation to be written off during several previous years.

(3) Expected useful Life of the asset

Having decided on the total amount of depreciation to be written off over several years, one must also set limit on periods within which the total amount is to be wiped off. It is for this reason, the commercial life of an asset is estimated. Whatever be the allocation of depreciable amount for any accounting year, it is to be ensured that the total amount of depreciation is written off within a period of estimated useful life of the asset. The estimation of useful life of an asset is a technical matter. It involves expertise. Exactitude cannot be expected of in such an estimation. Nevertheless, it is to be done. Estimated useful life of an asset is expressed in terms of various units of measurement. It may be expressed in terms of number of years for which the asset may be commercially fit, or number of machine hours a machine may last, or number of production units that may be manufactured within useful life of the machine and so on. The useful life of an asset is generally determined by its capacity to be fit for commercial use, say, sturdiness. But physical life of an asset is not always to be taken as estimated useful life of an asset. The useful life may still be shorter than the physical life of the asset. For example in case of leasehold right over an asset, the asset may be physically good to be exploited but the expiry of lease term may put an end to the period of use of an asset. Similarly there may be contractual restrictions or legal impediments which may shorten the physical life of an asset. The estimated useful life of the asset is dependent on various factors. They may be physical wear and tear, extent of use-number of shifts operated, quantum of extraction in case of quarry, mines, term of lease,— repair and renewal policy of management, skill and efficiency of operators of machines, contingency of the machine technologically becoming obsolete.

(4) Methods of providing depreciation

We have seen that how much in total is to be provided for depreciation and within how many years this is to be done. Now the question boils down to how much amount each accounting year, during the period of useful life of an asset must bear? We cannot allocate the total amount of depreciation among different years in a whimsical manner. These must be methodically determined. Different methods of depreciation are in vogue to ascertain the amount of depreciation to be allocated for a period. The principal methods of providing for depreciation are discussed below.

1. Fixed Instalment Method

This method is known by different names such as Straight Line Method, Original Cost Method, etc.

Under this method a percentage of the original cost of the asset concerned less the residual value, if any, is written off every year till the end of its estimate life. The percentage is fixed by taking into consideration the original cost of the asset, its estimated life and its residual value, e.g., a piece of machinery costs Rs. 1,000; its estimated life is 10 years while the residual value is thought to be Rs. 100 . Now by using the machinery for 10 years, the scrap will be sold for Rs. 100 at the end of 10 years. It means Rs. 900 worth of machinery would be consumed in 10 years, i.e., Rs. 90 per every year. Therefore, the revenue account will be debited for depreciation with Rs. 90 every year of 10 years. Repairs and renewals are debited to revenue account.

This method is very simple and easy to understand. The calculation of depreciation is not very complicated. This method is suitable for those assets the working life of which can be easily estimated, e.g., a lease, a patent, etc., but in the case of machinery its life cannot be estimated with accuracy as it depends upon its use. If the machinery is used for three shifts, the ear and tear will be more than in the case where it is used for one shift only. Again in the case of machinery, difficulty is felt when during the course of the year additions to the Plant and Machinery are made and thus calculations will be difficult unless a Plant Register is maintained.

Under this method, the deprecation charges remain the same while repair charges go on increasing when the asset becomes older. Thus the revenue account is debited with greater and greater amount year after year although every year takes the same amount of advantage from the asset.

This method of depreciation is used mostly in U.S.A. and Canada. The Institute of Chartered Accountants of England has also recommended it as the most suitable for general application. The general opinion is in favour of this method of depreciation.

2. The Reducing Instalment Method

This method is also known as Written Down Value Method or Diminishing Method, Declining Balance Method, etc.

Under this method a fixed percentage is written off every year on the diminished book value of the asset till the asset is reduced to its scrap value. Taking our previous example, if the rate at which depreciation is provided is ten per cent, the depreciation charges for the first year will be Rs. 100; in the second year it will be Rs. 90; in the third year it will be Rs. 81 and so on. Repairs and Renewals are debited to the revenue account every year. The annual depreciation charge decreases year after year while the repair charges go on increasing with the advancing age of the assets. Thus, the annual charge against revenue accounts becomes more or less the same every year. Under this method no separate calculation is necessary for any addition during the year as the percentage is calculated on the total book value of the asset at the end of the year, irrespective of the fact whether any addition has been made during the year or not. For income-tax purposes depreciation is allowed on the written-down value of the asset and not on the original cost of the asset. Hence this method is preferred. The Reducing Instalment Method is usually adopted in the case of Plant and Machinery.

The great drawback of this system is that it takes very long time to reduce the asset to its scrap value unless the fixed percentage is very high. In our above illustration, under this system, an undepreciated balance of cost of Rs. 348.68 would remain at the end of the tenth year, instead of Rs. 100 under the Straight-line method. But if 20 per cent instead of 10 per cent depreciation is provided, the undepreciated balance of cost of Rs. 107.38 would remain at the end of the tenth year. Thus we see that a very high rate of depreciation would have to be provided under this method to bring the value of the asset to its residual or scrap value. It would also mean that the revenue account will be debited with a very large sum of money in the earlier years of the life of the asset as compared with the later years of its useful life. If the fixed percentage is excessively high, the depreciation written off in the first year will be very high although the depreciation may not be so much.

Another disadvantage of this method is in case of cost accounts, e.g., a unit of goods is manufactured on 31st December when the depreciation charged is Rs. 100. The same kind of good is manufactured on the next day, i.e., 1st January, (the beginning of the next financial year) the depreciation charged will be of Rs. 90. It would mean reduction in the cost of production of the unit of goods in one day. This method, therefore, therefore, does not appeal.

3. The Depreciation Fund Method

This method is known by different names such as Redemption Fund Method, Amortization Fund Method, Sinking Fund Method, etc. Under this method, an equal amount is written off every year and the Profit and Loss Account is debited while the Depreciation Fund Account is credited during the estimated life of the asset. The amount of annual depreciation can be ascertained from the Depreciation Fund Tables. The instalment is calculated in such a way that if invested every year with compound interest, it will produce an amount equal to the cost of the asset, less its scrap value. The same amount is withdrawn from the business and securities are purchased. Investment Account is debited while Cash Account is credited with the cost of these securities. The asset is shown at its original cost in the balance sheet. When the interest is received on these securities, Cash Account is debited and Depreciation Fund Account is credited. At the same time interest so received is invested in the purchase of securities and Investment Account is debited and Cash Account is credited. This procedure is followed until the Depreciation Fund Account is credited. At the same time interest so received is invested in the purchase of securities and Investment Account is debited and Cash Account is credited. This procedure is followed until the Depreciation Fund Account to distinguish it from ordinary investment account. Then the investment will be sold, and with the help of the money, new asset will be purchased without drawing any money from the business. It may be remembered that the old asset amount will be shown during these years at full value when at the end of the life of the asset, it will be written off against the Depreciation Fund Account.

The advantage of this system is that when asset has to be purchased, funds are available by selling the securities while under the previous two methods, explained above, money is locked up in the business itself and it may not be available when the asset is required to be replaced. Another advantage is that one can know at any time the original value of the asset as it is always shown in the balance sheet at this figure. Moreover, one can know the exact amount written off in any year by comparing the Depreciation Fund Account of different years. This method is useful if the asset has to be purchased when it becomes a scrap.

The defects of this method are: (*a*) one is not in a position to know whether the investment will be sold for a price which will be sufficient to repurchase the asset and (*b*) so much amount is invested in securities, is withdrawn from business and working capital is reduced thereby.

4. The Annuity Method

This method of Depreciation is provided where it is also desired to retain the money in the business. Under this system, it is supposed that the money invested in the purchase of the asset earns interest at a fixed rate, which is debited to the asset account at reduced value and according to the annuity table a certain fixed amount of depreciation is charged every year for the estimated life of the asset which will be reduced to nil or its residual value by that year. The amount written off as depreciation remains the same while interest taken credit for will become less and less year after year.

This method is adopted where a large sum of money is required for the purchases of the asset, e.g., a lease where the life of the lease is definite. It is unsuitable where additions to the asset are made during the course of the year, e.g., in case of Plant and Machinery, because in that case calculations are difficult to be made. According to this method, the revenue account is debited for less amount year after year because rate of depreciation remains the same while the interest charges go on decreasing. Another defect of this system is that the asset is shown in the books of account at a higher figure than its worth in the initial stages of the life of the asset. The annuity method of depreciation, in practice, is very seldom used.

5. Insurance Policy System

According to this system, an Endowment Insurance policy is taken on the life of the asset, so that at the end of the definite period, the insurance company will pay the assured sum with the help of which the asset can be repurchased.

The advantage under this system is that the company need not worry whether the investments, as under the Depreciation Fund Method, will be sold at their face value or not. Under the Depreciation Fund Method, it is possible that due to a fall in the value of the securities, sufficient money may not be realised to enable the company to repurchase the asset worn out and thus the object of creating Reserve Fund may not be achieved. If an insurance policy is taken, the insurance company will pay the stipulated amount to enable the company to repurchase the asset. The company need not worry if the market value of the securities goes down. Moreover, the company has not to bother in the purchase of securities every year as in the case of Depreciation Fund Method. Of course, it is more expensive as the insurance company has to keep its margin of profit.

This method is not suitable for those assets to which many additions are made during the year and the life of which cannot be estimated with any precision. It is suitable for leases where the life of asset is definitely known.

6. Revaluation

Where it is not possible to provide for depreciation on mathematical basis, the asset is revalued at the time of the balance sheet, e.g., in the case of loose tools, livestock, jars, bottles, packages, patterns, jigs, etc., i.e., assets which have short life. This is so because it is not possible to estimate the life of such assets with any precision. The difference between the book value of such assets and the revaluation is the measure of depreciation. It must be remembered that appreciation in the value of such assets is never taken into account. The valuation must be according to "going concern" basis. Montgomery has suggested that the amount required to replenish or replace these assets at the end of each year is the amount of depreciation.

7. The Use or Mileage Method

The method is applied in the case of those assets the use of which can be measured in terms of miles and not in terms of time, e.g., a car, bus, a motor cycle, etc. For instance, it is estimated that a car worth Rs. 10,000 will run for about 40,000 miles and then it will become a mere scrap. This means, the depreciation is at twenty-five Paise a mile. Supposing the car runs for 5,000 miles in the first year, the depreciation charged will be Rs. 1,250. If next year the car runs for only 3,000 miles, the depreciation will be Rs. 750. This method appears to be fair as the depreciation charged will be according to the use to which the asset is put.

This method may be applied to other assets where life can be measured in terms of working hours, e.g., machinery, but the difficulty is that elaborate records will have to be maintained which is not practicable while in the case of cars, trucks, etc., meter shows the number of miles run in a year and, therefore, there is no necessity of keeping any record.

8. Efficiency Hours Method

This method of Depreciation is also known by different names such as Machine-hour Method, Unit of Production Method, Hours-of-Service Method, etc.

This method is exactly like the mileage method. Under this method, instead of counting the life of the asset in miles, it is estimated in terms of working hours. Supposing the life of the machine is estimated to be 10,000 hours and if the cost of the machine is Rs. 10,000, the cost per working hour is one rupee. If in the first year the machine was used for 2,500 hours, the depreciation for the first year will be Rs. 2,500. If the second year, on account of strikes, etc., the machine was worked for only 2,000 hours, the depreciation will be Rs. 2,000 only. We have assumed that the scrap value of the machine is nil. The drawback of the method is that it is difficult to estimate the expected amount of production or life of a machine.

This method is used for costly machines where a fair estimate of the life of the machine in terms of working hours can be formed.

9. Production Unit Method

Under this method the depreciation is provided according to the number of units of the goods manufactured. It is just like Efficiency Hours Method. But as has been described above, it is difficult to estimate the number of units of goods the machine will manufacture before it becomes a scrap. Again no comparison can be made between the two periods.

10. Global Method

Under this method the depreciation is provided according to the rate of depreciation is charged. The method is very unscientific and should not be adopted. It is not permissible under the Companies Act because fixed assets are to be distinguished from one another. Moreover, according to the Act, under each asset the original cost, the additions thereto and the deductions therefrom made during the year, and the total depreciation written off or provided up to the end of the year are to be stated.

11. Depletion Unit Method

This method is used in case of wasting assets such as mines, quarries, oil wells, etc. The contents of the mine are estimated in terms of tons, gallons, etc. Taking into consideration the cost of the mine, the value of one ton of the mineral raised is calculated. The depreciation in any year is calculated per ton according to the output of the year. This is considered as depreciation, for the value of the mine is reduced by so much as the contents of the mine, etc., have been depleted by so many tons or gallons.

Under this method a minimum annual charge is sometimes adopted irrespective of the fact that the production has not reached the minimum.

If an undertaking is formed for exploiting an asset of this kind and if it is decided to wind up the undertaking after the exhaustion of the mine, etc., no provision need be made. But in such a case it should be made clear in the profit and loss account to the shareholders that the dividend paid to them includes a return of part of the capital.

Again where an asset is used up such as when tree are felled on a forestry estate, it is known as depletion.

12. Single Charge Method

Under this method a definite sum of money representing a proper proportion of the total amount of depreciation and repairs over the life of the asset is debited to revenue account and credited to a Depreciation and Repair Reserve Account. Whenever any repairs are effected, they are debited to the Depreciation and Repairs Reserve account.

Investment of Depreciation Fund

We have seen from the discussion of different methods of providing for depreciation that sometimes the sum provided from depreciation is either retained in the business or sometimes it is invested outside the business. Now let us see the advantages and disadvantages of allowing the amount to be invested outside the business.

Advantages of Investing Funds Outside the Business

(*a*) If the amount is invested in gilt-edged securities, capital is safe and the money will be available when required; and

(*b*) A definite fixed amount of interest is earned and allowed to accumulate for a definite period when both capital and interest will be available for the repurchase of the asset.

Disadvantages of Investing Funds Outside the Business

(*a*) When money is withdrawn from the business, the working capital of the company will be reduced and this will hamper the expansion of the business.

(*b*) If the amount is invested in the purchase of investments, there is a danger of the capital being lost if the company, whose shares are held, goes into liquidation. Even if the amount is invested in the gilt-edged securities, there is a danger of the capital being lost, e.g., during the World War the value of Government Securities fell very heavily.

(*c*) If the funds are retained in the business which is earning more profit than the interest earned on securities it will be a loss, e.g., if the business makes a profit of, say, 6 per cent while interest earned on securities is 3 per cent, it is a disadvantage to withdraw the money from the business and invest it in securities.

(*d*) If the securities fall in value it will not be possible to realise sufficient money to replace the asset for which provision has been made.

Advantages of Investing the Amount in Taking up an Insurance Policy as against Depreciation Fund Method

1. No calculations are necessary for making the investments.
2. Interest has not to be reinvested.
3. It does not matter if there is a fall in the value of securities.
4. A definite amount for the repurchase of the asset will be paid by the Insurance Company.

Change in method of depreciation:

We have seen that there are different methods of providing for depreciation. Choosing a particular method suited to the entity is a matter of discretion left with the management of the entity. Different methods may be applied for different classes of asset. For example machinery may be depreciated on written down value method while building may be depreciated on fixed instalment method. Once a method of depreciation is chosen for class of assets, it is to be applied consistently year after year. It is wrong to apply a particular method for one year in respect of a class of asset and apply another method in next year in respect of that class of assets. If it is done so, the profits of different periods will not be comparable. But change from one method of providing depreciation to another method is made only if

(*a*) new method is required by a statute

(*b*) new method is necessary for compliance to any accounting standard

(*c*) the application of new method would result in more appropriate preparation or presentation of financial statements.

In the light of any of these three circumstances, if change in method of providing depreciation is contemplated, then the depreciation amount is to be recalculated using the new method. The recalculation is to done for the periods from the year of asset putting to use to the year of change. The total amount thus recalculated will have to be compared with the total amount of depreciation so far provided. If the recalculated amount exceeds the amount so far provided, the shortage is to be debited in P&L account in the year of change. If recalculated total depreciation falls short of total amount of depreciation so far provided, such excess will be credited in P & L account as profit in the year of change. Anyway, the debit or credit in this respect in P&L account should be distinctly disclosed. The effect of change in method of providing for depreciation on profit/loss is to be disclosed.

Revaluation of Fixed Assets:

Sometimes, fixed assets are revalued to reflect their values at market prices. The revaluation may result in increase in value of fixed assets or decrease in their value. While the decrease in value of fixed assets is recognised as a loss and is written off in P&L account, increase in value of fixed assets on account of revaluation is credited to revaluation reserve only. As a matter of conservatism, the unrealised gains are not recognised and taken to P&L account. The depreciation is always to be provided for with reference to the revalued figures. Full depreciation on the revalued figures of assets is charged in P&L account. Since the purpose of revaluing the assets is to reinstate the replacement cost of the asset in the place of original historical cost, it is always good to provide depreciation on the increased value of the asset. This would result in charging more depreciation in P&L account than what would have been charged, had revaluation not been made.Consequently available profits for distribution of dividend would be less and more money would accumulate to replace the asset. However, if the entity so desires, additional depreciation on account of revaluation may be charged against revaluation reserve and usual depreciation with reference to the original historical cost is to be charged in P&L account. If both normal depreciation and additional depreciation on account of revaluation are charged off to P&L account, the impact of additional depreciation on profit/loss of the entity should be distinctly disclosed in P&L account in the year of revaluation.

As discussed in previous topic in this chapter, depreciation should be charged only with reference to original cost of the asset and not with reference to the replacement value of the asset, unless replacement value is substituted for original cost or written down value of the asset on the basis of properly made revaluation. The basis of revaluation should be reasonable and the nature, and effect of revaluation on profit/loss should be adequately disclosed.

Writing Off Full Cost of the Assets :

Depreciation is allocation of original cost of the asset over a period of useful life of the asset. Can full cost be depreciated in one year itself ? Yes, if the value of asset is not materially significant. It is a matter of judgement of the management to decide what amount constitutes insignificant value for capital asset in the light of various factual circumstances including level of operations, money outlay in several other capital assets etc. For instance, under Income tax Act, full depreciation was allowed to be provided in respect of individual plant and machinery which cost not more than Rs 5,000 in the year of acquisition of assets.

Adjustment of Assets in the year of their disposal

When the asset is disposed of by way of sale or otherwise, the amount of depreciation so far accumulated against the asset in provision account should be transferred to the asset account. The netting of the cost of the asset against the transferred depreciation would result in the asset head reflecting the asset in its written down value. The amount realised in respect of the disposal of the asset is credited to the asset account. Depending on the sale value of the asset there may be excess or shortage over the written down value of the asset. These should be transferred to P&L account and should be shown in final financial statements separately as profit or loss on disposal of the assets.

(5) Compliance to Statutes :

If any of the enactments applicable to the entity stipulates rate of depreciation that should be applied in respect of various classes of the assets, then the entity should charge depreciation for an amount not below the amount specified in the Act. The Indian companies Act states that no dividend can be declared by the company unless depreciation (including arrears of depreciation, if any) is fully provided for. The Act contains separate schedule viz., schedule XIV specifying rates for various classes of the assets. There are rates for different classes of assets corresponding to written down value method of providing depreciation and straight line (fixed instalment) method of providing depreciation. The schedule also instructs that the depreciation is to be calculated pro-rata in case of addition or improvement effected during the year. That is, the depreciation is to be calculated from the date of addition or improvement to the date of closing of accounts at the rates mentioned in the schedule. The schedule also requires that the method of depreciation adopted should be disclosed in final financial statements. If the rates applied are different from those specified in the schedule, then the rates applied should also be disclosed in the final financial statements.

Plant Register :

The Plant Register contains the following information for each type of asset:

(*a*) Opening balance of the plant and machinery.

(*b*) Additions during the year.

(*c*) Nature of the plant, e.g., lathe, boiler, drilling machine, etc.

(*d*) Original cost price.

(*e*) Estimated life of the plant.

(*f*) Estimated scrap value.

(*g*) The rate at which depreciation is to be charged.

(*h*) The number of working hours per week.

(*i*) The number of non-working hours, e.g., breakdown of plant, strike, lack of work or lock-out, etc.

(*j*) Repairs effected during the year.

(*k*) Sale of any part of any plant.

The plant and machinery account in the General Ledger should be adjusted accordingly.

The advantages of Plant Register :

(*a*) The rate of depreciation is fixed on the advice of an expert possessing technical knowledge and, therefore, the auditor can be sure that the depreciation charged is fair and that the book value of the asset shown in the balance sheet is correct.

(*b*) The depreciation allowances can easily be checked by the Income Tax authorities.

(*c*) An exact amount for depreciation can be ascertained easily and, therefore, the exact cost of article manufactured can be known.

(*d*) Uneconomic repairs are revealed.

Auditor's duty with regard to Depreciation

1. The auditor should check that the cost of the assets are properly stated. He must check capitalisation entries keeping in mind the relevant accounting conventions. He must vouch the entries with such records as minutes of directors, purchase bills, delivery notes, expense vouchers, commencement certificate etc. Similarly when assets are disposed off, the auditor should vouch entries. He must check such evidences—authorisation of Board, sale invoice, copy of gate pass, amount received from the buyer and so on.
2. The auditor must bear in mind that adequate amount of depreciation is to be provided for in accounts. Regardless of non-availability of profits, availability of assets in market at a cheaper rate (*i.e.*, below book values), repair and renewal policy or non-user of asset during accounting year, the depreciation should be provided for. It is charge against profits of the company each year. It is equally important that no excessive depreciation has been provided for in the accounts. Any excess amount over adequate amount is an amount set apart in the nature of reserve and not a provision.
3. The auditor must ascertain that the scrap value and useful life of the asset are fairly estimated. He must also check that the method of depreciation adopted is suited to the entity. He must ensure the rates applied are not below the rates specified in relevant enactments applicable to the entity. For example, the company auditor should check that the rates of depreciation to be applied are not less than the rates stipulated in schedule XIV of companies Act.
4. Once a method of providing depreciation is chosen, it should be consistently applied. Change of method of providing for depreciation is allowed only on rare specific circumstances. The auditor should check that there are circumstances warranting change, if the entity desires to make change in method of providing for depreciation.
5. Now, the auditor must devise checks to ensure the accuracy aspect of depreciation. He must get a schedule of fixed assets from the client. He must compare the opening balances with previous year's figures, vouch additions, deletions and check the grouping of individual assets into such convenient classses of assets. He must test-check calculation of depreciation ensuring for all classes of assets, correct rate of depreciation is applied. The auditor should cross tally the total of balances of assets as appearing in the schedule with the balances appearing in control accounts in general ledger. The auditor should carefully check that the total depreciation calculated in the schedule gets reflected in P&L account without any discrepancy.

In the year of change in method of providing depreciation, the auditor must check calculations pertaining to recomputation of depreciation under revised method and its adjustment in accounts. The auditor must also check that entries passed in the year of disposal of the asset are correct.

6. Now the auditor should check that the depreciation is properly disclosed in financial statements. The provision of depreciation should be distinctly shown in P&L account and the total depreciation provision should be disclosed as a deduction from the cost of assets in the balance sheet. The method of providing depreciation for different types of assets should be disclosed. In the year of change of depreciation method, the quantum of impact on profit/loss of the entity due to adoption of changed method in the place of existing one, should be clearly disclosed by way of note to P&L account. In case of disposal of assets, the profit or loss on sale of asset should be separately disclosed if the amount is material.

   In short, the auditor has to ensure that a) correct principles are followed in determination of depreciation amount b) the depreciation is correctly calculated and c) that it is truly and fairly disclosed to the readers of financial statements.

2. Repairs and Renewals

Every year repairs and small renewals are to be effected in case of certain fixed assets, e.g., plant and machinery. This item appears to be an item of regular expenditure and, therefore, should be debited to revenue account. We also know that sometimes extraordinary repairs are to be effected. If the revenue account is debited whenever these extraordinary expenses are incurred the expenses are not properly spread over. For instance, when the asset is purchased, it being new, the expenses or repairs will be small while the cost of repairs will be high when the asset becomes older. All years have taken equal advantage of the asset during its life-time while the revenue account of the later years will be burdened more than the initial years. Therefore, such a system of repairs should be adopted which will do justice. This is the reason why some accountants prefer the Reducing Instalment System according to which depreciation provided will be higher in the initial stages and the repairs and renewals will be lower as the asset will be new. Hence the total of both the expenses, viz., depreciation and repairs will be practically the same in the initial stages new. Hence the total of both the expenses, viz., depreciation and repairs will be practically the same in the initial stages and the repairs and renewals will be lower as the asset will be as well as in the later years of the life of the asset. Those who oppose the adoption of the Reducing Instalment Method of Depreciation say that the depreciation of the asset is the same whether it is the initial stage or the final stage of the life of an asset. According to them, under the Reducing Instalment Method, more depreciation is shown in the books of account in the first stage of the life of an asset than is reasonable for the period. Therefore, they propose another method by which actual depreciation as well as the repairs effected in a year are shown. According to them the revenue account of every year should be debited with an average sum to be spent on repairs and Repairs and Renewals Maintenance Reserve Account should be credited. The Repairs and Maintenance Reserve should be debited and Cash Account credited with the actual amount spent on repairs. Thus the Profit and Loss Account of every year will be debited with the same account. Any debit balance on the Repairs Maintenance Reserve Account should be written off to revenue account as it shows that insufficient provision has been made for renewals in the past and, therefore, the reserve should be increased in the future.

While dealing with this item, the auditor should see that repairs and small renewals are not capitalised. Of course, if the repairs and renewals are of the nature of replacement and additions, such expenditure should be capitalised. We have already dealt with the question of allocation of expenditure to revenue and capital in one of the previous chapters and the reader is advised to refer to the chapter when dealing with such a problem.

Legal aspect of Depreciation

In the beginning of this chapter we indicated a difficulty which confronts a businessman as to how much depreciation should be provided for on an asset because it affects his divisible profit. In the case of an individual, there will be no difficulty as he himself is the proprietor. He may or may nor provide any depreciation. But in his case also, he cannot provide more depreciation beyond the rate allowed by the Income Tax Act for the purpose of calculating the assessable income because the Income Tax authorities will not permit him to do so, as less profit is shown, and , therefore, less income tax will be payable by him. On the other hand, if he does not make any provision for depreciation, the whole of the profit will be assessed and he will be liable to pay higher rate of income tax. Moreover, he might feel difficulty when replacing such an asset.

In the case of a partnership much will depend upon the agreement amongst the partners and the schedule of depreciation in the Income Tax Act.

In the case of Joint-Stock Companies and other statutory bodies, provision for depreciation will have to be made according to law, the Articles of Association of such companies and decisions by the law courts on such topics. Let us deal with some of the legal decisions. Till 28th December, 1960, the courts based their decision on the cases decided by the courts which laid down that it was not necessary to provide depreciation on the fixed and wasting assets but as has been mentioned previously a company is not allowed now to declare or pay any dividenduntil provision for depreciation has been made.

For the convenience of the reader we give below a few cases but with a word of warning that these cass have only an historical importance:

1. Lee vs. Neuchatel Asphalte Co. (1889)

It was held in this case that if a company is formed to work a mine, it may distribute the profits to the shareholders without making any provision for depreciation on the wasting assets where the articles of association of the company did not compel it to do so.

This case is not apllicable in India, as according to the Companies Act, it is incumbent upon a company to make provision for depreciation vide Section 205 (2). Moreover, according to this section, a dividend can only be paid out of profits of the company and, therefore, if a part of the capital in the form of dividend is returned to the shareholders, it will contravene the provisions of the Companies Act.

2. Crabtree vs. Crabtree (1912)

It was held in this case that depreciation must be provided on plant and machinery if the manufacturing business is to continue for an indefinite period. In other words if the manufacturing business is to be closed down after a few year no provision may be made for depreciation. But after the Companies Act was amended in 1960, it is necessary that depreciation should be provided irrespective of the fact whether the company is to continue for a definite period or not.

3. Wilmer vs. McNamara & Co. Ltd. (1895)

It was held in this case that a company cannot be restrained from declaring a dividend out of current profits because no provision has been made for depreciation on fixed assets.

This judgement does not hold good now in India vide Section 205 of the Companies Act, according to which depreciation must be provided on fixed assets before a dividend is declared.

QUESTIONS

1. Distinguish between Depreciation and Fluctuation. Discuss if it is necessary for a company to provide for the depreciation in respect of fixed assets both from commercial and legal points of view. State also the auditor's duties in this respect.

   (*Calcutta B. com. Hons., 1968*)

2. Discuss the legal position relating to the provision for depreciation on the fixed assets of a Company. (*Cal. B. Com.*)

3. In presenting the draft Balance Sheet and Profit and Loss Account of a company of which you are the auditor, you are informed that no provision has been made in the accounts for depreciation of plant and machinery since the Directors consider that —

   (*a*) The amount of Depreciation already written off has been excessive;

   (*b*) The market value of such assets is much in excess of their present book value;

   (*c*) The current year's profits are insufficient to cover provision for further depreciation.

   Draft a letter to the Directors of the company giving your advice on the matter.

   (*C.A. Int., Marathwada and Annamalai B. Com.*)

4. Why should Depreciation be provided on the fixed assets of business concern at the time of preparing the final accounts? What are the factors to be taken into consideration for measuring the extent of depreciation? (*Punjab B. Com. 1964*)

5. Should a reserve fund be necessarily invested in specific securities outside the business?

6. What are the different methods of writing off depreciation in respect of assets which are of depreciable nature? In the case of a Public Limited Company, what are the legal requirements about providing Depreciation in respect of such an asset? Which is the best method in your opinion? *(Delhi and Sardar Vallabhbhai Vidyapeeth B. Com. 1961)*

7. The profit and loss account of a company of which you are the auditor shows a huge loss even before taking into account the depreciation on the fixed assets. The Directors ask your opinion whether in the circumstances it is necessary to charge the depreciation to the profit and loss account. The Directors argue that the market value of these assets is higher. Give reasons for you answer. *(Delhi B. Com.)*

8. Enumerate the causes of depreciation. What factors should be taken into consideration for measuring the extent of depreciation?

9. Write short notes on —

(*a*) Efficiency Hours Method of Depreciation;

(*b*) Global Method of Depreciation;

(*c*) Mileage Method of Depreciation;

(*d*) Depletion Unit Method or Production Unit Method of Depreciation; and

(*e*) Single Charge Method of Depreciation."

10. What is a "Plant Register"? How would you keep this register? What information should be entered therein and how the question of depreciation should be dealt with?"

11. "It is supposed that there is no harm in showing the state of affairs of a Company worse than what it actually is, but the position should not be allowed to be shown better than what it is in reality."

Critically examine this statement. *(Bombay B.Com. 1958)*

12. As the auditor of a public limited company incorporated in 1955, you find that during the year 1970, the company which was previously following reducing balance method for providing depreciation on fixed assets, has recalculated the amount of depreciation, since inception on straight line method which showed that there was excessive depreciation provided in the past. The company proposes to transfer the difference to General Reserve and distribute dividend for the year 1970 therefrom. State your approach to this matter.

(C.A. Final, India 1971)

13. In auditing the accounts of a limited company you ascertain that no provision has been made for depreciation on wagons purchased on Hire-Purchase System. The directors contend that as the wages do not belong to the company, there is no need to make provision for depreciation and indeed such a course would be erroneous.

What would be your reply? Give reasons for your answer. *(Cal. M. Com. 1961)*

14. Having suggested the necessity for Depreciation of Machinery in the accounts of the Company, the Board of Directors raise objection on the following grounds respectively: —

(*a*) The cost of similar machinery having risen, nothing should be written off, as it is actually more valuable.

(*b*) Repairs done have fully maintained the machinery which is as good as new.

(*c*) To charge depreciation to the same extent as in a good year would prevent the declaration of a dividend with the result of dissatisfaction amongst the shareholders and a possible fall in the price of shares.

Criticise these arguments. *(Agra B. Com., 1966; Bombay B. Com 1958)*

15. Is it legally necessary to make provision for depreciation on fixed or wasting assets or floating assets before arriving at divisible profits of a limited company? Discuss this from the point of view of an auditor having regard to legal decisions on the subject.

(N.D. Com. 1968; Rajasthan B. Com. 1970)

16. The Accountant of XYZ co. Ltd.has given the following treatment in respect of the under mentioned accounting transactions. State with reason whether you can approve of his accounting treatment.

(*a*) The Chief engineer of the Company's plant visited Pune to make an on-the-spot inspection of a hydraulic pressing machine to be purchased by the company. Later, the same machine had been purchased. The travelling and other incidental expenses of the engineer in connection with his trip for inspection was accounted by debit to the machinery account.

(*b*) The same machinery had been purchased using term loan obtained from company's bankers. The loan was made at the disposal of the company since 16-08-1994. However, the purchase of machinery had been finalised on 15-10-94 and the machinery had been duly installed on 25-10-94. As on 31st March 1995, the company has paid interest for period upto 30th September 1994, quarters December 1994, March 1995. Since the loan is specifically to finance the purchase of machinery the accountant continues to debit all interest payments in machinery account.

17. The managing Director of ABC Ltd. wants to change the method of providing depreciation from straight line method to written down value method. However, he fears whether there would arise any audit objections if it is opposed to accounting practices and statutory provisions. You are contacted for your opinion. Raise up all issues in this connection and give your opinion on all those.

18. Give a check list for audit of depreciation.

Chapter 21

Reserves

Meaning

Generally one understands by the term "reserve" that something has been kept apart for future use for emergency. This is the definition by an ordinary man. But from the accountancy point of view, "reserve" means that part of the profits which is set aside for any known or unknown contingency, liability, diminution in the values of asset, etc. The American Institute of Accountants defines a reserve, in the Accounting Terminology Bulletin No. I (1953) as "The use of the term 'reserve' be limited to indicate that an undivided portion of the asset is being held or retained for general or specific purposes ...."

Generally speaking Reserves are of two kinds, viz., (1) A General Reserve which is not to meet any specific liability, and (2) A Specific Reserve which is to meet any specific liability or diminution in the value of an asset. But now the Reserves are classified as under:

(a) General Reserve ;
(b) Specific Reserve, or to be more appropriate "Provision" ;
(c) Sinking Fund ;
(d) Reserve or Development Fund ;
(e) Capital Reserve ;
(f) Secret Reserve ;

We shall discuss these different types of Reserves in detail.

(*a*) General Reserve

It is an amount set aside out of the profits or surplus of a business to provide additional working capital or to strengthen the liquid resources of the business or that they may be available for any unknown contingency or to equalise dividend or for expansion of business, etc. It is an appropriation of profit. It is usually treated as a revenue reserve. Such a reserve is also known as a "free reserve" or a "Revenue Reserve". This kind of reserve is not created to meet any known liability, contingency or commitment. This may considered as the "undistributed profit". The General Reserve can be created only when there is Profit and, therefore, there cannot be a debit balance of profit and Loss Account and a General Reserve at the same time. As in the case of an individual, he saves money out of his income for any expected and unknown contingency, a businessman also saves money out of profits for any unknown contingency, in which case it is called "Reserve". The whole of the profit is not distributed but a part of it is retained in the business. The money which would have been withdrawn from the business and paid to the shareholders, is not paid to them but is retained in the business. It is the surplus over the asset, minus the liabilities and the capital. Thus, the liquid resources of the business are improved. If, in future, there is any necessity, this reserve can be utilized or it may be distributed later on, provided the Articles of Association of the company do not prohibit such a course. Binnie and Manning have described the nature of a General Reserve when they say: "A general reserve, in effect, differs only in name from the 'carry forward' or 'surplus' as the balance remaining at the credit of Profit and Loss Account (after deducting dividends) is commonly called. The transfer of part of the profits to general reserve has the effect of setting aside a sum which thereupon ceases to be regarded as profit available for distribution under ordinary circumstances."

Although Part III of Schedule VI of the Companies Act does not give positive definition of the terms "reserve" and "capital reserve", etc., still it indicates the nature of these terms:—

7. (1)(*a*) The expression "provision" shall, subject to sub-clause (2) of this clause, means any amount written off or retained by way of providing for depreciation, renewals or diminution in value of assets, or retained by way of providing for any known liability of which the amount cannot be determined with substantial accuracy;

(*b*) The expression "reserve" shall not, subject as aforesaid, includes any amount written off or retained by way of providing for depreciation, renewals or diminution in value of assets or retained by way of providing for any known liability;

(c) The expression "capital reserve" shall not include any amount regarded as free for distribution through the profit and loss account; and the expression "revenue reserve" shall mean any reserve other than a capital reserve.

And in this sub-clause the expression "liability" shall include all liabilities in respect of expenditure contracted for and all disputed or contingent liabilities."

(2) Where —

(*a*) any amount written off or retained by way of providing for depreciations, renewals or diminution in value of assets not being an amount written off in relation to fixed assets before the commencement of this Act;

(*b*) any amount retained by way of providing for any known liability; is in excess of the amount which in the opinion of the directors is reasonably necessary for the purpose, the excess shall be treated for the purposes of this Schedule as a reserve and not as a provision.

Conversely, if there is a heavy loss in future, the General Reserve can be utilized for the purpose of wiping off the debit balance of Profit and Loss Account and the balance, if any, may be shown in the Balance Sheet.

The profits so withheld from distribution may be retained in the business if the turnover on such amount in the business itself is higher than if they were invested outside the business and provided further if there is any scope of expansion. Supposing the profit of the business is 6 per cent while the rate of interest outside the business is only 4 percent it would be advisable to retain the money in the business itself because the net income from such an investment will be 2 percent more, assuming that there is a scope for expansion of the business. On the other hand, if the business is not profitable on account of slump in that particular industry and the profit is less than the market rate of interest, it would be advisable to invest the money so set apart outside the business to earn more interest. Such investments can be drawn upon in case of emergency. This is a reserve on which the business can fall upon at any time.

If the money is invested in the business, it does not mean that the business is financially weak. On the other hand, it may mean that the business is progressive and that is why it requires more capital which can be more profitably employed in the business itself rather than invested outside the business.

It may be made clear here that it is not obligatory to set aside a certain sum of money for general reserve. If the profits permit and the management thinks it advisable, it may make provision for general reserve. It is not compulsory to do so. It is an appropriation of profit and not a charge against it. Hence it depends upon the discretion of the management to do so or not to do so. However, if there is any particular law to set aside a certain sum of money out of the profits, e.g., in case of banking companies or co-operative societies, a part of the profits according to the particular law has to be carried to reserve account. Similarly if the articles of association of a company lay down that a particular amount has to be carried to reserve account before distribution of the profit, the company must create a reserve.

The value of such a reserve depends upon the value of other assets. If they are overvalued because no or inadequate provision had been made for depreciation on the assets or doubtful and bad debts in the past, such a reserve will have no value. Similarly, if other assets are overvalued, it means general reserve is inflated or it may not be in existence at all.

The reader is warned here to avoid any confusion between the Reserve Account and the Reserve Fund. The latter denotes that the sum set aside out of the profits of the business is invested in readily realisable securities while Reserve Account denotes that the sum set aside out of the profits is retained in the business itself and the Reserve account is represented by the general asset of that concern.

It is no part of the duty of an auditor to see the adequacy or inadequacy of such a reserve. If the directors do not wish to provide for such a reserve, the auditor need not insist upon its creation. However he may be called upon to advise the directors on the desirability of creating such a reserve or whether the reserve be invested inside or outside the business. We have already discussed this question in the beginning of this chapter.

(*b*) Specific Reserve or Provision

The reserve which is a charge against revenue for the purpose of providing for losses and contingencies which may result in losses and which are known or expected at the date of making provision for such a contingency to occur at a future date, is known as Specific Reserve. Such a reserve must be created whether there is any profit or not and even if there is a loss, it is a must. The exact amount involved is not known. It is provided before the profits are distributed and is created for a definite object, *e.g.*, —

(*a*) To meet a known loss, e.g., depreciation, heavy repairs, and renewals, etc.

(*b*) To meet an expected contingency e.g., doubtful debts, discount on sundry debtors, liability for a disputed claim, contingent liability under Workmen's Compensation Act, etc.

(*c*) To meet an outstanding liability for expenses already incurred, *e.g.*, salaries and wages, commission, income tax and other accrued expenses.

Specific Reserve is not a surplus. It is not represented by any asset and, therefore, is not available for distribution amongst the shareholders. The amount is an estimate only at the date of making a provision. If provision is in excess of the need according to the directos, the excess amount should be treated as reserve.

Specific Reserve or provision is deducted from the assets as in the case of Depreciation, Reserve for Bad and Doubtful Debts, etc., while Reserves for outstanding liabilities are shown on the liabilities side of the Balance Sheet.

We have studied both General Reserve and specific Reserve, which are known to the accountancy profession in modern times as Reserve and Provisions respectively.

Let us now see the points of distinction between a "Reserve" and a "Provision" formerly known as "General" and "Specific" Reserves respectively.

"Reserve" which is an appropriation of profits.	*"Provision" which is a charge against profits*
1. 'The Reserve is created by debiting Profit and Loss Appropriation Account for the redemption of a known liability or to strengthen the liquid resources of the Company or for the equalization of dividends or for the redemption of debentures, etc.	1. A Provision is made by debiting the Profit and Loss Account for a specific contingency or expected loss, e.g., Provision for Bad and Doubtful Debts or Provision for Depreciation, etc.
2. The Reserve is created without taking into consideration the actual amount required except in the case of redemption of debentures when a definite sum is set aside.	2. A Provision is made for a definite amount and, therefore, a definite sum is set aside every year to meet the known contingency.
3. In the case of Reserves, the standing credit balance may be carried to Profit and Loss Account or may be distributed amongst the shareholders except in the case of Debenture Redemption Reserve which cannot be touched before the debentures are redeemed when it is carried to General Reserve Account.	3. When the loss occurs the Provision Account is debited.
4. It is usually shown on the liability side of the Balance Sheet as it is not Specific Reserve.	4. The Provision is generally shown on the assets side of the Balance Sheet by way of deduction from the Asset concerned, e.g., Reserve for Doubtful Debts is deducted from the Sundry Debtors Account.
5. Making of a Reserve is discretionary and is a matter of financial prudence except, (*a*) when the articles of the company so provide; or (*b*) in case of companies of special nature, e.g., in the case of a banking company where the Banking Companies Act, 1949, provides that 20 per cent of the profits must be credited to the General Reserve Account every year; or (c) when the terms and conditions of the issue of debentures provide that a Debenture Redemption Fund must be created and so on.	5. Making of a Provision is a 'must'.
6. A Reserve is created not with a view to meeting any definite liability and hence it is left to the Directors to make any provision or not to make any provision at all. The auditor need not interfere except when the Articles definitely lay down that the Reserve must be created, or according to the term of the issue of the Debentures, a provision for redemption has to be made.	6. The duty of an auditor in connection with the provision is to see that adequate provision is made to meet the loss. If it has not been done and he has not been able to persuade the Directors to make adequate Provision, he should refer the matter in his report. He must, therefore, consult the Articles, Minute book and the recommendations of the Directors.
7. The amount allocated for Reserve depends upon the profits of the company. If there are no profits, no Reserve need be created.	7. The amount allocated for Provision does not depend upon the profits of the company. Even if there is a loss, provision has to be made.

Let us now deal with some of the Specific Reserves or Provisions.

(*a*) Reserve for Bad Debts

This reserve is created to meet any future loss if the debtors fail to pay the whole or a part of the debt owing by them. When the amount of loss which will take place is known, provision should be made for the exact amount. The revenue account is debited and the account of the particular debtors are credited. This procedure is sometimes objected to on the ground that the loss will occur in future and hence the revenue account of the year in which the loss will actually occur, should be debited and not the revenue account of the year in which it is created. The argument appears to be sound but, to be conservative, it is considered that the future liability may be provided for out of the profits of the current year. Moreover, it is argued, that the debts were incurred during the current year and hence the reserve for any such bad and doubtful debt should be provided for out of the profits of the current year. If it is not provided, the profit and loss account and the balance sheet will not be correct. As regards the amount of the future loss and expense, a fair estimate formed on the basis of past experience, should be made. When the actual loss occurs, adjustment should be made.

But this is not the case with accrued expenses. The expenses have already been incurred and the amount ought to have been paid during the current year in order to show a correct statement of profit made or loss suffered during the year. Although it is not the duty of the auditor to see the adequacy or inadequacy of reserves, but if he thinks the reserve is inadequate and he cannot bring round the client to raise the amount, he should refer the matter in his report. Moreover, a balance sheet cannot be said to exhibit a true and fair view of the state of affairs of a company, if no or inadequate provision for bad and doubtful debts has been made.

(*b*) Reserve for Discount on Debtors and Creditors

In some business houses, it is the custom that when the debtors make payment within the prescribed period, a certain amount of discount is allowed to them. Similarly, the business house, when making payment to creditors, earns discount. At the date of closing the books, the book debts shown may not be worth the amount mentioned as some discount will have to be allowed to the debtors. Therefore, the debtors should not be shown at their book value but the actual amount realisable from them should be shown. If this is not done, the balance sheet will not show the correct position of the concern and, therefore, discount payable to the debtors should be deducted from the total debtors and net realizable figures should be shown in the balance sheet.

But there are accountants who argue that it is not necessary that provision should be made for discount at the close of the year as it may happen that the debtors may not take advantage of the discount and thus the full amount may be realized. Moreover, they say, a cash discount is granted to the debtors who make payment before the due date and hence the year in which such payment is made should bear the loss as that year has taken advantage of the cash payment.

Both the arguments appear to be sound but as an auditor has to certify the sundry debtors to be correct, he has to show the net worth of such debtors, i.e., whatever amount is expected to be realised at the date of the balance sheet. If such a reserve is not provided for, the balance sheet will not represent the correct state of affairs of the concern.

However, if it is decided to provide for discount on debtors, the amount can be calculated on the basis of past experience. The discount should be calculated on the debtors after deducting Bad Debts Reserve from the total debtors.

The auditor should also see that if no reserve for discount on debtors has been provided for in the past, it should not be done during the current year, as otherwise such a step will affect the comparison of the profit and loss accounts of the two periods.

Reserves for discount on creditors should not be provided unless discount on debtors has been provided. The rate of discount on creditors should be the same as in the case of discount on debtors.

(*c*) Sinking Fund

It is a kind of reserve by which a provision is made-

(*i*) to reduce a liability, e.g., redemption of debentures or repayment of a loan; or

(*ii*) to replace a wasting asset, e.g., a mine; or

(*iii*) to replace a depreciating asset; or

(*iv*) to renew a lease, etc.

Lancester defines it as "any fund which is created by the regular investment of such an amount as, with compound interest earned thereon will accumulate to a given sum at the end of a stated period."

Binnie and Manning define, "A Sinking Fund is a form of specific reserve set aside for the redemption of a long-term debt or the replacement of a wasting or a depreciating asset."

The main purpose of creating a Sinking Fund is to have a certain sum of money accumulated for a future date by setting aside a certain sum of money every year. It is a kind of Specific Reserve.

How is Sinking Fund Created ?

The Sinking Fund is created —

(*a*) by debiting the profit and loss account every year with a certain sum of money and investing it, at the same time, in gilt-edged securities to ensure the safety of capital and a regular rate of interest. In such a case the object is to provide against a loss which should naturally fall on revenue, e.g., in the case of a Depreciation Sinking Fund. This provision is a charge against profit. Whether there is any profit or not, provision must be made for such a fund;

(*b*) by debiting the Profit and Loss Appropriation Account every year with a certain sum of money and investing it at the same time in gilt-edged securities. In this case the object is the reduction of a liability or payment of a liability. The fund is created by allocation of profits.

Whatever the object or the method of creating such a reserve may be, every year a certain sum of money is interest in such a way that with compound interest, the exact amount to wipe off the liability or replace the wasting asset or to meet the loss, will be available. The amount to be invested every year can be known from the compound interest annuity tables.

Alternatively, an endowment policy may be taken out which matures on the date when the amount required will be paid by the insurance company. The advantage of this method is that a definite amount will be available while in the case of investment of funds in securities the exact amount may not be available on account of fall in the value of securities. If it is decided to take out a policy —

(*a*) Profit and Loss Account should be debited with the amount of the annual premium.

(*b*) A Sinking Fund Policy Account should be debited each year with the amount of the premium and a Sinking Fund Account credited, the respective balances being included in the Balance Sheet.

If no provision is made to meet the liability or the loss, money will have to be borrowed or certain assets will have to be sold to repay the loan or redeem the debentures at the time of maturity. It is, therefore, deemed advisable to set aside a part of the profits, when it is desired to redeem a liability or to charge the revenue account every year to meet a loss.

It must again be made clear that provision for depreciation for the wasting asset should be made by debiting the revenue account as it represents provision for the depreciation of the asset.

Again when any provision is made for the redemption of debentures or to repay the loans, the Profit and Loss Appropriation Account is debited. This type of provision is not a charge againt the revenue account. It is an allocation of the profits for a certain purpose, viz., the redemption of the debentures.

If any profit is made on selling the investments representing the Sinking Fund, it should be transferred to General Reserve. If any loss is incurred, such a loss may be debited to Profit and Loss Account.

Difference between Sinking Fund for the Redemption of a liability and Sinking Fund for the Replacement of an Asset

1. Provision for the former is made out of the divisible profits while in the latter case, provision is made by debiting the revenue account.
2. After the liability is redeemed, the Sinking Fund is no longer required and as it is the undistributed profit, it may be distributed to the shareholders or may be transferred to the General Reserve Account, while in the latter case when the asset is replace, the Sinking Fund no longer exists as it is transferred to the original assets to close that asset account.
3. After the expiry of the period, the gilt edged securities are sold and the cash so realised is applied for the payment of the liability or debentures while in the case of replacement of the asset, the cash realised by the sale of the securities is used to replace the existing asset.

Duty of an Auditor as regards Sinking Fund

As a matter of fact there is no legal obligation to create a Sinking Fund to meet a liability on a loan or debenture, but if the Articles of Association of a company or the Debenture Trust Deed lay down that such a reserve should be created, then it is incumbent to do so. In such a case a duty is cast upon the auditor to see that such a provision is made accordingly. If he fails to do so, he will be held liable as was decided in the case of Davar & Sons Ltd, vs. M S. Krishnaswami (1952). Sometimes the Articles are silent in regard to such a provision, but according to the terms of the issue of debentures Sinking Fund has to be created for the redemption of debentures. In such a case, the auditor should refer to the Debenture Trust Deed. He should not only see that Sinking Fund is created but also to see that adequate provision is made every year. He should also see that investment against Sinking Fund are clearly marked in the Balance Sheet to distinguish them from ordinary investments.

(*d*) Reserve or Development Funds

Practically there is no difference between a General Reserve, which has already been dealt with in the foregoing pages and a Reserve Fund. Both are created with the same object and are debited to Profit and Loss Appropriation Account. The only difference is that in the case of General Reserve, the surplus is retained in the business and is represented by the general assets of the company while in the case of the Reserve Fund, the surplus is invested outside the business in securities and is represented by such investments. Some accountants argue that the word "Fund indicates that the money is invested outside the business, and, therefore, it is but appropriate that such a reserve should be named Reserve Fund in order to distinguish it from the General Reserve. The Recommendations on Accounting Principles made by the Institute of Chartered Accountants of England also lay down "the term `reserve fund' should only be used where reserve is specifically represented by readily realisable and ear-marked assets". Formerly no such distinction used to be made but now a days some accountants prefer to make such a distinction in the Balance Sheet to make the position clear. They further suggest that investments which represent a Reserve must clearly indicate that they represent such and such reserve.

Some accountants are of opinion that Development Fund cannot be utilized for payment of dividend as a reserve can be, because it has been created for a specific purpose.

(*e*) Capital Reserve

The term "Capital Reserve" has not been defined by the Companies Act, except in a negative way in Part III of Schedule VI of the Companies Act as described in the beginning of this chapter. There is a considerable difference of opinion amongst accountants in regard to the definition of capital reserve. It has been defined as "any reserve which cannot legally be distributed amongst the shareholders". But this definition does not seem he quite correct. As we shall see later on, Capital Reserve may be distributed amongst the shareholders under certain circumstances. Capital Reserve is just like a General Reserve except that it is generally not distributable amongst the shareholders and that it is not created by debiting the Profit and Loss Appropriation Account.

The reader is warned here not to confuse Capital Reserve with Reserve Capital. The latter term denotes the uncalled capital which the shareholders cannot be called upon to pay unless the company goes into liquidation. According to Section 99 of the Companies Act, "A limited company may, by special resolution, determine that any portion of its share capital which has not already been called up, shall not be capable of being called up except in the event and for the purposes of the company being wound up, and thereupon that portion of its share capital shall not be capable of being called up except in that event and for these purposes." Reserve Capital is also known as Reserve Liability.

Capital reserve is created out of profits of a capital nature, *e.g.* —

1. If there has been an appreciation in the value of a fixed asset, the difference between the book value and the appreciated value is transferred to Capital Reserve provided other assets have been revalued and necessary adjustment has been made.
2. Selling a fixed asset at a higher price than its book value. As it is not regular profit it is not credited to the revenue account but is transferred to Capital Reserve Account.
3. Premiums received on the issue of shares and debentures.
4. Profit made on the Redemption of debentures in the market at a discount.
5. The balance standing to the credit of Forfeited Shares Account after such shares have been re-issued.
6. Profits of an exceptional nature which have not been earned in the regular course of business.
7. Profit made in purchasing a business, i.e., when the purchase price is less than the net assets acquired.
8. Profit earned prior to incorporation of a limited company.
9. Any profits including revenue profits, which are not represented by liquid asset or which cannot be distributed amongst the shareholders according to the Articles of Association of a Company.
10. Asset Replacement Reserve Fund.

As all such profits are either not earned in the regular course of business or such profits are prohibited to be distributed amongst the shareholders, they are set aside to strengthen the financial position of the company or to meet capital losses. They are carried either to Capital Reserve Account or to Capital Reserve Fund according to whether the amount is retained in the business or is invested in securities respectively.

If such a course is not resorted to, the capital profits may be utilized in the following ways :

1. Issue of Bonus Shares subject to Articles of Association of the company ; or

2. For writing off intangible assets, such as Goodwill, Preliminary Expenses, Cost of the issue of Debentures ; or

(3) The Premium received on the issue of shares, though credited to Capital Reserve Account, can be utilised only for the purposes mentioned in section 78 of the Companies Act, i.e.

(*a*) In paying up unissued shares of the company to be issued to members of the company as fully paid bonus shares ; or

(*b*) in writing off commission Preliminary Expenses; or

(*c*) in writing off commission or expenses or discount, etc., on the issue of debentures or shares; or

(*d*) in providing for the premium payable on the redemption of redeemable preference shares or debentures.

Duties of an Auditor in connection with the Reserve

1. The auditor should see that those capital profits which have been transferred to Capital Reserve Account are reaily surplus of capital over the assets and liabilities;
2. That the capital reserve is utilized according to the Articles and law;
3. Capital profits may be transferred to revenue account and distributed or utilised in writing off previous losses provided it is made clear in the accounts to distinguish such a profit from ordinary trading profits of the business, as was decided in the cases of Foster vs. The New Trinidad Lake Asphalte Company Ltd. (1901) and Lubbock. vs. The British Bank of South America Ltd. (1882). They can be distributed as dividends only.

(*a*) when the Articles of Association permit such a distribution;

(*b*) the surplus is realised; and

(c) such surplus remains after a revaluation af other assets.

4. Capital Reserve must be shown distinctly in the Balance Sheet and must be distinguished from the Revenue Reserve Account. Any additions and deductions since the last Balance Sheet should be clearly shown;
5. Capital Reserve may be invested either in the business itself or may be invested outside the business in easily realisable securities.

(*f*) Secret Reserves

Definition

It has been defined as "any reserve which is not apparent on the face of the Balance Sheet." It is sometimes called "Hidden Reserve or "Internal Reserve" or "Inner Reserve". "Secret Reserves" are an under-statement of assets or an overstatement of liabilities accompanied by a corresponding under statement of capital (Advanced Accountancy—Simon & Karrenbrook). 'This reserve represents the surplus of assets over liabilities and capital but it is not disclosed although the existence of such a reserve may be inferred from an intelligent perusal of the accounts of the concern even though the amount cannot be ascertained. It does appear in the Ledger. Secret Reserve is created usually by Joint Stock Companies especially the banking, insurance and financial concerns. The creation of Secret Reserve may not always be looked upon with suspicion.

How Secret Reserve is Created

A Secret Reserve is created by the following methods:

(*a*) By writing down the assets much below their cost or market value, such as investments, stock-in-hand, land and buildings, plant and machinery, etc.

(*b*) By not writing up the value of an asset, the price of which has permanently gone up.

(*c*) By providing more reserve than necessary for bad and doubtful debts or discount on sundry debtors.

(*d*) By providing excessive depreciation on fixed assets.

(*e*) By writing down the goodwill to a nominal value.

(*f*) By omitting some of the assets altogether from the balance sheet

(g) By charging capital expenditure to revenue account and thus showing the value of the asset to be less than its actual value.

(*h*) By overvaluing the liabilities.

(*i*) By inclusion of fictitious facilities.

(*j*) By showing contingent liabilities as real liabilities.

(*k*) By grouping dissimilar items on the liabilities side of the balance sheet, e.g., reserves, provisions and creditors, under a general heading, as "Sundry Creditors and other Credit Balances."

Objects of Creating Secret Reserve

A Secret Reserve is created with the following objects:

1. The reserve may be used in future to meet any extraordinary loss without disclosing this fact to the shareholders or the outsiders. If this were not done and if a very heavy loss occurs and consequently no dividend is declared, the value of the shares will go down in the market. If it is a banking company, there may be a "rush" on the bank for withdrawals and the bank might go into liquidation.
2. Secret Reserve is created to withhold information of the progress of the company from trade competitors. If the true earning position of the company is shown, it is possible that more rival companies may come into the field and compete with it, thus bringing down its profits.
3. Where the company has made an abnormal profit in a year and when it is intended that the whole of it should not be distributed, a Secret Reserve may be created to be utilized in a lean year.
4. The profits which have been utilized for the payment of dividend, remain in the business and increase the working capital and financial stability of the concern.
5. Such a reserve enables the company to equalise the payment of dividends.

Dangers of or Objections to Create Secret Reserve

1. The balance sheet does not show the correct financial position of the concern. This objection appears to be valid. But the position of the company *is not shown better than* what it actually is. If it is showing better that what it is, then there can be a charge of fraud or manipulation and, therefore, the objection is feasible. If Secret Reserve is created, the balance sheet does not show a true and fair view of the state of affairs of the company as is expected under the Companies Act.
2. The shareholders do not get their due share of the profit when Secret Reserve is created. This may not always be correct. The shareholders are entitled to the reserve later on. But if the shareholder ceases to be so by selling his shares, he loses the profit he would have got, had the Secret Reserve not been created.
3. Value of the shares goes down in the market. But if the dividend paid is the same as in the previous year, the value of shares will not go down in the market.
4. Low dividends and supposed bad position of the company may lead the company into crisis, especially if it is a banking concern as has been explained previously. Secret

reserve may not be created when the profits are insufficient. Thus the question of "supposed bad position" will not arise.

5. By creating Secret Reserve and thus lowering the dividend, the directors may indulge in speculation in the shares of the company.
6. If the fixed assets are undervalued for the purpose of creating Secret Reserve, and if there is a fire, the company will not be able to claim the full value of the assets because the insurance company will pay according to the book value of the asset destroyed or damaged and hence cause a loss to the company.
7. Secret Reserve may be used improperly by the directors and thus conceal their own weakness, e.g., if there has been a loss due to their negligence, such a loss may be drawn upon the Secret Reserve by appreciating the value of an asset which had been under valued in the past for the purpose of creating Secret Reserve. Thus if the position of the company is worse than it appears from the balance sheet due to the creation of Secret Reserve, the directors' policy of concealment cannot be upheld, *vide Newton vs. Birmingham Small Arms Co.* Ltd (1906). There are accountants who are of opinion that if such a reserve is utilized, the shareholders should not only be informed that such a step has been taken but the amount should also be disclosed to them. This change in the opinion of the accountants is due to the decision in the case of *Rex. vs. Kylsant in* 1931. There are others who argue that if this is done the object of creating a Secret Reserve will be frustrated. If an asset is altogether omitted from the Balance Sheet the auditor might omit to verify the asset and, in course of time, the asset might be spirited away. If, however, it is desired at all to reduce the value of an asset considerably, it may be reduced to a nominal amount, rather than omit it altogether from the books of account.
9. According to the Companies Act, creation of Secret Reserve is prohibited except in the case of banking, insurance or finance companies. The reasons are :

(*a*) The Act requires the full disclosure of the accounts relating to the reserves and provisions.

(*b*) The profit and loss account and the balance of a limited company must show *a true and fair* view of the state of affairs of the company. This *true and fair view* of the state of affairs of a company can be shown only when the accounts are not misleading, i.e., there is neither under statement nor over statement of the assets and liabilities of the company. Moreover, according to the proforma of the balance sheet prescribed by the Companies Act, it must show the reserves and provisions. Thus, no secret reserve can be created now except by banking, insurance, electricity, finance companies, etc.

Duty of an Auditor in connection with the Secret Reserve

From the above it would appear that as far as the audit of public companies other than banking, insurance, finance, electricity companies is concerned the position of the auditor is clear. He has to disclose the fact that secret reserve has been created, if it has been done so. If he does not disclose the fact that there is a reserve of such a kind and certifies the banance sheet as showing a *true and fair view* of the state of affairs of the company, he would be making a false statement as some of the assets are under-valued while some of the liabilities are over-valued.

In case of companies such as banking companies, etc.,the auditor should carefully enquire into the necessity of creating such a reserve. If he finds that the intention is honest and that it is in the best interest of the company to create a Secret Reserve, and that the amount is reasonable, he need not qualify his report. It is suggested by certain accountants that the auditor may make a statement like this in case secret reserve has been created: "The value of the assets is understated."

No doubt such a statement will indicate the existence of a Secret Reserve, but the extent of the reserve will not be shown. It is argued that if the shareholders so desire, they may eke out the information by putting questions to the directors. It is further argued that he cannot be accused of making a false statement because the statement which he makes does not mislead any person as was decided in the case of *Newton vs. Birmingham Small Arms Co., Ltd* (1906) where the learned judge said, "The purpose of the Balance Sheet is primarily to show that the financial position of the company is at least as good as there stated, not to show that it is not or may not be better." Moreover, the Balance Sheet does not show the position of the company as better than what it is. If any person deals with the company, which has created Secret Reserve, on the basis of the Balance Sheet he does not suffer any loss. On the contrary, he may gain if he purchases shares on the strength of such a balance sheet as the intrinsic value of the shares is more than what is indicated by the balance sheet. Although from the point of view of the purchaser of the shares this argument is sound but the balance sheet does not represent *the true and fair view of the state* of affairs of the company.

If the auditor finds that intention of the directors is not honest, e.g., to fabricate improper dealings in the shares of the company, he must disclose the fact in his report.

It may be mentioned here that a company cannot by its Articles of Association restrain its auditors from reporting to the shareholders the creation of Secret Reserve as was decided in the case quoted above.

It must be remembered that if any part of a Secret Reserve is utilised by the directors to meet bad and doubtful debts, it must be shown in the Balance Sheet and should not be concealed from the shareholders as was decided in the case of *Shamdasani vs. Pochkhanwala* in 1927, when their Lordships said: ". . . If any part of secret reserve is availed of to meet bad and doubtful book debts, it must be revealed in the Balance Sheet and not concealed."

"A very heavy or long, protracted utilization of the secret reserves, in order to keep the company going, is a serious matter which ought to be disclosed to the company" (*Lord Kylsant's* case, 1931).

"It (Secret Reserve) causes a misrepresentation of facts that may have been put deliberately or may be the outcome of an unintentional error. If the auditor is thorough in his examination of accounts and vigorously adheres to sound accountancy principles, he should discern a Secret Reserve of any substantial amount if it exists and he should endeavour to persuade his client to correct his records. In any event, the auditor should make full disclosure of his report in order to present to his client the final position clearly" (*Auditing-Silvoso & Bauer*).

In the case of partnerships, no Secret Reserve is created but when it is done, all the partners must be aware of such a reserve.

Now since an auditor has to certify a Balance Sheet to represent *a true and fair view* of the state of affairs of the Company, no secret reserve can be created by a limited company.

QUESTIONS

1. Distinguish between the following: —

(*a*) A General Reserve and a Specific Reserve.

(*b*) Capital Reserve and Revenue Reserve. (*Jabalpur B. Com. and N. D. Com.*)

2. What do you understand by the following, and what are the duties of an auditor in respect of these?

(*a*) Reserve Fund. (*b*) Specific Reserve;

(*c*) Depreciation Fund. (*d*) Sinking Fund.

(*Andhra Pb. Service Commission and Marathwada B. Com. 1961*)

3. Describe and contrast:

(*a*) A Reserve which is a charge against profits; and

(*b*) A Reserve which is an appropriation of profits. (*Punjab B. Com. 1962*)

4. What do you understand by "Secret or Internal Reserves"? How are they created in the books of a limited company? Give illustrations. Can such reserves be created under the Companies Act, 1956? What are the auditor's duties in this matter?

(*Gauhati M. Com. and Annamalai B. Com. Hons., Lucknow B. Com. 1971*)

5. Distinguish between.

(*a*) Sinking Fund for the redemption of a liability, and

(*b*) Sinking Fund for the replacement of an asset.

6. A company owning a lease decides to provide for depreciation by taking out a policy for leasehold redemption. How would you deal with the annual premium in the books and how would you adjust the accounts when the lease expires and the policy matures?

7. A company acquires property on a 50 years' lease for Rs. 10,00,000. A difference of opinion has arisen among the directors as whether the cost price of Rs. 10,00,000 should be provided by —

(1) writing off by equal instalments Rs. 20,000 per annum or

(2) the creation of a sinking fund by the company itself.

Discuss the advantages and disadvantages of each of these proposals. (*C.A. Inter. 1964*)

8. What is a Secret Reserve? What safeguards the auditor should observe with regard to their creation, existence and utilization? (*Nagpur B.Com. 1965*)

9. "There is no harm in showing the Balance Sheet worse than what it is in reality; but under no circumstances it may be shown better than what it is". Discuss.

(*Poona and Gujarat B. Com.*)

10. Show the difference between a Reserve and a Reserve Fund and suggest. when the reserve fund should be invested in the outside securities. (*Gujarat B.Com.*)

11. What is meant by capitalisation of Reserves and how Reserves can be capitalised? What are the merits and demerits if any of the policy? Discuss the duties of an auditor in case of capitalisation of reserves. (*Cal. B. Com. Hons. 1969;Annamalai B. Com. 1960*)

12. What is the difference between Capital Profits and Capital Reserve.

(*Calcutta.B. Com. Hons. 1968*)

13. Define the following terms in the Companies Act, 1956:—

(*a*) (*i*) Provision. (*ii*) Capital Reserve. (*iii*) Revenue Reserve.

(*b*) State giving reasons, to which of the above categories each of the following belong: —

(*i*) The amount set aside out of the profits to the anticipated liability of claim for delay in the delivery of goods.

(*ii*) The amount set aside out of the profits to defray the cost of an exclusive advertising campaign which the directors contemplate undertaking during the year subsequent to the date of the balance sheet.

(*iii*) Share premium account, created out of the issue of 20,000 ordinary shares of each at Rs. 150 per share. (*Annamalai B. Com.1961*)

Chapter 22

Audit of Limited Companies — Company Auditor

Introduction

So far we have been considering the general principles of auditing applicable to a concern irrespective of its constitution. In this chapter we shall consider the principles of auditing as applicable to joint stock companies.

Qualifications of an Auditor of a Limited Company

The necessary qualifications of an auditor who can audit the accounts of a limited company are given in Section 226 of the Companies Act which lays down that a person shall not be qualified for appointment as an auditor of a company (public or private) unless he is a Chartered Accountant within the meaning of the Chartered Accountants Act, 1949, and that provided a firm whereas all the persons practising in India are qualified for appointment as aforesaid may be appointed by its firm name to be auditors of a company, in which case any partner so practising may act in the name of the firm.

According to Section 226(2), a person who holds a certificate under the Restricted Auditors Certificates (Part B States) Rules, 1956, is also qualified to act as auditor of a company. However, the Central Government may by notification in the Official Gazette make rules providing for the grant, renewal, suspension or cancellation of such certificates and may prescribe conditions and restrictions for such purposes [Section 226(2) b.]

Disqualifications

The Companies Act, vide Section 226 (3), lays down that none of the following persons are qualified for appointment as auditors of a company —

(*a*) a body corporate;

(*b*) an officer or employee of the company;

(*c*) a person who is a partner, or who is in the employment of the officer or employee of the company;

(*d*) a person who is indebted to the company for an amount exceeding one thousand rupees, or who has given any guarantee or provided any security in connection with the indebtedness of any third person to the company for an amount exceeding one thousand rupees;

(*e*) a person holding any security (i.e., any instrument carrying voting right) of the company.

A person will also be disqualified to become an auditor of a body corporate if he is disqualified as above in relation to its holding company or its subsidiary company or subsidiary company of its holding company.

If an auditor becomes, subject to after his appointment, to any of the disqualifications specified in the foregoing paragraph, he shall be deemed to have vacated his office as such.

I. Appointment of First Auditor [(Section 224(5)]

1. Every company, even a private company, must appoint an auditor or auditors to audit its accounts.
2. The first auditor or auditors of a company shall be appointed by the Board of Directors within one month of the registration of the company and such an auditor shall hold office till the conclusion of the first annual general meeting. The company may, however, at a general meeting remove any such auditor or all or any of such auditors and appoint in his or their places any other person or persons who have been nominated for appointment by any member of the company and of whose nomination notice has been given to the members of the company not less than fourteen days before the date of the meeting.
3. If the Board fails to make such appointment, the company in general meeting may appoint the first auditor. Such an auditor is also automatically reappointed.

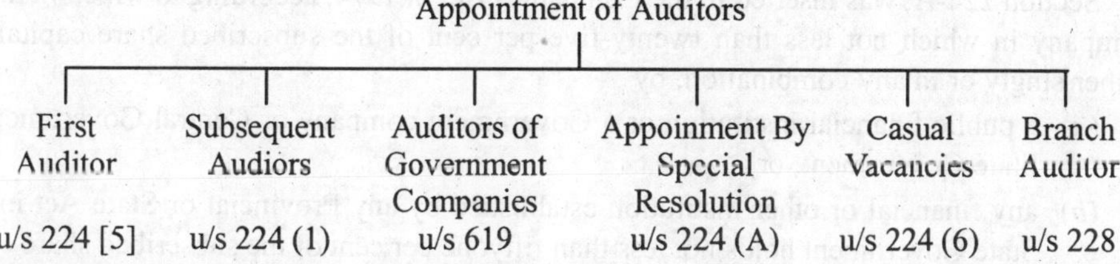

II. Subsequent appointments [(Section 224(1)]

1. Every company shall at each annual general meeting appoint an auditor or auditors to hold office from the conclusion of that meeting until the conclusion of the next annual general meeting and shall, within seven days of the appointment, give intimation thereof to every auditor so appointed, unless he is a retiring auditor.

   It may be stated here that though in theory an auditor is appointed by the shareholders, in practice the directors make the appointment because of the strong voting position exercised by the directors through block votes, proxies, etc., and the disinterest of many shareholders.
2. An auditor so appointed unless he is a retiring auditor shall, within thirty days of the receipt from the company of the intimation of his appointment, inform the Registrar in writing that he has accepted, or refused to accept, the appointment.
3. Where at an annual general meeting no auditors are appointed or re-appointed, the Central Government appoints a person to fill the vacancy.
4. The company shall within seven days of the Central Government's power under sub-section (3), becoming exercisable give notice of that fact to that Government. If the company fails to intimate this fact to the Central Government, the company and every officer who is in default, shall be punishable with a fine which may extend to five thousand rupees.
5. Where it is found that the appointment of the auditor at the annual general meeting was invalid ab initio, the new auditor in his place shall be appointed at the general meeting

of the shareholders.

6. The auditor appointed by whatever authority shall be reappointed at the annual general meeting unless —
   (*a*) he is not qualified for reappointment; or
   (*b*) he has given the company notice in writing of his unwillingness to be re-appointed; or
   (*c*) a resolution has been passed at that meeting appointing somebody instead of him or providing expressly that he shall not be reappointed; or
   (*d*) a notice has been given to the company of an intended resolution to appoint some person or persons in the place of a retiring auditor, and by reason of the death, incapacity or disqualification of that person or of all those persons, as the case may be, the resolution cannot be proceed with.

III. Appointment of auditor of Government Companies [Section 619]

1. The auditor of a Government company is appointed or re-appointed by the Central Government on the advice of the Comptroller and Auditor-General of India (Section 619).

IV. Appointment of Auditor by Special Resolution [(Section 224(A)]

Section 224-A, was inserted in the Companies Act in 1974, according to which in the case of a company in which not less than twenty-five per cent of the subscribed share capital is held, whether singly or in any combination, by-

(*a*) a public financial institution or a Government company or Central Government or any State Government, or

(*b*) any financial or other institution established by any Provincial or State Act in which a State Government holds not less than fiftyone per cent of the subscribed share capital, or

(*c*) a nationalised bank or an insurance company carrying on general insurance business, the appointment or the re-appointment of the auditor or auditors at the annual general meeting shall be made by a special resolution.

If a company does not pass the special resolution making the appointment of the auditor or auditors, it shall be deemed that no auditor had been appointed by the company, and the Central Government may appoint a person to be the auditor of the company.

V. Casual Vacancies [Section 224(6)]

1. Any casual vacancy in the office of an auditor, except one caused by prior resignation, may be filled by the Board but the remaining auditor or auditors may continue to act.
2. When a vacancy has been caused by the resignation of the auditor, it shall be filled only by the general meeting.
3. An auditor appointed to fill a casual vacancy shall hold office till the conclusion of the next annual general meeting.

VI. Appointment of Branch Auditor [Section 228]

1. The audit of the accounts of the branches of the company may be audited by the company statutory auditor.
2. The company may decide to have the accounts of the branches audited by a person other than the company auditor. In such a case, the appointment may be made by shareholders in a general meeting.
3. The Board of directors can appoint the branch auditor if the company has authorised the board of directors to appoint the branch auditors by a resolution passed in general meeting.

While appointing the branch auditor, the board of directors must consult the company statutory auditor.

Powers of the Board to appoint Auditor

As mentioned above, the first auditor of a company is appointed by the Board of Directors.

The Board may also fill any vacancy in the office of the auditor. Such an auditor will hold office till the conclusion of the next annual general meeting. If any vacancy has been caused by the resignation of the auditor, such a vacancy cannot be filled up by the Board. It can be filled up only by the general meeting of the shareholders.

Powers of the Government to Appoint Auditor

If the company does not appoint or re-appoint any auditor at the annual general meeting, the Central Government may appoint a person to fill the vacancy. The company must inform the Central Government within one week of the meeting of the shareholders when no appointment was made to enable the Central Government to appoint an auditor.

Ceiling on number of audits

To meet the demand for the rotation of auditors by the companies, the Companies (Amendment) Act, 1974, has made certain provisions in this direction. Under the new sub-section IB and 1C to Section 224 no individual and no partner of a firm shall hold office as auditor of more than twenty companies of which not more than ten shall be companies with paid-up share capital of rupees twenty-five lakhs or more. Thus it would be observed that a ceiling has been fixed on the number of audits which an auditor can hold simultaneously.

The ceiling, however, does not apply to a private company. This means that the firm or partner, as the case may be, can accept any number of audits of private company without attracting the ceiling limit. But there is a guideline issued by ICAI in this regard which must be adhered to. According to this notification, the total ceiling limit of audit assignment is 30 (including audits of private company). Of these 30, the audit of companies (public or private companies) whose paid up share capital is Rupees 25 lakhs or more should not exceed 10. The ceiling reckoning, will, as aforesaid will be computer per partner. Note the following-

- Where any partner of the firm of Chartered Accountants in practice, is also a partner in any other firm or firms of Chartered Accountants in practice, the number of audit assignments which may be taken for all the firms together in relation to such partner shall not exceed the specified number of audit assignments in the aggregate.
- Where any partner of a firm or firms of Chartered Accountants in practice accepts one or more audit assignments in his individual capacity or in the name of his proprietary firm, the total number of such assignments which may be accepted by all firms in relation to such chartered accountant and by him shall not exceed the specified number of audit assignments in aggregate.
- Where the audit is for head office and also for the branch/s, the assignments will be construed to be one only
- Where the audit is for one or more branches (without head office) of the same company, the audit assignments will be construed to be one only.
- The number of partners to be calculated for accepting an assignment will be as on the date of acceptance of audit assignment.

For example a firm has three partners A, B and C. as per section 224 (1B), it can accept 3 20 = 60 public companies. If some company has paid up capital equal to or more than Rs. 25 lakhs the number of such companies should not exceed $10 \times 3 = 30$ in the above overall ceiling of 60. It may be open to the firm to accept any number of audits of private companies as per section 224(1A).

But to comply the notification of ICAI, the firm must recalculate its overall ceiling thus- 30 × 3 = 90 companies in aggregate of which the public companies with paid up share capital equal to or exceeding Rs 25 lakhs cannot be more than 10 × 3 = 30 companies. Thus the total ceiling will be 90 consisting of these restrictions as under-

(i) The firm can accept audits of 90 private companies or

(ii) The firm can accept audits of 60 public companies and extra 30 private companies.

In case ii above, the audits of Public companies whose paid up capital is Rs 25 lakhs or more should be 30 or less.

The ceiling is subject to reduction in number by such number of units lapsed per partner due to his additional association as partner or proprietor etc., with other firms.

In computing the specified number of audits by a person, all company audits where a person or a firm is appointed as joint auditors, shall also be taken into consideration.

Auditors holding office in more than twenty companies as aforesaid, should within sixty days of the commencement of the Amendment Act, 1974, choose such companies as come within the above description, and notify his unwillingness to continue to hold office in others.

To ensure that the auditor of a company is acting within the above limits, a provision has been added to sub-section (I) which requires in the case of other companies at the annual general meeting, a certificate in writing from the auditor stating that the number of appointments he holds is in accordance with the limits prescribed by sub-section (1 B).

Removal of Auditor

No new auditor can be appointed in place of an existing auditor unless the latter has been given a due notice according to the Companies Act. The Companies Act does not lay down anything as to what will be the consequences if a due notice is not given to the retiring auditor or the members. However, according to law if a due notice has not been given the resolution regarding the removal of the auditor cannot be put before the general meeting. If still the auditor has to be removed, again a general meeting must be held and the auditor removed.

If any shareholder wishes to nominate another person in place of the existing auditor, he must give a special notice (14 days) to the company which in its turn must forthwith send a copy thereof to the retiring auditor. Such an auditor will have the right to send a representation (not exceeding a reasonable length) to the company which in its turn shall send it to the shareholders, provided such a representation was received in time. The company may refuse to send such a representation to the shareholders if the Court is satisfied on the application of the company or any other aggrieved person that this right of representation is being misused by the auditor. The Court may also order for the payment of the expenses incurred by the company in this respect, by the auditor.

In case it was not possible to send the representation to the shareholders if it had been received too late or because of the default of the company, such a representation might be read at the annual general meeting if it is so required by the retiring auditor. The auditor intended to be removed has also a right to attend the general meeting where his removal is to be discussed. He has also a right to speak at such a meeting.

The underlying idea is to prevent the directors to remove an auditor without the knowledge of the shareholders and to appoint another auditor who may readily accede to their wishes. Thus it would be seen that appointment of auditors is more or less in the hands of the shareholders.

An auditor can be removed only by the general meeting, as aforesaid, with the approval of the Central Government but the first auditor can be removed by the general meeting.

The first auditor who is appointed by the directors to hold office till the conclusion of the first annual general meeting may be removed before the expiry of his term by the general meeting even without the approval of the Central Government, provided at least a 14 days' notice before the holding of the meeting had been given to him.

If under any circumstance, it is desired to remove an auditor before the expiry of his term, the approval of the Central Government must be obtained before holding the general meeting at which a resolution removing him is passed. A due notice must be given to the auditor to enable him to make any representation if he so desires. He has a right to attend such a meeting and speak at the meeting.

Remuneration and Expenses of an Auditor

1. If the auditor has been appointed by the Board of Directors, it is the Board which fixes his remuneration.
2. If the auditor has been appointed by the Central Government under the circumstances mentioned above, the Central Government fixes his remuneration.
3. In case, the auditor is appointed by Comptroller and Auditor General of India under section 619 of the Companies Act, 1956, the remuneration shall be fixed company in general meeting or in such manner as the company decides in general meeting.
4. If the auditor has been appointed by the shareholders at the general meeting, it is the company which determines his remuneration unless the company in general meeting may delegate the power of fixing his remuneration to some one else, e.g., the Board of Directors. It is not necessary that the remuneration be fixed at the same meeting at which his appointment has been made.
5. The retiring auditor who is automatically re-appointed at the annual meeting, unless a resolution is passed refixing his remuneration, is entitled to get the same remuneration as he was getting previously.
6. If an auditor is asked to do any other work over and above his normal work of audit, e.g., preparing the final accounts or income-tax returns, he is entitled to get extra remuneration.

Any sum paid by the company in respect of the auditor's expenses shall be deemed to be included in the expression "remuneration." The profit and loss account shall contain detailed information regarding the payment to him in his capacity as an auditor and in any other capacity schedule Vl, Part II, Clause 4 B).

Different Classes of Auditors

(a) Joint Auditors

Section 2 (9) defines a branch as: "branch office" in relation to a company means-

(*a*) any establishment described as a branch by the company; or

(*b*) any establishment carrying on either the same or substantial the same activity as that carried on by the head office of the company; or

(*c*) any establishment engaged in any production, processing or manufacture;

but does not include any establishment specified in any order made by the Central Government under Section 8.

Thus this definition covers not only branches described as such by a company but also includes any establishment where production, processing and manufacture of goods is carried on.

Sometimes one or more auditors are appointed when the business of the company extends over a large area to enable the auditors to finish the work more quickly and efficiently. In such a case the auditors have a joint responsibility. In order to avoid a joint responsibility it will be better if the work between them is divided and the auditors make a declaration in their report as to what work has been performed by each one of them to avoid the responsibility of the work which was not performed by a particular auditor.

(b) Branch Auditors

According to Section 228 of the Companies Act, 1956, a company having a branch shall get the accounts of that branch audited by its auditor appointed under Section 224, or by any person qualified under Section 226. If the branch is in a foreign country, by the auditor of the company or by any person who is qualified under Section 226, or by an accountant duly qualified to act as an auditor of the accounts of the branch office in accordance with the laws of that country.

Where the accounts of any branch are audited by a person other than the company's auditor, the company's auditor —

(*a*) shall be entitled to visit the branch if he deems it necessary to do so for the performance of his duties as auditor; and

(*b*) shall have a right of access at all times to the books and accounts and vouchers of the company maintained at the branch office :

Provided that in the case of a banking company having a branch office outside India, it shall be sufficient if the auditor is allowed access to such copies of, and extracts from, the books and accounts of the branch as have been transmitted to the principal office of the company in India.

Whereas a company in general meeting decides to have the accounts of a branch audited otherwise than by the company's auditor, the company in that meeting shall appoint an auditor qualified under Section 226 or authorise the Board of Directors to make such appointment in consultation with the company's auditor. The auditor so appointed shall have the same powers and duties in respect of the audit of the branch accounts as that of the auditor of the head office, e.g., inspection of the branch account books, vouchers, etc., and ask for any explanation he may require. The branch auditor shall prepare an audit report on the accounts of the branch office and forward the same to the company's auditor who will incorporate the same in his report as he deems fit. A certificate should be attached with the balance sheet of the company for each year that there has been no change in the internal audit arrangement for the audit of the accounts of the branch office. This certificate should be signed by the same person who signed the balance sheet. The branch auditor shall receive such remuneration and shall hold office subject to such terms and conditions as may be fixed either by the company in general meeting or by the Board of Directors if so authorised by the company in general meeting.

The duty of the auditor of the head office is to see that the branch or foreign office accounts are properly incorporated in the head office books and he should mention in his report that he has accepted the returns from the branch office duly certified by the branch auditor. While examining the branch returns, the auditor of the head office should pay attention to the following points:

(*a*) that the branch returns have been signed by the branch manager and auditor ;

(*b*) that the branch returns contain full details of the sales and purchases, income and expenditure, and assets and liabilities ;

(*c*) that the assets and liabilities are grouped according to Schedule VI, Parts I and II of the Companies Act ;

(*d*) that the current account between the head office and the branch is correct ;

(*e*) that the stock-in-trade has been valued according to the accepted principles which have been followed in the past ;

(*f*) that adequate depreciation has been provided for on fixed assets ;

(g) that adequate provision has been made for bad and doubtful debts and that the outstanding advances for more than three months have been classified as loans ;

(*h*) that the bank balance has been confirmed by the bankers of the branch ;

(*i*) that cash in hand at the branch has been confirmed ;

(*j*) that the liabilities of the branch are correctly stated ;

(*k*) that the balances shown by the branch have been correctly converted into home currency according to rules.

He should also examine the report of the branch auditor.

Where an exemption has been granted to the company for the audit of its branch accounts under S. 228 (4), the auditor of the company should state that the branch office is exempt from the requirements of the compulsory audit by virtue of Rule 3 or that an exemption has been granted under Rule 4.

Exemption of Branch Audit

The Central Government may, however, exempt a company from the provisions of Sec. 228(4) of the Companies Act regarding the compulsory audit of branch accounts under certain circumstances, e.g., even an employee or an officer of the company may be appointed provided he is, otherwise, qualified as a branch auditor of the company or a branch auditor may not be employed if —

(*a*) the total amount of the goods manufactured or sold or the services rendered ; or

(*b*) the total amount of expenditure, whether capital or revenue, of the branch concerned does not exceed Rs. two lakhs or the two per cent of the average of the total turn over of the company including all its branches and the earnings from services rendered and from any other source during the same financial year, whichever is higher.

The quantum of activity shall be the average for the three years immediately preceding the financial year.

When a company wishes to apply for exemption, it must apply to the Central Government and state the grounds on which it claims exemption. The grounds may be :

1. that the company engaged in trading has made satisfactory arrangements for the scrutiny of the accounts of the branch office at regular intervals; or
2. that the company has made arrangement for the audit of the branch accounts by a person who is qualified to be the auditor of the branch even though he is an employee of the company; or
3. that having regard to the nature and the quantum of activity carried on by the branch office or for any other reason, a branch auditor is not likely to be available at a reasonable cost; or
4. any other reason.

If the application is made on the ground mentioned in (2), it must be accompanied by the following:

(*a*) a certificate by the company that satisfactory arrangements for internal audit for the branch office have been made;

(*b*) a certificate from the auditor of the company that arrangements for internal audit of the branch accounts are adequate and that the branch accounts are properly maintained.

If the application is made under (3) above, a statement showing the names of the auditors who had been requested to undertake the audit work of the branch and the fees quoted by them should be attached with the application.

If the Central Government is satisfied after making inquiries, it may grant the exemption sought for. It must be stated here that if exemption is granted the auditor of the company will have the right to visit the branch office and have access to the books of account and vouchers, etc., if he deems it necessary to visit the branch office.

The Central Government must send a copy of such a sanction to the statutory auditor of the company and it has to be read at the general meeting of the shareholders. The Central Government is empowered to withdraw this exemption if the terms and conditions of exemption have not been observed. The auditor appointed as stated above will have all those powers and rights as if he were a statutory auditor.

Powers and Duties of an Auditor

An auditor to perform his duties must have certain powers without which it may not be possible for him to perform his duties honestly and, thereby, he might be held liable for any loss which the company might suffer. In the case of the auditor of an individual or a firm, the question does not arise as the powers and duties of such an auditor depend upon the agreement which is entered in between him on the one hand and the private individual or the firm on the other, as the case may be. But in the case of the auditors of Joint-Stock Companies, the Companies Act has laid down the powers and duties of an auditor. We are concerned here principally with those powers, rights and duties which are detailed below:

Rights and Powers of an Auditor

1. *Right of access to books of account.* The auditor has a right of access at all times to the books of account and vouchers of the company whether kept at the head office of the company or elsewhere and also to the returns submitted by the branch offices to the head office [*Cuff vs. London and County Land Building Company Ltd. 1912)*] [Section 227 (I).] The term "books" includes not only those which pertain to accounts but also all the statutory, statistical and costing books while the vouchers include documentary evidence of any nature pertaining to the books and account under audit such as memorandum, minute books, stock books, share ledger, vouchers which include any documentary evidence in respect of a transaction in the books of account, contracts, correspondence, invoices, etc. Although the auditor has got right of access to the books of account, etc., *at all times* he generally does not exercise it. He informs or consults the directors as to which time will be suitable and convenient to them before he goes to check the accounts. But in case he has some suspicion, he need not contact the directors and must pay a surprise visit.

2. *Right to call information and explanations.* He has got a right to ask the directors and officers of the company, to give any information and explanations as may be necessary for the due discharge of his duty as auditor. [Section 227 (1).] The word "officer" includes Managing Agents, Secretaries and Treasurers or the Secretary, etc. If the Managing Agents, Secretaries, etc., is or are a firm, he can ask for an explanation from any partner of such firm. If such officers consist of a company, then he can question any director, managing director, etc., of such a company.

3. *Right to receive notice of and attend general meeting.* To receive a notice of and to attend every general meeting of the shareholders irrespective of the fact whether accounts are being discussed or not at such a meeting. He has a right to speak at such meeting when the accounts are being discussed (Section 231). It may be remembered that the auditor has such a right but he may or may not exercise this right if he so desires.

4. *Right to make statement at the general meeting.* He has a right to make any statement or explanation he desires at such a meeting in connection with the accounts but is not bound to do so. If an auditor is present at a meeting, he is not bound to answer any question unless he is asked to do so by the chairman of the meeting. He should answer only those questions which affect the accounts.

   If he finds that some wrong statement has been made by the directors relating to the accounts, he has the right to correct it. He cannot relieve himself of a responsibility for any omission in his report by making a verbal statement at the meeting to cover such omission. It must be remembered that according to Section 201, any provision, whether contained in the articles of the company, or in any contract with the company or otherwise, for affording to any auditor relief or exemption from or indemnity against any liability, shall be void.

5. *Right to indemnified.* He has a right to be indemnified out of the assets of the company against any liability incurred by him in defending himself against civil and criminal proceedings by the company provided he is acquitted of the charges or judgment is given in his favour or the court is of opinion that the auditor acted honestly. (Section 633). (Article 99 of Table A.)
6. *Right to visit the branches.* The auditor of a company has the right to visit the branches of the company to audit the accounts provided no qualified auditor to audit the accounts of these branches has been appointed and exemption to get the branch accounts audited has not been granted to the company by the Central Government. In case he has to audit the accounts of the branches, he will have the right of access to all the books of accounts and vouchers, etc., of the branches at all times. If the eompany is a banking company and has branches outside India, the auditor will have no right to visit such branches but will have the right of access to all the returns sent by the branch to the head office (Section 228).
7. *Right to take legal and technical advice.* He has the right to take legal, expert or technical advice but he must give his opinion in the report and not that of the experts, lawyers, etc. (Re London and General Bank, 1895).
8. *Right to remuneration.* An auditor has the right to have his remuneration paid to him provided he has eompleted the work he undertook to do. But if an accountant has been Employed at an annual fee and is dismissed during the currency of the year he is entitled to a full year's fee as was held in *Homer vs. Quilter* in 1908. Lancaster is of opinion that an auditor dismissed subsequently to his election would be entitled to a similar claim in respect of fees. Similar considerations apply in the case of an auditor to a partnership.
9. *Right to sign the audit report.* Only the person appointed as auditor of the company, or where a firm is so appointed, only a partner of the firm practising in India, may sign the auditor's report, or sign or authenticate any other document of the company required by law to be signed or authenticated by the auditor (Section 229).
10. *Right of Lien.*
    (*i*) The right of lien is possessory right available to a person to retain the goods belonging to others upon which he has worked or with respect to which he rendered service. During his audit work, the auditor works upon the books of accounts, documents, records etc., of his client. He also prepares working papers for his audit reference. The working papers prepared by him for his reference belong to him. As a owner he can refuse to part with his working papers when claimed by the client.
    (*ii*) The auditor works on the books of accounts, documents etc., belonging to the client if he has work on them. He acts as an accountant or as an auditor depending upon the terms of engagement. The accountant has right of lien on the books on which he worked. The right of lien of auditor over the books which he audited is a disputed one In the case of *Herbert Alfred Burliegh vs. Ingram, Clark Ltd* (1901), it was decided that the auditor had no lien on the books of account in respeet of the audit work. But if the work was of the nature of accountaney, lien could be exercised. The judgment of Justice Joyce runs as under:

"The affidavits filed show that the respondent claims a lien not as auditor, but as an accountant. In my opinion the question of an auditor's lien did not arise, and had it done so, I consider an auditor has no such lien; but that point I do not decide now. In respect of the Share Register, the accountant has no possible lien on that, he is entitled to a lien on such books as he had actually worked upon in respect of his proper remuneration for work upon those books only."

An accountant can exercise lien on correspondence and working papers as was decided in the case of *Sockockinsky vs. Bright Graham & Co.*, 1938.

On the other hand the case of *Arthur Francis Ltd*, Justice Swinfen Eady ordered the auditors who claimed lien on books of account in respect of accountancy and auditing charges to hand over such books to the Liquidators for the due discharge of the work of liquidation without prejudice to the right of lien by the auditors. The same decision was taken in the case of *Findle vs. Waddell* (1910). In the case of *Hoale, Smith & Field vs. Valattine Tingey*, 1926, it was a dispute as to the amount due to the plaintiffs, which was decided in their favour. The judgment on the subject of an accountant's lien in this case is quoted below:

"Now with regard to the books. The plaintiffs claim a lien for their work done upon the books and papers and the matter was dealt with by a sum being paid into court.... I think, a very weighty opinion and in principle it seems to me with regard to the papers and the books upon which the plaintiffs did work and on which they themselves made a considerable number of entries, their rights to a lien existed and the counter claim must be dismissed."

Again in the case of *Chantrey Martin & Co. vs. Martin* (1953), it was decided that the auditor has a lien on the working papers prepared by him for the purpose of producing the balance sheet but with regard to the correspondence between the accountant and the Inland Revenue regarding taxation belonged to the client.

From the above it can be appreciated that different views exist with respect to the right of lien of auditors. It stands to reason that the auditor may exercise right of lien if he renders service with respect to the books of accounts over which he claims the right.

(*a*) However the right of lien is exercisable only if the books come to the possession of the auditor in a lawful way during the course of his professional work.

(*b*) The remuneration or other out-of pocket expenses lawfully due to the auditor have not been paid.

(*c*) The books of account or other documents belong to the client.

(*d*) The exercise of right of lien should not hinder the operation of any of the provisions of statute. For example, under Companies Act, certain statutory registers must be kept with the registered office, similarly such books of account as prescribed in section 209 of the Companies Act must be kept in the registered office of the company only. The auditor, even though, might have worked on or with reference to them, cannot claim the right of lien defeating the requirements of the sections of statute.

(*e*) The right of lien of an auditor is not a general one. He has right of particular lien only. He can exercise lien over the books, papers etc., which have come to him for doing the work in respect of which the remuneration is unpaid. He cannot exercise lien over other records relating to some other engagement or work.

(*f*) The right of lien of the auditor does not extend to money left with him by the client. The reasons are :

1. The auditor has not worked on the money entrusted to him by his client.
2. The money belonging to his client is in trust with him and he is, therefore, a trustee of such money.
3. If he appropriates the money of the client, he would be guilty of breach of trust and is liable to be criminally punished.

4. If, however, the client has expressly or impliedly authorised him to use the money for the payment of his professional fees, the auditor is perfectly within his right to use that money.
5. The money with the auditor should be used strictly according to the instructions of his client and the money unspent should be returned to the client and he may sue him for the unpaid professional fee.

Duties of an Auditor

1. *Duty to make report.* An auditor is appointed to keep a check on the directors and therefore he has to send his report to the member even though he might have been appointed by the directors as we have already seen in the beginning of this chapter . He is the agent of the shareholders to examine the accounts maintained and supervised by the directors and to report to them whether the directors have properly maintained the accounts (*Spaceman vs. Eans*); (1868). Lindley J. said,.... "the auditors are to be appointed by the shareholders, and are to report to them directly and not to or through the directors. The object of this enactment is obvious. It evidently is to secure to the shareholders independent and reliable information respecting the true financial position of the company at the time of the audit." (*Re London and Central Bank,* 1895). It is not the duty of an auditor to see that his report has been sent or placed in the hands of the shareholders. After having signed his report and the balance sheet and having sent it to the secretary of the company, his duty is over, as was held in *Re Allen, Craig & Co. (London)* Ltd in 1934.

2. *Matters to be stated in the report*. The auditor will report to the shareholders about the accounts which have been audited by him. The report shall contain the following:

(*a*) whether or not he has obtained all the information and explanation which to the best of his knowledge and belief were necessary for the purposes of his audit;

(*b*) whether, in his opinion, the Profit and Loss Account referred to in his report exhibits a true and fair view of the profit or loss; and

(*c*) whether, in his opinion, the Balance Sheet referred to in his report is properly drawn up so as to exhibit a true and fair view of the state of affairs of the company according to the best of the information and explanation given to him as shown by the books of accounts;

(*d*) whether in his opinion, proper books of account as required by law have been kept by the company so far as appears from his examination of those books, and proper returns adequate for the purposes of his audit have been received from branches not visited by him;

(*e*) whether the report on the accounts of any branch office audited under Section 228 by a person other than the company's auditor has been forwarded to him as required by clause (c) of sub-section (3) of that section and how he has dealt with the same in preparing the auditor's report;

(*f*) whether or not the balance sheet and profit and loss account have been drawn up according to the requirements of the Companies Act. (Form and contents of the balance sheet and profit and loss account as required by Section 211 are given at the end of this chapter).

(*g*) Whether in his opinion, the profit and loss account and balance sheet comply with the prescribed accounting standards.

(*h*) The auditor has to report in thick type of italics, the observations or comments of the auditor which have any adverse effect on the functioning of the company.

(*i*) The auditor should also report whether any director is disqualified from being appointed as director under clause (*g*) of sub-section (1) section 274.

(*j*) Whether the cess payable under section 441 A

(*k*) has been paid and if not, the details of amount no paid.

The auditor shall also inquire, according to S. 227(1A) —

(*a*) whether the loans and advances by the company against security are properly secured and that the terms of the loan and advances are not against the interests of the company or its members ;

(*b*) whether the transactions of the company which are represented merely by book entries are not prejudicial to the interest of the company ;

(*c*) in the case of a non-banking company, whether the company has sold its investments, such as debentures, shares, etc., during the year at a price less than the purchase price ;

(*d*) whether loans and advances made by the company have been shown as deposits ;

(*e*) whether personal expenses have been charged to revenue account; and

(*f*) where the company has allotted shares against cash, whether the cash has actually been received and whether the position as stated in the account books and the balance sheet is correct, regular and not misleading.

If the answer to the above matters is in negative or with qualifications he shall report the reason for the answer.

How is an auditor to ascertain the true position of the company's affairs. The answer is, by examining the books of the company. But he does not discharge his duty by doing this without enquiry, and without taking any trouble to see that the books themselves show the company's true position. But his first duty is to examine the books, not merely for the purpose of ascertaining what they do show, but also for the purpose of satisfying himself that they show the true financial position of the company. (*Re London and General Bank*). Again, it was pointed out by Madras High Court in *Registrar of Companies, Bombay vs. Hegde (1954)* that the duty of the auditor is not merely to satisfy himself with the arithmetical accuracy of the balance sheet, as compared with the books of the company, but to enquire into and satisfy himself with the substantial accuracy of the balance sheet and to see that it contains a true and correct picture of the company's affairs. Similar view was expressed by the learned Judge in the cases of *Deputy Secretary to the Government of India, Ministry of Finance vs. S.N. Dasgupta in 1956 and Controller of Insurance vs. H. C. Das in 1957.*

The auditor has got the duty to mention in his report if he is not satisfied with regard to any point or if he could not get any information or explanation that in his opinion should be placed before the members.

If the system of book-keeping is bad the auditor should make a suggestion regarding the alteration and if the directors do not follow his suggestion, he should mention the fact in his report. Of course he cannot force the directors to change the system of book-keeping.

3. Duty to *assist Investigators*. It is the duty of an auditor to assist the Inspectors in every possible way when the affairs of the company are being investigated. He can be asked to produce the working papers for the purpose. [Section 240 (*v*)(*b*).]

4. It is the duty of the auditor to call for information on various points, such as (*a*) whether loans have been properly secured, (*b*) whether the shares, debentures securities, etc., have been sold at less than the purchase value, and (*c*) whether the personal expenses have been charged to revenue account, etc. It may be stated here in this connection that before the Companies Act was amended in 1965, the auditor was entitled to make such an inquiry but after the amendment, a duty has been cast upon the auditor to state in his report whether he has taken such steps or not. He has also to express his opinion as whether the loans advanced are secured or not. He should also state money deposited by the public with the company has been shown in the balance sheet as deposits.

In addition to the above duties of an auditor in connection with the audit of the annual accounts, the auditor of a limited company has to perform the following duties:

1. Duty to *certify the Statutory Report*. He has to certify the correctness of the Statutory report as far as:

(*a*) the number of the shares which have been allotted by the company whether against cash or for consideration other than cash;

(*b*) the total amount of cash received by the company in respect of all the shares allotted, distinguished as aforesaid;

(*c*) an abstract of the receipt of the company and the payments made there out, etc. (Section 165).

2. *Duty to certify Profit and Loss Account in a Prospectus*. If an existing company issues prospectus, it should contain a statement of profits and losses, year-wise for the previous five years showing the rate of dividends paid each year and a statement of assets and liabilities of the company. Such a statement has to be certified by the auditor of the company. (Section 56).

The statutory duties of the auditors mentioned above can be expanded but they cannot be restricted either by the Articles of Association or the Directors of the company as was held in the case of *Newton vs. The Birmingham Small Arms Co. Ltd* (1906).

Status of an Auditor

An auditor is appointed by the shareholders except in the case of the first auditor of the company who is appointed by its promoters or the Board of Directors or an auditor who is appointed by the directors during the currency of the year on account of the death of the auditor or by the Central Government in certain cases. It is the right of the shareholders to appoint an auditor. He is appointed by them to keep a check on the work of the directors, as far as accounts are concerned. He is to send a report to the shareholders even though he might have been appointed by the directors. The shareholders fix his remuneration if he is appointed by them. In cast he is appointed by the directors of the Government his remuneration is fixed by the directors or the Government respectively. The shareholdes may allow him to continue to act as auditor for the next year or may appoint another auditor with the approval of the Central Government. It is they who pay him, of course, out of the funds of the company. The question is whether he is the agent of shareholders or of the directors, or he is an officer of the company, just like the Secretary, Manager, Accountant, etc. Apparently it appears that he performs the functions of an agent as well as that of an officer of the company. Divergent views have been expressed even by the courts. Let us deal with some of these views.

Lord Cranworth in the course of his judgment in the case of *Spackman vs. Evans, said*, "The auditors may be agents of the shareholders, so far as it relates to the audit of the accounts. For the purposes of the audit, the auditors will bind the shareholders."

Lord Chelmsford said in the same case, "It seems to me that it would be an unreasonable conclusion from the mode of appointment of these officers that they were thereby constituted agents so as to conclude the shareholders by their knowledge of any unauthorised act of the directors."

As to how far the auditors are the agents of the shareholders, Turne J., said with respect to fraudulet representations made by the director of a company as to his position, "These were auditors of the company appointed by the shareholders. These auditors were within the scope of their duty, at least as much the Agent of the shareholders as the directors were, and the false and fraudulent representations were discoverable by them." *Nicols case, re Royal British Bank*.

From the above, it will appear that an auditor is an agent of the shareholders so far as it relates to the audit of the accounts of the company.

According to the law of agency the knowledge of the agent is the knowledge of the principal.' Although from the above discussion it would appear that an auditor is an agent of the principal (shareholders), but the shareholders are not bound for any information which the auditor might have acquired during the course of audit if he had not communicated it to the shareholders.

Again, if the auditor had given an information to the directors, it will not amount to giving the information to the shareholders (the principals). If they have to communicate anything to the shareholders, they must do it through their report to them.

Let us now see the other side of the picture. If an auditor is to be considered as an officer of the company, he will be held liable under Sections 477, 478, 539, 543, 545, 621, 625 and 633 of the Companies Act, 1956. These sections refer to the following matters respectively:

(*a*) Power of the Court in winding up to summon persons suspected of having property of the company, S. 477.

(*b*) Power of the Court to order public examination of persons guilty of fraud etc., in the promotion, formation or management of the company, S. 478.

(*c*) Penalty for the falsification of books, Section 539.

(*d*) Power of the court to assess damages against delinquent officers, Section 543.

(*e*) Prosecution of delinquent officers and members, Section 545.

(*f*) Cognisance of offences under the Act, Section 621.

(*g*) Payment of compensation in cases of frivolous or vexatious officers, Section 625.

(*h*) Power of the Court to grant relief to officers in proceedings for negligence, default, breach of duty, misfeasance, etc., provided that in a criminal proceeding, the court shall have no power to grant relief from any civil liability which may attach to an officer in respect of such negligence, default, breach of duty, misfeasance or breach of trust, Section 633.

It is, therefore, very important to know whether an auditor is or is not an officer of the company. Under the above-quoted sections, an officer includes an 'auditor' in the event of the company going into liquidation and in certain other cases. Again, in the case of *London and General Bank*, it was held that an auditor is an officer of the company when Justice Lindley said, "It seems impossible to deny that for some purpose, and to some extent, an auditor is an officer of the company. He is appointed by the company and his position is described in the section as that of an officer of the company. He is not a servant of the directors. On the contrary, he is appointed by the company to check the directors and for some purposes and to some extent, it seems to me quite impossible to say that he is not an officer of the company." It may be mentioned here that in this particular case, the Articles of the company specifically mentioned the auditor as an officer of the company. But in another case, viz., *Kingston Cotton Mills* case, though the auditors were not referred to as officers of the company, it was held that they were officers.

Again, in another case, viz., *The Western Countries Steam Bakeries and Milling Company Ltd* (1897), Lord Justice Lindley remarked: "If all person who did auditor's work for a company were officers of the company, the case would be easy but no decision has yet gone this length. An auditor may not be an officer of a company. So may anybody else— e.g., a banker or a solicitor. *Prima facie* such persons are not officers. To be an officer there must be an office and office imparts a recognised position with rights and duties annexed to it, and it would be an abuse of words to call a person an officer who fills no position either *de jure or de facto*, but who happens to do some of the work which he would have to do if he were officer in the proper sense of word." It was held, therefore, that casual auditors employed by a company to do a particular accounting work are not "officers". Similarly, an accountant to whom books have been handed over to prepare a balance sheet is not an officer. [*Findley vs. Waddell* (1910).]

In the case of *connel vs. Himalaya Bank*, 1895, it was held that "auditors" if appointed as such at a general meeting of the company and if also paid by the company, were officers of the company. Later on according to S. 2 (11) of the Indian Companies Act of 1913, it was held that auditors were not "officers" except for the purpose of sections mentioned therein. (*Hudson vs. Official Liquidating, Dehra Dun Mussorie Electric Tramway Company*, 1929).

What to talk of an auditor being an officer of the company, he is not even an employee of the company for he is at liberty to work for any one, even three or more companies at the same time. He need not perform the audit work himself and may entrust that work which he has undertaken to perform to his subordinates. Generally speaking an agent cannot appoint a subagent except under certain circumstances but an auditor generally gets the work done by his assistants. For the reasons stated above we may conclude that he is not even an employee of the company.

To know whether an auditor is an officer or an agent one has to decide the question according to the circumstances of each particular case.

Preliminaries to be gone through before the actual work is begun by the Auditor

1. Whether his appointment is in order

(*a*) If he has been appointed as the first auditor of the company by the directors before the annual general meeting, he should get a copy of the resolution by the directors about his appointment.

(*b*) If he is appointed in place of a retiring auditor, he should inquire whether due notice was given to the previous auditor. Even if a due notice was given to the retiring auditor, according to the provisions of the Chartered Accountants Act, 1949, he should inquire in writing from such an auditor the circumstances under which he retired and whether he should take up the new appointment and whether the requirements of Section 225 in respect of such an appointment had been complied with. If he does not communicate with the previous auditor in this connection it may be treated as breach of professional etiquette and therefore an action may be taken against him by the Council of the Institute of Chartered Accountants of India (*Kharwanidikar vs. Borker*, 1952).

(*c*) If he has been appointed by the shareholders at the annual general meeting, he should get a copy of the shareholders' resolution. He should within thirty days of the receipt of appointment letter, inform the Registrar in writing that he has accepted, or refused to accept the appointment. He should see that proper notice of nomination had been given, otherwise his appointment will be invalid.

(*d*) If he has been appointed to fill a casual vacancy caused by the death of the previous auditor he should get a copy of the minutes of the Board to see whether he was properly appointed. He should also get the confirmation of the death of the previous auditor.

(*e*) In case the vacancy was caused by the resignation of the previous auditor, the Board has no power to fill that vacancy. In such a case a general meeting of the shareholders should be held to appoint a new auditor in place of the auditor who has resigned. The auditor should see that these requirements of Section 224 (6) of the Companies Act have been complied with. He should also make inquiry from the auditor who had resigned as to the circumstances under which he resigned and whether he should accept the appointment.

II. Inspection of the Documents and Books

Before theauditor commences the work of audit, he should examine the following documents:"

(*a*) Memorandum of Association

He should examine the Memorandum of Association of the Company for the following objects:

(*i*) To see whether the company is carrying on the work according to the 'Object Clause' of the Memorandum. If it is not the case, the transaction will be void and it will be the duty of the auditor to bring that fact to the notice of the shareholders, otherwise he will be held guilty.

(*ii*) Whether the issue of the share capital is within the 'Authorised Capital', and that only two classes of shares have been issued as are mentioned in the Companies Act.

(*iii*) The Memorandum of Association is examined as far as it relates to the accounts of the company.

(*iv*) If authorised capital has been increased according to law, he should get a copy of the resolution.

(*b*) Articles of Association

The Articles of Association are examined to ascertain the following:

(*i*) The issue of share capital and its sub-divisions.

(*ii*) The payment of underwriting commission and brokerage on shares.

(*iii*) The amount of minimum subscription upon which the company may proceed to allot the shares. This amount is mentioned in the Articles. According to Section 69 of the Companies Act, the directors are restrained to allot shares until the amount fixed as the minimum subscription according to the articles of association of the company has been received. Minimum subscription is the amount which in the opinion of the directors must be raised. The minimum subscription is estimated by taking the following into consideration:

1. The purchase price of any property to be met out of the proceeds of the issue ;
2. The preliminary expenses and commission on shares payable by the company ;
3. Repayment of moneys borrowed for these purposes ;
4. working capital ;
5. and other expenditure.

If shares have been allotted before the minimum subscription has been received, the directors are liable to a fine.

(*iv*) To know the dates on which a call can be made and the amount thereof.

(*v*) Whether any interest is to be charged for calls in arrears, and interest payable for calls paid in advance which should not exceed 6 per cent unless the company decides otherwise.

(*vi*) The circumstances under which shares can be forfeited and re-issued.

(*vii*) Borrowing powers of the company and the directors, etc.

(*viii*) The recorganisation of the share capital.

(*ix*) Dividends and the reserves.

(*x*) Appointment, renunciation, powers and duties of the auditor in addition to the statutory powers and duties.

(*xi*) Meetings and how they can be called.

(*xii*) Voting powers of the shareholders.

(*xiii*) The appointment, remuneration and duties of the managing agents.

(*xiv*) Appointment, remuneration, etc., of the directors.

(*xv*) Accounts and audit of the company.

(*xvi*) Payment of interest out of capital.

(*xvii*) Rights as to dividends, etc., of various classes of shareholders if they are not indicated in the Memorandum of Association and the procedure to declare dividends and interim dividends.

These are a few items for which the Articles of a Company are to be referred to. In case the company has not adopted its own Articles, Table A of the Companies Act will apply.

It must be mentioned here that an auditor cannot escape liability on the plea that he was unaware of the Articles of the company or that he did not consult them as was held in the case of *Leeds Estate Building and Investment Society Ltd vs. Shepherd (1887).*

(*c*) Prospectus

The auditor must examine the Prospectus to ascertain almost all the points which have been mentioned above under the Articles of Association. He should persue the Prospectus in case of first audit of a Limited Company to examine the contracts entered into with vendors, if any; contracts entered into with third parties; underwriting commission and brokerage payable; whether the shares can be issued at a discount, the amounts payable on application, allotment, calls etc. In subsequent audits, it is not necessary to go through the prospectus.

(*d*) List of Books

He should ask the authorities to hand over to him a list of all the books of account, statistical and statutory books maintained by the company. Section 209 of the Companies Act lays down:

Every company shall keep at its registered office proper books of account, with respect to-

(*a*) all sums of money received and expended by the company and the matters in respect of which the receipt and expenditure take place;

(*b*) all sales and purchases of goods by the company; and

(*c*) the assets and liabilities of the company.

Statutorybooks are those books which a Limited Company is under a statutory obligation to maintain at its Registered Office, the list and details of which are given below:-

1. Register of Investments which are held in the name of its Nominees Section 49 (7)].

A company generally holds its investments in its own name but in case it makes investments in the names of its nominees, it has to maintain a Register which should record the following facts:

(*a*) The nature, value and such other particulars as may be necessary to identify fully the shares and securities in question, and

(*b*) The bank or the person in whose name or custody such shares or securities are held.

The auditor has to inspect this register while verifying the investments by the company and to see that the provisions of the Companies Act are being followed.

2. Register of Mortgages and Charges (Section 142).

Whenever a company mortgages its property or creates a charge, whether fixed or floating, on its assets, it must enter the following particulars in this Register:

(*a*) a short description of the property charged ;

(*b*) the amount of the charge ; and

(*c*) except in the case of securities to bearer, the names of the persons entitled to the charge.

The auditor has to examine this Register to find out whether any assets of the company have been charged, and if so, the nature of the charge.

3. Register of Members (Section 150).

This Register contains the names of the members of the company and the following particulars are entered in it:

(*a*) the name, address and his occupation, if any, of each member ;

(*b*) in the case of a company having a share capital, the shares held by each member, distinguishing each share by its number and the amount paid or agreed to be considered as paid on those shares ;

(*c*) the date on which each person was entered in the Register as member; and

(*d*) the date on which a member ceased to be a member.

The auditor examines this Register to find out the total amount of capital of the company whether the dividend has been correctly paid, etc.

4. Register and Index of Debenture-holders (Section 152).

When a company issues debentures, it has to record the following particulars in this Register:–

(*a*) the name and address, and the occupation, if any, of each debentureholder;

(*b*) the number of debentures held by each debenture-holder, distinguishing each debenture by its number, and the amount paid or amount to be considered as paid on those debentures;

(*c*) the date on which each person was entered in the Register as a debenture-holder; and

(*d*) the date on which any person ceased to be a debenture-holder.

5. Foreign Register (Sections 157 and 158).

If the members or the debenture-holders are residents in a State or in a country outside India, the company may, if so authorised by its Articles, keep in that State or country a branch register of members or debenture-holders residents in that State or country. Such a Register is called Foreign Register which will be deemed to be a part of the Company Register of Members (in such a case the latter Register is called the (principal register).

6. Register of Contracts with Companies and Firms in which the Directors are interested (Sections 297, 299 and 301)

Under Section 301 a company is required to maintain a Register of Contracts entered into by it with third parties but in which contracts the directors of the company are interested. The following particulars are entered in it:-

(*a*) the date of the contract;

(*b*) the names of the firms and the body corporates in which the directors are interested and of which a notice had been given by the director concerned;

(*c*) the date on which the Board met to consider the contract; and

(*d*) the names of the directors voting for or against the contract and the names of those remaining neutral, etc.

The auditor has to examine this Register to see whether contracts entered, in which the directors are interested, were duly sanctioned by the Board of Directors.

7. Register of Directors, Managing Agents, Secretaries, etc. (Section 303).

This Register has to be maintained by a company at its Registered Office. As the name indicates, this Register contains the names and addresses and other particulars required under this section in respect of directors, managing agents, secretaries and treasurers, etc. Any change in the officers or of their particulars has to be made in this Register and the intimation has to be sent to the Registrar within 28 days of such a change.

The auditor may have to examine this Register for the confirmation of any transaction and to find out whether such transaction have been sanctioned by the appropriate authority.

8. Register of Directors' shareholdings (Section 307).

Every company is required to maintain this Register which shows the number, description and amount of any shares in, or debentures of, the company or any other body corporate, being the company's subsidiary or holding company, or a subsidiary of the company's holding company, which are held by each director of the company or in trust for him, or of which he has any right to become the holder whether on payment or not.

This section is applicable to the managing agents, secretaries and treasurers and managers.

The auditor has to refer to such a Register while examining the transfer of shares to see whether the transactions have been properly recorded in this Register.

9. Register containing particulars? Appointment of Managing Agent, or Associate as Selling Agent of Goods produced by the Company (Section 356).

If a managing agent or his associate is appointed by a company as selling agent of goods produced by the company under certain conditions in pursuance of Section 35(2), all the particulars of such appointment shall be entered in this Register.

The auditor has to refer to this Register while vouching the payment of commission to such a person and also to find out whether the appointment has been according to the provisions of the Companies Act.

Readers may refer to Sections 357, 358, 359, 360 and 372 for some other statutory books which a joint stock company has to maintain.

(*e*) Contracts

He should inspect and examine the contracts which have been entered into by a company with others, e.g., with the vendors of any property, the underwriters and brokers for their commission, promoters for the preliminary expenses, etc. If any statement regarding these contracts has been made by the company in the Prospectus, the auditor should see that such statement is correct and that entries relating to such contracts are correctly recorded in the books of account.

(*f*) Minute Books

These are statutory books, *i.e.*, books which have to be maintained according to Section 193. They are of three types :

(*i*) Shareholders' Minute Book in which the proceedings of every kind of meeting of shareholders are recorded.

(*ii*) Directors' Minute Books in which the proceedings of the meetings of the Board of Directors are recorded.

(*iii*) Communities' Minute Books which contain the proceedings of the meetings of the Committees appointed by the Board of Directors.

The minute book should be in the form of a bound book and not loose sheet which might be removed or substituted as was held in the case of *Hearts of Oak Insurance Co. Ltd vs. Flower* (1935). The auditor should see that the minutes as recorded in the minute books have been certified by the chairman of the meeting.-

(1) *Shareholders' Minute Book*. The auditor has to examine this book for the verification of the following matters:

(2) *Adoption of the Annual Accounts*. Any resolution affecting accounts. Remuneration voted for the directors, managing agents, etc.

(3) Remuneration of the auditor.

(4) Appropriation of profits by way of dividends, reserves, etc.

(5)Directors' Minute Book. The auditor has to examine this book for the verification of the following matters:–

1. Allotment of shares and debentures.
2. Adoption of contracts.
3. Documents to which company's seal has been affixed.
4. Appointment of bankers and officers empowered to sign and endorse cheques and bills.
5. Calls on shares.
6. Forfeiture of shares.

7. Appointment and remuneration of managing director, manager, secretary or other officials.
8. Appointment of the first auditors or to fill a casual vacancy, fixing their remuneration and expenses.
9. Authorisation of capital expenditure.
10. Resolution to pay interim dividend, if this is permitted by the Articles of the company.
11. Directors' travelling expenses or special remuneration.
12. Adoption of Annual Accounts and Report to the Shareholders and recommendation as to dividend.
13. Any matter for which a resolution of the directors is specifically required by the Articles of the Company.

(*g*) Last Balance Sheet, Accounts and the last Audit Report

The last Balance Sheet is inspected to see that the balances therein are correctly recorded in the new books. Sometimes the companies, in order to commit fraud, or to manipulate accounts, open the accounts with incorrect balances. Moreover, according to the Companies Act, the corresponding figures of the previous year have to be given in the Balance Sheet. The last auditor's report is inspected to see whether the recommendations made therein are carried out or not. In order to have a rough idea about the company and its working, the auditor must inspect the previous audit report. He should also see the minute book of the shareholders about the adoption of the accounts.

He must also examine the directors' report of the previous year to see the appropriation of profits.

(*h*) List of the officers of the company and the books written by them

He should obtain a list of the officers of the company and their specimen signatures. This is done to ensure the quick disposal of queries, e.g., if there is any doubt about any transaction in the books of accounts that very officer may be sent for by him to clear the position instead of asking the manager or secretary to send for the officer, who keeps that books.

(*i*) Certificate of Incorporation

This certificate is required to be examined in order to see whether the company had been duly incorporated. The auditor will require such a certificate only when he is auditing the accounts of a newly registered company.

(*j*) Certificate entitling a Company to commence business

Inspection and examination of such a certificate is necessary as without the issue of such a certificate a public limited company is not allowed to commence business, borrow money, enter into contract, etc. Therefore, any contract which had been entered into by a company before it is granted the certificate of commencement of business, shall be regarded as provisional and not binding on the company until such a certificate has been granted to it.

(*k*) Written Statement about Internal Check

He should obtain a written statement from the directors of the company about the internal check system and internal audit in operation, the system of accountancy employed etc.

QUESTIONS

1. State the qualifications and disqualifications of a person to be appointed as company auditor.
2. Explain the procedure for appointment of a) first auditor of a company b) re-appointment of auditor of a company.

3. Can an auditor other than the retiring auditor be appointed in annual general meeting as company auditor? If so, state the procedures in connection therewith.
4. What are the rights available to a company auditor when he is sought to be removed by the company?
5. What are the powers of a statutory auditor according to the provisions of Indian Companies Act?
6. State the statutory duties of a statutory auditor?
7. "An auditor of a company, is sometimes, described as an agent of shareholders, sometimes, as an officer of the company. Still, essentially he is an independent reviewer and is expected to play fair." Discuss.
8. List down the important documents, books of accounts which are referred to by a company auditor on his being appointed.
9. Describe the procedure to be followed in order to appoint an auditor of a company in the following circumstances:
   (*a*) the shareholders failed to appoint an auditor in the annual general meeting
   (*b*) a notice has been received from a group of shareholders who intend to appoint a person of their choice in the place of retiring auditor.
   (*c*) the retiring auditor is appointed in general meeting. But he declines the offer.
   (*d*) The general meeting could not be held and therefore no auditor is appointed.
   (*e*) in a company where at least 25% of subscribed capital is held by public financial institutions, a person is appointed as company auditor in general meeting by an ordinary resolution.
10. Specify any five items for which you, a company auditor, would refer the minutes books of directors.
11. On being appointed as an auditor of a limited company, what steps would you take to ensure that your appointment is in order?
    What documents would you like to refer before commencement of your annual audit?
12. How will you decide:
    (*a*) You are the auditor of a private limited company in which the directors are the only shareholders. Due to financial stringency, the directors suggest you to accept a reduced audit fee and that you need not do a complete audit as you have done in the past. You are also told that you can avoid detailed vouching of all transactions as they have close watch over them.
    (*b*) The previous auditor of ABC Co. Ltd who has been re-appointed in annual general meeting resigned his office during the tenure of his service. You are appointed by the Board of directors vide their resolution passed in the board meeting.
    (*c*) You are appointed statutory auditor of a company. You are also offered a part-time employment in the same company to do internal audit by making visit to the company on all working days in the evening session. The terms and conditions regarding pay, service rules as applicable to executive category of the company will apply to you as well.
    (*d*) You are the auditor of a trading company in consumer durable products. The company has wide net work of branches all over India. You require the stock statements from all branches for your perusal. The management shows its unwillingness to produce them, as in their view, all the accounts of the branches have been audited by duly appointed branch auditor. You are informed to proceed for compilation on the basis of audited branch returns.

Chapter 23

Audit of Limited Companies — Audit of Financial Statements

Under section 216 of the Companies Act the profit and Loss Account shall be annexed to the Balance Sheet and the auditor's report shall be attached thereto. Under section 227 (2), the auditor of the company shall make a report to the members of the company on the accounts examined by him and on every balance sheet and profit and loss account and every other document which is a part of or annexure to the balance sheet or profit and loss account. It is therefore necessary that the auditor of the company must have thorough knowledge on the provisions of the companies Act dealing with accounts, or concerning the profit or loss of the company or assets or liabilities of the company.

Books of accounts to be kept by the company:

Under section 209 of the Act, every company shall keep at its registered office proper books of account with respect to

(*a*) all sums of money received and expended by the company and the matters in respect of which the receipt and expenditure take palace.

(*b*) all sales and purchases of goods by the company

(*c*) all assets and liabilities of the company

(*d*) Such cost records as may be prescribed by the Central Government in cases of companies engaged in production, processing, manufacturing of mining activities and is a class of company covered under the notification of central government in this behalf.

If the company has branches, it is enough if the branch maintains accounts in respect of the items stated above viz, cash book, purchase, sales registers, assets and liability accounts etc. However summarised return of the above should be sent to the registered office atleast once in a quarter.

It is necessary that proper books of accounts are to be kept. What is meant by proper books of account? Among other things as the term might imply it specifically includes the two important conditions mentioned in section 209(3), as amended by companies (amendment) Act, 1988.

(*a*) Such books as are necessary to give true and fair view of the state of affairs of the company must be kept. The books must adequately be maintained to explain the transactions of the company

(*b*) The books of accounts must be written following the (*i*) double entry principle of accounting and (*ii*) accrual basis of accounting for recording income and expenditure.

Annual accounts and balance sheet :

Under section 166 of the Act, each company has to conduct an annual general meeting in each year. In the meeting the annual accounts are to be laid for the purpose of their consideration by the members of the company. A copy of such annual accounts viz., balance sheet, its annexure P&L account and the auditor's, report to the attached to financial statement) must be sent to the members atleast 21 days before the annual general meeting. In case of companies whose shares are listed in any recognised stock exchange, it is enough if the company sends copy of abridged accounts, incorporating salient features of annual accounts therein, to the members. However detailed annual accounts must be kept for inspection for any member at its registered office atlest 21 days before the date of meeting.

Section 210 specifies what accounts are to be laid in annual general meeting for the consideration of members. In case of a company carrying on business for profit, annual accounts means balance sheet at the end of accounting period and profit and loss account for the period. In case of a company not carrying on business for profit, annual accounts means balance sheet as on last date of the accounting period and income and expenditure account for the accounting period. The period for which P&L account or Income and Expenditure account is to be prepared may be more or less than a calender year. But in no case it can exceed a period of fifteen months. However with the permission of Registrar of companies, the accounts may be prepared for a period upto eighteen months in exceptional difficulties. In case of first annual accounts the period of annual accounts must start from the date of incorporation and end with a date falling within a period of nine months preceeding the date of first annual general meeting. In case of subsequent annual accounts the date of accounting period must start from the date immediately following the period for which annual accounts were prepared and submitted in preceding annual general meeting and end with a date falling within a period of six months preceeding the date of annual general meeting in which these are to be laid. However, one must also note the provision requiring atleast 21 days time to be given to members for reading the accounts prior to annual general meeting.

Section 211 requires from every balance sheet and P&L accounts of the company true and fair view of the state of affairs of the company or profit or loss of the company. It stipulates that the balance sheet must be drawn up in the format set out in part I of schedule VI of the Act. Similarly the P&L account should be in the format set out in part II of schedule VI of the Act. However, exemptions are provided for banking, insurance and electricity companies for which specific format have been prescribed under special enactments concerning those class of companies. Therefore thorough understanding of disclosure requirements set out in part I and part II of schedule VI is necessary for company auditor. The relevant extracts in this regard are annexed to the chapter.

Under section 215 of the Act, the annual accounts have to be approved by the board of directors and signed as per the provisions of the Act before they are reported by the company auditor. Annual accounts are to be authenticated by atleast two directors (one of whom is to be a Managing director if there is one such person, and by manager or secretary of the company.

Under section 220 of the Act, the audited annual accounts laid before the annual general meeting are to be registered with the Registrar of companies within 30 days of the meeting.

Audit of Financial Statements

In auditing the final financial statements of a company the auditor must bear in mind the following:

(*a*) He must conduct compliance procedure to ensure the reliance he can place on the efficacy of internal control system. To check various assertions of financial data reflected in P&L account or balance sheet, he must perform substantive procedure to check the correctness, completeness and validity of the data. Various points to be checked in connection with it and principles to be followed thereof had been elaborately discussed in vouching, verification and valuation of assets and liabilities chapters.

(*b*) In addition to the above, the auditor should ensure that the transactions of the company do not violate the provisions of companies Act in as much as they get reflected in financial statements which he certifies. For this purpose, important provisions of companies Act affecting the financial transactions of the company are presented in the chapter.

(*c*) The auditor has to see that the items of revenue, expenditure and items of assets and liabilities do get reflected in P&L account and Balance sheet as per the information requirements specified in Schedule VI of the Act. The auditor has to check that the form in which these are presented and the assertions they signify. He must ensure that the financial statements reflect true and fair view of the trading results and financial status of the company pertaining to the period under audit.

Audit of Balance Sheet of Company

Schedule VI part I of the Act contains the following items of disclosure in respect of labilities viz.

(*i*) Share capital
(*ii*) Reserves and surplus
(*iii*) Secured loans
(*iv*) Unsecured loans
(*v*) Current liabilities and provisions
(*vi*) A foot note for contingent liability

Disclosure requirement for assets include the following broad areas viz."

(*i*) Fixed assets
(*ii*) Investments
(*iii*) Current assets, loans and advances,
(*iv*) Miscellaneous expenditure
(*v*) Profit and Loss Account (debit balance)

The schedule contains various specific information required to be disclosed in respect of each area of asset or liability mentioned above.

I. Share Capital :

A statutory auditor is concerned with checking of share capital item in balance sheet with regard to the truth and fairness of the various informations disclosed in the balance sheet about it. He verifies that there is no contravention of any provisions of the law. However, an internal auditor verifies beyond this. He deals in his audit various procedural aspects of share capital - procedures concerning issue, alteration of capital, transfer, transmission of shares, reorganisation of share capital and so on. Sometimes, an auditor is asked to carry out detailed share capital audit. In checking share capital, the auditor has to ensure, in a broad way, the following viz.

(*a*) The transaction viz, issue or alteration or transfer or reorganisation is properly authorised by memorandum of association, or articles of association of the company.

(*b*) In carrying out the transaction, the company has complied with the provisions of companies Act, the regulations and guidelines of Securities Exchange Board of India (SEBI).

(*c*) The transactions have been properly recored so as to truly and fairly explain the happening.

(*d*) The information required to be disclosed in annual financial statements are properly disclosed.

Audit of issue of share capital:

(A) Authorisation:

1. The auditor has to check that the issued capital is within the authorised capital of the company.
2. According to section 86 of the companies Act, the companies limited by shares can issue only two types of capital viz equity capital and preference capital. As per section 80 of the Act, the company cannot issue preference shares which are irredeemable or redeemable after a period of 12 years from the date of issue.
3. Where the company proposes to issue further capital within limits of authorised capital after first allotment, such subsequent issue must be offered first to the existing equity share holders. This offer is called rights issue. The shares can be offered to outsiders if the right is waived by the share holders by a resolution or is renunciated in favour of third party or is not exercised within the period allowed.

(B) Procedural compliance :

1. Shares may be issued at par or at premium or at discount.
2. Shares may be issued for cash or for consideration other than cash.
3. Shares may be issued to the existing share holders in addition to dividend, by way of bonus.
4. The auditor has to check that the company has complied with requirements of various provisions of the Act and SEBI guidelines with regard to pricing the issues, declaring bonus issues, inviting public subscription, allotment of shares and issuance of share certificates.

1. Pricing the issues:

Till 29th May of 1992, the Capital issues (control) Act 1947 regulated the issue of capital by companies. The Act had been repealed by Central Government. On the other hand, the Government had constituted the Securities and Exchange Board of India to protect the interests of investors in securities and to promote the development of and to regulate the securities, market and for matters connected therewith or incidental thereto. The SEBI is issuing guidelines with regard to issue of share capital from time to time. In this connection, it is important to note the contents of guidelines issued by SEBI as contained in SEBI (Disclosure and Investor Protection) Guidelines, 2000.

(*a*) **issue at par :** The issue may be made at par depending upon the pricing decision of the issuing company.

(*b*) **issue at premium:** According to section 78 of the companies Act, the premium amount raised must be kept in a separated account called 'securities premium account'. This accont is a kind of capital reserve and utilisation of fund for any other purpose other than those specified in the section is prohibited. The amount can be utilised for the following purposes only :

(*a*) for issuing bonus shares to the members of the company

(*b*) for writing off preliminary expenses of the company

(*c*) for writing off discount allowed, commission paid or expenses incurred in connection with the issue of shares or debentures

(*d*) for providing the premium payable on redemption of redeemable preference shares or debentures

(*c*) Issue at a discount:

According to section 79 of the companies Act, only existing company can issue shares at a discount, that too, in respect of class of shares already issued. Shares can be issued at discount only after one year had elapsed since the date of commencement of business. A resolution authorising the issue at discount has to be passed in general meeting. The sanction of company law board has to be obtained after resolution had been passed. The rate at which discount can be allowed shall have to be specified in the resolution. However, the rate cannot exceed 10% unless company law board specifically considers a higher percentage. The shares should be issued within 2 months of sanction by company law board.

Issue of sweat equity shares:

Section 79 contains provisions for issue of shares at a discount. Any issue of shares at discount should comply with the requirements of Section 79. However, one important exception is legislated by insertion of Section 79A. Issue of shares covered under Section 79A will not be hit by the provisions of Section 79. Such issue of shares shall only be governed by the provisions of Section 79A only, notwithstanding anything contained contrary to such issue in Section 79A.

Section 79A permits issue of shares at a discount or for a consideration other than cash. The section permits issue what is called as "Sweat Equity Shares" means equity shares issued by the company to its employees or directors at a discount or for consideration other than cash for providing know-how or making available rights in the nature of intellectual property rights or valuable additions, by whatever name called.

Section 79A (1) contains four important conditions to be fulfilled by a company in connection with the issue of sweat equity shares. They are—

(*a*) the issue of sweat equity shares is authorised by a special resolution passed by the company in the general meeting.

(*b*) the resolution specifies the number of shares, current market price, consideration, if any, and the class or classes of directors or employees to whom such equity shares are to be issued;

(*c*) not less than one year has, at the date of issue, elapsed since the date on which the company was entitled to commence business;

(*d*) the seat equity shares of a company whose equity shares are listed on a recognised stock exchange, are issued in accordance with the regulations made by the securities and Exchange Board of Indian this behalf.

However, where the shares are not listed on any recognised stock exchange, the issue of sweat equity shares shall be according to the guidelines as may be prescribed in this behalf.

2. Issue of shares for consideration other than cash:

In the following cases shares are issued by the company without receipt of cash:

(*a*) to pay the vendor for purchase price when running business had been taken over from him.

(*b*) to the nominee of the vendor if vendor had assigned his rights in favour of the nominee.

(*c*) to remunerate the underwriter to the issue

(*d*) to the promoters who have incurred preliminary expenses before the incorporation of the company

(*e*) to discharge the consideration payable to the shareholders of the companies which get merged with the company or amalgamate with it or in case of external reconstruction."

3. Issue of Bonus shares:

The SEBI has issued the following guidelines for issue of bonus shares vide their RMB (DIP series) circular number 2 of 15-4-94:

The SEBI (Disclosure and Investor Protection) Guidelines, 2000 have not changed the provisions of these earlier guidelines. The new provisions contained in chapter XV of the SEBI Guidelines 2000 are substantially the same as in old guidelines.

(1) The Board of directors of the company must take into consideration the relevant financial factors before deciding on bonus issue

(2) Articles of association of the company must permit bonus issue. If articles of association do not contain authorisation, the articles should be altered first to the effect.

(3) If the bonus issue may result in paid up capital of the company crossing the authorised capital, the authorised capital has to be increased before the bonus can be declared

(4) A company which has defaulted in payment of interest or principal to the deposit holder or debenture holders cannot issue bonus shares. Similarly if the default has been made in paying statutory dues to the employees of the company such as provident fund, gratuity bonus, the company cannot issue bonus shares.

(5) Bonus issue can be declared only if all shares existing are made fully paid up.

(6) If, at the time of declaration of bonus issue, there are convertible debentures (fully/partly convertible) pending conversion, the issue of bonus shares must give similar benefits by way of reservation to the debenture holders such number of bonus shares to which they are entitled in relation to their shareholding upon conversion of debenture into shares at future date.

(7) The bonus cannot be declared in lieu of dividend

(8) Bonus can be made out of free reserves built out of genuine profits or out of share premium account.

(9) Reserves created out of revaluation of fixed assets are not available for issue of bonus shares.

(10) The bonus issue must be approved by Board of directors. Freedom is given to Board to dicide bonus issue. Those resolutions stipulating financial test like residual reserve, yield on expanded capital etc. had been done away with. This is in keeping with the current trend of liberalisation of economy of the government. But these financial factors are left to be considered by board for the good of the company.

(11) Bonus issue must be made within 6 months of Board's approval.

4. Compliance with SEBI Guideline and Company Law Provisions:

So far we have seen various SEBI guidelines for issue of shares art pr, at premium, at discount, for consideration other than cash or by way of bonus. Let us have a brief introduction to certain other than cash or by way of bonus. Let us have a brief introduction to certain other SEBI guidelines and Company law provisions pertaining to issue and allotment of share capital

(*a*) **SEBI guidelines :** The parliament has enacted Securities and Exchange Board of India Act, 1992 to provide for establishment of a Board (*a*) to protect the interests of investors in securities and (*b*) to promote the development of the securities market and (*c*) to regulate the securities market. The Act also contains provisions for matters connected therewith or incidental thereto. Headquartered at Bombay, the Board consists of a Chairman and five members. Section 11 empowers the Board to do such acts and undertake such measures to achieve the objectives of this enactment. Again section 11A of this Act empowers the SEBI to specify by regulations the matters relating to the issue of capital, transfer of securities and the manner in which such matters shall be disclosed by the companies. However, such specification of disclosure requirements should not stand in contradiction to the provisions of company law if any, in respect of any such matters.

Deriving power from section 11 of the SEBI Act, 1992, the Board has issued Securities and Exchange Board of India (Disclosure and Investor protection) Guidelines 1992 in June 1992 detailing various matters connected with issue of share capital, debentures and certain other matters connected with and incidental to regulation and disclosure requirements of security market. Securities and Exchange Board of India (Disclosure and Investor Protection) Guidelines 2000 issued by the SEBI now replaces the original SEBI guidelines in these matters issued in 1992. As the guidelines are issued under delegated authority given to it by the Parliament, they shall have the force of law which must be complied with by the companies.

The Auditor while conducting the audit of share capital must have clear understanding of the requirements of SEBI guidelines, directions and instruction circulars issued by the Board from time to time. Although not exhaustive, the provisions of SEBI (Disclosure and Investor Protection) guidelines 2000 are presented hereunder.

1. Filing of offer document with Board. The company making public issue of capital shall file with the Board 21 days prior to filing of prospectus with the Register of Companies, the draft offer document. The same may require the company to incorporate in it such changes as are deemed necessary by it.

2. Companies prohibited from access to market. A company which is prohibited from accessing the capital market under any order or direction passed by the Board shall not make an issue of securities.

3. Compulsory lising. No company can make any **Public** issue (invitation through prospectus for subscription) unless it has made application for listing of those securities in stock-exchange(s).

4. Issue of securities in dematerialised form. No company shall make public or rights issue or offer for sale of securities unless it has made agreement with Depository for dematerialisation of its securities. The company should also give option to the securities-holders to keep the securities in certificate form (with distinct serial number and identification) or in dematerialised form (in account form without any such physical identification).

5. Eligibility criteria for Public issues by (a) unlisted company (b) listed company. An unlisted company (which has not listed its securities issued prior to this issue) can still go in for public subscription of its proposed issue. No unlisted company shall make a **public** issue of any equity shares (as such or any instrument convertible into equity shares in later periods) unless the company has:

(*i*) track record of distributable profits for atleast three out of five immediate preceeding years and

(*ii*) a pre-issue networth of not less than one crore rupees in three out of preceeding five years with the minimum networth to be met during immediately preceeding two years.

However, an unlisted company intending for going in public without such track-record of profitability or with less than adequate networth can make public issue if:

1. the project to be financed out of the issue is appraised by a public financial institution; and

2. not less than 10% of the project cost is financed by the said appraising bank or institution by way of *loan, equity, or combination of any of these two forms.*

3. the appraising bank shall bring in the minimum specified contribution atleast one day before the opening of the public issue.

A listed company shall be eligible to make a public issue of equity shares. However, where as a result of the proposed issue, the networth of the company becomes more than five times the networth of company prior to the issue, the company can go in for public issue only if it satisfies the cumulative conditions of track-record of profitability and adequacy of minimum networth or in the alternative participation of public financial bank or institution in its venture (as detailed supra).

However, these eligibility criteria — track-record of profitability cum adequacy of networth or participation in the venture by a public financial institution shall not apply to a banking company, infrastructure company, the rights issue by a listed company.

6. Compulsory credit rating for debt instruments. No public or right issue of debt instruments (like debentures) shall be made unless credit ratings have been obtained and disclosed in the offer document.

7. No public issue during the subsistence of partly-paid up shares. No company shall make a public or rights issue of equity shares or any security convertible into equity shares at a later date, unless all the existing partly paid-up shares have been fully paid or forfeited according to relevant provisions for forfeiture.

8. Pricing the issues. A listed company or an unlisted company may freely price its issues. Relevant provisions in the chapter III of the guidelines shall be complied with. No payment direct or indirect, in the nature of a discount, commission, allowance or otherwise shall be made either by the issue company or the promotors to the persons who have received firm allotment in such public issue. Firm allotment means allotment on a firm basis in public issues by an issuing company made to Indian and Multilateral Development Financial Institutions, Indian Mutual Funds, Foreign Institutional Investors including non-resident Indians and Overseas Corporate bodies and permanent/ regular employees of the company.

9. Promotor's contribution and lock-in period. The minimum contribution from promotors should be atleast 20% of proposed issue. It shall stand locked for three years. However detailed provisions as to quantum of contribution, manner of its computation, exceptions, etc., may be referred to in chapter IV of the guidelines.

10. Pre-issue and post-issue obligations. There are matters connected with pre-issue and post-issue of capital. Appointment of lead merchant bankers, the monitoring of the issue by the lead merchant bankers, appointment of co-managers to the issue, underwriting arrangement, the matters to be disclosed in offer document, the fixing up of mandatory collection centres for receiving application moneys, accompanying of adridged prospectus with the application are certain important matters connected with pre-issue of capital. The lead merchant banker shall exercise due diligence to verify the adequacy, veracity of the contents of the offer documents and offering procedures. The finalisation of allotment, proportionate allotment in cases of over-subscription, dealing with stock invests etc. are certain instances of matters in respect of post issues. Relevant provisions must be referred to in the guidelines by the auditor.

(*b*) **Provisions of Company Law:** Important provisions concerning issue and allotment of share capital are outlined below:

(*i*) **Prospectus:** The application for shares cannot be issued unless a prospectus is prepared and kept ready for furnishing to the person who may request for it. Every application must contain a memorandum of salient features specified in prospectus. The prospectus must incorporate all matters specified in part I of II schedule to the Act and must contain all reports specified in part II of the II schedule to the Act. The prospectus must be dated and duly signed. A copy of the prospectus must be registered with Registrar of the company before it is published and used. The prospectus should not contain misstatements in respect of matters disclosed therein.

(*ii*) **Statement in lieu of prospectus:** A company, not being a private company, which intends to raise capital not from public but from promoters and their relatives (i.e privately) must file with the Registrar of Companies a statement in lieu of prospectus. The statement in lieu of prospectus must contain the particulars specified in part I of schedule III and reports specified in part II of shedule III and reports specified in part II of schedule III.

(*iii*) **Minimum subscription:** No allotment shall be made unless the shares had been subscribed for such amount as is not less than the minimum amount specified in the prospectus to meet preliminary expenses etc. It is also necessary that the application money payable on such amount of shares has been fully received in cash. If minimum subscription is not received, the application money is to be refunded.

(*iv*) **Application money:** The application money payable on shares shall not be less than five percent of the nominal value of shares. All money received on application shall be kept deposited with a scheduled bank until minimum subscription has been received. If minimum subscription had not been received, on the expiry of 120 days all application money should be refunded within ten days without interest and thereafter with interest at the rate of six percent.

(*v*) **Listing of securities with stock exchange:** Every company intending to raise share capital from public by issue or prospectus must apply for permission for the shares to be dealt in stock exchange. If permission has not been granted, all money received in respect of shares should be forthwith refunded to the investors within eight days.

(*vi*) **Commission for subscribing or procuring subscription:** Commission in this regard cannot exceed five percent in case of shares and two and half percent in case of debentures.

(*vii*) **Restriction on purchase of its own shares:** The company cannot purchase its own shares nor can it finance anybody to enable him to purchase its shares. However, a banking company can advance loan in its ordinary course of business. Also, any company can give advances of an amount not exceeding six months wages to employees to enable them to purchase its shares to encourage workers' participation in equity.

However, the Companies (Amendment Act), 1999 has permitted buy back of its shares by company in accordance with the provisions of Section 77A which have been discussed elsewhere in this Chapter.

Audit procedures to check issue of share capital:

For the purpose of checking share capital in the case of a newly formed company, the following books, accounts and documents must be examined:

(*a*) Application for shares.
(*b*) Application Book
(*c*) Letters of allotment
(*d*) Allotment Sheets or Book
(*e*) Letters of calls
(*f*) Letters of regret
(*g*) Calls Book
(*h*) The Share Ledger Book
(*i*) The Cash Book
(*j*) The Pass book
(*k*) The Memorandum of Association
(*l*) The Articles of Association
(*m*) The Directors's Minute Books

The programme for checking the issue of shares for cash is given below:

1. The auditor should ensure that all legal provisions connected with issue of share capital has been complied with. He should check that the guidelines issued by SEBI have been followed.
2. He should check the Application and Allotment Letters with the Application and Allotment Sheets or Books.
3. He should check the Application and Allotment Books with the Share Ledger to find out the amount payable.
4. He should then check the amount received with the Cash Book or Pass Book and the Application and Allotment Book and Share Ledger.
5. He should check the payees' acknowledgment receipts.
7. He should check the Directors' Minute Book —
   (a) to see that the shares have been properly allotted;
   (b) to see that the Minimum subscription has been subscribed; and
   (c) to see that the calls have been made according to the Articles of Association.

8. He should check the amount received on account of calls with the counterfoils of the Receipt Book and the Cash and the Pass Books
9. He should see that the shares allotted do not exceed the nominal capital of the company.
10. Where shares have been issued for consideration other than cash, e.g. to the vendors of a business, he should examine the contract with the vendors, to see how many shares had to be allotted to them and whether such shares were to be fully or partly paid. He should also examine the Directors' Minute Book and see whether this fact had been mentioned in the Prospectus.
11. He should get a list of calls in arrear from the management and compare it with the Share Ledger and also compare it with the debit balances of the Calls and Allotment Account.
12. If calls have been received in advance, he should check the same with the Cash or Pass Book, counterfoils of the receipt book and see whether calls can be received in advance and whether any interest is payable on them according to the Articles sof Association. In any case such interest should not exceed six percent.
13. Such calls in advance must not be mixed up with the capital. They should be shown separately.

It may be mentioned here that the auditor should adopt the above procedure while auditing the accounts in the first year of the life of the company. In subsequent years, he should compare the total of the individual balances in the Share Register with the issued share capital of the company. If a fresh issue had been made during the year under audit, he should see whether the fresh issue is within he limit of the authorised capital of the company. If it is not, whether the legal formalities regarding the increase of capital have been gone through. He should also see that all moneys received against the application for shares have been deposited in a Scheduled Bank (Registar of Companies vs. P.M. Hegde, 1954) and that such a money has not been used for the business before the allotment of shares. If the prospectus of the company states that the company had made an application for permission to deal in and for quotation for the shares on any stock exchange the application money should be kept in a separate account in a scheduled bank. In case such permission has not been granted, application money should be returned to the applicants. He should note that the returns relating to allotment of shares have been filed with the Registar of Companies.

Duty of an Auditor in regard to shares issued at Premium

The auditor should examine the Prospectus, the Articles and the Minute Book of the directors to see whether the shares could be issued at premium and if so at what rate. He should vouch the amount of premium received. The auditor cannot raise any objection in regard to the use of the premium provided it is dealt with according to statute and the articles. At the most, he may advise the directors what they should do with the premium. He should see that the premium received has been carried to Security Premium Account and has not been carried either to Capital or Capital Reserve Account.

Duty of Auditor in regard to shares issued at discount

The auditor should see that the shares have been issued according to law. Every prospectus relating to the issue of such shares shall contain particulars of the discount allowed on the issue of the shares or of so much of that discount as has not been written off at the date of the issue of the prospectus. Such shares shall be shown in the balance sheet according to their nominal value. It is not legally compulsory to write off the discount but it is considered expedient to do so as early as possible and in the meantime shown on the assets side of the balance sheet under the head "Miscellaneous Expenditure."

Auditors duty in regard to the issue of sweat equity shares:

An auditor should check the following:

(1) Whether the issue could be brought within the meaning of sweat equity in the light of meaning given to such term in the section.

(2) The auditor should call for the scheme of issue and study the important terms of such scheme which provide for the principles and modalities of issue of shares to the employees or directions.

(3) If the shares of the company are listed in a stock exchange, the auditor should ensure that the issue conforms to the regulations made by SEBI. If the shares are unlisted, the guidelines prescribed by the Central government in this behalf have to be followed.

(4) The auditor should ensure that one year period has elapsed between the date of issue and the date of certificate of commencement of business.

(5) The auditor should call for the minutes of the general meeting and verify that the issue had been authorised by a special resolution passed to this effect.

(6) If the issue is to be made in consideration of acquisition of technical know-how or any intellectual property or any other valuable addition, the auditor should study the agreement, especially the terms governing the fixation of purchase consideration and mode of settlement.

(7) The auditor should also note that the sweat equity shares are to be subject to the same limitations, restrictions and provisions as are applicable to equity shares of the company. The sweat equity shares cannot claim any preference or be subject to any different treatment.

Duty of Auditor in regard to shares issued for consideration other than cash

The auditor should verify the entries in the Journal regarding the issue of such shares. He should inspect the details stated in the Prospectus or Statement in lieu of Prospectus in respect of such a contract with the vendors, promoters, etc., to who such shares have been issued. He should see that the copies of the contracts with vendors, promoters, etc., to who such shares have been issued, have been filed with the Registrar of Companies within one month of the allotment according to Section 75 (1) (b). If such a contract is not in writing, he should find out whether the Registrar has been informed of the particulars of the contracts. The amount of shares issued for consideration other than cash should be shown separately in the balance sheet.

In case the shares are issued for consideration other than cash in discharge of purchase consideration for acquisition of technical know-how or intellectual property rights or any other valuable additions, such issue will be in the nature of sweat equity shares and section 79A will accordingly apply to such issue. The auditor should ensure compliance in this regard.

Duty of auditor in regard to issue of Bonus shares

The auditor must inspect the minute book to see the resolution declaring the bonus. He should also find out from the articles of the company whether such shares can be issued. If the Articles of the company are silent, alteration must be made in them to enable the company to issue the bonus shares. If Table A has been adopted, the company to issue the bonus shares. If Table A has been adopted, provisions in Regulations 96 and 97 should be examined. He should see that such shares can be issued only out of the premium received on issue of shares [Section 78 (b)], undistributed profits, accumulated reserves, capital redemption fund [Section 80 (b)], etc., provided the Articles permit such an issue. The auditor should see that there is sufficient unissued capital and vouch the journal entries according to the Articles and the resolution. He should also examine the Share Ledger, and see whether the particulars about the issue of bonus shares have been included in the annual returns. He should also see that the balance sheet of the company shows the appropriation of the reserves and amount of bonus shares is included in the subscribed capital of the company.

He should further see that all the statutory requirements relating to the issue of bonus shares have been complied with.

Forfeited Shares

The auditor should examine the following:

1. The Articles of Association to ascertain the circumstances under which the shares can be forfeited and whether the forfeiture was in accordance with the regulations. Forfeiture of shares amounts to reduction of capital and hence forfeiture of shares except for nonpayment of calls would be illegal as was decided in the case of *Hopkinson vs. Martimer, Harley e Co.*, 1917. But this decision has not been accepted in India. Das J., in a Calcutta case *held* that the Indian Companies Act sanctions forfeiture of shares generally either on account of non-payment of calls or nonobservance of the rules and regulations of the company. He also observed that forfeiture of shares, otherwise than for nonpayment of calls, does not amount to an illegal reduction of share capital in contravention of the provisions of the Companies Act. He further remarked that such a step would not amount to the purchase of its own shares by the Company (Naresh *Chander Sanyal vs. Ramnikanto Roy*).
2. Whether the resolution passed by the Directors authorising the issue of a notice was given to the defaulting shareholders.
3. The Minute Book of the Directors to find out whether a resolution forfeiting the shares was duly passed.
4. Examine the entries in the books of account for the forfeiture.
5. If the forfeited shares have been reissued, he should see that the total amount realised (the amount received before the forfeiture and on the reissue) is not less than the nominal value of the shares otherwise it will amount to a reduction of capital. He should verify the receipt of money.
6. He should see that if more amount than the nominal value of the shares has been received, it should be carried to the Capital Reserve Account as it is a capital profit. (Part I Schedule VI to the (Companies Act).
7. If the shares had been forfeited and the premium on which the shares had been issued, had already been paid, he should see that such premium should remain to the credit of Share Premium Account and not included in the Forfeited Shares Account.

The amount received on account of shares forfeited should be credited to separate account called `Forfeited Shares Account' which should be allowed to stand in the Balance Sheet until written off. The total number of shares forfeited should be shown in the annual returns.

The forfeited shares may be reissued even at a discount which should not exceed the amount already received on such shares. Forfeited shares may be reissued as paid up to an amount not exceeding the amount paid by the previous holder and may be reissued in consideration of a sum less than1an the SUM1 credited as paid on them (*Morrison vs. Trustees, Executors and Securities Insurance corporation Ltd, 1898*). If the forfeited shares have been reissued and the total amount received in respect of such shares is in excess of the nominal value of the share,, the difference is to be carried to Capital Reserve Account.

The amount standing to the credit of forfeited shares account may, in the first instance, be applied to the discount on the reissue of shares. If there is still a balance, that may be utilised in reducing or writing off fictitious assets like goodwill, preliminary expenses or carried to Reserve Account. It is not illegal to transfer such a balance of forfeited shares account, after the reissue of such share to Profit and Loss Account provided the Articles do not prohibit such a procedure. But financially it is not a sound policy.

Audit of Share Transfer

The audit of share transfer is not compulsory. It is no part of an auditor's duty to do so. The auditor has only to see that the share capital as stated in the balance sheet agrees with the share capital. Sometimes the auditor is asked to undertake this work also for an extra remuneration, to ensure that there has been no error or fraud in the office of the secretary and that duplicate shares have not been issued. The auditor should follow the undermentioned procedure in connection with the sale transfer audit, if he is asked to undertake such a work:

(1) He should examine the Articles regarding the procedure to be followed in case of transfer of shares.

(2) He should see that the transfer fee is duly received and credited to Profit and Loss Account and whether money has been deposited in the bank.

(3) He should see whether the transfer is properly stamped.

(4) He should verify the signature of the transferor with the signature on application form. This is important because when a forged transfer is passed by the company, such a transferee does not get a good title and the company can remove his name from the register. The company will be liable to the true owner for any dividend which he had not received due to forged transfer. He is also entitled to have his name put on the register of members. If such a transfer or has transferred the shares to an innocent party, such an innocent party can hold the company liable, if it is deprived of the share by the true owner. However, such an innocent party does not get a good title to the shares.

(5) He should check the transfer with the Share Register and see that a share has not been transferred twice.

(6) He should find out whether the transfer has been notified to the transferor and in case the shares were held by joint holders, to each of them and that no objection has been raised against the transfer in order to prevent a forged transfer.

(7) He should find out whether the old share certificates have been cancelled so that they may not be issued to other persons.

(8) When a part of the holding has been transferred, the auditor should check; the balance certificates with the counterfoils of the certificates.

(9) He should examine the directors' Minute Book to' see that the transfers have been duly sanctioned by the Board of Directors.

(10) He should compare the total issued capital with the balances on the Shareholders' Account in the Share Book.

(11) He should inquire whether a notice as required by Section 110(2) of the Companies Act, was issued to the transferee in case of partly paid shares and the `no-objection' intimation had been received from such a transferee.'

(12) He should see that the transferee is not otherwise disqualified to hold shares in the company, e.g., no notice of trust has been entered on the Register of Members.

(13) If shares have been issued in the absence of shares certificate, the letter of indemnity should be examined.

(14) If the shares, which have been mortgaged, are transferred, he should see that due notice had been given to the mortgagee.

(15) If a share has been transmitted on account of the death bankruptcy of the holder, he should see—

(*a*) that the share has been transmitted according to the Articles,

(*b*) and examine the Succession Certificate granted by the Court, (*c*) the Certificate issued by the Controller of Estate Duty to find out whether Estate Duty has been paid,

(*d*) the application the executor or the legatee that the shares may be issued to him,

(*e*) order of the Court of Insolvency.

(16) Compare the transfer fees received with the number of the transfers lodged.

(17) Whether the blank transfer was current for more than six months. If so, transfer will be bad. The company ought not to have accepted such a transfer.

(18) Compare the Share Ledger balances with the Issued Share Capital.

(19) If the transfer has been executed by an agent, his signature should be compared with the specimen signature on the Power of Attorney.

(20) Signature of the transferor who is in a foreign country should be attested by the local Council, Attorney, etc.

(21) If shares have been issued to an incorporated company, he should examine its memorandum of associations as to whether it can hold such shares.

(22) He should see whether the restriction on the transfer of share imposed by the new section, viz., section 108A of the Companies (Amendment) Act, 1974, have been observed by the company.

Brokerage and Underwriting Commission on issue of Shares

According to Section 76 of the Companies Act, 1956, a company may pay a commission to any person who subscribes or agrees to subscribe for any shares or agrees to procure subscription for any shares in the company on the following conditions:

(*a*) The payment of commission is authorised by the articles of the company;

(*b*) The rate of commission does not exceed five per cent of the price of shares at which they are issued or the rate which is authorised by the Articles of Association of the company whichever is lower;

(*c*) If the rate of commission is left to the discretion of the directors, the rate should not exceed the one fixed by the Companies Act or the Articles; and

(*d*) The amount of commission payable is mentioned in the Prospectus or the Statement in lieu of Prospectus, as the case may be.

The above restrictions are applicable only when the commission is payable either in the form of shares or debentures. If the commission is payable out of profits, the above formalities need not be gone through.

The aforesaid requirements are also not applicable where brokerage is payable.

At this stage, it seems proper that distinction between *Underwriting Commission, Commission for procuring subscriptions or placing shares and brokerage* be clearly understood by the reader.

Underwriting Commission is a commission payable to a person or persons called underwriters who agree to take up all the shares or a proportionate number of shares issued by the company if the public does not subscribe for the shares offered by the company. It is a kind of an insurance contract between the company and the underwriters that the latter will take up all the shares which are not subscribed for by the public. The underwriters are entitled to the commission on all the shares whether subscribed by the public directly or through their efforts or even if they have to take them up in the event of their not being sold out. Thus it would be seen that the company is assured that all the shares which it has issued will be sold and that there would be no difficulty with regard to the minimum subscription.

Commission for procuring Subscription or Placing Shares. This is a commission which is payable to a person who agree to find out a buyer or buyers for the shares of a company. Such a person is entitled to get his commission only when he can find out a buyer otherwise he is not entitled to get commission (*Corrisen's case*). Such a person is not bound to take up any share or shares which could not be sold by the company. Thus

1. commission is usually payable to finance companies which often circulate copies of the prospectus amongst their clients to sell such shares to them.

Brokerage is a commission payable to a stock broker or banker whose clients apply for shares on the forms supplied by the former, and which forms bear their stamp. Such a broker is entitled to get brokerage on the shares sold against the forms which bear his stamp.

The distinction between the three kinds of commissions described above is of great importance as was held in *Andrae vs. Zinc Mines of Great Britain* (1918). In this case a commission was paid to a private individual who was neither a broker nor a banker. It was held that the amount paid was *commission* for procuring subscription and not brokerage.

Commission for placing shares should not be more than five percent according to Section 76 or articles of association or the prospectus whichever is less while brokerage may be any amount, "as it has heretofore been lawful for a company to pay."

Duty of the Auditor in connection with the Audit of Brokerage and Underwriting Commission

1. He should examine the Articles and Prospectus.
2. He should see that the commission payable is in accordance with the Articles and the statute.
3. He should examine the contract entered into between the brokers or underwriters and the company.
4. He should examine the applications for shares signed or stamped by the brokers to ascertain the brokerage payable to them.
5. He should examine the receipts for the commission paid to the brokerage and underwriters.
6. If shares have been issued to the underwriters in lieu of their commission, he should see that such a contract had been filed with the Registrar of the Joint Stock Companies, and that a note regarding the issue of the shares to underwriters is appended to the balance sheet.
7. He should see that the underwriters have paid the Application and the Allotment money on the shares which have been taken up by them or such sums have been set off against the commission payable to them. In case any such call has remained unpaid, he should state the fact in his report.
8. He should see that this item is shown separately on the assets side of the balance sheet under the head "Miscellaneous Expenditure" until it is written off.

Reorganisation of Capital

A company may, if authorised by its Articles, alter the share capital as mentioned in the Memorandum of Association in any of the following ways:

(*a*) Increase of Capital which may be effected:

(*i*) by the issue of new shares;

(*ii*) consolidation of all or parts of its capital, *i.e.*, divide its share capital into shares of larger amount;

(*iii*) conversion of all or a part of its fully paid up shares into stock;

(*iv*) reconversion of all or a part of its stock into paid up shares;

(*v*) subdivision of all or part of its capital into shares of small amounts; and

(*vi*) cancellation of any unissued shares (Section 94).

If such an alteration has been made it should be stated in the Memorandum and Articles of Association after the alteration has been made. Notice of such an alteration must be filed with the Registrar within one month of doing so. If the share capital has been increased beyond its authorised capital, information must be sent to the Registrar within 15 days of passing the resolution to that effect

Under S. 81(4) of the Companies Act, the Central Government can order the conversion of debentures issued by a company and the loan obtained by it, into the shares of such a company.

Now according to S. 94A added by the Companies (Amendment) Act, 1974, the conversion of debentures or loan under the direction of the Central Government as aforesaid, will have the effect of increasing the nominal share capital of the company equal to the amount of the value of the shares into which the debentures or loans or part thereof has been converted.

If any public financial institution wishes to convert its debentures or loan into shares of the company in pursuance of the option exercised by it, the Central Government may, on the application of such a public financial institution, direct that it may be done which will have the effect of increasing the share capital of the institution equal to the amount of such debentures and shares converted.

Where a conversion of the debentures or shares as stated above has been permitted by the Central Government, it shall send a copy of such an order to the Registrar and also a copy of the order to the company which in its turn will file a return with the Registrar regarding the increase of the share capital who will make the necessary changes in the memorandum of the company. The return shall be filed within 30 days of the receipt of the order.

(*b*) Reduction of Capital may be effected in the following ways:

(*i*) extinguish or reduce the liability on any of its shares in respect of share capital not paid up; or

(*ii*) either with or without extinguishing or reducing the liability on any of its shares, cancel any paidup share capital which is lost, or is unrepresented by available assets; or

(*iii*) either with or without extinguishing or reducing liability on any of its shares, pay off any paidup share capital which is in excess of the wants of the company (Section 100).

Capital can be reduced only (*a*) if authorised by the Articles, (*b*) by passing a special resolution, and (*c*) by confirmation of the resolution by National Company Law Tribunal.

Section 77 contains restrictions on purchase of its own shares by a company. Section 77(1) provides that no company limited by shares and no company limited by guarantee having share capital shall have power to buy its own shares, unless the consequent reduction of share capital is effected and sanctioned in pursuance of sections 100 to 104 or section 402.

Section 77(2) contains provisions to combat clandestine purchase of its own shares by a company. It prohibits a public company from giving any financial assistance including granting of loan or provision of guarantee for loan financed by any other person for the purpose of subscribing or purchasing its own shares or shares of its holding company. However certain normal course of transactions are excepted. They are:

1. A banking company can make loans for the purchase of its own shares if the lending of such loan is in its normal course of business;

2. A company can provide money for the purchase of its shares or for the subscription of its shares as fully paid by trustees of the employees (under trust deed or under arrangement for being held by or for the benefit of the employees). But the provision of money should be in accordance with any scheme for the time being in force;

3. A company can make loan to its employees (not exceeding six months salary or wages) with a view to enabling them to subscribe in or purchase the shares of its own company;

4. A company is not affected by provisions of section 77 in its redemption of preference shares in accordance with the provisions of section 80. Section 80 authorise redemption of preference shares. Such shares cannot be redeemed unless they are fully paid up. The shares may be redeemed out of profits available for dividend or out of the proceeds of fresh issue of shares made for the purpose of redemption. When shares are redeemed otherwise than out of the proceeds of fresh issue (*i.e.,* out of profits), a sum equivalent to nominal amount of shares so redeemed shall have to be transferred to an account called "Capital Redemption Reserve Account" from the profits available for dividend. The balance lying in the Capital Redemption Reserve account substitutes the security deficiency that might be cause to creditors by redemption of preference shares. The Capital redemption reserve account is treated as paid up capital of the company and all provisions applicable to it will equally apply to this account also. It may be noted that sub-section (5A) provides that a company cannot issue irredeemable preference shares or redeemable preference shares which may be redeemed after the expiry of a period of twenty years from the date of issue.

5. The buy-back schemes as contained in section 77A read with section 77B is outside the preveiw of section 77. A company can buy back its shares in accordance with the provisions of section 77A. The Companies (Amendment) Act has inserted sections 77A, 77AA and section 77B permitting and regulating buy back of shares by companies.

Buy-back of shares by companies. Section 77A of the Companies Act (as inserted by Companies (Amendment) Act 1999 permits a company purchase its own shares subject to the provisions contained in the Act in this behalf. The limited permission for the Company to purchase its own shares in accordance with the provisions of section 77A is called as buy-back of shares.

Conditions for buy-back of shares:

(A) Authorisation

1. The company can buy back its shares only if it is authorised by aıticles of association. If the articles of association do not provide for such permission, first the articles of association have to be so amended as to provide for such authorisation.

2. A special resolution is to be passed in the general meeting of the company authorising buy-back.

3. All the shares which are to be bought back are to be fully paid up. Parly paid up shares cannot be purchased back.

(B) Source for buy back

4. The shares can be bought back out of:

(*a*) free reserves of the company;

(*b*) the securities premium account;

(*c*) the proceeds of any shares or specified securities.

5. It is to be noted that when shares are to be bought back out of the proceeds of shares, the proceeds of any earlier issue of shares of the same kind cannot be utilised for buy-back. In other words, fresh issue of shares or specified securities should be made out to replenish the shares now being bought.

6. Where shares are to be bought back out of free reserves, (and not by replacing the shares purchased with a fresh equity capital issued for the purpose of purchase), then, a sum equivalent to the normal value of the shares so purchased shall be transferred to the capital redemption reserve account (Section 77 AA).

(C) Quantum of shares that can be purchased

The quantum of buy-back shares is conditioned by a simple absolute percentage and a relative ratio after buy-back is completed.

7. The buy-back is or is less than twenty five per cent of the paid-up capital and free reserves of the company.

8. Again, the buy-back, *in any financial year*, does not exceed twenty five per cent of its total paid-up equity capital in that financial year.

9. The ratio of debt owed by the company is not more than twice the capital and free reserves after such buy-back. That is the debt : aggregate of paid-up capital and free reserves < 2 : 1

However, the Central Government may prescribe a higher ratio of the debt for specified class or classes of companies.

(D) Timing of buy-back

10. Every buy-back is to be completed within 12 months from the date of passing special resolution in the general meeting of the company.

(E) Buy-back-how can be effected:

11. A company can purchase its own shares:

(*a*) from the existing shareholders on a proportionate basis; or

(*b*) from the open market; or

(*c*) from odd lots, that is to say, where the lots of securities of a public company, whose shares are listed on a recognised stock exchange is smaller than such marketable lot as may be specified by stock exchange; or

(*d*) by purchasing the securities issued to the employees of the company pursuant to a scheme of stock option or sweat equity.

In this connection, it is to be understood that section 77B prohibits buy-back in certain circumstances. It provides that no company shall directly or indirectly purchase its own shares or other specified securities.

(*a*) through any subsidiary company including its own subsidiary companies; or

(*b*) through an investment company or group of investment companies; or

(*c*) if a default, by the company, in repayment of deposit or interest payable thereon, redemption of debentures or preference shares or payment of dividend to any shareholder or repayment of any term loan or interest payable thereon to any financial institution or bank is subsisting.

Again the company which has not complied with the provisions of section 159 — filing of annual return; section 207 — failure to pay dividend within time allowed; section 211 — regarding presenting the accounts in the form with specified contents — shall not directly or indirectly purchase its own shares.

The duty of an Auditor in connection with the Reorganisation of Capital

1. The auditor should examine the Memorandum and Articles of Association and the resolution for the alteration of capital and see whether the resolution was passed according to law.
2. He should examine the confirmatory order of the court sanctioning the reduction of capital.
3. He should examine the registrar certificate which is a conclusive evidence that all the legal requirements regarding the reorganisation have been complied with.
4. He should verify the old share holdings and surrendered share certificates, if any, with the new holdings and certificates.
5. Journal entries must be vouched with other documentary evidence available.
6. Record in the register of members should be examined.
7. He must see that the legal requirements have been complied with.
8. If the capital has been reduced, the court may order the company to use the words "and reduced" after its name. The auditor should see that the provisions of Sections 100, 101, 102, and 103 have been complied with.

(c) Disclosure Requirement for Share Capital

Share capital is the first item in balance sheet of the company. The share capital is to be distinguished into different classes of shares and shown accordingly. (*i.e.* equity and preference shares). Authorised, issued, subscribed capital are to be disclosed. The paid up capital is to be shown as amount called up less calls unpaid. The calls unpaid is to be detailed as to due from directors and due from others. Where shares have been allotted for consideration other than cash, the total amount so allotted is to be indicated. Where bonus shares have been issued, the total amount in respect thereof and the source (capital reserve/premium account) from which they have been issued are to be specified. The forfeited share capital representing amount originally paid up on shares forfeited should be added to arrive at the figure of paid up capital. The addition is to be specifically shown in the balance sheet. In respect of redeemable preference shares, the terms of redemption are to be specified.

II. Reserves and Surplus :

The second item in liability side is reserves and surplus. The item is to be disclosed on the following lines:

1. (1) Capital reserves (2) Capital redemption reserve (3) Share premium account (4) Other reserves less debit balance in P&L account (5) Sinking fund. (6) P&L account (cr. balance) are to be distinctly shown.
2. The opening balance, additions made during the year, amount withdrawn during the year are to be indicated.
3. In respect of share premium account, the amount can be utilised only for the purposes specified. If the amount is utilised during the year the nature of utilisation must be indicated.
4. Debit balance in P&L account can be deducted only from free revenue reserves. If the amount cannot be deducted, it is to be shown in asset side under the relevant heading.

The vouching the accuracy, completeness, and validity of the balance in reserve accounts is to be made keeping in mind the principles enumerated in chapter on Reserves.

III. Secured Loans

This includes

(*a*) Debenture

(*b*) Loans and advances from banks

(*c*) Loans and advances from subsidiaries

(*d*) other loans and advances

In respect of the above, the nature of security offered by the company is to be indicated. Loans from directors or Managers are to be specified. Secured loans include, besides outstanding balance on account of principal, interest amount accrued and due on the loans. In case of debenture, the terms of conversion, if they are convertible and terms of redemptions should be disclosed.

Important provisions of Company Law with regard to debenture and creation of charges for securing the loans obtained by the company are discussed hereunder:

Debenture

Meaning

Debenture is acknowledgement of a debt given under the seal of the company containing a contract for repayment of the principal sum at a specified date and for the payment of interest at a fixed percent until the principal sum is repaid and it may or may not give the charge on the assets of the company as security of the loan. Debenture differs from share capital in many respects. The debenture holders are creditors of the company entitled for fixed interest rerespective of adequacy of profit. They have prior claim over share holders in case the company goes into liquidation. But share holders are owners of the company entitled for dividend only if there are profits.

Issue of Debenture:

Debentures may be issued at par and redeemable at par. They may be issued at discount and redeemable at par They may be issued at premium and redeemable at par. On the other hand, debentures may be issued at par or at discount but may be made redeemable at premium. When debentures are to be redeemed at par when issue is at discount or when debentures are to be redeemed at premium when the issue is at par /discount, the excess amount to be redeemed over issue price constitutes loss to the company. Such loss should be recognised at the time of issue itself by debiting the loss to the account called 'loss on issue of debenture'. This loss should be written off over the period of term of debenture.

Till the full loss is wipped off, the remaining loss will be shown in the balance sheet under the heading miscellaneous expenditure in asset side. Sometimes, the debentures are issued as collateral security for loan obtained by the company. The nominal value of debenture in such cases are generally stated at values higher than the loans for which they stand security. No cash is received in respect of such debenture. They are just nominal liability which becomes effective only if the loans are not paid on due dates. As such, they are not shown as liability in balance sheet but a note is included in the balance sheet to indicate the issue of such debentures.

Redemption :

Debentures are redeemed by (a) periodical drawings (b) by payment on fixed date or (c) by payment being made by company whenever it so desires after giving notice to the debenture holders. (d) by converting full or part portion of debenture into shares.

Securing debenture

Debenture may be made secured by creating fixed charge or floating charge. When a specific property is given to the debenture holders as security and when the company can deal with it only subject to the prior right of the debenture holders, a fixed charge is said to have been created. On the other hand, when the debenture holders have a charge on the undertaking of the company, i.e. on the whole of the property of the company, both present and future and when it can deal with the property in the ordinary course of business until the charge crystalises, i.e., when the company goes into liquidation or when a receiver is appointed, the charge is said to be floating charge. When the floating charge crystalises, the debenture holders have a right to be paid out of the sale proceeds of the assets subject to the right of preferential creditors but prior to making any payment to unsecured creditors. Charges created by the company are to be registered with Registar of companies as per section 125 the Act.

Power to reissue redeemed debentures:

According to Section 121 of the Companies Act, a company may re-issue the debentures which have been redeemed by it: —

1. if the Articles of the company do not prohibit such re-issue; or
2. if, according to the terms of the debentures, they could be re-issued after they had been redeemed; or
3. if the company itself passes a resolution to re-issue the redeemed debentures.

The company may re-issue the debentures which have been redeemed or may issue fresh debentures in place of the redeemed debentures. The holders of the re-issued debentures will have the same rights and privileges as if they were originally issued to them. the original debenture-holders will have a prior right to such re-issued debentures.

Particulars of debentures which have been re-issued must be given in the balance sheet of the company.

The auditor should examine the terms of the original debentures or the articles of association to see whether the redeemed debentures could be re-issued. He should also find out whether the company had passed a resolution to that effect. He should see whether fresh stamp duty had been paid on the re-issued be debentures according to law.

SEBI Guidelines for issue of Debentures

SEBI (Disclosure and Investor protection) Guidelines, 2000 (which replaces its earlier guidelines issued in June, 1992) provides for the following:

Chapter X of the guidelines 2000 provides that a company offering convertible/Non convertible debt instruments through an offer document, shall comply with the following provisions in addition to the relevant provisions contained in other chapter of the guidelines.

1. Mandatory credit rating. No public or right issue of debt instruments (including convertible instruments) irrespective of their maturity period or conversion period, shall be made unless credit rating from a credit rating agency has been obtained and disclosed in the offer document. Where credit rating is obtained from more than one credit rating agencies, all the credit ratings including the unaccepted credit ratings should be disclosed. For a public/rights issue of debt security of issue greater than or equal to Rs. 100 crores, two ratings from two different credit ratings agencies shall be obtained. All the credit ratings obtained during last three previous years proceeding the public issue shall also be required to be disclosed.

2. Appointment of Debenture Trustees. In case of issue of debenture with maturity of more than 18 months, the issuer shall appoint a debenture trustee.

The names of the debenture trustees shall be disclosed in the offer document.

A trust deed shall be executed by the issuer company in favour of the debenture trustees within six months of the closure of the issue.

Trustees of the debenture holders shall have to be vested with requisite powers for protecting the interests of the debenture holders including the power to appoint a nominee director on the Board of Directors in consultation with institutional debenture holders.

The merchant banker to the issue shall file with the Board, certificates from bankers of the company that the assets (on which debentures are to be secured) are free from encumbrance or where assets are subject to any prior charge in favour of bank/financial institution, that there is no objection on their part for the company creating a second or *pari pasu* charge in favour of debenture holders on such assets.

The debenture trustees shall ensure compliance of the following:

(*a*) lead financial institution shall monitor the progress in respect of debenture raised for project finance/modernisation/expansion/diversification/normal capital expenditure.

(*b*) the lead bank for the company shall monitor the debenture raised for working capital funds.

(*c*) Trustees shall obtain certificates from the company auditor regarding utilisation of the debenture proceeds for projects during implementation of projects and where debentures are issued to fund working capital requirements, trustees shall obtain year end certificates from the auditor for each and every accounting year.

Debenture issues by companies belonging to the groups for financing replenishing funds or acquiring shareholding in other companies shall not be permitted.

The Debenture trustees shall supervise the implementation of the conditions regarding creation of security for the debentures and debenture redemption reserve.

3. Creation of Debenture Redemption Reserve (DRR). In cases of issues of debentures with maturity of more than 18 months, a company has to create debenture redemption reserve (DRR). If debentures are issued for project finance, the reserve can be created upto the date of commercial production. In such a case, the amount to be transferred to the reserve may be in equal instalments or higher amounts if the profits permit. The company shall create DRR equivalent to 50% of the amount of debenture issue before the debenture redemption commences. Drawal from DRR is permissible only after 10% of the debenture liability has actually been redeemed by the company.

4. Distribution of Dividends. In case of new companies, the distribution of dividends shall require prior approval of the trustees to the issue and the lead institution, if any.

In the case of existing companies, where the company has not complied with terms for payment of interest or where debt service coverage ratio is not adequate, prior permission of the lead institution for declaring dividend in excess of 20% is necessary. Where loan covenants require obtaining of prior permission even otherwise, approval is to be obtained prior to dividend distribution. Dividend may be distributed out of profits of a particular year only after transfer of requisite amount of DRR.

5. Redemption. The issuer company shall redeem the debentures as per office document.

6. Creation of charge. The security shall be created within six months from the date of issue of debentures. A grace period of further six months is provided for and if still the company fails to create charge within such time (*i.e.,* 12 months), the company shall be liable to pay to the debenture holders a penal interest of 2% (in addition to the normal rate of interest). If charge is not created within 18 months from the issue, a meeting of the debenture holders shall be convened within 21 days. In the meeting the reasons for default shall be explained and the date within which such charge will be created will also be specified. Where the debentures are issued for a period of more than 18 months, it is incumbent upon the debenture trustees to look after creation of charges to protect the interests of the debenture holders. In cases where the company issues debentures of shorter period (less than 18 months) and also proposes to create charge in favour of the debenture holders, the company has to conform to complying the relevant provisions of the company law in creation of charges and should file with the Registrar of Companies, the necessary details. On the other hand, where the company does not propose to create charge (for shorter span debentures), the company has to ensure compliance with the provisions of the Companies (Acceptance of Deposits) Rules, 1975 as unsecured debentures are treated as deposits for the purpose of these rules.

The offer document shall contain the proposal or otherwise of the company to create charges and the implications of it.

7. Roll over, conversion. In case, the non-convertible portions of PCD (Partly convertible debenture) or NCD (non-convertible debenture), value of which exceeds Rs 50 lakhs, can be rolled over (*i.e.,* continued as debt without redemption on due date) without change in interest rates only if and after the following conditions are fulfilled:

(*a*) an option shall be compulsorily given to debenture holders to redeem the debentures as per the terms of the offer document.

(*b*) Roll over shall be done only in cases where the debenture holders have sent their positive consent and not on the basis of the non-receipt of negative reply from them.

(*c*) Before roll over of any NCD or non-convertible portion of FCD, a fresh credit rating shall be obtained within a period of six months prior to the due date of redemption and such rating communicated to the debentureholders before roll over:

(*d*) Fresh trust deed shall be executed at the time of roll over.

(*e*) Fresh security shall be created in respect of debentures to be rolled over.

(*f*) Fresh trust deed and cretion of fresh security may not be necessary if the existing deed providing for roll over take care of such situations.

In case, the convertible portion of any instrument such as PCDs or FCDs etc. issued by a listed company value of which exceeds Rs 50 lakhs and whose conversion price was not fixed at the time of issue, the holders of such instruments shall be given a compulsory option of not converting into equity capital. Conversion shall be made in such cases only if the positive responses for conversion have been received from the instrument holders. Where cap price for conversion had already been fixed and specified in the offer document, the conversion may be made within that cap price. In cases where price is left to be fixed at the time of conversion, option shall have to be given either to convert or not convert. Those who do not like to get the debenture or portion of it converted into equity at a price determined by shareholders, shall have to be paid at a price which is not less than the face value of the debentures held by them.

8. Interest rate. Interest rate for debenture may be freely fixed by the company.

9. Others. No company shall issue FCD having conversion period of more than 36 months unless conversion is made optional with put and call option.

If the conversion takes place at or after 18 months from the date of allotment but before 36 months, any conversion in part or whole of the debenture shall be optional at the hands of debenture holders. Conversion in such cases cannot be compulsorily converted.

The offer document shall contain such disclosures as are specified in the Guidelines.

Auditor's Duty in Checking Debentures:

1. The auditor has to check that the prospectus or statement in lieu of prospectus had been filed with the Registrar of the Companies before the issue of debenture.
2. He should vouch entries in application and allotment book with
   (*a*) application submitted by the applicants
   (*b*) directors minute book for allotment made
3. He should vouch the receipt of cash with regard to application and allotment money with counterfoils of receipt and entries in cash book and postings in application and allotment book.
4. Check the postings to each debenture holders account from application and allotment book in respect of persons to whom allotment has been made.
5. Vouch payment side of the cash book for refunds made to those applicants to whom allotment has not been made.
6. Check total of individual balances in debenture holders account tally with total control account of debentures in general ledger.
7. Where debentures are to be redeemed at premium when the issue price is at par, or when the redemption is to be made at par when the issue is at discount, the auditor has to see that the loss on issue of debenture in this regard is accounted and is written off during the life term of debentures.
8. The auditor should check that the terms and conditions of debenture issue are complied with especially with regard to creation of debenture redemption reserve, appointment of debenture trustees etc.
9. He must vouch the periodical interest payments with counterfoils of interest warrants issued and receipted vouchers from debenture holders. Unpaid interest if accrued should be provided. Interest accrued and due should be shown along with debenture in balance sheet. Interest accrued but not due should be shown in current liability in balance sheet.
10. The auditor has to check that transfer to debenture redemption reserve from P&L account is made each year according to SEBI guidelines.

11. Where the debentures are secured, the auditor has to verify that the charge has been registered with the Registrar and entries are made in register of charges.
12. When debentures are redeembed the auditor has to check the minutes of directors meeting. He should vouch payments made in respect of debentures from cash book entries and with cancelled debenture certificates duly signed by the debenture holders.
13. If debentures are purchased in open market for redemption, the auditor should verify the price at which they have been purchased and if there is any profit/loss, he should ensure that these have been duly accounted in P&L account.
14. If debenture redemption reserve is created in the form of sinking fund and the amount appropriated is invested in sinking fund investment, the company would sell the investment and utilise the money for redemption. In such a case the auditor has to vouch the sale of investment and ensure correct adjustment in sinking fund account in respect of profit or loss on sale of investment. After the redemption is completed, the amount at the credit of the sinking fund has to be transferred to general reserve.
15. Above all, the auditor has to ensure that the company has complied with all statutory provisions and SEBI guidelines in issue, allotment, creation of security, protecting the interests of debentureholders etc. In particular, the authority for issue of debenture with respect to quantum of amount that can be raised should be ensured at all relevant times.

IV. Unsecured Loans:

The fourth item in Liability side of a balance sheet is unsecured loans. It includes the following:

(*a*) Fixed Deposits,

(*b*) Loans and advances from subsidiaries

(*c*) Short term loans and advances from banks and others

(*d*) Other loans and advances from banks and others.

Loans obtained from directors and manager of the company are to be indicated. The amount stated in respective category should include besides balance in respect of principal amount, the unpaid interest which has accrued and had become due.

Fixed Deposits :

A brief outline on the audit procedure for checking fixed deposits accepted from public is given hereunder:

Provisions of Company Law regarding public deposit:

The auditor must be familiar with the provisions of company law while checking the public deposits. It is all the more important because the auditor makes specific comment about the compliance of rules regarding acceptance/renewal of deposit by companies in his MAOCARO 1988 (details follow in next chapter).

Under section 58A of the Act, the central government can prescribe the limits upto which and the manner in which public deposits can be raised by the company. The central government, accordingly, has issued Companies (Acceptance of Deposits) Rules 1975.

The important rules in this regard are:

1. The company cannot accept deposits repayable on demand. It can accept only term deposits. The term should be not less than 6 months and not more than 36 months.
2. The rate of interest cannot exceed the percentage prescribed (i.e. 14% p.a)
3. Brokerage payable for soliciting deposits should not exceed the percentages prescribed.
4. The total deposits that can be accepted should be within 10% of paid up capital and free reserves, in case of deposits from share holders and 25% of paid up capital and free reserves in case of deposits from public.

5. An advertisement in the prescribed format should be published in newspapers for inviting acceptance/renewal of deposits. The advertisement should be approved by the board of directors and a copy of it should be registered with the Registrar of Companies before its issue. The advertisement is valid until the expiry of six months from the end of financial year in which it is issued or until the date on which the balance sheet is laid before the general meeting subsequent to its issue. A fresh advertisement is to be issued once the advertisement has become invalid. A statement in lieu of advertisement is to be filed with the Registrar if deposit is raised privately.
6. The rule also prescribes matters to be specified in application form, time within which deposit receipt is to be issued to the depositor, maintenance of deposit register, filing of return of deposits as on 31st March of each year within last day of June.
7. The company should maintain liquid assets in the forms specified at the prescribed percentage on deposits.

Auditor's Duty in Checking Deposits

1. The auditor should check the borrowing power of the company by referring memorandum of association, articles of association.
2. He should check that the necessary advertisement has been filed before issue.
3. He should ensure that the terms of issue with regard to period of deposit, rate of interest etc are in conformity with rules.
4. The auditor should see that the quantum of total deposits is within the limits prescribed by Central government. (ie 25% of paid up capital and free reserves and 10% of paid up capital and free reserves in case of deposits from shareholders)
5. The auditor should vouch receipt of deposit amounts in cash book with counterfoils receipt issued to the depositors, and application form. He has to check that the postings are properly made to deposit registers.
6. The auditor has to check that the periodical interest payments are correctly paid. At the year end if any interest remains unpaid, necessary provision for interest accrued should be created.
7. Where deposit is paid prematurely, the interest for the period for which the deposit remained with the company should be paid at the rate relevant for that period after deducting penalty at the rate prescribed.
8. The auditor has to verify that the company maintains liquid assets in respect of deposits maturing during the year ending on the last day of March as per rules.
9. The auditor has to vouch payments made in respect of matured deposits with duly discharged deposit receipts from the depositors.
10. The auditor has to confirm that all other miscellaneous provisions of the Deposit rules are duly complied with.

V. Current Liabilities and Provisions:

The fifth item in liability side is current liabilities and provisions. This item includes (a) Current liability and (*b*) Provision.

Current liabilities are: acceptances, sundry creditors, subsidiary company dues, advance payments, unclaimed dividend, other liabilities, interest accrued but not due. Provisions include provision for taxation, provision for proposed dividend, for contingencies, for provident fund and pension and superannuation fund, others. Provision for depreciation should not be shown here but as a deduction from fixed assets. Provision should include only those amounts set apart to meet future liability, the quantum of which cannot be determined with substantial accuracy. Providing any amount in excess of liability is a reserve and is to be shown accordingly.

The amount due to sundry creditors is to be split into:

(*i*) Total outstanding due to small scale industrial undertaking and

(*ii*) Total outstanding dues to creditors other than small scale industrial undertakings.

The auditor should check the truth and fairness of each of the above item bearing in mind the principles discussed in verification of liability in a previous chapter.

VI. Contingent Liabilities:

A foot note on various contingent liabilities are to be given. Examples of contingent liability are: Claims against company not acknowledged as debts by the company, uncalled liability in respect of shares held as investment and which are partly paid up, arrears of dividend in respect of cumulative preference shares, others. By reference to various records of the company directors minute book, correspondence files, legal case-files etc; the auditor has to ascertain existence of contingent liabilities

Assets :

I. Fixed Assets :

Fixed assets are capital expenditure incurred in acquisition of assets of various types. The fixed assets are to be shown in terms of goodwill, land, building, leasehold, railway sidings, plant and machinery, furniture and fittings, development of property, patents etc, livestock, vehicles and capital work in progress. The original cost, additions, deletions, depreciation upto the date of the balance sheet are to be detailed. Where any asset is revalued during the year the balance sheet shall specify the revalued figure in the place of cost. The fact of revaluation should be indicated for next five years.

The auditor should check that the valuation of assets are properly done after providing for depreciation correctly. He should vouch additions, delections with the minute books of directors and cash vouchers, bills or invoices. In respect of additions, he should see that all connected expenses are duly capitalised. In MAOCARO 1988 (refer next chapter), the auditor has to comment on the maintenance of records for fixed assets, physical verification of fixed assets revaluation of fixed assets if any. The auditor should note the contents of the order and carry out necessary checks to comment on these areas.

II. Investments :

The investment are to be shown on the following lines:

(*a*) Investment in Government securities/trust securities

(*b*) Investment in shares, debentures (Details are to be given in respect of class of shares whether fully paid up or partly paid up, investments in subsidiaries, and others)

(*c*) Immovable properties

(*d*) Investments in capital of partnership firms

In respect of investment, the mode of valuation should be indicated. In respect of investment in shares and government securities, which are quoted, their market value should be indicated. In addition to this disclosure, the company has to annex a statement of investments showing the names of companies in which the investments had been made by the company during the year. The statement should give the details in a classified manner i.e. trade investment and other investment. Investment in companies under same management should be specified.

Auditor's duty with regard to Investment:

1. The auditor should check such details as are enumerated in verification of the asset- 'investment' detailed in a previous chapter. Important points in this connection are checking with respect to existence, valuation of investment.

2. The auditor should see that the provisions of company law relating to investment are complied with. For example, under section 49, the investments made by the company should be only in the name of companies. However, there are certain exceptions to this. Under section 292 the investment can be made only by passing a resolution in directors meeting.

   Section 372A as inserted by Companies (Amendment) Act, 1998 contains provisions for regulating inter-company loans as well investments. Prior to the insertion of this section, section 370 dealt with inter-company loans and section 372 dealt with inter-company investments. The auditor should check that the requirements of section 372A has been duly complied with the company before making any loan or investment to any other body corporate.

Power of the company to make inter-corporate loan or investment.

Section 372A (1) provides that no company shall directly or indirectly.

(*a*) make any loan to any other body corporate.

(*b*) give any guarantee or provide any security, in connection with a loan made by any other person to or to any other person by, any body corporate, and

(*c*) acquire by way of subscription, purchase or otherwise securities of any other body corporate exceeding 60% of its paid-up share capital and free reserves, or 100% of its free reserves whichever is more.

For example,

1. (*a*) If the paid-up capital of the company is Rs 30 lakhs and free reserves is 10 lakhs, the company can make inter-corporate loan or investments upto Rs 24 lakhs.

   (*b*) On the other hand, if the paid-up capital is Rs 10 lakhs and free reserves is Rs 30 lakhs, the company can make inter-corporate loan or investment upto Rs 30 lakhs.

2. (*a*) If the paid-up capital of the company is Rs 40 lakhs and free reserves is Rs 60 lakhs, the company can make inter-corporate loan or investments upto Rs 60 lakhs.

   (*b*) If the paid-up capital is Rs 60 lakhs and free reserves is Rs 40 lakhs the company can still make inter-corporate investments or loan upto Rs 60 lakhs.

   It means that the company can make inter-corporate loan or investment upto the prescribed percentages. The company management shall be entitled to make investments or loan without obtaining permission of the shareholders or government.

Where special resolution is to be obtained before making inter-corporate investment or loan:

Where the company makes inter-corporate loan or investment in excess of the above percentages, the company has to obtain previous authorisation of the company signified by a special resolution passed to this effect in the general meeting. However, previous authorisation by a special resolution can be dispensed with in cases of exceptional circumstances which prevent the management from obtaining authorisation by way of special resolution. In such cases inter-corporate loans or investments can be made by passing a resolution to this effect in the meeting of the Board. The resolution of the Board should however, be confirmed by a resolution (we opine it to be special resolution) passed by shareholders in a general meeting to be convened within 12 months of date of board resolution or in an annual general meeting held after the board meeting in reference, whichever is earlier.

Where prior consent of public financial institution is to be obtained:

1. Where there is a default in repayment of loan or payment of interest in regard to a term loan obtained from a public financial institution, any inter-corporate loan or investment shall have to be made only after obtaining prior permission from the public financial institution concerned.

2. Where the aggregate of inter-corporate loan or investment exceeds 60% of paid-up capital and free reserves the prior consent of public financial institution is always to be obtained so long the term loan obtained from such financial institution is subsisting Note in this connection while a company is free to make inter-company loan or investment in excess of 60% of its paid-up capital and free reserves (if the quantum of free reserves is still within 100% of its free reserves) without going in for obtaining shareholders consent (by way of special resolution), the company is obliged to obtain the prior consent of the public financial institution if the aggregate of inter-company loans and investments exceeds just 60% of paid-up capital and free reserves (but does not exceed its free reserves).

Prohibition as to making inter-corporate loan or investment:

A company which has defaulted in complying with the provisions of section 58A shall not make inter-corporate loan or investment till such default is subsisting. Section 58A contains, inter alia, power of Central Government to prescribe the limits upto which and the manner in which and the conditions subject to which the deposits can be accepted from the public. The relevant rules made in this behalf may be referred under the topic deposits in this chapter.

Inapplicability of the provisions:

In respect of the following cases, the section shall not apply:

(*a*) to any loan or investment made

(*i*) by a banking company or an insurance company, or a housing finance company in the ordinary course of its business or a company established with the object of financing industrial enterprises or of providing infrastructure facilities.

(*ii*) a company whose principal business is the acquisition of shares, stock, debentures or other securities.

(*b*) to investments made in shares allotted in pursuance of section 81 (1)

(*a*) — *i.e.,* investments in rights;

(*c*) to any loan made by a holding company to its cent percent owned subsidiary company;

(*d*) to any guarantee given or any security provided by a holding company in respect of loan made to its cent percent owned subsidiary;

(*e*) to acquisition by a holding company, by way of subscription, purchase or otherwise, the securities of its wholly owned subsidiary.

3. In the audit Report the auditor has to comment upon certain matters in respect of investments as per CARO 2003 in case of finance, investment, chit or nidhi or mutual benefit company. The areas of checking should cover matters in respect of such requirements also. (Refer next chapter for details of CARO 2003)
4. The auditor has to check that all details to be specified in balance sheet as per requirement are truly and fairly stated.

III. Current Assets, Loans and Advances

This head includes (a) Current assets and (b) Loans and advances.

Under current assets, the following items are to be disclosed:

(*a*) interest accrued on investments
(*b*) stores and spare parts
(*c*) loose tools
(*d*) stock in trade
(*e*) work in progress
(*f*) sundry debtors
(*g*) cash balance
(*h*) bank balance

With regard to checking stock in trade, the stock of raw materials, and stock of finished goods should be separately disclosed. The mode of valuation (like cost/cost or market value whichever is lower) should be indicated. Under CARO 2003, the auditor has to make specific comment in his report, about the physical verification of stock of raw materials, finished goods, stores, spares etc, about the valuation-its acceptability and consistency (refer next chapter for details). The checking of stock-in-trade should include the matters in this respect, in addition to usual points in connection with checking of the asset-stock'

With regard to sundry debtors, the auditor has to check the correctness, completeness and proper disclosure of the item in balance sheet. He must see that the total control account tallies with the individual balances of sundry debtors. The accuracy of individual balances must be supported by the confirmation of balances received from sundry debtors. The company might have sold goods but would not have despatched the goods. The auditor has to ensure that correct 'cut-off' procedure has been applied to increase the debtor balance and reduce the value of stock in such cases. Thus he has to ensure that all sales had been duly accounted and the debtor's balance is complete. In balance sheet the debtors has to be shown after deducting provision for doubtful debts distinctly. The debtors are to be classified into debts outstanding for a period exceeding six months and others.

Again, the debts are to be classified into debts considered good and debts considered doubtful. In respect of debts considered good, further classification into debts fully secured and debts secured on personal security of debtor only are to be shown. The debts due by director or officer and debts due from companies under same management are to be indicated. In case of debts due from directors or officers, the maximum outstanding balance at any time during the year is to be shown in addition to outstanding balance as on the last date of the accounting year.

IV. Loans and Advances:

Under this item the following are to be disclosed:

Loans and advances to subsidiary companies, loans and advances to partnership firm in which company holds share capital, bills of exchange, prepaid expenses, balances with port trust, customs etc. Loans and advances due from companies under same management are to be disclosed. Like sundry debtors, all disclosures viz age of loan (ie more than six months old/others), quality (good doubtful), security (fully secured/unsecured), due from interested parties (due from companies under same management, directors, officers) are to be disclosed. Provision for doubtful amount should be shown as a deduction distinctly.

In respect of loans and advances, the auditor is required to make specific comment in his report as per CARO 2003, about the terms of loans, recovery etc. (see next chapter for details). The auditor should cover these points in his checking.

The auditor should also ensure that the provisions of company law in respect of loans and advances has not been violated. Importantly the provisions of section 292, 293, 295, 372A are to be complied with. Under section 292 the board of directors must exercise the power to make loans only by passing a resolution in their meeting. Otherwise they can delegate this power to any committee of directors, or managing director or manager by a resolution. The resolution must specify the purposes for which loans may be given, the maximum amount that may be given for each such purpose in individual cases, and the total amount of loans that can be made. The committee or managing director, manager while acting on such delegated power has to strictly follow the directions of the resolution. Under section 293 the board of directors cannot remit or give time for repayment of any debt due by director. They can do so only after getting approval of shareholders by getting a resolution passed in their meeting. Section 295 prohibits the company from making loans to directors without prior approval of the central government. Similarly a company cannot give loans without previous permission of government to the director's relative or the director of its holding company, or the firm in which the director of the company is a partner or private company in which the director of the company is a member. This section is not applicable to a private company. The restriction of advancing loan shall also apply to a transaction represented by a book debt which from its inception was in the nature of loan or advance. While section 295 contains restriction in giving loans to directors or persons associated with directors section 372A provides restrictions with regard to inter-corporate loans. A company cannot make inter-company loans in excess of 60% of its paid up capital and free reserves or 100% of its free reserves whichever is more. Similar restriction shall also apply where the company wants to give guarantee or provide securities for and a loan obtained by another company from any other person. Similarly a company cannot give guarantee or provide security to another company for any loan obtained by any other person from a company. Any making of loan in excess of the specified percentage shall require prior approval of shareholders which shall be signified by passing of a special resolution in the general meeting. Prior consent of public financial institutions is to be obtained where there is default in complying terms of any loan agreement by a company with such financial institution, even if the quantum of inter-company loans does not exceed 60% of paid-up capital and free reserves. Where the quantum exceeds 60% of paid-up capital and free reserves, the prior consent of public financial institution is to be secured always so long as there is loan obligation subsisting with it. Detailed discussion on the section has been already presented under the topic investments which may be referred to.

V. MISCELLANEOUS EXPENDITURE:

The following nature of expenses, to the extent not written off, have to be disclosed:

(*a*) preliminary expenses
(*b*) expenses in connection with issue of shares/debenture-commission, brokerage etc.
(*e*) discount allowed on the issue of shares/debentures
(*d*) interest paid out of capital during construction period
(*e*) developmental expenditure
(*f*) others

Preliminary Expenses

Preliminary Expenses are those expenses which are incurred in the creation, floatation or incorporation of a company. These expenses are sometimes called Promotion, Floatation or Foundation Expenses. The Preliminary Expenses may be written off by and by in subsequent years, although it is not obligatory for a company to write them off unless the regulations of the company lay it otherwise. The share capital or debentures are issued in subsequent years, expenses incurred in the issue of such shares and debentures are not to be debited to Preliminary Expenses Account but are debited to 'Capital Issue Expenses Account' and are shown separately from the Preliminary Expenses'. The Capital Issue Expenses Account is also written off in subsequent years or written off' against the premium, if any, if the shares have been issued at a premium. If any loss has been incurred in the first year of the life of the company, it should not be debited to preliminary expenses. Once the company has begun to earn revenue, the current expenditure should not be debited to Preliminary expenses. (*Baidya Nath Biswas vs. Emperor, 1935*).

The following are the expenses which are generally debited to Preliminary Expenses Account:

1. Legal expenses incurred for drafting the Memorandum and Articles of Association, the Prospectus, and the Contracts entered into with the vendors, managing agents, etc.
2. Fees of accountants, the valuers, surveyors, engineers, etc.
3. Stamp duty, registration fees, etc., which is according to nominal capital.
4. Company's Sales, Statutory Books and Original Books of Accounts.
5. Cost of printing, stamping, etc., of the memorandum of and articles of association, prospectus, debentures and debenture trust deeds, if any, share certificates, etc.
6. Expenses incurred in entering into agreements, together with stamp duties thereon.
7. Cost of advertising the prospectus, etc.

Auditors' duty in connection with the Preliminary Expenses

The auditor should see that only those expenses which are connected with the incorporation of the company are debited to Preliminary Expenses Account. Sometimes, in order to show more profit in the very first year of the life of the company, the directors debit the ordinary revenue expenses to Preliminary Expenses. The auditor should see that this is not done as was decided in the case of *Baidya Nath Biswas vs. Emperor* (1933)

The preliminary expenses are not to be debited to Profit and Loss Account of the first year because the benefit of such expenses will be derived by subsequent years also and, therefore, it is but fair that those years must also bear the burden. Moreover, if the very first year of its incorporation is debited with such expenses, the result will be that very little or no profit will be left for distribution amongst the shareholders. The shares, therefore, might be quoted at a discount at the Stock Exchange. Again, these expenses are of non-recurring nature. To avoid all these consequences, the preliminary expenses are written off within three, five, or seven years.

The auditor should vouch as usual the cash payments in connection with these expenses by referring to vouchers, receipts, bills, etc. He should also examine the contract with the vendors of the business to find out whether they have to bear the preliminary expenses. If this is the case, their account should be debited with the amount. Sometimes the Preliminary Expenses are borne by the promoters and sometimes they are divided amongst the vendors, promoters and the new company. He should, therefore, see that such expenses are properly allocated. For this purpose he should refer to various contracts, agreements, correspondence, etc.

If the company has issued prospectus or a statement in lieu of prospectus and has stated the amount of Preliminary Expenses therein, the auditor should see that this amount is not exceeded. If the Preliminary Expenses have exceeded the amount stated in the prospectus, he should see whether the shareholders have sanctioned the excess amount.

The auditor should see that brokerage, commission, etc., for selling or underwriting or for placing shares is not debited to Preliminary Expenses but is shown as a separate item on the assets side to the Balance Sheet as per Schedule VI, Part I of the Companies Act.

Premiums received on the issue of shares may be utilised in wiping off the Preliminary Expenses (Section 78).

In the case of banking companies, the Banking Companies Act of 1949, prohibits the payment of dividends until all the preliminary expenses incurred have been written off.

The statutory report should set out, *inter alia*, an account or estimates of the Preliminary Expenses of the company.

Interest Paid out of Capital

Where a company has been formed to undertake some construction work or the provision of any plant or any other work where it will not be possible to earn any profit for some years, it may pay interest on the paid up capital according to Section 208 of the Companies Act, and may debit the same to construction account, etc., provided—

1. the payment of such an interest is authorised by the Articles or a special resolution. If the Articles are silent, a special resolution has been passed to that effect;
2. the previous sanction of the Central Government has been obtained for this purpose. The Central Government may hold an inquiry at the company's expense before granting the necessary sanction, and may require security for the cost of the inquiry. Such a sanction will be the conclusive evidence that the shares of the company have been issued for the purpose of construction, etc.;
3. the period for which interest is paid does not exceed the period sanctioned by the Government but in no case shall it exceed beyond the close of the halfyear next after the

halfyear during which the works have actually been completed or the plant provided, etc;

4. the rate of interest shall not exceed four per cent or SUCH other rate which may be prescribed by the Central Government by notification in the Official Gazette;
5. the payment of such interest and the rate at which it has been paid is clearly shown in the balance sheet of the year in which such interest is paid if it has not been shown in the Profit and Loss Account; and
6. the payment of such interest shall not operate as a reduction of the paid up capital of the company.

The above provisions of Section 208 do not affect any company to which the Indian Railway Companies Act, 1895, or the Indian Tramways Act, 1902, applies.

Interest paid on the debentures issued for the purpose of construction, etc., may also be treated as stated above.

The duty of an auditor is to see that all the legal formalities as shown above have been complied with and that the interest so paid is mentioned separetely in the balance sheet of the company under a distinctive head ``Miscellaneous Expenditure" unless it has already been debited to the Construction, Plantation accounts, etc. The rate at which such interest has been paid should also be stated.

VI. P&L account Debit Balance:

The last item in the asset side of a company balance sheet is debit balance in P&L account. The debit balance of P&L account pertaining to current year and earlier years are in the first instance adjusted against the credit balance of uncommitted (i.e., free) reserves appearing in liability side. To the extent the amount could not be adjusted there, it is shown in the asset side under this head.

Audit of Profit and Loss Account or Income and Expenditure Account

Entities doing business with the aim of earning profit prepare P&L account.and other non-profit organisations prepare income and expenditure accounts.

The P&L account should be prepared to disclose the result of the working of the company during the period clearly. In expenditure side various expenditure are to be disclosed, but they can be grouped and given under appropriate heads. Specifically, the following important expenses are to be distinctly shown:

(*a*) consumption of raw materials/purchases of goods
(*b*) opening stock of finished goods, work in progress
(*c*) consumption of stores, spares
(*d*) power and fuel
(*e*) staff expenses- salaries, wages, bonus
– contribution to provident and other funds
– welfare expenses
(*f*) rent
(*g*) repairs to building, machinery
(*h*) depreciation
(*i*) insurance
(*j*) taxes
(*k*) interest

(*l*) provision to meet specific liability

(*m*) reserves set apart

(*n*) miscellaneous expenditure

In income side, all income are to be disclosed but they may be disclosed after condensing them in convenient groupings. The following items of revenue are to be specifically disclosed:

(*a*) sales

(*b*) closing stock of finished goods/closing work in progress

(*c*) income from investments

(*d*) dividend from subsidiaries

(*e*) miscellaneous income

The profit and loss account shall also disclose by way of note or otherwise, the following:

(*a*) payment made to managerial personnel and computation of profit for determination of managerial remuneration payable

(*b*) payment made to auditor for his services in various capacities

(*c*) quantitative details of raw materials consumed, purchases, stocks of finished goods, and turnover of goods

(*d*) licensed, installed capacity and actual production

(*e*) C.I.F value o imports

(*f*) F.O.B. value of exports

(*g*) expenditure in foreign currency

(*h*) income in foreign exchange

(*i*) percentages of imported raw material consumed and indigenous raw materials consumed.

The auditor has to check that the items of income and expenditure appearing in trial balance by scrutinising the ledgers. Then he has to check that the items of expenditure and revenue are properly grouped as all and sundry item cannot be disclosed in P&L account.Where the Act requires certain item to be disclosed specifically, (as illustrated above) they are to be disclosed in P&L account itself or in the schedules accompanying them. The auditor has to check that items to be disclosed in notes to P&L account are properly disclosed. The auditor has to make a critical evaluation of result of the working of the company (ie profit/loss) by doing comparative studies or ratio anlysis to see that they reflect true and fair view

Managerial Remuneration:

While checking managerial remuneration the auditor should bear in mind the following:

1. The provisions of Company Law relating to ceiling on total remuneration payable to all managerial personnel together, ceiling on remuneration payable to whole time directors/ managing director, manager etc have been strictly adhered to. He has to check that various procedural requirement connected with sanctioning remuneration had been complied with by the company.
2. The auditor should check that profit calculated for the purpose of determination of managerial remuneration is properly arrived at as per Company Law sections.
3. He has to vouch the payments made to managerial personnel and in cases where there is amount unpaid, the auditor should ensure that the outstanding amount is suitably provided.
4. The expenditure of managerial remuneration and manner of computation of profit for determination of managerial remuneration should be disclosed in P&L account by way of note or otherwise. The auditor should ensure this.

A. Company Law provisions regarding ceiling on managerial remuneration:

Managerial personnel include whole time director, managing director, and manager (within the meaning of company law). The auditor should have thorough knowledge of the sections -198, 309, 310, 311, 348, 349, 350, 351, 381, 387 and 637AA.

1. Overall ceiling on managerial remuneration:

Under section 198 the total remuneration payable to managerial personnel for a financial year cannot exceed eleven per cent of net profits of the company for that year computed in the manner laid down in sections 349, 350 and 351. However, where the company has no profit or only insufficient profit, the remuneration can be paid to managerial personnel only after getting prior approval from central government.

2. Individual ceiling on managerial remuneration:

Section 309 provides restriction on the amount of remuneration payable to managing or whole time director, directors. Section 387 regulates remuneration payable to manager.

(*a*) Remuneration payable to whole time-Managing Director:

(1) The whole-time-Managing Directors should be properly appointed. Under section 269 of the Act, the appointment of these persons should conform to the conditions specified in schedule XIII to the Act. The schedule prescribes that no person who has committed certain offences under various enactments listed can be appointed as managing or whole time director or manager. It also specifies age limit i.e. the person should be of age not less than 25 years and not more than 70 years. The person should not hold appointment as full time director or manager in any other company, receiving remuneration.

(2) The total remuneration payable to managing director and whole time directors should be subject to ceiling laid down in section 309(3). If the company has only one such director, the remuneration may be paid upto 5% of net profits of the company. Where there are more than one such director, the amount payable to all of them should not exceed 10% of net profits of the company. Any amount in excess of the limits requires prior approval of central government. In case of no profit or inadequate profit, the company can pay minimum remuneration at the scales specified in part II of schedule XIII of the Act.

(*b*) Remuneration payable to other directors:

Section 309 (4) contains restriction in respect of remuneration payable to directors who are neither whole time directors nor managing directors. Generally no remuneration is admissible to them. They may be paid periodical (monthly/quarterly/annually) remuneration only with the approval of central government. They may be paid remuneration by way of commission if the same has been authorised by special resolution passed in shareholders meeting. However, the remuneration payable to them in any manner, whatsoever, for a year should not exceed 1% of net profits of the year in cases where there is a managing director or whole time director or manager for the company and 3% of net profits in cases where the company, does not have such person.

Section 309(2) allows the company to pay its directors fees for attending meetings. This payment will not be subject to restrictions specified in fixing ceilings on total managerial remuneration in sections 198 or 209.

(*c*) Remuneration payable to Manager:

Manager is an individual who, subject to superintendence, control and direction of board of directors has the management of whole or substantially the whole of the affairs of the company. A director or any other person may be appointed as manager. Hence it is to be carefully noted that the reference of the term manager is with reference to the person who has power substantially enough to manage the whole or near-whole of affairs of company, and not with reference to any person called as manager in the administration set up of the company. The manager may be paid remuneration by way of monthly payment or as percentage on net profit. The remuneration payable, in whatever manner, should not exceed the prescribed percentage (sec 387).

3. Payment of remuneration in case of loss/inadequate profits:

(*a*) Payment of remuneration to director who is neither whole time director nor managing director, is admissible by way of fixed periodical payments if the government approves it as per section 309 (4). Hence in case of loss, the question of payment of remuneration to them will have to be decided according to the terms of approval given by central government.

(*b*) Payment of remuneration to managing director/whole time director/manager is subject to ceilings calculated as a percentage on profits (overall and individual ceilings discussed above). Now what happens if the company incurs loss or earns very low profits. Can they be paid minimum remuneration in such cases? Yes, subject to ceilings specified in absolute amount in schedule XIII, part II. The schedule XIII, Part II (as amended by Ministry of Law, justice, & company affairs, department of company affairs dated 1-2-94), provides the minimum salary for managerial personnel with reference of effective capital of the company. Effective capital means total of capital, reserves, long term debts minus accumulated losses, preliminary expenses, investments made outside the business appearing in asset side. The above minimum remuneration in case of loss or inadequate profits is payable only if the remuneration is approved by remuneration committee of directors and the company has not defaulted in repayment of any of its debts (including public deposits) or debentures or interest payable thereon for a continuous period of thirty days in the preceding financial year before he date of appointment of such managerial person.

4. Remuneration in excess of ceiling:

Subject to overall ceiling (point number 1), individual ceiling (point number 2) and ceiling in case of inadequate profits, or loss (point number 3), the company can pay any amount of remuneration to its managerial personnel. The schedule XIII contains alternative scales of ceiling for managerial remuneration. A higher remuneration in accordance with alternate table is payable if the remuneration is approved by a special resolution in general meeting and Government's permission where the effective capital is in negative.

B. Computation of profit for the purpose of managerial remuneration:

The net profits for calculation of ceiling on managerial remuneration is to be ascertained according to the manner specified in section 349. Section 349 lists down expenses which must be deducted, which must not be deducted, income which must be added and which must not be added. The auditor should study the individual items in this regard. Importantly, the following income should not be taken into account:

(*a*) Profits on issue of shares or debentures (i.e. premium)

(*b*) profit on sale of forfeited shares

(*c*) profit on sale of immovable properties, undertaking etc.

Similarly the following expenses cannot be deducted viz.

(*a*) income tax

(*b*) compensation, damages or payments made voluntarily without legal liability

(*c*) losses of capital nature including loss on sale of undertaking or part thereof.

Dividend

Dividend may be defined as divisible profit distributed amongst the shareholders of a company in proportion to their shares in such a manner as is prescribed by the Memorandum of association and articles of association of the company. The word `dividend in ordinary sense means the sum paid and received or the quotient forming the share of the divisible sum payable to the recipients [Lamplough vs Kent Waterworks Proprietors (1904)].

The directors have right to recommend the rate of dividend. Its ultimate declaration, (subject to the maximum ceiling of rate recommended by directors) rests with the shareholders. That is, the shareholders need not approve the dividend recommended by the directors and declare less dividend. But they cannot declare more dividend than what has been recommended by the directors. The dividend, once declared by the shareholders in general meeting, becomes debt payable to the shareholders.

Statutory provisions regarding payment of dividend:

(1) Source from which dividend may be paid:

(*a*) Dividend may be paid out of current year profits

(*b*) Dividend may be paid out of accumulated past profits

(*c*) Dividend may be paid out of money provided by Central or State government for the payment of dividend in pursuance of guarantee given by that government

(*d*) Dividend may be paid in the form of interest out of capital in limited circumstances, as per section 208 of the Companies Act.

(2) Payment out of current profits or profits of prior years:

(*a*) Dividend may be paid out of current or past profits only if depreciation for that year or years has been fully provided. If the company has incurred losses in prior years, the loss to the extent it is due to charge of depreciation, must be set off against the profits available for dividend. Stated simply, the company charges depreciation each year in P&L account. The loss, if any, is arrived at after depreciation. The company must set off the quantum of depreciation debited in P&L account or the loss arrived at after debit of depreciation in P&L account, whichever is less.

For example to company wants to declare dividend for 1994-95

It has the following profit (losses) of prior years:"

Year	Profit (loss) before depreciation	Depreciation	Profit (loss) after depreciation
	Rs.	Rs.	Rs.
1991-92	(40,000) loss	15,000	(55,000) loss
1992-93	10,000 Profit	20,000	(10,000) loss
1993-94	40,000 profit	25,000	15,000 profit

It can declare dividend if depreciation or past losses after charge of depreciation, whichever is less, is set off. That is, it has to reduce form the profits of 1994-95 the following:

for 1990-91	Rs. 15,000
for 1991-92	Rs. 10,000
for 1993-94	Rs nil
	Rs. 25,000

If profits for 1994-95 is Rs 55,000 the company can pay dividend out of Rs. 55,000 minus Rs. 25,000 viz Rs 30,000.

The manner of providing depreciation should be in accordance with the provisions of company law. These have been discussed in chapter on Depreciation.

(*b*) Before a dividend is paid, the company must transfer such percentage of profits not exceeding 10% as is prescribed in Companies (Transfer of Profits to Reserve) Rules 1975, to reserve. The percentage of profits to be transferred to reserve is as under:

Rate of proposed dividend	Minimum Percentage of profits to be transferred to reserve
(*i*) more than 10% but not exceeding 12%	2.5% of current profit
(*ii*) more than 12.5% but not exceeding 15%	5.0%
(*iii*) more than 15% but not exceeding 20%	7.5%
(*iv*) more than 20%	10%

The company can transfer a higher percentage than 10 to the reserve if it desires. But if the company decides to declare dividend for a year, it can transfer the higher percentage to reserve only if it can ensure average rate of dividend (obtained from the past three years) could be declared for the year also.

3. Payment of Dividend out of past profits held in Reserves:

If the company cannot declare dividend out of current profits, it can as well use the accumulated profits of past years. But Companies (Declaration of Dividend out of Reserves) Rules 1975 contains certain restrictions on maximum rate of dividend that can be declared out of reserves. The rate of dividend proposed to be declared cannot exceed average rate of dividend (obtained from past five years) or 10% whichever is lower. The amount that can be withdrawn from reserves for payment of dividend should not exceed 10% of *paid up capital and free reserves*. The amount that should be left after in the reserve should be not less than 15% *of paid up share capital*.

4. Mode of payment of dividend:

Under section 205(5) the dividend may be paid in cash or by cheque or warrant and should be sent to the registered address of the shareholders entitled to dividend. In case of the share warrants, the dividend may be paid to the bearers of the warrant.

5. Time limit for payment of Dividend:

The dividend declared becomes debt against the company. If the dividend has not been claimed or paid within 30 days from the date of declaration, the amount of unpaid dividend should be transferred to a separate bank account called `Unpaid Dividend Account of ------ Company Limited/ Company Private Limited, within seven days after the expiry of 30 days. If still the payment is not made within the seven years from the date of opening of `Unpaid Dividend Account', the company must transfer the balance in the account to the Investo Education and Protection Fund. Any shareholder having claim can apply to central government. The default with regard to opening of Unpaid Dividend Account, Transfer to Investo Education and Protection Fund as aforesaid, will be treated as an offence punishable.

6. Income Tax Act provisions:

Under Income Tax Act, tax has to be deducted from payment of dividend if the amount of dividend exceeds the quantum prescribed under the law.

Dividend may be interim dividend or final dividend.

Interim Dividend

Interim dividend is a dividend which is declared between two annual general meetings. The Board has power to declare interim dividend if the articles of association permits declaration of interim dividend. The interim dividend once declared can be rescinded before payment of it as it does not become the property of the shareholders (Lagunas Nitrate Co., vs Schroeder (1901)). If interim dividend has been paid out of capital by a bonafide mistake, it can be recovered from the shareholders provided the money is retained by them (Towers vs African Tug Co. (1904)). The interim dividend may also be recovered from the shareholder if the shareholder knows that the payment is out of capital (Maxham vs Grant (1900)). If the divisible profits at the year end do not justify the payment of interim dividend during the year, the directors are liable for their negligence. The auditor should bear in mind the following while checking interim dividend:

(1) The articles of association empowers declaration of interim dividend.

(2) The board has authorised declaration of interim dividend in its meeting.

(3) Interim accounts have been prepared to ascertain the quantum of divisible profits.

(4) There are good prospects for declaration of final dividend. Declaration of interim dividend not followed by a final dividend may upset the share prices of the company.

(5) All provisions and contingencies are taken care of before determining amount of interim dividend.

(6) If there is a large amount of cash in hand, it does not mean that the company has made a large profit which justifies the payment of an interim dividend. A large cash balance in hand may be due to the following:

(*a*) Some fixed asset might have been sold for cash and that asset might not have been replaced.

(*b*) Goods might have been purchased on credit instead of cash basis as had been done in the past.

(*c*) Debentures might have been issued and the money so received might not have been utilised.

(*d*) Money might have been borrowed for some project but might not have been spent.

(*e*) No account might have been taken of the stock, debtors and creditors at the beginning and at the end of the interim period.

In fact a receipt and payment account does not take the place of Profit and Loss Account, as no account has been taken of depreciation, reserve for bad and doubtful debts, etc. It may be possible that a large cash balance in hand may go side by side with a trading loss. Similarly a small cash balance in hand may exist even though the company has made a large profit. To declare an interim dividend on the basis of cash in hand is a risky proposition as it may result in the declaration of dividend out of capital.

Cash resources must also be taken into account while deciding to declare an interim dividend. If small cash balance is left after the payment of interim dividend, working capital might be insufficient. Even if there is sufficient cash in hand and if funds are required to expand the business in future, interim dividend should not be declared.

Final Dividend:

Final dividend are recommended by directors after the compilation of annual accounts. The shareholders in annual general meeting declare the dividend. The deciding authority is with the share-holders but subject to the recommendations of the directors.

The shareholders cannot compel the directors to pay more dividend than has been recommended by the latter as was held in the case of *Bond vs. Barrow Haematile Steel Co., Ltd.* (1902) when Farwell J. said, "The court will be very relectant to compel directors to divide more than they thought proper and the courts will not compel a division of profit unto the hilt, as they regard it as perfectly proper and lawful for a company to carry forward a portion of year's profit to the credit of next year's Profit and Loss Account". *Also in Harisheshwar Idols vs. Khorooriah Zamindari Syndicate* (1944). The directors have the right to carry a part of the profit to next year and the shareholders cannot compel them to divide whole of the profit [*Burland vs. Earle (1902)*.].

In declaring final dividend there are certain factors which must be taken note of. They are (*a*) availability of divisible profits (*b*) statutory requirements (*c*) availability of liquid resources to meet the dividend obligations (*d*) the future needs of the company (*e*) the trend in rates of dividend by similar companies (*f*) stock market considerations (*g*) the dividend policy of the company and so on.

Capital profits are not available for payment of dividend unless (a) the articles of association permits it (*b*) such profits have been arrived at after revaluation of all assets and liabilities and (c) the profits are actually realised as held in Lubbock vs British Bank of South America (1892).

Final dividend once declared becomes debt against the company. Shareholders can sue for its payment (Severen and Wye Railway Co (1896) and Artisans Land Corporation (1904).Law of Limitation is applicable to it as it applies to other debts as was decided in A.Venkata Gurunatha R. Sheshayya vs The Tripurasundari Cotton Press and Re Lalitha vs Tata iron and Steel Co. Ltd. (1940).

Final dividend should be transferred to unpaid dividend account if the dividend has not been claimed or paid within 42 days of declaration of dividend. A company will not be deemed to have not paid the dividend in the following cases:

(*a*) where the dividend could not be paid because of the operation of any law;

(*b*) where the shareholder has given instructions to the company regarding the payment of dividend and those instructions cannot be complied with;

(*c*) where there is a dispute regarding the right to receive the dividend;

(*d*) where the dividend due has been adjusted by the company against any due to it from the shareholder; or

(*e*) where for any other reasonable cause, the dividend could not be paid within the aforesaid period. (Section 207, Companies Act).

In regard to the dividend payable, clause 88 of the Table A of the Companies Act runs as follows:

1. Subject to the rights of persons, if any, entitled to shares with special rights as to dividends, all dividends shall be declared and paid according to the amounts paid, but if and so long as nothing is paid according to the amounts of the shares.
2. No amount paid or credited as paid on a share in advance of calls shall be treated for the purposes of this regulation as paid on the share.
3. All dividends, shall be apportioned and paid proportionately to the amounts paid or credited as paid on the shares during any portion or portions of the period in respect of which the dividend is paid; but if any share is issued on terms providing that it shall rank for dividend as from a particular date such share shall rank for dividend accordingly.

Where the articles provide that the directors will declare a dividend "to be paid to the members in proportion to their shares" all the shares are entitled to participate equally in dividend without regard to the amount paid up on each. (Oakbank Pil Co. vs. Crum, 1883)

Dividend on Preference shares:

Holders of cumulative preference shares are entitled for arrears of dividend, if they have not been paid for any years. They can claim the arrears only if there are sufficient profits. Arrears of dividend in respect of cumulative preference shares should be indicated as a contingent liability in the balance sheet.

Unclaimed Dividends

Unclaimed or unpaid dividend within 42 days of declaration of dividend should be transferred to an account called Unpaid Dividend Account of — Co Ltd. This should be done within 7 days from the expiry of 42 days referred above. The account may be debited as and when claim is received. Any money transferred to unpaid dividend account of a company which remains unpaid or unclaimed for a period of seven years from the date of such transfer shall be transferred by the company to the "Investor Education and Protection Fund". Section 205C provides that the "Investor Education and protection Fund" shall be established by the Central Government and the amount forming part of such fund shall be utilised for promotion of investor's awareness and protection of their interests in accordance with such rules as may be prescribed.

The Duty of an Auditor in connection with the payment of Dividend

1. The auditor should examine the Memorandum and Articles of Association to ascertain the rights of different classes of shares in respect of which the dividends have been paid.
2. He should see that the profits available for dividends are really available according to Section 205 of the Companies Act and legal decisions as will be discussed in the chapter on Divisible Profits.
3. He should check the minute books of the directors and the shareholders in order to find out the rate of dividend and that the payment of dividends has been properly recommended by the directors and resolution for their payment has been passed by the shareholders.
4. Usually the total amount to be paid on account of dividends is transferred to a separate bank account called ``Dividend Account". When the shareholders present the Dividend Warrant to the bank for payment of dividend, the bank debits the ``Dividend Accounts" of the company. From the scrutiny of this account the auditor can know the amount of the unclaimed dividends. The auditor should check the Bank Pass Book of this account with the Dividend Warrants, which have been returned duly cancelled. He should also check the amount transferred from the General Bank Account to the Dividend Account.
5. He should examine the list of shareholders which has been prepared from the Register of Members. The list should show (*a*) the gross amount payable, (*b*) deduction of income tax at full rate, provided the dividend has not been declared "Free of Income tax", and (*c*) the net amount payable. The total of the net dividend payable according to this list should agree with the Dividend Account and the outstanding dividends with the balance of the "dividend Account" in the Pass Book.
6. He should check the unclaimed dividend amount from the Dividend Account Pass Book, the returned Dividend Warrants. etc.
7. He should see that the dividends are paid pro rata according to the amount paid on shares if the articles so provide.
8. He should see that tax has been duly deducted and deposited with government in respect of dividend payment in applicable cases.
9. The auditor should ensure that the quantum of divisible profit is properly ascertained. In particular, he should verify that the depreciation or past losses attributable to depreciation

has been duly set-off. He should also check that the Company Law Rules regarding transfer of profits to Reserves have been complied with. He should check that the requirements of Companies (Declaration of Dividend out of Reserves) Rules have been met in case the company utilises reserve for declaration of dividend.

Profit prior to Incorporation :

A company comes into existence only when incorporatede and, therefore, can act only then through its officers. Before the incorporation, a company cannot do any act because it has not come into being as yet.

It may so happen that the company might have entered into contract with the vendors of a business which has been purchased as from a date before the company was incorporated. The business might have made a profit since then but before the company was incorporated. Such a profit cannot be legally distributed in the form of dividends as it could not have earned anything before incorporation. Then the question is, what can be done with such profits under these circumstances? Such profits are carried to Capital Reserve and, therefore, are not distributed to the shareholders but can be utilised in the following ways:

1. In the payment of interest, if any, which was to be paid to the vendors for the purchase price. The interest is to be calculated only upto date of incorporation. the interest payable to the vendors after the date of incorporation should be debited to profit and loss account.
2. The balance, if any, may be utilised in wiping off good will, if any, which has been taken over from the vendors. Goodwill is the extra amount paid over and above the price of the net assets taken over.
3. The ramaining balance, if any, may be utilised in writing down fixed assets.
4. The balance, if any, should be carried to a capital reserve which is not available for distribution.

The difficulty arises in calculating such a profit specially when the stock of the business purchased is not taken on the date of incorporation. In such a case the profits may be apportioned between the two periods, viz., ante-incorporated and post-incorporated periods on the following basis:

(*a*) Gross profit on the basis of turn-over of the two periods;

(*b*) Direct expenses such as advertising, commission, etc., on the turn-over basis;

(*c*) Indirect expenses, e.g., salaries, rent, taxes, etc., on the basis of the time of each period.

If there is any loss prior to incoporation on such business it may be:

(*a*) debited to goodwill; or

(*b*) transferred to suspense account, which may be .... out of the capital profits later on or premium on the issue of debentures or forfeited shares account or any other capital profit.

It must be remembered that the date of division of the profit or loss should be the date of incorporation of the company and not the date entitling the company to commence business.

Duty of the Auditor in connection with Profits or Losses prior to Incorporation

He should examine the methods of apportionment and see that it is apportioned on the principles described above. He should also see that such profits are not distributed to the shareholders as they are in the nature of capital profits. This matter has been discussed in detail in the Chapter of Divisible Profits.

The audit of Private Limited Company

A private company is a company which consists of at least two members, and which by its Articles:

(*a*) limits the number of its members of fifty exclusive of its past or present employees who have been or are its members;

(*b*) prohibits any invitation to the public to subscribe for shares in, or debentures of, the company; and

(*c*) restricts the right to transfer its shares, if any.

It is in this connection the students must know that a private company ceases to be a private company and is deemed to be a public company in certain circumstances. Section 43A lists down the circumstances. They are :

(*i*) where not less than 25% of the paid up capital of private company is held by one or more body corporate.

(*ii*) where the average annual turnover of private company during the last 3 consecutive financial years exceeds or equals the turnover prescribed. (Rs 25 crore has been prescribed by the Central Government vide GSR 130(E) dated 23.2.1999).

(*iii*) where not less than 25% of paid up capital of a public company is held by the private company.

(*iv*) where a private company accepts after an invitation is made by an advertisement or renews deposits from public other than its members, directors or their relatives, with effect from 15-6-1988.

A deemed public company may retain its characteristics like ceiling on number of members, prohibitation as to invitation to subscribe for shares in or debenture of the company, and restriction on transferability of shares. But all provisions of law as are applicable to public company applies to deemed public company also.

The audit of private company is same as that of a Public Limited Company. However, the auditor must know that there are certain privileges enjoyed by a private company. These privileges may not apply to a private company if it is a subsdiary of a public limited company in most of the cases. The auditor should have an understanding of the privileges in so far as they relate financial matters. Important privileges are given hereunder :

1. The minimum number may be two instead of seven as in the case of a public (Section 12).
2. A private company limited by shares must register Articles of Association with the Memorandum of Association (Section 26)
3. A private company need not file a statement in lieu of prospectus before shares are alloted (Section 70).
4. The question of minimum subscription does not apply as the shares are not offered to the public (Section 149).
5. Restrictions as to the issue of different classes of shares, or shares with different kinds of rights in respect of dividends or voting, etc., as are applicable to public companies, do not apply to private companies.
6. Minimum number of directors must be two instead of three as in the case of public companies. Certain provisions with regard to the appointment of directors, limits of 20 companies which can be directed by a director, prohibition of loans to directors without the approval of the Government, voting by the interested directors at Board meetings,

provisions in regard to remuneration, acquiring of qualification shares by the directors, etc., which are applicable to public companies do not apply to private companies.

7. It need not hold the Statutory Meeting and submit the Statutory Report to the shareholders (Section 165).
8. It can commence business or exercise borrowing powers as soon as it is incorporated (Section 149).
9. The provisions regarding managerial remuneration (sections 198, 309, 311, 349 and 350) do not apply to private companies.

The audit of a Holding Company:

Definition

A company which

(*a*) Controls the composition of the Board of Directors of another company; or

(*b*) holds more than fifty per cent of the equity capital of another company or where the other company has equity as well as preference shares with the same voting rights, holding more than half of the total voting power;

is called a Holding company or a Parent Company. The company whose is called a Holding Company or a Parent Company. The company whose shares, etc., are so held is called a Subsidiary or an Associate Company. A company is deemed to control the composition of the Board of Directors of another company if it has the power to appoint or remove all or the majority of the directors of the other company.

It must also be remembered that a company, whose principal business is to invest funds in the purchase of the shares of other companies, is not to be considered as a Holding Company even though the purchasing company holds more than fifty per cent of the shares of another company. Such companies are called Trust Companies. Shares etc., so purchased by such companies are to be treated as fixed assets. The object of such companies is to average the profits and to divided the risk.

Similarly, a company which has lent money to another company on the security of the shares is not to be considered as a Holding Company.

The Companies Act lays down certain rules according to which a Holding Company must disclose certain particulars relating to the Subsidiary Companies in their report, Profit and Loss Account and the Balance Sheet so that the shareholders of the Holding Company may know the exact position (S. 212)

A Subsidiary Company may in its turn hold more than fifty per cent of the shares of another company or more than fifty per cent of the voting power, etc., of another company. This third company is called a Subsidiary Company of the Holding Company. Thus we see that a Subsidiary Company may be a Subsidiary Company of two or more different companies at the same time. This is why Mr. De Paula uses the word, "Children," "Grandchildren" and "Great-grandchildren." when he writes, "It will be appreciated that the holding company may have a large family including children, grandchildren and even great-grandchildren."

Balance Sheet of the holding Companies

The following documents in respect of each Subsidiary Company must be attached to the Balance Sheet of the Holding Company : —

(*a*) a copy of the latest balance sheet;

(*b*) a copy of the latest profit and loss account;

(c) a copy of the report of the Board of Directors;

(d) a copy of the report of the auditors;

(e) a statement of the Holding Company's interest, interest in the Subsidiary Company;

(f) a statement showing the changes which have occurred in respect of (i) the Subsidiary's fixed assets; (ii) its investments; (iii) the money lent by it; (iv) the money borrowed by it for any purpose other than that of meeting current liabilities since the last financial year of the Subsidiary and where it does not coincide with the financial year of the Holding Company ;

(g) a report where the Board of Directors of the Holding Company count not obtain information about Subsidiary's profit or loss (Section 212).

The balance sheet of the Holding Company must show separately secured loans and advances, unsecured loans and advances from Subsidiary Company, current liabilities due to Subsidiary Company, advances and loans to Subsidiary Company and investment in the shares and debentures of the Subsidiary Company and investment in the shares and debentures of the Subsidiary Company according to Schedule VI Part I of Companies Act given at the end of this chapter. However, the Central Government may, on the application of the Holding Company, permit it to forego provisions of Section 212 set out above.

When the financial years of the Holding Company and the Subsidiary Company do not coincide, the following information must be given respect of the Subsidiary : —

1. Where during the lapse of time (which should not exceed size months), there has been any change in the Holding Company's interest in the Subsidiary.

2. Where during the same period any material changes have occurred in respect of fixed assets, investments or loans of the Subsidiary.

The documents referred to in clauses (e), (f) and (g) above be signed by the persons who are required to sign the Balance Sheet of the Subsidiary Company.

If the Subsidiary Company has been incorporated outside India, the profit and loss account and the balance sheet of such a Subsidiary Company must be drawn up according to the Companies Act for the purpose of the above requirements.

A Holding Company may, by passing a resolution, authorise its representative to inspect the books of account kept by its Subsidiary.

The members of the Holding Company may apply to the Government to appoint a person to investigate into the affairs of the Subsidiary.

The signatories of the Balance Sheet of the Holding Company should state how the profits or losses of the Subsidiary Company have been dealt with in the Profit and loss Account of the Holding Company. If the report of the Subsidiary Company is a qualified one, the signatories must make a statement to that effect and mention the particulars thereof.

If for any reason, the Board of directors of the Holding Company is unable to obtain information on any of the matters required to be specified relating to the Subsidiary's profits or losses, a report in writing to that effect shall be attached to the balance sheet of the Holding Company, Section 212 (6).

Duties of an Auditor of a Holding Company

It may be mentioned here that the Companies Act does not specify any duty of an auditor of a Holding Company apart from the ordinary duties of an auditor except under Sections 212 and 213, regarding the preparation of the Balance Sheet but it is advisable that the auditor of such a company must pay particular attention to the following points :

1. He should pay attention to the inter-company transactions and he should verify such transactions.
2. He should examine the contracts for the purchase of the shares of the Subsidiary companies.
3. The share certificates should be examined.
4. He should see that the shares of the Subsidiary Company are held in the name of the company.
5. The Holding Company may hold shares of the Subsidiary Company in the name or names of its nominees to ensure that the number of members of the Subsidiary is not reduced, where it is a public company, below seven, and where it is a private company, below two.
6. He should vouch as usual the receipt of dividends from the Subsidiary Company.
7. In case any dividend has been declared by the Subsidiary after the preparation of the balance sheet of the Holding Company, it should not be included in that balance sheet.
8. He should also see that the profit and loss account of the Holding Company shows the dividends received from the Subsidiary and losses, if any.
9. He should see that if a consolidated Balance Sheet has been prepared, proper grouping, classification and valuation of the assets and liabilities has been done. In regard to valuation of the shares of the Subsidiary Companies they should be valued at cost price or the market price or the market price whichever is lower.
   (*a*) There will be no difficulty in the valuation of the shares of the Subsidiary Company, if they are quoted on the Stock Exchange.
   (*b*) If they are not quoted on the Stock Exchange, he should examine the Balance Sheet of the Subsidiary Company and from an idea of their value.
   (*c*) If he finds that the position of the Subsidiary Company is worse than when the shares were purchased, then such shares must be written down.
   (*d*) The auditor should examine the Articles of Association as regards the method of valuation of the shares of the Subsidiary Company.
   (*e*) If the shares of another company are held by way of permanent investment as in the case of a Trust Company, such investments are considered as fixed assets and, therefore, depreciation on such assets must be provided.
10. He should see that in the Balance Sheet of the Holding Company, the number of the shares of the Subsidiary Company is clearly mentioned.
11. The amount of indebtedness to and from the Subsidiary Companies should be stated in the Balance Sheet of the Holding Company.
12. He should see whether the Holding Company has made any provision for the losses of the Subsidiary Company; also whether the Balance Sheet of the Holding Company represents true and fair view of its state of affairs.
13. If the auditor is not satisfied on any of the above points, he must make reference to them in his report.

SCHEDULE VI
(Section 211)
PART 1
FORM OF BALANCE SHEET

The balance sheet of a company shall be in horizontal form or vertical form.

A. HORIZONTAL FORM

Balance Sheet of . . .. (Here enter the name of the company)

As at .... (Here enter the date as at which the balance sheet is made out)

Instructions in accordance with which liabilities should be made out	Figures for the previous year Rs. (*b*)	Liabilities	Figures for the current year Rs. (*b*)	Figures for the previous year Rs. (*b*)	Assets	Figures for the current year Rs. (*b*)	Instructions in accordance with which assets should be made out
*Terms of redemption or conversion (if any) of any redeemable Preference Capital to be stated, together with earliest date of redemption or conversion. †Particulars of any opinion on unissued share capital to be specified. ‡Particulars of the different classes of preference shares to be given.		Of the above shares, ... shares are allotted as fully paid up pursuant to a contract without payments being received in cash. *Of the above shares ... shares are allotted as fully paid up by way of bonus shares. *Less* : Calls unpaid: (*i*) By directors (*ii*) By others			CURRENT ASSETS, LOANS AND ADVANCES : A.Current Assets. (1) Interest accrued on Investments. ††(2) Stores and Spare Parts. (3) Loose Tools. (4) Stock-in-trade. **(5) Works in Progress.		and "Indian currency" shall have the same meaning respectively assigned to them under sub-section (1) of section 43-A of the Income Tax Act, 1961(43 of 1961), and *Explanation 2* and *Explanation 3* of the said sub-section shall, as far as may be, apply in relation to the said paragraph as they apply to the said sub-section(1). In every case where the original cost cannot be ascertained without unreasonable expense or delay, the valuation shown by the books shall be given. For the purposes of this paragraph such valuation shall be the net amount at which an asset stood in the company's

*Specify the source from which bonus shares are issued, e.g., capitalisation of profits or Reserves or from the Share Premium Account.			books at the commencement of this Act after deductions of the amounts previouslyprovided or written off for depreciation or diminution in value, and where any such asset is sold, the amount of sales proceeds shall be shown as deduction. Where sums have been written off on a reduction of capital or a revaluation of assets, every balance-sheet (after the first balance-sheet) subsequent to the reduction or revaluation shall show the reduced figures and with the date of the reduction in place of the original cost. Each balance-sheet for the first five years subsequent to the date of the reduction, shall show also the amount of reduction made. Similarly, where sums have been added by writing up the assets, every balance sheet subsequent to such writing up shall show the increased figures with the date of the increase in place of the original cost. Each balance sheet for the first five years subsequent to the date of writing up shall also show the amount of increase made. *Explanation*.- Nothing contained in the preceding two paragraphs shall apply to any adjustment made in accordance with the second paragraph. *Aggregate amount of company's quoted investments and also the market value thereof shall be shown.
†Any capital profit on reissue of forfeited shares should be transferred to Capital Rserve. Additions and deductions since last balance-sheet to be shown under each of the specified heads.	†[*Add* : Forfeited shares (amount originally paid-up)]. *RESERVES AND SURPLUS: (1) Capital Rserves. (2) Capital Redemption Reserve. (3) Share Premium Account (cc). (4) Other Reserves, specifying the nature of each reserve and the amount in respect thereof. *Less*: Debit balance in Profit and Loss Account (if any). *(h)* (5) Surplus, i.e., balance in Profit and Loss Account		

Instructions in accordance with which liabilities should be made out	Liabilities: Figures for the previous year	Liabilities	Liabilities: Figures for the current year	Assets: Figures for the previous year	Assets	Assets: Figures for the current year	Instructions in accordance with which assets should be made out
	Rs. (b)		Rs. (b)	Rs. (b)		Rs. (b)	
The word "fund" in relation to any "Reserve" should be used only where such Reserve is specifically represented by earmarked investments.		after providing for proposed allocations, viz., Dividend, Bonus or Reserves. (6) Proposed additions to Reserves. (7) Sinking Funds.			+(6) Sundry Debtors. (a) Debts outstanding for a period exceeding six months. (b) other debts. *Less*: Provision. (*7a*) Cash balance on hand. +(*7b*) Bank balances - (a) with Scheduled Banks; and (b) with others +B. Loans and Advances. (8) (a) Advances and Loans to Subsidiaries, (b) Advances and Loans to partnership firms in which the company or any of its subscribers is a partner,		Aggregate amount of company's unquoted investments shall also be shown. ††Mode of valuation ofstocks shall be stated and the amount in respect of raw material shall also be stated separately where practicable. **Mode of valuation of works in progress shall be stated. +In regard to Sundry Debtors particulars to be given separately of (a) debts considered good and in respect of which the company is fully secured, and (b) debts considered good for which the company holds no security; and (c) debts considered doubtful or bad. Debts due by directors or other officers of the company or any of them either severally or jointly with any other person or debts due by firms or private companies respectively in which any director is a partner or a director or a
*Loans from Directors, the Managing Agents, Secretaries and Treasurers, Manager should be shown separately.		SECURED LOANS: *(1) Debentures+ *(2) Loans and Advances from Banks *(3) Loans and Advances from subsidiaries. *(4) Other Loans and Ad-					

Interest accrued and due on secured loans should be included under the appropriate subheads under the head SECURED LOANS. 'The nature of the security to be specified in each case. Where loans have been guaranteed by managing agents, secretaries and treasurers, managers and or directors, a mention thereof shall also be made and also the aggregate amount of such loans under each head. ††Terms of redemption or conversion (if any) of debentures issued to be stated, together with earlier date of redemption or conversion. +Loans from directors, the managing agents, secretaries and treasurers, manager should be shown separately.	vances. UNSECURED LOANS: (1) Fixed Deposits +(2) Loans and Advances from subsidiaries. +'(3) Short Term Loans and Advances: (a) From Banks. (b) From others. +(4) Other Loans and Advances: (a) From Banks. (b) From others. CURRENT LIABILITIES AND PROVISIONS: A. Current Liabilities (1) Acceptances. (2) Sundry Creditors.	(9) Bills of Exchange. (10) Advances recoverable in cash or in kind or for value to be received, e.g., Rates, Taxes, Insurance, etc. (11) Balance with Customs, Port Trust, etc. (where payable on demand). MISCELLANEOUS EXPENDITURE (to the extent not written off or adjusted): (1) Preliminary expenses (2) Expenses including commission or brokerage or underwriting or subscription of shares or debentures. (3) Discount allowed on the issue of shares or debentures. (4) Interest paid out of capital during construction (also stating the rate of interest). (5) Development expenditure not adjusted. (6) Other items (specifying nature). †PROFIT AND LOSS ACCOUNT *Under each head, the original cost and the additions thereto	member to be separately stated. Debts due from other companies under the same management within the meaning of Sub-Section (1B) of S. 370 to be disclosed with the names of the companies. The maximum amount due by directors or other officers the company at any time during the year to be shown by way of a note. The Provision to be shown under this head should not exceed the amount of debts and any surplus of such Provisions, if already created, should be shown at every closing under "Reserves and Surplus" (in the Liabilities side) under a separate subhead "Reserve for Doubtful or Bad Debts." +In regard to bank balances, particulars to be given separately of - (a)The balances lying with the Scheduled Banks on current accounts, call accounts and deposit accounts; (b) The names of the bankers other than Scheduled banks and the balances lying with each such banker on current accounts, call accounts and deposit accounts and the maximum amount outstanding at any time during the year from each such banker; and (c) The nature of the interests, if any, of any director or his relative or the

Instructions in accordance with which liabilities should be made out	Liabilities		Assets		Instructions in accordance with which assets should be made out
	Figures for the previous year	Figures for the current year	Figures for the previous year	Figures for the current year	
	Rs. (*b*)	Rs. (*b*)	Rs. (*b*)	Rs. (*b*)	
Interest accrued and due on unsecured loans should be included under the appropriate subheads under the head "UNSECURED LOANS" Where loans have been guaranteed by managers and/or directors, a mention thereof shall also be made and also the aggregate amount of such loans under each head. See note (*d*) at foot of Form. ++The period for which the dividends are in arrear or if there is more than one class of shares, the dividends on each such class are in arrear, shall be stated.	(i) Total outstanding dues to small scale industrial undertaking(s); and (ii) Total outstanding dues of creditors other than small scale industrial undertaking(s); (3) Subsidiary Companies. (4) Advance Payments and Unexpired Discounts for the portion for which value has still to be given, e.g., in the case of the following classes of companies: Newspaper, Fire Insurance, Theatres, Clubs, Banking, Steamship Companies, etc. (5) Unclaimed Dividends. (6) Other Liabilities (if any). (7) Interest accrued but not due on		and deductions therefrom during the year, and the total depreciation written off or provided up to the end of the year to be stated. Where the original cost aforesaid and additions and deductions		Managing Agents, Secretaries and Treasurers of any associate of the latter in each of the bankers (other than the Scheduled Banks) referred to in (b) above. +The above instructions regarding "Sundry Debtors" apply to "Loans and Advances" also. +Show here the debit balance of profit and loss account carried forward after deduction of the uncommited reserves, if any.

loans.

B. Provisions

(8) Provision for Taxation.

(9) Proposed Dividends.

(10) For Contingencies.

(11) For Provident Fund Scheme.

(12) For Insurance, pension and similar staff benefit schemes.

(13) Other Provisions.

[A foot-note to the balance-sheet may be added to show separately:-

(1) Claims against the company not acknowledged as debts.

(2) Uncalled liability on shares partly paid.

+(3) Arrears of fixed cumulative dividends.

(4) Estimated amount of contracts, remaining to be executed on capital account and not provided for.

+(5) Other money for which the company is contingently liable.]

*FIXED ASSETS

Distinguishing as far as possible be-

thereto, relates to any fixed asset which has been acquired from a country outside India, and in consequence of a change in the rate of exchange at any time after the acquisition of such asset, there has been an increase or reduction in the liability of the company, as expressed in Indian currency, for making payment towards the whole or a part of the cost of the asset or for repayment of the whole or a part of moneys borrowed by the company from any person, directly or indirectly, in any foreign currency specifically for the purpose of acquiring the asset (being in either case the liability existing immediately before the date on which the change in the rate of exchange takes effect), the amount by which the liability is so increased or reduced during the year, shall be added to, or the case may be, deducted from the cost, and the amount arrived at after such addition or deduction shall be taken to be the cost of

Instructions in accordance with which liabilities should be made out	Liabilities		Assets		Instructions in accordance with which assets should be made out
	Figures for the previous year	Figures for the current year	Figures for the previous year	Figures for the current year	
	Rs. (*b*)	Rs. (*b*)	Rs. (*b*)	Rs. (*b*)	
	tween expenditure upon (a) goodwill, (b) land, (c) buildings, (d) leaseholds, (e) railway sidings, (f) plant and machinery, (g) furniture and fittings, (h) development of the property, (i) patents, trade marks and designs, (j) livestock and (k) vehicles, etc. INVESTMENTS: Showing nature of investments and				

The amount shall be stated before deduction of Income-tax except that in the case of tax-free dividends the amount shall be shown free of income-tax and the fact that it is so shown shall be stated.

+The amount of any guarantees given by the company on behalf of directors or other officers of the company shall be stated and where practicable, the

*SHARE CAPITAL

Authorised .... shares of Rs.....each

+Issued (distinguishing between the various classes of capital and stating the particulars specified below, in respect of each class)....shares of Rs....each.

++Subscribed (distinguishing between the various classes of capital and stating the particulars specified below, in respect of each class), (*c*).....shares of Rs.....each. Rs....called up.

mode of valuation, for example, cost or market value and distinguishing between:-

*(1) Investments in Government or Trust Securities.

*(2) Investments in shares, debentures or bonds (showing separately shares, fully paid-up and partly paid-up and also distinguishing the different classes of shares, and showing also in similar details investments in shares, debentures or bonds of subsidiary companies.

(3) Immovable properties.

(4) Investments in the capital of partnership firms.

the fixed asset.

Explanation I. - This paragraph shall apply in relation to all balance-sheets that may be made out as at the 6th day of June, 1966, or any date thereafter and where, at the date of the notification of the Government of India in the Ministry of Industrial Dvelopment and Company Affairs (Department of Company Law Affairs) G.S.R. No. 129, dated 3rd day of January, 1968, any balance-sheet, in relation to which this paragraph applies, has already been made out and laid before the Company in Annual General Meeting, the adjustment referref to in this paragraph may be made in the first balance-sheet made out after the issue of the said notification.

Explanation 2.- In this paragraph, unless the context otherwise requires, the expressions "rate of exchange", "foreign currency",

NOTES

General instructions for preparation of balance sheet — (*a*) The information required to be given under any of the items or sub-items in these Forms. If it cannot be conveniently included in the balance-sheet itself, shall be furnished in a separate Schedule or Schedules to be annexed to and to form part of the balance-sheet. This is recommended when items are numerous.

(*b*) Paise can also be given in addition to Rupees, if desired.

(*c*) In the case of subsidiary caompanies, etc., the number of shares held by the holding company as well as by the ultimate holding company and its subsidiaries must be separately stated.

The auditor is not required to certify the correctness of such share-holdings as certified by the management.

(c) The item "Share Premium Account" shall include full details of its utilization in the manner provided in section 78 in the year of utilization.

(*d*) Short term Loans will include those which are due for not more than one year at the date of the balance-sheet.

(*e*) Depreciation written off or provided shall be allocated under the different asset heads and deducted in arriving at the value of Fixed Assets.

(*f*) Dividends declared by subsidiary companies after the date of the balance-sheet should be included unless thay are in respect of period which closed on or before the date of the balance-sheet.

(*g*) Any reference to benefits expected from contracts to the extent not executed shall not be made in the balance-sheet but shall be made in the Board's report.

(*h*) The debit balance in the Profit and Loss Account shall be shown as a deduction from the uncommitted reserves, if any.

(*i*) As regards Loans and Advances, amountsdue by the Managing Agents or Secretaries and Treasurers, either severally or jointly with any other persons, to be separately stated; the amounts due from other companies under the same management should also be given with the names of the companies *vide* section 370; the maximum amount due from every one of these at any time during the year must be shown.

(*j*) Particulars of any redeemed debentures which the company has the power to issue should be given.

(*k*) Where any of the company's debentures are held by a nominee or a trustee for the company, the nominal amount of the debentures and the amount at which they are stated in the books of the company shall be stated.

(*l*) A statement of investments (whether shown under 'Investments' or under 'Current Assets' as stock-in-trade) separately classifying trade investments and other investments should be annexed to the balance sheet, showing the names of the bodies corporate indicating separately the names of the bodies corporate under the same management (in whose shares or debentures, investments have been made including all investments whether existing or not, made subsequent to the date as at which the previous balance-sheet was made out) and the nature and extent of the investments so made in each such body corporate; provided that in the case of an investment company, that is to say, a company whose principal business is the acquisition sufficient if the statement shows only the investments existing on the date as at which the balance-sheet has been made out. In regard to the investments in the capital of partnership firms, the names of the firms (with the names of all their partners, total capital and the shares of each partner) shall be given in the statement.

A "Trade Investment" means an investment by a company in the shares or debentures of another company, not being its subsidiary, for the purpose of promoting the trade or business of the first company.

(*m*) If, in the opinion of the Board, any of the current assets, loans and advances have not a value on realisation in the ordinary course of business at least equal to the amount at which they are stated, the fact that the Board is of that opinion shall be stated.

(*n*) Except in the case of the first balance-sheet laid before the company after the commencement of the Act, the corresponding amount for the immediately preceding financial year for all items shown in the balance-sheet shall also be giben in the balance-sheet. The requirement in this behalf shall in the case of companies preparing quarterly or half-yearly accounts etc., relate to the balance sheet for the corresponding date in the previous year.

(*o*) The amounts to be shown under Sundry Debtors shall include the amounts due in respect of goods sold or services rendered or in respect of other contractual obligations but shall not include the amounts which are in the nature of loans or advances.

(*p*) Current accounts with Directors and Managers, whether they are in credit or debit, shall be shown separately.

(*q*) A small scale industrial undertaking has the same meaning assigned to it under clause (*j*) of section 3 of the Industries (Development and Regulation) Act, 1951.

B. VERTICAL FORM Name of the company: Balance sheet at				
		Schedule No.	Current year figures (Rs)	Previous year's figures (Rs)
1	2	3	4	5

1. Sources of Funds

1. *Shareholders funds*
   (*a*) Capital
   (*b*) Reserves and surplus
2. Loan funds
   (*a*) Secured loans
   (*b*) Unsecured loan
   Total

II. Application of Funds

1. *Fixed assets*
   (*a*) Gross block
   (*b*) *Less:* Depreciation
   (*c*) Net block
   (*d*) Capital work-in-progress
2. *Investments*
3. Current assets, loans and advances
   (*a*) Inventories
   (*b*) Sundry debtors
   (*c*) Cash and bank balances
   (*d*) Other current assets
   (*e*) Loans and advances

Less : Current liabilities and provisions
   (*a*) Liabilities
   (*b*) Provisions

4. (*a*) Miscellaneous expenditure to the extent not written off or adjusted
   (*b*) Profit and loss account
   Total

Notes : 1. Details under each of the above item shall be given in separate schedules. The schedules shall incorporate all the information to be given under A. Horizontal From read with notes containing general instructions for preparation of balance sheet.

2. The schedules referred to above, accounting policies and explanatory statements that may be attached shall form part of the balance sheet.

3. The figures in the balance sheet may be rounded off to nearest' 000 or '00 as may be convenient or may be expressed in terms of decimals of thousands.

4. A footnote to the balance sheet may be attached to the above to show separately contingent liabilities.

PART II

REQUIREMENTS AS TO PROFIT AND LOSS ACCOUNT

1. The provisions of this Part shall apply to the income and expenditure account referred to in sub-section (2) of Section 210 of the Act, in the manner as they apply to a profit and loss account, but subject to the modification of reference as specified in that sub-section.

2. The profit and loss account:

(*a*) shall be so made out as clearly to disclose the result of the working of the company during the period covered by the account; and

(*b*) shall disclose every material feature; including credits or receipts and debts or expenses in respect of non-recurring transactions or transactions of an exceptional nature.

3. The profit and loss account shall set out the various items relating to the income and expenditure of the company arranged under the most convenient heads; and in particular, shall disclose the following information in respect of the period covered by the account:

(*i*) (*a*) The turnover, that is, the aggregate amount for which sales are effected by the company, giving the amount of sales in respect of each class of goods dealt with by the company, and indicating the quantities of such sales for each class separately.

(*b*) Commission paid to sole selling agents within the meaning of Section 294 of the Act.

(*c*) Commission paid to other selling agents.

(*d*) Brokerage and discount on sales, other than the usual trade discount.

(*ii*) (*a*) In the case of manufacturing companies:

(1) The value of the raw materials consumed, giving item-wise break-up and indicating the quantities thereof. In this break-up, as far as possible, all important basic raw materials shall be shown as separate items. The intermediates or components procured from other manufacturers may, if their list is too large to be included in the break-up, be grouped under suitable headings without mentioning the quantities, provided all those items which in value individually account for 10% or more of the total value of the raw material consumed shall be shown as separate and distinct items with quantities thereof in the break-up.

(2) The opening and closing stocks of goods produced, giving breakup in respect of each class of goods and indicating the quantities thereof.

(*b*) In the case of trading companies, the purchases made and the opening and closing stocks, giving break up in respect of each class of goods traded in by the company and indicating the quantities thereof.

(*c*) In the case of companies rendering or supplying services, the gross income derived from services rendered or supplied.

(*d*) In the case of a company, which falls under more than one of the categories mentioned in (*a*), (*b*) and (*c*) above, it shall be sufficient compliance with the requirements herein if the total amounts are shown in respect of the opening and closing stocks, purchases, sales and consumption of raw material with value and quantitative breakup and the gross income from services rendered is shown.

(*e*) In the case of other companies, the gross income derived under different heads.

Note 1: The quantities of raw materials, purchases, stock and the turnover, shall be expressed in quantitative denominations in which these are normally purchased or sold in the market.

Note 2: For the purpose of items (*ii*)(*a*), (*ii*)(*b*) and (*ii*)(*d*), the items for which the company is holding separate industrial licences, shall be treated as separate class of goods, but where a company has more than one industrial licence for production of the same item at different places or for expansion of the licensed capacity, the item covered by all such licences shall be treated as one class. In the case of trading companies, the imported items shall be classified in accordance with the classification adopted by the Chief Controller of Imports and Exports in granting the Import licence.

Note 3: In giving the breakup of purchases, stocks and turnover, items like spare parts and accessories, the list of which is too large to be included in the breakup, may be grouped under suitable headings without quantities, provided all these items, which in value individually account for 10% or more of the total value of the purchases, stocks, or turnover, as the case may be, are shown as separate and distinct items with quantities thereof in the break up.

(*iii*) In the case of concerns having works in progress the amounts for which such works have been completed at the commencement and the end of the accounting period.

(*iv*) The amount provided for depreciation, renewals or diminution in value of fixed assets.

If such provision is not made by means of a depreciation charge, the method adopted for making such provision.

If no provision is made for depreciation, the fact that no provision has been made shall be stated and the quantum of arrears of depreciation computed in accordance with Section 205 (2) of the Act shall be disclosed by way of a note.

(*v*) The amount of interest on the company's debentures and other fixed loans, that is, to say, loans for fixed periods stating separately the amount of interest, if any, paid or payable to the managing director, the managing agent, the secretaries and treasurers and the manager, if any

(*vi*) The amount of charge for Indian income tax and other Indian taxation on profits, including, where practicable with Indian income tax any taxation imposed elsewhere to the extent of the relief, if any, from Indian income tax and distinguishing where practicable, between income tax and other taxation.

(*vii*) The amount reserved for: (a) repayment of share capital; and (b) repayment of loans.

(*viii*) (*a*) The aggregate, if material, of any amounts set aside to reserves, but not including provisions made to meet any specific liability, contingency, or commitment known to exist at the date as at which the balance sheet is made up.

(*b*) The aggregate, if material, of any amount withdrawn from such reserves.

(*ix*) (*a*) The aggregate, if material, of the amount set aside to provisions made for meeting specific liabilities, contingencies or commitments.

(*b*) The aggregate, if material, of the amounts withdrawn from such provisions, as no longer required.

(*x*) Expenditure incurred on each of the following items separately for each item:

(*a*) Consumption of stores and spare parts.

(*b*) Power and fuel.

(*c*) Rent.

(*d*) Repairs to buildings.

(*e*) Repairs to machinery.

(*f*) (1) Salaries, wages and bonus.

(2) Contribution to provident and other funds.

(3) Workmen and staff welfare expenses to the extent not adjusted from any previous provision or reserve.

Note 1: Information in respect of this item should also be given in the balance sheet under the relevant provision or reserve account.

(*g*) Insurance.

(*h*) Rates and taxes, excluding taxes on income.

(*i*) Miscellaneous expenses:

Provided that any item under which the expenses exceed 1% of the total revenue of the company or Rs. 5,000 whichever is higher, shall be shown as a separate and distinct item against an appropriate account head in the Profit and Loss Account and shall not be combined with any other item to be shown under "Miscellaneous expenses."

(*xi*) (*a*) The amount of income from investments, distinguishing between trade investments and other investments.

(*b*) Other income by way of interest, specifying the nature of the income.

(*c*) The amount of income tax deducted if the gross income is stated under subparagraphs (*a*) and (*b*) above.

(*xii*) (*a*) Profit or losses on investments showing distinctly the extent of the profit or losses earned or incurred on account of membership of a partnership firm to the extent not adjusted from any previous provision or reserve.

Note: Information in respect of this item should also be given in the balance sheet under the relevant provision or reserve account.

(*b*) Profits or losses in respect of transactions of a kind, not usually undertaken by the company or undertaken in circumstances of an exceptional or nonrecurring nature, if material in amount.

(*c*) Miscellaneous income.

(*xiii*) (*a*) Dividends from subsidiary companies

(*b*) Provisions Gem losses of subsidiary companies

(*xiv*) The aggregate amount of the dividends paid and proposed and stating whether such amounts are subject to deduction of income tax or not

(*xv*) Amount, if material by which any items shown in the profit and loss account are affected by any change in the bash of accounting"

4. The profit and loss account shall also contain or give by way of a note detailed information, showing separately the following payments provided or made during the Financial year to the director (including managing directors), or manager, if any, by the company, the subsidiaries of the company and any other person

(*i*) managerial remuneration under Second 198 of the Art paid or payable during the financial year to the directors (including managing directors, or manager if any);

(*ii*) expenses reimbursed to the managing agent under Section 354;

(*iii*) commission or other remuneration payable separately to the managing agent or his associates under Section 356, 357 and 358;

(*iv*) commission received or received under Section 359 of the Act by the managing agent or his associate as buying or selling agent of other concerns in respect of contracts entered into by such concerns with the company;

(*v*) the money value of the contracts the sale or purchase of goods and materials or supply of services entered into by the company in the managing agent or his associate under Second 360 during the Financial year;

(*vi*) other allowances and commission including guarantee commission (details to be given);

(*vii*) any other perquisites or benefits in cash or in (stating approximate money value where practicable

(*viii*) pensions, etc.,

(*a*) pensions,

(*b*) gratuities,

(*c*) payment from the provident funds, in excess of own subscriptions and interest thereon,

(*d*) compensation for loss of office

(*e*) consideration in connection with retirement from office.

4A The profit and loss account shall contain or give by way of a note a statement showing the computation of the net profits in accordance with Section 349 of the Act with relevant details of the calculation of the commission payable by way of percentage of such profits to the directors (including managing directors), the managing agents, secretaries and treasurers or manager (if any).

4B. The profit and loss account shall further contain or give by way of a note detailed information in regard to the amounts paid to the auditor, whether as fees, expenses or otherwise for services, rendered

(*a*) as auditor;

(*b*) as advisor or in any other capacity, in respect of (*i*) taxation matter; (*ii*) company law matters;

(*iii*) management services; and c) in any other matter.

4C. In the case of manufacturing companies, the profit and loss account shall also contain, by way of a note, in respect of each class of goods manufactured, detailed qualitative information in regard to the following, namely:

(*a*) the licensed capacity (where licence is in force);

(*b*) the installed capacity; and

(*c*) the actual production .

Note 1: The licensed capacity and installed capacity of the company as on the last date of the year to which the profit and loss account relates, shall be mentioned against items (a) and (b) above respectively.

Note 2: Against item (*c*), the actual production in respect of the finished products meant for sale shall be mentioned. In cases where semiprocessed products are also sold by the company, separate details thereof shall be given.

Note 3: For the purposes of this paragraph, the items for which the company is holding separate industrial licences shall be treated as separate classes of goods but where a company has more than one industrial licence for production of the same item at different places or for expansion of the licensed capacity, the item covered by all such licences shall be treated as one class.

4D. The profit and loss account shall also contain by way of a note the following information~ namely:

(*a*) value of imports calculated on C.I.F. basis by the company during the financial year in respect of:

(*i*) raw materials;

(*ii*) components and spare parts;

(*iii*) capital goods;

(*b*) expenditure in foreign currency during the financial year on account of royalty, know how, professional consultation fees, interest, and other matters;

(*c*) value of all imported raw materials, spare parts and components consumed during the financial year and the value of all indigenous raw materials, spare parts and components similarly consumed by the percentage of each to the total consumption;

(*d*) the amount remitted during the year in foreign currencies on account of dividends, with a specific mention of the number of shares held by them on which the dividends were due and the year to which the dividends related;

(*e*) earnings in foreign exchange classified under the following heads, namely:

(i) export of goods calculated on F.O B. basis;

(ii) royalty, knowhow, professional and consultation fees;

(iii) interest and dividend;

(iv) other income, including the nature thereof.

5. The Central Government may direct that a company shall not be obliged to show the amount set aside to provisions other than those relating to depreciation, renewal or diminution in value of assets, if the Central Government is satisfied that the information should not be disclosed in the public interest and would prejudice the company, but subject to the condition that in any heading stating an amount arrived at after taking into account the amount set aside as such, the provision shall be so framed or marked as to indicate that fact.

6. (1) Except in the case of the first profit and loss account laid before the company after the commencement of the Act, the corresponding amounts for the immediately preceding financial year for all items shown in the profit and loss account shall also be given in the profit and loss account.

(2) The requirement in subclause (1) shall, in the case of companies preparing quarterly or halfyearly accounts, relate to the profit and loss account for the period which ended on the corresponding date of the previous year.

PART III
INTERPRETATION

7. (1) For the purpose of Parts I and II of this Schedule, unless the context otherwise requires

(*a*) the expression "provision" shall, subject to subclause (2) of this clause, mean any amount written off or retained by way of providing for depreciation, renewals or diminution in value of assets, or retained by way of providing for any known liability of which the amount cannot be determined with substantial accuracy;

(*b*) the expression "reserve" shall not, subject as aforesaid, any amount written off or retained by way of providing for depreciation, renewals or diminution in value of assets or retained by way of providing for any known liability;

(*c*) the expression "capital reserve" shall not include any amount regarded as free for distribution through the profit and loss account; and the expression "revenue reserve" shall mean any reserve other than a capital reserve;

and in this subclause the expression "liability" shall include all liabilities in respect of expenditure contracted for and all disputed or contingent liability.

(2) Where –

(*a*) any amount written off or retained by way of providing for depreciation, renewals or diminution in value of assets not being an amount written off in relation to fixed assets before the commencement of this Act; or

(*b*) any amount retained by way of providing for any known liability; is in excess of the amount which in the opinion of the directors is reasonably necessary for the purpose, the excess shall be treated for the purposes of this Schedule as a reserve and not as a provision.

8. For the purpose of aforesaid, the expression "quoted investment" means an investment as respects which there has been granted a quotation or permission to deal on a recognised stock exchange, and the expression "unquoted investment" shall be construed accordingly.

PART IV
BALANCE SHEET ABSTRACT AND COMPANY GENERAL BUSINESS PROFILE

I. Registration details:

Registration number ------------- State code --------- (refer code list)

Balance sheet ------------ (date) ------------(month -----------(year)

II. Capital raised during the year (amount in Rs thousands)

Public issue ------------- Right issue -------------

Bonus issue ------------- Private placement -------------

III. Position of mobilisation and deployment of funds (amount in Rs thousands)

Total liabilities ----------- Total assets -------------

Sources of funds :

Paid-up capital ------------- Reserves and surplus -------------

Secured loans ------------- Unsecured loans -------------

Application of funds :

Net fixed assets ------------- Investments -------------

Net current assets ------------- Miscellaneous expenditure -------------

Accumulated losses -------------

IV. Performance of the company (amount in Rs. thousands)

Turnover ----------- Total expenditure -------------

Profit (+) or loss (–) before tax (---) -------------

Profit (+) or loss (–) after tax (---) -------------

Earning per share in Rs. -------------

Dividend rate ------------- %

V. General names of three principal products/services of company (as per monetary terms)
Item code No. (ITC code) -------------
Product description -------------
Item code No. -------------
Product description -------------
Item code No. -------------
Product description -------------

(**Note.** For ITC code of products please refer to the publication. Indian Trade classification based on harmonised commodity description and coding system by Ministry of Commerce, Directorate of General Commercial Intelligence & statistics, Calcutta-700 001.

Annesure I

Code list — State codes

Students may refer the Companies Act, 1956 Schedule VI Part IV Annexure I for knowing the state codes for filling up the state code in relevant column of the registration details in Part IV information above. It is not reproduced here.

QUESTIONS

1. The auditor has to opine whether the company has maintained proper books of account. As such, discuss the statutory provisions that must be complied with regard to proper maintenance of books of accounts.
2. State the provisions of company law with regard to the following:
   (*a*) Form of annual financial statements
   (*b*) The period for which the P&L account should be prepared
   (*c*) The time limit with which the accounts are to be audited and presented in the annual general meeting
   (*d*) Authentication of annual financial stements
3. What are the basic audit aims in checking annual financial statements of a company?
4. List down the broad classification of liabilities and assets as per the disclosure requirements of Schedule VI to Companies Act in the Balance Sheet of a Company.
5. What are the duties of an auditor with regard to checking the issue of share capital of a company?
6. State the duties of auditor in respect of the following:
   (*a*) Shares issued at premium
   (*b*) Shares issued at discount
7. When can shares be issued for consideration other than cash? How is such an issue audited?"
8. What are the matters that are looked into when the issue of bonus shares is checked? Discuss in your answer the important SEBI guidelines.
9. Write short notes on: (*a*) forfeited shares (*b*) brokerage and underwriting commission on shares
10. Draft an audit programme for a share transfer audit
11. What are the duties of an auditor in checking the debentures?
12. Devise a suitable check list for audit of public deposits.
13. Mention the correct classification head for the following accounting balances in the company balance sheet:
    (*e.g.* public deposits - (ans) unsecured loan in liability side)
    (*a*) forfeited shares (*b*) sundry creditors (*c*) interest accrued and due on debentures (*d*) interest accrued but not due on debentures (*e*) proposed dividend (*f*) arrears of dividend on cumulative preference shares (*g*) company vans (*h*) stock of work in process (*i*) current account balances in scheduled banks (*j*) perliminary expenses amoritsed.
14. What are the special considerations to be given in checking the audit of the following in view of reporting requirements of company law: (you need not elaborate general principles of verification)

(*a*) fixed assets (*b*) investments
(*c*) stock in trade (*d*) sundry debtors

15. What are the restrictions of company law with regard to advancing loans to the directors of the company?

16. The management of ABC CO Ltd desires to revise the pay structure of its managing director. It is in this connection that you are contacted to appraise them with the ceiling if any under Companies Act with regard to quantum of remuneration to him. Draft the points for your advice.

17. Can the profits as per P&L accounts be taken for calculating ceiling on manageral remuneration? If not, mention important adjustments to be made thereto,

18. Explain the duties of a statutory auditor with regard to:
(*a*) Proposed dividend
(*b*) interim dividend declared and paid during the year
(*c*) unpaid dividend

19. A limited company having made sufficient profits to enable it to declare a dividend finds it difficult to pay it if declared, due to low cash balances. Suggest how it could be tackled.

20. A large reserve has been accumulated in a company out of profits. The directors seek your advice for distribution of part of it to the shareholders in the form of bonus issue of shares. Advise the managerment regarding the implications of such a move.

21. How will you deal with the following:
(*a*) The company has revalued its fixed assets recently. It has resulted in enormous gains. Since the gains are unrealised, the directors do not like to distribute them as dividend. Rather they resolve to issue bonus shares out of it.
(*b*) The company wants to declare dividend in its first year of operation itself. It does not have profits. It wants to make use of profits it earned prior to its incorporation.
(*c*) A company is facing severe cash crunche. Uptil least year it had been declaring dividend without break. This year too, it wants to declare dividend as profits are available. It proposes to obtain the permission of shareholders to place the amount of dividend declared with the company as a short term loan for a period of three months with interest. This would be achieved by a mere book entry once the dividend is declared.
(*d*) The directors of a company decide not to declare the dividend for the year. However certain group of shareholders, aggrieved over it, moved a resolution in the annual general meeting and got it passed by which a dividend of 6% was declared. The directors feel that it would not be binding treated in the coming year."

22. Can a company purchase its own shares ? As an auditor what special points would you like to check in case its own shares have been purchased by a company during the period covered by your audit ?

23. You are consulted to offer advice for the procedures to be followed to ensure statutory compliance in regard to the following transactions. Advise :
(*a*) A company with a paid-up capital of Rs. 20 lakhs and free reserves of Rs. 10 lakhs has advanced a loan of Rs. 15 lakhs to its subsidiary company.
(*b*) A company with a paid-up capital of Rs. 20 lakhs and free reserves of Rs. 10 lakhs and a term loan of Rs. 5 lakhs from SBI has invested 10 lakhs in shares of a company which supplies raw materials to it. The company is in arrears with regard to payment of two quarter interest to the Bank at the time of investment.
(*c*) A company has a paid-up capital of Rs. 20 lakhs and free reserves of Rs. 10 lakhs. It wants to purchase its own shares amounting in nominal value of Rs. 3 lakhs. The company wants to utilise its reserves for purchase of its own shares. It has external debt liability of Rs 14 lakhs at the time of purchase of won shares.

Chapter

24

Audit of Limited Companies — Audit Report

Lancester has defined a report as "a report is a statement of collected and considered facts, so drawn up as to give clear and concise information to persons who are not already in possession of the full facts of subject matter of the report."

Section 227 (2) of companies Act casts on company auditor the duty to make report to shareholders. It is not the duty of auditor to send the report to each and every shareholder (re, Allen Grigh & Co., (London) Ltd., (1934). The auditor should send his report addressed to shareholders to the secretary or a responsible official of the company. The auditor's report is to be read and discussed at the annual general meeting of shareholders.

Contents of Audit Report :

International Auditing Guideline 3, (IAG-3) `Basic Principles Governing an Audit' states that the auditor should review and assess the conclusions drawn from audit evidence obtained as the basis of expression of his opinion on the financial information. After review and assessment of conclusions, the auditor frames up an overall conclusion. The overall conclusion must concern matters with regard to the following:

(*a*) Whether the financial information disclosed in financial statements has been prepared using acceptable accounting policies;

(*b*) Whether the said policies are consistently applied year after year;

(*c*) Whether the financial information complies with relevant regulations and statutory requirements;

(*d*) Whether the view presented by the financial information as a whole is consistent with the auditor's knowledge of the business of the entity; and

(*e*) Whether there is adequate disclosure of all material matters relevant to the proper presentation of the financial information.

Thus, the overall conclusion of auditor concerns itself with the adherence to accounting policies, consistency in application of accounting policies, compliance to the provisions of statutes, truth and fairness of financial information and proper disclosure. The overall conclusion of the auditor in this regard, is reduced to clear written expression of opinion and expression of facts. The audit report contains these expressions.

In this connection, it is pertinent to understand the matters required to be reported by company auditor as per section 227(2) and 227(3) of the Act.

Under Section 227(3) of the Act, the audit report shall state :

(*a*) Whether the auditor has obtained all the information and explanations which to the best of his knowledge and belief were necessary for the purposes of his audit;

(*b*) Whether in his opinion, proper books of account as required by law have been kept by the company so far as appears from his examination of those books and proper returns adequate for the purposes of his audit have been received from branches not visited by him;

(*c*) Whether the report on the accounts of any branch audited by branch auditor (under section 228) has been forwarded to him and how the auditor has dealt with the same in preparing his final report.

(*d*) whether the company's balance sheet and profit and loss account dealt with by the report are in agreement with the books of account and returns.

(*e*) whether, in his opinion, the profit and loss account and the balance sheet comply with the accounting standards referred to in sub-section (3C) of Section 211.

(*f*) in thick type, or in italics, the observations or comments of the auditor which have any adverse effect on the functioning of the company.

(*g*) Whether any director is disqualified from being appointed as director under clause (g) of sub-section (1) of section 274.

(*h*) Whether the cess payable under section 441 A has been paid and if not, the details of the amount of cess no paid.

Where any of the matters referred to above (items a, b, c, d, e) is answered in negative, or with a qualification, the audit report shall state the reason for the answer.

Under section 227 (3) the auditor is given a responsibility to disclose whether any director is disqualified as per section 274 (1) (g). Section 274 (1) (g) provides that a person who is already a director of a public company, which

(*a*) has not filed the annual accounts and annual return for any continuous three financial years or

(*b*) has failed to repay its deposit or interest thereon due date or redeem its debentures on due date or pay dividend and such failure continues for one year or more.

shall not be eligible to be appointed as director of any other public company for a period of 5 years from the due date of filing return or due date for paying deposits etc., as the case may be.

To ensure that a director is not so disqualified the auditor should insist the company to take certificate from the directors that they are not so disqualified and the certification should be taken on record by the Board.

Under section 227(2) of the Act, the auditor has to state whether, in his opinion, and to the best of information and according to explanations given to him, the accounts give the information required by the Act in the manner so required and give a true and fair view - (i) in the case of balance sheet, of the state of affairs as at the end of company's financial year and (ii) in the case of profit and loss account, the profit or loss for its financial year.

On a reading of section 227(2) and section 227(3), it may be understood that the section 227 (2) contains opinion of the auditor (expression of overall conclusion) as to adequacy of disclosure of information required to be disclosed as per the Act and secondly as to the truth and fairness of assertions contained in balance sheet and profit and loss account. On the other hand, section 227(3) contains auditor's expression of opinion as well as expression of facts, concerning matters essential for his giving opinion under section 227(2). In a broad way, section 227(3) requires auditor's opinion as to maintenance of proper books of accounts and submission of proper returns by branches and auditor's expression of facts as to obtaining of sufficient information and explanation for audit, the manner of dealing with branch audit reports and the true and correct compilation of final accounts from books of accounts. Thus it is to be appreciated that the auditor's report under section 227 must include `fact' content and `opinion' content specified.

Opinion as to true and fair view:

Under section 227(2) the auditor gives opinion as to true and fair view of state of affairs of balance sheet as on the last date of financial year and true and fair view of profit or loss of the company for the financial year. The section 211 dealing with annual accounts of the company also makes mention of the word 'true and fair view'. It requires that the annual accounts are to be prepared in a manner to give true and fair view of the financial information. Prior to the enactment of companies Act 1956, the words 'true and correct' were used in section 145 of the companies Act 1913. The words 'true and fair view' were considered to be fair usage in the place of `true and correct view'. The expression 'true and correct' indicated exactitude or precision. Emphasising on accuracy (i.e. 'correctness'), these words did not throw required light on subjective assessment of financial information presented in annual accounts. On the other hand, subjective assessment of auditor (namely opinion of expert) is to be found in the report if the financial statements have to serve the purpose. It is for this reason, the words `true and correct view' had been substituted by the words `true and fair view'. An interesting comment was made by W.G. Campbell about the true and fair view under English companies Act 1948. "The question is sometimes raised to whom the presentation is to be fair, and the answer seems implicit in the Act, that the scale ought to be fairly held between the interests of the companies as a whole and the interests of those who are concerned with the accounts-the shareholders and creditors at the date of accounts."

Annual accounts may be said to be `true and correct' if they agree with the books of account. For example, if the assets were undervalued by passing the entries in the books of account, strictly speaking, the balance sheet was correct according to the books of the company and therefore the auditors could not be hauled up for a wrong statement even though the balance sheet did not give 'fair' picture of the state of affairs of the company. The purpose of audit would be served only if the report contains auditor's opinion as to fairness of the financial information disclosed in annual accounts. Again, it is impossible to include 'correct' amounts in respect of provisions. By definition itself, provisions are amount set apart to meet certain liabilities, the quantum of which cannot be ascertained with certainty. They are estimates only, e.g. depreciation provision. In such of those circumstances, the auditor can give opinion only on true and `fair' view of the financial data and not on true and `correct' view of them. All these points succinctly get reflected in the judgement of Deputy Secretary, Ministry of Finance vs S.N. Dasgupta by P. Chakravarthy, C.J., as follows. "It is the duty of the auditor to verify not merely the arithmetical accuracy of the balance sheet, but it is substantially accurate and to see that it includes the particulars required by the articles and the statute and contains the correct representations of the state of company's affairs". *Therefore, it can be summarised that the accounts give true and fair view of affairs of the company.*

(*a*) if the accounts are correct—i.e. in agreement with books of accounts,

(*b*) if they comply with accepted accounting policies and in a consistent manner

(*c*) if they give information in the manner required by statute and

(*d*) the transactions do not violate the provisions of statute, memorandum, articles of association.

Requirements of Section 211 as regards true and fair view of financial statements :

(1) Balance Sheet to be true and fair — Section 211(1) :

Sub-section (1) of Section 211 requires that every balance sheet of a company shall give a true and fair view of the state of affairs to the company as at the end of the financial year and shall be in the form set out in Part I of Schedule VI. Where Central Government permits the accounts to be prepared in any other form other than the form referred to above either generally or in any particular case, the balance sheet may, in such a case, be in such form as is approved by the Central Government. The Sub-section not only requires the balance sheet to be in Part I of the Schedule VI but also requires that while drawing the balance sheet notes to that Part contained therein must be given due regard to. This would mean that the Part I of the Schedule must be read in the light of the explanations and conditions contained in Notes coming down that Part.

Permission for drawing the balance sheet in any form other than one set out in Part I of the Schedule VI is contained in the sub-section if the Government approval is accorded for such form. But the requirement as to drawing of balance sheet in the format set out in Part I of the Schedule VI is excluded for four classes of companies. They are — (*a*) insurance companies (*b*) banking companies (*c*) companies engaged in the generation or supply of electricity and (*d*) any class of companies for which a form a balance sheet has been specified in or under the Act governing such class of company.

(2) Profit and Loss Account to be true and fair — Section 211(2) :

Sub-section (2) requires that every profit and loss of a company shall give a true and fair view of the profit or loss of the company for the financial year and shall comply with the requirements of Part II of the Schedule VI.

However, the Profit and Loss Account of an insurance company or a banking company or a company engaged in generation or distribution of electricity or a class of company for which a form of profit and loss account has been specified in or under the Act governing such class of company, is expected form the requirements of sub-section (2) of this section.

(3) Exemption in adhering to formats in the public interest — Section 211 (3) :

Sub-section (3) has delegated a blanket power for the Central Government to exempt any class of company from the compliance with any of the requirements in Schedule VI, if in its opinion, it is necessary to grant the exemption in the public interest. The Central Government may exercise its power by issuing notification to this effect. Any such exemption may be granted either unconditionally or subject to such conditions as may be specified in the notification.

(4) Profit and Loss Account and Balance Sheet to comply with the Accounting Standards — Section 211 (3A) and 3(B) :

Sub-section (3A) requires every profit and loss account and balance sheet of the company to comply with the accounting standard. Sub-section (3B) further provides that where the profit and loss account and the balance sheet do not comply with the accounting standards, such companies shall disclose in the profit and loss account and balance sheet, the following namely.

(*a*) the derivation from the accounting standards;

(*b*) the reasons for such deviation; and

(*c*) the financial effect, if any, arising due to such deviation.

Sub-section (3C) assigns meaning for the term accounting standard as used in sub-section (3A) and (3B). According to it, accounting standard means the standards of accounting recommended by the Institute of Chartered Accountants of the India constituted under the Chartered Accounts of India Act, 1949 (38 of 1949) as may be prescribed by the Central Government in consultation with the National Advisory Committee on Accounting Standards established under sub-section (1) of Section 210 A.

The provisions clause to Section 211 (3C) provides that the standards of accounting specified by the Institute of Chartered Accountants of India shall be deemed to be the Accounting Standards until the Accounting Standards are prescribed by the Central Government under this sub-section.

(5) Power of Central Government to modify any of the requirements of disclosure in annual accounts — Section 211(4) :

The Central Government may, on the application or with the consent of the Board of directors of the company, by order, modify in relation to that company any of the requirements of this Act as to matters to be stated in the Company's balance sheet or profit and loss account for the purpose of adapting them to the circumstances of the company.

(6) Certain matters need not be disclosed even if they are otherwise required for the purpose of true and fair disclosure — Section 211(5) :

The balance sheet and profit and loss account of a company shall not be treated as not disclosing a true and fair view of the state of affiars of the company merely by reason of the fact that they do not disclose:

(*a*) in the case of an insurance company, any matters which are not required to be disclosed by the Insurance Act, 1938;

(*b*) in the case of a banking company, any matters which are not required to be disclosed by the Banking Companies Act, 1949;

(*c*) in case of a company engaged in the generation or supply of electricity, any matters which are not required to be disclosed by both the Indian Electricity Act, 1910 and the Electricity Act, 1948.

Report *vs* Certificate :

At this stage, the difference between a report and certificate should be clearly understood. The report means simply an expression of opinion while a certificate means that the person issuing or signing it vouchsafes the truth of the statement he makes, i.e., what he states is cent per cent true and correct. If it is found later on that the certificate was wrong, he will be held responsible but in the case of a report, it is merely an opinion of the writer, and it is possible that he may be wrong in holding such an opinion. In such a case, he cannot be held responsible in such circumstances for the report which he has made. It may, however, be remembered that an auditor is not required to '*certify*' the accounts but is required to '*report*' that the balance sheet and profit and loss account are properly drawn up in accordance with the Companies Act so as to give a '*true and fair view*' of the state of the company's affairs and that the accounting and other records are properly maintained. He never certifies that the accounts depict a true and fair view. He reports that, *in his opinion*, the accounts represent a true and fair view of a company's affairs.Thus audit is *only a test* and not a *guarantee*. One cannot expect an auditor to examine each especially in case of a business where the number of transactions run into millions. Even if we presume that he checks each transaction, it would be difficult for him to detect an ingenious fraud committed by an employee, e.g., when a document is concealed from him. The auditor is not expected to guarantee the accuracy of the company's books. He is not to assume that frauds and errors have been committed in the books of account. As has been said: `he is a watch dog and not a blood hound'. His duty is to see that the financial position of the company is truly exhibited to the shareholders. In order to avoid unnecessary criticism against him, he should thoroughly check the internal check system in operation and apply test checks. He can be responsible only if it can be proved that he could have discovered the fraud or error had he been reasonably careful.

Basic Elements of Auditor's Report

The auditor's report should incorporate the following elements in it:

(*a*) title
(*b*) addressee
(*c*) identification of the financial statements audited
(*d*) a reference to the auditing standards, practices followed
(*e*) expression or disclaimer of opinion on the financial statement
(*f*) signature
(*g*) auditor's address
(*h*) the date of the report

The specific contents of the report will be according to the requirements of the Act if the report is mandatory in the Act. In companies Act, section 227 casts the duty on auditor to make report to shareholders. In addition to this report, the auditor makes out a long form audit report to the management. It contains detailed observation of auditors on various matters connected with financial areas of the company. It points out weaknesses, lapses and errors/frauds observed in the system. It suggests corrective measures. A good report must alteast meet the following qualifications:

(*a*) it should be based on factual information

(*b*) it should be convincing

(*c*) it should be forceful

(*d*) it should be unbiased

(*e*) it should point out mistakes

(*f*) it should be a constructive criticism and not be in reprimanding tone

(*g*) it should offer constructive and timely suggestions to the management

(*h*) it should be brief. If it is lengthy, the object of the report is defeated even if it is well written.

Singing of Auditor's Report:

Only the person appointed as the auditor of the company, or a partner in the firm of auditors (if all the partners of the firm are entitled to practise in India) may sign the auditor's report, or may sign or authenticate any other document of the company required to be signed or authenticated by the auditor (Section 229). In case it has been signed by a partner of the firm of auditors, he should inform the Registrar within a reasonable time that he has signed the report. This intimation should be sent preferably within seven days after the date on which the audit report was signed. If any auditor's report is made, or any document of the company is signed or authenticated, otherwise than in conformity with the requirements of Section 227 and 229, the auditor concerned and the person, if any, other than the auditor who signs the report or signs or authenticates the document, shall , if the default is wilful, be punishable with fine which may extend to not thousand rupees (Section 233).

Report of the auditor (including the auditor's separate, special or supplementary report, if any) shall be attached to every balance sheet placed before every annual general meeting (Section 216), while the report is to be annexed to every annual returns.

Types of Opinion

The auditor expresses his opinion about the financial information reported in annual statements of accounts. His opinion may be

(*a*) Unqualified or clean (*b*) Qualified (*c*) Adverse or (*d*) Disclaimer.

Unqualified opinion.

The auditor issues an unqualified opinion if he is satisfied in all material respects with the matters he reports to shareholders. Specifically, if he is satisfied in all material respect with regard to (*a*) preparation of accounts adhering to accepted accounting policies and application of accounting policies in a consistent manner; (*b*) the final accounts being in agreement with the books of account; (*c*) the final accounts being true and fair summary of the financial transactions of the company; (*d*) the disclosure of information in final accounts as per the requirements contained in the Act and; (*e*) the transactions of the company, in so far they get reflected in financial statements being not violative of the provisions of the companies Act, memorandum of association or articles of association. An unqualified opinion is also called clean or positive opinion.

Other than unqualified opinion :

On the other hand, when the auditor is not satisfied in material respects with matters concerning proper and consistent application of accounting policies, conventions, adherence to disclosure-requirement specified in the Act, truth and fairness of financial information reported in the statements, or compliance to the provisions of statute memorandum of association or articles of association, he may give 'other than unqualified opinion, Circumstances that, give rise to `other than an unqualified opinion' are categorised into (*a*) limitations on scope of audit (*b*) disagreement with management (*c*) uncertainty affecting financial statements (IAG13). For example, the accounting system or records may not be adequate for the auditor to conduct the audit in a manner which he feels necessary and thereby his scope of work may have to be curtailed. Or the auditor cannot agree with the management in certain respects concerning financial information. The selection of particular accounting policy or estimate made for provisions, or the manner of disclosing information in financial statements by the management - in such of those matters, for instance, the auditor may have valid grounds to disagree with the veiw points of management. similarly the financial information disclosed in statements may be subject to serious uncertainty which will be cleared in future only. Therefore, when the auditor is not satisfied with the financial statements in respect of matters of reporting in material respects due to limitation of scope of audit work, disagreement with management or uncertainty, he gives 'other than an unqualified opinion'. Depending on the nature of circumstances forcing forming up of an other than unqualified opinion, the opinion may be "qualified" or "disclaimer".

Qualified Opinion :

The auditor issues qualified opinion when

(*a*) He is not satisfied in material respects with matters concerning the areas of his report. (i.e. truth and fairness of financial information, proper disclosure of information, compliance to provisions of statute etc.).

(*b*) His non-satisfaction is due to circumstances such as limitations imposed on his scope of audit work, disagreement with management or uncertainty over financial information.

(*c*) The effect of his disagreement, uncertainty or limitation is not so material as to compel the auditor to give an adverse opinion or to state a disclaimer.

The auditor must be very clear as to when he should qualify his report and how he should qualify the report The directors sometimes, try to persuade the auditor to desist from giving qualified report as it is a slur on the work of the directors for the year under review. Moreover, a qualified report leads to bad consequences e.g., fall in value of shares in the market, non-renewal of appointment of directors, appointment of investigation etc. Unconcerned to these, the auditor must set out his qualifications to the report if it is necessary according to his professional judgement of circumstances.

When to Qualify :

The auditor should not use the weapon of qualifying his report on petty grounds. He must qualify the report only if his non-satisfaction in respect of matters vital for his reporting is very much great and the effect of circumstances (forcing him to qualify the report) on profit or loss or financial affairs of the company is material. For example, the following matters are examples requiring qualification in audit report:

(*a*) non-provision/inadequate provision for depreciation

(*b*) inadequate provision made for bad and doubtful debts

(*c*) valuation of investment at cost price when the market price is far below it.

(*d*) contingent liability not disclosed

(*e*) violation of provisions of company law-payment of remuneration to managerial personnel in excess of limits without approval.

In respect of the above examples, the auditor has justifiable grounds to disagree with what management has done. Certainly he must qualify the report as his disagreement has material effect on profit/loss reported or assets/liabilities shown in financial statements. Equally, the auditor must desist from using qualified opinion when the effect of his disagreement, uncertainty or limitation on his scope of work is so material as to render the whole of financial reporting to a naught. In such a circumstance, he must give an adverse opinion or a disclaimer.

How to Qualify :

In qualifying the report, the auditor proceeds to draft his report as though the report is an unqualified one (*i.e.* the statements 'give true and fair view), but suffixing the expression of clean opinion with such phrases as 'subject to" or "except that" and in continuation of such phrases, deftly mentioning the matters of his disagreement, uncertainty or limitation on the scope of work. While drafting a qualified report, the auditor should bear in mind the following points:

1. It should be clear and unambiguous so that the readers understand what the auditor wants them to know and they are left in no doubt as to the implications of the report.

Sometimes, the directors persuade the auditor to use such words and phrases as to soften the tone of the report. In the case of London and General Bank, the bank had advanced loans on insufficient securities. The auditor knew of the inadequacy of the security and qualified his report in these words. "The value of assets as shown on the balance sheet is dependent upon realisation". The auditor was held liable to pay damages as the phrase with regard to securities did not convey the true meaning. Part of the judgement reads as follows:

"It is a mere truism to say that the value of loans and securities depends upon their realisation. We are told that a statement to that effect is so unusual that the mere presence of so many words is enough to excite suspicion. But as already stated, the duty of an auditor is to convey information, not to arouse enquiry, and although an auditor might infer from an unusual statement that something was seriously wrong, it by no means follows that ordinary people would have their suspicion aroused by the similar statement if, as in this case, its language expresses no more than any ordinary person would infer without it."

The words or phrases used should convey a clear meaning which may be understood even by a layman or a casual reader. If this is not done, the auditor will be running a great risk. The auditor should make the report very clear and no ambiguous words should be used. We give another extract from the judgement in *London & General* Bank case:

"A person whose duty is to convey information to others, does not discharge that duty by simply giving them so much information as is calculated to induce them, or some of them to ask for more. Information and means of information are by no means equivalent terms .... an auditor who gives shareholders means of information instead of information in respect of a company's financial position, does so at his peril and runs the very serious risk of being held judicially, to have failed to discharge his duty."

2. It should be concise, but conciseness should not sacrifice clarity

3. It should be specific and to the point. The amount involved if any, should be clearly stated.

4. It should state the effect of matter under report on the accounts.

5. The opinion of the auditor expressed in the report should not be capable of misinterpretation.

Adverse Opinion:

The auditor issues an adverse opinion when

(*a*) He is not satisfied in material respects with matters concerning the areas of his report (e.g., truth and fairness of financial information, proper disclosure of financial information, compliance to provisions of stature etc., etc)

(*b*) His dissatisfaction is due to disagreement with management, in what they have done (both omission and commission) respecting preparation and presentation of financial information.

(*c*) His dissatisfaction is of such a magnitude as to force the auditor to frame up a negative opinion that the financial statements, taken as a whole, don't give true and fair view of the results of operations of the company or financial position of the company.

It has been said that the auditor should desist from issuing qualified opinion when he must issue adverse opinion. It, then. equally implies, that the auditor should desist from resorting to issue of adverse opinion when qualified opinion is sufficient. For example, when the matters over which the auditor is not satisfied are material in themselves, but not so serious as to make the whole of financial statements as untrue or unfair, the auditor should not give out adverse opinion, but give only qualified opinion.

Disclaimer :

The auditor issues an opinion of disclaimer when

(*a*) he is unable to express his opinion in respect of matters concerning areas of his report

(*b*) the inability to express opinion is due to limitations placed on the scope of his audit work or uncertainty affecting financial statements the resolution of which is dependent on future events.

For example, the whole set of company's books of accounts, might have been seized by income tax authorities and might not have been produced for his checking. In such circumstances, the auditor must not issue a qualified opinion or an adverse opinion. He must clearly state his inability through appropriately worded opinion of disclaimer. Think how ridiculous it would be if the auditor issues a qualified opinion in such a circumstance as "The financial statements give true and fair view of affairs of the company subject to our inability to check them".

Reporting Requirement Under Section 227 (1A) :

There is no mandatory reporting requirement under section 227 (1A) Under section 227 (1A), the auditor is specifically required to inquire in respect of six matters specified. He can report if results of inquiry so warrant. The matters to be inquired are:

(1) whether loans and advances made by the company on the basis of security have been properly secured and whether the terms on which they have been made are not prejudicial to the interests of the company or its members

(2) whether the transactions of the company which are represented merely by book entries are not prejudicial to the interests of the company

(3) in case of companies other than investment companies or banking companies, whether the shares, debentures, or other securities have been sold at prices less than the purchase prices.

(4) whether the loans and advances made by the company have been shown as deposits

(5) whether personal expenses have been charged to revenue account

(6) if shares have been allotted for cash, whether the cash has been actually received, if not whether the position is correctly stated in the balance sheet in a manner that is correct and not misleading.

Reporting Requirement Under Section 227 (4A) :

The main provisions of reporting requirements are contained in section 227 (2) and "227 (3). Section 227 (1A) requires auditor to make enquiry in respect of matters specified. On the other hand section 227 (4A) requires supplemental reporting by auditor in respect of matters specified for the class of companies covered under notification. The section gives only power to central government to issue order requiring auditor to include certain matters in the audit report of classes of companies notified.

In exercise of the powers contained in section 227 (4A) the Central Government has issued Companies (Auditor's Report) Order 2003. This order supersedes the earlier order viz., Manufacturing and Other Companies (Auditor's Report) Order 1988.

Applicability of the Order

The order apples to all companies except certain categories of the companies specifically exempted in this regard. The order also applies to foreign companies as defined in section 591 of the Companies Act, 1956. The Order applies to the branch audit report also.

Exemption from the Order

The order is not applicable to–

1. a banking company as defined clause (*c*) section 5 of Banking Companies Regulation Act, 1949
2. an insurance company as defined in clause (21) of section (2) of the Companies Act, 1956
3. a company licensed to operate under section 26 of the Companies Act, 1956
4. a private company with a paid up capital and reserves not more than Rs. 50 lakhs and has does not have outstanding loan exceeding Rs. 10 lakhs or more from any bank or financial institution and does not have turnover exceeding rupees five crores.

It is to be noted that this order applies to private company which does not fulfill all the three conditions specified above. If a private company satisfies any one or more but not all, then it would attract the applicability of this Order. If at any time during the year, the private company satisfies any of these three conditions, the Order would apply.

Matters to be included in the Order

The Auditor's Report shall include a statement of the auditor in respect of the following matters-

1. Fixed assets

(*a*) Whether the company is maintaining proper records showing full particulars including quantitative details and situation of fixed assets.

(*b*) Whether these fixed assets have been physically verified by the management at reasonable intervals. Whether any material discrepancies were noticed on such verification and if so whether the same have been properly dealt with in the books of account.

(*c*) If a substantial part of fixed assets have been disposed off during the year, whether it has affected the going concern;

2. Inventory

(*a*) Whether physical verification of inventory has been conducted at reasonable intervals by the management.

(*b*) Are the procedure of physical verification of inventory followed by the management reasonable and adequate in relation to the size of the company and the nature of its business. If not, the inadequacies in such procedures should be reported.

(*c*) Whether the company is maintaining proper records of inventory and whether any material discrepancies were noticed on physical verification and if so, whether the same have been properly dealt with in books of account.

3. Loans given and taken from interested parties.

(*a*) Has the company granted any loan secured or unsecured from companies, firms or other parties covered in the register maintained under section 301 of the Act. If so, number of parties and amount involved in the transactions.

(*b*) Whether the rate of interest and other terms and conditions of loans given by the company, secured or unsecured, are prima facie prejudicial to the interest of the company

(*c*) Whether the receipt of the principal amount and interest are also regular

(*d*) If overdue amount is more than one lakh rupees, whether reasonable steps have been taken by the company for recovery of the principal and interest

(*e*) Has the company taken any loan secured or unsecured from companies, firms or other parties covered in the register maintained under section 301 of the Act. If so, number of parties and amount involved in the transactions.

(*f*) Whether the rate of interest and other terms and conditions of loans taken by the company, secured or unsecured are prima facie prejudicial to the interest of the company.

(*g*) Whether the payment of principal amount and interest are also regular.

4. Review of internal control system

(*a*) Is there an adequate internal control procedure commensurate with the size of the company and the nature of its business, for the purchase of inventory and fixed assets and sale of goods and services. Whether there is a continuing failure to correct major weakness in internal control.

5. Related party transactions

(*a*) Whether the particulars of contracts or arrangements referred to in section 301, have been entered in the register in pursuance of the section.

(*b*) Whether each of these transactions have been made at prices which are reasonable having regard to the prevailing market prices at the relevant time. (this information is relevant for the transactions exceeding the value of Rs. 5 lakhs in respect of any party in any one financial year)

6. Contravention of rules regarding acceptance, payment etc., of public deposits

In case the company has accepted deposits from the public, whether the directives issued by Reserve Bank of India and the provisions of sections 58A and 58AA and other relevant rules framed thereunder, where applicable, have been complied with. If not, the nature of contravention should be stated. If an order has been passed by company Law Board, National Company Law Tribunal, or RBI, or any Court or other Tribunal, whether the same has been complied with or not.

7. Internal audit system

In case of listed companies and/or other companies having a paid up capital and reserves exceeding Rs. 50 lakhs, as at the commencement of the financial year concerned, or having an average annual turnover exceeding five crore rupees for a period of three consecutive financial years immediately preceding the financial year concerned, whether the company has an internal audit system commensurate with the size of the company and nature of its business.

8. Maintenance of cost records

Where maintenance of cost records has been prescribed by the Central Government under clause (*d*) of sub-section (1) of section 209 of the Act, whether such accounts and records have been made and maintained.

9. Payment of statutory levy

(*a*) Is the company regular in depositing undisputed statutory dues including provident fund, investor education and protection fund, employees' state insurance, income tax, sales tax, wealth tax, service tax, customs duty, excise duty, cess and any other statutory dues with the appropriate authorities and if not, the extent of arrears of outstanding statutory dues as at the last date of the financial year concerned for a period of more than six months from the date they became payable, shall be indicated by the auditor.

(*b*) In case dues of sales tax/ income tax/ custom/ wealth tax/ service tax/ excise duty/ cess have not been deposited on account of any dispute, then the amounts involved and the forum where dispute is pending. (a mere representation) to the department shall not be construed as a dispute)

10. Sick company

Whether in case of a company which has been registered for a period not less than five years, its accumulated losses at the end of the financial year are not less than fifty percent of its net worth and whether it has incurred cash losses in such financial year and in the immediately preceding financial year also.

11. Default in payment of loans to financial institutions

Whether the company has defaulted in repayment of dues to a financial institution or bank or debenture holders ? If yes, the period and amount of default to be reported.

12. Documentation for secured loans granted

Whether adequate documents and records are maintained in cases where the company has granted loans and advances on the basis of security by way of pledge of shares, debentures and other securities; if not the deficiencies should be pointed out.

13. Chit and Nidhi accounts

Whether the provisions of any special statute applicable to chit fund have been duly complied with ? In respect of nidhi/ mutual benefit fund/ societies

(*a*) Whether the net owned funds to deposit liability ratio is more than 1:20 as on the date of balance sheet,

(*b*) Whether the company has complied with the prudential norms on income recognition and provisioning against sub-standard/ doubtful and loss assets.

(*c*) Whether the company has adequate procedures for appraisal of credit proposals/ requests, assessment of credit need and repayment capacity of the borrowers.

(*d*) Whether the repayment schedule of various loans granted by the nidhi is based on the repayment capacity of the borrower.

14. Investment companies

If the company is dealing or trading in shares, securities, debentures or other investments, whether proper records have been maintained of the transactions and contracts and whether timely entries have been made therein; also whether the shares, securities, debentures and other investment have been held by the company in its own name except to the extent of the exemption, if any, granted under section 49 of the Act.

15. Guarantee given

Whether the company has given any guarantee for loans taken by others from bank or financial institutions, the terms and conditions whereof are prejudicial to the interests of the company.

16. End use of terms loans

Whether the term loans were applied for the purposes for which the loans were obtained.

17. Use of short term funds for long term investment

Whether the funds raised on short term basis have been used for long term investment. If yes, the nature and amount is to be indicated.

18. Share allotment to related parties

Whether the company has made any preferential allotment of shares to parties and companies covered in the Register maintained under section 301 of the Act and f so whether the price at which shares have been issued is prejudicial to the interest of the company.

19. Charge for issue of debenture

Whether security or charge has been created in respect of debenture issued.

20. End use of public issues

Whether the management has disclosed on the end use of money raised by public issues and the same has been verified.

21. Fraud on or by the company

Whether any fraud on or by the company has been noticed or reported during the year. If yes, the nature and amount involved is to be indicated.

Reasons to be stated for unfavourable or qualified opinion

Where in the auditor's report, the answer to any of the questions referred to is unfavourable or qualified, the auditor's report shall also state he reasons for such unfavourable or qualified answer, as the case may be. Where the auditor is unable to express any opinion in answer to a particular question, his report shall indicate such fact together with the reasons why it is not possible for him to give an answer to such question.

Events occuring after Balance Sheet date :

An auditor audits the accounts of a concern sometimes after the last date of the financial year on which date the balance sheet and the profit and loss account have been prepared by the client. A question which confronts an auditor is whether he should take note of those events which may have a material effect on the final accounts but which events took place after the preparation of the balance sheet and profit and loss account but before the actual audit. Distinction should clearly be understood between (*a*) events occurring after the balance sheet date which have no direct bearing on the accounts but are nevertheless important from the point of view of the true position, and (*b*) events occurring after the balance sheet date which have a direct bearing upon the items appearing in the balance sheet, e.g., the decision of the directors regarding the proposed dividend and the appropriation of the profits to be shown in the accounts. Such events have to be taken into accounts as required by Schedule VI of the Companies Act. As regards liabilities, provision for liabilities of contingent liabilities existing on the date of the balance sheet, information of the events occurring after the balance sheet date may be taken into account in order to provide a guide. Although the balance sheet is prepared on a particular date, any event occurring after such a date should be shown by way of a foot note or by the directors in their report to the shareholders. Liabilities are frequently estimated and for this purpose guidance may be obtained from the developments which have taken place since the balance sheet.

The Institute of Chartered Accountants of India has issued Accounting standard number 4 dealing with events occurring after the date of balance sheet but before the date of approval of accounts by board of directors. According to the standard, the events occurring after balance sheet date are to be categorised into two viz., events relating to the conditions existing on balance sheet date and events not relating to conditions existing on balance sheet date. In respect of events relating to conditions existing on balance sheet date, the additional information provided by them can be taken note of, and values of assets or liabilities can be adjusted accordingly. For example, the subsequent insolvency of a debtor after balance sheet date is an event related to the condition of collectibility of doubtful debt existing on balance sheet date. Hence the amount of debtor may be fully provided by taking note of this event. On the other hand, the ordinary fluctuation in market prices of investment after balance sheet date does not relate to condition of investment on balance sheet date. The fluctuation only reflects circumstances occurred subsequent to balance sheet date. Hence no adjustment has to be made of values of investment at balance sheet date. But, there are certain special events which, though occur after balance sheet date, get reflected in financial statements. Example is dividend proposed after balance sheet date which are provided in accounts Barring this, events which do not relate to condition existing on balance sheet date are not taken in to account for adjustment in accounts, but merely disclosed by board of directors if they are significant.

QUESTIONS

1. State the contents of audit report according to section 227(2) and 227 (3) of the Companies Act.
2. 'The auditor is concerned to opine as to the truth and fairness of financial statements, not merely as to the truth and correctness of them! - Discuss.
3. Bring out the difference between a certificate and a report.
4. Discuss the general and specific contents of an audit report of a limited company.
5. Explain the clean audit report
6. Mention the circumstances under which an auditor is required to issue an `other than unqualified opinion' in his report.
7. What are the types of `other than unqualified opinion? Briefly mention the grounds for giving each type of such opinion by the auditor in his audit report of a limited company.
8. How will you decide in the following cases with regard to giving clean or qualified opinion in your audit report:
   (*a*) The company desires to declare dividend during the period. But in view of small quantum of profit, it does not want to provide depreciation for the period under review. It, however, promises you that the arrears of depreciation will certainly be provided in the very next year which you can take as a quarantee from the management.
   (*b*) The total remuneration payable to managerial personnel (within the definition of Companies Act) is Rs. 12,75,000. The total profits of the company for the year is Rs 1 crore.
   (*c*) The figure in investment in assets side include investment in another company in excess of limits laid down by the companies Act in Section 372.
   (*d*) The company does not like to disclose the debts due by directors to it in the notes to the Balance Sheet.
   (*e*) A payment of Rs. 7500 to sales manager of the company in reimbursement of his travelling expenses is without supporting vouchers. The total profit of the company for the year is Rs. 35 lakhs.
   (*f*) The company values its stock consistently at cost for all the years. This year the market price is lower than the cost at the end of the accounting period. The company desires to stick to the practice hitherto followed. It argues that never in the past the market price had been lower than the cost. The decline in this year is a temporary phenomenon and the market price will surely pick up within a period of next 4 months.
9. How will you decide to report the following:
   (*a*) Three vouchers of capital expenditure are missing
   (b) Two errors were discovered in vouching the wages
   (c) A transfer of share submitted by a shareholder is irregularly passed for transfer.
   (d) A sum had been expended in contravention of one of the provisions of the Memorandum of Association of the company.

   In your answer, indicate the person to whom you will report each of the matter, and the salient points of your reporting matters. You can make use of hypothetical figures and assumptions needed.

10. What are the matters that are required to be inquired into by a company auditor as prescribed under section 227 (1A) of Companies Act?

11. State any five matters which are required to be commented by the company auditor under CARO 2003 ?

12. Mention the matters required to be reported in audit report under CARO 2003 with regard to the following:

(*a*) Fixed assets; (*b*) Stock in trade; (*c*) Investments;
(*d*) Public deposits; (*e*) arrears of statutory dues to government.

13. To what extent should the auditor of a limited company have regard to the events occurring subsequent to the date of balance sheet?

14. While auditing the books of Azhar & Sons Limited for a year the following are observed:

(*a*) A customer, who owed Rs. 75,000 to the company, had been adjudged as insolvent, subsequent to the date of Company's balance sheet date.

(b) The Company's building, which was not insured, the book value of which was Rs. 2,00,000 and the market value of which is Rs.8,00,000, was destroyed by fire which broke out on the very next date to Balance sheet date.

(c) A decree order had been passed against the company for damages for having breached the patent law. The decree had been passed within a week from the date of balance sheet date.

State whether it would be necessary for you to disclose the effect of a, b, c on the financial position of the company. If yes, state the manner of your disclosure.

15. (*a*) As an auditor of a holding company state what are your duties with respect to checking the accounts of subsidiarics.

(*b*) Your are an auditor of a subsidiary company the whole of whose shares are held by a single parent company and its nominees. You suggest the directors of the company that in view of certain transactions with the holding company, it is necessary to qualify your audit report. They reply that it is unnecessary because:

(a) the parent company is the major shareholder (practically single shareholder)

(*b*) The directors being the same persons in both the companies are aware of these.

(c) The auditor of the holding company has not thought it necessary to qualify his audit report for these. How will you react ?

16. Can the management of a company present its accounts which contain matters deviant from the accounting standards prescribed/specified by the Central Government or the ICAI ? Specify the duty of the Auditor of such a company in drafting his audit report.

Chapter 25

Audit of Banking Companies

The audit of Banks is made compulsory under the enactments governing the Banks. The Banking Regulation Act, 1949 deals with the matters including accounts and audit of various banking institutions. The Banking Companies (Acquisition and transfer of undertakings) Act 1970 regulate the functioning of nationalised banks. Certain provisions of Banking Regulations Act also apply to nationalised banks. The Companies Act also applies to Banking Companies if the provisions are not inconsistent with Banking Regulation Act. The Co-operative Societies Act 1912 deal with provisions applicable to co-operative banks. Regional Rural Banks Act 1976 govern regional rural banks. State Bank of India Act 1955 control the operations of State Bank of India and its subsidiaries. Besides these enactments, Reserve Bank of India has regulatory powers to regulate the functioning of all Banks under its statute. From time to time, it issues circulars and guidelines to be followed by banks.

The audit of banks is a specialised task. It requires the thorough knowledge of various enactments affecting banks, understanding the operations of banks, their accounting system, and above all appreciation of audit aims of bank audit.

Salient Features Of Enactments Affecting Banks :

(*a*) Restrictions on Business : According to Banking Regulation Act, a banking company is one which carries on the business of banking in India and includes foreign company carrying on banking business in India. Section 5 of the Act defines banking as 'the accepting for the purpose of lending or investment, of deposits of money from the public repayable on demand or otherwise and withdrawable by cheque, draft, order or otherwise'.

A banking company is not allowed to carry on any business except those permitted under section 6(1), besides the business of banking as defined. Section 6 permits banks to do the following business :

(*a*) borrowing and lending of money

(*b*) dealing in negotiable/quasi negotiable instruments

(*c*) issuing letters of credit/travellers cheques/circular notes

(*d*) buying and selling of bullions, foreign exchange

(*e*) underwriting, dealing in shares etc acting as managers to public issue of shares etc.

(*f*) providing safe deposit vaults.

(g) carrying on agency, guarantee and indemnity businesses

(*h*) managing, selling or dealing with property acquired in full or part settlement of its claims (non-banking assets) (*i*) acting as trustees, executors

(*j*) any other business notified by Government in this behalf

Section 8 specifically prohibits banks to deal in trading of goods.

Section 13 contains restriction on payment of brokerage or discount for remuneration on the sale of shares at a rate exceeding two and one half percentage.

Section 19 prohibits forming of subsidiary company except for the purposes specified.

Section 14 prohibits banks to create charge on unpaid capital. Similarly the banks cannot create floating charge on its undertaking or any property without the permission of RBI.

Section 15 puts ceiling in time up to which non banking assets acquired in full or part satisfaction of its claims could be held. It lays down that within a period of seven years such assets should be disposed off.

It is necessary that an auditor of banks must be aware of restrictions on the powers of banks. He must refer to various provisions of Banking Regulation Act for this.

(*b*) Capital Requirements: Section 11 and 12 of the Act contains minimum capital to be maintained by banks. The Act provides minimum amount of capital in terms of Rupees to be raised and kept for various banks. Section 12 further lays down that the subscribed capital of the banks should be not less than fifty per cent of authorised capital and paid capital should not be less than 50% of the subscribed capital. In addition to this, RBI has issued circular requiring banks to meet capital adequacy ratio. Capital adequacy ratio is nothing but expression of total capital of the Bank as multiple of funded and non funded assets and off-the-Balance sheet items. For this purpose, total capital includes share capital, reserves and subordinated debts. Assets and off-balance sheet items (like contingent obligations) are taken at values after adjusting them with prescribed factors applicable to each asset/item depending on its risk element. At present the ratio of capital adequacy i.e, total capital ÷ risk adjusted assets/items should be minimum of 8.

(*c*) Reserve Fund : According to Section 17 of the Banking Regulation Act, every banking company must transfer atleast 20% of its net profits to fund called reserve fund. This is a statutory reserve. It must be shown separately in the balance sheet. The banks must continue transferring 20% of net profit year after year till the balance in the reserve fund cross the aggregate of paid up capital and share premium account. This reserve must be kept intact. It is a kind of additional security available to depositors.

(*d*) Cash Reserve and Statutory Liquidity Reserve : According to Section 18 of the Banking Regulation Act, each banking company must maintain cash reserve with RBI for a sum equal to at lease 3% of its time and demand liabilities. Similar provision is found in section 42 of the Reserve Bank of India Act. It applies to scheduled banks only. Therefore, scheduled banks must maintain cash reserve with RBI for a sum not less than 3% of its time and demand liabilities. The RBI can increase the percentage up to 15% in this regard. In addition to this, every bank must maintain with RBI statutory liquidity reserve for a sum prescribed by RBI. The SLR is to be maintained in the form of cash, gold or unencumbered approved securities. The SLR should not be less than 25% of total demand and time liabilities.

(*e*) Restriction on Investments, Loans and advances : A banking company cannot hold shares whether as pledgee, mortgagee or absolute owner of other companies exceeding 30% of its own paid up capital and reserves or 30% of capital of other companies whichever is less.

A banking company cannot advance loans on the security of its own shares. It cannot give unsecured loan or advance to any of its director or firm or private company in which such director is interested. Again, permission from RBI is to be obtained for remitting the whole or part of debt due by director to it. RBI is empowered to give directions to banking companies in regard to advances granted to directors. RBI may require banks to obtain still more security or refuse further loans or recall the loans already granted to them. Monthly returns in the prescribed format regarding loans and advances to directors are to be submitted to RBI.

(*f*) **Dividend :** Banks cannot pay dividend unless all capitalised expenses are fully wiped off.

(*g*) **Accounts :** According to section 29, every banking company shall prepare its financial statements in the format prescribed in third schedule as of 31st March of each year.

(*h*) **Audit :** Section 30 of the Act deals with audit of the accounts. The accounts of the Indian Banking Companies shall be audited by Chartered Accountants. The appointment, powers, duties, removal and liabilities of auditor are as same as company auditor's. However, RBI's approval is to be obtained for appointment, re-appointment and removal. In case of audit of nationalised banks, the statutory auditor shall send his audit report to central government (i.e, President of India) with copies to RBI, and bank. The audit report shall state.

(*a*) Whether in his opinion, the balance sheet is a full and fair balance sheet containing all necessary particulars and is properly drawn up so as to exhibit true and fair view of state of affairs of the bank or not.

(*b*) Whether he has obtained satisfactory information and explanation or not.

(*c*) Whether the transactions which have come to his notice are within powers of bank or not.

(*d*) Whether the returns received from branches are found to be adequate or not.

(*e*) Whether Profit and Loss account give true and fair view of profit or loss of the bank for the period.

(*f*) Any other matter which auditor wants to bring to the notice of central government.

Accounting System of a Bank

The business of a bank generally consists of acceptance of deposits, lending, investment, doing agency and other utility functions. All these transactions occur in any of these modes viz. cash, transfer or clearing. Banks follow double entry system of accounting. If one effect of a transaction (debit or credit) involves cash, it is called cash transaction. Transfer transactions involve entries affecting two account heads of a bank other than cash. Clearing transactions involve transfer of funds into or out of branch to other members of clearing house. The banks categorise the transactions into three of these to have close check of items comprised therein.

The banks do not make use of journal vouchers. Rather, the slips used in ordinary business of a bank (like cheque, paying-in-slip, discharged deposit receipt etc.) are used to make entries in ledger. Based on these slips or vouchers, clerks make entries in subsidiary ledgers maintained for each type of deposits/loans. These slips are collected at the day-end and entries are made in supplementary day book. Main day book is written from these records. Daily supplementary day books are tallied with main day book. General ledger posting is made from day book. Periodically, the individual balances from subsidiary ledgers are extracted and are compared with the respective total control accounts, maintained in general ledger to check the accuracy. Thus slip system of posting and existence of sectional balancing are unique features of accounting system of a bank.

Internal Control System in a Bank

Good internal check is a pre-requisite in operating system of a bank for matters of convenience and control. Main internal controls operating in a bank are detailed hereunder:

(*a*) Division of work : No individual clerk has control over a transaction from origin to end.

(*b*) Slip system of posting: Original vouchers evidencing transactions are used for making records in ledgers.

(*c*) Job rotation among staff periodically.

(*d*) Existence of sectional balancing system ensures accuracy of data at any point of time.

(*e*) Joint custody: prescription of joint custody for dealing with vulnerable assets like cash, jewels pledged etc.

(*f*) Authorisation levels: existence of clear-cut authority level for incurring monetary commitments either by way of loans, investments or incurring of expenditure (capital or revenue).

(*g*) Monitoring: The transaction effected by an officer is put to well-laid monitoring system. Self monitoring and superior-monitoring occur in bank.

(*h*) Review: Independent review of operations by inspectors, internal auditors and statutory auditors periodically or at surprise intervals add effective control to the system.

(*i*) Reporting : Periodical control statements on various operational areas are often submitted to the controlling authorities by banks.

Bank Audit - Its Approach

The statutory auditor of a bank cannot carry out post and vouch audit. *It is sometimes, described as a balance sheet audit, a system audit and mostly an audit of advances*. Though a bank audit cannot be taken to be all those only, these descriptions do throw light on approach adopted in bank audit. As there are special features in accounting of banks, so too are audit approaches.

(*a*) Bank audit is a time-framed programme.

(*b*) The aim of statutory audit is to express opinion on truth and fairness of balance sheet items and profit/loss of bank.

(*c*) The transactions of a bank are voluminous, repetitive. An auditor cannot check all these. The auditor cannot be familiar with signatures of all deposit holders. No useful purpose is to be served in wasting time on checking routines.

(*d*) There exists well laid procedures to effect internal checks. What matters for an auditor is to apply checks and tests to ensure that the system actually functions effectively.

(*e*) As auditor gives opinion on items of balance sheet, his attention will be more drawn on item 'advance'. Because the item 'advance constitutes major item of assets in the balance sheet. *Hence the statutory audit of a bank can be described as an audit of balance sheet, system and advances*.

Steps in Bank Audit

Like any other audit, the auditor has to plan and proceed in bank audit. In particular, he may identify the following areas as important in his programming :

(*a*) evaluation of internal control system
(*b*) checking of advances
(*c*) checking of other items of assets
(*d*) checking of liabilities
(*e*) scrutiny of P&L items
(*f*) making audit report

To evaluate internal control system, the auditor can make auditing in depth in respect of certain transactions. He may study the reports of internal auditor and inspectors to identify areas of frauds or malfunctioning.

Checking of advances requires much time and energy of auditor. It is discussed separately in this chapter.

Checking Major Items of Assets:

Besides advances, the balance sheet contains the following assets viz.:

Cash, Balance with RBI

Balances with other Banks, money at call and short notice
Investments
Fixed assets
Other assets

The auditor should physically check the cash balance as on the date of his audit. He should get all records and scrutinise them. He should see that cashier's scroll, officer's scroll, balance in cash book and general ledger balance for cash-all tally with each other in respect of receipts, payments and balance. He should obtain certificate of balance from manager of the bank for his records.

Balances with other banks, money at call and short notice are checked by verifying confirmation of balances obtained from other banks/borrowers. If balance shown by them differs from that shown by books of the bank he should obtain reconciliation statement. He should scrutinise causes of difference and satisfy himself that nothing is unusual.

Investments : Auditor should check that efficient internal control operates with various aspect of investment viz - issuing order for purchase, decision to sell, custody, making entries in records etc. He should physically check all investments with bank to ensure ownership of bank and encumbrance if any. Where investments are with other party, say, brokers or safe deposit agency, he must ensure that there is nothing unusual in their having bank's investments. He must obtain written confirmation from them. The auditor should check that the valuation of investments is properly made. According to Gosh Committee (1982) recommendations the investments are to be classified into permanent or current investment depending on the intention of bank. The permanent investment can be shown at cost or market value on a consistent basis. But current investments must always be shown at cost or market value whichever is lower. The auditor should ensure that bank complies to this valuation policy.

Fixed assets and other assets are to be checked bearing in mind principles enumerated in valuation of assets. The auditor should check that proper depreciation is provided for fixed assets on a consistent basis.

Checking of Liabilities :

In capital and liability side of a bank the following appear: Capital, Reserves and surplus, Deposits, Borrowings and other liabilities.

In checking capital, the auditor should ensure that legal requirements as regards to capital are met by the bank. In checking reserves, the auditor should see that reserve fund is created as per section 17 of B.R. Act. He must see that no appropriations are made out of it without RBI approval. He must scrutinise various types of deposits and study the trend in their growth. He must satisfy himself that the deposit figure is not 'bloated' by adopting any window dressing methods. While checking borrowings, he must satisfy himself about the power of the bank to borrow, the terms and conditions attached to borrowings. The auditor should ensure that adequate provision is made in respect of interest accrued on deposits but not paid to deposit holders. Similarly it is to be ensured that all outstanding expenses, provision for bonus, gratuity etc., are correctly included in liability.

Scrutiny of P & L Items :

In income side, interest earned on advances constitute major revenue. Income from investments, discount on bills purchased etc. also constitute important sources of revenue. The auditor should ensure the income is properly recognised as per RBI guidelines. In respect of discount on bills, he must check rebate on unexpired discount had been created. In expenditure side, interest on deposits constitutes major expense. He must check few cases to ensure the accuracy. Unpaid interest should be adequately provided for. The auditor should test-check other items of expenditure like salary, depreciation, loss on sale of investments, miscellaneous expenses.

Making Report

The report by the auditor should be in the prescribed format. The requirement of report had been discussed already in audit of bank (salient features of enactments). In addition to this report, RBI has issued a questionnaire called long form audit Report (LFAR). It has prescribed LFAR for central auditor and LFAR for Branch auditor. The questionnaire contains various areas of banks-assets, liability, income, expenditure, internal control, accounting accuracy, inter-branch transactions, reports of internal auditor, inspectors, frauds etc. The auditor is required to make specific comments on each item in the questionnaire.

Audit Of Advances

Checking of advances is a major area of bank audit. In checking advances, an auditor is guided by the following aims in mind viz. :

(*a*) To check that there exists an effective internal control in various areas of credit management

(*b*) To check that the advance is shown in the balance sheet fairly in its realisable value

(*c*) To check that the income generated by the advance is properly recognised and measured and

(*d*) To check various informations required to be disclosed in financial statements are properly disclosed

Classification of advances :

Advances in a bank can be classified into -

facility-wise

(*a*) cash credit, overdraft, demand loans, bills purchased and discounted

(b) term loans

Cash credit, overdraft are drawal accounts with limit attached. Demand loans are loans repayable on demand or within a short period say, 36 months. Bills purchased and discounted are facility granted to drawer or holder of bills. Term loans mean loans repayable by instalments exceeding 36 months.

Security-wise

(*a*) Secured loans

(*b*) Unsecured loans

(*c*) Loans guaranteed by Bank/government

The security available for secured loan may be hypothecation, pledge, equitable mortagage

Sector-wise

(*a*) advances to priority sector like agricultural advances, advances to SSIs, or other priority industry, service or business

(*b*) advances to public sector

(*c*) advances to other sector

Prudential norms for income recognition

Depending on income generating capacity of advances, they can be categorised into performing asset (PA) or Non-performing Asset (NPA). The Narashimham committee, (1991) has laid down various criteria for determination of any advance into performing or non performing. Income in respect of non performing assets, can be taken to P & L account only if the income has been actually realised. Income on due basis (without actual receipt) can be recognised only if the advance is a performing asset. The criteria for determination of an advance into performing asset or non-performing asset for various facilities are given under :

(A) A cash credit or overdraft account is treated as NPA if the account remains out of order 90 days. Then what is meant by 'remaining out of order' ? An account is considered to be out of order if the outstanding balance in the account continously exceeds the limit or in cases where the balance is within limit, the credits in the account were insufficient to meet the debits towards interest remaining overdue for 90 days.

(B) A demand loan is considered as NPA if interest or instalment arrears remains uncollected even after the lapse of atlease 90 days from the it is overdue.

(C) A term loan becomes an NPA if the interest or instalment arrears are overdue for a period of 90 days.

(D) Bills purchased/discounted are considered NPA if the amount of bills remains overdue for 90 days.

Therefore it can be appreciated that generally an advance is taken to be NPA if the interest or instalment relating to the advance accumulates without collection beyond a reasonable period of time. In such of those cases, RBI has directed that the interest in such advances can be taken to P & L account only on the basis of actual collection and not on the basis of mere debits in the account.

Asset classification and provisioning

Another classification about which the auditor is concerned is categorisation based on realisability of advances. Accordingly advances are grouped into standard, sub-standard, doubtful and loss assets. Standard assets do not show any abnormal risks as to collection. Sub-standard assets are those which are non-performing assets in their initial stages. Any non-performing assets for a period not exceeding 12 months as on the date of balance sheet date are taken to be sub-standard asset. A doubtful asset is one which is non-performing for a period exceeding 12 months as on the date of balance sheet date. A loss asset is one where in the opinion of inspectors, internal auditors, the account is uncollectible and the security is not available/ is meagre. To guard against probable loss, the RBI requires banks to make provision for these assets. Ageneral provision @ 0.25% of total advances) is made for standard assets and substandard assets (10% of advances). In case of doubtful advances full provision for uncovered portion is made. In addition to this, additional provision on secured portion is to be made at percentages specified. The percentage increases as the years during which the account remains doubtful increase.

The provisioning of secured portion of doubtful advances is as under-

No of years for which asset is in doubtful category	Percentage of provision (secured portion)
Upto one year	20
Between one and three years	30
More than three years depending on identification dates of advances of this category. For doubtful assets identified on 31.3.2004-50%; 31.3.2005-60%; 31.3.2006-75%, 31.3.2007-100% (in a phased manner)	Range 50 to 100 (as per phasing provisions)

Loss assets should be fully provided or written off from books.

Points to be Checked in Audit of Advances

1. The auditor should check that efficient internal control operates in advance-management in the bank. He may select few major cases of advances to make audit-in-depth. He must evaluate controls operating various stages of advance administration - sanction, disbursement, security, execution of documents, custody of documents, recording of advances, follow up etc..
2. The auditor should ensure that the accuracy of figures of advances. He must see that the balances extracted party-wise in respect of different types of loan tally with the balances of respective total accounts in the general ledger.
3. The auditor should satisfy himself that the classification of advances into performing and non-performing is properly made. He must check that the interest in respect of non-performing assets are taken to P & L account only if they have been actually recovered. If interest in respect of NPAs are included in P & L account on the basis of mere debit in party account, the auditor should ask the bank to reverse the entries.
4. The auditor should check that facility-wise and sector-wise classification is fairly done.
5. The auditor should see that advances shown as secured or guaranteed by government/ Bank are really so. He must ensure that the security is available and is accessible to bank. In major cases he must study that the valuation of security is fairly made.
6. The auditor should ensure that adequate provision for sub-standard, doubtful and loss assets are made in P & L account.
7. The auditor must make a review of all major accounts. He must check that loan documents are complete and are not time-barred. Where the accounts show signs of sickness, he must draw the attention of bank for timely action. In cases of problematic accounts, he must see that timely steps are taken for recovery of loans. He must evaluate the position of suit-filed accounts.
8. The auditor can make physical inspection of security. Security in the form of jewels pledged will be with bank. He may check them at random. He may even visit the godowns of borrowers to check the adequacy of stocks in cases of hypothecation.
9. The auditor should ensure that all disclosure requirements with regard to advances in the balance sheet are fairly met.

Special Liabilities imposed on the Auditors of Banking Companies

According to Section 30 (3) of the Banking Companies Act, 1949, the auditor of a banking company incorporated in India is required to state in his report in addition to matters required by Section 227 of the Companies Act.

(*a*) whether or not the information and explanations required by him have been found to be satisfactory;

(*b*) whether or not the transactions of the banking company which have come to his notice have been within the powers of the company;

(*c*) whether or not the returns received from the branch offices of the company have been found adequate for the purpose of audit;

(*d*) whether the profit and loss account shows a true balance of profit and loss for the period covered by such account;

(*e*) any other manner which he considers should be brought to the notice of the shareholders of the company.

In case of a banking company incorporated outside India, the accounts of such a company must be audited by an auditor duly qualified under the Companies Act or by a person who is duly qualified to be an auditor under the law of the country in which the company has been incorporated.

The auditor of a banking company will have the same powers, duties, responsibilities and is subjected to the same penalties as that of an auditor appointed under Section 227 of the Companies Act.

The auditor should examine the provisions of bad and doubtful debts because the advances and loans in the case of a bank are other than those considered bad and doubtful. Again since a bank is allowed to create secret reserves, the auditor should see that such reserves are not misused by it.

If an auditor wilfully makes a false statement in any statement, return, balance sheet,etc., or wilfully omits to make a material statement, he is liable to be imprisoned upto a period of three years and is also liable to be fined [S. 46(1)].

Section 45G of the Banking Regulation Act provides for the public examination on oath of the auditors of banking companies if, during the course of winding up, it is found that a loss had been caused by any act or omission on the part of an auditor. The auditor has to answer on oath all such questions as may be put to him by the creditors and contributories, etc. If the High Court is satisfied that he is not fit to perform his duties as an auditor of a bank or a company, it may pass an order removing him from the office for a period not exceeding five years even though he may be quite innocent of any act of misfeasance.

The above procedure will apply even when a scheme of arrangement has been applied for on the report of the Reserve Bank.

Section 45H of the Banking Regulation Act further provides that if the High Court is satisfied, it may make an order against the auditor to repay or restore such money or property unless it is proved to the contrary.

The auditor of a banking company is deemed to be public servant under chapter IX of the Indian Penal Code.

PERFORMA OF BANK'S FINANCIAL STATEMENTS

Form 'A'

FORM OF BALANCE SHEET

Balance Sheet of ....(here enter name of the Banking Company)
as on 31 March (year)

(000's omitted)

CAPITAL AND LIABILITIES	Schedule	As on 31.3.... (Current Year)	As on 31.3.... (Previous Year)
Capital	1		
Reserves & Surplus	2		
Deposits	3		
Borrowings	4		
Othet liabilities and provisions	5		
	Total:		
ASSETS			
Cash and balances with Reserve Bank of India	6		
Balances with banks and money at call and short notice	7		
Investments	8		
Advances	9		
Fixed Assets	10		
Other Assets	11		
	Total:		
Contingent Liabilities	12		
Bills for Collection			

SCHEDULE 1 - CAPITAL

	As on 31.3... (Current Year)	As on 31.3... (Previous Year)
I. **For Nationalised Banks**		
Capital (Fully owned by Central Government)		
II. **For Banks Incorporated Outside India Capital**		
(*i*) (The amount brought in by banks by way of start-up capital as prescribed by RBI should be shown under this head)		
(*ii*) Amount of deposit kept with the RBI under Section 11 (2) of the Banking Regulation Act, 1949		
Total		
III. **For Other Banks**		
Authorised Capital		
(Shares of Rs. each)		
Issued Capital		
(Shares of Rs. each)		
Subscribed Capital		
(Shares of Rs. each)		
Called-up Capital		
(Shares of Rs. each)		
Less : Calls unpaid		
Add: Forfeited Shares		

SCHEDULE 2 - RESERVES & SURPLUS

	As on 31.3... (Current Year)	As on 31.3... (Previous Year)
I. Statutory Reserves		
Opening Balance		
Additions during the year		
Deductions during the year		
II. Capital Reserves		
Opening Balance		
Additions during the year		
Deductions during the year		
III. Share Premium		
Opening Balance		
Additions during the year		
Deductions during the year		
IV. Revenue and other Reserves		
Opening Balance		
Additions during the year		
Deductions during the year		
V. Balance in Profit and Loss Account		
Total : (I,II,III,IV and V)		

SCHEDULE 3 - DEPOSITS

		As on 31.3... (Current Year)	As on 31.3... (Previous Year)
A. I.	Demand Deposits		
	(i) From Banks		
	(ii)From others		
II.	Saving Bank Deposits		
III.	Term Deposits		
	(i) From Banks		
	(ii) From others		
	Total : (I,II,and III)		
B.	(i) Deposits of branches in India		
	(ii) Deposits of branches outside India		
	Total :		

SCHEDULE 4 - BORROWINGS

	As on 31.3... (Current Year)	As on 31.3... (Previous Year)
I. Borrowings in India		
(i) Reserve Bank of India		
(ii) Other banks		
(iii) other institutions and agencies		
II. Borrowings outside India		
Total :		
(I, II, III, IV and V)		

Secured borrowings included in I & II above - Rs.

SCHEDULE 5 - OTHER LIABILITIES AND PROVISIONS

	As on 31.3... (Current Year)	As on 31.3... (Previous Year)
I. Bills Payable		
II. Inter-Office adjustments (net)		
III. Interest accrues		
IV. Others (including provisions)		
Total :		

SCHEDULE 6 - CASH AND BALANCES WITH RESERVE BANK OF INDIA

	As on 31.3... (Current Year)	As on 31.3... (Previous Year)
I. Cash in hand (including foreign currency notes)		

II. Balances with Reserve Bank of India
(*i*) in Current Account
(*ii*) in Other Accounts

Total : ______ ______
(I,II,III,IV and V) ______ ______

SCHEDULE 7 - BALANCES WITH BANKS & MONEY AT CALL & SHORT NOTICE

	As on 31.3... (Current Year)	As on 31.3... (Previous Year)
I. In India		
(*i*) Balances with Banks		
(*a*) in Current Accounts		
(*b*) in Other Deposit Accounts		
(*ii*) Money at call and short notice		
(*a*) with banks		
(b) with other institutions		
Total :	______	______
(I, II, III, IV and V)	______	______
II. Outside India		
(*i*) in Current Accounts		
(*ii*) in other Deposit Accounts		
(*iii*) Money at call and short notice		
Total :	______	______
(I, II, III, IV and V)	______	______
Grand Total :		
(I and II)	==========	==========

SCHEDULE 8 - INVESTMENTS

	As on 31.3... (Current Year)	As on 31.3... (Previous Year)
I. Investments in India in		
(*i*) Government securities		
(*ii*) Other approved securities		
(*iii*) Shares		
(*iv*) Debentures and Bonds		
(*v*) Subsidiaries and/or joint ventures		
(*vi*) Others (to be specified)	______	______
Total :	______	______
II. Investments outside India in		
(*i*) Government securities (including local authorities)		
(*ii*) Subsidiaries and/or joint ventures abroad		
(*iii*) Other investments (to be specified)		
Total :	______	______
Grand Total :	______	______
(I & II)	==========	==========

SCHEDULE 9 - ADVANCES

	As on 31.3... (Current Year)	As on 31.3... (Previous Year)
A. (*i*) Bills purchased and discounted		
(*ii*) Cash credits, overdrafts and loans repayable on demand		
(*iii*) Term loans		
Total :		
B. (*i*) Secured by tangible assets		
(*ii*) Covered by Bank/Government guarantees		
(*iii*) Unsecured		
Total :		
C. I. Advances in India		
(*i*) Priority Sectors		
(*ii*) Public Sector		
(*iii*) Banks		
(*iv*) Others		
Total :		
II. Advances outside India		
(*i*) Due from banks		
(*ii*) Due from others		
(*a*) Bills purchased and discounted		
(*b*) Syndicated loans		
(c) Others		
Total :		
Grand Total : (C I and II)		

SCHEDULE 10 - FIXED ASSETS

	As on 31.3... (Current Year)	As on 31.3... (Previous Year)
I. Premises		
At cost as on 31st March of the preceding year		
Additions during the year		
Deductions during the year		
Depreciation to date		
II. Other Fixed Assets (including furniture and fixtures)		
At cost as on 31st March of the preceding year		
Additions during the year		
Deductions during the year		
Depreciation to date		
Total : (I and II)		

SCHEDULE 11 - OTHER ASSETS

	As on 31.3... (Current Year)	As on 31.3... (Previous Year)
I. Inter-office adjustments (net)		
II. Interest accrued		
III. Tax paid in advance/tax deducted at source		
IV. Stationery and stamps		
V. Non-banking assets acquired in satisfaction of claims		
VI. Others @		
Total :		

@ In case there is any unadjusted balance of loss the same may be shown under the item with appropriate footnote.

SCHEDULE 12 - CONTINGENT LIABILITIES

	Year ended on 31.3... (Current Year)	Year ended on 31.3... (Previous Year)
I. Claims against the bank not acknowledged as debts		
II. Liabilities for party paid investments		
III. Liability on account of outstanding forward exchange contracts		
IV. Guarantees given on behalf of constituents		
(*a*) In India		
(*b*) Outside India		
V. Acceptances, endorsements and other obligations		
VI. Other items for which the bank is contigently liable		
Total :		

From 'B'

FORM OF PROFIT AND LOSS ACCOUNT

Profit & Loss Account for the year ended 31st March (Year)

(ooo's ommitted)

	Schedule No.	Year ended on 31.3... (Current Year)	Year ended on 31.3... (Previous Year)
I. **Income**			
Interest earned	13		
other income	14		
	Total :		
II. **Expenditure**			
Interest expended	15		
Operating expenses	16		
Provisions and contigencies			
	Total :		

III. Profit /Loss

Net profit/loss (-) for the year

Profit/Loss (-) brought forward

Total :

IV. Appropriations

Transfer to statutory reserves

Transfer to other reserves

Transfer to Government/proposed dividend

Balance carried over to Balance Sheet

Total :

SCHEDULE 13 - INTEREST EARNED

	Year Ended on 31.3... (Current Year)	Year Ended on 31.3... (Previous Year)
I. Interest/discount on advances/ bills		
II. Income on investments		
III. Interest on balances with Reserve Bank of India and other Inter-bank funds		
IV. Others		
Total :		

SCHEDULE 14 - OTHER INCOME

	Year Ended on 31.3... (Current Year)	Year Ended on 31.3... (Previous Year)
I. Commission, exchange and brokerage		
II. Profit on sale of investments Less: Loss on sale of investments		
III. Profit on revaluation of investments Less: Loss on revaluation of investments		
IV. Profit on sale of land, buildings and other assets Less: Loss on sale of lands, buildings and other assets		
V. Profit on excange transactions Less: Loss on exchange transactions		
VI. Income caused by way of dividends etc. from subsidiaries/companies and/or joint ventures abroad/in India		
VII. Miscellaneous Income		
Total :		

Note: Under items II to V, loss figures may be shown in brackets."

SCHEDULE 15 - INTEREST EXPENDED

	Year Ended on 31.3... (Current Year)	Year Ended on 31.3... (Previous Year)
I. Interest on deposits"		
II. Interest on Reserve Bank of India/ Inter-bank borrowings		
III. Others		
Total :		

SCHEDULE 16 - OPERATING EXPENSES

	Year Ended on 31.3... (Current Year)	Year Ended on 31.3... (Previous Year)
I. Payments to and provisions for employees		
II. Rent, taxes and lighting		
III. Printing & Stationery		
IV. Advertisement and publicity		
V. Depreciation on bank's property		
VI. Directors' fees, allowances and expenses		
VII. Auditors' fees, allowances and expenses (including branch auditors)		
VIII. Law Charges		
IX. Postages, Telegrams, Telephones, etc.		
X. Repairs and maintenance		
XI. Insurance		
XII. Other expenditure		
Total :		

It may be noted that formats of Balance Sheet and Profit and Loss Account cover all items likely to appear in the statements. In case a bank does not have any particular item to report, it may be omitted from the formats. Figures should be rounded off to the nearest thousand rupees. Unless otherwise indicated, the banks in these statements will include banking companies, nationalised banks, State Bank of India, associate banks and all other institutions including co-operatives carrying on the business of banking whether or not incorporated or operating in India.

QUESTIONS

1. What special liability has been imposed by the Banking Companies Act, on the auditors of Banking Companies of India (*Rajasthan M. Com. 1961; Gauhati B.Com. 1969*)
2. How would you verify the "badness" or "doubtfulness" of a debt in the case of a Banking concern? (*Delhi B.A. Com. 1957*)
3. What are the special points to be kept in view while auditing the books of a commercial bank? (*Delhi B.A. Com. 1969*)
4. In what form should the book debts of a bank be shown in the Balance Sheet so that you, as an auditor, may pass them. State the main points you will take into consideration to verify them. (*Delhi B. Com. 1959*)
5. What special points would you bear in mind besides the normal audit routine, while conducting the audit of a Bank. (*Marathwada, Delhi, Annamalai and Cal. B.Com.*)
6. Draft Auditor's report to the shareholders of a Banking Company, incorporating therein any three qualifications. (*Bombay B.Com.*)
7. In auditing the accounts of a bank, what special points would engage your attention? (*Nagpur B.Com.*)
8. Discuss the special points which you would take into consideration while auditing the accounts of a bank. (*Annamalai and Varanasi B. Com*)
9. Having completed the audit of a Banking Company to your satisfaction, state in what form would you give an unqualified report to the shareholders? (*Gujarat B. Com*)
10. 'The audit of banks is the audit of systems, balance sheet and advances' - discuss.

11. State the main features of internal check that operates in a bank.

12. Briefly mention the points that you would check with respect to each specific item of assets of balance sheet of a bank. (mention matters of checking for any 4 assets only).

13. While checking advances, the auditor is concerned with correct classification of advances. Explain different categorisations of advances relevant for financial reporting.

14. Write short notes on :

(*a*) Performing assets Vs non-performing assets

(*b*) Doubfful asset Vs Loss asset

(c) Standard asset Vs sub-standard asset

(d) Secured advance Vs unsecured advance

15. Draw out an audit programme for checking advances of a bank.

Chapter 26

The Audit of Co-operative Banks and Institutions

Introduction

For the last few years, the Government has given much encouragement to the co-operative institutions because of the policy of establishing a socialistic pattern of society. Although the accounts of the co-operative institutions are audited by the staff of the Co-operative Departments concerned, a Chartered Accountant is often asked to audit their accounts. It is, therefore, deemed advisable that he should be familiar with the technique of auditing the accounts of such institutions. An attempt has been made in this chapter to lay down in broad outlines the procedure of auditing the accounts of co-operative societies.

The co-operative societies are established under the Co-operative Societies Act, 1912. Some States like Maharashtra, Madras, Bengal, Bihar, etc., have enacted Co-operative Societies Acts for their own States according to the provision of the Central Act. In such States, therefore, provisions of the State legislation will be applicable. We shall, for the purpose of this chapter, deal with the Co-operative Societies Act, 1912 and therefore the sections quoted in this chapter will be those of the co-operative Societies Act, unless otherwise stated. It may be stated here that the provisions of the Companies Act are not applicable to the Co-operative Societies.

Registration of Co-operative Societies

Any ten persons who are competent to enter into contract and who wish to form a co-operative society may make an application to the Registrar of Co-operative Societies of the State in which it is proposed to establish the society (Section 6). A registered society can also be a member of another co-operative society in which case a duly authorised member of the other society will sign the application. A central co-operative bank may be formed by one society and one individual.

No member can hold more than twenty per cent of the share capital of the society. To carry day-to-day work of a society, a managing committee is elected by the members. The managing committee, generally, consists of the chairman, the secretary and the treasurer. The members of the managing committee are elected annually at the general meeting of the society.

Liabilities of the Members

As regards the liability of the members, the societies may be divided into two categories, viz.,

1. Limited Liability Societies, and
2. Unlimited Liability Societies.

1. Limited Liability Societies

The liability of the members of such societies is limited. In the event of loss, no member can be called upon to pay more than the nominal value of the shares held by him. No member of such a society can hold more than the limit prescribed by the bye-laws of the Society but in no case more than twenty per cent of the share capital or more than one thousand rupees worth of shares of the society. At least ten persons above the age of 18 years can form such a society (Section 5). The word 'Limited' should be the last word in the name of the society. A past member is liable for the debts of the registered society for a period of two years after he ceases to be a member provided the debt was incurred when he was a member (Section 23). In case of the death of a member his estate shall be liable for a period of one year provided the debt existed at the time of his death (Section 24).

2. Unlimited Liability Societies

The liability of the members will be unlimited if the object of the society is to create funds in order to lend money to its members or where the majority of the members are creditors of the society. No registered society can be a member of such a society. A member of such a society cannot transfer his share unless he has held the share for not less than one year and the transfer or change is made to the Society or to a member [Section 14 (2)] or he resides in the same town or village.

Privileges of Registered Societies

The following are privileges which a registered society can enjoy :

1. It shall have the privilege of a body corporate.
2. It will have perpetual succession and a common seal.
3. It will have the power to hold property.
4. It can enter into contracts with others.
5. It can be sued by others and it can also sue others.
6. Its shares cannot be attached or sold under any decree or order of a court in respect of any debt or liability incurred by its members.
7. Under Section 27 of the Co-operative Societies Act, 1912, the Central Government may exempt a registered society or remit income tax payable in respect of the profits of the society of the dividend or other payments received by the members of the society on account of profits.
8. The Central Government exempts a registered society from any fee or stamp duty payable in respect of certain documents, under Section 28.
9. A registered co-operative society has a prior claim as against other creditors for the recovery of any amount due from a member or a past member in respect of the following debts :
   (*a*) For the supply of seed or manure or a loan advanced for this purpose (within 18 months from the date of such supply or loan); or
   (*b*) For supply of cattle, fodder, or for agricultural or industrial implements or machinery or raw material for manufacture (Section 19).
   It may be pointed out here that this section is not applicable to the debts due to Government in respect of land revenue or similar claims of the landlords.
10. The shares of a member of a registered society are not liable to be attached or sold against any decree or order issued by a court or by an assignee or official receiver under the Insolvency Act (Section 21).

1. Restrictions imposed on Co-operative Societies

1. *Restrictions on the Transfer of Shares.*

(*a*) A member of an unlimited society cannot transfer his share unless he has held that share for at least one year.

(*b*) A member can surrender his share to the society or to another member after the expiry of one year when he became a member (Section 14).

(*c*) A registered society may provide in its bye-laws for the refund of the share money when a member ceases to be a member either at his own instance or if he is disqualified to be a member or when he dies.

(*d*) A society may refuse to register a transfer if it is in contravention of Section 5.

2. *Restrictions on Loans.*

(*a*) A co-operative society is not allowed to advance a loan to a person other than a member of the society except with the general or special permission of the Registrar.

(*b*) It cannot advance a loan to another registered co-operative society without the permission of the Registrar of Co-operative Societies.

(*c*) A society with unlimited liability cannot lend money against the security of moveable property except with the permission of the Registrar of Co-operative Societies.

(*d*) The State Government may prohibit a registered society or a class of registered societies to lend money on the mortgage of immoveable property (Section 29).

3. *Restrictions on Borrowings.*

A registered society may receive deposits and loans from persons who are not the members of the society to such an extent and under such conditions as may be prescribed by the rules of the Co-operative Societies Act or the bye-laws of the society concerned (Section 30).

Investment of Funds

A registered society may invest or deposit its funds—

(*a*) in a Government Savings Bank; or

(*b*) in any of the securities specified in Section 20 of the Indian Trust Act, 1882; or

(*c*) in the shares or securities of other registered societies; or

(*d*) with any other bank or person carrying on the business of banking, approved for this purpose by the Registrar; or

(*e*) in any other mode permitted by the Co-operative Societies Act (Section 32).

Appropriation of the Profits of the Society

The profits of a co-operative society can be appropriated in the following order:—

1. The first 25 per cent of the net profit should be carried to the Reserve Fund (Section 33).
2. Of the remainder profit, not more than 10 per cent may be utilised for charitable purposes as defined in Section 2 of the Charitable Endowment Act, 1890, provided the sanction of the Registrar had been obtained. This money is usually utilised for educational, welfare, medical relief and entertainment purposes but not for any religious teaching or worship (Section 34).
3. Dividend can be paid to the members according to the rules and bye-laws but in no case it should exceed 6¼ per cent (Section 33).
4. No dividend can be paid to the members of a society with unlimited liability unless permitted by the State Government.

Enquiry and Inspection of a Co-operative Society

Enquiry

Enquiry into the affairs of a co-operative society may be held under Section 35 in the following circumstances:—

(*a*) At the instance of the Registrar of Co-operative Societies when he is of opinion that the affairs of the society are not satisfactory; or

(*b*) At the instance of the Collector of the district; or

(*c*) When a majority of the members of the Managing Committee apply to the Registrar of Co-operative Societies to hold an enquiry; or

(*d*) At the instance of at least one-third of the members of the society.

When an enquiry is being held, it will be the duty of every officer and member to furnish information in regard to the affairs of the society to the Registrar or any person authorised by him to hold the enquiry.

Inspection

Under Section 36, if an application is made by the creditors of the society to the Registrar for the inspection of the society, the Registrar shall inspec or direct some person to inspect the books of the society. He will take such a step only when he is satisfied—

(*a*) that the debt is due to the creditor;

(*b*) that the creditor had demanded the payment;

(*c*) that the payment has not been made within a reasonable time;

(*d*) that the creditor has deposited with the Registrar a sum of money which in his opinion is sufficient to cover the cost oi the inspection.

The result of the inspection shall be communicated by the Registrar to the creditor. As regards the cost of inspection, it is the Registrar who has to decide the proportion of cost to be borne by the creditor, the members, the officers and the society (Section 37).

Any money due to the Government from a registered co-operative society is recoverable under S.44(1)(2)—

(*a*) firstly from the property of the society;

(*b*) secondly in the case of societies of which the liability of the members is limited, from the members subject to the limit of their liability; and

(*c*) thirdly in the case of other societies, from the members.

Application of Banking Regulation Act to Co-operative Banks

It may be stated here that the provisions of Section 56 of Chapter V of the Banking Regulation Act, 1949, are applicable to Co-operative Banks, e.g.,

1. The bye-laws of the co-operative banks cannot over-ride the provisions of the Banking Regulation Act, i.e., they cannot be repugnant to those provisions. If they do so, they would be void to that extent.
2. No Co-operative Society can carry on banking business unless it uses the words "bank", "banker" or "banking" as part of its name. However, this provision will not be applicable to a primary society or a co-operative society formed for the protection of the mutual interests of co-operative banks or co-operative land mortgage banks.
3. Section 10 of Banking Regulation Act regarding the appointment of Managing Agents, employment of persons who had been adjudicated as insolvent or who had been convicted by a criminal court of an offence involving moral turpitude will not be applicable to a co-operative bank.

4. No co-operative bank can commence business of banking unless the aggregate value of the paid-up capital and reserve is not less than one lakh of rupees except under certain circumstances stated in Section 56(*h*) of the Banking Regulation Act.
5. Every co-operative society, except the State Bank of India, shall maintain by way of cash reserve at least 3% of its total time and demand liabilities in India with itself or with the Reserve Bank or the State Bank of India or the State Co-operative Bank or any other bank notified by the Government in this behalf. In the case of primary co-operative banks, they shall maintain the aforesaid reserve with the Central Co-operative Bank of the district or partly in cash with itself and partly in such account or accounts.
6. No co-operative bank shall hold shares in any other co-operative society except to such extent and subject to such conditions as the Reserve Bank may specify.

After having dealt with the general provisions of the Co-operative Societies Act, 1912, and the Banking Regulation Act as far as they are applicable to co-operative banks let us now proceed with the main subject, viz., the accounts and audit of co-operative institutions.

Audit of Co-operative Institutions

The responsibility of the audit of the accounts of the co-operative institutions primarily rests with the Co-operative Department of the State Government under Section 17 of Co-operative Societies Act, 1912, since 1925; when the 1912 Act was amended, unlike the joint stock companies whose auditors are appointed by the members except under certain circumstances. This procedure may be due to the following reasons:—

(*a*) A great majority of the members of the co-operative institutions are uneducated and ill-informed. They do not know the principles of accounting or law.

(*b*) Some District or Central Co-operative Banks or the State Co-operative Banks act as the agents of the Reserve Banks of India for the distribution of loans to the farmers or producers under the Agriculture Credit Scheme of the Reserve Bank.

(*c*) Finacially helping the society in an indirect way to save them from incurring an expenditure in the appointment of an external auditor.

(*d*) If there is a supervision on the accounts which are subject to audit by an official of the Co-operative Department, the members feel assured that there is no misappropriation of the funds or fraud. This will encourage the increase in the number of members and societies.

Under the circumstances and the reasons stated above, it is deemed advisable that the Registrar should come to the aid of these institutions to maintain proper records and prepare the final accounts. It is, therefore, necessary for the Registrar to audit the accounts of a co-operative society or get the accounts audited by some person authorised by him by special order under writing. The accounts of a co-operative society must be audited at least once a year. The annual accounts are prepared on 30th June. For this purpose the Registrar should have a full control over these institutions in respect of accounts by creating departmental audit.

We have seen that the audit of these institutions is conducted by the Co-operative Department at least once in a year. This type of audit is called Statutory Audit. The Co-operative Societies Acts of several States provide that the accounts of the societies shall be conducted by the Registrar Co-operative Societies of the State or his nominee. Thus this provision assures the members who do not have a hand in the management of the society that the affairs of the society are well managed. This involves the maintenance of a large number of qualified auditors and their assistants by the Co-operative Department of the State. In addition to that the Department prepares a panel of extemal auditors who are qualified persons. For this purpose the State is divided into divisions and the Registrar appoints auditors from the panel to audit the accounts of the co-operative institutions of that particular division.

Any person who is a Chartered Accountant or G.D.A. or a retired official of the Co-operative Department may apply to the Registrar for the inclusion of his name in the panel of the auditors of the co-operative societies. A society may, if it so wishes, appoint the statutory auditor from the panel of auditors maintained by the Registrar but such an appointment is subject to confirmation by the Co-operative Department. This right of appointment of statutory auditor is given to a society by taking into consideration the following factors:—

(*a*) Whether the society is well managed, and

(*b*) Whether the accounts are properly maintained.

This right of appointment of statutory auditor is denied to District or Central Co-operative banks and the State or the Apex Co-operative banks. If, however, any such bank so desires, it may appoint the statutory auditor who will act as the internal auditor of the bank.

The right of the person appointed as auditor of a co-operative institution or society will include access to the books of account, papers and securities of the institution. Every officer of the society or institution must furnish such information in regard to all the transactions and the working of the society as the person, making such inspection may require [S.17(3)].

Rights and Duties of the Auditor

The auditor of a Co-operative Society has a right to examine the books and vouchers of the business to enable him to satisfy himself whether or not the balance sheet is drawn up, so as to exhibit a true and fair view of the state of affairs of the business, according to the best of his information and explanation given to him. To enable him to perform his duty, the auditor should take the following steps:—

1. He should study the Co-operative Societies Act, 1912, and the bye-laws of the society concerned.
2. He should see that a member does not hold more than ten per cent of the capital of the society.
3. He should vouch the receipt of cash on account of deposits with the cash book, counterfoils of the receipt book and compare them with the relative accounts. It may be stated here that some societies permit non-members to deposit money with the society. In such a case, he should refer to the regulations of the society.
4. He should vouch the money borrowed from the Central Co-operative Bank with the Cash Book, correspondence and resolution passed by the Managing Committee of the Society to borrow money, the period, the rate of interest, etc.
5. Interest received from borrowers or return of loan from them should be vouched with the agreement entered into between the society and the borrower, regulations of the society, counterfoils of the receipt book, cash book, etc.
6. Loans to the members should be vouched with the agreement, regulations and the resolution passed by the Managing Committee, receipt issued by the member concerned, cash book, etc. If under any circumstance, loan has been granted to a non-member, he should see whether permission had been obtained from the Registrar of Co-operative Societies for the grant of loan. If a loan has been advanced by the Central Co-operative Bank to a Co-operative Society he should see whether the loan advanced is within the prescribed limit laid down by the Co-operative Department.
7. He should examine the over-due debts, if any.
8. He should vouch the expenses as usual.
9. He should see that first 25 per cent of the profits of the society are carried to the Reserve Fund and ten per cent are carried to the Welfare Fund.
10. Cash in hand should be vouched by actually accounting the cash and comparing it with the cash book.

11. Investments should be verified by inspecting them and comparing them with the Investment Account in the ledger.
12. Surplus funds of a co-operative society can be invested only in Government Saving Banks or any other bank which is on the approved list of the Registrar of Co-operative Societies. Such funds can also be invested in the securities specified in Section 20 of the Indian Trust Act, 1882 or in the shares and securities of other co-operative societies with limited liability. The auditor should see that the investments are in accordance with the rules.
13. If it is a consumers society, the auditor should check the sales summaries with the sales. He should check the purchases with the order book, the stock book, etc. He should verify the stock and examine the method of valuation.
14. He should see that the accounts of the society are prepared according to the Co-operative Societies Act and the provisions of the Income Tax Act as applicable to the Co-operative Societies have been followed.
15. The Balance Sheet and Profit and Loss Account are to be drawn up in accordance with the *pro forma* which is prepared by the chief auditor of Co-operative Societies of the State in which the society is registered, given under Part V, Third Schedule, S. 56 of Banking Regulation Act, 1949. The *pro forma* is given at the end of this chapter.
16. He should satisfy himself whether or not the balance sheet is properly drawn up so as to exhibit a true and fair view of the state of affairs of the business according to the best of his information and explanation given to him.
17. The Registrars of Co-operative Societies of certain States have prescribed a *pro forma* for drawing up the auditor's report and the final accounts. The auditor should see that his report, etc., is according to the *pro forma*.
18. He should see that the Cash Reserve is according to Section 56(*i*) of Banking Regulation Act.
19. He should see that the balance sheet and the profit and loss account are drawn up according to Forms *A* and *B* given under Section 56(21) of Banking Regulation Act or as near thereto as possible unless the Registrar of Co-operative Societies has prescribed another form.
20. Furniture and stationery should be physically verified and compared with the Stock Register.
21. He should pay attention to the over-due debts, if any, valuation of assets and liabilities of the Society [S. 17 (2)].

It may be stated here that the audit of co-operative banks is more detailed as compared to commercial banks because the internal check system is not in operation in the case of co-operative banks.

THE THIRD-SCHEDULE

FORM A

Form of Balance Sheet of a Co-operative Bank

CAPITAL AND LIABILITIES — **Rs. P. Rs.P**

1. Capital:
   - (*i*) Authorised Capital ... Shares of Rs. ... each.
   - (*ii*) Subscribed Capital ... Shares of Rs.... each.
   - (*iii*) Amount called up on ... Shares of Rs. ... each

   less calls unpaid of (*iii*) above, held by
   - (*a*) Individuals
   - (*b*) Co-operative Institutions
   - (*c*) State Government
2. Reserve Fund and other Reserves:
   - (*i*) Statutory Reserve
   - (*ii*) Agricultural (Credit Stabilization Fund)
   - (*iii*) Building Fund
   - (*iv*) Dividend Equalization Fund
   - (*v*) Special Bad Debts Reserves
   - (*vi*) Bad and Doubtful Debts Reserve
   - (*vii*) Investment Depreciation Fund
   - (*viii*) Other Funds and Reserves (to be specified)
3. Principal/Subsidiary State Partnership Fund Account: For share capital of:
   - (*i*) Central Co-operative Banks
   - (*ii*) Primary agricultural credit societies
   - (*iii*) Other societies
4. Deposit and Other Accounts:
   - (*i*) Fixed deposits**
     - (*a*) Individuals**

PROPERTY AND ASSETS — **Rs. P. Rs.P**

1. Cash: In hand and with Reserve Bank, State Bank of India, State Co-operative Bank and Central Co-operative Bank.
2. Balances with other Banks:
   - (*i*) Current deposits
   - (*ii*) Savings bank deposits.
   - (*iii*) Fixed Deposits.
3. Money at Call and Short Notice.
4. Investments:
   - (*i*) In Central and State Governments securities (at book value) Face Value Rs. ... Market Value ...
   - (*ii*) Other Trustees Securities
   - (*iii*) Shares in co-operative institutions other than in item (5) below.
   - (*iv*) Other investments (to be specified)
5. Investments out of the Principal Subsidiary State Partnership Fund In shares of:
   - (*i*) Central Co-operative Banks
   - (*ii*) Primary agricultural Credit Societies
   - (*iii*) Other Societies
6. Advances :
   - (*i*) Short-term loans, cash credits, over-drafts and bills discounted.

CAPITAL AND LIABILITIES — **Rs. P. Rs P.**

(b) Central Co-operative Banks
(c) Other Societies
(ii) Savings Bank Deposits
(a) Individuals**
(b) Central Co-operative Bank
(c) Other societies
(iii) Current Deposits
(a) Individuals**
(b) Central Co-operative Banks
(c) Other deposits
(iv) Money at call and short notice

5. Borrowings
(i) From the Reserve Bank of India/State/Central Co-operative bank :
(a) Short-term loans, cash, credits and over-drafts.
Of which secured against :
(A) Government and other approved securities
(B) Other tangible securities
(b) Medium-term loans of which secured against :
(A) Government and other approved securities
(B) Other tangible securities @
(c) Long-term loans
Of which secured against :
(A) Government and other approved securities
(B) Other tangible securities @
(ii) From the State Bank of India
(a) Short-term loans, cash credits and jdrafts
Of which secured against :
(A) Government and other approved securities
(B) Other tangible securities @
(b) Medium-term loans
Of which secured against :
(A) Government and other approved securities

PROPERTY AND ASSETS — **Rs. P. Rs P.**

Of which secured against:
(a) Government and other approved securities
(b) Other tangible securities @
Of the advances, amount due from individuals
Of the advances, amount overdue :
Considered bad and doubtful of recovery
(ii) Medium-term loans
Of which secured against :
(a) Government and other approved securities.
(b) Other tangible securities @
Of the advances, amount due from individuals
Of the advances, amount overdue:
Considered bad and doubtful of recovery
(iii) Long-term loans
Of which secured against :
(a) Government and other approved securities
(b) Other tangible securities @
Of the advances, amount due from individuals
Of the advances, amount overdue
Considered bad and doubtful of recovery
Interest Receivable: of which overdue
Considered bad and doubtful of recovery

8. Bills Recievable being Bills for Collection as *per contra.*
9. Branch Adjustments
10. Premises less Depreciation
11. Furniture and Fixtures less Depreciation

CAPITAL AND LIABILITIES	Rs. P. Rs. P.	PROPERTY AND ASSETS	Rs. P. Rs. P.
(*B*) Other tangible securites @		11. Profit and Loss	
(*c*) Long-term loans		Profit as per last balance sheet	
Of which secured against :		Less appropriations	
(*A*) Government and other approved securities			
(*B*) Other tangible securities @			
From the State Government			
(*a*) Short-term loans			
Of which secured against :			
(*A*) Government and other approved securities			
(*B*) Other tangible securities @			
(*b*) Medium-term loans			
Of which secured against :			
(*A*) Government and other approved securities			
(*B*) Other tangible securities @			
(*b*) Long-term loans			
Of which secured against :			
(A) Government and other approved securities			
(*B*) Other tangible securities			
(*iv*) Loans from other sources (Source and security to be specified)			
6. Bills for collection being Bills Receivable as *per contra*			
7. Branch Adjustments			
8. Overdue Interest Reserve			
9. Interest Payable			
10. Other Liabilities			
(*i*) Bills payable.			
(*ii*) Unclaimed dividends			
(*iii*) Suspense			
(*iv*) Sundries			

12. Other Assets (to be specified)
13. Non-Banking Assets acquired in satisfaction of claims (stating mode of valuation)
14. Profit and loss

CAPITAL AND LIABILITIES

PROPERTY AND ASSETS

Rs. .P Rs.P

Rs. .P Rs.P

TOTAL

Add profit for the year brought from the Profit and Loss Accounts

Contingent Liabilities

(*i*) Outstanting Liabilities for guarantees issued

(*ii*) Others

TOTAL

NOTES

*"Fixed deposits" will include reserve fund deposits of societies, employees provident fund deposits, staff security deposits, recurring deposits, cash certificates, etc.

**Under the item "individuals" deposits from institutions other than co-operative banks and societies may be included.

†"Borrowing" and "Advances".—Short-term loans will be for periods up to 15 months, medium-term loans from 15 months to 5 years and long-term loans over 5 years.

@"Other tangible security" will include borrowings against gold and gold ornaments, repledges of goods, mortgage of land, etc.

General Instructions—The corresponding figures (to the nearest rupee, if so desired) for the years immediately preceding the year to which the balance sheet relates should be shown in separate columns.

FORM B

Form to Profit and Loss Account of a Co-operative Bank

Profit and Loss Account for the Year ended .....

EXPENDITURE	Rs. P. Rs P.	INCOME	Rs. P. Rs P.
1. Interest on deposits, borrowings, etc.		1. Interest and discount	
2. Salaries and allowances and provident fund		2. Commission, exchange and brokerage	

3. Directors' and local committee members' fees and allowances		3. Subsidies and donations	
4. Rent, taxes, insurance, lighting etc.		4. Income from non-banking assets and profit from sale of or dealing with such assets	
5. Law charges		5. Other receipts	
EXPENDITURE	Rs. P. Rs. P.	INCOME	Rs. P. Rs. P.
6. Postage, telegrams and telephone charges		6. Loss (if any)	
7. Auditor's fees			
8. Depreciation on and repairs to property			
9. Stationery, printing and advertisement, etc.			
10. Loss from sale of or dealing with non-banking assets			
11. Other expenditure			
12. Balance of profit			
TOTAL		TOTAL	

General Instructions—The corresponding figures (to the nearest rupee, if so desired) for the year immediately preceding the year to which the profit and loss account relats should be shown in separate columns.

QUESTIONS

1. Outline the special features of the audit of :

(*a*) a Co-operative Union.

(*b*) a Central C-operative Bank. (*Gauhati B. Com.* 1969)

2. You are appointed the auditor of the Central Government Employees Co-operative Society Ltd. State the matters apart from verification of its trading transactions, which would receive your attention.

3. State the restrictions placed by the Co-operative Societies Act in the matter of powers and functions of a co-operative society.

4. Draft an audit-programme for a District Co-operative Bank.

(*C.A.Final,* 1964)

5. Draw out the Audit Programme of a Commercial Bank or a Co-operative Credit Society.

(*Cal. M. Com.* 1963)

6. (*a*) What is the statutory provision for the audit of a registered Co-operative Society?

(*b*) A creditor of a Co-operative Society wants to inspect its books. How should he proceed in the matter?

(*c*) In what manner and from whom can the Government recover moneys due to it from a refer Pg 356 of proof registered Co-operative Society? (*C.A. Final,* 1976)

Chapter

27

The Audit of General Insurance Business Companies

Introduction

The insurance is a contract of indemnity between insurer and insured. The insurance may be classified into life insurance and non-life or general insurance. The business of insurance is now well superintendented and coordinated by the Insurance Regulatory and Development Authority (IRDA). The IRDA regulates the insurance business on the following lines—

- Issuing, renewing, modifying, withdrawing, suspending, or cancelling the registration of an insurer—
- Controlling, regulating the rates, advantages, terms and conditions that may be offered by the insurers in respect of general insurance business not regulated by the Tariff Advisory Committee constituted under the Insurance Act, 1938.
- Promoting, regulating the professional organisations connected with insurance and reinsurance businesses.
- Promoting efficiency in the conduct of insurance business.

Enactments affecting the business of general insurance companies.

The following enactments matter for the general insurance companies.

(*a*) The insurance Act, 1938 (and also Insurance Rules 1939 issued thereunder).

(*b*) The IRDA Act, 1999

(*c*) IRDA Regulations 1999

(*d*) The General Insurance Business (Nationalisation Act) 1972 (and also Rules made thereunder.

(*e*) The Companies Act, 1956.

Entities eligible to start insurance business

As per Section 2C of the Insurance Act, 1938 the insurance business could be started by a public company, a cooperative society or a body corporate. The third proviso to Section 2C(1) persons other than Insurance company to begin to transact the insurance business after the commencement of IRDA Act, 1999. Thus apart from existing insurance entities, no new entity could start insurance business unless it is registered as an Indian Company after the coming into effect of IRDA Act,1999. The foreign companies are allowed to invest in Indian insurance companies in equity up to 26%.

Important IRDA Regulations affecting insurance business

IRDA is empowered to frame regulations affecting various realms of insurance business. The following IRDA regulations affect the insurance business in respective areas —

- Insurance Advisory Committee (Meetings) Regulations 2000
- IRDA (Registration of Indian Insurance Companies) Regulations 2000
- IRDA (Licensing of Insurance Agents) Regulations 2000
- IRDA (Meetings) Regulations, 2000
- IRDA (Assets, Liabilities, Solvency Margin of Insurance) Regulations 2000
- IRDA (Appointed Actuary) Regulations 2000
- IRDA (Actuarial Report and Abstract) Regulations 2000
- IRDA (Insurance, Advertising and Disclosure) Regulations 2000
- IRDA (General Insurance-Reinsurance) Regulations 2000
- IRDA (Obligations of Insurers to Rural or Social Sectors) Regulations 2000
- **IRDA (Preparation of Financial Statements and Auditor's Report of Insurance Companies) Regulations, 2000.**
- IRDA (Investments) Regulations 2000;
- IRDA (Investments) (.Amendment) Regulations 2001.
- Insurance Surveyors and Loss Assessors (Licensing, Professional Requirements and Code of Conduct) Regulations 2000
- IRDA (Third Party Administrators-Health Senices) Regulations 2001.

The auditor should acquaint knowledge on various provisions of the regulations

Registration of Indian Insurance Companies.

IRDA (Registration of Indian Insurance Companies) Regulations, 2000 requires that every Indian insurance company started after the passing of IRDA Act 1999 to get it registered with IRDA. The regulations provide for various regulations concerning submission of application, power of IRDA to call for information, Power of IRDA to issue, reject the registration certificate. Section 3A of the Insurance Act, 1938 requires annual renewal of registration by IRDA.

Minimum Paid-up Capital

The minimum paid up capital of an Indian insurance company carrying on general insurance business should be Rs 100 crore or more. This minimum amount should be exclusive of "Deposit" under section 7 of the Act and also preliminary expenses not written off.

Deposit under section 7 of the Act

As per section 7 of the Insurance Act, 1938, every insurer carrying a general insurance business to deposit and keep deposited for and on behalf of Government of India a sum equivalent to 3% of total gross premia written in India in any financial year. The deposit should be accumulated up to a maximum of Rs 10 crore (Rs 20 crore for reinsurance business). The amount will not be refunded to the insurance company till the business of the insurance company is closed and all the liabilities have been settled. According to section 8 of the Act the balance lying in deposit account shall not be susceptible to any assignment or charge. It is not available for discharge of any liability of the insurer other than those arising from the insurance policies issued and remaining undischarged.

Accounts and Audit of General Insurance business

Every insurance company after the commencement of IRDA Act, 1999 should keep separate accounts for shareholders fund and the policy holders fund. The insurance company is required to prepare a Balance Sheet, a P&L account, a separate account of receipts and payments a Revenue account for each year in accordance with IRDA (Preparation of Financial Statements and Auditor's Report of Insurance Companies) Regulations, 2000. The Schedule A to the Regulations contain provisions as applicable to companies carrying on Life Insurance business. The Schedule B to the Regulations lays down the accounting principles, disclosures forming part of financial statements, general insturction for preparation of financial statements, the management report, the format for the financial statements of the companies carrying on general insurance businees. Schedule C lays down matters to be covered in Auditor's report of both life as well as general insurance business companies.

Schedule B to IRDA (Preparation of Financial Statements and Auditor's Report of Insurance Companies) Regulations, 2000.

Schedule B to IRDA (Preparation of Financial Statements and Auditor's Report of insurance Companies) Regulations, 2000 contains 5 part.

- Part I deals with Accounting principles to be followed in preparation of financial statements.
- Part II deals with the disclosures forming part of financial statements.
- Part III gives general instructions for preparation of financial statements.
- Part IV specifies the contents of confirmation, declaration, certification or disclosure to be made in Management report.

Part V deals with the format of financial statements- Revenue Account, P&L account, and Balance sheet. It also lays down requirement to compile Cash flow (Receipt and Payment) statement.

Part I of Schedule B- Certain important matters

- **Accounting principles to be followed-** Every Balance sheet, Receipts and Payments Account (Cash flow statement), Revenue account should be prepared in confirmity with the Accounting Standards issued by the Institute of Chartered Accountants of India except AS13 (Accounting for Investments) is not applicable.

  Premium Revenue Recognition- According to section 64VB of the Insurance Act, 1938, no insurer should assume any risk in India in respect of any insurance business on which premium is oridnarily payable in India unless and until the premium payable is received or guaranteed to be paid in the manner prescribed. The premium is the matching income for the claims paid cost. The premium is recognised over the policy period. The policy period is the period during which the risk will be in force. The recognition of premium over the risk period is appropriate if the pattern of occurrence of events giving rise to claims is evenly distributed over the policy period. According IRDA regulations, the premium recognition should be based on the pattern of risk to which the insurer is exposed. Generally, the pattern of risk is uniform or evenly spread and hence recognition of premium as income based on passage of time over the policy period is acceptable. However, for some classes of insurance business, the pattern of risk may not conform to this assumption. In such a case, the premium is recognised based on events information of risks that had become known during or after the accounting period. Or where the nature of insurance is that the pattern of occurrence of risks could not be taken to be even, the regulations require the insurer to make an estimation, based on his experience, of recognition of premium which should be justifiable and also be supported by external evidence, say, a certification from an actuary. Adequate disclosure of the basis of revenue recognition in respect of premium income should be made in financial statements.
- **Unearned premium-** The policy period may not always fall within or by the accounting period. It may cross the closing date of the accounting year. Where the premium is recognised as income over the policy period (by passage of time method), some portion

of premium would be left without being taken to income. Such portion is called unearned premium and is shown as reserve for unearned premium as a current liability in the balance sheet.

- **Reserve for unexpired risks-** In cases where the premium income is not recognised in view of consideration that the pattern of risk not being even, the amount lying in premium account represents amount reserved to future years in which the risk is expected to happen. The amount is called reserve for unexpired risk. Reserve for unexpired risk is shown as a provision in the balance sheet.
- **Premium deficiency-** When unearned premium is kept in current liabilities, a duty is cast on insurer by IRDA regulations for making provision for premium deficiency, where applicable. The unearned premium represents amount not taken to income, but kept for future recognition as the claim period gets over. The Regulations require that on each balance sheet date to estimate for and make provision for any contingent loss on this score. It is incumbent upon the insurer to estimate the claim cost, related cost and maintenance cost in relation to unearned premium. If the sum total of estimated claim cost, related cost and maintenance cost is well within the unearned premium reserve, then nothing needs to be further done. If the sum total of estimated claim cost, related cost and maintenance cost exceeds the relative amount lying in unearned income, then the contingent loss should be immediately recognised and a provision should be made for this deficiency in financial statement. In respect of policies exceeding four years, the estimation of claim cost, related cost and maintenance cost should be done by an actuary. The assumptions made by actuary should be disclosed in the financial statements.

Part II of Schedule B- Disclosures forming part of financial statements

The following points are to be disclosed-

- Contingent liabilities.
- Encumbrances to assets in and outside India.
- Commitments made and outstanding for loans, investments and fixed assets.
- Claims less reinsurance paid in and outside India.
- Aging of claims outstanding- claims outstanding for more than 6 months and others.
- Premium less reinsurance written from business in and outside India.
- Extent of premium income recognised based on varying risk pattern, category wise with basis and justification therefor including whether reliance had been made on external evidence.
- Value of contracts in relation to investments for purchases where delivery is pending.
- Basis of allocation of operating expenses related to insurance business to various classes of businesses.
- Historical cost of investments valued on fair values
- Computation of managerial remuneration
- Basis of amortisation of debt securities.
- Unrealised gain/losses on account of changes in fair value of investments in shares and derivatives
- Fair value of investment in property
- Claims settled and remaining outstanding for more than 6 months as on balance sheet date
- Accounting policy should be disclosed; any departure from accounting policy should also be indicated.

- The following additional information should also be provided-
- Investment made in accordance with statutory requirements
- Segregation of investment into performing and non-performing as per directives issued by IRDA.
- Percentage of business by sector
- Summary of financial statements for the last five years
- Accounting ratios as may be prescribed by IRDA.
- Basis of allocation of investment income to Revenue account and P&L account.

Part III of Schedule B- Part III contains general instructions for preparation of financial statements. It requires disclosure of corresponding amounts of previous year. The amount are allowed to be stated rounding to nearest thousands.

Part IV- Management Report

Along with the financial statements a management report incorporating prescribed confirmation, declaration, certification and disclosure from/by management. The matters to be included in Management Report are as follows

- Confirmation regarding continuing validity of registration with IRDA.
- Certification that all statutory dues been paid to the authorities.
- Confirmation that shareholding pattern and transfer of shares is in accordance with the statutory requirement.
- Declaration that the funds received from the holders of policies issued in India had not been invested outside India.
- Confirmation that required solvency margin had been maintained.
- Certification that assets in balance sheet have been reviewed and they are shown at values not exceeding the relisable or market value under relevant heading as prescribed
- Disclosure with regard to overall risk exposure and strategy to mitigate the same.
- Operations outside country: management estimate of country risk, hedging strategy
- Aging of claims with average claim settlement for last 5 years.
- Certification as to how the investments have been valued.
- Review of assets quality and performance of items of portfolio.
- A responsibility statement regarding the preparation of financial statement in accordance with accounting standards, policies, principles, consistency in application of accounting policies, reasonableness and prudence of judgement in determination of estimates, maintenance of adequate accounting records in accordance wi:h applicable provisions of Insurance Act, 1938 and the Companies Act. 1956, preparation of financial statements on going concern basis and existence and operation of effective internal audit system.

The management report should be duly authenticated by a director authorised by Board, in this behalf.

Part V of Schedule B

The balance sheet should be in the form B-BS and Revenue Account in B-RA and P&L account in B-P:L. A cash flow statement in accordance with AS 3 of ICAI under direct method should be prepared.

Audit of Accounts

The accounts of the insurer are to be audited by a Chartered Accountant as provided in section 12 of the Insurance Act, 1938. Where the insurer is a company and hence is subject to statutory audit, the accounts shall be audited in terms of provisions of the Companies Act 1956. The auditor shall have rights and duties as provided in the Companies Act, 1956

The Schedule C of IRDA (Preparation of Financial Statements and Auditor's Report of Insurance Companies) Regulations, 2000 specifies the matters to be set out in Auditor's report. They are

1. FACT PART

(*a*) That they have obtained all the information and explanations, which, to the best of their knowledge and belief, were necessary for the purposes of our audit and whether they have found them satisfactory.

(*b*) Whether proper books of accounts have been maintained by the insurer so far as appears from an examination of those books.

(*c*) Whether proper returns, audited or unaudit from branches and other offices have been received and whether they have been adequate for the purpose of their audit.

(*d*) Whether the Balance Sheet, Revenue Account, and P&L account dealt with by the Report and Receipts and Payments Accounts are in agreement with the books of accounts and returns.

(*e*) Whether the actuarial valuation of liabilities is duly certified by the appointed actuary including to the effect that assumptions for such valuation are in accordance with the guidelines and norms, if any, issued by the Authority and/ or the Actuarial Society of India in concurrence with the Authority.

2. OPINION PART

(*a*) Whether the Balance Sheet gives a true and fair view of the insurer's affairs as at the end of the financial year/ period; Whether the Revenue Account gives a true and fair view of the surplus or the deficit for the financial year/ period; Whether the Receipts and Payments Account gives a true and fair view of the receipts and payments for the financial year/ period.

(*b*) The financial statements stated at (*a*) are above are prepared in accordance with the requirements of Insurance Act. 1938 (4 of 1938), the IRDA Act. 1999 (41 of 1999) and the Companies Act, 1956 (1 of 1956) to the extent applicable and in the manner so required.

(*c*) Investments have been valued in accordance with the provisions of the At and the regulations.

(*d*) The Accounting Policies selected by the Insurer are appropriate and are in compliance with the applicable Accounting Standards and with the accounting principles as prescribed in these Regulations or any order or direction issued by the Authority in this behalf.

3. THE AUDITOR SHALL FURTHER STATE THAT

(*a*) They have reviewed the management report and that there is no apparent mistake or material inconsistencies with the financial statements.

(*b*) The insurer has complied with the terms and conditions of the registration stipulated by the Authority.

4. A CERTIFICATE FROM AUDITORS IN RESPECT THE FOLLOWING MATTERS

(*a*) They have verified the cash balance and the securities relating to the insurer's loans, reversions and life interests (in case of Life Insurers) and investments.

(*b*) The extent, if any, to which they have verified the Investments and transactions relating to any trusts undertaken by the insurer as trustee and

(*c*) No part of the assets of the policy holders's funds has been directly or indirectly applied in contravention of the provisions of Insurance Act, 1938 (4 of 1938) relating to application and investment of policy holders' funds.

A careful reading of the requirements of audit report would reveal that onerous responsibilities have been imposed on auditors of insurance companies. They have to certify the truth and fairness of financial statements (including cash flow statements); Compliance with provisions for investments; Adherence to accounting standards; Opinion as to contents of Management Report; validity of registration; non-contravention of provisions as regards, investment of policy holder funds. The requirements of section 227 of Companies Act will also be applicable to the extent, they are not inconsistent with these. CARO 2003 is specified to be not applicable to the insurance companies.

Audit of Revenue Accounts of the insurance business

Part V of Schedule B to IRDA (Preparation of Financial Statements and Auditor's Report of Insurance Companies), Regulations, 2000 requires the preparation of Revenue accounts for each class of business-fire, marine and miscellaneous insurance business, a consolidated P&L account incorporating profit/loss from each revenue accounts and income and expenditure not related to any such class of business and a common Balance Sheet.

Audit of important items of income, expenditure in revenue accounts of insurance companies are now discussed.

Premium income

1. Premium is an important revenue item for insurance business. The auditor should check the internal control prevailing in the organisation for collection and recording of premium income. The efficacy of the functioning of internal control would affect the nature, extent and timing of audit procedures to be applied by the auditors.
2. The auditor should check that no risk is assumed without collection of premium or the collection of the same has been guaranteed in the prescribed manner.
3. The Revenue recognition policy of the insurer for booking premium income should be studied. It may be by passage of time if the pattern of occurrence of risk is even. The risks pattern as envisaged by the management should be examined and it is to be checked whether the same had been evidenced by certification from actuary.
4. Allocation of premium income between revenue account on one hand, and premium received in advance reserve (or unearned premium account), provision for unexpired risk on the other hand should be verified.
5. Premium deficiency should be ascertained for policies exceeding term of 4 years (backed by actuarial analysis) and if it exists, it must be provided for.
6. Substantial checking of the premium income should be done. The counterfoil of receipts issued, cover notes, policy copy, premium chart etc., should be cross referred to and amount of premium should accordingly be vouched.
7. Premium collected from branches should be remitted to the central office in accordance with the norms laid down by the company in this regard.
8. The Share of premium due to or due from other insurance companies in respect of reinsurance/ co insurance businesses should be checked. It should be ensured that they have been duly adjusted in the books.
9. The Collection from agents should be carefully vouched.
10. The risk commencement date should be particularly noted to ensure that no pre
11. He should check the schedule of outstanding premium and ensure that they are recoverable.
12. The subsidiary ledge of premium/ premium register totals should tally with the control account in G.L
13. Accounting control including charging and payment of service tax, if any, in collection of premium should be examined.

14. In case of cancelled policies, it is to be ensured that no risk is assumed for period between original issue date and cancellation date
15. Where premium has been refunded, it is to be ensured that commission allowed earlier in relation to premium is duly reversed and adjusted.

Claims

1. Claim is an important cost for an insurer. The internal control for admission of claim, claim estimation, claim determination, claim settlement etc., should be studied.
2. Based on total claims for the year, the auditor should make a substantial checking of claims selected on test basis (by a suitable statistical/judgement sampling). He should check the claims paid with the following- Claims register maintained as per section 14 of the Insurance Act, 1938, claims docket consisting of claim intimation, copy of policy, surveyor/ loss assessor's report, details of salvage, subrogation right exercisable, bank payment for settlement of claims, acknowledgement for payment made from the claimant etc.
3. The claims cost includes besides the amount of claim, such related expenses like surveyor's fees, legal expenses etc.
4. Provision should be made in current liabilities for claims admitted but not paid.
5. Similarly provision should be made for claims unreported but occurred before balance sheet date. Review of payments/transactions subsequent to balance sheet date would help find this information.
6. The claims admitted should be only in respect of such risks as are covered under policy and for which insurance company is liable.
7. Proper adjustment should be made for claims paid for which there are reinsurance.
8. Proper provision for claims to be admitted from co insurers where the company is not a leader/ or proper adjustment for claims to be shared by other co insurers where the company is a leader in co insurance should be made.
9. Long pending claims should be scrutinised. The disclosure of average claims settlement period of time is to be made as notes to financial statements in accordance with part II Schedule B to IRDA (Presentation of Financial Statements and Auditor's report of Insurance Companies) Regulations 2000.
10. The claims should be settled net of salvage and salvage register should be checked.

Commission

1. Commission is com-ensation paid to insurance agents. The payment of commission is allowed to person who are insurance agents. The relevant provisions of Insurance Act, 1938 in this regard should be referred to.
2. The internal control system prevailing for organisation of insurance agents, the business procured by them, the commission payable should be studied.
3. The payment of commission should be vouched with- agents register, Premium register -commission column, Commission chart, Commission bill copy, bank payment voucher, acknowledgement, copy of statement of account signed by agents.
4. Tax should be deducted at source where applicable and remittance of the same should be made timely.
5. An overall review of the commission amount should be made to ensure that it reflects with the levels of business transacted.
6. Commission due but not paid should be provided for.
7. Commission should be reversed in respect of policies which had been cancelled or premia had been refunded.

Operating Expenses or management Expenses

1. Management expenses refers to all operating and administrative expenses related with insurance business. Section 40C of the Insurance Act, 1938, Rule 17E of Insurance Rules, 1939 contains provisions affecting management expenses. These must be looked into.
2. The Internal control mechanism for authorisation for incurring, payment of management expenses should be checked.
3. The management expenses to be shown in Revenue account should be only such expenses as are relatable to the business of insurance. Expenditure not related directly or indirectly to the business of insurance should find place only in P&L account and not in Revenue account
4. The management expenses are first aggregatted and allocated to different revenue accounts on justifiable basis.
5. A certificate signed by chairman, two directors, principal officer and auditor should be incorporated in revenue account stating that all management expenses wherever incurred have been fully charged to the account without omission.
6. The disclosure of the management expenses should be on the following heads—
   - Employees remuneration and welfare benefits
   - Managerial remuneration
   - Travel, conveyance, and vehicle running expenses
   - Rent, rate, taxes
   - Repairs
   - Printing and stationery
   - Communication
   - Legal and professional charges
   - Medical fees
   - Auditor's fees and expenses
   - Advertisement and publicity
   - Interest and bank charges
   - Depreciation
   - Others
7. Where any expense constitute more than 1% of net premium or Rs 5 lakhs whichever is higher), it should be specifically indicated in a sub-head of schedule others
8. Provision should be made for expenses incurred but not paid.

Audit of certain items in Balance sheet

Agent balances

1. Obtain the schedule of agents balances and tally the total with control account figure.
2. Scrutinise the agent ledger accounts for originating debits and credits.
3. Where the agent's balances show credit balance, it represents generally dues on account of commission payable to them. Vouch the payments paid since the balance sheet date.
4. Where the agents balances are in debit, it may represent premium collected and unremitted. Obtain a aging schedule of the debit balances.
5. Determine the recoverability of debit balances and ensure that unrecoverables are duly provided for.

6. Obtain confirmation of balances for large balances. Check the reconciliation for differences. Ensure that entries in reconciliation which are material in amounts are duly adjusted.
7. Check that the agent's balances do not include balances not pertaining to this codelike outstanding premium, dues from employees, development officers, inspectors, other insurance companies.

Provision for unexpired risks

The matching concept requires that premia cannot be taken to income in full for a particular period when the risk attached to the policy remain unexpired. The policies are issued throughout the year and policy period may extend beyond balance sheet date. It implies that the risk exposure still remains in future period. In such case, it is incumbent upon the insurer to make a provision for such risk in accounts. But it is time consuming and cumbersome a procedure to compute unexpired risk portion for each policy and accordingly make provision for risk out of corresponding revenue by way of premium on them. A simple formulae based on percentage method has been prescribed by Insurance Act 1938 and also the same gets sanction for allowability under Income Tax Act, 1961. Accordingly, a percentage of premium is provided for in the accounts. It is 50% for fire, marine cargo and miscellaneous insurance business. It is 100% for marine Hull.

Investments

1. The internal control system for making investment, custody, accounting, disposal should be studied.
2. The relevant provisions of insurance Act, 1938, IRDA Act 1999 and regulations thereunder affecting investment should be noted.
3. The Reporting requirement for investments should be borne in mind. Schedule C of IRDA (Preparation of Financial Statements and Auditor's Report) Regulations, 2000 requires that the auditor should state his opinion as to whether investments have been valued in accordance of the provisions of the Act and regulations thereunder. It is also to be certified that no part of the assets of the policy holders' funds have been directly or indirectly applied in contravention of the provisions of the Insurance Act, 1938 relating to the application and investment of policy holders' funds.
4. As per section 27B of the Insurance Act, 1938, no insurer carrying on general insurance business can invest or keep invested any part of his assets otherwise than in approved investments mentioned in the section. However sub-section (3) allows for investment other than approved investment subject to certain conditions stipulated being fulfilled. The section provides that investment in other than approved investments can be made by approval of all directors upto a maximum of 25% of total investment portfolio.When investment in shares of other companies are made, 27B(4) restricts that such investment should not exceed 10% of the total assets of the insurer and 10% of the subscribed capital of the company in which amount is invested. If the invested company is an insurance company or investment company, the maximum amount that can be invested therein shall be reduced to 2% of the subscribed capital of that other company.
5. IRDA (Investment) Regulations 2000 and IRDA(investment) (Amendment) Regulations 2001 stipulates the minimum investment model. It says that 20% or more of total assets should be invested in Central Government securities; 30% or more of total assets should be invested in State government and guaranteed securities (including central government securities).10% or more of total assets should be invested in approved securities as specified in the schedule to the regulations.
6. The disclosure requirement for investment should be adhered to. All investment are grouped into long term investment and short term investment. Again the invesments are further classified into categorywise classification -

(*a*) Government securities,
(*b*) Other Approved securities

Other investments - classified into-

(*i*) Shares- Equity and Preference
(*ii*) Mutual Funds
(*iii*) Derivative instruments
(*iv*) Other Securities
(*v*) Subsidiaries
(*vi*) Investment property- real estate

7. The auditor should make substantial vouching of purchase, sale of the investment. He should examine contracts, copies of delivery orders, Investment register, cash book, brokers accounts, scrips etc.
8. The auditor should physically verify the investments on the closing date of the balance sheet. In respect of investments held in dematerialised form, the relevant record evidencing investments in dematerialised forms should be checked. Confirmation certificates should be checked.
9. The auditor should examine the income from the investments are properly measured accounted. Accrued income should be provided for. Contingent liability on partly paid up shares should be disclosed.
10. The auditor should verify that the investments are valued fairly and in accordance with the consistent accounting policy adopted in this regard.

Loans

1. The auditor should obtain a schedule of balances on loans account
2. The relevant provisions of the Act should be borne in mind. An insurer is prohibited from lending to its director, manger, auditor, actuary, or officer except against the life policics within surrender value
3. Loans should be valued as to its realisibility. Necessary provision for bad and doubtful debts should be created to cover impairment loss.
4. The loans should be disclosed in the balance sheet as follows- (*a*) Security-wise classification; (*b*) Types of borrowers (loans to Government, Banks, subsidiary); (*c*) Performing vs Non Performing (*d*) Maturity wise - Long term vs Short term
5. The interest accrued on loans should be provided for.

Catastrophe Reserve

The general insurance company should create a reverse called "Catastrophe reserve" to meet the future potential liability against insurance policies in force. Catastrophe reserve is not a provision for meeting any existing known specific liability on account of policies. It is a contingency reserve. The insurance company should make a fair estimation of the amount required to be accumulated in this account.

Solvency Margin

Solvency margin means the excess of assets over liabilities valued in accordance with the provisions of the Act. IRDA (Assets, Liabilities and Solvency Margin of Insurance) Regulations 2000 provide for the method of computation of solvency margin. First assets are valued as per regulations. Certain assets are taken to be zero value irrespective of the book values. For e.g. Agents's balances and outstanding premium beyond 30 days, sundry debts not realisable, furniture, fixtures, stock of stationery, deferred expenses. Reinsurer's balances outstanding for more than 3 months, Preliminary expenses, computers older than 3 years etc,. Liabilities are to be valued as per regulations. Reserve for unexpired risks at the rate of 50% of premium for fire, marine cargo, miscellaneous businesses, 100% of premia for marine hull should be taken as liability. Also, adequate provision for Outstanding claims, Claims incurred but not reported (IBNR)(based on date of occurrence of event giving rise. to claims) should be fully provided and taken to be liability. The margin should not fall below the limits prescribed. It is 20% of net premium incurred or 30% of incurred claim or Rs 50 crore (Rs 100 crore for reinsurance) whichever is higher. The statutory auditor should certify the quantum of solvency of margin.

Reinsurance, Co insurance

The insurer cannot absorb all the risks alone. The insurance company may like to transfer some of the burden of risk to another insurance company. Such passing over of the risk to another company is called reinsurance. The company passing the risk under a policy to another insurance company is called ceding company. The company accepting the risk transferred by an insurance company is called reinsurance company. The passing of risk may be in terms of specific contract for each risk in respect of each policy chosen to be transferred or under a general cover called treaty. In the forrner case it is called facultative reinsurance. In the latter case it is called treaty reinsurance. The ceding company pays premia to the reinsurance company. It gets commission from the reinsurance company for the premium paid. The claims are settled to the insured by the ceding company and gets its share of claim loss settled from the ceding company in terms of facultative arrangement or treaty. The transactions between ceding company and reinsurance company may entail due to or due from each others. The auditor must ensure that the reinsurance is in accordance with the regulations of IRDA in this regard. The balances of the reinsurance company must be scrutinised. The auditee company may deal both in reinsurance inward and reinsurance outward.

Co insurance, on the other hand, is arrangement where the insured gets insurance cover from more than one insurance company. In reinsurance the privity of contract is between insured and ceding company only. The ceding company again enters into another contract with reinsurance company to mitigate its burden. In co insurance one of the insurance company will act as a leader of the consortium and the premia, commission, claim settlement etc will involve sharing and resultant accounting adjustment.

QUESTIONS

1. How will you vouch the premium income of a general insurance company?

2. What is premium deficiency? How is to be treated?

3. What are the matters that an auditor should be concerned with in revenue recognition of premium?

4. What is reserve for unexpired risks? How does it differ from unearned premium?

5. Write a simple programme covering broad matters for vouching claims.

6. How will you verify/vocuh (*a*) claims incurred but not reported (IBNR) (*b*) commission to agents

7. State the reporting requirement on investments in auditor's report of insurance company.

8. State any six items of matters that must be bestowed attention while verifying investment of an insurance company.

9. What is solvency margin? How is it calculated?

10. Differentiate reinsurance from co insurance.

11. Write short notes on- (*a*) Management expenses (*b*) agent balances

Chapter 28

Audit of Partnership Accounts

The business firms have realised the advantages of getting the accounts audited even though it is not necessary according to the Indian Partnership Act of 1932 unlike the Joint-Stock Companies which must get their accounts audited by duly qualified auditors. Many firms, before they are established, make provisions in the Partnership Agreement to get their accounts audited by an auditor.

The Advantages derived by getting the Accounts of a Firm audited

1. The partners are satisfied with the accounts which have been maintained by one of the partners. This will avoid any dispute or friction amongst the partners. This is why usually provisions, regarding audit for the firm's accounts, are made in the Partnership Deed of many a firm.
2. Although there is no provision regarding the sleeping partner under the Partnership Act of 1932, all the partners do not take active part in the business. If the accounts are audited by an auditor, such a partner who did not take active part in the business, will be quite satisfied that there has been no fraud.
3. In case of death or retirement of a partner or when a new partner comes in, the valuation of goodwill or the settlement of accounts on the basis of audited accounts will become very easy.
4. An auditor can sometimes suggest better methods of keeping accounts.

In addition to the above mentioned particular advantages, a firm derives all the advantages which are usually derived in getting the accounts audited.

It may be mentioned here that even if a firm wants to get its accounts audited, it is not necessary to appoint a qualified auditor as is necessary in the case of the Joint Stock Companies. The Indian Partnership Act does not lay down the qualifications, duties, powers and liabilities of an auditor as has been done by the Companies Act. Therefore, it is left to individual firms to define the powers, duties, etc., of an auditor. Each case will have to be decided on the terms of contract entered into between the firm and the auditor. But it must be remembered that the main objects of an audit of the accounts of a firm are practically the same as those of a joint Stock Company, viz., the detection of frauds and errors, prevention of fraud and errors and the verification of the profit and loss account and balance-sheet.

Procedure to be followed by a newly appointed auditor of a Partnership

1. The auditor should get definite instructions in writing as to the work to be performed by him. If in his letter of appointment, no instructions are given he should write to his

employers as to the work he is expected to do. This point was emphasised in the case of *Smith vs. Sheard* (1906). It must be made clear as to whether the work to be performed by the auditor is of the nature of accountancy or auditing. In the latter case he must get it clarified whether the audit is to be "Partial Audit" or, "Complete Audit". In the absence of any instructions regarding the mode of audit, complete audit is implied. Therefore, the auditor will be liable to pay damages if he did not conduct complete audit.

2. Whether the work to be performed by him is of the nature of the preparation of Income Tax Returns. In this connection it may be mentioned here that the Central Board of Revenue has prescribed a form in which auditors should report on the accounts of concerns which are not Joint Stock companies. According to that form he must mention (*a*) in what capacity did he work; (*b*) whether the records of the concern appear to be correct and reliable; (*c*) whether he has been able to obtain all the information and explanation which was necessary for the work entrusted to him; and (*d*) whether any restrictions were imposed upon him to carry on the work and which restrictions would put a hindrance in forming an opinion as to whether the accounts give a true and fair view of the state of affairs of the business. The Central Board of Revenue has prescribed the Form in which Report of the auditor in the case of a non-company is to be given. The form of the report is given below:—

"We have audited the foregoing Balance-Sheet as at....... and the Profit and Loss Account for the year ended...... with the books and vouchers as maintained by the said...... and report that

(*i*) we have obtained all the information and explanation required,

(*ii*) the said Profit and Loss Account and Balance-Sheet are drawn up in accordance with the said books, and

(*iii*) in our opinion, the balance-sheet contains a correct summery disclosing the general nature of property and assets and capital and liabilities and the basis of valuation of fixed assets and stocks and it exhibits a true and correct view of the state of the affairs, according to the best of our information and the explanations given to us and as shown by the books of the said.............

Place ....

Date............. Chartered Accountant.

In this connection it would be interesting to note the recommendations contained in the "Members Handbook" issued in July 1973, by the Institute of Chartered Accountants of England with regard to the certificate issued by the auditor. According to this certificate, the auditor is relieved of his liability as an auditor of the firm. The wordings of the certificates are given below:

"In accordance with the instructions given to us, we have prepared, without carrying out the audit, the annexed accounts, from the accounting records of ... and from the information and explanation supplied to us".

The Institute also recommended to the members to make it clear in all cases to the client, both at the interview and in the form of engagement letter, the scope of the work to be performed. Other recommendations were that the accounts must always be submitted to the client for approval before the auditor's report is signed and written confirmation is obtained that all relevant information has been made available; that the accounts confirm to the accepted principles so far as practicable, and that professional charges are not described in correspondence or elsewhere as "audit fee".

3. He should read carefully the Partnership Agreement.
4. He should ascertain the powers and duties of each partner.
5. He should ascertain the amount of capital to be contributed by each partner, his withdrawals, loans to or by firms, profit sharing ratio, interest on capital or drawings,

salaries, commission, provision for depreciation and reserves and so on. It may be mentioned here that in the absence of a contract to the contrary the Partnership Act lays down that each partner is to contribute equal amount of capital, no interest is to be allowed on partner's capital, profits or losses are to be shared equally, no salary is to be paid to partners, if any loan has been advanced by a partner to the firm, he is entitled to six per cent interest and so on. Under these circumstances, it is necessary for an auditor to read carefully the Partnership Agreement and he should be well conversant with the Indian Partnership Act.

6. If there is any doubt in regard to the interpretation of any clause in Partnership Agreement, he should, with the permission of his clients, consult the solicitor or the pleader who drafted the agreement.
7. In case the firm has bought the business, the auditor should examine the contract and see whether entries have been correctly recorded in the books of account. If the business has been amalgamated, he should see that the entries are properly recorded.
8. The basis of the valuation of the business amalgamated, absorbed or purchased should be enquired into.
9. If the partners keep any minute book, the auditor should refer to it for any resolution passed regarding the accounts.
10. He should get a list of the books maintained by the firm and the system of internal check in operation should be enquired into.
11. He should obtain a list of the members of the staff and officials and inquire about their powers and duties.
12. If the firm is registered he should see that all the requirements of the Partnership Act are carried out.
13. If the firm has branches, either in the country or in a foreign country, he should
    (*a*) inquire from his clients whether he should visit these branches to check the accounts; or
    (*b*) inquire from his clients whether he should accept the returns duly certified by the branch managers or local auditors, if any.
14. He should examine the contract entered into by the firm with third parties.
15. How are the accounts to be prepared on, the death of a partner or his retirement from the firm.
16. What arrangement is to be made when the partners dissolve the partnership.
17. How the goodwill of the firm is to be computed in case of the death or retirement of a partner.

It is not necessary that he should make inquiry for every point mentioned above. His method of approach and the work to be done will depend upon the circumstances of each particular case and the agreement entered into between him and his clients as explained previously. He should, before his work begins, be definite as to what work is expected of him. If there is the slightiest doubt he should get the matter clarified. He might have been appointed to act as an accountant or an auditor. Therefore, he should know exactly in what capacity he is expected to work. If he does not do so, he runs a great risk. He might be held responsible to pay damages for negligence in the performance of his duties.

In the case of *Maritime Insurance Co. vs. William. Fortune and Son*, an action was brought against the auditors after the lapse of thirty years for the damages suffered by the plaintiffs on account of the negligence of the auditors. It was held that as the auditors were given the materials to prepare the accounts and not audit them, they (auditors) acted as accountants and hence they were not responsible.

In another case, *viz., Apfel* vs. *Annan Dexter & Co.* (1926), the plaintiff brought an action against the auditors that she was defrauded by her two sons, who acted as the managers of the firm. It was pointed out that had the auditors not acted negligently the fraud would have been. detected and, therefore, damages amounting to £28,600 were claimed.

The defendants, the auditors, proved that they were asked to prepare the accounts and not to audit them and, therefore, they were not nesponsible.

The certificate given by the auditors was worded: "Prepared from the books of Mrs. Apfel and in accordance therewith." It was, therefore, held that from the form of the certificate it was clear that the work was that of accountancy and not auditing.

The Institute of Chartered Accountants of England in its **Members Handbook**, issued in 1973, recommended to its members, **inter alia**, that professional charges should not be described in correspondence or elsewhere, as "Audit Fee".

Another very interesting case in connection with the duty of an auditor of a firm is that of *Leech* vs. *Stockes Bros. & Pim* (1937). The facts of the case were that the plaintiff was a member of a firm of solicitors. He instructed the defendants, a firm of auditors, to prepare annual profit and loss accounts for submission to the taxation authorities. The defendants were supplied weekly summaries of expenses incurred and the costs of rendering services to the clients. The auditors were also informed that these records contained all the information which they would require. The auditors prepared the profit and loss accounts from these records, from 1928 to 1937. Such a profit and loss account was approved each year by a partner of the plaintiff's firm and no question was raised as to the audit of accounts or the preparation of the balance sheet.

In 1934, one of the partners of the firm of the plaintiffs died and another partner was taken in. The new partner appointed another auditor to find out the financial position of the firm. The new auditor discovered that the cashier-book-keeper of the plaintiffs had misappropriated moneys received on account of rents for several years. Mr Leech paid the amount misappropriated to his clients but filed a suit against the firm of additors to recover damages for the loss which the firm suffered on account of negligence on the part of the auditors in not discovering such frauds. It was pointed out by the plaintiffs that the defendants were negligent in not comparing the cash book with bank pass book, vouchers or receipts. It was also found that the books of account had not been properly maintained.

The plaintiffs argued that the auditors ought to have verified the records before preparing the profit and loss account. They further said that had the auditors prepared the balance-sheet, they would have discovered the fraud and hence they, were guilty of negligence in the performance of their duty.

The defendants pleaded not guilty and said that they were engaged "to prepare,ay report of profits for the Inspector of Taxes" and that "there were no proper materials available for the preparation of the balancesheet". In fact there was neither a cash book nor a clients' ledger. The firm maintained only Costs Furnished Book in which costs charged to clients and the weekly summaries of the expenses were entered. They prepared only the profit and loss account. They further said that moneys which were misappropriated belonged to clients, the profit and loss account of the plaintiffs was not affected until the necessity arose to make good the loss suffered by clients. The defendants further pointed out that they were instructed to prepare accounts to be rendered to the Inspector of Taxes and in fact such accounts were correct and hence they were not negligent in the performance of their duty.

It was held by the court that the defendants were not negligent in preparing the profit and loss account from the material supplied to them and the instructions which were given to them as to what they were to do.

The journal, *Accountant* (England), commenting on the case *Leech* vs. *Stokes Bros. & Pim* (1937), wrote in its issue of 10th July, 1937:

"The opinion of an Irish judge on a matter of law is, of course, entitled to the highest respect......... but we can only say that...... *there is in fact all the difference in the world between the functions of an accountant and those of an auditor*. The one takes the material which is presented to him and uses his technical skill and experience in accounting to perform with that material whatever his instructions may direct; the other, that is the auditor, takes the material given to him but does not take it for granted, that is to say it is part of his duty to exercise his critical faculties in deciding whether an inference can rightly be drawn from the material in the form in which he finds it." (Quoted by Lancaster).

We have so far been considering the case of an auditor who has been appointed by mutual agreement by all the partners or where there was a provision in the Partnership Agreement. Auditors may also be appointed by :

(*a*) Sleeping partners.
(*b*) Retiring partners.
(*c*) A representative of a deceased partner.
(*d*) A partner who permanently resides abroad.

Let us now deal with these cases separately.

(*a*) Audit on behalf of a Sleeping Partner

A sleeping partner is a partner who has every right of a partner except that he does not take any active part in the business. He invests his capital he is entitled to profits, his liability is unlimited and so on. When his liability is unlimited and he cannot take active part in the business, naturally he would lille to know as to how the business is being carried on, and that his co-partners are not handling the business in such a way that ultimately he may lose his capital. Therefore, he may appoint an auditor to examine the accounts to safeguard his interest. Of course this is possible only when there is a provision in the Partnership Agree to that effect or all the other partners agree for such an audit. The auditor so appointed should see that the interest of his client, viz., the sleeping partner, is not sacrificed and that it is safe. He should pay particular attention to the following points:

1. No excessive reserve is created or over-depreciation is provided as it will reduce the amount of the profit to be distributed to the partners.
2. Capital expenditure is not charged to revenue account as it will have the same effect on the distributable profit.
3. The active partners do not withdraw more money on account of profit or capital than that which is allowed by the partnership agreement.
4. The active partners do not indulge in speculative transactions which do not form part of the ordinary business.

(*b*) Audit on behalf of a Retiring Partner

An auditor is appointed by a retiring partner to see that the assets and liabilities are properly valued and that his account is correctly prepared to show the amount due to him. The auditor so appointed must pay attention to the following points:–

1. He must read the agreement carefully especially the provisions relating to the retirement of a partner.

2. He should see that such provisions are properly carried out.
3. That the assets and the liabilities are properly and correctly valued and on a just basis.
4. That outstanding assets specially goodwill and liabilities are brought into account and that they are correctly valued, so that the amount of profit or loss arrived at on the date of retirement is correct and, therefore, the amount due to the retiring partner is correct.
5. After taking into consideration the above points, the auditor should see what amount is due to the retiring partner.
6. The amount so due to a partner, sometimes, is payable at once, or by instalments in subsequent years. The auditor should see that the terms of the original agreement relating to the repayment of money due to a retiring partner are properly carried out. If the amount is to be paid by instalments, he should see that it is transferred to the Loan Account and that the interest due on such loans is duly credited to the retiring partner's Loan Account.

(*c*) Audit on behalf of the representative of a Deceased Partner

The line of action by the auditor in such a case will be the same as in the case of an auditor appointed on behalf of a retiring partner. The deceased partner might have died during the course of the financial year and, therefore, the question of computation of the profit or loss, up to the date of the death, arises. Profit or loss may be calculated on the basis of the average profit or loss of the previous year or the books of account may be closed on the date of the death of the partner and Profit and Loss Account may be prepared up to that date. But which course should be adopted? For this he should refer to the terms of the agreement.

Again the question of computing the goodwill of the firm may arise. Goodwill item may not exist in the books of account. He will have to refer to the agreement in which usually a provision is made that goodwill is to be calculated on the basis of the average profits of the previous two or three years. He should see that it is computed correctly and that no capital expenditure is charged to revenue account as this step will reduce the net profit and consequently the share of the deceased partner will also be reduced.

He should also see that correct amounts are charged to revenue account so that the interest of the deceased partner is not sacrificed. Finally the auditor should see that the account of the deceased partner is correctly debited and credited and thus find out what amount is due to such a partner. He should also find out from the Partnership Agreement as to how the amount due to the representative of the deceased partner is to be paid and advise the representative accordingly.

(*d*) Audit on behalf of a partner who is permanently resident abroad

It is sometimes decided by the retiring partner, who does not withdraw his share of capital but allows it to remain in the business, to get interest on the amount standing to his credit; he may be given a right to appoint an auditor to see that his loan to the firm is safe. This will depend upon the terms of the agreement. Similarly, a creditor who advances a certain sum of money might insist upon appointing an auditor to see that his money is safe. Such an auditor is appointed until the liability is wiped off.

The auditor should ascertain whether he is to act for the creditors alone or for both the creditors as well as the firm. His duty will be to protect the interests of all the parties and to see that the provisions of the agreement are properly carried out. He should pay attention to the following points: —

1. He should get the instructions of his client.
2. He should see that the profit is correctly calculated.

3. That she assets are reasonably depreciated.
4. The drawings of the partner are not beyond the limit as laid down in the agreement.
5. The revenue expenditure is not charged to capital.
6. The partners have not indulged in speculative transactions.

QUESTIONS

1. What are the advantages of the audit of a partnership firm? What special points should be included in the audit report in respect of such an audit? *(Osmania B. Com).*

2. Explain how the position of an auditor to a sole trader or a partnership firm is different from that of an auditor to a joint stock company. In the case of partnership audit, on what points should you refer to partnership deed? *(Calcutta B.Com.)*

3. Messrs. Auto Agencies, a partnership firm, approaches you and inquires whether it is necessary for them, under any statute or otherwise, to get their accounts audited.

You are required to advise them, explaining briefly the objects and advantages of an audit of a partnership firm. *(C.A. Inter,* Nov. 1976)

4. A Chartered Accountant has been asked by the partners of a firm to take up the audit of their accounts. State what steps he will take before he actually commences the work. *(Calcutta B.Com.)*

5. "The auditor of an individual or a firm has no statutory obligation to comply with". Discuss briefly the implications and limitations of this statement. *(Jabalpur B.Com.)*

6. Set out the steps you would take at the first audit of a small trading concern (not a limited company) showing clearly the order in which you would proceed and explain the reasons why you would adopt that order. *(C.A. Int.* 1963)

7. You have been appointed auditor to a partnership under partnership deed. To what special clauses in the partnership deed would you direct your attention during your first audit? *(Poona B. Com.)*

8. What, in your opinion, are the essential clauses to be found in the Instrument of Partnerships?

State your decision with reasons in respect of the following transactions:

Commission received by Mr. X on the purchase of a property acquired for and in the name of the firm in which he is a partner. Mr. X feels that he is entitled to the commission since he negotiated the transaction. *(CA. Final)*

9. The partners in Black & Co. inform you that their present auditor Mr. J. White, an unqualified practitioner, will not be continuing as auditor as he is retiring from practice in December, 1959. They ask you to undertake the audit of their firm's accounts as from January 1, 1960.

You are required to state

(*a*) What action, if any, you would take (giving your reasons) before agreeing to undertake the audit?

(*b*) Assuming you have accepted the appointment, what information you would require from Black & Co. to enable you to draft a suitable audit programme?

(C.A. England Inter.)

10. Mention the special points that would require the attention of the auditor in the conduct of partnership audit. *(Rajasthan, Agra B. Com.)*

11. Does the audit of accounts of a partnership differ from Company audit? If so, in what respects? *(Marathwada and Cal. B.Com.)*

Audit of Government Accounts

It is deemed necessary that mention may be made about the system of Government accounts and their audit. The book-keeping system as is adopted by the commercial concerns is not followed in Government offices although their objectives may be the same. The audit system in Government offices is, therefore, not similar to that of the commercial concerns. Let us deal with the objectives of the Government audit.

Objectives of Government audit

The following are the objectives of Government audit:—

1. To set whether there is a provision of fund for the expenditure and whether such a fund has been duly authorised by competent authority and to see that the amount spent is reasonable.
2. To see whether the expenditure is not more that the occasion demands.
3. To see that the expenditure has been properly sanctioned according to the rules and regulations.
4. To see whether the sanctioned expenditure has been incurred by an officer competent to incur such an expenditure.
5. To see whether the official has exercised his power to benefit him directly or indirectly.
6. To see that the payment has been properly and correctly classified.
7. To see whether the Government servant has exercised the same amount of care and vigilance in the matter of the expenditure as he would have done in the case of his own money.
8. To see whether the payment is to be debited to the personal account of a contractor or an employee or any other individual and whether such a payment is recoverable from such a person under any rule or order. If such an amount is recoverable, it is to be recorded in the prescribed account.
9. To see while checking the receipt—

   (*a*) that the money due from others is regularly recovered and checked against payment already made, and

   (*b*) that the amount received is duly credited to the account concerned.
10. To see while auditing the stores and stocks, whether they are properly and accurately valued, if priced accounts are maintained. It should also be seen that the rates for such goods and articles fixed initially are revised from time to time according to the market rates.

11. To see that the stock taking of the stores is periodically done or such stores are verified with the balance as shown in the Stock Register.
12. To see that the expenditure conform to the general principles—
    (*a*) that the expenditure is not more than what is necessary every Government servant has exercised reasonable care to spend the money;
    (*b*) that no authority must sanction expenditure which results in an advantage to the sanctioning authority itself;
    (*c*) that public money is not utilised for the benefit of a person or section of the community unless—
        (*i*) the amount involved is insignificant; or
        (*ii*) the claim for the amount could have the sanction of the Court behind it; or
        (*iii*) the expenditure involved is in pursuance of a recognised policy or custom.
13. To see that the amount of allowances such as travelling allowance is permissible according to the rules and such allowance is so regulated that it may not become a source of income to the recipient,
14. Mr. Ashok Chander in his book "Aspect of Audit Control" says "The purpose of Government audit is to bring to the notice of the administration lacunae in the rules and regulations, and to suggest, wherever possible, ways and means for the execution of plans and project with greater expedition, efficiency and economy.

Distinction between the Audit of Government Accounts and Commercial concerns

Having discussed the audit of Government Accounts, let us now examine the points of distinction between the audit programme of government accounts and that of the commercial concerns.

1. The audit of Government transactions whether in or outside India, is entrusted to the Audit and Accounts Department which department is quite independent of the spending department but which also compiles the major portion of the accounts which it audits. Such a procedure appears to be unreasonable in as much as the department which prepares the accounts is also entrusted with the audit work. It may be remembered that in the case of commercial concerns, the auditor never prepares the accounts which he has to audit later on.

2. The spending department in the case of Government offices itself performs a part of the work incidental to audit and thus the Audit Officer has no knowledge of the quantity or quality of the goods supplied by the supplier or the number of the workers on a particular day and so on. On the other hand, in the case of commercial concerns, the audit work is never performed by the department spending the money. Even in the case of internal audit the work of audit is undertaken by separate departmental officers who have nothing to do with either writing the accounts or spending money.

3. Treasury Officer who is not a member of the Accounts and Audit Department in a large number of cases, makes the payment on Government accounts. It is he who makes the preliminary examination of the bills which are either paid by him or by a disbursing officer of another department while in the case of commercial firms, the cashier has nothing to do with the audit or preliminary examination of the bills which are paid by him.

4. A Government audit is continuous audit because of very large number of transactions and also because a. large part of the work is concerned with the personal claims of the Government officers and others which claims have to be finalised and adjusted with greater speed but on the other hand commercial audit is, in a great majority of cases, periodical and not continuous.

GOVERNMENT ACCOUNTS AND THEIR AUDIT

The Role of Comptroller & Auditor General of India in accounts and audit of Government accounts

The Comptroller & Auditor General of India is an authority appointed by and under the constitution of India. The Constitution guaranatees his independence. He shall be appointed by the President of India; and he shall not be removed except in the manner prescribed. The approval of both the houses of Parliament signified by 2/3 majority of persons present and voting is required to remove him. His salary, terms of service are governed by The Comptroller & Auditor General's (Duties, Powers and Conditions of Service) Act, 1971. According to article 149, the C&AG shall perform such duties and exercise such powers in relation to the accounts of the Union and the States and of any other authority or body as may be prescribed by or under any law made by the Parliament. Article 150 specifies that his report shall be submitted to the President/ Governor who shall cause them to be laid before the House of Parliament/ State Legislature.

Duties and Powers of C & AG

1. **Duty to compile accounts of Union and States.** The C & AG shall be responsible for compilation of accounts of the Union and each State from the initial and subsidiary accounts rendered by them. The C & AG shall prepare the Appropriation accounts showing the receipts and disbursements for and on behalf of the Union or State concerned. The C & AG may also render such assistance or provide such information as may be necessary to the Union or States in preparation of the financial statements.
2. **Duty to audit the expenditure from the Consolidated Fund of India.** The C & AG shall be responsible for making audit and submitting report on all expenditure from the Consolidated Fund of India, Contingency Fund and Public Accounts (Audit of expenditure- audit against rules and orders, audit of sanction, audit against provisions of funds and, propriety audit, performance audit).
3. **Duty to audit the financial statements of Departmental undertakings.** The C & AG shall also be responsible for auditing the trading, manufacturing, Profit and Loss Accounts and Balance sheet and other subsidiary accounts kept in any department of the Union or State.
4. **Duty to audit the accounts of body or authority substantially financed by Government.** Where any authority or body is substantially financed by grants or loans from the Consolidated Fund of India or of any State, the C & AG shall audit the receipts and expenditure of such bodies or authority.
5. **Duty to audit the Grants or Loans.** Where any grants or loans is given from the Consolidated Fund of India, the C& AG shall scrutinise the procedures by which the sanctioning authority satisfies itself as to fulfillment of the conditions subjiect to which such grants or loans are given.
6. **Duty to check Receipts into Consolidated Fund.** The C & AG shall audit that the rules and procedures are designed and are followed to secure an effective check on the assessment, collection and proper allocation of revenue.
7. **Duty to audit stores and stocks.** The C& AG shall audit the accounts of stores and stocks kept in any office or the department of Union or State.
8. **Audit of Government Companies and Corporations.** The audit of Government companies shall be done in accordance with the directives of C & AG.

To accomplish his task effectively, the C & AG has enormous powers such as right of access, right to information, explanations, right to make reports.

I Audit of Expenditure

***(a)* Audit against Rules and Orders.** To ensure accountability for public money, it has been provided that the expenditure out of Consolidated fund should be in accordance with the rules framed under constitution or any law made thereunder. The C& AG shall examine whether the relevant rules, regulations or order dealing with incurring, claiming, sanctioning, disbursement of tih expenditure out of Consolidated Fund of India have been adhered to.

***(b)* Audit of Sanctions.** The expenditure should be one that can be incurred out of Governmental funds and the sanctioning authority should have financial powers to allow for it. The Financial powers of the sanctioning authority may be prescribed under rules, regulations, orders or delegation orders.

***(c)* Audit against provision of funds.** This audit aspect covers that the expenditure incurred is one the purpose of which is covered within the grant or appropriation and the amount incurred is well within the amount provided for in this respect.

***(d)* Propriety audit.** The audit of rules, sanction and provision is called regularity audit. An expenditure may be properly incurred and may hence be regular. The auditor should not be content with it. He should go beyond these. The necessity to incur such expenditure, the wisdom in decision, the integrity and morality in utilising the funds, etc should all be inquired into. Such an examination beyond what it looks apparently regular is called propriety audit. In propriety examination of expenditure the auditor sees that the expenditure is incurred economically and the demands of the occasion justifies the expenditure. Again the personal pecuniary benefit had not enured in incurring such expenditure. The expenditure should be for the common good and no personal or caste-biased profiteering should be involved in it.

***(e)* Performance Audit.** The perfortnance of projects, activities or operations should conform to the parameters of economy, efficiency and effectiveness. The objectives, in the form of goals, targets etc should be achieved with minimum cost, resources and without waste. The means of attaining them should also involve efficient utilisation. The optimum results within the constraints of available resources should be achieved. The effectiveness in achieving results and efficiency in utilisation of resources are critically examined in this aspect of auditing phase.

II Audit of Receipts

The objective of checking the receipts into the Consolidated Fund of India is to ensure that the system to ensure that revenue due to the Government is fairly assessed, collected and there is no leakage of income in this respect. The audit of receipts encompasses the a critical examination as to—

1. Whether there is a system involving adequate regulations and procedures to secure an effective check on the assessment, collection and proper allocation of revenues.
2. Whether the system is effectively working throughout the period without break and in effect.
3. Whether all the receipts including recovery towards debts have been correctly received, recorded and reported.
4. Whether there is a system involving checks to ensure prompt detection and investigation of irregularities, double refunds, fraudulent or forged refunds, other loss of revenue, or wilful omission to levy or collect taxes or issue refunds.
5. Whether the system of internal procedures are adequate, secure and accounting of the Demand, Collection. Refunds are in order and whether they require any improvement in any areas.

The receipts cannot be checked in full. The auditing in depth of transactions selected will give an idea to the auditor to frame a judgement as to the overall efficiency and effectiveness with which receipt operation and accounting is functioning in the Government organs. The approach will be focussing more on general review; yet the scrutiny of individual cases of demand, collection or refund is not ruled out.. Based on the test design the C & AG may like to make use of in the situation, necessary directives will be issued to the audit officers for selection and scrutiny of the cases.

III Audit of Commercial Accounts of the Government

The contemporary Government is not merely functioning as a laissez faire onlooker, protector of law and order alone but is a pro active participant in economic transactions of the economy. It does the business of commercial transactions. The Government takes the following entity forms while doing commercial transactions-

(*a*) Departmental enterprises engaged in commercial transactions subject to departmental rules and regulations.

(*b*) Statutory bodies, Corporations, established under special statutes.

(*c*) Government Companies set up under the Companies Act 1956

The audit of departmental enterprises shall have to be done in accordance with the rules and regulations of the department concerned. The enactments to which the Statutory Corporations, Bodies owe their genesis prescribe the provisions relating to the audit of accounts of such entities. The Companies Act, 1956 stipulates the audit of the government companies by qualified Chartered Accountants in accordance with the directives, superintendence of the C&AG.

Audit of Government Companies

Section 617 of the Companies Act, 1956 defines a Government company as a company in which not less than 51% of the paid up capital is held by Central Government or one or more State Governments or partly by Central Government and partly by State Government.

As per section 619B stipulates that the following companies will also be covered by the Audit as if they are Government companies— They are the companies in which not less than 51% of the paid up share capital is held by one or more of the following or any combination thereof.

(*a*) the Central Government and one or more Government companies.

(*b*) any State Government or Governments and one or more Goverment Companies.

(*c*) the Central Government, one or more State Governments and one or more Government companies.

(*d*) the Central Government and one or more corporations owned or controlled by the Central Government.

(*e*) the Central Government one or more State Governments and one or more corporations owned or controlled by the Central Government.

(*f*) one or more corporations owned or controlled by the Central Government or the state government.

(*g*) more than one government company.

Section 619 of the Companies Act, 1956 contain the provisions relating to the audit of government companies. The auditor of the government company is appointed by the Comptroller and Auditor General of India. The audit is conducted by qualified Chartered Accountants appointed by C&AG. The audit is on line with the audit of limited companies. In addition to the regular audit report, the auditors have to submit a separate report on matters to be reported by the directives of C&AG. As per section 619 (3) the C&AG shall have power -

(*a*) to direct the manner in which the company's accounts shall be audited by the auditor and give instruction in regard to any matter relating to the performance of his function as such.

(*b*) to conduct a supplementary or test audit of the company's accounts by any person authorised by him in this behalf and require the information to be provided to the person so authorised to conduct the supplementary or test audit.

The audit report will be submitted to the C&AG who shall have power to comment upon or supplement the report. The report with comments, supplementary shall be laid before the annual general meeting of the company. An annual report on the working of the company shall be prepared and it along with the auditor's report, comments, supplementary of C&AG shall be laid before both the houses of Parliament where the Central Government is a member of the Company and or before the State Legislature where the State Government is a member of the company.

QUESTIONS

1. What are the respects in which the audit of government transactions differ from the audit of commercial entities?
2. What are the different perspectives of audit of government expenditure?
3. The audit of expenditure of government involves audits of both regularity and propriety-discuss.
4. State the points that are covered in audit of receipts of the Government.
5. What are the duties and powers of the C & AG as enshrined in the Constitution of India?
6. How the commercial transactions of the Government are examined?
7. How is the auditor of a government company is appointed? What are the powers of C&AG in relation to the audits of government company?
8. Give the objectives of audit of Government accounts and compare them with those of the audit under the Companies Act, 1956. (*Gauhati M Com.*)

Cost Audit

Introduction

Cost Audit is auditing of cost records to comment whether they are properly maintained so as to give a true and fair view of the cost of production, cost of sales and margin of product. The cost audit is a critical examination on maintenance of cost records to express an opinn on their adequacy, truth and fairness, compliance to cost accounting principles. The audit involves elements of propriety in as much as the report contains the auditor's observation and suggestions on matters required to be commented.

Relevance of Cost Audit

Cost audit is mandatory for certain companies as have been so ordered. Besides, the conducting of cost audit ensures benefits to the entity, government, consumers, workers etc. The cost audit benefits on many counts.

1. Mandatory cost audit. Under Section 209 (1) (d) of the Companies Act, 1956, the Central Government may notify certain classes of companies to maintain the cost records prescribed. Under Section 233B (1), the Central Government may order the audit of such accounts in respect of any company. Thus the cost audit is mandatory in respect of such companies for which the audit has been ordered by Central Government.

2. For pricing decisions. In competitive market environment, the entity will be anxious that it does not price the product more than what it should be as any overprice may price the entity out of the market. The evils with underpricing is obviously known to anybody. The management may like to ensure that correct pricing procedure from cost considerations is followed. Again, in cost plus contracts, the contractee may require the contractor to submit his cost particulars of the job done to an auditor so as to ensure that the total cost is fairly computed without any undue artificial loads.

3. For consumers. The cost audit may sometimes be conducted to make known that cost of production and hence the price is truly and fairly computed. The consumers may themselves require the seller to show the audited cost of the product if the consumer is in an advantageous position to dictate such arrangement. Sub-contractors as suppliers of components to a big industry may be required to accumulate cost in accordance with the terms of agreement and subject to audit prescribed.

4. For Government. The Government may like the know the correct cost of production of certain goods or service in the interests of public. Also the grant of subsidy, concessions may require the correct data about cost of production.

5. For trade union. The trade unions may like to maintain the audited cost details of various products and services. Again settlement of certain trade disputes in relation to wage revision, increments, productivity linked bonus etc. may require analysis of cost data, which if, audited are reliable.

6. For taxation. Certain tax assessment requires correct details of cost of production. Especially, the indirect taxes like excise duty, service tax etc. require correct cost of production or cost of input used in production. Cost audit helps in this direction.

7. For managerial decisions. Cost audit helps the management in taking various strategic decisions. Decisions involving rehabilitation or restructuring of sick units also require careful analysis of cost data which are reliable.

Definition of Cost Audit

The terms "Cost Audit", "Management Audit" and "Efficiency Audit" have been used synonymously by many authors. However, we give a few definitions used by different writers. Smith and Day in their book 'Advanced Cost Accountancy' define it: "By the term 'Cost Audit' is meant the detailed checking of the costing system, technique and accounts to verify their correctness and to ensure adherence to the objective of cost accountancy". Another writer defines it as "Cost Audit is systematic and accurate recording of detailed transactions and operations of manufacturing, contracting, extracting, transporting, supplying, etc., so as to show the actual cost of each individual piece of work, service or separate process comprised in the operations of the business". The definition appears to be that of Cost Accountancy rather than that of Cost Audit. R.W. Dobson in his book "Introduction to Cost Accountancy" defines it: "Cost Audit is the verification of the correctness of cost accounts and of the adherence to the cost accountancy plan". According to the terminology of the Institute of Cost and Works Accountants of England it is "Verification of the correctness of cost accounts and of the adherence to the cost accounting plans". In brief cost audit is the verification of cost records.

From the above definitions, it would be observed that the auditor of cost accounts has to examine the accounts of a manufacturing or a mining company, etc., in order to see the correctness of their accounts as far as the cost of manufacture or turnover is concerned and also to see whether the plans regarding the costs have been adhered to or not.

Purpose of Cost Audit

The following are some of the purposes for which Cost Audit is undertaken:

1. To verify the arithmetical accuracy of cost accountancy entries in the books of account.

2. To find out whether the cost accounts have been properly maintained according to the principles of costing employed in the industry concerned.

3. To verify that the cost statements are properly drawn up as per the records and that they represent a true and fair views of the cost of production and marketing.

4. To find out whether each item of expenditure involved into the relevant components of the goods manufactured or produced has been properly incurred or not.

5. To find out whether the cost accounting procedures prescribed by the management have been adhered to or not.

6. To detect any error or fraud which might have been committed intentionally or otherwise.

7. Sometimes a contract is entered into between the Government and producers or manufacturers, etc., that the latter will charge such and such amount or percentage on the cost of production. Such contracts are called 'Cost plus percentage contracts'. This is done when the cost of production cannot be estimated with exactitude because of uncertain conditions, as for instance during the war. During the last Great War such contracts were entered into by the Defence authorities of the governments of several countries. Even in this country Cost Plus Percentage contracts were entered into with the manufacturers of locomotives. To determine the actual cost of production

when the goods are ready, the services of the Cost Auditor are required to see whether the chargeable expenses as recorded by the cost accountant of the manufacturer are correct or not.

8. To assist in reducing the amount of detail checking by the external auditor where the internal Cost Audit system is in operation.

L.R. Dieksee in his book, **Auditing**, now edited by Brian Mayer, says "The existence of cost accounts assumes importance for two seasons: First, the structure of cost accounts involves cost-analysis of the extent (viz., under "unit of production" as distinguished from "normal" headings) and so tends to bring to light any errors existing in the original material or the analysis thereto. Second, it is only the light of cost accounts that a reliable valuation of manufacture of cost, or work-in-progress, can be arrived at for the purpose of the balance sheet".

Distinction between Financial Audit and Cost Audit

It is very difficult to make a distinction between Financial Audit and Cost Audit from the practical point of view though in principle the difference does exist. As a matter of fact, in Cost as well as in Financial Audit, the auditor is ultimately concerned with the financial aspect of every business transaction. Of course, in the Cost Audit he does not examine the financial ledgers such as debtors, creditors, capital etc., except the stock records. However, a few points of distinction between the two audits are given in the following lines:

1. Financial Audit is compulsory under the Companies Act but Cost Audit is not compulsory except in the case of companies carrying on manufacturing or mining business, etc., and which companies have been specifically asked by the Central Government to maintain cost accounts under Section 209 (d) and get their accounts audited under Section 233 B.
2. The objects of Financial Audit are to find out whether the accounts of the company have been properly maintained and whether the balance sheet and the profit and loss account represent a true and fair view of the state of affairs of the company while in the case of Cost Audit the objects are to find out whether the expenditure involved has been wisely incurred or not and to find out the cost of manufacture of each unit of goods.
3. In the case of Financial Audit, the auditor does not go into the details of the cost records which can be made to manipulate the facts while on the other hand the Cost Auditor's duty is not only to bring to light the errors of omission and commission but also to detect manipulation in the cost accounts.
4. In the case of closing stock the auditor has to see whether it has been correctly shown and has been property valued for the purpose of the balance sheet while on the other hand the Cost Auditor has to see whether the stock is excessive or inadequate for the needs of the factory.
5. An auditor has to see whether the ledger entries and castings are arithmatically correct while the Cost Auditor has to take into account the storage cost.
6. An auditor is not concerned whether the raw materials are issued according to the programme or not but a Cost Auditor has to see to this aspect of the cost accounts.
7. The field of audit is limited but in the case of Cost Audit it is wider.
8. In the case of audit, the auditor examines the financial aspect of the accounts while the Cost Auditor is concerned with the cost aspect of the accounts.
9. The Financial Audit is primarily concerned to serve the interests of the shareholders while the Cost Audit is concerned to serve the interests of the management.
10. In the case of Financial Audit, the auditor sends the report to the management while in the case of Cost Audit, the report is sent to the Company Law Board and also to the company.

11. The role of the Financial Auditor is in the office while that of Cost Auditor is in the factory.
12. The Financial Auditor has to certify the arithmetical accuracy of the entries in "proper books of account" in respect of (a) the sums of money received and the expenditure which took place; (b) all sales and purchases of goods; and (c) the assets and liabilities of the company, while the Cost Auditor has to go through all the subsidiary ledgers"regarding facts relating to the utilisation of material, labour or other items of costs as may be prescribed."

Integration of financial and cost records

The cost records and financial records are maintained to serve the differing disclosure requirements and uses. The reconciliation of profits as shown by these two records would add additional corroboration as to proper upkeep of records under these two systems. Instead of maintaining two sets of records, an integrated accounting system which encompasses such accounting heads as are required to incorporate both the systems may also be maintained in which case, the reconciliation matters automatically get reflected through well designed account heads.

Conditions under which Cost Audit is conducted

Cost Audit was introduced in India in October 1965, when the Central Government added Clause (*d*) to Sections 209 and 233B to Section 233. These Sections have been given in the beginning of this chapter. By reading these sections, it would be observed that the audit of cost accounts of only those companies which are to maintain cost accounts under Section 209(*d*) and which companies are engaged in manufacturing, processing, mining activities, etc., can be ordered. Again the accounts of all such companies engaged in such types of business are not subject to cost audit but only those companies which may specifically be ordered to do so. Thus all the companies engaged in manufacturing processing, mining, etc., do not come under the orbit of Section 233B except those companies which have specifically been asked to do so. More and more companies are being ordered under Section 233B to get their cost accounts audited. The Central Government has framed rules regarding the audit of cycle; caustic soda, cement industries, etc. The Cost Auditor should examine these rules for general appraisal before he begins the audit of a particular industry.

OBJECTIVES OF COST AUDIT

From the point of view of Government

1. To find out whether any particular industry should be given any prize or subsidy in order to encourage, develop and expand that industry. It is not only from the point of view of the investors, producers, consumers that a reasonable price should be fixed, but since the Government is interested in the export of goods to earn foreign exchange, it is important that the goods should be priced reasonably to compete in the world market.

2. To determine whether differential pricing within the industry is desirable.

3. To determine whether a particular unit requires protection and if such protection has already been given to it, should it be removed or should it continue or curtailed.

4. To assist the Tariff Board to consider the extension or removal of protection.

5. For the purpose of comparison of cost between two companies engaged in the manufacture of identical goods to find uneconomic units and also to bring certain industries under the mischief of sections 209 and 233-B of the Companies Act.

6. To find out the accuracy of the cost accounts to see that only chargeable items are debited to the cost accounts in the case of "Cost plus Percentage Contracts" to be entered into between the Government and the manufacturers.

7. To curb the profiteering by the manufacturing concerns.

8. To reduce the cost of essential commodities.

9. To fix the selling price in order to protect the interests of the consumers.

10. To avoid waste and unnecessary expenditure by the manufacturers and thereby reduce the cost of production to make available consumers goods at reduced rates.

11. To bring to light the fraudulent intentions of the management.

12. To decide whether excise duty should or should not be reduced or removed on the finished goods.

From the point of view of manufacturers

1. To aid the management to regulate production.

2. To enable the management to choose economic methods of operations and thus earn profits to satisfy the shareholders and the investing public.

3. To enable the management to reduce the working costs by avoiding wastes.

4. To enable the management to chalk out the future policy on the basis of the report by the cost auditor especially in regard to labour, raw material, plant, etc. to maximise production and reduce the cost of production.

5. Cost analysis furnishes useful information in respect of such important matters, such as, gross margin, differential costs, replacement costs, etc.

6. To find the profitability of different units of the factory. In other words, the system is a study of the productivity or measurement of efficiency of different products manufactured by the company.

7. To fix the price when tenders or quotations have to be sent, especially in times of competition.

8. To give up the production of less economic units and pay more attention to the more profitable lines of manufacture.

9. To see the efficiency of the cost procedure introduced to avoid leakage of resources of the company, their thefts, fraud and negligence.

10. To test the effectiveness of cost control techniques and to evaluate their advantages to the enterprise.

11. To test check the evaluation of inventory and work-in-progress at various stages of completion especially at the close of the financial year.

12. To have internal control and check which may in their turn be helpful to the financial auditor.

13. To check wastage of materials and labour.

14. To fix the responsibility of an individual or of the management wherever inefficiency or wastage is found.

15. To get the up-to-date information whenever required for any purpose.

16. To value correctly the work-in-progress and the closing stock.

17. To test check important items of cost to find the accuracy of the cost figures and their reliability.

Steps taken to achieve the objectives

1. Rules have been prescribed by the Government for the maintenance of separate records relating to cost of production in the case of certain industries, such as cycle, cement, caustic soda, tyres and tubes, etc.

2. The Government requires the industries to maintain books of account in such a manner that the cost of production and cost of marketing are shown separately in order to calculate the cost of production, marketing and profit earned without any difficulty.

3. The accounts have to be prepared in such a manner that expenditure on each item, like raw materials, stores, wages, overhead charges, etc. can be ascertained.

4. If a company prepares or manufactures two kinds of goods, viz., one which is covered by the rules framed by the Government and the other does not come under this head, separate accounts should be prepared and the expenses are properly allocated to two different types of goods.

Qualifications and appointment of Cost Auditor (S. 233B)

Section 233B of the Companies Act, 1956, has been amended by the Companies (Amendment) Act, 1974, regarding the qualification of the person who can conduct cost audit, the mode of appointment, the report to be submitted by him and so on. We give below the summary of the relevant section for the benefit of the reader:—

1. The cost audit is to be done by a cost accountant only within the meaning of the Cost and Works Accountants Act, 1959.
2. However, in the event of sufficient cost accountants not being available, the Central Government may, by notification in the Official Gazette direct that Chartered Accountants possessing the prescribed qualification may be permitted to do cost audit.
3. It is only the Board of Directors with the prior approval of the Central Government which is competent to appoint cost auditor.
4. The qualifications and disqualifications prescribed for a statutory auditor under S. 226(3) and (4) are applicably to the cost auditor. It may be mentioned here that a person competent to audit the accounts of a company under S.224, is not competent to conduct cost audit. No relative of a director can be appointed as the cost auditor of the company.
5. If a person, appointed for conducting the audit of cost accounts of a company, becomes subject, after his appointment, to any of the disqualifications specified in clause (*a*) or clause (*b*) of S. 233B(5), he shall, on and from the date on which he becomes so subject, cease to conduct the audit of the cost accounts of the company.
6. If a cost auditor becomes, subject, after appointment, to any disqualification specified in S. 226(3), he shall be deemed to have vacated his office as such.
7. On receipt of an order from the Government for the appointment of a cost auditor, it shall be the duty of the company to render every assistance to such a cost auditor to conduct the cost audit.
8. The cost auditor has to submit his report to the Central Government instead of to the company. The Government may send a copy to the directors of the company.
9. The Government may call upon the company to furnish any further information and explanation on the report submitted by the cost auditor. Such information and explanation must be furnished by the company within thirty days of the receipts of the copy of the report by the company. After considering the explanation submitted by the company, the Central Government may ask the company to furnish further information and explanation within the prescribed time.
10. The Central Government may allow the company to circulate the whole or such portions of the audit report as it may specify in this behalf.
11. The company has to send the copy of the report or portions of it along with the notice of the next annual general meeting of the shareholders after the submission of the report.
12. If any default is made by the company in this regard, it shall be punishable with a fine up to rupees five thousand and every officer of the company who is in default, may be

punishable with simple imprisonment which may extend to three years or with a fine which may extend to fifty thousand rupees or both.

The Companies Act does not lay down the method of filling the vacancy by the cost auditor if he resigns; how can he be removed for misconduct, etc. Perhaps all these things depend upon the Central Government which will have to be approached in such cases.

It may be pointed out here that the Cost audit is in addition to the statutory audit of the company.

Rights and Powers of Cost Auditor

The Cost Auditor will have the same rights and powers which can be exercised by an auditor under Section 227 (1) of the Companies Act, 1956.

Cost Audit Programme

The auditor should clearly understand the cost system in operation in the company concerned. The Companies Act has not laid down the procedure in which the cost audit is to be conducted and what the Cost Auditor is expected to do. It appears that it has been left to the discretion of the Government or the company concerned to issue necessary instructions covering these points in each individual case at the time of the appointment of the Cost Auditor. The auditor should study these instructions if they have been issued.

The Cost Auditor should pay his attention to the following records:

(*a*) Records of Materials.

(*b*) Labour Records.

(*c*) Records of Overhead Charges.

(*d*) Depreciation.

(*e*) Work-in-Progress Records.

(*f*) Incomplete Contracts.

(*g*) Stores and Spare Parts Records.

We shall take each of these points separately in detail and the duties of the Cost Auditor in connection therewith.

(*a*) Records of Materials

1. The auditor should inquire whether the management has fixed the maximum quantity of raw materials which can remain in stock at any time to avoid over-stocking and thus locking up of the funds and consequently increasing the cost of production and whether the instructions in this respect have been followed faithfully.

2. He should also inquire whether the minimum quantity or the ordering level has been fixed so that orders for raw materials should be placed in time to avoid shortage of materials required for the manufacture of goods and thus causing bottlenecks with the result that the machines and labour remain idle resulting in less production. He should see that the minimum or the ordering level has been rigidly adhered to. This minimum or ordering level should be changed from time to time according to experience.

3. He should examine the authority for making purchases and inquire whether tenders or quotations are invited by the Purchasing Department before any order is placed to ensure purchases at competitive rates and whether orders are placed by authorised officials.

4. He should compare the standard costs of different items in the Stores with the purchase price. If he finds that the purchase price is higher than the standard costs he should inquire into the reasons for the purchases at higher price.

5. He should check the stores and raw materials ledger with the Delivery Notes or Goods Received Book and also with the Gate-Keeper's Book, if one is in use.

6. Adequate records should show the receipt, issue and the balance, both in quantity and value of various items of materials which are required for manufacturing or processing to enable the auditor to assess the correct value of the goods manufactured, semi-finished goods and the closing stock of materials, etc. The value of these materials should include direct and indirect charges.

7. He should see whether the materials received as per Delivery Notes have been correctly recorded in the Bin Cards as well as the stock register.

8. He should see whether the size of inventory is adequate or excessive as compared to the production programme.

9. He should compare the Stores Requisitions with the Bin Cards to see that there is no fictitious entry in the Bin Cards. He should also see that the requisitions are according to schedule to avoid unnecessary piling up of materials in the production department.

10. He should check the postings of the Stores Requisitions for direct materials with the cost sheets.

11. He should compare the total costs of the direct materials as per the various cost sheets with the direct material consumer according to consumption statements.

12. He should reconcile the total materials consumed with the cost sheets as certified by the management and the Stores Ledger.

13. He should compare the cost of production of goods with that of the previous year and if he finds an increase, he should analyse the causes of the higher costs of production which may be due to either negligence on the part of the management or it may be due to higher cost of raw materials or labour, etc.

14. Any wastage in storage, transit or for any other reasons, should be shown separately. The method of dealing with such losses in the calculation of costs should be indicated in the cost records or in a footnote, explanatory notes or in any other suitable manner.

15. He should enquire whether the system of receipt of requisitions and issue of material involves lot of paper works, filling the forms, etc., which result in bottleneck.

16. He should see that there is no possibility of pilferage in the Production Department.

17. He should see that any surplus or scraps are returned to the Stores Department from the Production Department without delay so that the job or process may not be unnecessarily debited with the whole of the cost of materials issued for the job, thus artificially increasing the cost of production.

(*b*) Labour Records

1. The Cost Auditor should compare the Attendance Register of the Workers and the operational staff kept at the gate of the factory with the Attendance Register maintained by the foreman of each Department or Section. He should compare the worker's attendance cards with the Attendance Register and the Foreman's Register. He should also examine the Leave Register.

2. If the wages are paid on piece rate basis, he should see whether proper records are maintained for the work done by the workers.

3. He should compare the piece work cards of the workers with the stock register and the wages sheets.

4. He should inquire into the system of over-time work put in by the workers, e.g., who is authorised to ask the workers to put in overtime work, how are the records for the over-time work kept, who sanctions the payment for the over-time work, the rate at which the wages are paid for

the over-time work, whether there was really the necessity of over-time work. Double the wages are payable for the over-time and hence he should see that the workers are not asked to put in over-time work unless there is an urgent contract.

5. He should inquire whether extra payments are made in regard to incentives in the form of bonus, etc. If such incentive payments are made, he should see whether such incentive payments are genuine. He should inquire as to who sanctions such payments and what records are maintained in respect of such incentives.

6. He should see whether wages and salaries paid are properly allocated to various departments, units or jobs in the factory. He should check these allocations.

7. He should check the wages and salaries, being expenditure on additions to plant, machinery or any other asset, have been allocated to the asset concerned.

8. He should inquire the reason for idle time, if any. Such idle time should be recorded separately. If the reasons for idle time are not satisfactory, he should mention this fact in his report.

9. The method of treating the idle time in calculating the cost of the product should be shown by way of a footnote.

10. He should check the time summaries with the attendance cards and the job tickets.

11. He should check the postings of the job tickets with the cost.

12. He should see that proper allocation has been made in regard to the direct and indirect labour to the different jobs and units.

13. He should compare the total direct labour cost as per the various cost sheets with the time summaries.

(*c*) Records of Overhead Charges

After having examined the relevant records relating to the materials and wages directly applicable to each job, the Cost Auditor should now proceed to examine the overhead expenses like power consumed, rent, salaries, etc., in order to ensure that they have been correctly allocated to the jobs concerned. Overheads relating to manufacture, administrative and selling and distribution activities should be distinguished from each other as he has to certify that overhead charges have been properly and correctly allocated to each job or unit.

1. He should inquire into the principles of allocation of overhead charges.

2. Whatever system of allocation of overhead charges is followed, he should see that it is consistently followed. He should inquire the principle or basis on which the overheads are allocated. He should satisfy himself that the principle or the basis of allocation is fair and equitable.

3. In order to see the accuracy of the overhead charges and their allocation to different jobs, the auditor should check a few items.

4. If the overhead expenses have not been allocated according to the principle laid down or the actual indirect expenditure has exceeded the budget or the standard expenditure significantly, he should make inquiry as to why there has been a divergence. If he is not satisfied with the explanation, he should mention this fact in his report.

5. He should reconcile the total overhead expenses as per the different cost sheets with the actual overhead expenses and if there is any difference or discrepancy, he should make inquiry.

6. He should examine the method of apportioning factory costs to ensure that it is equitable to different jobs according to the principles laid down by the management.

7. He should see that the overhead expenditure is allocated between finished and unfinished products according to the correct principles.

(*d*) Depreciation

The auditor should see that proper records have been maintained in respect of each asset over which depreciation has been provided for. The records should show the cost of each asset, the date of its acquisition, additions during the year, if any, the rate of depreciation and the total amount of depreciation written off. If expenses have been incurred on special repairs or renovation of any asset and if such expenses have been added to the value of the asset concerned, he should see that they are separately recorded indicating the basis of allocation of depreciation charges thereon.

The rate of depreciation on the assets in different departments or units should be according to Section 205(2) of the Companies Act. He should see that whatever rate of depreciation is adopted, it is followed consistently year after year. If the company has not allocated depreciation to each Department separately, the auditor should see that the total amount of depreciation on the assets may be allocated at the end of the year according to a pre-determined percentage basis.

He should pay special attention to the depreciation of plant and machinery. He should inquire whether the method of depreciating plant and machinery is suitable and sufficient for the type of plant. Whether the basis used for costing purposes differs from that used in the financial accounts? If so, he should see which method has greater merit. He should also see whether any provision has been made for the replacement cost. He should also take into consideration the risk of the plant becoming obsolete.

(*e*) Work-in-Progress Records

Work-in-Progress is that work which has not been completed at the date of the balance sheet. In order to value this asset at the date of the balance sheet; all expenses incurred, whether directly or indirectly, should be debited. Incomplete work should be treated as Work-in-Progress only when the work is nearly completion. The profit on such incomplete contracts is calculated only when two-thirds of the work is completed.

1. The Cost Auditor should inquire into the principle of allocation of the overhead charges to the work-in-progress.

2. He should inquire the basis on which the Work-in-Progress has been valued. What method has been used to find the stage of the completion of the Work-in-Progress? Whether the method employed is satisfactory.

3. He should see that there has been no under or over-valuation of the opening Work-in-Progress which may result in showing more or less profits than actually they are.

4. He should see that whatever system of allocation of overhead charges had been adopted, it is followed consistently year after year.

5. He should compare the overhead charges used with the actual rate for the year.

6. If there is any change in the basis of allocating the overheads to the Work-in-Progress during the year as compared to the previous years, he should inquire into the reasons for such a change. The resulting effect of such a change should be brought to the notice of the clients.

7. Test check the new items of overhead charges with the cost sheets to see that the allocation has been correctly done.

8. Lastly he should see that the total value of the Work-in-Progress is not disproportionate to the finished goods. If it is so, he should ask for an explanation. If he is dissatisfied with the explanation he should mention this fact in his report.

(*f*) Incomplete Contracts

1. The auditor should inquire whether measurement of works had been regularly obtained.

2. Whether there is any hazard which may cause a set-back or even cause a loss instead of the expected profit.

3. He should inquire whether raw material at the site had been lying there for unnecessarily long time before being used for the work.

(*g*) Stores and Spare Parts Records

1. He should see whether appropriate records of stores and spare parts which are required for manufacturing purposes as regards their receipt, issue and balances, both in quantity and value, have been maintained.

2. He should reconcil the value of issues and the balances of the stores and spare parts with the purchases.

3. He should see whether the value of stores and spare parts have been debited to proper heads such as manufacture, repairs to plant and machinery, repairs to buildings, etc.

4. He should check whether the value of stores and spare parts debited to manufacture have been further debited to different departments or manufacturing units or jobs or not.

5. If there has been any wastage either in storage, transit or otherwise it should be shown separately.

6. The method of dealing with such wastage or loss in the calculation of costs of the spare parts and stores should be shown in the cost records by way of a footnote or explanatory note.

7. He should check whether all charges up to the work such as carriage, customs, octroi, insurance, etc., are included in the value of the stores and spare parts while valuing them at the date of the balance sheet.

8. He should check the stores physically and compare the balance with the stores stock book. Any discrepancy should be inquired into.

9. If any items of stores are obsolete, they should be written off, Inquiries should be made as to why such stores became obsolete and why were they not used earlier.

Cost Audit Report

A duty is cast upon the cost auditor appointed under Section 233B to submit his report to the Central Govrnment. A copy of the report will also have to be given to the company. Within thirty days upon the receipt of the report, the company has to furnish information and explanation for every point of reservation or qualifications referred to in the report. It has to provide such information as may be required by the Central Government. The Central Government may also require the whole or part of the report to be circulated among the members of the company. The Central Government is empowered to take such action as it deems necessary in relation to the report.

Deriving power under Section 233B(4), the Central Government has made the Cost Audit Report Rules, from time to time. The rules were made in 1969, 1977, 1982, 1986, 1996, 2001. The Cost Audit Report Rules suppresses its earlier 1996 Rules.

Cost Audit Report Rules, 2001

The Rules require the Cost Auditor to submit his report within 180 days from the end of the closing of the year to which the report relates. The company and its evry, officer shall make available to the Cost Auditor the cost records, cost statement, annexures and proforma referred to in Cost Auditor's Report duly filled in within 135 days from the end of the year so that the cost Auditor Can do his audit upon and in relation to them. The Cost Auditor should set out his report in the format along with his observations and suggestions and also annexures and proforma as prescribed.

Reporting requirement in Cost Audit Report

The cost audit report should be in the form as prescribed in rule 4. The form should be as follows:

I/ we having been appointed as Cost Auditor's under Section 233B of the Companies Act, 1956 (1 of 1956) of .... Company Limited., having its registered office at ...., have examined the books of account prescribed under clause (*d*) of subsection (1) of Section 209 of the said Act, and other relevant records in respect of the unit .... for the period/ year .... relating to the.................. (product/activity) maintained by the company and report, in addition to my/our comment in para 3 relating to the auditor's observations and suggestions, that

1. (*i*) I /we have / have not/ obtained all the information and explanations, which to the best of my / our knowledge and belief were necessary for the purpose of this audit.

   (*ii*) Proper cost accounting records, as prescribed under clause (*d*) of sub-section (1) of section 209 of the Companies Act, 1956 have/ have not been kept by the company.

   (*iii*) Proper returns adequate for the purpose of my/our audit have/ have not been received from the branches not visited by us.

   (*iv*) The said books and records give/ do not give the information required by the Companies Act, 1956 in the manner so required.

   (*v*) The cost statements in respect of the product or activity, under reference as specified in the Annexure/ Proforma of Schedule I, Schedule II, or Schedule III of the concerned Cost Accounting Records ( ) Rules duly audited by me/us are kept in the company.

2. In my/our opinion, the company's cost accounting records have/have not been properly kept so as to give a true and fair view of the cost of production, cost of sales and margin of the product under reference as prescribed under the rules.

3. Based on my/our information of the records of the company, subject to aforesaid qualifications, if any, I/we give my/our observations and suggestions on the following :

   (*a*) The adequacy or otherwise of the cost accounting system including inventory valuation in vogue in the company and suggestions for the improvement thereof. The Cost Auditor shall also indicate the persistent deficiencies in the system as pointed out in the earlier reports but not rectified.

   (*b*) The adequacy or otherwise of the budgetary control system, if any vogue in the company.

   (*c*) Matters which appears to him to be clearly wrong in principle of apparently unjustifiable.

   (*d*) Cases, where price charged for related party transactions as defined in the respective Cost Accounting Records Rules is different from normal price, impact of such lower/ higher price on margin of the product under reference shall be specified.

   (*e*) Areas where the company is incurring losses or where there is considerable decline in profitability, the Cost Auditor shall comment on the reasons thereof including indicative break even point. The Cost Auditor shall also comment on the default, if any on the payments due to the Government, financial institutions and banks penal interest levied thereon and its impact on the cost of sales and profitability.

   (*f*) Steps required to strengthen the company under the competitive environment especially with regard to need for protection from cheaper imports, if any.

   (*g*) Export commitments of the company, vis a vis actual exports for the year, under review. Also comment on the comparative profitability and pricing policy of the company for domestic and export sales. Give impact of exports benefits/incentives offered by the Government on export profitability.

   (*h*) The scope and performance of internal audit of cost records, if any,

   (*i*) and comments on its adequacy or otherwise.

4. The Cost Auditor shall suggest measures for making further improvements in the performance in respect of cost control and cost reduction.
5. The Cost Auditor may also give his other observations and suggestions if any, relevant to the cost audit.

Dated .... Signature & Seal of Cost Auditor

Membership number

The reading of the cost audit report would suggest that the reporting requirement consists of the following :

1. The statement of facts : as to obtaining of information, maintenance of cost records, the receipt of returns from branches, the disclosure, the fact that he audited the cost records prescribed under relevant "Cost Accounting Records (product name) (e.g. cement) Rules". The Government prescribes the records to be maintained by certain type of companies under the rules. The auditor should state that he had checked them a copy of the same is with the company. Unlike in financial audit where P&L account and Balance sheet are attached to the report, the cost audit report, the cost records audited are not attached to the report in cost audit.

2. A statement of opinion that cost of production, cost of sales, margin have been reflected in such records as it appears from the examination of cost records.

3. Certain observations and suggestions on 8 areas as specified to be reported.

4. The particulars in annexure and proforma to the Report should also be certified by the Cost Auditor.

The annexure contains details as to (1) General information, (2) Cost accounting system, (3) Process of manufacture, (4) Quantitative details, (5) Major input- materials, components, consumption pattern, (6) Imported inputs, (7) Power, fuel, utilities, (8) Labour cost, (9) Repairs and maintenance, (10) Depreciation and fixed assets, (11) Gross block, depreciation, lease rent, (12) Overheads- factory, administration, selling, distribution, (13) Research and development expenses, (14) Royalty, technical know-how charges, (15) Quality control expenses, (16) Pollution control expenses, (17) Abnormal non-recurring costs, (18) Non-moving, writing off inventory, (19) Inventory valuation, verification, (20) Sales, (21) Margin, (22) Comparative margin against import, (23) Value addition and distribution of earnings, (24) Financial position and ratio analysis, (25) Capitalisation of revenue expenditure, (26) Related party transaction, (27) Central Excise reconciliation, (28) Profit reconciliation between cost and financial records.

QUESTIONS

1. What is Cost Audit? What is the principle behind it? How does it differ from Statutory Audit?

2. What do you understand by the term "Management Audit"? Discuss in brief the scope of such an audit and the benefit which the management can derive therefrom.

3. State the provisions of the Companies Act, 1956, regarding Cost Audit in the case of limited companies. Do these provisions of the Act apply to all companies engaged in manufacture or similar activities? What is the justification for a Cost Audit? Give reasons. (*Cal. B. Com. Hons.* 1968)

4. Write a note on "Cost Audit. (*Bombay B. Com.* 1968)

5. What are the qualifications of a Cost Auditor? How is he appointed? What are his powers?

6. State the points which should be borne in mind by the Cost Auditor before he commences the Cost Audit.

7. Describe a typical Cost Audit Programme.

8. What is the role of Cost Audit in the manufacturing and trading business?

9. Do you think that the statutory provision for Cost Audit in the selected industries in India is justified? Give reasons for your answer.

10. "Cost Audit of industries should follow a uniform pattern". Do you agree?

11. What points should be incorporated in the Cost Audit Report?

12. As Cost Auditor to a group of factories, describe the procedure how would you adopt the record of labour and material costs. *(I.C.W.A. Final, England)*

13. Give your reasons as to why a company or any large organisation should incur expenses of an Internal Auditor, when in fact it has to employ professional auditors to audit its annual accounts. *(C.A. England)*

14. In which direction, the costing records are of value to the auditors of the financial accounts? To what extent do you consider an independent audit of the cost accounts is necessary?

15. You are Cost Auditor to a limited company which manufactures and repairs cycles. Upon attending at the Stores Department, you find:

(*a*) That invoices representing goods purch gased are handed to the, Store-keeper when the goods arrive.

(*b*) That particulars of goods received and issued are entered by the Store-keeper in a 'Store book', no other records being kept.

(*c*) That stores are issued to foreman upon verbal request.

(*d*) That the Store-keeper is allowed to order goods direct, if under Rs. 100 in value.

(*e*) That stores 'left over' from jobs are replaced in the Store-room bins by the foreman concerned.

If you do not approve of the system of Store-keeping described above make suggestions for its improvement.

16. Compare and contrast the procedure for verification of capital work-in-progress and production work-in-progress (stock-in-progress). *(C.A. Final, May, 1969)*

Chapter 31

Management Audit

Importance of Management Audit

When the profession of accountancy developed, the management used to requisition the services of auditors to detect errors and frauds. Later on they were asked to suggest ways and means to prevent the commission of errors, frauds and manipulation of accounts. By and by the area of the functions of the auditor expanded and the statutory auditor was required to state whether the balance sheet and the profit and loss were properly drawn up according to the Companies Act and that they represented a true and fair view of the state of the affairs of the company. Now-a-days the Act enjoins the auditor, in addition to what has been stated in the foregoing lines, to state in his report whether or not the personal expenditure has been charged to revenue account; whether the prices paid for the 'stores, raw materials or other components exceeding the specified value purchased from the subsidiaries in which the directors are interested are reasonable or not; whether the rate of interest and other terms of loan in the case of concerns engaged in manufacturing, mining, processing if reasonable or not and so on.

But in spite of all these enactments and precautions, the statutory auditor never goes into the question whether the policies laid down by the management are properly carried out or not; whether any improvement in running the business can be made in order to maximise the profits or to eliminate the wastes; he is not expected to make any suggestion as to whether centralisation or decentralisation of the management is advantageous or disadvantageous; he is not concerned whether a change in the system of running the business is beneficial to the concern.

It is argued by some people that the internal auditor who is appointed by most of the large companies, fulfills all these functions as stated above. It may be pointed out that the internal auditor confines his attention to the financial aspect for the prevention and detection of errors, frauds and manipulations, etc. But today the business has become so large and complicated that many of the unhealthy situations which arise as a consequence can be attributed to the basic defects of the organisational structure and the ineffective type of the organisation. Here lies the necessity of the management auditor who pays attention to all the factors of production and to the elements of costs which are very important in the business world of today.

Due to keen competition in the business world today, the management of the industrial organisations want to minimise the cost of production which is possible by eliminating wastes, avoid bottlenecks and to utilise fully the manpower as well as the plant and machinery and so on. In order to achieve these objectives, management now-a-days recruit auditors from the fields other than that of accountancy. Such a person is called management auditor.

The area of management consultancy services has been receiving growing attention from auditors in recent years. Highly specialised techniques as operational research, statistical sampling, electronic data processing and production control, etc. has made it difficult for business concerns to maintain competent staffs for all these spheres. Mostly the limited companies are governed by the Board of Directors whose duties are onerous. If the company is successful, the directors get a vote of thanks and a word of praise. If anything goes wrong, they are invariably criticised in spite of the carefully laid down plans which their shrewdness and experience could conceive. The directors cannot pass on the blame on any other person when the things go wrong for the Board could not possibly have control on the events which no one could have forseen, e.g., the information furnished to them by the management may not be sufficient or may even be incorrect. There is only one channel of communication between the Board and the rest of the organisation and this is the managing director. Again the directors have to take immediate decision on the information or the figures furnished and they have to accept such information. As such, there is no time to investigate the correctness or otherwise of the information furnished. Thus whatever information is given to them, has to be accepted. Under the circumstances they cannot delay a full discussion and take the decision which may ultimately go wrong.

The auditors are often called upon to advise the firm as to how to minimise waste, bottlenecks, breakdowns and maximise the production of quality goods. The fees paid for these consulting services by the auditors are attractive because the client is benefitted much more than the consulting fees he pays.

Taking into consideration the above facts, the management consultancy is deemed to be a necessity. The question is what is meant by consultancy, and what are its functions. The object of management consultancy services is to imrpove the organisational operations. The management now-a-days recruit auditors from the field other than that of accountancy. This is what is called management consultancy. It is claimed that the presence of management service amount to a practical guarantee that the work will be satisfactory. The management consulting firm has to make recommendations after which its responsibility is over.

Management audit is a new concept in the sphere of auditing. It was the United States of America which coined this term. In that country the professional accountants have a management services wing which is designated as Management Audit. We have already seen while dealing with the audit of Government companies, that the auditor has to answer a questionaire relating to the management of the company in addition to the audit report, pertaining to the financial matters, which he has to submit. That is what is meant by management audit. The questionaire relates to the appraisal of the efficiency of the management.

We are also familiar with the internal audit which is an independent appraisal of the activity within the organisation for the review of accounting, financial and other business practices as a protective and constructive arm of the management. The management audit is an expansion of internal audit and which is now called Management Audit. Management Audit is the latest development of internal audit. It may be pointed out that there is some difference between Internal Audit and Managerial Audit though sometimes it is considered to be the same thing. John A. Eddy, in **The Chartered Accountant** of Canada in its March 1975 issue states "Since 1966 decidedly there is a shifting trend towards using the term management auditing in place of operational auditing."

Definition of Management Audit

Management Audit is an independent appraisal activity for the review of control of managerial functions so as to ensure compliance with the organisational objectives, policies and procedures and the management methods and purposes.

William P. Leonard defines Management Audit in his book "Management Audit" as "A comprehensive and constructive examination of an organisational structure of a company, institution or branch of Government, or of any component thereof, such as a division or department, and its plans and objectives, its means of operations, and its use of human and physical facilities".

This is a long definition but a comprehensive definition has been given by Leslie R. Howard who defines it: "Management audit is an investigation of a business from the highest level downward in order to ascertain whether sound management prevails throughout, thus facilitating the most effective relationship with the outside world and the most efficient organisation and smooth running of internal organisation". Yet another clear definition is given by Taylor and Perry who say: "Management auditing is a method to evaluate the efficiency of management at all levels throughout the organisation, or more specifically, it comprises the investigation of a business by an independent body from the highest executive level downwards, in order to ascertain whether sound management prevails throughout, and to report as to its efficiency or otherwise, with recommendations to ensure its effectiveness where such is not the case".

Thus it would be observed that the Management Audit is an examination, review and appraisal of the various policies and actions of the management. It is a tool for the evaluation of methods and performance in all the areas of the enterprise.

Objectives of Management Audit

1. The object of management audit is to reveal defects or irregularities in any of the elements examined by the management auditor and to indicate what improvements are possible to obtain the best results of the operations of the concern.
2. To assist the management to achieve the most efficient administration of the operations.
3. To suggest to the management the ways and means to achieve the objectives if the management of the organisation itself lacks in the knowledge of efficient management.
4. The management audit aims at achieving the efficiency of the management.
5. To help or aid the management, the management auditor is concerned with any phase of business activity which can be the basis of service to the management.
6. To aid the management at all levels in the effective and efficient discharge of their duties and responsibilities.

Criticism of Management Audit

There has been a certain amount of criticism against management audit. The critics of the system point out that instead of serving any useful purpose, it would discourage the initiative and dynamism of the management. The management thinks that there is bound to be some criticism and hence they will shirk doing anything new which may perhaps ultimately prove useful for the organisation. The management will not pay any attention to higher production because they will always try to keep the books of account and other data up-to-date. The management will not take any risk because their decision may prove to be wrong even though the intentions were for the good of the organisation. The critics also point out that the management auditor will always try to find out some fault or another in order to justify his appointment and existence.

The supporters of the system, however, say that the fear on the part of the management is uncalled for and is based on wrong notion. They say that the management auditor simply states as to how far the actual performance has reached, and if the target, as was laid down, has not been achieved, what were the causes of such a slackness which might have been due to unforseen circumstances or the target might have been too ambitious The management auditor suggests as to how to achieve that target. We hear a lot about the "sick textile mills". The Government may, in such a case, order the management audit with a view to examine the efficiency of the management of a particular mill. Some public enterprises are not showing good results as was expected of them.

The Government may order a management audit of such enterprises in order to find out as to where does the snag lie. Similarly a banking company would like to get management audit conducted of a prospective borrowing concern before advancing a large loan to it in order to find out whether its management is efficient and therefore it could expect to get back the money advanced. Again, some Indian companies want to set up factories in collaboration with foreign companies and therefore they would be able to persuade the foreign companies that the proposition is attractive and financially sound provided the management audit had been conducted of its business.

Under the circumstances, stated above, we may safely say that the criticism of management audit is uncalled for and if it is properly conducted, it would prove to be a good tool of management control in many a case.

Distinction between the Statutory Audit and Management Audit

1. The statutory auditor examines the historical records of the past performance while the management auditor appraises and reviews of the past as well as looks to the future with a view—

(*a*) to the assessment of the policy and planning, whether these are best and suitable for attaining the objective;

(*b*) to see whether the policy as laid down was or was not followed;

(*c*) to appraise the performance of the executives;

(*d*) to measure the performance of the business and compare the actual results with the targets;

(*e*) to analyse the data and various variations to find the cause of such variances; and

(*f*) to suggest remedial and appropriate action to achieve the target.

2. The statutory auditor reports as to the financial position of the organisation on a particular date and whether the financial statements show a true and fair view of the state of affairs of the company while the management auditor reports the performance of the management during the particular period and suggests ways and means to achieve the objectives in future, if they have not already been reached.

3. The statutory auditor does not go into the question whether the management has been active or not while the management auditor appraises the activities of the management and to find out whether they have been inefficient.

4. The statutory auditor or the financial auditor looks only at the history of financial transactions while the management auditor goes beyond the financial records into the operating areas with the aim of improving the future business operations.

5. "Management auditor's work begins where the work of the statutory auditor ends", as has been put by a writer.

6. The management auditor's duties include critical examination of the organisational structure and charts, manufacturing process, production planning and schedule, adherence to the prescribed overall efficiency as a result thereof while the statutory auditor is mainly concerned with the financial aspects of the organisation.

Who should conduct Management Audit?

The question is whether the internal auditor should carry out the appraisal of the systems and procedures or should this work be entrusted to what is known as "Organisation and Methods Study", (O & M), in case the concern has no separate O & M department of its own. The aim of both is to appraise the management. There are two views on this point. One view is that the management audit should be assigned to the internal auditor because of the following reasons:

1. The term management audit and operational audit means the same thing.

2. The internal auditor goes over the question of the performance of the management

3. The internal auditor also states whether the management control system is effective or not.

4. The internal auditor examines the short-comings of the personnel or the department of the organisation.

5. The internal auditor examines the plans and policies of the business with a view to find out the inefficiency or the effectiveness of controls and operations and he therefore suggests a change or organisational structure which will have greater flexibility and control.

Those who suggest the work to be assigned to O & M personnel advance the following arguments to support their suggestion:

1. O & M study both organisation and also the method. They study the organisational workings in order to remove the bottlenecks.

2. O & M study, of course is concerned with the appraisal of the performance by the organisational personnel as to how far they have reached the goal of the organisation.

3. O & M personnel has an analytical bent of mind in regard to the organisational structure and the methods of operations.

4. O & M personnel are technical hands and are, therefore, in a position to study the organisation more effectively.

Arguments in support of both the views appear to be sound and it is rather difficult to decide as to who should conduct management audit-internal auditor or the O & M personnel. In any case management audit is not considered to be within the purview of the professional auditor.

In any case it will depend upon the circumstances of each particular case but while taking the decision one should take into consideration the technical proficiency required of the management auditor and assign the management audit work to that particular person who is more suitable for the job irrespective of the fact whether he is an internal auditor or an C & M personnel.

Preliminaries to the Conduct of Management Audit

To achieve better results of management audit, it should be conducted by a team of experts because a variety of skills cannot be possessed by one individual. Therefore the members of the team of management auditors should consist of an accountant, an industrial engineer, a social scientist and so on and who should have proper training. Such a team should have a full backing by the top management to enable it to fully appraise the various areas of management.

Before the management auditor commences the work, he should study the details of the organisation and its plans, if any. After having studied the plan, he should cover the following matters:

1. He should see whether the plan, as laid down by the management, is suitable and practicable to achieve the objective in the circumstances of the case.

2. If he finds that the plan, as laid dawn by the management, is suitable and practicable, whether it has been able to achieve the objective.

3. He should study the position of the organisation vis-a-vis other organisations in the same field.

4. He should ask relative questions to collect the necessary information, such as :

(*a*) what is the economic outlook;

(*b*) whether the organisational structure is adequate;

(*c*) whether the controls are efficient and accurate;

(*d*) whether the protective methods are adequate;

(*e*) whether the compliance with the plans, policies, procedures, etc. are being followed;

(*f*) whether there are variances between the plans laid down and the actual , performance , or there are variances between the results of the previous year and the current year, and if so, what are the causes of such variances;

(*g*) whether the manpower and equipment is properly utilised;

(*h*) whether there are bottlenecks, and if so, what arc the causes thereof;

(*i*) whether there has been any breakdown, and if so, what were the causes thereof;

(*j*) whether the methods of operations are satisfactory;

(*k*) whether any irregularities have been committed, and if so, who committed such irregularities;

(*l*) whether there is any internal friction between the executives, and so on.

5. He may have to examine documents or other information in writing so as to confirm the information which he has already collected by asking questions.

6. After obtaining the necessary information it should be corelated so that he may be able to draw conclusions.

7. He has to compare the actual performances of the organisation

(*a*) with the actual standards laid down by the top management;

(*b*) with the performance during the previous year.

8. While corelating the relative information, he should be very careful in doing so, that he may arrive at meaningful conclusions.

9. Above all what has been stated in the foregoing paragraphs, he may have to rely on his own observation regarding the activities and conditions of the organisation. For this purpose, he may have to prepare charts and flow charts.

Management audit programme

Before the management auditor begins his work, he should chalk out the audit programme. It may be pointed out here that it is not necessary that he should rigidly adhere to the audit programme which he had chalked out. Sometimes it may perhaps be necessary to deviate here and there according to the exigency. He has to use his imagination and judgment according to the circumstances of each case.

Outlines of management audit programme

1. Organisation. He should study the structure of the organisation in the area of the management audit work assigned to him. In this connection he should compare the company's organisation chart, if any. He should ascertain whether careful attention has been paid to the principles of good organisation.

2. Plans and objectives. He should discuss the plans and objectives, of the concern with the management.

3. Policies and practices. He should find out whether the policies as laid down are properly adhered to. Whether any improvement can be made to the existing policies and practices so that they may be more effective.

4. Systems and procedures. He should study the systems and procedures with a view to find out whether there are certain defects in them. If he finds such a thing, he should suggest improvements to the existing systems and procedures.

5. Controls. He should find out whether these controls are adequate and effective. If not, he should make suggestions to make them more effective.

6. Operations. He should ascertain whether there is any loophole in the working of the organisation in connection with the manufacturing process which hinders the achievement of the maximum production. If this is the case, he should suggest ways and means to overcome these drawbacks and difficulties.

7. Layout and physical equipment. He should study the existing layout and see whether any improvement can be made therein in order to take maximum advantage of it. Similarly in regard to the physical equipment, whether better and greater use of modern physical equipment can be derived.

8. Personnel. He should see whether manpower is fully utilised and if not, what can be done to increase productivity. He should see whether there is co-operation between the workers and the management. How can better and improved relationship between them be established?

9. Regulations. He should ascertain whether the concern complies with not only its own rules and regulations and the Companies Act but also those of the municipal and local authorities.

The efficiency of the management audit will depend upon the management auditor as to how he handles the audit work; how cleverly and tactfully he extracts information; how he conducts investigation and how he analyses the data collected by him. He should bear in mind the following points while conducting audit:

1. He should look for irregularities which might have been committed.

2. He should see whether there has been any conflict and any disagreement amongst the members of the management about the planning, objectives and functions.

3. He should pay special attention to the cost element and obtain complete details in regard to this element.

4. He should be alert for weaknesses in the organisation, systems, methods, controls, objectives and personnel.

5. He should go deeper into details if he comes across any incomplete, inaccurate or inadequate data or statement.

6. He should see whether procedures, policies, etc., are properly followed.

7. He should ascertain whether or not duties and responsibilities are being carried out.

8. He should pay attention that the manpower, equipment materials, etc. have been fully utilised.

9. He should pay attention to any bottlenecks, wastes, unnecessary work, lack of coordination and other defects in all the areas of his study.

Work and Duties of the Management Auditor

In this small book it is not possible to deal in detail of the work to be done by the managing auditor in regard to different transactions. However, we shall deal with a few items in the form of synopsis. If the management auditor is satisfied as to the conditions of the general management of the business he may proceed to check the items on the following lines:

1. Production

(*a*) *Buying:* Materials of right specification, right quantities, right time, right prices.

(*b*) *Planning:* Receipt of customers orders; execution of their orders.

(c) *Processing:* If he is not a technical hand, he should be very careful in the critical analysis of the manufacturing process. He should inspect the factory or the workshop and see whether it is clean, materials are not lying in the gangways as to hinder the free movement of the workers and thus causing delay.

(*d*) *Storage:* Proper inspection of materials before storage; storage conditions; whether storage conditions will damage or deteriorate the materials; whether placed properly; safety measures; etc.

(*e*) *Internal transport and despatch:* Movement of materials; whether quick or delayed; packing problems; whether packing cases regularly supplied or not.

2. Distribution

(*a*) *Sales Records:* Whether adequate sales records are maintained; whether sales service is satisfactory; selling costs.

(*b*) *Sales Policy:* Critical examination of sales policy; sales agents; sales depots; sales reports from the agents and depots.

(*c*) *Services:* Whether there have been complaints from customers; after sale service; whether interest of customer is waning whether goodwill of the concern is maintained.

(*d*) *Publicity*: Whether scrap book is maintained in regard to publicity; is media for publicity satisfactory; whether results of advertising analysed.

(*e*) *Sales control*: Whether orders are executed promptly; whether there are complaints by customers re-delays; whether there are complaints regarding quality of goods and so on.

For want of space in this small book, we have not dealt with the work involved regarding market research, accounts, finance, personnel, etc.

Management Auditor's Report

1. Essentials of good management auditor's report

(*a*) The report should be correct, i.e., the statements which he makes in the report should be correct and should be based upon definite information he receives while engaged in the audit work.

(*b*) It should be concise, but clear-cut and comprehensive of facts.

(*c*) It should be courteous, i.e., even if it has to criticise the management, it should be so worded as to avoid unnecessary sharpness or implication.

(*d*) It should contain the recommendations if any, which should be constructive and not condemning in nature.

2. Matters to be dealt in the report

(*a*) Is the return on the investments of the shareholders poor, adequate or above average.

(*b*) Comparison of the rate of return on investment between the current year and the previous year/years.

(*c*) Comparison of the operating costs of the concern with other concerns conducting the same type of business.

(*d*) Whether plant and machinery in use is suitable or otherwise to get the maximum amount of production.

(*e*) Whether the relationship between management and the staff and the workers has been cordial.

OPERATIONAL AUDIT

Many professionals in the field view the operational audit as a tail end of the management audit. The management audit encompasses the operational audit in its fold, whether both are same or different, one may look into the philosophies and principles involved in operational audit ignoring semantic differences. In management audit, the goals, aims and strategies of management is critically looked upon for continuous improvement. On the other hand, operational audit seeks to examine the effectiveness and efficiency in achieving the goals, objectives within a given management systems. The performance of the entity is tested in operational audit in terms of attaining objectives, cost effectiveness in attaining objectives, value addition in process of attainment, growth acceptable to employer and employee and so on.

Objectives of Operational audit

1. The operational audit seeks to ensure that the business is carried on with good business control system in existence.
2. The performance of the entity is measured against models developed. Key Performance Indicators to evaluate the specific areas of performance are developed. Measurement of performance is done against these indicators. The overtime bill of a particular department the time pattern of overtime payments say, last days of month etc. may throw open certain operation Development Concerns (ODC). The planning as regards production scheduling, levelling production traffic, sub-contracting etc. are few relevant or alternative areas of concern, for example, in regard to containing overtime wages.
3. Technical costing of operations performance is done to examine cost-benefit factors associated with operations. The cost centres are accumulated for every major operations. The overall profits is not just relevant. The profit contribution from each segment of operations should be optimal. The leg should not be dragged by an operation while another operation lifts a height the goal of the entry. The operational auditor examines the cost effectiveness of the operations.
4. The organisational structure involving authority-responsibility lines, accountability staffing, co-ordination should be examined to ensure that they operate on lines contemplated.

Performance Audit

Performance Audit seeks to examine that the resources of the enterprises are put to optimal use against the parameters of efficiency, economy and effectiveness. The performance audit is an important sub-sect of Operational audit. Tile wastages in resources including time (delay) are the cost-related constraints that deter the effectiveness of the attainment of the goal. These inefficiencies must be spotted rectified by correction, changes and adaptations.

Propriety Audit

E.L. Kohler defines the propriety as that which meets the tests of public interest, commonly accepted customs and standards of conduct and particularly as applied to professional performance, requirements of law, government regulations, and professional codes. The Propriety audit is an examination that verifies whether the standards of propriety are met in transactions of the entity. Instead of limiting the auditing to verification of records, the wisdom behind the decisions are checked as it matters to common good. For example, as regards government spending, the propriety elements that need to be considered are as follows:

- The expenditure should not be prima facie more than what the occasion demands. The public money should be spent as one's own money in his pocket.
- No authority should order for expenditure which, will inur benefit directly or indirectly to him with tacit approval for private profiteering.
- The funds should not result in benefit for the particular person or persons against the denial of benefit to others.

The elements of examination of propriety in certain matters are enshrined in Companies Act, 1956. Section 227 (lA) require investigation of certain matters (like-whether personal expenses have been charged to revenue; whether loans and deposits have been camouflaged as deposits; whether fictitious entries are made in books etc.) CARO 200 3 also requires matters requiring auditor's comments on certain matters (like whether the transactions with related parties (persons specified in Section 301 register) are genuine; whether statutory dues have been remitted duly with authorities; whether the company has defaulted in repayment of loans taken from financial institutions or banks; whether the term loans obtained have been utilised for the purposes for which they were taken Section 619 (3) (a) gives power to C&AG to perform supplementary or test audit for government companies. Section 233 B gives power to Central Government to order cost audits for certain companies.

Behavioural problems associated with management audit

The management audit a whole set involving subsets of operational audit, performance audit, propriety audit may have to encounter certain behavioural problems associated with it in its performance. Few among them are

(*a*) Line and staff conflict. The line managers are doers of the function while staff advises and suggests. The management auditor's advice may sometimes provoke the ego balance between line and staff relations.

(*b*) Resistance to change. Change is often resisted and it is quite time consuming to win the others to accept and adapt for change.

(*c*) Fear of criticism, fear of penalty, fear of loss of face etc. may force the field staff to ignore the management audit and the cooperation may not be forthcoming.

These problems should be tactfully managed by the management auditor. He should bear a friendly approach. He should develop a participative style. He should not air around a scent of scepticism in his approach. He should develop empathy, realising practical difficulties in performing things. He should not build castle in air. He should devise good communication channel between him and the auditees. He should brush aside from the minds of the auditees the unfounded fears. He should work as team member for the overall well being of the entity as a whole.

Questions

1. Define management audit. State the objectives of management audit.
2. What are the aspects covered in propriety audit?
3. The Companies Act requires, though not explicitly the consideration of elements of propriety items in auditing Elucidate.
4. State the objectives of operational auditing.
5. What are the problems that may surface in implementing auditing of managerial decisions? Suggest ways to tackle them.

Chapter 32

Tax Audit

An auditor certifies the profit and loss account and balance sheet of an entity in his regular audit. Such financial statements are called general purpose financial statements. The audit report of general purpose financial statements vouchsafe the truth and fairness of operating results and financial position of the entity. They are meant to be referred by owners of the entity and others who have interest with the entity. These financial statements provide information to the readers which are necessary for proper appreciation or understanding the operating results or financial status of an entity in a general way. These statements cannot cater to the individual information requirements of varied groups of users of financial statements.

In this context, it is to be understood that the Income-Tax authorities require specific information about the accounting data of an entity. As is well known, income tax is a levy on the income of an entity. But the profit for accounting and the profit for taxation are not one and the same. Though true and fair, the profit certified by the auditor in general purpose financial statement cannot be taken for levy by Income Tax authority. The accounting profit and tax profit differ due to varied reasons. According to accounting policies, the accounting profit is to be ascertained. But tax profit is to be computed according to the provisions of the Income Tax Act and Rules. Certain expenses are allowed to be deducted under Income Tax Act though they are against accounting principles. These are allowed on various considerations like providing incentive for growth of industry. For example, the capital expenditure are not to be deducted in P & L account. But for tax accounting, capital expenditure on scientific research activities can be fully deducted. Similarly the accounting profit is arrived at after allowing certain expenses which may be disallowed under Income Tax Act. For example, a genuine revenue expenditure incurred by an entity will be allowable for computing accounting profit. But the same may not be allowable under Income Tax Act, if the payment for such expense is made by cash and not by crossed cheque or draft in cases where the amount of expenditure exceeds the specified limit. Again, for companies there may be restriction under Companies Act for incurring certain cash out-gos. There are ceiling on amount to be contributed to the charitable or other funds, for example, under Section 293 of Companies Act. Any expenditure in excess of the limit, strictly speaking, cannot be debited in P & L account and is to be shown as amount recoverable from the management who has violated the provisions. But, interestingly, the Income Tax Act may permit deductions at prescribed percentages for the full amount if the contribution is according to Income Tax Act. In addition to this difference in accounting profit and tax profit, there are procedural requirements to be complied with under Income Tax Act. For example, the tax is to be deducted according to the Income Tax Act before paying dividend, rent, interest, contractor charges etc. The amount so deducted is to be reported to the Income Tax Authorities and the same has to be remitted within the prescribed time limit. Again, for claiming certain deduction under Income Tax Act, certain conditions are to be fulfilled. These and the like reasons have created specific information requirements for tax administration. Since the Income Tax Authority cannot devote its limited time on the minutest details on various aspects including correctness of tax profit, compliance of provisions of Income Tax Act, and fulfillment of conditions for claiming deductions etc., it was felt that the expertise of the auditors could be utilised to be of assistance to Income-Tax administrators. It is in this context that the attest function of auditors in matters of income tax gained utility and significance.

Scope of Auditor's Role Under Income Tax Act

The auditor's role under Income Tax Act can be broadly summarised into (a) Conducting tax audit under section 44AB (b) Certifying in prescribed form for claiming various deductions under Income Tax Act (c) Conducting selective audit under Section 142 (2A) (d) Giving tax advice and tax planning consultancy

I. Compulsory Tax Audit (Sec 44AB)

Under section 44AB, the Income Tax Act stipulates that it is necessary to get the accounts audited in the manner provided under section 44AB in respect of specified persons. The Tax audit under section 44AB is to be carried out in respect of the accounts of a person carrying on any business or profession if a) in case of business the total sales, turnover or gross receipts exceed Rs. 40 lakhs in the previous year and b) in case of a profession if the gross professional receipt in the previous year exceed Rs. 10 lakhs. The salient features of compulsory tax audit is given below:

(1) Applicability of the section

The tax audit is applicable to persons who carry on either business or profession during the year. Even in respect of such persons, the audit is compulsory only if their turnover or professional receipt as the case may be, during the previous year exceed the specified limit. Certain exceptions are provided under the section in respect of businessmen even if their gross receipt etc., exceed the specified limit. The Income Tax Act provides for presumptive taxation (i.e, tax at a flat rate without ascertaining profit from accounts) in respect of certain classes of business. Those will be outside the purview of compulsory tax audit. Examples of the persons enjoying presumptive taxation are: Non residents deriving income from shipping business, (sec 44B), Non residents deriving income from the business of exploration of mineral oils (sec 44BB), foreign companies engaged in the business of civil construction in certain turnkey projects (sec 44BBB), persons engaged in civil construction business (sec 44AD) persons engaged in the business of plying, leasing or hiring trucks etc., (sec 44AE).

(2) Manner of Measuring Turnover etc. :

The tax audit is applicable only if the turnover or gross receipts or sales exceed the specified limit in case of businessmen. The terms sales, turnover or gross receipts have not been defined in the Income Tax Act. However, guidance is available from the pronouncement of the Institute of Chartered Accountants of India. Accordingly, these terms have to be understood by reference to their ordinarily accepted commercial meaning and in accordance with the method of accounting followed by the assessee. Sales include amount realised from the sale of scrap and by-products. It includes excise duty, sales tax, service charges for freight and forwarding etc., if and only if the sale price quoted is a composite one without specifying the details as to these extra charges. However, if the excise duty, sales tax, service charges etc. are separately indicated in the invoice and are accounted separately, they will not form part of the turnover or the sales. Again, sales or turnover does not include amount due on sale of fixed assets. The term gross receipts include all receipts arising from business or profession. It includes the receipt from sale of products or services, cash subsidies, duty drawback, insurance settlements etc.,. It does not include receipts which are not assessable as income under the head 'profits and gains of business or profession' under I.T. Act. For example, the rent receivable on house property which is assessed under the head 'income from house property' will not form part of gross receipts.

(3) Duty of the assessee under Section 44AB

The assessee has, importantly, three duties to be performed under section 44AB. They are (i) the assessee must get his accounts audited (ii) the assessee must obtain a report of audit as required under the section within the specified time. (iii) he must furnish the audit report along with the return of income to the income tax authority. Failure to comply with the provisions may attract levy of penalty. The quantum of penalty under section 271B is one half percentage of sales or gross receipts or Rs. 1,00,000 whichever is less.

(4) Tax Auditor

The tax audit report is to be given by an 'accountant' as defined in the Income Tax Act. 'Accountant' means a practising Chartered Accountant within the meaning of the Chartered Accountants Act 1949. Where the accounts of the entity are audited under any other law, the person appointed to conduct such audit can conduct tax audit also. The Institute of chartered Accountants of India has prescribed a ceiling of 30 tax audits per Chartered Accountant as a self regulatory measure among Chartered Accountants.

(5) Tax Auditor Report

The tax auditor has to submit (a) tax audit report and (b) statement of particulars. The relevant regulations are contained in Rule 6G of Income Tax Rules. In case of any person who carries on any business, the audit report should be in the form 3CA if his accounts are to be audited under any law and in the form 3CB if his accounts are not required to be audited under any law. In either case, the statement of particulars should be in the form 3CD. The form 3CA refers to the fact that statutory audit has been conducted in accordance with law and a copy of the report is attached to the tax audit report. The form 3CB contains assertions of the auditor with regard to the truth and fairness of the accounts as these have not been audited already. The contents of the form 3CD (i.e, statement of particulars) are given at the end of this chapter for reference of the students. In case of a person who carries on the profession the, the tax audit report should be in form 3-CC and the statement of particulars should be in form 3 CE. Form 3CC gives the tax auditor's opinion as to the truth and fairness of financial statements. The contents of form 3 CE are similar to the contents of form 3 CD (vide clauses 1, 2, 4, 5, 6 and 7 of form 3CD) with appropriate deletions that are not applicable to persons engaged in profession.

II. Certification For Claiming Exemptions/Deductions

The Income Tax Act provides for various exemptions and deductions. As regard, exemptions, the income as expressed to be exempted will be outside the purview of levy of income tax. For example section 10, 11 provide for exemption of certain income. As regards deductions the amount, subject to ceiling if any, provided in the Act, will be allowed to be deducted from taxable income either at the stage of computing income under various individual head or from gross total income according to the nature of deduction. For claiming certain exemption or deduction, the Act provides for fulfillment of certain conditions and compliance with certain procedures. The Act requires the audit of accounts and submission of certificate from Chartered Accountant to avail certain of these exemptions and deductions.

While tax audit under section 44AB is compulsory in respect of specified persons, the audit and obtaining of auditor's report for claiming these deductions/exemptions is optional. While non-compliance with section 44AB attracts levy of penalty, non-obtaining of auditor's certificate as provided in the relevant sections of exemption/deduction forfeits the right of the assessee to avail the deduction/exemption in his assessment of income. Though the assessee suffers tax liability, he breaches no provisions and makes no offence. Few instance wherein the Income Tax Act requires certification by Chartered Accountants for claiming exemption/deduction are listed hereunder for general appreciation of certification work under Income Tax Act.

(*i*) Audit of Public Trusts :

According to section 11 of the I.T. Act certain income of public charitable and religious trusts or the institutions are exempt from income tax. But availing of this exemption is subject to fulfillment of certain conditions specified in section 12 A. Section 12A (b) provides that where the total income of trust or the institution(before claiming exemption) exceeds Rs. 50,000 during the previous year, the accounts of the trust/institution are to be got audited by a Chartered Accountant. The auditor's report with annexure of statement of particulars is to be submitted along with the return of income. The audit report should be in form no. 10B. The form 10B contains essentially two parts. The part one deals with certification of auditor with regard to proper maintenance of books of accounts and truth and fairness of financial statements. The other part specifies list of particulars in the form of an annexture to be duly signed by the 'accountant' (i.e.,the auditor). While certifying the report the auditor has to express his opinion as to the truth and fairness of the financial statements, the auditor has to make a reasonable checking before attesting the statement of particulars as contained in annexure to his certificate.

(*ii*) Deduction Under Section 35D :

Section 35D of the Act provides that the preliminary expenses incurred by a company or a resident assessee in connection with setting up or extension of industrial undertaking are allowed to be deducted over a period of ten years. The section further provides that the deduction is admissible only if the accounts of the undertaking are audited by a Chartered Accountant and his audit report with statement of particulars in the prescribed format is forwarded to Income Tax authority along with the return of income. However, for company or co-operative assessee, the audit is not stipulated as their accounts are subject to audit under enactments.

(*iii*) Deduction Under Section 35E :

Section 35E provides for deduction of expenditure incurred by company or resident person engaged in any operation relating to prospecting for, or extraction or production of any mineral specified in seventh schedule to the Act. The expenditure specified in the Act is allowed to be deducted over a period of five years starting from the year of commercial production. The deduction is admissible only if the accounts are audited by qualified 'accountant'and his report in the prescribed format, is forwarded to I.T. authority along with the return of income. No audit needs to be conducted separately for company or co-operative assessees whose accounts are subject to audit under the relevant Acts governing them.

(*iv*) Deduction Under Section 80HH :

Section 80 HH provides for deduction from gross total income for an amount equal to 20% of profits and gains from the business of an industrial undertaking or an approved hotel set up in a backward area. The deduction is admissible for a period of 10 years starting from the year in which the industrial undertaking commenced manufacture or the hotel starts functioning. The deduction is admissible only if the accounts relevant to the previous year for which the deduction is claimed are audited by an `accountant' and his report is forwarded to the I.T. authority along with the return of income of the relevant previous year.

(*v*) Deduction Under Section 80 HHA :

Section 80HHA provides for deduction from gross total income for an amount equal to 20% of profits and gains derived from a small scale industrial undertaking within the meaning of the section. The deduction is allowed for 10 years starting from the year in which the industrial undertaking begins to manufacture or produce articles. The deduction is admissible only if the accounts are audited by an 'accountant' and his report in the prescribed format is forwarded to I.T. authority along with the return of income of the year for which deduction is claimed.

(*vi*) Deduction Under Section 80HHB :

Section 80 HHB provides for deduction from gross total income for an amount equal to 50% of the profits and gains derived from the business of execution of foreign projects in pursuance of a contract entered into by the assessee or of the execution of any work undertaken by the assessee in pursuance of a foreign project contract entered into by some other person. The deduction is admissible only if the assessee maintains separate accounts in respect of profits and gains derived from the business of execution of foreign project or the work forming part of foreign project as the case may be. In addition to that, the accounts are to be audited by a qualified 'accountant', and his report in the prescribed format is forwarded to I.T. authority along with the return of income.

(vii) Deduction Under Section 80HHC:

Where the assessee, being an Indian company or person resident in India is engaged in the business of export out of India any goods or merchandise (which the section allows for deduction), he shall be allowed from his gross total income a deduction for an amount equal to the profits derived from the export of such goods or merchandise. The person may, instead of exporting directly to a foreign country, may sell the merchandise or the goods to the export house or the trading house. In such a case too, the person will be treated as supporting manufacturer. He will be allowed deduction if he gets a certificate from the export house or trading house in the prescribed format. In such a case the export house or trading house can claim deduction only in respect of export turnover as reduced by the turnover in respect of which certificate had been issued in favour of supporting manufacturer. The profits attributable to the business of export is found by applying on the total profits of the business the proportion of export turnover to total turnover, if the goods are manufactured or processed by the assessee. On the other hand, if the goods are trading goods, the profits attributable to the export of such trading goods, is found by deducting the direct and indirect costs attributable to the goods from the export turnover. If the person makes export of trading and manufacturing goods, the profit on export of trading goods is first ascertained as above and the same is deducted from the total profits of the business and the total turnover is taken net of export turnover pertaining to the trading goods. Then the profits on export of manufactured goods is arrived at by applying on the adjusted profits the proportion of export turnover of manufactured goods to the adjusted total turnover. One of the conditions for allowing the claim is that the assessee furnishes in the prescribed form (form 10 CCAC) along with the return of income, the report of Chartered Accountant, certifying that the deduction has been correctly claimed in accordance with the section.

(*viii*) Deduction Under Section 80HHD :

Section 80 HHD provides deduction to a company or resident person engaged in the business of a hotel or of tour operator or of a travel agent for an amount specified. The amount of deduction is equal to fifty percent of profits derived from rendering such services and so much of the remaining profits as is kept apart in a special reserve to be utilised for development of the business in the manner specified. The deduction is claimable only if the receipts for services from the foreigners are in convertible foreign currency. Deduction can also be claimed if the receipts are in Indian Rupees provided the amount of Rupees had been obtained by surrendering convertible foreign currency to the authorised dealer by the foreign tourists. The profits derived from rendering services to the foreign tourists is obtained by applying on the total profits of the business, the proportion of receipts from foreign tourists to the total receipt of the business. One of the conditions for allowing the claim of deduction under this section is that the assessee furnishes along with the return of income the report of a Chartered Accountant that the deduction has been correctly claimed as per the section.

(*ix*) Deduction Under Section 80HHE :

Section 80HHE provides deduction from gross total income in respect of persons being a company or a resident engaged in the business of export of computer software or providing technical services outside India in connection with the development or production of computer software. The amount of deduction is equal to the profits attributable to the business of export of software or providing technical services outside India as the case may be. The consideration in respect of export etc., should be in convertible foreign currency and it should be brought into India within the specified time. The profit attributable to the business of export of software etc., is obtained by applying on the total profit of the business, the proportion of export turnover on this account to total turnover. One of the conditions for allowing the claim of deduction is that the assessee should furnish the report of a Chartered Accountant that the claim has been correctly made in accordance with the section in the prescribed form along with the return of income.

(*x*) Deduction Under Section 80-IA:

Section 80-IA provides for deduction to any assessee who derives profits and gains from the business of an industrial undertaking or business of a Hotel or of operating cold storage or ship provided the business has been started after Ist April 1991 but before 31st March, 1995. However, the small scale industries can commence business uptill 31st March, 2000. The amount of deduction is 30% of profits for corporate assessees and 25% for non-corporate assessees. The deduction is available for 10 years and in case of co-operative Societies the deduction is for 12 years. One of the conditions for allowing the claim of the deduction is that the accounts are to be audited and the assessee furnishes along with the return of income, the report of the auditor in the prescribed form.

III. Selective Tax Audit

Audit Under Section 142 (2A)

Under section 142 (2A), the assessing officer has power, at any stage of proceedings before him, to direct the assessee to get his accounts audited by an 'accountant' nominated by the commissioner of Income Tax Act. This direction can be given by the assessing officer if he is of the opinion that it is necessary to get the accounts audited in view of the nature or the complexity of the accounts of the assessee or in the interest of revenue. Before giving direction the prior approval of the commissioner of Income Tax has to be obtained. The commissioner will fix the remuneration and expenses payable to the auditor which is to be paid by the assessee. The audit report should be in the prescribed format and must set forth such particulars as may be prescribed and as may be required by the assessing officer.

Tax audit under section 44AB is compulsory for all cases of specified persons. Audit for claiming deductions is optional. But audit under section 142 (2A) applies to cases which are ordered by the assessing authority. Failure to comply with the direction regarding audit under section 142 (2A) entails levy of penalty. Similar is the case with non-compliance with provision regarding compulsory audit under section 44AB. In case of selective audit under section 142 (2A) the assessing officer can direct the audit of accounts even if the accounts have been audited under any law in force. But in case of the compulsory audit, if the accounts have been audited under any law in force, the audit need not be conducted again. It is enough that the report in the prescribed format in such case together with the statement of particulars as authenticated by the auditor are submitted to the I.T. Authority.

IV. Tax Consultancy And Representation

It is within the permissible realm for the tax payer to so arrange his affairs in such a manner that his tax liability is fully avoided or reduced to the minimum by resorting to lawful devices. He can so plan his affairs as to avail the maximum exemptions and deductions. He can avoid the burden of interest and penalty by complying with the procedures prescribed in the Act and Rules and adhering to time-schedule provided therein. An auditor is an expert in income tax matters by virtue of his professional knowledge and his services are often sought after. Besides tax consultancy, the auditor acts as an authorised representative of his clients before income tax authorities, in various proceedings connected with assessment, appeal etc.

FORM NO. 3CA

[See rule 6G (1) (a)]

Audit report under section 44AB of the Income-tax Act, 1961, in a case, where the accounts of the business of a person have been audited under any other law.

I/We have to report that-the statutory audit of .... (Permanent Account No............) (name and address of the assessee) was conducted by me/us/M/s........................ ......, in pursuance of the provisions of the ....Act, and I/We annex hereto a copy of my/our audit report dated........ along with a copy each of the audited profit and loss account for the year ended on .... and a copy of the audited balance sheet as at .... along with the documents declared by the relevant Act to be part of, or annexed to, the profit and loss account and balance sheet.

A further report as required under the provision to section 44AB is furnished in Form No. 3CD annexed hereto.

In my/our opinion and to the best of my/our information and according to explanations given to me/us, the particulars given in Form No. 3CD, are true and correct.

Place: ....

Date : .... (Signature)

QUESTIONS

1. Explain the provisions of Income Tax Act regarding compulsory tax audit.
2. State any five matters which are to be certified by verification in respect of statement of particulars to be attached to tax audit report of a limited company carrying on trading business.
3. What is selective tax audit under section 142 (2A) of Income Tax Act?
4. Explain generally the certification of auditors for claiming certain deductions under Income Tax Act.
5. Can auditor suggest ways to minimise tax burden of his clients. Will such a planning be construed as unethical?

Chapter 33

Divisible Profits

What are Profits

The question of the determination of profits is of great importance. The true profits of a concern not only affect its proprietors but also the Income Tax authorities as well as the Managers; Directors, etc., who are to be paid a percentage of the net profits. Therefore the question is, what are profits? It is not so easy to answer this question. Law has not defined the "profits". Even the accountants ,are not unanimous on the matter. Different authorities have defined profits in different ways. Some writers say, "Generally speaking, the profit of a business during a given period is the excess of income over expenditure for the period". Others have defined it: "It is the excess of the assets over the liabilities and the capital between the two periods." "Profits are ascertained by setting against the income earned, the cost of earning it." (Lord Herschell in *Gresham Life Assurance Society* vs. *Styles*, 1892). Profits means profits realised. (*Union Bank of Allahabad*, 1925). Profits may arise from trade as well as other sources. What is profit has been well answered in the judgment in the case of the *Spanish Prospecting Co. Ltd.*, (1911). We are, therefore, tempted to quote extracts from the decision of the learned Judge:—

". . . If the total assets of the business at two dates be compared, the increase which they show at the later date as compared with the earlier date (due allowance, of course, being made for any capital introduction into or taken out of the business in the meanwhile), represents, in strictness the profits of the business during the period in question. The strict meaning of the 'Profit' is rarely observed in drawing up the accounts of firms and companies. . . Certain assumptions have become so customary in drawing up balance-sheets and profit and loss accounts that it may almost be said to require special circumstances to induce parties to depart therefrom. For instance, it is usual to exclude gains and losses arising from causes not directly connected with the business of the company. ... The value assigned to trade buildings and plant is usually fixed according to arbitrary rule, by which they are originally taken at their actual cost and are assumed to have depreciated by a certain percentage each year, though it cannot be pretended that any such calculation necessarily gives their true value either in use or exchange. . . It is better to underrate than to overrate the profits since it is impossible for you to see all the risks to which a business may in future be exposed. . . .But though there is a wide field for variation of practice in these estimation of profits, this liberty ceases at once when the rights of third parties intervene. . . .In the absence of certain stipulation to the contrary, 'profits', in cases where the rights of third parties come in, mean actual profits and they must be calculated as clearly as possible, in accordance with the definition to which I have referred".

Problems which arise in the Determination of Profits

But the determination of profits is not so easy as it may appear to be at first sight. There may be lot of complications, e.g.,

1. *The valuation of fixed assets*—how to value the assets at the close of the period? At what rate they should be valued? If they are not valued at uniform rates, the profits of the concern may fluctuate from year to year. In case of fixed assets, what should be the rate of depreciation? The charge for depreciation is always an estimate. The life of an asset cannot be correctly computed. It is only a guess work. Again, it is not possible to estimate correctly the scrap value of the asset. Should not sufficient provision for depreciation be made to replace the fixed asset in view of the rising prices? The fixed assets are valued at cost price *less* depreciation. The market value of such assets is ignored. It is argued that the market value is taken into consideration while valuing the current assets, why should not the fixed assets be valued according to the same principle?
2. *Deferred Revenue Expenditure*. Again some of the revenue expenses might have been incurred, the advantage of which will be derived in the subsequent accounting period, i.e., Deferred Revenue Expenditure. They might have been debited to the current year's profit and loss account with the result that the profit for the current year will be shown at a lower figure than what it actually is. Even if they have not been debited to revenue account, the question is, over how much period they should be speard over? Successful companies write them off sooner than less successful companies. Why should then be such differentiation?
3. *Stock-Valuation*. There is a divergence of opinion in regard to the valuation of stock-in-trade. Of course, the accepted principle followed in the valuation of stock is "cost price or market price whichever is the lower" but the question is what is meant by the "cost price". We have already dealt with this question in the Chapter 'Verification and Valuation of Assets and Liabilities'. Cost or market value may mean different things for different companies, It is generally said that profit must be taken into account only when the goods have been sold. If this is so, what about those companies which are engaged in long-term contracts, i.e., construction companies. In practice they do take into consideration the profits on uncompleted contracts.
4. *Intangible Assets*. Again in regard to intangible assets like goodwill, patent rights, there is no uniform opinion about their valuation. There are accountants who say that such assets should not appear at all in the books of account while others argue that they should be retained in the business.
5. *The Valuation of Liabilities*. The same remarks as under (a) above apply to the valuation of liabilities and their effect on the profits.
6. Some of the expenses which ought to have been incurred during the current year might not have been defrayed or, in other words, the business might have been starved of legitimate expenses with the result that more profit is shown during the year under review than what actually it is.
7. *Taxation*. There are unexpected changes in the Income Tax Act off and on. Therefore no exact estimate regarding the provision for income-tax payable can be made. It is only an estimate.
8. *Allocation of Expenditure*. Again, capital expenditure might have been treated as revenue expenditure and *vice versa* which will affect the profit.
9. *Provision for Reserves, etc*. Whether it is necessary that reserve, provision for depreciation and similar other contingencies must be provided for or not before the determination of profits.

Profit an Uncompleted Contracts

Again another problem regarding the ascertainment of correct profits may arise in the case of companies which carry on business as contractors, ship-builders or constructional engineers, etc. In such cases, it takes years to complete the contracts or build a ship. If the principle 'no profit should be brought into account until the contract is completed' is rigidly applied, it will create lot of complications and hardships, e.g., in some years no profit will be distributed because no contract was completed in that year while on the other hand in some years a large amount of dividend will be paid because some important contracts were completed in those years. This brings us to a question whether profits should or should not be distributed in the case of uncompleted contracts.

The following will be the consequences if the profits on uncompleted contracts are not taken into consideration.

1. The profits of the company will fluctuate from year to year.
2. No comparison of the profits of the company can be made between two periods.
3. The market value of the shares of such companies will widely fluctuate in the stock-exchange.
4. People may hesitate to indulge in speculation in the shares of such companies.
5. Investing public may not like to invest their funds in the purchase of the shares of such companies.
6. Certain classes of shareholders may be very unfairly treated, e.g., holders of non-cumulative shares may be deprived of the profits in some years although the average profits had been sufficient for the period to enable the company to pay the dividends to such shareholders.
7. Even the, cumulative preference shareholders and ordinary shareholders suffer to a certain extent, for although they get the same amount of dividend in the long run, they are deprived of the use of cash in those years when owing to important contracts being uncompleted, no dividend was paid.

In order to avoid the complications ensumerated above, it is necessary to take profits for the years when the work is still incomplete but the following precautions should be taken into consideration:

1. Profits on an uncompleted contract should be taken only when the work has reached a sufficiently advanced stage or completion.
2. Sufficient reserves should be made for contingencies such as increase in the cost of materials and labour or for fines which may be imposed for any delay in completing the contract.
3. When the contract is undertaken with a Government Department, the possibility of price refund should also be taken into consideration while calculating the profit.
4. It is usually deemed prudent not to take credit if the work has not reached to two-thirds of the book value of the contract and as certified by the contractor's architect, surveyor, etc.
5. Where a proportion of the amount certified is retained by the contractor, as a margin, until the completion of the contract, the two-thirds profits as ascertained above is reduced by the same proportion that the retention monies bear to the total amount certified.

In case the work is very nearly completion, the profit is calculated by estimating the total amount of material, labour and overhead charges which will be required to complete the work and by deducting the total expenditure which has been so arrived at from the contract price. The whole of the profit thus arrived at should not be credited to the profit and loss account but a proportion of it (bearing the same value to the total profit with the work certified to date bears to the contract price) should be considered as earned to date subject to the carrying forward of a proportion thereof in reserves as explained in the previous paragraph.

Above are some of the problems which are faced by an auditor. Unless they are properly solved and a guidance is given to the chartered accountant, the complicated problem of calculating the current profit will create difficulties.

Consequences of Incorrect Valuation of Profits

From the above, it will be clear how difficult it is to calculate correct profits. If the profits are not correctly arrived at, it may result in the following consequences:—

1. If more profit is shown than what actually it is, it would mean capital is being distributed. It amounts to reduction of capital without the sanction of the Court in contravention of Section 100 of the Companies Act. In such cases the directors are jointly and severally liable to the company to the extent of such dividend as has been so paid out of capital together with interest at 5 per cent, if they have paid such dividend knowingly. However, if such dividend has been paid on a *bona fide* valuation of the company's assets or by relying on the trusted officials of the company, they are not liable.
2. If capital is distributed it will mean the assets will be reduced and hence the security, which the creditors and the debenture-holders had, will be reduced. If the assets are reduced it may ultimately result in the company going into liquidation.
3. Understatement of profit may deprive the present shareholders of dividends to which they are entitled and the employees, etc., who get commission on profits will get less commission than what they are entitled to.
4. Understatement of profits will lower the value of shares in the market.
5. Overvaluation or undervaluation of assets and liabilities will mean creation of secret reserve which is prohibited by Companies Act.
6. The auditor has to give a report according to Section 211, that the balance-sheet and profit and loss account show a true and fair view of the state of affairs of the company and if the profit arrived at is incorrect, such a report will be misleading and the auditor will be held liable.

Profits and Divisible Profits

At this stage, one must clearly understand the difference between *profits* and *divisible profits*. Even if we arrive at correct profits, we may say that all those profits are not divisible as we shall see in the following pages. Therefore, we may say that 'divisible profits' are those profits which can be *legally* distributed to the shareholders of a company in the form of dividend.

Although one has to face the above problems in arriving at correct profits, it does not matter much to a proprietor of business or to a partnership. The proprietor or the partners are the owners of the business. They can withdraw whole of the profits or even the capital if he or they so desire. The difficulty arises in the case of a joint-Stock Company. Till 1955 the Companies Act did not contain any provision defining the divisible profits except Regulation 97 of Table A. The present Companies Act does not define what are "divisible profits". It also does not say that only "true profits" can be divided. Section 205 of the Companies Act simply lays down that, no dividend shall be declared or p d except out of profits of the company arrived at after providing depreciation or out of the moneys p ovided by the Central or State Governments for the payment of the dividend in pursuance of a gu antee given by such Governments. The law still does not lay down the meaning of "profits".

On account of th above mentioned difficulties, there is always a dispute and controversy as to the definition of "div ible profit". Under such circumstances one has to depend upon the legal decisions. Going through the previous decisions of the courts, one finds that different judgements have been given in different cases, i.e., rulings given in different cases do not entirely agree with one another. Therefore, each case will have to be decided on its own merits.

"Profits available for dividend" means "net profits after making any deductions which the directors can duly make". (*Fisher* vs. *Black and White Publishing Company*, 1901).

"Profits of the Company" means profits available for recommendation and distribution as dividends after setting aside to reserve or after carrying forward such amounts as the directors deem fit; even the whole of the profits for the year can be carried forward. (*In re Buenos Aires Great Southern Railway Co., Ltd.* vs. *Preston*, 1947). Profits mean profits realised (*The Union Bank of Allahabad Ltd.*, 1925).

Another, interesting case in connection with "what are profits?" was that *Stewart* vs. *Sashalite Ltd.*, which was reported by *The Times* in its issue of 30th July, 1936, and quoted by Binnie and Manning. The facts of the case are that the plaintiff was to be paid in consideration of the services rendered by him to the company in its floatation. According to the agreement dated 20th December, 1930, the company agreed to pay to the plaintiff £ 1,000 "out of the *first profits* of the company and in priority to all dividends payable in respect of any share in the capital of the company". The company's balance-sheet for the year ended 31 st March 1935, showed a balance of £698, 11s. l0d., to the credit of profit and loss account. The directors of the company wanted to write off the Preliminary Expenses to the extent of about £393 and the balance of about £304 was to be carried to the Patents Reserve Account. The plaintiff claimed the whole of the money on account of £1,000 due to him under the agreement, i.e., "the first profits". The defendants contended that "on a true construction of the agreement the plaintiff was to be the first person to benefit out of profits which if he had not been there, would have gone to the shareholders".

The company argued that it was a prudent course for the directors to write off the preliminary expenses and carry something to the reserve and that if there was any balance which was to be distributed to the shareholders, the plaintiff had the prior right over the shareholders. It was further stated that since it was not proposed to pay any dividend to the shareholders, the question of paying anything to the plaintiff did not arise. Further the words used in the agreement indicated that sense. The words were: "When the directors came to consider the payment of a dividend they must first pay the plaintiff his £1,000 out of the money which would otherwise be available for dividend".

The plaintiff argued that if this were the case, the directors would always postpone paying dividend and he could never get anything. To this argument, the directors replied that a company is formed to earn profits and to distribute them to the shareholders and hence they could not always postpone the payment of dividends.

The court gave judgment in favour of the defendants.

As to whether depreciation should be provided before ascertaining the divisible profits, the judgments in the case of *Crabtree*, *Thomas* vs. *Crabtree* was confirmed in the case of *Edward* vs. *Sounton Hotel Co. Ltd.*, (1942) where a director of the company was entitled to 20 per cent of the profits "available for distribution each year". Atkinson, J., during the course of judgment said: "Of course, there is no dispute that depreciation properly ascertained must be, and ought to be deducted from the sum earned in order to arrive at the true profits which a company has made". It was further laid down that depreciation should be provided on fixed instalment method, and not on the reducing instalment method.

"Divisible Profits" are those profits which are arrived at after deducting all the expenses including the taxes payable to the State by the Company. In this connection it will be interesting to state the case of the *Commissioner of Income Tax, Delhi*, vs. *Delhi Flour Mills Co. Ltd.* (1959).

The facts of the case are that the assessee company entered into a contract in 1936 with its Managing Agents. Regarding the remuneration payable to them the agreements provided:

"In consideration for acting as managing agents the company should pay to the firm remuneration at Rs. 750 per month on such principal sum as may from time to time be deemed reasonable by the directors and in addition a commission equal to 10 per cent of the annual net profits. Such net profits will be arrived at after allowing the working expenses, interest on loans and due depreciation, but without setting aside anything to reserves or other special funds."

The assessee company wanted to deduct the commission payable to the Managing Agents before arriving at the profits on which the excess profit tax could be calculated. The Supreme Court of India held that net profits as provided in the agreement with the Managing Agents meant those profits which were arrived at after the deduction of all expenses and taxes and which could be distributed to the shareholders and on which the commission payable to the Managing Agents should be calculated.

Therefore, distinction between "profits" and "divisible profits" must clearly be understood. All profits are not divisible. Only those profits which can be legally distributed amongst the shareholders are "divisible profits."

The following principles must, however, be kept in view while declaring dividends by a joint Stock Company:—

(a) Dividends must be paid according to Section 205 of the Companies Act.

(b) Dividends must be paid according to the Articles of Association of the Company. If the company has no Articles of its own, then it must be paid according to Regulations 85 to 94 of Table A of Schedule I appended to the Companies Act.

(c) The Article of Association of the Company must not be *ultra vires* the Company Law.

(d) Dividends must not be paid so as to deprive the creditors or debenture-holders of their security.

Factors to be considered before recommending Dividend

1. *Transfer to Reserve.*
   - (*a*) Statutory Reserve, i.e., the reserve which is legally required to be created, e.g., in the case of banking companies twenty per cent of the profits must be transferred to reserve account or in the case of electricity companies contingency and tariff reserve has to be created.
   - (*b*) Provision for reserve according to the Articles of Association.
   - (*c*) Contractual Requirements, e.g., if the terms of the issue of debentures or redeemable preference shares provided that reserve should be created for their redemption, it must be provided.
   - (*d*) Other considerations. The directors should transfer a portion of the profits to the general reserve having regard to the fact that purchase of some fixed asset was to be financed out of the profits of the year or some will be required for future development of the company.
2. *Dividend Equalisation Reserve.* Sometimes the profits of the company fluctuate violently from year to year. In such circumstances, it is desirable to transfer a part of the profits, before declaring dividend, to the Dividend Equalisation Reserve to maintain a uniformity in the declaration of dividends.
3. *Cash Requirements.* If the working capital is just sufficient, it is not advisable to declare a dividend. If it is declared it will have to be paid to the shareholders within 42 days and thus the working capital will be reduced.
4. *Past Policy.* While declaring dividend, the directors should follow a consistent policy. On account of fluctuation in the rate of dividend, the value of the shares in the market will be very much affected.

5. *Preference Shares*. Before declaring dividend to the equity shareholders, preference shareholders must be paid dividend.

In determining what profits are to be distributed to the shareholders, the courts have to take into consideration the following points:—

1. That the interest of the minorities is not sacrificed;
2. That the interest of creditors, debenture-holders and third parties is not adversely affected;
3. That no dividend should be paid out of capital except under certain circumstances, which will be discussed later on. Dividends are considered to be paid out of capital when
   (*a*) a company pays dividend in spite of the fact that it has not made any profit during the year under review and there is no balance of undistributed profits;
   (*b*) revenue expenditure is charged to capital account; or
   (*c*) a fixed asset is sold and is treated as an ordinary sale.
4. That the requirements of the Companies Act and the Articles and Memorandum of Association are complied with. It must be mentioned here that even if the Articles of Association and Memorandum of Association permit the payment of dividends out of capital, such payment will be illegal.

The legal decisions have laid down the following principles for the distribution of profits:—

(*a*) the shareholders' capital cannot be used to pay dividends, and

(*b*) a dividend can only be paid out of *bona fide* surplus.

The complications for ascertaining the profits available for dividends arise under the following heads:—

1. Whether capital profits are available for dividends.
2. Whether all the surplus made by a company engaged in working a wasting asset is available for dividends.
3. Whether the loss of fixed assets must be made good before distribution of the surplus.
4. Whether profits made prior to incorporation are available for dividends.

Let us deal with these questions separately.

(1) Whether Capital Profits are available for Dividends

Those profits which are not earned during the regular course of business are called capital profits. Profits which are not earned on account of trading are called capital profits. Non-trading profits are capital profits. The examples of capital profits are:—

1. Profits made from a business which has been purchased and before, the certificate of commencement of business has been granted to the company.
2. Premium received on the issue of shares.
3. Profits made on the resale of the forfeited shares.
4. Profits made on the redemption of debentures in the open market, i.e. purchasing them at a discount.
5. Profit made on the sale of a fixed asset.

Thus, it would be seen that unusual trading profits are capital profits. The question is whether such profits can be distributed to the shareholders of a company.

Ordinarily such profits should not be distributed because these are not trading profits and hence are not normal profits, e.g., if premiums are received on shares, the first year of the life of the company will show more profits than the subsequent years when no shares will be issued. The result will be that less dividend will be payable to the shareholders in the subsequent years; the price of shares will go down in the market, the shareholders might think that the directors have become negligent or dishonest and so on.

It would be seen from the following decisions that the courts have allowed the distribution of capital profits under certain circumstances: —

(i) Foster vs. The New Trinidad Asphalte Co., Ltd. (1901)

The facts of the case were that the defendant company took over the assets of another company. Amongst the assets, one debt was also taken over. At that time it was considered that the debt amounting to 100,000 dollars was irrecoverable. Hence, it was not recorded in the books. Later on, the debt was recovered in full together with interest and the directors wanted to treat it as profit and distribute it to the shareholders. Thereupon, the debenture-holders and a shareholder moved the court to issue an injunction against the directors restraining them from distributing the capital profits.

It was argued by the directors that the debt, when it was taken over, was considered worthless and was not recorded in the books. When the amount of the debt was unexpectedly paid it was to be considered as a windfall and hence the directors could distribute such a profit. But Justice Byrne did not accept this argument and said:

"It appears to me that amount in, question is *prima facie* capital, and that I have no evidence which would justify me in saying that it has changed its character because it has turned out to be of greater value than had been expected. I must not, however, to be understood as determining that this sum or a portion of it may not properly be brought into profit and loss account or be taken into account in ascertaining the amount available for dividend. It is clear, I think, that an appreciation in the whole value of capital assets if duly realised by sale or by getting in of some portion of such assets, may in proper case be treated as available for purpose of dividend. This, I think, is involved in the decision in the case of *Lubbock* vs. *British Bank of South America* (1892) cited with approval by Lord Lindley in *Verner* vs. *General and Commercial Investment Trust* (1894) where he says, 'Moreover, when it is said, and said, truly, that dividends are not to be paid out of capital, the word "Capital" means the money subscribed pursuant to the memorandum of association or what is represented by that money. Accretion to that capital may be realised and turned into money which may be dividend amongst the shareholders, as was decided in *Lubbock* vs. *British Bank of South America*'. If I rightly appreciate the true effect of the decisions, the question of what is profit available for dividend depends upon the result of the whole accounts fairly taken for the year, capital as well as profit and loss, and although dividends may be paid out of earned profits in proper cases, although there has been a depreciation of capital, I do not think that a realised accretion to the estimated value of one item of the capital assets can be deemed to be profit divisible amongst the shareholders without reference to be result of the whole accounts fairly taken".

Conclusion

It was held that capital profits could not be distributed as dividends unless (a) all the other assets had been revalued, (b) depreciation in the value of other assets was set off against the appreciated value of the asset, (c) such profits had been actually realised, and (d) that the Articles of Association of the company permitted such a step.

(ii) Lubbock vs. British Bank of South America (1892)

The facts of the case were that the Bank was carrying on business of banking in Brazil and other countries: It sold its business in Brazil to another Brazilian Bank for a sum of £875,000 on the condition that the British Bank would not carry on the business in Brazil. After a few months; the British Bank purchased the business from the Brazilian Bank for a sum of £75,000. The net surplus out of the deal amounted to £205,000 (deducting £500,000 Paid-up Capital and £75,000 paid to the Brazil Bank and a few other odd amounts). The Directors of the British Bank wanted to credit the Profit and Loss Account with the sum of £205,000 and to pay dividend to the shareholders.

The plaintiff, on behalf of himself and other shareholders, brought an action against the directors to restrain them from distributing this surplus in the form of dividend on the ground that the distribution would mean payment of dividend out of capital.

It was stated that the suit was of a friendly character in order to find out the opinion of the court. The plaintiff did not wish to prevent the dividend being paid. The action was brought to elicit the opinion of the court.

It may be stated here that the Articles of the British Bank were silent on the point with regard to the method of calculating divisible profits.

Mr. Justice Chitty gave the decision in favour of the directors on the ground that any surplus left after deducting the paid-up capital and liabilities out of the sale proceeds of the assets, represented profits and was, therefore, available for dividend provided Articles of the company did not prohibit such a procedure. Mr. Justice Chitty, therefore, held that the directors were justified in distributing such a surplus, after carrying a part of this surplus to Reserve Account which they thought proper.

Conclusion

If a company's Articles of Association so provide, a profit made on the sale of a part of the-undertaking is available for dividend.

We have discussed the case from the legal point of view. From the financial point of view, the following points must be kept in view while deciding to distribute capital profits.

(*a*) Capital profit should not be distributed, though legally permissible, if working capital is not sufficient for carrying on business.

(*b*) If it has already been decided to expand the business and consequently more money will be required, capital profit should not be distributed even though such a course is permissible by law.

(*c*) Capital profit should not be distributed when the asset has not been sold, as it may not be possible in such a case to pay any dividend because money has not been realised by the sale of the appreciated asset.

(*d*) But where the appreciation in the value of the asset is due to the, fact that asset in question had been excessively, depreciated in the past-with a view to creating secret reserve the book value of the asset may be appreciated and the surplus may be credited to the Profit and Loss Account as the excessive depreciation represents the amount withheld from being distributed to the shareholders in the past to which they are entitled now as was decided in *Stapley* vs. *Read Bros., Ltd.*, (1924).

(*iii*) Stapley vs. Read Bros., Ltd,, (1924)

The facts of the case were that the defendant company had written off its goodwill in the past at a very excessive rate with the result that the whole of the Goodwill amounting to £40,000 had been wiped off from the books of accounts. The Profit and Loss Account of the company showed a debit balance in 1922. The company showed a credit balance of Profit and Loss Account in 1923 to the extent of £13,430 The directors of the company proposed to pay dividends to Cumulative Preference Shareholders who had not been paid anything in the years 1921, 1922 and 1923. In order to do so they proposed to write up the Goodwill to the extent of £40,000 by debiting goodwill account and crediting the Reserve Account and then writing off the debit balance of Profit and Loss Account by transfer to the Reserve Bank Account.

This was a motion for restraining the Directors from (1) paying any dividend out of the credit balance of Profit and Loss Account as on 31st December, 1923 until the debit balance of Profit and

Loss Account as on 31st December, 1922, had been written off, and (2) from treating the profits as available for dividend (a) any profits originally applied in writing off or writing down the book value of any of the assets, and subsequently written back on the ground that such assets stood in the company's books at less than their true value; (b) any unrealised profit arising from an estimated increase in the value of any capital asset.

The defendants argued that the goodwill had been written off in the past out of the profits and that the present value of the goodwill was more than what they proposed to write up. Therefore, they argued that there was nothing wrong in the proposed action.

It was held by justice Russel that a company which had, in the past, written down the assets excessively out of profits may subsequently write them up to the extent of such excess and apply the amount thereof to pay dividends. He, therefore, refused to grant the injunction sought for. During the course of his judgment, Russel J., said:

"The sole question was whether profit and loss was to be treated as a continuous account, so that no dividend could be declared out of one year's profits until any debit to profit and loss in respect of prior years had been made good: His Lordship said that this point was covered by the decision in *Ammonia Soda Co., Ltd., vs. Chamberlain* (1918).

In dealing with the second part of the motion his Lordship said that the point was not covered by direct authority. Had the company retained the goodwill as an asset in the balance-sheet, and, instead of writing off its value out of profits, had carried those profits to a goodwill depreciation reserve fund, it could distributed those profits at any time to the extent by which the amount of the reserve fund exceeded the amount of actual depreciation. It was admitted that the value of the goodwill was at least £40,000, and if, therefore, there had been £40,000 to the credit of that reserve fund the company could have distributed £40,000 of that reserve as profits. In his opinion the shareholders, if they thought fit, write back to the profit account the £40,000 which was admitted to be the amount by which the depreciation written off goodwill exceeded the proper requirements. There was no provision in the Companies (Consolidation) Act, 1908, or in the constitution of the company, to prevent this course, which was further more prejudicial to the creditors.

Conclusion

If a company has written down excessively its assets out of profits in the past, it may write up such assets again to the extent of such excess and apply such an amount in payment of dividends.

(*iv*) Re Spanish Prospecting Co., Ltd., (1911)

The facts of the case were that two employees of the company, viz., Messrs. Punchard and Vivian, were to receive their salaries subject to the condition that they were not to withdraw them "except only out of profits" and that any arrears of salaries could be paid out of future profits.

The Prospecting Company went into liquidation showing a debit balance of Profit and Loss Account. The object of the company was to purchase and sell shares and debentures. The company had a few debentures which had been acquired by it during the course of business. At the time of the liquidation of the company, these debentures were considered worthless and were treated in the accounts of the company as of no value. The Liquidator realised these debentures. He paid off all the creditors of the company except Punchard and Vivian and also returned the capital to the shareholders. After these disbursements, the Liquidator had still some money in hand. Punchard and Vivian claimed this money as the arrears of their salaries. They argued that the surplus was the profit and that they were entitled to be paid their arrears of salaries out of the surplus.

The lower court dismissed the case on the ground that the surplus was not the profit as on the date of liquidation, the company had a debit balance of Profit and Loss Account and that the company ceased to, function on that date and, therefore, the employees were not entitled to receive the arrears of their salaries which were to be paid only out of profits.

Punchard and Vivian, thereupon, appealed to the higher court which reversed the judgments of the lower court, and it was held that when a salary is payable out of profits, such profits are not necessarily the profits shown by the company's annual accounts, but may include accretions to capital.

The judgment dealt with the question of 'what are profits'. We shall quote a few extracts from the judgment:

"The word `profits' has, in my opinion a well-defined meaning and this meaning coincides with the fundamental conception of 'profits' in general parlance, although in mercantile phraseology the word may at times bear meanings indicated by the special context, which deviates in some respects from the fundamental signification. 'Profits' implies comparison between the state of a business at two specific dates, usually separated by an interval of a year. The fundamental meaning is the amount of gain made by the business during the year. This can only be ascertained by a comparison of the assets of the business of the two dates.

"We start, therefore, with this fundamental definition of 'profits', viz., if the total assets of the business at the two dates be compared, the increase which they show at the later date as compared with the earlier date (due allowances, of course, being made for any capital introduced into or taken out of the business in the meanwhile) represents in strictness the profit of the business during the period in question. . . . In the absence of special stipulation to the contrary, 'profits' in cases where the rights of third parties come in, mean actual profits, and they must be calculated as closely as possible in accordance with the fundamental conception, or definition to, which I have referred. I would have it clearly understood that these remarks have no bearing upon the vexed question of the fund out of which dividends may legally be paid in limited companies."

Conclusion

When a salary is payable out of profits, such profits need not necessarily be the profits shown by the company's annual accounts but may include accretions to capital. Moreover, a distinction must be made between profits and profits which can be legally distributed to the shareholders

(*v*) Lee vs. Neuchatel Asphalte Co., Ltd., (1889)

The facts of the case were that the company was formed to purchase mines and work them in Switzerland. The company wanted to distribute profits to Preference Shareholders without making provisions for depreciation on the fixed assets, viz., the mines.

Thereupon, Mr. Charles John Lee on behalf of himself and other ordinary shareholders brought an action against the company and the directors, with a view to obtaining an injunction restraining the directors to pay any dividend to the Preference Shareholders without first making provision for depreciation on the mines. It was argued by Lee that every ton of mineral raised from a mine which was brought with capital, represented a portion of capital and if that mineral was sold out and the sale proceeds, after deducting the expenses, was distributed amongst the shareholders, it would amount to the return of capital to the shareholders, which action was prohibited by the Companies Act.

Lee lost the case on the following grounds:

(*a*) That the Articles of Association of the company did not compel the directors to set aside any money for the renewal or replacement of any lease or concession.

(*b*) That the assets of the company were of greater value than at the time of its formation.

(*c*) That if a company was formed to work out a wasting asset and to go into liquidation when such an asset was exhausted, it was not necessary to make any provision for depreciation.

Let us quote relevant extracts from the judgement:

"... It has been very judiciously and properly left to the commercial world to settle how the accounts were to be kept. The Acts do not say what expenses are to be charged to capital account and what to revenue account; such matters were left to the shareholders; they may or may not have a sinking fund or a deterioration fund; the Articles of Association may or may not contain regulations on these matters; if they do, the regulations must be observed; if they do not, shareholders can do as they like so long as they do not misapply their capital. In this case, one of the articles provides that the directors shall not be bound to reserve moneys for the renewal or replacing of any lease or of the company's interest in any property or concession . . . but if a company is formed to acquire, or work property of wasting nature, e.g., a mine, quarry or patent, the capital expended in acquiring the property may be regarded as sunk and gone, and if the company retains assets sufficient to pay its debts, and excess of money obtained by working the property over the cost of working it may be divided among the shareholders; and this is true, although some portion of the property itself is sold, in one sense the capital thereby is diminisehed. If it is said that such a course involves payment of dividends out of capital, the answer is that the Act nowhere prohibits such a payment as is here supposed. The proposition that it is ultra aires to pay dividends out of capital is very apt to mislead and must not be understood in such a way as to prohibit honest trading. But it is true if working expenses exceed the current gains, profits cannot be divided and that if in such a case capital is divided and paid away as dividend, the capital is misapplied, and the directors implicated in the misapplication may be compelled to make good the amount misapplied...."

Conclusion

If a company is formed to work a mine, it may distribute the profits to the shareholders without making any provision for depreciation on the wasting assets where the articles of association of the company did not compel it to do so.

It must be pointed out here that though Mr. Lee lost the case, from the viewpoint of sound financial and commercial policy, provision for depreciation of assets, whether of fixed or wasting nature, must be made before declaring any dividend. If any dividend is paid without making provision for depreciation it would amount to distribution of income as well as a part of capital. Moreover, according to the Indian Companies Act, as amended in 1960, depreciation must be provided on assets before the profits are distributed to the shareholders.

(*vi*) Crabtree Thomas vs. Crabtree (1912)

The facts of the case were as under:—

The testator authorised the trustees, by his will, to carry on his business and to pay 7½ % of the profits to his wife during her life-time. The trustees provided depreciation on plant and machinery before arriving at profits. Thereupon, the wife of the testator brought an action on the ground that no depreciation should be provided on the plant and machinery.

The testator's wife lost the case. It was argued by the defendants that, no doubt, legally it was not necessary to provide depreciation on fixed assets, but it was supposed to carry on the manufacturing business indefinitely, the necessity for replacing the plant and machinery would be felt when it would be worn out. Hence it was stated, depreciation on plant and machinery must be provided before arriving at the profits.

Conclusion

Depreciation must be provided on plant and machinery of a manufacturing concern if the manufacturing business is to continue for an indefinite period. It may be remembered that in this case no joint stock company was involved. Even if the company is not to continue its business for an indefinite period, depreciation must be provided in India according to the Companies Act as amended in 1960.

From the above decisions, it would appear that the capital profits can be distributed under the following circumstances;

(*a*) when all the other assets have been revalued;

(*b*) when depreciation in the value of other assets has been set off against the appreciated value of the assets; and

(*c*) when the Memorandum and Articles of Association of the company permit such a step.

It may be pointed out here that due to the decisions by the Courts in two cases in 1960 and 1961, doubts have arisen as to whether capital profits may be distributed even though such profits might not have been realised.

(2) Whether all the surplus made by a company engaged in working a wasting asset, is available for dividends.

Wasting assets are properties of a fixed nature which are used up by depletion or exhaustion, e.g., a mine, an oil well, a quarry, etc. The question arises whether all the surplus made by a company engaged in the working of such an asset is available for dividends. Different views have been expressed on the subject.

There are accountants who are of the opinion that this surplus is the capital and therefore the division of such a surplus will amount to payment of dividend out of capital. They base their argument on the ground that the surplus represents a part of the capital, e.g., if a coal mine is purchased, say for Rs. 75,000 and, supposing for the sake of simplicity, it contains 75,000 tons coal, the cost of which is Re. 1 per ton. Supposing in the first year the output is 10,000 tons which realises Rs.15,000 after, deducting all the expenses and if these Rs. 15,000 are distributed to the shareholders of the company, it means a part of the capital is being returned to the shareholders. But it has been held in the following cases that if a company is formed to work a mine and after exhaustion it is to be wound up, the company may distribute this surplus. We have already seen in one of the legal cases cited earlier that it is not necessary for a company to provide depreciation on wasting assets before distributing dividend, provided the company is formed mainly to work the wasting asset and provided further, the Articles of Association of the company do not prohibit such an action (*Lee* vs. *The Nauchatel Co. Ltd.*, 1889). If in such a case dividend is paid to the shareholders it will not amount to "dividend paid out of capital".

It will not be out of place to mention here that if no depreciation is provided, the balance-sheet will not show the true and fair view of the state of affairs of the company. Under these circumstances, the auditor will do well to refer this matter in his report to the shareholder Moreover, the Companies Act in India definitely lay down that depreciation must be provided on assets, before any dividend is paid. Thus, this case does not hold good now-a-days.

(3) Whether the loss of fixed assets must be made be good before distribution of the surplus.

The question is whether a company can declare dividend even though there may be a loss of fixed assets which fact has not been taken into consideration while arriving at the profit of the year. Let us discuss a few cases to arrive at a correct decision.

(*i*) Bolton vs. Natal Land & Colonisation Co., Ltd., (1892)

The facts of the case were as under:—

A bad debt amounting to £70,000 was debited to Profit and Loss Account of the company while appreciation in the value of the land amounting to £70,000 which was above the cost price of the land and at which it stood in the books of accounts, was credited to Profit and Loss Account, in the same year, viz., 1882. The result was that profit and loss account of the year was balanced. In 1885, the company having earned a profit, wanted to distribute it in the form of dividends. The plaintiff brought a suit against the company to restrain it to pay any dividend without bringing down the face value, of the land to the true value.

The plaintiff argued that the value of the land was far below its true value and hence it was but fair that the depreciation in the value of the land must be brought to its real value in order to arrive at the true profits. It was further argued by the plaintiff that when an increase in the value of the land was credited to Profit and Loss Account in 1882, the decrease in its value should also be debited to the same Account in 1885.

The plaintiff lost the case. It was held that even assuming the loss in the value of the assets, it was not necessary that the directors must take into consideration the decrease in the value of the land while estimating the profit or loss. Therefore, it was held that a company might declare a dividend out of current profits without being obliged to show that all its capital was intact.

Conclusion

A company may pay a dividend out of the current profits without making good the previous loss of capital assets or in other words the capital of the company need not remain intact.

It may be pointed out here that payment of dividend out of unrealised profits of this type would hamper the working of the business as the working capital would be reduced and hence the declaration of such a dividend is inadvisable, even if such payment is not illegal.

Again, payment of the dividend without writing off the previous losses is prohibited according to Section 205 of the Companies Act.

(*ii*) Verner vs. General and Commercial 1nvestments Trust Ltd,, {1894)

The facts of the case were as under:—

The company was formed in 1888 with a capital of £600,000 and it also issued debentures worth £300,000. This amount was invested in the purchase of securities, stock and shares according to the Memorandum of Association. The objects of the company, according to the Memorandum of Association, were "to receive the dividends, income, profits, bonuses and advantages of every description from time to time payable or receivable in respect of the company's investments and to apply the same respectively according to the-provisions of the Articles of Association in force for the time being".

The Articles of the company provided that "subject to the rights of members holding share capital issued upon special conditions, the receipts of the company from the dividends, income, profits, bonuses and advantages payable or receivable in respect of the company's investment shall be applicable as follows. . . The trustees may before recommending any dividend, set aside out of the profits of the company such sums as they think proper as a reserve fund to meet contingencies or for equalising dividends, or for any other purposes of the company; and may from time to time apply the whole or any part of such fund for any purpose of the company".

The market value of the Securities on 28th February 1894, the balance-sheet date, was estimated to be £657,776 although their book value was £894,776. Thus there was a deficiency or loss of £240,000. It was estimated that of this deficiency £75,000 would be a dead loss. In other words there was absolutely no hope of making up this loss. The company had made profit of £23,000 from these investments during the year under review. The company wanted to distribute the whole of this amount, viz., £23,000 in the form of dividend to the shareholders without making good the loss in the value of assets.

Mr. Willian Henry Verner, a shareholder, on behalf of himself and all the shareholders except the directors, brought a suit against the company and the directors, restraining them from distributing £23,000 without providing for depreciation in the value of investments.

Mr. Justice Sterling, taking into consideration the objects of the company, held that there was no legal obligation on the part of the company, to make good the loss in the value of investments before declaring dividend. He, therefore, dismissed the case.

The plaintiff thereupon appealed to the higher court.

It was an interesting case of company law as to whether a company could pay dividend in spite of the fact that there had been: a loss of capital through depreciation in the value of its assets. The appeal was dismissed. Let us'quote a few extracts from the judgment delivered by Lord justice Lindley in collaboration with Lord Justice Smith;

"The broad question raised by its appeal is whether a limited company which has lost part of its capital can lawfully declare or pay a dividend without first making good the capital which has been lost. I have no doubt it can—that is to say, there is no law which prevents it in all cases and under all circumstances. Such a proceeding may sometimes be very imprudent, but a proceeding may be prefectly legal and may yet be opposed to sound commercial principles. We, however, have only to consider the legality or illegality of what is complained of. As was pointed out in *Lee* vs. *Neuchatel Asphalte Company*, there are certain provisions in the Companies Acts relating to the capital of limited companies; but no provisions whatever as to the payment of dividends or the division of profits. Each company is left to make its own regulations as to such payment or division. The statutes do not even expressly and in plain language prohibit a payment of dividend out of capital.

Conclusion

A company can pay dividend out of the current profits without making good loss of capital provided (a) that the assets are sufficient to pay off the liabilities, and (b) subject to the terms of the articles of the company.

But now whether the articles provide for depreciation or not, it has to be provided according to Section 205. Thus the judgment does not hold good now in India.

(*iii*) Wilmer vs. McNamara & Co., Ltd., (1895)

The facts of the case were that the defendant company was conducting a business of carrying mails, etc. The company used to provide depreciation on its assets, viz., leases, goodwill, premises, horses, vans, etc., in the past before arriving at the distributable profits. The company passed a resolution at the annual general meeting, declaring a dividend to the preference shareholders without providing any depreciation on the assets. Therefore, Mr. Wilmer an ordinary shareholder, brought an action against the company and requested the court to issue an injunction against the directors, restraining them from paying dividend without providing any depreciation on the assets. This was a friendly action.

It was argued on behalf of the plaintiff if no depreciation was provided, it would mean the capital of the company would not remain intact, and that the assets as valued at the balance-sheet date would not represent the, prim state of the company's affairs: Moreover, the company, in fact, had always provided for depreciation in the past and that it should also do so during the year under review.

The question, therefore, before the court -was whether it was lawful for a company to pay dividend without providing for depreciation on its assets.

Sterling, J., while delivering the judgment, said:—

"Article 117 provides that 'no dividend shall be payable except out of the profits arising out of the business of the company'— what are these profits?" Upon this point his Lordship referred to the judgment delivered by Lindley, L.J., in the case of *Verner* vs. *General Investment Trust* and continued: "Apart from the use of the word 'profits' in article 117 there is nothing in the articles to show that the capital of the company (or, rather, assets of the value of those acquired by the company at its formation) must be kept up. Further, the articles appear to contemplate 'profits' as the excess of receipts over all expenditure properly attributable to the year. It is necessary, however, to consider whether the depreciation in goodwill and leaseholds is to be treated as loss of 'fixed' capital or of 'floating' or 'circulating' capital and on this point I am of opinion that it is to be treated as loss of 'fixed' capital. It very closely resembles the loss which a railway company may be said to suffer if it be found that their line, which was made, say; ten years ago, at a certain cost, could now be made at a much smaller cost. Having regards to the remarks of Lindley, L.J., in *Lee* vs. *Neuchatel Asphalte Co.*, I think the Balance-Sheet cannot be impeached simply because it does not charge anything against revenue in respect of goodwill. I feel much more doubt whether £200 is a sufficient sum to allow in respect of depreciation of leaseholds, but I think under the circumstances that a case has been made out for an injunction and the motion must be refused".

Conclusion

The conclusion is that a company cannot be restrained from declaring a dividend out of current profits because no provision has been made for depreciation on fixed assets.

The judgment does not hold good now in India *vide* Section 205 of the Companies Act, according to which depreciation must be provided on fixed assets before a dividend is declared.

(*iv*) Ammonia Soda Company Ltd. vs. Arthur Chamberlain and Others (1918)

The facts of the case were that Mr. Chamberlain and Mr. Cocking were the directors of the company. They were entrusted with the work of valuing the land of the company. The company had a debit balance of Profit and Loss Account. The company wrote up the value of the land on the report of the directors; the defendants. This appreciation in the value of the land was utilised in wiping off the debit balance of the Profit and Loss Account, etc. In subsequent years when the company made a profit, it declared a dividend. It may be pointed out here that the value of the land had appreciated because a new shaft of rock salt was discovered while the land was being bored for the supply of water to the company's works.

The case was brought by the company against the directors on the ground that the appreciation in the value of the land was not genuine but was manipulated with a view to wipe off the previous losses (the debit balance of Profit and Loss Account) and that the dividend was paid out of capital. It was further pointed out by the plaintiffs that the previous loss ought to have been paid out of the subsequent profits before any dividend was declared.

The plaintiff company brought this action requesting the court to make the defendants, who were the directors of the company when such dividends were paid, liable to refund to the company dividends wrongfully paid in the past.

It was pointed out by the plaintiffs that the directors ought not to have valued the land as they were interested parties and they valued the land in order to conceal the losses and that they were not experts in the valuation of the land and hence their valuation was not genuine. It was further alleged that the land was over-valued by the directors with an indirect and improper motive. It was further pointed out by the company that the amount standing to the debit of profit and loss should have been wiped out before dividends were paid, and as that had not been done the amount paid as dividends were paid out of capital and, therefore, the directors who misapplied the assets of the company were liable to replace such assets.

The defendants argued that the company should prove that the action of the directors was *ultra vires* the company and that the dividends were paid out of capital. The defendants further argued that assuming that they (defendants) were wrong in the valuation of the land, but if the court found that they acted honestly and *bona fide* it was not proper to make them liable.

It was decided by the court that the company might write up its assets as a result of a *bona fide* revaluation and might divide current profits without first making good prior losses.

A few extracts from the judgment are given below:—

". . . But there is no rule of law which requires directors to obtain assistance in such matters or prevents them from valuing the property themselves, provided, of course, they act honestly in doing so....."

"There is not any ground for suggesting that any facts were concealed from the shareholders by the directors. In these circumstances it is not, in my opinion, open to the company to attack the directors for an honest, though it may be erroneous, estimate which has been expressly adopted by the company in general meeting after the attention of the shareholders had been pointedly called to the resolution by the auditor's certificate which was attached to the balance-sheet. . . .

"But where a company had made losses in the past years and then makes a profit out of which it pays a dividend, the question is a different one. Such a dividend is not paid out of paid-up capital. If it were, paid-up capital would be still further reduced by the payment. In fact, the assets representing the paid-up capital remain the same or of the same value as before the payment of the dividends. It may be that, the balance to the credit of profit and loss account ought to be applied in making up lost capital, and it may be that the directors are liable for neglecting to apply it in this way. But such a payment does not involve a reduction of capital, it involves a failure to make good capital which has already been lost.

"I am satisfied that the directors acted honestly. What they proposed to do was clearly shown in the balance-sheet and the auditors' report, which were submitted in the general meeting of the company in October, 1911. Most, if not all, of the shareholders who attended that meeting were commercial men, and they unanimously approved of the proposal.

"In my judgment, then, the, present action fails and must be dismissed with the usual consequences".

Conclusion

Held that a company may write up its assets as the result of a *bona fide* revaluation, and may divide current profits without first making good prior losses.

Held further, (*a*) there is no rule of law which forbids a company from setting off an appreciation in value of its capital assets as ascertained by a *bona fide* valuation against losses on revenue accounts and, (*b*) the dividends in this case were not in fact paid out of capital but out of current profits.

In regard to the point that dividend may be paid without writing off the the previous losses, it may be pointed out, that according to Section 205(I)(b) of the Companies Act, if a company has suffered any loss in the previous year or years, such a loss must be set off against profits of subsequent years. Thus the decision does not hold good now in India.

(*v*) Drown vs. Gaumont British Picture Corporation, Ltd., (1937)

The facts of the case were that subsidiary companies of the holding company had suffered a heavy loss. The company had a reserve which was composed of the share premiums. The reserve was more than the loss of the combined companies.

The directors wanted to declare a dividend on cumulative preference shares out of this reserve.

The plaintiff filed a suit to restrain the company from paying any dividend to the preference shareholders on the ground that there were no profits and hence there was no justification to declare a dividend.

The court refused to interfere in the case as the plaintiff could not show that "the directors, in paying the dividend, would be encroaching upon that part of the assets which represented the subscribed capital". It was further stated that subject to any provisions in the articles of the company to the contrary, legally it is not wrong to pay dividends to the shareholders out of the premiums received by the company as long as the money so paid does not form part of the subscribed capital.

Commenting on the decision, *The Accountant*, of England, wrote in its issue of 26th June, 1937:

"The decision appears to us to break no new ground but emphasizes and confirms the very old-established principle that where directors are acting honestly, the court will not step in to interfere with their discretion, exercised within the articles unless the company would be left with less than twenty shillings in the pound as representing its paid-up capital".

Conclusion

A holding company need not provide depreciation on its investments in its subsidiary companies before payment of dividends, on cumulative preference shares as such investments are like fixed assets. The decision does not hold good now as depreciation has to be provided on the assets of the company.

(*vi*) Dovey and Others vs. Cory (National Bank of Wales, 1901)

In this case John Cory was a director of the bank, which was under liquidation. The liquidator brought an action against the director to make him liable—not to creditors who had been paid in full—to the contributories in respect of misfeasance: (1) in paying dividends out of capitals; (2) in making improper advances to directors; and (3) in making improper advances to customers, who were reputed to be insolvent. Mr. Cory was the director for about seven years.

The counsel representing Cory disclaimed the imputation of any moral turpitude on the part of his client. He dealt with the question of negligence and failure to discharge his duty as a director holding a fiduciary position. He said that the number of transactions were so many not only in respect of the head office but of its thirty-three branches and over a period of many years, that it was not possible to look into every transaction. The dividend so wrongly paid amounted to £52,986, while the advances which were improperly made amounted to £1,20,818.

Mr. Justice Wright ordered, the director to pay the sum of £54,787, being the amount of dividends wrongly-paid together with interest at 5 per cent per annum. The learned judge held that the dividends were, in fact, paid out of capital and the director was liable to refund that amount. As regards improper advances to customers and directors, his lordship declined to make the respondent liable.

Cory appealed to the Court of Appeal which reversed the judgment of the lower court and exonerated the respondent from liability. This decision was affirmed by the noble and learned lord of the House of Lords. A part of the judgment runs as follows:—

". . . .and the argument; raises a serious question as to the responsibility of all persons holding position like that of directors—how far they are called upon to distrust and be on their guard against the possibility of fraud being committed by their subordinates of every degree. It is obvious if there is such a duty it must render anything like an intelligent devolution of labour impossible. . . . . It is easy to lay down as an abstract proposition that you must not pay dividends out of capital, but the application of that very plain proposition may raise questions of the utmost difficulty in their solution. . . . in one ship being last out of a considerable number, and the question whether all dividends must be stopped until the value of that lost ship is made good out of the further earnings of the company or partnership, is one which one would have to deal with. On the one hand, people put their money into a trading concern to give them an income and the sudden stoppage of all dividends would send down the value of their shares to zero and possibly involve its ruin. On the other hand, companies cannot at their will and without the precautions enforced by the statutes reduce their capital; but what are profits and what is capital may be a difficult and sometimes an almost impossible problem to solve. . . . . . "

Conclusion

It was held that a director, if he acts bona fide, in entitled to rely on officers of the company to prepare true and honest accounts.

(4) Whether Profits made prior to incorporation are available for Dividends

Sometimes a company takes over the running business of a firm or an individual. The purchase price is fixed according to the balance-sheet at a particular date which is prior to the date of incorporation. It is possible that the vendor might have made some profit between the two dates, viz., the date on which the balance-sheet had been prepared and the date of agreement, e.g a company was registered on lst April, takes over a business on that date from the vendors according to the balance-sheet which had been prepared as on l st February. The profit, if any, made by the vendor between lst February and lst April, is called "profits prior to incorporation."

The question is whether such a profit is available for distribution as dividend to the shareholders. Legally speaking, the shareholders have no right to share such profits as the company had not come into existence when such profits were made and hence it could not earn any profits.

Under such circumstances, the correct basis of the purchase consideration will be the Balance-Sheet as at the date of incorporation, i.e., the purchase, consideration (plus any interest till the date of formation of the company) would be set off against the assets and liabilities at that date and any goodwill (or Capital Reserve) figure computed on the new facts. The net assets would have been increased by any interim profit or decreased by an interim loss, if any. The correct procedure would be to adjust such a profit to the goodwill account or other assets.

Sometimes permission is sought according to Articles and Memorandum of Association to distribute such profits. This distribution will be illegal especially when it is found that the assets had been unduly inflated as it will mean distribution of capital profits.

Again, some accountants argue that apportionment of such profits should be made *as at the date of certificate of commencement of business* and *not as at the date of incorporation.* They argue that as a company is not allowed to do business before the certificate to commence business is granted to it, it is not possible for it to earn any profit. It is submitted that the argument appears to be sound but even though the company is not allowed to commence business, it has come into existence and hence the contract entered into after the date of incorporation can be ratified after the certificate to commence business is granted to it. Therefore, such profits should be calculated from the date of incorporation of the company rather than the date of the commencement of business by the company as any transaction between the incorporation date and the commencement of business date can always be ratified.

Having come to the conclusion that profits prior to incorporation are not available for distribution amongst the shareholders, the difficulty arises as to how to calculate such profits. Of course, no difficulty would ărise if stock is taken and Balance-Sheet of the firm or the individual taken over is prepared on the date of the incorporation of the company. However, if this is not found convenient and practicable, the profit prior to incorporation may be ascertained by apportioning over two periods, viz., pre-incorporation and past-incorporation periods, the profits shown at the end of the first financial period of the company.

There are three methods of apportionment:—

(*a*) On the basis of turnover, i.e., by taking the gross profit on a percentage basis of sales.

(*b*) On the basis of time, i.e., by apportioning the profit into "pre-" and "post-" incorporation periods.

(*c*) On the combined basis of turnover and time. Under this method gross profit is taken according to turnover while expenses are apportioned according to time. This method seems to be more accurate and logical.

It will not be out of place to mention something about the "Loss Prior to Incorporation". Such a loss may be dealt with in any of the following ways:—

(*a*) it may be debited to the goodwill account because, as a matter of fact, it amounts to increases in the purchase price. However, even if nothing is paid for goodwill, the loss prior to incorporation must be debited to a newly opened goodwill account. If this method is adopted, Goodwill Account should, later on, be written off as soon as possible; or

(*b*) it may be debited to an account called "Loss Prior to Incorporation" which may be written off by and by; or

(*c*) it may be debited against the profits earned after incorporation, i.e., no separate figure should be shown in the accounts; or

(*d*) the amount should be debited to a newly opened "Suspense Account" which may be written off out of capital profits made in subsequent years, e.g., Premium on Issue of Debentures, Credit Balance of Forfeited Shares, if any, after they have been reissued; or

(*e*) the amount may be debited to the construction account if the business was taken over during the construction period.

General Summary of the Rules relating to the Distribution of Profits

1. Dividends are to be paid out of trading profits which mean excess of income over expenditure.
2. Shareholders, capital may, in no case, be used for the payment of a dividend.
3. The Companies Act does not lay down that the capital should remain intact but the law does not permit any part of capital to be returned to the shareholders.
4. No dividend should be paid if the security of the creditors is jeopardised in any way.
5. A dividend should not be paid without providing any depreciation on fixed assets.
6. A dividend may be paid out of current profits without making good a loss of fixed capital, provided there are sufficient assets to pay off liabilities.
7. No dividend can be paid without providing depreciation on floating assets.
8. Capital profits may be distributed if (a) articles permit such a payment, (b) the capital profits have been realised, and (c) if the surplus remains after the revaluation of all the other assets.
9. A dividend should not be paid if there is a debit balance of profit and loss account.
10. A company formed to work a wasting asset should provide depreciation on such an asset before declaring a dividend.
11. If goodwill or other assets have been excessively written down in the past, the excess may be written back to profit and loss account and distributed to the shareholders in the form of dividend.
12. Directors or auditors who are parties to the improper payment of a dividend are criminally liable but if they acted honestly and *bona fide*, they are not guilty.
13. A company need not divide the whole of the profit amongst its shareholders.

QUESTIONS

1. 'A company can declare dividend out of current profits without making good depreciation of fixed assets'. Examine the validity of the statement under the current law.

(*Gauhati M.Com.*)

2. What are Capital Profits? Discuss the legal and commercial view-points regarding distribution of capital profits. (*Lucknow B.Com. 1974*)

3. (*a*) A company sold its branch and goodwill in a foreign country for Rs. 15,000. The Directors propose to distribute this as dividend.
   (*b*) After two years of continuous loss of Rs. 5,000 in trading, a company made a profit of Rs. 6,000 which the Directors propose to distribute as dividend without making good the past revenue loss.
   (*c*) A recently floated company earned a profit of Rs. 10,000 and the Directors decide to transfer Rs. 8,000 to Reserve, leaving Rs. 2,000 as divisible profit which is not enough even to pay the preferential dividend. The preference shareholders object to this and demand that their preferential claim to profit should first be met in full before any transfer is made-to the Reserve.

   Give your opinion in the above proposals of the directors. Discuss fully from the legal and commercial prudence point of view. (*Rajasthan B. Com.*)
4. State briefly, with reasons, whether it is permissible for a company to pay or declare dividends
   (*a*) out of a profit arising from redemption of its debentures at a discount;
   (*b*) out of the past year's profit a further dividend after the declaration of final dividend in respect of that year;
   (*c*) out of the current profits without making good a debit balance on profit and loss account brought about by losses in the past years. (*Col. B. Com.*)
5. (i) Company 'A' has had a valuation made of its fixed assets which show an excess over book values which it has taken to the credit of Profit and Loss Account.
   (*ii*) Company 'B' has also had a valuation of its fixed assets which show a decrease on book values and proposes making no amendment to financial figures.

   Give your comments on both these cases from the financial and legal aspects. (*C.A. Inter.*)
6. "No dividend shall be payable except out of profits". Discuss. (*Gujarat B. Com.*)
7. Is it permissible for a company after having written down in the past, some of its Assets excessively out of profits, to write them up again on a subsequent occasion and credit the excess to Profit and Loss Account for the purpose of Dividend?

   (*Andhra Pb. Service Commission*)
8. Can a company declare dividend out of current year's profit without providing for arrear of depreciation and trading losses of previous years? Under what circumstances can a company declare dividend out of "Capital profit" arising on sale of plant and machinery which were used in business? (*Gauhati M. Com.*)
9. The ABC Co., Ltd., incorporated five years ago, took over at ,that time a patent which was then considered valueless and it was not shown in the accounts. Recently the patent was sold for Rs. 9,500 and the directors propose to distribute this as dividend. Is this legally correct? Quote decisions, if any, in support of your answer.
10. As an auditor, will you recommend the payment of dividend out of the following:—
    (*a*) Capital.
    (*b*) Realised capital profits.
    (*c*) Current years' profits, but before writing off past losses.
    (*d*) Past accumulated profits in a year of loss. Give reasons. (*Lucknow 1971*)
11. A limited company was registered on 31st March, 1977, for the purpose of taking over the existing business of ABC as from lst January 1977. According to the agreement, the company was entitled to the profits or responsible for the losses of the firm prior to incorporation. How would you ascertain and deal with the loss made prior to incorporation? What principles would guide you in dealing with such a loss?

12. What is the legal position as regards divisible profits. Is there any legal bar on a company against distribution of its current profits by way of dividends, without providing for depreciation on its fixed assets? Cite case law in view of your answer. *(Delhi B. Com.)*

13. What are 'divisible profits'? Discuss, in the light of legal decisions, whether profit on revaluation of assets can be distributed as dividend. *(Nagpur B.Com.)*

14. While examining the accounts of X Co. Ltd., you find that the following items appear on the credit side of Profit and Loss Account:—

(*i*) Profit on revaluation of Land and Building Rs. 50,000;

(*ii*) Profit arising from forfeiture and reissue of shares Rs. 15,000;

(*iii*) Premium on issue of shares Rs. 20,000; and

(*iv*) Bounties received from the Central Government by the company, Rs. 75,000.

Would you have any objection as an auditor to passing the accounts? Give reasons. *(Cal. B. Com. Hons.)*

15. Section 205 of the Companies Act, 1956, states that no dividend can be declared or paid except out of the profits of the company. Discuss whether this provision has in any way modified the earlier law on divisible profits. *(Delhi B. Com.)*

16. What do you understand by the term 'Divisible Profits?' Discuss the question with the help of at least three case laws bearing on the subject. *(Gauhati, Varanasi and S. V. Vidyapeeth B. Com.)*

17. Briefly summarise the legal position of profits available for dividend. *(Madras B. Corn.)*

18. (a) What do you understand by the term "Interim Dividend"? The directors of a company of which you are the auditor, consult you as regards the payment of an "Interim Dividend" on the Company's shares. What information would you require and what general advice would you give to the directors? *(Rajasthan M.Com.)*

19. What do you mean by "Divisible Profits"? What consideration and legal decisions would weigh with you before declaring dividend? *(Madurai, Poona, Punjab, Bombay, Cal. B. Com.)*

20. When consulted by Directors as to whether it would be desirable to pay interim dividend, on what points would you, as an auditor, direct your enquiries before giving your opinion? *(Nagpur B. Com.)*

21. As auditor, you find that the company has made a profit of Rs. 10,000 including a capital profit of Rs. 3,000 during the year under review. In the preceding two years the company has suffered revenue losses to the tune of Rs. 6,000. The directors propose that the entire profits be utilised by declaring a dividend without making good the past losses. Give your views. *(Marathwada B. Com.)*

Chapter 34

Investigation

Definition

Investigation means an inquiry into the accounts of a business for a special purpose. It is an examination of the books of accounts of a business to know its actual financial position or earning capacity, etc. Taylor and Perry have defined it thus: "Investigation involves inquiry into facts behind the books and accounts, into the technical, financial and the economic position of the business or organisation". It is a kind of special audit with a limited or extended scope according to the purpose for which it is conducted. Investigation is neither accountancy nor auditing as we shall see later on. Investigation may be conducted with many objects which will be discussed in the following pages.

Difference between 'Investigation' and 'Auditing'

1. Audit is conducted on behalf of the shareholders or proprietors; while investigation is usually carried out on behalf of outsiders who intend to purchase the business or who wish to lend money and thus want to know the earning capacity or the financial position of the concern. However, it may be carried out on behalf of the proprietors where they suspect any fraud, or by the Central Government at the instance of the shareholders or the court.

2. Accounts of a Joint Stock Company *must* be audited according to law while investigation is *not compulsary*.

3. Investigation may be conducted even though the accounts have been audited while audited accounts are not audited again except in the case of special audit under Section 233A.

4. The audit of accounts is usually for a year or six months, while investigation may cover a period extending over three to seven years.

5. The accounts are audited with a view to ascertaining whether or not the Balance-Sheet is drawn up according to law and that the Profit and Loss Account and the Balance-Sheet exhibit a true and fair view of the state of affairs of a business, while investigation is conducted with a particular object in view, viz., to know the financial position of the concern or its earning capacity, etc.

6. Audit is a kind of test checking while investigation is a thorough examination of the books of account for a particular year or a number of years.

7. Audit includes an examination of the books of accounts of a business while investigation is not only an examination of accounts but it is also an inquiry into other factors affecting the business such as the extent of fraud, who committed it, the causes of the fall of the profits, and so on and the investigator has, therefore, to go beyond the books of account.

8. In the case of investigation, the net profit or the actual earning capacity of the concern is ascertained by making certain adjustments in the net profit as calculated by the accountant or the auditor while this is not so in the case of an audit.

9. The report of the investigator is sent to the party which appointed him for the purpose of investigation while the report of the auditor is sent to the managing director/chairman of the company who places it before the shareholders.

10. The report of the investigator is a positive report while the auditor's report is generally in short-form and somewhat negative as it refers to the shortcomings, if any, but does not refer in detail to the audit methods or approach.

11. The report of the investigation is in detail and refers to (a) the instructions given to him, (b) the method of approach, (c) the work carried out, (d) the documents relied upon, and (e) his findings and often his recommendations to the client while the report of the auditor is stereotyped except when he mentions the points on which he is not satisfied with regard to the accounts of the client.

12. The investigator is not concerned whether the financial policy of the company is being followed or not but in the case of the auditor he has to state that fact, e.g., whether the method of the valuation of stock is being consistently followed or not, or whether there has been a change in the method of providing depreciation and its effect on the profits, etc.

Points to be noted while conducting an Investigation

Before dealing with the different classes of investigation, it is desirable to lay down here certain principles and rules to guide the investigator in drafting his report. His liability depends upon his report. To be on the safe side, he should keep in view the following points while conducting an investigation:

1. He must get in writing the objects or the purpose of investigation and the period to be covered.
2. He should chalk out a programme, taking into consideration the nature of the business, the method of keeping the books of account, system of internal check, etc. If the accounts have already been audited, very little work of checking regarding the verification, etc., will have to be done though it has been held in the case of *Soakot Compton* vs *Bracket* (1908) that an auditor while investigating on behalf of an incoming partner is entitled to, assume that the figures in the books of account are correct. Again it was held in the case of *Mead* vs. *Ball, Baker & Co.* (1911), that an auditor was not expected to check errors in the stock sheets and the omission of liabilities, if he was appointed by his client to act as an investigator in a limited company. But still he must enquire from his client whether he could rely upon the accuracy of the audited accounts or should, he go through them again.
3. He should be honest and must not be influenced by any interested party, e.g., the vendors or promoters of a company.
4. He should show as much skill and diligence as is expected of such an investigator.
5. Where it is desired, he should get the opinion of the experts in case of valuation of stock and other assets.
6. If the accounts had already been audited, he should consult the auditor of the company to get opinion about the state of affairs of the company.
7. If he has relied upon the audited accounts without verification of assets, he must mention that fact in his report.
8. He should keep a proper record of inquiries, explanations given and so on for future reference, so that he may have a proof against any charge of negligence levelled against him in future. Such a record will be a good documentary proof.

9. The report should be simple, unambiguous and concise, but not at the cost of clarity.
10. He should be very careful in drawing up the report. It should be absolutely correct; if it is not and his client relying upon such a report suffers any loss, he will be held liable for damages. Legal cases regarding his liability will be taken up at the end of this chapter.

Objects of Investigation

Following are some of the particular purposes for which investigations are conducted:

1. Investigation on behalf of an individual or a promoter of a joint-Stock Company which wishes to purchase a private running business in order to ascertain the financial position and the earning capacity of the concern proposed to be taken over.
2. Investigation on behalf of an incoming partner, who wants to know the earning capacity of the firm, the financial position of the concern and whether it is advisable to become a partner.
3. Investigation on behalf of a client who wishes to lend money to a concern to know its financial position.
4. Investigation where fraud is suspected by the proprietor.
5. Investigation on behalf of a client who wishes to purchase the shares of a company
6. Investigation under the Indian Companies Act
7. Investigation to ascertain the amount of compensation payable on the compulsory removal of business.
8. Investigation for claims under an insurance policy covering consequential losses, e.g., in the ease of fire, burgalary, etc.
9. Investigation on behalf of the company or an individual for alleged negligence or lack of skill by the Auditors.
10. Investigation on behalf of the liquidator of a company where the directors are suspected of fraud or misfeasance.
11. Investigation on behalf of beneficiaries where trustees are suspected of fraud or misappropriation.
12. Investigation on behalf of Income Tax authorities for tax liability or for detection of undisclosed income.

We shall take up these cases separately and discuss them in detail.

1. Investigation on behalf of a Purchaser, to ascertain the earning capacity of the concern and whether the assets have been properly valued.

The investigator should pay attention to the following points when called upon by his client who wishes to purchase a, running business to conduct an investigation:

1. Why does the vendor sell the business? Is it a genuine case of sale?
2. Whether it is worthwhile to purchase the business?
3. What is the trend of the business? This may be known by preparing a columnar statement for the past several years, showing the expenses, sales, gross profits, net profits and the percentage of their rise or fall to show whether the business is on the road to prosperity. Extraordinary profits must not be included. Similarly capital profits should be excluded. He should also see that the business had not been starved of necessary expenses in the past. He should not rely on the average annual profits as they may be misleading. The Trading and Profit and Loss Account should be prepared on a uniform basis for easy comparison.
4. Whether the assets have been properly valued and sufficient depreciation has been provided on these assets and whether the goodwill is properly valued; whether sufficient provision has been made for bad and doubtful debts.

5. Whether the liabilities have been properly valued and that they have not been shown at lower figure.
6. Whether the accounts have been previously audited? If so, he should examine the Auditor's Report.
7. Whether the working capital is adequate.
8. Whether the plant and machinery are old or new.
9. Whether any technical knowledge or skill is required for the business to be taken over. If so, whether his client possesses such a skill.
10. Whether trade restrictions have affected recent purchases and sales.
11. Whether there is much competition in the business which is proposed to be taken over.
12. Whether the vendor will be allowed to carry on the same type of business.
13. Whether the customers are a set of friends of the vendor who will cease patronising the business after it has been sold to his client.
14. The Deferred Revenue Expenditure should receive special attention as some of the amounts which ought to have been written off in the past might not have been so treated and thus the Profit and Loss Account might not have been debited with the result that more profit was shown than the actual one.
15. Capital and revenue expenditure should be properly vouched and he should find out whether proper allocation had been made between the two.
16. Profits of the previous years might have been inflated by—
   (*i*) Inflation of closing stock
   (*ii*) Inclusion of fictitious sales.
   (*iii*) inclusion of goods on 'sale or return' basis in the sales.
   (*iv*) Omission of purchases.
   (*v*) Starving the business of necessary expenditure.
   (*vi*) Less provision for bad and doubtful debts.
   (*vii*) Less provision for depreciation.

   Therefore necessary adjustment must be made.
17. Whether the goodwill is properly valued. What has been the basis of its valuation and whether it is fair to his client?
18. Whether reserves are adequate.
19. Whether contingent liabilities have been provided for or not and whether all such liabilities have been taken into account.
20. Whether the forward contracts will result in profit or loss.

If the business proposed to be acquired is a limited company, attention should be paid to the following points:—

1. The authorised, issued, called-up and paid-up capital of the company should be ascertained.
2. What is the amount of the uncalled liability, reserved liability and the calls in arrears?
3. The rights of different classes of shareholders should be enquired into.
4. He should enquire as to what was the rate of dividends which had been paid in the past and whether there is any arreass of dividends to be paid.
5. The Memorandum and Articles of Association of the company should be carefully examined.
6. The value of the shares of the company quoted in the Stock Exchange should be inquired into.

7. If the price of the shares is not quoted in the Stock Exchange, shares will have to be valued according to the method described in the following pages.
8. The assets and liabilities of the company proposed to be taken-over should be valued and he should see whether all liabilities have been included in the balance-sheet and whether any loan is secured or unsecured.

Assuming that the profits shown by the books of accounts of the concern proposed to be taken over are correct, still certain adjustments will have to be made in order to arrive at the profits the purchaser will be able to make after the business has been acquired.

The following items should be added to the profits of the vendors:

1. Rent, if the purchaser is going to purchase the land or premises which the vendor had not owned and was paying rent for it.
2. Interest on Partner's Capital and Current Accounts, Partner's salaries, if any, as they will not have to be paid after the purchase.
3. Interest on loans and over-draft, if any, if the purchaser is not going to take over the loan or over-draft.
4. Discount on purchases, if the vendors had not taken advantage of the cash discount on purchases on account of inadequacy of working capital with the vendors, provided the purchaser will have sufficient working capital.
5. Exceptional losses, e.g., loss by fire which was not covered by insurance, costs and damages incurred by litigation, etc., which do not normally occur and which might have been debited to revenue account.
6. Excessive reserve for bad and doubtful debts or depreciation, etc.
7. Capital losses if they had been debited-to-profit and loss account.
8. Capital expenditure which was debited to profit and loss account.

The following items should be deducted from the profits:

1. Income from assets not taken over by the purchaser.
2. Rent, if the purchaser is not going to purchase the premises which the vendor owned.
3. Capital profits, e.g., profits on sale of fixed assets as such profits do not usually occur.
4. Exceptional profits, e.g., speculative profits, which had been credited *to* profit and loss account by the vendor.
5. Director's fees payable by the purchasing company, but if the purchaser is a limited company, the fees will not be deducted as the company will have to pay the director's fees.
6. Interest on partner's drawings which was credited to profit and loss account by the vendor.

The question of depreciation will have to be tackled as the company will have to provide depreciation on the value at which they have been acquired. After making these adjustments, the investigator will be in a position to find out the profits which the purchaser will be able to earn after purchasing the business.

If the purchasing company wishes to incorporate the report relating to the profits in the prospectus of the company it may safely do so. The investigator must be very careful to give a true picture. He must not express any opinion about the future earning capacity of the business. If it is found later on that the business purchased was not making so much profit; any shareholder who had purchased the shares on the faith of such a statement by the investigator in the prospectus, will be entitled to get compensation from the investigator if the shareholder has suffered any loss.

2. Investigation on behalf of an Incoming Partner

In addition to the points which have been considered above in connection with the purchase of a business the following points must be taken into consideration:

1. The reason why a new partner is to be taken in.
2. If the new partner is admitted in place of a deceased or retiring partner, whether the business will suffer for want of skill, experience or influence of the deceased or the retiring partner and which skill and experience his client does not possess.
3. What is the financial position of the proprietor, partner or partners who wish to take his client as a partner as, on account of the principle of unlimited liability, his client's interest will be affected, in the event of heavy losses, if the other or others are financially weak.
4. While computing the future profits of the business the investigator should take into consideration any salary which the retiring partner was getting.
5. He should find out whether the amount of goodwill which is to be paid by his client is reasonable one.
6. Whether the capital to be introduced by his client will be used for paying off any liability or paying back the capital of the retiring or deceased partner or will be utilised as additional working capital. In the former case, whether sufficient amount will be left as working capital. If not, it may affect the business and the profit. In case his client's contribution will be used as working capital, whether the amount will be sufficient to expand the business and Whether there is any further scope for expansion of the business.
7. Whether the proposed share of profits to be paid, to his client is reasonable, taking into consideration the capital and labour of the other partners.
8. Whether the incompleted contracts which will be transferred to the reconstituted firm will be a liability or a loss.
9. He should thoroughly study the old as well as the proposed Partnership Deeds to see that they do not adversely affect the interest of his client.
10. He should see that the goodwill has been properly valued.

3. Investigation on behalf of a Lender of Money

Sometimes a bank is asked by its customer to lend him heavy amount or allow an overdraft or to pay bills even though his credit balance may be insufficient. Hence, the bank would like to know the financial position of the borrower before it grants an overdraft or gives a loan, etc. Even if the bank examines the audited balance-sheet of the would-be borrower, it may not be in a position to know the true financial position and may hesitate to lend money especially when the amount involved is a heavy one. Under such circumstances the bank may requisition the services of an investigator before it grants the necessary loan. It may be mentioned here that such an investigation is conducted only when the amount involved is a large one. Investigations may also be conducted on behalf of a private money-lender. Such an investigator should pay attention to the following points:

1. Why is additional finance required?
2. Whether the loan will be utilised productively.
3. Whether any other party in the past has refused to give the loan. If so, what were the reasons.
4. The nature of the security offered and its true value.
5. Whether the security offered is adequate.
6. Whether the security has already a prior charge, and if, so what is the value of the charge,

7. If the loan is proposed to be advanced on the general assets of the company, a statement of the assets and liabilities should be prepared and he should ascertain the net value of the assets, viz., whether the assets are already charged or whether some of the debts are over-due or time-barred.
8. What is the ratio of the current liabilities to liquid resources?
9. What is the normal earning capacity of the borrower? This can be ascertained by scanning the profit and loss accounts for the past several years. If the earning capacity of the borrower is good, there is greater possibility of the loan being re-paid in time.
10. He should also make enquiries about the ability, experience, character, etc., of the borrower. If he is an able man, is of a high character, and is honest, he will deem it his moral duty to repay the loan in time.

4. Investigation when Fraud is Suspected

When the investigator is called upon to investigate into a suspected fraud, he should study the system of accountancy and internal check followed in the business. If he finds that there is any loophole and there is a possibility of fraud, he must go deep into the question. It is very difficult to lay down the different methods of fraud as human ingenuity has and will ever devise various and peculiar ways to commit frauds. Each case must be handled on its own merits. But it must be remembered that fraud is usually committed by those who handle cash and goods. Fraud may also be committed by manipulating the accounts. Thus fraud is usually committed in the following ways:—

(*a*) By misappropriating cash—(usually committed by the employees).
(*b*) By misappropriating goods—(committed by the employees).
(*c*) By manipulating the accounts—(committed by the proprietors or those at the helm of affairs).

Let us deal with each item separately and see how such a fraud is committed and what should be the line of action by the investigator.

(*a*) Misappropriation of Cash

Cash may be misappropriated in any of the following ways:

(*i*) Omitting to enter the receipt of cash.
(*ii*) Entering less amount in the cash book than what has been received.
(*iii*) Entering fictitious payments.
(*iv*) Entering more amount than what has actually been paid.

The investigator should follow the line of action as detailed below especially when the cashier had an access to the books of account:

(*i*) Permission should be obtained from his client to issue a circular to the debtors asking them to confirm the balance owing by them. The letters of confirmation should be sent direct to the investigator.
(*ii*) Examine the internal check system regarding cash sales and see whether there is any loophole. If so, he must probe into the matter.
(*iii*) Similarly sales of goods might have been omitted from the books so that when cash is received from the buyers, it is misappropriated.
(*iv*) He should compare the counterfoils of Paying-in-Slips with the entries in the Cash Book and the Pass Book to see that less amount than that stated in the counterfoils might not have been deposited in the bank.
(*v*) Enquire as to who signs and endorses the cheques.

(*vi*) List of bad debts should be examined and enquiry should be made whether the bad debts are really bad debts or in fact money might have been received from the debtors and misappropriated and the amount written off as 'Bad Debt'.

(*vii*) What is the system of payment of salaries and wages. It is possible that payments might have been made to fictitious employees or over-payment might have been made.

(*viii*) Petty cash transactions should be verified and vouchers obtained as far as possible. Special attention should be paid to Petty Cash transactions as they are usually a source of fraud.

(*ix*) He must pay attention to bill transactions. It is possible that some bills might have been paid, proceeds misappropriated and the transactions might have been passed as if the bills had been dishonoured for non-payment. Such supposed 'dishonoured bills' and other bills must be examined. Bills in hand must also be examined. Similarly bills might have been discounted and cash proceeds misappropriated but the bills might be shown as if they are still in hand. The supposed 'dishonoured bills' must be examined. Since they have not been dishonoured, they would not be available.

(*x*) Duplicates must be obtained for missing vouchers.

(*xi*) Cash received on account of unusual receipts, such as sale of waste materials, cash received from debtors who might have been written off as 'bad' in the past, allowances received, etc., might have been misappropriated.

(*xii*) Pay attention to misappropriating cash by the 'Teeming and Lading' method which means that cash received from one customer is misappropriated and the cash received from another is credited to the first customer's account and later on when cash is received from a third customer it is credited to the second customer and so on.

(*xiii*) Misappropriating cash by showing more discount allowed than actually is the case. Examine the rules regarding granting of discount.

(*b*) Misappropriation of Goods

Pilfering of goods is very difficult to detect especially when they are small in bulk and are very costly. Proper stock accounts should be maintained. The Investigator should check the receipt and issue of goods and the Stock Accounts. He should compare the Order Received Book, Sales Book, Godown-keeper's Book, Gate-keeper's Book and invoices, etc. (*Rez* vs. *Hinds, Musgrave and Steven,* 1950).

(*c*) manipulation of Accounts

Accounts may be manipulated by (a) the proprietors of a business, (b) the partners of a firm, (c) the employees, or (d) the: directors of a company. The object of manipulation of accounts may be to

(*i*) show less profits in order to pay less income tax;

(*ii*) show more profits to earn more commission, if it is payable to the manager, employees, etc., on the result of the rate of dividends.

(*iii*) show more profits than actually they are in order to maintain the rate of dividends.

(*iv*) show more profits when the business is going to be sold.

Less profits are shown by recording more or fictitious expenses, less sales, undervaluation of closing stock, omission of accrued income, debiting of capital expenditure to revenue, and so on.

On the other hand, more profits may be shown by omitting to enter expenses or debiting *the* revenue expenditure to capital accounts, suppressing of purchase invoices, overvaluation of closing stock, showing fictitious sales or treating goods sent on 'sale or return' as sales, etc.

The investigator should study the Internal Check System. He should thoroughly check the purchases and sales transactions especially those which took place at the close of the financial year.

He should also examine the profit and loss account transactions taking place at the end of the year. He should use tact and his experience.

He should compare the gross profit ratio and the ratio of the net capital with those of the previous years. If there is an appreciable change or variation he should go deeper into the matter. He should also examine whether there has been any change in the accounting method during the years or in any previous years for which investigation is being carried out. He should not only point out the amount of fraud committed and the person responsible for it, but he should also suggest ways and means to prevent the commission of such frauds in future.

If the investigator has been very careful in following the above suggestions and if he has been able to detect the fraud he will be in a position to give evidence against the defaulting party

5. Investigation on behalf of a client who wishes to purchase the shares of a company

The subject of valuation of shares has always been controversial in the accounting profession. There are people who are of opinion-that there is no scientific method of valuation of .shares of a company, but it is, a wrong notion.

Sometimes the Articles of Association of a Private Company lay down that the members wishing to sell their shares must offer them in the first instance to the shareholders of the company at 'fair value' which has to be determined by the auditors of the company. The auditor is, therefore, asked to fix the 'fair value' of the shares to be paid by the shareholders. Again, sometimes a client seeks the advice of the auditor when purchasing the shares of a company. In such a case the client is not only interested to find out the dividends payable but also in the security of the amount invested in the purchase of the shares. The purchaser would also like to know whether the same rate of dividend will be maintained.

It may be stated here that the Central Board of Direct Taxes have framed the following rules for the valuation of the shares of private limited companies other than investment companies and managing agency companies:—

The shares will be valued at the break-up value—the difference between the book value of the assets and liabilities of the company.

From the break-up value a discount of 15 per cent will be allowed. This discount may be increased to 25 per cent, if dividends have not been declared by the company in earlier years.

Thus no difficulty will arise in valuing the shares of private companies and will obviate the necessity of a large number of appeals regarding the valuation of such shares.

In the case of the valuation of the shares of public companies, the auditor should find out at what price the shares of the company were purchased and sold in the past. This will give a rough idea of the value of the shares. More correct methods of estimating the current value of the shares of the company are the following:—

(*a*) On the basis of the average profits in the previous years, i.e., the "Yield" or "Profits" Basis Method. To ascertain the value of the shares according to this method, the profit and loss accounts of the previous few years, say three to five years, be taken into consideration. Necessary adjustments in respect of reserves should be made. He should also find out the interest payable on first class securities and the earnings of other companies carrying on the same class of business. Let us take an example to make the point clear. A company has 50,000 equity shares of the nominal value of Rs. 10 each and 50,000, 5% Preference Shares, of the nominal value of Rs. 10 each. The company makes an average annual profit of Rs. 61,000 after making the necessary adjustment as described above. The average income from investments in other companies of similar nature is 6 percent according to Stock Exchange quotations. The value of the shares, will be calculated as under :

	Rs.
Average Profits	61,000
Less dividend payable to preference shareholders	25,000
Profit available for equity shareholders	36,000

The capitalised value of the equity shares at the rate of 6 per cent is

$$= \frac{36,000 \times 100}{6}, \text{ i.e., } 6,00,000.$$

Therefore, the value of each , share will be $\frac{6,00,000}{50,000}$

i.e., Rs. 12.

Hence the fair value of each share will be Rs. 12.

(*b*) On the basis of the net assets of the company. Under this method the total value of liabilities including the prior claims of other classes of shareholders is deducted out of the total value of the assets including the goodwill, if any. It may be stated that here some accountants are of opinion that goodwill should be excluded from the assets. Others say that it should be included only when a large number of shares are to be purchased. The balance so arrived at is divided by the number of shares. It may be mentioned that this method is applicable only in the case of the equity shares as only the equity shareholders are entitled to all the surplus after the satisfaction of the claims of the other class of shareholders.

In this connection, the question is: how are the assets to be valued? The Institute of Chartered Accountants of India has issued a pamphlet "Study on Share Valuation", which states, "For the purpose of the assets basis of valuation, generally they are valued at market price and in some cases the book value is used".

The meaning of the market price has been given in the judgment given in the case of *Gajapatiraju, V. N.* vs. *Revenue Divisional Officer,* (1939): "Market value means the value at which the shares will be sold in the market. Market value assumes to the a willing transaction between the buyer and the seller and not a faced sale when a seller is-willing to sell and the buyer is in urgent necessity to buy".

The investigator should make the necessary adjustments in the book, value of the assets and liabilities. Conventional value of certain assets is ignored in certain cases, e.g., market value of the premises, investments, etc., is taken-, into consideration rather than original price less total depreciation as is the convention.

He should also examine the trend of the business as has been pointed out previously. The conditions prevailing in the money market, likely legislation which will affect that business in the future, etc., must be taken into consideration while valuing the shares: The Memorandum of Association and Articles of the company must be scrutinised in order to ascertain the rights of the different classes of shareholders. The accountant should be rather conservative in the valuation of shares. He should mention in his report the basis on which he has computed the value of shares in which case the court can question his findings (*Dean* vs. *Prince and Others,* 1953). If he values the shares as an expert, he need not give any reason for his findings.

6. Investigation under the Provision of the Companies Act

Investigators or Inspectors may also be appointed under the Companies Act by the Central Government in the following circumstances:

I. In the case of companies having share capital if at least 200 members or those who hold at least one-tenth of the total voting power apply to the Government [S. 235 (*a*)].

II. In the case of companies which have no share capital, when at least one-fifth of the total number of the members apply to the Government [S. 235 (*b*)].

Under the above two cases, the Central Government may require evidence to prove good reasons for requiring the investigation and may also call for security up to Rs. 1,000 for payment of the cost of investigation (S. 236).

III. The Registrar of Joint-Stock Companies may apply to the Central Government for the appointment of Inspectors—

(*a*) if the company has failed to send any information or explanation which he required the company to furnish; or

(*b*) if the documents filed 'by the company disclose an unsatisfactory state of affairs; or

(*c*) if it has been represented to the registrar that the affairs of the company have been carried on fraudulently (S. 234).

IV. The Central Government may also appoint inspectors if it appears to it—

(a) that the business of the company is conducted fraudulently or to commit fraud on creditors or on minority or that the company was formed with fraudulent or unlawful objects; or

(b) that the persons connected with the management of the company are guilty of fraud, misfeasance, or misconduct towards the company or its members; or

(c) that full information regarding the method of calculation of the commission payable to managing agents, managing directors, etc., is not given (S. 237).

It may, be pointed out that the Government cannot appoint the investigator unless one of the circumstances mentioned above exists.

V. The Government shall appoint Inspectors, if—

(*a*) the company passes a special resolution for their appointment;

or

(*b*) the court issues an order that the affairs of the company ought to be investigated by an inspector appointed by the Central Government (S. 237).

VI. The Central Government must appoint one or more inspectors to investigate and report on the membership of a company for the purpose of determining the true persons—

(*a*) who are or have been financially interested in the success or failure, whether real or apparent, of the company; or

(*b*) who are or have been able to control or materially to influence the policy of the company (S. 247).

The expenses of this type of investigation will be borne by the Central Government out of moneys provided by Parliament unless the Government directs that the expenses or any part thereof should be paid by the persons on whose application the investigation was ordered.

Such Inspectors or investigators are usually accountants. No firm, body corporate or association can be appointed as an inspector under Section 235 or 237. They have wide powers to examine any book of account, documents, vouchers, etc., and can examine any officer of the company on oath. (S. 240). If such an officer refuses to answer any questions an oath or refuses to show the books of accounts, or documents etc., he is liable to be punished as if he has been guilty of contempt of court. (S. 240). The inspectors have also right to examine any director, managing director, managing agents, secretaries and treasurers, etc., who are or have been connected with the company, its holding or subsidiary company. If the inspector has no legal power to examine any person, he may apply to the court which may order that person to appear before the inspector.

The investigator should pay special attention-to the following points:

1. Whether the remunerations of the director, managing agents, etc., have been paid according to the Companies Act and shown in the profit and loss account accordingly.

2. Whether the funds of the company are properly or profitably invested.

3. Whether loans advanced to Directors of the company, interest charges thereon, and the security offered by such a director are according to the Companies Act and shown in the balance-sheet accordingly

4. The current account of the managing agents with the company should be examined.

5. The contracts entered into by the managing agents with other companies in which such managing agents or directors are interested should be examined.

6. The assets and liabilities should be verified and valued.

Powers of the Inspector under S. 240

1. He can demand the production of any books, papers, etc., from any officer, employees or the agents of the company or the related bodies corporate.

2. He can, with the prior approval of the Central Government, demand any information, production of any books, documents etc., if he thinks it necessary for the purpose of investigation, from any other body corporate.

3. He can examine on oath any officer, employee or the agent of a related body corporate.

4. He can, with the prior approval of the Central Government, summon any other person and examine him on oath.

5. He can seize, if so authorised by a magistrate, the books, papers, etc., of the company or of any related body corporate and retain them if he is of opinion that these books, papers etc. will be destroyed, falsified, altered, mutilated or removed. He can retain them till the conclusion of the investigation.

If any officer, employees or the agent of the related body corporate fails to produce the books of account, document, papers etc. or fails to furnish any information sought by the inspector, he will be punished with fine up to two thousand rupees or imprisoned up to six months or may be awarded both the punishments.

The Inspector may submit an interim report, if so directed by the Central Government, and on the conclusion of the investigation shall make a final report to the Central Government which shall send a copy of the report to the following:

(*a*) The Registrar of the Joint Stock Companies;

(*b*) The registered office of the Company;

(*c*) Any body corporate, managing agents, secretaries and treasurers who have been dealt with under section 239;

(*d*) Any applicant, if he so desires on prescribed fees;

(*e*) The court at whose direction the Inspector was appointed;

(*f*) Any body corporate which was subjected to examination.

The Central Government may cause the report to be published.

On the receipt of the report from the Inspectors the Central Government—

(*a*) may launch criminal proceedings against the officers who have been found guilty of any criminal offence; or

(*b*) may order for the winding up of the company; or

(*c*) may institute criminal proceedings against any party on behalf of the company and recover damages; or

(*d*) may make an application to the court for an order under S. 397 or S. 398.

Expenses of investigation shall be incurred by the Central Government in the first instance but it will have the right to be reimbursed by persons convicted or found liable for damages, etc., or by the applicants, if it appears that there was no reasonable cause for such an investigation, etc.

Duties of the Investigator

If an auditor is appointed under the above circumstances to conduct an investigation, he should get instructions in writing regarding the scope of enquiry, its objects and the time limit by which the report has to be submitted. The auditor so appointed should proceed on the following lines:—

1. Whether there has been any breach of duty by any officer.
2. Whether any loss has been caused by the negligence on the part of directors, etc.
3. Whether contracts entered into were fair deals especially those entered into with directors and officers of the company.
4. Whether the assets and liabilities have been properly valued. He should also verify them.
5. He should interrogate directors and officers of the company, and if need be, he may seek legal advice. He may, if he thinks necessary, interrogate directors and officers of related companies.
6. If there are subsidiaries, he should direct his attention to the inter-company dealings.

VI. According to Section 233A of the Companies Act, the Central Government may get the accounts of a company audited by a special auditor for a period of one or more years. Although such an audit is termed as special audit, it is more or less a kind of investigation with special object in view. We shall deal with the provisions contained in Section 233A which has been added to the Companies Act in 1960.

The Central Government may appoint special auditor under the following circumstances when in the opinion of the Central Government—

(*a*) the affairs of any company are not being managed in accordance with sound business principles or prudent commercial policy; or

(*b*) any company is being managed in a manner likely to cause serious injury or damage to the interests of the trade, industry or business to which it pertains; or

(*c*) the financial position of any company is such a way as to endanger its solvency.

The Central Government may, under the aforesaid circumstances, appoint—

(*a*) a Chartered Accountant as defined in clause (b) of sub-section (1) of Section 2 of the Chartered Accountants Act, 1949, even though such a Chartered Accountant is not in practice; or

(*b*) the company's auditor himself to conduct such special audit. The Government may order the conduct of special audit for any period or periods it thinks advisable.

The Chartered Accountant so appointed, whether he is the company's auditor or any other Chartered Accountant, will be designated as special auditor. He will have the same powers and duties in relation to the special audit as an auditor of a company appointed under Section 227 except that instead of submitting his report to the member of the company, he will have to submit it to the Central Government.

In addition to the powers conferred on the inspector under S. 227, he will have the following powers:

If he thinks it necessary for the purpose of his investigation to investigate also the affairs of any other body corporate which is, or has at any time been, company's subsidiary or holding company or a subsidiary of the holding company or holding company or its subsidiary or has been its managing agents, he may examine any person who had been their managing director, or managing agent or secretaries and treasurers or manager.

The Central Government may direct any person to furnish any information in connection with such an audit to the special auditor as may be required by him. If such a person refuses to furnish the information within the prescribed time, he is punishable with a fine up to five hundred rupees.

The report prepared by the special auditor shall incorporate almost all the points which are usually incorporated in the auditor's report under Section 227, in addition to a statement on any other matter which may be referred to him by the Central Government. On receipt of the report from the special auditor, the Central Government may take such action on the report as it considers necessary in accordance with the provisions of the Companies Act, 1956

If the Central Government does not take any action on the report within four months from the date of receipt, it shall send to the company either a copy of or relevant extracts from the report with its comments thereon and require the company to send a copy of such a report or extracts to the members of the company or to have such a copy or extracts read before the company at its next general meeting.

The expenses, incidental to such a special audit including the remuneration of the special auditor, shall be determined by the Central. Government and paid by the company. In default, the amount will be recoverable as if it were an arrear of land revenue.

The auditor in such a case will have to follow the same line of action as has been mentioned in the foregoing pages but he may have to face certain difficulties in carrying out his duties. He should, therefore, get the precise nature of the enquiry from the Government when called upon to undertake such an investigation.

As stated above, the Government may appoint Special Auditor, if in its opinion the affairs of the company are not managed on;

(*a*) "Sound Commercial Principles"; or

(*b*) "Prudent Commercial Policy".

The Act has not defined what are "Sound Business Principles" and "Prudent Commercial Policy". Transactions which may appear to one against. "Sound Commercial Principles" and "Prudent Commercial Policy" may appear to be sound to another person. There can be differences of opinion. *Bona fide* transactions may result in a loss. Again an auditor is not a technical hand to decide whether the purchase of foreign made machinery or home made machinery was in the best interest of the company or whether electrical or mechanical power used was in the interest of the company and so on.

Again special auditor appointed may happen to be the statutory auditor of the company in which case he will not like to point out his own negligence in not pointing out the wrong and wasteful policy pursued by the directors.

In any case, if an auditor is appointed as a Special Auditor, he should know what is the precise nature of his investigation.

7. Investigation to ascertain the amount of compensation payable on the Compulsory Removal of Business

Sometimes the property of a concern is acquired by a public body like Railway, Municipal Corporation, Electricity Company, Port Trust, Improvement Trust, etc. In a case like this such a concern has to shift to another place or permanently close down its business and consequently it suffers a monetary loss. Naturally it will have the right to claim compensation from such a public body.

The question is as to how much compensation is to be paid to such a concern. The efforts of the concern will be to get as much compensation as possible while the public body will try to pay the minimum possible amount of compensation. To arrive at a fair amount of compensation payable, an investigator, who is usually an accountant, is appointed to assess the correct amount of compensation. The accountant should, in such a case, take into consideration the following points to arrive at a decision:—

1. *The actual expenses incurred in the removal of the business.* He should vouch these expenses as usual by examining the vouchers, cash book, etc.

2. *The actual loss suffered on account of compulsory slae of stock fixtures, etc.* This loss can be found out from the difference between the book value and the sale price, by referring to correspondence or auctioneer's statement of account..

3. *The loss in the earning capacity of the concern.* As the business will have to shift to another place or locality, it may not get the same number of customers. It will have to establish its reputation in that locality and it would take some time to do so. In the meantime, it would suffer some loss. To assess this loss, the investigator will have to find out ;he average net profits earned during the last few years. The claim for compensation would be the difference between the profits earned during the, past, and the estimated average profits of the next three or five years.

4. *The loss suffered on account of forfeiture of the lease.* If the concern had a leasehold property, it would loss that lease. The loss in this respect is assessed by adding ten to twenty per cent to the book value of the lease.

Now it would not be difficult for the investigator to find out the total amount of the claim for compensation. All the losses suffered or to be suffered will be added together.

The investigator will have to prepare report which must show as to how he arrived at the figure for compensation. The report should be clear and convincing.

8. Investigation for Claims under an Insurance Policy covering Consequential Loss

If the premises of a business house is burnt down by fire, the owner not only suffers the loss due to destruction of goods, machinery, fixtures, etc., but he suffers another loss also, viz., the profit which he would have earned from the date when the fire - destroyed the premises till the insurance claim is settled and the business is set up again. Therefore, he can take an insurance policy to cover this loss. The insurance policy in such a case lays down certain rules according to which the "loss of profits" is calculated. Usually an accountant is appointed to assess this "loss of profits". While doing so, the accountant has to take into consideration the turnover of the previous year, the increased cost of working and the period for which this loss is to be calculated. If the amount of the loss is greater than the insured sum, the principles of average will be applied and only a percentage of the loss will be borne by the insurer. The claim cannot exceed the insured sum.

The assessment by the auditor in such a case is taken as conclusive unless it is proved by the other party (1) that the auditor has misdirected himself in point of law, (2) that he had omitted to take into consideration some material fact, or (3) that the auditor had omitted to take into consideration the fact that losses of turnover were wholly or in part due to other causes than the fire. The insurance company cannot dispute the findings of the accountant as was held in *Rechter Co.* vs. *North British and Mercantile Insurance Co.* (1915) except under the circumstances mentioned in the beginning of the paragraph.

Under these circumstances the special auditor or the investigator must be very careful in assessing the damages on the principles stated above and according to the terms of Insurance Policy.

9. Investigation on behalf of the company or an individual (or alleged negligence or lack of skill by the Auditor

Sometimes a company whose accounts have been audited by its auditor alleges that due to his negligence or lack of skill certain types of frauds which had been perpetrated by its employees have not been detected by him. Therefore, the company wishes to appoint an investigator to prove such an allegation against the auditor.

Thus it becomes a very delicate position for the investigator so appointed. The investigator, who is usually an auditor, is reluctant to give evidence against his professional brother even though the latter may be at fault. But the public have a right to get help of these professional people and get evidence to prove their case. It is, therefore, necessary that those whose services are required must render the best possible service irrespective of the fact that the report to be submitted is against their fellow professionals.

10. Investigation for Auditor's Report for Prospectus Purposes

An auditor is sometimes asked by an already established company which wants to issue more shares, to give a report regarding the profits earned by the company in the past years so that his report may be incorporated in the prospectus to be issued to the public inviting applications for the purchase of its shares. According to the Companies Act, 1956, the profits or losses earned by the company during the previous five years must be certified by the auditor of the company. The profits or losses, whatever the case may be, should be stated year-wise and 'not the average profits or losses'. If the company has been in existence for less than five years, then the profits or losses for all those years should be stated in the report. Sometimes a company asks its auditor to certify the profits for more than five years, say seven years, in which case he should act accordingly.

The auditor should see that the profits are not inflated. He should make necessary adjustments in the profit and loss account of the previous years in arriving at the correct figure of the profits or losses as has been explained in the beginning of this chapter. He should pay attention only to the facts which directly concern the figures of normal profits earned during the period under investigation. While submitting his report, the auditor should refrain from expressing any opinion about the future earning capacity of the company.

The Companies Act requires the Auditor to state in his report as to what adjustments he had made to arrive at the figures of profits or losses. Such a report involves heavy responsibilities on him as was decided in the case of *Regina* vs. *Wake & Stone* in 1954. In this connection the Institute of Chartered Accountants of England has issued its recommendations Nos. 13 and 16 for the guidance of its members.

Investigator's Report

As has been stated earlier, the investigating auditor has to submit his report to his client and, therefore, it is deemed advisable to state here the form and technique of writing his report.

Form of investigator's report

1. The introduction should mention the instructions to him regarding the investigation, matters on which he relied and the work he has carried out.

2. He should then briefly deal with the history and the nature of business.

3. The report should, thereafter, briefly state the structure of the organisation, officials, their duties and responsibilities, etc.

4. The summary of the report, his findings and recommendations, if any, should be concluded in his report.

What factors should be taken into consideration will depend upon the purposes for which the investigation is being conducted, e.g., in the case of investigation for the valuation of a business for its purchase and sale, the following factors are taken into consideration:

The availability of labour, ages of the technical staff, transportation facilities available, dependance of regular supply of a particular raw material, whether the customers of the old firm will continue patronising the new firm, the amount of goodwill demanded (whether it is reasonable), and such like factors will have to be taken into consideration.

Technique of investigation

The most common and useful technique to be followed is the use of ratios, e.g., the gross profit percentage on sales as a measure of two periods, i.e., profit for the current year with that of the previous year or years. Other ratios which may be applied are—

1. Outstanding creditors to purchases of last three months.
2. Outstanding debtors to sales of last three months.
3. Current liabilities to current liquid assets (to see the liquidity and solvency of the firm).
4. Current liabilities to current assets.
5. Equity ratio, i.e., the ratio of capitalisation including loans.
6. Stock value to turnover, etc.

Let us deal with a few legal cases and discuss the duties of the investigators.

Short and Crompton vs. Brackett (1904)

The facts of the case were that the plaintiffs, the accountants, were employed by Brackett, who intended to take a partner, to prepare accounts from his books which would show the amount of the profits and the goodwill. After the work was over, the plaintiffs, i.e., the auditors claimed their fees while the defendant put in a counter claim to recover damages alleging that the plaintiffs were negligent in the discharge of their duties, because during the period, a certain clerk had committed frauds by preparing incorrect wages sheets and misappropriated money which frauds were not detected by the plaintiffs.

The plaintiffs pleaded that they were employed to arrive at the results as shown by the books of accounts and not to audit the accounts. They further pointed out that the defalcations were due to the negligence on the part of the defendant who kept his books of account in such a manner. Mr. C. W. Carnish, Fellow of the Institute of Chartered Accountants, during the course of his evidence said that in the case of preparation of a balance-sheet from books the totals in the books would be assumed to be correct without investigation, and it would not be the duty of an accountant to examine vouchers, in which term he included wages books. The judgment was given in favour of the accountants. His Honour, Judge Tindal Atkinson, held that, having regard to the object for which they were employed, the plaintiffs were entitled to assume that the amount appearing in the defendant's books as paid for wages was correct, and in view of the fact that at the time there was no suspicion of any defalcations by the defendant's clerk alluded to, he thought there was no negligence on their part. Therefore, judgment would be for plaintiffs on the claims with other costs and the counter-claim would be dismissed with costs.

Colmer vs. Meerrett, Son & Stret (1914)

The facts of the case were that Colmer who was an engineer wanted to invest £2,500 in F. Bradley Ltd. This company had already got its balance-sheet duly audited by the defendant as at 28th February 1910, showing a profit of £700. The plaintiff wanted to know the *interim* profit earned by the company from lst March, 1910 to 31st October, 1910. The auditors, the defendants, were asked to do so. Colmer wanted to get this information within three days. The defendants showed that the company had made an interm profit of £1,363. Thereupon, the plantiff invested the money and lost most of it. On investigation it was found that the company had suffered losses instead of making profits in both the periods. The plaintiff sued the defendants for the loss he had suffered on account of negligence of the auditors in not detecting the losses and then by indirectly inducing him to invest his money in a worthless company.

The defence of the auditors was that with regard to the first period, viz., from lst June, 1910 to 28th February, 1910, they owed no duty to the plaintiff as there was no privity of contract between him and the plaintiff. As regards the second, viz., from 1 st March to 31st October, 1910, when their services were requisitioned by the plaintiff, the time at their disposal to audit the accounts was very short, i.e., only three days were given to them to let the plaintiff know the amount of profit the company had earned during eight months. The report submitted by Mr. Meerrett, a partner of the firm of the auditors, had said that he had extracted the balances as on 31st October, 1910, from the Bought and Sold Ledgers, but that he was unable to vouch for their accuracy as owing to the short time at his disposal, he had been unable to call for statements from suppliers or send out enquiries to debtors, but that they might be taken as approximately correct. He further added, "With reference to the stock, as arranged with Mr. Colmer, I have taken the figures supplied by Mr. Bradley".

The jury returned a verdict for the plaintiff and assessed the damages at £250. During the course of judgment, Lush, J., said:

"Negligence meant in law breach of duty which one person owed to another who paid him to render certain services by not bringing to bear that reasonable skill and care which a professional man impliedly undertook that he would use.

"The burden was on the plaintiff to prove that the work that the defendants did in the preparation of the October balance-sheet was negligent. The defendant did not suggest that he undertook a full audit, which the plaintiff said in substance that he did. One of the first questions for the jury, therefore, was what was the real duty the defendant undertook. There was, of course, no charge of fraud against him. The report furnished by the defendant was of the greatest importance in the case, and it seemed to him actually set out what was undertaken to be done. That was never demurred to. The plaintiff's solicitor did not write back and say that was not what the defendant agreed to do. The defendant said, that he ,had taken the figures as supplied by the Managing Director, and that again was not objected to either by the plaintiff or by his solicitor. The plaintiff also must -have known from the report of the shortness of time in which the statement was prepared. It was begun on Saturday and finished on Tuesday and as to that the defendant had stated that a full audit would have taken three weeks. The question of time seemed very important, and if the auditor was employed to check the Managing Director, and to make a full audit, then two or three days did not seem a long time to do it in. But if the jury were of opinion that the defendant undertook to act as a check upon the Managing Director and advise the plaintiff what the position of the company was as an auditor did when he made a full audit, they might properly think that the duty had not been fulfilled and there had been a breach of it. It was very unfortunate that a gentleman who was going to invest a considerable sum in a business should have been content with having the result of two or three days' work from an auditor authorised to accept from the Managing Director his own view of what the stock was worth, instead of having the thing done with full care. The result was that he had lost between £1,900 and £2,000."

As mentioned previously, the jury returned the verdict for the plaintiff and assessed the damages at £250.

Regina vs. Wake & Stone, (1954)

The facts of the case are that a company, Wake & Dean Ltd, issued Prospectus in 1951, which contained a report in regard to the valuation of stock and work-in-progress duly certified by the auditor. The statement regarding the stock was worded "stock and work-in-progress" as valued by the company's officers *at the lower of the cost or market value* as at 30th June, 1950, amounted to £641,607.

The case was filed against the managing director and the auditor of the company for having inflated the figures of work-in-progress and the stock. It was admitted in the Court that the figure in respect of stock and work-in-progress was "false, deceptive and misleading". It was proved that the method of valuation of the timber in which the company dealt with was wrong and the stock sheet did not show as to how the figure of £641,607 was arrived at which in fact should have been £495,000.

The auditor defended himself by saying that he had asked for an explanation of the altered figure but it was found that he never held any independent corroboration except by asking for an explanation from the managing director who said that the alteration had been made because of an error in the original figure in respect of stock and work-in-progress.

The managing director who pleaded guilty was sentenced to imprisonment. The auditor pleaded not guilty and was sentenced to pay a fine of £200 or in the alternative six months imprisonment for having signed the report recklessly.

QUESTIONS

1. On behalf of the Pigmy Bank Limited you are required to investigate the affairs of the Giant Limited, which has applied for a loan on the security of its stock-in-trade. What are the special points you would examine? *(Madras B. Com.)*

2. The Directors of a Private Limited Company of which you are an auditor call upon you to fix the value of its Equity shares. State the main points you would take into account in arriving at such a value dealing particularly with the question of goodwill. *(Bombay B. Com.)*

3. What is investigation? Distinguish Investigation from Audit.
(Marathwada Cal., Punjab, Madras, Poona, B. Com., Cal. B. Com., Hons., Cal. M. Com.)

4. (*a*) Distinguish between audit and investigation. State the principles you would bear in mind before taking up an investigation.

(*b*) Mention five business situations in which an investigation into the affairs of business would be required. *(Madurai, Cal., Guahati B. Com.)*

5. Your client is contemplating joining an established firm of architects as a partner. He has given you an introduction to the firm and has handed to you a draft of the proposed terms. He has instructed you to make such an investigation of the affairs of the business as you think fit and to advise him generally.

State the matters to which you would direct attention when carrying out the instructions. *(CA. Final* 1966; *Lucknow* 1974)

6. What points would you bear in mind in conducting an investigation on behalf of an individual proposing to buy a running trading concern? *(Rajasthan, Poona B. Com.)*

7. You have been instructed by a client to investigate into the books of a business which has been offered for sale to him. Assume your own details and write a report to your client advising him to reject the offer, giving detailed reasons in support of your advice. *(Rajasthan M. Com.)*

8. Your client is a retailer who informs you that he uniformly prices his goods 10% over cost. The Profit and Loss Account shows a gross profit of *6%*. Give reasons for shortfall and indicate the enquiries you would make in your capacity as auditor in these circumstances. *(Delhi B. Com.)*

9. Govinda Hazarika wants to join Sarma Brothers as a partner. He requests you to carry out an investigation into the business on his behalf. Indicate the points to which you will pay special attention before you can give a favourable report to Hazarika in this connection. *(Gauhati B. Com.)*

10. (*a*) What consideration should be borne in mind by Auditors when reporting for the purpose of the prospectus?

(*b*) Indicate adjustment to be made for the above purpose to the profits of a partnership proposed to be converted into a public company. (*CA. Final, May*)

11. The Articles, of Association of a Private Limited Company provide that the shares of the company may be transferred only at a valuation to be made by the auditors of the Company. You are called upon to value the shares on the death of a member. State the main points you would take into account in arriving at the fair value of the shares. (*Gujarat B. Com.,* 1958; *C.A. Final May*)

12. The profit of a firm for the half year ended 31-12-69 is nearly double-as compared with the preceding half year although the turnover remains practically the same. Enumerate the points that would be examined by you to explain the disparity. (*C.A. Final, Nov.*)

13. According to the Companies Act as amended in 1960, the Central Government is empowered to direct "Special Audit" of a Limited Company. Under what circumstances and how can such an audit be conducted? Do you agree with such a provision in view of the fact that the Central Government can get the accounts of a company investigated under S. 235 of the Companies Act? (*Andhra Pb. Service Commission*)

14. The term "Investigation" implies an examination of accounts and records for some special purpose. State as to how would you conduct an investigation where fraud is suspected or known to have taken place. (*Varanasi, Gujarat and Bombay B. Com.* 1968)

15. You are asked to investigate into the reasons for a considerable fall in the trading profits of a manufacturing concern for a particular year. What line of procedure will your investigation take? (*I.A.S.*)

16. A client informs you that he is contemplating advancing a considerable sum to a private limited company on terms which appear to him very attractive. He instructs you to investigate the matter fully on his behalf. You are required to:

(a) give concise details of the information you would require; and

(*b*) draft a detailed programme of the work involved in the investigation. (*Agra B. Com.*)

17. "The principal duty of the auditor of a company is to report to the members on the Annual accounts examined by him". Explain and state what are further statutory duties of a Company Auditor. (*Bombay B. Com.*)

18. If you are asked by a bank which proposes to lend a large sum of money to an existing business, to make investigation of the accounts of that business, state briefly how would you do so? (*Annamalai B. Com.*)

19. You are asked as an investigator into the affairs of a concern by a creditor as to whether the debtor concern is 'good' for the sum already advanced by him. Detail the points which will require consideration. (*Annamalai, Lucknow, B. Com*)

20. Your client suspects that there has been theft of stores from the warehouse with the collaboration of the store-keeper. Suggest a programme of investigation to be carried out to determine the extent of theft, if any. (*Cal. B. Con Hons.*)

21. State how you would proceed to investigate when you are called by taxing authorities who suspect that a well-known film actor-cum-producer has evaded huge amount of taxes and has large amount of unaccounted money. (*Poona B. Com.*)

22. The management of a company offers a share in the profits instead of three months bonus, given in earlier years to the labourers. The secretary of the labour union to which the workers of the said company are attached, request you to investigate the proposal. Give your report in the form of a letter. (*Annamalai B. Com.*)

Chapter 35

Typical Audit Programmes

Having studied the theoretical side of auditing, let us now proceed with practical side of an audit, i.e., how should an audit be conducted? We shall discuss the answer of this question in the following pages. There are certain common features with all types of audits. The auditor should have the following programme:

Preliminary Work

1. See that your appointment is in order and examine the relevant resolution about your appointment.

2. Ascertain the accounting year.

3. Enquire into the system of book-keeping followed by the business concern.

4. Get a list of the books of accounts maintained by the concern.

5. Find out the names of the directors and their powers.

6. Enquire the names of the persons who write those books of account and also obtain the specimen signatures of these officers.

7. Enquire into the system of internal check and see whether it is efficient. If it is not, be more cautious.

8. If it is a partnership audit, examine the Partnership Deed.

9. If it is the audit of a limited company, examine its Memorandum and Articles of Association, and Prospectus, if any.

10. Enquire into the nature of the business of the concern.

11. Examine the profit and loss account, balance-sheet, auditors' and directors' reports of the previous year. If the business is of a technical nature, acquaint yourself with the technical side of the business.

Cash Book

1. See whether the opening balance agrees with the cash balance as shown by the balance-sheet of the previous year.

2. Compare the cash sales with National Cash, Register if that is in use. If it is not in use, enquire into the internal check system regarding the cash sales and compare the copies of cash memos with the cash sales.

3. Check a few transactions regarding receipt of cash from debtors with the counterfoils of the receipt book and with any other documentary evidence available.

4. If any asset has been sold out, examine any documentary evidence which may be available and see that the sale has not been treated as sale of goods.

5. Check the discounts in the nominal ledger and enquire the system of granting loans.

6. Check the cash purchases with the cash memos received.

7. Check cash payments to the creditors with the receipts received from the payees.

8. Check the payments into the bank with the Pass Book and the counterfoils of the paying-in-book.

9. Prepare a bank-reconciliation statement to agree the balance as per the Cash Book and Bank Book.

10. Check carefully the receipts and payments just before the close of the year to ascertain any fictitious receipts or payment.

11. Ask the banker to send statements of balances on different accounts, if necessary.

12. Total both the sides of the cash book in order to find out whether the balance as shown by the cash book is correct.

13. Verify the cash in hand by actually counting it and see whether it agrees with the balance as shown by the cash book.

14. If there are many cash books in use, verify all the cash in hand at the same time.

15. Pay attention to cash-in-transit.

16. Carefully examine the I.O.Us.

Petty Cash Book

1. Vouch the debit side of the petty cash book with the credit side of the cash book paying particular attention to the dates on which the receipt and payments were recorded.

2. Check the petty cash book with postage book.

3. Check the total of the different columns and cross-additions.

4. Verify the cash balance of the petty cash book by actually counting the cash.

Purchases Book or Purchases journal

1. Enquire into the internal check system regarding purchases and see that they are made by a responsible officer.

2. Vouch the purchases books with the invoices.

3. See that the goods which have been entered in the stock book have also been entered in the purchases book and vice versa.

4. If a columnar purchases book is used, see that the invoices are properly entered into.

5. See that the discount is deducted from the invoice before it is posted.

6. Test the purchases order book with the goods inward book and the godown-keeper's book.

7. See that the entries in the purchases book have been correctly posted to the ledger.

8. Check the additions of the purchases book and see that the total loss has been correctly carried to the trading account.

9. See that the purchases do not include the purchase of fixed assets.

Purchases Returns (Returns Outwards)

1. Enquire into the internal check system regarding the returns outwards.

2. Check the returns outward book with the godown-keeper's book and gate-keeper's book, if any.

3. Compare the returns outward book with the credit notes and examine correspondence.

4. Check the additions of this book and find out whether the amount has been correctly posted to the ledger.

Sales Books or Sales journal

1. Enquire into the internal check system regarding sales.

2. Compare the entries in the sales book with the orders received book, carbon copies of the invoices, the godown-keeper's book and gate-keeper's book, if any.

3. Check the additions of the sales book.

4. See that the total of the sales book has been correctly posted to the ledger.

5. See that the sales do not include sales of assets.

6. See that sales do not include goods sold on 'sale or return' basis or consignment outwards.

Sales Returns (Returns Inwards)

1. Enquire into the internal check system regarding the returns inwards.

2. Check the returns inward book with the godown-keeper's book and gate-keeper's book, if any.

3. Compare the returns inwards book with the counterfoils or the carbon copies of the credit notes and goods outward book.

4. Check the additions of this book.

5. Check the postings to the ledger.

6. Examine the correspondence regarding the goods returned.

Wages Book

1. Enquire into the system of preparation of the wages sheets or wages book.

2. Find out the method of employment of casual workers.

3. Ascertain the system of payment of wages.

4. Test the additions and extensions of the wages book or wages sheets.

5. Check the deductions made on account of fines, sickness insurance, provident fund, etc.

6. Compare the wages book or sheets with the time and piece work records maintained by the gate-keeper or time-keeper, foreman and the godown-keeper or the Time Recording Clock, if in use.

7. Check the wages book with the Cost Sheets.

8. Check the wages sheets with the Employees State Insurance cards.

9. Compare the amount of wages payable as per the wages sheets and the amount of cheque drawn for payment of wages.

10. See that there is no loophole in the method of unpaid wages.

Bills Receivable Book

1. Compare the opening balance in the ledger with the balance sheet of the previous year.

2. Check the entries in the bills receivable book with correspondence and any other documentary evidence available.

3. See that the proceeds of the bills are properly accounted for and the account of the acceptor is credited with the amount.

4. If any bill is dishonoured, see that the account of the individual is debited with the amount of the bill together with the noting charges, etc., and examine the returned dishonoured bill.

5. Check the additions in the Bills Receivable Book and verify the bills in hand.

6. Check the postings to the accounts concerned.

Bills Payable Book

1. Compare the opening balance in the ledger with the balance-sheet of the previous year.

2. Check the entries in the bills payable book with correspondence and any other documentary evidence available.

3. Compare the bills payable book with the cash book for the bills which have been honoured and see the returned bill.

4. Check the additions of the Bills Payable Book and verify the bills in hand.

5. Check the postings to the accounts concerned.

6. Check the balance with the ledger.

Journal Proper

1. Check the opening entries with the balance-sheet of the previous year.

2. Vouch the entries with the documentary evidence, e.g., correspondence, agreement, memorandum and articles of association, minute books of the Board of Directors and shareholders' meetings, etc.

3. Check the additions of the book.

4. Check the postings to the purchases, sales and nominal accounts or ledgers, etc.

5. Check the closing entries with the Trading and Profit and Loss Account.

Purchases Ledger (Ledger containing the accounts of Creditors)

1. Check the opening balance with the balance-sheet of the previous year.

2. Vouch the entries passed in the individual accounts with correspondence, cash book, purchases book, journal, returns outward book, bills payable book and other books of original entry.

3. Compare the individual balances with the- schedule of creditors supplied by the management.

4. Test a few balances by getting statements of account from a few creditors, of course, with the permission of the client.

5. Check the balances in the ledger and see whether the totals of all these balances agree with the total of the schedule of the creditors.

Sales Ledger (Ledger containing the accounts of debtors)

1. Check the opening balance with balance-sheet of the previous year.

2. Vouch the entries passed in the individual accounts with correspondence, cash book, sales book, journal, returns inward book, bills receivable book and other books of original entry.

3. Compare the individual balances, with the schedule of the debtors supplied by the management.

4. Test a few balances by getting statements of account from a few debtors, with the permission of the client.

5. Check the balances in the ledger and see whether the totals of all these balances agree with the total of the schedule of the debtors.

6. Scrutinise the list of the debtors duly certified by a responsible official of the concern to find out the doubtful and bad debts.

7. See that sufficient provision is made for bad and doubtful debts.

8. If the debtors include Director, Managing Agents, etc., see that such debtors are shown in the balance-sheet according to the Companies Act.

Nominal Ledger

1. Check the different accounts from the cash book, journal, etc.

2. Check the balances of the accounts in the ledgers.

3. Ascertain that necessary adjustments have been made for the following:

(*a*) Expenses incurred but not yet paid.

(*b*) Expenses paid in advance.

(*c*) Income receivable but not yet received.

(*d*) Income received in advance.

4. Verify the entries with the subsidiary books.

5. See that the balances are correctly carried to the concerned accounts.

Audit Programme for the Statutory Report

1. Examine the memorandum and Articles of Association, prospectus, or a statement in lieu of prospectus in regard to authorised capital, its division into different classes of shares, etc.

2. Check the applications and allotment letters with the application and allotment books and share ledgers.

3. See whether the allotment is in order by referring to the minute book of the Board of Directors.

4. See that the minimum subscription had been subscribed before the allotment was made.

5. Check the share applications to find out the brokerage payable on the sale of shares.

6. Vouch the cash received on application with the application forms and see that entries have been made in the share ledger when the shares have been allotted.

7. Vouch the cash received on allotment with letters of allotment and see that entries have been made in the share ledger.

8. If shares have been issued to the promoters or vendors of the business taken over by the company for consideration other than cash, examine the contract and see the letters of authority nominating the allottees. See that the entries have been made in the share ledger in regard to such shares.

9. If the shares have been allotted to the vendors for consideration other than cash, whether the contract with the vendors has been filed with the Registrar of the Joint Stock Companies.

10. See that the directors have taken up and paid for their qualification shares.

11. If the debentures have been issued, see that they are issued according to the prospectus and Articles of Association.

12. Vouch the receipt of cash pertaining to the debentures in the cash book or bank pass book.

13. See that the money received in respect of shares and debentures, etc., has been banked in a scheduled bank and that it has not been utilised till the grant of Certificate of Commencement of business.

14. Check the cash book with the pass book and prepare a bank reconciliation statement. Get a certificate of the balance at bank, if there is any suspicion.

15. If any shares have been forfeited, see that it has been done according to the articles and a resolution to that effect had been passed by the directors.

16. Whether the necessary returns have been sent to the Registrar according to the Companies Act.

17. If redeemable preference shares have been issued, see that the articles permit such an issue.

18. Vouch the underwriting commission with the agreement with the vendors and see that it does not exceed the amount permitted by the Companies Act.

19. Vouch the preliminary expenses and see if any of them had to be paid by the vendors. If so, see that the vendor's account is debited with such amounts. See that the revenue expenditure is not debited to Preliminary Expenses account.

20. Scrutinise the capital expenditure.

21. Examine the register of mortgages and charges and vouch the receipts of loans against mortgages and debentures, if any. See that mortgages have been registered with the Registrar of Companies and examine the Certificate of Registration issued by the Registrar.

22. Ascertain the borrowing powers of the company from the articles and see that such powers are not exceeded.

23. Vouch all the receipts and payments up to and within seven days of the report. The receipts should be shown under distinctive headings such as receipt from shares, debentures and other sources and payment thereout and the balance in hand.

The certificate should be worded: "I hereby certify that the annexed statutory report of the . Co. Ltd., so far as it relates to the shares allotted by the company and to the cash received in respect of such shares and to the receipt and payment of the company is correct."

General Audit Programme of a Limited Company

We have already considered in detail the steps in general to be taken by an auditor while conducting an audit of a limited company. We have also considered the audit programme in connection with the Statutory Report. In addition to these steps, the auditor of a joint-stock company should proceed on the following lines:

1. Examine the memorandum and Articles of Association, prospectus or a statement in lieu of prospectus, etc., with a view to find out the following:
   (*a*) qualification and remuneration of the directors;
   (*b*) purchase price to be paid to the vendors of business, if any, and the form in which the payment is to be made;
   (*c*) the powers of the directors or managing director to delegate their powers;
   (*d*) the borrowing powers of the company and how they can be exercised.
2. Examine previous year's auditor's and director's report.
3. Examine the minute books of the Board of Directors and the shareholders to see the following:
   (*a*) the remuneration of directors and other officers;
   (*b*) the dividend recommended by the directors;
   (c) the appointment of auditors;
   (d) issue and transfer of shares and debentures;
   (*e*) the treatment of underwriting commission and brokerage for placing the shares in the market;
   (*f*) whether shares have been issued at a premium and if so, how is that premium treated in the books of accounts;
   (*g*) if the shares have been forfeited and reissued, how is the balance of the forfeited shares account treated.
4. See that the necessary returns, etc., have been filed with the Registrar of Joint-Stock Companies.
5. Compare the total issued capital with the shareholders accounts in the share ledger.
6. Examine the share transfer and see that there is no mistake.
7. See whether the loans to the directors of the company are authorised according to the articles and whether they have been shown separately in the balance-sheet according to the Companies Act.

8. See that the balance-sheet is drawn up in conformity with law.

9. Examine the preliminary expenses, discount on debenture, discount on issue of shares, heavy expenses on advertising, etc., and see whether they are shown separately in the balance-sheet.

10. See that the dividends have been paid according to Section 205 and the memorandum and Articles of Association.

Special features of the Audit of Non-Trading Concerns

Charitable Institutions

1. Examine the constitution, rules and regulations of the charitable institution or the Trust Deed, if any.

2. See that the funds for specific purposes have been dealt with according to the rules.

3. Vouch the receipts of donations and subscriptions as shown on the debit side of the cash book with the counterfoils of the receipt book, register of the subscribers, list of the donors notified in the newspapers from time to time, correspondence and any other documentary evidence available.

4. Vouch the income from investments from the Investments Register and see that income tax deducted from dividends received is recovered from the income tax authorities, if the charitable institution is not liable to income tax.

5. Vouch the receipt of rents from the properties belonging to the charitable institution, with the rent roll, agreements with the tenants, etc.

6. Vouch the payment with the minute book of the trustees or the managing committee regarding important payments.

7. Verify the purchase of investments by referring to the Bought Notes and physically examine such investments. In case such investments are lodged with the bank, get a certificate from the bank.

8. Verify the cash and bank balance.

9. See that the accounts are drawn up in accordance with the regulations.

10. If any special Act has been passed by any State relating to the Charitable Institution, e.g.; the Bombay Trust, Waqf, etc., see that the form of accounts and the auditors report are drawn up according to the special laws.

Clubs

1. Study the constitution and bye-laws of the club particularly in regard to the powers of the officials, operation of the bank account, etc.

2. Examine the minute books of the club.

3. Vouch the receipt of cash on account of admission fees and subscriptions with the counterfoils in the receipt books and list of the members.

4. See that the life membership fee is carried to Income and Expenditure account over a number of years or is treated as capital income according to rules of the club.

5. See that the subscription received in advance or in arrears are properly appropriated.

6. Enquire into the system of supplying meals, refreshments, drinks, etc., to the members and vouch the receipt of cash.

7. Vouch the payments on account of purchase of crockery, furniture, provisions, etc.

8. See that expenditure is properly allocated between capital and revenue.

9. Verify the assets, particularly stock in hand in the usual manner.

Educational Institutions (Schools, Colleges or Universities)

1. Examine the University Act, the rules and regulations, trust deeds, charters, etc., to ascertain the management of the institution and especially the rules, etc., which affect the accounts.

2. Study the minute books of the Board of Management, Governing Body or Managing Committee of the educational institution or the Senate of the University as the case may be.

3. Check the cash receipts on account of fees, etc., by referring to the counterfoils of the fee receipt books and the register of the students.

4. Irrecoverable fees should be written off by the person authorised by the Managing Committee.

5. Fee outstanding or paid in advance must be adjusted and accounted for.

6. Ascertain the system of the recovery of fines and extras such as examination fees, fees for duplicate copies of diplomas, hostel rent, electricity charges, building fund, etc., and their recovery and treatment in accounts.

7. Receipt from admission fee should be compared with the Application Forms for Admission duly signed by the Head of the Institution.

8. See that the free studentship has been granted by a responsible officer.

9. Vouch the income from the landed property, endowments and securities, etc.

10. Vouch the grant from the government or the local authorities by examining correspondence. Receipts on account of caution moneys or securities is shown on the liability side of the balance-sheet.

11. Vouch the payment of salaries to the members of the staff by reference to the salary register, the cash book, the receipts, the counterfoils of the cheque book and the pass book. Particular attention should be paid to any increment earned by the members of the staff and see whether they have been sanctioned by the Managing Committee. Reference may also be made to the copies of letters of appointment or agreements.

12. Capital expenditure should be vouched as usual but see that the necessary sanction is there.

13. See that the internal check system regarding the purchase of provisions, linen, etc., for the boarders is efficient.

14. See that a donation for a particular purpose is spent accordingly.

15. Distinction should clearly be made between capital and revenue income and expenditure.

16. Verify the balance at bank and cash in hand as usual.

17. Verify the stock of provisions, linen, furniture, stationery etc., as usual. See that proper record has been maintained for such articles.

18. See that the outstanding assets and liabilities are taken into account.

19. See that investments representing prize endowment funds are kept apart and that they are, not mixed: up with ordinary investments.

20. Moneys relating to Provident Funds should be invested in securities and should be shown separately as liabilities. Investments representing Provident Fund should be shown separately on the assets side.

21. See that refund of Income tax deducted from the dividends or interests on securities has been claimed as educational institutions are usually exempted from the payment of income tax on such income.

Hospitals

1. Examine the internal Check System.

2. Vouch the receipts with counterfoils of the receipt books.

3. Subscriptions and donations, if any, must be vouched with correspondence, counterfoils of receipt books, register of the subscribers and other documentary evidence and the cash book.

4. Receipt of rent, dividends, etc., may be vouched as usual.

5. See that the grants from local authorities are properly spent according to rules. Vouch the grant by referring to the correspondence.

6. Vouch the payment of salaries to the members of the staff and other expenses as usual.

7. See that income tax paid on interest and dividends received on securities and shares at the source, is reclaimed if the hospital is exempt from the payment of such income tax, etc.

8. Payments should be vouched with vouchers.

9. Vouch the Bill Register of patients with the carbon copies of the bills sent to patients.

10. Compare the bills with the attendance register of the patients.

11. Collections from patients should he compared with the copies of the bills, cash book and patients account.

12. See that legacies, donations, etc., made for a particular purpose are applied accordingly.

13. Examine the system of receipt and issue of stores, drugs, linen, clothes, instruments from the suppliers and to the different wards, operation theatre, etc.

14. See that adequate depreciation has been provided for on fixed assets.

15. Verify the closing stock.

16. See that the expenditure under different heads does not exceed the budgeted amounts.

Special features of the Audit of Trading Concerns

Branches

1. Examine the system of accounting maintained by the branches and if there are more branches, he should see that a uniform system of accountancy is employed by all the branches.

2. See whether the returns from the branches are duly certified by the branch managers or the local auditor. If he has accepted such returns, he must mention that fact in his report.

3. See that the goods and cash in transit are incorporated in the books of accounts.

4. See that such returns are properly incorporated in the head office books.

5. If it is a foreign branch, see that the returns are converted into home currency according to the set rules.

6. Pay proper attention to the question of depreciation, reserves for bad and doubtful debts, repairs and renewals, outstanding assets and liabilities, etc.

7. If the goods are supplied to the branches at market price, see that proper adjustments are made to arrive at the correct profit or loss.

8. See that the assets and liabilities are grouped according to Schedule VI, Parts I and II of the Companies Act.

9. See that the bank balance at the branch has been confirmed.

10. See that the cash in hand at the branch has been confirmed.

Bus Companies

1. Study the method of collection of fares from passengers.

2. Compare the conductors' way bills with the traffic book and check a few entries with the passengers' receipts.

3. Vouch the receipts from advertisement in the buses with the returns from the agents and contracts.

4. Check the purchases of buses with the agreement with the sellers' invoices, Stock Register, etc.

5. If the buses have been purchased on hire-purchase system see that the interest payable along with, the instalment is debited to the revenue account.

6. See that if free service was to be given by the company from which busses and motors, etc., had been purchased, full advantage is taken of that free service.

7. See that expenses of repairs, etc., are debited to revenue account and that they are duly certified by the engineer.

8. If repairs and renewals are of variable nature, see that repairs and renewals reserve account is maintained.

9. See that a proper system in regard to the purchase and issue of petrol, tyres, tubes, parts, etc., exists.

10. Examine the system of the payment of salaries and wages to the engineers, clerks, drivers, conductors, etc.

11. See that proper provision is made for depreciation of motors and buses.

12. Verify the stock of stores, spare parts, petrol, tyres, tubes, etc.

13. Vouch capital and revenue expenditure.

Cinemas, Theatres, Circuses, etc.

1. Check the daily receipts as shown in the cash book with the Daily Returns of the tickets sold and the counterfoils of the tickets. See whether there is a good- internal check regarding the sale of tickets of different classes.

2. Money received on account of advance booking should be carried over.

3. Check the receipts on account of the sale of tickets with the amount of entertainment tax paid.

4. Check the receipts from the sale of drinks, refreshments, programme books, etc.; and see that the sales are supervised by a responsible official. These accounts should be separately maintained to see what profit is made on account of these items.

5. Enquire whether the unused tickets are kept under lock and key by a responsible official.

6. Vouch the receipts on account of advertisements, etc., by reference to correspondence, contracts, etc.

7. Check the payments on account of salaries, wages, electricity, purchases, etc.

8. See that distinction has been made between capital and revenue expenditure.

9. Vouch the payments on account of advertisements with the agreements entered into with the advertising agents.

10. See that proper depreciation is provided for on assets like films, scenery, machines, dresses, furniture and other equipments.

11. Check the entertainment tax account with the counterfoils of the tickets sold.

12. Verify the closing stocks.

13. In the case of a theatre, all expenses incurred in connection with a production, such as dresses, scenery, etc., should be spread over a period till the show lasts and all the receipts by sale of tickets should not be credited to profit and loss account till the expenses are recouped.

Collieries

1. Enquire into the system of preparation of wages sheets and the payment of wages.

2. Enquire into the capital expenditure such as sinking of pits, construction of tramways and railways, construction of workmen's cottages, purchase of machinery and plant and other fixed assets.

3. If the wagons have been purchased on hire-purchase system see that proper allocation is made between capital and revenue (interest).

4. Inspect the arrangements in regard to leases, royalties, dead rent, short-workings, etc.

5. Verify the sales with the accounts of the agents.

6. Verify the income (rent) from workmen's cottages, etc.

7. See that proper provision is made for depreciation on fixed assets such as rolling stock, machinery, etc.

8. Refer to the articles of the company in regard to provision for depreciation on leases and concessions.

9. Any development expenses should be treated as capital expenditure and written off over a number of years.

10. Compare the cost of production per ton with the previous year. If there is any difference, enquire into its causes.

11. Enquire into the basis of the valuation of the closing stock. If the cost of production is more than the selling price, it should be valued at the lower price.

Contractors and Builders

1. Enquire into the system of recruitment of labour, fixing their wages, account of wages payable to the labourers and the method of payment of such wages.

2. Enquire into the system of purchases of materials, etc.

3. Enquire into the system of the issue of materials of different jobs-direct or through the Central Stores Department.

4. What is the system of allocating establishment expenses such as manager's salary, rent of godown, carriage, etc., to different jobs and contracts.

5. The method of depreciation of fixed assets and the allocation of such depreciation to different jobs and contracts should be enquired into.

6. See that separate record is maintained for each contract or job and that a proper record is maintained for the transfer of plant from one job to another.

7. Ascertain the mode of valuation of stock and work-in-progress.

8. Enquire into the method of the ascertainment of profits on incomplete contracts. For this purpose inspect building agreements, architect's certificate, etc. See that the profit ascertained is on very conservative basis, taking into consideration any future contingency, higher wages, cost of materials going up, etc.

9. Enquire into the method of the valuation of the closing stock of materials, and, incomplete contracts. See that all the purchases have been debited to the work-in-progress.

10. Examine the costing system and compare it with the financial records.

11. Vouch the receipts on account of contracts.

Co-operative Societies

1. The auditor of a Co-operative Society is appointed by the Registrar of Co-operative Societies.

2. Study the Co-operative Societies Act, 1912, and rules and regulations as far as they concern the accounts. In case such an Act has been replaced by state legislation, examine the provisions of such a special legislation.

3. See that a member does not hold more than 10 per cent of the share capital of the society.

4. Vouch the receipt of cash on account of share capital with the register of the shareholders, counterfoils of the receipts, etc.

5. Vouch the receipts on account of deposits with the cash book and the counterfoils of the receipts and compare the relative accounts. Deposits from non-members can be accepted only according to the terms and conditions of the Society.

6. Vouch any money borrowed from the central co-operative bank with cash book, correspondence and any other documentary evidence available.

7. Vouch the receipt of interest and return of loans from the borrowers with the agreements for the grant of loans and the relative rules and regulations of the Society.

8. Vouch the loans granted with agreements. Loans can be granted only to the members but in special cases they may be granted to non-members with the general or special sanction of the Registrar.

9. Vouch other expenses as usual.

10. See that at least 25 per cent of the profit is carried to the Reserve Fund and 10 per cent is carried to Welfare Fund.

11. Verify the cash in hand and investments. The surplus funds of Co-operative Society can be invested only in Government Savings Banks or any bank which is on the approved list of the Registrar. It can also invest its funds in the securities specified in Section 20 of the Indian Trust Act, 1882, or in the shares and securities of other Co-operative Societies with limited liability.

12. If the Society is consumers' society, check the sales with the summaries and the sales account.

13. Check the purchases with the order book, purchases book, stock book, etc.

14. Verify the stock and examine the method of the valuation of stock.

15. See that the dividends are paid to members according to the rules and regulations of the society and the Co-operative Societies Act. The rate should not exceed $6\frac{1}{4}$ per cent.

16. See that the accounts are prepared according to the Co-operative Societies Act. The special provisions in the Income Tax Act concerning the Co-operative Societies should be noted.

Electric and Gas Companies

1. Study the special Acts concerning such companies and particularly the provisions of the Electricity (Supply) Act, 1948, and the Indian Electricity Act, 1910, relating to the accounts of the company.

2. Enquire into the internal check system regarding the records of the consumption of electric current by the consumers—whether, individuals or municipality, etc.

3. Compare the consumers' tabular ledger with the original records.

4. Examine the receipt of cash from consumers with the bills and counterfoils of the receipts.

5. See whether the consumers have taken advantages of the cash discount by paying the bills within the prescribed period.

6. See whether arrears have been recovered in the subsequent period.

7. Whether bad debts have been written off on the advice of a responsible official and whether the connections of such delinquent consumers have been cut off.

8. Inspect the contracts for the supply of current to the municipality and whether any special rate is to be charged from it.

9. See whether the allocation of wages between capital and revenue has been done on the advice of the chief engineer,

10. See that the salaries of the engineers, managers, accountants, etc., are allocated between generation, distribution and management departments on proper basis.

11. When assets are replaced, see that the cost of replacement is properly allocated between capital and revenue.

12. See that repairs and renewals are charged to revenue-account.

13. See that proper depreciation is provided on plant and machinery, mains, meters, stores, etc.

14. Check the stores book.

15. See that the accounts and balance-sheet are prepared according to the prescribed forms, given in the Electricity (Supply) Act, Indian Electricity Act and the Companies Act as is applicable.

16. The auditor should see whether the annual accounts of the company have, been submitted to the State Government or such authority as is appointed by the State Government in the prescribed manner and on or before the prescribed date.

Executors and Trustees

1. Before the commencement of the audit obtain the following documents:—

(*a*) Copy of the Trust Deed.

(*b*) List of the books of account.

(*c*) A schedule of the Investments.

(*d*) A Statement of Account.

2. Examine the system of Internal Check in operation.

3. Examine the will and codicils, or the Trust Deed as the case may be, paying particular attention to the points affecting the accounts, the powers of the executors and, trustees, the instructions regarding the carrying on of the business, treatment of the annuities, creation of trusts for the minors and others, beneficiaries, etc.

4. Examine the Estate Duty Account and the Affidavits in order to see what assets and liabilities were left by the deceased. If possible, examine the private books of accounts of the deceased and see whether the Estate Duty Account is correct.

5. Examine the minute books of the trustees in regard to any transactions affecting accounts.

6. See whether rents from estates, income from investments, etc., have been duly accounted for. Vouch such receipts in the usual manner.

7. See whether trustees have committed any breach of duty and whether they have made the necessary amendment to the default.

8. Verify the assets and see that the income and rents, etc., which had accrued on the date of the death of the deceased have been brought into account and capitalised.

9. See that the debts of the deceased have been paid off and vouch such payments.

10. Vouch the purchase of investments with the bought notes sent by the brokers.

11. Vouch the purchase of estates, etc., with the title deeds, etc.

12. Payments to the beneficiaries should be vouched with vouchers and see that the payments are according to the trust deed or the will.

13. If the estate of the deceased consists of several buildings which have been let out, see that proper rent rolls are maintained.

Finance and Trust Companies

1. Study the Memorandum and Articles of Association of the company in order to know the aims, objects and limitations of the company.

2. Vouch the purchase and sale of securities, stocks, shares; etc., with the brokers' bought and sold notes, correspondence and any other documentary evidence available.

3. If shares, etc., have been allotted to the company for consideration other than cash, examine the agreement or correspondence, etc.

4. If shares, etc., have been purchased and sold "cum-dividend", see that dividend is subsequently received and see that the net value of the investment is treated as the cost of the investment concerned.

5. See that the interest, dividends, etc., accrued but not paid at the date of the balance-sheet is credited to the revenue account at the date of the balance-sheet.

6. Vouch the receipt of dividends and interest.

7. Verify the cash in hand, at bank and investments.

8. Verify the valuation of the investments at the close of the period. It must be noted that for a trust company, though the investments are to be treated as fixed assets, there is no necessity to provide any depreciation on such investment for the purpose of the balance-sheet unless the articles of the company so provide.

9. If there is a loss on the sale of investments, such a loss need not be met out ;of profits of the current year, for such a loss is to be treated as a capital loss. Similarly if there is a profit on the sale of investments, it is a capital profit. However, such a profit may be distributed amongst the shareholders —

(*a*) if the Articles of Association permit this;

(*b*) such a profit has been realised in cash; and

(*c*) other assets have been revalued.

10. If there is any liability in regard to partly-paid shares held by the company, make a note on the face of the balance-sheet to that effect.

11. Examine the minute book of the directors.

12. If certain investments are held for the purpose of resale, any profit or loss on such resale must be carried to revenue account:

Hotels

1. Ascertain the system of book-keeping in vogue in the hotel.

2. Enquire into the internal check system regarding the following:

(*a*) purchase and issue of provisions, stores, wines, linen, crockery, etc.

(*b*) payment for provisions, stores, wines, etc.

(*c*) receipt of cash, on account of daily sales, room rent; meals, wines, billiards, etc.

3. Verify the stocks.

4. Check the cash book with the window ledger.

5. Visitors' Ledger should be carefully examined to see whether all charges against them are entered in their accounts.

6. Check the postings from the window ledger into the personal ledger.

7. Vouch wages and salaries, etc.

8. See that proper distinction is made between capital and revenue expenditure.

9. Ascertain whether proper provision has been made for depreciation on crockery, furniture, linen, etc. The method for depreciation should be applied consistently. Sometimes these articles are revalued. In some hotels, expenditure on these items is capitalised and a Renewal Account is created with an amount based on previous experience by debiting the Revenue Account.

Newspapers and Periodicals

1. Enquire into the system of issue of the paper to newspaper agents and subscribers.

2. Enquire into the system of returned newspapers if the system of unsold copies to be returned prevails.

3. Vouch the receipts on account of subscription and advertisement charges and see that the unexpired subscription or advertisement charges paid in advance is taken into consideration on the balance-sheet date.

4. Payments made to contributors should be vouched with vouchers.

5. See that provision is made for damages, for defamation, if any, payable for any article published in the paper.

6. See that the advertisement journal showing advertising booking for each edition is properly maintained.

7. See that the advertising revenue has been received in advance for a number of editions and whether provision has been made for revenue received in advance at the time of closing the books of account.

8. Check the advertisement journal with the advertisement accounts.

9. See that the outstanding amounts due to contributors are brought into account.

Publishers

1. Agreement with authors and royalties payable to them should be examined.

2. Examine the cost accounts of each book. The unsold books at the date of the balance-sheet should be valued at cost price, and if the book has not been popular, it may be valued even at below the cost price.

3. See that proper provision is made for libel or infringement of copyrights in, case a suit against the company is still pending at the date of the balance-sheet.

4. Copyrights should be revalued from time to time.

5. If heavy expenses have been incurred in advertising a book, such expenses should be treated as deferred revenue expenditure.

6. If the sale of the book is very slow, see that sufficient provision has been made for the unsold stock of that book.

Railway Companies

1. Examine the internal check system and study the Act according to which the railway company has been established.

2. Vouch the cash receipts with the monthly summaries sent by the station masters and agents in regard to the sale of tickets, freight, etc.

3. Examine the railway clearing house statements and check them with ledger.

4. See that proper distinction is made between capital and revenue expenditure.

5. See that proper provision is made for depreciation on locomotives, rolling stock, buildings, permanent ways, etc., and examine the chief engineer's certificate in this respect.

6. Test a few items of expenditure with vouchers, etc.

7. Verify the investments.

8. See that the stocks of stores, etc., are duly certified by a responsible officer and check a few items.

9. Examine the outstanding assets and liabilities.

10. See that interest payable on loans and debentures is debited to the revenue account.

11. See that the final accounts are prepared in accordance with the Statute.

Retailers

1. Examine the internal check system regarding the cash and credit sales.

2. See whether National Cash Register is used to record cash sales.

3. Enquire into the system of credit sales.

4. Check the summaries of the salesmen with the returns of the cashier and the gate-keeper, if any.

5. Vouch the debit side of the cash book with the National Cash Register or the automatic till.

6. Vouch the payments in the usual way.

7. Check the credit sales with invoices, ledger accounts, order, received book, godown-keeper's book, etc.

8. If there are several departments, see that establishment expenses are allocated to different departments according to a set principle.

9. Verify the closing stock.

Rubber, Tea and Coffee Plantations

l. If it is the first audit of the plantation, verify the purchase of 'estates by examining the title deeds and study the terms on which the estates are held. See that the estates are free from any encumbrance.

2. Scrutinise the expenditure and see that expenses such as purchase of property, buildings, plant, machinery, rubber or the plantations not bearing, clearing expenses, etc., are charged to capital account while expenses such as upkeep of the plant and machinery, cultivation, picking of leaves, manufacturing expenses are debited to revenue account.

3. See that the general expenses have been allocated in proportion to the acreage of the area which is bearing and which is not bearing to the total area.

4. Vouch the payment of wages.

5. Vouch the total production with the production sold as per the returns of the agents and the stock in hand as per the certificate of the Estate Manager.

6. See that the returns are properly incorporated in the Head Office books. If the estates are in a foreign country, see that the figures are converted into home currency according to the set rules.

7. Verify the stock and see that it is properly valued.

Shipping Companies

1. See that a separate account is maintained for each voyage.

2. See that a separate ledger account is maintained for each ship.

3. Compare the money received on account of freight and passage with the certified summaries and the journal or cash book.

4. See that each voyage account is debited with the expenses and proportionate insurance premium. If any provisions, coal and stores are in hand at the conclusion of the voyage, such expenses should be adjusted and carried to the next voyage account.

5. Outstanding liabilities should also be adjusted.

6. If return tickets have been issued, see that each voyage account is not credited with the full price of the return ticket but necessary adjustment is made.

7. Examine the insurance policies in regard to the insurance premium and the period for which the policy is taken.

8. See that proper provision is made for depreciation on ships, linen, crockery, etc.

9. Pay particular attention to the foreign currencies.

10. Verify the stores ana examine the method of their valuation.

11. See that proper distinction is made between capital and revenue expenditure.

12. See that the usual repairs and renewals are debited to revenue account while heavy expenses such as overhauling expenses are spread over a number of years.

Solicitors

1. See that a separate bank account is maintained in respect of cash received or paid on behalf of the clients.

2. Examine the payments made out of the client's banking account and see that only moneys payable by the client is withdrawn except—

(a) any money payable by the client to pay off the money borrowed by him from the solicitor;

(b) any money which might have been deposited in the client's account by mistake; and

(c) any money which might have been paid by the solicitor to open the client's bank account.

3. Compare the balance shown by the client's bank account with the client's account in the ledger.

4. Examine the bills of costs sent to the clients and see that the amounts have been debited to the client's accounts in the ledger. See that the amount of the bills of costs is also recorded in the client's ledger.

5. See that outstanding costs are taken into consideration while preparing the final accounts.

6. Similarly see that any money paid in advance by the client is shown as a liability.

7. See that premiums received from articled clerks are spread over the duration of their articles.

QUESTIONS

1. Discuss special points to which you would give attention while auditing the accounts of an electric supply company. *(Rajasthan M. Com.)*

2. Draft an audit programme for any two of the following, concerns:

(*a*) Branch of a nationalised bank.

(*b*) Travel Agent.

(*c*) Sundry creditors for goods supplied. *(CA. Final, India 1971)*

3. What are the special points to which you, as an auditor, would direct your attention, while auditing the accounts of any two of the following:

(*i*) Club. (*ii*) Branch Account. (*iii*) Newspapers. (*iv*) Builders.

4. Draft an audit programme for the audit of the accounts of a High School. (CA. *Int.* 1971)

5. State the special points to which you would pay your particular attention in auditing the accounts of a Tea or Sugar Company. Also draft your report. *(Rajasthan. M.Com.)*

6. Harekrishna Charitable Dispensary of Dubri is a very useful institution. It derives its income from Government and Municipal Grants as well as public donations.

You have been asked to audit the accounts of the Dispensary for the year ended 31st March, 1964. Draw up a suitable audit programme covering all essential points. *(Gauhati B.Com.)*

7. Outline a suitable programme for auditing the accounts of a college having three departments, namely, Arts, Science and Commerce. (*Rajasthan, Calcutta B.Com.*)

8. Mention the special points in auditing the accounts of any one of the following:

(*i*) A big hotel.

(*ii*) An Insurance Company doing general business.

(*iii*) A Co-operative Bank. *(Punjab B.Com.)*

9. The executors of a deceased person request you to carry out an audit of the estate account prepared for a period of three years from the date of death. The estate consisted of freehold property and investments, and the Will provided that the deceased's wife, who is still living, should have a life interest in the estate, after payment of estate duties and certain legacies therefrom.

Set out the work you would perform in complying with the executor's request. *(C.A. Final)*

10. Draw up an audit programme mentioning the special points in respect of the following:—
(*a*) A cinema theatre.
(*b*) A coal company. (*Osmania B.Com.*)

11. Outline the special matters to be taken into consideration in doing the audit of one of the following:
(*a*) A colliery;
(*b*) A shipping company. (*C.A. Final*)

12. What are the special points to which the auditor should devote his attention while auditing the accounts of a firm of solicitors or the accounts of a charitable institution? (*C.A. Final*)

13. Give the audit programme for any three of the following:—
(*a*) Cinema Theatre
(*b*) Retail Chemist.
(*c*) School run by a Trust.
(*d*) Hospital. (*Annamalai B.Com.*)

14. Draft an audit programme for a Recreation Club. (*Annamalai B.Com.*)

15. What are the special points to be borne in mind while auditing the accounts of a Public Trust registered under the Bombay Public Trust Registration Act. (*S. V. Vidyapeeth*)

Chapter

36

Liabilities of an Auditor

Legal Position of an Auditor

The present Company Law imposes a wide responsibility upon the practising auditor not only to his client but also to third parties whom he never met or who had never employed him. Charges are often, levelled against them for the following:—

1. For not detecting misappropriation of money by the employees of the client because of incorrect accounting procedure.
2. Errors in preparing the final accounts.
3. Dishonesty or carelessness on the part of the audit or articled clerk of the auditor.

The liabilities of an auditor from the legal point of view may be discussed under two heads, viz.,

(*a*) When he is appointed by a private concern; and

(*b*) When he is appointed by a Joint Stock Company under the Companies Act, 1956.

We shall discuss these points separately.

(a) The Liability of an Auditor when he is appointed by a Private concern

It is not obligatory for a private concern to appoint an auditor. But if he is appointed by a private concern, his duties and liabilities are not defined by any Act. His duties, powers and responsibilities depend upon the agreement which is entered into between him and his client. In other words his liability is contractual liability. As was pointed out in one of the previous chapters, it would be in his interest that he should get definite instructions in writing from his client as to the scope of his duties so that he may not be held responsible for the work which he never undertook io perform.

If, according to instructions, the auditor does not examine any books of account or any document which he was not required to examine and if consequently his client suffers any loss, the auditor is not liable. The reason is that he was not instructed to do any particular work,, but such is not the case with the auditor of a joint Stock Company where his duties are definitely laid down by statute and no agreement limiting such duties will be valid.

In any case-he must adhere to the instructions given to him. He must show As much diligence as was expected of him. He must be honest in the, performance of his duties. Whenever there is anything to arouse his suspicion, he must probe into the matter. He must not sign the balance-sheet which he does not believe to be correct. He must not be negligent in the performance of his duties.

If he has followed the above instructions, he is free from any liability. He can be sued only under the Contract Act in failing to perform his duties as laid down in the agreement which was entered into between him and his client. In case no agreement was entered into, and even though full audit was not intended, the auditor should regard himself under as much responsibility as if he were conducting a complete audit. Even if no agreement was entered into, he must show as much diligence and skill as is expected of such a person otherwise he will he responsible for the damage or loss suffered by those who employed him. The essential elements to constitute such a liability are: (a) he must be negligent, (b) as a result of negligence, a loss is caused, and (c) the loss is suffered by the person who employed him.

As to what constitutes negligence, will depend upon the circumstances of each particular case. But it must be mentioned here that the standard of skill, knowledge and diligence expected of an auditor has gone under lot of changes. He is expected to show more skill and diligence than a few decades back. Hence some of the decisions given in the past do not hold good now, e.g., in the *Kingston Cotton Mills* case the auditor could defend himself against the charge of negligence if he depended upon the certificate regarding the value and quantity of stock given by the trusted officials of the company but such is not the case today.

(b) The Liability of an Auditor under the Companies Act

The case of an auditor of a limited company is different. He is appointed under the Companies Act which defines his -duties and liabilities, etc. The liability of an auditor under this heading may arise from any one or more of the causes given below:—

1. Liability for Negligence under the Law of Agency.
2. Liability under the statute (misfeasance).
   (*a*) The Companies Act, 1956, —either civil or criminal
   (*b*) The Indian Penal Code.

1. Liability for Negligence under the Law of Agency

The auditor may be sued in a civil court for damages arising out of negligence in the performance of his duties, e.g., when the dividend has been paid out of capital.

An auditor is appointed, amongst other things, to detect frauds, defalcations, errors, etc. If on account of negligence in the performance of his duties, he has failed to do so and consequently the company suffers a loss; the auditor is held responsible for damages. He is an agent in regard to his duties as an auditor and, therefore, must show reasonable skill and diligence in the performance of his duties. In the case of an agent who does not show as much skill and diligence in the performance of his duty and as a result of his negligence, the principal suffers a loss, the agent must compensate his principal under the Law of Agency. Similarly, if an auditor fails to show as much skill and diligence as is expected of *a* man of ordinary prudence, he must suffer the consequences, as was decided in the case of *Hudson* vs. *Official Liquidator, Dehra Dun Mussorie Electric Tramway Company*. Again in the case of *Commissioner of Income Tax* vs. *G. M. Dandekar,* the auditor was held liable for negligence in not verifying the cash in hand. In the case of *Martin* vs. *Isitt,* the monthly audit of the client was delayed unreasonably. It was held that the auditor was liable for the loss suffered by the client. In another case when the auditor did not submit the audit report in time to enable the client to fulfil the statutory requirements, he was held guilty of gross professional misconduct *(Lakshmi Narain Saxena's case)*.

An auditor is not liable even though the company has suffered a loss if it can be proved that he was not negligent in the performance of his duties. On the other hand, even if it is proved that the auditor was negligent in the performance of his duty, he cannot be held liable for damages, if the company has not suffered any loss due to his negligence, as was held in the case *of Liverpool and Wigan Supply Association Ltd,* 1907. In such a case he cannot recover the fees payable to him on the ground that he was negligent. If the auditor has failed to detect any fraud or embezzlement, he would have to compensate the client if it can be proved that he could detect such a fraud, etc., by exercising reasonable skill and diligence. A question may arise as to whether an auditor will be liable for consequential losses, i.e., losses which may be caused on account of his previous negligence. For example, on account of the negligence on the part of the auditor, a defalcation could not be detected. As a consequence of this negligence the employees were emboldened and committed more defalcations. Now the question arises, (1) whether the auditor is liable for the previous losses, and (2) whether he is also liable for the consequential losses. As a matter of fact, damages which are the direct result of negligence are only recoverable. Remote damages are not recoverable and the courts are inclined to take into account contributory negligence by directors and other officers in assessing the damages due from the auditors.

On the question of consequential damages; *The Accountant* of England, referring to the *Armitage* vs. *Brewer & Knott,* wrote: The case gives a profit and loss account exhibit a true and fair view of the state of affairs of the company and. are drawn up according to the Companies Aet, etc. If he does not comply with these requirements, he is guilty of misfeasance, and is liable to be fined up one thousand rupees.

According to Section 229, the report has, to be signed only by the person who is appointed as, auditor or by a partner of the firm if the appointment is in the name of the firm. Such a partner who signs the report must inform the Register of Companies within a reasonable time of his having done so. Failure to comply with the requirements of this section may make an auditor liable to a fine up to one thousand rupees provided the default is wilful.

The court may relieve an auditor under Section 633 under certain circumstances. Section 543 of the Companies Act lays down that to the event of the winding up of a company, if it appears that any promoter director or any officer of the company has misapplied or retained any money belonging to the company or has been guilty of misfeasance or breach of trust in relation to the company. The Court may compel such promoter, director or officer to repay or restore the property or any part thereof with interest at certain rate or to contribute any such sums by way of compensation. The word 'officer' referred to in this section includes an auditor of the company as has been discussed in the Chapter on "The Audit of Limited Companies'. If the dividends have been improperly declared or paid or commission on net profits has been improperly paid on the faith of the accounts audited by him and which did not show a true and fair picture and were incorrect and misleading, he will be liable to refund such an amount. Mr. Mukerjee, J., in the case of *Indo-Burma Industries Ltd,* (1957), remarked: "It is a section which has required rather inadequate description of being called 'misfeasance section'." Thus the law has saddled an auditor with liabilities for misapplication or fraud, misfeasance, breach of trust, etc.

It must be remembered that if a company has suffered any loss, it is only the company which can sue the auditor for damages and an individual shareholder has no right to do so. If the company has gone into liquidation and it is found that on account of the negligence of the auditor, the company had suffered any loss, it is the Liquidator who can bring a suit in the name of the company against the auditor.

Under Companies Act (Criminal Liability)

Criminal liability of an auditor arises out of an act constituting a crime, e.g., when an auditor wilfully makes a false statement either in the balance-sheet or any other document, destroys or mutilates any voucher or document.

Section 628 of the Companies Act lays down: "If in any return footing disadvantage to the profession in applying the principle of consequential damages to audit claims.. . . Thus, if an auditor omits to detect the defalcation by an employee and in the following, year, before there is a chance of any further audit, the employee emboldened by having escaped detection, embezzles, a larger sum, is the auditor liable both for the original embezzlement which he failed to detect and for the subsequent losses to the employer as well?

"A mere mistake will not render a professional man liable for its consequence, but if the negligence was of the type where omission was to detect a fraud which by the exercise of a reasonable care an accountant would have detected, then we are inclined to think that a jury would take into account the consequential losses in their award of damages. On the other hand, if the auditor's failure to detect defalcation was not blameworthy, and he could not reasonably be expected to detect such a defalcation, then he might not, in our opinion, be liable."

It may be remembered that any provision in the articles of association of a company or in a contract by the company to indemnify the auditor against any liability arising from negligence, breach of duty, etc., of which he may be found guilty is void. The company may, however, indemnify the auditor for any expense which he might incur in defending himself provided the judgment is in his favour.

Therefore in order to hold the auditor liable for negligence, it must be proved (a) that he was negligent, (b) that as a result of his negligence the client suffered a loss and (c) that the loss was suffered by the person to whom the auditor owed a, duty. It must also be remembered that an auditor of a company cannot restrict his liability by entering into an agreement as his duties are defined by statute and an agreement against law will be void. He will be liable for damages in spite of such an agreement as was held in the case of *Newton* vs. *Birmingham Small Arms Co., Ltd* in 1906. An indemnity clause in an agreement between a company and an auditor, whereby which an auditor is freed from liability, has now been declared void as per Section 201 but, as will be explained in the following pages, a Court has the power to relieve an auditor from liability under S. 633 of the Companies Act, under certain circumstances.

2. Liability under Statute (Misfeasance)

(a) Under Companies Act (Civil Liability)

Misfeasance means breach of duty imposed by law. A duty has been imposed on the auditor of a limited company according to Section 227 (3) of the Companies Act to state in his report (i) whether he has obtained all the information and explanations required by him which were necessary for the purpose of audit, (ii) whether in his opinion the balance-sheet and report, certificate, balance-sheet, prospectus, statement or any other document; required by or for the purpose of any of the provisions of this Act, any person makes a statement—

(*a*) which is false in any material particular, knowing it to be fales;

or

(*b*) which omits any material particular, knowing it to be material; he shall, save as otherwise expressly provided in this Act, be punishable with imprisonment for a term which may extend to -two years and shall be liable to fine". This provision of law is applicable to an auditor of a company.

An auditor may be prosecuted if it is proved that he has been guilty of any criminal offence in relation to the company under S. 539 of the Companies Act which lays down: "If with intent to defraud or deceive any person, any officer or contributory of a company which is being wound up—

(*a*) destroys mutilates, alters, falsifies or secrets or is privy to the destruction, mutilation, alteration, falsification or secreting of any books, paper or securities; or

(*b*) makes, or is privy to the making of, any false or fraudulent entry in any register, book of account of document belonging to the company.

he shall be punishable with imprisonment for a term which may extend to seven years, and shall also be liable to fine.

If a prospectus has been issued by a company which contains a false statement, every person who authorised the issue of such a prospectus, will be liable to be punished with imprisonment up to a period of two years or fined up to five thousand rupees or both (S. 63). For the purpose of Section 63, an auditor may be punished if he authorised the issue of the prospectus.

An auditor being an officer of the company under Section 545, can be prosecuted by the liquidator during the course of winding up for delinquency.

In order to hold an auditor criminally liable the following must be proved:

(*a*) That the statement made was false in material facts;

(*b*) That the auditor wilfully made such a false statement; and

(*c*) That the statement complained of has been made in any return, report, balance-sheet, certificate or any other document required to be made under any provisions of the Companies Act.

It may be stated here that the Court has power to relieve an auditor under S. 633, either partly or wholly if a case is proceeding against him for negligence, default or breach of duty or trust provided it is satisfied that the auditor acted honestly and reasonably by taking into consideration all the circumstance of the case. However, the court has no power to relieve the auditor from his liability as stated in the foregoing lines unless it has served a notice on the Registrar to show cause why such relief should not be granted to the auditor.

The Court, however, has no power to relieve the auditor in case of any civil liability in a criminal case against the auditor.

(b) Under the Indian Penal Code

Section 197 of the Indian Penal Code lays down: "Whosoever issues or signs any certificate required by law to be given or signed or relating to any fact which such' certificate is by law admissible in evidence, knowing or believing that such certificate is false in any material point, shall be punishable in the same .manner as if he gives a false evidence."

Liabilities of an Auditor to Third Parties

So far we have been considering the liability of an auditor to the company, the accounts of which he has audited. The question arises, whether an auditor can be held liable for damages to third parties, if they have suffered any loss by relying on any balance-sheet or any financial statement signed by him. It is argued that as there is no privity of contract between the auditor and the third party, the auditor owes no duty to such third parties and hence he cannot be held liable. He is never appointed by the third party and, therefore, he has nothing to do with such a party as was decided in the case of *Le Lievere and Dennes* vs. *Goudd* (1893). This question came before a United States Court in the case *of Ultramares Corporation* vs. *Touche, Niven & Co.*, in 1921. In this case a banker advanced loans to a company on the strength of the balance-sheet of the company which had been signed by the auditor. The lender lost the money as the balance-sheet was defective and fraudulent. Thereupon, the lender sued the auditor for damages. The case, however, was compromised. It may be pointed out here that the auditor did not know that the accounts were required for the purpose of obtaining financial assistance and would be shown to the plaintiff. In giving its decision, the Court realised that it would be quite wrong to expose the auditor to a potential liability in an indeterminate amount for an indefinite time to an indefinite class. The *Accountant* of England still maintained that the auditors would be protected firstly because there was no privity of contract between the auditor and the third party and secondly because the plaintiff must prove all the points discussed under the *Derry* vs. *Peek* case, viz.,

(*i*) that the statement was untrue in fact;

(*ii*) that the person making it -knew that it was untrue, or was recklessly and consciously ignorant whether it was true or not;

(*iii*) that the statement was made with intent that the plaintiff should act on it;

(*iv*) that the plaintiff did act in reliance in it and suffered damages; and

(*iv*) that the auditor gave his consent for the inclusion of such a statement in the prospectus.

The *Accountant* argued that in that case (*Ultramares*), the auditors did not believe that the statement which they made was wrong and that they never had any intention that the plaintiff should use and act on the statement. In these circumstances the auditors should not be held liable for damages.

There has been a change in the opinion of the courts regarding the auditors' liability to third parties, after the Ultramares's casts in America in 1921. New York's highest Court of law ruled in *State Street Trust Co* vs. *Earnest* in 1938: "Accountants.... may be liable to third parties evenwhere there is lacking, deliberate or active fraud. A representation certified as true to the knowledge of the accountant when knowledge there is none, a reckless misstatement, or an opinion based on grounds so flimsy as to lead to the conclusion that there is no genuine belief in its truth, are all sufficient upon which to base liability". (*Quoted , from Accountants' Digest, p.* 228, June 1967).

In another case where it was made known to the auditors that their findings will be utilised by the plaintiff, but with whom they had no contractual relation, it was held that the auditors were not liable for negligence to the plaintiff if he suffered any damages. (*Candler* vs. *Crane*, *Christmas & Co., Ltd*, 1951). The reasons given by the learned judge were (a) that because the defendants were not employed by the company and were not under the plaintiff, and (b) that the plaintiff could not claim damages from the defendant in tort for negligence because it did not recognise tortious liability for negligent misstatements.

This case was followed by another peculiar case, viz., *De Savvary* vs. *Helden, Howard & Co.* (1961), where it was decided that the auditor was not liable to third parties where there is no privity of contract between the two. The plaintiff was the managing director of a company receiving substantial financial assistance from the bank. The bank was requested to advance further loan to the company. The bank asked the company to get its account investigated by an independent auditor on their behalf to find out the financial position of the company. The costs of investigation by the auditor was to be incurred by the plaintiff. The accounts prepared by the investigating auditor and showed a profit of £ 14,000 (due to the inclusion of incorrect figures of stock and work-in-progress). Had this negligence on the part of the investigating auditor been not committed, the accounts would have shown a loss. Later on the plaintiff himself used these audited accounts and suffered a loss. He, thereupon, sued the auditor for damages.

It was held that the investigating auditor was employed by the bank and there was no contractual relationship with the plaintiff even though he had paid the cost of investigation. Thus the plaintiff had no case against the auditor. However, it was held that if the auditor is guilty of fraud, he can be held liable to third parties. Howard F. Stettler in his book *Auditing Principles* states: "Fraud and gross negligence are, the usual basis for action by third parties against the auditor. Courts in America have awarded compensation to injured parties if it had been proved that the loss was caused to such a party by gross negligence or fraud by the auditor"

Again, in the case of *Commissioner of Income Tax, Madras* vs. *G. M. Dandekar,* (1952), it was held that an auditor does not owe any duty to the third party when Venkatarama Ayyar, J, said: " ... The charge is that he (auditor) owed a duty to the department (Income Tax Department), to himself investigate the truth and correctness of the accounts of the assessees and not merely to act as their post office in transmitting them. We do not agree that the respondent (Auditor) is under any such duty to the department and, therefore, no question of negligence arises." It may be stated here that the auditor in this case was appointed by A. *Mohamed* & Co., to audit the accounts of the firm and the Income Tax Officer was informed of such an appointment. After having examined the accounts, the auditors sent a letter together with certain statements relating to the profits of the firm and duly checked by them, to the Income Tax Office. It was found later on that the profit shown by the books was not correct.

However, the decision by the House of Lords in the case of *Hedley, Byrne & Co., Ltd vs. Heller & Partners Ltd,* (1963), set at rest the doubts about the liability of the auditor to third parties. The House of Lords decided, that the *Candler* case was decided wrongly and agreed with the dissenting view of Lord Denning in that case. Although this case (Hedleys) did not directly concern the auditors, it is considered that it applies to them as well and they can no longer consider themselves immune to the actions by third parties who have sustained losses through reliance on their services.

In this connection it would be interesting to read: the recommendations of the Institute of Chartered Accountants of England embodied in Statement No. S. 8, "Accountants' liability to third parties—The Hedley Byrne decision". We give below a few extracts from the "Council's Advice" for the benefit of the readers:

"In Council's view that third parties entitled to recover damages under the Hedley Byrne principle will be limited to those who by reason of accountants' negligence in preparing reports, accounts of financial statements on which the third parties place reliance suffer financial loss in circumstances where the accountants knew or ought to have known that the reports, accounts or financial statements in question were being prepared for the specific purpose or transaction which gave rise to the loss or that they would be shown' to and relied on by third parties in that particular connection. There is no general principle that the accountants may be liable for damages if a report of statement which proves to have been prepared negligently by them is shown casually or in the course of business to third parties who suffer loss through reliance on the report or statement.

"The position of clients' creditors, where clients seek financial assistance—here proof of negligence and knowledge of use for the purpose would be needed.

"Shareholders and their judgment of the company's affairs by the use of annual accounts—no action would lie by an individual shareholder but if the company collectively suffered loss due to reliance on accounts negligently prepared, the auditors could be liable. The auditors could also be liable if the accounts were used as an effective part of a document and the auditor knew of or should have known that they were intended to be used. On the other hand, where an individual shareholder might use them for investment decisions, then the auditor would not be liable as the accounts are not normally prepared for such a purpose.

"Where taxation is concerned, although the accountant might know that the accounts would be used for assessment purpose, no action would lie, in case of reliance upon accounts negligently prepared, since in fact any ultimate loss suffered by the Revenue through failure to recover tax loss must be attributed to the death, decamping or insolvency of the tax payer, not to the negligence of his accounting.

". . . .Council has further advised that where an accountant specifically restricts the scope of his report or expresses appropriate reservations in a note attached to and referred to in the Financial statement he has prepared or the report which he has made thereon, this can constitute a disclaimer which will be effective against any action for negligence brought against him by third parties."

But if a misleading statement is made in a prospectus issued by a company, the auditor of a company, *if he had authorised the* issue *of such a prospectus,* can be held liable for damages to a third party which has purchased the shares of the company on the strength of such a misleading statement even though there might not have been privity of contract between the auditor and the shareholders, under S. 63 (1) of the Companies Act, but he may be freed from his liability under sub-section (2) of the same section when his statement was included in the capacity of an expert. To save himself, the auditor must prove, (1) that he withdrew his consent in writing before delivery of the prospectus for registration, (2) that after the delivery of the prospectus for registration and before allotment thereunder, he on knowing the untrue statement withdrew his consent and gave, a public notice, or (3) that he was competent to make the statement and that he had reasonable grounds for believing the statement to be true., [S. 62 (3)].

No doubt the argument that there is no privity of contract between the auditor and the third party is true but the third parties, hold the auditor liable for any fraud in tort even though there is no privity of contract between the two. Moreover, the auditor has a moral responsibility to third parties. The auditor should realise that the balance-sheet, statements, etc., which are signed by him will be read by third parties and if they rely upon such statements, etc., and consequently suffer any loss because such statements were misleading he will be responsible to them.

Thus, we see that the present law has imposed a great responsibility on auditors to third parties as well as to his client. The claims against the auditors arise because of the following reasons:

1. Improper accounting procedure which failed to detect embezzlement of an employee of the client.
2. Negligence on the part of the employees of the auditor.
3. Errors in preparation of the financial statement.

To avoid liability to third parties, it has been suggested by a leading accountant that while drawing up his audit report, the auditor should either

(*a*) enter into an agreement with his client that the report is furnished without responsibility to any person other than his client, or

(*b*) incorporate in his report a disclaimer of responsibility to third parties.

The question is whether such an attitude by the auditor will not shake the confidence or the investing public or the financing companies. It is further argued that even if the auditor is sure of the correctness of the accounts, he might insert such a clause in his report or the agreement with his client to be on the safe side. Will not such an attitude be detrimental? If the answer is yes, it will mean a great loss to the economic system of the country.

In order to save their skin, the auditors take taxation cases rather than those of auditing. But will his liability be the same as a professional accountant. In india the judgment has gone in favour of the auditor when it was decided in the case of *Commissioner of Income Tax* vs. *G.M. Dandekar* that an auditor does not owe any duty to third party. This case was decided in 1953 but in the case of *Bancraft,* vs. *Indemnity Insurance Company of America,* it was decided in 1962 that an auditor is as much responsible as if he were acting as an auditor. The auditor had in this case prepared the accounts for income tax purposes. Whether the courts in India will take this judgment into consideration while deciding such cases, has yet to be seen.

The amount of damages follows the ordinary rule of the law of contract. "The, damages should be such as may fairly and reasonably be considered either arising naturally, i.e., according to the usual course of things from such breach of contract itself, or such as may reasonably be supposed to have been in the contemplation of both parties at the time they made the contract as the probable result of the breach of it", *Hadley* vs. *Baxendale* (1854). The party must try to mitigate the loss as far as possible.

An auditor's duty is to keep strictly confidential all financial matters of the company of which he is the auditor. If he discloses any financial matter and his client suffers a loss the auditor is liable for damages.

The auditor must examine all the documents of the company: If he does not do so, he is liable for damages. He cannot plead ignorance of the existence of any documents. (*Oxford Benefit Building & Insurance Society,* 1887).

Law of Limitation can be pleaded by an auditor in case of assessment of damages *(Oxford Benefit, etc., Society)*. The period of limitation is five years from the date of appointment of the liquidator.

We may summarise that an auditor will be held liable under the Companies Act under the following circumstances:

(1) If he fails to exercise reasonable care and skill in the performance of his duties.

(2) If he knowingly contravenes the provisions of S. 227.

(3) If he does not disclose material facts in the financial statements which he knows are material and that the non-disclosure of such facts will make the financial statements as misleading.

(4) If he knows that a material statement has not been made in the financial statements and in spite of that he does not report.

(5) If he falsifies or is privy to the falsification of any books or papers of the company with a view to deceive any person.

(6) If he destroys, mutilates, secretes, etc., any documents, vouchers, books, etc., with a view to deceive any person.

Liability of an Honorary Auditor

An honorary auditor, is as much responsible for negligence or misfeasance as a paid auditor. An honorary auditor cannot relieve himself of liability on the ground that the agreement between him and his client was not supported by consideration and hence it was void. If he wishes to be free from liability he should not commence the work. But having done the work and submitted his report, he is as much responsible as a paid auditor. (*Fairdeal Corporation, Bombay* vs. *K Gopalkrishan Rao,* 1957).

Liability of Joint Auditors

In the case of large companies, they generally appoint two or more auditors or firms of chartered accountants with a view to expedite the audit work so that the audited accounts may be presented to the shareholders soon after the close of the financial year. Moreover, the appointment of joint auditors gives an opportunity to younger auditors to do a part of the audit work of large companies. Such auditors am called joint auditors. The necessity of the appointment of joint auditors may arise—

1. where the company is a very large one with several departments, e.g., textile, coal, jute, sugar, paper, etc.; or

2. where the company has several branches in different cities; or

3. where the company has some subsidiary companies.

The question of the responsibilities and liabilities of the joint auditors arises in such cases. The problem of assigning the responsibilities may not arise in some cases, such as—

1. when the organisation is such where the audit work of the concern does not overlap; or

2. when the organisation has several branches in which case the audit work of each branch is assigned to different auditors.

On the other hand a problem may arise where the nature of the work is such when the audit work cannot be divided between the joint auditors.

To overcome some of the difficulties in such cases, a particular company or a particular area of the company is assigned to each of the joint auditor by mutual consent. However, there are cases in which the work of audit involved is such that both the auditors have to do the work jointly because of the importance of the work. The problem in such a case may be (*a*) what will be the position when there is a difference of opinion between them and (*b*) whether the liability of the auditors will be joint or joint and several. In this connection, the Council of the Institute of Chartered

Accountants of India has issued Statement No. 210 under the title "Responsibilities of Joint Auditors". This Statement has made the following recommendations to its members:

1. In such a case, the joint auditor should divide the work as far as practicable between themselves. Therefore, an auditor should not be held responsible for the work done by the other joint auditor. Each auditor should be held liable for the work he has performed under such arrangement.

2. The client should be informed as to which area or portion of the work is to be performed by each auditor.

3. In case a company has different branches and the audit work has been divided mutually by the joint auditors between themselves, each one of themselves should prepare his report on the financial statements of the branch concerned, the accounts of which have been examined by him.

4. Whenever any branch auditor has to refer to the joint auditor, he should do so in writing.

When mutual division of work is not possible

Now let us deal with the situation when division of work between the joint auditors is not possible. In such a case, the joint auditors should inform the client as to the mutual division of work, as far as has been practicable, has been made between the two auditors; e.g., receipt and payment of cash will be examined by one auditor while the purchases and sales will be the jurisdiction of the other auditor. Again, the work may be divided between the joint auditors according to time, e.g., one auditor will check the accounts from lst April to 30th September while the other auditor will check the accounts for the remaining period of the financial year. Again, the assets and liabilities will be examined by one or the other joint auditor and so on. This system may also be applicable in the case of partnership of a firm of chartered accountants: However, the client should be informed by the joint auditors about the mutual arrangement but each of them will have to write a separate audit report.

If the above arrangement is made by the joint auditors, it is the duty of each of them to determine the extent of audit tests to be applied in relation to the area of the audit work undertaken by him: Thus it would a kind of separate audit by each joint auditor and therefore he should inquire into the system of accounts prevalent, the tests to be applied, the consideration at the outset, whether to undertake depth audit or complete audit of the area of audit allocated to him.

Of course, the final audit report will have to be prepared jointly and each of them will be responsible for his own work.

Audit of large units with several branches, divisions or zones

In the case of a very large unit which has several branches, divisions or zones, etc., separate auditors are generally appointed for for different areas, branches, zones, etc. In such a case, it is the duty of the individual auditor to get and rely upon the reports submitted by each branch to see that they are properly incorporated in the account books of the division or the zone, as the case may be. If the individual auditor deems it necessary, he may visit the branch or the zone under his jurisdiction to take necessary action.

In case the work of a zone or branch is common and consequently does net fall within the jurisdiction of a particular auditor, both the auditors may agree between themselves as regards the division of work pertaining to the returns submitted by the branch or the zonal offices. In such a case, i.e., where the assignment is handled jointly by both the auditors, the responsibility will be shared by them' jointly unless they are able to agree upon a specific pattern of distribution of responsibility between themselves.

To conclude, we may say

1. that each joint auditor is entitled to assume that his co-auditor has carried out the audit of the books of account in accordance with the normal practice and standards laid down by the Institute of Chartered Accountants;

2. That while drawing up, the report, if, there is any difference of opinion between the joint auditors, they may submit a separate report to the client;

3. that in case there are more than two joint auditors of the concern and if differences of opinion have cropped up, each one of them may submit separate report expressing his opinion about the state of affairs of the company and therefore there cannot be a question of majority or minority in regard to the joint audit report.

Liability of auditor of holding company/subsidiaries

As a subsidiary company is considered to be separate legal entity whose accounts may be audited by a separate auditor, the Council of the Institute of Chartered Accountants of India is of opinion that no responsibility is cast upon the auditor of the holding company in respect of the work performed by the auditor of the subsidiary company.

Moreover, the Companies Act does not compulsorily require the holding company to compile consolidated accounts or group accounts of the subsidiaries. Section 212 simply requires that the accounts of the holding company shall have attached thereto the balance sheet, profit and loss account, directors' and auditor's reports of different subsidiary companies. Besides this, certain additional information regarding the subsidiaries is also required to be given. Thus the auditor of the holding company is not responsible for the audit work performed by the auditor of the subsidiary unless he has been entrusted to do the audit work of the subsidiary company.

Liability of auditor for branch audit

Even though the statutory auditor is not responsible for the work performed by the branch auditor, it is suggested that there should be sufficient liaison between the two auditors to ensure that the work is performed expediously. To achieve this objective, the statutory auditor may often have to communicate with the branch auditor. Though the branch auditor is under no obligation to prepare the returns, viz., balance sheet, profit and loss account etc., to be submitted to the head office which the auditor may require to enable him to incorporate these returns in the final accounts without any difficulty, he (branch auditor) should express his opinion on the accounts in such a way that the statutory auditor may be Able to express his own opinion that the accounts show a true and fair view of the state of affairs of the company as a whole, e.g., according to para 4 of Part II of Schedule VI.

Liability of Local Auditors

In case of a concern, which has branches in foreign countries where local auditors are appointed, the auditor of the Head office is not liable for the work done by the local auditor provided he makes it clear in his report that he had relied upon the figures supplied by the local auditor and that there was nothing to arouse his suspicion and that the figures of the branches were properly incorporated in the Head Office books. For details, the reader is referred to the chapter on The Audit of Limited Companies.

Liability of Auditors for Libel

If an auditor has, in his report, made a statement which' turns out to be libelous or slanderous, he will not be held guilty, if it is proved that such a statement was made *bona fide* and without any malice as was decided in the case of Lawless *vs. Anglo Egyptian Cotton & oil Co.* (1843) But if the auditor while making such a libelous statement went beyond the scope of his duties, he would not be protected even though such a statement was made *bona fide*. No such case has been decided by any court in India and it would depend upon the view held by the court.

Liability for unaudited accounts

Auditors are sometimes asked by their clients to prepare financial statements from the books of account without being asked to undertake the audit of accounts. The report issued by the auditor in such a case may be required for several purposes, e.g., showing to the prospective partner about the financial position of the firm or for the purpose of borrowing money from a lender, etc. Such a report or the statement which has been prepared and signed by a qualified auditor creates an impression that the statement is quite correct since it has been signed by an auditor. These statements are called unaudited statements. The auditor who signs such a statement runs a great risk in being held liable in case his client suffers a loss as was held in the case of *Apfel* vs. *Annan Dexter & Co* (1926) or even to a third party which relied upon the statement signed by the auditor.

To safeguard the interests of its members, the Institute of Chartered Accountants of England issued "Members' Handbook" in July 1973, which recommended that the report to be issued by the auditor for an unincorporated company be as follows:

"In accordance with instructions given to us, we have prepared without carrying out an audit, the annexed accounts, from the accounting records of...... and from information and explanations supplied to us"

(From Accountants Digest, P. 11, September 1973 Issue)

The Institute recommended that in such cases, the auditor should make it clear to the client both at the time of interview arid is the form of engagement letter, the scope of the work to be performed. Other recommendations were that the accounts should be submitted to the client for approval before the auditor's report is signed and written confirmation is obtained that all relative information has been made available; that the accounts conform to the accepted principles so far as practicable; that the professional charges are not described in correspondence or elsewhere as "audit fee"; the report should be headed "Accountant's Report" and should not include any opinion or expression on the accounts, etc.

In the United States of America, the accountants clearly state in such cases that the financial statements were not audited by them and therefore they do not express any opinion on them. They also take a further precaution by adding the words "Unaudited" on each page of the report to the client.

Though the recommendations were made by the Institute of Chartered Accountants in England to its members and the precautions taken by the American accountants, such advice if followed by the auditors in India will free the auditors from their liability which might be due to a little negligence by wording the report carelessly.

The readers may refer to the chapter on "Audit of Partnership Accounts" for details.,

Legal Decisions as regards Auditor's Liabilities

(*i*) Leeds Estate Building and Investments CO. vs. Shephered, 1887 (for negligence)

The company was established in 1862. The Articles of Association of the Company provided that the Directors were to be paid bonuses in proportion to the dividends paid and that both dividends and bonuses were to be paid out of profits. The Articles further provided that the Auditor of the company was to state whether in his opinion the balance-sheet was a full and fair balance-sheet properly drawn up so as to exhibit a true and correct view of the state of the company's affairs.

The company made no profit except in the year 1876. The company went into liquidation. During the course of liquidation proceedings, it was discovered that the company had made no profits, and that by including fictitious items, it was shown that the company had made profits and, therefore, dividends were declared and bonuses paid. The Articles of the company were not shown to the Auditor.

The Auditor was sued for damages. The defence put forth by the Auditor was that he was unaware of the existence of the Articles of Association and that the action was time-barred by the Law of Limitations.

It was argued by the Liquidator that the Auditor was negligent in the performance of his duties. Had he referred to the Articles, he could have seen that the Directors were to be paid bonus on the payment of dividends. In this case there were no profits and hence no, dividends and bonuses to Directors could be paid. Moreover, the balance-sheet did not exhibit a true and correct view of the state of the company's affairs.

It was held that the Auditor was liable to pay damages. He ought to have seen what exceptional duties were cast upon him. Ignorance of the provisions of the Articles was no excuse to relieve him of any responsibility. In regard to the plea of Law of Limitation, relief was given to some extent.

It would be interesting to read apart of judgment of J. Sterling:

"It is the duty of the auditor not to confine himself merely to the task of ascertaining the arithmetical accuracy of the balance-sheet, but to see that it is true and accurate representation of the company's affairs. It is no excuse that the auditor had not seen the Articles when he knew of their existence":

Conclusion

The duty of an auditor is not only to verify the arithmetical accuracy of the balance-sheet but to inquire into the substantial accuracy. If he failed to do so, he was negligent in the performance of his duties and therefore liable for damages.

(ii) Irish Woollen Co. vs. Tyson and Others (1900) (for negligence)

In this case the accounts of the company had been manipulated and falsified in respect of the following points:—

(*a*) The stock had been over-valued;

(*b*) The book debts had been over-valued; and

(*c*) The trade liabilities had been understated by suppressing the purchase invoices and carrying them to the following period while including the goods in the stock of the current year.

As a result of the above, more profits were shown and consequently dividends were paid out of capital.

The auditor had entrusted the work of audit of his assistant and he himself did very little work.

It was argued by the company that on account of the negligence on the part of the auditor fraud had been committed: It was stated that:

(*a*) had the auditor taken care that the stock was properly valued;

(*b*) had the auditor seen 'that sufficient provision was made for bad and doubtful debts;

(*c*) had the auditor himself done the major part of audit work; and

(*d*) had the auditor sent for statements of account from the creditors; the fraud would have been discovered.

It was stated in the judgment:

in regard to (*a*), it was no part of the duty of an auditor to take stock unless there was something" to arouse his suspicion as was held in the *Kingston Cotton Mills case*;

in regard to (*b*), there was no ground for alleging negligence against the auditor;

in regard to (*c*), it was considered that an auditor was entitled to get the work done by his assistant; and in regard to (d), it was held that 'the auditor was negligent in the performance. of his duties in not getting statements of accounts from the creditors. Had he done so, the fraud would have been discovered.,

On the last score, the auditor, was held guilty and was asked to pay damages

A few extracts from the judgment are given below for the benefit of the readers:

"Mr. Kevans(auditor) seems to have done little of the actual-work himself, and the evidence varies as to the nature of the supervision which he gave to it the investigations of the books he deputed to his assistants... and it must be on the faith of their representations that he certified the balance-sheets. I presume this course is not unusual and that an accountant with a large business is not supposed to do everything himself. The auditor is bound to give reasonable care and skill and this can also be exercised by his deputy. He is entitled to see the company's books and the materials for their books, and also to ask for explanations. But he is not called on to seek for knowledge outside the company, or to communicate with customers or creditors. He is not an insurer against fraud or errors; and if fraud is alleged, it must be shown with precision the acts of negligence for which he is said to be responsible. . .There was certainly no duty on the auditor to take stock. . . As to the provisions for the 'bad debts', if there is any one thing upon which an auditor is. dependent upon the officers it is the writing off or the making of a prospective allowance for bad debts. He has no personal knowledge of the customers. . .There is no doubt that both the suppression and carrying over of invoices would have been detected, if the auditor had called for the creditors' statements of accounts upon which payment was ordered and compared them with the ledger. I should have thought this was part of the auditor's duty for many reasons. ....."

Conclusion

That when the accounts of a company have been falsified and dividends improperly paid out of capital in consequence, the auditor is liable if the falsification could be discovered by the exercise of reasonable care and skill.

It may be mentioned here that this decision was given more than half a century back. There has been a great change in the standard of work expected of an auditor. Today the plea put forth by the defendant that he is not a stock taker or valuer or that he could rely upon the trusted officials of the company regarding the list of the bad or doubtful debts will not hold good.

(*iii*) London Oil Storage Co. vs. Seear, Hasluck and Co. (1904) (for negligence)

In this case, the auditors failed to verify, an asset, viz., Petty Cash in hand which amounted to £796, but actually only £30 were in hand. The clerk of the auditor. compared the Petty Cash with the accounts where it was shown as £796; but he did not verify the actual petty cash in hand. The difference, viz., £766 had been misappropriated by the Petty Cash-keeper.

It was argued on behalf of the company that had the auditor verified the petty cash in hand, the fraud would have been discovered.

The defence plea put forth was that it was mainly due to the negligence on the part of the directors by keeping such large sums of money with the Petty Cashier and in not checking the Petty Cash Book from time to time that the fraud had been committed and, therefore, the directors were. responsible for the damage and not the auditors.

Lord Alverstone, C. J., while delivering judgment said that it was valid argument to say that the directors were guilty of negligence and hence the auditors were free from their liability. His Lordship said that by omitting to verify petty cash in hand, the auditors committed a breach of duty and hence were liable to pay damages. But only nominal damages of five guineas were awarded as the directors were considered to be also guilty of gross negligence and were a contributory cause of the loss.

Conclusion

Held that it is the duty of the auditor to take proper steps to verify the existence of assets stated in the balance sheet.

(iv) Wilde and Others vs. Cape and Dalgleish (1897) (for negligence and misfeasance)

In this case the plaintiffs, a firm of solicitors, sued the auditors for negligence and breach of duty and claimed damages amounting to about £1,750, which the cashier of the plaintiffs has defalcated and which defalcation was not discovered by the auditors as they had not checked the Pass Book. The defendants' Plea was that they were simply to prepare the Profit and Loss Account and the Balance-Sheet. Lord Russel, C. J., found that there was misunderstanding between the auditor and the plaintiffs but held the auditors guilty in negligently performing their duties. The suit was compromised, and the auditors agreed to pay £850 as damages.

Conclusion

Held that an auditor is liable to pay damages if his client suffers a loss occasioned by his not fulfilling his contract.

(v) Arthur E. Green & Co. vs. The Central Advance and Discount Corporation Ltd. (1920) (for negligence)

In this case the plaintiffs, the firm of auditors, claimed their fees due to them by the defendants. There was a counter-suit by the defendants, a money-lending company, claiming damages from their auditors in not reporting that insufficient provision had been made for bad and doubtful debts as a consequence of which profits were inflated and more commission was paid to the manager. Furthermore, some of the debts were time-barred, which fact had not been pointed out by the auditors. The defendants, thus, contended that the auditors were negligent in the performance of their duty and hence liable for damages.

The auditors' plea was that although some of the debts were time-barred, they did not point out this fact as from past experience they found that the customers did pay the time-barred debts in order to get more advances.

It was held that the auditors were negligent in the performance of their duty in not reporting to the shareholders regarding the insufficient provision for bad and doubtful debts.

Part of the judgment reads as under:

"The duty of the auditors was quite clear as to statutory duties. They had to make a report, and state whether in their opinion the balance-sheet was properly drawn up so as to afford a true account or statement of the company's affairs .... that they (auditors) were not only to be hornest, but were bound to exercise an extraordinary skill but there was a standard..... The case for the auditor was that from time to time there was a bad debts meeting of the directors to consider a certain list which was prepared by the managing director .... and that they were entitled to rely upon the directors; that they had no reason to suspect Mr. Foot (manager of the company). The auditors said that when the list of bad debts came back to them for them to settle the balance-sheet, Mr. Foot had struck out some of the people they had put in respect of bad debts. Mr. Foot had been described as a man who would brook no interference, and I cannot help thinking that when the directors struck these names out of the list it was upon the instructions or advice of Mr. Foot... There was an article which gave the company power, after 15 per cent had been earned, to declare a bonus to the managers, and for four years such a bonus had been voted by the directors in this way. Obviously, it was to Mr. Foot's advantage to show large balances in order that the director's discretion might be exercised by awarding such a bonus to Mr. Foot himself. . .

"This satisfied my mind that the auditors deliberately concealed that from the shareholders which they had communicated to the directors. It would be difficult to say this was not a breach of duty. Auditors must not be made liable for not tracking out ingenious and carefully laid schemes of fraud, when there is nothing to arouse their suspicion and when those frauds are perpetrated by tried servants of the company and are undetected for years by the directors. So to hold would make the position of an auditor intolerable."

Conclusion

An auditor is guilty of negligence when he accepts a list of the debtors prepared by the management as correct although it is clear from the list that some of the debts are bad and irrecoverable.

(*vi*) The Westminster Road Construction Co. Ltd. (1932) (for misfeasance)

The facts of the case were that the auditors did not point out to the shareholders that the work-in-progress was overstated while the liabilities were understated by suppressing some invoices for the purchases. As a result of this, profits were shown as £3,458 while actually they amounted, to £297. Thus, in fact, the dividend was paid out of capital.

It was held that the duty of the auditor was to see that no invoice pertaining to the period under review was omitted. If he did not do so he failed to perform his duty and was, therefore, guilty of misfeasance.

In regard to the valuation of "Work-in-progress" it was held that the duty of the auditor was "to check the figures at which work-in-progress was brought into balance-sheet".

The auditors were found guilty of misfeasance and were ordered to refund the amount of dividend, wrongly paid, with interest to the company.

During the course of his judgment, Bennett, J., remarked:

"The liquidator had proved that the company did not earn a profit of £3,458 during the period in question. No charge of dishonesty was made against any of the respondents. It was settled law that an auditor did not discharge his duty if he merely saw that the balance-sheet accurately represented what was shown by the books on the material date. His duty with regard to the ascertainment of unrecorded liabilities must depend upon the facts of each particular case ...If the auditor found that a company in the course of its business was incurring liabilities of a particular kind and that the creditors sent in their invoices after an interval and the liabilities of the kind in question must have been incurred during the accountancy period under audit, and that when he was making his audit a sufficient time had not elapsed for the invoices relating to such liabilities to have been received and recorded in the company's books, it became his duty to make specific enquiries as to the existence of such liabilities and also, before he signed a certificate as to the accuracy of the balance-sheet, to go through the invoice files of the company in order to see that no invoices relating to liabilities had been omitted. . . .

"... With regard to the over-valuation of the work-in-progress, the expert evidence was that it was the duty of the auditor to check the figures at which work-in-progress was brought into the balance-sheet. It was the duty of Mr. Buckle (the accountant of the Westminster Co.), to satisfy himself that nothing was included in the work valued as in progress on 31st March which was in fact done after that date. He had also to satisfy himself that all expenses and liabilities incurred by the company in connection with the work so valued had been brought into account".

Conclusion

An auditor is guilty of misfeasance

(*a*) if he fails to detect the omission of liabilities from the balance-sheet even when such omission is apparent; and (*b*) if he fails to detect the over-valuation of work-in-progress when ample evidence is available for checking the accuracy of the figures given to him.

(*vii*) Rex vs. Kylsant (1931) or the Royal Mail Steam Packet Company case

This case is more commonly known as the Royal Mail Steam Packet Company case.

The facts of the case were that the company created excessive secret reserve in boom years under the heading "Taxation Reserves" and such reserves were not shown on the face of the balance-sheet. Later on the company suffered heavy losses for several years, and during these years the losses were concealed and instead it was shown as if the company had made profit by utilising the secret reserves. Thus the shareholders were kept in darkness and they were made to believe that the company was running profitably.

The chairman of the company, Lord Kylsant, and the auditor, Moreland, were criminally prosecuted on the ground that the Chairman issued false annual reports with the intention of deceiving the shareholders and that the auditor of the company aided and abetted in the issue of false reports and accounts.

The company was, in fact, running at losses for the past several years. The accounts were manipulated to show considerable profits. During the years from 1921 to 1927, the profit and loss accounts were credited with £5,000,000 after adjustment of "Taxation Reserves", which they showed had been accumulated in the past and which they did not require. These "Taxation Reserves" were actually Secret Reserves which had not been shown in the books of account.

The contention of the auditor was that the auditor need not disclose the fact that the Secret Reserves had been utilised in order to augment the profit of the lean years, and that if he did so the object of creating secret reserve would be frustrated. It was further argued that as a matter of fact secret reserve is created to fall upon in lean years, especially in banking, financial and insurance companies where there is the question of public confidence. Hence, if the auditor did not disclose the fact that secret reserve was being utilised to augment the profit, he was not guilty of a criminal offence.

In this case the accused were acquitted in the criminal case against them. However, the auditor who had committed a breach of duty in connection with the account of the company was made liable under civil liabilities to pay damages for the dividends which were paid out of capital. The lesson drawn from this case is that if excessive reserve is created or where there is a suspicion that such a reserve will be improperly utilised it would be the duty of the auditor to mention that fact in his report. In the same way, if excessive amount is drawn from such a reserve to conceal losses, the shareholders must be informed of the fact. Of course, each case will have to be considered on its own merits. According to the Companies Act, no secret reserve can be created by any company except banking, insurance and financial companies, etc.

Conclusion

While the accumulation of secret reserves might in many cases be quite proper and not open to objection, the utilization at a later date of such reserves, or any part of them (if the amounts were relatively large) to increase the profits, should be specifically disclosed in the accounts. If an auditor commits a breach of such a duty he may have a civil liability but he cannot be held criminally liable.

But as has been pointed out above, such a decision will not hold good in India as the companies except banking, insurance and financial companies, etc., are not allowed to create secret reserves and hence such a case will not arise.

(*viii*) The Kingston Cotton Mills Company Ltd., (1896) (for negligence in valuation of stock)

The facts of the case were that the accounts of the company had been falsified by its manager by over-valuation of stock-in-trade for a number of years and thus profits were inflated and consequently dividend was paid out of capital.

The auditor of the company was sued for negligence in having relied upon stock sheets as prepared by the officers of the company and which were signed by the manager of the company.

The contention of the auditor was that there was nothing to arouse his suspicion and that he relied upon the stock sheets which were signed by a responsible official of the company, viz., the manager. He further pleaded that while signing the balance-sheet he put the remark "as per manager's certificate".

It was held that it was no part of the auditor's duty to take stock and that in the absence of suspicious circumstances he could not be regarded guilty of negligence for having accepted the certificate of a responsible official of the company.

In the course of the judgment, Lopes, J., said:

". . It is the duty of an auditor to bring to bear on the work he has to perform that skill, care, and caution which a reasonably competent, careful and cautious auditor would use. What is reasonable skill, care and caution, must depend on the particular circumstances of each case. An auditor is not bound to be a detective, or as was said, to approach his work with suspicion or-with a foregone conclusion that there is something wrong. He is a watch-dog, but not a blood hound. He is justified in believing tried servants of the company in whom confidence is placed by the company. He is entitled to assume that they are honest and to rely upon their representation, provided he takes reasonable care. If there is anything calculated to excite suspicion, he should probe it to the bottom but in the absence of anything of that kind, he is only bound to be reasonably cautious and careful. . .The duties-of auditors must not be rendered too onerous. Their work is responsible and laborious, and the remuneration moderate. . Auditors must not be made liable for not tracking out ingenious and carefully laid schemes of fraud, when there is nothing to arouse their suspicion and when those frauds are perpetrated by tried servants of the company and are undetected for years by directors. So to hold would make the position of an auditor intolerable".

Lord Justice Lindley, in the same ease, said, "....... I protest, however, against the notion that an auditor is bound to be suspicious as distinguished from being reasonably careful. It is no part of an auditor's duty to take stock. No one contends that it is. He must rely on other people for details of stock-in-trade in hand. In the case of a cotton mill, he must rely on some skilled person for the materials necessary to enable him to enter the stock-in-trade at its proper value in the balance sheet."

Conclusion

In the absence of suspicious circumstances, an auditor is not guilty of negligence if he relies upon the statements made by trusted and responsible officials of the company.

By this decision, the auditor of a company has been relieved of a great deal of responsibility. But this judgment has been criticised by many an accountant on the ground that if an auditor can be relieved of his responsibility by accepting certified lists of the stock-in-trade, why should he not be relieved of his responsibility by accepting certified lists of the debtors, bills receivable, cash in hand and so on.

Since the McKesson and Robins case, it is the practice in America that the auditor or his representative shall be present at the time of taking stock. Even in India, the decision in the *Kingston Cotton Mills* case has not been accepted as was held in *Deputy Secretary, Ministry of Finance* vs. *S. N. Dasgupta's* case. Though this decision was in connection with cash in hand and not stock-in-trade but the underlying principle will be applicable to stock-in-trade also. Thus the decision in the *Kingston Cotton Mills* case does not hold good in India now. For full discussion in regard to the duties of an auditor in connection with the stock-in-trade, readers may refer to the chapter on "Verification and Valuation of Assets and Liabilities".

(*ix*) Republic of Bolivia Exploration Syndicate Ltd., (1913)

The facts of the case were that the company was incorporated in March, 1907. The company had no special Articles of its own and therefore Table A of the Companies Act was applicable. Thus the directors had no power to enter into contract with the company but they did so and payments were made to them by the company under these contracts. The company went into liquidation and the iiquidator took out summons against the auditors for having committed negligence or misfeasance for having certified certain payments in respect of commission and profit costs which payments were alleged to be ultra vires. The aleged wrongful payments were as under:—

(1)Payments for commission (not to a director) for placing shares, for £330 10s.

(2)Payments of profits-costs to a Solicitor Director for £169.

(3)Payment to a director not accounted for by him,amounted to £36.

As regards (1), the auditor did not point out about such a payment in his report of the first year but with regard to the balance-sheet of the ;second year he stated, "Commission paid for obtaining subscribers for shares, £338 10s". But no qualification was appended to auditors's certificate.

No question regarding the payment was raised in the first meeting. In the second meeting an objection was raised to such a payment. The auditor admitted that the Companies Act did not permit such a payment but the memorandum of the company did so and the matter was not pursued any further by the shareholders.

On this point the judge said:

"I am not satisfied that respondents failed in their duty to the comuany in not knowing or ascertaining that the payments were made under the circumstances improper in law before they passed them in the first audited balance-sheet, especially having regard to the facts that the balance-sheet states in terms for what the sums in quest ion were paid... and I do not think that they ought to be held guilty of breach of duty for passing the same entry as to these sums in the second audited balance-sheet; nor do I think, that having regard to the fact that the shareholders approved them after discussion, the liquidator has established that any damage resulted to the company from the auditor having acted as they did."

As regards (b), the solicitor was elected as a director of the company after he had been appointed as solicitor. The payment to him was shown on the first of the two balance-sheets as "Preliminary Expenses for the incorporation of the company, duty, fees and other disbursements, £250". Out of this amount, £150 were alleged to be ultra vires payment. While giving evidence, the auditor said that the amount was duly sanctioned by the directors according to the minute book of the Board, but he admitted that he did not see as to whether the Solicitor-Director was counted for the purpose of forming the quorum.

His Lordship, during the course of his judgment, remarked:

"To the question as to how far the auditors were bound to ascertain that in this company no authorisation existed for directors to contract with the company and to appreciate that the profit-costs of the solicitor's bill were not authorised in law. I do not think I ought to make any order for payment of these sums by the auditors, although I am far from satisfied with the way in which this part of their audit was conducted."

As regard (c), a cheque for £100 was drawn in favour of "Army and Navy Stores or Bearer". A director, Myring, received the balance of £36 but he never accounted for it.

His Lordship did not see any reason to make the auditors liable with any breach of duty on this count as whole of the amount was entered in the audited balance-sheet. But according to Companies Act any amount advanced to the Directors must be stated in the balance-sheet.

Conclusion

Disckse has summed up the conclusion as under:

The Company auditors are bound to know or make themselves acquainted with their duties under the companies articles and under the Companies Act; and if the audited balance-sheet does not show the true financial condition of the company and damage is thereby occasioned the onus is on the auditors to show that this damage is not the result of any breach on their part.

Auditors are prima facie responsible for the ultra vires payments made on the faith of their balance-sheets, but whether and to what extent they are responsible for not discovering and calling attention to the illegality of payments made piror to the audit must depend on the special circumstances of each case.

(x) Re Joseph Hargreaves Ltd. (1900)

This is a very peculiar case. The auditor was properly appointed but he never signed the balance-sheet because of its incorrectness. Again, dividends were paid although no resolution was passed by either the directors or the shareholders authorising such a payment. The auditor refused to sign the balance-sheet because the payment of dividend was being made improperly. The auditor could not communicate this fact to the shareholders, either through his report or by communicating directly to the shareholders, for he never signed the balance-sheet because of its inaccuracy and as no general meeting of the shareholders was held. This state of affairs continued for several years.

The auditor was sued by the liquidator of the company for misfeasance. It was argued by the liquidator that the auditor ought to have resigned when he saw that such illegal actions were being taken by the directors. The auditor pleaded that he had no powers either to hold a general meeting of the shareholders or to communicate directly with each shareholder. He further said that he never signed any balance-sheet and, therefore, he could not be liable for wrong payments. He further added that as no meeting of the shareholders was held, he could not convey the information to them. The suit was dismissed. Cozens-Hardy, J., said:

"It would be startling, I think, to say that an auditor who knows that dividends have been improperly paid out of capital is to be rendered liable because he does not commence an action, on behalf of himself and all the other shareholders, I suppose, against the directors who have improperly paid these dividends, or does not do that which he really had no power to do—get the general meeting together and inform them of the fact."

Conclusion

It was held that an auditor who refuses to certify the accounts of a company due to their incorrectness cannot be held liable if no general meeting was held before which such incorrect accounts could be placed.

(xi) Re Union Bank of Allahabad (1925)

The auditor of the bank blindly signed the balance-sheet. He was held liable for the refund of the previous two years' dividends in having signed false balance-sheet by blindly trusting a dishonest Manager and Secretary of the bank. The judgment of Wallis, J., provides interesting reading:

"Unless auditors are to be held strictly to their legal liability, however honest they may be, the object of legislature in requiring certificate from them is absolutely defeated. . . . I hold that he (auditor) was utterly reckless and indifferent in his conduct as an auditor. He was trusted to discharge his duty. It is nothing to an auditor whether the business of a company is being conducted prudently or unprofitably. It is nothing to him whether dividends are properly or improperly declared, provided he discharges his own duty to the shareholders. His business is to ascertain and state the true financial position of the company at the time of the audit and his duty is confined to that. He is to ascertain that position by examining the books of the company. But his first duty is to examine the books not merely for the purpose of satisfying himself that they show the true financial position of the company... In my opinion he allowed Kedar Nath (Secretary) to throw dust in his eyes and to deceive him in the most obvious manner. Mr. De (auditor) says that if he had examined the books and asked for an explanation about the Tata Industrial Bank's liability, he would have discovered in two minutes that the affairs of the bank were in a very critical state and that the depositors and creditors were being defrauded. He never asked a question and he signed a statement in the Balance-sheet saying that he had received all the needed information and explanation. These words are put in for the reason that an Auditor is not a mere arithmetical machine to check the figures in the books. He should have satisfied himself not only that the accounts were correct, but that the books represented the true state of affairs of the fact."

Conclusion

If an auditor blindly signs a balance-sheet simply because it had been signed by the trusted officials of the company, and if such a balance-sheet turns out, later on, to be incorrect, the auditor must . suffer the consequences.

(*xii*) L. Hudson vs. Official Liquidator, Dehradun Mussoorie Electric Tramway Co., Ltd., (1929)

Robberies were committed by the management. The auditor did not examine the documents. Even where there was doubt about any transaction, he did not make any enquiry about the particular transaction. Consequently some illegal payments were made and were passed by the auditor as correct.

The auditor was held guilty of misfeasance, as he refrained from performing his clear duty. An extract from the judgment of the Allahabad High Court is given below:

"Wilful default, therefore, is, indicative of some misconduct in the transaction of business or in the discharge of duty or omitting to do something either deliberately or by reckless disregard of the fact and whether the act of omission was or was not a breach of duty.... Under the Act where the auditors pass over illegal payments without demanding explanation and the facts disclose that there was deliberate abstention from performing plain and manifest acts and there was absolute duty cast upon them to enquire into the illegal payments and think over the real meaning of dubious transactions; they are guilty of misfeasance unless there is anything to the contrary in the Articles of Association."

Conclusion

When an auditor passes over illegal payments and does not ask for any explanation, he is guilty of misfeasance and must compensate the company for any loss it might have suffered.

(*xiii*) The City Equitable Fire Insurance Co. Ltd., (1924)

The facts of the case were that the balance-sheet of the Company for the years as at 28th February, 1919, 29 th February, 1920, and 28th February 1921, contained misdescription of debts due by Company's brokers and by the manager. The Company went into liquidation and the official receiver as liquidator of the company took out summons against Mr. Beavens, the Chairman of the Board of Directors and other directors and Messrs. Longton and Lepine, the auditors of the Company. The charges against the auditors were:

(1) The debts due by Ellis & Co., the stock brokers of the Company, and Mr. Mansel (Company's General Manager) were misdescribed as "Loan at Call and Short Notice" or "Loans" and a part of the debt owing by Ellis & Co., was described as "Cash at bank and in hand".

(2) The sums due by Ellis & Co., were more than what was shown in the balance-sheet.

(3) A few securities were, in the custody of Ellis & Co., who had pledged these securities but the auditors did not detect that to report to the shareholders.

It may be mentioned here that Mr. Beavens, the Chairman of the Board of Directors was also a senior partner of the firm of Ellis & Co., the stock-brokers of the Company. The court found all the accused except Mr. Beavens, not guilty of the charges.

The auditors were acquitted of all the charges. Mr. Justice Romer made good remarks about the way the audit was conducted and said that the auditors showed skill, care and industry. He expressed these views on the basis of the reports, memoranda, etc., prepared by the auditors and produced in evidence and the time they took in the audit of these accounts.

As regards the charge against the auditors under (1) above, Mr. Justice Romer said that misdescription of the debt owing by Messrs. Ellis & Co., and Mr. Mansel in the balance-sheet did not involve any damage to the Company and that it was not the duty of an auditor to draw the attention of the directors and the shareholders regarding the debt owing by Beavens or Mansel. He also said that there was nothing to raise any doubt in the minds of the auditors that the debts were not good.

Regarding the charge against the auditors under (2) above, the court held that the transactions were of a "window dressing" nature and, therefore, the auditors were not guilty of negligence in the performance of their duty in not actually inspecting the securities, held by the stockbrokers, Messrs Ellis & Co., who had pledged these securities. If the auditors had insisted upon inspecting these securities, the fraud would have come to light and the auditors would have been found guilty on that count, but for the protection given to them under Article 150 of the Company which provided that the directors, etc., should be indemnified by the Company against any liability attaching to them unless the liability arose out of wilful negligence on their part. It may be stated here that such protection is not given now to the auditors under S. 201 of the Companies Act.

The Official Receiver appealed against this decision as against the auditors but the Court of Appeal dismissed the appeal with costs.

Romer, J., during the course of his judgment said:

"That it is the duty of a company's auditor in general to satisfy himself that the securities of the company in fact exist and are in safe custody cannot, I think, be gainsaid. If authority for the proposition be required, it may be found in the passage from Lord Justice Lindley's judgment in the *London & General Bank* case, which has already been referred to. The auditor in that case, amongst other things, 'saw that the bills and securities entered in books were held by the bank' and this the Lord justice plainly treated as being part of an auditor's 'legal standard of duty', though he did not of course mean that in all cases the bills and securities should be lodged with the bank. He meant 'with the bank or in other proper custody'.........."

The Master of the Rolls said:

"Now I come to the last point, part of which is contained in the third charge, and that is the failure to detect the fact that much larger sums were in the hands of Ellis & Co., at the date of the balance-sheet, and the failure to detect and report that the securities were in the hands of Ellis Co."

"Now upon the matter, I want to say a, word or two about the evidence. In fact, Mr. Lepine enquired from the bank and got a certificate from the bank that a certain number of securities were there, and then he turned to Ellis & Co., and he got from Ellis & Co., under the signature of Ellis & Co., a certificate attached to the document apparently not by Mr. Beaven, but by one of the partners a certificate that a number of securities were in the hands of the stock brokers. It is said it was quite wrong to accept the certificate of the brokers, and we me asked to accept the evidence of Mr. Cash and Mr. Van de Linde as meaning this, that you may accept the certificate of a bank apparently in all cases, but you may never accept the certificate of the stock brokers. I cannot agree that the evidence is so to be read, as is intended by the witnesses to be so understood."

The auditors were acquired. They were protected by the Articles of Association of the Company. As a matter of fact, as the law stands today, any provision in the Articles of a Company, which aims at restricting the liability of an auditor, is **ultra vires.**

Conclusion

An auditor is liable where assets are misdescribed in the balance-sheet if damage is caused to the company as a result of such misdescription. He is also liable if he fails to personally inspect the securities which are in the hands of a third party in whose custody such assets are not usually kept.

(*xiv*) Armitage vs. Brewer and Knott (1932)

The facts of the case were that Miss Harwood, the book-keeper, had embezzled a large sum of money by manipulating the wages sheets. She was completely in charge of the books, vouchers, wages sheets and other documents. There was no system of internal check. The auditors were appointed to conduct a continuous and a detailed audit. The charge against them was that they failed to exercise reasonable care and skill in the course of examination of documents, e.g., wages sheets, that is, they failed to vouch and verify book entries. The defence put forth by the auditors was that the frauds could not have been detected by the exercise of ordinary and reasonable care but the learned judge said:

". . . The documents at the beginning set out that the defendants would vouch all payments with receipts in petty cash, check calculations of all wage sheets, check totals of wage sheets into wages book and check weekly totals with other detailed provisions, and accountants undertaking duties of that kind could not be heard to excuse themselves on the ground that this or that was a small matter; they undertook rigorous check, and they did so because that was what their client wanted.... It was doubtless true that to detect the fraud, required minute examination of larger number of documents but that was exactly what the defendants (auditors) undertook to do.... As to the suggestion that some things were too trivial to notice, audits differed greatly as to scope and special instructions. A 6s. 1d. had been altered 16s. 1d. That was passed in what purported to be a meticulous examination. The most casual inspection would detect the discrepancy on the voucher; both figures were there..... It was the duty of the auditor to bring that l0s—which was indicative not only of fraud but of forgery— at once to the notice of the principal. That one piece of paper raised a grave suspicion. It was of critical importance. It was by little things like that that forgeries and frauds were found out".

The case was decided in favour of the plaintiff and the auditors were ordered to pay damages amounting to £1,259 to the plaintiff. It may be remembered that according to the instructions issued to the auditor, it was clear, that there was a suspicion that fraud had been committed and hence the auditor ought to have been extra careful.

Conclusion

It is the duty of an auditor to examine the vouchers, wages sheets and other documents very carefully especially when he is 'informed that there was a suspicion about a fraud having been committed. If he fails to do so, he will be held liable for negligence.

(xv) Apfel's Trustees vs. Annan, Dexter and Co. (1926)

The trustee in bankruptcy of the property of Mrs. Adele Apfel, a bankrupt, brought a suit against the auditors that they had failed to discover that large sums had been converted to their use by the sons of the bankrupt. The trustee alleged that the defendants were employed as auditors while the defendants pleaded that they were employed as v accountants to prepare income-tax returns and not to audit the accounts. The bill which was submitted by the defendants ran as under, thereby indicating that they acted as auditors:

"Professional services rendered for auditing your accounts for the eight months ending 31st December, 1922.

The certificate appended to the balance-sheet by the defendants ran as under:

"Prepared from the books of Mrs. Adele Apfel and in accordance therewith."

It was suggested that the accountants could have discovered the fraud, if they had looked into the accounts of the period following that to which the accounts were made up. The judge did not agree to this suggestion on the ground tliat the accountants were not bound to do any work which they had not undertaken. The learned judge came to the decision that the defendants acted as accountants for a special purpose and dismissed the suit filed by the trustee.

Conclusion

It was held that the auditors were appointed to do the work of accountancy in preparing certain returns and therefore they did not act as auditors of Mrs. Apfel, though inadvertently a bill of charges was prepared as if they acted as auditors. The auditors were freed from their liability.

(*xvi*) The Blue Band Navigation Co. Case (1934)

Originally the current account between the company and Mr. Whittal, a director of the company, showed a debit balance amounting to 25,000 dollars. In order to conceal the fact, this debit balance together with another sum of 12,000 dollars was transferred to the debit of the Western Trading Syndicate, a fictitious concern. The auditor asked for an explanation regarding such a transaction. The explanation was refused by Mr. Whittal on the ground that the circumstances were "extremely confidential". When the auditor persisted, Mr. Whittal gave personal security for the repayment of the debt. Mr. Whittal informed the shareholders at one of their meetings that he stood as surety for the repayment of the debt. The company could not recover a single dollar in respect of the debt. The suit was brought against the auditor for negligence in passing the debt of 37,000 dollars in the balance-sheet without any comment.

It was held that the auditors were not negligent in the discharge of their duty inasmuch as they honestly believed the debt to be a good one, even though such a debt turned out to be a bad one. Mr. Dicksee says, "The case makes no new law, but is a useful reminder that an auditor is not guarantor; after taking reasonable precautions by way of enquiry and weighing of the fact he must come to an honest conclusion and report it."

Commenting on this case, Mr. F.R.M. de Paula writes in the *Principles of Auditing*:

"The case makes clear the fact that an auditor is not an insurer, he is not concerned with the wisdom or unwisdom of an investment, and he is in no way responsible for the management. His responsibilities are confined to taking reasonable precautions, making proper enquiries, coming to an honest opinion and reporting it clearly to the shareholders."

The court absolved the auditors of their liability.

Conclusion

An auditor, who honestly believes a debt to be a good one, is not guilty of negligence, if it afterwards turns out to be a bad one.

(*xvii*) Newton vs. Birmingham Small Arms Co. Ltd., (1906)

The facts of the case were that the defendant company passed a special resolution whereby which the directors of the company were empowered to create Internal or Secret Reserves in addition to two Reserve Funds, etc. They were further empowered to utilize these reserves in any way in the interest of the company, without disclosing this fact. It was also resolved that these facts might be disclosed to the auditor who were not to disclose the existence and the disposal of such reserves to the shareholders.

Thereupon, Sir A: J. Newton on behalf of the shareholders moved the court to declare the special resolution as ultra vires and invalid.

It was argued by the plantiff that the new article was inconsistent with the duties of an auditor as to auditing a company's accounts under S. 23 of the Companies Act, 1900. It was further argued that the result of the new article would be to enable the directors to create a-secret reserve which was subject to no supervision and they might use it as they thought fit.

It was held in this case that provisions in the Articles of the company limiting the powers of the auditors were ultra vires.

Buckley, J., in his judgment, said:

"It is, I think, inconsistent with the Act of Parliament that the auditor should be bound, even when he thinks that the true state of the company's affairs is affected by facts relating to the internal reserve fund upon investments which might involve the company under certain circumstances in enormous loss, the Act, I think, requires that the auditor shall be at liberty and to be bound to report that fact. . .But the special resolutions do not stop there. They provide that it shall be the duty of the auditor not to disclose any information with regard to this fund to the shareholders or otherwisc... Any regulation which precludes the auditors from availing themselves of all the information to which, under the Act, they are entitled as material for the report which under the Act they are to make as to the true and correct state of the company's affairs are, I think, inconsistent with the Act."

Conclusion

An auditor cannot be deprived of his statutory right even by an express provision in the Articles of Association of the company. (For false statement by auditor).

(*xviii*) Superintendent and Rememberancer of Legal Affairs vs. Akhil Bandhu Guha and others (1936)

The facts of the case are that the Managing Directors of a Cotton Mill which did not carry on banking business but received deposits from its customers to augment its working capital; issued a balance-sheet which did not show the real position of the company and concealed certain facts. There was an item in the balance-sheet as "Deposit by others". As a matter of fact the amount against "Deposit by others" was not the real amount of deposits but actually these were *Deposits less a Loan and Interest thereon* This loan had been advanced by the Managing Director to another mill in which he was interested. This loan to another mill was not shown separately or specifically in any part of the balance-sheet. The auditors had given a certificate that in their opinion the balance-sheet had been properly drawn up. It was held that a loan and a deposit, being obviously items differing completely in principle from a balance-sheet point of view, ought to appear on different sides, one as an asset and the other as a liability and that the act of consolidating the two and presenting them as one item in the balance-sheet was a striking case of non-disclosure amounting to suppression of the truth and being a statement false in material particulars, the Managing Directors were guilty of an offence under S. 282 (now S. 628). According to this Section, any person who makes a false statement in any returns, balance-sheet, etc., is liable to be imprisoned up to two years and fined.

A balance-sheet which does not disclose the true state of affairs of a company is not a properly drawn up balance-sheet. The opinion of the auditor that it has been properly drawn up is of no value whatsoever

A part of the judgment runs as under:

"A balance-sheet need not be, in fact it must not be, a mere inventory. It is supposed to be a pictorial representation of the trading of the company, easily appreciated not by ignorant people but by persons who are reasonably able to understand commercial expressions and commercial conditions."

(*xix*) Baidya Nath Biswas vs. Emperor (1935)

"Where, after the company had begun to earn revenue, current expenditure has been debited to organisation expenses when it ought to have been debited in revenue accounts in the balance-sheet, the balance sheet contains a wilful false statement and a technical offence under S: 282 (now S. 628) is committed. It is not necessary that the statement should be such as to deceive any one or that it should even be dishonestly made."

(*xx*) Official Liquidator of Karachi Bank Ltd. vs. Directors, Manager and Auditors of Karachi Bank Ltd. (1932)

"Where the directors of a bank show in the balance-sheet a cash profit for the year by adding bad debts or doubtful debts which were never paid and which are never likely to be paid, it amounts to making a false statement and a very material one. The fact that no dividend is declared makes no difference.

"Auditors signing the Auditors' Report in the false balance-sheet to the effect that in their opinion the balance-sheet is drawn up in conformity with law and exhibits a true and correct view of the company's affairs wilfully make a false statement in the report which by S. 131(2) has to be attached to the balance-sheet and are liable to prosecution under S. 282. (now S. 628)."

(xxi) Lawless vs. Anglo-Egyptian Cotton and Oil Co. (1943) (Action for libel)

The facts of the case were that the company had its head office in Manchester while it had a branch in Egypt. The company received the statement of account from its Egyptian branch wherein there was a "Deficiency in stock of £1,306 1s. 7d". This item was explained to the Auditors that as a matter of fact, it was not a deficiency but "depreciation of stock", for which the manager of the branch was not responsible. The auditor was not satisfied with this explanation and reported:

"We certify that the accounts as above stated are correct. Shareholders will observe that there is a charge of £1,306 Is. 7d. for deficiency of stock, which the manager is responsible for. His accounts have been badly kept, and have been rendered to us very irregularly."

The report was submitted to the shareholders at the annual general meeting as usual. The report was later on printed and sent to the shareholders, and this report was used at an adjourned meeting of the shareholders. Thereupon the manager of the branch brought an action for libel against the company. It was contended by the company that it did nothing but its usual duty in submitting the report to shareholders.

It was held by the court that the directors to the company were bound to circulate the report containing the alleged libelous statement amongst the shareholders and, therefore, printing and circulation of the auditor's report amongst the shareholders were privileged and that there was no evidence of malice on the part of the company.

(xxii) In re G. M. Oka (1952)

The facts of the case were that the Assistant Controller of Insurance required from the Trinity Mutual Assurance Company Ltd., to supply certificate from the auditor certifying the number of Government and approved securities held by the company as on 31st December, 1949. The auditor,

Mr. G. M. Oka, issued a certificate on 16th January, 1950, showing the position of the company as at 31st December, 1949.

The certificate showed that the company held securities of the face value of Rs.5,98,400. The book value of these securities was Rs.5,98,65,3-2-6 and the market value was Rs.58,915-4-0. It appeared that on that date the company had already deposited Bombay Municipal Debentures of the face value of Rs. 1,00,000, with the Saraswat Bank as security against an overdraft. Thus strictly speaking these Debentures did not form part of the securities held by the company, as they were encumbered and were with the Saraswat Bank. Therefore, the company did not comply with the provisions of the Insurance Act of 1938, which required an assurance company to have a certain minimum value of the Government and approved securities.

To overcome this difficulty, the management of the company sold Conversion Loan 1946, on 13th January 1950 and with the proceeds paid off the overdraft and redeemed the Bombay Municipal Debentures which had been pledged with the Saraswat Bank. The Debentures were shown to the auditor by the Managing Director of the company. Therefore, the auditor made the following remarks on 16th January, 1950, against this form of security:

"Purchased on 28th September, 1949. Lodged as security with bankers for overdraft; repaid in full on 13th January, 1949. Actual bonds seen".

Thus it would appear that though the certificate indicated that the company had so many securities on 31st December, 1949, but in fact securities worth Rs. 1,00,000 had been pledged with the Saraswat Bank against an overdraft and therefore could not be said to be the property of the company. The certificate, showing the position of the company as on 31st December, 1949, was misleading and false.

The Debentures pledged with the Saraswat Bank were redeemed on 13th January, 1950, by selling Conversion Loan of 1946 although Conversion Loan formed part of the Government and approved securities held by the company according to the requirements of the Insurance Act, 1938. Thus if the Conversion Loan was sold out the amount of the securities held by the company had fallen below the requirements of the Insurance Act.

The certificate issued by the auditor was sent to the Assistant Controller of Insurance who found later on that the Conversion Bands which had been included in the total number of securities held by the company as on 31st December, 1949 had been sold and, therefore, the certificate issued by the auditor was false. Though the certificate was issued on 16th January, 1950, the number of securities was short on that date. The Assistant Controller of Insurance, therefore, made a complaint to the Council of the Institute of Chartered Accountants of India. The Council found the auditor guilty in the performance of his duty in not verifying the securities. The case went to the Bombay High Court.

It was argued by the Council that the Conversion Bonds included in the list of securities as on 16th January, 1950 were not existent on that date. Moreover, the certificate showed that the company had the Municipal Bonds in hand on 3st December, 1949.

The defence put forth by the auditor was that Mr. Nadkarni who was a justice of Peace and a Municipal Corporator and the Managing Director of the company had told him on 16th January, 1950, that the encumberauces on the Municipal Bonds had been cleared out of other funds of the company., The auditor further added that Mr. Nadkarni showed him the Municipal Debenture Bonds and therefore he (auditor) was satisfied that the Municipal Bonds had been redeemed and that they were no longer in the possession of the Saraswat Bank as security as they had been redeemed.

It was argued by the Council of the Institute of Chartered Accountants that had the auditor verified the securities on 16th January he would not have found the Conversion Bonds and a false and misleading certificate would not have been issued by him. Moreover, the Bombay Municipal Bonds were not in the possession of the company on 31st December, 1949.

The High Court of Bombay found Mr. Oka, the auditor, guilty in the performance of his duty in not verifying the securities before issuing the certificate. A few extracts from the judgment of Chagla, C. J., are given below:

"Now the only answer which the respondent (the auditor) can give and has been given through his counsel is that he was very credulous that he accepted the statement made by Mr. Nadkarni that the overdraft had been repaid from the company's other funds, and acting on this statement he did not verify whether all the securities were there on the 16th of January, but merely saw the Municipal Bonds which had been released from the Saraswat Bank and issued the certificate. The case of the respondent that he issued this certificate on a misrepresentation made to him by Mr. Nadkarni rests solely on the word of the respondent. It is very easy when you are charged with misconduct to throw the blame upon someone else who is not present to defend himself. It is true that Mr. Nadkarni is convicted out of his own mouth by his letter he had written to the Assistant Controller of Insurance on the 17th January, 1950, but that letter does not show that Mr. Nadkarni made a false statement to the respondent. We fail to understand how any auditor can seriously put forward in his defence that he was gullible, that he accepted some one's statement at its face value and failed to discharge his duty of verifying the securities. The very defence and the very explanation renders the respondent unfit to continue as a member of the Institute of Chartered Accountants. His certificate, his signature, his verification carry great weight, and they are usually accepted as correct and genuine.....

In our opinion, this is a serious case and we agree with Sir Jamsedji Kanga, who is appearing on behalf of the Council and who asks us to take a serious view of the conduct of the respondent.

"Under the circumstances, we think that the proper order we should pass is that the name of the respondent shall be temporarily removed from the Register of Chartered Accountants for a period of six months. The respondent should pay the costs of the case."

(xxiii) The Registrar of Companies vs. P. M. Hegde (1954).

The respondent was the auditor of the Rural Bank of India Ltd. Amongst other charges, the auditor was sued for failure to discharge his duty to the shareholders on the following counts:

(*a*) That he did not verify the cash in hand at the head office on the date of the balance-Sheet in each of the years 1945, 1946, 1947, 1948 and 1949.

(*b*) That he did not report to the shareholders on the noncompliance of the provisions of S. 101 (2-B) of the Indian Companies Act, 1913 (*now Section* 69 *of Companies Act*, 1956).

Therefore, the auditor was charged with gross negligence in the discharge of his duty as auditor of the Rural Bank of India Ltd.

The auditor explained that he verified the cash in hand on the several dates he visited the Bank for audit in each of the years but these dates were later than the dates of the balance-sheet concerned. He stated that he actually checked the cash on 15th December, 1945 for the balance-sheet as at 31 st October, 1945, and so was the case of verification of cash in regard to other balance-sheets. He admitted that he had not verified the intermediate transactions between the several dates of the balance-sheet and the actual amounts of cash found by him at the head office on the several dates he made the check. Their Lordships quoted Lord Alverstone, C.J., in the *London Oil Storage Co., Ltd* vs. *Seear, Hasluck & Co.*:

"It cannot be disputed that when an auditor returns to the shareholders an entry of cash in hand, he must have taken reasonable steps to ascertain that the cash was in hand". Their Lordships said, "cash in hand is verified either by production of actual cash balance or if the date of the accounts has gone by, by exhaustively vouching the cash count up to the date of audit and then counting the balance of cash in hand. It is, of course, obvious that in the case of cash at distant branches a satisfactory certificate from responsible officers of the branches that the balance exists may generally be accepted in lieu of actual counting. . . In our opinion, it is the duty of the auditor, except in special circumstances, to verify the cash in hand on the material date. . . .The respondent admittedly did not verify the cash on the material date, and ever when at a later date he made a check he did not examine the intermediate transactions. We, therefore, agree with the finding of the Council that the respondent who was required to satisfy himself by actual verification that the cash did exist on the date of the balance-sheet and Profit and Loss Account exhibited a true and correct view of bank's affairs, had failed in his duty to satisfy, the asset was there."

The second charge against the auditor was that he did not report to the shareholders that the provisions of Section 101 (2-B) [*Now Section* 69 (4) *of Companies Act*, 1956] of the Indian Companies Act, 1913, had not been complied with. The section lays down that all moneys received from applicants for shares should be deposited in a scheduled bank until the company is allowed to commence business or it is returned to the applicants for want of minimum subscription before a particular date.

The auditor defended himself by stating that when he came to know about the non-compliance of the provisions of Section 101 (2-B), at the time of the audit of accounts, he asked the managing director to explain. He added that the explanation given was that the bank was 100 miles away, that it could be reached only by bus and that within a week the certificate to commence business would be obtained. Their Lordships remarked:

"Even assuming that the managing director did give this explanation, it was the duty of the respondent to have mentioned that there was non-compliance with the statutory direction. . .the very failure to deposit the moneys should have roused his suspicion, and very probably a searching enquiry would have revealed the fact that the major allottees of the shares had not paid a pie for the large number of the shares allotted to them:"

"We, therefore, agree with the Council of the Institute of Chartered Accountants that the respondent failed to discharge his duty as an auditor of the Rural Bank of India Ltd., and he was guilty of gross negligence. . .", remarked their Lordships.

(xxiv) Commissioner of Income. Tax, Madras vs. G. M. Dandekar of Messrs. G. M. Dandekar and Co., Madras (1952)

The facts of the case are: A. Mohamed & Co., of Madras, engaged the services of Messrs. G. M. Dandekar & Co., Chartered Accountants, Madras, to audit the accounts and prepare income tax returns of the firm. The Income Tax Officer was informed of the appointment by A. Mohamed & Co. Messrs. Dandekar & Co. examined the books of account and signed a few statements, including the Trading and Profit & Loss Account, Profit and Loss Adjustment Account and Balance-sheet. All the statements were signed by the respondent and the balance sheet bore the following words:—

"Valued and found to be correct"

However, quantitative statement of opening stock, purchases, sales and closing stock was signed by A. Mohamed & Co.

In the covering letter the respondent stated:

"The books and account are kept in Gujrati style in the usual course of business and the statements of schedules prepared therefrom represent, in our opinion, correct income of the firm",

A. Mohamed & Co. had two separate set of books of account (one for the regular business and the other for the black market transactions which were never shown to the auditors).

The Income Tax Officer got suspicious and examined the books of account and found that the income of the assessees was more than what had been certified by the auditors.

The charge against the auditors by the Commissioner of Income Tax was that the auditors were negligent in the discharge of their duties:

(1) that their certificate that the books of accounts of A. Mohamed & Co., for the year ended 29th October 1943, were kept in the. usual course of business was unwarranted;

(2) that they failed to report the omission of the cost which was debited in the main book and which was not accounted in sales or the closing stock;

(3) that their subscribing to the unsubstantiated plea that some of the sales recorded in the separate book were from and out of the unaccounted purchase debited in the main book was misleading.

Mr. G. M. Dandekar, the partner of the firm of the auditors, had audited the accounts. The respondent, viz., Mr. G. M. Dandekar, argued that the work done by him was not that of audit. He said that it was an examination of the assessees' books with a view to present it to the Income Tax Officer and that it was not a certificate but it was an opinion that he had given about the books. He further said that he was not expected to go beyond the books of account if he was appointed to prepare the returns for the purpose of income tax because he was not appointed to audit the accounts. He added that he never signed the statement regarding the stock and that he never undertook examination of the transactions in the separate book in which black market transactions were entered.

The judgment was given in favour of the auditor. A few extracts from the judgment of Venkatarama Ayyar, J., are given below:

"....The point for decision is whether on the facts mentioned, the respondent can be held to be guilty of gross negligence. There can be no negligence unless there is a duty cast upon the person to do a particular act and he fails to do it.

"It is, therefore, necessary to ascertain what the duties of the auditors are as the auditor of Messrs. A. Mohamed & Co. It is contended by the respondent that when an assessee engages him for auditing his accounts and preparing the income tax returns for him, his duty is only to prepare the statements on the basis of the accounts produced by the assessee and that he is under no obligation to go further and enquire whether the account books maintained by the assessee are reliable".

Ayyar, J., continuing said:

".... But if the duty of the respondent was only to prepare a correct statement from the accounts of the assessees and not to investigate whether those accounts are correct or not, this charge must fall on the ground. The respondent did not state that the figures mentioned in the statement represented the real profits made by the assessees. He only stated that the balance-sheet represented the correct position according to the accounts of the assessees.

"There is no charge against the respondent that he connived at the assessees putting forward false statement or that he had in any manner associated himself with the attempt of the assessees to mislead the department. The charge is that he owed a duty to the department, to himself investigate the truth and correctness of the accounts of the assessees and not merely to act as their post office in transmitting them. We do not agree that the respondent is under any such duty to the department and, therefore, no question of negligence arises.

"In the result we hold that the respondent is not guilty of any conduct which renders him unfit to be a member of the Institute."

(xxv) Davar and Sons Ltd vs. M. S. Krishnaswami (1952)

The facts of the case are: The Amalgamated Coffee Estate Ltd., Madras, had issued debentures which were secured on the properties of the company by the Deed dated 8th January 1945, executed by the company in favour of Mr. B. N. Viswanathan, the managing agent, as trustee of the debenture-holders. One of the terms of the issue of debentures was that the company shall establish a special fund called sinking fund for the redemption of the debentures and shall each year provide Rs. 33,000 *out of the profits of the* ***company*** *or other resources*.

Davar & Sons Ltd., who had purchased a number of debentures, complained that in spite of the fact that the Amalgamated Coffee Estate Ltd. had made profits during the financial year ending 30th April 1945, according to the published accounts, it had not transferred anything to the contemplated sinking fund. Again the company made profits during the years ending 30th April 1946, 1947 and 1948 and it was alleged that not a single pie was transferred to the sinking fund and none of the published balance-sheets of the company exhibited any sinking fund. Therefore, these balance-sheets did not exhibit a true and correct view of the state of affairs of the company and were calculated to mislead whomsoever they concerned, more especially the debenture-holders of the company.

The defendant, Mr. M. S. Krishnaswami of the firm of Messrs. M. S. Krishnaswami and Jagannathan, Chartered Accountatns, who had audited the accounts of the Amalgamated Coffee Estate, pleaded that clause 13 of the trust deed did not oblige the company to transfer the sum of Rs. 33,000 each year out of the profits to the "sinking fund". He added that the clause in question consisted of two parts—the first part relating to the "sinking fund" was a mere statement as it was left indeterminate as to the point of time at which appropriation of the profits was to begin and as to the quantum of profits to be apportioned. He further stated that there was no obligation cast on the directors to create a sinking fund out of the profits every year as there were no specific provisions in the debenture trust deed that the net profits ought not to be distributed before the specific sum out of the net profits of the year was apportioned to the sinking fund. On the other hand, he argued, the appropriation to the sinking fund was entirely a matter within the discretion of the directors. They might create a sinking fund at any time, e.g., in the year when there was bumper profit but not every year.

The auditor contended that he was appointed as the auditor of the Company by the Shareholders and his duty, therefore, was primarily towards them. The debenture-holders were like any other creditors of the company and, therefore, he did not owe any duty to the debenture-holders. He said that he was concerned with the correctness of the balance-sheet which was correct and that he was not concerned whether the Company paid to its creditors or not, whether the company set aside any sum or did not redeem the debentures. It was for the creditors, in this case, the debenture-holders, to see that the terms of the issue of debentures were carried out.

The case was decided against the auditor by the Madras High Court. A few extracts from the judgment are given below:

"We do not think it is necessary to decide the question whether the directors of the Company were or were not under an obligation to create a sinking fund, though we are inclined to take the view that the trust deed did contemplate such an obligation. But we are clearly of the opinion that it was the duty of the respondent as an auditor to have mentioned the fact that in spite of the company earning the profits no part thereof had been set apart towards the sinking fund and that on the other hand the company had borrowed Rs. 33,000 from the managing agents for the purpose of sinking fund investment. A sinking fund primarily denotes `moneys set aside for the purpose of sinking or wiping out a corporation's debt by degrees'. Such a fund is-created by periodically debiting instalments against profits arid crediting the amount of such instalments to the sinking fund account.... The duty of the auditor in respect of a sinking fund is thus set out in the same text book (Dicksee's Auditing, sixteenth edition) :

'The sinking fund instalment must in all cases receive the Auditor's close attention; he must satisfy himself as to their sufficiency for the redemption of the loans within a period prescribed and verify the investments of the 'fund, both as to principal and interest'.

"Having regard to the nature of the sinking fund and its purpose, it strikes us extremely strange that the company instead of allocating the prescribed sum from and out of the profits should have borrowed that amount from the managing agents..... But surely it was incumbent on the auditor to have drawn the attention of the shareholders to this extraordinary action of the directors.... It is taken as an axiom in auditing that no sum which is not set aside out of profits can properly be called a reserve.

"We, therefore, hold that the respondent failed in his duty as an auditor in not drawing the attention of the shareholders to the fact that the sinking fund was not created as contemplated by the debenture trust deed and in not making clear the fact that the amounts shown as towards the sinking fund were borrowed from the managing agents.

"We agree with the finding of the committee that the respondent was guilty of gross negligence in accepting as correct during the course of his audit the journal entries which were mere book entries and that he was guilty of passing the balance-sheet as on 30th April 1946, 30th April 1947, and 30th April 1948, which contain material defects and misleading entries as regards the sinking fund investments and the cash described as being with the debenture trustee or the managing agents. We hold that the respondent must have known or with the exercise of due diligence could have known that no investments existed and there was no cash of Rs. 33,000 with the managing agents as shown in the balance-sheet as on 30th April 1948 but nevertheless he certified to the correctness of the relative entries".

(*xxvi*) Dumbell's Banking Company Ltd. (1900)

The facts of the case are that Dumbell Banking Company issued balance-sheet which contained an item of a credit of £65,000 obtained from the London City and Midland Bank Ltd., under the heading "Cash in hand". The auditors drew the attention of the managers regarding the overdraft but they did not make any change in the balance-sheets. The auditors did not mention anything about this matter in their reports to the shareholders.

The auditors together with the directors were prosecured' under the Manx Criminal Code, 1872, identical to Section 628 of the Companies Act, 1956, and sentenced to various terms of imprisonment for concurring in the publication of the balance-sheets knowing them to be false and with intent to deceive.

(*xxvii*) McKesson & Robins Incorporated, Maryland (1939)

The facts of the case are that the President of McKesson & Robins in league with other high officials of the company manipulated the accounts and fictitious set of records of purchases, sales and stock were presented to the auditors of the company. As a result of this manipulation, the total assets were over-valued by about $21 millions.

The defence of the auditors was that the verification of inventories should be confined to records presented to them by the company and that they were not expected to actually verify the stock and other assets. They further stated that they had followed the accepted practice by the Certified Public Accountants.

The Securities and Exchange Commission held investigation to find out:

(1) whether the auditor conducted the audit according to the accepted practice; and

(2) whether the recognised audit procedure was adequate or not.

The Commission published its report in 1941 and stated that they found divergent views were expressed with regard to the duties and responsibilities of the auditor in connection with the physical verification of quantities, etc., of the stock. They added that a majority of the accountants expressed the view that the verification of assets should be confined to the records. On the other hand a large number of accountants were of opinion, that the auditor should physically verify the assets either:

(1) by test counts; or

(2) by observation at the time the assets are being verified; or

(3) by a combination of these two methods.

The Commission endorsed the above views.

As described in the Chapter 'Verification of Assets and Liabilities' the American Accountants have accepted the recommendations of the Commission and the present practice is stated in the following extracts from the *"Audits by Certified Public Accountants"* published in 1950 by the American Institute of Accountants:

"The C. P. A. is required by generally accepted auditing practice to be present at the inventory-taking to observe the effectiveness of the count procedure when it is practicable and reasonable to do so and the amount of the inventory is significant".

(xxviii) Ultramares Corporation vs. Touche, Niven & Co. (1931) (For Liability to Third Parties)

The facts of the case are that the plaintiff had advanced sums of money to Fred Stern & Co., Inc., on the basis of the balance sheet certified by the auditors. They lost the money. It was found that though the balance-sheet of the company showed a net worth of 1,070,000 dollars, as a matter of fact the liabilities of the business exceeded the assets by some 200,000 dollars. Assets had been over-stated by inclusion of fictitious assets to the tune of 950,000 dollars and by the omission of liabilities to the extent of 300,000 dollars from the balance-sheet.

The auditors had supplied thirty-two copies *of* their report, who were presumably aware that these would be shown to banks and other creditors. The auditors were held liable. Justice Cardozo gave the decision in the Court of Appeal as under:

"The defendants owed to their employers a duty imposed by law to make their certificate 'without fraud, and a duty growing out of contract to make it with the care and caution proper to their calling. Fraud includes pretense of knowledge when knowledge there is hone. The creditors and investors to whom the employer exhibited the certificate, the defendants owed a like duty to make it without fraud, since there was a notice in the circumstances of its making that the employer did not intend to keep it to himself".

(*xxix*) Re Thomas Gerrard & Sons, Ltd. (1967)

The facts of the case are that the auditors of the company noticed some alterations in the invoices. While verifying the stock, the auditors asked the Managing Director for an explanation regarding the alterations in the invoices. They were assured by the Managing Director, who was also the Secretary of the company and a justice of Peace and a well-known and a responsible figure in the district, about the correctness of the procedure of the stock taking. The auditors accepted such assurances and desisted from making any further inquiry. It was found later on that stock was over-valued.

On being sued, the defence put forth by the auditors was that they accepted the assurances given by a responsible person (Managing Director) who was a justice of Peace and an important figure of the district. The question before the Court was whether the auditors acted in an irresponsible manner and were guilty of misfeasance.

A witness (an expert) said:

"If the invoices were altered, then undoubtedly a complete examination should be made of all purchase invoices and, where alterations were seen, the suppliers should be communicated with as to the correct valuation. At the same time, as this would be a very serious matter, the completion of any report on the accounts should be held over and the board of directors should be informed"

The learned judge said that though it was no part of the duty of an auditor to take stock, it was incumbent on them, when once material alterations affecting the valuation came to their notice, to take all reasonable steps to verify that the supporting vouchers and records relating to the taking of stock were in order. When the attention of the court was drawn to the decision in the leading case of the *Kingston Cotton Mills Co.*, Peunyenick, justice, said: "The standard of reasonable care and skill are, on the expert advice, more exacting today than it prevailed in 1896, when the *Kingston Mill* case was decided".

The accountants in England have not accepted the procedure accepted by the American Accountants but Spicer and Pegler in their book 'Practical Auditing', 12th edition, observe on page 139: "The American practice is to be recommended wherever possible but it is obvious that such considerable technical knowledge is required to take the stock of certain business that an auditor would not be competent to make the physical inventory. It is considered, however, that the auditor should, on occasions, be present at the stocktaking in order to satisfy himself that the procedure laid is being observed."

QUESTIONS

1. (*a*) What do you understand by 'Criminal Liability' of an auditor? Name the criminal offences of which an auditor may be guilty under the Indian Companies Act, 1956.

(*b*) In the Kingston Cotton Mills case (1896), in the course of his judgment, the learned judge remarked: 'An Auditor is not bound to be detective, or as was said, to approach his work with suspicion or with a foregone conclusion that there is something wrong. He is a watch-dog but not a blood-hound'.

In the Armitage vs. Brewer and Knott case (1932), in the course of hearing, the learned judge declared 'that it was the duty of auditors to be suspicious: that was what they were there for. If every body was honest and careful, there would be no need for auditors'.

How would you reconcile the two conflicting views? (*Rajasthan M. Com.*)

2. (*a*) 'An auditor is not an insurer; he does not guarantee that the books do correctly show the true position of the company's affairs; he does not guarantee that the balance-sheet is accurate according to the books to the company'.

(*b*) 'Auditor is a watch-dog and not a blood-hound'.

Elucidate the above two statements stating legal cases.

(*Bombay, Varnnas:' S. V. Vidyapeeth B. Com.*)

3. When can an auditor be held liabte for damage to third party? What points third party should prove to hold the auditor liable when the third party has not appointed the auditor?

(*Gujarat B. Com., Cal. B. Com., Hons., C.A. Inter.*)

4. Outline the extent of an auditor's liability for non-detection of frauds and defalcations. Illustrate your answer by citing the relevant case law. (*Poona B.* Com.)

5. An auditor of' a limited company did not verify the investments but he inserted a note in the Balance-Sheet— "Investments not verified".

The shareholders approved and adopted the accounts at the annual general meeting. Subsequently, it transpired that the investments were misappropriated and the company suffered a loss.

Can the auditor be sued for damages, negligence or otherwise in the discharge of his duties? Give your answer with reasons. (*Cal. M. Com.*)

6. What is the liability of an auditor of a public company with regard to the stock-in-trade of a manufacturing business? Quote legal decisions. (*Jabalpur B. Con.*)

7. Discuss briefly the liabilities of an auditor to a Public Company and mention some legal decisions you know of in this connection.

(*Andhra Pb. Service Commission*; *Lucknow,* 1974)

8. Distinguish between a Civil and Criminal Liability of an Auditor and illustrate your answer by referring to legal cases. (*Punjab Pb. Service Commission*, 1963; *Cal. B. Com.*)

9. Section 231 of the Companies Act provides that an auditor of a company shall be entitled to receive notice of and to attend any general meeting of the company at which any accounts which have been examined or reported by him are to be laid before the company and may make any statement or explanation he desires with respect to the accounts.

(*a*) In what circumstances should this right be exercised?

(*b*) Would any explanation made by the auditor relieve him in respect of omissions from his report or from his balance-sheet?

(*c*) Should an auditor, so attending, answer questions put by shareholders?

(*d*) If an auditor is present and wrong information is given by a director in regard to an item in the balance-sheet, would it be proper for him to correct that information in the absence of explanation by the director concerned?

(*e*) Would an auditor incur any liability for absenting himself from an annual meeting? Give reasons for your answers.

10. "An auditor has no liability for negligence in the conduct of an honorary audit". Discuss.

11. On wanting to inspect your clients' investments, you are told that many of them are in the custody of their brokers for which the latter have furnished a certificate. How would you react? Cite the leading case on the point, stating how the court eventually decided therein as regards the Auditor's liability. Would the court's decisions have been the same in the light of the present Law in India. (*C A. Final*)

12. Discuss the Auditor's liability to third parties for (a) Fraud, and (b) Negligence: (*Annamalai, Bombay, Poona, Punjab, Cal., B. Cum. and CA. Final* 1971)

13. "An auditor's duty is to convey information". Explain how you would distinguish between "information" and "means of information". (*Cal. B. Com.*)

14. Discuss the liabilities of auditor under the Companies Act, 1956. Is an auditor personally liable if it is subsequently proved that his audit assistants were negligent and as a result the accounts he has certified are false or fraudulent. (*Cal. B. Com. Hons.*)

Professional Conduct and Ethics

Introduction

This chapter is intended for the students who are preparing for the final examination of the Institute of Chartered Accountants of India.

We have already discussed in general the duties of an auditor in Chapter IX. It would have been observed that an auditor owes duties not only to his clients but also to his professional brothers and third parties in some cases. He has to observe certain rules—rules which are written and those which are not written. In the former category we include the rules under the Chartered Accountants Act, 1949, while the unwritten rules are those which in the course of time have come to be regarded as professional code, the breach of which is considered to be professional misconduct by professional accountants. In India, however, an auditor's conduct is regulated only by the Act.

The word 'Ethics' means moral philosophy which teaches men their duties and the reason for it—duties which are voluntarily self-imposed. The word "ethics" has been defined in Oxford Dictionary as "science of morals, moral principles, whole field of moral science". Generally it refers to all standards of behaviour. Originally these ethics were formulated with the object of putting an end to malpractices. We may say that these are precedents and conventions which should be honoured not by the force of law but by moral force. Thus the expression '*professional ethics*' refers to the behaviour of a member of a professional body towards the other members of his profession and towards the members of the public. The code of *professional ethics* is a voluntary assumption of self-discipline above and beyond the requirements of the law. Ethics provide standards of conduct by which all members of an organisation are guided in their daily activities. They establish one's official responsibilities to society in contrast to one's personal responsibilities as owner, supervisor, employer or employee.

All professions such as those of law, medicine, accountancy, etc., have formulated rules and regulations for the guidance of the members of their respective profession and also in the interest of the public. The Institute of Chartered Accountants of India has also formulated such rules and regulations for the members to win the confidence of the public and their clients since they possess a great deal of information of the business of their clients and which information can be used by them to the detriment of their clients. It is the duty of the auditors that the information which they give about a public company is correct. If the information given is incorrect as a result of which the investing public suffers, it may not rely on the accounts certified by the auditors. The members are expected to be under certain obligations to the members of the public while performing their professional duties. The rules of professional conduct are given in the Chartered Accountants Act, 1949. We shall deal in this chapter with some of the important sections concerning a public accountant **vis-a-vis** his professional conducts. All references made will be in respect of Chartered Accountants Act, 1949, unless otherwise stated.

Professional misconduct has been defined by Section 22 of the Chartered Accountants Act, 1949, as "For the purposes of this Act, the expression 'professional misconduct' shall be deemed to include any act or omission specified in any of the schedules, but nothing in this section shall be construed to limit or abridge in any way the power conferred or duty cast on the Council under sub-section (1) of Section 21 to enquire into the conduct of any member of the Institute under any other circumstances". Thus this definition is inclusive and not exhaustive because the Council has been given powers to enquire into the conduct of any member under any circumstances which are not specified in the schedules.

The expression "professional negligence" should not be confused with the expression "professional misconduct". It means any failure to perform a duty according to accepted professional standards, which may result in a loss, damage or detriment to the client who has engaged the professional man. Such a negligence gives rise to a civil liability to pay damages to the party which has suffered the loss or damage.

Similarly distinction between "negligence" and "gross negligence" should be clearly understood. "Negligence" means carelessness or accidental or inadvertant failure to perform a duty incidental to the work of the auditor, e.g., if an auditor failed to point out remuneration of the managing agents having been paid without obtaining the sanction of the Central Government, it would amount to "negligence". On the other hand, "gross negligence" means failure to perform, what was fundamentally, the duty cast upon the auditor, will amount to "gross negligence", e.g., if more remuneration was paid to the managing agents and the auditor knowingly did not point out this fact to the shareholders in order to accommodate the managing agents, it would amount to "gross negligence". Again where the auditor informed the shareholders of a bank that he had not verified the cash in hand and that he had signed the balance-sheet in anticipation of the receipt of confirmation letters from the banks in respect of the cash said to be lying with them, it was held that the auditor was guilty of "gross negligence" *(Deputy Secretary, Ministry* of *Finance*, vs. *S.N. Das Gupta)*.

Formerly a distinction was made between 'members in practice' and 'members not in practice' but now every member of the Institute is designated as 'Chartered Accountant' irrespective of the fact whether he practises the profession of accountancy or not. However, for some purposes, the distinction is still important as we shall see later on. Section 2 (2) clarifies the expression 'to be in practice' as follows:—

"A member of the Institute shall be deemed 'to be in practice' when individually or in partnership with chartered accountants, he, in consideration of remuneration received or to be received,—

(*i*) engages himself in the practice of accountancy; or

(*ii*) offers to perform or performs services involving the auditing or verifications of financial transactions, books, accounts, or records or the preparation, verification or certification of financial accounting and related statements or holds himself out to the public as an accountant; or

(*iii*) renders professional services or assistance in or about matters of principle or detail relating to accounting procedure or the recording, presentation or certification of financial facts or data; or

(*iv*) renders such other services as, in the opinion of the Council, are or may be rendered by a Chartered Accountant in practice; and the words 'to be in practice' with their grammatical variations and cognate expression shall be construed accordingly."

Thus if an associate or a fellow of the Institute is employed by a practising chartered accountant or a firm of chartered accountants, he will be deemed to be in practice for the purpose of the training of articled clerks.

The Council of the Institute decided in the meeting on 15th September, 1964:—

"A member will be deemed to be in practice during the period he renders service with Armed Forces".

If a Chartered Accountant who is suspended from practice under the orders of the High Court, appears before the Income Tax authorities as Income Tax Practitioner, legal position being not clear, benefit of doubt was given and he was therefore held not guilty of any misconduct. [Re. *A. C. Kaher* (1959)].

Again a chartered accountant who renders part time service will be deemed to be in practice under Regulation 167 of Chartered Accountants Regulations.

From the above definition it would appear that it is not necessary that a member must be practising and have clients in order to be styled as "member in practice". Any member who sets up an establishment and who offers to perform various accounting functions even though he might not yet have any client, will also be considered as a "member in practice".

Entry of names in the Register

Section 4 1ays down:

1. Any of the following persons shall be entitled to have his name entered in the Register, namely:—

(*i*) any person who is a registered accountant or a holder of restricted certificate at the commencement of this Act;

(ii) any person who has passed the examination and completed such training as may be prescribed for members of the Institute;

(*iii*) any person who has passed the examination for the Government Diploma in Accountancy or an examination recognised as equivalent thereto by the rules for the award of the Government Diploma in Accountancy before the commencement of this Act, and who, although not duly qualified to be registered as an accountant under the Auditor's Certificate Rules, 1932, fulfils certain conditions as the Central Government may specify in this behalf;

(*iv*) any person, who at the commencement of this Act, is engaged in the practice of accountancy in any acceding State and who, although not possessing the requisite qualifications to be registered as an accountant under the Auditors' Certificate Rules, 1932, fulfils certain conditions as the Central Government may specify in this behalf;

(*v*) any person who has passed such other examination and completed such other training without India as is recognised by the Central Government or the Council as being equivalent to the examinations and training prescribed for members of the Institute:

Provided that in the case of any person who is not permanently residing in India, the Central Government or the Council, as the case may be, may impose such further conditions as it may deem fit;

(*vi*) any person domiciled in India, who at the commencement of this Act, is studying for any foreign examination and who is at the same time undergoing training whether within or without India, or who having passed such foreign examination, is at the commencement of this Act undergoing training, whether within or without India:

Provided that any such examination or training was recognised before the commencement of this Act for the purposes of conferring the right to be registered as an accountant under the Auditor's Certificate Rules, 1932, and provided further that such person passes the examination or completes the training within five years after the commencement of this Act.

2. Every person belonging to the class mentioned in clause (i) of sub-section (1) shall have his name entered in the Register without the payment of any entrance fee.

3. Every person belonging to the class mentioned in clauses (ii), (iii) , (iv), (v) and (vi) of sub-section (1) shall have his name entered in the Register on application being made and granted in the prescribed manner and on payment of the prescribed fee, which shall not exceed rupees three hundred in any case.

4. The Central Government shall take such steps as may be necessary for the purpose of having the names of all persons belonging to the class mentioned in clause (i) of sub-section (1) entered in the Register.

The Act has also made distinction between two different classes of members—Associates and Fellows. According to Section 5(2) as soon as a person is enrolled as a member of the Institute, he becomes an Associate Member of the Institute and can use the letters A.C.A. after his name. On the other hand, if an Associate Member has been in continuous practice in India for a period of at least five years, he becomes a Fellow and is entitled to use the letters F.C.A. after his name. By a recent amendment, a person, who has been a member for a period of at least five years although he has not been in practice, may be admitted to the Fellowship if the Council of the Institute is of opinion that the member has experience equivalent to the experience gained by a member in practice for a period of five years.

A member practising the profession of accountancy is not allowed to use any designation other than that of "Chartered Accountant" according to Section 7. If a member is also a member of other Institutes of accountancy is England or America etc. provided such Institutes are recognised by the Institute of Chartered Accountants of India, he may also use other designations and letters. The Council of the Institute has recognised the following foreign accountancy Institutes:

1. The Institute of Chartered Accountants of England and Wales.
2. The Institute of Chartered Accountants of Scotland.
3. The Institute of Chartered Accountants of Ireland.

However, a member who is not in practice and does not use the designation other than that of a chartered accountant may use any other description.

It may be stated here that a member cannot designate himself as a Cost Accountant but he can use the letters A.C.W.A. after his name provided he is a member of that Institute.

If a chartered accountant is found to have forged the Will of a relative, he would be liable to be excluded from the membership of the Institute even though *this action of his* was not connected with his professional duties vide Section 8 of the Chartered Accountants Act, 1949. The reason advanced that such an action on the part of the chartered accountant is that he is dishonest and therefore will not be relied upon by the public when he signs the balance-sheet and profit and loss account of a company.

Disabilities

Notwithstanding anything contained in Section 4, a person shall not be entitled to have his name entered in or borne on the Register if he-

(*i*) has not attained the age of twenty-one years at the time of his application for the entry of his name in the Register; or

(*ii*) has been adjudicated by a Competent Court to be of unsound mind; or

(*iii*) is an undischarged insolvent, or

(*iv*) being a discharged insolvent, has not obtained from the Court a certificate stating that his insolvency was caused by misfortune without any misconduct on his part; or

(*v*) has been convicted by a competent court whether within or without India, of an offence involving moral turpitude and punishable with transportation or imprisonment or of an offence, not of technical nature, committed by him in his professional capacity unless in respect of the offence committed he has either been granted a pardon or on an application made by him in this behalf the Central Government has, by an order in writing, removed the disability; or

(*vi*) has been found on enquiry to have been guilty of conduct which renders him unfit to be a member of the Institute.

Failure on the part of a person to disclose the fact that he suffers from any one of the disabilities mentioned above would amount to professional misconduct. The name of such a person can be removed from the Register of Members by the Council (S. 20).

A person who is not a member of the Institute and falsely represents that he is a member of the Institute or uses the designation 'Chartered Accountant' or a member who has not obtained the certificate of practice, practises, he is liable to be punished with a fine which may extend to one thousand rupees.

If a chartered accountant in practice or a firm of chartered accountants has more than one office in India, each one of such office should be in the charge of a member of the Institute (Section 27).

Failure on the part of a member of a firm not to have a member incharge of its branch and a separate member in case of each of these branches when these are more than one, would constitute professional misconduct.

It is necessary that the chartered accountant incharge of a branch should be associated with him or with the firm either as a partner or as a paid assistant. In the latter case he must be a whole time employee.

Removal of the name of a member from the Register

Disciplinary powers over the auditors are vested in the Institute under Sections 21 and 22. Section 22 deals with acts and omissions which render a member unfit to be a member of the Institute. Section 21 deals with the procedure in inquiries into the misconduct of members. We shall first deal with Section 22 which contains an inclusive, though not exhaustive, definition of "Professional Misconduct". These are the principal professional rules of conduct for a member of the Institute.

For the purpose of finding out whether a member is guilty of misconduct or not, whether the Council of the Institute or the High Court is to punish the member guilty of misconduct, whether a member who is not in practice can be punished, etc., the Act has two Schedules. The First Schedule deals with misconduct by a member whose case can be decided by the Council. This Schedule has three parts. Under Part I of the Schedule various acts and omissions which amount to misconduct committed by "members in practice" are enumerated. Part II deals with "members not in practice" and Part III is applicable to all members. Second Schedule of the Act deals with certain other important rules of conduct the breach of which requires. a decision by the High Court after the Council has considered the case of a member.

Before we deal with the contents of the two schedules, let us understand the meaning of the word 'misconduct' on the part of a Chartered Accountant. In a paper read by Mr. P.K. Lahiri at the third Conference of Chartered Accountants of India, he said: "A Chartered Accountant acting as an auditor will be deemed guilty of misconduct if he—

1. fails to disclose a material fact known to him which is not disclosed in a financial statement;
2. fails to report a material mis-statement known to him to appear in a financial statement;
3. fails to obtain sufficient information to warrant the expression of opinion or his exceptions are sufficiently material to negate the expression of an opinion;
4. fails to invite attention to any material departure from the accepted procedure of audit applicable to the circumstances.

First Schedule

Part I—which deals with professional misconduct by a member in practice and which case is to be decided by the Institute.

Clause 1 :

"If he allows any person to practise in his name as a chartered accountant unless such person is also a chartered accountant in practice and is in partnership with or employed by himself."

This clause prohibits a member to allow any unqualified or non-member to practise on his behalf or in his name. The object is to safeguard the public against unqualified persons in the guise of qualified accountants. But the rule permits a member to allow a person to act on his behalf provided such a person is also a member of the Institute and is a partner of the member. There seems to be no objection as both of them are members or the Institute. There is an exception to this rule which allows an employee of a member to work on his behalf provided such an employee works directly under his control and supervision. In this context it may be mentioned here that if a firm of chartered accountants has a branch, it must be supervised by one of the partners and not by an employee (Section 27).

Clause 2 :

"If he pays or allows or agrees to pay or allow, directly or indirectly, and share commission or brokerage in the fees or profits of his professional business, to any person other than a member of the Institute or a partner or a retired partner or the legal representative of a deceased partner."

This clause prohibits a member to share his fees directly or indirectly with any non-member but a member may agree to pay a share of his fee, commission etc., earned during the course of his professional business to any partner, or a retired partner or even to the legal representative of a deceased partner. In this connection it may be stated that the Council of the Institute is of opinion that a retired partner or the widow of a deceased partner should not be entitled to share the profits unless such share was payable to them according to the provisions of the partnership agreement.

The legal representative or the widow of a single-member firm will not be entitled to share the profits if the business has been purchased by another person. If the partnership agreement does not contain any provision that the widow or the legal representative of the deceased will be entitled to share the profits, such person will not be entitled to share the future profits. However, she may continue to receive the goodwill of her husband by instalments provided the goodwill was to be sold to the new firm.

Clause 3 :

"If he accepts or agrees to accept any part of the profits of the professional work of a lawyer, auctioneer, broker or any other agent who is not a member of the Institute."

This clause does not allow a member to share any fees, brokerage of commission earned by a non-member. The underlying idea of such a clause is that a member may not take undue advantage of his position as the auditor of a client. Sometimes an auditor is asked by his client to suggest or recommend the name of a legal adviser or an auctioneer. In such a case the auditor might manage for the appointment of a legal adviser or an auctioneer with an understanding to share their fee or commission etc. As a member cannot share his fee with, a non-member, similarly he cannot share the fee or commission earned by a non-member, (K. *V: Narasimhan, In Re* 1952).

Clause 4 :

"If he enters into partnership with any person other than a chartered accountant in practice or a person resident without India but who for his residence abroad would be entitled to be registered as a member under clause (v) of sub-section (1) *of Section 4 or whose qualifications are recognised by the Central Government or the Council for the purpose of permitting such partnerships, provided*

that the chartered accountant shares in the fees or the profits of the business of the partnership both within and without India."

According to this clause a chartered accountant in practice cannot take any person as a partner unless such a person is also a chartered accountant in practice. But according to Clause 4, a chartered accountant may take a person as a partner who is not in practice provided (a) he is resident abroad, (b) he could be enrolled as a member of the Institute if he had been in India, and (c) if the member shares the fees and profits of the partnership earned both in India as well as abroad.

Clause 5 :

"If he secures, either through the services of a person not qualified to be his partner or by means which are not open to a chartered accountant, any professional business. "

According to this clause, a member is not permitted to secure professional business through a non-member. In other words touting is prohibited. Thus all forms of anvassing directly or indirectly are prohibited.

Clause 6 :

"If he solicits clients or professional work either directly or indirectly by circular, advertisement, personal communication or interview or by any other means."

According to this clause a member is not allowed to contact or interview people or to advertise or send circulars, etc., in order to secure professional business *(Gadre vs. Ambekar)*. When a chartered accountant wrote to the Ministry of Commerce and Industry that the name of his firm may be included in the panel of the auditors it was held that he was guilty of professional misconduct *(Re. K.C* f. *Satyavadi*, 1955). If, however, it has been ascertained in advance that a panel is being maintained, it will not amount to canvassing and therefore will not tantamount to misconduct.

It is permissible to quote fees on enquiries received from the co-operative banks, societies and other institutions which maintain a panel of approved auditors. Such scales of fees should not be printed or cyclostyled to be sent in reply to enquiries.

Publication of the name or the firm's name in the Telephone Directory, in Bold Type and/or under a classified list is prohibited by making special request or by means of additional payment.

Responding to Tenders. Advertisement or Circulars, the Council of the Institute is of opinion that the members should not

(*a*) respond to tenders;

(*b*) respond to advertisements inviting applications for appointment of auditors;

(*c*) respond to circulars inviting quotations for professional services of a chartered accountant; and

(*d*) respond to enquiry asking to send quotations if the enquiry indicates that such an enquiry has also been made from other members but if the letter received does not indicate that such enquiry has been made from other members, quotation for fees may be made.

Issuing of handbills apparently for the guidance of assessees re income tax, sales tax etc., by a member is prohibited.

A chartered accountant may publish an article or a book provided he does not indicate his connection with the firm of chartered accountants with which he is associated.

The Council of the Institute does not approve of sending of Greeting Cards or personal invitations by members indicating their professional designation, status or qualifications, etc. Similarly when a chartered accountant sent a letter with a request that he may be appointed as auditor, it was held that it amounted to professional misconduct (*In Re B.K Swain*, 1960). The profession of accountancy is not ordinary business where a businessman advertises his wares or sends circulars to customers or to prospective customers to sell goods. The profession should be carried on in a dignified manner. If this prohibition were not imposed, there would be under-cutting and competition among the members. Moreover the public will lose its confidence in the profession.

No doubt this clause might cause difficulties to the newly enrolled young accountants but the clause is enforced to upkeep the dignity of the profession. With the development of industries and opening of more business houses, and if their work is honest and satisfactory, young accountants will not find any difficulty in securing more business. An honest work and satisfied client in itself is a good advertisement.

Although an auditor in England is not allowed to advertise about his business, as is the case in India, a question was raised sometimes back as to whether an auditor should be prevented to advertise about his business. The Monopolies Commission in U.K. went into the question and came to the following conclusion:—

1. that these restrictions operate against the public interest, innovation and development of new practices; and

2. that these restrictions have given rise to procuring business by less desirable ways.

The Commission, under the circumstances, made the following recommendations :—

(*a*) The advertisements by the auditors may be permitted provided such advertisements do not claim superiority over others.

(*b*) Such advertisements should not be inaccurate.

(*c*) Such advertisements are such that "could reasonably be regarded as not likely to bring the profession into disrepute."

However, *The Accountant*, of England, in its issue of 12th August, 1976, editorially criticised these recommendations on the following grounds :

1. The present restrictions do not in any way create a difficulty for the clients in obtaining professional services since the list of the members, etc., are available.

2. Moreover, accountancy services are secured on the basis of 'personal recommendations.

3. That the British Institute of Management thought that advertising would substantially increase the cost of professional services.

4. That the accountancy bodies in U.K. were also of the opinion that advertising runs counter to the professional and traditional impartiality in its advisory and reporting role.

Clause 7 :

"If *he advertises his professional attainments or services, or uses any designation or expression other than chartered accountant on professional documents, visiting cards, letter heads or sign-boards, unless it is a degree of a university established by law in India or recognised by the Central Government or a title indicating membership of the Institute* of *Chartered Accountants or of any other Institution that has been recognised by the Central Government or may be recognised by the Council.*"

Under this clause, as stated in the previous clause, a Chartered Accountant should not advertise his professional attainments or use any designation except that which is permitted by the institute and the University degrees on his sign-boards, letter heads, visiting cards, etc. He may use any title, words or letters permissible by any Institute of Accountancy of England, provided they are recognised by the Central Government or the Council. For example, he should not advertise or use such phrases as "Specialist in Income Tax or Sales Tax", "Recognised auditor of the Co-operative Banks", etc., on his letter heads, visiting cards or sign-boards, etc. Again, the Council is of opinion that it is improper for a chartered accountant if he states in his letter heads, etc., the date on which his firm established or if he uses the designation Municipal Counsellor or any functionary after his name in the letter heads, etc., as it would amount to advertising.

A member may advertise in the press under the following circumstances even though his address or name as chartered accountant is given:—

1. Advertisement for staff in his office;
2. Advertisement on behalf of his client for the recruitment of staff or disposing of the property of his client if a request in this respect is made to him;
3. Advertisement in the capacity of a trustee for the sale of business or property of his client.

When he advertises for staff or Article clerk for his own office, he must not use expressions such as 'a well known firm of chartered accountants' as it would amount to advertising one's attainments.

The Council of the Institute has recommended that the following words is telegraphic address would amount to advertising and therefore the members should not use such words:

Tax Expert; Tax Consultant; Consultants; Audit Experts; Company Audit; All-Audit; Free Advice ; Audit Advice; Tax Advice; Tax Audit; Faithful; Fearless; Carefree, etc.

If a letter is sent to the editor to be published in the newspapers; the writer should not write his designation as chartered accountant after his name. He may simply use *nom de plume* or "Chartered Accountant", or "A.C.A." or "F.C.A.", or give his name without the words Chartered Accountant.

In books or pamphlets on professional subjects, the name and designation may appear. But not the name of the auditor's firm if he is in practice.

The Council has advised the members that in case any one has used these words, he should substitute any other suitable words as soon as possible.

In the case of *Mirza M. Hussain* (1955), where the Chartered Accountant used the designation "Incorporated Accountant", London, and Registered Accountant, India, in the Balance-Sheet, it was held that he was guilty under this clause.

If a telephone directory has a separate section for particular group of subscribers such as doctors, advocates, property dealers, etc., a chartered accountant may have his name inserted in such a list provided that the name is not in bold type. It is immaterial whether any extra payment has to be made to the telephone company are not for such an insertion.

Clause 8:

"If he accepts a position as auditor previously held by another chartered accountant or a restricted state auditor without first communicating with him in writing"

The clause is self-explanatory. An auditor who is appointed by a limited company in place of an existing auditor, should not accept the appointment unless he has communicated with the existing or retiring auditor to enquire as to the reasons which compelled the existing auditor to resign or as to why his services were dispensed with *(Kharwandikar* vs. *Borkar,* 1952). This clause has been framed with a view to prevent the unscrupulous directors of a company to remove an honest auditor who could not fall prey to the wishes of such directors. This clause thus safeguards the interest of the shareholders of the company as well as that of the profession and the public. This clause also safeguards the interest of the new auditor by enabling him to know the reasons of his appointment in place of the existing auditor.

Sometimes it is argued that a company may replace an auditor because (a) the existing auditor was careless and therefore the company was not satisfied with his work, or (b) the company could not afford to pay the exorbitant fee or wanted to reduce the expenses of audit, or (c) that a company has a right to appoint any person to act as its auditor subject to the provisions of the Companies Act, or (d) sometimes when a company changes its place of business, it may change its auditor because it would prefer the local auditor who may be available for consultation, etc., at any time; or (e) when a partner of the firm of the auditors retires or dies and who had been dealing with the accounts of the company, the change is advisable. Therefore, it is argued that whenever it is sought to replace an auditor, it should not be presumed that the directors are dishonest persons or the auditor is being removed with certain ulterior motives. In some cases it may be correct but experience has shown, it is argued, that in most of the cases the existing auditor is removed because he is considered to be as "inconvenient" by the directors.

It may be mentioned here that this clause is also applicable to an auditor who has been appointed to render special services such as financial adviser, liquidator, trustee or a receiver although he is not to act as statutory auditor of the company.

Clause 9 :

"If he accepts an appointment as auditor of a company without ascertaining from it whether the requirements of Sections 224 and 225 of the Companies Act, in respect of such appointment, have been duly complied with".

According to this clause an auditor is prohibited to accept an appointment as auditor of a company without first ascertaining whether his appointment is in order, according to Sections 224 and 225 of the Companies Act. Section 224 lays down that the first auditor is to be appointed by the directors within one month of the registration of the company. If they do not make the appointment, the shareholders of the company should do so at their general meeting. A casual vacancy can be filled up by the Board but a vacancy caused by resignation by the auditor has to be filled up by the shareholders. In case the directors or the shareholders do not appoint an auditor, the Government will fill up the vacancy. In case an auditor is appointed in place of an existing auditor, certain formalities under Section 225 are to be followed, viz., a special notice (14 days) has to be given to the company by the shareholder who intends to move such a resolution at the general meeting. The company in its turn has to immediately inform the existing auditor of the proposed resolution. The existing auditor. has a right to put a defence orally or in writing at or before the holding of such a meeting. Before he accepts the appointment, the auditor should, therefore, see that all these formalities had been observed. As a matter of fact, it has been made obligatory on the incoming auditor to ascertain from the company whether appropriate procedure has been faithfully followed. For details, the reader may refer to the chapter on "Audit of Limited Companies".

A Chartered Accountant was appointed by the Board because the company had failed to appoint the auditor at its annual general meeting. The Chartered Accountant wrote to the previous auditor of the company about the appointment but finished the work of audit on the same date before the receipt of any reply. It was held that the auditor was guilty but since it was found that there was some misapprehension as to the true legal position, the auditor was given a warning (*U.C. Majumdar* vs. *J.N. Saika*, 1954).

Clause 10 :

"If he charges or offers to charge, accepts, or offers to accept in respect of any professional employment fees which are based on a percentage of profits or which are contingent upon the findings, or results of such employment, except in cases which are permitted under any regulations made under this Act."

This clause has been framed in keeping with rules and regulations of professional bodies that the remuneration of the professional men should not be based on the results of their work (*R.B. Basu* vs. *P.K Mukherjee,* 1956). Whatever the fee may be, a chartered accountant is expected to show as much skill and diligence as is expected of a man of his status. Thus if such "Contingent fee" is not paid to him he might not show as much skill and diligence as he ought to have shown. Again, if the public finds that the quality of the work of the auditor is according to what he is paid, it may not have so much confidence in such an auditor. This practice may impair his independence. The rule has made provision for exceptional cases, e.g., fee payable to the liquidator, receiver or valuer (Regulation 168 of C.A. Regulation), who may be a chartered accountant, according to the amount distributed to the shareholders or according to the amount realised on the sale of the assets of the company. The Central Government Department, of Revenue has prescribed a scale of fees to be charged in connection with the Estate Duties, Wealth Tax, etc.

Clause 11 :

"If he engages in any business or occupation other than the profession of chartered accountants unless permitted by the Council so to engage: Provided that nothing contained therein shall entitle a chartered accountant from being a director of a company unless he or any of his partners is interested in such company as an auditor."

This rule prohibits a chartered accountant to engage in any trade or occupation other than that of a chartered accountant. The underlying idea of this clause is to keep up the dignity of the profession. If this rule were not there, a chartered accountant might engage in such a business or occupation which might inherently be dishonourable. There might be misapprehension that if a chartered accountant were permitted to take up any other profession he might take advantage of his position while advertising for the other business.

It may be noted here that Rule 167 of Chartered Accountants Regulations permits a chartered accountant to act as director, liquidator, trustee, executor, administrator, arbitrator, etc. This rule also permits members by a general resolution of the Council to engage themselves in the following occupations:—

1. Employment under a chartered accountant or a firm of chartered accountants.
2. Private tutorship.
3. Authorship of books.
4. Attending classes and appearing for any examination, either academic or Accountancy or any examination relating to other professions.
5. Part-time lectureship under the Coaching Organisation of the Institute.
6. A part-time tutorship under the Coaching Board of the Institute of Chartered Accountants of India.
7. Holding of Life Insurance Agency Licence for the limited purpose of getting renewal commission.
8. Acting as Notary Public.

A specific resolution by the Council is required to permit a member to engage in the following occupations:—

1. A full-time or part-time employment in business concerns, e.g., banks, insurance companies, factories and other commercial firms.
2. A full-time or part-time employment in non-business concerns, e.g., Government or semi-Government Departments, clubs, associations, etc.
3. Family business provided he does not take any active part in the management of the concern.
4. Part-time or full-time lectureship for courses other than those relating to the Institute's examinations conducted under the auspices of the Institute or the Regional Councils.
5. Proprietorship of an educational institution.
6. Part-time or full-time tutorship under any educational institution other than the Coaching Organisation of the Institute.
7. Editorship of professional journals.

8. Holding part-time public elective office, e.g., Member of Parliament, Member of Legislative Council, Municipal Commissioner.

In addition to the above occupations the Executive Committee may pass a specific resolution allowing a member to engage himself in other occupations. The Council is, however, empowered to refuse permission in individual cases to allow a member to engage in any of the above occupations.

Clause 12 :

"If he accepts a position as auditor previously held by some other chartered accountant or a restricted State auditor in such conditions as to constitute under- cutting."

The object of this clause is to prevent competition among the members and therefore prohibits them to accept a position held by another auditor under such circumstances which may amount to under-cutting. It may be stated that each case will have to be considered on its own merits, e.g., an auditor of a long standing shall charge higher fees while a young auditor may charge less fees. It also depends upon the client who may not be able to afford to pay high fees which he had been paying so far and therefore may like to appoint an auditor of less standing. Thus it would appear that such a regulation is difficult to be observed in practice.

Clause 13 :

"If he allows a person not being a member of *the Institute or a member not being his partner to sign on his behalf or on behalf* of *his firm, any balance-sheet, profit and loss account, report or financial statements."*

According to this clause a member is not permitted to allow a person who is not a member of the Institute or who even though he is the member of the Institute but is not a partner of the member, to sign on his behalf or on behalf of his firm any balance-sheet, profit and loss account, a report or any financial statement. An auditor is appointed because of his qualifications, integrity, etc., and therefore, it is he who should audit the accounts and sign the balance-sheet and profit and loss account. Similarly in the case of the appointment of a firm of auditors, one of the partners who has audited the accounts should sign the balance-sheet and profit and loss account and no one else. Again, Section 227 lays down that the auditor shall make a report *to the members of the company* on the accounts examined by him. Therefore, the report must be presented by that person who was appointed by the shareholders and not by any other person on his behalf.

Moreover,. Section 229 of the Companies Act lays down: Only the person appointed as auditor of the Company or where a firm is appointed, only a partner in the firm practising in India may sign the auditor's report.

PART II

This Part, as stated previously, deals with acts and omissions which give rise to an action against those members of the Institute who are not in practice, i.e., members who are employees of an individual firm or a company.

Clause 1. The first clause prohibits a member who shares or agrees to share directly or indirectly his remuneration with others.

Clause 2. The second clause prohibits a member to receive any share of commission or remuneration of others such as a chartered accountant, an advocate, a broker, etc.

Clause 3. The third clause prohibits a member to disclose any confidential information obtained during the course of his employment except when the employer himself permits him or law compels him to disclose such confidential information to others.

PART III

This part is applicable to all the members of the Institute whether they are in practice or not. According to this part:

Clause 1. Members are prohibited to furnish false information whether in the form of statements, returns, etc., to the Institute knowing it to be false. (*J.R. Chathrath, In Re* 1952).

Clause 2. Members are prohibited to style themselves as Fellows of the Institute when in fact they are not so.

Clause 3. If a member fails to furnish information asked for or does not comply with the requirements asked for by the Council or any of its Committees, he is guilty of misconduct.

Section 24 of the Chartered Accountants Act lays down various penalties to which a person is liable if he fraudulently claims to be a member of the Institute or uses the designation, of "Chartered Accountant". If an Associate Member uses the designation of "Fellow" he would be dealt with under the above section.

If a partner of the firm of auditors has signed the report he should within a reasonable time of his signing the report, inform the Registrar, of Companies that he has signed the report or any other document of the company, stating the year for which he has signed it.

Second Schedule

After having described the acts and omissions which amount to misconduct and which are decided by the Council of the Institute, we now proceed to discuss those rules the breach of which gives rise to an action against a member to be decided by the High Court. Whenever any complaint against a member is made to the Institute, it makes an enquiry and forwards its findings to the High Court for adjudication.

This Schedule has two parts, viz., Part I which deals with the rules which are applicable to Chartered Accountants who are in practice while Part II deals with the rules which are applicable to members in general.

PART I

Which deals with cases of professional misconduct by a member in practice which are to be decided by a High Court.

Clause 1 :

"If he discloses information acquired in the course of his professional engagement to any person other than his client, without the consent of his client or otherwise than as required by any law for the time being in force..

A businessman has his own secrets—financial as well as others. When his accounts are audited by an auditor who may also be auditing the accounts of a competing concern, there is a possibility of the secrets and information of confidential nature being disclosed by the auditor to the competing concern. Confidence reposed in the auditor might be betrayed. Therefore the client may not have any confidence in the integrity of the auditor. The public might not employ auditors because of the danger of secrets leaking out. To avoid any such contingency, this rule has been framed which prohibits an auditor to disclose any information of the confidential nature gained by him during the course of his professional work unless the client himself permits him to do so or law compels him to disclose the information. This clause has been framed in the interest of both the client and the chartered accountant as well as to keep up the dignity of the profession.

Clause 2 :

"If he certifies or submits in his name or in the name of his firm a report of an examination of financial statements unless the examination of such statements and the related records has been made by him or by a partner or an employee of his firm or by another chartered accountant in practice "

This rule requires a chartered accountant to certify or submit only those financial statements, records, etc., which have been examined by him or by one of his partners or an employee or by any other chartered accountant. Thus, this rule prohibits a chartered accountant to sign or submit any financial statement, etc., which has been examined by an unqualified person. This clause thus ensures the audit by a qualified person.

Clause 3 :

"If he permits his name or the name of his firm to be used in connection with an estimate of earnings contingent upon future transactions in a manner which may lead to the belief that he vouches for the accuracy of the forecast:"

Sometimes a running concern is taken over by a company which issues prospectus and in order to make them more attractive and to sell shares quickly, the auditor is asked to certify not only the profit which the concern had been making but also to express an opinion about the future profits and prospects of the company. If the auditor does so, the prospective shareholder might think that the estimates are correct as they have been certified by a chartered accountant. The estimate may prove to be incorrect. Therefore, this clause prohibits a member to express any opinion about the future profits of the company. The rule also prohibits a member to allow his name to be affixed to such a certificate.

Clause 4 :

"If he expresses his opinion on financial statement of any business of any enterprise in which he, his firm or a partner in his firm has a substantial interest, unless he discloses the interest also in his report."

Under this clause a chartered accountant must not express his opinion on financial statements of any business in which he is directly or indirectly interested, e.g., opinion about a business in which one of the partners of his firm has interest because if this were allowed, the opinion might be biased. If he expresses an opinion in such a case, he must make it clear in the certificate about his interest. Thus this rule will ensure an independent opinion of the chartered accountant. A chartered accountant must be above suspicion and that is why such a clause has been framed.

The question might arise as to what is meant by the expression "substantial interest". If the chartered accountant is entitled to a share of say two per cent of the profits of the concern the accounts of which he is auditing, has he a "substantial interest" or not in the concern and whether he is precluded from expressing any opinion about the financial position of the concern or not? Law does not define "substantial interest" Each case, therefore, will have to be decided on its own merits.

If we refer to Sections 226(3) and 224(4) of the Companies Act, we find that a person is not qualified to be appointed as auditor of a limited company, (i) if he is a partner, or he is in the employment, or an officer or an employee of a company; or (ii) if he is a member or a director of a private company or partner of a firm which is the managing agent of the company, etc. The reader should study this Section carefully. It will be observed from this Section that whatever interest a chartered accountant has in a concern, he cannot act as the auditor of that concern if that is a limited company and hence the question of "substantial interest" does not arise. But what will be the position if he is the auditor of a partnership firm in which he has some direct or indirect interest. Thus each case will have to be considered on its own merits.

Clause 5 :

"If he fails to disclose a material fact known to him which is not disclosed in a financial statement, but disclosure of which is necessary to make the financial statement not misleading."

A chartered accountant must disclose in his report any material fact which has been suppressed in the financial statements when the disclosure of such facts is necessary so that such statement may not mislead the public provided he is aware of the suppression or non-disclosure of the facts

(*S Ganesan* vs. *A.R ,Joscelyne,* (1956) also (*Davar & Sons Ltd.* vs. *M.S. Krishnaswamy,* 1952). The chartered accountant was found guilty in giving a false certificate regarding the circulation of *"Amar Ujala"*, a magazine, and was debarred to practise for three months under Section 21(5)/ Regulation 11A of Chartered Accountants Act, 1949 (*Audit Bureau of Circulation Ltd, Bombay* vs. *Kailashi Lall Aggarwal,* 1967, Allahabad).

Clause 6 :

"If he fails to report a material fact known to him to appear' in financial statement with which he is concerned in a professional capacity".

According to this clause, if an auditor, during the course of his professional duties, comes across any material mis-statement which has been made in the financial statements, he must disclose this fact in his report (*Registrar of Companies* vs. *S.S. Iyer,* 1960).

What is "material mis-statement", will depend upon judgment of the auditor in both of the clauses stated above.

Clause 7 :

"If he is grossly negligent in the conduct of his Professional duties."

As a matter of fact an auditor must show as much skill and diligence as is expected of a man of his status. The question is what is that "skill and diligence". This is very difficult to decide. The court will have to decide as to whether the auditor showed that much of "skill and diligence" as was expected of haim. If he did not he will be held guilty of negligence. The word "gross negligence" indicates reckless, carelessness or utter carelessness, i.e., if one has been a little careful he could have found the facts (*Davar & Sons Ltd* vs. *Krishnaswami,* 1952).

If the auditor does not complete the work of audit and does not submit the audit report in time to enable the clients to fulfil the statutory requirements, he is guilty of professional misconduct under this clause (*Lakshmi Narain Saxena's* case). Again, in the same case Mr. Saxena was held guilty of professional misconduct in that he exercised undue influence and coercion in securing from the clients fourteen hundred rupees and a letter of appointment.

Clause 8 :

"If he fails to obtain sufficient information to warrant the expression of an opinion or his exceptions are sufficiently material to negate the expression of an opinion".

An auditor has to state in his report "whether he has obtained all the information and explanations which to the best of his knowledge and belief were. necessary for the purposes of his audit." Therefore, he must obtain all the information and explanations. If he fails to obtain such information either because he himself did not care to obtain such information or the management did not supply him with sufficient information even though he required it, he must not express any opinion about the correctness of the financial statements of the concern even with any proviso, e.g., "the balance-sheet and the profit and loss account represent a true and fair view of the state of affairs of the company subject to the remarks that we have not been able to verify the existence of the investments or their valuation." When the auditor could not verify the existence of the investments or their valuation how could the balance-sheet represent a true and fair view of the state of affairs of the company. In the case of bank audit, if the auditor could not get sufficient information regarding the cash in hand, he must mention the fact in his report in spite of the assurance by the management about the existence of cash in hand. If he does not do so, how can he report that the balance-sheet represents a true and fair view of the bank. Under this rule, therefore, the auditor will be held guilty of misconduct. The right step in such a case should have been for him to state "since we could not verify the existence of the investments or their valuation on account of........ we are unable to verify the correctness of the balance sheet and profit and loss account." (*Deputy Secretary, Ministry of Finance* vs. *S.N. Dasgupta,* 1955).

Clause 9:

"If he fails to invite attention to any material departure from the generally accepted procedure of audit applicable to the circumstances."

If the auditor has departed from the normal procedure of audit, he must state this fact in his report. If he does not do so, he will be considered guilty of misconduct under this rule *(Audit Bureau of Circulation Ltd., Bombay* vs. *Kailashi Lall Aggarwal, Allahabad,* 1967).

It may be submitted that law has not prescribed any procedure for the audit of the accounts by an auditor as has been done in America. So far the auditors have followed their own procedure which they may change from time to time according to the experience gained by them. It is, therefore, not clear as to how can an auditor be held guilty in the circumstances stated above.

Clause 10:

"If he fails to keep money of his client in a separate banking account or to use such moneys for purpose for which they are intended."

This rule is quite clear. An auditor is sometimes entrusted with the moneys of his client, e.g., if he has been appointed as liquidator of a company, he must not misuse this money. If he commits a breach of trust or misuses the money belonging to his client he will be guilty of misconduct under this rule *(National Insurance Co., Ltd* vs. *B. Mukherjee,* 1957). He should use the money belonging to his client only for the purpose for which it is meant. He should not mix up the moneys belonging to his client with his own money, e.g., depositing his client's money in his own bank account. 'Clients money' means money received by the chartered accountant for the discharge of his duties as Chartered Accountant and for purposes connected therewith.

PART II—which deals with the clauses, the breach of which amounts to misconduct and is applicable to the members in general. The cases arising under this Part are to be decided by the High Court.

Clause 1 :

"If he contravenes any of the provisions of this Act or the regulations made thereunder."

According to this rule if a member contravenes the provisions of the Chartered Accountants Act, 1949 or any regulations made thereunder, he will be deemed to be guilty of misconduct. A chartered accountant certified that an audit clerk was in service with him although the clerk was employed elsewhere between 11 a.m. to 5 p.m. but worked under the chartered accountant between 5 p.m. to 8 p.m. It was held that the auditor made a mis-statement to the Institute and therefore was guilty of misconduct and hence his name was removed from the Register of Members for a year and a half (*J.K. GhoshIn Re* 1953).

Clause 2 :

"If he is guilty of such other act or omission as may be specified by the Council in this behalf, by notification in the Gazette of India."

The list of the acts and omissions enumerated in the foregoing pages is not exhaustive, e.g., if a chartered accountant engages a clerk without notifying the fact to the Institute; if he uses the designation of Chartered Accountant before enrolment; (Joint Secretary *to the Government of India* vs. *A.C. Kaher,* 1954); Auditor of a Co-operative Society issuing a false certificate of verification of cash in hand (*Paradise Co-operative Housing Society Ltd., Bombay* vs. *R. Viraswamy,* 1955), and so on. Therefore, according to this rule, the Council of the Institute is empowered to formulate other rules for the guidance of the members, which rules may be notified from time to time in the Gazette of India. For instance, according to a Notification No. C.A. (7)/65, issued by the Institute of Chartered Accountants of India, a member of the Institute who is an employee shall be deemed to be guilty of professional misconduct if he is grossly negligent in the conduct of his duties as such an employee.

According to a notification dated 6th May 1910 issued by the Institute of Chartered Accountants of India,

"A member of the Institute shall be deemed to be guilty of professional misconduct if—

1. he accepts as Cost Auditor of a Company under Section 233B while he—

(*a*) is an auditor of the company appointed under Section 224 of Companies Act; or

(*b*) is an officer or an employee of the Company; or

(*c*) is a partner, or is in the employment of an officer or employee of the company; or

(*d*) is a partner or is in the employment of the company's auditor appointed under Section 224 of the Companies Act, 1956; or

(*e*) is indebted to the company for an amount exceeding one thousand rupees, or has given any guarantee in connection with the indebtedness of any third person to the company for an amount exceeding one thousand rupees; or

2. after the appointment as Cost Auditor, he becomes subject to any of'the disabilities stated in the items 1 (*a*) to (*e*) above and continues to function as a Cost Auditor thereafter.

Procedure for Inquiry of Misconduct by a Member

We have already dealt with the acts and omissions which amount to professional misconduct on the part of a member of the Institute, whether in practice or not, and the breach of which gives rise to disciplinary action against the member. In addition to the professional misconducts enumerated in Section 22, the Council is also empowered to enquire into any misconduct of a member even though it may not arise during the course of his professional duties, e.g., a chartered accountant knowingly files false income tax returns in respect of his own profession. We have also stated the cases where the matter is to be decided by the Council whose decision is final (misconducts under the First Schedule) and also the cases of misconduct where the matter has to be referred to the High Court for its decision (misconducts under the Second Schedule).

Procedure in Inquiries re misconduct of Members

We shall now describe the procedure to be followed when a complaint is received against a member till the case is decided. The procedure is laid down in Section 21 of the Chartered Accountants Act, 1949.

Whenever any information or a complaint against a member is received by the Council and if it finds that a *prima facie* case has been made against a member for professional or *other misconduct* it must refer the matter to the. Disciplinary Committee. The Committee holds an inquiry and forwards its conclusions to the Council. The words "other misconduct" used above includes any conduct in his private capacity and not in the capacity of a Chartered Accountant, e.g., a chartered accountant was found guilty for having forged the Will of a relative even though the forgery had not been committed in his capacity as a chartered accountant. It will be deemed to be a professional misconduct and disciplinary action may be taken against him.

If the Council finds from the report of the committee that the member is not guilty, the case is dropped. If, on the other hand, it is found that the member is guilty of a professional misconduct described in the First Scheduled, it sends a "show cause" notice to the member as to why an action should not be taken against him. The member concerned may give a written explanation or plead orally in his defence. Such a member may be represented by a legal adviser or another chartered accountant. On receipt of the explanation or the evidence, the Council may

(*a*) reprimand the member; or

(*b*) remove his name from the Register for a period not exceeding five years.

If the Council decides to remove the name of the member from the Register for a period exceeding five years or permanently remove his name, it should forward the case together with its findings and recommendations to the High Court.

The decision of the Council in such a case is final except in the following circumstances:—

(*a*) when the aggrieved member prefers an appeal to the High Court; or

(*b*) when the High Court on its own initiative or otherwise revises the decision of the Council; or

(c) where the Council decides to remove the name of the member for a period exceeding five years.

If on receipt of the report from the Disciplinary Committee, the Council is of opinion that the misconduct on the part of the member is that which is stated in the Second Schedule, it must refer the case together with its recommendations to the High Court for its decision. If on the other hand the Council finds that the member is not guilty the case is dropped and the complainant is informed accordingly.

The High Court, on receipt of reference from the Council, will cause a notice of the hearing to be given to the member concerned, the Council and the Central Government to give them the opportunity for pleading. After hearing the afore-stated parties the High Court may

(*a*) dismiss the case; or

(*b*) reprimand the member; or

(*c*) remove his name from the Register permanently or for such period as it thinks fit; or

(*d*) refer the case to the Council for further enquiries and report.

A member has a right to appeal to the Supreme Court against the order of the High Court.

After having dealt with the procedure to be followed for enquiry in the misconduct of a member, we proceed now to state the power of the Council.

The Council has also the power to enquire into the conduct of a person who had been a member of the Institute but who has ceased to be a member on the date of the enquiry, Section 21 (7). The powers of a Civil Court are vested in the Council as well as in the Disciplinary Committee under the Code of Civil Procedure, e.g.,

(*a*) to summon and enforce attendance of any person and to examine him on oath;

(*b*) to ask any person to produce any document;

(*c*) to receive evidence on affidavit; etc.

A few important cases on professional misconduct decided by the various High Courts in India are given below:—

(*i*) J.K. Joglekar in re (1957)

The facts of the case are that Mr. J.K. Joglekar of the firm of Messrs: J.K. Joglekar & Co., Chartered Accountants of Poona, sent a letter dated 22nd September, 1954, to the Chairman, Laxmi Mills Employees Cooperative Credit Society Ltd., Sholapur, for appointment as auditor of that society for the year 1954-55. In the application Joglekar had stated that his name was included in the panel of auditors kept by the Registrar of Co-operative Societies for the purpose of auditing the accounts of Co-operative Societies. He also stated in the letter that he was a Fellow of the Institute with considerable experience of auditing the accounts of Go-operative Societies. He added: "should your Management and General Body choose to select me for the auditorship of the Society for the year ending 1954-55, I shall be glad to accept it on such remuneration which will be within the scale laid down by the Department and the budget provision of yours in that behalf."

The Vice-Chairman of the Society forwarded this letter to the Institute of the Chartered Accountants in compliance with a request made by the latter to the society.

The Institute issued a notice to Joglekar to show cause. He sent a statement dated 28th November 1955 admitting that the application dated 22nd September 1954 to the Chairman of the Society was signed and sent by him but he denied the charge that he attracted the provisions of clause (e) of the Schedule to the Chartered Accountants Act, viz.,

"If he solicits clients or professional work either directly or indirectly by circular, advertisement, personal communication or interviews or by any other means."

He further stated that he had written the letter to the Chairman of the Society in pursuance of an enquiry from a member of the Society and therefore it did not amount to 'soliciting any work'.

Later on, a letter dated 23rd May 1956 was sent by Joglekar to the Disciplinary Committee that he had realised that by writing the letter dated 22nd September 1954, to the Chairman of the Society, he had contravened the provisions of the Chartered Accountants Act but that was done under wrong advice tendered to him by his legal adviser. He also stated that it was a general practice by co-operative societies to ask the auditors to make applications for appointment as auditors and therefore he had made that application which he should not have written. He gave an undertaking that he would not commit any breach of the provision of the Act in future and that the breach he had committed be condoned.

The Disciplinary Committee found him guilty and referred the case to the Bombay High Court. An extract of the judgment of Shah, J., is given below:—

"The respondent (Joglekar) is an accountant of 12 years' standing. He has appeared before us and he has stated that he did not realise that he was, when he wrote the letter dated 22nd September 1954, doing anything which was improper. In our view, the infringement is a serious breach of the code of professional ethics, and we cannot permit this sort of conduct to go unpunished with merely a warning. We are of the view, taking into consideration all the circumstances, that the respondent be suspended from practising for a period of three months from this date. The respondent do also pay the costs of the Institute which we quantify at Rs. 250".

Conclusion

If an auditor solicits clients for professional work by communication, he is guilty of professional misconduct.

(ii) Sunderlal Fatehpuria, in re (1958)

The facts of the case are that one Kantilal G. Shah, proprietor of the firm of Messrs. 'New Dye Stuff Corporation, Bombay, approached Sunderlal Fatehpuria, a Chartered Accountant, with a request for a certificate for betelnuts turnover, as was required to obtain an import licence. Two certificates showing the turnover amounting to Rs. 43,299 and 53,345 for the years 1951–52 and 1952-53 respectively were signed and issued by the respondent, Sunderlal Fatehpuria.

Shah was, however, not successful in getting the licence and therefore refused to pay the fee to the respondent. The respondent after reminders for payment issued the following threatening letter:

"If I do not get the same (i.e., the fee) at an early date by Monday, I will see that you will also not get the licence and on the contrary you will be put into trouble by the import office."

The respondent was prosecuted under Section 193 I.P.C. for having issued a certificate knowing it to be false but due to some technical legal point he was acquitted while Shah was convicted for misrepresentation and fraud.

The Superintendent of Police reported the matter to the Institute of Chartered Accountants which treated it as information.

During the course of hearing by the Disciplinary Committee, the respondent pleaded that he had entrusted the work of checking the books of account of Shah to his articled clerk and relying on his report he signed and issued the certificate.

It may be noted that it was found during the course of evidence that the articled clerk had a few months' experience and that he never maintained any audit notes. It was also found that the articled clerk never checked the purchases, sales or stock books which in fact had never been maintained by Shah.

The Council of the Institute was of opinion that the threatening letter which the respondent sent to Shah showed that the respondent knew that the certificate issued by him was false.

The respondent defended himself by stating that since he was acquitted under Section 193, I.P.C... by the Additional Presidency Magistrate, he was not guilty but the Council did not accept this plea on the ground that the respondent was acquitted under a technical legal flaw. Another plea put forth by the respondent was that he acted *bona fide* in relying upon his articled clerk. The Council of the Institute gave the following verdict:

"The respondent was grossly negligent in the conduct of the professional duties and, therefore, he was guilty of the charge of gross negligence under item (q) of the Schedule to the Chartered Accountants Act which would render him unfit to be a member of the Institute under Section 21 of the Chartered Accountants Act, 1949."

During the course of proceeding in Bombay High Court, the respondent expressed regret stating that he was not guilty of such negligence or gross negligence which would deserve an order against him and which would render him unfit to be a member of the Institute and practise as a Chartered Accountant, Justice Desai gave the following judgment:—

"Mr. Kantawala, learned counsel for the Council of the Institute of Chartered Accountants, has taken up a very fair and reasonable attitude before us and he says that his clients do not press for any serious action against the respondent. We also feel that this is not a case in which any strong action should be taken against the respondent. We think the ends of justice will be met by accepting the regrets expressed by the respondent and giving him a warning not to repeat any such act in future.

"The respondent to pay the costs of the Council."

An auditor is guilty of professional misconduct if he is grossly negligent in the conduct of his professional duties.

(*iii*) Mrs. Indramani Singhania vs. Messrs P.L. Tandon and A.L. Talwar (1954)

The facts of the case are that Mrs. Singhania leased the Baijnath Bankeybeharilal Woollen Mills to Messrs. J.K. Woollen Manufacturers. According to lease agreement Mrs. Singhania was to be paid the lease rent @ 7 annas 9 pies per rupee of the net profits which the lessees would earn. J.K. Woollen Manufacturers were a partnership firm in 1947 but thereafter it was converted into a Private Limited Company.

Mrs. Singhania made complaint against the Chartered Accountant that he was negligent in the performance of his duties in computing the net profits incorrectly as some of the items debited to profit and loss account ought not to have been there. The following complaints were made:—

1. That a person with no technical qualification but who was related to one of the directors was appointed the manager of the firm on a high salary. The contention of the complainant was that had he not been appointed, the firm would have shown more profits and thus the lease rent payable on the basis of the net profits would have been more. Her complaint against the auditor was that he was negligent in not pointing out this fact.

The Hjgh Court held that since in 1947, the firm was not a joint stock company and therefore, if all the partners agreed to the appointment of the technician, it was not the duty of the auditor to point out this fact. Moreover, it was held that the auditor owed no statutory duty to third parties as , in the case of a joint stock company. The High Court based this view on the decision by the Madras High Court in the case of *Commissioner of Income Tax vs. G.M. Dandckar*, 1952.

2. Another charge by the complainant was that the directors were paid excessive fees and remuneration, allowances and entertainment expenses, etc.

The High Court held that these fees and allowances, etc., were allowed according to a resolution by the Board of Directors of the company in pursuance of Article 86 of the Company's Articles of Association.

3. Payment of gratuity to the widow of the manager was objected to by the complainant,

The High Court held that it was no part of the duty of the auditor to question the reasonableness of the payment.

4. The complainant objected to the contribution made by the company to the Mahatma Gandhi Memorial Fund. The company had contributed the amount according to the direction issued by the Federation of the Woollen Manufacturers of India of which the company was a member.

The complaint was dismissed by the High Court.

Conclusion

It is not the duty of the auditor to question the employment of a manager or reasonableness of the payment of gratuity to the widow of an employee so long as the partners of the firm agreed to such payments.

(*iv*) M. N. Bhargava, In re (1958)

The facts of the case are that two persons, viz., Tehsildar Sinha and S.P. Sinha, ex-articled clerks of M.N. Bhargava, a chartered accountant of Lucknow, the respondent, reported to the Council of the Institute that the respondent issued certificates of service under Articles stating that he had refunded the entire premium to them under regulation 34 of the Chartered Accountants Regulations, 1949, but in fact, they alleged, full premium was not refunded to them and therefore the certificates were false. It was reported that a part of the premium alleged to have been refunded represented food and halting allowances paid to them while on duty to places other than the headquarters.

The respondent was asked by the Institute to send a written statement regarding the complaint. After the receipt of the statement from the respondent the Council of the Institute referred the matter to the Disciplinary Committee which heard both the complaints as well as the respondent at two sittings.

The charges against the respondent were that he had infringed clause (u) of the Schedule to Chartered Accountants Act and clause (v) of the said Schedule for having included particulars knowing them to be false in the certificates of service and also for having violated the provisions of regulation 34 in not having refunded the entire premium to the articled clerks.

The defence put forth by the respondent was that since the clerks were taking food with his clients they could not charge the same from him.

During the course of hearing it was found that the respondent had billed the clients for the food charges for the articled clerks. It was also found that the respondent threatened the articled clerks that unless they signed a receipt certifying that they had received back the entire premium he would not issue the certificate regarding their moral character. A few extracts from the findings of the Disciplinary Committee are given below:

"He (respondent) was clearly exploiting their (articled clerks') helpless position as they were at his mercy for their certificates of completion of service in order to enable them to appear for the Final Examination.

"We would mention, however, that at a late stage in the enquiry before us, the respondent realised the wrong attitude he had taken towards the articled clerks and sent the Institute cheques drawn in favour of the articled clerks for the balance amounts of the premiums refundable to them.

"In conclusion we find that the respondent is guilty of misconduct in that (1) he issued false certificates to the two articled clerks stating that he refunded the entire premiums money due to them whereas part of the amount represented a set off of the food and halting allowances re-imbursed to them while they were on outstation work; (2) he violated Regulation 34 of the Chartered Accountants Regulations 1949 by not refunding the premiums charged by him from the articled clerks within such time as specified in the said Regulation; and (3) in the case of one clerk (T-Sinha) he did not refund any instalments as specified by him in the certificate. .. . However, the payment, made by him to the articled clerks subsequently for the balance of the premia claimed by them, may be taken into account in extenuation of the misconduct committed by him when judging whether his conduct was such as to render him unfit to be a member of the Institute."

The Council agreed with the findings of the Disciplinary Committee and found the respondent guilty of misconduct.

The matter was referred to the Allahabad High Court which found the respondent guilty of misconduct. A few extracts from the judgment are given below:—

"The integrity of the members of the profession of chartered accountants is a matter of very great importance to the commercial community. The progress of industrialisation depends in no small measure on accurate accounting, and an unquestioned honesty appears to us an essential qualification of a chartered accountant.... In the present case the respondent has himself been guilty of dishonest behaviour, both as regards his clients and his articled clerks. We do not consider that he is fit to be a member of the Institute.... After giving the matter our most careful consideration, we are of opinion that the respondent's name should be removed from the register for five years; and we direct accordingly.

"The respondent will pay the costs in this Court." The respondent appealed to the Supreme Court against the judgment of the Allahabad High Court but the appeal was rejected.

Conclusion

A member of the Institute is guilty of professional misconduct, if he includes in any statement, return or form to be submitted to the Council any particulars knowing them to be false or contravenes any of the provisions of the Chartered Accountants Act, 1949, or the Regulations made thereunder.

Paul David Keassley whilst a clerk under articles was convicted on 14th July 1967 in stealing 3/4 gallon petrol valued 4s. 3d. and was fined £ 20. He was found guilty of an offence so as to render him unfit to become a member of the Institute.

David Raymond Carston, F.C.A., England had been found guilty of acts or defaults discreditable as he had signed the Accountant's Certificate relating to the practice of a solicitor for the accounting records of about three years which he knew or ought to have known were not correct so as to render himself liable to be excluded or suspended from membership of the Institute.

The Committee ordered that Carston be reprimanded.

S. Ganesan vs. A.K. Joscelyne (1956)

The facts of the case are that the respondent was the auditor of Deccan Sugar and Abkari Co. Ltd. The company had entered into an agreement with the managing agents that they would receive "by way of remuneration for their services, (a) an allowance of five thousand rupees per month ... and (b) a commission of ten per cent on the annual profits of the company...."

In another paragraph of the agreement it was also provided that the managing agents "shall also receive commission on sales of the company's products elsewhere than Madras City, at or through the branches or agencies."

The profit and loss account signed by the auditor disclosed only the allowance paid to the managing agents @ five thousand rupees per month and also a commission of ten per cent on the net annual profits of the company.

However, a sum of Rs. 35,400 paid, to them as commission on sales was not shown as expenditure in the profit and loss account either under the particular heading or as sales expenses. The amount of Rs. 35,400 paid to the managing agents as commission on the sale of the products, was deducted out of the gross receipts in respect of the sales at branches and therefore the net amount so arrived at was shown as gross profit.

The charges against the auditors, on the complaint to the Institute of Chartered Accountants made by a shareholder, were —

(*a*) that the profit and loss account did not show the commission on sales amounting to Rs. 35,400 paid to the managing agents and thus the shareholders were misled;

(*b*) that a mis-statement was made in the trading account in as much as the commission on sales was deducted from the sales and thus the correct gross income was not shown as the commission on sales paid to the managing agents was deducted from sales; and

(*c*) the auditor failed to show the total amount paid to the managing agents as a distinct item in the profit and loss account with a view to accommodate the managing agents and directors to conceal the payment of commissions on sales and thus the shareholders were kept in dark as regards the commission paid to the managing agents and, therefore, went to the extent of giving a misleading report that the accounts were in conformity with law.

The opinion of the majority of the Disciplinary Committee was in favour of the respondent, whereas the opinion of the Council was against him. The High Court did not find the respondent guilty of gross negligence. A few extracts from the judgment of the learned judge are given below:—

"... I am unable to hold that the respondent acted in this case with reasonable care. The difficulty, however, is that he has been charged only under items (*o*) and (*p*) of the Schedule, but has not been charged under item (*q*) which is concerned with 'gross negligence' in the conduct of professional duties ... there might have been a ground for proceeding against the respondent if it could be established against him that he had been a willing party to or at least had connived at the concealment of the payment of the selling commission by the Directors.

"Our difficulty in dealing with this reference is increased by the fact that the opinion of the majority of the Disciplinary Committee was in favour of the respondent, whereas the opinion of the Council is against him . . . but where the conclusion of the Council is the opposite of the conclusion of the Disciplinary Committee, this Court is placed at a disadvantage, unless it is informed of the reasons which weighed with the Council in coming to a contrary conclusion.

"For the reasons given above, we must hold that in spite of the evidence of negligence and imprudence in acting on his own responsibility in matters beyond his province and certifying the Profit and Loss Account without obtaining any explanation from the Directors which was obviously called for in view of the terms of the Agreement and of the difficulty of reconciling the entries in the Account with even his own view of the meaning of 'gross income', the particular charges laid against the Respondent had not been established against him. No orders on the Reference are, therefore, necessary and there will be no order for costs."

It may be stated here that the charge of "accommodating the managing agents" was withdrawn during the pendency of the case. Again, the Council of the Institute did not advance any reason as to why it differed from the findings of the Disciplinary Committee. These facts weighed with the High Court in giving the above judgment.

Deputy Secretary to the Government of India, Ministry of Finance vs. S.N. Dasgupta (1955)

The facts of the case are that the respondent was the auditor of the Aryan Bank Ltd. during the years 1942, 1943 and 1944. The bank went into liquidation later on. The charges against the respondent (auditor) were—

(*a*) that he failed to verify cash in hand for the years 1942 and 1943. Thus he was negligent in the performance of his duty under the law and the approved audit procedures;

(*b*) the loans and overdrafts of branches as stated by the auditor were "good", but in fact they were not.

As regards the first charge under (a) above, the defence of the respondent was that he had stated in his report that he had not personally verified the cash and, therefore, he was not guilty because he did not certify the cash in hand at the branches.

As regards the second charge under (b) above, the respondent defended himself by stating that he had in his special report regarding the loans and advances inserted "all the loans and overdrafts of branches are shown in the balance-sheet as good". He stated that he inserted this statement as he had some doubt as to some of the loans.

As regards the loans which were shown in the balance-sheet as "fully secured", the special report contained the following sentence:—

"These have been granted to aid parties against the fixed deposit receipts of debtors."

The Disciplinary Committee found that if the respondent felt some doubt as to some of the loans, overdrafts and fixed deposits, as he had felt that if he found it necessary to qualify his report by certain reservations made in the special reports, he should have expressed himself unequivocally on the suspected items instead of making cryptic statements which might mean anything or nothing. The Committee stated that his duty was to give information and not merely means of information.

As regards the first charge, the Committee found that the alleged verification of cash in hand at the end of the year 1944 was falsified by the fact that the confirmation letters from other banks had been received after the respondent had already signed the report.

Held: If an auditor does not do what it is his duty to do, it is no defence for him to say in disciplinary proceeding that he had told the shareholders that he had not done it. His failure to perform his duty is not excused by giving information of the means to the shareholders.

The High Court found the respondent guilty of misconduct. The learned judge held that "Authorities, both legal and professional, are unanimous that in a bank audit, the cash balance claimed by the management must be verified by the auditor". The Court made an order that the respondent should be suspended from the membership of the Institute of Chartered Accountants and from practice for two years from the date of the order.

R.B. Basu vs. P.K. Mukerji (1956)

The facts of the case are that the respondent was employed by the complainant to represent him in an income tax case before the Income Tax Appelate Tribunal. The remuneration to be paid to the respondent on certain percentage of the relief the complainant would get as a result of the appeal. The complainant's case against the respondent was—

(*a*) that the respondent failed to appear at the hearing of the appeal before the appelate Tribunal;

(*b*) that in addition to having received a large sum of money by false representations, the respondent threatened to get more money from the complainant; and

(*c*) that the respondent had charged his fee at a certain percentage of the accepted relief (this charge was added by the Disciplinary Committee of the Institute when the matter was referred to it though the complainant had not included this charge in his complaint).

Decision

(*a*) As regards the first charge, the Court did not accept it on the ground that the respondent who was very busy on the day of hearing as he was to appear in another court and therefore he had entrusted this work to another advocate which is usually the practice prevalent amongst the busy advocates and thus the respondent was not found guilty on this charge.

(*b*) As regards the second charge, the Court did not find him guilty as no evidence could be produced that the respondent exhorted money by threats from the complainant.

(*c*) It was on the third charge, viz., that he charged fee at a certain percentage of the accepted relief, the Court found him guilty of misconduct under Clause 10, Part I of the First Schedule of the Chartered Accountants Act, 1949, and he was suspended from practice for a period of three months.

B.M. Mohan vs. K.C,J. Satyawadi (1955)

In this case the chartered accountant applied in response to an advertisement in a newspaper for appointment as auditor and so was appointed but he failed to ask the previous auditor to ascertain from the company whether the provisions of Ss. 224 and 225 of the Companies Act, regarding the appointment had been complied with. It was held the respondent was guilty under Clauses 8 and 9 of Second Schedule, Part I.

Company Law Administration vs. D.B. Kulkarni

In this case the chartered accountant did not verify the reconciliation of the bank balance with the Pass Book and called for certificates of balances from the bank in respect of the balances at the bank. The Council of the Institute found him guilty of misconduct under Clauses 7 and 8 of Part I of the Second Schedule. It was held that there was no proof of dishonesty or *mala fide* on the part of the chartered accountant and in view of the circumstances of the case, the High Court did not take a serious view except to express disapprobation of the conduct of the chartered accountant in the form of admonition.

Directors of Accounts, Gujarat State, vs. K.D. Patel (1968)

In this case the chartered accountant gave clean reports on the balance-sheets but later on when the special audit was conducted, it was revealed that there were certain irregularities which amounted to failure to examine the Pass Book and to verify the cash balances. The chartered accountant was found guilty under Clause 7 of Second Schedule, Part I.

Qaroon Trading & Finance (Pt.) Ltd. vs. Lakshmi Narain Saxena and others

The chartered accountant did not complete the audit work of the company and consequently did not submit his audit report in due time to enable the company to comply with the statutory requirements in this connection. He was held guilty of professional misconduct under Clause 7 of Second Schedule, Part I.

Again, in the same case, Mr. Saxena was held guilty of professional misconduct in that he exercised undue influence and coercion in securing from the clients fourteen hundred rupees and a letter of appointment.

J.R. Chatrath, In re (1952)

J.R. Chatrath applied on lst January, 1948 that his name may be included in the list of Registered Accountants entitled to train article clerks. In his application, he stated "From April, 1944 onwards I was employed as manager of the firm of B.M. Chatrath, Registered Accountants (B.M. Chatrath & Co.) on a fixed salary plus percentage of the firm's earnings. From 21st October, 1948 onwards I am full-fledged partner of the firm of Registered Accountants holding two-fifths share."

Later on he modified his statement in the previous letter and stated "in short I was paid assistant of the status of a partner of the firm next to Mr. B.M. Chatrath."

On 15th September, 1949, J.R. Chatrath applied to be enrolled as a Fellow of the Institute and in his application he stated "Practised as a partner all through." In reply from a letter to the Institute, he stated that he was a partner of BIM. Chatrath & Co. with effect from lst April, 1944 and that he was getting a salary plus a share of the profits and also a share of the goodwill.

It was found that there was no written partnership agreement and that it was only a verbal one. He also could not prove that he had a share in the goodwill of the firm. The Committee of the Institute argued that by signing the balance-sheet of B.M. Chatrath & Co. did not mean that he was a partner of the firm and that it might have been understanding and arrangement that he would sign the balance-sheet.

The High Court held that Chatrath understood the difference between a partner getting a share of the profits and the manager. However, Chatrath persisted that he was a partner. It was also found that his name was not included in any agreement which had been entered into between B.M. Chatrath and other partners of the firm.

J.R. Chatrath was found guilty of misconduct in making a false statement to the Institute knowing it to be false, that he was a partner of the firm of B.M. Chatrath & Co. and was therefore suspended for one month from practice under First Schedule, Part I, Clause 1.

QUESTIONS

1. Discuss the important rules of professional conduct for Chartered Accountants, the breach of which requires eventual reference to the High Court. *(CA. Final)*

2. Discuss the rule of conduct which prohibits a Chartered Accountant to be engaged in any business or occupation other than the profession of chartered accountant unless permitted by the Council, stating the categories and occupations which are permitted by the general resolutions of the Council. *(C.A. Final Nov.* 1962)

3. Enumerate the various instances of professional misconduct of a Chartered Accountant in practice which however do not require action by a High Court. *(CA. Final Nov.)*

4. What is misconduct according to the Chartered Accountants Act, 1949? Name at least eight instances of misconduct defined in the said Act. (*C.A.*; Cal. *M. Com*)

5. Examine the provisions of the Chartered Accountants Act and Schedules thereto with regard to the conduct of members. Can a Chartered Accountant be charged with professional misconduct in respect of any matter not mentioned in the Act or Schedules? *(Gauhati B.Com.)*

6. Mr. K who had passed the Final examination of the Institute of Chartered Accountants of India, applied to the Institute to be enrolled as a member. Before his name was registered, he issued certificates to certain firms of importers, certifying the amount of their imports. Do you think that Mr. K acted properly? Give reasons.

7. X, Y and L, were three Chartered Accountants who were partners under the name and style of XYZ & Co., Chartered :Accountants. X died of heart failure. Y and Z decided to carry on the business and agreed to pay 10 per cent of the future profits, for a period of five years, to the widow of X in lieu of the share of goodwill of X. Will such a decision be in order?

8. How far do you think the charges of breach of rules of professional conduct brought against an auditor on the following grounds are appropriate:—

(*a*) that he has accepted an appointment immediately after intimating his appointment over the phone to the previous auditor, who, in due course, made an objection;

(*b*) that he has accepted an appointment at a fee lower than the feedemanded by the previous auditor, whose demand was on the ground that the volume of work had substantially increased;

(*c*) that he has charged an excessive fee for auditing the accounts of a particular year;

(*d*) that he has charged a fee for representing in income tax appeals proportionate to the relief that may be obtained as a result of the appeal. (C.A. *Final)*

9. Discuss the reasons as to why conduct of a Chartered Accountant in practice is considered unethical if he—

(*a*) solicits professional work;

(*b*) engages in undercutting;

(*c*) accepts appointment as an auditor without communicating with the retiring auditor;

(*d*) charges fees which are contingent upon the results. *(C.A. Final)*

10. Outline the procedure that is to be followed, under Section 21 of the Chartered Accountants Act, 1949, on receipt by the Council of the Institute of a complaint against a member. (C.A. *Final*)

11. Enumerate the possibilities mentioned in Section 8 of the Chartered Accountants Act, 1949, which disentitle a person from having his name entered in the Register of Members mentioned in the Act. (C.A. *Final*)

12. In view of the provisions of the Chartered Accountants Act, 1949, state and justify your views on the following cases:—

(*a*) whether you would accept offer of appointment as auditor of a firm in which your brothers are partners;

(*b*) whether the chartered accountant employee in your firm can sign the balance-sheets of a concern in the name of your firm;

(*c*) whether you can put up a sign board showing your designation as a Chartered Accountant, Income Tax Practitioner and Company Law Consultant. (CA. *Final*)

APPENDIX

Questions and Model Answers

Q.1. What is an audit? What are its advantages?

Ans. Definition of Audit

The word "audit" is derived from the Latin word "*audire*", which means to hear. In middle ages, whenever the owners of a business suspected fraud, they appointed certain persons to check the accounts. Such a person sent for the accountants and "heard" whatever they had to say in connection with the accounts. It was an Italian, Luca Pacialo, who first published his treatise on double entry system of book-keeping for the first time in 1494. He mentioned and described the duties and responsibilities of an auditor. Since then there have been lot of changes in the scope and definition of audit and responsibilities of an auditor.

As has been mentioned above, the original object of an audit was principally to see whether the accounting party had properly accounted for the receipts and payments of cash. In other words the object of audit was to find out whether cash had been embezzled and if so, who embezzled it and what amount was involved. Thus, it was only an audit of Cash Book but with the development and expansion of business activities, the principal object of modern audit is to see whether the balance-sheet exhibits a true and fair view of the state of affairs of a company and whether it is drawn up according to the Companies Act, in the case of the audit of a company. Detection of fraud is an incidental object of modern audit.

Spicer and Pegler have defined an audit as "such an examination of the books, accounts and vouchers of a business as will enable the auditor to satisfy himself that the balance-sheet is properly drawn up, so as to give a true and fair view of the state of the affairs of the business, and whether the Profit and Loss Account gives a true and fair view of the profit or loss for the financial period, according to the best of his information and explanations given to him and as shown by the books; and if not, in what respect he is not satisfied."

L.R. Dicksee defines : "An audit is an examination of accounting records undertaken with a view to establishing whether they correctly and completely reflect the transactions to which they purport to relate."

From the above definitions, it would be seen that an auditor has not only to see the arithmetical accuracy of the books of account but has to go further and find out whether the transactions entered in the books of original entry are correct or not.

Advantages of an Audit

1. Errors and frauds are located at an early date and no attempt is made in future to commit such frauds or one is rather careful not to commit any error or fraud as the accounts are subject to audit at regular intervals and hence they would be detected.

2. The auditing of accounts keeps the accounts clerks regular and vigilant as they know that the auditor would complain against them if the accounts are not prepared up to date or if there is any irregularity.

3. The audit of accounts of a firm by an independent person minimises the chances of dispute amongst the partners.

4. If a new partner is to be taken in or one of the partners retires or dies, the audited balance-sheet will be a good basis to estimate the value of the goodwill thus avoiding the chances of dispute.

5. In the case of the Joint Stock Companies the shareholders, who have no hand in the actual management of the business, are assured that the accounts have been properly maintained and that the directors have not taken any undue advantage of their position.

6. In the case of a fire, the insurance company may settle the claims on the basis of the audited accounts of the previous year.

7. Money can be borrowed easily on the basis of the audited balance-sheet.

8. If the business is to be sold, price can be fixed on the basis of the audited balance-sheet.

9. Income Tax, Sales Tax, Wealth Tax authorities generally accept the profit and loss account as more reliable which has been audited by a qualified auditor and they do not go into the details of the accounts.

10. The auditor may sometime give valuable advice though it is not his duty.

Q.2. Briefly explain the difference between Book-keeping, Accountancy and Auditing.

Ans. Book-keeping

Book-keeping is the art of recording the transactions on the books of original entry and the ledgers. This work is usually performed by junior clerks who are sometimes called book-keepers or accounts clerks. This work is more or less of mechanical nature and does not require any specialised knowledge of the principles of accountancy. The work of such clerks is supervised by a man who is called an Accountant.

Accountancy

Accountancy involves the preparation of the final accounts to show the result of the business at the end of the financial period. The man who is entrusted with this work is called an accountant. His work is not only to supervise the work of the book-keepers but also to analyse, review and draw conclusions from the final accounts. His work is of a specialised nature and he must be well-versed with the principles of accountancy.

Auditing

Auditing is quite a different thing from book-keeping and accountancy. It has nothing to do with the writing of the books of account or the preparation of the final accounts. Auditing is a careful and critical examination of the books of account to find out their accuracy whether the profit and loss account and the balance-sheet have been properly drawn up and whether they exhibit a true and fair view of the state of affairs of the business.

Distinction between accountancy and auditing is of great importance. An auditor must clearly know as to whether he is working in the capacity of an accountant or an auditor. In the case of *Apfel* vs. *Annan, Dextor & Co.* (1926), it was sought to prove that the auditors has acted in the capacity of auditors and, therefore, they were liable for negligence in not detecting a fraud. The auditors' contention was that they were employed to prepare the books of account for income tax purposes and not to do the work of an audit. The certificate given by the auditors was "... prepared from the books of Mrs. Adele Apfel and in accordance therewith". But they (auditors) had sent the bill for costs which was worded as "for services in connection with the preparation and audit of your accounts."

From the certificate given by the auditors, it is clear that work done by them was of a purely accountancy nature while the bill sent by them indicated that the work done by them was both of accountancy and auditing. Astbury, J., gave the judgement in favour of the auditors taking into consideration the object and the purpose for which the auditors were employed.

In the case of *Commissioner of Income Tax, Madras* vs. *G.M. Dandekar,* 1952, it was held by the Madras High Court that the auditor was employed to prepare income tax returns and did not act in the capacity of the auditor of his employer.

Distinction between Accountancy and Auditing

We may briefly lay down the points of distinction between accountancy and auditing :

1. The book-keeper record the entries in the original books of account, the accountant analysis the accounts, prepares the trial balance, profit and loss account and balance-sheet while the auditor checks the books of account.

2. Accountancy means keeping the books of account in such a way that one is in a position to know the state of affairs of the business, while auditing means the checking of such accounts to find out their accuracy.

3. The spadework is done by the accountant while the finishing touch is given by the auditor or, as has been said, the work of an auditor begins where the work of an accountant ends.

4. An accountant has to record the transactions in the books of account while an auditor has to check and verify such transactions and accounts prepared by an accountant.

5. The book-keepers or the accountants have not to find out whether there have been any errors or frauds while the auditor has to detect such errors and frauds, and to see whether the balance-sheet and profit and loss account represent a true and fair view of the company.

Q.3. Briefly state the main objects of auditing.

Ans. 1. To verify statements. The auditor has to verify the accounts and the financial statements prepared by the client and his staff.

2. To discover errors and frauds. The auditor has to discover errors and frauds which might have been committed intentionally or unintentionally. As a matter of fact this was the originally object of auditing but now it is considered to be the incidental object.

3. To prevent errors and frauds. When the members of the staff of the accounts department know that the accounts prepared by them are subject to audit and hence they are rather very careful to see that no error or fraud is committed as it would be detected by the auditor and they might be taken to task.

Q.4. What are the main classes into which errors in the books of accounts are divided? Briefly explain and illustrate such errors.

Ans. The following are the various types of errors :-

I. Clerical errors which may be sub-divided into

(*a*) Errors of Omission; and (*b*) Errors of Commission.

II. Errors of Principles.

III. Compensating Errors.

IV. Errors of Duplication.

It may be noted here that all errors except errors of principles are known as technical or clerical errors.

Let us explain these errors, separately.

I. (*a*) Errors of Omission

An error of omission is one where a transaction has not been recorded in the books of account either wholly or partially. In the former case, it will not be detected by the trial balance, though it may be apparent in some cases, e.g., the rent for the last month of the year might not have been recorded in the books of account as it had not been paid to the landlord. In case the transaction has been partially recorded, e.g., if one aspect of the purchases or sales had been entered in the books, it will affect the trial balance and ultimately the profit and loss account.

(*b*) Errors of Commission

When a transaction has been recornded but has been wrongly entered in the books of original entry or in the ledger, error of commission is said to have been made, e.g., incorrect entries in the original records, wrong castings, calculations, extensions, carry forwards etc. Some of such entries will be detected by the non-agreement of the trial balance. On the other hand, if a mistake has been committed in the invoice for the sale of goods, the error will not be detected as the mistake will appear both in the original books as well as in the ledger.

II. Errors of Principles

Such errors arise when the entries are not recorded according to the fundamental principles of accountancy, e.g., wrong allocation of expenditure between capital and revenue, ignoring the outstanding assets and liabilities, valuation of assets against the principles of book-keeping.

Such errors may be committed either intentionally or unintentionally. If they are committed intentionally, the object is to falsify and manipulate the accounts either to show more profits or less profits than they actually are. Such errors actually effect thye balance-sheet. Therefore, it is very important for an auditor to pay particular attention towards this type of error. Such an error is not disclosed by the trial balance or by routine checking. It can be detected only by searching enquiry and independent checking.

III. Compensating Errors

A compensating error is one which is counter-balanced by any other error or errors, e.g., if A's account was to be debited for Rs. 100 but was debited for Rs. 10 by mistake B's account was to be debited for Rs. 10 was debited for Rs. 100 by mistake, such a mistake will not affect the trial balance. Such an error may or may not affect the profit and loss account.

Similarly an over-casting of an account may be counterbalanced by the under-casting of another account to the same extent. This type of error will not affect the trial balance and will be detected easily. Such errors may or may not affect the profit and loss account.

IV. Errors of Duplication

Such errors arise when entry in a book or original entry has been made twice and has also been posted twice.

Q.5. Explain and illustrate "manipulation or falsification of accounts."

Ans. By manipulation or falsification of accounts we mean to say that the accounts are prepared in such a way as to show more profits or less profits or even to show a loss when in fact there is no loss. This type of fraud is difficult to discover. It is usually committed by directors or managers with certain objects.

Objects of Manipulation

(*a*) The objects of manipulation of accounts may be to show more profits than actually what they are—

(*i*) so that if the employees get commission on profits or bonus they may get more commission or bonus; or

(*ii*) their services may be retained by showing to the shareholders that because of their efficiency they have shown more profits and thus maintain the confidence of the shareholders; or (*iii*) if they hold shares, they may sell them at a high price by declaring higher dividends; or

(*iv*) to obtain further credit by showing that the position of the concern is better than what actually it is; or

(*v*) to attract more subscribers for the sale of the shares of the company, etc.

(*b*) The objects of manipulation of accounts may be to show less profits than actually it is—

(*i*) in order to purchase shares in the market at a lower price; or

(*ii*) to reduce or avoid the payment of income tax; or

(*iii*) to give a wrong impression about the success of the business to the competitors in order to ward off competition, etc.

Methods of Manipulation of Accounts

Manipulation or falsification of accounts may be resorted to :

(*a*) by not providing any depreciation or providing less depreciation or providing more depreciation; or

(*b*) by undervaluation or overvaluation or assets and liabilities; or

(*c*) by including fictitious sales or purchases or return in order to show more profit or less profit or even a loss, etc.; or

(*d*) by the utilization of secret reserves during a period when the concern has made less or no profit, without disclosing the fact to the shareholders; or

(*e*) by charging revenue expenditure to capital account or *vice versa;* or

(*f*) by crediting the revenue account with the income which will be received next year or not crediting the profit and loss account with the income which has accrued but which has not been received.

Such frauds are difficult to detect as they are committed by the people at the helm of affairs who are presumed to be trust-worthy, honest and responsible, and, therefore, no suspicion falls on them. Such frauds are very cleverly committed and, as such, the auditor should be very careful in detecting them. He should carry out the routine checking and vouching more carefully and make searching enquiries intelligently and tactfully.

Q.6. What is meant by Continuous Audit and to what class of business is it especially applicable? State briefly the advantages of and the objections to an audit of this nature.

Ans. Definition of Continuous Audit. A Continuous Audit or a Detailed Audit, as it is sometimes called, is an audit which involves a detailed examination of the books of account at regular intervals of say one month or three months. The auditor visits his clients at regular or irregular intervals during the financial year and checks each and every transaction. At the end of the year he checks the remaining transactions which have not been checked, the profit and loss account and the balance-sheet.

Applicability of Continuous Audit

This type of audit is specially applicable to the following businesses :

(*a*) when the business is very large and consequently the whole of the audit cannot be completed in a short time; or

(*b*) where it is desired that the monthly results be prepared to find out the trend of the business; or

(*c*) where a good and efficient system of internal check does not exist; or

(*d*) where the volume of transactions is very large.

Advantages of Continuous Audit

(*a*) Errors and frauds can be discovered easily and quickly as the auditor checks the accounts at regular intervals and in detail.

(*b*) A thorough and exhaustive checking is possible and hence the work done is more efficient.

(*c*) The audited accounts can be presented soon after the close of the financial period.

(*d*) The chances of fraud are minimised as the clerks know that the auditor will check the accounts in detail at short intervals.

(*e*) This type of audit keeps the clerks up-to-date and vigilant.

(*f*) Since the auditor remains more in touch with the business, he knows its technical details and hence can make valuable suggestions.

(*g*) Where the directors of a company wish to declare interim dividend, continuous audit will be helpful in the preparation of the interim accounts without much delay.

Objections to a Continuous Audit

(*a*) Figures in the books of account which have already been checked by the auditor at his previous visit, may be altered by a dishonest clerk and the frauds may thus be perpetrated.

(*b*) The frequent visits by the auditor may dislocate the work of his client and may cause inconvenience to the latter.

(*c*) It is an expensive system of audit.

(*d*) The audit clerk may lose the thread of his work and the queries which he wanted to make may remain outstanding as there may be long interval between the two visits.

The following precautions may be taken to guard against the objections to a Continuous Audit :

(*a*) No alteration should be allowed to be made after the transactions have been checked by the auditor, without his permission.

(*b*) If any alteration is to be made, it should be done by means of a rectifying entry.

(*c*) Checking of a book should be complete as far as possible at each visit to avoid lose ends. However, if this is not possible, the auditor should check the transactions up to a particular date and make a note of it in his diary, and if possible he should make a note of the totals up to that date in his diary or note-book and compare them at his next visit.

(*d*) Any queries which could not be satisfactorily answered must be noted in the diary so that the matter may be settled at the next visit.

(*e*) If any alteration in a figure had already been made, the auditor should put a secret tick against such a figure or in the alternative he may enter inset, in coloured pencil, the correct figure or he may re-write the correct figure in a different coloured ink and tick it as usual.

(*f*) Before he begins the work at the next visit, he should glance over any alteration which does not bear his secret tick.

Q.7. Differentiate between

(*a*) the fundamental principles of auditing, and

(*b*) the technique of auditing.

Explain why the latter must be subject to change though the former may remain constant.

Ans. By fundamental principles of auditing we mean the chief rules and principles according to which the books of account of a business concern are audited. They are the set principles of auditing and hence they cannot be changed at the sweet will of the auditor.

On the other hand, by the technique of auditing we mean to say the methods of procedure adopted by an auditor in checking the accounts. This technique of auditing is different with different auditors according to their experience. If his experience shows that the technique or the procedure adopted by him in the past was not satisfactory, he may adopt a different technique, but the principles of auditing will remain the same and he cannot make any change in them.

Q.8. What do you understand by the term "Internal Check"? Has an auditor any responsibility in regard thereto? Show by illustration under what circumstances and to what extent, if any, he is justified in relying upon it in the course of an audit.

Ans. Internal Check is a method of organising the accounts system of a business concern or factory where the duties of different clerks are arranged in such a way that the work of one person is automatically checked by another and thus the possibility of fraud or error or irregularity is minimised unless there is a collusion between the clerks, e.g., the receipt of cash is entered by the cashier on the debit side of the cash book; this is carried to the ledger by another clerk; the statement of account relating to this transaction is sent to the customer by a third clerk and so on. Thus, we see that the same transaction has passed through three different hands and the work of one is checked automatically by the other. This minimises the possibilities of fraud and errors unless all the three clerks join hands in defrauding their employer. Again if an error or fraud has been committed, it will be detected very soon by another clerk while the transaction is being automatically checked.

To what extent should an auditor depend upon the Internal Check system will depend upon the magnitude of the concern whose accounts he is auditing. In the case of a big concern where there is a good internal check system, the auditor may rely upon it and may, to a great extent, presume the accuracy of the accounts. But he must not be negligent. He should apply a few test checks, *i.e.,* he should check a few transactions here and there at random or check fully the accounts for a few months, say for January, April, July, etc., and carry out a thorough check of the whole of certain classes of transactions for 'test checks.' The auditor should see that such sample transactions are representatives and true specimens of such entries throughout the year.

If he finds that there is no mistake and there is nothing to arouse his suspicion, he may presume that the accounts are correct. It must be remembered that in such a case, the auditor is not relieved of his responsibility. Therefore, it would be better for him to probe the matter thoroughly if there is the slightest suspicion. If, later on, it is found that a fraud had been committed which the auditor failed to detect as he had not checked all the transactions, he will be held liable. The existence of a good internal check system reduces to a great extent the work of the auditor but does not reduce his liability. To what an extent should an auditor depend upon the internal check system will depend upon the circumstances of each particular case and the efficiency of his audit will depend upon his tact, skill, experience and judgement.

Q.9. What steps would you take before commencing the actual work of audit upon being appointed an auditor ?

Ans. An audit is generally performed with some definite object in view. This object should be clearly kept in mind constantly in the initial stages of the audit.

1. He should satisfy himself that his appointment is in order.
2. He should obtain definite instructions from his clients about the nature and scope of his work and duties; whether he is to do the accountancy work or audit work or both; by which date the work is to be completed; his honorarium, etc. This type of clarification is necessary in case he is appointed by an individual, a firm or a trust, etc. In the case of the audit of a joint stock company, the question does not arise as the scope of his work, his duties, powers, liabilities, etc. are embodied in the Companies Act.
3. He should see that his appointment is in order in the case of a Joint-Stock Company (*U.C. Majumdar* vs. *J.N. Saika,* 1954).

4. He should examine the system of accounting employed by his client.
5. He should get a list of all the books maintained in the office, the names of the keepers of such books and their specimen signatures.
6. If internal check system is in operation, he should get a written statement to that effect.
7. He should get a list of the officers of the company and should enquire about their duties and powers.
8. If the business is of a technical nature, he would do well to read a book dealing with the technical side of the business or visit the works, if possible.
9. He should ask his client to close the books of account, draft the profit and loss account and balance-sheet, prepare a list of the debtors and creditors, keep the legal papers, contracts, list of securities and other documents ready for his inspection.
10. He should inspect the Auditor's Report, audited profit and loss account and the balance-sheet of the previous year, and see that the books for the current year have been opened according to the balance-sheet of the previous years.
11. He should read carefully the Memorandum of Association, Articles of Association, partnership deed, will or trust deed, etc., as the case may be.
12. If it is the first audit of the company he should also go through the prospectus, contracts with vendors, promoters, etc.

Q. 10. What is an audit programme and how should it be considered? State the advantages and disadvantages of audit programmes.

Ans. Before the work of an audit is commenced, the auditor should chalk out a programme as to what work is to be done by his assistants and by himself and the time by which the work is to be finished. The assignment for each of the assistants is to be laid down in the Audit Note Book of the assistants. There are three methods by which the programme is carried out, viz.

1. There is a complete programme on the file from which the items to be completed by a particular assistant are ticked off and thus the assistant knows what he has to do and by which date each item is to be completed.
2. In other cases the auditor chalks out a programme for each assistant according to the nature of the business of the client. In this case there is no previous chalked-out programme.
3. In the third case, the auditor never prepares a programme in advance but may allow it to go as the work progresses.

While preparing the audit programme, the auditor should bear in mind two points, viz., the points which are common to all kinds of audits and the special points relating to a particular type of audit. The example of the first is the verification of assets while in the second case, payment of insurance policies, annuities, surrender value, etc., in the case of the audit of insurance companies.

Each assistant should sign for the work he has performed so that the responsibility may rest upon him for the work he has done. This is very important.

Advantages of Audit Programme

1. The auditor is in a position to know about the progress of the work done by his assistants.
2. The uniformity of the work can be attained as the same programme will be followed at subsequent audits.
3. Work of the audit can be divided amongst the different assistants who will be responsible for their work. In case a clerk goes on leave, his work can be resumed by another clerk who is in a position to know what has already been done.

4. In case of a charge of negligence against the auditor for not having done some work, the auditor can defend himself by producing the Audit Programme and the Audit Note Book.
5. It is a kind of guidance to the audit clerk for the work he has to perform. It is also an assurance to the auditor that the junior will not overlook essential points while checking the accounts.
6. In case any fraud or an error has remained undetected, the responsibility for negligence can be fixed on the clerk who had performed that work as his initials are affixed on the audit programme.

Disadvantages of Audit Programme

1. The assistant does not apply his common sense. He performs the work mechanically. This disadvantage may be overcome by insisting upon the assistants that the programme laid down by the auditor may be amended if so desired by the assistants and it need not be rigidly adhered to if the exigency of the work so requires.
2. Again, in case of small audits, an audit programme may be unnecessary.
3. Even if the audit programme is well chalked out, it may not cover everything that might come up during the course of audit.
4. Each business may have a separate problem of its own and hence a rigid programme cannot be laid down for each type of business.

Q.11. What is an Audit Note Book? What is your opinion as to the value of an Audit Note Book? State the usual contents of Audit Note Books.

Ans. During the course of an audit, an auditor has to make several queries which might not have been satisfactorily answered, he might have taken down the totals of different books of account, and certain other points which he would like to incorporate in his audit report. Lest he might forget these points, he notes them down in a book which is called an Audit Note Book. This book is sometimes called Memoranda Book. It may be a bound or loose leaf book.

Value of an Audit Note Book

This book is of great value to an auditor at the time of preparing the report to be submitted to the shareholders. In case a charge of negligence is levelled against the auditor, the Note Book may prove to be a good evidence. Such a book is kept for future reference and guidance when the accounts of the same company will be audited next year. A separate Audit Note Book is required for each client. The auditor knows what work has been done by his assistants or clerks at each audit. The importance of such a Note Book was emphasised by Lord (then Mr.) Justice Vaughan Williams in the *London and General Bank* case.

The Audit Note Book which contained detailed information proved to be very helpful to the auditor in the case of *City Equitable Fire Insurance Company*.

Contents of an Audit Note Book

1. A list of the books of account maintained by the client.
2. The names of the principal officers, their powers, duties and responsibilities, etc.
3. The technical terms used in the business.
4. The points which require further explanation and clarification.
5. The particulars of the vouchers and invoices which could not be produced at the time of audit.
6. Points which must be incorporated in the Audit Report.
7. Explanations received during the course of audit.
8. A record of the work done on each visit.

9. Schedules of investments, debtors, creditors and important legal points affecting the rights of the directors, shareholders, partners, etc.
10. Points which require discussion with the senior or the auditor.
11. The method of stocktaking, provision for bad and doubtful debts, allocation of expenditure between capital and revenue followed by the client.
12. Particulars of missing vouchers, the duplicates of which have to be obtained.
13. Date of commencement and completion of audit.
14. A few particulars of the Memorandum of Association, partnership deed, trust deed, etc., which affect the accounts.

It must be remembered that large number of notes must not be made in the Note Book. Efforts should be made to settle the queries, etc., on the spot. Only important points and unsatisfactory explanations need be put in the Audit Note Book. Such books should never be destroyed because they will prove to be of immense legal value if there is a dispute later on, or a suit is filed against the auditor for negligence, etc.

Q.12. Your client, who conducts an extensive Ready Money Business (not Mail Order) requests you to advise him how to protect himself against losses of cash sales. Outline your recommendations.

Ans. In case of sales against cash in a big business house, there is a great possibility of misappropriation of cash as the salesmen may sell the goods and pocket the money, without issuing a cash memo. Hence, it is necessary that a good internal check system should be in operation to avoid any fraud. The following system for the sale of goods against cash is recommended:

Salesmen should not be allowed to receive cash when the goods are sold. Cash memos with four copies may be prepared. One copy may be retained by the salesman for his record. Three copies of the cash memo may be handed over to the customer. The goods purchased by the customers should be sent to the gate-keeper.

The customer should then go to the cashier to make the necessary payment. The cashier having received the price of the goods makes an entry in the cash book and puts a rubber stamp 'Cash Received' on the three copies of the cash memo, one of which is retained by him for his record.

The customer should then go to the gate-keeper who will deliver the goods to the customer after collecting one copy of the cash memo which shows that the payment had been made.

At the end of the day, each salesman sends a report to the general manager as to the total amount of goods sold by him during the day.

The cashier sends a report to the general manager at the end of the day that he has collected so much money against cash memos issued by different salesmen.

Similarly the gate-keeper sends a report to the General Manager that he had delivered goods worth so much against cash memos issued by such and such salesmen.

If the General Manager finds that all the reports sent by the salesmen, cashier and the gate-keeper tally, there is no fraud. If any fraud is committed, it can be quickly detected.

If the above suggestions are followed, there will be no possibility of misappropriation of cash.

Q.13. What do you understand by the term "vouching"? What is the object of vouching?

Or

"In vouching payments, the auditor does not merely seek proof that money has been paid." Discuss.

Meaning of Vouchers

Ans. A voucher is a documentary evidence in support of a transaction in the books of account. The act of establishing the accuracy and authenticity of an entry in the original books of account is called vouching. Vouching means not only to substantiate an entry in the books of account with any documentary evidence, such as agreements, receipts counterfoils of a receipt book or paying-in-book, contracts, but also to see that the transaction had been properly authorised, recorded and entered in the books of accounts, e.g., verification of entries in the invoices book with the invoices, checking of the cash receipts with the counterfoils of the receipt book, the checking of the cash payments with the receipts issued by the payee and so on. Vouching means testing the truth of the entry appearing in the books of original entry. The success of an auditor in vouching depends upon his intelligence, critical bent of mind, common sense, observation and tact with which he handles his work. He should go beyond the books of account and go to the source of a transaction. He should not only see that the payment has been made but he should see that the payment has been made— (*a*) to the right person or the party; (*b*) for the business itself; (*c*) and properly recorded in the books of account; (*d*) and sanctioned by a competent person; and (*e*) that it has not been fraudulently made. If he simply compares the entry, say, on the credit side of the cash book with the receipt, it is possible that he might be deceived, e.g., the purchase might not have been made for the business or the receipt might have been for the previous year. If it is the receipt side entry and if he compares the entry in the counterfoil of the receipt book, it is possible that less amount might have been entered on the counterfoil than the money which has actually been received. Clever frauds can be discovered only by proper vouching. Therefore, it is very important that the auditor should vouch the entries with great care and intelligence. It is through vouching that an auditor can satisfy himself as to the authenticity and completeness of transactions in the books of account. In case he is negligent, he will be held guil as was decided in the case of *Armitage* vs. *Brewer & Knott* (1932).

Vouching also means checking of additions, ledger postings, extracting of balances in the ledger, etc. The extent to which the auditor should check will depend upon the size of the business, the accounts of which he is auditing. If it is a big business, efficient internal check system will be in operation and hence the auditor will be justified in relying upon a few test checks, while on the other hand in a small business internal check may not be in operation and hence the auditor will have to check every entry. To be on safe side, the auditor will do well to check in detail because the curtailment of work will not in any way reduce his responsibility.

From the above discussion, it would be clear that the object of vouching is to find out the accuracy of the entries appearing in the books of account.

Q.14. Give examples of voucheres you would refuse to accept although properly stamped and signed. Explain clearly the reasons of your refusal.

Ans. The following vouchers though properly stamped and signed should be refused by the auditor :

1. If the date of the voucher does not correspond with the date of the payment as recorded in the Cash Book because an old voucher might have been produced to conceal the misappropriation.
2. If the voucher is in the personal name of an officer of the company, as it is possible that goods might have been purchased by that officer in his personal capacity.
3. If the voucher has not been passed by a responsible officer it may mean an unauthorised payment.
4. A cancelled voucher should not be accepted as it has already served its purpose and hence there is a danger of double payment.
5. If the nature of the payment indicates that it does not concern the business, it should not be accepted as it is not a regular payment for the business.

6. If the amount stated in the voucher differs in words and figures because one cannot be sure as to which one is correct.
7. Where the amount mentioned in the voucher does not agree with the corresponding entry in the cash book for there is a danger of more receipt or payment to have been made.
8. If the amount of the voucher is more than twenty rupees and if it is not stamped, it should not be accepted as such a voucher cannot be accepted in a court of law.
9. Receipted invoice should not be accepted as a voucher as there is a danger of the payment being made twice—once as a credit purchase and again as a cash transaction.

Q. 15. A client of yours suspects that cash is misappropriated by his employees. He seeks your advice to suggest to him a good system of receipts dealing with the receipts and payments of cash to avoid such misappropriations.

Ans. There are lots of chances of misappropriation of cash if there is no well organised system of internal check. As regard the receipt of cash, the following method of dealing with it is suggested :

1. As soon as cash is received, it should be entered in a rough cash book or diary in the presence of a responsible person.
2. Remittances should be opened by the cashier in the presence of a responsible official.
3. All cheques received should be immediately crossed 'Not negotiable, A/c Payee only.'
4. When cash is received, it should be acknowledged by means of a printed receipt which should have a counterfoil or a carbon copy.
5. The receipts should be signed by a responsible official of the concern but the cashier should countersign it.
6. The receipts should be consecutively numbered.
7. Unused receipts should be kept under lock and key.
8. Spoiled receipts should be cancelled and must not be detached from the counterfoils.
9. No blank counterfoils should be accepted.
10. Automatic Tills or Cash Registers are very useful for checking receipts.
11. All the receipts of the day should be deposited in the bank at the end of the day or the next morning.
12. Bank Reconciliation Statement should be prepared frequently by the cashier and some other persons.
13. The cashier should not have any control over the ledgers.
14. Petty cash should be organised under the Imprest System.
15. Before a cheque is issued it should be presented along with the account of the payee to a responsible official for his signature.
16. Cheques should always be crossed 'A/c Payee', before they are deposited in the bank.
17. Unused cheques always be kept under lock and key by a responsible officer lest they may be used by forging the signature of the officer concerned.
18. Internal control over the preparation of wages sheets to prevent fraud and manipulation should be exercised.
19. All payments, as far as possible except for petty expenses should be made by cheques.
20. Attention should be paid to the cash sales and purchases.
21. The cashier should not sanction the payment of special nature.

The Directors should do so.

Q.16. You are informed by the management of a factory that they suspect the existence of 'ghost' workers. How may payment to such 'ghost' workers be avoided?

Ans. It appears that the factory had no internal check system regarding the record of the workers employed and the payment of wages to them. The following internal check system regarding wages may be introduced to avoid the existence of 'ghost' workers in the wages sheets:

1. The attendance of workers should be taken by the Gate-keepers and the Foreman of each Department or Section of the factory. The attendance may be taken either in a register or by a Time Recording Clock maintained at the gate.
2. The same procedure should be followed by the Foreman of each Department or Section.
3. The Wages Sheet or Book should be prepared at the end of the week or month from the Attendance Register by a third man who had no hand in taking the attendance of the workers.
4. Thus, the Gate-keeper will not include the name of a 'ghost' worker as he knows that a record of the workers is maintained by the Foreman of the different departments also unless he joins hands with the Foremen.
5. Similarly a Foreman cannot include the name of a 'ghost' worker as he knows a record is maintained by the Gate-keeper unless both of them join hands to deceive the management.
6. In case the payments of wages are to be made to the piece wage workers, their record of work done will be maintained by the Foreman of the department and the Godown-keeper. The wages sheets will be prepared by a clerk from the records maintained by the Foreman and the Godown-keeper.
7. Wages must be paid to the workers in the presence of the Foreman who will certify each worker when the latter receives payment. Wages should be paid only to the workers who are present and not to their nominees. Thus, even if the Gate-keeper had joined hands with the Foreman, the payment would not be made to the Foreman for a 'worker' who never worked. If an outsider is brought in to receive the payment on behalf of the 'ghost' worker, the other workers will at once point out that the man was not working in their section.

The payment should be made in the presence of the Works Manager or his nominee and the Foreman of the Department or Section concerned.

The cashier should have no hand in the preparation of the Wages Sheets. A list of the 'Uncollected Wages' should be prepared and signed by the Cashier, Foreman of the Department concerned and the Works Manager.

If the above-mentioned system of the preparation of the Wages Sheets and the payment of wages is followed, the danger of the existence of 'ghost' workers will not be there.

Q.17. How do you audit a Petty Cash Book and Petty Cash Account? To what extent should you examine the Petty cash transactions?

Ans. There is a great possibility of misappropriation in the case of petty cash transactions as usually vouchers for small payments are not available. Therefore, there should be a good internal check system. If the petty payments are organised on the imprest system, the chances of fraud will be minimised. If the auditor finds that there is a good internal check system, he should proceed on the following lines.

1. The auditor should check the receipt of money by the Petty Cashier with the Cash Book and also compare the dates.
2. He should check the totals of the columns of the Petty Cash Book.
3. He should check some of their items with the vouchers which are available.

4. He should enquire as to whether a new cheque is issued only after the expenses already incurred by the Petty Cash Keeper have been checked by the cashier.
5. He should see that the totals of different columns have been correctly posted to the ledger.
6. He should compare the postage expenses with Postage Book.
7. He should verify the cash with the Petty Cash Book. If he does not do so and if there is any discrepancy in the balance as per the Petty Cash Book and actual cash in hand, he would be held responsible to pay damages as was held in the case of *London Oil Storage Company Ltd.* vs. *Seear, Hasluck & Co.* (1904).

   If he is unable to be present on the balance-sheet date to count the cash in hand, he should ask the client to deposit it in the bank.
8. While counting the petty cash balance the auditor should see that it does not include any I.O.U.'s. If there are such acknowledgements, he should get confirmation of such I.O.U.'s from the officers who had signed these documents.

Q.18. In the audit of the accounts of a company having a considerable volume of transactions with its bankers, it is sometimes considered unnecessary to check all the entries in the cash book with bank pass book, and, therefore, you are asked to describe a form of "test check" which would, in your opinion, result in saving of time without loss of efficiency.

Ans. If there is a good internal check system in operation and the bank reconciliation statement is often prepared by his client, the auditor may agree to the proposal for the application of "test check". He should, therefore, work on the following lines :

1. He should check a few transactions at random.
2. He should compare a few counterfoils of the 'paying-in-slips' with the pass book and the cash book paying special attention to the dates of the 'paying-in-slips', the pass book and the cash book.
3. The auditor should prepare a bank reconciliation statement, or check a few of those which had already been prepared by his client.
4. There have been cases when fictitious pass books have been produced. Therefore, a certificate from the bank about the balance should be obtained directly, but this step may be taken with the permission of the client.

In spite of this, it must be mentioned here that if any error or fraud remains undetected because the auditor did not check all the transactions, the auditor will be held liable. It was held in the case of *Fox & Sons* vs. *Morris Grant & Co.* (1918), that it is the duty of the auditor to check the bank pass book irrespective of the fact whether he is engaged in auditing the accounts or to prepare the accounts.

Q.19. How would you vouch the following payments :

(*a*) Salaries; (*b*) Insurance Premium; and (*c*) Entertainment Expenses.

Ans. (*a*) Salaries

The auditor should examine the salary book. He should see that the total in the salary book for a particular month agrees with the cheque drawn for salaries or the item in the cash book under the cash column should be examined.

There may be some variation in the salary of an employee during the course of a year, possibly because of the increment which falls due in a particular month or some spacial increment or allowance might have been given. The auditor should see whether the increments was actually due or it is a fictitious entry. To ascertain this he should examine the agreement or a copy of the letter of appointment, or the minute book of the Directors sanctioning such increment, etc.

(*b*) Insurance Premium

In the case of a new policy, the receipt or the Cover Note from the Insurance Company and the policy itself should be examined. In case of renewal, receipt for the premium should be examined. The auditor should also find out whether the goods or the property insured belongs to his client and whether the policy stands in the name of his client. The date on the receipt and the period for which risk is covered should be examined.

(*c*) Entertainment Expenses

The auditor should see whether such expenses have been sanctioned by a responsible official, or the managing agent or directors, etc. He should examine for this purpose the resolution, minute books, etc., sanctioning such a payment. In certain cases, a fixed monthly allowance is sanctioned to the manager, etc., to spend the amount for entertaining the customers. In such cases, the auditor should examine such a permission.

Q.20. Write a short note on "teeming and lading" process of fraud and state what steps you will take to detect such frauds.

Ans. Teeming and Lading Method of Fraud.

This is a method by which deficiencies of cash (misappropriation of cash already committed) are concealed for some time in the following way :

When cash is received from some debtor, it is not recorded in the cash book and is misappropriated. Later on, when cash is received from any other debtor, his account is not credited but the account of the first debtor is credited, and cash is debited. Again, later on when cash is received from a third debtor, his account is not credited but that of the second debtor is credited, and the cash is debited. This process goes on for some time till the cashier is in a position to pay back the money embezzled or the fraud is discovered. This method of fraud is known as "Short Bankings" or "Delayed Accounting of Money Received". This is a method by which the past defalcations are covered up by the present receipts. This method of fraud is also known as "teeming and lading," or "Lapping." "Lapping" has been defined by Professor Meigs as "concealment of a shortage by delaying the recording of cash receipts."

So far we have presumed that all remittances have been received in cash. But in case remittances are received by means of cheques, then the cheques will have to be split up. This process is known as "Splitting cheques." Let us make this point clear by an example. *A* sends one hundred rupees in settlement of his account. The cashier misappropriated the amount and does not either debit cash or credit *A*'s account. But there is a danger that if *A* does not receive a receipt for the amount, he will write to the company for the receipt or the company itself may remind *A* for the settlement of the account. Suppose another cheque for two hundred rupees from *B* is received. The whole of the amount will not be credited to *B*'s account, but one hundred rupees will be credited to *A*'s account, in order to close it and to send a receipt to him for one hundred rupees and one hundred rupees only will be credited to *B*'s account. The cheque for Rs. 200 will be sent to the bank for collection. Suppose later on *C* sends a cheque for Rs. 300. *B*'s account will be credited for Rs. 100, thus, closing his account while *C*'s account will be credited with Rs. 200 instead of Rs. 300. Thus, this process goes on and the defalcation is transferred from one account to another till the fraud is discovered or the cashier, having embezzled a large sum of money, absconds.

These are the methods by which the past defalcations are covered up by the present receipts. These methods of fraud are known as "teeming and lading" or "lapping"

Such frauds are very difficult to discover unless the internal check system in regard to the receipts and bankings is efficient.

Duty of the Auditor

1. The auditor should find out what is the internal check system regarding cash. If there is any weak point he must probe into the matter. The cashier should not have access to the ledger.

2. He should check the counterfoils of the receipts with the cash book paying particular attention to the dates.
3. He should check the counterfoils of the paying-in-book, the entries in the cash book, the bank pass book and the rough cash book, if any, paying particular attention to the dates.
4. He should compare the details of the cheques received and sent to the bank and the accounts of the parties to find out if any "Splitting up" of cheques has been done.
5. He should carefully examine the debtor's balances in the ledger and see whether there are accounts which appear to be falling more and more into arrear.
6. He should see whether the accounts are being settled by several instalments especially in cases where the customers have been settling the accounts regularly and not instalment-wise.
7. He should, with the permission of the client, send for the statements of account from the debtors and compare them with their balances in the ledger.

Q. 21. In auditing the accounts of a business you find a number of receipts upwards of Rs. 20 without revenue stamp affixed.

(*a*) What do you consider your duty as an auditor to be?

(*b*) Would it make any difference if the unstamped receipts were on the back of cheques?

(*c*) Has a customer who buys goods for cash a right to demand a stamped receipt when the purchase exceeds Rs. 20?

Ans. (*a*) If the auditor is satisfied as to the genuineness of the voucher, he may pass it but in case he is doubtful, he must draw the attention of the directors.

(*b*) Cheques are not to be taken as receipts and hence whether the stamp is there or not makes no difference.

(*c*) The customer has no right to demand a stamped receipt when he purchases goods against cash, the value of which exceeds Rs. 20. It is a cash sale and he has the right to demand a cash memo only.

Q.22. During the course of an audit, it has been observed that :–

(1) a number of documents constituting a particular record, all the fourth copies, show certain figures that are more distinct than the rest,

(2) three tenants' rent cards were missing from those produced in connection with the examination of the income derived from rental properties,

(3) the initials of the clerk placing orders were the same as those that appear on some of the invoices as indicating authorisation for payments, and

(4) certain expenses paid in cash against initial vouchers prepared by the cashier show tendency to increase without any known special reason.

You are asked to state the principal ways in which fraud could have occurred in each of the above circumstances, and to tabulate the steps you would take to satisfy yourself that no irregularity has taken place.

Ans. (1) The fact that the fourth copy of the document shows distinct figure as compared to the other two or three copies shows that a fraud had been committed. The method of doing so might have been by placing a paper above the fourth copy but below the carbon paper. Later on another figure on the carbon might have been written after removing the plain paper from below the carbon to give an impression on the fourth copy of the document. This is why the impression on the fourth copy is distinct from others. This might have been done with a view to commit fraud, e.g., if a sale had taken place, the less amount on the fourth copy of the invoice (maintained for office use) might have been entered and thus the goods might have been misappropriated.

The auditor in such a case should take the following steps to discover the fraud :—

(*a*) He should make inquiries about the system prescribed for the creation of the particular document and their associated carbon copies.

(*b*) In the case of sale of goods on credit, he should make direct inquiries from the customers for the confirmation of their accounts.

(2) It appears from the question that a separate card for each tenant is prepared and whenever the tenant pays the rent, and entry is made in his card and his signature is obtained thereon. Under such circumstances the non-availability of the cards shows that the rent might have been collected, entry made on the cards but the agent might have embezzelled the money so received and that is why he has not produce the tenants' cards.

The auditor should take the following steps in such a case:—

(*a*) He should inquire into the exact reason for the missing tenants' card.

(*b*) He should examine the copies of the agreements with the tenants to find out the rent payable, the date on which it is payable and whether the amount has been banked.

(*c*) If he is not satisfied after making the above mentioned inquiries, he should write direct to the tenants asking them to inform him whether they have paid the rent and if yes, he should see whether it has been deposited in the bank. If no such amount has been deposited, it is a clear proof of fraud.

(3) The fact that the initials of the clerk placing the order and authorising the payment for the same, happen to be the same may show that neither the goods were ordered nor received, but payment made to a fictitious supplier who shared it with the clerk concerned unless incidentally the initials of the two different clerks tallied. It is also possible that the clerk might have purchased these goods for his personal use and the payment might have been made by the company.

In such a case the auditor should examine the Order Book, Gate-keeper's Book, Stock Register, etc. If the goods had been purchased recently, physical checking of the stock should be resorted to.

(4) Increases in the cash expenditure supported by initial vouchers by the cashier may show misappropriation of the cash by the cashier. Such initial vouchers might be fictitious as no expenditure was incurred for the business. It may also be possible that the expenditure might have been incurred by some other employee not for the business but payment might have been made out of the company's funds.

The auditor should make inquiries from the cashier and the chief accountant as to the actual items of expenditure. He should examine in depth the items of expenditurte to find out the correctness of the initial voucher.

Q.23. The cashier of a trading firm has also control of all the financial books. He also opens all letters. Receipts comprise cash and cheques. Under these circumstances, what malpractices are open to the cashier in respect of both receipts and payments and what checks would you, as an auditor, adopt to locate such irregularities?

Ans. Under the circumstances mentioned in the question, the cashier has the opportunity of committing frauds in the following ways :

1. Misappropriation of Cash Receipts

When cash is received no entry might be made in the cash book but as the cashier has a control over other books of account, he credits the customer's account. If he has control over blank receipt books, he may issue a forged receipt in acknowledging the receipt of money from the customer although no cash is debited.

Such a fraud may be detected by examining carefully the counterfoils of the receipts, entries in the cash book, and the money sent to the bank for deposit by referring to the counterfoils of the paying-in-book to find out any evidence of "teeming and lading."

2. Manipulation of discounts

Cashier might show that more discount was allowed to customers for cash payment although less cash discount was granted and the difference might be misappropriated, e.g., ninety-five rupees were received and five rupees were allowed as discount. The cashier might debit ninety rupees only and show as if ten rupees were allowed as discount.

This can be detected by enquiring the rate of discount, counterfoil of the receipt and by referring to correspondence, etc.

3. Misappropriation of Cash Sales Proceeds

If there is no good internal check system regarding cash sales, misappropriation of cash may take place. If there is internal check system, the auditor should find out its efficiency and compare the Cashier's Summary, Salesmen's Extracts and the Gate-keeper's Extracts in the case of a big departmental store. (*For details refer to the Answer to Question* 12.)

4. Cash Proceeds of the Sale of fixed assets, Bills Receivable, etc.

The correspondence, auctioneer's note, broker's note and bank pass book must be examined.

5. Misappropriation of payments in respect of fictitious Purchases and Expenses.

The cashier might show fictitious purchase and later on may show that the payments have been made to these fictitious sellers but in fact money is misappropriated.

This type of fraud can be detected by referring to the Order Book, Purchase Book, Goods Inward Book and the Gate-keepers' Book, if any. He should also refer to the receipt sent by the purchaser to whom the payment for the goods is supposed to have been made.

6. Fictitious Returns Inwards

The cashier might show that the goods have been returned by the buyers which in fact have never been returned. Later on, cash purported to be paid to the buyer, is misappropriated.

To detect such a fraud, the auditor should refer to the gate-keeper's inward book, godown-keeper's inward book, correspondence, etc. Since it was a fictitious transaction no entry will be found in any of the above-mentioned books.

7. Miscellaneous

Wages might have been paid to dummy workers. The auditor should examine the wages sheets, time and piece wage records and the amount of the cheque drawn, etc.

Q.24. Describe a good internal check system regarding credit purchases.

Ans. The system of internal check will depend upon the size of the business and the staff available. Whenever goods are required in a particular department, its head should send to the Purchasing Department the "Purchase Requisition" which should show the quality, price, if possible, or the maximum price at which they may be purchased, the time by which the goods must be supplied, etc.

1. All the orders sent out should be recorded in the Purchase Order Book which should have carbon copies—one to be sent to the supplier of the goods and the other to be retained for reference purposes.

2. When the goods are received, the Gate-keeper or the Store-keeper should make an entry in the Goods Inward Book.

3. The invoice should be checked with the Goods Inward Book maintained by the Store-keeper to see that the goods are correctly recorded in the stock-register according to the invoice.

4. A clerk should check the invoice regarding calculations.

5. Then the invoice should be sent to the head of the department who placed the order for the goods to see whether the prices and qualities are correctly recorded in the invoice.

6. The departmental head will now poss on the invoice to the clerk who will record the same in the Purchases Book.

7. Every person who has to deal with the invoice and the goods should initial the invoice.

8. Goods Inward Book should be compared with the Purchases Book.

9. He should see that the name of the creditor is the same as has been entered in the "Particulars" column of the Purchases Book.

Q.25. Describe an efficient system of internal check regarding credit sales.

Ans. 1. Whenever an order is received, it should be recorded in the Order Received Books, giving details regarding the date on which the order was received, the name of the customer, the particulars about the goods, date of delivery, mode of transport, etc.

2. The order or a copy of it should be sent to the Despatch Department.

3. Another clerk should check the goods ready to be packed with the order to see that only those goods which have been ordered are being packed.

4. A responsible officer should fix the rates at which the goods are to be charged.

5. A clerk should then make the extensions.

6. The invoice should be prepared in duplicate or triplicate by means of carbon paper—one copy to be sent to the buyer, another to the invoice clerk or the Account Department for debiting the account of the customer and the third copy is sent to the Gate-keeper who will record in the Goods Onwards Book that such and such goods have left the premises.

7. If the orders are booked by the travelling agents, they should be supplied with Order Books with triplicate copies—one to be given to the customer, second to be sent to the head office for necessary compliance and the third is to be retained by the travelling agent for his record.

Q.26. How could a dishonest Book-keeper defraud his employer in connection with the Sales Ledger entries? How would you, as an auditor, endeavour to discover whether such fraud has taken place?

Ans. 1. The book-keeper may not make an entry in regard to the sales and thus the account of the buyer would not be debited. Thereafter, when cash is received from the buyer, it would be misappropriated and no entry—neither in the cash book, nor in the ledger—will be passed.

2. Even though no goods might have been returned by the buyer, his account is credited and a fictitious entry is made in the Returns Inward Book. Thereafter, it is shown in the books that cash has been sent to the customer although it has not been sent to him but is misappropriated.

3. Similarly fictitious rebates, allowances, discounts are allowed to customers and the amount is misappropriated.

4. When full amount is sent by the customer in settlement of his account, some money is credited to his account and the balance is written off as "bad debt" although this amount is misappropriated or the whole of the amount received is misappropriated and it is shown as if it is a "bad debt."

5. Money received from customers is misappropriated by the process of "teeming and lading" as explained in Question 20.

The auditor should take the following steps to discover whether such a fraud has been committed.

1. He should find out whether the book-keeper has access to Ledger, Cash Book, Sales Book, Goods Outward Book. If so, it would be difficult to detect the fraud. In no case should the book-keeper write the Goods Outward Book, Returns Inward Book, issue the Credit Notes or receive or pay cash at the same time.

2. He should vouch the sales with the Sales Book, Invoice Book, Gate-keeper's Outward Book, etc.

3. Similarly Returns Inward Book, Gate-keeper's Inward Book, carbon copies of the Credit Notes, Correspondence, etc., should be compared.

4. He should enquire as to who sanctions rebates, discount, etc., and the rates thereof.

5. Correspondence in regard to bad debts should be examined with a view to find out the amount of bad debts dividends.

6. He should vouch the cash received from customers with the help of counterfoils of the receipts and correspondence, etc.

7. He should check the deposits in the bank with the counterfoils of the paying-in-book, pass book and the cash book paying particular attention to dates and particulars of cheques deposited to see if the process of "teeming and lading" has been resorted to.

Q. 27. Your clients suspect that its manager receives unlawful gratification (monetary benefit) from the suppliers while purchasing goods for the company. State how will you detect such a fraud.

Ans. In such a case there will be no direct evidence to detect the fraud. The auditor will have to depend upon indirect evidence. The unlawful gratification might have been given to him—

(*a*) by supplying sub-standard goods; or

(*b*) by supplying less quantity of goods than what had been stated in the invoice or cash memo.

The auditor, in such a case, should follow the following procedure :—

1. He should inquire into the internal check system prevalent in the business, e.g., whether the goods, which are purchased, are inspected by a technical officer to see whether goods of standard quality have or have not been received. If the goods received are not subject to inspection, it is possible that goods of inferior quality might have been supplied and the difference between the standard quality and the inferiority quality might have been given to the manager.

2. He should inquire whetherd any complaints have been received from the departmental or the production manager or the material controller regarding the sub-standard quality of goods supplied.

3. He should inquire whether tenders or quotations are invited while purchasing the goods.

4. He should inquire whether any tenders were rejected and if so, what were the reasons thereof.

5. If the lowest quotations or tenders were accepted (which is usually the case) he should pay particular attention to the quality of the goods received as in such a case there is a possibility that the lowest quotations were accepted but the quality of the goods was of sub-standard.

6. The auditor should compare the prices of the same kind of goods which were purchased during the absence of the purchase manager when he was on leave.

7. He should find out whether the purchase manager is related to the suppliers, and if so, he should see whether the goods are reasonably priced and they are of standard quality.

Q. 28. In the course of an audit of a firm's accounts, you notice

(*a*) that the sales entered in the Day Book in the last month before stock-taking are abnormally large;

(*b*) that the purchases in the same period are usually small;

(*c*) that the stock after allowing for inflated prices is much greater than usual.

What steps would you take to satisfy yourself in regard to the above particulars?

Ans. (*a*) The auditor should compare the sales with the corresponding months of previous years. It is possible that the business might be seasonal one and hence there is great demand for the sale of goods in the last month, e.g., in December, an account of X-mas, if the financial year closes on 31st December. It is also possible that "Clearance Sale" might have been organised in the closing month of the year and hence the sales are large.

It is also possible that the prices of the goods might have gone up abnormally high and hence the total amount of sales might be higher than the previous months although the quantity of the goods sold remained the same. If none of the above causes of abnormally large sales is there, the auditor should proceed on the following lines :

1. He should vouch the sales of the last month with the Order Received Book, Gate-keeper's Outward Book and the Godown-keeper's Book.
2. He should see that the sales for the succeeding period are not included in the sales of the previous months.
3. He should see that the sales do not include sale of a fixed asset.
4. He should see that the sales do not include sale of goods received on consignment.
5. He should ascertain that the sales do not include the "Sales on Approval" when the date for approval has not expired.
6. He should find out whether "Consignment Sent Out" has been treated as sales.
7. He should check the Returns Inward Book for the following months with the carbon copies of the Credit Notes lest the sales might be fictitious ones.

(*b*) The auditor should pay attention to the following :

1. Compare the Purchase Book with the Orders Received Book, Godown-keepers' Inward Book, Invoices, and the Gate-keeper's Inward Book.
2. Check the purchases for the succeeding months as purchases for the previous month might have been suppressed and recorded in the following month in order to inflate profits of the year.

(*c*) It appears to be a serious matter when the purchases for the last month are small, the sales for the same period are large and in spite of this the closing stock is much greater. As a matter of fact, under the circumstances mentioned, the stock should be much less. It appears that attempt has been made to inflate profits. The auditor should be very careful and pay attention to the following points to find out the fraud:

1. He should find out the mode of the valuation of the stock. The correct principle for the valuation of the closing stock is 'the cost price or the market price whichever is the lower.'
2. The auditor should check the stock sheets, paying attention to calculations, prices, etc.
3. He should see that the stock does not include the goods received on consignment.
4. Similarly he should see that the goods which have been received on approval are not included in the closing stock if such approval has not been sent to the supplier.
5. He should see that goods which have been sold out but have not been despatched to the buyer, are not included in the closing stock as the ownership in the goods has been transferred to the buyer.
6. If the goods have been sent out to branches at selling price and some goods remain unsold at the date of the balance-sheet, proper adjustment should be made in regard to such unsold stock to be included in the closing stock, i.e., stock at the branches should be valued at selling price.
7. If the firm maintain a Quantity Stock Record, check some of these items with the Stock Sheet.
8. Get a certificate pertaining to the closing stock from a responsible official.

Q.29. For what purpose is the Journal utilised? How is it audited?

Ans. Use of Journal. The Journal is used for recording all those transactions which cannot be passed through any other book of prime entry. In some continental countries, all the entries are passed through the Journal. The use of the Journal is compulsory in some of these countries. In certain countries the totals of the subsidiary books are passed through the Journal. The use of the Journal will depend upon the size of the business and consequently the number of entries, e.g., where very few entries relating to bills of exchange take place, there will be no necessity of having separate books for Bills Receivable and Bills Payable. Similarly where there are few transactions relating to returns inwards and returns outwards, there will be no necessity for maintaining Returns Inwards or Returns Outwards Book. In such a case all such entries are passed through the Journal.

The following transactions are generally passed through the Journal :

1. Opening entries;
2. The acquisition of different assets from the vendors or liabilities taken over;
3. The issue and allotment of shares;
4. Forfeiture of shares;
5. Adjusting entries such as provision for bad and doubtful debts, outstandings, depreciation, interest on capital, rectification of entries, etc.;
6. Closing entries, i.e., transfers from nominal accounts to the profit and loss account;
7. Consignment entries;
8. Entries relating to the dishonour of bills, etc.

From the above, it would appear that these entries are of a varied nature. They affect the Profit and Loss Account. The Auditor should insist upon narration being given after each entry. There are lot of chances for committing frauds through the journal, e.g., writing of a good debt as bad and misappropriating the cash received in respect of such a debt. Hence, the auditor should pay particular attention to the transactions passed through the journal.

The evidence to vouch each transaction will depend upon its nature, e.g., the opening entries will be vouched with the previous year's audited balance-sheet or the working papers of the previous year; the acquisition of assets from the vendors can be vouched with the contract entered into with the vendors; the issue of shares can be vouched with the prosectus, directors' minute book, copies of application and allotment letters; forfeiture of shares can be vouched with the prospectus, Articles of Association, minute book of the Board of Directors, correspondence, etc., and so on. The auditor should also pay particular attention to the allocation of expenditure between capital and revenue and obtain certificate from a responsible officer to that effect. The auditor should check the totals of the journal entries consisting of more than one item. He should not pass any entry in the journal until he is quite satisfied with regard to its validity and correctness. In short while vouching the entries in the journal the auditor should see that (*a*) the entry has been properly authorised, (*b*) the entry is within the powers of the company, and (*c*) the entry is supported by documentary evidence.

Q.30. What are the special points to which an auditor should direct his attention for the proper valuation of book debts with a view to ascertaining the adequacy of Reserve for Bad and Doubtful debts?

Ans. Reserve for Bad and Doubtful Debts.

For the purpose of valuation of book debts, the auditor should ask his client to give him a list of the good, doubtful and bad debts. He can verify this list by applying the following test to each account :

1. Whether the account is regularly settled and the advantage of cash discount taken by the debtor. In such a case, the debt is good.
2. Whether the debt is outstanding beyond the period of credit allowed. If so, it *may* mean that the debt is doubtful.
3. Whether the payments are on account and the balance tends to increase. If it is so, it means the party is financially weak.

4. Whether an old balance is being carried forward and the new goods are supplied for cash. If so, it may mean the debt is doubtful. It is also possible that the old balance may be due to a dispute. The possibility of the old balance having been paid and the cash misappropriated should also be considered in such cases.
5. Whether cheques or bills received against a debit balance have often dishonoured. If it has been the case, it shows the party is not financially sound and that the debt may be doubtful or may prove bad some day.
6. Whether any note regarding non-payment, like 'account stopped', 'in liquidator's hands', 'in bankruptcy', 'in liquidation', or 'disappeared and address unknown', etc., is made on the ledger account. If so, he should thoroughly scrutinise the case to find out whether the debt is doubtful or bad.
7. The law of Limitation allows three years to recover a debt and if the debt is outstanding for a longer period, it means the debt is bad.
8. If the bills are constantly renewed, the party is financially unsound and the debt may be treated as doubtful.
9. If payments are irregular, the debt may not be good and may prove to be bad some day.
10. Whether there is any unusual item of discount or allowance.

The list should be prepared in a columnar form to find out 'good', 'doubtful' and 'bad' debts. The experience of previous years should also be taken into consideration to find out whether adequate reserves have been created.

Q.31. What is the legal position of an auditor of a company regarding the adequacy of the Reserve for Bad and Doubtful debts? Quote the relevant case law in support of your answer.

Ans. Legal position of auditor re Reserve for Bad Debts.

The auditor has to report to the shareholders whether the balance sheet exhibits a true and fair view of the state of the affairs of the company or not. If no or inadequate provision for bad and doubtful debts is made, the balance-sheet will not exhibit a true and fair view of the state of affairs of the company and if he reports on the balance-sheet as stated above, it would be a misleading report and he might land himself into difficulty. Moreover, the verification of the assets is one of the most important duties of an auditor. If he does not verify the book debts which are the assets of the company, he will be held negligent in the performance of his duties. Therefore, it is very necessary that an auditor should see that sufficient provision is made for bad and doubtful debts.

Again, if no or inadequate provision is made for bad and doubtful debts, the profits and loss account which he has to certify will also be incorrect.

It is the duty of the auditor to pursuade the directors of the company to make sufficient provision for bad and doubtful debts and if they do not agree to his suggestions, he should report the fact to the shareholders. If he does not do so, he will be held liable as was held in *re The London and General Bank* (1895). In another case, the auditors relied upon the manager's estimate of the reserve for bad debts which was wrong and the profits were overstated. The auditors were held liable even though they relied upon the trusted officials of the company.

(*Arthur E. Green & Co.* vs. *The Central Advance and Discount Corporation Ltd.*, 1920).

Q.32. In the annual Balance-Sheet of a Limited Company the creditors are understated, in consequence of goods purchased not having been brought into the Purchases Day Book and the Ledger, though the goods were included in the Stock. Could an auditor, under such circumstances, be held responsible for not discovering the omission?

Give reasons for your reply.

What checks can an auditor apply to avoid such errors?

Ans. It appears that the auditor has not checked the accounts carefully. If he had compared the Gate-keeper's Inward Book with the Invoices, Purchase Book and the Store-keeper's Book he would have detected this fraud. He could have detected this fraud by comparing the ledger accounts and the statements of account sent by the creditors. It appears he was negligent in the performance of his duty and hence is responsible as was held in the case of the *Irish Woollen Co.,* vs. *Tyson & Others* (1900) and *re. Westminster Road Construction Co.*

In order to discover such a suppression of purchases (probably it was done with a view to inflate profits), the auditor should apply the following checks :

1. He should check the Invoices with Purchases Book, Gate-keeper's Inward Book, Store-keeper's Inward Book especially for a few weeks before the close of the period under audit.

2. He should, with the permission of the client, send for the statements of account from the creditors and compare them with the ledger accounts, whenever there is any suspicion.

3. He should examine invoices for a few weeks after the close of the period under audit with a view to find out whether the invoices relate to the previous period.

Q.33. In the course of audit of

(*a*) proprietorship concerns,

(*b*) partnership firms, and

(*c*) limited companies, you find that there are occasional purchases of controlled materials without vouchers. Your clients do not want qualified reports. State the steps in each case you should take in order to give unqualified report, if possible.

Ans. Goods are sometimes purchased at a higher price than the controlled price. In other words they are purchased in the "black market". In such a case, the seller does not issue a cash memo or an invoice because if he does so, he might be put into trouble for illegally charging higher price than the controlled price.

In case the proprietors do not want that the auditor should write a qualified report the auditor should take the following steps :

(*a*) Proprietorship Concerns

The auditor should get a certificate from the proprietor that a cash memo or invoice could not be obtained for the purchases and that the goods were purchased with his consent and with his permission at the price stated in the books of account.

(*b*) Partnership Firms

He should prepare a list of such purchases and get a certificate from each partner to the effect that they had agreed to the purchase of the goods at such a price.

(*c*) Limited Companies

He should obtain the signature of all the Directors on the list of purchases made at a higher price or resolution passed by the Board of Directors to that effect which will be sufficient.

Q.34. Vouching is the very essence of auditing.

(*a*) When auditing Bought Day Book to what points should attention be given in the examination of invoices?

(*b*) How should an auditor satisfy himself that all invoices are included in the Bought Day Book at the date of the Balance Sheet?

(*c*) Is an auditor legally liable if the state of affairs as shown in the Balance-Sheet is falsified owing to the suppression of invoices?

Ans. Vouching means to substantiate an entry in the books of account not only with any documentary evidence such as agreements, receipts, counterfoils of a receipt book or paying in book, contracts, resolutions, correspondence but also to see that the transaction has been properly authorised, recorded and entered in the books of account. Vouching means testing the truth of the transactions appearing in the books of original entry. Hence vouching is considered to be the essence of auditing. It is through vouching that an auditor can satisfy himself as to the authenticity and completeness of transactions in the books of account. In case he is negligent, he will be held guilty as was decided in the case of *Armitage* vs. *Brewer & Knott* (1932).

The auditor should pay attention to the following points while examining vouchers :

(*a*) 1. Whether the invoice is made in the name of the concern.

2. Whether the date of the invoice corresponds with the entry in the Bought Day Book.

3. Whether the goods purchased relate to the business.

4. Whether the goods purchased are of capital nature. If so, the goods account should not be debited but the particular asset account should be debited.

5. Whether the invoice has already been cancelled. If so, it should not be accepted.

6. Whether it is a "duplicate" copy of the invoice. If so, he should scrutinise the transaction.

7. Whether the invoice has been initialled by the clerks who has checked the accuracy of the prices charged, quantity and quality of the goods, the calculations, etc.

8. Whether trade discount has been deducted while debiting the goods account and crediting the supplier's account.

(*b*) 1. He should compare the Purchases Book with the Order Received Book. Invoices, the Gate-keeper's Inward Book, and the Godown-keeper's Book.

2. He should check the purchases for the succeeding months as the purchases made at the close of the month might have been suppressed and recorded in the following month.

3. He should get the statements of Accounts from creditors, with the permission of the client.

(*c*) An Auditor is legally liable if the state of affairs, as shown in the Balance-Sheet, is falsified owing to the suppression of invoices as was held in the case of *Westminister Road Construction Co.* However, if he can prove that he applied all the tests stated under (*b*) above, he is free from the liability.

Q.35. As an auditor, how would you satisfy yourself that the following have been duly provided :

(*a*) Reserve for Doubtful Debts;

(*b*) Outstanding Liabilities for Expenses; and

(*c*) Provision for Depreciation.

Ans. (*a*) Reserve for Doubtful Debts. ***See Answer to Question* 30.**

(*b*) Outstanding Liabilities for Expenses

It is the duty of an auditor to see that all liabilities including the outstanding ones, are brought into account before ascertaining the net profit and loss for the current year. If he fails to do so, he would be held liable as was held in *re The Westminster Road Construction and Engineering Co. Ltd.,* (1932). He should examine the cash book for the succeeding month as to whether any amount has been paid for an outstanding liability. He should examine the Purchases Book, Goods Inward Book, etc., regarding the purchases by the close of the period under audit. But it may not be easy for an auditor to know whether all liabilities have been brought into account or not. Some of the expenses might have been suppressed and this may not be clear from the books of account. But there are some outstanding liabilities, e.g., expenses of a regular nature like the rent, which usually occurs and, therefore, the auditor can easily find out such liabilities. Moreover, the auditor will learn about the existence of such outstanding liabilities by experience. It would be better if the auditor gets a certificate from a responsible official that there are no outstanding expenses for the period under audit.

(c) Provision for Depreciation

The auditor should work on the following lines :

1. He should enquire :

(i) Who estimated the probable life of the asset?

(ii) Who fixed the rate of depreciation to be charged?

(iii) Whether the rate of depreciation so fixed will bring down the value of the asset to zero or scrap or residual value at the expiry of that particular period.

2. He should see that correct principles of depreciation are followed and that the depreciation is provided on consistent basis.

3. If excessive reserve has been provided in the past, Part III of Schedule VI of the Companies Act lays down—

(2) where

(a) any amount written off or retained by way of providing for depreciation, renewals or diminution in value of assets, not being an amount written off in relation to fixed assets before the commencement of this Act; or

(b) any amount retained by way of providing for any known liability; is in excess of the amount, which in the opinion of the directors is reasonably necessary for the purpose, the excess shall be treated for the purposes of this Schedule as a reserve and not as a provision.

4. If he thinks insufficient provision has been made for depreciation to inflate the profits of the current year, he should pursuade the directors to raise the amount and if they do not agree with him, he should have the courage to mention the fact in his report.

5. Above all he should find out whether provision for depreciation has been made according to the Companies and Income Tax Acts.

Q.36. What are the principal considerations in determining whether any item of expenditure by a manufacturing and trading company should be allocated to capital or revenue? State the importance of allocation between Capital and Revenue.

Ans. Capital Expenditure.

It is that expenditure which is incurred in purchasing new property which will help the production of goods and hence increase the earning capacity of the business. This type of expenditure is "incurred in acquiring assets for the purpose of earning income or increasing the earning capacity of the business." If heavy expenditure is incurred on repairs which ultimately increase the efficiency of the plant or machinery, such an expenditure is of capital nature. Similarly expenses incurred in erecting plant and machinery should be capitalised as such expenses increase the value of machinery.

Sometimes a wrong idea is formed that if a heavy expenditure is incurred, it is of the nature of capital expenditure and when a small expenditure is incurred, it is revenue expenditure. It may or may not be so. It depends upon the circumstances of each particular case.

The auditor should, therefore, see the basis on which expenditure has been allocated and should not be guided by the amount of expenditure alone.

Revenue Expenditure

It is an expenditure which is periodically incurred to *maintain* the revenue-earning capacity of the business, e.g.,

1. Expenditure incurred to maintain the value of any existing asset, e.g., ordinary repairs, whitewashing of the building, etc.

2. Expenditure incurred in the ordinary conduct and administration of the business, i.e., rent, salaries, wages, etc.

3. Expenditure incurred in connection with the administration and distribution of the goods manufactured or sold, e.g., commission, travelling expenses, advertising and so on.

It is not easy to classify a particular expense as revenue expenditure, e.g., wages during the ordinary course of manufacturing business will be of a revenue nature, while on the other hand wages paid for erecting and fitting a new machinery will be of a capital nature. Carriage paid for buying a new machinery, interest paid during the construction of work, legal charges incurred for purchasing a building, etc., will all be considered as expenses of capital nature and will be debited to the particular asset account while on the other hand carriage expenses, interest on money borrowed or debentures, etc., will be considered as revenue expenditure and will be debited to the revenue account.

Importance of Allocation between Capital and Revenue

The correct allocation of expenditure between capital and revenue is of great importance as it will affect the profit and loss account and the balance-sheet of a concern.

Improper allocation of expenditure between capital and revenue will have far-reaching results on the accounts of a concern. The auditor should very carefully see that proper allocation is made. He should get a certificate regarding the allocation of expenditure from a responsible official and mention that fact in his report especially when the expenditure involved is very heavy. He should state in his report that he has relied upon the certificate from a responsible official about the allocation of expenditure between capital and revenue, but he should not be negligent and cannot absolve himself from liability behind the cloak of the certificate.

Q.37. Contingent liabilities may be divided conveniently into two main classes :

(*i*) those involving a loss, should be liability materialise; and

(*ii*) those involving the acquisition of an asset of corresponding amount.

Give an example of each class and state how you would require each to be dealt with in the Balance-Sheet of a company.

Ans. A Contingent Liability is a liability which may or may not arise. It materialises on the happening of a certain event. Contingent Liabilities may be of two kinds, viz.,

1. A liability involving an ultimate loss, e.g., a liability in a disputed case where damages may have to be paid; a guarantee given for debts owing by third parties; speculative transactions; forward contracts, etc.
2. A liability which will involve the acquisition of an asset of corresponding value, e.g., when goods have been purchased for future delivery or under an agreement of service. No note should be made in the balance sheet in respect of this type of contingent liability but if the amount involved is considerable, a note should be inserted at the foot of the balance-sheet.

The auditor should see that the requirements of the Companies Act of 1956 regarding the contingent liability are complied within the balance-sheet on the liability side.

Contingent liabilities of a limited company are shown in the balance-sheet according to the Companies Act as under :

1. Contingent liabilities for which provision has been made in the balance-sheet, e.g., where the directors think that the liability will definitely arise in connection with a suit filed against the company though the amount may be uncertain, will be shown under the "Current Liabilities and Provisions."
2. Contingent liabilities for which no provision has been made, will be shown under the "Contingent Liabilities not provided for", e.g., arrears of Fixed Cumulative Dividends. The amount of such a liability is not extended in the amount column.

The information required to be given under any of the items or sub-items in this form if not included in the Balance-Sheet because they are numerous should be furnished in a separate schedule or schedules to be annexed to and form part of the Balance-Sheet.

Q.38. What do you understand by "Outstanding Assets", and "Outstanding Liabilities", and what are the duties of an auditor in relation thereto?

Ans. Outstanding Assets

Outstanding assets are those assets over which the company has no immediate claim but which are recoverable at a later date or which cannot be converted into cash immediately.

Following are a few examples of different classes of outstanding assets :

1. Income Receivable

Rent might have accrued but might not have been received by the time when the books are closed; the borrower might not have paid the interest at the date of the balance-sheet; commission, shipping rebates, taxation claims, etc., might not have been received.

2. Prepaid Expenses

Insurance premium, rent, rates and taxes, subscriptions, telephone rent, etc., might have been paid in advance and the period for which they have been paid might not have expired at the date of the balance-sheet.

3. Deferred Revenue Expenditure

Sometimes heavy expenditure is incurred, the advantage of which will be derived in subsequent years, e.g.,

(*a*) Expenditure incurred in launching an advertisement campaign;

(*b*) Development Expenditure;

(*c*) Experimental Expenditure;

(*d*) Research Expenditure, and so on.

Outstanding Liabilities

Outstanding Liabilities are those liabilities which have not been paid at the date of the balance-sheet. The examples of outstanding liabilities are given below :

1. Unearned Income

Income received though a part of it is not applicable to the current year but will be earned during the following year is called Unearned Income. The auditor should examine the vouchers to find out how much amount is to be credited to the profit and loss account of the current year and how much is to be carried forward and which will be earned during the following period.

2. Unpaid Expenses

Expenses incurred during the year but for which payment has not been made and will have to be made next year are called Unpaid Expenses, e.g., rent, rates, taxes, electricity charges, audit fee, salaries, etc. The auditor should examine vouchers, receipts, invoices, demand notes, etc., to ascertain whether expenses ought to have been debited to the current year's profit and loss account and whether any payment has been made.

In all these cases, the auditor should ask his client to get an Outstanding Memoranda Book prepared. Such a book should be signed by a responsible official. He should see that proper adjusting entries have been made. The auditor will not be relieved of his responsibility if there is any mistake in the outstanding memoranda book or he relied upon such a book even though it was signed by a responsible official. He must, therefore, exercise reasonable skill and diligence while examining such a book.

Q.39. What is the meaning of a note on a Balance-Sheet 'Contingent Liability on Bills Receivable discountable, Rs. 25,000'? If you were the company's auditor, would you consider it necessary to verify this item; and if so, how would you proceed?

Contingent Liabilities

Ans. A contingent liability is one which may or may not arise at a future date, e.g., the result of a litigation about the assessment of damages; a bill receivable which has been discounted may be dishonoured at the due date and hence become a liability because the amount will have to be paid to the banker with whom the bill was discounted. A contingent liability may or may not involve the payment of money. If the bill is honoured, the question of payment of money will not arise.

The phrase in the question indicates that Bills Receivable had been discounted during the year but at the balance-sheet date such bills amounting to Rs. 25,000 have not matured and there is a chance that they may be dishonoured at the due date. The company being the previous endorser, will, in such a case, be called upon to pay that amount to the endorsees. Thus such a liability will arise only in the event of the bills being dishonoured. Hence, such a liability is called contingent liability.

The auditor should see that the requirements of the Companies Act of 1956, regarding the contingent liabilities are complied with in the balance-sheet on the liabilities side.

The auditor should verify this liability by referring to the Cash Book, Bills Receivable Book, paying particular attention to the date of discounting the bills, date of maturity and the date of audit.

Q.40. In what way does the omission of liabilities affect (*a*) Profit and Loss Account; (*b*) Balance-Sheet?

Ans. The omission of liabilities will affect the Profit and Loss Account as well as the Balance-Sheet. The following illustrations will make the matter clear :

1. Goods might have been purchased but the account of the seller might not have been credited while the goods were taken into stock. This omission of liability will affect the revenue account as the profits will be over-stated and the balance-sheet will also be incorrect for the creditors are under-stated (*Westminster Road Construction Co.*)

2. Similarly, the workers might not have been paid for the last month of the financial year and, consequently, neither wages account was debited nor cash account was credited. This would affect the profit and loss account as profit would be over-stated and the balance-sheet will also be incorrect as liabilities are under-stated. Same is the case with salaries and other expenses.

3. If any asset has been purchased on credit and no entry has been passed, it would affect the balance-sheet. The name of the seller of the asset will not be put on the liability side of the balance-sheet and the asset will also not be recorded on the asset side of the balance-sheet.

Q.41. At the date of the Balance-Sheet, a manufacturing concern has outstanding forward contracts for the supply to it of its principal raw materials at a price substantially higher than the market price. No reference to the matter appears in the Profit and Loss Account and the Balance-Sheet presented to you for audit. What would you do?

Ans. Usually manufacturing concerns purchase raw materials to be supplied at a later date. Such forward contracts are entered into so that there may be a continuity of supply of raw materials. The rate at which forward contracts are entered into may not be the same as the rate prevailing in the market at the date of delivery.

In case of a trading concern which has entered into another forward contract for the sale of the same goods, it may not make any provision for any loss. But it is different with a manufacturing concern which does not cover the purchase by a forward sale and thus a loss may occur. Hence a provision should be made for such a loss as was recommended by the Institutes of Chartered Accountants of England, "where goods have been purchased forward and are not covered by forward sales, provision should be made for the excess, if any, of the purchase price over the market value and should be shown as such in the accounts." (*Recommendations to Accounting Principles,* Paragraph 132).

Although the presents market price is much below the forward contract price, it is also possible that the market price may go up by the date of the delivery of the goods. The loss may or may not occur. Therefore, it is a contingent loss. A note may be appended at the foot of the balance-sheet regarding this contingent loss.

But in case it appears that the fall in price is a permanent one and that there is no likelihood of the price going up, provision for reserve for such a loss must be made to the extent of the difference between the contract price and the market price on the date of the balance-sheet.

Q.42. Explain what is meant by the expression "Audit in depth" and illustrate your answer by the verification of payments made to a creditor for the goods supplied.

Ans. The Institute of Chartered Accountants of England issued a Statement on the General Principles of Auditing on 16th August, 1961, which shows the meaning of "Examination in depth" when it states : "Examination in depth" involves tracing a transaction through its various stages from origin to conclusion, examining at each stage to an appropriate extent the vouchers, records and authorities relating to that stage and observing the incidence of internal check and delegated authority. The examination in depth is sometimes called "Auditing in depth."

In simple language, the process of checking a transaction from its initial stage to its conclusion is known as "Examination in depth". It may be stated here that there is no difference between Examination in Depth and Auditing in Depth. Both the terms mean the same thing. The examination of a tranaction, of course, will depend upon the effectiveness of the internal check system in operation in business. For instance, if payment has been made to a creditor for the goods supplied, not only the cash book, receipts issued by the creditor and the counterfoil of the cheque issued will be examined as is normally done but the following documents in connection with the payment are also to be examined :—

(*a*) Order Book to see whether an order had been placed with the creditor.

(*b*) Gate-keeper's Book, if any, regarding the entry of the goods received at the premises.

(*c*) The Delivery Note to see the quantity of the goods received.

(*d*) Stock Book to see whether the goods stated in the Delivery Note had been entered in the Stock Book.

(*e*) Comparison of the invoice received from the supplier with the Delivery Note, Stock Book and the Ledger to see whether the account of the creditor had been credited with the correct amount.

It is a sound practice to reduce progressively the number of transactions selected for examinations as the depth of the examination increases.

This process of examining a transaction at its different stages from the beginning to the conclusion is known as "Examination in Depth" or "Auditing in Depth".

Q.43. What is meant by verification of assets and liabilities? What is the object of such a verification? How far is an auditor responsible for the verification of assets appearing in the balance-sheet?

Meaning of Verification

Ans. Verification means 'proving the truth', or 'confirmation.' An auditor has not only to see the arithmetical accuracy and **bona fides** of the auditor has not only to see the arithmetical accuracy and *bona fides* of the transactions in the books of account by vouching only, but has also to see that the assets as recorded in the balance-sheet actually exist. The fact that there is an entry regarding the purchase of an asset and which entry has been found to be correctly recorded, is not a proof that the asset is in the possession of the concern at the date of the balance-sheet. It is possible that after the asset had been acquired and the necessary entries made in the books of account, the asset might have been disposed of or pledged or mortgaged and no entry had been made regarding these facts in the books of account before the closing of the financial year. He has also to see whether a particular asset as recorded in the balance-sheet on the day of the closing of the books of account exists or not.

Verification of liabilities is also important as is the verification of assets. If the liabilities are over-stated or under-stated, the balance-sheet will not represent a true and fair view of the state of affairs of the company.

Auditor's duty re verification

If the auditor fails to verify the assets, he will be held liable as was decided in the case of *London Oil Storage Co., Ltd.* vs. *Sear Hasluck & Co.* (1904), when Alverston, C. J., said : "It is the duty of an auditor to verify the existence of assets stated in the Balance-Sheet and he will be liable for any damage suffered by the client if he fails in his duty ...."

Of course, it is not possible for an auditor to inspect each and every asset, e.g., stock. If this duty was imposed on him, it may take weeks and months for him to actually inspect every asset. It was held in *re Kingston Cotton Mills* case that "it is no part of an auditor's duty to take stock. No one contends that it is. He must rely on the other people for the details of the stock-in-trade in hand ......"

Thus it would appear that it is not possible to verify each and every asset. From the decisions of the courts it appears that the auditor should actually inspect certain assets like cash in hand, cash with petty cashier, investments, etc., to verify them, while assets like buildings, plant and machinery, stock, etc., need not be actually inspected as the auditor may not possess technical knowledge and, therefore, it may not be possible for him to inspect them. But in such a case if he examines the ledger accounts pertaining to these assets, depreciation account, Mortgage Register, certificate regarding Registration of Mortgages issued by the Registrar, he will be able to find out the existence and valuation of the assets.

Since the decision in the *Kingston Cotton Mills* case quoted above there has been a great improvement in the standard of audit expected of an auditor. The auditor must physically check the stock-in-trade or be present when the stock is being taken as was decided in the *Mckesson* vs. *Robbin's* case in America in 1940.

It may be stated here that it would be sufficient if the auditor inquires into the system of stock taking and examines the stock sheets and the stock book. He is not expected to physically check the closing stock.

Q.44. In the balance-sheet of a limited company the following item appears under the heading shown :—

1964 Rs.		1965 Rs.
	Capital Reserve :	
16,000	**Reserve against increased cost of materials consumed**	**19,500**

This reserve has been created by annual appropriation from profit and loss account.

You are required :

(*a*) to state exactly what you understand this item to represent and the reason for its creation;

(*b*) to state how you would verify this item;

(*c*) in regard to the 'Reserve against increased cost of materials consumed' to discuss whether, in your opinion, it is correctly shown as a capital reserve, it having been created by appropriation from revenue surpluses.

Ans. (*a*) The reserve against increased cost of materials consumed represents the amount set aside out of the profits for the stock of material consumed which had been purchased at less cost than the cost of the materials prevailing when they have been consumed because of the inflationary tendency. The step is taken during inflation as when the materials wil have to be purchased later on for further production of goods, the materials will cost more.

(*b*) The auditor can verify this reserve by referring to the minute book of the Board of Directors for creating such a reserve. He need not pay attention to the adequacy or otherwise of the reserve as it is a reserve and not a provision. The amount of the reserve is left to the discretion of the directors.

(*c*) As this reserve has been created out of profits, it would appear that this reserve is a revenue reserve and not a capital reserve and thus it can be distributed to the shareholders. But the purpose for which it has been created, it seems, it is a capital reserve as it is to be permanently retained in the business. According to Part III to Schedule VI of the Companies Act, the expression 'Capital Reserve' shall not include any amount regarded as free for distribution through the profit and loss account, and the expression 'revenue reserve' shall mean any reserve other than a capital reserve. However, if the directors think that this reserve is no more required, they may transfer it to the Profit and Loss Account and distribute it to the shareholders provided they transfer the amount from the capital reserve to the revenue account and make it clear to the shareholders.

Q.45. State how the investments by a limited company should be (*a*) valued, and (*b*) stated in the published Balance-Sheet when they are held for the following purposes :—

(*a*) Investments for the Reserve Fund;

(*b*) Interest in Subsidiary Companies for trade purposes;

(*c*) Temporary investments of working capital otherwise unemployed;

(*d*) Pledged Securities for a loan from a bank.

Ans. (*a*) Investments for the Reserve Fund.

(*i*) These Investments should be shown on the assets side of the balance-sheet and should be clearly shown that they are held against a particular Reserve Fund.

(*ii*) As regards their valuation, they should be shown at cost price. Temporary fluctuations in their value should be ignored. The important thing in such a case is their realisable value on a particular date in future. If, however, it is found that the fall in the value of the Investments is a permanent one, provision or reserve should be made and an Investment Fluctuation Fund Account should be opened and credited with the difference in the market value and the cost price. This account should appear on the liability side of the balance-sheet.

(*b*) Interest in Subsidiary Companies for trade purposes

Such assets are considered as fixed assets. They do not depreciate by use in the business. Therefore, they should be shown in the balance-sheet at cost price. They should be shown in the balance-sheet of a Company according to the *pro forma* given in the Companies Act, 1956, distinguishing the partly paid shares from the fully paid shares and shares of each individual subsidiary company must be shown separately. The mode of the valuation of these investments should also be indicated.

(*c*) Temporary Investments of working capital otherwise unemployed

If the investments represent a temporary investment of the surplus funds, they should be shown at cost price or market price whichever is lower. If the total market value of the investment is less than the total cost price, the whole of the difference may be debited to Depreciation Account and credited to Investment Fluctuation Account. Depreciation Account should be debited to the Profit and Loss Account while the Investment Fluctuation Account should be deducted from the original cost of the investments on the assets side of the balance-sheet, thus showing the net figure in the outer column. If there is any appreciation in the value of the investments, such an appreciation should be ignored. Credit may be taken only when the investment is sold out.

***(d)* Pledged Security for a Bank Loan**

Such a security should be shown at cost price.

According to the Companies Act, the aggregate amount of company's quoted investments and also the market value thereof shall be shown. Aggregate amount of company's unquoted investments shall also be shown.

The mode of valuation of investments, *i.e.,* cost price or market price should be shown. Investments should be classified in the balance-sheet according to their nature.

Q.46. State briefly how you would verify the following :—

***(a)* Cash in hand; *(b)* Cash at Bank; and *(c)* Petty Cash**

Ans. *(a)* Cash in hand

The auditor should visit the business house at the close of the financial period or on the following morning and actually count the cash in hand and compare it with the balance in hand as shown by the cash book. If there are different kinds of cash balances, e.g., petty cash balance, cash in till, etc., they should be counted simultaneously so that shortage in one account may not be made up from cash in hand from another account, i.e., one cash balance may not do 'extra duty'. He should also count cash, stamps, and I.O.U's in hand. He should make searching enquiry to find out the genuineness of I.O.U.'s. If there are cheques and drafts in hand, the auditor should see that a receipt for them has already been issued. If any advance has been made to a director or any officer of the company, an acknowledgement should be obtained.

If it is not possible for the auditor or his assistant to pay visit to actually count the cash in hand, he may pay a visit on a subsequent day and count the cash in hand and exhaustively vouch the petty cash and cash books up-to-date and compare the cash in hand with the balance as shown by the books of account. If he does not do so, he will be held guilty of negligence as was held in the case of *Registrar of Companies, Bombay,* vs. *P.M. Hegde* in 1954. In case of continuous audit, all balances should be counted frequently say at an interval of a month or so, i.e., at each visit.

Another method of verification of cash in hand is to ask his client to deposit the whole of the cash in hand including petty cash etc., into the bank on the closing day and then drawing a cheque on the following day for expenses to reopen the cash book with cash drawn from the bank. In this way whole of the cash will be automatically counted and the auditor will be saved of the cumbersome task of counting the cash in hand. The difficulty in such a case is that stamps, I.O.U.'s etc., cannot be deposited in the bank.

The auditor should preferably pay a surprise visit to count cash in hand to prevent the cashier to borrow money and make up the deficiency which was due to embezzlement in the past.

As regards cash in hand and at different branches, the auditor should get a certificate from the auditors of these branches to that effect and mention in his report that he has relied upon the certificates from the local auditors.

In respect of cash in transit reference may be made to documentary evidence which may be available. He should also see whether such an amount has been recorded in the cash book in the succeeding period.

***(b)* Cash at Bank**

The auditor should compare the balance as shown by the bank column of the cash-book with the bank pass book. It is possible that there may be difference between these balances due to several factors, e.g., cheques might have been issued but not presented at the bank; cheques might have been sent to the bank for collection but might not have been realised; the bank might have debited the client's account for interest charges, bills receivable dishonoured, etc. Under these circumstances the auditor should prepare a bank reconciliation statement.

But even if the pass book balance agrees with the cash book, it is no proof of the correctness of the bank balance as there have been cases where fictitious pass books have been presented to the auditors although it was found later on that the real pass book showed less balance. To prevent this type of fraud, the auditor will do well to get a certificate regarding the balance at the bank directly from the bank. The auditor should take this step with the permission of his client. Here again, the danger is that the cashier might borrow money to deposit the same in the bank a few days before the year closes in order to conceal the misappropriation which he had committed in the past. Thus even if a certificate is obtained from the bank, the fraud will not be disclosed as happened in the case of the *Brighten Eden and Empire Syndicate Ltd.* vs. *London and County Bank Ltd.* (1904).

The auditor should see that the cheques not yet collected are genuine and not made up in order to conceal the deficiency.

Cash in Fixed Deposit with the bank can be verified by examining the deposit receipt or getting a certificate from the banker as described above.

(c) Petty Cash

The same considerations apply as in (*a*) above. *See Answer to Question* 17 *also.*

Q. 47. State briefly how you would verify and also what evidence you would require of the value of the assets appearing in a limited company's balance-sheet :—

(*a*) A policy of life assurance held by assignment;

(*b*) A mortgage of Rs. 25,000 on freehold property;

(*c*) Patents;

(*d*) Goods on Consignment; and

(*e*) Bills Receivable.

Ans. (*a*) Life Assurance Policy

1. The policy should be examined to see tha value. The value of this form of security should not be taken as the assured sum but the surrender value of the policy—which value can be ascertained from the assurance company—should be taken as the value of the security. The reason is that if the borrower does not pay the premium, the policy will lapse and the amount payable by the assurance company at the same time will be only the surrender value as the assured sum is payable only at the death of the policy-holder provided he had been paying the premiums regularly.

2. Last receipt for the payment of the premium paid, should be examined. If the receipt is not available, the insurance policy might have lapsed.

3. He should also find out whether the notice of assignment to the assurance company had been given by the assured.

(*b*) Mortgage of Freehold Property

1. The auditor should find out from the memorandum of association whether the company can lend money against the security of landed property.
2. He should examine the loan account. If possible, he should get the amount of the loan confirmed by the borrower.
3. He should find out whether the mortgage has been properly executed.
4. If it was a second mortgage, he should enquire whether the first mortgagee had been duly informed of the creation of the second charge. He should, in such a case, find out whether the loan advanced in fulle or partly secured.
5. He should examine the title deeds relating to the property.
6. In the case of a second mortgage, the title deeds relating to the property will be the first mortgagee in which case the auditor should ask the first mortgagee whether he has got the title deeds relating to the property and see whether there is sufficient margin between

the residual value of the property and the loan. The interest payable but not paid should be added to the amount of the principal.

7. The value of the property can be verified from architect's or valuer's certificate. The amount advanced should not exceed two-thirds of the value of property.
8. He should find out the possibility of recovering the loan.
9. He should also see that the property is insured against fire and should examine the last receipt for the premium paid.
10. He should see that the mortgage is duly registered.

(c) Patents

1. The patents should be examined. If they have been purchased, the auditor should examine the assignment deeds and see that they have been registered.
2. The auditor should ask his client to prepare a schedule of the patents giving the (*i*) description of the patent, (*ii*) registered number, (*iii*) date, and (*iv*) the unexpired period.
3. He should examine the receipt for the payment of the fee for the renewal of the patent. If it has not been paid, the patent will lapse.

With the lapse of time, the patents lose their value. Therefore, the patents should be revalued at the date of the balance-sheet. Their value should be estimated according to the unexpired period. In no case they should be valued at a higher price than that at which they were purchased.

(d) Goods on Consignment

1. The auditor should ask for a certificate from the consignee to ascertain the amount of unsold stock with the consignee.
2. He should examine the Consignment Outward Book and Accounts Sales, if any, and correspondence with the consignee.
3. The unsold should be valued a cost price *plus* the proportionate expenses, e.g., freight, dock dues, customs duty, godown rent, etc.
4. The unsold stock with the consignee should never be valued at higher price than the market price of similar goods.
5. Due consideration should be paid to damaged and obsolete unsold stock with the consignee while valuing it.

(e) Bills Receivable

1. He should examine the Bills Receivable Book and the bills in hand.
2. He should enquire from the bank in respect of the bills which have been sent for collection and which have not matured at the date of the balance-sheet.
3. While examining the bills, the auditor should see that they are properly drawn, stamped and that they are not overdue.
4. Bills which have been dishonoured before the date of the balance-sheet should not be included in the 'bills receivable in hand' as they are no longer assets of the company.

Q.48. When examining the stock sheets of a manufacturing business, you notice three items which appear to you to be unusual, viz.,

(*a*) Goods on consignment outwards—valued at market price to which 5 percent has been added as representing a proportion of the profit which will be made when goods are sold.

(*b*) Goods on consignment inwards—valued at invoice price.

(*c*) Goods sold but not delivered—valued at selling price.

What special enquiries would you make in regard to each of the three cases, and if you do not agree with the methods of treatment, what would you suggest how the items should be shown?

Ans. (*a*) Goods on Consignment Outwards

Such goods should be valued at cost price, plus proportionate expenses which had been incurred for the whole consignment, e.g., customs duty, freight, etc. In no case anticipated profits should be added to the cost as has been done in the present case. If the market value of such goods has gone down, they should be valued accordingly. If it appears that the goods are unsaleable, reserve should be made for them. If the client does not agree, the auditor should refer the matter in the report. Account sale or certified copies of the stock with the consignee should be examined.

(*b*) Goods on Consignment Inwards

They should not be included in the stock sheets as they do not belong to the client. If such goods are taken in stock, profits will be inflated. Such goods should be entered in a Memoranda Book. It is immaterial to the client whether they are valued at selling price or cost price etc. Correspondence, Memoranda Book, Pro Forma Invoice, etc., should be examined.

(*c*) Goods sold but not delivered

If the contract of sale is complete, they should not be included in the closing stock. On the other hand, if they have been sold on a forward contract, they should be included in the stock sheets and valued at sale price provided there is no dispute regarding their sale.

Q.49. State how you would verify the following assets in the balance-sheet of a company :—

(*a*) Loans against the security of land;

(*b*) Loans against the security of stocks and shares;

(*c*) Loans against the security of goods; and

(*d*) Loans against the personal security of the borrower.

Ans. (*a*) Loans against the security of land

(*i*) The auditor should examine the Memorandum and Articles of Association to see whether the company is empowered to lend money against the lended property.

(*ii*) The auditor should not only examine the loan account in the ledger but he should also examine the documents relating to the security.

(*iii*) If the land or the property has been mortgaged, the auditor should examine the mortgage deed and find out whether the mortgage is properly executed.

(*iv*) If it is a second mortgage, he should see whether the first mortgagee has been informed of the second mortgage and whether he (the first mortgagee) has the title deeds relating to the property.

(*v*) The date of the mortgage should be enquired into.

(*vi*) He should enquire whether the borrower has a right to borrow money.

(*vii*) If possible he should get the amount of the loan confirmed by the borrower.

(*b*) Loans against the security of stock and shares

(*i*) The auditor should get a list of the stock and shares which have been held as security.

(*ii*) He should enquire whether such stock and shares have been transferred in the name of his client.

(*iii*) The auditor should get confirmation from the borrower regarding the amount of loan on the date of the balance-sheet.

(*iv*) The auditor should enquire whether the shares are fully paid or partly paid. As a matter of fact, partly paid shares should not be accepted as security because when partly paid shares are transferred, the transferee will be liable to pay the unpaid amount whenever the company makes a call.

(*v*) He should enquire the value of the stock and shares and the amount of the loan. There should be sufficient margin between the two.

(*vi*) He should inspect such shares and if they have been lodged with the bank for safe custody, a certificate to that effect should be obtained from the bank.

(*c*) Loans against the security of goods

(*i*) Where the loan has been advanced against a Godown-keeper's Receipt, such a receipt should be examined. If they are at docks or in bonded warehouse, the dock warrant or the warehouse certificate duly endorsed in favour of his client should be examined. In case dock warrant or warehouse certificate has been issued, delivery not in favour of his client should be examined.

(*ii*) He should see that the rent for the warehouse or godown has been paid by the borrower. If it has not been paid it should be added to the amount of the principal.

(*iii*) If the loan has been advanced against the goods in transit, railway receipt, or bill of lading together with letter of hypothecation, insurance policy and invoices as the case may be, duly endorsed in favour of his client, should be inspected.

(*d*) Loans against the personal security of the borrower

(*i*) The auditor should make an enquiry regarding the financial position of the surety, if any, as the value of the security depends on his financial position.

(*ii*) He should see that no change in the terms of the loan has been made as such a course will discharge the surety, if any, and the client loses that security.

(*iii*) Promissory Note should be examined paying attention to the date of maturity.

Q.50. A company had a large surplus bank balance. It purchased Rs. 9,00,000 worth of securities at Rs. 85. Afterwards Rs. 3,00,000 worth were sold at Rs. 80. The market price at the date of the balance-sheet was Rs. 87, and the investment appeared at Rs. 5,25, 000. How would you deal with this item?

Ans. Such investments being current assets, the formula 'cost price or market price, whichever is the lower', should be followed in valuing the investments in hand at the date of the balance-sheet.

The company sold a number of securities at a loss of Rs. 5 per security and thus suffered a total loss of Rs. 15,000. This loss should be debited to the revenude account of the year under audit.

As regards the balance of the securities in hand, at the date of the balance-sheet, they should not be valued at a higher price than the cost price, *i.e.*, they should be valued at Rs. 85 per security. They should be valued at Rs. 5,10,000 and not at Rs. 5,25,000. If the directors do not agree to this, the auditor should refer the matter in his report to the shareholders.

The auditor should vouch the purchase and sale price by referring to the Bought and Sold Notes respectively and the market quotations of the Stock Exchange. He should physically verify the security in hand.

Q.51. The Cotton Mill Company places before you their stock sheets showing the stock at the end of the year. State how you would proceed to check them and what information you would call for before including the figures of stock on the balance-sheet you are called up to sign.

Ans. The auditor has to take the utmost precautions in connection with the stock-in-hand. Following suggestions may, therefore, be adopted by him with advantage :—

1. While verifying the quantity of stock, he should find out whether the internal check system in connection with stock-taking is efficient enough to prevent any manipulation.

2. If a Stock Book has been maintained, he should compare it with the Purchases and Sales Books in regard to quantity. He should also check the Gate-keeper's Outward Book lest any fictitious sale has been entered in the Sales Book.
3. He should check the stock sheets. If he does not do so, he will be held responsible.
4. He should check the calculations, additions and castings.
5. He should check a few items in the stock sheets, especially the bigger ones.
6. He should see that the goods which have been sold but not delivered to the buyer on the stock-taking day, are not included in the stock-in-hand.
7. He should see that the goods which have been purchased and the relative invoices of which have been entered in the Purchase Book, are included in the closing stock.
8. He should see that goods received from others to be sold on their behalf are not included in the stock-in-hand.
9. He should see that assets like furniture, tools, etc., are not included in the stock-in-hand.
10. He should compare the balance as per the Stock Book and the Stock Sheets.

For the purpose of the valuation of stock of a cotton mill, the goods may be of the following categories and they should be valued accordingly :

(*a*) Raw materials; (*b*) Semi-finished goods;
(*c*) Finished goods; and (*d*) Stores.

(*a*) Raw materials

Such goods should be valued at cost price but not at a higher price. Reasonable and proportionate expenses like freight, duty, etc., may be added to the cost price of such goods.

If they have been purchased in different lots and they cannot be identified from each other, average price of purchases may be taken as the cost price of the closing stock.

(*b*) Semi-manufactured goods

It may so happen that at the date of the balance-sheet, some goods might be in the course of manufacture, *i.e.,* they, have not been completely manufactured, *e.g.,* yarn in a spinning and weaving mill. In such a case, they are valued at cost price of the raw materials used, plus a proportionate amount of wages, other manufacturing expenses, and a percentage to cover establishment charges relating to manufacture as per the certificate given by the departmental manager and as shown by the Cost Accounts. He should examine the Cost Accounts.

(*c*) Finished goods

The goods which have been manufactured by the mill, should be valued like the semi-manufactured goods as explained above, *i.e.,* the cost of the raw materials, plus proportionate expenses of manufacture and the establishment charges. He should examine the Cost Sheets. The auditor should refer to the Cost Accounts if they are maintained. He should also see that such finished goods are not valued at a higher price than the price of such goods prevailing in the market. Sometimes it so happens that the cost of manufacture is very high in the initial stages of the establishment of a factory and consequently the cost of production of such goods may be higher than the same kind of goods available in the market. As aforesaid, such goods must be valued at the lower price, viz., the market price.

(*d*) Stores

There are goods other than those described above, which may be in hand at the date of the balance-sheet. Stores are not held for sale in the original form. Such goods are oil, tallow, grease, dyes, fuel, etc. These stores must not be included in the list of the stock-in-trade. They should be shown separately.

As regards the valuation of such stores, it may be pointed out here that the general practice is that they are valued at cost price. If the market price of such stores has gone down, it is suggested by some accountants that they must be written down. There are others who say that the stores should be valued at cost price even if their market price has gone down.

Q.52. In the course of an audit you find that the item "Sundry Debtors" includes charges made for packing cases and the like.

Discuss the correctness or otherwise of this.

Ans. Where customers are supplied with packages, e.g., casks, jars, bags, etc., which they have to return, a good system of records should be maintained. It would be better if a separate column is provided in the Sales Journal for packages and empties.

It is not desirable to include the cost of these empties and packages amongst the debts owing by the debtors. These packages are with the customers and are returnable. The cost of these empties and packages is not the amount owing by the customers. Of course, when the customers do not return these empties, etc., their account may be debited. Therefore, these empties, etc., should be shown in the balance-sheet on the asset side as 'Packages and Empties with Customers' and should be valued at cost price less depreciation.

Q.53. In auditing the balance-sheet of a company, state what steps you would take to verify the Sundry Debtors and what is your duty regarding these?

Ans. The auditor should verify the debtors in the following ways :

1. He should ask his client to supply him with a schedule containing the names of the debtors and the amount due from them. Such a schedule must be certified by the Manager, Secretary or any other responsible official of the company.
2. He should check the Sales Ledger with this schedule.
3. The accuracy of the sales ledger can be checked from the subsidiary book, such as Sales Journal, Sales Returns Book, Cash Book, Journal, Allowance Book, Bills Receivable Book, etc. He should pay special attention to the credit entries in the Sales Ledger as there is a possibility of commission of fraud by passing fictitious entries regarding credit notes, cash discounts, allowances and bad debts.
4. To avoid any fraud, it would be better, if he, in consultation with his client, sends the Statements of Account to all the debtors to confirm the balance and that the replies from these debtors are sent direct to the auditor so that the clerks may not make any alteration in the statements so received. Such statements of account should be sent to the debtors under the supervision of the auditor of his assistants.
5. If the number of such debtors is very large, such letters may be sent only to major debtors, *i.e.*, debtors who owe large sums of money and who should be selected at random.
6. Either a full statement of account or only the balance owing by the debtor should be sent to the debtor concerned.
7. If no confirmation or reply is received from a few debtors after the lapse of a reasonable time, a reminder should be sent to the debtors.
8. If such letters or reminders are returned having been not delivered to the addressees the auditor should inquire whether the address of the debtors was correct and he should be very cautious in such a circumstance.

It is possible that some balances as shown by the debtors and the schedule of debtors prepared by the client may not agree. It may be due to some reasons, e.g., the debt may be under dispute between the parties or any incidental omission of an entry in the books of account, etc. However, if the balance is due to a dispute between the client and the debtor, due allowance must be made for such a balance in the books of account.

After having verified the book debts, he should ascertain their value. For the purpose of valuation of debts, he should ask his client to give him a list of the good, doubtful and bad debts. He can verify this list by applying certain tests to each account.

He should see that the book debts in the balance-sheet of the company are shown according to Schedule VI, Part I of the Indian Companies Act of 1956 as under :—

(*a*) Debts considered good in respect of which the company is fully secured;

(*b*) Debts considered good in respect of which the company hold no security other than the debtors' personal security;

(*c*) Debts considered doubtful or bad; and

(*d*) Less provision for bad and doubtful debts.

Debts due by a director or other officers of the company or any of them either severally or jointly with any other person or debts due by firms or private companies respectively in which any director is a partner or director or member, are to be separately stated.

Debts due by other companies under the same management should be indicated with the names of the companies (*vide* Section 370).

The maximum amount due by directors or other officers of the company at any time during the year should be shown by way of a note.

Q.54. State how you would value stock in trade and give reasons for the same.

Ans. Stock is a current asset and is meant for resale. The accepted basic principle of accounting is to value current assets *at cost price or the market price, whichever is the lower*. In no case should, therefore, the stock be valued at a higher price than the cost price even if the rise in the price is a permanent one. The reason is that profits are taken into account only when the goods are sold. Although on the date of the balance-sheet, the value of the stock is higher than the cost price, profit and loss account cannot be credited with the difference as the goods have not been sold as yet. Moreover, unsold stock when sold in the subsequent period after the date of the balance-sheet may not be sold at a higher price either because the prices have gone down or the goods have gone out of fashion, obsolete, etc.

On the other hand, if there is a fall in the price of the goods it must be valued accordingly. As stock is a floating asset, it must be brought into account at its realisable value at the date of the balance-sheet, if it is lower than the cost price. It may be questioned that when we ignore the realisable value of the stock which is higher than the cost price on the date of the balance-sheet, why should not the realisable value, which may be lower than the cost, be ignored in this case. It is argued the goods have been bought for the purpose of selling at a profit and if there is any probability or possibility of a loss on the date of the balance-sheet, it must be taken into account.

As the price has gone down, there is a probability or possibility of a loss during the subsequent period and it must be provided for out of the profits of the current year by bringing such stock into account at its reduced value. It must be mentioned here that even if the price has gone down due to obsolescence or staleness, that fact must be taken into consideration.

It the goods have been purchased in different lots and they can be identified as to which lots they belong to, there will be no difficulty in finding out the cost price of such stock as the invoices or the cash memos will show the cost price of different lots which have remained unsold at the date of balance-sheet. The method is known as the 'unit cost' method of valuation.

Where goods have been purchased from time to time and they are so mixed up that it is not possible to identify a particular consignment, *e.g.,* oil purchased from time to time and stored in bulk in tanks, one of the following methods may be adopted to find out the cost price of such an unsold stock :—

1. *Average price system.* The merit of this method is that violent fluctuations in the purchase price of goods are taken into consideration.
2. *Fifo system.* The whole of the stock is valued at the rate of the latest consignment purchased or up to the quantity which is in hand at the time of taking the stock on the

assumption that the latest purchases have not been sold, *i.e.,* the goods are sold in the order in which they are purchased. This method is known as *'fifo'* method, *i.e.,* 'first in, first out'. Under this system the unsold stock has a reasonably close relation to the replacement price or the price prevailing on the balance-sheet date.

3. *Lifo system.* The whole of the stock is valued at the rate at which the earliest purchases were made on the assumption that the latest purchases are sold first and the unsold stock represents the earliest purchases. This method is known as *'lifo'* method, *i.e.,* 'last in, first out'. This method does not appeal to common sense. Every business man would try to sell those goods which were received first so that they may not become stale. Another defect of the *'lifo'* method is that the stock appears in the balance-sheet which has no relation to its realisable value or replacement cost. This method is very little used in the United Kingdom but it is widely used in the U.S.A.
4. *'Base stock system'.* This system is that where it is supposed that a fixed quantity of stock is retained in the business at a fixed price like a fixed asset. It is just like the 'lifo' method.

In regard to the valuation of raw materials, semi-finished goods, finished goods, and stores, etc., *see* the answer to Question No. 51.

Q.55. What inquiries and tests should be made by an anditor to satisfy himself that at the date of the balance sheet—

(*a*) the balances on continuous stock records can be relied upon to provide accurate figures of stock quantities;

(*b*) the cost figures appearing in stock sheets are correct; and

(*c*) the valuation placed on by-products can be expected?

Ans. (*a*) Re: the reliability of the Continuous Stock Records

The auditor should follow the under-mentioned procedure to satisfy himself regarding the reliability of the balances as shownd in the stock sheets :

1. He should obtain a written statement from his client regarding the procedure for recording the stock in order to find out whether the method of the receipt and issue of stock in foolproof.
2. He should test check the entries in the continuous stock records by referring to the Order Book, Delivery Notes, Requisitions for the issue of stocks, etc. He should pay special attention to any heavy receipt or issue of stock just before the balance sheet date to find out whether the accounts have been manipulated.
3. Co-relation of stock, purchases and creditors, sales and debtors should also be examined to ensure that the accounts of the creditors have been credited when the goods have been purchased or the accounts of the debtors have been debited for the goods which have been sold and the entries have been made at the same time in the stock records.
4. He should see that the goods sold but not delivered to the customers have not been included in the stock records.
5. Similarly the goods purchased but not delivered at the date of the balance sheet should not be included in the stock records. He should also see that the accounts of the suppliers have not been credited for such goods.
6. Purchases and sales for next year should not be recorded in the stock records of the current year.

(*b*) Re: the Correctness of the Valuation of Stock

1. The auditor should inquire about the method of valuation of stock, e.g., whether it has been valued on the Lifo, Fifo, Standard Cost, Average Cost system or on any other system of valuation.

2. He should see that whatever system of valuation has been adopted, it is followed consistently year after year.
3. If there has been a change of the method of valuation, he should inquire the reason thereof and see whether it will have any effect on the profit and loss account. He should inquire the authority of such a change.
4. He should compare a few items in the stock records with the invoices.
5. He should see whether pricing of stock include such elements as direct expenses, overhead charges, etc., and if so, he should examine that such expenses have been properly allocated according to the policy of the management.
6. If some of the items of closing stock have been written down because they are slow-moving or obsolete or are damaged, he should inquire as to who ordered the writing down of such items and whether such a person has an authority to do so.

(*c*) Re: Valuation placed in By-products

1. The auditor should inquire about the system of valuation of by-products. He should verify the basis of allocating the expenses to different products to find out that no cost is charged to more than one main or by-product.
2. He should see that the valuation of these by-products is not more than its realisable value.

It may be noted here that sometimes the sale price of the by-product is treated as profit or it is deducted from the cost of the main product to fix its cost price.

Q.56. How should investments be verified and valued for the purpose of company's balancesheet?

Verification of Investment

Ans. If there are a large number of investments as in the case of banks and insurance companies, the auditor should ask for a schedule of investments held by his client. The schedule should give full particulars of the investments, e.g., name of the investment, the cost price, the market price, book value, etc., and compare those with records in the books of his client.

The auditor should examine all the investments simultaneously and compare them with the schedule. If the number of the investments is large and they cannot be inspected at one sitting, the investments which have been checked must be locked and sealed in a box so that they may not be produced again at the time of the next inspection. If these investments are held by any trustee on behalf of the company, the Trust Deed executed by such a nominee should be examined. If there is no Trust Deed, he should get a certificate from the Trustee that the latter holds those securities in trust and that they are free from any charge, and that they are in favour of the nominee or any other person. In such a case, he should advise his clients that Trust Deed should be obtained as soon as possible.

If the securities have been entrusted to the bankers for safe custody, the auditor should get a certificate from the bank that so many securities are held by it for safe custody and that they are free from any charge; but will such a certificate be sufficient in all cases? The answer is in most cases it will be sufficient but in the light of the judgement in the case of the *City Equitable Fire Insurance Company Ltd.* (1924), where a large number of Treasury Bonds were held for safe custody by the Company's Stock Brokers, who in their turn pledged these bonds, it would be better to go beyond this step. Their lordships in this case were of opinion that in all cases, an auditor should personally inspect all securities wherever or by whomsoever held.

If at all a certificate is to be accepted, the auditor should examine the date and enquire whether it is usual to deposit such securities with banks, etc., for safe custody.

If some of the securities have been sold since the date of the balance-sheet but prior to the date of audit, the auditor should vouch the proceeds either in the cash book or the bank pass book and refer to the Sold Note.

Valuation of Investments

The basis of the valuation of investments in the Balance Sheet will, to a great extent, depend upon the purpose for which they are held. If they are held by a Trust Company the object of which is to earn dividends and interest and distribute them amongst the shareholders, such investments are to be treated as fixed assets and, therefore, even a permanent fall in their value may be ignored, of course, subject to the Articles of Association and the Memorandum of Association of the Trust Company.

On the other hand, if the investments are held by a Finance Company as current assets to be sold whenever found necessary, the basis of their valuation should be cost price or the market price whichever is the lower.

For the underwriters, if they have to purchase the shares, which had been underwritten by them, the 'cost price' will be the face value, less the underwriting commission.

Q.57. Enumerate the causes of depreciation. What factors should be taken into consideration for measuring the extent of depreciation?

Ans. The causes of depreciation may be enumerated as follows:

1. Wear and tear

If a machine is used, there will be wear and tear and, therefore, naturally it will not be of the same value after some time. Therefore, depreciation is due to the use to which the asset has been put into.

2. Effluxion of time

Decrease in the value of an asset due to effluxion of time, as in the case of a lease when at the end of the period, the lease terminates, the lease becomes valueless. The premium paid for the lease is capitalised value of rent paid in advance and, therefore, it should be written off by and by during the period of lease. Same is the case with patent rights.

3. Obsolescence

This is a kind of loss on account of new inventions coming into the market. Use of such an invention will make the goods cheaper, better and in larger quantity. A businessman may, therefore, purchase the latest type of machinery and sell the old one and thus suffer some loss. This loss is the depreciation of the asset by obsolescence.

4. Exhaustion

If by using an asset, it is exhausted, e.g., a mine, where the mineral is taken out of it and ultimately the whole of the mine is exhausted, the reduction in its value is the depreciation.

Measure of Depreciation

It is not easy to measure exactly the amount of depreciation of a particular asset during the year. Only a reasonable and fair estimate can be formed. The auditor should, therefore, take into consideration the following factors while deciding the total amount of depreciation which is to be provided:

1. The original cost of the asset.
2. The additions to the asset during the year, taking into consideration the dates on which these additions were made for the purpose of calculations.
3. The interest that could be earned if the sum spent in the purchase of the asset had been invested outside.
4. The estimated efficiency of the life of the asset.
5. The scrap, break-up or the residual value of the asset.
6. Obsolescence, i.e., the chance of the asset going out of fashion.
7. Depreciation should be provided according to the Income Tax Act and the Companies Act.

Q.58. In the course of your audit of the accounts of a limited company, you find that no provision has been made for Depreciation of Plant and Machinery. The Director's objections to making any provision are that

(*a*) owing to rise in the cost of similar machinery, it is actually worth more than the book value;

(*b*) the repairs and renewals charged against revenue have fully maintained it and that it is as good as new;

(*c*) the past year had been a bad one as far as trading was concerned and that to charge depreciation would be to prevent the declaration of a dividend, cause dissatisfaction amongst the shareholders and bring about a fall in the price of the company's shares.

Criticise these objections.

Ans. (*a*) The plant and machinery is a fixed asset for a manufacturing concern. During the course of its use, there is bound to be wear and tear of the machinery. The loss in the value of the machinery has to be debited to the revenue account. The machinery in this case is not for the purpose of resale, i.e., it is not a floating asset. Hence the market value of the machinery has to be ignored. Moreover, the rise in the value of the machinery may be a temporary one and, therefore, such a rise has not to be taken into consideration. Again, the loss suffered by using the machinery is according to the original price of the machinery. The argument put forth by the directors in not providing for depreciation does not hold good. They must remember that according to Section 205, depreciation has to be provided on fixed assets before any dividend can be paid.

(*b*) Whatever the repairs and renewals may be, there is bound to be some depreciation of the plant and machinery. Heavy repairs and renewals may make the machinery more efficient and its life may be increased but depreciation is bound to be there. The value of the machinery would be reduced on account of wear and tear. Therefore, depreciation must be provided. In such a case rate of depreciation may be less. The argument of the directors does not appear to be sound.

(*c*) If the past year had been a bad one as far as trading was concerned, there is no reason why legitimate expenses (depreciation) should not be debited to the revenue account as other expenses are dealt with. Dividend is paid out of profits only according to Companies Act and, therefore, the directors are not bound to recommend the payment of a dividend when there is no profit left after debiting the amount of depreciation to the revenue account whatever the consequences may be. If the directors pay dividend without providing for depreciation, it would amount to payment of dividend out of capital in certain cases and contravention of the provisions of Section 205 of Companies Act, and therefore, the directors are liable to be punished. Moreover, if depreciation is not provided for, the assets in the balance-sheet will be over-valued and it will not represent a true and fair view of the state of affairs of the company. Therefore, the argument of the directors is unsound. Hence it is necessary, that depreciation should be provided on Plant and Machinery.

It may be pointed out that no dividend can be paid to the shareholders unless depreciation has been provided on fixed assets according to S.205 and depreciation has been provided according to Income Tax Act.

Q.59. What considerations would guide you in advising whether the amount of Depreciation Fund should be invested inside or outside the business?

Ans. The advantages of allowing the amount of Depreciation to be invested outside the business are given below:

(*a*) If the amount is invested in gilt-edged securities, capital is safe and the money will be available when required;

(*b*) A definite fixed amount of interest is earned and allowed to accumulate for a definite period when both capital and compound interest will be available for the repurchase of the asset; and (*c*) At the time of replacement of the asset, it may be difficult to withdraw money from the business as it might have been locked up in stock and fixed assets.

The disadvantages of investing the funds outside the business are:

(*a*) When money is withdrawn from the business, the working capital of the company will be reduced and will hamper the expansion of the business.

(*b*) If the amount is invested in the shares of other industrial companies, there is a danger of the investments being lost, if those companies whose shares are held, go into liquidation. Even if the amount is invested in the gilt-edged securities, there is a danger of the money being lost, e.g., during the war, the value of Government Securities fell very heavily.

(*c*) If the funds are retained in the business which is earning profit and which is more than the interest earned on securities it will be a loss, e.g., the business makes a profit of, say, 6 per cent, while interest earned on securities is 3 per cent, it is a disadvantage to withdraw the money from the business and invest it in securities provided there is scope for the expansion of business.

(*d*) If the securities fall in value, it will not be possible to raise sufficient money to replace the asset.

Under the abovementioned circumstances, it is difficult to decide whether Depreciation Fund should be invested inside or outside the business. Each case will have to be considered on its own merits.

Q.60. At a general meeting of a company, a share-holder rises and criticises the company's annual accounts as follows:–

(*a*) He objects to the fact that goodwill has appeared in the Balance-Sheet for the last ten years at the same figure and holds that it should be written down annually.

(*b*) He states that Plant and Machinery standing at Rs. 2,00,000 after deduction of depreciation is wrong because, in his opinion, it would not realise more than Rs. 1,50,000.

(*c*) He objects to premiums received on shares during the time prior to the date of the Balance-Sheet being taken to Profit and Loss Account and to the Managing Director's commission on these premiums.

Give your views on these criticisms.

Ans. (*a*) Goodwill is an intangible asset. Its value depends on the earning capacity of the business and fluctuates accordingly, i.e., it increases with the rise in profits and decreases with the fall of profits. But in practice, its value is not shown in the balance sheet according to the profits earned by the concern. As a matter of fact, it is not valued at the date of the balance-sheet like other assets. It does not depreciate even with the lapse of time.

The Company Law does not compel to show goodwill at its realisable value. It is usually shown at cost less any sum written off. Legally goodwill need not be written off, but from the sound financial point of view, it must be written off within a reasonable period out of the current profits or out of capital profits in certain cases. However, if the Articles of Association of the Company lay down that goodwill must be written down, the shareholder is right in criticising the annual accounts.

(*b*) The realisable value of the plant and machinery for a manufacturing concern is not to be taken into consideration for valuing it for the purpose of balance-sheet. It is a fixed asset and is not meant for resale. Therefore, the market value has to be ignored. However, if the difference between the book value and the market value amounting to Rs. 50,000 is due to insufficient provision for depreciation in the past, the book value of the machinery may be reduced by providing more depreciation. But this step will mean debiting the revenue account with a very large amount of depreciation in a particular year as compared with the previous years. This may amount to showing less profit or even a loss. Again the higher rate of depreciation than what is permitted by the Income Tax and Companies Acts cannot be debited to the revenue account.

(*c*) Although the premium received on the sale of shares is a profit but it is not a trading profit and hence should not be credited to revenue account. It is a kind of capital profit which cannot be distributed to the shareholders except by way of issuing bonus shares according to Section 78. According to Section 349 of the Indian Companies Act of 1956, premiums received on the sales of shares cannot be credited to the revenue account for the purpose of calculating the commission payable to the Managing Directors. Hence, the objection raised by the shareholders is reasonable.

Q.61. The directors of a company of which you are the auditor consult you regarding the charging of double depreciation during the year as no depreciation was charged last year. Write a letter giving your views and your reasons for the same, and stating if you consider it necessary to qualify your report to the shareholders.

Ans.

New Delhi

9th October, 1974

The Directors,

Star of India Manufacturing Co., Ltd.,

Lucknow.

Dear Sirs,

With reference to your letter No. 572 66, of 2nd October, 1974 we give below our views on the subject :–

If no depreciation was provided for during the past year, you must debit the revenue account of the current year with the amount of depreciation this year. Of course it would result in less profit to be distributed to the shareholders during the current year and may even result in showing a loss. This may mean the fall in the value of shares in the market and the shareholders might take into their head that the directors have become negligent or dishonest.

We may add that according to the Companies Act, as amended in 1960, if no depreciation had been provided for during the past year, it will have to be provided for during the current year according to Section 205 an extract of which we quote below for your ready reference:–

Privided that :–

(*a*) If a company has not provided for depreciation for any previous financial year or years which falls or fall after the commencement of the Companies (Amendment) Act, 1960, it shall before declaring or paying dividend for any financial year provide for such depreciation out of the profits of that financial year or out of the profits of any other previous financial year or years.

We may also point out here that you will have to transfer not more than 10 per cent of the profits to the reserve account before dividend can be paid to the shareholders.

Yours faithfully

Ranbir Singh & Son,

Chartered Accountants

Q.62. The Directors of a company made no provision for depreciation on plant and machinery in a particular year on the ground :

(1) that the cost of similar machinery has increased and that it is worth an amount in excess of that at which it stands now in the books of the company;

(2) that the year had been bad one for the company and to charge depreciation would mean that it would not be in a position to declare any dividend thereby causing discontentment amongst the shareholders and a fall in the market value of the shares in the Stock Exchange; and

(3) that the charges for repairs have been regularly made against revenue and that the company's plant and machinery have been fully maintained and are as good as new.

Do you agree with the view of the Directors? Give reasons for your answer.

Ans. *See* answer to Question No. 58.

Q.63. It is the practice of some companies to provide for reserves for repairs and renewals by creating a reserve account with equal annual instalments, debiting the amounts to Profit and Loss Account.

If, in your opinion, this is legitimate accounting, describe the circumstances which would justify the procedure and detail the facts you, as auditor, would take into consideration before passing the entries in the accounts.

Ans. Every year repairs and small renewals are to be effected in case of certain fixed assets, e.g., plant and machinery. This item appears to be an item of regular expenditure and, therefore, should be debited to revenue account. We also know that the expenditures on repairs vary from year to year. If the revenue account is to be debited whenever these expenses are incurred the expenses are not properly spread over. For instance, when the asset is purchased, it being new, the expenses on repairs will be small while the cost of repairs will be high when the asset gets old. All the years have taken equal advantage of the asset during its life-time but the revenue account of the later years will be burdened more than the initial years. Therefore, such a system of repairs should be adopted which will do justice. This is the reason why some accountants prefer the Reducing Instalment System of Depreciation according to which depreciation provided will be higher in the initial stages and the repairs and renewals will be lower as the asset will be new. Hence both the expenses, viz., depreciation and repairs, will practically be the same in the initial stages as well as in the later years of the life of the asset. Therefore, the revenue account of every year should be debited with an average sum to be spent on repairs, and Repairs Maintenance Reserve Account should be credited. The Repairs Maintenance Reserve Account should be debited and cash account credited with the actual amount spent on repairs every year. Thus, the Profit and Loss Account of every year will be debited with the same amount year after year. Any debit balance on the Repairs Maintenance Reserve Account should be written off to revenue as it shows that insufficient provision had been made for renewals in the past, and, therefore, the reserve should be increased in the future.

The auditor should see that repairs and small renewals are not capitalised. Of course, if repairs and renewals are of the nature of replacement and additions, such expenditure should be capitalised. He should also see that the amount debited to the revenue account is a reasonable one, i.e., it will be equivalent to the average expenses for repair.

Q.64. A Depreciation Fund has been started with the object of replacing an asset at the end of its life of usefulness. The annual instalments have been calculated on the basis of a growth of 5 per cent per annum of the Fund. In the course of your audit, you find that the Fund does not earn more than 4 per cent per annum. Please advise your client, in the form of a letter, as to what course of action he should now adopt.

Ans.

Delhi,
9th October, 1977

The Directors,
Bharat Engineering Works Ltd.,
Kanpur
Dear Sirs,

During the course of the audit of the books of account of your company, we found that a Depreciation Fund had been started with the object of replacing an asset at the end of the life of the asset. The annual instalments have been calculated on the basis of a growth of 5% per annum of the fund but we find that the fund does not earn more than 4% per annum. Therefore, it would not be possible to accumulate sufficient amount to replace the asset concerned unless the provision for replacement is increased so as to yield the amount required to replace the asset at the end of the life of the asset concerned. We would, therefore, suggest that more funds should be invested in the purchase of securities to replace the asset at the end of its life.

Yours faithfully,
Vijay Khosla & Sons,
Auditors.

Q.65. Describe and contrast :–

(*a*) A Reserve which is a charge against profits; and

(*b*) A Reserve which is an appropriation of profits.

Give an illustration of a reserve of each class and state how they would appear in the accounts of a limited company, and describe an auditor's duty in relation thereto.

Ans. (*i*) A Reserve which is a charge against profits is created by debiting the Profit and Loss Account for making provision for Bad and Doubtful Debts or Depreciation, etc., while a Reserve which is an appropriation of profits is created by debiting the Profit and Loss Appropriation Account for the redemption of a known liability or to strengthen the liquid resources of the company or for the equalisation of dividends or for the redemption of debentures, etc. According to S. 205, a company must transfer not exceeding 10 per cent of the profits to reserve account before it can pay any dividend to the shareholders. Such reserves are called free reserves.

(*ii*) A Reserve which is a charge against profits is created for a definite amount and, therefore, a definite sum is set aside every year to meet the known contingency while a Reserve which is an appropriation of profits is created by debiting the Profit and Loss Appropriation A/c for a known contingency without taking into consideration the exact amount required except in the case of redemption of Debentures.

(*iii*) A Reserve which is a charge against the profits is debited whenever the loss occurs while the credit balance of the Reserve which is created by debiting the Profit and Loss Appropriation A/c may be distributed amongst the shareholders except in the case of Debenture Redemption Reserve which cannot be touched before the debentures are redeemed.

(*iv*) In the case of (a) it is shown on the asset side of the balance-sheet by way of deduction from the asset concerned, e.g., Reserve for Doubtful Debt is deducted from the Sundry Debtors' Account while in the case of (b) it is usually shown on the liability side of the balance-sheet.

(*v*) In the case of (a) it is compulsory to create a reserve while in the case of (b) it is discretionary as it is a matter of financial prudence.

(*vi*) In the case of (a) it is the duty of an auditor to see that adequate provision is made to meet the loss while in the case of (b) it is left to the discretion of the Directors to make any provision or not to make any at all. The auditor need not, therefore, interfere except when the Articles definitely lay down that such a Reserve must be created or, according to the terms of the issue of debentures, a provision for redemption has to be made.

(*vii*) In the case of (a) the amount allocated for reserve does not depend upon the profits of the company. Even if there is a loss reserve has to be created. On the other hand, the amount allocated for the Reserve in the case of (b) depends upon the profits of the company. If there are no profits, no such reserve need be created.

Q.66. Distinguish between :–

(*a*) Sinking Fund for the redemption of a liability; and

(*b*) Sinking Fund for the replacement of an asset.

Ans. The following are the points of distinction between a Sinking Fund for the redemption of a liability and a Sinking Fund for the replacement of an asset:

1. Provision for (a) is made out of the divisible profits while in the case of (b), provision is made by debiting the revenue account.
2. After the liability is redeemed, the Sinking Fund is no longer required and as it is undivided profit, it may be distributed to the shareholders or may be transferred to the General Reserve Account, while in the case of (b), when the asset is replaced, the Sinking Fund no longer exists as it is transferred to the original asset to close the asset account.
3. After the expiry of the period, the gilt-edged securities are sold and the cash so realised is applied for the payment of the liability or the debentures while in the case of replacement of the asset the money realised by the sale of securities is used to replace the existing asset.

Q.67. What is a Capital Reserve? What is the duty of an auditor in relation thereto?

Ans. The term 'Capital Reserve' has not been defined by the Companies Act except negatively in the Part III of Schedule VI as "a reserve which shall not include any amount regarded as free from distribution through the Profit and Loss Account". In other words, profits which cannot be distributed in the form of dividends shall be treated as Capital Reserve. The following are some of the incomes which are credited to Capital Reserve:

1. Profits prior to incorporation.
2. The excess of the net value of the assets taken over the purchase price paid to a vendor.
3. Appreciation in the book value of the fixed assets on revaluation.
4. Share premiums, Capital Redemption Reserve Funds, etc.

The Act also does not lay down as to how this Reserve can be utilised but it may be inferred from the definition that it can be used only for writing off losses, issue of bonus shares, etc., which do not involve the distribution of dividend through Profit and Loss Account.

The following are the duties of an auditor in connection with the Capital Reserve:

1. The auditor should see that these capital profits which have been transferred to Capital Reserve Account are really surplus of capital over the assets and liabilities.
2. That the Capital Reserve is utilized according to the Article and the Company Law.
3. Capital Reserve must be shown distinctly in the Balance-Sheet. Additions and deductions since the last Balance-Sheet must also be shown.

Q.68. The Directors of a Limited Company decide for the redemption of an issue of Rs. 3,00,000 worth of 8 per cent Debentures, repayable at the end of 20 years by one of the following method :–

(*a*) By taking out a Capital Endowment Policy with an Assurance Company; or

(*b*) **By investing in gilt-edged securities annually a sum estimated to produce with compound interest and the amount necessary to pay off the Debentures at the due date.**

You are requested to submit a report placing before them the advantages and disadvantages of either of the methods.

Ans. (*a*) Capital Endowment Policy

Advantages

The followings are the advantages of taking an Endowment policy:

1. The company need not bother itself about the purchase of securities and investing the interest accrued thereon every year.
2. The company will be paid a definite sum of money for redemption of the debentures after the expiry of the period.
3. The company will get the definite sum of money at the end of 20 years even if the value of investment goes down.

Disadvantages

1. The cost of the policy is expensive as the Assurance Company will also get profit and expenses for its establishment.
2. The company cannot take advantage of the rise in the market value of the assets when the debentures are to be redeemed.

(*b*) Debenture Redemption Fund or Sinking Fund

Advantages

Money will be available for the redemption of the Debentures at the end of 20 years without disturbing in any way the finances of the company as the gilt-edged securities will be sold, money realised and paid off the debenture-holders.

Disadvantages

1. If at the end of 20 years, the market value of the gilt-edged securities falls down, it would be difficult for the company to redeem the debentures.
2. The company will have to bother itself to invest the funds every year in the purchase of the securities.
3. The company will have to invest every year the interest received on the securities.

Q.69. What are the provisions of law relating to the qualifications, disqualifications and appointment of the auditors of a company?

Ans. Qualifications of auditor

1. Only a person who is a chartered accountant within the meaning of the Chartered Accountants Act, 1949, can be appointed as auditor of a company.
2. The Central Government or the Council of the Institute of Chartered Accountants of India are empowered, according to S.4 of the Chartered Accountants Act, to recognise any foreign qualifications for the purpose of enrolment of the member of the Institute.
3. A firm whereof all the partners practising in India are qualified for appointment as aforesaid may be appointed by its firm name to be the auditor of a company and may act in the name of the firm.

Disqualifications of auditor

Section 226(3) lays down that none of the following persons are qualified to act as an auditor of a company :–

(*a*) a body corporate;

(*b*) an officer or employee of the company;

(*c*) a person who is a partner, or who is in the employment, of an officer or an employee of the company;

(*d*) a person who is indebted to the company for an amount exceeding one thousand rupees, or who has given any guarantee or provided any security in connection with the indebtedness of any third person to the company for an amount exceeding one thousand rupees;

(*e*) a person who is a director or member of a private company, or a partner of a firm, which is the managing agent or the secretaries and treasurers of the company;

(*f*) any person who is a director, or the holder of shares exceeding five per cent in nominal value of the subscribed capital of any body corporate or which is the managing agent or the secretaries and treasurers, of the company.

Note : Although the words, managing agents, secretaries and treasurers, still exist in the section, they have no meaning as the institution of such an institution has been abolished since 1970.

Appointment of auditors

1. The first auditor of a company shall be appointed by the Board of Directors within one month of the registration of the company.
2. Such an auditor shall hold office till the conclusion of the first annual general meeting of the shareholders.
3. If the Board fails to make the appointment, the company in general meeting may appoint the auditor.
4. If neither the Board of Directors not the shareholders make the appointment , the Central Government/Company Law Board shall make the necessary appointment.
5. The appointment of auditor other than the first auditor is always made by the shareholders at the annual general meeting and the auditor so appointed shall hold office till the conclusion of the next annual general meeting.
6. The company shall intimate to the person appointed as auditor within seven days of such appointment.
7. Before the appointment or re-appointment of an auditor is made by the company, a written certificate shall be obtained from him that if appointed, he shall not hold more than twenty auditorships out of which not more than ten shall be companies whose paid-up share capital is more than rupees twenty-five lakhs or more.
8. Within thirty days of the receipt of the intimation of the appointment or re-appointment, the auditor so appointed shall inform the Registrar that he has accepted or refused to accept the appointment.
9. The auditor of the following companies shall be appointed or re-appointed only a special resolution :–

Where the Central Government or a State Government or a public financial institution, nationalised banks or general insurance companies holding 25 per cent or more of the subscribed capital of the company either singly or in any combination.

The Act further lays down that if a company, does not make the appointment or re-appointment of the auditor by a special resolution, it would be deemed as if no appointment of the auditor had been made by the company at the annual general meeting. In such circumstances, the Central Government is empowered to appoint the auditor of such a company [S. 224(3)].

Re-appointment of retiring auditor

The retiring auditor, by whatever authority appointed, shall be re-appointed unless

(*a*) he is not qualified for re-appointment; or

(*b*) he has expressed his unwillingness to be re-appointed; or

(*c*) the company has passed a resolution appointing some one else instead of him; or

(*d*) a notice has been given to the company of an intention to pass a resolution to appoint another person as auditor either because of the death, incapacity or disqualification of the existing auditor.

Q.70. State the law relating to the removal of the auditor of a company.

Ans. (*a*) Only by the company in general meeting. The first auditor of the company appointed by the Board of Directors can be removed only by the general meeting of the company [S. 224 (5) (*a*)].

(*b*) Previous approval of Government. Except with regard to the first auditor, any auditor appointed under the provisions of the Companies Act, can be removed only after obtaining the previous approval of the Central Government in that behalf [S. 224 (7)].

(c) Notice for removal. If an auditor is not to be re-appointed at the annual general meeting a fourteen days notice must be given to him to enable him to defend himself.

Q.71. How are the remuneration of an auditor fixed?

Ans. (*i*) If the auditor has been appointed by the Board of Directors, it is the Board which fixes his remuneration.

(*ii*) If the auditor has been appointed by the Central Government under the circumstances mentioned in the answer to the previous question, it is the Central Government which fixes his remuneration.

(*iii*) If the auditor has been appointed by the shareholders at the annual general meeting, it is the company which determines his remuneration.

Any sum paid by the company in respect of the auditor's expenses shall be deemed to be included in the expression "remuneration."

The payments made to the auditor should be shown in detail in the profit and loss account, such as (a) payment as auditor, (b) payment as advisor, e.g., regarding tax, company law matters, etc., (c) payment in any other capacity.

Q.72. May any of the following be appointed as auditor of a public limited company?— (i) Mrs. Jones, Chartered Accountant (England), but not a member of the Institute of Chartered Accountants of India; (ii) a person of unsound mind who is a member of the Institute of Chartered Accountants of India, (iii) a Partner of a Director of the Company; (iv) a firm of Chartered Accountants of India of which the Secretary of the Company is a member.

Ans. (*i*) Mrs. Jones cannot be appointed as an auditor of a company unless she is a member of the Institute of Chartered Accountants of India and holds a Certificate of Practice.

(*ii*) Although the Companies Act is silent on the appointment of an auditor who is of unsound mind, the Chartered Accountants Act, 1949, will not enrol such a person as member. Therefore, such a person cannot be a member of the Institute of Chartered Accountants.

(*iii*) A partner of a director of the company cannot be appointed as an auditor under Section 226 (3).

(*iv*) A Secretary, being an officer of the company, the firm of Chartered Accountants whose partner he is cannot be appointed as auditor of the company.

Q.73. You are the auditor of a private company in which there are only three shareholders who are also directors. In view of bad trade, efforts are made to reduce expenses in all directions.

You are asked to accept a reduced fee and are told that it is not necessary for you to do such a full audit as you have done in the past, because the directors keep in touch with all the

transactions. Give your views on the proposal and state your position as an auditor in regard to the suggestion of the directors.

Ans. I will not agree to the suggestion of the directors. It is immaterial whether the company is a private or a public limited company. The statutory duties of an auditor cannot be restricted as was held in the case of *Newton* vs. *The Birmingham Small Arms Co., Ltd.*, (1906). In accepting their suggestion, I will be running a great risk. I should rather resign than accept the suggestion of the directors.

Q.74. (*a*) Can an auditor once appointed for a particular term be removed during the currency of the term and in the event of his removal as such would he be entitled to any fee?

(*b*) Has an auditor (duly appointed) any lien on the books of the company for his fees?

Ans. (*a*) Yes. The first auditor of the company appointed by the Board of Directors can be removed by the general meeting of the Company. Section 224 (5) (a).

If the auditor has been appointed by the directors to fill a casual vacancy he can be removed if the shareholders pass a resolution to that effect.

It must be remembered that if an auditor is to be removed in this case, sanction of the Central Government is necessary as per Section 224 (7) except in the case of the first auditor of a company.

An auditor who is removed before the expiry of his term is entitled to get his full fee provided he had actually commenced the audit work before his removal. But if an auditor resigns before the term of his appointment expires, he is not entitled to get any fee unless it could be proved that failure to do the audit work was due to the fault of his client.

(*b*) The right of lien of an auditor is a disputed one. It would appear that an auditor who has done some work on the books of account must have the right to exercise lien as a tailor who has stitched a suit has such a right. But this is not the case with an auditor. The statutory books must be kept at the head office of a company for inspection by the public and the shareholders. If the books of account are removed by the auditor who has exercised the right of lien, the object of keeping them at the head office will be frustrated. It has been definitely held that an auditor has got no lien on the books of account which he has audited. But an accountant who has done accountancy work in writing these books has been given the right of lien. In the case of *Herbert Alfred Burligh* vs. *Ingram Clark Ltd.*, it was decided that the auditor had no lien on the books of accounts in respect of the audit work.

Q.75. You have been approached by the directors of a public limited company, which has been in existing for some time past, with a view to your name being proposed as the auditor of the company. They inform you that the existing auditor will not seek re-appointment at the forthcoming annual general meeting. You are requested to state, what, if any, steps you would take before agreeing to your name being proposed for appointment as auditor.

Ans. Before the auditor gives his consent to his name being proposed for the appointment in place of an existing auditor.

1. He should ascertain whether the existing auditor had actually given his consent in writing to retire from the company.
2. If the existing auditor has voluntarily agreed to retire, the auditor should inquire from the existing auditor the reasons of his retirement; it may be that the management was not co-operating with him while performing his duty or his audit fee was not paid in time or the audit fee was being reduced, etc.
3. He should get in writing from the existing auditor whether the latter had any objection in accepting the offer of appointment.
4. He should inquire whether a fourteen days notice required under S.225 (2) to the retiring auditor had been given that he would not be re-appointed.

5. He should also ascertain that he is not being offered lower fee than what was being paid to the existing auditor; if he accepts lower fee, he would be guilty of professional misconduct.
6. He should also see that he does not hold twenty auditorships of other companies.

Q.76. What preliminary work would you as auditor do before commencing the regular audit of a newly started limited company?

Ans. Before I commence the audit of a newly started company, I would pay attention to the following:

1. Whether my appointment is in order. I would ask the directors to send to me the copy of the resolution appointing me as the auditor. I would inform the Registrar within thirty days of the receipt of the letter of appointment that I have accepted the offer to act as the auditor of the company.
2. I would ask the directors to give me a list of the books maintained by the company.
3. I would get a list of the officers together with the specimens of their signatures.
4. I would examine the Memorandum of Association of the Company with a view to find out whether the company is carrying the business according to its "Object Clause", whether the issue of share capital is within the "authorised capital", and anything which effects the accounts.
5. I would examine the Articles of Association of the company with a view to find out (a) the commission payable to the brokers or underwriters on the sale of shares, (b) the minimum subscription, (c) the dates on which the call can be made and the amount thereof, (d) whether interest can be paid on calls paid in advance, (e) circumstances under which shares can be forfeited, (f) borrowing powers of the company, (g) the amount which must be carried to reserves, (h) appointment, remuneration and duties of the auditors in addition to the statutory powers and duties, (i) appointment, remuneration and duties of the managing directors, directors, etc. (j) the method of convening the meeting and the voting powers of the shareholders, (k) rules and regulations about the accounts and audit, etc.
6. I would examine the prospectus of the company.
7. I would also inspect the contracts which have been entered into by the company with others, e.g., the vendors of any property, the under-writers and brokers for their commission, promoters for the preliminary expenses, etc.
8. I would inspect the minute books of the Board of Directors and the shareholders to vouch the issue of capital, allotment of shares, calls made by the company, forfeiture of shares, issue of debentures, declaration of dividends, etc.

Q.77. When conducting the audit of a limited company, how would you check the items of

(*a*) forefeited shares, (*b*) shares issued at a premium,
(*c*) shares issued at a discount, and (*d*) shares issued for consideration other than cash?

Ans. (*a*) Forfeited Shares

The auditor should examine the following:

(*i*) The Articles of Association should be examined to ascertain the circumstances under which the shares can be forfeited and whether the circumstances justified the forfeiture. Shares can be forfeited only for non-payment of a call otherwise the forfeiture would be illegal as was held in the case of *Hopkinson* vs. *Mortimer, Harley & Co.*, 1917. In India, however, Das, J., in a Calcutta case after an exhaustive review of authorities, both Indian and English, held that the Indian Companies Act sanctions forfeiture of shares generally, that is to say, as a means to get rid of a member who is in default, either in payment of calls or observing or performing other rules and regulations of the company. (R.H. Pandia, *The Companies Act,* 1956).

(*ii*) He should enquire whether due notice, according to the Companies Act, was given to the defaulting shareholders.

(*iii*) The minute book of the Directors should be examined to find out whether a resolution forfeiting the shares was duly passed.

(*iv*) He should see that the returns relating to the re-allotment are filed with the Registrar if the forfeited shares have been re-issued.

The auditor should find out how the amount received on the forfeited shares has been utilized. According to law this amount should be carried to Capital Reserve Account as it is a capital profit (Part I, Schedule VI of Companies Act). It should be shown on the liabilities side of the balance sheet.

(*b*) Shares issued at a premium

The auditor should examine the Prospectus, the Articles and the Minute Book of the directors to see whether the shares could be issued at a premium and if so, at what rate. He should examine the bank pass book about the receipt of the premium.

The amount received as premium on the issue of shares should not be credited to profit and loss account as it is not a trading profit and, therefore, should not be credited to revenue account. Such a premium, being in the nature of capital profit, may be utilised in writing down fictitious assets like preliminary expenses, brokerage or underwriting commission on issue of shares or debentures or issue of bonus shares, etc., according to Section 78 of the Companies Act.

(*c*) Shares issued at a discount

Generally speaking, the shares cannot be issued at a discount but according to Section 79 of the Companies Act, a Company may issue shares at a discount under the following conditions:–

(*a*) such an issue is authorised by the shareholders in the general meeting by a resolution specifying the rate of discount which should not exceed ten per cent and is sanctioned by the Company Law Board,

(*b*) the share can be issued within two months from the date of the sanction of the Court, or within such extended time as the Company Law Board may prescribe;

(*c*) the rate of discount is to be fixed by the shareholders but it should not exceed 10% or at higher percentage as may be permitted by the Company Law Board;

(*d*) such discount must be shown on the face of the Balance-Sheet until it is written off;

(*e*) the shares to be issued at a discount are of a class already issued; and

(*f*) such an issue can take place only after a year after the commencement of the business by the company.

(*g*) bonus shares can be issued according to the Companies Act and the rules made thereunder.

The auditor should see that the shares have been issued at a discount according to the above conditions. It is not legally compulsory to write off the discount but it is considered expedient to do so as early as possible. Receipt of cash in connection with the issue of shares may be vouched as usual. Such shares should be shown in the balance-sheet at their nominal value.

(*d*) Shares issued for consideration other than cash

(*i*) If the shares have been issued to the vendors, the auditor should examine the contract entered into between the company and the vendors. He should also examine the Directors' Minute Book regarding the allotment of such shares. He should see that the returns regarding such shares have been filed with the Registrar.

(*ii*) If the shares have been allotted to the underwriters, he should examine the contract with the underwriters, the prospectus, the Articles of Association, the minute book of the directors, etc., in order to ascertain the commission payable.

(*iii*) If the shares have been allotted to the promoters or the shareholders of the company which has been taken over, he should examine the contract, minute book, etc., to find out the particulars.

(*iv*) If the shares have been allotted to the existing shareholders of the company as Bonus Shares, he should examine the Articles of Association as to whether such shares can be issued and if so under what circumstances. He should examine the minute books of the Board of Directors, Shareholders, etc. He should see that there is sufficient unissued capital to enable the company to issue more shares.

The auditor should see that the copies of the contracts with the vendors, promoters, etc., to whom such shares have been issued, have been field with the Registrar of Companies. If such a contract is not in writing, the auditor should find out whether the Registrar has been informed of such contracts.

Q.78. State four matters to which you, as auditor, would be likely to refer in the Articles of Association of a limited Company?

Ans. The following are some of the matters to which the auditor may have to refer to the Articles of Association of a Company:–

1. The various classes of share capital, the respective rights of these classes of shares and the manner in which these rights may be varied.
2. The powers and duties of the directors, provision as to their remuneration, and their rotation and their disqualifications.
3. The provision regarding the payment of dividend, e.g., whether or not the power is given to distribute surplus on the realisation of the company's fixed assets or provision regarding the transfer to the reserve account, etc.
4. Any limitation on the company's borrowing powers and the power of the directors to pledge the company's property as security for debentures and other loans.

Q.79. In what circumstances does an auditor of a Company find it necessary to qualify his report to the members of the company?

Ans. Whenever the auditor of a company is not satisfied with any explanation and information given to him, or if he thinks that the profit and loss account and the balance-sheet do not exhibit a true and fair view of the state of the company's affairs or if the accounts presented by the directors call for further elucidation, he must ask the directors to set the matters aright and if he is unsuccessful in persuading the directors to do so, he must mention that fact in his report. Such a report is called "Qualified Report" as distinct from a "Clean Report."

A qualified report may be in respect of the following matters and the auditor should use appropriate words or phrases:

(*a*) Insufficient provision has been made for depreciation.

(*b*) No provision for depreciation has been made on fixed assets on the ground that the assets have been efficiently maintained by heavy repairs and renewals.

(*c*) Inadequate provision has been made for Bad and Doubtful Debts.

(*d*) Investments have been valued at cost price which is in excess of the market price.

(*e*) The stock-in-trade has been valued at market price which is more than the cost price.

(*f*) There is a contingent liability in respect of bills discounted amounting to Rs. 1,00,000 which have not matured.

(*g*) No provision has been made for taxes payable to the extent of Rs. ......

There may be so many other points. If the auditor wishes to report on any of these points, he should write a separate report below the balance-sheet:

"The Balance-Sheet and the Profit and Loss Account of the ... Co., Ltd., above set forth and dated .... 19 ..... should be read in conjunction with my report to the shareholders dated ....19..... attached herewith."

Q.80. You are appointed auditor of a newly incorporated public company and are instructed to examine the books for the purpose of certifying the Statutory Report of the company. State the particulars that you are required to certify under the Companies Act, and the steps you would to verify them.

Ans. The directors of a newly started company have to forward to the shareholders and the Registrar, twenty-one days before the holding of the Statutory Meeting, a report called the Statutory Report. Among other things, the report should contain the following:

1. Number of shares allotted as fully or partly paid.
2. The amount received in respect of such shares.
3. The number of shares which have been allotted for consideration other than cash and the consideration thereof.
4. An abstract of cash receipts in respect of shares, debentures and other sources and payments thereout, up to seven days before the submission of the Statutory Report.

The auditor has to certify the report so far as it relates to the shares allotted by the company and to the cash received in respect of such shares and to the receipts and payments of cash.

The auditor has to give a certificate in connection with the report as follows:

"I hereby certify that the part of the above Report which relates to the shares allotted by the Company, and to the cash receipts in respect of such shares, and to the receipts and payments of the company is correct.

Vijay Dhawan
Chartered Accountant

In certifying the number of shares allotted, and cash received, and payments made thereout, etc., he will have to examine the following:

(*a*) The Memorandum of Association.
(*b*) The Articles of Association.
(*c*) The Prospectus.
(*d*) The Cash Book.
(*e*) Bank Pass Book.
(*f*) The Minute Book of the Board of Directors.
(*g*) The contracts entered into with vendors, brokers, and underwriters.
(*h*) The Application and Allotment Books, Register of Share-holders, etc.

From the above stated facts, it would be seen that an auditor has to certify the receipts and payments in connection with the issue of shares, debentures and brokerage and underwriting commission, which has to be incorporated in the Statutory Report. He should therefore vouch the receipts and payments as usual.

Q.81. How should profits earned by a limited company prior to incorporation be treated in its accounts?

Ans. Sometimes the promoters or directors of a company enter into contract with the vendors of a business which has been purchased as from a date before the company was incorporated. Such a profit called 'Profits prior to incorporation' cannot be legally distributed in the form of dividends as the company cannot earn anything before it is incorporated. Such profits are, therefore, carried to Capital Reserve and can be utilised in the following ways:–

1. In the payment of interest, if any, which was to be paid to the vendors for the purchase price. The interest is to be calculated only up to the date of incorporation.
2. The balance of such a profit, if any, may be utilized in wiping off goodwill, if any, which has been taken over from the vendors.
3. The remaining balance, if any, may be utilized in writing down fixed assets.
4. If there is still a surplus of the profit, it may be carried to a capital reserve which is not available for distribution, until the company goes into liquidation.

In regard to the computation of the "Profit prior to Incorporation", in case the final accounts had not been prepared, the following methods have been suggested:–

(*a*) Gross profit on the basis of turnover.

(*b*) Direct expenses such as advertising, commission, etc., on turn over basis;

(*c*) Indirect expenses, e.g, salaries, rent, taxes, etc., on the basis of the time, i.e., period prior to and after incorporation.

The auditor should examine the methods of apportionment of such profits. He should see that such profits are not distributed to the shareholders as they are in the nature of capital profits.

Q.82. As auditor of a limited company, you are asked by the directors whether you think they would be justified in paying as interim dividend. What points would you take into consideration in advising the directors?

Ans. Interim Dividend is a dividend which is paid before the Final Dividend is declared or it is a dividend which is paid in between the two final dividends. It is a dividend which is paid between the two annual general meetings. It is paid when the directors think that they have made sufficient profit for such a dividend to be paid.

I would take the following points into consideration while advising the directors to pay an interim dividend:

1. Whether the Articles of the company permit the payment of such a dividend. If the Articles are silent, I would suggest that a special resolution must be passed to alter the Articles permitting the company to pay interim dividend.
2. Whether interim accounts have been prepared to find out the profits available for distribution.
3. Whether necessary adjustments, such as reserve for bad and doubtful debts, depreciation, etc., have been made before arriving at the figure of the profits.
4. If the turnover and the gross profits have been constant for the previous few years, interim dividend may be declared, even without the preparation of interim accounts on the basis of the previous records. In such a case, estimate of the profit should be on conservative basis.
5. I would ask the directors to take into consideration the general conditions and prospects of the trade, orders in hand, any seasonal element in business before advising payment of interim dividend.
6. I would also bear in mind that the proposed rate of interim dividend is lower than the expected rate of final dividend because if the final dividend is lower than the interim dividend, the value of the shares in the market might go down.
7. I would suggest that the cash account should not take the place of profit and loss account, i.e., if there is more cash in hand, it should not be assumed that the company has made a large profit.

8. The directors should also take into account the cash in hand. If cash is insufficient, the dividend should not be declared. If dividend is paid in such a case, working capital would be reduced thereby.
9. If it is desired to expand business, interim dividend should not be paid.

Q.83. The directors of a trading company present to their shareholders a statement of cash receipts and payments and on the strength of the excess shown thereby, they resolve to distribute the whole of such surplus in dividends. Criticise their action and point out the risk they run in looking upon such excess as profits available for dividend.

Ans. The directors are running a great risk if they resolve to pay dividend on the basis of an excess of cash receipts over cash payments. If there is a large amount of cash in hand, it does not mean that the company has made a large profit which justifies the payment of dividend. A large cash balance in hand may be due to the following:–

(*a*) Some fixed asset might have been sold for cash and that asset might not have been replaced.

(*b*) Goods might have been purchased on credit instead of cash basis as had been done in the past.

(*c*) Debentures might have been issued and the money so received might not have been utilized.

(*d*) Money might have been borrowed for some project but might not have been utilized.

(*e*) No account might have been taken of the stock, debtors and creditors at the beginning and at the end of the interim period.

In fact a receipt and payment account does not take the place of profit and loss account as no account has been taken of depreciation reserve for bad and doubtful debts, etc. It may be possible that a large cash balance in hand goes side by side with a trading loss. Similarly a small cash balance in hand may exist even though the company has made a large profit. To declare a dividend on the basis of cash in hand is a risky proposition as it may result in the declaration of dividend out of capital.

Under the circumstances explained above, I would not advise the directors to declare a dividend on the basis of surplus of cash in hand.

Q. 84. If a company's accounts show sufficient profits to pay dividend which the directors have duly declared but the cash balance is insufficient to pay the dividend, what would be your attitude as auditor? State the expedients of overcoming such shortages of funds.

Ans. The auditor should enquire as to the cause of insufficient cash which fact prevents the directors from paying dividend which has been declared in spite of there being sufficient profit. Insufficiency of cash under the circumstances may be due to the following causes:

1. (*a*) Inflation of stock-in-trade by over-valuation or including fixed assets in stock.
(*b*) Fictitious sales.
(*c*) Under-valuation or omission of liabilities.
(*d*) No provision or inadequate provision for depreciation.
(*e*) No provision or inadequate provision for bad and doubtful debts.
(*f*) Omission of purchases, etc.

2. Expenditure might have been incurred on the purchase of fixed assets for expanding the business.

Shortage of cash under (1) above shows that the profits shown are not actual profits and there can be no question of payment of dividend.

In case the insufficiency of cash in hand is due to the clause (2) above, there is no harm if the company raises loans in order to enable it to pay dividend. The following methods may be adopted to overcome the shortage of funds:

(*a*) To borrow money from the bankers of the Company.

(*b*) To issue debentures.

(*c*) To issue more shares provided there is sufficient unissued capital.

(*d*) To issue bonus shares to the shareholders instead of paying the dividend in cash but since the dividend has already been declared, it has to be paid in cash and not in scrips.

The method to be adopted will depend upon the circumstances of each case. The question does not make it clear whether the shortage of the cash is a temporary phase or money has been sunk in permanent expansion of business.

Q.85. Is it essential that dividends be paid in cash? If not, what conditions, and in what form, may they be paid?

Ans. Dividends must be paid only in cash, according to Section 205(3). If the Articles so provide, a company, if it has made profit, may issue fully paid-up shares or paying up any amount for the time being unpaid on any shares held by members of the company. No dividend can be paid unless the company has made profit during the financial year. It may also do so out of the profits of the previous years after providing for depreciation. A company may also pay dividends in the form of Bonus Shares when there is insufficient cash although the Company has made profit or when the company wants to expand business and thus capitalises the profit earned.

According to Section 205(3) of the Companies (Amendment) Act, 1960, no dividend shall be payable except in cash provided nothing in that Section shall be deemed to prohibit the capitalisation of profits or reserves of a company for the purpose of issuing fully paid-up bonus shares or paying up any amount for the time being unpaid on any shares held by the members of the company.

The auditor should consider the following points when requested to advise the company for the issue of Bonus Shares:–

1. Profits in future should be enough to enable the company to pay the same rate of dividend to the shareholders of the company in spite of the increased amount of capital by the issue of Bonus Shares.
2. That there is sufficient authorised unissued capital to enable the company to issue Bonus Shares over and above the shares which have already been issued by the company.
3. If there remains no unissued capital, a resolution may be passed altering the Memorandum to increase the Authorised capital of the company.
4. Dividends are usually payable in cash but if they are to be paid in the form of Bonus Shares the Articles will have to be altered to enable the company to do so.

Any dividend payable in cash has to be paid by cheque or a warrant sent through the post directed to the registered address of the shareholders entitled to the payment of the dividend.

Q.86. State the law regarding the treatment of unclaimed dividends.

Ans. Unclaimed Dividends

If the dividend has been declared but some of the shareholders have not claimed the money, the amount so unclaimed shall be transferred to the "Unclaimed Dividend Account".

If the company after having declared a dividend, has not paid or has not posted the Dividend warrants for forty-two days, such unpaid dividend together with the unclaimed dividends by the shareholders, must be deposited in a scheduled bank in a separate account called "Unpaid Dividend Account of .... Co., Ltd.", within seven days after the expiry of the period by which the dividend ought to have been paid. If the company fails to deposit the unclaimed or unpaid dividend to a separate account, as aforesaid, it will have to pay interest at 12 per cent and also be liable to be fined at rupees five hundred per day till the default continues. However, the company will not be entitled to the interest on the balance of the unclaimed dividends with the scheduled bank. The Government is entitled to the interest so earned.

Untill the unclaimed dividends are paid, they must be shown as the liability of the company in the balance sheet.

Whatever amount remains unpaid or unclaimed after the expiry of three years from the date of such a transfer to the scheduled bank, it should be transferred to the general revenue account of the Central Government from which it may be claimed by the person entitled thereto as provided by S. 205-B, i.e., an application will have to be made by the shareholder concerned to the company which will forward it to the Government for necessary payment.

The auditor should see that the above requirements are completed before the unclaimed dividends are paid to the shareholders.

Q.87. What are "Contingent Liabilities"? Give examples of different types of such liabilities and how they should appear in a company's balance-sheet? What would be your duty as auditor in connection with these liabilities?

Ans. A Contingent Liability is one which is not an actual liability on the date of the balance-sheet. Though it is not an actual liability on the date of the balance-sheet, it may become an actual liability later on, on the happening of an event which is not certain. Such a liability may be due to past dealings or action which may or may not become a legal obligation. The uncertainty as to whether there will be any legal obligation differentiates a contingent liability from an actual liability. A contingent liability may or may not involve the payment of money. Examples of contingent liabilities are given below:

1. *Bill Receivable discounted but not matured.* A company might have discounted a bill with its bankers, a few days before the closing of the books of account. Supposing at the date of maturity, which is after the balance-sheet has been prepared, the bill is dishonoured, the company will be liable to the bankers. This liability of the company has become actual liability although on the balance-sheet date, the company was not sure as to whether the bill will be met or dishonoured. Hence such a liability on the balance-sheet date was a contingent liability.
2. *Guarantee given on behalf of others.* A company might have given a guarantee for the payment of the principal and interest in respect of debentures issued by its subsidiary company. Supposing the subsidiary company commits a default in the payment of the debentures at the due date, the company having given a guarantee, will be liable for the payment to the debenture-holders. On the date of the balance-sheet, such a liability is contingent liability.
3. *Law suits pending against the company.* A company may have law suits pending against it at the date of preparing the balance-sheet. The company does not know whether the case would be decided in its favour or against it. The company may or may not have to pay damages. It is a contingent liability on the date of the balance-sheet but it might become an 'Actual Liability' later on, if the court gives judgement against the company.
4. *Arrears on Cumulative Preference Shares.* Such a liability depends upon the profits available next year. If sufficient profits are available next year, the company will have to pay the arrears of the dividends to the Cumulative Preference Shareholders when it would become an 'actual liability' but at the balance-sheet date, it would be a contingent liability.

The above contingent liabilities would appear as a note on the company's balance-sheet as under:–

The company is under a contingent liability:

1. in respect of a bill discounted, amounting to Rs.....
2. in respect of guarantee of principal and interest for Rs. .... 3½% Debentures of XYZ Co., Ltd.
3. in respect of claims against the company for breach of contract but not admitted by the company, which claims are the subject of a law-suit.
4. in respect of arrears on Cumulative Preference Shares amounting to Rs. ....

Each of the above contingent liability will be verified as follows:

1. *Bill Discounted.* Examine Bills Receivable Book, Cash Book, paying particular attention towards the date of the maturity of the bill. If any information has been received that the bill has been paid it is not a contingent liability any more. If there is any possibility of the bill being dishonoured at the due date, sufficient reserve should be created.
2. *Guarantee on behalf of others.* Documentary evidence such as the Guarantee Deed, Correspondence, etc., should be examined. Memorandum of Association and Articles should be examined to see the powers of the directors to give such a guarantee. The minute book of the directors should also be examined to find the amount of guarantee. The age of the debtor and his financial position should be examined. Pay attention to the date of the termination of the guarantee. See whether it is a continuing guarantee. Whether any security has been lodged with the client.
3. *Claims against the company not acknowledged as debts.* The auditor should examine the contracts, correspondence, minute book of the directors to find out the nature of the dispute and the claim.
4. *Arrears on Cumulative Preference Shares.* The Memorandum and the Articles of the company should be examined to find the nature and the percentage of dividend to be paid to the Preference Shareholders. The minute book of the directors should be examined in respect of the years for which the dividends have not been paid to such shareholders.

Q.88. During the course of an audit you come across the following matters. State how would you deal with them.

(*a*) The directors hand you a list of the work they want you to carry out stating that it is not necessary for you to do any thing outside the list to certify the balance-sheet and accounts.

(*b*) The Articles of Association provide that any voucher signed by two directors shall be evidence of payment chargeable against the company and shall be accepted by the auditors as such.

(*c*) At a meeting when a proposal to buy another business for cash was approved and subsequently carried out, was later on found that a quorum was not present.

(*d*) The minute book is in the form of a loose leaf book, the Chairman signing the last page of the minutes of each meeting.

Ans. (*a*) An auditor has to certify that the profit and loss account and the balance-sheet represent a true and fair view of the state of the affairs of a company. For that purpose he has the power to have access to all the books of accounts, vouchers, correspondence, etc. Unless he examines the necessary books, etc., he cannot give such a certificate. If he does not examine any book or voucher, etc., and later on if it is found that an error or fraud had remained undetected he would be held guilty in the performance of his duty. Therefore, it is necessary that he should examine any and everything pertaining to accounts. If he meets with the wishes of the directors to omit vouchers, books, etc., from checking he would be running a great risk. Moreover, according to the Companies Act, the scope of the work of the auditor can be increased but cannot be reduced as was decided in the case of *Newton* vs. *The Birmingham Small Arms Co., Ltd.*, (1906). Hence, the auditor should not agree to the proposal of the directors.

(*b*) The Articles of Association of a company cannot impose any restriction on the statutory duties of an auditor. According to the Articles, the auditor should accept a voucher signed by two directors as a proof of the payment which procedure is fundamentally wrong. The Articles are, therefore, void and the auditor should ignore such a regulation.

(*c*) If the transaction is correct but the quorum was not complete when the proposal was approved at the meeting of the Board of Directors, the auditor need not object to such an irregularity.

(*d*) The minute book and the method of signing it is not satisfactory. Any leaf of the book may be removed and a new one substituted. Thus, it may not be an authenticated record as was decided in the case of *Hearts of Oak Insurance Company Ltd.* vs. *Flower* (1935). Therefore, the auditor should not accept such a minute book as authentic one. If at all a loose-leaf minute book is used every page must be signed by the chairman.

Q.89. A firm of auditors accepts two audits, one that of a partnership firm and the other of a public joint-stock company. Is there any difference in principle between the two audits? Indicate the directions in which such divergence lies and briefly describe how the duties of auditors are affected thereby.

Ans. The following are the points of distinction between the audit of a partnership firm and a public joint-stock company:

1. The audit of a partnership firm is not compulsory while the audit of a public company is compulsory under the Companies Act.
2. The auditor of a partnership firm need not hold those qualifications which an auditor of a public company must hold under Section 226 of the Companies Act, 1956.
3. The duties, powers, rights, liabilities, etc., of an auditor of a partnership firm are not defined by the Partnership Act but they depend upon the agreement between the firm and the auditor and the law of agency, while in the case of a public company they are defined by the Companies Act, 1956.

Duties of an auditor of a partnership will, therefore, depend upon the agreement while in the case of an audit of a Joint Stock Company these will depend upon the Companies Act.

Q.90. "The character and the structure is one of the factors that determine the scope of audit". Explain the significance of this statement by reference to the requirements of a co-operative society and a joint stock company.

Ans. The auditor has to report to the shareholders whether the accounts show the true and fair view of the state of affairs of the concern. For that purpose, he must define the scope of the audit that he considers necessary to carry out. In order to determine the scope of his audit, he has to take various factors into consideration. For instance, he has to consider the nature and character of the management of the concern. Every concern has its own character and structure of the management and that is why the scope of his audit work will be different in different concerns.

The character of management would imply the determination of the fact as to how far there is separation of management, with the ownership. In the case of proprietary concerns, the proprietor himself manages the entire show and therefore, the scope of his audit would definitely be different from the scope of the audit of a concern like a joint stock company. In the case of a joint stock company, the management is the trustee and agent of the shareholders. The management manages the concern on their behalf. The auditor while drafting the audit programme must keep in view that no transaction entered into by the company is prejudicial to the interests of the shareholders. The management must not take undue advantage of its position at the cost of the company. Again, the work at lower level is carried out by the hired employees who may not care much in the interests of the company. The auditor, therefore, must be very careful while examining the transactions. But he must not go into detail checking and may apply test checks in the case of a big company where there is an efficient system of internal check and control.

But if, on the other hand, it is a co-operative society, the work would normally be carried out by the members themselves, i.e., the proprietors themselves. In such a case the management and the owner are almost the same. There would be less possibility of fraud and dishonesty at lower level. If, however, it is a big co-operative society, the shareholders will not manage the affairs of the society. The work could be carried out by hired employees. In such a case, the character of the co-operative society will be the same as that of a joint stock company. The only difference will be that the auditor will have to draft his report according to the directions of the Registrar of Co-operative Societies and the pro forma set out by the Co-operative Department. Thus the character of the management definitely affects the scope of the audit work that should be carried out to make the report to the members.

The structure of the management would also affect the scope of the audit that would be carried out. The structure of the management will include the delegation of powers, e.g., who is authorised to sign cash vouchers; who is authorised to sign petty cash vouchers; who is authorised to sanction the capital expenditure; who is authorised to place orders for goods and so on. In the case of a joint stock company certain things have to be sanctioned by the shareholders, others by the directors while in some cases the managing directors are empowered to do the things. Still in some cases the sanction of the Central Government is necessary. In the case of co-operative societies, the advance of loans depends upon the bye-laws of each society and sometimes the maximum limit for the loan is fixed by the Registrar of Co-operative Department. In the case of banking companies, the Banking Regulation Act, 1949, defines the scope while in the case of insurance companies, it is the Insurance Act, 1938, which defines the scope of the work of an auditor. Thus all these things will affect the scope of the work of the auditor.

We may, therefore, conclude that the character and the structure of management is one of the factors that determine the scope of audit.

Q.91. "The auditor of an individual or a firm has no statutory obligation to comply with." Discuss briefly the implications and limitations of this statement.

Ans. The auditor of an individual or a firm is not appointed under any Act and hence his duties and liabilities are not laid down by any statute. He is appointed under an agreement between him and his client. His duties and liabilities are, therefore, laid down in the agreement and if he commits a breach of any of the terms of the agreement he is liable to pay damage for any loss which his client might have suffered due to such a breach.

On the other hand an auditor of a joint-stock company has certain duties, liabilities and responsibilities which are laid down in the Companies Act. If an auditor enters into an agreement with the company that he would not perform a duty which is imposed upon him by the Companies Act, such an agreement would be void.

The statement in question is not quite correct. For example, if the auditor of an individual or a firm is negligent in the performance of his duty, he would be liable under tort or the Contract Act. Therefore, we may say that to some extent he is under statutory obligation. For example, if he does not show the amount of professional skill or degree of care as is expected of him while auditing the accounts, he would be held guilty. He cannot plead that he was unaware of the principles of accountancy or law or partnership agreement between the partners. He must perform his duties, so far as the audit of accounts is concerned, as is expected of a man of his status.

Q.92. You have been appointed auditor to a partnership under partnership deed. To what special clauses would you direct your attention during your first audit?

Ans. 1. The auditor should get definite instructions in writing as to the work to be performed by him. If in his letter of appointment, no instructions are given, he should write to his employers as to what work he is expected to do. This point was emphasised in the case of *Smith* vs. *Sheared* (1906). It must be made clear as to whether the work to be performed by the auditor is of the nature of accountancy or auditing [*Apfel* vs. *Annan Dexter & Co.* (1926)]. If he is to perform the work of auditing, he must enquire whether the audit is to be "Partial Audit" or "Complete Audit."

2. Whether the work to be performed by him is of the nature of the preparation of Income Tax Returns.

3. He should carefully read the Partnership Deed.

4. He should ascertain the powers and duties of each partner.

5. He should ascertain the amount of capital contributed by each partner, his withdrawals, loans to or by the firm, sharing of profits and losses, interest, if any, payable on capital or drawings, salaries, commission, provisions for depreciation and reserves and so on.

6. If the partners keep any minute book, the auditor should refer to it for any resolution passed regarding the accounts.

7. If the firm is registered, he should see that all the requirements of the Partnership Act are compiled with.

8. He should examine the contracts entered into by the firm and third parties.

His method of approach and the work to be done will depend upon the circumstances of each particular case and the agreement entered into between him and his client.

Q.93. Explain briefly what is implied by the following expressions:–

(*a*) Management Auditing. **(*b*) Management Consultancy.**

(*c*) Efficient Auditing. **(*d*) Operational Auditing.**

Ans. (*a*) Management Auditing. William P. Leonard defines it: "Management Auditing is a comprehensive and constructive examination of an organisational structure of a company, institution, or branch of a Government, or of any component thereof, such as a division or department and its plans and objectives, its means of operations and its use of human and physical facilities".

Taylor and Perry define it: "Management Auditing is a method of evaluating the efficiency of management at all levels throughout the organisation, or, more specifically, it comprises the investigation of a business by an independent body from the highest executive level downwards, in order to ascertain whether sound management prevails throughout, and to report as to its efficiency or otherwise, with recommendations to ensure its effectiveness where such is not the case".

(*b*) Management Consultancy. It is an investigation of an organisation by an independent body in order to evaluate its organisation with a view to facilitate its more efficient working.

(*c*) Efficient Auditing. This type of auditing is generally conducted in case of public enterprises to see whether the return on the capital outlay justifies the existence of the enterprise. Efficient audit is sometimes called propriety audit. Kohler defines it : "Propriety audit is that which meets the tests of public interest, commonly acceptable customs and standard of conduct". It is that auditing in which the various positions and actions of the executive of a concern are examined to find out whether they are in the interest of public and whether they meet the standards of conduct.

(*d*) Operational Audit. It is an extension of internal auditing to all the operations and the activities of a concern. The object of such an audit is to include the examination of control structure and of the relation of departmental control to the general policy of the company.

Q.94. What do you mean by 'divisible profits"? What legal considerations would weight with you before declaring dividends ?

Ans. "Divisible Profits" means those profits which can legally be distributed to the shareholders of a company in the form of dividends. The Companies Act does not define as to what is meant by divisible profits. It also does not say that only "true profits" can be divided. Section 205 of the Companies Act as amended in 1960 and subsequently in 1974, lays down that

"No dividend shall be declared or paid by a Company for any financial year except out of the profits of the company for that year arrived at after providing for depreciation in accordance with the provisions of sub-section (2) or out of the profits of the company for any previous financial year or years arrived at after providing for depreciation in accordance with those provisions and remaining undistributed or out of both or out of moneys provided by the Central Government or a State Government for the payment of dividend in pursuance of a guarantee gives by that government. The Companies (Amendment) Act, 1974, also provides that no dividend shall be declared unless a sum not exceeding 10 per cent of the profits is transferred to the reserves of the company. However the Government may allow a company to transfer a higher percentage if it thinks fit.

While computing the profits a company must bear in mind the following points :

If a company has not provided for depreciation for any previous financial year or years, it shall provide for depreciation and shall transfer not more than 10 per cent of the profits to the reserve account before declaring any dividend after the commencement of the Companies (Amendment) Acts, 1960 and 1974.

If a company has suffered any loss in any previous financial year or years, after the commencement of the Companies (Amendment) Act, 1960, the amount of such a loss or an amount which is equal to the amount provided for depreciation for that year or years whichever is less shall be set off against the profits of the company of the year for which dividend is proposed to be declared or paid (Section 205). The Central Government may, however, if it thinks necessary to do so in the interest of the public, allow any company to pay dividend for any financial year or years without the provision of depreciation in any of the previous years.

Depreciation referred to above will be calculated in accordance with Section 205 (2) and 350 of the Companies Act and Indian Income Tax Act or rules made thereunder by the Central Government. Thus, it is left to the discretion of the management of a company to decide as to what amount is to be distributed to the shareholders. Of course, the company must bear in mind two principles while determining the amount of divisible profits, viz., (1) That under no circumstances a dividend should be paid out of capital, (2) That there is no contravention of the provisions of the Companies Act, the Memorandum of Association and the Articles of Association of the company provided they are not **ultra vires** of the Companies Act.

Q.95. What are the Capital Profits ? Are such profits available for distribution as dividends? Give cases and discuss briefly.

Ans. Capital profits are those profits which are not earned during the regular course of business or in other words which are not trading profits. Such profits are (1) Premium received on the issue of shares or debentures, (2) The difference between the amount received on the forfeited shares and the amount at which they are reissued, (3) Profits prior to incorporation, (4) Profits earned by the redemption of the company's own debentures at a discount in the market, (5) Profits realised on the sale of fixed assets, and so on.

Legally speaking, there is no objection if some of the capital profits enumerated above are distributed to the shareholders provided the Articles of the company do not prohibit such an action and that sufficient working capital is retained in the business after the distribution of such profits. But from the sound financial and business point of view such capital profits should not be distributed as strictly speaking they are not trading profits and they are not a regular feature of the business.

As regards profits earned prior to incorporations, we may say that they are not the profits of the company to which it is entitled as the company was not in existence when these profits were earned. Hence, such profits may be utilised in wiping off the intangible assets like goodwill or bringing down the value of some of the assets which have been acquired.

In regard to profits made on the redemption of its debentures by a company, it has been held in the case of *Wall* vs. *London and General Provincial Trust Co. Ltd.*, (1932), that a company which adopts the Double Accounts system should not treat profits made on the redemption of its own debentures in the market as profits available for dividend.

In case capital profits have been made on account of appreciation in the value of assets, such profits may be distributed under the following conditions :

(*a*) when all the other assets have been revalued;

(*b*) when depreciation in the value of other assets have been set off against the appreciated value of the asset;

(*c*) when such a profits has actually been realised;

(*d*) when the Articles of Association of the company permit such a step.

Such decisions were laid down in the *Lubbock* vs. *The British Bank of South America* (1892), and *Foster* vs. *The New Trinidad Lake Asphalte Co. Ltd.*, (1901).

There are, however, certain capital profits like premium received on the issue of shares which cannot be distributed to the shareholder except in the form of bonus shares.

Q.96. Is a company formed to work a wasting property bound to set apart a sinking fund to meet depreciation of such property? What is the legal position of the auditor of such a company in this connection and what are his duties?

Ans. Wasting assets are properties of a fixed nature, which are used up by depletion or exhaustion, e.g., a mine, an oil well, a quarry, etc. Such assets are fixed assets but of wasting nature. The question is whether all the surplus made by a company engaged in the working of such as asset is available for dividends. Different views have been expressed on the subject.

There are accountants who are of opinion that this surplus, without providing any depreciation, is a part of the capital of the company and therefore, division of such a surplus will amount to the payment of dividend out of capital. They say that the surplus represents a part of capital. But it has been held by a court that if a company is formed to work a mine and after the mine is exhausted it is to be wound up, the company may distribute this surplus (*Lee* vs. *Neuchatel Asphalte Co.*, 1889). It may be remembered that since the passing of the Companies (Amendment) Act in 1960, it is obligatory for a company to provide for depreciation on fixed assets. Since a mine is a fixed asset, depreciation must be provided for before the distribution of profits (Section 205).

If, however, no depreciation is provided, the balance-sheet will not represent the true and fair view of the company's position. Moreover, the capital of the company is not kept intact, and when the mine is exhausted, the company will go into liquidation unless it borrows money to replace the exhausted mine. Supposing the company was formed only to work that mine and go into liquidation, nothing or very little will be left to be returned to the shareholders. To this objection, it is argued that capital had already been returned to the shareholders, when all the surplus, without providing any depreciation, was returned in the form of dividend to the shareholders. Even if we accept such an argument, there is another objection. In the event of the company going into liquidation capital having been returned to the shareholders, it will be the creditors who depended upon the security of capital will suffer.

Duty of the Auditor

It may be noted that according to Section 205 of the Companies Act, depreciation has to be provided on assets. The Act does not distinguish between a fixed asset and a wasting asset. But depreciation has to be provided on assets at a particular rate according to S. 350 of the Companies Act, the Income Tax Act and the rules made thereunder. These acts do not prescribe any rate of depreciation for wasting assets. If one reads through all these sections, a company need not provide depreciation on assets like wasting assets, goodwill, leases, etc. Therefore, from the legal point of view no depreciation need be provided on such assets but from the sound financial point of view, depreciation must be provided on wasting assets before the distribution of profits to the shareholders.

Hence, it is necessary that depreciation should be provided on all assets. Therefore, the auditor should see that depreciation has been provided for on all the assets before the declaration of any dividend.

Q.97. In what circumstances, if at all, can a company, which has written down its assets excessively out of profits, write them up again to the extent of such excess and apply the amounts thereof in payment of dividends?

Ans. It was decided in the case of *Stapley* vs. *Read Bros. Ltd.*, (1924), that a company which had excessively depreciated its fixed asset (in this case, the goodwill) in the past, may write it up in a subsequent year to the extent of such excess and apply the amount in payment of the dividend provided :

1. there is nothing against the procedure in the Memorandum and Articles of Association of the company; and
2. the amount by which the profit and loss account is credited, is not in excess of the present value of the asset.

The court, in the case quoted above, was of the opinion that if a fixed asset had been written off in the past out of the profits, it did not mean that the company had permanently capitalised the profit and that such profits could be utilized in the payment of dividend in subsequent years, if there was no provision to the contrary in the memorandum or articles of association of the company.

Q.98. Can a company divide its current profits without making good past losses? Discuss any decided case on the subject.

The question which often arises is whether a company which had suffered loss in the past can pay dividend out of the profits of subsequent years without wiping off the previous loss. There are different opinions on the subject. Sometimes back, it was opined that the current profits could not be distributed unless the previous losses had been written off. The argument put forth was that when a loss occurs, capital of the company is lost. Therefore, it would not be proper to pay dividends out of profits in subsequent years unless the lost capital was replaced by subsequent profits. If that was not done, the dividend proposed to be paid would amount to the payment of dividend out of capital which is against the company law.

On the other hand, there are accountants who are of opinion that it is not necessary to wipe off previous loss before a dividend is declared in the subsequent year. The argument put forth by them is that this action does not among to "payment of dividend out of capital". They say that when a loss is suffered, the capital is gone. Shareholders invest their money and they know that it might be lost. If it has been lost, it need not be made good in subsequent years. They add that it would not amount to payment of dividend out of capital because the capital is already lost. They further say that the only thing that the law lays down is that it should not be touched, i.e., if a company has not made any profits in any year, nothing should be paid in the form of dividend out of capital. They further argue that law does not lay down that if a part of capital has been lost on account of losses, the deficiency of such capital should be made up out of subsequent profits. This view has been confirmed by the courts in *Ammonia Soda Co. Ltd.*, vs. *Chamberlain and other* (1917), and *Steplay* vs. *Read Bros. Ltd.* (1924).

But according to the Companies Act as amended in 1960, past losses must be written off before any dividend can be declared by a company. It also lays down that previous loss or depreciation of that year when such a loss was incurred, *whichever is less,* should be deducted out of the profits of the subsequent year is which it is proposed to pay dividend.

So far we have considered the question from the legal point of view but from the commercial point of view, the previous loss must be made good out of the subsequent profits. Unless that loss is made good out of subsequent profits, the capital of the company permanently remains depleted which fact will affect the earning capacity of the business. Thus from the commercial point of view, the previous loss must be made good out of the current profits. Moreover, it appears a contradictory thing to pay dividend where there is a debit balance of Profit and Loss Account.

Q.99. In each of the following cases, state whether payment of profits is legal or illegal :–

(*a*) When there is excess of current income over current expenditure after making good depreciation on floating assets and retaining sufficient funds to pay liabilities but without taking into account depreciation of fixed assets.

(*b*) Distribution of capital profit which has been realised, there being a surplus after making good all capital losses.

(*c*) Distribution of revenue profits after making good revenue losses but without making good all capital losses.

(*d*) Payment of dividends out of the current profits without writing off previous year's losses.

(*e*) Payment of dividends out of current profits without making good deficiencies in paid-up capital.

Ans. (*a*) According to Section 205 of the Companies Act, it is mandatory that depreciation should be provided for on assets irrespective of the fact whether they are current or floating assets. Hence the company cannot distribute profits without providing depreciation on fixed assets. Therefore, the payment of the dividend is illegal.

(*b*) The payment is not legal as Capital Profits can be divided amongst the shareholders on the following conditions :

(*i*) They have been realised.

(*ii*) Articles of Association of the company permit the division of capital profits.

(*iii*) When *all the other* assets have been revalued and deficiency, if any, has been made up out of the capital profits.

From the question it does not appear as to whether the Articles permit such a payment. If they are silent, payment may be made.

(*c*) The payment is not legal. (*See* answer to Question No. 95).

(*d*) The payment is not legal. (*See* answer to Question No. 98).

(*e*) The payment is legal. (*See* Question No. 98).

Q.100. The directors of a limited company which has been making heavy losses in several successive years are desirous of issuing new shares with a view to providing fresh working capital. They are anxious to assure the new shareholders that dividends will be paid to them as soon as profits are available irrespective of past losses.

Can they legally give such an assurance? Are there any legal decisions bearing on the point?

Ans. From the question it appears that directors want to assure the new shareholders that as soon as profits are available in future they would be paid dividend. The question is whether they can give preference to such shareholders over the existing shareholders. The answer is that they cannot differentiate between the two kinds of shareholders unless the new shareholders are preference shareholders as to profits in which case the new shareholders are entitled to get dividends before the existing (equity) shareholders are paid any dividend. But if preference shares have already been issued, there can be no preferential treatment for the proposed new preference shares.

Again the directors cannot give an assurance to the new shareholders that if in future there are profits, they would declare dividends without writing off the past revenue losses as according to Section 205 of the Companies Act, previous losses must be written off before any dividend can be paid except under certain conditions.

Q.101. A limited company was registered on 31st March, 1967, for the purpose of taking over the existing business of ABC as from 1st January, 1967. According to the agreement, the company was entitled to the profit or responsible for the losses of the firm prior to incorporation. How would you ascertain and deal with the loss made prior to incorporation? What principles would guide you in dealing with such a loss?

Ans. The company was registered on 31st March, 1967, and hence, it could not work before that date. Any profit made or any loss suffered before a company is registered is called "Profit or Loss Prior to Incorporation."

If the profit and loss account of the firm could be prepared for the period ended 31st March, 1967 there would be no difficulty in the ascertainment of the profit or loss prior to incorporation.

In the absence of the preparation of such a profit and loss account the company may adopt any one of the following methods to ascertain the profit made or the loss suffered by the firm up to 31st March, 1967, from which date the company could conduct business :

(*a*) On the basis of the turnover, i.e., by taking the gross loss on a percentage basis of sales.

(*b*) On the basis of time, i.e., by apportioning the *loss into* "pre" and "post" incorporation period.

(*c*) On the combined basis of turnover and time. Under this method gross loss is taken according to turnover while expenses are apportioned according to time. This method seems to be more accurate and logical.

The "loss prior to incorporation" may be dealt with in any of the following ways :

(*a*) It may be debited to goodwill account because, as a matter of fact, it amounts to increase in the purchase price. However, even if nothing is paid for goodwill, the loss prior to incorporation must be debited to a newly opened goodwill account. If this method is adopted, Goodwill Account should be written off as soon as possible; or

(*b*) it may be debited to an account called "Loss Prior to Incorporation" which may be written off in the course of time; or

(*c*) it may be debited against the capital profits after incorporation, i.e., profit on the sale of a fixed asset, balance of forfeited shares account after they had been re-issued, if any, etc.; or

(*d*) the amount should be debited to a newly opened "Suspense Account" which may be written off out of capital profits made in subsequent years, e.g., Premium on Issue of Debentures, credit balance of forfeited shares, if any, after have been re-issued.

Q.102. How should profits earned by a limited company prior to incorporation be treated in its accounts?

Ans. Profits which have been earned by a business which has been taken over by a company before it was incorporated are of the nature of capital profits. As the profits were earned before the company was incorporated they could not be credited to its profit and loss account. Distribution of such profits amounts to payment of dividend out of capital. The best course for the company would be to utilize such profits for the following purposes :

(*a*) if one of the assets taken over was goodwill, it may be written off out of the profit prior to incorporation; or

(*b*) the assets taken over may be written down to their real value out of such profits; or

(*c*) if the assets taken over are properly valued, the profit prior to incorporation may be credited to the General Reserve Account.

Q.103. What is meant by investigation of accounts of a business and how does it differ from an audit? Mention some of the purposes which may necessitate investigation of accounts of a business.

Ans. Investigation means an enquiry into the accounts of a business for a special purpose. It is an examination of the books of account of a business to know its actual financial position or earning capacity. Taylor and Perry have defined it thus : "Investigation involves enquiry into facts behind the books and accounts, into the technical, financial and economic position of the business or organisation." It is a kind of special audit with a limited or extended scope according to the purpose for which it is conducted. Investigation is neither accountancy nor auditing.

Difference between "Investigation" and "Auditing"

1. *Audit* is conducted on behalf of the shareholders or proprietors, while *investigation* is usually carried out on behalf of outsiders who intend to purchase the business or who wish to lend money and thus want to know the earning capacity or the financial position of the concern. It may also be carried out on behalf of the proprietors when they suspect any fraud or by the Central Government at the instance of the shareholders or the court.
2. Accounts of a Joint-Stock Company *must be audited* according to law while the accounts of a Joint-Stock Company *may or may not be investigated into.*
3. The *Audit* of accounts is usually for a year or six months while *investigation* may cover a period extending over three to seven years.
4. The accounts are *audited* with a view to ascertain whether or not the balance-sheet is drawn up according to law and that the profit and loss account and balance-sheet exhibit a true and fair view of the state of affairs of a company, while *investigation* is conducted with a particular object in view, viz., to know the financial position of the concern or its earning capacity, etc.
5. *Audit* is a kind of test checking while *investigation* is a thorough examination of the books of account for a particular year or a number of years.
6. *Audit* includes an examination of the books of account of a business while *investigation* is not only an examination of accounts but it is also an enquiry into several factors affecting the business such as the extent of fraud, who committed it, the causes of the fall of the profits and so on and the investigator has, therefore, to go beyond the books of account.
7. In the case of *investigation,* the net profit or the actual earning capacity of the concern is ascertained by making certain adjustments in the net profit as calculated by the accountant or the auditor while this is not so in the case of an *audit.*
8. Investigation may be conducted even though the accounts have already been audited while audited accounts are not audited again except in the case of special audit under Section 233A.
9. Investigation of accounts may be conducted even though the accounts have already been audited but the audited accounts are never re-audited unless special audit is conducted under S. 233-B.

Purposes which may necessitate investigation of accounts of a business

1. Investigation on behalf of an individual or a promoter of a Joint-Stock Company which wishes to purchase a private running business in order to ascertain the financial position and the earning capacity of the concern proposed to be taken over.
2. Investigation on behalf of an incoming partner, who wants to know the earning capacity of the firm, the financial position of the concern and whether it is advisable to become a partner.
3. Investigation on behalf of a client who wishes to lend money to a concern whose financial position he wants to know.
4. Investigation where fraud is suspected by the proprietor.

5. Investigation on behalf of a client who wishes to purchase the shares of a company.
6. Investigation under the Indian Companies Act, 1956.
7. Investigation to ascertain the amount of compensation payable on the compulsory removal of business.
8. Investigation for claims under an Insurance Policy covering consequential losses, e.g., in case of fire, burgalary, etc.
9. Investigation on behalf of a company or an individual for alleged negligence or lack of skill by the auditors.
10. Investigation on behalf of the liquidator of a company where directors are suspected to be guilty of fraud or misfeasance.
11. Investigation on behalf of beneficiaries where trustees are suspected to have committed fraud or embezellement.

Q.104. Nut and Bolt is a small firm of wholesale ironmongers for whom you prepare the annual accounts. You receive a call from the senior partners that his cashier and book-keeper, who was entrusted with the responsibility for the receipt and payments of cash and the payment of wages, has not returned for work and, furthermore, that there appear to have been some irregularities with regard to both the receipt and payment of cash.

Tabulate a programme of investigation of the possibility and extent of any defalcation of cash that may have taken place.

Ans. The cashier who keeps books of accounts might have misappropriated cash in any of the following ways :

1. Omitting to enter the receipt of cash.
2. Entering less amount in the Cash Book than what has been received.
3. Showing fictitious payments amongst others, to the workers.
4. Entering more amount in the Cash Book than what has actually been paid.

Before he begins his investigation, the auditor should inquire from his client the period for which the investigation is to be carried out. After having done so he should follow the line of action as detailed below :

1. Permission should be obtained from his client to issue a circular to the debtors and creditors asking them to confirm the balance owing by them or to them respectively.
2. He should pay attention to the Cash sales and see whether there is a loophole. If so, he must probe into the matter.
3. Similarly sales of goods might have been omitted from the books so that when cash is received from the buyers, it is misappropriated.
4. He should compare the counterfoils of Paying-in-Slips with the entries in the Cash Book and the Pass Book to see that less amount than that mentioned in the counterfoils has not been deposited in the bank.
5. He should enquire as to who signs and endorses cheques.
6. List of bad debts should be examined and enquiry should be made whether the bad debts are really bad debts or in fact money might have been received from the debtors and mis-appropriated and the amount written off as 'Bad Debt'.
7. What is the system of payment of salaries and wages. It is possible that payment might have been made to 'dummy' employees or overpayment might have been made.
8. Petty cash transactions should be verified and vouchers obtained as far as possible. Special attention should be paid to Petty cash transactions as they are usually a source of fraud.

9. He must pay attention to bill transactions. It is possible that some bills might have been paid, proceeds mis-appropriated and the transactions might have been passed as if the bill had been dishonoured for non-payment. Such supposed 'dishonoured bill' and other bills must be examined. They would not be there if they had been paid. Bills in hand must also be examined. Similarly bills might have been discounted and cash proceeds misappropriated but the bill might be shown as if it is still in hand or has been sent to bank for collection.
10. Duplicates must be obtained for missing vouchers.
11. Cash received on account of unusual receipts, such as sale of waste materials, cash received from debtors who might have been written off as 'bad' in the past, allowances received, etc., might have been misappropriated.
12. Attention should be paid to misappropriation of cash by 'Teeming and Lading' method which means that the cash received from one customer is misappropriated and the cash received from another is credited to the first customer's account and when later on cash is received from the third customer, it is credited to the second customer and so on.
13. Misappropriating cash by showing more discount allowed than actually is the case. He should enquire what is the usual rate of discount allowed. He should pay attention to the date on the receipt.
14. The wages and cash book should be cast and the latter should be vouched with a view to find out the possibility of any fictitious payments.
15. The existence of the workers shown in the wages book should be certified by the partners.
16. He should compute the wages payable to the workers and compare them with the cash book.

Q.105. You are asked to investigate into the reasons for a considerable fall in the trading profits of a manufacturing concern for a particular year, although the sales of that year are well on a level with those of the preceding year. What line of procedure will your investigation take?

Ans. A considerable fall in the trading profits of a manufacturing concern in a particular year although the sales have been practically the same as in the previous year may be due to one or more of the following causes :

1. The price of raw materials might have increased although the selling prices of the manufactured goods might have remained the same.

The auditor should examine the invoices and if possible enquire about the prices of raw materials prevailing in the market during the year under review.

2. The wages might have gone up due to certain legislation or a decision by the Labour Tribunal or bonus might have been paid during the year.

   The auditor should go through correspondence and other relevant papers. He should properly vouch the payment of wages. He should also examine the resolution passed by the Board of Directors, sanctioning increase in the rate of wages or payment of bonus.
3. Purchases might have been entered twice in the Purchases Book either fraudulently or otherwise.

   The auditor should vouch the purchases by referring to the Invoices, Gate-keeper's Book, Order Book, etc.
4. Entries might have been passed in the Purchases Book relating to the goods, the Invoices of which might have been received but goods might not have been included in the closing stock as they have not been received.

The auditor should see the Gate-Keeper's Book and Store-keeper's Inward Book. If the goods purchased have not been entered in the closing stock no entry need be made in the Purchases Book.

5. The sale price of the goods might have gone down while the prices of raw materials might have remained the same or might not have gone up proportionately.

   The auditor should refer to the copies of the invoices and enquire whether a responsible officer fixed up the prices to be charged from customers.

6. Sales might have been affected but no entry might have been passed in the books. When the price of the goods sold was received, it might have been misappropriated.

   The auditor should examine the Order Received Book, Invoices Book, Gate-keeper's Outward Book, the Store-keeper's Outward Book, Customers' Account and the Cash Book.

7. Closing stock might have been valued at a lower rate than in the past.

   The auditor should enquire into the mode of the valuation of the closing stock. He should see that closing stock is valued every year according to the set principles of accountancy and that there is no change in the principle of the valuation of closing stock from the previous year.

8. Goods with the agents or at branches might not have been included in the closing stock.

   The auditor should examine the accounts of agents, branches, etc.

9. Some of the goods might have been sold at a very heavy reduction because they were either damaged or gone out of fashion, etc.

   The auditor should enquire as to who authorised the clearance sale or auction sale.

10. Goods might have been stolen.

    The auditor should check the Stock Registers, Gate-keeper's Book, etc.

Q.106. The accounts of Very Clever & Co. are submitted to you for examination for the purpose of certifying the profits of the past five years for publication in the prospectus of a proposed company.

The profits of the business as shown in the accounts prepared by the firm, appear as follows :

			Rs.
Year	**1964**	**Profit**	**18,223**
Year	**1965**	**Profit**	**17,934**
Year	**1966**	**Profit**	**19,650**
Year	**1967**	**Profit**	**17,340**
Year	**1968**	**Profit**	**25,236**

The comparison of the accounts of year 1967 with year 1968 reveals the fact that the increased profit, as between these two years, is accounted for thus

(*a*) Decrease in the provision for depreciation Rs. 750.

(*b*) Decrease in the Returns Inward, Rs. 1,260.

(*c*) Increase in sales (Chiefly in November and December, 1968) Rs. 3,636.

(*d*) Decrease in trade charges, Rs. 1,600.

If you are of opinion that these items need any special investigation, how should you proceed?

Ans. From the question it appears that all these items requires special investigation.

(*a*) The auditor should inquire the total amount of assets in 1968 as compared to 1967, whether some of the assets have been sold and that is why there is a reduction in the total amount of depreciation written off. If he finds that there is no reduction in the total assets, he should enquire whether the rate of depreciation provided has been reduced in the year 1968. As a matter of fact, the rate of depreciation should be consistent year after year.

(*b*) The auditor should enquire in which month of 1968 the returns were less. It is possible that the normal Return Inwards for 1968 might have been entered in the books of account in order to show more sales and profit in 1968. For this purpose, he should refer to the Return Inwards Book, the Gate-keeper's Book, correspondence with the customers regarding the return of goods.

(*c*) It appears that probably the firm has inflated the profit for 1968 by showing more sales. He should enquire whether the sales were actually more or whether they were fictitious sales and were mere book entries. He should, therefore, examine the Order Received Book, Sales Book, Gate-keeper's Book, etc., to find the genuineness of the sales in 1968. He should also compare the prices of the goods sold in earlier months of 1968 with the prices in November and December. It is possible that the prices might have gone up in these months as a result of which the value of sales had increased.

(*d*) There may be several reasons for the decrease in the trade charges. In order to show more profit in 1968, the proprietors of the firm, Very Clever & Co., might have starved the business of the legitimate expenses or he might have paid some expenses out of his own pocket. It is also possible that the expenses due for 1968, e.g., rent, taxes, salaries payable, might not have been paid and these liabilities might have also been omitted from the balance sheet. The auditor should compare the expenses for 1968 with 1967 and especially those which are normally incurred in the last months of the year. Thus it will enable him to discover whether any expenses have been omitted to be recorded in the books of account.

Q.107. A private firm is to be converted into a public company. To enable a public issue of shares, you are required to give a certificate as to the average past profits of the firm for inclusion in the prospectus. What adjustments would you have to make in the profits as shown by the firm's books and how would you qualify the certificate by reason of the adjustments?

Ans. Assuming that the accounts of the firm were subject to audit or that the profits shown are correct for the previous 3 or 5 years, the following adjustments will have to be made in order to arrive at the profits the company will be able to make after the firm has been converted into a public company.

The following items should be added to the profits as shown by the firm :—

1. Rent, if the company is going to purchase the land or premises which the firm had not owned and was paying rent for it.
2. Interest on Partners' capital and current accounts, Partners' salaries, if any, as they will not be payable to the shareholders after the business is taken over except the fee which will have to be paid to the directors.
3. Interest on loans and overdrafts, if any, if the company is not going to take over the loan or overdraft.
4. Discount on purchases, if the firm had not taken advantage of the cash discount on purchases on account of insufficiency of working capital with the firm, provided, the company will have sufficient working capital.
5. Exceptional losses, e.g., loss by fire which was not covered by insurance, costs and damages incurred by litigation, etc., which do not occur normally and which might have been debited to revenue account.

6. Excessive reserves for bad and doubtful debts or depreciation, etc.
7. Capital losses which had been debited to revenue account.
8. Capital expenditure which might have been debited to profit and loss account.

The following items should be deducted from the profits of the firm :

1. Income from assets not taken over by the company.
2. Rent, if the company is not going to purchase the premises which the firm owned.
3. Capital profits, e.g., profits on sale of fixed assets if they had been credited to the revenue account of the firm as such profits are not normal profits.
4. Exceptional profits, e.g., speculation profits which had been credited to profit and loss account by the firm.
5. Directors' fees payable by the purchasing company as the firm had not to pay the fees to the Directors.
6. Interest on partners' drawings which was credited to profit and loss account by the firm.

The question of depreciation will have to be tackled. The firm must have provided depreciation on the book value of the assets while the company will provide depreciation on the value of the assets at which they have been acquired from the firm.

The certificate in regard to the profits should be for every year. Average profits may give a wrong impression, e.g., if the profits have been Rs. 25,000, Rs. 20,000, Rs. 15,000, Rs. 10,000, Rs. 7,500 for the previous five years the average profits will be Rs. 15,500. The certificate that the firm has been making an average profit of Rs. 15,500 per year is misleading. If the figure of profit for each year is given, it would show that the business is on the decline and the company will not be able to make a profit of Rs. 15,500. The auditor must not express any opinion about the future earning capacity of the business. If it is found later on that the business purchased was not making so much profit, any person who has purchased the shares on the faith of such a statement in the prospectus, will be entitled to get compensation from the investigator if the purchaser of the shares has suffered any loss. The investigation should, in such a case, cover a period of five years.

The Report should be clear and in unambiguous terms. If the Report is wrong or is misleading, the auditor will be held liable to pay damages to the company. Therefore, the Report should be very clearly drawn up.

Q.108. If you are appointed by Government, under Section 235 of the Companies Act, 1956, as an Inspector to investigate the affairs of an industrial company, what powers are given to you by law for the purpose and how would you carry out your investigation?

Ans. The Inspector who has been appointed by the Government under Section 235 of the Companies Act to investigate the affairs of an industrial company has the following powers :

1. He can examine any book of account, document, voucher, etc.
2. He can examine any officer of the company on oath. (*Minakshi Mills,* 1959).
3. He can hold any officer of the company liable as if the latter had committed a contempt of court in case such an officer refuses to answer any question on oath or refuses to show the books of account, etc., if asked to do so, (Section 240). The punishment in such a case can be imprisonment for six months and/or fine up to one thousand rupees.
4. If during the course of investigation the inspector wishes to examine on oath a person whom he has no power to examine e.g., an ex-managing agent, secretaries and treasurers or any other person not connected with the company, and if such a person refuses to furnish information or to be examined on oath, he may apply to the Court which may, if it thinks fit, order that person to attend and be examined on oath before it. During the course of Court proceedings, the inspector may take part therein personally or by a legal practitioner.

5. The inspector has a power to call upon any company even if such a company had no connection with the company whose accounts are being investigated into to furnish information and to produce books of account and other papers.
6. The inspector may delegate his power to receive the information and papers, etc., as stated in the foregoing paragraph to any person of course, with the approval of the Central Government.
7. This right can be exercised against companies but not against individuals or firms. (*S. Prakash Chopra* vs. *Bennet Coleman & Co. Ltd., Bombay*).

The Investigator should pay special attention to the following points :

1. Remuneration of the directors, managing directors etc.
2. Whether the funds of the company are properly and profitably employed.
3. Loans advanced to the directors of the company, interest charges thereon, and the security offered by such a director.
4. The current account of the managing agents with the company.
5. The contracts entered into by the managing agents with other companies in which such managing agents or directors are interested.
6. The assets and liabilities should be verified and valued.

After having critically examined the accounts, the Inspector should submit the report to the Central Government which in its turn will send a copy of it to the company or any other person who had been examined by the inspector.

Q.109. Distinguish between the Civil and Criminal Liability of an auditor and illustrate your answer by reference to legal cases.

Ans. The liability of an auditor of a company may be considered under two heads, viz., (*i*) Civil Liability; and (*ii*) Criminal Liability.

(*i*) Civil Liability

The auditor may be sued in a civil court for damages arising out of negligence in the performance of his duties, e.g., where the dividend had been paid out of capital.

An auditor is appointed to report whether the balance-sheet and profit and loss account of the company show true and fair view of the state of affairs of the company and incidentally to detect frauds, defalcations, errors, etc. If on account of negligence in the performance of his duties, he has failed to do so, and consequently the company suffers any loss, the auditor is held responsible for damages. He is an agent in regard to his duties as an auditor and, therefore, must show reasonable skill and diligence in the performance of his duties. If he fails to do so, he must suffer the consequences. What is reasonable care and skill, will depend upon the circumstances of each particular case.

An auditor is not liable even though the company has suffered a loss if he can prove that he was not negligent in the performance of his duties. On the other hand, even if it is proved that the auditor was negligent in the performance of his duty, he cannot be held liable for damages, if the company has not suffered any loss due to his negligence as was held in the case of *Liverpool and Wigan Supply Association Ltd.*, 1907. In order to hold an auditor liable for negligence, it must be proved (a) that he was negligent, (b) that as a result of his negligence, the client suffered a loss, and (c) that the loss was suffered by the person to whom the auditor owed a duty.

The following cases in connection with the civil liability of an auditor are worth studying :

1. *Leeds Estate Building Society vs. Shephered* (1887). In this case it was held that an auditor, who did not examine the Articles of the company and as a result of this negligence, the dividends were paid out of capital, was liable to pay damages to the company.

2. *Irish Woollen Co.* vs. *Tyson and Others* (1900). In this case the accounts of the company had been manipulated and falsified and as a result of the manipulation of accounts, the dividend was paid out of capital. Purchases were not properly vouched and thus liabilities were under-stated. It was held that the auditor was negligent in the performance of his duties in not getting statements of account from the creditors. Had he done so, the fraud would have been discovered. Hence he was held guilty and was asked to pay damages.
3. *London Oil Storage Co.* vs. *Seear, Hasluck and Co.* (1904). In this case the auditors failed to verify an asset, viz., petty cash in hand which amounted to £796, but actually only £30 were in hand. Had the auditors verified the cash in hand with the Petty Cash-keeper, the fraud would have been discovered. The learned Judge said that by omitting to verify petty cash in hand, the auditors committed a breach of duty and hence were liable to pay damages.

There are other cases also, viz., *Wild and Others* vs. *Cape of Dalgleish* (1897), *Arthur E. Green & Co.* vs. *The Central Advance and Discount Corporation Ltd.* (1920), *London & General Bank Case* (1895), *Republic of Bolivia Exploration Syndicate* (1913), *The Westminster Road Construction Co. Ltd.*, (1932), *Union Bank of Allahabad Case* (1925), *Dehra Dun Mussoorie Electric Tramway Co., Case* (1930), *Davar & Sons* vs. *M.S. Krishnaswami,* 1954, *Commissioner of Income Tax* vs. *G.M. Dandekar,* 1952.

(*ii*) Criminal Liability

Criminal liability of an auditor arises out of an act constituting a crime, e.g., if an auditor wilfully makes a false statement either in the balance-sheet or any other document, destroys or mutilates any voucher or document.

Section 628 of the Companies Act lays down : "If in any return, report, certificate, balance-sheet, prospectus, statement or any other document, required by or for the purposes of any of the provisions of this Act, any person makes a statement :—

(*a*) which is false in any material particular, knowing it to be false; or

(*b*) which omits any material particular, knowing it to be material; he shall, save as otherwise expressly provided in this Act, be punishable with imprisonment for a term which may extend to two years and shall also be liable to fine."

The word 'person' used in this Section is also applicable to the auditor of a company.

Similarly, an auditor may be prosecuted if it is proved that he had been guilty of any criminal offence in relation to the company under Section 539 of the Companies Act which says that any person who with intent to defraud or deceive, destroys, mutilates, alters, falsifies or secretes or is privy to the destruction, mutilation, alteration or falsification or secreting of any books, papers or securities or makes or is privy to the making of any false or fraudulent entry in any register, book of account or document belonging to the company, shall be punishable with imprisonment for a term which may extend to seven years and shall also be liable to fine.

If a prospectus has been issued by a Company which contains a false statement, any person who authorised the issue of such a prospectus, will be liable to be punished with imprisonment up to two years or fined up to five thousand rupees or both (Section 63). For the purpose of Section 63, an auditor may be punished if he authorised the issue of the prospectus.

In order to hold an auditor criminally liable the following must be proved :

(*a*) That the statement made was false in material facts;

(*b*) That the auditor wilfully made such a false statement; and

(*c*) That the statement complained of has been made in any return, report, balance-sheet, certificate or any other document required to be made under any provisions of the Companies Act.

It may be mentioned here that the court has powers to relieve an auditor under Section 633 if a case against him is proceeding for negligence, default, breach of duty or breach of trust, if the court is satisfied that the auditor acted honestly and reasonably:

Provided that in a criminal proceeding under this Section, the Court shall have not power to grant relief from any civil liability which may attach to an officer in respect of such negligence, default, breach of duty, misfeasance or breach of trust.

Under Section 197 of the Indian Penal Code any person who issues or signs any certificate required by law to be given or signed, or relating to any fact and which certificate is by law admissible in evidence, knowing and believing that such a certificate is false in any material point, shall be punishable in the same manner as if he gives false evidence.

Q.110. Section 231 of the Companies Act provides that an auditor of a company shall be entitled to receive notice of and to attend any general meeting of the company at which any accounts which have been examined or reported on by him are to be laid before the company and make any statement or explanation he desires with respect to the accounts.

(*a*) In what circumstances should this right be exercised?

(*b*) Would any explanation made by the auditor relieve him in respect of omissions from his report or from the balance-sheet?

(*c*) Should an auditor, so attending, answer questions put by shareholders?

(*d*) If an auditor is present and wrong information is given by a director in regard to an item in the balance-sheet, would it be proper for him to correct that information in the absence of explanation by the director concerned?

(*e*) Would an auditor incur any liability for absenting himself from an annual meeting? Give reasons for your answers.

Ans. (*a*) It is not obligatory for the auditor to attend the annual general meeting of the shareholders. He has been given a right to attend such a meeting. He may or may not exercise this right. But if he thinks that the directors might give misleading information relating to accounts to the shareholders at the meeting, he should attend such a meeting.

(*b*) The Companies Act requires that the report of the auditor should be comprehensive and self-explanatory. If it is not so, he might be held guilty. Any explanation made by the auditor will be for the benefit of the shareholders *present* at the meeting. The shareholders who have read the report which was not comprehensive and who might not have attended the meeting might remain under a misconception. Therefore, any statement made by the auditor at the meeting will not relieve him of his responsibility.

(*c*) Although an auditor is appointed by the shareholders whose agent he is, he should refrain to answer any question put to him by them at the meeting. He is not bound to answer any question. However, if the Chairman of the Board of Directors, who is presiding at the meeting, asks him to do so, he should answer the question put to him.

(*d*) If a wrong information is given by the directors relating to the accounts at the meeting and the auditor is present at such a meeting, the auditor should intervene and correct the statement. If he does not do so, it might be presumed that the statement is correct. If the auditor receives any information subsequent to the submission of the report, and if that information was necessary for incorporation in the Report, the auditor should speak at the meeting to give such information to the shareholders.

(*e*) It is not necessary that the auditor should attend the annual general meeting though he has a right to do so. By absenting himself from attending the meeting, the auditor does not incur any liability. It is not his duty to attend the annual general meeting.

Q.111. Are there any circumstances in which under the Indian Companies Act, the auditor may be held to be an officer of a company, and in such cases, what are his liabilities?

Ans. An Auditor may be held liable as an officer of a company under Sections 477, 478, 539, 543, 545, 621, 625 and 633 of the Companies Act, 1956. These Sections refer to the following matters respectively :

(*a*) Power of the Court in winding up to summon any officer of the company or person suspected of having property of the company (Section 477);

(*b*) Powers of the court, to order public examination of any officer or person guilty of fraud, etc., in the promotion, formation or management of the company (Section 478);

(*c*) Any officer or person found guilty for the falsification of the books (Section 539);

(*d*) Power of the Court to assess damages against delinquent officers (Section 543);

(*e*) Prosecution of delinquent officers and members (Section 545);

(*f*) Any offence committed by any officer or person and complained of by the Registrar or a shareholder or any person authorised by the Central Government (Section 621);

(*g*) Payment of compensation in case of frivolous or vexatious prosecution (Section 625); and

(*h*) Power of the Court to grant relief to officers in proceedings for negligence, default, breach of duty, misfeasance, etc. (Section 633).

Under the above quoted sections an officer includes an 'auditor' in the event of the company going into liquidation and also in certain other cases.

Q.112. Discuss the liabilities of an auditor for misfeasance or breach of trust under the Companies Act, as an officer of the Company.

Ans. Misfeasance means breach of duty. The Companies Act imposes certain duties on the auditors of the companies. If an auditor commits a breach of such a duty, he is guilty of misfeasance and is, therefore, liable to pay damage if his client has suffered any loss on account of his negligence in the performance of his duty. An auditor of a company is not only liable for misfeasance when he is acting as the auditor of the company but he is also liable in certain cases when he is no more the auditor of the company or even when the company is under liquidation. In case the company has gone into liquidation, it is the liquidator who can proceed against the past or the present auditor for having committed a breach of duty otherwise the company can proceed against him.

Q.113. The auditor of a company issued the necessary certificate about the correctness of the accounts of a company without proper or reasonable verification, while in fact they were erroneous, as a consequence of which dividends were paid out of capital. What is the remedy available to the liquidator?

Ans. Section 205 (3) of the Companies Act lays down that dividends can be declared *only* out of the profits of the financial year or out of the undistributed profits of the previous years after having provided depreciation on fixed assets and also transferring not more than 10 per cent of the profits to the reserves or out of both or out of the moneys provided by the Central or State Governments in pursuance of a guarantee given by the Governments.

From the above it would appear that dividends can be paid only out of the profits. In the problem given in the question, the auditor never verified the accounts and as a result of that the dividends were paid out of capital which action amounts to reduction of capital which is against the provision of Section 100 of the Companies Act.

Having found that the dividend was wrongly paid, let us see how far is the auditor liable in this case. Section 543 provides that if in the course of winding up of a company, it is found that any director or any officer had misapplied its funds, the court may, on the application of the liquidator, order such a person to refund that money.

The auditor in this case had certified the accounts as correct which in fact were not and on the basis of such certificate the directors recommended the payment of dividend which otherwise would not have been possible. Thus the auditor was guilty for misfeasance and he would be liable under Section 543 to refund the amount wrongly distributed to the shareholders in the form of dividend. The liquidator may, therefore, bring an action against the auditor to recover the amount.

Q.114. What do you conceive to be the liability of an auditor to a third-party, who has advanced money on the faith of a certified balance-sheet in regard to the audit of which there has been negligence?

The certificate was given by the auditor with the knowledge that in the usual course of business the certified accounts would be exhibited to banks, creditors, etc., according to the needs of the occasion.

Ans. The question arises whether an auditor can be held liable for damages to third parties, if they suffered any loss by relying upon any balance-sheet or any statement signed by him. It is argued that as there is no privity of contract between the auditor and the third party, the auditor owes no duty to such a third party and hence he cannot be held liable. He is never appointed by the third party and, therefore, he has nothing to do with such a party as was decided in the case of *Le Lievre and Dennes* vs. *Gould* (1893). This question came before a United States court in the case of *Ultramares Corporation* vs. *Touche, Niven & Co.,* in 1931. In this case a banker advanced loans to a company on the strength of the balance-sheet of the company, which had been signed by the auditor. The lender lost the money as the balance-sheet was misleading and fraudulent. Thereupon, the lender sued the auditor for damages. The case, however, was compromised.

The Accountant of England still maintained that the auditors would be protected firstly because there was no privity of contract between the auditor and the third party and secondly because the plaintiff must prove all the four points discussed under the *Derry* vs. *Peek* case, viz.,

(*i*) that the statement was untrue in fact;

(*ii*) that the person making it knew that it was untrue;

(*iii*) that the statement was made with intent that the plaintiff should act upon it; and

(*iv*) that the plaintiff did act in reliance in it and suffered damages.

In the question given, it is clear that the auditor knew that the balance-sheet which he would sign would, in the usual course of business, be exhibited to banks, creditors, etc., according to the needs of the occasion. In the circumstances the auditor is liable to pay damages to a third party which has suffered a loss on account of his negligence even though there is no privity of contract between him and the third party which has advanced the money on the faith of the balance-sheet.

Again, in the case of *Commissioner of Income Tax* vs. *G.M. Dandekar,* it was held by Ayyar, J., that the auditor does not owe any duty to the third party.

But it may be stated here that since the decision in *Hedley Byrne & Co., Ltd.* vs. *Heller and Partners Ltd.* in 1963, the auditors can be held in tort for negligent statements. Thus the decisions in previous cases that auditor does not owe any duty to third parties do not hold good now.

Again, if a misleading statement had been made in a prospectus issued by a company, *and if the auditor had authorised the issue of such a prospectus,* he can be held liable for damages to the third party which had purchased the shares of the company on the basis of such a misleading statement even though there might not have been privity of contract between the two (Section 63).

Q.115. The annual audit of a Banking Company has just been over and the auditor has given his usual certificate. It is afterwards discovered that some of the paper securities held by the bank against some overdraft accounts are forged documents, the forgery consisting in the alteration of the number of shares covered by individual share scrips. The securities had been lodged with the bank with blank transfer deeds.

What precautions could the auditor have taken to detect forgery himself and what are his liabilities in the present case?

Ans. If the number of shares was mentioned only in figures and the figures were altered, the auditor would not be held liable provided the forgery was very cleverly committed and the auditor was not negligent. If, however, the number of shares was indicated both by figures as well as in words, the auditor would be guilty of negligence in not comparing the figures as well as the words and he would be liable to pay damages. Had he compared both the figures as well as the words, he would have discovered the forgery and the loss would not have been caused. Moreover, he should have compared the figure relating to the number of shares as mentioned in the share certificate and the Transfer Deed.

Q.116. What is the liability of an auditor of a public company with regard to the stock-in-trade of a manufacturing business?

Ans. The liability of an auditor in connection with the stock-in-trade is two-fold, viz.,

(*i*) When the management has manipulated the accounts by showing more or less stock-in-trade than what actually it is; and

(*ii*) When the stock-in-trade is over-valued or under-valued by the management.

If the auditor has not detected the above manipulations which he could be showing reasonable skill and diligence, he would be held guilty in the performance of his duty. There are, of course, certain difficulties on account of which an auditor may not be able to discover the frauds in connection with stock-in-trade

An auditor has no time to inspect the stock-in-trade. If such a duty was cast upon him it would take months for him to take stock in certain trades. Moreover, he is not a technical hand to know every item of stock-in-trade of each class of business. It is, therefore, very difficult for him to verify the stock. He has to depend upon the stock sheets prepared by the management. If the following precautions are taken by him in connection with the verification of the stock, he is free from any liability:

1. He should find out whether the internal check system in connection with the stock-taking is efficient enough to prevent any manipulation.
2. He should check the stock sheets. If he does not do so he will be held responsible.
3. He should check the calculations, additions and castings in the stock-sheets.
4. He should see that the goods which have been sold but not delivered to the buyer on the stock-taking day are not included in the stock-in-hand.
5. He should see that the goods which have been purchased and the relative invoices of which have been entered in the Purchases Book, are included in the stock.
6. He should see that assets like furniture, tools, etc., are not included in the stock-in-trade.
7. It is suggested that the auditor should be present at the time of taking stock to see that it is being properly taken.
8. He should check the Stock Book with the Purchases Book. Purchases Returns, Sales Book, Sales Returns and compare the balance of this book with the Stock Sheet.

In regard to the valuation of stock, the auditor should see that it is valued according to the set principles of accountancy. For this purpose, he should find out the cost price and the market price of the similar goods. He should enquire as to who fixed the prices as indicated in the stock sheets. He should check a few calculations, castings, etc. He should see that proper provision is made for obsolete, damaged goods, etc. Goods with consignee must be included in the closing stock.

If he has taken the precautions as enumerated above and there was nothing to arouse his suspicion, he may certify the stock and even if later on it is found that the stock was not properly valued or that quantity of the stock was not correct, he would not be liable. Though in the famous *Kingston Cotton Mills* case it was held that an auditor is not a valuer but there is a change in the view of the accountants especially after the decision in the *McKesson and Robins* case in America where it was held that the auditor was negligent in accepting the stock sheets as prepared by the management. Even in India a doubt was expressed in this connection by P. Chakravarty, C.J., in the case of *Deputy Secretary, Ministry of Finance* vs. *S.N. Dasgupta,* though it was in regard to cash in hand.

Q.117. What do you understand by Internal Audit? What should be the main functions of an internal auditor? Under whom should he work and to whom report his findings? What powers should he have for the successful performance of his duties?

Ans. Arnold W. Johnson has defined Internal Audit: "Internal Auditing is the independent appraisal activity within an organisation for the review of the accounting, financial and other operations as a basis for protective and constructive service to management." Business or undertaking of a very big size like banking and insurance companies engage a certain set of people who conduct a kind of continuous audit during the whole of the year. They check the accounts which have been maintained by book-keepers. As a matter of fact, the nature of work of such a set of people who are called Internal Auditors, is more or less the same as that of professional auditors who are appointed by the shareholders. The Internal Auditors are appointed by the Directors. The Internal Auditor checks the entries after they have been passed by the accounts clerks. He checks the accounts before the Auditor of the Company conducts the annual or six-monthly audit as the case may be. Internal audit is a device which detects any error or fraud which might have been committed while the internal check prevents the commission of an error or fraud. The reader may refer to Chapter II regarding the points of distinction between Internal audit and Internal check for details. The Internal Auditor has advisory functions as well while on the other hand it is no part of the duties of an auditor to give advice. The Internal Audit Department should be quite independent of the main office to enable the auditor to submit his independent report without any pressure or influence. He should work under an officer of high rank or the Board or Management to whom or to which he should submit his report.

He should have the same powers as a professional auditor has in order to enable him to perform his functions efficiently.

How far the professional accountant should depend upon the work of an Internal Audit Department will depend upon the circumstances of each case. The auditor should not delegate any part of his responsibility to the Internal Audit Department. It is the auditor who will be responsible for any fraud which remained undetected if he relied upon the Internal Audit Department. Of course, if he can prove that he showed reasonable care and skill he may be relieved of the liability. If the auditor is satisfied that a good Internal Audit system prevails, he may apply test checks and need not go into details. As mentioned before, it is he who is responsible for any error or fraud which remained undetected due to his reliance on the Internal Audit.

Q.118. A Statutory Corporation recently purchased a large number of shares of various industrial undertakings, prices of some of which were quoted in the market while others were unquoted. The question having been raised as to whether fair prices were paid or not, you are called upon to value them.

State the usual basis for the valuation of shares and illustrate how you would proceed to value them by using hypothetical figures.

Ans. In the case of quoted shares, there will be no difficulty to find out whether fair prices were paid or not as the auditor can refer to the quotations of such shares at the Stock Exchange and compare the prices paid by the Corporation. The problem of the valuation of the shares which are not quoted by the Stock Exchange can be solved in the following ways:

The two main elements in the valuation of shares are :

(1) Surplus of assets; and

(2) Profit earning capacity.

(1) Valuation according to Surplus assets

To ascertain the value of the shares according to the surplus of assets including the goodwill, the balance-sheet for the previous year may be prepared on the basis of the real and conventional values. If the assets had been valued by experts, there is no need to disturb the balance-sheet. Out of the assets, all the liabilities should be deducted and the quotient should be divided by the number of shares so that the net value of the shares is ascertained. Thus, it would be possible to calculate the value of each share. Such value is called "Break-up value."

(2) Valuation according to earning capacity

To ascertain the value of the shares according to the profit earning capacity, the profit and loss accounts of the previous few years be taken into consideration and necessary adjustments be made therein in order to know the future earning capacity of the business. Adjustments may be made in respect of reserves, depreciation, goodwill and so on.

Let us take an example to make this point clear. A company has 50,000 equity shares of the nominal values of Rs. 10 each and 50,000, 5 per cent preference shares of the nominal value of Rs. 10 each. The company makes on an average annual profits of Rs. 61,000 after making the necessary adjustments as described above. The average income from investments in such companies in 6 per cent according to stock exchange quotation. The value of the shares will be calculated as under :

	Rs.
Average profits	61,000
Less Dividend payable to preference shareholders	25,000
Profit available for equity shareholders	36,000

The capitalised value of the equity shares at the rate of 6 per cent is $= \frac{36,000 \times 100}{6}$ i.e., 6,00,000. Therefore, the value of each share will be $\frac{6,00,000}{50,000}$, i.e., Rs. 12. Hence the fair value of each share will be Rs. 12.

While valuing the shares, the auditor should also take into consideration the question of goodwill, fashion of the commodity manufactured by the company, competition, restrictions, or controls imposed by the State, possible nationalisation of the industry, supply of and demand for the shares, the reserves created out of profits in the past, etc.

The auditor, by applying the above tests, can find out the values of the shares as to whether fair and reasonable prices were paid for them or not.

Q.119. When auditing a company's books state for what reasons you would —

1. **scrutinise payments made after the end of the financial year;**
2. **check bank paying-in-book counterfoils with cash book;**
3. **examine leases of premises occupied by the company;**
4. **examine the Articles of Association**
5. **examine minutes of :**
   (*a*) Directors' Meetings;
   (*b*) Annual General Meetings;
6. **request a certified from the company's bankers.**

Ans. 1. The auditor should scrutinise the payment side of the cash book after the financial year is over to find out what were the outstanding expenses for the previous year. In order to show more profits the management of the company might not have debited the expenses account and credited outstanding expenses account. Thus more profits might have been shown during the year under audit. The amount payable to such persons will be paid in the beginning of the next year and the revenue account of the next year will be debited although it ought to have been debited in the previous year. By scrutinizing the payment side of the cash book, the auditor will be able to detect such a fraud.

He should find out whether the dividends on shares sold or purchased "ex-dividend" or "cum-dividend" respectively had been received in the subsequent period.

Again, if the auditor did not go on the last working day to verify cash, he should check the cash transactions from the date of the balance-sheet and the date on which he pays the visit in order to find out the accuracy of the cash in hand on the closing day of the year.

2. The counterfoils of the Bank Paying-in-Book are compared with the cash book to find out whether the amounts supposed to have been paid into the bank according to the cash book were really paid on that date or not and whether the amount was actually paid or not. Sometimes the cashier retains the money with him and does not deposit it in the bank but passes an entry in the cash book as if the money had been deposited. If the auditor compares the counterfoils of the Paying-in-Book with the cash book and pass book, he will be able to detect such a fraud. Moreover, the counterfoils are examined to find out whether the process of 'splitting up' cheques had been adopted to commit a fraud.

3. Leases of premises occupied by the company are examined to find out—

(*a*) The value of the lease.

(*b*) The terms of the lease because if there is any breach of any terms of the lease, the lease would terminate.

(*c*) The period of the lease so that appropriate provision should be made for their renewals, etc.

4. He should examine the Articles of Association for the following purposes:

(*a*) Whether the shares have been issued according to the rules and regulations laid down in the Articles.

(*b*) Whether any underwriting commission or brokerage, etc., was to be paid and if so at what rate.

(*c*) If it is the first year audit, whether the minimum subscription had been applied for before the shares were allotted.

(*d*) To know the dates on which a call could be made and the amount thereof.

(*e*) Whether interest is to be charged on calls in arrear.

(*f*) To know the circumstances under which shares can be forfeited.

(*g*) To know the borrowing powers, appointment, remuneration, powers and duties, etc., of the managing agents, directors, etc.

(*h*) To know about accounts and audit of the company.

5. Minute Books of the Directors and shareholders are examined to vouch the following transactions:

(*a*) Directors' Minute Book. The auditor has to examine this book for the verification of the following matters:

(*i*) Allotment of shares and debentures.

(*ii*) Adoption of Contracts.

(*iii*) Documents to which the Seal of the company has been affixed.

(*iv*) Appointment of bankers and officers empowered to sign and endorse cheques and bills.

(*v*) Calls on shares.

(*vi*) Forfeiture of shares.

(*vii*) Appointment and remuneration of managing director, manager, secretary or other officials.

(*viii*) Appointment of the first auditors or to fill a casual vacancy, fixing their remuneration and expenses.

(*ix*) Authorisation of capital expenditure.

(*x*) Resolution to pay interim dividend, provided it is permitted by the Articles.

(*xi*) Directors' travelling expenses or special remuneration.

(*xii*) Adoption of Annual Accounts and Report to the shareholders and recommendation as to dividend.

(*xiii*) Any matter for which a resolution of the directors is specifically required by the Articles of the company.

(*b*) Shareholders' Minute Book. This book is examined by auditor in connection with the following matters :—

(*i*) Adoption of the Annual Accounts.

(*ii*) Any resolution affecting the accounts.

(*iii*) Remuneration voted for the directors, managing agents, etc.

(*iv*) Remuneration of the auditors.

(*v*) Appropriation of profits by way of dividends, reserves, etc.

6. A request would be made to company's bankers to find out.

(*a*) The balance to the credit of the client in case there is a doubt about certain transactions.

(*b*) Whether the securities, stock and shares, etc., which are alleged to have been lodged with the bankers, are really with them and that are free from any charge.

(*c*) Whether the bills receivable discounted with the bank have been dishonoured to find the contingent liabilities.

Q.120. Mention the several ways in which Goodwill Account would find its place in the books of a company. What steps would an auditor take to satisfy himself as to its correctness?

Ans. Goodwill is an intangible asset. In the case of a company, the goodwill may be due to two reasons, viz., either (1) it has been purchased from the vendors whose business has been taken over or (2) it has been raised in the books of accounts by spending a large sum of money on experiments or research which enable to company to have a monopoly. We shall take up these separately and discuss them.

(1) Purchased Goodwill

When a running business is purchased its assets and liabilities are taken over for a certain sum of money. If the value of the net assets acquired is less than the purchase price, the difference is paid for the goodwill as more price is paid than the value of the net assets acquired. This extra amount is debited to goodwill account. The auditor should examine the agreement with the vendors to find out the original amount paid for the goodwill and the assets and liabilities taken over.

Now the question arises as to whether goodwill, being one of the assets, should be depreciated like any other asset. The answer is that it is not necessary to write off the goodwill unless the Articles of Association lay it otherwise. Goodwill depends upon the profits of the company. If the profits increase, it shows that the goodwill of the company has increased. If the reputation of the company suffers, profits will go down. But in practice goodwill of a company is never valued according to the profits of a business. As a matter of fact, goodwill being an intangible asset, it is usually written off out of abnormal profits or capital profits. Sometimes to create secret reserve, a company writes it off at a very high rate. The auditor need not object to such a procedure.

(2) Created Goodwill

This kind of goodwill is sometimes called "Deferred Goodwill". Sometimes a very heavy expenditure is incurred in making experiment or doing research work which result in acquiring a new invention or a patent which enables the company to have a monopoly. Whole of such expenditure is debited to goodwill account. The auditor should see that only that expenditure which is directly connected with research or experiment is debited to the goodwill account. Sometimes in order to show more profits, the directors debit such an account with ordinary revenue expenditure. The auditor should pay his attention to this matter.

Moreover, such a goodwill should be shown in the balance-sheet in such a way as not to be confused for "Purchased Goodwill". This kind of goodwill *should* be written off within a reasonable time.

Q.121. "An auditor to a limited company is not responsible for undetected errors or frauds in a Balance-Sheet, where there is nothing to excite his suspicion." Comment on this statement, giving reasons for your answer.

Ans. An auditor is appointed by the shareholders of a company to check the accounts and to find out whether the balance-sheet and the profit and loss account of the company are drawn up according to Companies Act and that they exhibit a true and fair view of the state of affairs of the company. Incidentally he has to find out whether there is any error or fraud. He thus acts in the capacity of an agent. As an agent is expected to show as much skill and diligence as is expected of a person of his status, the auditor is, therefore, expected to show the same amount of care and skill as is expected of a person of his status. If in spite of showing so much care and skill there is nothing to arouse his suspicion, he is not liable, if later on it is found that some error or fraud remained undetected. But the auditor will have to prove that (*i*) the fraud was so skillfully executed that it was not possible for a man of his status to discover that, (*ii*) the system of book-keeping and internal check was so defective that it was not possible to detect the fraud, (*iii*) there was nothing to arouse his suspicion to probe into the matter very deeply, and (*iv*) he showed the same amount of care and skill which was expected of him.

An auditor is not a detective. He does not approach his work with suspicion that there is something wrong unless there is something to arouse his suspicion or unless he is told that there is a suspicion of fraud as was in the case of *Armitage* vs. *Brewer and Knatt.* "He is a watch-dog and not a blood-hound" as has been said by Justice Lopes in the *Kingston Cotton Mills* case.

Q.122. What is a 'Branch Office' of a company for the purposes of the Companies Act, 1956? State the duties and responsibilities of auditors regarding Branch Accounts.

Ans. Section 2 (9) of the Companies Act, 1956, defines a "Branch Office" of a company as "branch office" means any establishment described as a branch by the company, or any establishment carrying on either the same or substantially the same activity as that carried on by the head office of the company or any establishment engaged in any production, processing or manufacture but does not include any establishment specified in any order made by the Central Government under Section 8.

Section 8 referred to above lays down: "The Central Government may, by order, declare that in the case of any company any establishment carrying on either the same or substantially the same activity as that carried on by the head office of the company, or any establishment engaged in any production, processing or manufacture shall not be treated as a branch office of the company for all or any of the purposes of this Act."

Accounts

Section 209 (2) of the Companies Act lays down that where a company has a branch whether in India or outside India proper accounts shall be maintained at the branch relating to all the transactions effected there and summarised returns shall be submitted to the registered office of the company or wherever books of accounts of the company are maintained at an interval of not more than three months.

Audit

The accounts of the branch office shall be audited by the company's auditor appointed under Section 224 or by a person qualified for appointment as auditor of the company under Section 226, (Section 228).

Where the branch office is situated in a foreign country, the accounts of the branch shall be audited by the company's auditor or a person who is qualified to audit the accounts of a company according to the law of that country.

In case the accounts of a branch office are audited by a person other than the company's auditor, the company's auditor shall have the right to visit the branch office, if he deems it necessary to audit the accounts and to have access to the books of account, vouchers, etc., maintained at the branch office.

In case of a banking company, having a branch office in a foreign country, it shall be sufficient for the auditor to have access to such copies of, and extracts from, the books and accounts of the branch as have been transmitted to the head office of the company in India.

The Central Government may, however, exempt a company from the provisions of Section 228 (4) of the Companies Act, under certain circumstances, e.g., even an employee or an officer of the company may be appointed to act as the auditor of the branch provided he is otherwise qualified or even a branch auditor may not be employed.

The Duty of an Auditor

In case the accounts of branch office have been audited by a qualified auditor as described above, the duty of the auditor is to see that (a) the returns submitted by the branch are adequate for the purpose of his audit, (b) the returns have been sent at an interval of not more than three months, (c) the returns are properly incorporated in the books of accounts of the head office. He should also see whether the assets and liabilities of the branch are grouped according to Schedule VI, Parts I and II of the Companies Act; that the stock in trade is valued according to the set principles of accountancy, etc. If he sees to all these things his responsibility is over.

If a qualified person has not been appointed at a branch, it is the right and duty of the auditor of the head office to visit the branch to audits accounts.

Q.123. Distinguish between "Contingent Liabilities provided for" and "Contingent Liabilities not provided for." Give instances for each type of these liabilities and state how these will be dealt with in the final accounts of a limited company. What entries will be passed in the books of the company?

Ans. A Contingent Liability has been defined as one which may or may not arise at a future date after the preparation of the balance-sheet. The element of uncertainty makes a liability as Contingent Liability. It is a possible future liability arising from one or more business acts preceding the date of the balance-sheet. For instance some of the contingent liabilities are given below :—

1. **A liability involving an ultimate loss.** A liability in a disputed case where damages may have to be paid. This type of liability may be of two kinds, viz., firstly where it is certain that the company would lose the case and will have to pay damages, the amount of which may not be certain, and secondly, where the company has a strong case but there is *possibility* of the case-being lost resulting in a loss.
2. **A guarantee for third parties.** If the principal debtor does not pay, the liability will arise.

3. **A liability on a bill discounted.** If the bill is dishonoured at the due date, the company being the previous endorser will be liable to the endorsee. This liability will arise only when the bill is dishonoured.
4. **A liability in case of partly-paid shares.** If the company has held partly-paid shares in another company, a liability may arise in case a call is made.
5. **A liability which will involve the acquisition of an asset.** For instance where goods have been purchased for future delivery.
6. **A liability in respect of unfinished contracts.** If the contract is not completed in time and; therefore damages have to be paid.

From the auditing point of view, the contingent liabilities may be divided into two main classes, viz., (1) contingent liabilities for which provision has been made, and (2) contingent liabilities for which no provision has been made.

(1) *Contingent liabilities for which provision has been made.* Such liabilities are those which the directors think are more likely to become legal obligations and hence they make provision for them, e.g., claims against the company which the directors think that the company will have to pay although nothing has been decided at the date of the balance-sheet or liability in respect of partly-paid shares held by the company and on which a call may be made very soon.

The directors make provision in respect of such liabilities. The entry in the books is passed as under:

Appropriate Expenses A/c. Dr.
To Contingent Liability Provided for A/c.

(2) *Contingent Liabilities for which no provision has been made.* Such liabilities may or may not arise and consequently the company may or may not be called upon to pay anything, e.g., liabilities on bills discounted which have not matured at the due date. There is a possibility that the bill may be dishonoured at the due date and the company as the previous endorser may be called upon to pay the amount when such a contingency happens; liability in respect of guarantee given by the company for loans or overdrafts granted to managed companies. The liability will arise in case the debt is not paid at the due date. One is not sure whether such a contingency will arise or not. Under the circumstances no provision is made for such a contingent liability. Such liabilities are shown by way of a footnote in the balance-sheet.

Q.124. As the auditor of a Holding Company, what are your duties with regard to Subsidiary Companies?

Ans. The Companies Act does not specify any duty of an auditor of a Holding Company apart from the ordinary duties of an auditor except under Sections 212 and 213, regarding the preparation of the balance-sheet. According to the Act, the Holding Company must disclose certain particulars relating to the subsidiary companies in their report, Profit and Loss Account and the Balance-Sheet so that the shareholders of the Holding Company may know the exact position. According to Section 212, the following documents in respect of the subsidiaries must be attached to the Balance-Sheet of the Holding Company:

(*a*) a copy of the balance-sheet of the subsidiary:
(*b*) a copy of the profit and loss account;
(*c*) a copy of the report of the Board of Directors;
(*d*) a copy of the report of the auditor;
(*e*) a statement of the holding company's interest in the subsidiary in respect of the following particulars:
  (*i*) the extent of the interest in the subsidiary at the end of the financial year and if the end of the financial year of both the companies does not coincide, then the interest in the subsidiary at the end of the previous year also;

(*ii*) the amount of profits and losses of the subsidiary calculated in the same way as in (i) above, etc.

(*f*) a statement showing the changes which have occurred in respect of (i) the subsidiary's fixed assets; (ii) its investments; (iii) the money lent by it; (iv) the money borrowed by it for any purpose other than that of meeting current liabilities since the last financial year of the subsidiary and where it does not coincide with the financial year of the Holding Company;

(*g*) a report where the Board of Directors of the Holding Company could not obtain any information about subsidiary's profit or loss (Section 212).

In addition to the above requirements of the Companies Act, the auditor should pay attention to the following :

1. If the auditor of the Holding Company has not audited the accounts of the subsidiary company, he should examine the statements of accounts of the subsidiary company and pay attention to the qualifications of the report by the auditor of the subsidiary company.
2. He should pay attention to the inter-company transactions and should verify such transactions.
3. He should see that if a consolidated profit and loss account and balance-sheet have been prepared (the Companies Act does not require), proper grouping, classification and valuation of the assets and liabilities are done. In regard to the valuation of shares of the subsidiary companies they should be valued at cost price as they are fixed assets of the Holding Company. However, if the subsidiary has suffered a heavy loss and consequently the value of its shares has gone down, a provision should be made in the books of the Holding Company for such losses. The auditor should see that these investments are segregated in the balance-sheet of the Holding Company according to Part I or Schedule VI of Companies Act.
4. He should see that in the balance-sheet of the Holding Company, the number of shares of the Subsidiary Company is clearly mentioned.
5. The amount of indebtedness to and from the subsidiary Companies should be mentioned in the Balance-Sheet of the Holding Company.
6. He should see whether the Holding Company has made any provision for the losses of the Subsidiary Company and whether the Balance-Sheet of the Holding Company represents a true and fair view of its state of affairs.

If the auditor is not satisfied on any of the above points, he must refer the matter in his report.

Q.125. A company has a large balance to the credit of General Reserve Account built up out of the following:

(*a*) Appropriation from Profit and Loss Account;

(*b*) Profit on sale of fixed assets from time to time;

(*c*) Liabilities waived voluntarily by creditors due to the company's financial conditions in earlier years.

The year under review has made a small profit and the directors decide to recommend the payment of a Dividend involving an amount exceeding the profit of the year. For this purpose they propose to transfer from the Reserve Account sufficient balance to meet the dividend payment.

Consider the propriety of the above proposal.

Ans. Generally speaking, the credit balance of a General Reserve Account shows the undistributed profits and such profits may be carried to the credit of profit and loss account and distributed to shareholders provided the Articles of Association do not prohibit such an action. The credit balance of the General Reserve Account is credited with such amounts which in normal course of business are distributable to the shareholders. That money belongs to them and there can be no objection if that is returned to them in the form of a dividend later on. But in the question under consideration we find that the General Reserve Account has been credited with revenue as well as capital profits and hence whole of the credit balance cannot be carried to the profit and loss account of the current year. Let us take each item separately. But it must be made clear to the shareholders that the past profits are being distributed as the profits of the year under review are insufficient.

(*a*) *Appropriation from Profit and Loss Account.* The amount representing appropriation from the previous Profit and Loss Accounts may be carried to the Profit and Loss Account as it represents the profit which would have been distributed to the shareholders in the past but which had been withheld. It should be seen that the Articles of the company do not provide otherwise and the shareholders are informed of the fact.

(*b*) *Profit on sale of fixed assets from time to time.* Such a profit is capital profit and it ought not to have been credited to General Reserve Account. However, the amount representing capital profits cannot be carried to the credit of Profit and Loss Account unless the following conditions are fulfilled:

(*i*) Articles of the company permit such distribution.

(*ii*) The profit is realised.

(*iii*) The surplus exists after the revaluation of the other assets and liabilities of the company.

(*c*) *Liabilities waived voluntarily by creditors due to the company's financial conditions in earlier years.* This amount credited to the General Reserve Account is not a revenue profit but represents capital profit and hence cannot be distributed to the shareholders. Therefore, this amount should not be credited to the Profit and Loss Account.

Q.126. (*a*) Mr. R. E. Taylor, a partner in Taylor and Co., whom you have known for some years, tells you that he wishes you to take over the audit of the books of his firm. He says that his firm's accounts have, in past year, been audited by Vouch & Co., Chartered Accountants, but that Mr. Vouch, Senior, who had always attended to the work personally, has died recently and that he and his partners do not wish to entrust the work to any of the surviving partners in Vouch & Co.

(*i*) State what steps you would take before deciding to accept appointment.

(*ii*) State if any different action would be taken by you if neither Mr. Vouch nor Vouch & Co. had a professional qualification.

(*b*) Assuming that Mr. Taylor had approached you to take over the audit of his company, Taylor & Co. Ltd., what action additional to that given in answer to (a) (i) above would have to be taken by you or by Taylor & Co. Ltd.?

Ans. (*a*) (*i*) The auditor, a member of the Institute of Chartered Accountants, to whom the work of audit of Taylor & Co., whose accounts had been audited in the past by Vouch & Co., has been offered, should write to Vouch & Co., asking them whether there is any professional reason why he should not accept the offer. He should do so before he accepts the offer to audit the accounts of Taylor & Co. (*S. V. Kharwandikar* vs. *D. K. Borkar,* 1952).

(*ii*) Even though neither Mr. Vouch nor Vouch & Co. had professional qualifications, the auditor should, out of courtesy and in his own interest, write to Vouch & Co. before he accepts the offer whether he should take up the work of audit though legally speaking it is not necessary to communicate the fact to the previous auditor.

(*b*) If Taylor & Co. was a limited company, the auditor should, in addition to the above steps, see that the requirements of Section 225 of the Companies Act have been complied with by the company. Under this section, the company must have taken the following steps in removing the previous auditors.

1. Special notice of at least 14 days for a resolution at the annual general meeting, appointing an auditor in place of the existing auditor, must be sent by a member to the company.
2. A copy of such a resolution must be sent to the existing auditor by the company immediately on the receipt of such a notice but if it is not practicable a public notice regarding the resolution will serve the purpose.
3. The auditor proposed to be removed has a right to send a representation to the company. If this representation has been received in time, a copy of it must be sent to each shareholder unless the representation was either received too late to be sent to the shareholders or it is defamatory or it is vexatious. The cost is to be borne by the auditor.
4. If the representation could not be sent to the shareholders either on account of default by the company or on account of its being received too late the representation must be read at the annual general meeting without any prejudice to the right of the retiring auditor to give an oral explanation.

Q.127. XYZ Ltd., has made loans to—

1. **P, who is a director of the company,**
2. **Q & Co., in which Q a relative of P, is a partner, and**
3. **AB Private Ltd., which is the subsidiary of XYZ Ltd.**

Discuss briefly your duties as the statutory auditor of XYZ Ltd.

Ans. Section 295 of the Companies Act, 1956, provides:

No company shall, without obtaining the previous approval of the Central Government, make directly or indirectly any loan to—

(*i*) any director of the company or of its holding company or to any partner or relative of such a director,

(*ii*) any firm in which such director or relative is a partner,

(*iii*) a private company of which such director is a director or member,

(*iv*) any body corporate of which 25 per cent of the voting power is capable of being exercised or controlled by such director or more than one such director together,

(*v*) any body corporate, whose Board of Directors, managing directors, managing agent, secretaries and treasures or manager, is "accustomed to act in accordance with the instructions" of the Board of any director or directors of the lending company.

Such restrictions do not apply to—

(*i*) a private company unless it is subsidiary of a public company,

(*ii*) a banking company,

(*iii*) a holding company for loan advanced to its subsidiary.

(*iv*) a company which is the managing agent or secretaries or treasurers to the managed company (Section 295).

From the above, it would be clear that

1. Loan made by XYZ Ltd. to P, who is a director of the company, is against the provisions of the Companies Act, 1956.
2. Loan to Q & Co. in which Q is the relative of P, the director of XYZ Ltd., is also against the provisions of the Companies Act, unless the previous sanction of the Central Government had been obtained by XYZ Ltd. to advance such loans in both (i) and (ii)

above. From the question, it is not clear whether XYZ Ltd. is a Banking Company. If it is a banking company the loan advanced will not be against the provisions of the Companies Act.

3. Regarding the loan to AB Private Ltd., which is the subsidiary of XYZ Ltd. such a loan is in order and there can be no objection.

It is the duty of an auditor to see that such loans or advances to directors, directly or indirectly, are clearly mentioned on the assets side of the balance-sheet. He should also see that the rate of interest charged from the directors is not less than what is usually charged. If a director has borrowed money from the company and repaid it before the date of the balance-sheet the fact must be mentioned by way of a footnote. The maximum amount due by directors at any time during the year is to be shown by way of a footnote. The auditor should see that the sanction of the Central Government in case of (i) and (ii) had been obtained before the loan was advanced.

Q.128. How should an auditor deal with loans to companies under the same management?

Ans. Generally speaking, a company is not allowed to advance loans to other companies which are under the same management according to Section 370 except when a special resolution is passed to that effect with a condition that the amount of the loan should not exceed 20 per cent of the subscribed capital and the free reserves of the company and that also with the prior approval of the Central Government. The total amount of the loans to more than one company under the same management should not exceed 30 per cent.

Section 370 further lays down

(*a*) that the loan advanced should be entered in a register within three days of the advance;

(*b*) that such a register should be kept at the registered office of the company; and

(*c*) that the register should remain open for inspection to any member of the company who may be allowed to take extracts from such a register.

The auditor while auditing the accounts should, therefore inquire :-

(*a*) whether the loans advanced is within the limits;

(*b*) whether a special resolution had been passed;

(*c*) whether prior approval of the Central Government had been obtained; and

(*d*) whether the requirements regarding the maintenance of the register had been complied with or not.

He should vouch the payment or advance of loan to the company as usual.

Q.129. To what extent do you consider that counterfoils of receipts are of value for audit purposes? Describe the conditions which you would impose in order to render the counterfoil system effective as check upon cash receipts.

Ans. Counterfoils of receipts are of value for audit purposes if there is a good internal check system in respect of receipt of cash. If the internal check is not in operation or is inefficient they are of no value to the auditor, e.g., if cash has been received, less amount might be inserted in the counterfoil than in the receipt or a receipt might have been issued to the sender of the money but the word "cancelled" might have been put on the counterfoil and the whole of the money received might have been misappropriated. This is the reason why carbon copy receipts are preferred. However, if it is desired to use counterfoil receipt books, the following precautions must be taken to make the counterfoils more reliable from the audit point of view :

1. The cashier should not sign the receipts and the counterfoils when cash is received. They should be signed by a responsible official after comparing the rough cash book (if any) and the cash book with the receipts, counterfoil and the account of the debtor. However, the cashier must countersign the receipt.

2. Receipts should be consecutively numbered so that a blank form may not be removed by a dishonest clerk to use it improperly.
3. The spoilt receipts should be cancelled but must not be detached from the counterfoils.
4. No blank counterfoils should be accepted.
5. Unused receipt books should be kept under lock and key.

Q.130. An interim dividend was paid by the Directors of a Company on the basis of its half-yearly accounts, but when the final accounts were drawn up for the year, the Company had incurred a loss. The Directors propose to utilise secret reserves to make up the deficiency. Also, the Managing Director of the Company waived a large portion of his salary to reduce the loss.

State your comments laying special emphasis on the liability, if any, arising therefrom of the Directors and Auditors of the Company.

Ans. When at the end of the year is found that the company had suffered a loss although it had paid an Interim Dividend on the basis of the half-yearly accounts, it means the dividend had been paid out of capital. In such a case both the directors and auditors would be held liable to refund such an amount to the shareholder with interest at 5 per cent. If the directors can prove that the interim dividend was paid on the basis of a **bona fide** valuation of assets which subsequently turned out to be too high, they would be free from any liability. (*Re Mercantile Trading Co., Stringer's case,* 1869). In the absence of any suspicion, the directors are entitled to rely upon trusted officials of the company in the preparation of the company's accounts (*Dovey* vs. *Cory,* 1901). A Court has the power to relieve a director of his liability in such a case under section 633 of the Companies Act, 1956.

It may be mentioned here that the shareholders who had received such a dividend knowing it that it was being paid out of capital, have no right to claim any refund from the directors. Besides, such shareholders can be asked to refund the money. (*Maxham* vs. *Grant, 1900*). If the interim dividend was paid out of capital by a *bona fide* mistake, it must be recovered from the recipient shareholder provided he has retained the money as was held in the case of *Towers* vs. *African Tug Co.* (1904).

In case the directors wish to make up the loss by utilising the Secret Reserves, they may do so but this fact must be made clear in the profit and loss account of the company [*Shamdasani* vs. *Pochkhanwala* (1927)]. Again, if the Managing Director waives a part of his salary to reduce the loss, it may be done but a resolution to this effect must be passed by the directors and this source of income must be made clear in the accounts. It is the duty of the auditor to see that his information is given to the shareholders.

If the auditor had not audited the accounts for the first half year, he is not liable for the interim dividend which had been paid out of capital. In case he had audited the accounts for the interim period, he would be held guilty for misfeasance. In such a case he ought not to have advised the directors to pay the interim dividend.

Q.131. A company has a debit balance on the profit and loss account of Rs. 1,00,000, and a credit balance of Rs. 6,00,000 and Rs. 1,40,000 in the general reserve and the Development Rebate Reserve, respectively. The directors do not wish to show the debit balance of the profit and loss account on the assets side of the balance sheet and propose instead to show it on the liabilities side under "Reserve and Surpluses" by way of deduction from the Development Rebate Reserve. Advise the directors.

Ans. According to the prescribed form of the balance-sheet vide Schedule VI of the Companies Act, a company is allowed to deduct the debit balance from the General Reserves but not from the specific reserves, such as Development Rebate reserve.

If the directors resort to the latter course, the Income Tax authorities will not allow the company the deduction from Development Rebate admissible under S. 34 (3) of the Income Tax Act. If such Development Rebate reserve is utilised by the company for distribution to the shareholders in the form of dividends, the rebate allowed will be withdrawn.

Under the circumstances, the directors are advised not to take such a step and the debit balance of the profit and loss account may be shown on the liabilities side of the balance sheet by way of deduction from the profit and loss account under "Reserves and Surpluses" instead of a deduction from the Development Rebate reserve as in proposed by the directors.

Q.132. The Directors of a Company suggest that in view of the efficient system of internal check by the Company's employees and in view of the urgency to have the audited Balance-Sheet it would be enough if you abridge your programme of Audit and let them have the Balance-Sheet early.

State to what extent would you be prepared to comply with the requests.

Ans. The duty of an auditor is to report to the shareholders of the company whether the profit and loss account and the balance-sheet of a company are drawn up according to the Companies Act and exhibit a true and fair view of the state of affairs of the company. But how can he do so. The answer is by examining the books of accounts to which he has access at all times. If he is asked to abridge his programme of audit in order to submit the balance-sheet earlier, he would have to curtail his work. This means certain restrictions are being imposed on his statutory duties which action is against the provisions of Companies Act. The power and duties of an auditor can be expanded but cannot be limited as was held in *Newton* vs. *Birmingham Small Arms Co. Ltd.* Even if there is an efficient system of internal check by the company's employees, the auditor should not agree to the suggestion. Efficient internal check system lightens the work of an auditor but does not reduce his responsibility and liability.

In the light of the above discussion, the auditor should not agree to the suggestion of the directors. In case he does so, he runs a great risk. Even if an agreement is entered into between him and the company whereby he is relieved of his liability such an agreement will be void as per Section 201 of the Companies Act, 1956.

Q.133. Do you consider the following chargeable to capital expenditure or revenue account?

- **(*a*) Compensation in respect of loss of office paid to the directors of a company absorbed by another.**
- **(*b*) The cost of pulling down an old factory preparatory to building a new one.**
- **(*c*) A premium paid for a lease.**
- **(*d*) Interest paid to date of completion of the purchase of freehold Property.**
- **(*e*) Costs incidental to the raising of a mortgage.**
- **(*f*) Discount on issue of debenture stock.**
- **(*g*) An amount received as compensation for loss of goodwill to a business, the premises of which are acquired for road widening.**

Give your reasons for dealing with the amount in the way you propose in each case.

Ans. (*a*) The whole of the compensation which is a loss to the business should not be debited to the revenue account in one year. This loss should be spread over a number of years. It is an expense which is in connection with the absorption of the company like the preliminary expenses which are incurred at the time of formation of a company. Moreover, the directors' fees payable by the new company will be less than the fees paid by the two companies together before the absorption. Thus, it would mean a permanent saving. Therefore, as stated above, the compensation paid should be treated as revenue expenditure and be written off over a reasonably short period.

(*b*) The cost of pulling down the building should be debited to the new building account if the building was purchased with the object of renovating it.

However, if one of the old building has been pulled down, the cost of demolition should be debited to the revenue account or it may be spread over a number of years as it is a capital loss. In no case, should it be debited to the buildings account as it would mean showing the value of the buildings at a higher price than their actual value.

(*c*) The premium paid for a lease is capital expenditure for the purpose of acquiring the lease. Hence, it should be written off to revenue accounts for the period for which the lease stands. The revenue account of the first year should not be debited with the whole of the amount.

(*d*) Interest paid up to the date of the completion of the purchase of the freehold property should be debited to the revenue account as it is not a part of the purchase price or expenses directly connected with the purchase of property.

(*e*) Costs incidental to the raising of a mortgage is capital expenditure as these expenses have been incurred in acquiring capital. Therefore, such a cost should be spread over a number of years for which the mortgage is to run. The revenue account of each of these years should be debited with a proportionate amount.

(*f*) Discount on issue of debenture stock is directly connected with the raising of funds through debentures. It is not an ordinary expense and hence it should be spread over the period for which these debentures have been issued and the revenue account of every year should be debited with a proportionate amount.

(*g*) The amount received as compensation for the loss of goodwill is not a trading profit earned during the regular course of business and, therefore, it should not be credited to revenue account. However, the amount may be utilised in writing off the goodwill account, if such an account still exists, or credited to a Capital Reserve account or General Reserve account.

If the loss of goodwill is a temporary one, the compensation received may be credited to the revenue account over a number of years.

Q.134. (*a*) In what circumstances do you think it may be desirable for the auditor of a limited company to attend at the company's stock-taking?

(*b*) For what purpose should he attend?

(*c*) How should he ensure that the management does not misunderstand his duties if he does attend?

Ans. (*a*) It may be desirable for the auditor of a limited company to attend at the time of the company's stock-taking in the following circumstances :–

(1) As a matter of fact it is not the duty of the auditor of a company to be present at the time of annual stock-taking. The management of the company takes the stock and values it. The auditor has to apply certain tests to verify the assets including the stock. For this purpose he has to find out whether the directors have properly taken and valued the stock. If he is present at the time of stock-taking, provided it is reasonable and practicable, he can be sure that the procedure in regard to stock-taking is correct.

(2) If there is any material alteration in the method of stock-taking it may effect the valuation of stock and hence it may help him to some extent.

(3) In case it is the first audit of the company by the auditor, he may know the technicalities of the business, as no auditor is expected to know the technicalities of every business. The knowledge of such technicalities of business will be helpful to him in the subsequent audits even though he may not be present in future at the time of stock-taking.

(4) If during the course of the year no stock records were maintained and the management depended entirely on the annual physical stock-taking, it is desirable that he should be present at the time of taking stock.

(*b*) The auditor should attend at the company's stock-taking for the following purposes:–

(1) To find out whether stock is being taken according to the procedure laid down, if any.

(2) To find out whether the existing procedure for taking stock is adequate for the purpose of internal control.

(3) To test some of the stock-sheets if the thinks desirable.

(4) To find out the cause of any difference between the stock book and the stock-sheets after physical verification.

(*c*) Lest any misunderstanding might arise on account of his presence at the time of stock-taking he should make it clear to the management :–

(1) that his presence at the stock-taking time is necessary to enable him to assess whether the procedure for stock-taking is adequate and effective;

(2) that his presence will not relieve the management of any of their responsibilities;

(3) that he is neither a valuer nor stock-taker and therefore he has no responsibility for supervising the stock-taking.

Q.135. What more information and explanations, other than those supplied as stated below, would you require in verifying the following entries:

1. Cash received from a customer credited to Bad Debts Dividend Account:

Documents Supplied: Counterfoil of the receipt issued in favour of the customer.

2. Payment on account of legal charges debited to Preliminary Expenses Account:

Documents supplied : Acknowledgement by the lawyers.

3. Cost of repairs to Buildings debited to Buildings Account:

Documents supplied: Contractor's Bill.

Ans. The necessary documents and explanations which will be required to verify the different transactions are given below:—

1. *Cash received from customer credited to Bad Debts Dividend Account:*

(*a*) Enquire as to who authorised the writing of the debts as bad in the past and what was the amount due and written off.

(*b*) If the customer had been adjudicated as insolvent what was the amount of the claim which was filed with the Official Receiver or the Assignee. Compare the amount of the claim with the customer's account.

(*c*) Find out the amount of the claim admitted by the Official Receiver or the Assignee by examining the letter from him.

(*d*) Ascertain the amount received, if any, by examining the covering letter;

(*e*) Check the amount which was received and the balance outstanding against the customer.

(*f*) Check the letter from the Official Receiver or the Assignee intimating the amount of instalment sent.

2. *Legal charge debited to Preliminary Expenses:*

(*a*) Examine the bill submitted by the lawyer in connection with the formation of the company and see that only those expenses which can legally be debited to Preliminary Expenses, e.g., cost for the preparation of Memorandum and Articles of Association, Prospectus, Registration fee, etc., are debited to Preliminary Expenses Account.

(b) See that the total amount of the Preliminary Expenses has not exceeded the amount as stated in the Articles and the Prospectus. For this purpose examine these documents.

(c) If the amount of the Preliminary Expenses has been exceeded, examine the resolution passed by the share-holders sanctioning the excess amount.

3. *Cost of the repairs to building debited to Building Account:*

(a) Find out whether the expenses which have been debited to Buildings Account are ordinary expenses of repairs or they have been incurred for any extension to the buildings which will increase the rental value of the buildings. In the former case the amount should not be debited to the Revenue Account. In the latter case the expenses should be capitalised.

(b) Examine the agreement with the contractor as to the nature of the work which was to be done by him and the amount payable therefor.

(c) If the capital expenditure was to be incurred, examine the Board's resolution sanctioning such an expenditure.

Q.136. "An auditor is not a valuer and yet he is intimately connected with values." Discuss.

Ans. An auditor is not a valuer. This statement is quite correct. He is only an accountant. An auditor is not a technical hand. He has no knowledge of the quantity of the goods and especially when a concern has a variety of goods. He does not know the value of each and every kind of asset. In spite of all this he has to certify the value of the assets as stated in the balance-sheet. Again, market value and the cost price may be quite different. But will the auditor be in a position to find out the market price of every article? In the case of fixed assets, they are valued at cost price less depreciation while current assets are valued at cost price or the market price whichever is the lower.

The assets are valued by the management. The auditor has only to see that the principles of valuation stated above are applied while valuing them. In case he is not satisfied with the method of valuation of any particular asset he may seek the advice of an expert. Thus it will be observed that he does not value the assets as he depends upon the management or experts in the valuation of assets.

The principles at which different assets are valued and the duty of the auditor in that connection are given below:

1. *Tangible Assets.* Such assets are Buildings, Plant and Machinery, etc. They are valued at cost price less depreciation written off. It is the duty of the auditor to see that the cost of the assets stated in the balance-sheet is correct. For this purpose he should refer to the invoices. He should also see that the depreciation written off is according to the rules and regulations, e.g., Income Tax Act, Companies Act, etc.
2. *Intangible Assets.* Such assets are those which cannot be seen or touched, e.g., goodwill. It should be valued at cost price at which it was acquired, less the amount written off, if any. The auditor should examine the agreement with the vendor to find out its cost price. The amount written off from time to time can be ascertained from the previous balance-sheets and profit and loss accounts.
3. *Stock-in-trade.* This asset is valued at cost price or market price whichever is lower. The cost price can be ascertained from the original invoices while the market price can be ascertained by referring to the copies of the invoices relating to the goods sold recently. The quantity of the stock-in-trade can be ascertained by referring to the stock accounts, stock sheets or by physical check of a few items of the stock.

4. *Book Debts.* This item should be valued at the amount which can ultimately be realised from the debtors. To ascertain this, the auditor should examine the accounts of the debtors, cash book, bills book, allowances book, statements of account received from the debtors, etc. By applying certain tests, he can form an idea as to whether the debtors are good, bad or doubtful. He should see that adequate provision for bad and doubtful debts is made.
5. *Investments.* Cost price can be found by referring to the Bought-Notes while the market price can be found by referring to Stock Exchange quotations and the Sold Notes relating to investments sold recently. If the market price is lower than the cost price provision should be made for depreciation.
6. *Cash in hand and at Bank.* He should physically verify cash on the last working day but if it is not possible for him to do so he should count the cash at the visit subsequent to the balance-sheet date and vouch the cash transactions from the balance-sheet date to the day of his visit. In regard to cash at bank, bank pass book should be compared with the cash book and if there is any difference, bank reconciliation statement should be prepared.

From the above discussion it would be clear that the auditor verifies the fixed assets by referring to certain documentary evidence. He does not verify the actual physical condition of the assets or the market value of the assets concerned. On the other hand in the case of current assets, market value is taken into consideration for the purpose of the valuation of these assets. In certain cases he has to depend upon the opinion of the experts, e.g., in the case of plant and machinery, buildings, etc.

Thus it would appear that the auditor is not a valuer in determining the value of the assets by taking into consideration their physical condition. Nevertheless he verifies the value of the assets in the balance-sheet by depending upon the documentary evidence, opinion of the experts and so on. Therefore, we may say that though he is not a valuer yet he is intimately connected with values.

Q. 137. "The auditors are neither stock-takers nor values, not have they any responsibility for supervising the stock-taking." Discuss this statement.

Ans. This quotation has been taken from the guidelines issued by the Institute of Chartered Accountants of England and Wales regarding the duties of the auditors in connection with stock-taking. This statement had been issued with a view to clarify the position of the auditors **vis-a-vis** stock-taking as many an auditor, largely under the influence of American standards which have required auditors to attend at clients' stock-taking since the *McKesson & Robins case* in 1939.

It is clear from the statement that it is not the duty of the auditors to take stock or even to supervise the stock-taking. It is the duty of the management to do so. If the auditor is present at the time of stock-taking, he may be there only to see the procedure for taking stock and to advise the management about the stock-taking. He is not expected to be there to see the physical accuracy of stock in hand.

The auditor may physically check a few items of stock provided he is satisfied that the method of stock-taking is satisfactory. In cash he is not satisfied with the system in operation regarding the stock-taking, he may suggest rechecking of the stock but it must be remembered that it is no part of the duty of the auditor either to take stock or even to be present while stock is being taken.

Q.138. To what extent is the work of an audit modified by the institution of a mechanised system of accounting, whereby the whole of the ledgers and subsidiary books are written up by means of an accounting machine?

Ans. The basic principles of audit are not affected by the institution of mechanised accounting in a business house. The work of the auditor will be modified as follows:

1. The auditor need not check the arithmetical accuracy of the books of account and thus he saves time.
2. Since the records will be more neat and clean and legible, he has not to waste his time in going through these details. It will also result in saving of his time.
3. Alteration in figures is not possible and hence the detail checking is not necessary.
4. Since the code numbers are used in mechanised accounting, the auditor might miss detecting some errors unless he has a copy of the code with him.
5. The auditor will have to be more careful to see that the duplicates of the loose sheets are not used. For that purpose, he should ask the authorities to keep the blank loose sheets under lock and key.

Q.139. You are asked by the executors of XYZ, deceased, to audit their accounts covering the period from the date of the death to the ascertainment of the residue. Describe briefly the steps you would take in the course of your work in this connection.

Ans. The auditor should pay attention to the following points when auditing the accounts of the executors of XYZ:

1. He should get a copy of the will together with codicils, if any, to find out the property left by the deceased.
2. He should examine the assessment of the estate duty, the amount paid therefore and the expenses in connection therewith incurred by the executors. He should vouch these expenses.
3. He should find out from the will whether any provision had been made in it about the appointment, powers, remuneration, etc., of the executors and the auditors.
4. He should ascertain the names of the beneficiaries.
5. If a trust had been created he should find out whether the investments left by the deceased had been converted into Trustee Securities.
6. He should find out whether the beneficiaries have been paid according to the will. He should vouch the payments.
7. He should verify the assets and liabilities as usual.
8. He should see that the executors have not misused their powers an mixed up their own property with that of the deceased.
9. He should see that the accounts prepared by the executors represent a true and fair view of the transactions and that they have been signed by the executors.

Q.140. Suggest a suitable system of internal control over stores in the case of big textile mills.

Ans. In order to have a satisfactory system of internal control over the stores in the mills following methods should be adopted with advantage:

1. Satisfactory control over the purchase of the stores.
2. Satisfactory control over the issue of stores.
3. Satisfactory arrangement for the physical verification of the stores from time to time.

1. *Purchase of Stores*

With the previous experience the 'minimum level' or the 'order level' should be fixed in advance, This 'minimum' is recorded in the stores ledger as well as the Bin Cards. The underlying idea is that the stores may be obtained in time so that the mills may not run short of the stores if they are not purchased in time. Similarly "maximum" is also fixed to avoid over-stocking and thus locking up capital. Therefore stores should never be purchased beyond this limit.

Whenever the store-keeper finds that the 'minimum' has been reached prepares a requisition in duplicate—one copy is retained by him and the other is sent to the Purchase Department. The requisition contains the particulars of the goods the quality, quantity, etc.

The Purchase Department then asks for quotations or invites tenders from the suppliers. For small purchases, stores are purchased according to price lists.

After the receipt of the tenders or quotations, the Purchase Department prepares the Purchase Order in triplicate—on copy is sent to the suppliers, the second copy is sent to the Account Department and the third copy is retained by the Purchases Department for its record.

The store-keeper receives the stores when they are received from the suppliers and signs the Delivery Notes. He should prepare the Goods Received Report in triplicate—one copy should be sent to the Accounts Department, the other to the Purchase Department which compares it with the invoice and the third copy is retained by him from which he should make entries in the Bin Cards. Packages containing stores should be opened and inspected in the presence of a responsible official who should verify the quantity and quality of the stores. Accounts Department should credit the account of the suppliers after comparing the invoice and the Goods Received Report. The Purchase Department should make the necessary entry in the Stores Ledger.

2. *Issue of Stores*

No store should be issued by the store-keeper unless there is a Requisition giving the details of the stores required by the department or section concerned. It should be prepared in triplicate–one copy is to be sent to the Store Department, the second copy is to be sent to the Purchase Department for record in the Stores Ledger after the issue of the stores and the third copy is to be retained by the section concerned for its record. The store-keeper will make an entry in the Bin Card when the stores are issued.

3. *Physical Verification*

The stores in hand should be verified from time to time by comparing them with the balances as shown by the Bin Cards and the Stores Ledger.

If there is a small shortage, it may be due to evaporation, spillage, etc., and, therefore, it may be written off. If the shortage is big it may be due to pilferage and therefore enquiry should be made.

Damage, unserviceable or state stores may be written off by a responsible person and not the store-keeper.

If the above procedure for the purchase, issue and verification of the stores is followed in the mills, wastage, pilferage, over-stocking will be avoided.

Q.141. What are the difficulties which are encountered by an auditor of a concern where mechanised accountancy system is in operation? What suggestions would you make to overcome these difficulties?

Ans. Following are some of the difficulties which an auditor might experience in a concern where mechanised accounting system is in operation:–

1. Since the entries are made in the ledger directly from the original documents like Invoices Bought and Sold Notes, etc., it is difficult to check the totals of the Purchases or sales in the nominal accounts. To resort the original documents for checking purposes will entail wastage of time.

   To overcome these difficulties, the original documents should be sorted out in different bundles before the commencement of audit. For example if all the invoices relating to the purchases are sorted, bundled together and totalled, no difficulty will be experienced for checking purposes at the time of audit.

2. The clerk of the concern might, intentionally or unintentionally, miscode the documents. Thus if miscoding has been done, the mistake will not be discovered until the final accounts are prepared and compared.

   To guard against miscoding the codes should be translated and kept by the clerk for ready reference so that he might not commit a mistake while using the code.

3. Since the account book consist of loose sheets and cards, there is a danger of sheets or cards being removed, substituted or destroyed.

   To guard against the substitution or destruction of cards, there should be an efficient system of internal check. The original documents should be consecutively numbered.

4. As the entries are made from the original documents directly in the ledger, there is no cross reference between the ledger, the original documents and the books of prime entry.

   This difficulty can be overcome by introducing a suitable system of cross-reference so that the prime entries can be certified easily and without any difficulty.

Q.142. What are the special liabilities imposed by the Banking Companies Act, 1949, on the auditors of banking companies?

Ans. In addition to the matters required under Section 227 of the Companies Act, the auditor of a banking company incorporated in India, under Section 30 (3) of the Banking Companies Act, 1949, has to state in his report—

(*a*) whether or not the information and explanations required by him have been found to be satisfactory;

(*b*) whether or not the transactions of the company which have come to his notice have been within the powers of the company;

(*c*) whether or not the returns received from branch officers of the company have been found adequate for the purposes of his audit;

(*d*) whether the profit and loss account shows a true balance of profits and loss for the period covered by such accounts;

(*e*) any other matter which he considers should be brought to the notice of the shareholders of the company.

The auditor must examine the provision for the bad and doubtful debts as the advances and loans stated in the balance-sheet of a banking company are other than those considered bad and doubtful for which provision has been made to his satisfaction.

As the banks are allowed to create secret reserves, the auditor must see that such reserves are not misused.

If in the course of winding up proceedings of a banking company, the liquidator finds that the bank had suffered a loss due to any act or omission on the part of the auditor, he shall submit a report to the High Court. If the High Court is satisfied on this count, it may direct public examination of the auditor (Section 45G of Banking Companies Act).

At such a public examination, the auditor has to answer on oath any question put to him by the Court, any creditor or a contributory, etc., and such evidence may be used against him in any further legal proceedings instituted against him. On examination of such an auditor if the High Court is of opinion that the auditor is not fit to hold the office of an auditor of a company, it may pass an order removing him from the office for a period not exceeding five years even though he may be quite innocent of any act of misfeasance.

Section 45H of the Banking Companies Act further provides that if the High Court is satisfied, it may make an order against the auditor to repay or restore such money or properly unless it is proved to the contrary.

Q.143. (*a*) What is the statutory provision for the audit of a registered co-operative society?

(*b*) The creditor of a co-operative credit society wants to inspect its books. How should he proceed in the matter?

(*c*) In what manner and from whom can the Government recover moneys due to it from a registered co-operative society?

Ans. (*a*) The following are the statutory duties of the auditor of a registered co-operative society:–

1. He should examine the over-due debts by its members.
2. He should value the assets and the liabilities of the society.
3. He should satisfy himself that the balance-sheet exhibits the true and fair view of the society.
4. For verifying his duty efficiently, he has a right to ask for any information and explanation regarding the working of society which he may require and if he is not satisfied with the information or explanation given to him, he should mention such a fact in his report to the members.

(*b*) The creditor of the society should take the following steps:–

1. He should make an application to the Registrar for the inspection of the books of the society.
2. The application should contain the following information:–
   (*a*) The amount due.
   (*b*) The age of the debt due to him.
   (*c*) The due date of the repayment of the debt.
   (*d*) Whether a reminder to the society for the repayment was sent, and if so, on what date, etc.
3. He should deposit with the Registrar a sum of money, as the Registrar may deem necessary, as security for the cost of the proposed inspection of the books by the Registrar.
4. The information stated in (2) above is to enable the Registrar to satisfy himself that the applicant has a reasonable case for the inspection of the books of account.
5. If the Registrar is satisfied, he himself may inspect the books of account or he may delegate the work of inspection to any other person who will submit his report to the Registrar.

It may, however, be stated here that a creditor himself has no right to inspect the books of account.

(*c*) The Government can recover its due from the society in the following ways:–

1. The Government can recover the moneys together with the costs incurred, from any officer, member (past or present) as if the amount due is an arrear of land revenue, i.e., the land of the person can be sold by auction in order to recover the amount due.
2. The order of recovery will be as under:–
   (*a*) Firstly out of the property of the registered co-operative society.
   (*b*) Secondly, from the members of a limited liability society according to the maximum limit of the liability.
   (*c*) Thirdly, in the case of other societies from the members.

Q.144. State the duty of an auditor of a company which has changed the descriptive pattern of profit and loss account.

Ans. Although the Companies Act has prescribed a **pro forma** of the balance sheet of a company vide Part I of Schedule VI to the Act, no such *pro forma* for the profit and loss account of a company has been prescribed. Therefore a company is at liberty to prepare its profit and loss account in any form it likes as long as all the information regarding the different items of income and expenditure, as is required to be shown in the profit and loss account according to Part II of Schedule VI, is shown and that no such item of income and expenditure is withheld. If such is the case, the auditor need not report to the shareholders regarding the changed form of the profit and loss account.

In any case the auditor should inquire from the clients the reasons for the change in the pattern of the profit and loss account. He should also see, as stated above, that no information, as is required, is withheld by preparing the profit and loss account in the altered form. He should inquire whether the changed form of the profit and loss account shows an improvement in its presentation to the shareholders.

Again, he should see whether the comparison between the figures of different items of profit and loss account of the current year with the previous year is possible or not according to the altered form. He should further see that the figures for the current year are not misleading because of the changed form of the profit and loss account. If he is satisfied on the above points, he need not take note of such a change in the descriptive pattern of the profit and loss account.

Q.145. " It is worth remembering that the primary responsibility for running a company and preparing its accounts is of the directors. The auditor is supposed to shout when something is wrong. When a watch-dog barks, you do not shoot him. You buy a better pad-lock. Only if he sleeps you replace him." Discuss.

Ans. One has to remember that the primary duty of the directors is to get the accounts of the company, of which they are the directors prepared. Of course, they themselves do not prepare the accounts. They get them prepared by the accountant but it is their responsibility to see that the accounts are ready for being audited by the auditor as will appear from the following section of the Companies Act :–

Section 215 (8) lays down "The balance sheet and the profit and loss account shall be approved by the Board of Directors before they are signed on behalf of the Board in accordance with the provisions of this section and before they are submitted to the auditor for their report thereon".

Again, S. 209 (6) (d) states "Where the company has neither the Managing Agent ... nor a Managing Director, and a Manager, every director of the company" if he fails to see that the compliance of this section is observed, is liable to be punished with imprisonment up to six months or with a fine up to one thousand rupees or with both.

Thus it would be observed that it is the duty of the directors of the company to get the accounts prepared and sign the balance sheet and the profit and loss account. Up to this stage the auditor of the company does not come into the picture. It is the directors who organise the accounts department; it is they who have to see that the internal check system is efficiently organised and that the accounts are ready for submission to the auditors of the company for audit at the right time.

After that, it is the duty of the auditor to report to the shareholders, after having audited the accounts, whether the balance sheet and the profit and loss account are drawn up according to the Companies Act, and whether they represent a true and fair view of the state of affairs of the company. If the auditor finds that they are all right, he keeps quiet and gives a clean report regarding the balance sheet and the profit and loss account.

Thus it would be observed that the auditor is like a watch-dog and keeps quiet and does not shout (barks) if he finds that there is no thief (accounts are correct). On the other hand, if he finds that there is something wrong with the accounts and in spite of that he does not report to the shareholders (does not shout or bark), it is the duty of the directors to see that another auditor is appointed and proceed against him for negligence in the performance of his duty. In other words they appoint a better auditor (buy a better pad-lock).

Q.146. During the course of audit of accounts of a company having a paid-up capital of Rs. 10 lakhs and its profits exceeding Rs. 5 lakhs you observe :

(*a*) that a salesman had misappropriated various amounts aggregating to Rs. 5,000;

(*b*) that a contribution of Rs. 5,000 has been paid by the company to a political party and the amount has been debited to miscellaneous expenses account;

(*c*) that the company during the year has been working only single shift instead of double shift as had been done in the previous year due to some negligence on the part of the management as a result whereof profits have been reduced considerably.

State whether it would be necessary for you to qualify your report on the accounts of the company in respect of any one or more of these matters. Give your reasons therefor.

Ans. (*a*) An auditor has to verify whether the profit and loss account of a company exhibits a true and fair view of the state of affairs of the company. From the question it is not clear whether the loss caused by the misappropriation of amounts aggregating to Rs. 5,000 by the salesman had been stated in the profit and loss account or not. Moreover, it is also not clear whether any action had been taken by the directors against the salesman. In case an action had been taken against the salesman, the directors have done their duty and, therefore, it is not necessary for the auditor to qualify his report. On the other hand; if the directors did not make any effort to recover the loss from the dishonest salesman, in spite of the fact that they knew about the misappropriation, the auditor should qualify his report.

(*b*) According to Section 293 A of the Companies Act, a company is prohibited to contribute to any political party or for any political purpose to any individual or body, any amount or amounts which will in any financial year exceed twenty-five thousand rupees or five per cent of its average profits of the previous three years, determined according to Sections 349 and 350. Thus it will be found that the contribution is in order but the amount cannot be debited to miscellaneous expenses account. According to Section 293A, the amount so contributed must be clearly stated in the profit and loss account, indicating the name of the party or individual to which or to whom the amount has been contributed. The directors should be asked to put the matter aright and if they do not do so, the auditor must qualify his report. It may be stated here that by a recent decision by the Allahabad High Court it has been held that such a contribution cannot be treated as an expense for the purpose of calculating the income tax payable by the company.

(*c*) In the past it was held that it is no part of the duty of the auditor to state in his report whether the business of the company is carried on prudently or imprudently. He was not expected to sit in judgement of the acts of the directors. Justice Lindley said in 1895: "It is no part of the auditor's duty to give advice either to directors or shareholders as to what they ought to do. An auditor has nothing to do with prudence or imprudence of making loans with security or without security..." But there has been a big advance in the industrial field since 1895 and therefore it is the duty of the auditor to express his opinion as to whether the business is conducted prudently or imprudently. From the practical point of view it may not be easy for an auditor in all cases to find lapses on the part of the directors. However in this case, if the auditor thinks that the directors were negligent in not running the double shift and as a result of their negligence, a loss has been caused to the company, it is his duty to qualify his report.

Q.147. Enumerate the various instances of professional misconduct of a Chartered Accountant in practice which however does not require action by a High Court.

Ans. Section 22 of the Chartered Accountants Act, 1949, defines the term Professional Misconduct as "Professional misconduct shall be deemed to include any act or omissions specified in any of the Schedules."

The Act has two Schedules. The First Schedule deals with professional misconduct of a chartered accountant. Such cases can be decided by the Council of the Institute. The Second Schedule deals with professional misconduct of a Chartered Accountant. Cases of such misconduct have to be referred to the High Court by the Council.

The First Schedule has three Parts. The First Part deals with misconduct by a member in practice. We are, according to the question, concerned here with such cases. We shall deal with a few cases of acts and omissions by a chartered accountant whose case can be decided by the Council without any reference to the High Court.

1. If a member accepts or agrees to accept any part of the profits of the professional work of a lawyer, auctioneer, broker or any other agent who is not a member of the Institute, he will be deemed to have committed professional misconduct.

Example. A lawyer has been appointed to prepare Memorandum and Articles of Association and Prospectus of a proposed company. The lawyer asks a friend, a chartered accountant, to prepare the necessary documents on the terms and conditions that the fee receivable will be shared between the two. If the chartered accountant has agreed to undertake the work, he is deemed to be guilty of professional misconduct and the Council of the Institute is to decide the case without any reference to the High Court (*K.V. Narsimhan, In. Re.* 1952).

2. A chartered accountant is deemed to be guilty of misconduct if he solicits clients or professional work either directly or indirectly, by circular, advertisement, personal communication or interview or by any other means.

In this connection we shall cite the case of *Gadre* vs. *Ambekar.* Ambekar, a chartered accountant, had sent circular letters among others to the managers of a school and a firm with a request that he might be appointed as an auditor. The complainant, Gadre, was the auditor of both the school and the firm. It was held that the respondent was guilty of professional misconduct in sending circular letters to solicit clients. The Council took a lenient view of the matter because of the extenuating circumstances—lack of professional experience than any wrong motive or dishonesty and ignorance of the rules on the part of the respondent. His name was removed from the Register but with a permission to him to apply immediately thereafter for reinstatement.

3. If a chartered accountant accepts a position as auditor previously held by another chartered accountant without first communicating with him in writing he will be deemed to be guilty of professional misconduct (*Kharwandikar* vs. *Borkar,* 1952).

The reader may refer for further cases of professional misconduct enumerated in the First Part of the First Schedule of the Chartered Accountants Act referred to in the Chapter "Professional Conduct and Ethics."

Q.148. Describe the procedure for taking an action against a chartered accountant, suspected of being guilty of a misconduct, under the Chartered Accountants Act, 1949.

What are the different types of punishments which may be awarded and by whom?

Ans. When a complaint is made to the Institute against a member or the Institute itself gets the information that a member has committed an act which amounts to professional or other misconduct under the First Schedule and if the Council of the Institute is satisfied that a **prima facie** case has been made against the member, it refers the case to the Disciplinary Committee. The Committee holds an inquiry and forwards its conclusions to the Council.

The "other misconduct" used in the previous paragraph means non-professional misconduct, conduct which does not arise out of his professional work. For instance, if a chartered accountant has forged the signature of a person on a cheque, he is considered to be guilty of misconduct although such an act is not connected with his professional duties. Again, when a chartered accountant forged the will of a relative, he was found guilty of having committed misconduct although the act had nothing to do with his professional work. Such acts are considered to be misconduct because a chartered accountant is expected to maintain a very high standard of integrity in his personal conduct.

If the Council finds from the report by the Committee that the member is not guilty of misconduct, the matter is dropped. If, on the other hand, it finds the member guilty of professional or other misconduct specified in the First Schedule, it issues a notice to the member to show cause why action should not be taken against him. The member may plead his own case or may be represented by a lawyer or by another chartered accountant. After hearing the case, the Council.

(*a*) may reprimand the member; or

(*b*) may remove his name for a period not exceeding a period of five years.

If the Council decides to remove his name for a period exceeding five years, the case has to be forwarded to the High Court which may decide the case as it deems fit. The decision of the Council is final except in the following cases:–

(*a*) when the aggrieved member prefers an appeal to the High Court;

(*b*) when the High Court on its own initiative or otherwise revises the decision of the Council;

(*c*) when the Council decides to remove the name of the member for a period exceeding five years.

If, however, the misconduct of a member falls within the scope of the Second Schedule to the Act, the Council has to refer the case with its recommendations to the High Court for its decision unless the Council has found from the report of the Disciplinary Committee that the member is not guilty.

It may be mentioned here that the Council of the Institute and the Disciplinary Committee are empowered to exercise the same powers which are vested in a Civil Court, viz., (*a*) summoning or enforcing attendance of any person and examining him on oath; (*b*) discovery and production of any document; and (*c*) receiving evidence on affidavit.

Q.149. State the fundamental differences between an internal audit and an audit under the Companies Act.

Ans. Arnold W. Johnson has defined internal audit: "Internal audit is the independent appraisal activity within an organisation for the review of accounting, financial and other organisations as a basis for protective and constructive service to management." Internal audit is a part of the internal control which is introduced in a big business house to detect any error or fraud at an earlier stage. In other words, it indirectly prevents the commission of errors or frauds.

Distinction between internal check and internal audit must be clearly understood to avoid any confusion between the two. Internal check is a device which prevents the commission of an error or fraud while on the other hand internal audit is a device to detect an error or fraud which has already been committed.

We are, however, concerned here with the distinction between internal audit and statutory audit.

1. Internal auditor is appointed by the management while the statutory auditor is appointed by the shareholders except in certain cases.

2. Internal auditor need not possess the qualifications as are laid down under Section 226 of the Companies Act but a statutory auditor must have those qualifications.

3. Internal auditor is an employee of the company while statutory auditor is an independent person.

4. The scope of the work by the internal auditor is determined by the management while the scope of the work by and the responsibilities of the statutory auditor are determined by law.

5. An internal audit is a kind of continuous audit while a statutory audit is generally conducted after the preparation of the final accounts.

6. An internal auditor has to find out whether any error or fraud has been committed while the statutory auditor has to report whether the balance-sheet and the profit and loss account of a

company have been drawn up in conformity with law and whether they show a true and fair view of the state of affairs of the company. Detection of errors and frauds are incidental duties of an auditor.

7. The internal auditor has not to submit any report to the shareholders of the company while a statutory auditor has to do so.

8. Internal auditor has to make suggestions to the management as to how to run the business economically, efficiently and to avoid wastage but a statutory auditor need not do so unless he is especially asked.

9. The internal auditor can be removed by the management while the statutory auditor cannot be removed by it.

10. The internal auditor has to go through all the transactions while the statutory auditor may apply a few test checks.

11. The internal auditor cannot be prosecuted for professional misconduct unless he is a chartered accountant while a statutory auditor, who is so, can be prosecuted.

Q.150. State the steps you would take if you were asked to undertake a full share transfer audit.

Ans. It is not the duty of an auditor to audit the share transfer but sometimes he is asked by the management to do so as a special case with a view to check against a clerical error or the issue of duplicate shares. If he is asked to do so, he may charge additional fee and should take the following steps:–

1. He should examine the Articles of Association regarding the procedure to be followed in case of the transfer of shares.
2. He should enquire whether intimations were sent to the transferors or to each shareholder in case of joint holders whether he had any objection against the transfer. If "no objection" letters were received, they should be checked with the transfer instruments.
3. In case the shares transferred were partly paid, enquire whether a notice under Section 110 (2) of the Companies Act has been given to the transferee that the shares were partly paid and that "no objection" letters had been received from the transferee.
4. In case the shares were mortgaged, he should see whether a notice regarding the proposed transfer had been given to the mortgagee.
5. He should see that the transfer is properly executed.
6. He should see that the transfer is properly stamped and that the share transfer fee received had been credited to the profit and loss account. Count the number of shares transferred, the fee payable and see whether it has been correctly credited to profit and loss account.
7. He should compare the signature of the transferor with his specimen signature on the original application form or the previous transfer form, if any, kept in the office of the company or with any recent transfers.
8. He should examine the Board's Resolution to see the approval of the directors regarding the transfer.
9. He should see that the transferee is not disqualified to hold shares.
10. He should see that the share certificates which have been transferred have been duly cancelled to prevent the issue of shares against such shares certificates.
11. In case of transmission of shares,
    (*a*) he should see that the transmission is according to the Articles of Association;
    (*b*) he should find out whether the estate duty had been paid by the transferee before the shares were transferred;

(c) he should examine the succession certificate in the case of the death of the shareholder or the order of the court in the case of the insolvency or bankruptcy of the shareholder.

12. When a part of the holding has been transferred, the auditor should check the balance certificates with the counterfoils of the certificates.

13. He should compare the total issued capital with the total balance on the Shareholders' Account in the Share Book.

14. He should see whether the blank transfer was in currency within the prescribed time.

For the share transfer the auditor is required to issue a certificate which may be on the following lines: "We have examined the Share Register with the Transfer Deeds, the cancelled share certificates and the counterfoils of the shares issued and certify them to be in order. We have agreed the Share Register with the shares issued."

Q.151. One of the recommendations made by the O. & M. Department of a large company is: "Thatin the interest of economy, the Internal Audit Department should be dispensed within view of the soundness of accounting system and the existence of the External Audit." State with reasons whether you agree with such a recommendation.

Ans. An Internal Audit Department is maintained by a company as a means of internal control. Such a department is primarily established to assist the management rather than external auditor. This department, is; therefore, responsible to the management. Its function is to ensure that the information which is passed to the management is both correct and according to the requirements of the management. Its function is to see whether there has been any waste, whether there has been any variance from the standard cost and, if so, why, whether stock-taking system is satisfactory and so on. In short, the Internal Audit Department is not a substitute of the External Audit.

Internal Audit Department, therefore, should not be dispensed with especially when the company is a large one as given in the question.

Q.152. What is meant by 'generally accepted auditing practices'?

Ans. Auditing is a professional exercise. It is a process involving various accepted procedures. The auditor cannot give snap opinion on a financial statement. Accepted auditing practices are to be observed. In a broad manner it implies the following:

(a) The person conducting the audit must be professionally competent and independent.

(b) The audit work must be well planned and documented.

(c) Sufficient and appropriate evidence must be gathered and evaluated to form a basis for opinion-giving.

(d) The professional opinion must be pronounced after a proper judgement of facts. In giving the opinion the auditor must ensure the truth, fairness and adequate disclosure of financial information in the financial statements.

(e) The audit should be conducted with due regard to the accepted accounting conventions, special enactments applicable to a particular case, pronouncements of professional bodies.

Q. 153. Explain the compliance procedure and substantive procedure of testing evidence?

Ans. For forming an opinion, the auditor requires sufficient and appropriate audit evidence. For evaluation of audit evidence the auditor makes use of compliance procedure and substantive procedure tests.

The auditor cannot check all transactions of an organisation. He test-checks certain transactions. Yet he requires an assurance that other transactions occur within an, inbuilt control system. By employing compliance procedure test, the auditor seeks to test that (i) there exists an internal control system for the organisation (ii) it functions effectively and (iii) it operates without break till the end of audit period.

Auditor makes test checking of certain transactions. The transactions of the organisation get reflected in P & L account or Balance Sheet. These reflections reveal one or more of the following assertions viz., existence, rights and obligations, occurrence, completeness, valuation, measurement and disclosure. The auditor is concerned to ascertain the correctness of these assertions. He accomplishes this by resorting to substantive procedure of checking evidence. He does substantive checking of transactions by inspection, observation, inquiry, confirmation computation and analytical review.

Q.154. What are the various types of audit evidence?

Ans. The audit evidence may be gathered from within the organisation or from outside the organisation. The audit evidence may be in the form of written records, oral representations, events, physical existence, operation of a system or analytical results. Written evidence are in the form of bills, invoices, pass book, subsidiary ledgers, ledgers, agreements, etc., Oral evidence is obtained from discussion with employees and other people concerned with the organisation. The happening of events, for e.g., events occurring after balance sheet date but before signing audit report may provide clues as to the assertions of certain transactions. The physical existence of say, building is an evidence as to the assertion of existence represented by capital expenditure on building. The results arrived at from using analytical tools may point to correctness or otherwise of certain assertions reflected in financial statements.

Q.155. Explain the requirements of MAOCAR order 1988 with regard to (a) fixed assets (b) Stock in trade.

Ans. Auditor has to comment under requirements of MAOCARO 1988 in respect of the following items, the matters mentioned against them:

Fixed assets :

(*a*) Whether the company maintains proper records showing full particulars including quantitative details and situation of fixed assets.

(*b*) Whether physical verification has been conducted at reasonable intervals for fixed assets.

(*c*) If material discrepancy is noticed in verification, whether the same has been properly adjusted.

(*d*) If fixed assets have been revalued during the year, the basis of revaluation should be indicated.

Stock in trade:

(*a*) Whether physical verification has been conducted at reasonable interval.

(*b*) Whether the physical verification procedure is reasonable and adequate in relation to the size, nature of the business.

(*c*) If material discrepancies are observed in verification, whether the same has been properly adjusted in the accounts.

(*d*) Whether the valuation of stock is proper and is on consistent basis. If a change in method of valuation is adopted, the effect of change in method on profits or loss of the company should be indicated.

Q.156. Briefly mention the duties of auditor in checking advances of banks.

Ans. 1. The auditor must check the internal control prevailing in banks with regard to credit department.

2. The auditor should ensure the accuracy of figures reported under advances.

3. The auditor should check that the advances are classified into performing and non-performing assets as per RBI guidelines. He must ensure that only income on performing assets are recognised in P & L account. Income on non-performing assets can be taken to P & L account only if it is actually realised.

4. The auditor has to check that the classification of advances (facilitywise, sector-wise and security-wise) has been properly made.

5. When advances are stated to be secured, the auditor must evaluate the nature, value and enforceability of securities.

6. The auditor should review major accounts for the adequacy of documentation, proper credit appraisal, disbursement and follow-up of accounts.

7. The auditor has to ensure that adequate provision for bad and doubtful debts has been created for doubtful and loss assets. He should also see that ad hoc provision is made for sub-standard assets.

8. He should ensure that advances appear in balance sheet with adequate disclosures prescribed under Banking Regulations Act.